ADDENDUM

Because there is some disagreement on whether members of the Democrat-Farmer-Labor (D-F-L) Party of Minnesota should be considered Democrats, four governors belonging to this party were excluded from the list of Minnesota governors. Their names are noted below. Please see page 413 for a full list of Democratic Minnesota governors.

FREEMAN, Orville Lothrop. May 9, 1918–; Jan. 5, 1955–Jan. 2, 1961; Secy. of Agriculture Jan. 21, 1961–Jan. 20, 1969.

ROLVAAG, Karl Fritjof. July 18, 1913–Dec. 20, 1990; March 25, 1963–Jan. 2, 1967.

ANDERSON, Wendell Richard. Feb. 1, 1933–; Jan. 4, 1971–Dec. 29, 1976; Senate Dec. 30, 1976–Dec. 29, 1978.

PERPICH, Rudolph George "Rudy." June 27, 1928–; Dec. 29, 1976–Jan. 1, 1979; Jan. 3, 1983–Jan. 7, 1991.

THE ENCYCLOPEDIA

of the

DEMOCRATIC PARTY

Volume Three

THE ENCYCLOPEDIA
of the
DEMOCRATIC PARTY

Volume Three

Edited by

GEORGE THOMAS KURIAN

JEFFREY D. SCHULTZ
Associate Editor

Sharpe Reference

An imprint of M.E. Sharpe, INC.

1997 Library Reference Edition published by Sharpe Reference
Sharpe Reference is an imprint of M.E. Sharpe INC.

M.E. Sharpe INC.
80 Business Park Drive
Armonk, NY 10504

Copyright © 1997 by *M.E. Sharpe* INC.

Library of Congress Cataloging-in-Publication Data

Kurian, George Thomas.
[Encyclopedia of the Republican Party]
The encyclopedia of the Republican Party ; The encyclopedia of the Democratic Party /
George Thomas Kurian.
p.   cm.
Includes bibliographical references (p.   ) and index.
Contents: v. 1–2. The encyclopedia of the Republican Party — v. 3–4. The encyclopedia of the Democratic Party.
ISBN 1-56324-729-1 (set)
1. Republican Party (U.S. : 1854–)—Encyclopedias.
2. Democratic Party (U.S.)—Encyclopedias.
I. Kurian, George Thomas. Encyclopedia of the Democratic Party.
II. Title.
JK2352.K87   1996
324.2734'03—dc20
96-12187
CIP

Printed and bound in the United States of America

The paper used in this publication meets the minimum requirements of
American National Standard for Information Sciences—Permanence of
Paper for Printed Library Materials,
ANSI Z 39.48-1984.

∞

EB (c)   10   9   8   7   6   5   4   3   2   1

CONTENTS

Editor
George Thomas Kurian

Contributors

Bruce E. Altschuler
Department of Political Science,
State University of New York,
Oswego, New York

Monica Bauer
Iona College,
New Rochelle, New York

Stephen D. Van Beek
Department of Political Science,
San Jose State University,
San Jose, California

Arthur Blaser
Political Science Department,
Chapman University,
Orange, California

Steve D. Boilard
Department of Government,
Western Kentucky University,
Bowling Green, Kentucky

Robert J. Bookmiller
Millersville University,
Millersville, Pennsylvania

Robert E. Dewhirst
Department of Government,
Northwest Missouri State
University, Maryville, Missouri

William E. Dugan
Border Research Institute,
Las Cruces, New Mexico

J. David Gillespie
Department of Political Science,
Presbyterian College,
Clinton, South Carolina

Christian Goergen
College of DuPage,
Glen Ellyn, Illinois

Douglas Harris
Department of Political Science,
The Johns Hopkins University,
Baltimore, Maryland

David Hatchett

Paul S. Herrnson
Department of Government and
Politics, University of Maryland,
College Park, Maryland

Steve Hoenisch

Rogan Kersh
Department of Political Science,
Yale University,
New Haven, Connecticut

Quentin Kidd
Department of Political Science,
Texas Tech University,
Lubbock, Texas

Melvin A. Kulbicki
Department of History and Politics,
York College, York, Pennsylvania

Tom Lansford
Old Dominion University,
Virginia Beach, Virginia

Cynthia J. Levy

W. Adam Mandelbaum

Janet B. Manspeaker
Department of Political Science,
Cheyney State University,
Cheyney, Pennsylvania

Michael E. Meagher
Department of History and Political
Science, University of Missouri,
Rolla, Missouri

Jack J. Miller

Tim Morris

Kimberly J. Pace

Russell L. Riley
Political Science Department,
University of Pennsylvania,
Philadelphia, Pennsylvania

John S. Robey
Social Sciences Department,
University of Texas,
Brownsville, Texas

Robert Allen Rutland

Frauke Schnell
Department of Political Science,
West Chester University,
West Chester, Pennsylvania

Diane L. Schultz

Jeffrey D. Schultz
Colorado College,
Colorado Springs, Colorado

Larry M. Schwab
Political Science Department,
John Carroll University,
Cleveland Heights, Ohio

Edward W. Siskel

Daniel Stanhagen

B. Kim Taylor

Susan L. Thomas
Department of
Political Science,
Hollins College,
Roanoke, Virginia

Michael J. Towle
Department of Government,
Mount St. Mary's College,
Emmitsburg, Maryland

Jessamyn West

John F. Yarbrough

PREFACE

There can be but two great political parties in this country.
—Stephen A. Douglas, 1858

Exactly 200 years ago, in 1796, Thomas Jefferson became a candidate for the presidency of the United States on the Jeffersonian Republican (later Democratic-Republican) ticket, and this event marks the beginning of party politics in the United States. *The Encyclopedia of the Democratic Party* and *The Encyclopedia of the Republican Party* are designed to mark the bicentennial of parties and party politics in the United States.

Although the definitions of Republican and Democrat have changed over the years, the United States is one of the few countries in the world where a strict two-party system has flourished. It was not always so. The history of political parties is filled with paradoxes. Parties are not mentioned at all in the Constitution, and the framers did not consider them essential, or even desirable. George Washington himself often spoke of "the baneful effect of parties" and condemned the Democratic-Republican groups as "self-created societies."

Yet, parties have become the primary mechanism outside the Constitution for transforming the perceived popular will into legislative acts and executive policies and programs. During the early years, parties coalesced around issues rather than personalities, and their labels and names changed as these issues lost urgency. Party labels were always fluid and sometimes misleading. It is interesting that Democratic and Republican are among the blandest political labels in the world. In one sense, they are perfectly interchangeable and neutral. Party symbols are even more meaningless: one is a jackass, the other an elephant.

There are at least two reasons why these two parties have flourished whereas more conventional political parties have not. The first is structural. The United States is not a fertile ground for extremism of any kind. Americans are not essentially apolitical, but they are uncomfortable with ideology-driven political activism. Barry Goldwater was dead wrong when he said that "extremism in the defense of liberty is no vice," and his statement reveals a common but perni-

cious confusion between ends and means. Extremism is not justifiable in defense of anything. The last time Americans espoused extremism in the defense of liberty was in the Civil War, an avoidable conflagration that cost tens of thousands of lives. As a corollary, Americans have not encouraged ideological purity in their parties or leaders. George McGovern was one of the most logical and ideologically consistent political personalities in recent times. Adlai Stevenson II was one of the most articulate and eloquent champions of a rational and just society in the twentieth century. Yet, both of them, like many others of their ilk, have ended on the wrong side of the ledger of American history. Another corollary is that whenever members of an extremist faction or peripheral group try to take over a party, they lead it into political wilderness. This happened when the limousine liberals took over the Democratic Party in the 1960s and converted it into their playground. It happened again when certain extremist factions tried to take over the Republican Party in the 1980s and early 1990s. It has been said that the middle of the road is only for armadillos and road kills. But the strength of both the Democratic and Republican parties is in the middle, and it is when they return to the middle that they are able to renew their vision and communicate with the American people on the right wavelength.

The second reason for the durability of the Democratic and Republican parties is historical. The early political leaders followed the Westminster model of binary politics, in which there are only two camps: Conservative (Tory) and Liberal (Whig). William Gilbert (the better-known half of Gilbert and Sullivan) wrote:

> I often think it's comical
> How Nature does always contrive
> That every boy and every gal
> That's born into the world alive
> is either a little Liberal
> or else a little Conservative.

The success of the Democratic and Republican parties and the relative failure of third parties to strike deep roots illustrate Gilbert's insight into the biology of politics. This is in contrast to the Continental model of multiple parties. In Italy at one time there were 46 political parties, each a fiefdom for some unemployed or disgruntled politician. The election ballot papers would run into many pages. Multiple parties would require runoffs after the first elections, something that is constitutionally impossible in the United States.

This encyclopedia is not only high history but high drama. It tries to capture the sweep of electoral and convention history. The quadrennial political paroxysm that begins with the primaries and ends on election night is more Barnum and Bailey than strict Constitution. Even before the advent of television, American politics was part spectacle and part carnival. The encyclopedia also presents the varied tableau of ideas, rivalries, issues, conflicts, identities, and movements that the campaign rhetoric often hides. While many issues have changed, may others have endured. For most of the twentieth century, the driving themes in the party platforms of both parties have been the linkages between politics, on the one hand, and, on the other, economy, religion, foreign policy, immigration, society, law, environment, finance, crime, race, women's rights, civil rights, education, and social values. That these issues should recur every four years is a tacit admission that they have no easy solutions.

In many cases party positions on these issues undergo subtle shifts. Sometimes parties completely reverse themselves and adopt contradictory positions, trusting in the public's short memory to overlook these somersaults and U-turns. One of the most ironic is how the Democratic Party evolved over the years from a viciously racist party willing to shed blood rather than give civil rights to black slaves into a doughty champion of African Americans. The changes in the Republican positions have been less dramatic but nonetheless striking. After waging a Civil War to enforce federal authority over the states, Republicans have become strong defenders of states' rights.

In his *Cycles of American History*, Arthur Schlesinger has provided a broadbrush framework for aligning the fortunes of the two major political parties with social, economic, and political cycles. Since 1860, the Republicans have been in the White House for 84 years and the Democrats for 52 years. The Democrats have controlled the House for 80 years and the Republicans for 56 years. The Democrats have controlled the Senate for 62 years and the Republicans for 72 years. (They were equally divided in the Senate of the 47th Congress.) All the four major wars of this century (World Wars I and II, the Korean War, and the Vietnam War) have been under the Democrats; the Great Depression, under the Republicans.

In trying to weave history, issues, biography, and party platforms together, this encyclopedia tries to give perspective and depth to the political moment. Writing about politics cannot be separated from interpretation. In the Issues and Ideology section there is a wide range of significant interpretations. Reference books are expected to provide accurate and definitive information consistent with the highest standards of scholarship. This encyclopedia attempts to meet this expectation. But it goes beyond that to offer vibrant, cutting-edge analysis and to convey the vitality and excitement that drive party politics.

THE ENCYCLOPEDIA OF THE DEMOCRATIC PARTY

The Encyclopedia of the Democratic Party chronicles the evolution of the Democratic Party, the older of the two major parties and also one of the oldest political parties in the world. Although strictly dating from 1828, it traces its lineage to Jefferson's Democratic-Republican Party. Political parties were a novelty at that time. No one knew exactly how to finance and organize campaigns, how to choose candidates and leaders, or how to hold conventions and decide party positions. The concept of majority rule was new and the threat of a return to a monarchic form of government ever present. The functioning of the political system in the United States is entwined with the Democratic Party's experiments in democracy and its triumphs and disasters. The Democratic Party has survived while its early rivals, the Federalists and the Whigs, have perished because of its extraordinary ability to project certain factional values and also to produce the right leaders at the right time. The first was Andrew Jackson, who may rightly be called the founder of the Democratic Party. He was the first to identify the party with the populist, as opposed to the elitist, strain of politics. For many decades after Jackson, the Democratic Party was the party of the South pitted against the northeastern establishment. Nearly wiped out after the Civil War, the Democratic Party managed to cling precariously to life for nearly 70 years until the rise of FDR, who may be considered the rebuilder of the party. FDR managed through sheer political magic to convert a southern conservative agrarian party into a northern liberal and intellectual party. He also managed to pull the rug from under the Republicans by winning the loyalty of blacks, whose enslavement was the official creed of the party a century earlier.

The twentieth century has been remarkably kind to the Democratic Party. Its seven presidents in this century have included two great ones: Woodrow Wilson and FDR, although no Democratic president appears on Mount Rushmore. (The conventional wisdom is that a party must produce at least one great president a century to maintain its effectiveness.) However, as the century draws to a close, the party finds itself in the process of redefinition. The twenty-first century will change the rules and armaments of political warfare, and the Democratic Party finds itself ill prepared to meet the uncertain challenges ahead. The next generation of voters will be empowered not so much by political parties and governments as by technology and electronic communications. Political constituencies will become more fragmented and not even an avatar of FDR can build another Rainbow Coalition, bringing disparate interest and ethnic groups together. Social value systems and preferences are changing rapidly, and political behavior is becoming more un-predictable. As a result, the Democratic Party is discovering that in politics there are no permanent successes and no permanent failures and that voters have no permanent loyalties either.

My list of acknowledgments begins with Evelyn Fazio, vice president and publisher at M.E. Sharpe. Her perseverance, enthusiasm, and commitment to the creation of solid reference books were strong assets for the project and sustained it during its gestation. The production department, headed by Carmen Chetti, did a superb job in record time. Eileen Gaffney, who handled production, was a model of efficiency and tact. Also at M.E. Sharpe, Aud Thiessen helped the project to move along smoothly. The encyclopedia also benefited immeasurably from the efforts of associate editor, Jeffrey D. Schultz, who handled many of the major entries and provided important leads.

Above all, I must thank my wife, Annie Kurian, who has been, as always, a wellspring of encouragement and support.

George Thomas Kurian

Harry S. Truman, the "One Man Band." Democratic Candidate for President, 1948. *Source:* Truman Library.

HISTORY

EUROPEAN ROOTS OF AMERICAN PARTIES

Political parties are a phenomenon that developed out of the struggles in Europe between monarchs and their subjects over power and money. Most notably, the history of England after 1600 is a chronicle of the rise of Parliament, an old but weak institution until Charles I overreached himself, was dethroned by parliamentary leaders, and finally was executed. The resulting English Revolution changed the nation into a constitutional monarchy, with power shared by the monarch and Parliament; and in time two factions or parties, one supporting the king and the other opposing royal power, coalesced into the Tory and Whig parties. These parties offered candidates at parliamentary elections, chose prime ministers and cabinets, and represented a spectrum of ideas ranging from conservative to extremely liberal views on social, economic, and political questions of the day.

Thus, when British North America was colonized in the seventeenth century, the emigrants brought with them the system already established in the home country, but without the party mechanism. The royal appointees were either royalists or apolitical, and though each colony developed a legislature the lines drawn were on local issues without any ties to the Whigs or Tories in Parliament. The king formally appointed governors, who could call a legislature into session or force it to adjourn, and all loyalty was centered on the Crown, rather than any political allegiance to ideas or leaders.

This was the situation existing in the 13 British colonies stretching from Massachusetts southward to Georgia in 1774. There had been earlier troubles, particularly after Parliament passed the obnoxious Stamp Act in 1765. But generations of Americans gloried in their ties to the home country and the monarchy. All this was changed dramatically after disguised colonists dumped a cargo of tea into Boston Harbor.

The Boston Port Act, passed by Parliament to punish Boston for the antiestablishment "tea party," galvanized the colonial leaders into action. If war came, they insisted, the blame would fall on a Parliament more interested in party politics than colonial welfare.

During the ensuing months, colonists favoring resistance to British domination began to call themselves *patriots* and spoke of the pro-British leaders as *tories*. In time, the patriots became intolerant of their fellow colonists, who clung to the British standard; in some areas they were jailed, while in others they took flight to Canada, Bermuda, or the Bahamas—wherever they could find a British sanctuary. Thus, from the beginnings of the new nation, there was a partisanship created by political differences.

Even before the shooting started, most of the leaders involved in the American Revolution believed that the breakup of the British Empire was owing to "factionalism" in a Parliament dominated by jousting Whigs and Tories. A few Americans spoke of themselves as Whigs, meaning they were more liberal than the Tories who backed George III as the crisis in colonial relations grew apace.

The rising American leaders—the Adamses, Jeffersons, and Henrys—were also students of ancient history, and in their reading they became convinced that governments ancient and modern become corrupt when party allegiance overcomes national interest. Well read in ancient history, they could cite writers from Plato to Plutarch to show that factionalism had preceded the downfall of Greece and Rome. Even closer to home, the American patriots could point to a contemporary, the French writer Montesquieu. The French nobleman's work had enormous influence on their thinking; his *The Spirit of Laws* was regarded as a textbook on how a viable nation could achieve stability and prosperity through the workings of a constitutional monarchy. Happily for his Anglo-American admirers, Montesquieu had taken the English concept of a constitution as his model and professed to show how the English system, with its executive, judicial, and legislative branches, had created a model government.

From 1775 until the peace treaty signed in Paris in 1783, the United States was dominated by patriotic fever, and in its legislative councils no political factions of any importance developed. After 1783, however, when the 13 new states began operating in a peacetime atmosphere, animosities arose over public policy under the system created by the Articles of Confederation. Adopted in 1777 by the Continental Congress, the Articles provided for a loose-knit Republic that had no executive or judicial branches. But the Continental Congress was not all-powerful, for it took the unanimous consent of all the states (voting as delegations) to pass any major legislation dealing with finance. With no taxing powers, the congressional government was headed toward bankruptcy (a large foreign debt had been created to finance the war), and the states began to quibble over customs fees, boundary lines, and contributions or assessments to the empty national treasury.

As the crisis mounted, a taxpayers' protest in western Massachusetts blossomed into a skirmish known as the Shays's Rebellion. State troops quickly squelched the fracas and the leaders were arrested, but the incident was used by a small band of articulate leaders as proof that the Confederation was a failure. Washington was told of the uprising and dolefully asked whether the Revolution had been "a blessing or a curse." Pessimism reigned as newspaper essayists decried the depressed state of farm prices, the mortgages that went unpaid, and tax gatherers who could auction off cattle and implements when no cash was available.

Creditors in Rhode Island were appalled by paper-money laws passed by a farmer-led legislature that made debts difficult to collect, and wildfire inflation sent prices skyrocketing.

THE DEMON "FACTIONS" APPEAR

Factions arose, with the sympathetic farmers supporting leaders who wanted "cheap money" to pay debts and merchants eager for laws that prevented runaway inflation. As more paper money appeared, silver and gold coins all but disappeared; in many communities, nearly all transactions were made on credit terms. In some states, the city-merchant faction fought with the farmer-debtor faction for control of the legislature.

This background gave the founding fathers cause to doubt the useful role of parties in the Republic, and in their deliberations in Philadelphia in 1787 there was a strong assumption that political factions would not, or should not, become dominant in the government they were creating. In the ratification battle of 1787–1788, however, two opposing forces organized, used newspapers to espouse their views of the Constitution, and even took distinctive names: Federalist and Antifederalist.

Even before the Constitution went into operation, James Madison had warned in *The Federalist*, No. 10, the causes of faction were "sown in the nature of man." In some cases, Madison wrote, religious or political differences or personality clashes "divided mankind into parties." "This propensity of mankind to fall into mutual animosities," Madison warned, had often resulted in violent battles over "the most frivolous and fanciful distinctions."

> But the most common and durable source of factions has been the various and unequal distribution of property. Those who hold and those who are without property have ever formed distinct interests in society. . . . A landed interest, a manufacturing interest, a mercantile interest, a moneyed interest, with many lesser interests, grow up of necessity in civilized nations, and divide them into different classes, actuated by different sentiments and views.

So parties are going to arise, Madison admitted, and to keep one party from dominating and oppressing its opposition became a key to the operation of a just government. Regulating "various and interfering interests forms the principal task of modern legislation and involves the spirit of party and faction in the necessary and ordinary operations of government." Nobody has ever expressed the dilemma of a republican government better.

Once the Constitution had been ratified, Madison's blueprint turned into reality. Within months, two opposing views drew support from members of the newly created Congress, state politicians, and a handful of newspaper publishers. Federalists were not eager to keep the name used during the ratification struggle, but the strongest supporters of a program to bring in federal taxes and outlaw state currency acts were soon willing to accept the fact that the Federalists had a goal and the votes to achieve it in Congress. Some congressmen resisted the rush to create a federal financial structure, but they had no visible leadership and no informal name. Some factions tended to room and board with like-minded members of the House of Representatives, but there was no "boardinghouse" party as such.

"There is nothing I dread so much as the division of the Republic into two great parties," Vice President

John Adams lamented as the new government went into operation. Soon it was evident that the United States of America was in fact a stretched-out union of conflicting interests—slavery was the most apparent—but a nation of farmers also was suspicious of bankers, merchants, and tax gatherers.

As Madison had warned, early debates on the House floor indicated that it would be difficult to keep every interest group from becoming so dominant that exploitation of one group by another would be prevented.

WASHINGTON FEARS PARTY SYSTEM

President George Washington spoke often of the "baneful" effects of parties, yet within his cabinet the seeds of party strife were planted early. Secretary of State Thomas Jefferson worked out an arrangement with Secretary of the Treasury Alexander Hamilton in 1789–1790 that fixed the permanent capital of the Republic on the Potomac River in return for a financing plan that created a national debt based on government security markets. Later, Jefferson said he had been duped in the deal, but Hamilton's system led to a public credit arrangement that stablized the young nation's financial markets.

Thus the problem of taxes and a national debt laid the groundwork for a party system in the earliest days of the Republic. "A national debt, if it is not excessive," Hamilton wrote, "will be to us a national blessing." Jefferson and his friend James Madison took the opposite view. "I go on the Principle that Public Debt is a Public curse," Madison retorted, "and in a Re[publican] Govt. a greater than in any other."

Jefferson looked at Hamilton's plans and thought he saw a scheme to weaken the Constitution until it became a piece of meaningless paper. "The ultimate object of all this is to prepare a way for a change," Jefferson warned Washington, "from the present republican form of government, to that of a monarchy." Hamilton's minions, Jefferson added, had seized control of Congress but an opposition had formed. "The republican party, who wish to preserve the government in its present form, are fewer in number," Jefferson admitted, but there was hope if Republicans could gain control of Congress.

Despite Jefferson's fears, the Federalists kept their majority in Congress for a decade. Once the new government was in full operation, a wave of growth and prosperity followed, so the Federalists under Hamilton came to dominate Congress and were committed to elect a president in 1796 who would carry on the financial policies at the heart of the Federalist program.

THE DEMOCRATIC PARTY EMERGES, 1796

The 1796 presidential campaign came in the midst of a crisis, out of which the Democratic-Republican Party emerged. Angered by Hamilton's dominance in Washington's administration, Jefferson resigned and vowed he was through with politics. But the French Revolution, after drawing much praise in America, created a political split in the country as the conservative Federalists viewed the Reign of Terror and Louis XVI's execution with horror, while Jefferson and his friends saw the French experience as an offshoot of the American rejection of monarchy in 1776.

By 1795, Jefferson was encouraging the formation of Democratic-Republican societies across the country; these local groups were formed by supporters of the French Revolution who also found their clubs useful as meeting places to discuss local problems, elections, and petitioning programs. Prodded by Hamilton, Washington went out of his way to condemn these critics as "self created societies." Jefferson seethed at the suggestion that the Republicans were unpatriotic, for he had warned Washington in 1792 that there was in the nation a "republican party," and more than any other citizen he nurtured the seedling faction into a full-fledged political party committed to oppose the "monarchism" of Hamilton's supporters. Now, Jefferson spoke to his friends of a "Republican interest" that must fight against Hamilton's program for more taxes, a larger army, and a friendly relationship with Great Britian.

FROM FACTION TO PARTY

The crisis came to a head when the treaty John Jay negotiated in London was supported by Washington in 1795–1796. The treaty provided for the British to abandon forts they still occupied in the western United States, but was so tilted toward the commercial interests of Englishmen that the French were outraged and Jeffersonian Republicans denounced the treaty as a betrayal of American interests. Thus Jefferson, who in 1789 had said that "if I could not go to heaven but with a party, I would not go there at all," became the focus of the Republican effort to elect him president against Federalist John Adams in 1796.

Washington, eager to escape the presidential office, said he would not accept a third term and at the same time took pains to decry "the baneful effects of the Spirit of Party." He had set the style for presidential candidates by not exerting himself in any way during the campaign, and this precedent was followed until 1896, but supporters of Adams and Jefferson used the newspapers and political rallies to criticize the opposition unsparingly. A key factor in the campaign was the work of Virginian John Beckley, a Jeffersonian supporter who had several secretarial jobs in the new government and had made friends in New York and Pennsylvania. Jefferson knew of the campaign to elect him, but in public he only acknowledged his commitment to certain principles he held as fundamental. The strength of Jefferson's opposition to the Federalists was tested in the fall balloting, which showed that Adams was popular in the North and Jefferson in the South. The vote was close, and in the electoral college, Adams won, 71 to 68. By law, as the second-largest vote-getter, Jefferson, who had professed to yearn for retirement from public affairs, became the vice president.

PARTY WARFARE INTENSIFIES

During Adams's presidency (1797–1801), the Federalists raised taxes to support an expanding army and navy and showed hostility toward Napoleon and the French, who were fighting England and most of Europe in a series of bloody battles. Federalists in Congress also passed an anti-French set of laws, the Alien and Sedition Acts, which curbed freedom of the press by making critics of the president liable for fines or imprisonment. All of the prosecutions under the Sedition Act were aimed at Republicans—even a member of Congress was convicted of violating the law because of a letter he wrote critical of the Adams administration. Jefferson seethed as he saw vindictive federal judges guide juries to convictions of newspaper editors who had Republican leanings.

THE "REVOLUTION OF 1800"

During the 1800 campaign, Republicans had a kind of party platform because of a public letter Jefferson wrote explaining what he called "my political faith." In effect, Jefferson said, he wanted a party committed to preserving the Constitution against those who were trying to "monarchize" it by subtle pressures. Jefferson also favored "preserving to the States the powers not yielded" by the Constitution, eliminating the national debt, supporting only a small army and navy, with "little or no diplomatic estab-

lishment." Mindful of the recent prosecutions of Republicans, Jefferson also insisted that his party be pledged to the preservation of every citizen's civil liberties.

The battle lines were now drawn. Republican rallies were held in Philadelphia, New York, Richmond, and other Jeffersonian strongholds, and in the voting Adams came in third behind Jefferson and Aaron Burr. Burr was also a Republican, but he reneged on a deal that would have made him vice president in the regular way. Instead, a 73-to-73 deadlock was resolved in the House of Representatives when Jefferson was chosen as president.

PROMISES TO KEEP

Once in office, Jefferson made his political lieutenant, James Madison, secretary of state and picked a cabinet that would remain intact for eight years. As he promised, Jefferson (supported by an overwhelming Republican majority in Congress) cut taxes, reduced the size of the army and navy, and whittled down the national debt year after year. During his two terms in the White House, Jefferson's control of his party was also apparent in the number of vetoes—zero—as he favored low-key federal programs while trying to keep the country out of war. A vigorous advocate of religious liberty, Jefferson also declared that "a wall of separation" must exist between the church and the state, and he expected the Bill of Rights to keep the wall intact.

Looking back on the era, Jefferson was fond of calling the whole experience "The Revolution of 1800."

By the time Jefferson left the presidency, the Republican Party was capturing statehouses and local elections in every section of the nation. Jefferson had said farmers were God's "chosen people" and in a nation overwhelmingly populated by farmers they responded by giving Jefferson's party sanction in elections at every level, so Madison became the president's hand-picked successor. Chosen as the Republican nominee in a congressional caucus (another innovation, like the two-party system), Madison was elected by the solidarity of the New York–Pennsylvania–Virginia alliance that combined wealth, population, and popularity to exert a political control that lasted for a generation.

While the nation expanded its shipping fleets and cotton and tobacco fields, and began a modest industrial program, the Republicans held on to power as the Federalist Party declined. During the War of 1812 the

Federalists in New England tried to embarrass the Madison administration by holding a convention in Hartford that shaped an arrogant set of demands and threatened a splintering of the Union if Republicans held back. But the sudden and unexpected news from Europe of a peace treaty, followed by General Andrew Jackson's stunning defeat of a crack British army at New Orleans, left the Federalists in an embarrassed crisis of their own making. Thereafter, the Federalists held some important offices in New England, but were clearly a minority party elsewhere and offered only token opposition in presidential elections.

THE ERA OF GOOD FEELING

The Republicans had flourished when embattled, but the election of James Monroe in 1816 was also a peaking of power. Although even a Federalist editor in Boston hailed the coming of "an era of good feeling" under Republican Monroe, sectionalism created a shifting majority for the party in Congress. The Missouri Compromise, hammered out in Congress over the admission of a slave state, showed seams in the party structure that would be tested anew every four years.

The congressional caucus system of nominating a presidential candidate was the first old Republican trapping to go. The Federalist Party offered only token opposition, but the animosities that rose out of sectional and regional differences took a new form within the changing Democratic-Republican majority party. A rising tide of immigration, particularly from Ireland, caused a resentment among some established Americans who thought the Irish Catholics were riffraff. Moreover, the growth of such cities as Buffalo, New York, Philadelphia, and Baltimore left many citizens with little political power because of antiquated property qualifications for voting.

THE FIRST DEMOCRATIC PARTY CONVENTION, 1828

After John Quincy Adams became president in 1824 as a National Republican, his critics formed a phalanx behind the popular Andrew Jackson and declared themselves ready to mobilize voters behind a candidate chosen in open debate. The result was the first political convention, held in Baltimore in 1828, where Jackson was declared the candidate of the

Democrats, who had taken over the old Republican Party in a bloodless coup. These men gloried in their name for the party of Jefferson, and as "Democrats" wanted an expansion of the franchise so that city dwellers who owned no landed property could vote, and they appealed to the new wave of immigrant voters.

The Federalist Party was dead, but resentment among frustrated voters surfaced as parties formed not to urge progressive programs but to give a voice to tensions exacerbated by the religious differences of immigrating hordes. Sporadic violence occurred and was well publicized, giving new life to anti-Masonic cliques and a strong faction that wanted to restrict political activity to native Americans. Religious factionalism grew apace, and as splinter parties flourished in politics, the Mormons and other minority church groups found themselves persecuted and forced to move frequently owing to intolerance exhibited by their neighbors.

The First Political Poster. Andrew Jackson. *Source:* Library of Congress.

Jackson at First Inauguration on Steps of Capitol, 1829. Mural in U.S. Capitol. *Source:* National Archives.

JACKSONIAN "DEMOCRACY" TRIUMPHS

Andrew Jackson appealed to voters eager for a change. His campaign themes included charges that the moneychangers were running the country, and he vowed to wrest control of the nation's banking system from the federally chartered Bank of the United States.

Jackson won handily in 1828 and, like Jefferson, believed in living up to his campaign promises. Jackson vowed he would destroy the hated Bank of the United States, which had become a political football with denunciations regularly expressed by the party faithful except on Wall Street in New York and Beacon Street in Boston, where money power exceeded voting power. In New York, the Tammany organization took form as a local enclave dedicated to electing Jacksonian Democrats and then distributing minor offices to party supporters. With the Federalist Party dead, opposition to the Democrats was sporadic but loud. The antislavery movement had few adherents, but bigoted pleas for anti-Catholic or anti-immigrant votes found a response.

Ultimately, the Whig Party formed out of a coalition of anti-Jackson Democrats, voters who feared the power of the Masonic order, and politicians who exploited anti-Irish sentiment along the Atlantic seaboard.

Neither party, Whig or Democrat, knew how to handle the slavery issue successfully. Senators were chosen by the state legislatures, and in the South the Democrats became the dominant party and through the seniority system exerted controls that were resented by northerners, even those within their party. When a northern spokesman complained about slavery, a southern apologist would remind his colleagues that one of the prices of growing industrialism in the North was unemployment, slum housing, and rising crime rates.

THE WORKINGMAN'S PARTY

Within the Democratic Party a faction grew that championed the laboring man against the bankers and mill owners. In New York state the "barnburners" and

"Locofocos" factions challenged the conventional party members to wrestle with old problems of wealth, poverty, and social justice. "The men of wealth . . . labor, it is said, as well as the farmer and the mechanic," a New York Locofoco Democrat complained. "They do labor . . . but *it is laboring to collect that which others have earned.* . . . If houses are to be erected, it is to be done by the hard hand of labor, in sweat, and toil, and fatigue. The legislature grants no charters for the *workingmen* to build houses without labor and to grow rich without being industrious." Northerner lawmakers listened to such pleas and enlarged the voting rolls by ending the property qualifications for voting, with liberal rules on residence and citizenship that added thousands of Irish and northern European immigrants to the Democrats' strength at the polls. In popular parlance, the party was called "The Democracy"—partly in derision—for the Jacksonians courted voters recently arrived in the country as well as the backwater farmers whose great-grandfathers had crossed the Atlantic a century earlier.

Unlike most of the world in 1830, Americans boasted a high degree of literacy for a nation of farmers. Reading skills were related to religion, for Bible reading was considered a normal part of life on American farmsteads; and thus the ease with which a newspaper could be started in a small community soon made the United States a nation of newspaper readers. Foreign visitors often commented on the variety of newspapers available to the Americans, but most of the travelers also thought the quality of Yankee journalism low or nonexistent. "I read newspapers from all parts of the Union," a visitor from Scotland wrote, "and found them utterly contemptible in point of talent, and dealing in abuse so virulent, as to excite a feeling of disgust, not only with the writers, but with the public which could afford them support."

ROLE OF NEWSPAPERS EXPANDS

In fact, the crossroads town that had a newspaper usually was a hotbed of Democratic sentiment, with a journal that annually blasted the opposition (Whig, Federalist, or Independent) unmercifully until the elections were held. Then quiet resumed, so foreigners were fooled by the outspoken editors. But the American voters were not. No president up to

President Jackson on His Way to the White House. Wood Engraving from *Harper's Weekly,* 1881. *Source:* Library of Congress.

Jackson's time had taken full advantage of the press, although Jefferson knew how to exploit readership in swaying public opinion. But with former editor Amos Kendall at his elbow, Jackson appointed publishers to a variety of petty jobs, including postmasterships, and used newspapers as allies in his battle with bankers and wealthy merchants who loathed the Jacksonian "mobocracy." When James Gordon Bennett made his *New York Herald* into the country's leading daily newspaper with Jacksonian ties, the days of nonpartisan journalism in America were ended.

Although the nation was still barely 60 years old, voters in some areas resented the constant reelection of incumbents and talked of "term limits" as a device to control entrenched politicians. For a time, Jackson was sympathetic to the movement and even suggested that he would support a constitutional amendment limiting presidents to one term, but once in office Jackson dropped the idea. Under Jackson's leadership, the Democrats became unashamedly the party committed to a spoils system. His New York ally, William Marcy, is said to have answered critics of the wholesale ouster of petty bureaucrats from their jobs by saying, "To the victors belong the spoils." The anti-Jackson *National Intelligencer* printed a list of 57 Democratic newspapermen appointed to federal jobs as proof that merit no longer counted when Jackson's crony Amos Kendall handed out "the loaves and fishes of federal office." Kendall, a firebrand newsman who handled Jackson's patronage, dismissed the charges as the complaints of chronic losers.

PARTY COMPOSITION CHANGES

Indeed, the character of the Democratic Party changed during the Jackson years as a new crop of men with little formal education came to dominate the party at local and state levels. By concentrating his attack on the Second Bank of the United States as a demonized institution erected to keep most Americans in debt, Jackson rallied voters to his standard. Wealthy bankers who ate off imported china and drank wine from silver decanters became the villains in Jackson's drama. Perhaps overconfident, the bank's managers decided to seek a new charter through an early maneuver on the eve of the 1832 presidential election. The bank's president, Nicholas Biddle, was a man of uncommon abilities as a financier but a poor judge of political opportunities. Biddle saw to it that many editors of influential newspapers received loans from the bank, hoping to cash in his political capital during the campaign.

THE BATTLE OVER THE BANK

Exposure of the bank's loans backfired, and when Jackson's veto message was printed in nearly every newspaper in the country, the bank was all but finished. The *Boston Post* summed the drama up with its epitaph: "Biddled, Diddled, and Undone."

Encouraged by his victory, Jackson demanded an independent treasury and never got it, but in the meanwhile wildcat banking schemes flourished and helped touch off a panic that would catch Jackson's successor, Martin Van Buren, in the White House. Van Buren, a New York Democrat who was an early booster on the Jackson bandwagon, had been secretary of state briefly in the Jackson cabinet. But Jackson tried to send Van Buren to London as the American minister, and vindictive Whigs in the Senate resolved to block the nomination and humiliate Van Buren—"kill him dead," one Whig said with glee. The Senate rejected Van Buren's nomination, but paid a price. Democrats reacted by making Van Buren a hero second only to Jackson in stature, and at their nominating convention in 1832 they placed the overweight New Yorker (his enemies called Van Buren "his rotundity") on the ticket with Jackson.

During his second term, Jackson stared down the South Carolina Democrats who talked about "nullification" (they would overturn unpopular laws or secede from the Union) with a curt vow that disunion would be met with a hemp rope and scaffold. At the same time, Jackson played to the land hungry in the South and West who wanted the Indian tribes removed beyond the Mississippi. Jacksonian Democrats also flexed their power in statehouses, defeating an antisaloon measure in Massachusetts and pushing bankruptcy laws through in states where banking lobbies had long succeeded in killing such debtor-friendly legislation.

THE WHIG CHALLENGERS

Clearly the Democrats had popular support for these programs, but Jackson's Whig opponents took their name from English history and gloried in being aligned against "King Andrew I." The Whigs accordingly viewed Van Buren as the crown prince, and they made him their target for a political vendetta that concentrated on the outgoing president. Van Buren made it easy for the Whigs to make Jacksonian Democracy the main issue, for early on he declared that he would "tread generally in the footsteps of President Jackson."

The Whig campaign proved to be more sound than

substance. A coalition party at best, the Whig Party allied the Clay Diehards with a strange collection of anti-Jackson merchants and bankers in the northeast, the leftover dissenters from the Anti-Masonic Party, and a rabid band of southerners who thought John C. Calhoun was the smartest man they had ever seen. In time, Daniel Webster threw his hat in the ring from Massachusetts, Hugh White was nominated by the Jackson haters in the Tennessee legislature, and William Henry Harrison's supporters won for him the nomination of the fading Anti-Masonic Party.

Against this field of would-bes and never-wases, Van Buren had no real difficulty. The "Little Magician" proved he still had a mysterious knack at the polls by winning more popular votes than his three opponents combined (761,549 to 736,250 for the other three contenders), and in the electoral college it was all Van Buren, a total of 170 to 124 for the ragtag opposition.

Now Van Buren was on his own, and at his inauguration the new president reviewed the past glories under Jackson and saw a vision of greatness for the United States, under the guidance of the redeeming Democrats. But his basking in glory proved to be short lived.

THE PANIC OF 1837

Van Buren's problems came not only from the depression that hit the country in 1837 but from the growing sentiment that the Democrats had been in power far too long—since Jefferson's triumph in 1800 no Democratic opponent had resided in the White House, and the Whigs were eager to reverse the trend. During that long tenure, Democratic presidents had appointed the territorial officers in the old Northwest Territory and the new lands included in the Louisiana Purchase. Most minor officials in the territories, starting in Ohio and going westward to Iowa, owed their jobs to their Democratic affiliation. These plums of office had been too long out of their hands, the Whigs and old Federalists moaned.

Despite the problems that longevity in office brings,

Van Buren Inauguration. *Source:* Library of Congress.

Van Buren might have survived his tumultuous tenure and held on to the presidency had not the Panic of 1837 deepened day by day. Washington was still a sleepy village except when Congress was in session, but newspapers from around the country told a recurring story of unemployment, falling farm prices, and a drastic shortage of cash. Respected banking houses in the country's largest cities went bankrupt and left thousands of dazed depositors in their wake. Van Buren was a spectator to these portents, but saw no role for the federal government in the worsening crisis. "The less government interferes with private pursuits," Van Buren said, "the better the general prosperity." He did issue an executive order, remarkable for its timing, that established a ten-hour workday on federal projects; but beyond his endorsement for an independent treasury, Van Buren had no nostrums in his magical closet.

Van Buren, the first truly professional politician ever to sit in the White House, faced a crisis after the Panic of 1837 struck the nation. There were bread riots in New York City, where unemployed workers roamed slum streets in search of food. On the wharves from Baltimore southward, thousands of cotton bales stood untouched as cotton prices fell to the unheard quotation of eight cents a pound. The price for tobacco and other farm products also fell to new lows. To suggestions that the federal government should make a gesture by helping the jobless and near-bankrupt, Van Buren said the purse strings of the nation could not be loosened to "help the people make a living." Jackson's dream of an independent treasury bill finally passed Congress, but offered no relief to the hard-pressed merchants or speculators flattened by the contraction of prices and the Democrats' hard-money policies.

THE TROUBLESOME SLAVERY PROBLEM

Approaching the election, Van Buren also had his problems in 1840 compounded by the festering slavery problem. After the Texan Revolution in 1836, the successful rebels—mostly Americans who had been born or raised in the South—courted annexation by the United States. Southerners in the Senate were eager to comply with the Texans' request, but northern sentiment was beginning to take shape, so the question of Texas's admission was postponed. This probably suited Van Buren, for although he was touted as "the Northern President with Southern Principles" in campaign literature, Van Buren was not eager to bring another slave state into the Union. And the slavery issue

was heating up in the North, as evidenced by the formation of the antislavery Liberty Party, which ran a candidate in the 1840 race in an act of symbolic defiance (in the South, the Liberty Party candidate was not mentioned on the ballot).

Henry Clay, the Democratic turncoat who directed the Whigs and was their perennial candidate for president, offered voters an alternative but never a party victory. In contrast to the Democrats, Clay favored the use of federal money for internal improvements such as canals and turnpikes and a protective tariff. Democrats lampooned the Clay program and did their best to imply that Clay was the tool of banks and stockjobbers who pulled strings from their eastern offices. Even though some of the worst of the 1837 panic was over, Clay had no appeal for the Whigs, who desperately wanted to win.

With some reluctance, the leading Whigs finally turned their backs on Clay in 1840 and nominated a military hero, William Henry Harrison, for president. Just as the Democrats had done in 1832, when they had adjourned their convention without proposing a party platform, the Whigs in 1840 made no platform commitments but centered their whole campaign on Harrison. Almost 30 years after he had been made into an Indian fighter and hero, Harrison was offered to voters as the man of the hour. Old-line Whigs were perplexed. To make matters worse, the convention chose a sometime Democrat, John Tyler of Virginia, as Harrison's running mate.

ERA OF SLOGANS BEGINS

Neither Harrison nor Van Buren made any personal effort in the 1840 campaign, but their supporters and newspaper editors in particularly made the race memorable. Led by the energetic Whig editor of the *New York Tribune*, Horace Greeley, Harrison's partisans clamored their slogan, "Tippecanoe and Tyler, Too!" and left Van Buren frustrated by mass defections. Voters were told Harrison was another Jackson—a frontier fighter, an Indian hater, and a friend of the farmer who wanted to move westward and find a place to begin life anew. Democrats tried to meet the slaveowners' pleas for support by issuing campaign literature that vowed Van Buren was committed to the constitutional proposition that "Congress has no power . . . to interfere with or control" slavery. The Democrats issued their platform, which took a swipe at abolitionists ("all efforts" by those opposing slavery, it said, "are calculated to lead to the most alarming consequences") and decried nativist movements aimed at making citizenship harder for immigrants to attain. The United States was "the asylum of the oppressed of every nation" and all efforts "to abridge the present privilege of becoming citizens . . . ought to be resisted with the same spirit which swept the alien and sedition laws from our statute-books."

Van Buren, relying on the voters' sense of history, took that platform plan so seriously that he had the Kentucky and Virginia resolutions of 1798 reprinted and distributed as campaign literature. The Whigs insisted Harrison would restore prosperity and welcomed the remnants of the Anti-Masonic Party into their fold with enthusiasm. Van Buren, ever the professional politician, could look at the map and count the electoral votes, and thought he saw a sweeping victory in his crystal ball.

But nothing could stop the Harrison–Tyler ticket, not even the Democrats' willingness to give away as much hard cider as the Whigs offered near polling places on election day. The outcome was full of surprises, for Illinois (then considered part of "the West") went for Van Buren, but "the little Magician" lost his charm at home, and New York was captured by Harrison. Pennsylvania, once the keystone in the Democratic alliance, gave its electoral votes to Harrison by a mere 239 ballots. In the final electoral voting, it was not even close (234 for Harrison, 60 for Van Buren), and it seemed to Greeley and his Whig friends that the Democrats' hold on the presidency had been broken.

Harrison's health was a factor the Whigs had not counted on; he died after only a month in office, and for the first time a vice president was sworn in to succeed the man elected to hold office for four years. John Tyler, like Harrison a native of Virginia, was in some ways more of a Democrat than many of the delegates at the Baltimore convention where Van Buren was nominated; but with this difference: Tyler was not ashamed of his proslavery feelings—and if the Senate wanted to add a slave state to the Union, that was no problem for Tyler.

True to his origins, Tyler was too much of a states' right politican to be embraced by the Whigs, and much to his annoyance, both Democrats and Whigs in Washington began to call him "His Accidency." Clay, still a leading power in the Senate, pushed through bills creating another nationally chartered bank, and twice Tyler vetoed the measures. After the second veto, Whigs in Congress held a caucus and voted Tyler

Democratic Campaign, 1844. *Source:* New York Public Library.

out of their party, and most of his cabinet turned in their resignations.

Democrats saw the Tyler presidency crumbling and in high glee predicted a victory for their party in the 1844 contest. Tyler, hoping perhaps he could return to his old place in the Democratic Party, decided to risk his chances by working for the annexation of Texas. In the regular fashion, a treaty of annexation required a two-thirds majority in the Senate, but Tyler hoped for a compromise.

TEXAS QUESTION DIVIDES PARTY

Southern leaders wanted no part of Tyler, but they did want Texas in the Union as a slave state. Van Buren, too much of a man of principle to be a good politician, wrote a damaging letter opposing Texas annexation and was soon out of the running for the presidential nomination in 1844. James K. Polk, a former speaker of the House of Representatives, had returned to Tennessee but lost the governor's race and openly solicited the vice presidential nomination. Tyler had some friends in the Baltimore convention hall, but the two-thirds rule (which required that a candidate be approved by 66% of all the delegates) was revived to stop the Tyler bandwagon and ruin Van Buren chances too. On the first ballot, Van Buren was ahead, but there were scattered votes for Tyler and Lewis Cass (who had much western support).

Ballot after ballot at the Democratic Convention produced no nominee, until Polk's name suddenly was thrust forward and for the first time in history a "dark horse" was nominated. Polk's name had not been mentioned until the eighth ballot, but when the New Hampshire delegation swung his way on the ninth ballot, a stampede followed. In derision, the Whigs shouted, "Who is James K. Polk?" Clay was their nominee, and they confidently believed the Kentuckian's third try for the presidency would be successful.

Party men, including Andrew Jackson, thought otherwise. Polk had a reputation for hard work and was that singular kind of candidate who believed that campaign promises were a pact with the people who elected him. The Texas question became moot, too, because President Tyler had managed to sidestep the Senate by maneuvering Texas into the Union by a joint resolution of Congress (which only required a simple majority) on his last day in office.

Polk was all for the Texas statehood boom, even if it meant that eventually Texas might split itself into four separate states. But Polk and the Democrats were riding the crest of an expansionist wave, and if the bel-ligerent Mexicans were afraid, their threat that annexation meant war was not taken too seriously on Capitol Hill.

President Polk made it clear in his acceptance speech that if elected, he was going to serve only one term and step down. Unique as that gesture was, Polk never minced words. Anxious to avoid a shooting war, Polk sent an emissary to Mexico, with an offer to buy the disputed territory; but the incumbent Mexican president was overthrown in a coup, and anti-American sentiment made any kind of deal with the United States impossible for practical politicians in the Mexican republic. Frustrated, Polk then sent American troops to Texas, to take positions in territory that the Mexicans claimed was part of their republic. Soon the shooting started (April 1846), and when Polk reported to Congress that "American blood has been shed on American soil," the rush to declare war was on.

The Mexican War was brief, but costly. Over 10,000 American troops died of disease, while less than 2,000 were casualties on the battlefield. But the aftermath of the war was the addition of all the Mexican lands above the Rio Grande and Gila River including parts of New Mexico, Colorado, and Wyoming, plus all of Arizona, Nevada, Utah, and California. Thus the Manifest Destiny regaled in newspaper editorials and on the floors of Congress became a reality, for by the treaty of 1848 the United States stretched from the Atlantic to the Pacific and from the Gulf of Mexico to the finally settled Canadian boundary. Democrats claimed the credit, of course, for implementing Manifest Destiny, but there were critics who denounced the whole affair as an unconstitutional business, among them Whig congressman Abraham Lincoln.

Lincoln proved to be a one-term congressman, not by choice; but Polk was a one-term president by choice. John Quincy Adams, now a congressman, said Polk was a president who worked "like a galley slave." Bernard DeVoto, a historian of the era, said Polk was more than a hard worker. "His integrity was absolute," DeVoto wrote. "He was the only 'strong' president between Jackson and Lincoln."

There was only one fly in the Mexican treaty ointment. When Congress debated the Treaty of Guadalupe Hidalgo, an antislavery Democrat from Pennsylvania, David Wilmot, had borrowed language from the Northwest Ordinance to call for the banning of slavery in the newly acquired western territory. "Neither slavery, nor involuntary servitude," would be allowed in any of the former Mexican territories except Texas. The provision was voted down, but the cat was out of the bag—the Democratic Party had a serious sectional split that would fester for more than a decade before it finally tore the party apart.

Typical of the southern wing's attitude was the idea fostered by a Senate faction, and prodded by Secretary of State James Buchanan, that the United States ought to go all the way and grab Mexico while the grabbing was good. The northern delegations could not stomach such a blatant attempt to extend slavery; but serious lawmakers in both parties let it be known that in time Manifest Destiny would bring Cuba and Santo Domingo into the orbit controlled by Uncle Sam.

Slavery issues thus began to dominate national politics and made other issues secondary. In the 1848 election, as Democrats took Polk at his word and let him retire, they nominated a northern man who had a southern following, General Lewis Cass, as his successor. Cass was now a senator from Michigan and a strong believer in the new-fangled doctrine of "squatter sovereignty" that the expansionists (and proslavery crowd) pushed. The point was to drop the Missouri Compromise boundary line that forbade slavery above the 36°30′ limits approved in 1820, which the northern leaders considered as a permanent fixture. "Squatter sovereignty" would allow the inhabitants of a territory to decide whether their country was to come into the Union free or as a slave state. The issue was too hot a potato for the platform committee to swallow, so the 1848 party program simply denied that Congress had any power to interfere with slavery in the existing states, and the delegates rejected a plank that would have tied Congress's hands regarding slavery in the territories.

THE NORTH–SOUTH DIVISION

The Whigs were unable to pass a party plank asserting that Congress *could* control slavery in the territories, but their candidate was General Zachary Taylor, who was once a slaveholder and now a war hero. Between Cass and Taylor, the citizens who worried about opening the western territories to slavery had little to choose. Antislavery Democrats, called "barnburners" by the press, walked out of the Democratic convention and held a rump meeting of their own that proceeded to nominate Van Buren as their candidate. Ultimately the dissenting Democrats, antislavery Whigs, and other northern voters who were disgusted with both the major parties combined to form the Free Soil Party, and before their patchwork convention Van Buren's nomination was ratified.

As the Democrats had seen in 1840, a military hero can tickle the American voter into rationalizing that

battlefield leadership is an immense asset for a presidential candidate. In 1848 "Old Rough-and-Ready," as the troops had called Taylor, was the darling of voters, who seemed indifferent to the bitter quarreling on Capitol Hill. Taylor won the popular vote and bested Cass, 167 to 123, in the electoral college, where Van Buren received not a single vote.

Although his electoral count was nil, Van Buren had indirectly helped elect Taylor, who kept silent about the slavery in the territories issue. In New York, Van Buren and Cass had a combined vote 16,000 better than Taylor, but the split allowed the Whig to win the Empire State; Pennyslvania also defected to Taylor. Democrats knew they could not win without those key states, even though they had a firm grip on the southern results. Indeed, the "Little Magician" had lost his touch, but the former president fired a last shot by denouncing the southern extremists who were insisting that the Missouri Compromise was unconstitutional and a hindrance to western development.

To worsen matters, southern Democrats (led by Calhoun) called for explicit ways to end "acts of aggression" against the South. The immediate excuse for the southerners' manifesto ("An address of the southern delegates") presented by 69 members of Congress (all but two were Democrats) blasted a pending bill that would prohibit slave trade in the District of Columbia. The aggressive acts, the manifesto claimed, were the prohibition on slaves in western territories and stumbling blocks thrown in the way of slaveowners who tried to recover runaway slaves in the North.

To some Democrats, the southerners were seen as mere gadflies who bothered party harmony but could not damage the party permanently. After all, Iowa had recently been admitted as a free state, and most of the state's major officeholders carried on as before, because they had been appointed by Democratic presidents. California and Utah were gaining population rapidly, and if precedent were followed, these western states would send four more Democratic senators to Washington to solidify the party base in the upper chamber. Wisconsin and Minnesota were also ready to enter the Union, and they had Democratic appointees ready to make the leap to statehood. At the time, however, there were 15 free states and 15 slave states, so the Senate seats were a prize worth fighting for and every politician, North and South, well knew it.

A SAVING COMPROMISE

The scene was set for the greatest debates ever held in the Senate. Clay was back in the chamber, ready to shape a compromise that would please both sections and anxious to avoid an impasse that would damage the national prosperity following in the wake of the California gold discoveries. Late in January 1850 Clay introduced a series of conciliatory resolutions, with the objective of removing the sectional tension, and for the next seven months the Senate battle waxed and waned. Southerners were already grumbling about seceding from the Union, and their spokesman was the aged John C. Calhoun. Daniel Webster, a Whig like Clay, was also ready to enter the fray, not as a belligerent, "not as a Massachusetts man, not as a Northern man, but as an American." Webster's position was that there was no need to dredge up the volatile issue of legislative exclusion of slavery because the soil and climate in the western states made slavery there a practical impossibility.

Southern leaders ignored Webster's main point and seemed to welcome a constitutional crisis. While Clay's compromise was discussed, first Calhoun died and then President Taylor was in his grave. Democratic Senators Cass and Stephen Douglas came forward in favor of Clay's compromise, and in September 1850 the total package was enacted piecemeal with the blessing of Whig President Millard Fillmore. California was admitted as a free state, but New Mexico and Utah as territories were left to be "received into the Union, with or without slavery, as their constitutions may prescribe." These provisions angered many southerners, who were soothed by passage of a Fugitive Slave Act, which toughened laws dealing with the return of runaway slaves, but upset by a companion law that abolished the slave trade in the District of Columbia.

Within days, friends and foes of the Fugitive Slave Act learned that passage of the law, as a compromise measure, had settled little. Whig editor Horace Greeley blasted the law, which he blamed on northern "Doughfaced Democrats" who lacked principle, while *De Bow's Review* in New Orleans saw the law as an entering wedge that would lead to full-scale emancipation. "The final act is not yet, but soon," the southern journal predicted. "There is a precedent in the British [emancipation]. . . . *They will use the precedent. We know the rest.*"

Although the firebrands in Congress condemned the settlement as a sellout of the South, voters below the Mason–Dixon Line soon showed they approved of the measures by rejecting radical candidates in Alabama, Georgia, and Mississippi who had denounced the 1850 compromise. Moderate Democrats and proslavery Whigs seemed to be gaining the upper hand as they made more gains in the 1852 elections,

Winfield Scott Handbill in German. Because of the Large Numbers of German Immigrants, Political Posters Were Often Issued in English and German. *Source:* Smithsonian Institution.

when the Democratic convention nominated Franklin Pierce on the 49th ballot—a clear victory for those who wanted explicit endorsement of the compromise legislation. Whigs went for another military hero, Winfield Scott, and also endorsed the compromise. And for the first time at a national political gathering—the Free Soil Party convention—there was support for homestead legislation that would allow settlers to earn free farmsteads on public lands. Soon the so-called Homestead plank was stolen by the Whigs and condemned by the southern Democrats, but the idea of "voting yourself a farm" became a political issue with strong appeal to landless voters.

HARMONY—AT A PRICE

After Pierce triumphed over his Whig opponent, crushing Scott in the electoral college by 254 to 40 and carrying 27 states to 4 from Scott, a temporary lull in the sectional tension settled on the land. The over-heated political rhetoric of the sectional drama gave way to a speculative boom in real estate as railroad building took the center of the national stage. Chicago, a prairie outpost in 1832, was a burgeoning metropolis 20 years later as the hub of a rail network linking eastern markets to western farms. Canal building suddenly became old-fashioned as iron rails created a dramatic and swift way to move people and goods at speeds of up to 50 miles an hour on solid roadbeds.

Lawmakers were aware of the transportation revolution taking place, and one Democratic senator was ahead of the pack—Stephen A. Douglas of Illinois. Short of stature (he was five feet, four inches tall) but an adroit politician, Douglas was eager to help the Illinois Central Railroad extend its reach through subsidies, and as chairman of the Senate committee on territories he supported plans for a Pacific railroad that would link California with a Mississippi terminal. Unlike the southern Democrats, Douglas favored action on a homestead bill and had ardently supported the Compromise of 1850.

Douglas believed that the tinderbox threatening the Union was the status of slavery in the western territories, and as chairman of a powerful committee he was able to promote the "squatter sovereignty" that Cass and other northern Democrats had pushed after the Mexican War ended. Using the more dignified title of "popular sovereignty," Douglas sought to make self-determination in the territories a cardinal issue within the Democratic Party, for he knew that southern extremists would never accept the idea that any territory had a constitutional right to prohibit slavery.

THE LID COMES OFF: THE KANSAS–NEBRASKA ACT

Confident that he knew where the necessary votes could be found, early in January 1854 Douglas introduced his Kansas–Nebraska bill, hardly aware of the bombshell he was tossing into the nation's political lap. President Pierce realized that the issue was touchy, but was convinced that the Douglas solution deserved his support. Northern Democrats, however, quickly perceived the implications of Douglas's bill, for it would repeal the Missouri Compromise and thus rip the lid off the ban on slavery above the 36°30' that leading northern men considered sacrosanct. All hell broke loose inside the Democratic Party as a group labeling themselves "Independent Democrats" broadcast an appeal for defeat of the pending bill because it destroyed the truce they believed had been permanently set in place by the 1820 compromise.

Leading Democrats and Free Soilers, including Salmon P. Chase and Charles Sumner, castigated Douglas and his bill in "An Appeal of the Independent Democrats," which hundreds of northern newspapers printed. Soon bonfire rallies were fashionable in many northern cities, where Douglas and his proposal were burned in contempt. Although the firestorm of protest in the North alarmed moderates, southern extremists were also upset, and Douglas and the moderate Democrats found themselves assailed from all sides. As professional politicians with thick skins, Douglas and his northern allies thought that once the bill passed and the new territories decided on their own whether they would be free or slave states, the public outcry would wither away.

Instead, the Kansas–Nebraska Act, though it passed and was signed by President Pierce in May 1854, proved to be a watershed event in American history. Opponents held mass meetings in Michigan, Wisconsin, Ohio, and all the way up the coast in New England, so that by the fall of 1854 a new political force was created out of the Democrats' misjudged policy. Former Free Soilers, antislavery Whigs, and splinter groups from the nativist Know-Nothing Party banded together to elect state governors, legislators, and a handful of congressmen—all committed to overturning the "popular sovereignty" concept that Douglas had carefully guided into law. Within a year, the newly named Republican Party was gaining converts from the northern Democrats and talking about running a presidential candidate in 1856.

A PARTING OF COMPANY

Sectional politics now dominated every move in Washington. The northern Democrats favored a railroad route to the Pacific that would begin in Illinois, while southern Democrats wanted a link to the West starting from New Orleans. William Cullen Bryant, long a Democratic stalwart with his *New York Evening Post*, led an exodus from the party of Jefferson and Jackson to promote the Republican candidates. Already in the Republican camp, Whig editor Horace Greeley used his *New York Tribune* and its weekly edition to castigate "the Democracy" for the party's reactionary defense of slavery—or so it seemed to northern citizens who had never felt threatened before by the abstraction of distant slavery.

The moderate *New York Times* told readers a fundamental shift had occurred and blamed the Democrats. "The political equilibrium between Slavery and Freedom is to be destroyed, and the slave-holding interest is to dominate in public councils with perpetual and relentless sway," the *Times* predicted. "When the present members of Congress were elected, no human being in the Union *dreamed* that they would be required to vote for, or against, the repeal of the Missouri Compromise. The project has been sprung on the country suddenly and treacherously."

What made the Kansas–Nebraska Act such a castastrophe for the Democrats? In the United States, almost from the outset, political questions had hinged on the effect policies had on the future. Jefferson and Madison formed a political party to keep the new nation from becoming a carbon copy of the British government, and all through its history up to 1854, the Democrats had appealed to the new voters who wanted their government to be low key, low tax, and noninterfering in ordinary affairs. The Kansas–Nebraska Act was viewed as a threat because it seemed to give new life to slavery, at the time when popular ideas held that slavery had become an anachronism, except in the South. In the rest of the world, slavery had been outlawed by nation after nation; and what disturbed many southerners was the recent announcement in Madrid that slavery would soon be prohibited in Cuba. That was coming too close for comfort, leading southerners decided, and they began a public discussion of plans to annex "the pearl of the Caribbean" either by purchase or by conquest.

In short, the Democrats appeared to have stopped being a party committed to future progress and had become a haven for reaction. A farmer in remote Maine who had voted for Democrats all his life now had to consider what his party stood for.

AN UNCERTAIN FUTURE

Faith in the Democratic Party was not dead, however, for the 1856 presidential campaign provided a temporary lull in the sectional political struggle. Despite troubling news from the Kansas frontier, where guerrilla warfare surfaced, the Know-Nothing Party was not ready to merge with the Republicans, and they nominated former President Millard Fillmore as their standard-bearer. The Republicans met in Philadelphia and drew up a platform that urged the admission of Kansas as a free state, endorsed the Pacific railroad plans, and insisted that Congress had the power to prohibit slavery in the territories. In the nominating process, dominated by former Democrats and Whigs, the new party chose John C. Frémont, the "Pathfinder" who was now a California senator, as their nominee.

Eager to get on with the business of railroad building and the export of American cotton to Europe, the Democrats looked for a safe candidate and found one in the bachelor minister to Great Britain, James Buchanan.

THE CRITICAL 1856 ELECTION

The campaign battle was far from pretty. Republicans concentrated their attack on the extremists who were talking about seceding from the Union if Frémont were elected. Firebrand editors in Charleston and other southern cities urged lawmakers to prohibit Frémont's name from appearing on their ballots (and in some cases they succeeded). Democrats promised that Buchanan would be a peacemaker, for he came from a northern state and had been in England when all the fuss over the Kansas–Nebraska Act had tormented the nation. In fact, however, Buchanan proved to be another "northern man with southern principles," and despite the campaign issues of "Bleeding Kansas" and "Black Republicanism," Buchanan carried all the slave states except Maryland (plus five free states), and thus he won the election with 174 electoral votes to 114 (all from free states).

Buchanan tried to calm southern fears and northern anxieties in his inaugural address by appealing for calm deliberations and support for popular sovereignty. He might have kept the nation on an even keel with his hands-off policy (the federal government was to take a neutral stance on the slavery issue, since the Kansas–Nebraska Act had settled the territorial question). But in 1857 the Supreme Court handed down its mandate in the *Dred Scott* decision, by declaring that the Missouri Compromise had always been a usurpation and that slaves "had no rights the white man is bound to respect." This judicial slap at the antislavery movement and the Republican Party caused another uproar and ranks as one of the most political and harmful decisions ever made by the High Court.

Suddenly the fighting in Kansas, the John Brown raids on Harper's Ferry, and the financial panic in 1857 upset all the good intentions of the Buchanan administration. In the off-year elections for Congress, Republicans made huge gains in the North, and Democrats living above the Mason–Dixon Line left the party in droves. When Senator Douglas, up for reelection in Illinois, agreed to debate the Republican Abraham

Buchanan Inauguration. *Source:* Library of Congress.

Lincoln in 1858, national attention focused on their campaign. How many Democrats left their party after Lincoln's "House Divided" speech cannot be known, but the victory of Douglas was not dazzling. Instead, Lincoln became a converted Whig who was now a leading spokesman for the Republican Party.

AFTERMATH OF LINCOLN–DOUGLAS DEBATES

In fact, Douglas had opened a fissure in his party support when he said at the Freeport debate that "slavery cannot exist a day or an hour anywhere, unless it is supported by local police regulation" created by a state legislature. Douglas's "Freeport doctrine" was widely denounced in the South as backtracking, and from that time onward, Douglas's southern support declined until it almost disappeared.

Buchanan proved to be an ineffective leader, for he sympathized with the slaveholders but realized that the North was fed up with any policy that would permit slavery to expand in the frontier territories. So Buchanan filled his cabinet with southerners or southern sympathizers and let the fight continue in Congress. There, in February 1860, Democratic Senator

Jefferson Davis from Mississippi introduced a set of resolutions guaranteeing a foothold for slavery in the West, with a pledge that the federal government would provide "all needful protection" for slavery in the territories. Bitter debates ensued, with northern Democrats shouting at southern colleagues, and though the resolutions passed, the anger did not subside. More Democrats switched their allegiance to the Republicans, cutting down the majorities that had once been safely Democratic.

Buchanan lacked the courage needed to help mend the growing splits within his party. Well intentioned but inept, he watched the proceedings from the safety of the White House, while southern "fire-eaters" warned the North that any disturbing of the status quo would cause wholesale secession by every slave state from Delaware to Florida. Greeley, eager to play an influential role in the 1860 Republican convention, assured readers that the southern talk was "all bluster" and decided that a former Democrat from Missouri (Edward Bates) would be the best choice for his party as the Republican nominee.

Meanwhile, the Democrats favoring Douglas found they had made a strategic mistake in the selection of Charleston for their nominating convention. Angry southern Democrats believed they had been betrayed

Buchanan Riding the "Slavery Monster." *Source:* National Archives.

by Douglas's commitment to squatter sovereignty, since that doctrine implied that slavery could be denied by territorial conventions seeking admission to the Union. Radical Democrats blamed Douglas for a law that indicated slavery was not an absolute possibility in the admission process, and they proceeded to make such an uproar that no final action on a presidential nominee was possible. The Douglas faction created a platform favoring nonintervention by Congress in territorial constitutions, praised the *Dred Scott* decision, and held out the peace pipe to the South by stamping approval on a plan to annex Cuba (still in Spanish hands, but threatened by a revolt).

SPLITTING INTO TWO CAMPS

Nothing could appease the southern fire-eaters, however, and after 57 ballots without a presidential nominee, they stormed out of the convention hall, determined to pick a candidate who would endorse their hard line on slavery. The Douglas delegates reassembled in Baltimore in mid-June and proceeded to nominate the "Little Giant," thus entering a wedge in the party structure that was confirmed ten days later when the dissenters nominated John C. Breckinridge as their candidate. Slavery in the territories was con-

sidered a *sine qua non* in their platform, and, of course, the hasty annexation of Cuba was urged.

The Cuban annexation crisis never occurred, for the Spanish put down the rebellious local militia and proceeded with their own program of slave emancipation. But the presidential election was clouded further by the third convention of former Whigs, former Know-Nothings, moderate Democrats, and Unionists-at-any-price who called a convention of their newborn Constitutional Unionist Party. Their platform condemned any political party that favored a sectional split and called for a reconciliation program that would leave the status quo in place.

Meanwhile, Republicans had convened in May, where the leading candidates proceeded to drop by the wayside until a boom for Lincoln swept the Chicago Wigwam (built specially for the Republican convention). Lincoln won on the third ballot at a convention where the platform explicitly denied western territories the right to enter the Union as slave states. Taking the opposite view from that of Democrats at their Charleston meeting, the Republicans said that the Missouri Compromise was the only proper solution for their sectional conflict. Moreover, the Republican platform called for the building of a Pacific railroad, endorsed the "free farm" homestead bill, and gave backhanded support to a protective tariff.

The ensuing campaign was unlike anything the country had ever seen. Douglas defied tradition and made speeches, but the other candidates let friends and supporters do their talking. In the South, the legislatures prevented the Republican ticket from appearing on ballots for the presidential race. William Lowndes Yancey and other extremists loudly proclaimed that if Lincoln were elected, the entire South should secede from the Union immediately after the results were known.

"The Democratic Party has utterly fallen to pieces," the pro-Lincoln *New York Times* proclaimed on July 3, 1860. A day later the *Times* insisted that President Buchanan "has given the finishing touches to the degradation of his party, and has made respectable persons ashamed to confess that they ever belonged to it." The candidacies of Douglas and Breckinridge, the *Times* insisted, caused sensible voters to realize "that worse things might happen than the election of Lincoln."

Traditionally, highly partisan newspapers carried the main brunt of the campaign, but the three-way split of opponents to the Republican ticket made Lincoln's victory in the electoral college a virtual certainty. An avalanche of northern support overwhelmed the moderates and the fire-eaters, but left Lincoln with far less than a majority of the popular vote. Douglas led the opposition, but Lincoln had l,866,000 votes to 2,811,000 for his three rivals. In the electoral college, however, Lincoln carried most of the North and garnered 180 votes; Breckinridge had 72 (every slave state), while Douglas had only 12. John Bell, the Constitutional Unionist, won the border states and 39 electoral votes.

FIRE-EATERS THREATEN UNION

Reckless talk forced leading men in South Carolina to either "put up or shut up." President Buchanan offered nothing in the way of leadership and thus consigned his presidency to the dustbin of history. But more important than the ineptitude of the Democratic president was the chimera of Charleston citizens, who huzzahed when South Carolina went out of the Union as soon as Lincoln's election was confirmed. On December 20 the firebrand state legislature voted to quit the Union, and by February 1 South Carolina had been joined by six other slave states, and public attention in the North centered on President-elect Lincoln. Buchanan pouted in the White House, content to see the Union dissolve and offer nothing in the way of leadership. Douglas, exhausted by the campaign, was ill and soon in his grave. Former Democrats in the Congress resigned *en masse* as the Confederate States of America was proclaimed to exist from an Alabama base, and in New York business tycoons worried about their investments in southern properties and cotton bales in particular. Democrat August Belmont bemoaned Lincoln's election as local newspapers predicted the loss of over $200 million if the wounds of secession were not quickly healed.

No such healing process took place. Instead, the crisis exacerbated as Lincoln issued cautious but moderate statements, Buchanan did next to nothing, and the secessionists pushed plans for a war by mobilizing men and resources, including vast hordes of arms held in seized federal arsenals. Northern Democrats, shaken by the election results, looked to Virginia as a key to the dilemma. If Virginia would not join in the seceding procession, leading Democrats in Pennsylvania, Indiana, and Illinois predicted, the whole crisis might blow over without a single shot ever fired.

There matters stood when Lincoln was inaugurated. In his first speech as president, Lincoln held out the olive branch. Lincoln reminded the South that he had repeatedly said he had no intention of interfering "with the institution of slavery in the Sates where it exists." He added: "I believe I have no lawful right to do so, and I have no inclination to do so." Whether Lincoln's words penetrated far in the South is problematical. The decision to leave the Union and fight had too much appeal to the hotheads in control, and public opinion supported them.

Thus the Democratic Party lost its base, and some of its best men, and slipped out of its major role in American politics from 1861 until 1933. For despite an occasional election that gave control of Congress to Democrats over that 72-year period, and even with Cleveland and Wilson in the White House for 16 of those years, the Democratic Party was on the defensive, and its Jeffersonian roots withered and almost died.

The chief factors in the party's near-demise were the Civil War and its aftermath. Initially, the Republicans were a new party without a positive philosophy but enormous support at the northern polls. The 1860 platform, with its Homestead and Pacific Railroad planks, had great appeal to citizens eager to expand their horizons in an atmosphere of economic betterment. Able Republican congressmen guided the platform into law, unfettered by southern obstructionists, so that a railroad network soon created a northern transportation system of vast potential. Buffalo, Cleveland, and Chicago became major cities and Republican strongholds, and as the party solidified urban support, it secured the loyalties of an overwhelming farm vote.

THE WAR STARTS
WITH DEMOCRATS IN TROUBLE

The Democrats were in disarray after the firing on Fort Sumter. Republicans successfully exploited latent fears that Democrats might be disloyal, and once-solid Democratic groups in Iowa, Illinois, Wisconsin, Indiana, and Ohio dissolved when attacked by a phalanx of Republican newspapers. In Iowa, the *Des Moines Register* was eager to castigate Democrats as "copperheads," devious men who secretly favored a Confederate victory. "All Democrats may not be copperheads," an Iowa newsman wrote, "but all copperheads are Democrats!" Thus branded, Democrats switched parties in midwestern states by the thousands, particularly after the length of casualty lists grew and Republican candidates at every level proclaimed the Democratic Party was "the party of treason."

Lacking a strong leader, the Democrats failed to fight back effectively. The overwhelming number of northern Democrats soon spoke of themselves as "Peace Democrats," loyal to the Union but ready to criticize the conduct of the war. When Democrats made inroads in the 1862 congressional elections, alarmed Republicans renewed their charges of disloyalty. To give their accusations force, Republicans saw to it that Democrats who might have a following were discredited. A former Democatic senator from Iowa came back from a diplomatic post in South America and was thrown in jail as a suspected traitor. Also in Iowa, a Democratic candidate for Congress in the 1862 election was arrested and quickly moved to Washington, where he was jailed on an unspecified charge.

"COPPERHEAD" LABEL
HURTS DEMOCRATS

Other midwestern Democrats, some of them former officeholders or newspapermen, including a recently elected congressman from Illinois, were treated similarly and jailed in the notorious Old Capitol prison in the nation's capital. In an era when fistfights often punctuated a campaign, the editor of the Circleville, Ohio, *Watchman* found himself on a bread-and-water diet after he lambasted the local Republican postmaster as "a traitor, a thief, to the extent of his very limited brains, and if he has any of that article, they are the brains of a slimy viper!" Name-calling, once a rather harmless appendage of every election, became cause for sending an outspoken legislator or editor to jail.

Then the election of 1862 was over, the Republicans won a safe majority in Congress, and the jailed Democrats were released, most of them never having been charged with a crime or allowed bail under habeas corpus.

Such events undermined the Democrats, and by the end of 1863, the once-safe majorities in the Old Northwest were gone and would not return for three generations. Republican leadership in Congress, still committed to a liberal, progressive program as outlined in their 1860 platform, continued with a reform agenda. A landmark piece of legislation, passed in July 1862, was the Morrill Act, which created financing for all state agricultural colleges. Added to the Homestead Act, which allowed settlers to claim 160-acre farms for a nominal filing fee, and the Pacific Railroad Act, the first Congress when Republicans had full control passed laws that made it one of the most progressive sessions ever held.

DESPITE WAR, AN ELECTION IS HELD

The only thing that kept the Democratic Party from total dissolution by the time of the 1864 presidential elections was the course of the war. Lincoln had tried to find a successful general, and one by one they had proven to be inert, or loudmouthed, or drunk and deficient. This led Republicans to worry, and some even suggested that the 1864 election might be suspended under the War Powers implied in the Constitution. Lincoln would not encourage their cowardly plans, however, and his main politicking was the draft of an Emancipation Proclamation—an order that freed slaves in the territories already under Union control. In December 1862 the Confederate army led by General Robert E. Lee slipped out of a Union trap with Union losses double those inflicted on Lee's smaller army. Stung by public criticism, on January 1, 1863, Lincoln issued the proclamation, to become effective immediately.

Lincoln's proclamation had little practical effect in freeing slaves, and none at all beyond Union lines, but the statement gave heart to Republicans who saw the war as an ideological battle on behalf of human freedom. Democrats could only reply that they wanted "the Constitution as it is, the Union as it was," and with that rallying cry they held a nominating convention in Chicago and nominated ousted General George B. McClellan as their presidential candidate. In a bow to their own extremists, the Democrats adopted a platform plank that called for immediate cessation of hostilities and resurrection of the Federal Union as it existed in 1860. McClellan accepted the nomination but disavowed the "Peace Now" plank and found a solid base of support in areas where the long casualty lists and resistance to draft laws stirred hopes for a Democratic victory. Indeed, Lincoln himself is said to have predicted to intimate friends that he would lose the election.

But Lincoln did not lose. The Union Army shook off its plague of repeated defeats in the spring of 1864 when General William Tecumseh Sherman led his forces from Chattanooga toward Atlanta. Sherman's army entered the rubble of Atlanta on September 1, 1864, for a sorely needed Union victory; voting in the presidential election during the ensuing weeks was influenced by Sherman's triumph, which offset the heavy losses of Grant's troops as Richmond remained a Confederate stronghold under Lee's command.

Democratic hopes were buoyed by dissension within the Republican ranks. Angry congressmen called for a second Republican convention to replace Lincoln on the party ticket, after the president had used a pocket veto to pigeonhole a bill that would have provided harsh terms for reconstruction of the shattered Confederacy. And Republican leaders, fearful that war weariness might cause voters to defect, had called their convention a National Union gathering, soft-pedaled the obvious Republican format, and added a War Democrat to the ticket as Lincoln's running mate—Andrew Johnson.

JOHNSON TOO LENIENT FOR REPUBLICANS

The presidential election then was reduced to an issue of loyalty. Union campaigners stressed the need for a message to troops at the front—insisting that a vote for McClellan was little more than a stab in the back. Whole battalions of troops were furloughed by Union commanders to return home and vote, and the so-called soldier vote was a strong factor in McClellan's defeat, for he lost by 400,000 votes in the popular count and perhaps 600,000 soldier ballots were counted. A regular visitor at the telegraphic offices in Washington, Lincoln learned that he had won in a close popular ballot but had easily triumphed in the electoral college, 212 to 21.

Events of the next four years set up a Republican bastion that left Democrats on the defensive well into the next century. After the war ended and Lincoln was assassinated, the Radical Republicans soon ended their brief "honeymoon" with the former Democrat, Johnson. Both Lincoln and Johnson favored a mild series of measures to bring the old Confederacy back into the Union with little delay or punishment for the

southern miscreants. To the Radicals, who were eager to keep the Republicans in power, the idea of amnesty and quick restoration had no place in their plans. A running battle between President Johnson and Congress finally settled into an impeachment struggle, centering on General Ulysses S. Grant. Grant, a former Democrat, was appointed by Johnson as his secretary of war, but Congress made the molehill into a huge mountain by insisting Johnson had violated their law dealing with cabinet succession.

Johnson was barely vindicated by the Senate in mid-May 1868, when his conviction on the trumped-up charges was avoided by a single vote. A few days later, the Republican nominating convention met in Chicago and chose Grant as their presidential choice. Democrats wanted nothing to do with Johnson and met in New York City to select Horatio Seymour, former governor of New York, as their presidential choice. Francis Blair, a former slaveholder, was added to the ticket as Seymour's running mate.

The Democrats immediately fell into the kind of trap that became a political morass for the rest of the century—their platform took one direction and the delegates would nominate a candidate headed in the opposite direction. In July 1868 the Democratic platform tried to accentuate the differences in the two parties by repudiating the "hard-money" Republican plank that called for redemption of federal war bonds in gold, while the "soft-money" Democrats called for redemption of the national debt in paper money "Greenbacks" that often sold at a discount. Congressman George Pendleton of Ohio became the spokesman for Democrats, who suggested that Wall Street was running the Republican Party to please the rich and the well born.

WALL STREET ENTERS PARTY BATTLES

The trouble was that Seymour was a New York hard-money man, friendly to the banking interests that held millions of dollars in government bonds and eager to redeem them in gold. So in one sense the Republicans had their opponents on the run from the start of the campaign.

For the first time in a presidential campaign, the Republicans began to wave "the bloody shirt" and claim that Democrats were, in general, a bunch of traitors who had brought on the war and now wanted to ruin the peace. "The Democratic party may be described as a common sewer and loathsome receptacle," the Radical Republican governor of Indiana asserted, "into which is emptied every element of

Democratic Parade, 1868. *Source:* Smithsonian Institution.

treason North and South, and every element of inhumanity and barbarism which has dishonored the age."

This was strong stuff, but the Republicans were frightened that the Democrats might win the White House and undo all the programs and particularly the Reconstruction laws passed by the Radicals in Congress. And the whole western area, with its territorial governments and enticing patronage, was by no means secure. So they launched a nationwide campaign to discredit the Democrats and attach to every Democratic candidate the suspicion that he had been a lukewarm Union man during the war.

To make sure that the South was not a factor in the contest, the army occupied most of the old Confederacy—three southern states were not allowed to vote at all. The new factor in the election was the vote of blacks, and an estimated 500,000 went to the polls, often with blue-uniformed soldiers standing guard over the ballot boxes. Helpful Republicans saw that black men were ushered to the polls, certified to vote, and shown how to mark the ticket for Republican candidates. That a black man might vote for a Democrat was deemed unthinkable in 1868.

What the election of 1868 confirmed was the end of Democratic domination in the presidency for most of the next 44 years. West Virginia and Nevada were now in the Union, dragged in by the Radicals to fortify their hold on the Senate. But Maine, once a firm Democratic stronghold, switched its allegiance with a convincing 68% vote for Grant and stayed away from Democrat majorities until the eve of World War II. The vote in California, which had been sending Democrats to the Senate, went for Grant by a 56% count, and countless other western states followed suit. No longer were Democratic editors arrested during the election, but rallies attended by Union veterans heard speakers denounce "the Democracy" as a pitiful collection of Peace Democrats, Confederate sympathizers, and draft-dodgers.

The excessive campaign rhetoric did not overwhelm every voter. In Boston, John Quincy Adams II was a citizen of unquestioned loyalty who was "so repelled by the policies of the Black [Radical] Republicans who took over national leadership after Lincoln's death . . . he switched to the Democratic party." In the following years Adams, the descendant of two presidents, ran for governor five times and was resoundingly defeated in each contest.

Harsh words in the campaign were part of Horace Greeley's *New York Tribune* diet for readers. Greeley, who began to think of himself as a kingmaker, continued to exert great influence in the midwestern states with his weekly edition, and Greeley assured farmers in Ohio, Indiana, and Illinois that Seymour's election would undo all the good that the peace terms at Appomattox epitomized. Grant would save the country, Seymour would ruin it, the bewhiskered Greeley told the thousands who had cast their first Republican vote in 1860. What worse tragedy could befall the nation than the triumph of "the Democracy"?

The campaign, nerve-racking as it was, had a lighter side. A northern humorist, David Ross Locke, started writing humorous doggerel during the war, attributing its authorship to "Petroleum V. Nasby," the fictional postmaster of "Confedrit X. Roads, Stait of Kentucky." Locke teased the Democrats for the broad umbrella the party offered to candidates with widely differing opinions. "The Democracy" had so many positions, Nasby suggested, that "in it every sole may find rest. . . . Would he pay the [national] debt, but pay it in Greenbax? Look at [Congressman] Pendleton. Wood he pay it in gold? Reed Seemore's Cooper Institoot Speech. Is he a war Dimokrat? Blare is our candidate. Is he a secessionist? Wade Hampton and Booregard [both Confederate generals] run the Convenshun. Ther is an assortment uv principle—let every one choose for hisself."

CLOSE, BUT NO VICTORY: 1868

The last laugh, in 1868, belonged to the Republicans. Grant won a popularity majority of 306,000 votes out of the 5.7 million cast, but in the electoral college he had 214 votes to Seymour's 80. The combined vote of northern veterans and the newly franchised blacks made Grant's victory a certainty. Perhaps of equal importance was the decline of Democrats in Congress. The 40th Congress elected in 1866 had a Republican majority of 174 to 49 in the House of Representatives and 55 Republicans in the Senate with only 8 Democrats "across the aisle." Now, with a Republican in the White House and Congress still overwhelmingly dominated by the Radicals, the main business was party entrenchment through constitutional amendment and the continuance of a hard-money policy.

During the decade following the Civil War, the Democrats retreated on many fronts but survived because of Republican blunders and strong local organizations. The Republican efforts to bring the old Confederacy back into the Union on humbling terms with black officeholders quickly alienated large numbers of whites in the South. Midwestern farmers, on the other hand, saw their destinies linked to the Republicans and in the corn belt there were more votes than in the cotton belt, even after Reconstruction ended in 1877. Before the sectional splits crystalized, however, the scandals of the Grant administration (in the Whiskey Ring tax frauds, the gold crisis of 1869,

and the greedy Crédit Mobilier episode) tested Republican loyalties.

A PARTY ON THE DEFENSIVE

The Democrats were on the defensive because the big issues—a low tariff or a high one, and a gold certificate or a greenback—roused public opinion but not public indignation. The growing urban areas in Boston, Chicago, New York, Philadelphia, Pittsburgh, and Cleveland were all in the North and with the exception of Tammany Hall in Manhattan and a variety of Boston enclaves, they were dominated by Republicans hungry for patronage. Nepotism was often replaced by party loyalty as the chief qualification for a job as a schoolteacher or city clerk.

Another factor in the changing face of American politics after 1865 was the Iron Horse. Railroad building became the driving force in the national economy, and Republicans were given the credit for starting the "gravy train" that took greed in many forms. The Crédit Mobilier scandal, which the New York Sun exposed in 1872, revealed that a coterie of Republican leaders, ranging from Vice President Schuyler Colfax on down to some venal congressmen from New England and New York, had voted vast sums to build the Pacific railroads and had accepted stock in the construction company organized by officials of the Union Pacific Railroad. Speaker of the House James G. Blaine, who was implicated, was forced to appoint a special committee to investigate the scandal after the Sun exposé. Profits of 50% per annum, and dividends on a similar scale, were revealed, and Blaine was permanently tainted, but only two Republican lawmakers were actually censured—and nobody was expelled from Congress as the public interest waned as the 1872 presidential election took center stage.

THE TAMMANY SCANDAL

In city and state governments, corruption was not unknown but was unreported. Unless a desperate source talked with a reporter, the secret dealings for streetcar franchises, utility contracts, or street construction contracts often involved bribes and graft of vast proportions. These shady aspects of urban life were carried on without public awareness unless a reporter, such as the Sun correspondent or the New York Times writer singled out by a disgusted Tammany "contractor," wrote a series of articles revealing the avarice of councilmen, aldermen, supervisors, police captains, sher-

Something That Did Blow Over, November 7, 1871. Nast's Triumphant Comment on the Election
Results That Destroyed Tammany Hall. The Mayor Is Still Clinging to the Remains of the Building.
Source: Library of Congress.

iffs, and state legislators. Because most of the North
was safely in the Republican column, the party
claimed the allegiance of a horde of culprits who used
black bags and cash payments to defraud taxpayers of
millions. That Tammany Hall was the largest, and
most greedy—and also Democratic—only indicates
that in the so-called Gilded Age when the term "millionaire" first came into popular usage, the crooks
were using convenient labels, and had no real loyalty
to the ideals of either party.

Amid all the cries for reform, the Republicans most
distressed by the miseries of the Grant administration
called for action. In part, these men disagreed with
their party's Reconstruction program, too, but they
were eager to break with the domineering Senate
Republicans who were in control of the regular party.
They called like-minded dissenters to a Liberal
Republican convention, nominated by a fluke the
fiesty Horace Greeley as their candidate, and called for
a variety of reforms ranging from civil service programs to public land policy.

If the Liberal Republican convention was a fluke, the
Democratic meeting in July 1872 was a disaster from
one viewpoint and a comic opera from another. Greeley,
who had spent most of his life whipping the Democrats,
was chosen as their candidate as the convention delegates adopted a me-too attitude and sold themselves on
the notion that with help from the Liberal Republicans,
the New York editor could carry the election.

AN UNLIKELY CANDIDATE: GREELEY

Full of nervous energy, Greeley actually tried to do
some campaigning and worked himself into a flurry of
activity. Grant stood aloof, after he was renominated,
and let Greeley do all the talking. The irony of the farce
was noted by General William Tecumseh Sherman,
who told his Republican brother: "Grant who never
was a Republican is your candidate and Greeley
who was never a Democrat . . . is the Democratic
candidate."

With many of the southern states still occupied by
federal troops, and the midwestern farmers puzzled
by the antics of Greeley (whose word had once been
treated as Gospel truth), the Republicans depended on
the increasingly powerful Grand Army of the Republic
to help straighten matters. The 400,000 members of the

GAR were solidly aligned behind Grant, and at their encampments revived the "bloody shirt" and brooked no whispers of scandal in high places.

Disgusted by the Greeley candidacy, a band of "straight" Democrats held their own convention in Louisville early in September 1872 and rejected the Greeley ticket. After condemning the Liberal Republican-Democratic alliance as unworthy of the party of Jefferson and Jackson, the Louisville delegates nominated Charles O'Connor, an almost unknown senator from New York, as president. The faithful John Quincy Adams II of Massachusetts was tacked on the ticket as the vice presidential candidate. The delegates adjourned with more prayers for than hopes of a victory.

The outcome was another Democratic shambles. Grant swamped the Democrats in a humiliating contest that found Greeley barely clinging to life in the last days of the campaign. He died on November 29, so that most of his 66 electoral votes were cast for a variety of Democrats simply to protest Grant's overwhelming victory—3.6 million votes for Grant to 2.8 million for Greeley.

Grant's second term was in some ways a repeat of Van Buren's experience. A financial panic struck in the fall of 1873, and farms were among the first to feel its effects as wheat, corn, and other grain prices tumbled on the eve of what became a worldwide depression. Nothing akin to the famine and misery felt in Europe was known in the United States, but a genuine protest movement gained momentum in the Midwest. State legislatures became the battleground for protests against railroad rates, tightened credit, and market problems exacerbated by the depressed grain market.

The Democrats capitalized on the voters' distress and in the off-year elections of 1874 they captured a 60-vote majority in the House of Representatives. The Senate stayed in Republican hands, but a statehouse revolt also took place to gain governorships for a host of Democratic candidates. Two years earlier, the Democratic Party looked as if it was headed the way of the dodo bird, but the Congress meeting in 1875 was full of energetic young men who looked forward to the coming battle for the presidency. The Republicans were embarrassed, too, when one of Grant's appointees was exposed as the key figure in a St. Louis tax scandal involving revenues presumably paid on whiskey but never collected. Similar conspiracies between distillers and tax collectors eventually surfaced

Mixing Day at *Harper's*, Making Mud to Fling at Greeley. Editor Curtis: "Don't spit in it Thomas; it is not gentlemanly." A Cartoon in Opposition to Nast's and Curtis's Treatment of Greeley. *Source:* Library of Congress.

until 238 federal employees were indicted. Grant's secretary of war, implicated in a trading-post bribery scandal, resigned on the same day Congress voted to impeach him. He escaped conviction, barely.

REPUBLICANS HAVE SCANDALS, TOO

When the smoke of the Whiskey and War Department scandals cleared, even Grant's personal secretary had been named among the wrongdoers, but Grant was not accused of anything but poor judgment. With all the damage done, Democrats sought a presidential candidate who could seriously challenge Grant's successor, and they finally settled on another New York governor, Samuel J. Tilden, to carry the presidential banner. Tilden had gained national attention as a reform Democrat who helped bring down the rotten Tweed Ring in New York City, along with a number of corrupt party hacks who held judgeships. Democrats wanted to stress Tilden's role as a prosecutor of corruption, and the recent Republican scandals were offered as a distinct contrast to Tilden's image as a fair-minded man who exposed evil wherever he found it.

Republicans used the two-term tradition to turn Grant out and welcomed an Ohio governor with a good war record as their candidate. Rutherford B. Hayes was no spellbinder, but he had solid party credentials and was beloved by the GAR veterans, who once again talked about "the bloody shirt" and hooted down the band when someone suggested they play "Dixie" in the spirit of reconciliation.

But the real Dixie was not quiet in 1876. The South was still harboring some federal troops, and the reconstructed states came back in the Union bearing a grudge against the Republicans, who were accused of bringing "carpetbag" government below the Mason–Dixon Line.

THE PROSTRATE SOUTH

Initially, the Republicans hoped to use a constitutional amendment, the federal troops occupying the old Confederacy, and a variety of strategems to create a sizable vote block in the errant eleven states. But circumstances ruled otherwise, for white southerners resented the "blue-back" soldiers, hated the opportunists who came South to make quick fortunes, and denied the legitimacy of the carpetbag rulers. Radical Republicans slowly revised their plans. Unlike the attitude after World War II, when the Marshall Plan was devised to rebuild war-torn Europe, there was no

scheme in Congress to help the South get back on its feet. Instead, a wrenching deflation kept land prices low, farm products were never near their prewar demand or prices, and the crossed bayonets over southern ballot boxes for a decade was a bitter drug.

Every calculation the Radical Republicans made seemed to end in failure. Besides the enormous increase in state debts brought on by excesses of the carpetbag governments (Arkansas's public debt rose from $3.5 million to $15.7 million in seven years; in Louisiana the debt skyrocketed from $11 million to $50 million in the same period), the Radicals stoked the railroad-building process in the North and left the South floundering for transportation links. Democratic congressmen were so outvoted, their hopes for a Southern Pacific route from New Orleans to the West Coast floundered.

None of this might have mattered if the nation's economy had not faltered. But the Panic of 1873 caused massive unemployment and sent farm prices so low that some farmers complained they could not afford to pay for their vital seed crop. "Hard times is our deadliest foe," the Republican governor of Ohio admitted. Even the GAR rallies were dismal replays of the past excitement, and voters sent their own message in the fall of 1876. When all the results were in, Tilden had 250,000 more votes than Hayes. Thunderstruck Republicans shook their heads and turned off their kerosene lamps, retiring in a gloomy atmosphere.

But the Democrats could not celebrate too much, for there was a flaw in the election process. Disputed election returns from Oregon and three southern states left the electoral college outcome in doubt. Outraged Democrats threatened to march on Washington if Tilden was "robbed" of his election. In Kentucky, Henry Watterson used the columns of the *Louisville Courier* to call for 100,000 Democrats to volunteer for a force that would converge on Washington to ensure an honest count. In South Carolina, Wade Hampton's rifle clubs (reorganized after a presidential order outlawed informal militia groups) were renamed musical clubs and members promised to arm with "four-pound flutes" to make sure the election returns were counted fairly, that is, for Tilden.

FORCE THREATENED IN 1876

The situation was getting nasty. Inauguration day approached, with no president legally entitled to take office. Congress stepped in and appointed a special election commission to sort out the various claims of fraud and impropriety, with eight Republicans and seven

Democrats authorized to make a final judgment. Predictably, the vote went eight to seven for Hayes on all the disputed ballots, and the announced tally was 185 electoral votes for Hayes, 184 for Tilden, with the March 4 deadline met but the Democrats in a dither. Historian C. Van Woodward, sifting through all the evidence in a more dispassionate time, wrote that if the votes had been counted honestly, Tilden would have won, 188 to 181.

"Thieves, crooks, and rascals!" Democrats shouted, but the deal was done. And it was a deal, as events soon proved. Southern threats of a congressional filibuster were rewarded in a variety of ways. Most important, the Republicans gave up on their effort to establish their party in the South and agreed to withdraw federal troops forthwith. Hayes appointed a southerner to serve in his cabinet. Plans for a southern railroad route to the West emerged in Congress. Not a single member of the commission ever admitted to any shenanigans, but a few members of Congress were candid. "The Democratic business men of the country are more anxious for quiet than for Tilden," Representative James A. Garfield of Ohio observed, "and the leading southern Democrats in Congress . . . are saying they have seen war enough."

By default, a mixed bag of "Redeemers" took over in the South. A coalition of former Whigs, bourbon Democrats, and the last of the old Democracy from the Jefferson–Jackson mould moved to take control. Within three months, a variety of carpetbag administrations quietly packed and headed North. Within a year, the Democrats had their "Solid South" in place, and would keep it there for almost a century.

In 1992, candidate Bill Clinton kept repeating to his staff, "It's the economy, stupid!" Perhaps that motto came from a staff member with a sense of history, for in 1877 a president not elected by a majority of the voters had won office because the leaders in both parties were more concerned about the economy than fairness. News from abroad revealed the deepening of a worldwide agriculture depression. After the bonanza from California gold fields in the 1850s and 1860s turned to realistic levels, an infusion of new capital was needed by railroad financiers, bankers, and builders.

TARIFF ISSUE CROWDS AGENDAS

On Wall Street, the Republicans were entrenched and the financiers looked to the Grand Old Party to protect the high tariffs believed essential for continued growth in heavy industries. Hard-money policies promised low inflation and a deflationary effect on the job market.

These were subtle matters not used by campaign orators when on the hustings in farm communities in Indiana or Illinois, but Democrats were forced into defending legislation that would curb the power of railroads and keep tariffs within reasonable limits. And as mortgages became more burdensome during hard times, farmers rallied behind protest movements that neither party could handle. Populist forces swept through local elections in the Midwest, forcing lawmakers to attempt regulation of railroad rates, and the Greenbackers in Iowa and Illinois wanted an inflationary "soft-money" policy that would help them climb out of debt.

The result of all these controversies was that the nation expanded, but at a heavy price. Between Grant's administration and the end of the nineteenth century, Republican Congresses passed laws subsidizing railroad building, more laws to ease the pathway for mining companies to exploit mineral properties, and timber companies had almost *carte blanche* to cut down forests at a devastating rate. In this process, Democratic votes helped big businesses become bigger, to be sure, but unless the country slipped into a recession, both houses of Congress remained safely in Republican hands. Castles for millionaires were built in Newport as the slum lords of Manhattan charged outrageous rents on cold-water flats. A steady stream of immigrants from Europe kept the industrial workforce from any kind of organized protest as prices outran wages, 12- or 14-hour workdays were normal for millions of laborers, and public funding for education was still minimal.

WHERE ARE THE REFORMERS?

Indeed, the Gilded Age had its romantic side, but most of the American people never saw it. Neither the Democrats nor the Republicans offered much encouragement to reformers, and loyalty to a party overrode practical considerations, even common sense. In Boston, the recent Irish immigrants looked to the Democrats for help, but in the rest of New England the Democrats often gave up elections by default, for no candidate was willing to be a sacrifical lamb in lopsided contests. In the Midwest, the "bloody shirt" campaigns still brought cheers from Civil War veterans, and the GAR became a lobbying wing of the Republican Party. An estimated $2 billion was voted by Republican Congresses for Union Army pensions, always with encouragement from the GAR hierarchy; but for Confederate veterans, unless their localities made some gestures, there was no relief. To a Congress dominated by men who still called Lee's veterans "traitors," aid for former Confederate soldiers was unthinkable.

So the Democrats became two parties for a long time span. In the North, the Democrats were the outsiders, always pinched for campaign funds and hard-pressed to find editors who would plead their causes. The election of a Democrat to a northern congressional seat was often a mere "upset" that could be corrected in two years and was caused mainly by recessions that hit pocketbooks harder than ideology. In the West, the power of combined mining, ranching, and railroad interests bought legislators in California and other key states; rarely was a Democrat allowed to become a governor or senator unless he was "on the right side" of conservatives who believed that maintaining the status quo was holy territory. Ronald Reagan often said his Eleventh Commandment was "Speak no evil of a fellow Republican." The nineteenth-century version was "Don't tinker with the economy."

Splinter protest groups came and went. The Grangers wanted railroad regulation, and won a few battles. The Greenbackers wanted inflation to help pay off mortgages and other debts, and they won virtually no battles. None of these protesters could merge with the Democrats, in part because of the "bloody shirt" label and because Democrats had little to offer in return. The major newspapers were solidly Republican, ranging from the overwhelming *Chicago Tribune* to the *Portland Oregonian* in the West and the *New York Herald* in the East.

Millions of readers learned of the Tweed Ring scandals through the *New York Times*, but it was the cartoonist Thomas Nast who brought the message nationwide through *Harper's Magazine*. Nast, a devout Republican, gave his favorite party its symbol—the raging elephant—in a cartoon showing how comebacks might be fashioned. Where the first depiction of Democrats as stubborn donkeys came from is uncertain, but both labels stuck. Except in the South, it was a rare newspaper that assailed Republican candidates until Joseph Pulitzer took over the derelict *New York World* in 1883 and made it the newspaper of the underdog, the downtrodden, and the Democrats. Within a decade, the *World* managed to change the role of journalism and set in motion the wave that brought Lincoln Steffen's *Shame of the Cities* and Jacob Riis's *How the Other Half Lives* into the nation's conscience.

UNDERDOGS AND PROTESTERS

Underdogs and protesters are not good at winning elections, as George McGovern learned in 1972. A century earlier, those active groups on the fringe of society did no better, except when the nation was hit by a shattering depression. The Tweed Ring's bold theft of $9 million for bogus courthouse repairs could upset the voters temporarily, but when Republicans kept their house in order, they held on to the White House and all the power that follows. The assassination of President James A. Garfield threw the Republicans into disarray, however, for they had never expected Chester A. Arthur to be more than a low-key vice president. Arthur surprised his party chieftains by showing that he had some ideas of his own. Civil service reforms were demanded by public opinion after Garfield's death, and Arthur was willing to consider merit instead of party affiliation as a qualification for office.

President Arthur paid for his independence by alienating the New Yorkers who had tried to shelve him. A New Yorker himself, Arthur learned that his days in the White House were numbered. The conservative leadership had long wanted to promote Senator James G. Blaine, and now they had their chance. Arrogantly, they dumped Arthur (from New York, with its preponderance of 44 electoral votes) for a canny senator from Maine (with 3 electoral votes). Republicans can shoot themselves in the foot, too, as the 1884 election proved.

New York had long been the linchpin of the Democratic Party's hold on the White House, dating back to Jefferson's time. The slavery battle obscured this key factor somewhat, but New York governors Tilden and Seymour had been great campaigners and almost won against stiff odds. Thus when a Democrat held the New York governor's post, he automatically became presidential timber. In 1882 the Democrats sent to the statehouse in Albany Grover Cleveland, who was something of a rising star in party circles. In 1881 the ex-sheriff was elected mayor of Buffalo, and a year later was chosen governor in a Democratic sweep.

GOING TO THE PROMISED LAND: GROVER CLEVELAND

Cleveland looked like the messiah needed to lead the Democrats to the land of milk and honey. He was young (47), a reformer who had tightened the purse strings of a spendthrift state, and he was unmarried. True, he had not served in the Civil War and had paid for a substitute when his draft number came up, but he did it because his widowed mother needed him. Cleveland was perfectly frank about all these matters, and he also told the business community he was no wild-eyed liberal. In fact, he gained respect for his vetoes of popular bills, including one that would have cut streetcar fares in New York City to five cents.

The reason Cleveland gave for his veto of the car-fare bill, and a similar refusal to approve public aid for Catholic schools, was that he had no powers under the state constitution to sign such bills. When a bill passed that cut the working hours of streetcar operators from 16 hours to 12, Cleveland also vetoed it. This infuriated the Tammany Hall crowd, but Cleveland stuck by his guns and weathered an intense personal attack led by Tammany Boss "Honest John" Kelly. In short, Cleveland showed himself to be a maverick Democrat.

While Cleveland's vetoes gained the headlines, the nation was plunged again into a severe recession in 1884. Republican leaders were confident they could dismiss President Arthur and go with their choice, Blaine, without trouble from the rank and file. A slight ripple came when the Greenback Party, disgusted with the antics surrounding the dump-Arthur movement, held their own convention in late May and nominated Benjamin F. Butler, once the darling of the Radical Republicans, as their presidential candidate committed to inflationary monetary policies. These defections from the Old Guard Republicans were dismissed by the Republican convention, which met a week later, as mere gadfly disturbances that would not hinder the party at election time.

There was one other embarrassment for the Republicans, stemming from Blaine's involvement in the Credit Mobilier mess. He had tried to exonerate himself from any wrongdoing, but left behind an unfortunate letter that reeked of a cover-up. For this and other reasons, a group of independent Republicans distanced themselves from Blaine and declared themselves ready to run their own candidate. Labeled *Mugwumps* by regular Republicans, their numbers included Charles Francis Adams and Carl Schurz, the intellectual giants of the party and men committed to civil service reforms far beyond those already proposed. In a pinch, they were so opposed to Blaine they were ready to leap over to the Democrats.

STOPPING THE "PLUMED KNIGHT"

Supremely confident, the Republicans ignored the fractious elements in their party and proceeded to nominate Blaine. For Blaine's running mate, the Republicans chose John A. Logan, a chief organizer of the GAR and a former Union general. The Mugwump Republicans were ignored.

Cleveland had his troubles, too. Because of his fight with Boss Kelly, the New York delegation at the Democratic Convention was lukewarm for the gover-

nor but was finally won over when it was obvious that the mainstream delegates wanted Cleveland as their nominee. Kelly bided his time, and did as much as he could to block Cleveland's path to the White House. Kelly's outspoken opposition caused one enthusiastic Cleveland delegate to shout, "We love him for the enemies he has made!" The Tammany boss's remarks boomeranged, as Cleveland won the nomination on the second ballot. Once again, Thomas Hendricks of Indiana was picked for the vice presidential spot.

Through the summer months and into the fall, the campaign was waged with unusual ferocity. Blaine, hailed by his party as the "Plumed Knight," had to ward off blows from critics about the damning "Mulligan letters" that made Blaine's past look shady. To worsen matters, a friendly clergyman called on Blaine and as spokesman for his fellow Protestant ministers he condemned the Democrats as the party of "Rum, Romanism, and Rebellion." In one breath the preacher, in his widely quoted remark, had insulted the moderate drinker, Catholics, and the entire South. Called on to repudiate the remark, Blaine stood pat, and thereby alienated voters across the land, but more particularly in New York, where the Irish Catholics were a major voting block.

Nor was Cleveland spared. During the campaign Blaine supporters learned that many years earlier, Cleveland had fathered a baby but never made the child's mother "into an honest woman." Cleveland

Frank Beard's Cartoon Refers to Cleveland's Illegitimate Child, a Major Campaign Issue in 1884. *Source:* Library of Congress.

met the charge head on, admitted his indiscretion, but said he had been paying for the child's upkeep for ten years. A leading Republican newspaper said the admission was an insult to the American people. Cleveland's election, said the *Independent*, "would argue a low state of morals among the people," for his candidacy itself was "a disgrace to the nation."

Democrats counterattacked by claiming Blaine's corrupt past was a blight he could not escape. "Blaine! Blaine! Continental liar from the state of Maine!" was the cry hurled at the Maine senator while his supporters chanted: "Ma, ma, where's my Pa? Gone to the White House, Ha! Ha! Ha!"

But the Mugwumpish *Nation* decided that between the two candidates, Cleveland had some minor blemishes while Blaine was a disreputable crook. "Blaine's vices are those by which governments are overthrown, states brought to naught," the magazine editorialized, "and the haunts of commerce turned into dens of thieves."

By late October both sides were slugging away, and the final outcome promised to be as close as the 1876 contest. And it was close, for Cleveland's popular vote total was 4.9 million to 4.8 million for Blaine, but Cleveland managed to carry New York (by only 1,100 votes), Connecticut, and the entire South. In the electoral college, Cleveland had 219 votes, Blaine 182. Dazed but defiant, Blaine said he would have won if the "rum and Romanism" comment had never been uttered.

Elections sometimes hinge on strange, small matters; but the fact was that Cleveland had broken the Republicans' seven-term tenure in the White House, and more important, the Democratic Congress elected in 1882 was pretty much returned. Cleveland thus could count on, he assumed, the support of Congress for the reforms he favored. Civil service reform was at the top of most agendas, but the pickings in 1885 were not even close to what the federal bureaucracy would become in the twentieth century. If all the customs house collectors, postmasters, and pension office clerks were counted, the number of federal officeholders nationwide came to about 130,000.

In his inaugural address Cleveland stressed his commitment to a meritocracy, but to be sure that Democrats showed more merit than the other office seekers, Cleveland placed Adlai E. Stevenson of Illinois in charge of his replacement program. In fact, Cleveland showed considerable contempt for the clamoring mob that claimed to be deserving of a federal job because of their loyalty to the Democratic Party. To reinforce his determination to root out political hacks, Cleveland appointed as his secretary of the navy William C. Endicott of Massachusetts, an outspoken enemy of the old-time spoils system. Other cabinet posts were filled by moderates. Stevenson, as assistant postmaster general, gently guided around 8,000 Democrats into postmasterships, but Cleveland

Cleveland as Hercules Facing a Host of Obstacles. *Source:* Library of Congress.

took some matters in hand personally. When Tilden came calling and was known to seek the plush customs collector's job in New York harbor, Cleveland kept the 1876 candidate cooling his heels and gave the $50,000 job (the same salary paid to the president) to another.

CLEVELAND NO REFORMER

Perhaps Cleveland overreacted to cries for reform. After Cleveland had been in office long enough to make his policy clear, even his vice president felt discouraged. "I had hoped that Mr. Cleveland would put the Democratic party into power in fact as well as in name," Hendricks lamented. When a senator complained that too many Republicans still held jobs that Democrats wanted, Cleveland exploded. "Should I," Cleveland exclaimed, "appoint two horse thieves a day, instead of one?"

Meanwhile, the financiers on Wall Street began to relax. Cleveland was acting in many ways like a good Republican, for he watched over the federal treasury like a mastiff. Congress fell into the habit of passing private bills to create pensions for Union veterans who did not qualify in the ordinary way. Some were piddling, and few ran to more than several hundred dollars. But Cleveland thought the whole process was unconstitutional, and despite advice to the contrary, he vetoed these bills right and left. Recall that Jefferson had never vetoed a single bill. Now Cleveland set a record (in his two terms) of 304 regular vetoes and 110 pocket vetoes. The GAR howled, the veterans screamed about the "bloody shirt," but only two of Cleveland's vetoes were overridden by Congress.

Veterans were disappointed, and in time so were farmers in the areas hit by a drought. Congress passed an appropriation bill that committed $10,000 for the purchase of seeds to be distributed to Texas farmers in the parched region. Cleveland vetoed this bill, too. "Though the people support the Government," Cleveland said in his veto message, "the Government should not support the people."

When the Republicans regained the Senate in midterm, Cleveland let it be known that he would not veto a bill lowering the tariff. For one thing, a surplus was piling up in the federal treasury from the customs income. For another, Cleveland's chief loyalty to his party was a steadfast belief that protective tariffs were a bane on the common man, who was forced to pay higher prices for domestic manufactures so that American industry could be protected from foreign competition.

FALLOUT FROM THE HAYMARKET BOMBING

Domestic violence became a national concern in 1886 after a bomb exploded in a Chicago confrontation between police and a radical group of anarchists. The Haymarket Massacre, as newspapers termed it, left 7 policemen dead and 70 officers and civilians wounded. At a sensational trial in September, seven defendants received death sentences. Before the executions, a nationwide appeal was made for commutation or pardons; Cleveland would not interfere, and late in 1887 four were hung. Labor groups were disappointed and kept up the pressure for pardons, claiming the trial was a farce. Cleveland was adamant, believing that what happened to criminals in Illinois was none of his business.

The president had other things on his mind. In 1887 Cleveland decided to dramatize the tariff issue, and breaking with precedent sent his annual message to Congress based on a single issue: tariff reduction. Senate Republicans saw their chance to embarrass the president, and when the House passed a bill along the lines Cleveland favored, the Senate Republicans rejected it.

Cleveland was upset, but determined to carry on the fight. But within the Democratic Party, he found defections in unexpected places. Pennsylvania Democrats, ever mindful of the steel and iron industries benefiting from higher tariffs, deserted Cleveland on the issue. In New York City, the Tammany mayor declared open warfare. "I don't believe in his re-election," the Tammany catspaw declared. Cleveland's successor as governor in Albany also took a potshot at the president, and was quoted as saying that if Cleveland were a one-term president, he would not be sorry.

These defections were mainly soreheaded remarks caused by Cleveland's refusal to let party bosses arrange patronage in their bailiwicks, but loyalty is the lifeblood of party politics. Every vote controlled by disloyal party workers contributes strength to the opposition, as Cleveland well knew. But Cleveland thought he was winning the battle for public opinion, so he stayed on course. Let the party hacks snarl about patronage; he would stay above their petty fights and keep battling for lower tariffs.

Some presidents have delegated power, others have used power with a heavy hand, and a few presidents have been too concerned with day-to-day trivia. Cleveland tried to keep his hand in everything, and his failure to delegate responsibility hurt him. But Cleveland was not always in a negative mood. He signed the Indian Emancipation and Interstate Commerce Acts in 1887, both hailed by reformers as statesmanlike measures.

A WHITE HOUSE WEDDING

Whether political advisers played a hand is not known, but late in his term Cleveland wooed the lovely Frances Folsom, and his bachelorhood ended in a White House wedding. One newspaper wag commented that the marriage was the only popular thing Cleveland did in his four-year tenure.

Surely Cleveland did not listen to his counselors when he decided to make his 1888 presidential bid by hammering on the tariff issue. Early in June 1888 the Democrats renominated Cleveland but bumped Hendricks off the ticket and added Allen G. Thurman of Ohio for the vice presidency. To accentuate their differences, Republicans at their Chicago convention approved a strong plank commending the protective tariff. They also approved another plank promising generous pensions to Union veterans, in an attempt to exploit Cleveland's many vetoes. Another former Union general, Benjamin Harrison, was nominated for the presidency, and the bunting was placed on the rafters while the strains of "Battle Hymn of the Republic" resounded in the convention hall.

The campaign was probably too high-minded to attract lackadaisical voters, for the tariff issue was about all that separated Harrison from Cleveland. Harrison was for a sound dollar, but so was Cleveland. Cleveland wanted to push civil service reform, but so did Harrison. Ultimately, and for the second time in history, a Democrat had more popular votes than the Republican but wound up on the losing side. Cleveland had nearly 100,000 votes more than Harrison, but Harrison carried New York and Indiana and that was the whole story, for in the electoral college the Ohioan had 233 votes to Cleveland's 168 count.

UNION VETERANS' VOTE INFLUENTIAL

Old soldiers rejoiced, and they had reason to jump with joy. With Cleveland's pen swept aside, the Republican Congress moved with haste to reenact a bill that offered a pension to every Union veteran with at least 90 days of service who was either disabled or "unable to earn a livelihood." A $60 million treasury surplus soon disappeared after Harrison signed the measure, and in four years the pension rolls carried the names of 970,000 Union veterans. In the century that followed, never again would the federal treasury show a surplus.

Parade Painting, 1892. Adlai Stevenson Campaigning for the Vice Presidential Spot under Grover Cleveland. *Source:* Smithsonian Institution.

The tariff issue was fought out in Congress, and the Democrats lost again. Representative William McKinley, an Ohio Republican, offered a tariff bill that increased the duties on a long list of imported goods, enough to warm the hearts of the most rabid protectionists. Congress swallowed McKinley's bill, along with the Sherman Antitrust Act, which was meant to curb the powerful combinations and mergers that created near monopolies in sugar, refined petroleum, and railroads. Hailed as a reform measure of vast significance, the act failed to stop the merging process or create real competition in the marketplace.

Discontent on the farms in nearly every section of the country was fomenting early in 1892. Republican hard-money programs aggravated attempts by farmers to stabilize the price for wheat and corn and caused desperate critics to turn away from the Democrats and create their own third party. A groundswell of public opinion in the Midwest helped feed the discontent. First, the People's or Populist Party convened in 1891 to discuss remedies, and when thousands flocked to their regional meeting a full-fledged convention was held in July to nominate a presidential candidate and adopt a reform platform. The Populists called for direct election of senators, a postal savings system, a graduated income tax, and a long list of innovations in government and commerce. James B. Weaver of Iowa was nominated for president, and the Populists were off and running a full year and four months before there would be any voting.

NEW LIFE FOR OLD ISSUES: THE POPULIST AGENDA

The Populists forced public discussion on questions that the Democrats had long discussed and long deferred. The demand for unlimited coinage of silver (16 silver dollars for one gold one) was inflationary, but perhaps a better approach than the Greenback idea of printing money fast and then faster. Election of senators by the state legislature was enshrined in the Constitution, but an amendment could take every voter into the process. Income taxes had been tried during the Civil War and declared unconstitutional, but another amendment might handle that effort and create a second source of federal revenue (besides the customs). Many Democrats, particularly in Nebraska, Kansas, the Dakotas, Minnesota, and Wisconsin, found these Populist planks appealing. In the South, however, the Democratic Party was in the hands of controlling cliques in nearly every state, and the last thing the Old Guard Democrats wanted was the ap-

pearance of startling reform. The ancient dream of an agrarian alliance between the cotton South and the wheat Midwest had expired in 1860 and would not be revived.

Certainly, Cleveland was not going to try and turn the clock back. His nomination was never in doubt, but the tariff issue was a hot potato. Meeting in Chicago in June 1892, the platform committee tried to please everybody but wound up with a plank that alienated the few protectionists left. The resolution had a ring of the 1830s about it, as the final plank stated that "the federal government has no constitutional power to impose and collect tariff duties, except for purposes of revenue only." And, of course, the Republican plank said the opposite, that tariffs to protect American industry from harmful foreign competition were one of the blessings showered on Columbia's shores by an all-wise-and-benevolent band of dedicated Republicans.

Although Cleveland wanted an all-out war on the Republicans over the tariff in 1888, he was only mildly interested in the issue in 1892. Instead, he now confessed that keeping the United States on a gold standard (that is, basing all government financing on the premise that currency and gold were interchangeable) would ensure four more years of prosperity. Wall Street loved such a pronouncement, even if the Greenbackers in Iowa felt betrayed.

TARIFFS, AND MORE TARIFFS

Cleveland's conservatism, the backlash of the harsh McKinley tariff in the Midwest, and Harrison's colorless personality helped forge a second term for the Democratic standard-bearer. Cleveland won again in the popular voting, 5.5 million to Harrison's 5.2 million, but this time New York stuck with her native son and altogether Cleveland had 277 electoral votes to 145 for Harrison. In the South, Cleveland won solidly, but the results in Mississippi gave a hint of how far down the Republicans had fallen. There, Cleveland won 40,288 votes; Harrison had 1,395. If a single black man voted, it was unrecorded.

For all their bluster and hopes, the Greenback candidate had not been a spoiler, but Weaver did win 22 electoral votes and had over a million popular votes. In Congress, Democrats carried elections for both the House and Senate.

In 1995 the British banking firm of Baring Brothers failed, and except for the six o'clock financial news on television channels, the U.S. markets hardly noticed. How times had changed, for in 1893 the Baring

Brothers failure in London and the ensuing collapse of credit in Europe and America brought on a financial panic in America. Cleveland had hardly settled into his second term when the crisis hit, triggering a collapse of stock prices on Wall Street.

WHERE IS ALL THE GOLD?

Gold reserves seemed to be the key to the unexpected collapse of credit. Gold bullion was removed from the federal treasury until Cleveland called a special session of Congress to stop the panic. Congress repealed the Sherman Silver Purchase Act, which was causing the drain, but the Senate vote was close (48 to 37) and many western senators nursed a grudge over the incident.

Meanwhile, the panic left the country swimming in bankruptcies, farm prices plunged, and jobless men roamed the streets in New York and Chicago. A Populist leader called on the unemployed to join in a march on Washington, to focus national attention on their plight. This was "Coxey's Army," and although they gained publicity for their demands (including immediate issuance of $500 million in greenbacks), the ringleaders were arrested in Washington and the tiny "army" of 400 disbanded.

Presidents can change their minds. In the Haymarket affair, Cleveland took a "hands off" attitude toward the bombing and subsequent trial in 1886–1887, but in the summer of 1894 he decided that a strike in Illinois deserved federal intervention. Workers at the Pullman plant called a strike, crippling rail service because sleeping cars were involved. First, Cleveland saw to it that 3,400 special federal agents were dispatched to keep the trains running. Then the president decided that the strike was interfering with the mails and interstate commerce, so he supported a motion for an injunction against the striking union. Eugene Debs, a perennial thorn in the side of Wall Street, was jailed, and the strike called off.

Cleveland had little sympathy for the strikers, and his attitude toward unions was akin to that of banker J.P. Morgan or industrialist Mark Hanna. These men thought alike on the matter of the gold standard, and reverence for gold bullion in a government vault was perhaps ahead of their allegiance to the stars and stripes. A host of Democrats, however, thought the gold standard was becoming a political football. As the government's gold reserves continued to fall, loans were arranged with Morgan and other wealthy New York financiers to keep the government solvent.

Enormous profits were linked to these "bailout" loans, and among the most vocal critics of Cleveland's policy was Representative William Jennings Bryan from Nebraska. Bryan was serving his second term in the House and became an outspoken opponent of the Gold Democrat wing of his party, but failed when he tried to win a Senate seat in 1894. Cleveland was too conservative to consider the merits of a proposal to revive the free coinage of silver. Bryan was only 35 years old when he lost his bid for the Senate, and he was soon organizing the liberal Democrats for an effort to restore the Bland–Allison silver act.

Republicans decided to draw the line of demarcation between the parties clearly. Guided by the clever manipulations of Mark Hanna, the Republicans nominated William McKinley—author of the much-assailed McKinley tariff—as their presidential candidate at their June 1896 convention. What better way to stress the party differences than to pit McKinley, the high-tariff darling, against the president who embraced a low tariff above all other things?

Cleveland's popularity plunged like the stock market, and even the Democratic-leaning *New York World* decided it was time for the president to relax his hard-money policy or step aside. More than a few Democrats looked to Cuba and decided that this crumbling Spanish colony, with its sporadic rebellions, ought to be annexed and allowed a *Pax Americana*. But Cleveland watched as Germany, France, and Great Britain grabbed colonies around the globe and decided that the United States did not need to indulge in the imperial game; the president threw cold water on any effort to create a rival empire. The high point of Cleveland's second term came when the British were picking a fight with Venezuela over boundaries. The president reminded the British minister of the Monroe Doctrine, and subtly warned that he saw one of two solutions: arbitration or war. The public applauded Cleveland's forceful action, particularly after the British decided talking was preferable to shooting.

GOLD VERSUS SILVER

But the main issue plaguing Cleveland and his party was the decision to stick with the gold standard. A South Carolina demagogue, Ben Tillman, campaigned for the Senate and distanced himself from the president, whom he called "a bag of beef" who needed to be deflated by a pitchfork. Thereafter "Pitchfork Ben" made Cleveland, Wall Street, and the gold standard his favorite targets, and he carried his battle into the Democratic convention in Chicago in July 1896.

Of all the Democratic conventions ever held, the mass meeting on the shores of Lake Michigan in 1896 was the most electrifying and dramatic. Cleveland had served two terms and was out of the running, so the convention was open to new ideas, new men, and a new direction. To the idealists, the chance to run against McKinley and all the money power he stood for seemed like an opportunity—certainly "golden" in this case—because the main issue was the gold standard they believed was keeping the country on its knees. Desperately searching for a leader, the Democrats were stunned by the speech Bryan gave on the second day. Bryan made no bones about it: he was a Silver Democrat and he wanted the gold standard abandoned before it ruined the nation.

"CROSS OF GOLD" SPEECH

An enthralled audience heard Bryan's speech with a mixture of rapture, admiration, and enthusiasm. When the Nebraskan pleaded, "You shall not press down on the brow of labor this crown of thorns, you shall not crucify mankind on a cross of gold," the crowd was in a frenzy. The steamroller of opinion carried Bryan into the nominating process and before the dust settled, the Democrats had a 36-year-old presidential candidate who was ready to slay the Gold Dragon in its lair.

He failed, of course, but those present in Chicago never forgot the magic moment when the "Cross of Gold" speech made them believe that nothing was impossible. Promising a crusade against the corporations he insisted were strangling the country with their greed, Bryan took off the gloves. The polite campaigning of the past, from the candidate's front porch or parlor, was left to McKinley—Bryan scheduled an arduous campaign tour that took him to major cities for tabernacle meetings that bespoke a religious fervor. Populists caught the fever and also nominated Bryan as their candidate. In late July 1896 it appeared that only a miracle could derail the Bryan candidacy and prevent him from moving into the White House.

BRYAN DENOUNCED AS "RADICAL"

Not every Democrat was pleased by Bryan's steamroller nomination. The *New York World*, usually a reliable supporter of Democratic candidates, rebelled. "Lunacy having dictated the platform," a *World* editorial noted, "it was perhaps natural that hysteria should evolve" a candidate as weak as Bryan. The Democratic Party had survived other disastrous nominations, the newspaper suggested, but "there is peril in making it ridiculous" by nominating a political upstart.

Much can and often does happen between July and November in a presidential election. For Bryan, the old-fashioned front-porch campaign was simply another tradition that needed abandonment. Nicknamed by the press the "Boy Orator of the Platte," Bryan made whistle-stops and major speeches on a tour that carried him 18,000 miles. The more Bryan lambasted the Republicans, the more McKinley smiled benevolently from his front porch and spoke in homilies.

BACK TO THE "BLOODY SHIRT"

Born in 1860, Bryan had been playing with toy soldiers during the Civil War, but the GAR was reminded that McKinley (while not becoming a general) had served with an Ohio regiment with honor if not distinction. Waving the "bloody shirt" as a campaign practice was not the emotional rouse it had been in 1868, but in a close contest, any trick that worked was still useful.

Frightened Republicans thought Bryan was a radical and predicted the stock market would never recover if the Democrat won. The Gold Democrats, disgusted with Bryan, held their separate convention, nominated candidates, and drew up a platform affirming support for the gold standard; but this proved to be a meaningless gesture. Meanwhile, McKinley's astute campaign manager told friendly newspapers to remind readers that a vote for Bryan was a vote for anarchy. Perhaps some readers believed Mark Hanna, and assuredly his pals on Wall Street did.

So in the end, the staid conservative Republican won handily. In the popular vote McKinley had 7 million votes, some 500,000 more than Bryan, and in the electoral college it was no contest as the Republican counted 271 votes to Bryan's 176. Bryan lost New England, New York, and much of the Midwest. Only in the South and West was his message heard and accepted. In Congress, the Republicans added on to the gains they had made in the 1894 off-year elections.

UNDERLYING PHILOSOPHY BEGINS TO CHANGE

Little noticed at the time was the fundamental shift of emphasis in the Democratic Party philosophy. From Jefferson's time onward, the common thread holding the Democrats together was a commitment to "stand aside" government, based on the idea that the government's main role was negative—not to overtax, not to interfere with business, not to help labor, and not to shoulder any responsibility for the unemployed, sick, or aged. Bryan preached a new philosophy and was clearly ahead of his time. The Bryan Democrats saw government intervention as a positive force, a legitimate means of balancing the competing forces of capital, labor, industry, and agriculture through legislation and executive action. That view of government as a helpful agency was anathema to the conservative interests in 1896 and may still be a century later.

Bryan was down, but not out. Nor would presidential campaigning ever be the same, for although he had lost, Bryan showed a new conception of how a candidate ought to act by traveling across the land, shaking hands by the thousands, and speaking from the rear of a special railroad car with a crowd of newspapers ready to telegraph speeches back to their home bases. Some reporters thought they saw a crack in Bryan's armor. He could excite a crowd, but his message had a moralistic, almost evangelical fervor. He would make a great preacher, but would he make a great president?

No answer came, but the Democrats were willing to take a chance on Bryan, even after he became a party relic divorced from the promising leadership role thrust on him in 1896.

McKinley was the ideal man for the Republicans in 1897. He was a veteran, a former congressman and governor, and if his party wanted a gold standard, that was all right with him. He gladly signed the Gold Standard Act, and when rebels in Cuba made life miserable for their Spanish overlords, McKinley supported diplomatic intervention (extensive sugar and mineral interests were involved). As every schoolboy knows, the nation went to war when the USS *Maine* blew up in Havana harbor. A brief war ensued, and suddenly the United States was an imperial power, with Puerto Rico added to its territories and protectorates arranged for the Philippines and (in part) Cuba. Democrats in the Senate, and Bryan on the stump, criticized the McKinley policy as un-American, and the Democrats' foot-dragging slowed down the process, but by 1900 the United States was a colonial power.

NEW CENTURY, NEW CHALLENGES

The opening year of the twentieth century was also an election year, and in newspapers and magazines much speculation centered on the opportunities that lay before the American people. For five cents readers could choose from over a dozen magazines full of stories about technological improvements that would add to the easy life already brought by electric lighting, electric trolleys, subway systems, and elevated railroads. Motion pictures were not yet a craze, but Thomas A.

Edison was the subject of many articles that depicted technological wizardry as the key for a future dedicated to the pursuit of happiness in a manner undreamed of in 1776. Glossed over were the long working hours in most industries, the sweatshops where women and children worked 12- and 14-hour days, and the vast depletion of eastern forests.

The Republican Party was now solidly entrenched, having lost only two presidential elections since 1856 and usually in control of Congress as well. Democrats, except in the South, were becoming a minority party on a permanent basis. Even in a staunch Democratic stronghold such as Louisville an editorial writer could ask: "Is the Democracy dead?" Democrats were hard pressed to furnish a denial.

Bryan would not quit, however, and he kept hammering the Republicans for their hard-money policies. At a time when most workers were paid weekly wages in cash, shopkeepers still had trouble cashing a $20 bill and during periodic recessions they accepted scrips issued by cash-strapped employers. Yet the trusts were still dictating the costs for a gallon of kerosene (used for home lighting), a pound of sugar, or a box of matches. And the most gigantic merger in the nation's history was only months away, as Andrew Carnegie began his move toward creating the industrial giant, U.S. Steel, with its billion-dollar price tag. Financing a political campaign was never a problem for the rising corporations, and few if any dollars were ever earmarked for the critical Bryan or his party.

ROLE OF LOCAL
MACHINES ENLARGED

Still, the Democrats persisted. Reform candidates came and went, but in New York, Pittsburgh, and Chicago the Democratic machines took on a unique role. A poor family that needed coal during a harsh winter on Manhattan could go to the precinct captain and probably receive a burlap sack filled with fuel. A struggling family of Irish immigrants could hope that the oldest boy would be recommended for a job on the police force by the precinct captain. A Jewish girl who wanted to be a teacher could hope to be hired if the precinct boss knew her father. Another immigrant family from Italy, if they had Democratic connections, might have a son working on the municipal garbage detail. On upper Park Avenue, the builders borrowed from Republican bankers but had to take care of Democratic inspectors when the newfangled electric elevators were installed. "All politics are local," House Speaker Thomas "Tip" O'Neill once intoned. In America's big cities from 1900 to 1930, that was truer than true, and nobody knew this better than the Democrats warming their hands in a precinct headquarters.

So there was a two-tiered level of American politics, and both parties recognized the reality and lived with it. Poverty and crime exist in every society, and the muckraking movement in the five-cent magazines began to expose it, while Bryan worried about the gold standard. But the United States sailed into the twentieth century with a confidence that was lacking when the century drew to a close.

Democrats sounded hopeful at their 1900 nominating convention, after Republicans had endorsed a McKinley–Roosevelt ticket with much pomp and circumstance at Philadelphia. In Kansas City, Bryan welcomed a second chance and was offered it by the cheering delegates, who reached back and gave Adlai E. Stevenson (Cleveland's last vice president) the second place on the ticket. The platform committee took aim at the Republicans' love affair with gold and wrote a plank condemning the Gold Standard Act. Another and more controversial plank assailed the McKinley administration for its imperialistic intru-

sions in the Pacific and Caribbean. As for silver, the Democrats repeated their old 16-to-1 formula and urged the adoption of an inflationary program that could flood the country with silver dollars.

Only 40 years old and full of the same vinegar he had exhibited in 1896, Bryan went after the Republicans with more whistle-stopping, hand-shaking, and bonfire rallies. The Republican claim that Bryan was still an incipient anarchist had lost its sting, for the nation knew Bryan better this time, but he was no longer a fresh face. Carefully guided by Mark Hanna, McKinley stayed in the background most of the time and the Republicans never tired of reminding voters that the last four years had seen workers enjoy "a full dinner pail."

No longer the boy wonder, Bryan lost by close to a million votes in the popular count and was soundly beaten in the electoral college, 292 to 155. Disheartened Democrats, if they gave it much thought, realized their party was still talking to farmers and the voters were moving into the cities by the thousands. Bryan's speeches foresaw a role for government in the citizens' lives, but he was directing his call toward a diminish-

WILLIAM J. BRYAN
Democratic Candidate for President

ADLAI E. STEVENSON
Democratic Candidate for Vice-President

DEMOCRATIC PLATFORM

ADOPTED IN NATIONAL CONVENTION

AT KANSAS CITY, MO., JULY 5, 1900.

Democratic Presidential and Vice Presidential Candidates, 1900: Bryan and Adlai Stevenson. *Source:* National Archives.

ing breed, the American farmer. "You come to us and tell us that the great cities are in favor of the gold standard," Bryan said, but "I tell you that the real cities rest upon . . . fertile prairies. Burn down your cities and leave our farms and your cities will spring up again as if by magic. But destroy our farms and the grass will grow in the streets of every city in this country."

POPULATION SHIFTS TOWARD CITIES

Politicians did not need historian Frederick Jackson Turner to tell them that the old frontier was gone, the farmers were fast becoming a minority, and the city dwellers were the future source of political power in the United States.

The political equilibrium was upset further by the third murder of a president. McKinley had served only a few months in his second term when an assassin's bullet brought the brash young vice president, Theodore Roosevelt, into the White House in September 1901. Two years older than Bryan, Roosevelt was not the darling of the New York bankers, but had been placed in cold storage by them at the convention when they forced Roosevelt on the ticket. A blueblood with Harvard connections and a limited experience in western cattle raising, Roosevelt energized the reluctant Republicans. He also changed the presidency by becoming an activist in trust busting, environmental concerns, and naval building. Roosevelt used his office, as he said, as "a bully pulpit" to give Americans a new kind of presidency that was warm, relaxed, and full of confidence.

Roosevelt's popularity left the Democrats agape. Never before had a president become so friendly with the press, or the press so friendly with a president. Bryan retreated into the background and his departure left the Gold Democrats in control. The muckraking newsmen fired salvo after salvo at local bosses and corrupt senators, but spared Roosevelt from the fire. Gingerly, Roosevelt supported reforms in railroad regulation and signed Republican legislation that created a department of commerce. But he was not an easy target for anybody, and the Democrats despaired of finding a competent challenger as 1904 appeared on the calendar.

As it turned out, they never came close. A jubilant Roosevelt accepted the Republican nomination in June, then waited to see what the Democrats could find. After great soul searching, the Democrats settled on a Gold Democrat for their candidate. Colorless, shy, and in some ways more Republican than Roosevelt,

Alton B. Parker was the choice. A New York judge may have been chosen because he had fewer enemies on the convention floor than any other candidate. For whatever reason, the Democrats were stuck with the judge and he was stuck with them. With a Gold Democrat at their helm, the Democrats avoided the gold–silver issue and concentrated their platform's fire on the big trusts and the railroads. The nation apparently yawned and went about its business.

ROOSEVELT LANDSLIDE ENGULFS DEMOCRATS

The disparity between Roosevelt and Parker was so obvious that no pollsters were needed to turn predictions of a GOP sweep into reality. "TR" (as the newspaper headlines conveniently now called Roosevelt) won in a landslide, with 2.6 million votes more than Parker. Was Roosevelt popular? His 336 electoral votes were far ahead of Parker's 140. Roosevelt might have won by a bigger margin, but his White House luncheon with the black leader Booker T. Washington had infuriated the South. So the South stayed solidly with the Democrats, but not to Roosevelt's discomfort.

The Democrats had one piece of luck. Roosevelt said he would not run for a third term and thus removed himself from the 1908 contest. Bryan's friends perked up at this news, and given a financial setback here and a minor recession there, Democrats began planning for a comeback. Then a huge stock market drop in March 1907 seemed to be a down payment on a deep depression, and Republicans worried more than Democrats for the first time in years. A currency act passed in 1908 pushed the federal government closer to a bank regulatory role, but the drastic surgery needed was postponed.

Bubbling with confidence, Roosevelt picked his cabinet member William H. Taft as his anointed successor, and the Republican convention confirmed the choice at its June convention. Searching for a new base, the Democrats moved their convention site to Denver, and there they called Bryan back for one last try. Bryan could still make a rousing speech, and the crowds roared their approval, but the old fire was missing when the "Great Commoner" hit the campaign trail. For one thing, business was recovering from the 1907 collapse, and the platform committee merely came up with the usual suspects by condemning trusts, monopolies, and railroads for the people's problems.

Taft, able and rotund, was not interested in a whirlwind campaign, but let others do most of the talking. Bryan did most of the talking and actually provided lots of excitement in what might have been a dull election. But the end result was never in real doubt, as Taft had 7.6 million popular votes to 6.4 million for Bryan. The electoral college count was Taft 321, Bryan 162.

BRYAN FOUND THIRD TRY NO CHARM

So Bryan was through, and Taft was to carry on the trust busting that Roosevelt had promised but never quite got around to doing. Instead, Roosevelt went to Africa to hunt lions.

Bryan was too professional a politician to try and hold on to the party that had embraced him three times in vain. Taft was moving in the same direction as Roosevelt, actually was more effective in trust busting, but lacked TR's dramatic flair. There was much talk of running a southerner who could make an impression in the North, but all discussion grew more intense when Roosevelt began to criticize Taft, until an open rift occurred. Then a number of Republican governors asked Roosevelt to seek a third term, despite his pledge not to run again.

Indeed, things began to look up for the Democrats and in the midterm elections of 1910 they gained control of the House. The Senate was still Republican, but many pro-Roosevelt men were more friendly to Democrats than men on their side of the aisle.

Democrats began looking for a new face to offer voters on the national scene, and appeared to have found it when Woodrow Wilson left the presidency of Princeton University to run as a reform candidate for governor in New Jersey. In November 1910 Wilson was elected and his name suddenly sprang to the foreground of Democratic candidates for the 1912 race, although as yet Wilson was untried as a political figure.

WILSON RISES IN PARTY SPECULATION

Instead of being a passive governor, Wilson plunged into the business of reform and persuaded the state legislators to pass a progressive set of measures on taxes, schools, and transportation issues that drew more national attention to his competency. But Speaker of the House Champ Clark from Missouri had some new ideas, too. As leader of the Democratically controlled House, Clark had encouraged debate on issues the Republicans kept buried in pigeonholes. A graduated income tax, direct election of senators, and votes for women were openly discussed, and ultimately the constitutional amending process was implemented to bring real action.

Even the Senate was not immune to the blowing winds of change. Early in 1912 the Senate, stung by repeated charges that the body had become a mere "rich man's club," voted to send the amendment for direct election of senators to the states for ratification. Things really were changing!

In this heady atmosphere, with Roosevelt encouraging his friends to create a third party, the Democrats sensed victory. As Speaker Clark and House Majority Leader Oscar Underwood jostled for position, Wilson's friends wondered if they could nominate their man in the face of the archaic two-thirds rule (a nominee could not be elected by a simple majority, but needed two-thirds of all the delegates for his support). Meanwhile, a favorite-son boomlet for Governor Judson Harmon of Ohio loomed, and it seemed that the convention floor would see more banners than at any time since the disastrous 1860 Charleston convention—when everybody went home in an ill humor.

Roosevelt's supporters failed at the regular Republican convention, which nominated Taft, and went it alone by calling a second convention—for a Progressive, or Bull Moose, Party—and duly named TR as their standard-bearer.

Finally, the Democrats met, heard the long and boring nominating speeches, and then began to vote. After ten ballots, Clark was ahead but stymied by the two-thirds rule, yet his 556 loyal delegates seemed determined to stop the Wilson boom in its tracks. They might have succeeded if Bryan, now busy working in the smoke-filled rooms at hotels and on the convention floor, had not decided that the party could not win with Clark. Bryan shifted to Wilson and let delegates know his feelings. On the 46th ballot, Wilson was nominated by an exhausted bunch of Democrats.

With the usual chest-thumping manifest, the Democratic platform promised voters to clean up "corruption, fraud, and machine rule" from top to bottom. Wilson, with his neatly starched collar and pince-nez, ripped into that old Democratic bogeyman, the tariff, and assured voters he would batter down tariff walls built as "the entrenchments of Special Privilege." He linked high tariff rates to the trusts, hoping to convince voters that when they lighted a lamp they paid a double tax for high-priced kerosene in a device made by protected lampmakers. His first order of business as president, Wilson promised, was an "immediate downward revision" of the obnoxious tariff schedules. And, Wilson said, the Democratic Party was still the only place for the common man who needed a friend in the White House.

THE CRITICAL 1912 ELECTION

The divided Republicans provided most of the fireworks in that watershed election of 1912. The nation itself was at a pivotal point, for the population was more urban than rural, and small-town America was at its peak. In 1912 the nation boasted about 12,000 weekly newspapers, with their folksy editorials, rural community news, and loyal readership reaching an all-time peak. Taft and Roosevelt forces wrestled publicly, while the Democratic candidate said the contest was really "Wall Street versus Wilson."

Wilson picked up the challenge to old-fashioned, time-honored Democratic strategy that was first sounded in Bryan's 1896 campaign. When a disaster struck, the federal government had an obligation to help the victims, whether the trouble came from a flood or a financial blizzard. The government could be a positive force, Wilson insisted, and should be when its citizens suffered. From the rear platform of a railroad car, Wilson said that only the federal government had the power to tame the trusts, prevent greedy employers from exploiting low-paid workers, and weed out corrupters in high places. If Bryan had opened the way for a new path that Democrats might follow, Wilson turned it into a high road for a positive role for government. The old Democratic approach was traditional, but under Wilson the party followed its instincts and would find a "New Freedom" from special interests and other roadblocks to progress. People must trust the government to do the things that needed to be done, the one-time college professor told his audiences.

SPLIT MAKES WILSON WINNER

The message might have never been received if the Republicans had not been so divided. Roosevelt, who barely concealed his disdain for Democrats (TR had an inborn feeling that a Democrat probably used his sleeve instead of a handkerchief), showed even more bitterness for Taft. Taft had betrayed his trust, the hero of San Juan Hill implied, and had gone over to the financiers lock, stock, and barrel. Left on the defensive, Taft wanted to continue his programs—he actually had done far more trust busting than Roosevelt—and was hailed by the regular Republicans.

The 1912 campaign titillated the nation and left the exhausted Roosevelt wondering, on election night, if he had swung hard enough to keep Republican votes and still win over urban Democrats. He came close, but the final returns proved that the divisive campaign

had allowed Wilson to win. The combined Taft–Roosevelt popular vote was 7.6 million, Wilson trailed with 6.2 million, but where it counted, in the electoral college, Wilson had 435, Roosevelt 88, and Taft a humiliating 8.

Wilson, brimming with energy, was off to a running start. "No one can mistake the purpose for which the nation now seeks to use the Democratic party," Wilson said at his inauguration. "Hang on to your hats" was the president's implied message to Congress. Part of his vision of a "New Freedom" was a break with the traditional messages to Congress. Jefferson, unlike his two predecessors, had sent his messages by a clerk, and they were read to Congress. From 1801 to 1912, no president had broken Jefferson's rule of presidential conduct. Nonsense, Wilson said, the president has to go up Capitol Hill and speak to Congress—and the nation—in a face-to-face confrontation. At first, Congress thought this was brash, but Wilson made his fellow Democrats like it, and in time the Republicans decided it might be a good idea, too.

Speaking to a joint session of Congress, Wilson called for a whirlwind of activity, and because voters had given the Demcrats control in both the House and Senate, major reforms came fast and furious. Most notable was the Federal Reserve Act, which took the old independent treasury and revamped its powers and duties to create a system that is still in place. The Clayton Anti-Trust Act was an honest-to-God reform

Woodrow Wilson Campaigning in 1916. *Source:* Library of Congress.

measure that gave the government far more powers than the decrepit Sherman Act and led to a series of lawsuits to break monopolies that would keep federal court dockets crowded for years.

CONSTITUTIONAL AMENDMENTS RATIFIED

So far, so good. The law allowing injunctions to restrict the power of labor unions was relaxed. These gains, added to final ratification of the 16th and 17th amendments to the Constitution (one permitting an income tax, the other calling for direct election of the Senate), establishment of a Federal Trade Commission (aimed at unfair business dealings), and low tariff rates all made the heady days of 1913 memorable and boosted Wilson's stock with the voters. To be sure, the amendments came out of efforts by earlier Congresses, but Wilson was now ready to take all the credit.

Or most of it, for Bryan was still around and in fact was in Wilson's cabinet as secretary of state. The anti-imperialist Bryan was eager to undo some of the Republican outreach for colonies, and before he left the cabinet Congress passed legislation conferring "home rule" on the Philippines and Puerto Rico.

The euphoria lasted for a year, not even dampened by a new law that cut down on liquor shipments into those states where the sale of distilled spirits was banned by law. Much more of the same was on the plate when in August 1914 a Balkan shooting incident erupted into a full-scale world war. Reacting to the nation's shock, Wilson was quick to say that the United States would not be involved in a war brought on by imperialism and sword-rattling gone out of control. American ships would create their own neutrality zone and should be free to plow the seas everywhere. "Free ships make free goods" in 1915 echoed Jefferson's views a century earlier. The U.S. Navy was placed on the alert as Secretary of the Navy Josephus Daniels took on more responsibilities, as did his assistant, Franklin D. Roosevelt.

In the midterm elections held in the fall of 1914, the Democrats kept control of Congress, adding to their Senate majority but losing almost 60 seats in the House.

Wilson tried to keep the nation a spectator in the conflict that dragged on, cost the belligerents millions of lives in combat, and brought more misery to civilians. Except for areas where old ties made German Americans root for the Central Powers, there was an undercurrent of sympathy for the Allies. After his offer to mediate a peace was rejected by the warring powers, Wilson realized that outside intervention was a waste of time.

"HE KEPT US OUT OF WAR"

Meanwhile, the Republicans looked to 1916 as their year of the great comeback. The year began with the president urging Congress to spearhead a national preparedness program, with increased funding for a larger army, and legislation authorizing a force of 223,000 men passed only days before the Democratic National Convention renominated Wilson. Early in June, the Republicans had nominated Charles Evans Hughes, a brilliant lawyer and Supreme Court justice. The bloodbath waged on French battlefields continued as Americans jostled Wilson's or Evans's banner in the late summer: the Battle of the Somme cost the British 400,000, the Germans 450,000, and the French 200,000—one of the bloodiest and most futile battles in history and little ground gained or lost when it was over.

For all his expressed concern for the common man, Wilson showed little feeling for blacks, whose northern migration included a large portion of the nation's capital. Negro leader Booker T. Washington complained that the "New Freedom" Wilson promised apparently did not include the black community. Blacks working on federal payrolls were segregated from white workers. Another minority also felt left out. Women organizers of a suffragette movement found fault with Wilson and their "Votes for Women" marches drew little sympathy from Wilson. Delegates at the Democratic Convention were of a different mind, for in 12 states women still were denied the ballot, so a party platform plank called for a constitutional amendment to end the male monopoly. As it turned out, the 1916 election would be the last where women would be denied the ballot.

Wilson started his bid for reelection in 1916 and ended it on the same note: "He kept us out of war" was a slogan that appealed to a broad spectrum of voters, including the sizable German American block in the Midwest that had been critical of Wilson's pro-Allied policies. Irish Americans also defected from Wilson because he soft-pedaled his regret over the Easter Day "massacre" by British troops in Ireland. Hughes was a formal sort of man and found it hard to unbend on the hustings.

The final days of the campaign, with Hughes confident and Wilson pleading, left close observers saying that the contest was "too close to call." Big business was definitely hostile to Wilson, and although there was a modicum of prosperity in the wheat and corn belts because of wartime prices, there was much doubt that Wilson could hold his own in the Midwest and Far West. The South, of course, was Wilson's by default.

CLOSE CALL FOR WILSON

Telegraph lines hummed through the election night. Hughes won New England and was holding on to the big states, but Wilson had the lead in some key midwestern states and looked strong in the West. More than one newspaper had the headlines already set—*Hughes Elected!*—but press deadlines came and went in New York with no definite result. Not until the California vote was counted, and Wilson declared the winner by a mere 3,773 vote, could the Democrats breathe a sigh of victory.

Overall, Wilson had 9.1 million votes to 8.5 million for Hughes. The electoral vote was similarly close: 277 to 254. A swing of 2,000 votes in California would have elected Hughes. Congress also stayed Democratic, but the margin in the House was cut to six votes.

A WINTER OF DISCONTENT BUT NO DISASTER

The winter of 1916–1917 was certainly one of discontent. The Battle of Jutland left the British in control of the surface sea lanes and German submarines menaced American shipping, causing Wilson to ask Congress for authority to arm merchant ships. The House moved swiftly to pass the Armed Ship Bill, but a bipartisan clique of senators filibustered the bill into oblivion. Angered by this "little group of willful men," Wilson was frustrated until advised he could permit the armaments through an executive order. But Wilson's troubles with "willful men" were not over.

Winter snows were still melting when news from Russia told of a collapse of morale and a revolt against the czarist regime. U-boat sinkings in the Atlantic increased, and in early March five American ships were torpedoed by the Germans (including an oil tanker off the neutral Dutch coast). In early March newspapers were handed copies of an intercepted message from Germany to Mexico, where General Pershing had been chasing Pancho Villa along the Rio Grande. The so-called Zimmerman note offered Mexico the return of Arizona, Texas, and New Mexico if it would declare war on the United States.

Now things began to move. The Wilson cabinet met, deliberated, and advised the president to ask for war against the Germans. Finally, Wilson called for a special session of Congress to meet on April 2, and on the fateful day the president asked for a declaration of war against Germany because of its submarine campaign. The goal was world peace, the president said, as he coined his phrase: "The world must be made safe for Democracy."

RESHAPING THE PRESIDENCY

During the next two years, Wilson remade the presidency, and he had a vision to reshape the world. Eventually, more than 2 million American fighting men helped overwhelm the Germans by November 1918. In the process, the United States was mobilized out of a Washington headquarters that placed labor, industry, and most aspects of American life under a central control. The federal bureaucracy expanded as the war was nourished by Liberty Bond campaigns and an army of workers in munitions factories, textile plants, and the rising industrial complex around Detroit. Censorship descended, particularly in areas where German Americans were concentrated, and the nation underwent an orgy of senseless attacks on German American schools and churches.

Wilson was not afraid to use Republican talent as he sought a war footing for the whole country. He appointed Herbert Hoover, a California Republican, to head an emergency food effort and approved the rationing of vital commodities. The nation grew accustomed to "meatless Tuesdays" and "sugarless Fridays" as headlines told of starvation and famines in war-torn Europe.

Europe was bled white by the fighting. Allied propaganda made much use of Wilson's rhetoric, including his "14 Points" promising a just peace that would allow a redrawing of boundary lines along linguistic and ethnic, rather than political, grounds. The president, in his program made public in January 1918, also sought creation of an international body to make sure that this was "the war to end all wars."

EUROPE SURRENDERS TO WILSON

As Wilson became more popular in Europe, his appeal at home was weakening on several domestic fronts. Russia was out of the war and had accepted a humiliating German peace offer, but the new regime was so radical, conservative Americans wanted no part of it. When the moderate wing of the Russian government collapsed and the Bolsheviks took over and proclaimed a victory for "Soviet Communism," Wall

Street shuddered. While the last big offensive of the war embattled over a million American troops, the off-year elections were held. Trying to shore up the Democratic majority in Congress, Wilson asked voters to endorse his policies by sending more Democrats to Washington. Voters respounded by giving the Republicans control, though barely, of both the House and Senate.

Rebuffed, Wilson turned his attention to Europe, for as the election results came in, so did news of an armistice. In the peace that followed, Wilson took a leading role and became the first president to visit Europe while in office. For his diplomatic mission to Paris, Wilson made a tactical mistake by ignoring foreign policy experts in the Senate. At the time, this slight did not seem as much of a blunder. Hailed on the Champs-Elysées Boulevard as "the saviour of mankind," Wilson beamed and talked of a just peace, but on America's Main Streets his support was slipping.

The war ended with dramatic suddenness, and the people let off a lot of steam. Prohibition had been approved in the 18th Amendment to the Constitution, but nobody took it seriously until it was at length enforced (nominally, anyway, begininng in January 1920). Business was good, farmers had money in their pockets, and factory workers had savings built up during the wartime shortages. A binge of spending for Model-T Fords, fur coats, and fancy furniture gave a temporary lift to the economy. The stock market, hesitantly at first, joined in the boom.

THE LEAGUE VERSUS ISOLATIONISM

Wilson returned from Europe to face a Republican Congress that was in no mood to give the Democrats credit for winning the war or anything else. The main thing on Wilson's mind was the League of Nations he had helped create, and he was impatient when Congress dawdled and showed more interest in enforcing the upcoming "ban on booze." Congress passed the Volstead Act, giving the federal government the power to enforce the 18th Amendment, and Wilson vetoed it. A Calvinist with great moral convictions, Wilson was also a Democrat; and the mainstream of the Democratic Party had never liked the Prohibition amendment from the day of its origin. But now the Republicans ran over his veto with all the force of a Mack truck. In the halls of Congress, acceptance of Prohibition by the citizenry apparently was assumed.

Soon it was clear that on the byways and alleyways of the nation, the Prohibition amendment was a travesty. A new word, *bootlegger*, entered the nation's vocabulary. Who did not know bootleggers, those who trafficked in illegal whiskey and beer?

Domestic problems were not bothering Wilson. He wanted the Democrats to help him nudge the nation into a new international role, mainly through membership in the League of Nations. Wilson's gaffe at ignoring the Senate during the treaty negotiations was compounded when the 268-page document landed on the Foreign Relations Committee's desk. Senator Henry Cabot Lodge insisted that the whole treaty be read, line for line, and if boredom could not kill the treaty, he would. When Wilson realized the Republican attacks on the treaty ("We will lose our sovereignty as a nation" was strongly hinted in the committee hearings), he decided to go to the people directly.

WILSON COLLAPSES ON TOUR

In September Wilson scheduled a series of talks across the nation, where he planned to explain the treaty and urge its ratification without strings attached. A latent streak of isolationism, particularly strong in the Midwest, fed the fires of an anti-League movement. Lodge found Republican allies in Hiram Johnson and William Borah, two senators with a formidable combination of seniority and energy.

Wilson's audiences were polite, but in the West he aroused emotions when he alluded to his visits to French military cemeteries where American heroes were buried, and he asked for an outpouring of sentiment for the League and thus make future wars impossible. Suffering from fatigue, Wilson kept pushing until his campaign train stopped briefly in Colorado. Wilson started to go for a walk, but was stricken by a paralytic stroke. The rest of the tour was canceled and the train sped back to Washington.

Looking back, Wilson's collapse was also the end of the debate over the League. Place two mule-stubborn politicians at odds, and compromise becomes a near-impossibility. With Senator Lodge healthy and Wilson sick, it was no contest.

Now we know how ill Wilson really was, but at the time various White House schemes were employed to keep the truth hidden. The "willful little group" he had attacked proved adamant, and they were joined by too many Democrats. Wilson made a final appeal from his sickbed, and in the March 1920 crucial Senate vote the treaty fell seven votes short of the required two-thirds majority. As Wilson predicted, without the United States as a member, the League never had the necessary force to become a major deterrent of war.

The Democratic Party was in even worse shape after the fight, however, and in the 1920 presidential election, the torn seams of party unity were highly visible.

IN SEARCH OF "NORMALCY"

A few Democrats saw the treaty vote as only a minor setback and began scrambling for delegates headed for the San Francisco convention. In the suites of the Palace Hotel, it seemed that William Gibbs McAdoo might win on the first ballot. McAdoo was Wilson's son-in-law and secretary of the treasury, well known in party circles and a good campaigner. But there were others who thought they could distance themselves from Wilson and run an independent course. Governor Alfred E. Smith of New York was one—and he made no bones about his opposition to Prohibition. William Jennings Bryan was still around, and he begged the delegates to write in a platform plank pledging to dry up the nation. But Bryan was no longer a candidate, and the Ohio favorite son, Governor Cox, began to gain ground and won the nomination after 42 roll calls. In a bow to the New York Democrats, Franklin D. Roosevelt was picked as the vice presidential candidate—mainly because he bore a popular name and was only 38 years old and brimming with health.

BURIED IN A LANDSLIDE: THE 1920 ELECTION

Feeling cocky, the Republicans nominated Senator Warren Harding for president and Calvin Coolidge for vice president. Like Cox, Harding was a newspaper publisher in Ohio before entering the political arena. The election of 1920 thus pitted two Ohioans, neither of them well known or distinguished, in an election campaign summed up by Harding's phrase: "Back to Normalcy." In other words, Harding seemed to say, let us forget the war and the League mess and go back to a time when the most popular places in town were the post office and the ice-cream parlor.

The Cox–Roosevelt ticket took a terrible drubbing. The Harding landslide counted 16.1 million votes, while Cox lost with 9.1 million—or more votes than Wilson gained in losing only four years earlier. What made such a difference? Women now could vote in every state, and perhaps their overwhelming vote was for the handsome Harding instead of colorless Cox. For whatever reason, Democrats ran so poorly that their numbers in the House fell to a pitiful 131 to the

GOP's 303, and in the Senate Harding had a majority of 59 to 37 to work for his programs.

A DISMAL TIME FOR DEMOCRATS

Actually, Harding had no programs. A business downturn late in 1920 may have hurt Cox, but the recession did not slow down, and in 1921 a record 4.7 million workers were looking for jobs. As prosperity slowly returned, the stock market started an upward swing that took Wall Street favorites into record highs, week after week. A new kind of public hero emerged, too, as Babe Ruth and Jack Dempsey drew far more attention than the president in the *New York World* and the *San Francisco Chronicle*. Radio moved rapidly from its shortwave stage into the nation's parlors as more stations were licensed and the powerful stations could reach listeners 100 miles away (sometimes further) from their transmitters.

Immensely popular, Harding had troubles in his official family and went on vacation in the summer of 1923. On a return trip from an Alaskan vacation, Harding stopped in San Francisco and died suddenly. The suddenness of the president's death stunned the nation, but Calvin Coolidge was quick to reassure citizens that he would be just as quiet as Harding had been. Despite some joking about his tight-lipped manner by comedian Will Rogers, Coolidge left most of the government in the hands of Congress and the bureaucracy. Except for the rise of crime in big cities, where gangs fought over the territory where they sold bootleg whiskey and beer, the nation approved of Coolidge's reserved manner.

BUSINESS IS GOOD—TOO GOOD

The scandals that began to leak, ranging from embezzlement by Harding's appointee as alien property custodian to bribery and fraud in the Teapot Dome oil company mess, were all blamed on the dead president's easy relationship with crooked friends. Coolidge stood apart from the disgrace meted out to a former cabinet member and a handful of oil company grafters. Democrats could not attack the dead president, nor could they count on an easy win over Coolidge. After Coolidge repeatedly said "the Business of America is Business," the stock market jumped into higher ground. Auto sales also boomed, and new oil discoveries kept pace with the growing demand for gasoline. As a newspaper wag said, "the flow of bootlegged booze and gasoline carried the nation along on a tidal wave of prosperity."

Democrats were uneasy. William G. McAdoo (Wilson's secretary of the treasury) was not able to crow much about corruption in government, for he had been an attorney for one of the chief oil magnates in the Teapot Dome mess. Al Smith still wanted the nomination, and Senator Underwood of Alabama was interested in running against Coolidge, who was easily nominated by the Republicans at their great Cleveland love-fest that was more of a celebration than political convention.

The New York site of the 1924 Democratic Convention seemed to give Governor Smith a head start toward the nomination, but his liberal views on Prohibition hurt him in the South. Underwood had the southern vote but was not as aggressive in condemning the revived and racist Ku Klux Klan, even though the platform contained a plank repudiating the KKK. McAdoo looked good on paper, but as an oil company lawyer, he carried some of the Teapot Dome taint into his bid.

103 BALLOTS—AND DISASTER

Ultimately, the Democrats would again shoot themselves in the foot. Instead of a meeting to pick a president, the delegates indulged in an endurance contest. After a record 102 ballots, caused by the two-thirds rule, Democrats tried one more time and chose John W. Davis, the former congressman and ambassador to England who was now a Wall Street lawyer. In view of Coolidge's popularity, perhaps the party leaders were only looking for a sacrificial lamb; in any event, they found one in Davis.

Davis was not a pushover, but he was not the "dark-horse" candidate that Polk had been in 1844. Instead, Davis was the white horse nominee, ready to ride into battle as a former solicitor general who had been championing the underdog. As solicitor general Davis had successfully fought the Alabama convict-leasing system and in the Supreme Court he had won an overturn of the Oklahoma "grandfather clause" used to deny black voters their franchise. More recently, Davis had joined a Wall Street law firm and was considered one of the nation's leading corporation attorneys.

THE MAKING OF A DISASTER

Ordinarily, boardrooms are not the best place to look for a Democratic candidate, but in 1924 the Democrats became desperate. Smith was too "wet," Underwood

was too "dry," and McAdoo was too close to a smelly oilwell. Davis wore a very white shirt and well-tailored suit—the same qualities that had won for Harding in 1920.

Davis proved to be no Harding. Treasury Secretary Andrew Mellon, probably the wealthiest man ever to serve in the cabinet, tossed a bombshell when his department released a list of the wealthiest taxpayers in the country. The implication was that if Davis won, the incomes of everybody would be in the daily newspapers. That was bad business, for if Americans like anything, they like their incomes kept secret. On top of that, Republican maverick Senator Robert La Follette entered the race as the Progressive Party nominee. A constant embarrassment to the regular Republicans, La Follette proved to be a spoiler as he carried his home state (Wisconsin) and ran behind Coolidge in California, where Davis wound up in third place.

Democrats had a millionaire candidate but not much money in their campaign coffers. With gifts from corporations unrestricted by law, the Republicans suffered from an embarrassment of riches. But where could the money be spent, except on full-page newspaper ads or intermittent radio commercials? By and large, the campaign was boring and preordained. When the shouting ended, the nation heaved a collective sigh of relief, and few were surprised when the Wednesday headlines proclaimed Coolidge a landslide winner. Coolidge's 15.7 million votes were a ringing testimonial to his popularity, and Davis's 8.3 million only meant he was one of the "also rans" who became a footnote in history. Congress, of course, remained safely in Republican hands.

On the surface, everything looked bad for the Democrats. Farm prices began to slide, but Coolidge confidentially vetoed farm relief bills. When a jury found Nicola Sacco and Bartolomeo Vanzetti guilty at a 1920 murder trial in Massachusetts, who could have thought their conviction would arouse an international storm of protest? After appeals were exhausted and international pleas came for their pardon (their claim was that they had been convicted because of their anarchist backgrounds, not evidence presented at the trial), Coolidge refused to intervene, and they were executed in 1927. A second attempt at a farm relief bill was again vetoed by Coolidge.

DEMOCRATS DECIDE TO GO "WET"

Coolidge's popularity was an insurmontable barrier the Democrats did not have to cross, for the president issued a statement that he did not "choose to run for

President" in 1928 and created a temporary quandary in both parties. The Republicans recovered first, and a small boom emerged for Herbert Hoover, the secretary of commerce with strong alliances in the financial community. At their Kansas City convention, Hoover was nominated by the GOP delegates on the first ballot.

Democrats were almost as harmonious. There was a mood of defeatism rippling through the convention hall in Houston because of the country's prosperity and the smug confidence exuded by Republicans at their convention as they reaffirmed their support of Prohibition and a high tariff and rejected direct help for hard-pressed farmers. Governor Al Smith blasted away at the Republicans, pledged his support for the repeal of Prohibition, and endorsed the platform plank favoring direct aid to struggling farmers.

Smith had several problems. His accent, nursed by his East Side origins in Manhattan, made his radio remarks sound crude to nationwide radio audiences. A Catholic and a "wet," Smith had difficulty when reassuring southern audiences he was a Democrat who shared their concerns. The addition of Senator Joe Robinson of Arkansas to the ticket did little to mollify the evangelicals, whose whispering campaign ("Do we want the pope advising the White House?" was the whisperers' rhetorical kiss-of-death) promised trouble for Smith in the ordinarily reliable South. The Ku Klux Klan was gone, but the root cause of its popularity was still around in the Deep South.

SMITH HAD DRAWBACKS APLENTY

Another problem facing Smith was his limited vision. He was a New Yorker, born and bred, and knew little about the rest of the country. When a reporter asked Smith how he viewed his chances of winning the western states, Smith's rejoinder was, "What are the states west of the Mississippi?"

Hoover, projecting a public image of competence because of his record on war relief and as secretary of commerce, let others do most of the talking. The more Smith talked, the deeper his campaign sank in popular esteem. There were not many hopeful signs for Democrats that fall, except that in New York Franklin D. Roosevelt was running to succeed Smith as governor. After a crippling disease struck him, Roosevelt had exercised rigorously and was encouraged by his wife to try again for public office. From a wheelchair Roosevelt acted as Smith's floor manager at the convention, then returned home to run for governor in New York.

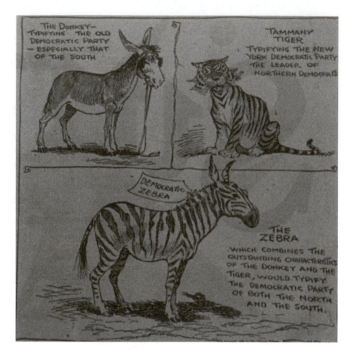

Democratic Campaign, 1928. "The New Symbol." Depiction of the Combining of the South Democrats and the North Democrats. *Source: Chicago Tribune,* June 25, 1928.

Roosevelt won in New York; Smith lost in the 48 states. And Smith lost badly. In fact, landslide margins were becoming a Republican habit. The total popular vote gave Hoover a 6-million vote plurality, but perhaps even worse for the Democrats was the earthquake rendering the Solid South into a crippled South. Seven southern states, led by Texas, marched into the Hoover column.

DEMOCRATS "NOT AN ORGANIZED PARTY"

The Democrats needed a poultice, and humorist Will Rogers gave them a humorous one in his newspaper column. "For Sale—would like to sell, trade, dispose of or give away to right parties franchise of what is humorously known as Democratic party. . . . Under present management they have killed off more good men than grade crossings have." Democrats shook their heads but laughed, and saw some truth in Roger's sheepish confession: "I am not a member of an organized party—I'm a Democrat."

Humor helped, but more than one editorial writer pondered the question asked so often since 1868: Has the Democratic Party become a permanent minority?

If bedrock Democratic states such as Virginia and Texas would vote for a Republican presidential candidate, perhaps the answer was yes.

The South defected, but in Chicago, Jersey City, Kansas City, and Boston the Democratic machines survived. In New York the Tammany crowd helped elect Roosevelt as governor in 1928 to buck the national trend, and Mayor Jimmy Walker was popular in speakeasys and on the lower East Side, if not on Park Avenue. The Kansas City Pendergast machine was heavy-handed, but had a few honest men whom Tom Pendergast liked and promoted, including an obscure county judge from Independence, Missouri, named Harry S. Truman. These local pockets of resistance were able to weather without huge discomfort the Hoover landslide.

HARD-PRESSED FARMERS SEEK RELIEF

Even the farmers whose prices were slipping lower month by month had voted for Hoover. Smith's popular votes in Iowa, Nebraska, Kansas, and the Dakotas were embarrassingly few in number. Yet within the Republican Party a "farm bloc" of senators from the wheat and corn belts complained that some kind of federal aid to tillers of the soil was needed, and quickly. They sought a government subsidy, to be financed by duties on exports. A bitter debate between House and Senate Republicans early in 1929 saw the Democrats mainly spectators at a bitter intraparty fight. The subsidy plan died after Hoover promised to veto any such federal giveaway.

By June the farm crisis was growing. Then Democrats joined in the passage in June of a Federal Farm Marketing Act, which set aside $500 million for low-interest loans based on crops of cotton, corn, and other commodities.

As farmers tightened their belts, speculators on Wall Street loosened theirs. A speculative boom, touched off by low margin requirements, allowed stocks to soar in unprecedented fashion from 1922 onward.

General Electric common stock soared to 394, but smart money was on the Auburn Automobile Corporation shares, quoted at 419 in August 1929. Railroad stocks, public utility shares, and oil company common stocks climbed to unprecedented highs, fed by the speculative fever in "bucket shops" where $100 was collateral for a $1,000 stock purchase. The Empire State Building was among the skyscraper projects announced for a buying public with an insatiable appetite. Or so it seemed.

BEGINNING OF THE GREAT DEPRESSION

Then came October 1929. A sharp sell-off in stocks was followed by a brief recovery. Black Friday ended the reverie with a loud bang as $30 billion (mostly in paper profits) vanished, margin calls ruined the small speculators, and bankers nervously assured reporters the problems were only temporary. General Electric stock, after a 4-for-1 split in 1926, sold for 245 before the crash—and would hit bottom at 22. Financier Jacob Raskob, a New York Catholic who was chairman of the Democratic National Committee, sought to make no political capital out of the calamity. "My friends and I are all buying stocks," Raskob answered, when reporters sought informed advice.

The whistling in the dark continued briefly. Inventories in factories piled higher, a Chevrolet sedan cost $750 but still automobile sales slumped, and farm prices took another downward plunge. Then in the spring of 1930, the banks began to fail, until 1,352 went under by the year's end. Depositors were sometimes left destitute, as job layoffs continued apace. President Hoover believed that relief for the unemployed was a local problem demanding a local solution, but he did seek lower interest rates from the Federal Reserve Board to help stimulate business.

Prices and morale tumbled apace. The *New York Times* cut its street-sale price to two cents, and before long a quarter-pound Butterfinger candy bar sold for a nickel. A nickel also bought an apple from any of hundreds of street vendors—some holding signs *Help a Veteran—Apples 5 cents*. In contrast to the misery in the marketplace, the steel skeleton of the luxurious Waldorf-Astoria Hotel rose skyward on Park Avenue.

The Democrats were suffering everywhere but at the polls in the off-year elections in 1930. Disspirited voters left the Republicans with a 1-vote margin in the Senate, but in the House the Democrats gained control, 220 to 214. Republican leaders saw no wake-up call in the results, however, and proceeded to pass a tariff bill calling for the highest duties in history.

Stopgap measures were not working. In 1931 bank failures continued at the rate of 7 a day, reaching 2,294 by Christmas. The Waldorf-Astoria Hotel opened, but was not crowded. A Chevrolet with a "rumble seat" was priced at $628, but buyers were scarce. One million auto workers lost their jobs, and the Ford plant managers discussed closing down the Model-A assembly line if sales did not pick up. Stagnant markets continued, and Ford closed down the plant. Detroit was staggered by the layoffs, but there was no city in

America immune from the wave of despondency that followed a plant closing or factory shutdown.

CRISIS DEEPENS, DEMOCRATS NEED MIRACLE WORKER

Early in 1932 it was clear that the depression was worldwide and that nothing in American history had ever reached such dimensions. Home foreclosures were rampant. Angry farmers dumped their milk on highways as an act of defiance, because milk selling at nine cents a quart did not pay their feed bills. Official reports on the jobless showed that 10 million Americans were unemployed.

Nevertheless, the Democrats came forth with no panacea. The Republicans, at their convention, called for a lower federal budget and adhered to a deflationary gold standard. The controversial Prohibition amendment was supported, but without notable enthusiasm. Democrats offered only one outstanding dif-

Democratic Sheet Music, 1932. *Source:* Smithsonian Institution.

ference in their platform—a pledge to get rid of Prohibition. But the candidates were different; Hoover offered more of the same, while Franklin D. Roosevelt offered hope. Roosevelt finally was nominated after newspaper tycoon William Randolph Hearst tried his best to make Speaker of the House John Nance Garner the candidate. Garner graciously took the second spot on the ticket, and all precedents were set aside.

Roosevelt, eager to jump into the fray, rode an airplane to Chicago to accept the nomination (tradition said that candidates waited until a formal notice came from a committee). By a deceptive effort to shield his handicap from the delegates, Roosevelt stood erect and told the convention: "I pledge myself to a new deal for the American people." Radio audiences overlooked his Harvard accent, reporters discounted his health problems, and disillusioned Republicans greeted his whirlwind tour with large crowds at every stop. Placards proclaiming "No More Hooverism" and "Give Us a New Deal" flourished in the whistle-stops, but left the voters in Plymouth Notch, Vermont, unmoved.

FDR BRINGS NEW DEAL TO WASHINGTON

Elsewhere, the story was different. Hoover carried Maine and Vermont, but not much else. He polled 15.7 million votes, but Roosevelt took 42 states with his 22.8 million ballots, and won in the electoral college by a landslide (472 to 59). The long wait from November to March was a grueling time and helped hurry along a constitutional amendment to bring a winning president into office much sooner. Many an American cupboard was bare, but there was a "New Deal" ahead. So citizens waited, and hoped.

The March 4, 1933, inauguration thus was to be the last before the Lame Duck amendment decreed that future presidents would take office on January 20. After the swearing-in ceremony, Roosevelt held on to the podium and gave a message of hope to the nation (radio reception had improved, so the president was clearly heard in San Diego as well as on the capitol steps). Roosevelt promised he would be a man of action and told Americans that "the only thing we have to fear is fear itself."

Once in office, Roosevelt stirred the country with his rapid-fire program during the famous "100 days" when more significant legislation came to his desk than probably at any time in history. Aided by his bright staff, full of Ivy League lawyers and "braintrusters," Roosevelt declared a bank holiday to sus-

Roosevelt/Garner, 1932. *Source: Washington Post.*

pend business for four days while all gold and silver exports were forbidden. On March 12 Roosevelt held his first of many "fireside chats" that drew millions of radio listeners as he explained his actions and told Americans what they wanted to hear—better times were coming. In quick order Congress met in special session and passed the New Deal laws that dealt with banks, reduced federal salaries, permitted the sale of beer and wine, abandoned the gold standard, created

This Bumper Plate Showed the Voters How FDR Liked His Name to Be Pronounced. *Source:* Stanley Wise Collection.

a Civilian Conservation Corps for 250,000 young unemployed men, and appropriated $500 million for direct relief through state-run work projects.

EVERY DAY A NEW LAW PASSED

That was just the beginning. The languishing Tennessee Valley Authority was revived to bring cheap electricity to surrounding states and exercise control of a multiple-dam system in seven southern states. Other laws gave relief to farmers, homeowners, and small businesses. Regulation of the stock market was turned over to a federal commission with watchdog powers. By the time the special session ended on June 16, a Public Works Administration was authorized to spend up to $3.3 billion to create jobs by building schools, post offices, armories, sidewalks.

Before the whirlwind of 1933 was over, Roosevelt had made one significant move in foreign affairs. Because of the bloody revolution in 1917 and other factors, three Republican presidents had refused to extend diplomatic recognition to the Soviet Union. Without fanfare, Roosevelt recognized the USSR, probably in the hope that Soviet gold might be spent on machinery and food that was piling up in warehouses and silos.

Roosevelt was no miracle man, but he came close. Wall Street perked up, and so did Main Street. More changes came in 1933, including the 21st Amendment to end Prohibition, "the glorious experiment." Ratified before Christmas, the repeal allowed legalized rum in voters' eggnog for the first time since 1919.

NO EASY WAY OUT

The depression was too deeply embedded for the New Deal to pull the country out of the doldrums hurriedly. The stock market fell back to new lows, and prices barely rose as unemployment persisted. The Democrats kept control of Congress for the next 20 years, but the laws of the marketplace gave way only slowly to the laws of Congress.

Roosevelt was probably the best party president since Jackson. He took the national committee structure created during the Hoover administration, when party fortunes were at a low point, and made his postmaster general, James A. Farley, also serve as chairman of the national committee. Alliances with city machines were nurtured. The Jefferson–Jackson dinners were used to feed a party war chest, and as Roosevelt looked longingly at the cherry blossoms south of the White House, he visualized a memorial to the founder of his party. After all, the Republicans had built their monument to Lincoln on the Mall; with deft moves in Congress, a park for the Jefferson Memorial in a fitting rotunda was funded and opened in 1939.

BLACK VOTERS TURN TO ROOSEVELT

In only one area was Roosevelt near-sighted. He never showed great concern for the segregation existing in the armed forces or in the federal workforce. Perhaps this oversight was part of an implicit compromise Roosevelt needed to keep his southern congressmen behind the New Deal. Despite this lapse, however, Roosevelt proved to be enormously popular in black communities. Blacks who had voted for Republicans for decades began defecting to the New Deal in 1936. For the next 50 years, black voters tended to favor Democrats so steadily that Republicans finally surrendered heavily black precincts by default.

Blacks suffered during the depression, but no group seemed to be harder hit than the farmers. Prices for grain and cotton fell, but in the decade beginning in 1931, the hardship of farm life was deepened by the forces of nature. Dark, billowing dust clouds swept across the plains and prairies, ravaging fields and leaving behind thick layers of dust on farm equipment and everything else standing in their pathway. The Dust Bowl became a metaphor for a destitute people whose farmers would not produce a living, so between 1932 and 1936 thousands of penurious citizens migrated to the West in search of jobs and "a new start."

The only good news seemed to come out of Washington. A second round of the New Deal was promoted by Congress as it created a program of rural electrification, passed a Social Security bill for "old-age pensions," and enacted a work-relief program for jobless young citizens. The National Labor Relations Act passed in July 1935 vastly strengthened the negotiating powers of labor unions.

PARTY REFORMS, DROPS TWO-THIRDS RULE

During the dark days, some Republicans joined the New Deal as the country's economy sputtered and sometimes almost stopped cold. Senator George Norris, a progressive Republican from Nebraska, was able to cross the aisle on key votes. But the key figures were all Democrats, ranging from Speaker Sam Rayburn in the House to a small band of Senate Democrats from the South (with overwhelming seniority) who kept party discipline intact. These same men also pushed for reforms in the Democratic Party, and at the June convention they forced a repeal of the old "two-thirds" rule that had plagued conventions time and again. Thereafter, a presidential nominee would need only a simple majority of delegates' votes to win.

FDR WINS IN 1936 LANDSLIDE

The 1936 presidential race settled down to a slow trot when Republicans chose Governor Alfred Landon of Kansas as their presidential nominee, and Roosevelt was easily renominated by Democrats. Although some Republicans attacked the New Deal as "socialist planning," Roosevelt exuded confidence in his public appearances, often riding in a convertible sedan. Polling techniques were still in their infancy, as the *Literary Digest* magazine proved when it predicted a Landon victory. The outcome was one of the most lopsided in history as Roosevelt beat Landon by a 11 million plurality and a 523-to-8 electoral college count. In the Senate, Democrats had a 76-to-16 majority and the House was nearly as overwhelming, 331 to 89.

The voters' endorsement of the New Deal was all the more surprising, for a majority of the nation's newspapers had endorsed Landon. Was the age-old power of newspapers during presidential elections crumbling?

"COURT-PACKING" BACKFIRES

Roosevelt, perhaps too cocky because of election returns, stubbed his toe in 1937. Upset with a conservative Supreme Court that was overturning many New Deal programs, Roosevelt asked Congress to expand the court from 9 to 15 (if judges reaching age 70 did not retire). A stick of dynamite in the Senate could not have produced a louder boom as many loyal New Dealers roared their disapproval. The "Court-packing bill" drew fire from every direction as radio commentators and newspaper editors condemned the plan as an assault on the nation's most sacred institution. The Supreme Court was suddenly embraced by a phalanx of supporters who vowed a fight to the death. Surely Roosevelt was surprised by the outburst of congressional defiance.

Some sparks of anger were doused when a staunch Republican justice announced his retirement. The sudden death of Senate Majority Leader Joe Robinson also frustrated the dwindling band of supporters, and in late July the bill was sent back to committee, where it died.

Through his first six years in the White House Roosevelt's attention was focused on the domestic crisis, but in the fall of 1938 it seemed that war clouds were gathering in Europe. The rise of Chancellor Adolph Hitler from 1933 onward marked the rearmament of a rejuvenated Germany. A crisis in September was resolved when the British and French diplomats allowed Germany to swallow the neighboring republic of Czechoslovakia. Hitler's broken promises, use of thugs for book burnings, and the humilation of Jews made the specter of a German threat that Roosevelt noted with dismay. Early in 1938, Roosevelt had supported a bill that called for a $1 billion expansion of the U.S. Navy, and a program of ship and submarine building was under way when the congressional elections were held.

As with other presidents before and since, Roosevelt campaigned against several rebel Democrats who had opposed his programs. And most of his efforts to "purge" dissenters failed, but the Democrats still held on to their majority in both houses. Indeed, Roosevelt would see that his attempts to help candidates also could backfire, as happened in Nebraska when he tried to aid the Republican Norris and was a helpless spectator when "the father of TVA" was defeated.

WAR COMES TO EUROPE

Recovery was still moving at a slow pace when World War II began in September 1939. Roosevelt proclaimed the United States a neutral power, but after a German *blitzkreig* knocked France out of the war in May and Great Britain was left alone, a surge of public opinion for some kind of aid to the British became evident.

"NO THIRD TERM" SLOGAN FAILS

In this ominous atmosphere, the 1940 presidential campaign started with Roosevelt informing the Democratic Convention that he was ready to step down. Two days later, the convention brushed aside "No Third Term" banners and nominated FDR and chose Henry Wallace for vice president. Now it was time for Republicans to plead that the two-term tradition should be honored, and a dark-horse candidate and former Democrat, Wendell Willkie, became their nominee. A national group calling itself "America First" held rallies, sometimes with Charles Lindbergh

FDR Poster, 1940. *Source:* Smithsonian Institution.

on the podium, pleading for the United States to stay out of the European war. Pro-Allied groups sprang up along the Atlantic coastline; but midwestern America clung to a vision of the Atlantic moat as the nation's best protection from foreign wars. The nation's first peacetime draft bill was debated in Congress and finally passed by a single vote in the House. Roosevelt stayed close to the White House and let others carry on the 1940 campaign, which ended in a 5 million plurality for Roosevelt and a resounding electoral college victory (449 to 82).

Roosevelt feuded with the press lords but enjoyed his frequent press conferences in the White House, where his sense of humor often delighted reporters but infuriated newspaper publishers. With prodding from the president, a wealthy Illinois Democrat started the *Chicago Sun* in an attempt to challenge the power of the arch-Republican *Chicago Tribune* in December 1941. As the *Sun* rose, the "empire of the rising sun"—Japan—attacked Pearl Harbor. Suddenly, all of Roosevelt's energy and attention were focused on winning World War II.

ALL-OUT MOBILIZATION FOR WAR

As commander in chief, Roosevelt turned aside party loyalty to appoint Republicans to organize the war effort (two Republicans already held key cabinet posts) and appealed to the GOP for a bipartisan effort to defeat the Axis powers. Wartime elections kept the Democrats in control of Congress; the energies of the nation were concentrated on industrial production and support for the 12 million soldiers, sailors, and marines. Dewey never seriously challenged Roosevelt, despite all the "No Fourth Term" banners waved amid the usual campaign rhetoric heard on the radio.

In 1944, while the Allies pushed Italy out of the war and invaded German-held France, the end of the European fighting seemed in sight. Roosevelt, now 62, wanted to serve a last term and see the war brought to a victorious conclusion; the Democratic convention complied, but interparty infighting led to the dumping of Wallace. Senator Harry S. Truman, the prodding investigator of corporate skulduggery, took Wallace's

place. Republicans made a half-hearted attempt to switch horses in the middle of a war, but Thomas E. Dewey was overmatched. Few knew how ailing Roosevelt really was, and to prove he was fit, the president rode to a rally in a downpour while waving from his open-topped convertible. He won with 25 million votes to Dewey's 22 million. The electoral college vote was 432 to 99.

Indeed, old Republican strongholds voted against Roosevelt all four times, and in certain corporate boardrooms it was easy to find men who detested Roosevelt as "a would-be dictator in the White House!" But among younger professionals, blacks, and citizens living on pension checks, FDR was considered the equal of Washington or Lincoln in popularity polls taken by reporters to fill a place in Sunday supplements.

Roosevelt's sudden death in April 1945 shocked the nation, for obliging reporters had not told the public how ill the president really was. Harry Truman came into the presidency prepared by his Senate service but with no intimate knowledge of White House secrets, including work on the atomic bomb project. After the war in Europe ended, Truman gained more assurance and took on his own shoulders responsibility for dropping the atomic bomb on Japanese targets in

Democratic Campaign, 1944, New York City. President Roosevelt Rides Through a Shower of Paper.
Source: Office of the War Information, October 21, 1944.

August 1945. Told by his staff that a planned invasion of Japan might cost 250,000 American casualties, Truman chose to have the bombs dropped as a means of ending the war quickly. Two weeks after the last bomb was dropped, the war was over.

THE GI BILL OF RIGHTS

Thereafter, Truman showed a firmness that confounded his opponents but pleased Democrats in the 79th Congress. Americans, as always, were eager for a demobilization "to get the boys home," and the few signs of tension between the United States and the Soviet Union were all but ignored in the rush to make former conquerors civilians. Congress, told by economists a depression and much joblessness must come with rapid demobilization, passed a landmark bill offering educational subsidies for veterans, as well as guarantees on home loans. This "GI Bill of Rights" provided for the peacetime transition of millions of veterans and created an educated workforce, and thus is always cited when critics of the federal government claim "Washington never does anything right."

Events soon proved that Truman loved the Democratic Party more than it loved him. The end of price controls, massive layoffs brought on by strikes, and memories of FDR's way of working with Congress were problems Truman faced. Educated at a public high school and possessed of a sharp midwestern twang, Truman was a far different leader from Roosevelt, but he had much of FDR's confidence, and he was not afraid of bucking public opinion after voters elected a Republican-controlled Congress in 1946.

Thwarted by a Senate with 51 Republicans and 45 Democrats, Truman was an embattled president in 1947 and 1948. He threatened to take over the steel industry, then had to back down.

The president paid a price for his liberalism. Truman's popularity sank as the first postwar pollsters began to gain much public attention. Truman's approval rating in 1947 sank to less than 30% of the polled citizens, and Republicans began to shuffle toward the White House with optimism early in 1948.

Democratic Campaign, 1948, Los Angeles. Thousands of People Lined Broadway as President Truman Slowly Paraded Down Los Angeles's Streets on His Way from the Train Station to Ambassador Hotel. Here Is Where He Made a Major Address. *Source:* Acme Photo, June 14, 1948.

Domestic politics had the center stage, but a bipartisaned vote had given Truman funds for the Marshall Plan forged by his secretary of state to combat the communists' inroads in Western Europe. American aid was pledged to rebuild Europe, and Winston Churchill called the plan "an unsordid act" of American altruism. Between 1948 and 1951, $13 billion was spent; communist parties in France and Italy were weakened, and the money seemed well spent.

TRUMAN UPSETS SOUTHERN DEMOCRATS

All hell broke loose in July 1948 when Truman issued Executive Order 9981 ending segregation in the armed forces. Truman had promised voters a "Fair Deal," and blacks applauded, but southern conservatives threatened to bolt the party. (Looking back, the long journey of the South from its Democratic moorings into the Republican Party may have begun with Truman's order for integration of the nation's military force.)

Two weeks earlier, Democrats had nominated Truman after some spoilsports suggested General George Marshall would be a better candidate, but Marshall gave them no encouragement whatever. So the ticket was Truman for president, Senator Alben Barkley for vice president. Barkley made himself popular with his convention blast at Republicans who promised to "clean out the bureaucracy in Washington." "What is a bureaucrat?" the Kentucky senator asked. "A bureaucrat is a Democrat who holds a job a Republican wants!"

Polls during the fall of 1948 gave the Truman–Barkley ticket no chance. Southerners resented the armed forces integration order, and in some states Truman's name would not be on the ballot. Truman fought back, rode around the nation, and from the rear of an observation car lambasted the "good-for-nothing 80th Congress," which he claimed was thwarting the liberal programs needed to keep the country prosperous. The postwar depression predicted by academicians never materialized, and the pent-up demand for consumer goods kept factories humming. A new Chevrolet sedan was priced at $1,285, a box of corn flakes cost 45 cents, and there were no homeless persons wandering the streets in 1948. Republicans had done so well with their "Had Enough?" slogan in 1946, however, they nominated Dewey again and were assured Truman was finished.

POLLSTERS PREDICT DEWEY VICTORY

Polls by news magazines and the Gallup group were of one voice as Election Day neared—Dewey would be elected, perhaps in a landslide. On election eve, pollster Elmo Roper told a nationwide radio audience that "barring a major miracle, Thomas E. Dewey will be elected president tomorrow." The *Chicago Tribune* was so confident, it printed an early edition with the headline *Dewey Defeats Truman!*

Of course, the last laugh was Truman's. To the pollsters' amazement, Truman lost New York, Pennsylvania, and half of the South but still managed to carry 28 states and win 303 electoral votes (Dewey had 189). Rebellious southern Democrats had placed their own "Dixiecrat" candidate in the fray, probably hoping to throw the election into the House. Their efforts fizzled. A Democratic Congress was also assured, but it would be dominated by southern conservatives. In his State of the Union address in 1949 Truman called for repeal of the controversial Taft–Hartley labor law and staked out a liberal agenda for the 81st Congress. The *Washington Star* reacted in horror and declared Truman had made "the most frankly socialist [speech] ever presented by a president." Congress was lukewarm to the president's "wish list" and refused to repeal the Taft–Hartley bill. Truman took what he could get, including a wage law fixing a 75-cents-an-hour minimum, but a commission to investigate civil rights violations was rejected.

Meanwhile, the constitutional amendment aimed at FDR wound its way slowly through the ratification process. The 22nd Amendment barred a president from serving more than two terms and had been offered by the 80th Congress as a gesture of contempt for Roosevelt. The amendment did not apply to Truman, however, and was officially ratified on February 26, 1951.

COLD WAR OVERRIDES OTHER ISSUES

By then, Truman had others things on his mind. The Cold War with the Soviet Union heated up, and war almost came in 1950 when South Korea was invaded by communist North Korea. Truman ordered American troops into action as part of a UN command, and after initial successes under General Douglas MacArthur the UN troops were pushed back. A brilliant naval maneuver forced the North Koreans into retreat, but then China sent in division after divison, and a stalemate ensued. MacArthur sent an ill-timed letter to the Speaker of the House—Truman was angry at being the butt of a political ploy—and he fired MacArthur. Public opinion, nursed by orchestrated television coverage, condemned Truman initially, but MacArthur overplayed his hand and faded away, like the old soldier he was.

Truman's other outspoken adversary was Senator

Joseph McCarthy of Wisconsin. After the Soviet Union exploded their own atomic bomb, the Republican senator accused the administration of being responsible for communists in key government posts. In time, McCarthy became a problem for the Republicans, too, but as the Korean War dragged on, McCarthy and his following kept up a drumfire of criticism that Truman resented. Perhaps because of these critics, Truman did authorize a "loyalty" check of federal employees and approved plans for a counterintelligence agency (CIA) to subdue claims he was "soft on communism."

Truman had other ideas, but his second term was more embattled and less productive than the first. The Korean stalemate was accentuated when casualty figures rose and no peace seemed in sight. A Senate investigating committee found widespread evidence of racketeering and some corrupt federal officials were tied in with criminal bosses. A member of Truman's White House staff caused embarrassment when his wife accepted a fur coat from a government contractor. Republican hints that another Teapot Dome scandal was coming never materialized, but Truman's personal popularity again plunged. A budget surplus, one of the last to be recorded over the next 50 years, was almost ignored by the voters.

PRIMARIES AND TELEVISION CHANGE THE RULES

Presidential primaries had long existed without much attention focused on them, but television quickly made them into national news events. In February 1952 Senator Estes Kefauver won the New Hampshire primary (Truman's name was on the ballot, but he ignored the contest), and presidential politics have never been the same. The media frenzy probably had nothing to do with Truman's decision, but on March 30 he announced, "I shall not be a candidate for re-election." A madcap race was on, with the Republicans nominating General Dwight Eisenhower and the Democrats choosing a somewhat reluctant Governor Adlai Stevenson of Illinois, who had Truman's endorsement.

Eisenhower, affectionately called "Ike," drew enormous crowds on his whistle-stop tour and led the polls consistently. Witty and articulate, Stevenson fell behind, although his campaign was a model in that he talked about issues and "took the higher ground." The result: an Eisenhower landslide. The Republican had 33 million votes to 27 million for Stevenson, and a 442–89 electoral college count. Congress was returned to the Republicans' control by the slimmest of margins (48–47 in the Senate).

Adlai Stevenson in New York Parade, 1952. *Source:* United Press International.

So the New Deal and Fair Deal ended with Inauguration Day, January 20, 1953. It had been a long ride and seen drastic changes in America's role in the world; the depression had finally ended, but it took a war to bring the country out of the doldrums. None of the doleful predictions for a postwar depression had proved true, so the return of a Republican to the White House after 20 years came as the country was prosperous, and the Korean War soon ended with a conference and compromise.

During the eight years when Ike was president, Democrats had control of Congress most of the time, but the most bitter partisanship came in Republican circles. Senator McCarthy was finally silenced by his Senate colleagues, but Vice President Richard Nixon was a controversial figure who nurtured his anti-communist image and courted the party faithful regularly. Democrats began to make gains in areas once strongly Republican (Maine and Minnesota), while a few reactionary southern Democrats moved into Republican ranks. The most notable domestic legislation, passed by the Democrats and signed by the president, created a huge national highway network.

DEMOCRATS CONTROL CONGRESS

Far more publicity was given to the 1954 decision of the Supreme Court in *Brown* v. *Board of Education*, which legally ended segregation in public schools. White Citizens' Councils, aimed at thwarting the transition, sprang up across the South.

Adlai Stevenson Poster. *Source:* Library of Congress.

KENNEDY'S "NEW FRONTIER"

In his acceptance speech Kennedy spoke of a "New Frontier" and welcomed a television debate with the Republican nominee. Republicans chose Richard Nixon on their first ballot, and the race shifted into high gear with a series of debates where the youthful Kennedy appeared to outdistance the vice president. The race proved to be extremely close—68 million votes cast and yet Kennedy had only 112,000 more than Nixon. In the electoral college, however, Kennedy won handily, 300 to 219.

At 43, Kennedy was a handsome and articulate Bostonian whose Senate career had been undistinguished. But Kennedy spoke boldly in his inaugural speech of a vision for America as a world leader. The Cold War was neither won nor lost, but in the end America would prevail. "Let us never negotiate out of fear, but let us never fear to negotiate," he told

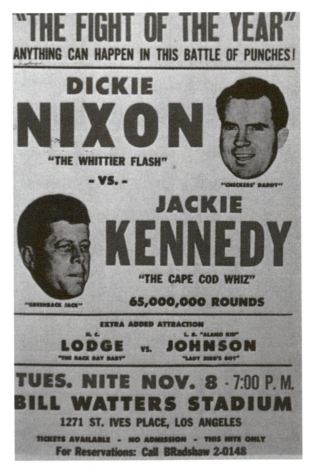

Nixon–Kennedy Poster. *Source:* Smithsonian Institution.

In the 1956 presidential election, a rematch of 1952 with Eisenhower running against Stevenson, Ike's popularity created another landslide. The president had a 457–74 majority in the electoral college, but Democrats continued to dominate Congress.

Eisenhower called federal troops to Little Rock in 1957 to ensure that the public schools would admit blacks, and the Cold War kept the defense budget boiling, but Democrats held on to control of Congress in the off-year elections, and in 1960 passed a Medical Care bill for the aged.

Democrats smelled blood in July 1960 at their Los Angeles convention. The presidential primaries had shown Senator John F. Kennedy to be a front-runner, but doubts were expressed because Kennedy was a Catholic. Kennedy was nominated on the first ballot and took Senator Lyndon B. Johnson as his running mate.

Senator Kennedy Campaigning in Los Angeles in 1960. *Source:* Wide World.

Americans *and* Russians. The Bay of Pigs fiasco in Cuba was a setback, but in domestic matters Kennedy supported a space program aimed at a visit to the moon, pushed for civil rights legislation, created a Peace Corps to aid Third World countries, and, in the time-honored Democratic tradition, slashed tariffs in pursuit of a free-trade policy.

The assassination of Kennedy in November 1963 ended an era in American history. That killing, along with a similar shooting of black leader Dr. Martin Luther King Jr., caused the nation to slide into a decade filled with self-doubts, new inner-city problems compounded by drugs, rising crime rates, and no let-up of a Cold War that cost over $1 trillion. Budget surpluses disappeared and the national debt climbed, but Kennedy's successor was as much a Cold Warrior as any of his predecessors.

Lyndon Johnson took office by reviewing Kennedy's programs and said, "Let us continue." He had been the Senate majority leader and was a skillful legislator, so once-doubtful civil rights bills went through Congress without difficulty. Voting rights for blacks and full integration for blacks in public places (on public transportation, hotels, restaurants, theaters) came quickly

Kennedy and Jacqueline Bouvier Kennedy. *Source:* Frank Muto, Capital.

President Johnson and Humphrey at the Convention in 1964. *Source:* Wide World.

after the 1964–1965 bills were signed. In strong contrast to the Harvard-trained Kennedy, with his New England accent, Johnson was a wheeler-dealer president who sometimes used crude language to force home a point.

Had there been no Vietnam, Johnson might have been listed among our best presidents. But the Asian conflict turned from a civil war into an American disaster, and Johnson was among its victims. He won reelection in 1964 against a conservative Republican who seemed no more warlike than Johnson. In another landslide, Johnson won 43 million votes to Barry Goldwater's 27 million, with the electoral count of 486 to 52.

THE GREAT SOCIETY STUMBLES

Except for the war, Johnson showed his commitment to bettering life for millions of Americans. During his "Great Society," programs for health care, education, and the environment were funded by Congress and carried on by his Republican successors for the next 30 years. But in the end, the staggering losses in Vietnam and concern over the nation's role in fighting communism everywhere on the globe forced Johnson into retreat. He chose not to seek reelection in 1968 and turned the party reins over to Vice President Hubert

Humphrey, an avowed liberal who relished a battle with conservatives.

Finally, Humphrey met his match. The Republican candidate, Richard Nixon, said the contest revolved around "my character" and he proceeded to campaign as a trustworthy Cold Warrior. The race really turned on the third candidate's abilities, however, as Governor George Wallace of Alabama, a segregationist, had immense appeal in blue-collar voting areas in both North and South. The popular vote was almost a dead heat for Nixon and Humphrey, 31.7 million to 31.2 million, but Wallace's 9.9 million votes hurt the Democrat and helped Nixon win easily in the electoral college, 301 to 191 (Wallace also had 46 votes from the South).

The seeds of integration Truman sowed in 1948 seemed to blossom into a bonanza for the Republicans 20 years later. Voting patterns in northern blue-collar precincts carried a strong message that unions would ignore at their peril. Even in prosperous times, working voters carry their prejudices to the polls. The swing toward a Republican candidate, begun in 1968, would accelerate until confirmed by the elections of 1980, 1984, and 1988. Lobbying organizations for lax firearms laws, sale of public lands, and relaxed environmental rules took note and began to cultivate these former Democrats. In a short period, the word *liberal* was turned from a compliment into a cuss-word in many circles.

VOTERS START SHIFT TO CONSERVATISM

From 1969 forward, the American voters continued their slow migration from the Democratic Party. In 1933, three in five voters considered themselves Democrats when polled on party preference, but by 1983 the major parties were neck and neck. The Democrats would usually control Congress, but no Republican president called for drastic reforms or tried to kill social programs that came out of Democratic administrations.

As the selection of Humphrey showed in 1968, candidates were still selected by delegates chosen by traditional methods: party service, precinct or district meetings, national or state committee service. But before the 1972 campaign the Democrats tried to meet the demands of reformers who insisted the old methods were archaic. These reformers succeeded in creating a quota system for minorities (blacks, women, Hispanics) who had been pretty much ignored in the traditional selection of delegates.

Presidential primaries gained more time on evening telecasts, but the reform movement carried Senator George McGovern into the 1972 convention as the

Senator McGovern Running for Democratic Party, 1972. *Source:* Associated Press.

odds-on favorite. Reports of a break-in at the national headquarters in an office building, Watergate, in Washington, D.C., were easily dismissed. City machines, already in disrepute, suffered from the reforms, and some former bosses decided to stay on the sidelines instead of working for the McGovern ticket.

The Nixon–McGovern race was over before it began. The Republican candidate swamped McGovern

Democratic Party Presidential Candidate Humphrey and Vice Presidential Candidate Muskie. *Source:* Staff/Pinto.

with over 47 million votes to the Dakotan's 29 million. The electoral count was a Democratic embarrassment: Nixon 520, McGovern 17.

Nixon found he could work with a Congress controlled by Democrats, particularly the southern Democrats, and he scored some diplomatic coups such as the recognition of the Communist People's Republic of China that a Democratic president would have avoided. The resignation of Vice President Spiro Agnew brought Gerald Ford into the vice presidency, and when Nixon resigned in August 1974, the American people had a president they had not elected to the high office.

During the Watergate investigations and on through to Nixon's final wave from the helicopter pad, television coverage of national politics was overwhelming. Thus the 1976 presidential primaries took on a new dimension, as Georgian James E. "Jimmy" Carter proved. A former governor and peanut grower, Carter was the first of the self-nominated candidates ever to go into primaries without any organizational backing whatever and emerge the winner. In the process, the Carter sweep of primaries made the convention delegates' vote into nothing but a confirmation of the primary process.

CARTER WINS THE PRIMARIES

Carter pressed his campaign against President Ford as a new face who was not allied to the "Washington Establishment." Running as an outsider ("beyond the Beltway") Carter convinced voters of his personal honesty and brought back to the Democrats thousands of workingmen and women who had defected in the 1968 and 1972 campaigns. Nevertheless, the race was close. Carter had 40.8 million votes, Ford 39.1 million, and the outcome was in doubt until early on the morning after Election Day when Ohio was safely in the Democratic column. Senator Walter Mondale of Minnesota was elected vice president.

Mainly because of the high cost of national television commercials, the Democrats spent around $55 million to elect Carter. The Republicans spent more, but in a lost cause (perhaps made inevitable by Ford's early pardon of Nixon).

Carter Campaigning in Newark, New Jersey. *Source:* Carter Library.

The first governor of a southern state to be elected president since 1844, from the outset Carter showed that he was perhaps too much of an outsider. Moreover, Carter had not used the Democratic national organization to much advantage—neither had Kennedy or Johnson—but Carter's staff was personally loyal and not party oriented. The Carter White House staff, mainly consisting of young Georgians without many acquaintances on Capitol Hill, was unable to establish a working rapport with Congress. One result was that although Carter carried out pledges to stop a wasteful B-1 bomber program and promoted the extension of voting rights in slow-moving southern regions, he could not count on a solid block of votes in a Democratically controlled Congress.

By bringing together the leaders of Egypt and Israel at his Camp David retreat for a peace accord, Carter scored one important diplomatic triumph. This was overshadowed when a group of terrorists seized the American Embassy in Iran and held the Americans captive through the summer and fall of the 1980 election year. After an American attempt to rescue the hostages failed miserably, Carter was fighting for his political life.

Presidential primaries took the center stage from February on as Carter defeated a feeble challenge from Senator Ted Kennedy in New Hampshire and Hollywood film star Ronald Reagan smashed his Republican opponents. The California governor, once a New Deal Democrat, had made a ideological shift of 180 degrees and now sailed into the Republican convention as the predetermined candidate. Inflation became a key issue in the campaign, and business slowed down in the summer after the Federal Reserve Board (with Carter's support) raised the prime interest rate to 12%—an all-time high.

TELEVISION TAKES OVER

In the now-traditional television debates, Reagan's good looks and easy manner contrasted with Carter's earnest but mild demeanor. Polls predicted Reagan would win big, and he did, carrying most of the South and the northern industrial strongholds. Labor, once able to develop a whopping majority for a Democratic candidate, was unable to muster members into Carter's column. Jewish urban voters, blacks, and non-skilled workers either did not vote or defected from their usual Democratic voting habits. All these factors added up to one thing: another landslide for Republicans. Reagan won with 43.8 million votes to 36.4 million for Carter, and 489 electoral votes to Carter's 49. Few had predicted a Republican victory of such dimensions.

Carter Smile. *Source:* Smithsonian Institution.

TWELVE YEARS ON THE OUTSIDE

For the next 12 years, Republican presidents lived in the White House but with a few exceptions Democrats controlled one or both houses of Congress. Reagan's landslide intimidated Congress, and tax cuts were passed that boosted the national debt from $8.3 billion in 1980 to $3.5 *trillion* when Reagan stepped down in 1989. Meanwhile, Reagan increased the defense budget, assailed the Soviet Union as an "evil empire," and rejuvenated the Republican organization that Nixon had allowed to sleep softly. Polls rated Reagan's popularity in the same category once used for Eisenhower, as the Democrats began jostling in the presidential primaries. Early in 1984 former Vice President Walter Mondale stumbled in New Hampshire when Senator Gary Hart came out of nowhere to win with 37% of the vote.

The combination of good balloting and media attention could work wonders, for Hart had been a weak second in Iowa. Eight days later, helped by around-the-clock media attention, Hart leaped ahead and won New Hampshire, and appeared headed for a preconvention victory until his personal life (some spent on a yacht named *Monkey Business*) was exposed and he withdrew. The media could make and break, the 1984 campaign proved.

After Hart dropped out, Mondale won the nomination, and the Democratic candidate committed the unpardonable sin (in American politics) of suggesting taxes might have to be raised to cut the federal deficit. That was the end of Mondale's brief bid, and in that disastrous Democratic year Reagan's popularity soared. He beat Mondale in the popular vote 54 million to 37 million, and by an overwhelming 525 to 14 in the electoral college.

Republicans took credit for the meltdown of the Cold War as the USSR became more friendly at the atomic weapons treaty talks. Reagan was even invited to speak in Moscow, and as the "evil empire" faded, the political atmosphere for Democrats was bleak. The soaring federal deficit was not a great issue, but environment and arms control were much discussed after the Republicans promoted George Bush toward the White House. An easy winner in the primaries, Bush made television commercials his chief campaign tool. Massachusetts Governor Michael Dukakis was nominated by the Democrats to confirm the primary results. The conventions were becoming television spectaculars, with long-winded speeches and glamorous interviews, but no power remained in the old process that had brought the likes of Theodore Roosevelt and Woodrow Wilson to the nation's attention.

AN UNBEATABLE CANDIDATE—ALMOST

President Bush had to recant on a no-new-taxes pledge, but business held up well until 1990, and Democrats once again took control in Congress. Then a border incident in the Middle East erupted into a full-scale war, with Bush leading the way for a UN force (mainly American troops and ships) that had its own *blitzkrieg* on an outmanned Iraqi army. Bush's popularity in polls soared to 83%, and a *New York Times* columnist suggested the Democrats had lost the 1992 presidential race before it started.

The young governor of Arkansas, William Jefferson "Bill" Clinton, had other thoughts. He dashed to Iowa and New Hampshire and took a commanding lead in the polls, despite some harmful allegations concerning his personal life. In 1984 such rumors had ruined Gary Hart's chances, but in 1992 Clinton's youthful exuberance and promise to remake the federal bureaucracy (as an outsider looking in) won him the nomination. In the summer of 1992, suddenly the Bush campaign was in trouble, and the television debates did nothing to help the incumbent president.

The other presidential candidate in 1992 was Ross Perot, a Texas gadfly millionaire who finally ran as an Independent with a "plague on your houses" attitude toward both Bush and Clinton. Perot's followers managed to place their man's name on the ticket in all 50 states. Both Republicans and Democrats assumed Perot would hurt the other side, and let it go at that.

By late October, it was clear that the Bush campaign had floundered, that Clinton had forged into the lead, and that Perot had spent about $40 million of his fortune in a doomed quest for the presidency. All this was confirmed by the outcome, as Clinton had 44 million votes to 39.1 million for Bush and 19 million for Perot. The electoral college count was even more lopsided: Clinton 370, Bush 168, Perot 0. Democrats also kept control in both houses of Congress.

PARTY 200 YEARS OLD

On an overcast January day, Clinton was inaugurated with almost 400,000 citizens looking on as the bareheaded 47-year-old president took the oath. The scene reminded onlookers of two earlier presidents in their 40s who had become national icons: Teddy Roosevelt and Jack Kennedy. Thereafter, Clinton sent Congress plans for deficit reduction (which meant more taxes), measures for gun control, and a treaty striking down trade barriers in all of North America.

Congress passed all of these, but in one case by only a single vote. So far, so good, even though the margin of victory was scary. The abortion issue, never settled despite a favorable Supreme Court decision in 1973, was kept alive by shootings at clinics by religious zealots. Democrats were reminded that preserving religious freedom had been one of Thomas Jefferson's highest priorities and were reassured by Clinton's actions to safeguard and uphold the *Roe* v. *Wade* decision in the face of verbal sniping in Congress and gunfire in the streets.

Then the first lady came forward with a national health care program that was immediately attacked by Republicans, plus lobbying groups involved in the health industry, and an estimated $200 million was spent in a television crash effort to defeat the president's health plan. Hillary Clinton suddenly became a lightning rod for criticism from both mild Republicans and the far right Christian Coalition. The campaign that had started with a such a loud bang ended in a bitter whimper.

Thus encouraged, in the fall of 1994 Republicans unleashed a full-scale attack on the incumbent congressmen who had helped Clinton pass his program. The outcome was devastating for Democrats; not a single Republican incumbent lost, while even senior senators from once-safe southern states fell victim to the GOP landslide. When the dust settled, Republicans had control of Congress for the first time in 40 years.

Exuberant Republicans forgot, temporarily, that the Constitution gave the president veto power, but Clinton gave them a lesson in civics in late 1995 and early 1996 as he thwarted plans for cuts in medical and social programs recently attacked as "holdovers from the New Deal and Great Society." Clinton reminded voters that despite criticism, the federal government was still a last refuge for many aged and ill citizens, for children in broken homes, and for costly educational programs. Republicans had also sought to change or abolish environmental protection programs, but Clinton and the Democrats in Congress held their ground as the nation swung into the 1996 presidential and congressional races with much at stake.

Whatever the outcome of the 1996 election, the Democratic Party would be charged with carrying the traditional role laid out at its founding in 1796 by Thomas Jefferson. Two hundred years earlier, Jefferson had been instrumental in forming the party, and when he left the White House he set forth the party's cardinal principle: "The care of human life and happiness, and not their destruction, is the first and only legitimate object of good government." From Jefferson's day to Clinton's, nobody had come up with a better idea. Whatever the outcome of the 1996 election, the Democratic party still has its historic mission, unchanged since Jefferson first conceived it.

Robert Allen Rutland

SEE ALSO Andrew Jackson, Martin Van Buren, James K. Polk, Franklin Pierce, James Buchanan, Grover Cleveland, Woodrow Wilson, Franklin D. Roosevelt, Harry S. Truman, John F. Kennedy, Lyndon B. Johnson, Jimmy Carter, Bill Clinton

BIBLIOGRAPHY

Agar, Herbert. *Pursuit of Happiness: The Story of American Democracy.* Boston: Houghton Mifflin, 1938.

Andersen, Kristi. *The Creation of a Democratic Majority, 1928–1936.* Chicago: University of Chicago, 1979.

Ansom, Robert S. *McGovern: A Biography.* New York: Holt, Rinehart and Winston, 1972.

Arden, Caroline. *Getting the Donkey Out of the Ditch: The Democratic Party in Search of Itself.* New York: Greenwood, 1988.

Baker, Jean H. *Affairs of Party: The Political Culture of Northern Democrats in the Mid-19th Century.* Ithaca, NY: Cornell University Press, 1983.

Banning, Lance. *The Jeffersonian Persuasion.* Ithaca, NY: Cornell University Press, 1978.

Beard, Charles A. *Economic Origins of Jeffersonian Democracy.* New York: Macmillan, 1915.

Berman, Larry. *Lyndon Jonson's War: The Road to Stalemate in Vietnam.* New York: Norton, 1989.

Brown, Stuart G. *The First Republicans.* Syracuse, NY: Syracuse University Press, 1954.

Bryan, William J. *A Tale of Two Conventions.* New York: Funk and Wagnalls, 1912.

Burner, David. *The Politics of Provincialism: The Democratic Party in Transition, 1918–1932.* New York: Knopf, 1967.

Burns, James MacGregor. *The Democrats Must Lead: The Case for a Progressive Democratic Party.* Boulder, CO: Westview Presser, 1992.

Carter, Jimmy. *A Government as Good as Its People.* New York: Simon and Schuster, 1977.

Chambers, William N. *The Democrats, 1789–1964.* Princeton, NJ: Van Nostrand, 1964.

Chambers, William N. *Political Parties in the New Nation: The American Experience, 1776–1809.* New York: Oxford University Press, 1963.

Chase, James S. *Emergence of the Presidential Nominating Convention, 1789–1832.* Urbana: University of Illinois Press, 1973.

Cohn, David L. *The Fabulous Democrats.* New York: G.P. Putnam's Sons, 1956.

Colton, Elizabeth, O. *The Jackson Phenomenon: The Man, the Power, the Message.* New York: Doubleday, 1989.

Conkin, Paul K. *Big Daddy from the Pedernales: Lyndon Baynes Johnson.* Boston: Twayne, 1986.

Cunningham, Noble. *The Jeffersonian Republicans: The*

Formation of Party Organization, 1789–1801. Chapel Hill: University of North Carolina Press, 1957.

David, Paul T., et al. *The Politics of National Party Conventions.* Washington, DC: Brookings Institution, 1960.

Dell, Christopher. *Lincoln and the War Democrats.* Rutherford, NJ: Fairleigh Dickinson University Press, 1975.

Donovan, Robert J. *Conflict and Crisis: The Presidency of Harry S. Truman.* New York: Norton, 1977.

Eisele, Albert. *Almost to the Presidency: A Biography of Two American Politicians.* Blue Earth, MN: Piper, 1972.

Ferguson, Thomas. *Right Turn: The Decline of the Democrats and the Future of American Politics.* New York: Hill and Wang, 1986.

Flick, Alexander C. *Samuel Jones Tilden: A Study in Political Sagacity.* New York: Dodd Mead, 1939.

Freidel, Frank. *Franklin D. Roosevelt.* Boston: Little Brown, 1952.

Garraty, John A. *Woodrow Wilson: A Great Life in Brief.* New York: Knopf, 1956.

Garson, Robert A. *The Democratic Party and the Politics of Sectionalism, 1941–1948.* Baton Rouge: Louisiana State University Press, 1974.

Gillon, Steven M. *The Democrats' Dilemma: Walter F. Mondale and the Liberal Legacy.* New York: Columbia University Press, 1992.

Glad, Paul W. *The Trumpet Soundeth: William Jennings Bryan and His Democracy, 1896–1912.* Lincoln: University of Nebraska Press, 1960.

Goldman, Ralph N. *The Democratic Party in American Politics.* New York: Macmillan, 1966.

Goldman, Ralph M. *Search for Consensus: The Story of the Democratic Party.* Philadelphia: Temple University Press, 1979.

Gorman, Joseph B. *Kefauver: A Political Biography.* New York: Oxford University Press, 1971.

Grossman, Lawrence. *The Democratic Party and the Negro: Northern and National Politics, 1868–1892.* Urbana: University of Illinois Press, 1976.

Guterbock, Thomas M. *Machine Politics in Transition: Party and Community in Chicago.* Chicago: University of Chicago Press, 1980.

Hamby, Alonzo L. *Beyond the New Deal: Harry S. Truman and American Liberalism.* New York: Columbia University Press, 1973.

Hammond, Jabez D. *The History of Political Parties in the State of New York.* Syracuse, NY: Hall, Mills, 1852.

Harbaugh, William H. *Lawyer's Lawyer: The Life of John Davis.* New York: Oxford University Press, 1973.

Henggeler, Paul R. *In His Steps: Lyndon Johnson and the Kennedy Mystique.* Chicago: I.R. Dee, 1991.

Hershowitz, Leo. *Tweed's New York.* New York: Anchor, 1977.

Holcombe, Arthur N. *The Political Parties of Today.* New York: Harper and Brothers, 1924.

Hollingsworth, J. Roger. *The Whirligig of Politics: The Democracy of Cleveland and Bryan.* Chicago: University of Chicago Press, 1963.

Johannsen, Robert W. *Stephen A. Douglas.* New York: Oxford University Press, 1973.

Kent, Frank R. *The Democratic Party: A History.* New York: Macmillan, 1928.

Koenig, Louis W. *Bryan: A Political Biography.* New York: Putnam, 1971.

Kucharsky, David. *The Man from Plains: The Mind and Spirit of Jimmy Carter.* New York: Harper and Row, 1976.

Kuttner, Robert. *The Life of the Party: Democratic Prospects in 1988 and Beyond.* New York: Viking, 1987.

Lengle, James I. *Representation and Presidential Primaries: The Democratic Party in the Post-Reform Era.* Westport, CT: Greenwood Press, 1981.

Leuchtenburg, William E. *Franklin D. Roosevelt and the New Deal, 1932–1940.* New York: Harper and Row, 1963.

Link, Arthur S. *Woodrow Wilson and the Progressive Era, 1910–1917.* New York: Harpers, 1954.

Martin, John B. *Adlai Stevenson and the World.* New York: Doubleday, 1976.

McCoy, Charles A. *Polk and the Presidency.* Austin: University of Texas Press, 1960.

Merrill, Hoarace S. *Bourbon Democracy of the Middle West, 1865–1896.* Seattle: University of Washington Press, 1967.

Merrill, Horace S. *Bourbon Leader: Grover Cleveland and the Democratic Party.* Boston: Little, Brown, 1957.

Mileur, Jerome M., ed. *The Liberal Tradition in Crisis.* Lexington, MA: Heath, 1974.

Morrison, Chaplain W. *Democratic Politics and Sectionalism: The Wilmot Proviso Controversy.* Chapel Hill: University of North Carolina Press, 1967.

Murray, Robert K. *The 103rd Ballot: The Democrats and the Disaster of Madison Square Garden.* New York: Harper and Row, 1976.

Myers, Gustavus. *The History of Tammany Hall.* New York: Boni and Liveright, 1917.

Nevins, Allan. *Grover Cleveland: A Study in Courage.* New York: Dodd Mead, 1932.

Nichols, Roy F. *The Democratic Machines, 1850–1854.* New York: Columbia University Press, 1923.

Nichols, Roy F. *The Invention of the American Political Party.* New York: Macmillan, 1967.

O'Connor, Richard. *The First Hurrah: A Biography of Alfred E. Smith.* New York: Putnam, 1970.

Parmet, Herbert S. *The Democrats: The Years After FDR.* New York: Macmillan, 1976.

Peterson, Merrill. *The Jefferson Image in the American Mind.* New York: Oxford University Press, 1960.

Remini, Robert V. *Martin Van Buren and the Making of the Democratic Party.* New York: Columbia University Press, 1959.

Sanders, Arthur B. *Victory: How a Progressive Democratic Party Can Win and Govern.* Armonk, NY: M.E. Sharpe, 1992.

Schlesinger, Arthur M., Jr. *The Age of Jackson.* Boston: Little, Brown, 1948.

Schlesinger, Arthur M., Jr. *A Thousand Days: John F. Kennedy in the White House.* Boston: Houghton Mifflin, 1965.

Silbey, Joel H. *A Respectable Minority: The Democratic Party in the Civil War Era, 1860–1868.* New York: Norton, 1977.

Solberg, Carl. *Hubert Humphrey: A Biography.* NY: Norton, 1984.

Stewart, John G. *One Last Chance: The Democratic Party, 1974–76.* New York: Praeger, 1974.

Thompson, Hunter S. *Better than Sex: Confessions of a Political Junkie.* New York: Random House, 1994.

Van Buren, Martin. *Inquiry into the Origins and Course of Political Parties in the United States.* New York: Hurd and Houghton, 1867.

Ware, Alan. *The Breakdown of Democratic Party Organization, 1940–1980.* Oxford: Claredon Press, 1985.

Wicker, Tom. *JFK and LBJ: The Influence of Personality upon Politics.* Baltimore: Penguin, 1976.

Wooten, James T. Dasher: *The Roots and the Rising of Jimmy Carter.* New York: Summit, 1978.

I THINK WE'VE GOT ANOTHER WASHINGTON

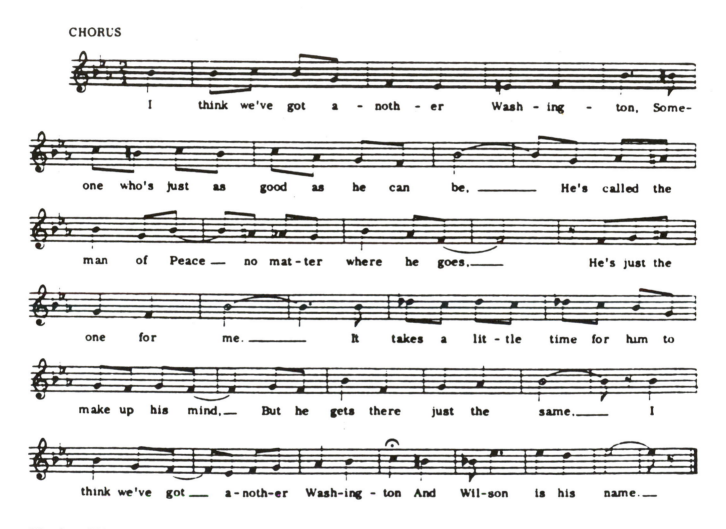

Woodrow Wilson Campaign Song, 1912. *Source:* National Archives.

ISSUES AND IDEOLOGY

Abortion

The legal status of abortion has been the subject of heated and divisive political debate ever since the Supreme Court decided, in *Roe* v. *Wade* (1973) that women have a constitutional right to abortion and states cannot therefore prohibit doctors from performing this procedure. This ruling unleashed onto the American political scene some of the strongest, least compromising factions in American history, generating a level of commitment and intensity among activists that has seldom been seen in American history. Over the past 30 years, few other political issues have inspired marches, civil disobedience, and violence similar to that of the abortion issue. The effects of this divisive and inflammatory issue on partisan politics have been noticeable, with the Democratic Party taking a diametrically opposite position from the Republican Party. The Democratic Party, generally regarded as more liberal, has unsurprisingly come to be identified with the pro-choice cause; however, the actual relationship between the Democratic Party and the right to abortion is not as simple as party formulations might suggest. Initially, the right to abortion was championed by a Republican-dominated Supreme Court and opposed by a Democratic president (Carter). It was only during the Reagan presidency, when the Republican Party adopted a strong and proselytizing "traditional family values" position, that the various elements of the Democratic Party coalesced around the right to abortion as a central party principle.

In the Supreme Court, at least, the abortion issue has always been decided by Republicans. The *Roe* Court was dominated by Republican appointees (only three of the nine justices had been appointed by Democratic presidents), but many of these justices were liberal, whose tendency, under the leadership of Eisenhower-appointed Chief Justice Earl Warren, had been to extend the sphere of protected liberties, often by direct judicial intervention. The Warren Court had under-taken a broad and ambitious plan of judicial activism that centered much of the social change of the 1950s and 1960s right in the Supreme Court. The Warren Court not only held that the Bill of Rights, specifically the First, Third, Fourth, Fifth, and Ninth amendments, constituted a "penumbra" of protections that could be contained under a broad "privacy" right, it used the 14th Amendment to apply the protections afforded by this "right" to state as well as federal legislation. By the time *Roe* was heard by the Supreme Court, Warren had been replaced by the more conservative Warren Burger, but the weight of Warren-era precedents and the continued presence on the Court of the liberal justices that had made these precedents led to the decidedly unconservative outcome that established abortion as a "privacy" right (by a 7-to-2 margin).

The strength of this decision, and the determination of the *Roe* justices to back up that ruling persistently and consistently, meant that for nearly 16 years after *Roe*, the Supreme Court consistently struck down attempts by the states to restrict access to legal abortions, overturning measures allowing the prospective father a veto over a woman's abortion decision and requiring parental consent for the abortions of minors. The Court also struck down a variety of state laws designed to discourage women from having abortions: exposure to mandatory, detailed descriptions of fetal development; descriptions of the risks and possible psychological traumas; and reminders about the availability of support from the father or from social service agencies. The only important exception to this slew of rulings that protected nearly unlimited access to abortions came in *Maher* v. *Roe* and *Harris* v. *McRae*, in which Congress was allowed to restrict Medicaid funding for abortions.

The Courts that were responsible for these rulings were still dominated by Republican appointees, but over the 16 years during which the original abortion cases were heard, the liberal majority on the Court was declining as the original justices from *Roe* retired and were replaced by the decidedly antiabortion Reagan appointees. The only Democrat-appointed members after 1975 (when William O. Douglas retired after 36 years on the Court) were Thurgood Marshall and Byron White, the latter of whom had been one of the two justices in the minority in the *Roe* decision and who was staunchly against the "right to abortion." Carter, the only Democratic president for the 20 years following the *Roe* ruling, was also the only president in the twentieth century who did not get the opportunity to appoint a member of the Supreme Court—and as an antiabortionist, any appointment he made would likely have continued the slow dissolution of the *Roe* majority. By 1989 the two dissenters in *Roe*, Rehnquist and White, were reinforced by the Reagan appointees, and with the makeup of the Court thus, the string of rulings in support of abortion was interrupted in 1989 in the case of *Webster* v. *Reproductive Health Services*. In *Webster* the Court ruled, by a 5-to-4 margin, that some state-imposed restrictions on abortion are constitutionally permissible. The issue in *Webster* was a preamble to a Missouri law that declared that human life begins at the moment of conception. *Webster* did not overturn *Roe*, though Republican-appointed Justice Antonin Scalia urged the Court to do so, but it did invite state legislatures to write restrictive abortion laws that might pass constitutional muster.

By the time of the *Webster* ruling, the two sides of the abortion issue, outside the Supreme Court, were almost wholly identifiable by party affiliation. While the Court itself had only two Democratic appointees—one of whom, Justice White, not only voted with the majority in *Webster* but had been an opponent of the "right to abortion" since *Roe*—support for and against the "right to abortion" in the Congress and the presidency had increasingly fallen out over party lines, and by 1989 this identification was almost absolute. Of the 23 senators who signed the antiabortion *amici* briefs sent to the Supreme Court, only one was a Democrat, and of the 25 senators who signed a pro-choice brief sent in 1989, only three were Republican. While the 1988 Republican national platform affirmed "that the unborn child has a fundamental individual right to life which cannot be infringed," the Democratic national platform read: "We further believe that . . . the fundamental right of reproductive choice should be guaranteed regardless of ability to pay."

But the Democratic Party had come late to its position of unequivocal support of the right to abortion. Republican President Ford had equivocated on the abortion issue, cautiously opposing *Roe* by saying that the Court had "gone too far," declaring that the states should have the power to decide, but opposing any constitutional amendment that would limit or overturn *Roe*. Ford was criticized by both sides of the abortion debate for his fence straddling. The Democrats missed the opportunity to galvanize support of pro-choice voters by not opposing Ford with a strongly pro-choice candidate. Carter, a deeply religious southern Baptist who personally opposed abortion, campaigned to end federal funding for abortions. Like Ford, however, he opposed a constitutional amendment to overturn *Roe*. Carter's nomination by the Democratic Convention in 1976 meant that the party's first post-*Roe* platform was a lukewarm concession to the pro-choice forces within the party; it read that "it is undesirable to amend the U.S. Constitution to overturn the Supreme Court decision [on abortion]." As the campaign progressed, Carter changed his position on the constitutional amendment, cutting the one thread that connected him to abortion rights elements of the Democratic Party.

As president, Carter, like Ford before him, did little either to legitimize or to oppose the ruling in *Roe*. He mainly restricted himself to fighting federal funding of abortion by supporting the Hyde Amendment's restrictions on the use of Medicaid funds to pay for abortions. Carter maintained throughout his presidency that though he was personally opposed to abortion, he had taken an oath to uphold the laws and Constitution of the United States, which included the Supreme Court's ruling in *Roe*. In support of this position, he stated that "I don't see the need for a constitutional amendment on the subject . . . what the Supreme Court has ruled is adequate for our country. . . . But it doesn't seem right to me for the Federal Government to collect taxes from those who have deep religious feelings against abortion and use that same tax money to finance abortions."

Carter's middle-of-the-road stance on abortion was typical of not only *Roe*-era presidents but also, with the exception of Ronald Reagan, the presidential hopefuls of the time. George Bush took the typical line at the time, trying to downplay the abortion controversy by opposing both federal funding of abortions and a constitutional amendment overturning *Roe*. Pro-choice forces within the Democratic Party, however, were more active than they had been at the 1976 convention, and they managed to get a plank into the 1980 platform that more strongly supported abortion; the platform recognized "the belief of many Americans that a woman has a right to choose whether and when to have a child." This language, which was still not as strong as the "reproductive freedom as a fundamental human right" clause that would appear in later Democratic platforms, was a compromise between

Carter and a faction led by the feminist Gloria Steinem, who had called for support of federal funding of abortions through Medicaid.

Reagan's strong position on the abortion issue, and the dominating rhetoric and strategy of that administration, helped bring the Democratic Party, during the 1980s, to a more solidly pro-choice position. Congressional Democrats consistently opposed Reagan's attempts to cut funding to clinics that performed abortions and provided abortion counseling, though the Republican majority in the Senate, which gave Strom Thurmond control of the Senate Judiciary Committee, precluded Democrats from successfully blocking the slew of antiabortion judicial appointees. When the Democrats regained a senatorial majority in 1987, however, the Senate rejected Reagan's Supreme Court nomination of Robert Bork, an outspoken opponent of *Roe* who had called that ruling "an unconstitutional decision, a serious and wholly unjustifiable judicial usurpation of state legislative authority." This rejection forced Reagan to appoint a less controversial justice, but after the Bork battle, the Democrats in the Senate were in no mood for a fight, and the Senate approved Anthony Kennedy, who would vote party line with the conservative majority that Reagan had forged on the Rehnquist Court.

The Democratic majority in Congress was often unable to block the Reaganite assault on abortion rights, and by the late 1980s, a significant portion of congressional Democrats were decidedly antiabortion. In April 1989, 50 House Democrats sent a letter to the chairman of the National Democratic Committee seeking a change in the party's platform. In language reminiscent of Carter's position, they wrote that "it is politically wrongheaded for our party to be on the record as favoring the use of taxpayer dollars to fund an alleged 'fundamental right' which is so strongly opposed in conscience by millions of Americans and by ourselves." Traditionally, the Democratic leadership, secure in a congressional majority, had not put any pressure on antiabortion Democrats to vote the party line, but with the increasing number of antiabortion members, the party's ability to promote itself as the party of abortion rights was being undermined. With an increasing number of House Democrats voting with the Republicans on abortion issues, and a new Republican majority in Congress, the abortion rights elements in the Democratic Party faced strong opposition.

The election of Bill Clinton in 1992, the first Democrat in 12 years and the only post-*Roe* president to support the right to abortion, signaled a possible resurgence in the strength of the abortion rights groups in the government. Two days after his inaugu-

ration, Clinton issued an executive order repealing the Reagan and Bush administrations' bans on abortion counseling. Clinton also rescinded a ban on fetal tissue research. With the potential of Clinton's appointments to federal judgeships to alter the balance achieved during 12 years of Republican appointees, Republicans geared up for battles over Clinton's nominees.

Early in Clinton's first term, long-time *Roe* opponent Justice White retired, giving Clinton the opportunity once again to shift the balance on the Court, this time in favor of abortion rights. In this and a subsequent appointment to the Supreme Court, Clinton chose not to confront directly the antiabortion forces in the Senate with a strongly pro-choice nominee. Ruth Bader Ginsburg, who replaced White, has a reputation as a centrist, although her record is strong on women's rights issues. Prior to nomination, Steven Breyer had not expressed any public view on the constitutionality of abortion. As a judge, Breyer had voted to strike down federal regulations that barred federally funded clinics from engaging in abortion counseling. These two appointments served to strengthen the moderate forces on the Court but reversed the Republican-era trend that was gradually but steadily undermining *Roe*. The Clinton-affected Rehnquist Court is unlikely to make any radical moves on the abortion issue, particularly regarding the overturning of *Roe*. The near future of the abortion issue will likely be settled in Congress and between the president and the new Republican congressional majority.

Jessamyn West

SEE ALSO Women

BIBLIOGRAPHY

Cook, Elizabeth Adell, Ted G. Jelen, and Clyde Wilcox. *Between Two Absolutes: Public Opinion and the Politics of Abortion.* Boulder, CO: Westview Press, 1992.

Craig, Barbara Hinkson, and David M. O'Brien. *Abortion and American Politics.* Chatham, NJ: Chatham House, 1993.

Tribe, Laurence H. *Abortion: The Clash of Absolutes.* New York: Norton, 1990.

Affirmative Action

Affirmative action programs were developed by federal agencies given the authority to make rules and regulations under the Civil Rights Act of 1964 for desegregating activities receiving federal funding. President Lyndon Johnson issued an executive order in 1965 that promoted affirmative action for employment and promotion in the federal government and for businesses contracting to do work for the federal government. In 1972 the U.S. Office of Education issued guidelines that contained "goals" for university admission and hiring policies for both African Americans and women.

Progress in affirmative action is generally measured in terms of the number of minorities or women admitted to a university or employed or promoted at a company. In order to retain federal funding many companies and universities have felt pressured to show "progress." This pressure can lead to preferential treatment and challenges to the traditional methodologies that have been used for school admissions (e.g., the scholastic aptitude test, or SAT). Some minority groups have argued that these tests are not good predictors of academic success. For example, women score lower on the SAT than men, but women have higher graduation rates. In addition, it is alleged that the SAT is culturally biased in favor of middle-class Anglos.

The main constitutional issue posed by affirmative action is whether these programs discriminate against whites and violate the Equal Protection Clause of the 14th Amendment. This has led to a string of decisions but unfortunately not a clear-cut answer.

In *Regents of the University of California v. Bakke* (1978) the Court struck down a special admissions program at a state medical school because it excluded a white applicant on the basis of his race. Bakke had applied to the University of California–Davis medical school twice and had been rejected both times. African American applicants with significantly lower grade-point averages and medical aptitude text scores had been admitted through a special admissions program that reserved 16 places in the class of 100 for minority applicants. The University of California argued that its use of race was "benign." That is, it was designed to help minorities, not hurt them. The special admissions program was designed to counter the effects of past discrimination and increase the number of underrepresented minorities in the medical school. In addition, the university argued that it would obtain those benefits that are derived from having an ethnically diverse student body.

The Supreme Court held that the objectives of the university were legitimate but that maintaining a *separate* admissions program with a quota of openings not available to white applicants violated the Equal Protection Clause. The mandate to provide equal protection could not mean one thing to one individual and something else when applied to another individual. As a consequence, the Court ordered that Bakke be admitted to the medical school and that the special admissions program be eliminated. It also recommended that the university examine the Harvard program, which considers an applicant's ethnicity a "plus" but does not have a numerical quota that excludes persons from competing for all positions.

This line of thinking was the guiding force in determining a more recent case in the U.S. 4th Circuit Court of Appeals. The court held in *Podberesky* v. *Kirvin* (1994) that the University of Maryland may *not* fund a scholarship program that awards aid only to African American students. The decision is binding only on the states in the 4th district (i.e., Maryland, North and South Carolina, Virginia, and West Virginia), and it is probable that the case will be appealed to the Supreme Court. Nevertheless, it may be indicative that the courts continue to look with disfavor on programs that entirely exclude a racial group or that create a quota.

Some cases have upheld the practice of affirmative action. In *United Steelworkers of America* v. *Weber* (1979) the Supreme Court approved of a plan developed by the Kaiser Aluminum Corporation and a union that reserved 50% of higher-paying jobs for minorities. Only 2% of skilled technical jobs were held by African Americans, but they comprised 39% of the workforce. Weber was excluded from a training program that would have led to a higher-paying job, but African American employees with less seniority and fewer qualifications were accepted. Weber could not claim that his rights to equal protection under the 14th Amendment had been abridged, since the 14th Amendment applies only to the "state." Instead, he argued that the affirmative action program violated provisions of the 1964 Civil Rights Act, which forbade discrimination on the basis of race.

The Supreme Court ruled that the 1964 Civil Rights Act did not prohibit affirmative action plans and that it would be "ironic" if private efforts to deal with the vestiges of past discrimination were to be found impermissible based on a piece of legislation passed with the goal of assisting the minority groups that had experienced the past discrimination.

The Supreme Court has continued to express concern about whites adversely affected by affirmative action programs. In *Firefighters Local Union* v. *Stotts* (1984) the Court held that a city could not lay off white firefighters in favor of African American firefighters with less seniority. And in *Richmond* v. *Crosen* (1989) the Supreme Court held that a minority set-aside program that allotted 30% of all city construction contracts to minorities violated the Equal Protection Clause.

In a 1995 decision the Supreme Court cast doubt on the constitutionality of affirmative action programs that award federal contracts even for "benign" purposes. In *Adarand* v. *Pena* the Court examined a law that mandated that at least 10% of federal money spent on highway projects go to businesses owned by "disadvantaged individuals." A job in the San Juan National Forest in southern Colorado was awarded to Mountain Gravel and Construction, a firm owned by an alleged disadvantaged individual. Adarand Contractors, owned by a white man, submitted a bid for the work that was $1,700 less than the bid of Mountain Gravel but Adarand was still not awarded the contract. The company sued, challenging the constitutionality of the set-aside program.

Justice Sandra Day O'Connor, writing for the majority, found that federal programs that classify people by race, even for ostensibly a benign purpose such as increasing opportunities for minorities, are unconstitutional unless they are subject to the most searching judicial inquiry, "narrowly tailored," and accomplish a "compelling governmental interest." The Court stopped short of voiding federal affirmative action entirely, but it did establish a formidable obstacle with the "compelling governmental interest" standard.

Justices Scalia and Thomas would have gone further and wrote in their concurring opinions that affirmative action programs can *never* be justified. The ruling cast doubt on the validity of *Fullilove* v. *Klutznick* (1980), which had upheld a 10% federal set-aside program for minority contractors. Mr. Justice Thomas, the court's only African American, wrote that he found "benign discrimination" every bit as noxious as "malicious prejudice."

The change in attitude of the "Court is dramatic when comparing the *Adarand* decision with that of the *Metro Broadcasting* v. *Federal Communications Commission* (FCC) just four years earlier. In the *Metro* case the Court ruled that the federal government may use "benign racial classifications" to give a preference to African Americans in awarding radio and television licenses. Because fewer than 1% of the nation's radio and television stations were owned by minorities in 1978, the FCC said that it would consider it a "plus factor" in awarding future licenses if the application was submitted from a minority.

Metro Broadcasting, a predominately white Florida firm, lost a bid for a new television station license in Orlando to a company owned by a Hispanic and sued. The Court upheld the FCC's use of "benign racial classifications" not just to remedy past discrimination but also to give African Americans and other minorities a greater share of federal benefits.

By the mid-1990s the makeup and thinking of the Court, and perhaps much of the nation, regarding affirmative action had changed. Congress had amended Title VI of the Civil Rights Act to make it clear that employers were not required to meet statistical quotas reflecting the available workforce. In addition, several

Republican leaders (e.g., Phil Gramm, Bob Dole, Lamar Alexander, and Pat Buchanan) believe that affirmative action should be curtailed.

Governor Pete Wilson of California announced that California's state universities were abandoning affirmative action as a tool to guarantee the diversity of the student body and employees. Governor Wilson made his opposition to affirmative action the cornerstone in his short-lived presidential campaign. But he did highlight the issue in the minds of the electorate.

In October 1995 President Clinton announced in a major address on racial harmony at the University of Texas that he did not like affirmative action but that it was still necessary in order to remedy the lingering effects of past discrimination. The same day that the president spoke at the University of Texas, Louis Farrakhan led a "million man march" in which he called for African American men to take greater control of their lives and responsibility for their families. He presented a vision of the future where civil rights organizations would free themselves from reliance on white funding sources, bureaucratic decisions and legal opinions (e.g., those that deal with promoting the welfare of African Americans through affirmative action programs). His view was that the system has been built on the wrong idea (i.e., white supremacy) and that there is really no way that African Americans could integrate into white society, be it through affirmative action or other programs, and maintain their self-respect.

On the other hand, President Clinton presented a defense of affirmative action and governmental assistance that should be linked to greater personal responsibility among African Americans. How can the decisions and opinions of divergent views found in the courts, among African American leaders and politicians regarding affirmative action be reconciled? Perhaps they cannot. Rather than look for consistency in the law or among politicians, we may need to resign ourselves to some uncertainty about how far affirmative action programs can go. At some point they do indeed become "reverse discrimination," but that point may vary from program to program, and each of those programs may have to be judged separately.

If the courts want to announce a clear-cut national policy, they will shortly have the opportunity. A case that it being appealed to the U.S. Supreme Court involves an affirmative action program at the University of Texas Law School. In 1992 the law school admitted 41 African Americans and 55 Mexican Americans using a separate committee to evaluate the credentials of Anglo applicants and another committee to evaluate the qualifications of minority applicants. Use of the "Texas Index" resulted in a white applicant's having a

1% chance of being admitted to the law school and a Mexican American applicant's having a 90% chance.

Four white students who were denied admission but who had better Law School Admission Test scores than most of the minority applicants that were admitted sued. The university responded that if they had not used the "Texas Index" the number of African Americans admitted would have dropped from 41 to 9 and the number of Mexican American students in the law school would have declined from 55 to only 18. The "Texas Index" called for the use of separate admission committees and the use of a formula based on standardized test scores and grade-point averages. White and minority applicants had separate cutoff points.

The lower court ruled that the Texas use of separate admission committees and separate cutoff scores was not permissible but that the goal of achieving student population diversity and the need to rectify the lingering effects of past discrimination did warrant considering race as a factor in admissions decisions.

This decision may be threatening to similar programs at other universities. For example, the University of Wisconsin's law school admits all minority applicants thought to be able to succeed in the law school program. If there are additional seats, then Anglo applicants may compete for them. The Texas decision is being appealed, and if the Supreme Court grants it a hearing, the Court will have an opportunity to reconcile many of the ambiguities that currently surround affirmative action programs.

John S. Robey

SEE ALSO African Americans, Other Minorities

BIBLIOGRAPHY

Glazer, Nathan. *Affirmative Discrimination.* Cambridge: Harvard University Press, 1987.

Hacker, Andrew. *Two Nations.* New York: Charles Scribner, 1992.

Hero, Rodney E. *Latinos and the U.S. Political System.* Philadelphia: Temple University Press, 1992.

Sigelman, Lee, and Susan Welch. *Black Americans' View of Racial Inequality.* Cambridge, MA: Cambridge University Press, 1991.

African Americans

The Reverend Jesse Jackson's strong run for the Democratic Party's presidential nomination in 1984 was a milestone in the history of that party. The former aide to Dr. Martin Luther King Jr. shook the party to its foundations and forced the Democrats to respond to the demands of an African American power broker as they never had before.

Spending just $1.7 million, Jackson registered 183,000 voters in the South, won Mississippi and Louisiana, and made a strong showing in a number of other states. There was a 10% increase in the number of African American mayors as a result of Jackson's effort, according to a report by the Joint Center for Political and Economic Studies. An April 1984 poll found that 31% of all Democrats gave Jackson a favorable rating.

Jackson did even better in the 1988 Democratic presidential primaries. He won 6.6 million votes to finish second to Massachusetts Governor Michael Dukakis, the eventual Democratic nominee. Jackson won 92% of the African American vote and doubled his share of the white vote to 12%.

Jackson won Michigan, Mississippi, Delaware, Alabama, Virginia, and a number of other states. He got the Democrats to eliminate the "superdelegate" and other antidemocratic candidate-nomination procedures and had a number of his campaign themes included in the 13 final platform planks at the party's nominating convention.

Jackson's meteoric rise had been predated by a generation of rock-solid African American support for the Democrats. From 1952 to 1984, African Americans gave Democratic presidential nominees an average of 84% of their votes. This figure swelled to over 90% in the 1980s. The Democrats, in turn, helped to usher in all the major civil rights gains of the post–World War II period.

But it was not always that way. For most of their 195-year existence, the Democrats have been the party of racial exclusion and reaction that African Americans have shunned almost reflexively. The transformation of this relationship is one of the great sagas of American history.

Andrew Jackson's old Republican Party changed its name to the Democratic Party at its 1840 national convention. Since the 1820s, elements of its "liberal" wing had called themselves Democrats to express solidarity with the ideas of the French Revolution.

Among other things, they opposed any form of strong central government. And in this, they attracted the allegiance of southern slaveholders. By the 1850s, the South had come to dominate the party. Catholic immigrants in the northern cities were the Democrats' only major nonsouthern constituency.

By 1854, the Democrats had won control of Congress. They pushed forth the Kansas–Nebraska Act permitting the expansion of slavery into territories west of the Mississippi. The widespread anger over the passage of that act led to the formation of a new Republican Party to fight the Democratic agenda.

In 1860 this party won control of Congress and got Abraham Lincoln elected to the White House. One of the new administration's goals was to prevent the further expansion of slavery. Within months, the southern states had seceded from the Union and the Civil War had begun.

The Democrats followed the pattern of the rest of the country. Southern Democrats joined the rebellion. Northerners mostly chose to remain with the Union. But they fought for a negotiated peace and a "conciliatory approach" toward the slaveholders. And they were defeated only by the narrowest of margins.

Only a series of Union victories at Atlanta and in the Shenandoah Valley together with the transportation of thousands of Union veterans from the front lines to voting booths sealed a 2.3 million to 1.8 million Lincoln victory over Democratic "peace candidate" George McClelland in the 1864 presidential election.

After the war, the Democrats fought as hard to shape a peace that would be favorable to the South as they had to stop the war. They were helped in this by Lincoln's assassination just before the war ended in 1865 and his vice president, Andrew Johnson, taking over the White House.

Johnson was an implacable opponent of black equality. He allowed southern Democrats to seize control of state governments and implement a series of laws that effectively reduced the newly freed African Americans to a state of semislavery. Travel and employment restrictions were placed on them. Employers were given wide latitude to chastise their African American employees physically.

Only a Republican-engineered counterattack gave African Americans some temporary respite. Using their control of Congress, the GOP wrested control of postwar Reconstruction policy from Johnson. In the summer of 1866, the Congress passed a civil rights bill over a Johnson veto, giving African Americans the same citizenship rights as other Americans. This was followed by the 14th Amendment forbidding any state from depriving "any person of life, liberty, or property without due process of law." It also stopped them from denying "any person within its jurisdiction equal protection of the law." In 1869 the Republicans pushed through the 15th Amendment outlawing racial discrimination.

These events set the stage for a period of unprecedented African American political power. Over the next 30 years, 16 African Americans were elected to Congress, two of whom became senators. And 800 African Americans were elected to state legislatures.

Southern Democrats fought back with every means at their disposal—both legal and illegal. Voting booths were placed on islands, in swamps, barns, or fodder houses. Election days were marred by violence. Pitched battles were even common, as armed groups of African Americans and whites sparred over access to the voting booths.

The impact of the Democratic onslaught was so great that only South Carolina, Florida, Mississippi, and Louisiana were still in the Republican column by 1874. But this was only the beginning.

In 1876 the GOP was only able to retain the White House and break an electoral deadlock over disputed elections in South Carolina, Louisiana, and Florida by promising to withdraw federal troops from the South. Ohio Governor Rutherford B. Hayes became president. But the Democratic counterrevolution gained an almost unstoppable momentum.

The Democrats were aided in their efforts by the emergence of a new, more conservative national mood. Northern business interests realized they did not have to go through the trouble of trying to maintain African American rights in the South to integrate the region into the country's nascent urban industrial economy. In 1883, the Supreme Court declared the 1875 Civil Rights Act unconstitutional. Then in 1896 it supported the *Plessy* v. *Ferguson* "separate but equal" doctrine opening the way for legal apartheid in the United States.

Concurrent with this, Democrat-dominated southern state legislatures began to rewrite their constitutions, denying African Americans and many poor whites the right to vote. In Alabama, for instance, the 181,000 African Americans who had been eligible to vote in 1900 had been reduced to a mere 3,000 just two years later.

And with the demise of African American voting, the final vestiges of African American political power were eliminated. The last Reconstruction-era black congressman—North Carolina's George White—left the House of Representatives in 1901.

A system like that of the Democratic South could only be held together by terror. And in this the Democrats and their white vigilante supporters were well versed. More than 2,000 blacks were lynched in the United States between 1882 and 1903, the vast majority of them in the South.

African Americans responded to this by leaving the South in record numbers for the urban areas of the Northeast and Midwest. Over 3 million blacks took the journey between 1900 and 1950. They carried with them the seeds of a new era of African American politics. In 1928 blacks in Chicago made Oscar De Priest the first black elected to Congress since George White.

Though De Priest and most other African American political leaders of his generation were Republicans, the party's links to the African American community were becoming increasingly strained. After Herbert Hoover's victory in the 1928 presidential election, he dismissed Republicans from positions of influence in the party all over the South. Hoover still won most of the African American vote, but significant numbers of blacks voted for the Democratic nominee, Franklin Delano Roosevelt.

Once in office, Roosevelt began to implement his New Deal—the most extensive social welfare program in the country's history. Desperately poor—even in the best of circumstances—and suffering horribly from the Great Depression, African Americans benefited more than any other group from the Civilian Conservation Corps, the Federal Emergency Relief Administration, and other New Deal programs. The number of African American federal employees increased from 50,000 in 1933 to 200,000 by 1944.

And with this, Roosevelt finally wrested most African American voters away from the Republicans in 1936, 1940, and 1944. Following on the coattails of their constituents, African American political leaders also began to change parties. In 1934, Chicago's Arthur Mitchell became the first African American elected to Congress as a Democrat.

The Democratic-facilitated buds of the African American political resurgence also began to sprout in the South during the New Deal years. African Americans in South Carolina formed the Progressive Democratic Party in 39 of the state's 46 counties in 1944 to get African Americans registered to vote. By the spring of 1946, there were 75,000 African American registered voters in Texas and 100,000 in Georgia.

In one of the great political sleight-of-hand efforts in U.S. political history, Roosevelt also kept the segregationist southern wing of the party securely within his New Deal coalition. He did this by keeping his support for African American issues at a moderate level, while turning the New Deal's programs in the South over to the segregationist Democrats. This bolstered their positions and actually strengthened the Jim Crow apartheid system. Roosevelt even refused to sign an antilynching bill. He only agreed to desegregate defense industries during World War II, when African American labor leader A. Philip Randolph threatened a march on Washington.

After Roosevelt's death, his successor, Harry Truman, continued the New Deal policies toward African Americans. He supported moderately paced racial reform. But he kept the patronage largess flowing to southern Democrats and gave prominent political leaders from the region important positions in his administration. But this was not enough.

Fearful of even the most tepid moves toward African American equality, prosegregationist southern politicians bolted from the Democrats during the 1948 presidential election and formed their own States' Rights Party. With South Carolina Governor Strom Thurmond at the head of the ticket, the party won Mississippi, Alabama, South Carolina, and Louisiana and 1.7 million votes.

Seeing this, African Americans gave Truman two-thirds of their votes in the 1948 presidential election and formed a significant portion of his 2-million-vote margin of victory.

The struggle to placate the growing number of African American voters in the North with the recalcitrant white South tied the Democratic Party in knots in the 1950s. The number of African Americans living outside the South had grown to 6.4 million by the early part of the decade. Even there, over 1 million African Americans were on the voter rolls. But the more prominent African Americans became in the Democratic Party, the more southerners became uneasy.

Republican Dwight Eisenhower's election to the presidency in 1952 and 1956 was partly the result of southern Democratic leaders encouraging their constituents to vote for the GOP in presidential elections and Democrats in state and local contests. This cost the Democrats Florida, Virginia, and a number of other southern states in the two elections.

By the 1960 presidential election, African Americans were demonstrating all over the country for an end to segregation and social and political equality. The election featured Richard Nixon, Eisenhower's vice president, as the Republican nominee and Massachusetts Senator John Kennedy as the Democratic stalking horse.

Neither candidate had been closely identified with civil rights issues in his political career. But Kennedy actively solicited the African American vote. The high point of this activism was his telephoning civil rights leader Martin Luther King's wife, Coretta Scott-King, to check on her husband's welfare while he was serving a jail stint in Atlanta for leading a demonstration. African Americans responded by casting 68% of their ballots for Kennedy. This made up a critical portion of the New Englander's narrow 100,000-vote margin of victory.

Propelled by brutal southern vigilante and police attacks on civil rights activists, Kennedy came out in support of civil rights like no president had since Reconstruction. In September 1962, he sent federal marshals to Oxford, Mississippi, to protect civil rights activist James Meredith's efforts to integrate the University of Mississippi. In June 1963, Kennedy delivered a strong civil rights bill to the Congress.

After Kennedy's assassination, Lyndon Johnson, his vice president, continued his efforts. On July 2, 1964, Congress passed the Civil Rights Act, ending segregated public accommodations. On July 2, 1965, Johnson signed the Voting Rights Act, ending the law and practices that prevented African Americans from voting in the South.

But by the summer of 1964 the country was literally being torn apart at the seams. Civil rights demonstrations were joined by African American riots in northern and western cities. Faced with this, Johnson began his famous War on Poverty program, funneling hundreds of millions of dollars into aid for minorities and the poor.

This fueled what has been become known as the "white backlash." Johnson won the majority of the white vote in 1964. But the next seven Democratic presidential candidates would fail to do so. And the traditionally Democratic South would be lost altogether.

Nixon rode the wave of conservative reaction into the White House in 1968, determined to preserve the racial and social status quo. He won again in 1972, crushing liberal Democrat George McGovern.

But the white flight from the Democratic Party left a void African Americans were only too glad to fill. The 500 African American elected officials in 1965 grew to over 3,500 by 1975—nearly all of them Democrats. They included mayors of Detroit, Gary, Los Angeles, Newark, and Atlanta. By 1976, there were 17 African American members of Congress. They were organized into the Congressional Black Caucus, the body's most consistently liberal voting block.

In 1977 the Democrats recaptured the White House, as Georgia Governor Jimmy Carter became the first president from the Deep South since Zachary Taylor. Carter appointed an unprecedented number of African Americans to high positions. These included Andrew Young as UN ambassador and Patricia Harris as secretary of housing and urban development. But, like Roosevelt and Truman before him, the former Georgia governor could not bring himself to embrace fully an agenda that would address the needs of the African American community, despite winning around 90% of the African American vote.

The African American community seethed with anger when the new administration announced in May 1977 that there would be no new spending initiatives on social programs. In August 1977, Jesse Jackson, NAACP head Benjamin Hooks, and a number of other prominent African American leaders met in New York City and declared that Carter had "betrayed" African Americans. They described his policies toward African Americans as little more than "callous neglect."

The rumblings of discontent in the presidents's strongest base of support continued into the 1980 election. At one point, Jackson told the press that "the black community has the responsibility and obligation to listen to what both parties have to say." Running against archconservative Ronald Reagan, Carter still won nearly 90% of the African American vote. But only 40% of eligible African American voters bothered to turn out, against just under 50% of the electorate as a whole.

These and other factors led to a Reagan landslide, as Carter won only five states and the District of Columbia, and the Republicans took control of the Senate.

This began the eight years of the Reagan "revolution," during which over $100 billion were cut from federal social programs. These and other factors drove Jackson into the 1984 presidential race. But the results were even worse than in 1980, as Reagan annihilated Walter Mondale, Carter's vice president, in a 49-state, 17-million-vote sweep.

After the election, the Democratic National Committee commissioned a $250,000 study of 5,000 Democratic defectors to the Republican Party in the South and among urban "white ethnics" to find out why they had switched parties. It found that many of them believed that the Democrats had abandoned them for African Americans, Hispanics, and the poor.

Shaken moderate Democrats decided the time had come to move the party back in line with the "mainstream." In 1985 Georgia Senator Sam Nunn, Virginia Governor Charles Robb, and a number of other mostly white southern Democratic leaders formed the Democratic Leadership Council. One of its primary goals was recapturing the white vote for the Democrats in national elections.

But even as the DLC's influence in the party grew over the rest of the decade, the Democrats continued to depend heavily on the African American vote. Harold Washington became mayor of Chicago in 1983 after a bitterly contested election in which the city's 1 million African Americans turned out in overwhelming numbers to support him.

The southern African American vote helped the Democrats regain control of the Senate in 1986. White moderates like Terry Sanford in North Carolina and Richard Selby in Alabama won because African Americans voted up to 88% Democratic, against 35%–40% for whites.

There were more than 7,400 African American elected officials by 1990. This included more than 300 mayors and 26 members of the House.

Despite all the internal maneuvering within the party, the 1988 presidential election was no different than 1984. Massachusetts Governor Michael Dukakis lost 40 states to George Bush, Reagan's vice president, and won only 41% of the white vote.

By the 1992 presidential election, the DLC had become the most powerful force in the Democratic Party. Nearly 3,000 local, state, and national elected officials had joined the group. It had chapters in 27 states, 19 full-time staff members, and a $2.5 million annual budget. Arkansas Governor Bill Clinton, who chaired the organization from 1990 to 1991, won the Democratic nomination for president.

Early on, Clinton let it be known that the party would distance itself from African American, labor, and other "special interests." But in many respects, Clinton ran on the same type of social welfare platform that had attracted African Americans to the Democrats since the days of the New Deal. He called for a $65 million increase in federal appropriations for education and increased aid to cities.

This combined with African American disillusionment with the Reagan–Bush years brought 1 million more African Americans to the polls in 1992 than had voted in 1988. Their 82% support for Clinton was the highest of any group in the country. They also elected 16 new African American members of Congress and 40 southern state legislators—almost all of them Democrats.

But Clinton's ambivalent attitude toward the African American community continued into his presidency. He angered African American leaders by withdrawing support for the nomination of Lani Guinier for assistant attorney general for civil rights because of her support for proportional representation to ensure minority rights. And the former Arkansas governor pointedly told African Americans they could not depend on government to solve all their problems during a speech at an African American church in Memphis in November 1994.

These and other events have Jackson hinting at possibly challenging Clinton in the 1996 Democratic primaries or forming an independent third party, while many African Americans are looking toward yet another reassessment of African American support for the Democrats.

David Hatchett

SEE ALSO Affirmative Action

BIBLIOGRAPHY

Bennett, Lerone, Jr. *Before the Mayflower: A History of Black America*. New York: Penguin Books, 1984.

Boller, Paul F., Jr. *Presidential Campaigns*. New York: Oxford University Press, 1984.

Edsall, Thomas Byrne, with Mary D. Edsall. "Race." *Atlantic Monthly*, May 1991, pp. 53–86.

———. *Chain Reaction: The Impact of Race, Rights and Taxes on American Politics*. New York: Norton, 1992.

Frisby, Michael K. "The Democrat's Identity Crisis." *Focus*, October 1991, pp. 3–4.

Hagerstrom, Jerry. *Beyond Reagan: The New Landscape of American Politics*. New York: Penguin Books, 1988.

Henry, Charles P. "Jesse Jackson and the Decline of Liberalism in Presidential Elections." *Black Scholar*, January–February 1989, pp. 2–12.

Hicks, John D., George E. Mowry, and Robert E. Burke. *The American Nation: A History of the United States from 1865 to the Present*. Boston: Houghton Mifflin, 1965.

Kazin, Michael. *The Populist Persuasion: An American History*. New York: Basic Books, 1995.

Lusane, Clarence. *African Americans at the Crossroads: The Restructuring of Black Leadership and the 1992 Presidential Elections*. Boston: South End Press, 1994.

Marable, Manning. *Race, Reform and Rebellion: The Second Reconstruction in Black America, 1945–1982*. Jackson: University of Mississippi Press, 1984.

———. *Black American Politics: From the Washington Marches to Jesse Jackson*. London: Verso, 1985.

Piven, Frances Fox, and Richard A. Cloward. *Why Americans Don't Vote*. New York: Pantheon Books, 1988.

"Political TrendLetter." *Focus*, October 1991.

Polsby, Nelson W., and Aaron Wildavsky. *Presidential Elections: Strategies and Structures of American Politics*. Chatham, NJ: Chatham House, 1996.

"A Question of Competence: The Lani Guinier Fiasco Raises Distressing Questions about How Clinton Makes Decisions." *U.S. News & World Report*, June 14, 1993, pp. 40–47.

Reichley, James A. *The Life of the Parties: A History of American Political Parties*. New York: Free Press, 1992.

Tryman, Mfanya D. "Blacks and the Democrats: Dissolution of an Irreconcilable Marriage." *Black Scholar*, November/December 1986, pp. 28–33.

Arms Control

During the first 20 years of the Cold War, the Congress of the United States anxiously reinforced the policies of the executive on national security matters, particularly with regard to nuclear strategy and arms-control policies (Stoeffer 1980, 1). Although different schools of thought on arms control were reaching maturity, these differences did not emerge in the policy debate until the middle of the 1960s. The Vietnam War profoundly changed the congressional role in national security policy (Levine 1990, 113). The war in Southeast Asia polarized the country, increased the public awareness of defense policy, and ended the era of relatively unquestioned congressional support for the policies of the executive branch.

Issues once considered too sensitive for public consumption and debate rapidly moved into the political arena. The ensuing empowerment of a conglomerate of special interests, including think tanks, defense contractors, universities, scientists, and public-interest lobbies, dramatically changed the formulation of U.S. security policy. A permanent arms-control community representing the varying schools of thought on arms control was established.

The anti-ballistic missile (ABM) system debate represented the first manifestation of these changes. The executive's desire to build and deploy an ABM system in the late 1960s was met by staunch, open opposition by some members of Congress (Stoeffer 1980, 4). Supported by an increasingly influential group of eminent scientists, civilian military experts, public-interest lobbies, and academics who doubted the viability of the system and warned of its destabilizing effect on U.S.–Soviet relations, Congressional critics were able to limit ABM research and development severely. The initial round of the ABM debate marked the end of exclusive reliance on executive branch control of national security affairs.

The next two decades saw a divisive debate over arms-control policy. The spectrum of opinion varied from the liberals' push for a "nuclear freeze" to the conservative crusade against the "evil empire." The disagreements between Congress and the executive over ABM led to the independent congressional policy evaluation of all areas of national security. To this day, the debate over the strategic impact of the funding, research, and deployment of an anti-ballistic missile system remains the defining impetus for arms-control policy. Look no farther than a legislator's position on ABM and his position on any aspect of arms control seems somewhat predetermined.

Although the end of the Cold War has left the arms-control process void of any clear direction, the prevailing attitudes that existed during the Cold War remain. The Republican takeover of the houses of Congress in 1994 was won at the expense of moderate Democrats. Many of the Jacksonian Democrats who had espoused conservative positions on defense issues lost their seats to more conservative Republican opponents. The 1994 election left the Democratic minority solidly in the liberal camp.

The current Democratic position on arms control traces roots back to the spiral model of international relations (Jervis 1976). The belief is that arms races are fueled by fear and mutual distrust. The spiral of ten-

sion leads to massive arms buildup and eventual war. Likewise, if one side would unilaterally disarm or at least cease weapons production, the spiral of tension would be halted and the risk of war reduced. The clearest evidence of this thinking took the form of the nuclear freeze movement of the 1980s. A vast majority of the Democratic members of the 104th Congress supported the freeze movement (information available on the Internet).

The Soviet invasion of Afghanistan and the election of President Ronald Reagan in 1980 marked the end of détente. The Senate refused to ratify SALT II, and President Reagan announced a complete review of arms-control priorities. These events effectively marked a suspension of arms-control negotiations and a resumption of the arms race. The liberal Democrats and arms-control lobbies responded with a movement to freeze the U.S. strategic arsenal at existing levels. Unilaterally freezing the nuclear arsenal would diffuse the spiral of nuclear tension between the United States and the Soviet Union. The movement failed due to lack of support by conservative Democrats and Republicans alike. The freeze movement illustrates the congressional Democrats' perspective on arms control.

The uncertainty of the direction of the former Soviet Union and the failure of the United States to develop a clear strategic vision of the future has resulted in little substantive action in the arms-control arena. The largest area of contention remains the funding of the Strategic Defense Initiative.

According to the House Democratic minority leader, Richard Gephardt, the official Democratic position on defense spending is as follows: "Established priorities for defense spending that emphasize sustaining readiness of our troops and critical combat systems over deployment of an outdated Star Wars missile defense system" (information available on the Internet).

The Democrats' objection to an additional $7 billion in funding for the Strategic Defense Initiative (SDI) formed the impetus for President Clinton's veto of the 1996 Defense Authorization Bill. At the core of the dispute is the interpretation of the 1972 ABM treaty with the former Soviet Union. Democrats favor a strict interpretation of the treaty, which prevents the testing or deployment of "exotic weapons." Democrats assert that many of the systems funded under SDI constitute violations of the treaty.

Agreed Statement D of the ABM treaty prevents the development and deployment of "exotic weapons" for use in missile defense systems. According to Democrats, the SDI clearly demonstrated a breakout from the ABM treaty. Violation of the treaty would damage U.S. credibility and disable efforts to negotiate future agreements. Furthermore, the Soviets' fear of the SDI could destabilize deterrence and escalate the arms race.

The origins of the Democratic opposition to SDI can be found in the spiral model. Many Democrats believe that deployment of SDI would exacerbate tensions with the Soviet Union. Fearing the deployment of a credible ABM system could actually result in a Soviet first strike. At best, the SDI would act as impediment to the serious negotiation of reductions in the strategic arsenal. Although the rise of Mikhail Gorbachev and the collapse of the Soviet Union have resulted in dramatic reduction in the strategic arsenals of both nuclear superpowers, the Democrats still maintain that SDI is unfeasible, unnecessary, and destabilizing.

More important, Democrats contend that SDI represents a "Boondoggle in the Sky" (information available on the Internet). According to Democrats, SDI is technically impossible and politically destabilizing. The United States should not invest its resources in the "budget-busting fantasy called Star Wars."

The U.S. Congress is moving toward consensus on several arms-control issues. The Senate recently ratified the START II treaty, which will reduce U.S. and Russian strategic arsenals to less than 3,500 warheads each. Congress favors a rapid negotiation and implementation of a comprehensive Nuclear Test Ban Treaty, ratification on the Chemical Weapons Convention, and extension of the Non-Proliferation Treaty. Although both Republicans and Democrats favor the concept of these agreements, their fundamental differences on arms control will likely produce heated debate over the details.

The chaotic nature of the post–Cold War environment provides a very uncertain future for arms-control negotiations. Foreign policy experts are struggling to develop solutions to the proliferation of weapons of mass destruction, the move from bilateral to multilateral deterrence, assurance of environmental security, and the containment of terrorism. The complexity of multilateral negotiations and enforcement has delayed any substantive move in these areas. The key to understanding the Democratic position on future issues lies in understanding the history of arms control, particularly the debate over the development and deployment of an anti-ballistic missile system.

Cynthia J. Levy

SEE ALSO Defense

BIBLIOGRAPHY

Jervis, Robert. *Perceptions and Misperceptions in International Politics*. Princeton: Princeton University Press, 1976.

Levine, Robert A. *Still the Arms Debate*. Brookfield, VT: Dartmouth, 1990.

Stoeffer, Howard. *Congressional Defense Policy Making and the Arms Control Community*. Ann Arbor, MI: University Microfilms, 1980.

Big Government

In his State of the Union address in 1996, President Clinton said, "The era of big government is over." With these words, a Democratic president seemed definitively to announce a historic reversal of Democratic Party sentiment toward the U.S. national government. But had an "era" in fact ended? And how historically accurate are contemporary generalizations about big-government Democrats and devolutionary Republicans?

Questions surrounding big government invoke a variety of related topics: federalism, public administration, and so forth. Given this literally encyclopedic forum, discussion here focuses specifically on Democratic Party approaches to the size and growth of the U.S. federal government, particularly with respect to national efforts at taxing, spending, and regulating.

JACKSONIAN DEMOCRATS: RESISTANCE

Andrew Jackson had characteristically strong opinions about federal government activity: he didn't much like it. Jacksonian politics ushered in novel—and enduringly Democratic—themes, centered on the rejection of oligarchy in favor of egalitarian, populist policies. On these grounds Jackson staunchly opposed most of the limited federal activities undertaken by his predecessors, notably internal improvements (appropriations for canals, roads, and other major structures) and the fledgling national banking system. He also championed a balanced federal budget, to the point of reacting with horror at "the unnecessary accumulation of public revenue" when the United States marked its first-ever budgetary surplus during his tenure (Wildavsky 1987).

Thus the origins of the modern Democratic Party were suffused with antigovernment rhetoric. Indeed, the first national party platform in America, produced by the Democrats in 1840, resolved at its outset "the federal government is one of limited powers . . . it is inexpedient and dangerous to [exceed these]," and went on specifically to enumerate limits on those powers in seven of its eight other planks. Certainly this spirit existed among the wider American public at least since the Revolution, but Jackson captured and symbolized it. Democrats' salutes to the "common man" translated into support for individual, not government, initiative.

Traveling through Jacksonian America, Tocqueville recorded this ethic. The national government, his informants reported, threatened to "cover the surface of society with a network of small complicated rules, minute and uniform . . . it compresses, enervates, extinguishes, and stupefies a people, till each nation is reduced to nothing better than a flock of timid and industrious animals, of which the government is the shepherd" (Tocqueville 1945, 2:321).

A separate and familiar theme in the history of American national government also appears initially in Jackson's administration. Though the first president to emphasize opposition to federal activity, Jackson also presided over tremendous expansion in national government activity. Federal civilian employment rose by nearly 60% during his tenure, while budget receipts and expenditures both doubled (Bennett and Bennett 1990, 5–6). Part of the impetus came from a rapidly expanding national economy, but Jackson's own efforts to root out corruption and streamline government functions, especially in the executive, were major contributors.

Thus, as Republican and Democratic administrations alike would attest, antebellum efforts to restrain the growth of big government in the United States were severely bounded. Burgeoning westward expansion and spiraling international trade, combined with a spoils system of patronage that encouraged both parties to add federal positions filled with their supporters, all translated into a steadily growing national state.

Jackson's balanced-budget, limited-government ideal nonetheless remained the rhetorical law of the land, among both Republicans and Democrats alike, into the Civil War. Wartime mobilization swelled the civilian and military establishments to by far their greatest extent to date. This mini Leviathan was swiftly diminished after 1865, but a period of Republican-dominated federal activity ensued. And it was a Democratic president, Grover Cleveland, who sought strenuously to stem the tide, making "retrenchment" the centerpiece of his victorious 1884 campaign. Cleveland's insistence on economy, efficiency, and decentralization fit comfortably with the *laissez-faire*, business-dominated Gilded Age then under way.

Hence the first national figures gaining notoriety as against big government were Democrats, while especially during Reconstruction, the Republican Party was closely identified with federal largess in such areas as pensions for soldiers and their widows. And this historical "anomaly" was by no means permanently reversed in the twentieth century.

PROGRESSIVE REFORM: DEMOCRATIC EXPANSIVENESS

During Cleveland's first term, future Democratic leader Woodrow Wilson published "The Study of Administration," which became a hallmark of Progressive-style administrative reform. Wilson urged sensitivity to increasing complexity in government and called for expanded administrative powers to match. In his words: "Large powers and unhampered discretion [are] the indispensable conditions of responsibility. There is no danger in power, if only it be not irresponsible" (Wilson 1941, 497).

Though most closely associated with Theodore Roosevelt (a Republican), a host of "responsible" Progressive reforms were enacted during Wilson's presidency. Principal among these were the first progressive income tax; creation of new regulatory agencies, including the Federal Reserve Board and Federal Trade Commission; and varied labor regulations. Also worth mentioning is the 19th Amendment to the Constitution, which established Prohibition. Among its effects were a vast expansion of federal investigative and crime-fighting capabilities.

Inasmuch as Progressives sought aggressively to expand national government capacities in order to regulate big business, Wilson stands as the first Democrat to positively support more active federal government. Wilson's efforts to this end were marked by caution and even ambivalence, however, as was public support for national regulatory and spending activity: interest groups had begun widely seeking particularized federal benefits by Wilson's tenure, but traditional opposition to a more powerful central state remained.

TO THE NEW DEAL

Today we routinely associate the coming of Franklin Roosevelt's New Deal in 1933 with the birth of an activist U.S. federal state. This canard is questionable on various fronts: as one scholar has recently demonstrated, American social policy directed by the federal government originally emerged toward the end of Reconstruction. Moreover, the Democratic outlook in Roosevelt's campaign and initial months in office was hardly an unmitigated paean to big-government virtues. The 1932 Democratic platform, on which Roosevelt was elected, demanded as its first point "an immediate and drastic reduction of governmental expenditures," and Roosevelt remained a rhetorical champion of austerity and private-sector initiative well into his first term.

Still, the New Deal, and its Democratic purveyors, soon became indelibly identified with the growth of a positive welfare state. The political and economic exigencies brought about by the depression coincided with a growing body of sophisticated public administration analysis, joining urgent need and ideology in the service of vastly expanded and reorganized national government.

Democratic legislative initiatives, especially during Roosevelt's two "100 days" of lawmaking in 1933 and 1935, were unprecedented in their collective import for federal regulatory and spending authority.

Such enduring New Deal legacies as Social Security and the minimum wage, among other forces for national administrative expansion and reorganization, engendered bitter conflict over the perceived growth of a federal Leviathan. Republicans within and outside the government went on the warpath: a characteristic view comes in the GOP's 1940 party platform, which lamented that New Dealers had "failed America . . . by seducing our people to become continuously dependent on government, thus weakening their morale and quenching the traditional American spirit." The sentiment echoed the U.S. revolutionary and constitutional founders, to be sure, as well as no few Democratic leaders of the past. Yet, fueled still further by World War II, big government grew. And by 1945, "for the first time in American history, government was perceived as a positive good by a large proportion of the voting public" (Chandler 1987, 24).

GREAT SOCIETY, GREAT GOVERNMENT

Such perceptions remained intact over the next three decades. Republicans' sporadic control of Congress (1947–1948, 1953–1954) and return to power in the White House under Eisenhower yielded a slow but continued rise in federal civilian employment and the budget. This trend was exponentially hastened with the Great Society programs of Lyndon Johnson. Government-enhancing programs passed at a rate rivaling that of Roosevelt's reign, in areas as diverse as welfare, health care, housing, civil rights, the environment, and education.

Owing largely to the "liberal" character of Great Society programs, the surge in federal responsibilities during the 1960s is typically associated only with the Democratic Party. But the record of regulatory and legislative expansion continued steadily into Richard Nixon's presidency. In both his first and abbreviated second terms, Nixon oversaw tremendous growth in the welfare state: new social and environmental programs ranged from the first publicly financed jobs for unemployed Americans since the New Deal to a host of urban aid programs. As for regulatory activity, more new federal agencies and statutes regulating business and state/local government activity were established under Nixon than in Johnson's term—indeed, more than in the Truman, Kennedy, Johnson, and Carter administrations combined.

By the early 1970s, it appeared that this era of expansive welfare state government, dating from the New Deal with merely a slowdown under Eisenhower, might last indefinitely. Federal benefits to individuals, groups, and society at large were widely supported and, evidently, politically untouchable. The only political party urging major retrenchment and states' rights in 1972, judging from party platforms, was the Prohibition Party. (And, of the two major party candidates, it was McGovern, the Democratic standard-bearer, who sounded most alarms against overbearing national authority.)

DEMOCRATS REGROUP . . . AND RETRENCH

A subsequent series of jolts to this American equilibrium, from the Vietnam War's aftermath to the Watergate investigation and Nixon's impeachment to oil-price driven inflationary pressures, profoundly affected national attitudes toward government. It was a Democratic presidential candidate, Jimmy Carter, who successfully tapped public misgivings, campaigning and later governing as an anti-Washington outsider.

Democrats, controlling both executive and legislature from 1977 to 1980, compiled a record dominated by deregulation and other reductions in federal authority. As one analyst notes, contrasting this record with that of Nixon's first term, Democrats "defeated labor-law reform, voted against the establishment of a Consumer Protection Agency, restricted the power of the Federal Trade Commission, deregulated oil prices, delayed the imposition of automobile-emission standards, reduced price controls on natural gas, and enacted two tax bills, the first of which primarily benefited the wealthy . . ." (Vogel 1989, 13). Carter's infamous "malaise" speech in July 1979 and the Iranian hostage crisis dominating the news during the last year of his term inaugurated a new portrait of the national government as an ineffectual, swollen giant.

Successfully impugning such a view, and identifying it with Carter and fellow Democrats who had in fact struggled to rein in federal activities, was Ronald

Reagan. Carter's administration marked the opening of an antigovernment trend culminating in Reagan's sustained attacks on big government. The two must be understood as yoked in this regard, much as Johnson and Nixon "shared" the period of Great Society expansion.

Yet, despite Reagan Republicans' legion efforts, the Leviathan state continued to grow. Federal budgets topped the trillion-dollar mark in 1983, ominously shadowed by a mounting deficit. Americans' attitudes toward the public sector actually improved during Reagan's tenure, with opinion polls demonstrating a significant shift toward preference for bigger government by the end of his presidency (Bennett and Bennett 1990, 141).

Democrats claimed credit for the lion's share of this shift. Led by House Speaker Thomas "Tip" O'Neill, Democrats spurred popular hostility toward Republican efforts to cut highly popular programs, particularly Social Security. The 1988 campaign, partly in consequence, saw neither Reagan successor George Bush nor Democratic standard-bearer Michael Dukakis mount a high-profile drive against big government. Bush's presidency, moreover, included notably expansive acts in environmental (Clean Air Act) and social (Americans with Disabilities Act) arenas.

ERA OF BIG GOVERNMENT OVER?

The superficial distinction between "tax and spend" Democrats and limited-government Republicans was further muddied with the Democrats' return to the White House in the person of Bill Clinton. One centerpiece of Clinton's campaign was the idea of "reinventing government," formally introduced early in his presidency. Revolving around a "shift from top-down bureaucracy to entrepreneurial government," the initiative included a mix of proposals to devolve fiscal and programmatic authority to the states, adopt "performance standards" for executive bureaucrats, and "reform and streamline" the regulatory process. Clinton's program recalled efforts since Andrew Jackson's at reorganization of the federal bureaucracy.

Unlike most would-be administrative reformers, moreover, including Democrats and Republicans from Jackson to Reagan, Clinton's early years in office marked a real reduction in national government. Both federal spending and civilian employment declined slightly between 1990 and 1994.

Party stereotypes had not entirely been abandoned. Clinton's 1993 proposal for sweeping health care reform, though unsuccessful, represented a federal-centered effort, as did such programs as national service

and proposed regulations on telecommunications technologies. Such initiatives, particularly health care, were pilloried by Republicans and other foes as a return to Great Society legislating.

Big government—cast as ineradicable budget deficits, unfunded mandates, inefficiency, overregulation, and the like—was the GOP foil in the Contract with America, underpinning their astonishing 1994 midyear election victories. Despite Clinton's genuine efforts at "reinvention," Democrats were successfully portrayed as old-style liberals, promoting public spending and government action as a panacea for social and economic problems.

Reduced to minority status in both houses of Congress for the first time in 40 years, Democratic leaders after 1994 initially renounced any identification with national government initiatives. The party's position was most starkly presented by Clinton's 1996 State of the Union address, when he pointedly repeated, "the era of big government is over."

And yet, congressional Republicans' initial thrusts toward deregulation and devolution bogged down within the first months of the 104th Congress. As in Reagan's presidency, Democrats identified popular federal programs slated for elimination, from environment to Medicare, spurring public disapproval for cuts. Though hardly halted, Republicans' efforts to slash national government were stalled as the 104th Congress moved toward 1996 adjournment.

CONCLUSION

Beginning with Woodrow Wilson and epitomized by Roosevelt's New Deal and Johnson's Great Society, the Democratic Party chalked up over a half century of confident support for expansive national government. The party's 1968 platform exemplified this view, opening "For the first time in the history of the world, it is within the power of a nation to eradicate from within its borders the age-old cause of poverty. . . . It remains to implement and adequately fund the host of practical measures [required]." Yet Democratic leaders before Wilson and after Johnson advertised a different, even opposing view, that Americans should "expect less" from government, as President Carter warned in 1979.

Present-day Democrats seem divided on the question of federal provision of regulation and services. Remaining members of the party's liberal wing support expansive government on principle, as a vital source of social progress; Americans' evident attachment to entitlement programs, many originally established by Democrats, provides strategic fodder for such views. Others, including self-styled "new Demo-crat" Bill Clinton, seek to move the party in the direction of "reinvented" entrepreneurial government, with streamlined federal responsibilities and expanded fiscal and programmatic power devolved to the states.

The term *reinvention* also applies to the late-twentieth-century Democratic Party, especially where views on big government are concerned. As Democratic leaders continue to mark out broad new positions, it is worth recalling the history spelled out earlier. Forces superseding partisan differences—budgetary limits and other economic exigencies, "public moods," war—have recurrently altered the terms of debate over the presence of the federal government in American politics and society.

Rogan Kersh

BIBLIOGRAPHY

Bennett, Linda L.M., and Stephen Earl Bennett. *Living with Leviathan: Americans Coming to Terms with Big Government.* Lawrence: University Press of Kansas, 1990.

Chandler, Ralph Clark, ed. *A Centennial History of the American Administrative State.* New York: Free Press, 1987.

Tocqueville, Alexis de. *Democracy in America.* 2 vols. Edited by Phillips Bradley. New York: Knopf, 1945.

Vogel, David. *Fluctuating Fortunes: The Political Power of Business in America.* New York: Basic Books, 1989.

Wildavsky, Aaron. "On the Balance of Budgetary Cultures." In *Centennial History,* ed. Ralph Clark Chandler. New York: Free Press, 1987.

Wilson, Woodrow. "The Study of Administration." *Political Science Quarterly* 55 (1941; originally published 1885).

Campaign Finance and Campaign Finance Reform

Running for office has always meant spending money. Even before the American Revolution, there are records of candidates spending money to gain elected office. There is an account of George Washington's race for the Virginia House of Burgesses in 1757, which required that he offer "the customary means of winning votes," which included rum punch, wine, beer, and other libations (Thayer 1973).

Almost immediately, campaign money and where it came from became a hot issue in American politics. As early as 1832, President Andrew Jackson spoke to Congress on the topic, stating that "it is to be regretted that the rich and powerful too often bend the acts of government to their selfish purposes . . . the humble members of society . . . who have neither the time nor the means of securing like favors to themselves, have

the right to complain of the injustices of their government" (Bauer 1994).

Machine politics in the urban areas of the nation honed political fund raising to a fine art in the nineteenth century. Such organizations as Tammany Hall in New York, the Pendergasts in Kansas City, Frank Hague in Jersey City, "Big Bill" Thompson of Chicago, and Mayor James Curley of Boston were known for their corruption scandals, often revolving around campaign money. Campaigns could be funded from kickbacks due from patronage employees into the party's coffers or from those who, desiring to build, buy, or sell to the state or local government, were obliged to contribute to the party in power in order to stay in business.

SCANDAL LEADS TO REFORMS

After the Civil War, with the federal government now in the position to help or hinder numerous business interests, money from persons interested in legislation poured into federal and presidential campaigns. An example was the fund raising done by Marcus Alonzo "Dollar Marc" Hanna, an Ohio businessman who raised money for William McKinley for president in 1896. Because of the Teapot Dome scandal that flowed from Hanna's fund-raising practices, Congress passed a law prohibiting corporate donations to political campaigns in 1907 (the Tillman Act) and followed that up in 1910 with a law mandating disclosure of the sources of federal campaign funds (Beck and Sorauf 1992).

The 1925 Corrupt Practices Act banned corporate contributions to political candidates and limited expenditures for House races to $5,000 and Senate races to $25,000. Under the 1925 act, all expenditures directly under the control of the candidate must be reported to the clerk of the U.S. House, but any amount spent by committees without the express knowledge of the candidate need not be reported. The act contained no provisions for enforcement: no mechanism to compel the filing of reports or to scrutinize them for their accuracy. It was the first of many campaign finance reforms containing loopholes and omissions.

In 1943 the Tillman Act ban on contributions from corporations was extended to labor unions. In response to the ban, the Congress of Industrial Organizations developed the first political action committee. This PAC allowed union members to pool their voluntary donations into a fund that could be used to disburse funds to political candidates, thus circumventing the letter of the 1943 reform. Eventually business and other organized interest groups adopted the same practice.

Before 1950, most campaigns were a matter of radio

Table 1

Total Political Costs for All Offices in the United States During Presidential Years

Year	Total expenditures in millions		Percentage change since past election	
	Actual	Adjusted	Actual	Adjusted
1952	$140	$140	—	—
1956	155	151	+10.7	+7.9
1960	175	157	+12.9	+4.0
1964	200	171	+14.3	+8.9
1968	300	229	+50.0	+33.9
1972	425	270	+41.7	+17.9
1976	540	252	+27.1	−6.7
1980	1,200	388	+122.8	+54.0
1984	1,800	470	+53.3	+18.9
1988	2,700	666	+48.3	+41.7

Note: The largest increase occurs between the 1964 and 1968 elections, and again between the 1976 and 1980 elections. The largest increase in the safety margin for House incumbents also took place during this period of time, with the number of competitive House seats dwindling. The logical explanation for this is that by the 1968 campaign, the use of expensive television advertising was becoming the norm even in congressional races. Because of television ads, new, and expensive, consultants were added to campaigns in order to create tailored spots to best fit the circumstances of each campaign.

There is a dip in expenditures in 1976, which was the first election held under the new Federal Election Campaign Act rules. Campaigns were struggling to understand and comply with new rules, and the number of political action committees had not yet exploded to take advantage of the new legal routes of obtaining large amounts of campaign money. There were only 608 PACs operating in federal elections. Since this was also the first post-Watergate election, campaign managers were extremely cautious in their fund raising and were careful to stay within the confines of the law. If there was a doubt as to the meaning of the Federal Elections Campaign Act, the campaigns were more likely to err on the side of caution in 1976.

By the 1980 election, the number of PACs had increased, a new profession of campaign law had sprung up, and campaigns were more confident of their abilities to raise money while remaining technically within the boundaries of the Federal Elections Campaign Act.

How are such vast sums of money spent? A look at the 1988 contest, where there were no major independent candidates for the presidency, shows what a typical two-party contest costs and for what services the money is spent (see Table 2).

Sources: Alexander and Bauer 1988; Beck and Sorauf 1992.

and newspaper advertisements, followed by grass-roots volunteer efforts to get out the vote. After the advent of television, first used in a 1948 Connecticut Senate race, campaign costs began to soar, and the costs of running for president tripled between 1960 and 1968 (see Tables 1 and 2).

By the 1950s, a majority of states also had laws limiting campaign expenditures on the books, but these laws also applied only to spending done by the candidate, exempting committees spending on the candidate's behalf. Also exempted from these statutes were expenditures for such key campaign tools as printing, stationery, and postage (Clapp 1963). In a study on the attitudes of congressmen conducted by the Brookings Institution in 1959, a congressman pointed out the inadequacies of the prevailing campaign finance laws: "I don't believe you can be elected in some of these districts, mine included, within the spirit of the law. You can do it within the technicalities. What we had to do was technically legal: we created a whole slew of committees, each of whom would take over a portion of the campaign" (Clapp 1963).

Table 2

Costs of Nominating and Electing a President, 1988
(in millions)

Prenomination		
Spending by candidates for major party nomination	$199.6	
Compliance costs	12.4	
Independent expenditures	4.1	
Communication costs	0.2	
Labor spending	15.0	
Spending by minor party candidates	2.1	
Delegate candidate expenditures	0.1	$233.511
Conventions		
Republicans' expenditures	$18.0	
Democrats' expenditures	22.4	$40.4
General election		
Spending by major party candidates	$92.2	
Spending by minor party candidates	3.0	
Compliance costs	6.1	
Party committee spending	61.6	
Republican National Committee media	5.8	
Expenditures by labor, corporations, and associations	27.5	
Independent expenditures	10.1	
Communication costs	2.0	$208.3
Miscellaneous expenses		17.8
		$500.0

Note: The term *communication costs* indicates the monies spent by organizations such as labor unions and corporations, to urge their members or employees to vote for a particular candidate. Compliance costs are monies spent to hire accountants and attorneys to prepare and file the campaign finance disclosure forms required by the Federal Election Commission on a quarterly basis for all federal campaigns. In addition to the federal requirement, many states have their own campaign finance laws, which also require compliance.

Source: Alexander and Bauer 1991.

THE MODERN REFORM ERA

In 1971, Common Cause sued the Republican and Democratic national committees under the 1925 Corrupt Practices Act. It had long been common knowledge that the parties received large amounts of money from contributors who could remain behind the scenes, while the voters were unable to discover whose money was financing American politics. Under pressure of this suit, the Federal Elections Campaign Act of 1971 was born. As both Democrats and Republicans scrambled to finish their fund raising for the 1972 elections before the new law took effect, Common Cause struck again, this time suing the Committee to Re-Elect the President (Nixon's reelection campaign) under the 1925 law still in effect. This lawsuit led to the discovery of slush funds and money laundering of huge campaign contributions made by big business, all illegal under the 1925 act.

The last unregulated presidential campaign in American history seemed to the reform lobby proof that campaign finance was in desperate need of regulation. The Republicans raised the largest campaign treasury in American history for the 1972 reelection campaign of Richard Nixon. Over $60 million was raised, most of it before the April 7, 1972, deadline when the new election law took effect. One of Nixon's chief fund raisers that year, Maurice Stans, was subsequently convicted for his role in funneling cash to pay for the illegal actions in the Watergate scandal.

THE 1971 FEDERAL ELECTION CAMPAIGN ACT

The Federal Election Campaign Act was the first major reform of campaign finance since 1925. It mandated reforms in four categories. The first category of reforms concerned the actions of candidates, the second concerned the actions of individual donors, the third regulated donations by multicandidate committees, and the fourth applied to donations given by groups other than multicandidate committees. Every candidate for federal office since 1972 has filed reports according to its provisions. It was the single most important campaign finance reform of the twentieth century.

Federal Candidates

1. Candidates for federal office must disclose the names, addresses, employers, and occupations of any donor giving a cumulative total of over $200 to the campaign, in reports submitted to the Federal Election Commission at specified intervals in and between election cycles.
2. Party and PAC contributions, no matter what the amount, must be reported.
3. Reports of all campaign receipts and expenditures must be submitted in reports to the Federal Election Commission at specified intervals; these reports must also be filed locally, normally with the state election commissioner.
4. Campaign contributions from businesses, corporations, and labor unions are not allowed.

Individuals

1. Individuals wishing to influence elections are limited to donating $1,000 to any candidate or candidate committee per election in any given year (so an individual could double their contribution by contributing $1,000 in the primary and $1,000 in the general election).
2. Individuals are allowed to donate no more than $20,000 to any national party committee in any calendar year.
3. Individuals are allowed to give up to $5,000 per year to a PAC or political committee.
4. Individuals may contribute no more than $25,000 in total to these sources in any calendar year.

Actions of Political Action Committees

1. All political action committees must submit detailed reports quarterly to the Federal Election Commission that disclose contributions and their sources and disbursement to candidates or groups.
2. Committees that support fewer than five candidates and have fewer than 50 contributors may contribute $1,000 per election (primary and general elections counting as separate elections) to any particular candidate; they are limited to donating $20,000 to any national party committee and $5,000 to any other political committee. There is no limit on what the committee may contribute in a calendar year or election cycle.
3. Multicandidate committees (defined as any group that gives to more than five different candidates, has more than 50 contributors, and has been registered as a group for at least six months) may donate $5,000 per election (primary and general counting as separate elections) to individual campaigns. They may contribute up to $15,000 to the national party and $5,000 to any other political committee. There is no limit on what the multicandidate committee may contribute in a calendar year or election cycle.

This last provision in the law led to an explosion in the number of political action committees (PACs), from 600 in 1974 to more than 4,000 in 1996. Since the FECA severely limited individual contributions, the PAC became a handy mechanism for raising the large sums of money needed in modern congressional campaigns, but it has been widely criticized for contributing to incumbents over challengers. Nine out of every ten PAC dollars go to a congressional incumbent. Some political scientists believe this has led to higher reelection rates and safer seats for House incumbents in particular (Bauer and Hibbing 1989).

THE FEDERAL ELECTION COMMISSION

To correct a major flaw in the 1925 Corrupt Practices Act, the 1974 legislation created the Federal Election Commission. The FEC is made up of six members appointed by the president, with equal representation from the two major parties to keep the commission from becoming a tool for partisan advantage. Commissioners serve six-year staggered terms.

The commission has been frequently criticized for timidity in the enforcement of campaign laws. With each party represented by three members, it is easy to see how controversial actions that would put either party in a bad light could be blocked by a tie vote. As a result, most of the penalties meted out in the first 20 years of its existence have been relatively minor, most often calling for the payment of fines long after the campaigns are over.

Along with an enforcement function, the commission plays an important role in collecting and disseminating information to the public. Statistical reports are published before and after each round of federal elections, allowing the media to report on the ways campaigns are raising and spending their money. Individuals may request copies of the disclosure forms for any federal candidate, allowing anyone willing to pay a modest fee the chance to see exactly where individual candidates got their funds and how these funds were spent. This has allowed ordinary citizens to track campaign funds in a way not possible before 1974, while opening up new areas of inquiry in fields such as political science, history, and journalism. These reports may be accessed by contacting the Public Records Office of the Federal Election Commission at 999 E. Street Northwest, Washington, DC 20463.

Disclosure forms for any candidate for federal office may also be viewed by computer at terminals in many state election commission offices at no charge, or on-line at a home personal computer for a fee of $20 per hour. In addition to individual disclosure forms, FEC bulletins may also be downloaded to personal computers, allowing anyone with the right equipment the chance to become thoroughly educated on all aspects of campaign finance.

THE 1974 FECA AMENDMENTS

In response to the Watergate scandal, the FECA was amended to create a system of public funding of presidential campaigns, through a voluntary $1 check-off on the income tax form. By 1992, the federal treasury was supplying over $55 million each to the Republican and Democratic nominees for president. Only 19% of taxpayers in 1995 were contributing to the public financing of presidential campaigns, and by 1996 the fund was having trouble paying matching funds to candidates in the Republican primaries in a timely manner (Dye and Zeigler 1996).

This reform was designed to take special-interest money out of presidential elections, by fully funding the general election campaigns of both major party candidates with an equal amount. Here is how it works. In the contest for the nomination, campaign contributions of $250 or less given by individuals would be matched, dollar for dollar, by federal money, according to the following rules:

1. The presidential candidate must raise at least $5,000 in 20 states, from small donations.
2. After qualifying, the candidate would continue to receive matching funds until they received less than 10% of the vote in two primaries in a row.

The amendments included a set amount to be given equally to fund the Republican and Democratic National Conventions.

THE SUPREME COURT AND CAMPAIGN FINANCE

The FECA had to be amended again in 1976, when certain provisions of the law were ruled unconstitutional by the Supreme Court in the case of *Buckley* v. *Valeo*. In the Buckley ruling, the Court said that spending on campaigns was a form of free speech. Therefore the law could not simply limit spending; this would be limiting speech. It would be legal to grant a benefit, such as public financing, only to those who abided by the spending limits, thus ensuring that most candidates would spend within the limits of the law. If a candidate wanted to spend over the limit, however, there was no constitutional way to prohibit it.

The first presidential candidate to spend over the legal limit was a multimillionaire businessman who did not need federal funds to mount his campaign. Texan H. Ross Perot spent $59 million of his own money and garnered 19% of the vote in 1992. In the 1996 Republican presidential primary contest, multimillionaire publisher Steve Forbes ignored spending limits to fund his campaign from his own pocketbook.

In the same ruling, the Court also declared unconstitutional any limitations placed on independent groups wishing to spend money in behalf of a candidate. The 1976 FECA amendments allowed such "independent expenditure" committees to raise and spend unlimited funds in behalf of candidates. By the 1988 election, such groups had become a factor in American politics, raising and spending money in behalf of both major party candidates.

SOFT MONEY

In 1979, the FECA was amended once again, this time to create a category of campaign money that would not be limited or recorded. "Hard" money must be reported to the FEC by amount and donor. Unregulated funds are considered "soft money" and were allowed as a tool for political parties to engage in "party-building activities," activities meant to help the entire party instead of a single candidate. The amendments were adopted at the urging of leaders of both political parties, who argued that the political parties had been marginalized by the strict funding limits of the 1974 act. Although soft money may be subject to state laws, it is currently unregulated at the federal level.

The 1979 amendments allowed the following monies to be raised in unlimited amounts, without public disclosure of donors: funds for printing, preparation, and distribution of lists of endorsed candidates, including the distribution through the mail; campaign materials such as yard signs, bumper stickers, and brochures, paid for by local party committees; and voter registration and get-out-the-vote activities to benefit their party's nominees for president and vice president, including funds for telephone banks designed by professionals but utilized by volunteers.

Soft-money contributions allowed individuals, corporations, and labor unions to give large sums of money to political parties, often in contributions of $100,000 or more. Corporations, which had been prohibited from direct contributions to campaigns since 1907, were once more able to give direct contributions.

Table 3		
Soft-Money Expenditures (in millions)		
Year	Republicans	Democrats
1980	$15.1	$4.0
1984	$15.6	$6.0
1988	$22.0	$23.0
1992	$49.6	$35.3

Source: Citizen's Research Foundation and the Center for Responsive Politics.

Managers of presidential campaigns contend that without soft money, they would be unable to mount adequate campaigns. For example, the amount given to the campaigns of George Bush and Bill Clinton in 1992 by the federal check-off program provided only about 36% of the amount actually spent in the election (see Table 3; Greenberg and Page 1996).

Soft money could come from groups and individuals simply interested in improving government as a function of their being good citizens. Or it could come from individuals and groups with a strong motivation to influence government policy for their own benefit. It is this second category that alarms some political analysts. The major donors of soft money seem to fall almost exclusively into the second category, giving large contributions, often to both parties, while seeking benefits from the federal government for their companies.

RECENT ATTEMPTS AT REFORM

In 1990 two important attempts were made at campaign finance reform, and both attempts failed to produce tangible results. The leader of the Republican and Democratic parties in the Senate appointed a bipartisan Campaign Finance Reform Panel made up of experts, academics, and party activists. They proposed the following reforms: reduced broadcast and postal rates for candidates, free broadcast time for parties to allocate to candidates, and exemptions from the spending limits for a percentage of funds raised in the candidate's home state (Beck and Sorauf 1992).

The second attempt was made through the political process, when campaign finance reform bills were passed in the House and Senate. This attempt failed, in large part, because the House and Senate bills disagreed on fundamental issues and were impossible to reconcile. Even if the bills had been reconciled in Conference Committee, the bill faced a probable presidential veto from President George Bush. The debate on these proposals showed clear partisan positions on

Table 4

Receipts of the Major Parties (in millions)

	1978	1980	1982	1984	1986	1988	1990	1992	1994
Democrat	$26.4	$37.2	$39.3	$98.5	$64.8	$127.9	$85.7	$177.7	$139.1
Republican	$84.5	$169.5	$215	$279.9	$255	$263.3	$206.3	$267.3	$245.6
Total	$110.9	$206.7	$254.3	$396.4	$320	$391.2	$292	$445	$384.7

Source: Federal Election Commission.

campaign finance reform, with Republicans objecting to spending caps and Democrats objecting to the elimination of PAC money. The 1990 debate showed the partisan interests on display, and led to a legislative deadlock (Beck and Sorauf 1992).

When President Bill Clinton was elected in 1992, his campaign speeches promised campaign finance reform. But bills passed separately in the House and Senate were never reconciled, and the Clinton administration was unable to pass campaign finance reform legislation while the Democratic Party held both the White House and both houses of Congress.

By 1995, the Republicans were in control of both the House and the Senate, and campaign finance reform did no better in the atmosphere of a divided government. During a joint speaking engagement in the summer of 1995, Speaker of the House Newt Gingrich shook hands with President Bill Clinton, pledging to appoint yet another joint commission to study campaign finance reform. As this volume goes to press, months after the historic handshake, no commission members have been appointed, and the only campaign reform legislation to be signed into law was a bill that mandated that all lobbyists register as such, which limited the ability of lobbyists to pay for gifts and meals for legislators.

By 1996, the group that formed around Ross Perot's surprisingly effective third-party presidential candidacy in 1992, United We Stand America, had placed campaign finance reform at the center of their efforts. At a campaign forum held in Concord, New Hampshire, on January 20, 1996, the executive director of United We Stand America, Russell Varney, described the current campaign finance system as "organized graft" (Randolph T. Holhut, "Getting Big Money Out of Politics," from an Internet posting February 1996, The Written Word, mdle@primenet.com Michael Lewis).

One of the obstacles to an overhaul of campaign finance has been the lack of consensus among groups lobbying for changes in the system. Three nonpartisan public-interest lobbies have focused on campaign finance reform: Common Cause, the group that began reform by suing the political parties in 1971; Public Citizen, a Ralph Nader–sponsored group of public-interest lobbyists; and the Center for Responsive Politics, the youngest reform organization, founded in the late 1980s to research and report on campaign finance. Only the Center for Responsive Politics calls for full public financing of all federal campaigns, while the older groups take more moderate positions.

Monica Bauer

SEE ALSO Fiscal Policy

BIBLIOGRAPHY

Alexander, Herbert, and Monica Bauer. *Financing the 1988 Election*. Boulder, CO: Westview Press, 1991.

Bauer, Monica. "Money and Politics: In Pursuit of an Ideal." In *Presidential Campaigns and American Self Images*, ed. Arthur H. Miller and Bruce E. Gronbeck. Boulder, CO: Westview Press, 1994.

Beck, Paul Allen, and Frank J. Sorauf. *Party Politics in America*. 7th ed. New York: HarperCollins, 1992.

Clapp, Charles L. *The Congressman: His Work as He Sees It*. Washington, DC: Brookings Institution, 1963.

Dye, Thomas R., and Harmon Zeigler. *The Irony of Democracy*. 10th ed. Belmont, CA: Wadsworth, 1996.

Greenberg, Edward S., and Benjamin I. Page. *The Struggle for Democracy*. New York: HarperCollins, 1996.

Thayer, George. *Who Shakes the Money Tree*. New York: Simon and Schuster, 1973.

Campaign Materials

SYMBOLS

Unlike the Republican Party and its long identification with the elephant, a variety of animals have symbolized the Democratic Party. These have included the tiger and the rooster. Both were utilized before the donkey gained popular acceptance as the party's emblem in the early 1900s.

Harper's Weekly political cartoonist Thomas Nast is credited with negatively associating the party with a tiger in 1871. His tiger was a fearful and nasty beast. Originally drawn to depict Boss William Tweed of New York City's powerful Tammany Hall political machine, by 1872 Nast was using the tiger to illustrate Democrats on the national level as well. The animal was employed to portray the presidential bids of *New York Tribune* editor Horace Greeley in 1872 and New York's Governor Samuel Tilden in 1876. Both candidates were affiliated at one point with the Tammany machine, although later, Tilden had actually prosecuted Tweed. Nast, as a zealous Republican and a great critic of Tammany corruption, tended to personify Democrats and the party as animals with unflattering characteristics. In addition to the tiger, he utilized dogs, snakes, and assorted other creatures.

Following Tilden's narrow and contested electoral vote loss in March 1877, Nast buried both Tammany's influence and the tiger. His illustration pictured a tombstone engraved "Here Lies the Democratic Tiger." This cartoon also contained a battered and injured elephant (the Republicans), symbolizing the extreme controversy surrounding Tilden's loss. Except, ironically, for a few Tammany items issued in celebration of Grover Cleveland's 1893 inauguration, the tiger was never employed by the Democrats as their own symbol, perhaps because it was identified too heavily with Nast's poison pen. Yet another animal designated by the cartoonist to represent Democrats eventually would be adopted by the party.

In December 1879, Nast penned the first cartoon that jointly depicted both the Republican elephant and the Democratic Party, now characterized by a donkey. The donkey (or more specifically, the "jackass") had appeared in 1830s anti-Jackson cartoons drawn by others and was used to represent the Whig Party at times in the 1850s. But Nast's marriage of the Democratic Party with this animal would give rise to its popular usage as other illustrators—and then the party itself—emulated his choice. Nast's selection of a new symbol coincided with the Democratic capture of both congressional chambers in the 1878 election after decades of Republican dominance. By the century's end, the donkey was still largely evoked as a negative image by others. In the 1896 race, for example, Republicans utilized a half-donkey, half-goose creature to represent the William Jennings Bryan coalition of Democrats and Populists.

While others saw the Democrats as tigers or donkeys, the party preferred the rooster. Some of the earliest badges designed for James Buchanan's 1856 campaign used this image. The rooster can be found adorning many Democratic candidates' political artifacts throughout the latter part of the nineteenth century. One prominent example was utilized by Winfield Scott Hancock during the 1880 race. Over a portrait of the candidate can be found an open palm with a rooster; a rebus puzzle for "hand" + "cock" (Hancock).

First Appearance of the Democratic Donkey with Jackson Aboard. *Source:* Library of Congress.

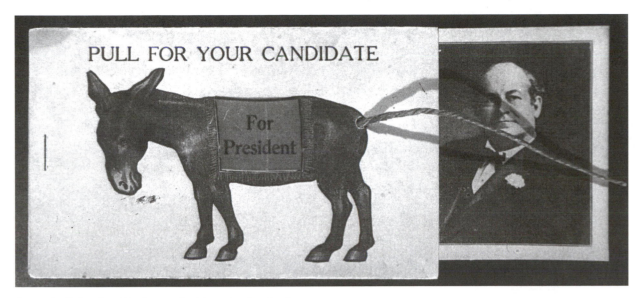

Bryan Pull Card, 1908. *Source:* Smithsonian Institution.

By the early 1900s, the rooster was gradually replaced by the donkey as the party's animal of choice. Bryan's 1908 run for the presidency employed both creatures. In addition, a popular series of postcards had Bryan riding a donkey racing William Howard Taft atop an elephant. James Cox employed the rooster in 1920 along with the slogan "I Will Crow in November," and in decreasing frequency the bird can be found on artifacts as late as Franklin Roosevelt's campaigns. One isolated usage even surfaced in 1964. On a button noting that the rooster was "the Democratic Party's first national emblem," the bird crows, "Cock-A Doodle Doo! Johnson and Humphrey Too!" While no longer utilized on the national level, today some statewide Democratic parties such as Kentucky still employ roosters on some of their campaign items.

The donkey ascended as the party's sole national symbol in the early 1900s. By 1932, it had firmly replaced the rooster as the chief party image. The animal had become a "depression buster," and one widespread button had it booting an elephant and the logo "Kick Out Depression with a Democratic Vote." Democrats now warmly embraced as their own powerful symbol an image that began as an object of scorn drawn by Thomas Nast.

SLOGANS

The 1828 election produced the first president from the newly constituted Democratic Party. This election was a rematch of Andrew Jackson against John Quincy Adams. Four years earlier, despite having a plurality of both the popular and the electoral vote, Jackson lost when the election was decided by the House of Representatives. Jackson's 1828 victory owes much to the expansion of male suffrage, when three times as many voters were eligible to vote than in 1824. The proliferation of eligible voters also coincides with the expanded use of campaign items to solicit support for candidates. Medal tokens and cloth ribbons (which later doubled as bookmarks) made much of Jackson's nickname "Old Hickory" as well as his military victories during the War of 1812: "General Jackson/Hero of New Orleans." The 1832 race revived these ideas and produced a number of items centering on the issue of paper currency. A popular slogan of the day was "No Bank! Down with Rag Money," which referred to Jackson's opposition to both a second national bank and the issuance of paper currency. Jackson's image also adorned three-dimensional items such as thread, snuff and pill boxes, flasks, pitchers, and glassware. These items, however, were expensive and were more for personal usage then for mass advertising of the candidate. Opposition retorts of the period painted Jackson as "King Andrew" and were critical of his monetary policies as well as those of Martin Van Buren, Jackson's vice president, who won the 1836 contest. Generally, material items prior to the 1840 campaign featured portraits of the candidates, with very little sloganing. But Van Buren lost his 1840 reelection bid to the twin challenges of economic depression and the clever imagery of the Whig's William Henry Harrison whose supposed down-home roots

Jackson as "King Andrew I." *Source:* Library of Congress.

were popularized by using the log cabin among his political objects on campaign. Harrison's logo, "Tippecanoe and Tyler Too," references to his 1811 military victory and running mate John Tyler, became one of the best-known slogans of any presidential contest.

The 1844 race centered on issues of territorial expansion. Phrases such as "Oregon, Texas and Democracy" and "Alone but Not Deserted," featuring the Lone Star of Texas, decorated ribbons made for James K. Polk, who advocated enlarging the United States. Polk articles portrayed the candidate as an heir to Jackson's legacy and labeled him "The Young Hickory." Indeed, Jackson had prevented the Democrats from renominating Van Buren in 1844 because of Van Buren's opposition to the annexation of Texas. Polk campaigned on a Jackson reform platform and

made much of his opponent, Henry Clay's, role in denying Jackson the presidency in 1824. The victorious run of Franklin Pierce in 1852 used catchy phrasing, such as, "We Polked 'em in '44; We'll Pierce 'em in '52," to capture the White House.

Between 1856 and 1876, the issues of slavery, preservation of the union, and eventually Reconstruction dominated presidential politics. James Buchanan ("Old Buck") emphasized "The Union, It Must Be Preserved," and "One Country, One Constitution, One Destiny." An uglier side of this campaign came as Republicans were demonized as radicals who would free the slaves. Unfavorable images of blacks adorned numerous artifacts. On the lighter side, Democrats pledged: "We Polked 'em in '44/We Pierced 'em in '52 and We'll Buck 'em in '56." Rebus puzzle items pictured an antlered-deer and a cannon (Buck + cannon).

Stephen Douglas, known as the "Little Giant," secured the national (northern) Democrat nomination in

Van Buren Pull Card, 1836. Second Expression—Repugnance from Drinking Harrison Cider. *Source:* Smithsonian Institution.

1860. He stumped on a platform of union and as "The Champion of Popular Sovereignty." Douglas's opposition came not only from the nascent Republican Party's candidate Abraham Lincoln but also from within his own party. The divisive issues of the day led southern Democrats to nominate Buchanan's vice president, John C. Breckinridge, as a presidential candidate as well. His slogan, "Our Rights, the Constitution and the Union," sounded lofty, but it clearly indicated a states' rights approach popular in the pre–Civil War South. The campaigns of Douglas, Breckinridge, and Lincoln were enhanced by the introduction of new types of material items in 1860. Advances in photography allowed for the politicians' pictures to be reproduced for partisan artifacts. The use of these ferrotype lapel pins made their debut during the 1860 election.

From 1864 through 1880 the Democrats nominated a series of standard-bearers who ultimately would go down in defeat. General George B. McClellan was the first of these candidates selected to challenge Lincoln's reelection bid in 1864. The retired general advocated prosecuting the war only to save the union and not for emancipation of slaves or other issues. New York Governor Horatio Seymour was the party's choice in 1868. Saddled with a running mate, Francis Blair, who opposed Reconstruction and black suffrage, Seymour's team lost to the popular Civil War hero Ulysses S. Grant. In 1872 Grant's reelection was opposed by *New York Tribune* editor Horace Greeley, who took on Grant's military background with the slogan "The Pen Is Mightier Than the Sword." Nicknamed the "Sage of Chappaqua," after his New York home, Greeley advocated tariff protection and national reconciliation. In the wake of a series of scandals that plagued the Grant administration, in 1876 another New Yorker, Samuel J. Tilden, urged honesty, reform, sound money, and prosperity in his campaign. Although Tilden won more popular votes than his rival, Rutherford B. Hayes, Republican maneuvering in the electoral vote count secured the win for Hayes. In the 1880 race, ribbons became more colorful and ornate as new production techniques replaced the dull black-on-white designs. Lapel studs that could be placed through jacket buttonholes emerged at this time as well. Even though Winfield Scott Hancock lost his bid for the presidency, imaginative campaign items picturing a palm and a rooster (hand + cock) were popular among the Democratic faithful.

Grover Cleveland reversed a quarter century of Democratic defeats by capturing the White House in 1884. Four years later, perhaps to counter the revelation that in his youth he had fathered a child outside

Democratic Candidates for President and Vice President, 1888: Cleveland and Thurman. Frances, Cleveland's Wife, Appears in the Middle. *Source:* Library of Congress.

wedlock, a variety of artifacts promoted his new wife, Frances, whom he married in June 1886. The party designated Frances as "The Nation's Favorite Belle," and her image could be found on plates, playing cards, napkins, and tokens. This widespread promotion was the first such effort for a first lady. Despite the emphasis on the first lady, political cards with the rhyme "Ma, Ma, Where's My Pa? Fired from the White House, Ha, Ha, Ha" surfaced during 1888 and foreshadowed Cleveland's defeat. In this race and the 1892 rematch with Benjamin Harrison, however, the main issue was free trade versus protective tariffs. Both Cleveland–Harrison contests coincided with a momentary return of textile usage as well. Candidate portraits and slogans appeared on red bandanas, which were a hallmark of this campaign.

The 1896 race not only is noteworthy for its lively "Battle of the Standards," where Democrats advocated the silver standard to the Republican support of gold, but was also significant for the inception of the celluloid pinback button. With its combination of bright colors and candidate pictures covered with a thin layer of transparent celluloid placed over a metal pin, these buttons revolutionized campaign artifacts. They were relatively inexpensive to produce and became a colorful staple of contesting elections. Items associated with William Jennings Bryan heralded his support of silver at a ratio of 16 parts to 1 part gold. Artifacts reading "16-to-1" were commonplace. Less common, but inspired, was a button featuring a face of a clock. The positioned hands reflected a time of 12:44 (16-to-1). Bryan's impassioned convention speech with its maxim, "No crown of thorns/No cross of gold," could be found on many items as well.

Bryan's 1900 race rejuvenated many of the themes from 1896. Chief among them was again his advocacy of the silver standard. Many artifacts appeared with silver as a background color. Bryan's opposition to big business was highlighted with "Democracy Stands for People Not Trusts" and "A Friend to All: True Democracy Against Monopoly." For the first time in fifty years, foreign policy was also an important election issue in the wake of the Spanish-American War. The candidate was critical of U.S. imperialism associated with the U.S. capture of Cuba and the Philippines during that conflict. This view was reflected in his "Anti-Expansionism," "Republic, Not Empire," and "No Foreign Alliances/No Trusts/No Imperialism for U.S." buttons.

The party's nominee in 1904, Alton B. Parker, did not campaign for election and instead followed a then-common practice among many candidates by retreating to his home after the convention to await the people's verdict. Few items from Parker's run carry any slogans. While most buttons merely pictured Parker and his running mate, Henry Davis, one interesting artifact profiled an elephant shackled by protectionism and trusts. While poking fun at the GOP as the "Grand Old Pirate," this "white elephant" highlights the national deficit that occurred under Theodore Roosevelt's administration. Bryan was the Democrat's choice once more in 1908. His third try for the White House corresponded with the previous year's economic downturn. Bryan tried to make the most of it by classifying the Republican "Full Dinner Pail" strategy as the "Empty Dinner Pail" or "The Bottom Is Out of the Full Dinner Pail," but he lost again.

In 1912, Woodrow Wilson ran a rather bland campaign as the incumbent William Howard Taft brawled with his former mentor, Teddy Roosevelt. The team of Wilson and Thomas Marshall used as one of its slogans "I Wood/row Wilson and Marshall to Victory." In 1916 Democrats emphasized "America First," "He

Parker–Davis Campaign Button. *Source:* Library of Congress.

Had Kept Us Out of War" and "War in Europe/Peace in America/God Bless Wilson," references to American neutrality at that time toward World War I. Another theme of Wilson's reelection bid centered on the enactment of the eight-hour working day. The theme "8-Hour Wilson" and "Wilson's 8-Hour Day" were designed to appeal to blue-collar voters.

Despite the introduction of lithograph materials, which enabled a photograph to be printed directly on tin, thus making items more inexpensive, Democratic materials for the 1920 and 1924 elections are scarce. Indeed, items picturing the 1920 nominee James Cox and his running mate, Franklin Roosevelt, are some of the most valuable campaign items. For this race, Democrats recycled old slogans, such as "Peace! Progress! Prosperity!" A few articles did emphasize Cox's opposition to Prohibition: "Vote for Cox and Cocktails," but in general the offerings were slim. John Davis's 1924 run made frequent references to the Teapot Dome Scandal of the Warren G. Harding administration. One novel piece employed was a doorhanger in the shape of a teapot. The party highlighted an honesty theme that included "Honesty at Home/Honor Abroad," "Back to Honesty with Davis," and "Better Days with Davis," but voters opted to stay with the Republicans. In 1928, Alfred Smith, the "Happy Warrior," made history as the first Catholic to be nominated by a major party. Smith's campaign was among the first also to highlight a candidate's first

Wilson Campaign Truck. *Source:* United Press International.

name. Numerous articles contain "Al" phrases: "Better Times with Al" and "Goodbye Cal/Hello Al," a reference to the retiring Calvin Coolidge. In the end, Smith was unable to deflect the perceived dual loyalty issue in a widespread anti-Catholic campaign.

With the lingering effects of the Great Depression, Franklin Roosevelt accentuated economic issues in 1932. His trademark "Happy Days Will Come Again" was buttressed with "Roosevelt or Ruin." Voters were encouraged to "Get Rid of the White Elephant/Turn Democratic," as buttons highlighted the donkey as a "depression buster." Democrats also advocated repealing the 18th Amendment regarding the Prohibition of alcohol: "Repeal with Roosevelt" and "For Repeal and Prosperity." In addition, supporters also stressed his famous last name with "America Calls Another Roosevelt," and similar to cousin Teddy, the campaign manufactured rebus puzzle buttons picturing a rose followed by "velt." In 1936, New Deal references abounded on Roosevelt items. Buttons heralded that "He Saved America" and urged "Follow Through with Roosevelt" and "Forward with Roosevelt." Taking on Alfred Landon's prevalent sunflower motif, one prominent offering read "You Can't Eat Sunflowers/

Disgusted Republican/Let's Lose with Landon." In FDR's bid for a unprecedented third term in 1940, one banner heralded "To Keep the Nation Firm; Give Him Another Term," while other objects intoned "Better a Third Termer than a Third Rater" and "I Want Roosevelt Again." Similarly in 1944 the issue was addressed by "Three Good Terms Deserve Another," and "Go 4th to Win the War." Sloganing associated with FDR's prosecution of World War II was widespread. Except for the Civil War, 1944 was the only other time an election had been held during a conflict. Themes included "Finish the Job" and "Roosevelt and Truman for Lasting Peace/Security for All." Harry Truman in 1948 ran against the Republican-controlled Congress with "The Won't Do Congress Won't Do," as much as he ran against Thomas E. Dewey, that party's nominee. Most items featured only pictures of Truman and his running mate, Alben Barkley, but a few contained the phrase "Give 'em Hell Harry," or emphasized Truman's domestic program, called the "Fair Deal."

Adlai Stevenson in 1952 and 1956 tried to rejoin arguably the most effective slogan of all time—Dwight Eisenhower's "I Like Ike." Campaign items from the Stevenson camp included "I Like Adlai Better,"

Repeal of Prohibition Was a Democratic Pledge in 1932. *Source:* Franklin Delano Roosevelt Library.

"Gladly for Adlai," "I'm Madly for Adlai," "We Believe in Steve," and "Adlai and Estes [Kefauver] are the Bestes." In 1956, utilizing the new medium of the automobile bumper sticker, one prominent message read, "FDR—The New Deal/Harry—The Fair Deal/Ike—The Ordeal," while another had in red "I Switched to Adlai" superimposed over a white "I Like Ike" sign.

John Kennedy's quest in 1960 featured slogans such as "Let's Back Jack" and "I'm Gone for John," while *PT-109* lapel pins noted his World War II naval heroism. Flasher buttons alternated between Kennedy's image and the logo "The Man for the '60s." In 1964 one could find "All the Way with LBJ" and "LBJ for the USA." Lyndon Johnson punctuated his Texas roots with items featuring the state outline and Stetson hats. Democrats spoofed Barry Goldwater's slogan, "In Your Heart You Know He's Right," with the retort, "In Your Guts, You Know He's Nuts." The negative aspects of Johnson's campaign also produced "Bury Goldwater" and "Goldwater in '64/Hot Water in '65/Bread and Water in '66/Under Water in '67." The Republican nominee was painted as a warmonger with "Barry G. and World War III," "Help Goldwater Wipe Out Peace" and spoofing the popular *Dr. Strangelove* movie about nuclear armageddon: "Doctor Strangewater for President." Johnson's vice president, Hubert H. Humphrey, was the party's choice in 1968. Although 1968 was a dramatic political year, the Humphrey camp tendered few unusual buttons. A series alluding to his father's pharmacist profession did offer "HHH fills the Prescription" and "Humphrey—Rx for a Better World."

The anti-Vietnam themes of George McGovern's 1972 run were evident in the colorful images of peace signs, doves, olive branches, and slogans such as "Come Home America/Elect McGovern in '72" and "Make America Happen Again." Voters were encouraged both to "Make America McGovernable" and to "Let's Help Nixon OUT." In 1976, playing off his famous toothy smile and his past occupation as a peanut farmer, Jimmy Carter offered "The Grin Will Win" and "I'm Nuts about Carter." The peanut motif was widespread as was Carter's use of green as a background color on buttons instead of the traditional red, white, and blue. Carter's southern roots and his running mate Walter Mondale's nickname were combined in a popular set of buttons with "Grits and Fritz." In attempting to capitalize on the Watergate scandal and the less than enthusiastic support for Gerald Ford's accidental presidency, the overall Carter campaign theme was "A Leader, for a Change." Negative items included "Remember the Watergate Burglars, Vote Carter," "Ford Is an Edsel," "Happiness Is Trading in an Old Ford," and "Vote for Carter/Ford Will Pardon You." Another item issued in support of Carter—but certainly not sanctioned by the candidate—made reference to the nominee's controversial *Playboy* interview: "I'm a Bunny for Carter," portrayed the head and ears of the rabbit shaped as the magazine's trademarked logo. In their failed 1980 reelection bid, Carter and Mondale were heavily featured jointly as "A Tested and Trustworthy Team." Americans were counseled to "Keep Them Working for You."

In 1984, as the party's standard-bearer, Mondale

made history by selecting Geraldine Ferraro to be his running mate. Many items highlighted the first woman to be on a national ticket. These included: "A Woman's Place Is in the House/in the Senate/and the Vice Presidency" and "Why Not a Woman?/Ferraro 1984." Competing against the popular incumbent Ronald Reagan, the Mondale–Ferraro team campaigned on the theme "America Needs New Leadership" and "America Needs a Change." Michael Dukakis's 1988 contest against George Bush played heavily on his nickname "Duke." Similar to Mondale in the 1984 campaign, Dukakis seemed to be overshadowed by his running mate, Lloyd Bentsen. One item from this race played on fears of a less than adequate Republican vice presidential candidate: "Quayle—A Heartbeat Away."

Bill Clinton's 1992 campaign cleverly capitalized on his saxophone playing by issuing pins in the shape of the instrument as well as items proclaiming "Clinton, a Cure for the Blues." The predominant theme tied Clinton to the "year of the woman" sentiments, which saw an unprecedented number of women running for political office. Buttons proclaimed "Pro Choice/Pro Family/Pro Clinton." Numerous items pictured "Rosey the Riveter" from World War II fame, with the 1992 refrain "We Can Do It/Clinton–Gore" In addition, the presidential nominee was pictured alongside many of the female candidates for Senate. One such coattail button portrayed Clinton with Diane Feinstein and Barbara Boxer, who were contesting the two open seats in California: "As California Goes/So Goes the Nation." And it did.

Robert J. Bookmiller

BIBLIOGRAPHY

Fischer, Roger A. *Tippecanoe and Trinkets Too: The Material Culture of American Presidential Campaigns, 1828–1984.* Urbana: University of Illinois Press, 1988.

Hake, Ted. *Hake's Guide to Presidential Campaign Collectibles.* Radnor, PA: Wallace-Homestead, 1992.

Keller, Morton. *The Art and Politics of Thomas Nast.* New York: Oxford University Press, 1968.

Melder, Keith. *Hail to the Candidate: Presidential Campaigns from Banners to Broadcasts.* Washington, DC: Smithsonian Institution Press, 1992.

Schlesinger, Arthur M., Jr., Fred L. Israel, and David J. Frent, eds. *Running for President: The Candidates and Their Images.* New York: Simon and Schuster, 1994.

Campaigns and Elections

Electioneering activities always have been critical aspects of the Democratic Party, since the major purpose of a political party is to gain political power through contesting and winning elections. Nomination processes, voting procedures, and campaign regulations directly influence campaign practices. The general trend in U.S. elections has been from party-centered nominations and campaigns to candidate-centered campaigns. Electoral modification and capital-intensive campaign technology have severely limited the power of party elites since the beginning of the twentieth century. Nonetheless, Democratic state and local parties and national party committees continue to provide critical electioneering services.

In the early 1790s nomination practices varied from state to state. In some states, committees of correspondence nominated and campaigned for candidates. In many states nominations were solicited at outdoor mass meetings. Consequently, many candidates competed for each elective office. From 1792 to 1800, patriotic societies such as the German Republic Society and fraternal organizations such as the Society of St. Tammany began to perform electioneering functions, primarily for the Democratic-Republican Party. Nominations were garnered at the societies' monthly meetings, usually held in public buildings. Congressional and state legislative caucuses nominated statewide and national candidates. State central committees soon developed to supervise local party committees. Before 1800, suffrage was extremely limited, and most voting was done by the viva-voce method. Poll officials required voters to announce their selections publicly. This method was time-consuming and open to fraud. Governments also held their elections at different times.

Partisan electioneering methods conformed to the nomination and voting procedures. One of the first electioneering activities of the nascent political parties was to acquire auxiliaries among the press. In 1792 Alexander Hamilton used U.S. Treasury Department funds to subsidize a friendly Philadelphia paper, *Gazette of the United States*, to promote the Washington administration. Thomas Jefferson quickly responded and hired Philip Freneau as a State Department "translator clerk" to publish a rival paper, the *National Gazette*, which became the leading Democratic-Republican paper. Tammany and patriotic societies also began to develop systematic electioneering practices. By the 1800s, Aaron Burr and Tammany societies used card indexes of voter names and several Democratic-Republican state managers employed a hierarchical county, district, and town-manager voter canvassing system. Pennsylvania Governor Thomas McKean initiated the patronage system as he appointed state officials on a partisan basis and expected contributions in return.

Democratic-Republican societies in several states campaigned vigorously for Thomas Jefferson in 1800, resulting in the first party-centered presidential campaign. Partisan papers engaged in negative campaigning, accusing John Adams of being a monarchist. But electioneering was primarily directed at state legislators who chose the electors. The Democratic-Republican Party pressed its members to cast a straight party vote for state and local elections. One major electioneering practice during this time was for party activists to give voters alcoholic beverages at the voting place.

By 1824, almost all white males could vote, and electoral processes were modified to accommodate the increased number of voters. States reduced the size of electoral districts and started to use paper ballots, which were printed and distributed by the parties. As suffrage expanded, the Democratic-Jeffersonian Republican Party became very organized at the local and state levels. Rural school district and township committees, city ward and county committees met frequently, sponsored local candidates and produced political information. State party committees performed a wide range of functions including distributing literature, collecting funds, printing ballots, preparing lists of eligible voters, measuring voter preferences, and organizing rallies.

During President Monroe's administration, Senator Martin Van Buren and others believed that a two-party system was essential for a stable representative government. Van Buren organized opponents of the National Republicans into regional central committees to support the 1828 campaign of President Jackson and conduct state and local campaigns. In the 1828 election Democratic committees refined existing campaign practices designed to attract the popular vote. Party leaders conducted rallies, parades, and grand barbecues. Democrats put hickory leaves in their hats, carried hickory canes, and erected hickory poles in central locations. Campaign memorabilia such as jugs, campaign buttons, and plates were also distributed to voters. Jacksonian Democratic leaders also established a chain of newspapers aimed directly at voters.

The Democratic Party continued to refine the art of mass politics in the mid-1800s. Elected officials became more systematic about giving jobs to loyal party men and demanding contributions in return. Leaders continued to rely on a partisan network of penny papers and often subsidized unprofitable weeklies. Democratic machines developed where a strong party leader maintained control with close ties to a popular newspaper. At the local level, Democratic postmasters served vital electioneering functions. They distributed campaign material, raised money, often became editors of local papers, and habitually trashed campaign material from opponents. Postmasters were also a key source of campaign contributions since they represented two-thirds of national patronage jobs. For example, after the 1844 election, the new Democratic postmaster replaced 11,000 out of 14,000 postmasters with loyal party men.

Democratic parties staged monster rallies during the mid-1830s. In the morning a partisan parade was organized complete with bands, glee clubs, honor guards, and floats. Organizers held a picnic at midday accompanied by speeches, the raising of a huge campaign pole, and distribution of campaign memorabilia and literature. Democratic candidates also conducted individual or joint canvasses with their opponents, usually consisting of long speeches and debates. After 1840, Democrats usually adopted a platform at the national convention that candidates used during their campaigns.

These partisan electioneering methods were very effective, and voter turnout routinely surpassed 70%. The Democratic Party was portrayed as the main vehicle for self-government, and members became loyal soldiers fighting for a noble cause, rather than supporting candidates. The party-centered nature of electioneering practices was reflected in presidential campaigns as party managers conducted the campaign with the assistance of state and local leaders, while the candidate stayed at home and appeared unconcerned by the election.

Illegal electioneering practices flourished during the mid-1880s. Democratic machines recruited armies of recent immigrants and hired men to act as repeaters, hauling them to many polling places in carts. Party activists also printed their party's ballots on distinctive colored paper, paid or intimidated voters, and stuffed ballot boxes.

From the late 1860s to the end of the 1890s, parties had their greatest influence on election outcomes. In 1868 Samuel J. Tilden, a wealthy New York politician, instituted a new style of Democratic electioneering. Tilden believed that systematic campaigns based on analytical methods and voter education were more effective than traditional rallies. He created a Literary Bureau to write, print, and distribute political pamphlets in several different languages. Tilden also hired a private advertising agency and used informal pre-election polls of voters to discover undecided regions. Tilden applied his methods on a national scale during his presidential campaign in 1876. His staff sent a campaign textbook of more than 700 pages to state Democratic committees and mailed out more than 27 million campaign fliers. After Tilden won the popular

Bryan Campaigning in 1896. *Source:* Smithsonian Institution.

vote in 1876, Democratic state and local leaders supplemented mass politics with educational political campaigns. Managers still primarily conducted presidential campaigns, but candidates gave "front porch" speeches. In 1896, however, William Jennings Bryan broke with tradition and traveled more than 18,000 miles to take his message to voters in 26 states. Though Bryan received an unprecedented number of votes, William McKinley, who stayed home, won the election, and presidential hopefuls returned to their porches for a little while longer.

Election frauds also became more systematic in the Gilded Age. Machine workers quickly naturalized recent immigrants so that they would be loyal Democrats and often transported repeaters from city to city and across state boundaries in substantial numbers. Political operatives also purchased votes in large numbers, and party bosses systematically levied campaign assessments among their political appointees.

Electoral reforms such as voter registration, the Australian ballot, voting machines, civil service laws, and primary elections were widely adopted by the end of the nineteenth century. Democratic machines continued to produce many votes in the early 1900s by using patronage, services, and fraud but gradually lost power. Concurrently, candidate-centered electioneering practices began to replace party-centered methods. For example, Woodrow Wilson believed that the party was an instrument designed to mobilize voters for its candidates. As an illustration, the Democratic presidential campaigns of 1912 and 1916 used mass advertising techniques, movies, and recordings to publicize Wilson's characteristics and accomplishments, rather than rally the party faithful behind a cause. Regional tours became commonplace for state and national candidates and presidential aspirants began to canvass voters. Nevertheless, party officials continued to solicit candidates and dominate presidential nominations at party conventions.

During the interwar period, candidates began to rely on professional expertise and technology. Radio advertisements became standard campaign tools in the 1920s, and the use of public relations firms and opinion polls started in the early 1930s on a limited scale. Since the 1950s, campaigns and other electioneering activities have become increasingly capital in-

Democratic Campaign, 1948, York, Pennsylvania. President Truman Addresses a Huge Crowd That Turned Out to Greet Him as His Train Passed Through York on the Way Back to Washington from a 9,000-Mile Coast-to-Coast Tour. Source: Acme Photo.

tensive as a result of the use of expensive technology and professional consultants. In 1952 Adlai Stevenson and Dwight Eisenhower used regional television ads, and in 1960 televised candidate debates were initiated. The commercialization of campaigns spread rapidly to state and local elections in the 1960s. Television made it possible for candidates to communicate directly with their constituents, rather than rely on party activists to distribute political information. The use of opinion polls and computerized voter and contributor lists replaced traditional partisan canvasses and fundraising activities. Presidential candidates including incumbent presidents entered the campaign process. President Truman's famous whistle-stop campaign in 1948 covered 31,700 miles and was a major factor in his victory. Airplanes soon allowed presidential candidates to campaign in distant locations.

While the cost of campaigns escalated, the new-style campaign methods freed candidates from labor-intensive party campaigns. For the past 45 years, candidates have developed their own campaign organizations to conduct electioneering activities. Party power in the nomination process has also eroded during the past 25 years. For example, in 1968, Democratic Party leaders could ignore public opinion polls and primary election

results and nominate Hubert Humphrey for president. Democratic reforms initiated after the 1968 election, however, resulted in the increase in the number of presidential primaries, dramatically decreasing the power of state and city party leaders.

Despite the party's loss of power, Democratic Party leaders continue to be involved in electioneering activities. County parties are the primary center of campaigns in many areas and distribute literature, post signs, place newspaper advertisements, and issue press releases in conjunction with candidates' campaign efforts. Local parties are also very effective in conducting voter registration drives and get-out-the-vote campaigns. Many state parties provide research and polling data as well as campaign literature and seminars to candidates.

Since 1981, national Democratic committees have expanded their resources, staffs, and campaign activities. Though Democratic national organizations have lagged behind their Republican counterparts, they provide significant campaign assistance. Under the 1979 campaign finance law amendment, contributions to parties, rather than candidates, are virtually unlimited (soft money). Soft money is used for party-building activities such as creating voter and contributor lists, polling, conducting campaign schools, promoting the party as a whole, preparing media packages, and contributing to state and local parties. Therefore, though the Democratic Party has lost much of its control over electioneering activities, party leaders continue to influence elections and campaigns. If interest-group contributions are limited in the future, the Democratic Party may become an important source of campaign funds and expertise. Nevertheless, primary elections, professional consultants, and television ads will continue to weaken the Democratic Party's ability to influence election outcomes.

Janet B. Manspeaker

SEE ALSO The Presidential Nomination Process, Presidential Nominations and Elections

BIBLIOGRAPHY

Goldman, Ralph. *Search for Consensus*. Philadelphia: Temple University Press, 1979.

Kovler, Peter B., ed., *Democrats and the American Idea*. Washington, DC: Center for National Policy Press, 1992.

Reichley, A. James. *The Life of the Parties*. New York: Free Press, 1992.

The Cold War

The term *Cold War* was first used in 1947 by Bernard Baruch, one of President Harry Truman's initial appointees to the United Nation's Atomic Energy Commission. The phrase was soon picked up by the popular press and came to describe the outwardly hostile but nonlethal relationship following World War II between the United States and the Soviet Union. For Democrats, the emerging Cold War between the Soviet Union and the West revealed a painful division in their New Deal coalition. Democrats found themselves divided between, on the one hand, pacifists who wanted to find a middle ground with the Soviet Union and end tests of atomic bombs and on the other hand those who saw the necessity for a strong defense to contain the spread of communism around the world. This uneasy division between Cold War Democrats and more pacifist Democrats would characterize the party's internal struggle over the direction of America's foreign policy for decades and would become most pronounced during the Vietnam War.

The split in the New Deal coalition proved to be very politically damaging to the Democratic Party early in the Cold War and helped contribute to the American public's lasting impression that Republicans were better able than Democrats to handle issues of national defense and foreign affairs. On one side of the New Deal coalition stood Henry Wallace, Franklin D.

Roosevelt's vice president from 1941 until 1945 when he was replaced by Harry Truman. Wallace feared that trade and commerce would be needlessly disrupted if relations with the Soviet Union were allowed to turn sour. He felt that rather than react in a hostile way toward communism, the United States should reach a political understanding with the Soviet Union so that the East and West could engage in friendly economic competition. On the other side, Truman was convinced that the Soviet Union was never going to be content with playing by Western rules and that the only way to deal with the rising tide of communism was to confront it with a superior military force.

Truman had been weakened by his party's infighting, and in order to overcome Republican isolationism in Congress just after World War II and win support for the Marshall Plan and the Truman Doctrine, he had to engage in scare tactics. Truman raised the specter of international communism and the threat it could pose to internal security by arguing that the Soviet Union had expansionist ideas and that the United States was the only nation that could possibly stand up to the communist threat. While this strategy proved to be successful for Truman in the short run, it also gave the Republicans, especially Senator Joseph McCarthy of Wisconsin, the opportunity to exploit the division in the Democratic Party by using the issue of domestic security to bash pacifist and New Deal Democrats within the government and throughout society.

In the 1950s, the Democratic Party tried to walk a fine line between its ideals of a free world without armaments and the realization of the need to confront with equal or greater force the expansion-minded Soviet Union. At their 1952 convention, Democrats noted their support for increases in the military and civil defense forces but also called for limitations on the production of armaments, especially nuclear weapons. Throughout the 1950s, Democrats complained that the Eisenhower administration had not been working hard enough to achieve peace but instead had engaged in brinkmanship that unnecessarily subjected the American people to the risks of atomic war. They argued for an expanded role for the United Nations in international security and peace and a universal, effective, and enforceable disarmament policy to control the spread of war.

By the 1960s, the tone of the Democrats had changed somewhat. Arguing that the Eisenhower administration had lost ground to the Soviet Union in terms of military power and technology, Democrats talked in terms of gaps—missile gaps, space gaps, and limited-war gaps. While still arguing for further arms-control agreements with the Soviets, Democrats faced the

Cold War realization that preeminent military strength was the ideal position from which to bargain. President John F. Kennedy increased the military budget by 15% in 1961 and in 1962 took the world to the brink of nuclear war over Soviet missiles in Cuba. Bowing to his party's less aggressive tendencies, Kennedy used the Cuban missile crisis not to push for a greater expansion of military capabilities but to ease Cold War tensions through negotiations. The fruits of Kennedy's efforts were the nuclear test ban treaty, the establishment of the Washington-to-Moscow "hotline," and an agreement to keep outer space free of nuclear weapons.

Yet Kennedy also allowed the United States to become deeply involved in Vietnam, a quagmire that would tear the Democratic Party apart in years to come. President Lyndon Johnson continued Kennedy's Vietnam policy, seeing the war as both an experiment in the flexible response doctrine and as a foreign policy version of his Great Society vision of imposed stability. As the Vietnam conflict became more costly in both lives and dollars, and as opposition to the war expanded, Johnson's view toward Vietnam diverged more and more with the view held by many congressional Democrats. Responsible for holding the reins of power, the Democratic Party struggled within itself for an answer to the Vietnam conflict but found it a difficult burden to bear. It was, in the end, Johnson's great disappointment that the revolt against the Vietnam conflict was led by Democrats, especially by Senator J. William Fulbright of Arkansas, and the division within the party helped convince Johnson not to seek reelection in 1968.

After 1968, with a Republican in the White House, Democrats found it somewhat easier to speak with a unified voice on Cold War issues. Still frustrated with their inability to end the Vietnam War, though, Democrats in Congress began an institutional struggle with President Richard Nixon over the control of foreign affairs. Vietnam represented a failed Cold War policy, and many Democrats, while acknowledging their own party's responsibility for initiating U.S. involvement in the conflict, nevertheless felt that the time had come to change course and leave Southeast Asia. In 1972 Democrats called for the cessation of all military action in Vietnam and the complete withdrawal of U.S. troops from the region. They called the war a distortion of America's international priorities and advocated a reduction in the military budget that would allow for a more efficient and moral military. Along with these reductions, Democrats continued to push for a comprehensive ban on nuclear weapons testing and improved relations with the Soviet Union and China.

Largely as a result of the way that the United States had conducted the Vietnam War, but also in response to Henry Kissinger's "realist" approach to foreign policy, Democrats began to express concern in the 1970s over the moral implications of America's Cold War policies. Congressional Democrats such as Donald M. Fraser of Minnesota and Tom Harkin of Iowa began to argue that America's foreign policy should reflect as best as possible the values and ideals of American society and that under Kissinger's realist approach this was not being done. Especially troublesome to many Democrats was the large amount of foreign aid that the United States provided to countries with very poor human rights conditions. Both the Nixon and Ford administrations, and later the Reagan administration, argued that the geopolitical balance of power with the Soviet Union was more important than the condition of human rights in any single country.

Several times in the 1970s and 1980s, Democrats tried to pull America's foreign policy toward a more humanitarian direction by linking the allocation of foreign aid, especially military aid, to human rights. President Jimmy Carter came into office having argued that the general character of America's foreign policy should not be tied solely to Cold War concerns revolving around relations with the Soviet Union but instead should be bound to more fundamental and far-reaching American ideals of democracy and individual freedom. Despite concerns about communist guerrilla activity, Carter attempted to implement such a foreign policy by limiting military aid to countries such as El Salvador that were known to have poor human rights records. In the end, the Carter administration found it difficult to carry out its foreign policy from such a perspective and was not as successful as it had hoped in making the condition of human rights a litmus test for foreign aid. Critics of the Carter administration's foreign policy argued from one end that it was too soft on communism and from the other end that it paid only lip service to the moral issues.

Human rights continued to dominate the Democrats' concerns in the 1980s as President Ronald Reagan began what would prove to be the final phase of the Cold War by repudiating détente and engaging in a massive military buildup and pursuing a more aggressive approach toward the Soviet Union. Whereas the Carter administration had cut foreign aid to El Salvador because of the condition of human rights there, Reagan contended that the threat of another Cuba in Central America was a more immediate concern for the United States than human rights. The Reagan administration poured hundreds of millions of dollars into El Salvador and began funding the contra rebels, a CIA-backed army based in El Salvador that was aimed at overthrowing the Marxist Nicaraguan government. Concerned about getting involved in a Central American version of the Vietnam conflict and concerned about reports that the contras were no better than the government they were trying to overthrow, Democrats in Congress began to question whether the United States should be funding such an army at all. Beginning in 1982, Representative Edward P. Boland of Massachusetts, chairman of the House Intelligence Committee, began attaching amendments to defense-related appropriations bills that banned all U.S. aid to the contras beyond that specifically approved by the Congress. The Boland Amendments, as they became known, were designed to prevent the Reagan administration from circumventing normal budgetary channels to provide covert support behind Congress's back for the contras.

Not content to have its foreign policy dictated by a Democratic Congress with different priorities than its own, the Reagan administration started to provide funding to the contras through other avenues. In a highly secretive deal, and without the proper approval, several members of Reagan's National Security Council worked out a deal by which arms would be sold to Iran at inflated prices in exchange for the release of American hostages in the Middle East, and the profits would be funneled to the contra operations in Nicaragua. Congressional Democrats were enraged after learning of the illegal operation and launched a series of investigations that resulted in charges that the Reagan administration had broken the law by ignoring the wishes of Congress. In what became known as the Iran–contra scandal, criminal charges were eventually brought against National Security Council head Admiral John Poindexter, staff member Lieutenant Colonel Oliver North, and others.

The Iran–contra scandal proved to be one of the last partisan battles between Democrats and Republicans over Cold War policy. Mikhail Gorbachev became the leader of the Soviet Union in 1985 and began reforms that ultimately led to the demise of communism across Eastern Europe and led to the reduction of tensions with the West. Democrats in Congress continued to press for a foreign policy that reflected American ideals and found less resistance from President George Bush. Bush came into office claiming that the fall of communism had ushered in a "new world order" that allowed the United States to carry out a foreign policy that focused primarily on promoting capitalism and democracy around the world. In 1992 the Democratic governor of Arkansas, Bill Clinton, ran for the presidency with a campaign that centered on domestic pol-

icy and criticized the Bush administration for paying too much attention to foreign affairs. While Clinton tried as president to focus much of his energy on domestic renewal, he found it difficult to ignore the international scene even in the post–Cold War world.

Quentin Kidd

SEE ALSO Foreign Policy

BIBLIOGRAPHY

Beschloss, Michael R. *The Crisis Years, Kennedy and Khrushchev 1960–1963.* New York: Edward Burlingame Books, 1991.

Crockatt, Richard. *The Fifty Years War.* London: Routledge, 1995.

Gaddis, John Lewis. *Strategies of Containment.* Oxford: Oxford University Press, 1982.

———. *The United States and the End of the Cold War.* Oxford: Oxford University Press, 1992.

Kofsky, Frank. *Harry S. Truman and the War Scare of 1948.* New York: St. Martin's Press, 1993.

LaFeber, Walter. *America, Russia, and the Cold War 1945–1984.* New York: Knopf, 1985.

Levering, Ralph B. *The Cold War, 1945–1972.* Arlington Heights, IL: Harlan Davidson, 1982.

McCormick, Thomas J. *America's Half-Century, United States Foreign Policy in the Cold War and After.* Baltimore: Johns Hopkins University Press, 1995.

Congressional Elections

The Democrats dominated congressional elections from the 1820s, when they began using the name "Democrat", until the Civil War. During the Civil War and Reconstruction, the Republicans controlled Congress. With the end of Reconstruction, the Democrats established their base in the South and became competitive again in congressional elections, especially in House races. The Democrats won all but three of the House elections from 1874 to 1894.

A new era of Republican dominance in congressional elections began in the mid-1890s and lasted for more than 30 years. During this period, the Democratic Party won the majority of both the House and Senate only in the 1912 and 1914 elections. One of the Democrats' main problems was their inability to win consistently the majority of seats in regions outside the South.

Then the major political bombshell of the century hit the country in the 1930s. A Democratic realignment occurred as voters replaced hundreds of Republicans with Democrats on the national, state, and local levels. As part of this realignment, the Democrats won back control of Congress. The shift toward the Democrats began in the 1930 election when they increased their seats by 53 in the House and 8 in the Senate. Then in 1932, they added 97 more seats in the House and 12 more in the Senate. After the 1936 election, the Democrats held 333 of the 435 seats in the House and 75 of the 96 seats in the Senate. These huge majorities allowed the Democrats to pass the historic New Deal legislation. So this landmark shift in congressional voting patterns produced a fundamental change in national public policies.

The Democratic dominance continued through the late 1930s and into the 1940s as the Democrats won the 1938, 1940, 1942, and 1944 congressional elections. But the Republicans started to cut into the Democrats' large majorities. In the 1944 election, the Democratic majority was down to 243 in the House and 57 in the Senate.

Then, in the 1946 election, the Democrats' winning streak ended. In a landslide victory, the Republicans gained 56 seats in the House and 13 in the Senate. So in 1947 the Republicans controlled Congress for the first time since 1932.

The Democrats, however, came roaring back in the 1948 election. They picked up 75 seats in the House and 9 in the Senate. During the campaign, President Truman and the congressional Democrats attacked the record of the Republican-controlled Congress.

The Democrats lost seats in the 1950 election but retained their majority in both chambers. The outcome followed the usual pattern in midterm elections in which the party of the president (or the party of both the president and the majority in Congress) loses seats in Congress. The party fortunes were reversed again in 1952. The Republicans won the presidency and recaptured both houses of Congress. Some political analysts at the time concluded that this election ended the Democratic era that had started in the 1930s. But this conclusion turned out to be untrue. The Democrats won the 1954 election and began another long string of victories in congressional elections. The Republicans did not win the majority in both houses of Congress again until the 1990s.

In 1956 the Democrats maintained their congressional majorities despite President Eisenhower's landslide reelection. The results indicated that the presidential coattail effect was weak. This pattern occurred in several elections over the next 40 years in which Republican presidential candidates would win, and sometimes by landslides, but Democrats would again win the House and Senate.

Congressional Democrats won another landslide victory in 1958. This election was one of the biggest Democratic victories in Congress since 1936. A key feature of this election was the success of the Democrats

in the Midwest and the Northeast. They were less dependent on their southern base than they had been in many previous elections. This pattern of the Democrats winning more northern seats became a significant aspect of their congressional victories over the next several decades.

The Democrats won all the congressional elections of the 1960s. The huge victory (295 House seats, 68 Senate seats) in 1964 was especially significant. This election provided the moderate and liberal congressional Democrats and President Johnson with enough votes to pass several major social programs (e.g., Medicare) and laws (e.g., the 1965 Voting Rights Act). While some progress had been made on the Democratic majority's agenda in the 1961–1964 period, the increase in Democratic seats from the 1964 election significantly improved the chances that the legislation would be enacted. In another typical midterm contest, the Democrats, as the party of the president and the majority in Congress, lost seats in the 1966 election. Their majorities were reduced to 248 representatives and 64 senators. The 1968 election ended the decade with only a few changes in the partisan makeup of Congress.

The Democrats also won all the congressional elections in the 1970s. After President Nixon's enormous reelection victory in 1972, some pundits were again predicting that the end of the Democratic era was at hand. But yet again, these predictions, at least for congressional elections, were wrong. The Republicans lost the momentum they gained from the 1972 presidential race when the Watergate scandal hit the Nixon administration. The Democrats won the 1974 election by a landslide. Their victory was almost as big as their triumph in 1964. This election brought into the House a large number of young liberal Democratic freshmen. Political commentators began calling them the "Watergate babies." These new Democrats had an important impact on debates on policy issues and procedural reforms during the remainder of the decade. Some of them became influential leaders in Congress during the 1980s and 1990s. The Democrats maintained their huge lead over the Republicans in the 1976 congressional election. And Jimmy Carter's victory in the presidential race ended divided party control in the national government. But, as would be expected, the Democrats lost congressional seats in the 1978 midterm election.

An important change occurred in the power structure of Congress in the 1970s as a result of election trends. Northern moderate-to-liberal Democrats began replacing southern moderate-to-conservative Democrats as committee and subcommittee chairmen.

The southern Democrats dominated these chair positions through the 1940s, 1950s, and much of the 1960s. The lack of party competition in the South allowed the southern Democrats to become the largest regional group among congressional Democrats and to acquire the most seniority. These advantages provided the southerners with opportunities to hold the top leadership positions. But northern Democrats started to acquire large amounts of seniority through the high reelection rates of all incumbents. And they became a bigger part of the Democratic membership in Congress as Republicans, starting in the 1960s, began winning seats in the South. So a large number of northern Democrats with many years of seniority were available to move into leadership positions.

In 1980 the Democrats finally lost another congressional election. The Republicans gained 12 Senate seats and became the majority party for the first time since 1955. A major aspect of the Republican victory was success in winning almost all the close races. While the Democrats also lost a large number of seats in the House races, they still kept their House majority. But in 1982 the House Democrats came back and won almost as many seats as they had lost in 1980. One factor in the Democrats' victory was the decline of the popularity of President Reagan and congressional Republicans caused by the huge recession of the early 1980s. Although the Senate Democrats won the majority of the national vote in 1982, they gained no seats and remained in the minority. The increase in Democratic House seats had a significant impact on the overall policy struggle in Congress. The greater voting strength put the House Democrats in a much better position to combat the Reagan administration and the congressional Republicans.

The same pattern of split victories continued in 1984. The Republicans kept their majority in the Senate, and the Democrats maintained their control of the House. Presidential coattails were short again as President Reagan won reelection by a landslide, but the Democrats won 58% of the House seats and gained two Senate seats.

Then in 1986, the split-party pattern ended as the Democrats regained the Senate majority and won again in the House. In contrast to what happened in 1980, the Senate Democrats won, at least partly, because of their ability to win close races. With control of both chambers again, the Democrats' position was strengthened enormously in the partisan legislative battles.

Divided party control of the executive and legislature continued with George Bush's victory in 1988 and the congressional Democrats' victories in 1988 and 1990. House and Senate Democrats were aided in these elections, just as in many previous elections, by the high reelection rates of incumbents. As long as most of the majority party's incumbents seek reelection, the majority party will benefit from high reelection rates.

The Democrats won a big victory in 1992 as Bill Clinton defeated President Bush and House and Senate Democrats maintained their majorities. House Democrats won even though several incumbents faced difficult races because of either changes in their district from the 1990 redistricting or bad publicity from being implicated in a check-writing scandal. Another important aspect of the election was the success of women and minority candidates. Although their total numbers were still relatively small, a record number of women and minorities were elected to Congress. And most of the successful women, African American, and Hispanic candidates were Democrats.

In 1994 the Democrats finally lost their majority in the House and Senate. This was the first time that the Republicans had won a House election and combined House and Senate elections since 1952. The Democrats' loss surprised many political analysts. The conventional view was that the Democrats would lose seats in the typical midterm pattern, but not enough to cost them their majority. Democratic losses in the South were a key factor in the Republican victory. Republicans won the majority of southern congressional seats for the first time in this century.

Larry M. Schwab

BIBLIOGRAPHY

Abramson, Paul R., John H. Aldrich, and David W. Rohde. *Change and Continuity in the 1992 Elections*. Rev. ed. Washington, DC: CQ Press, 1995.

Baker, Ross K. "The Congressional Elections." In *The Election of 1988*, ed. Gerald Pomper. Chatham, NJ: Chatham House, 1989.

Duncan, Philip D., and Christine C. Lawrence. *Politics in America 1996*. Washington, DC: CQ Press, 1995.

Erikson, Robert S. "The Puzzle of Midterm Loss." *Journal of Politics* 50 (1988): 1011–1029.

Herrnson, Paul S. *Congressional Elections: Campaigning at Home and in Washington*. Washington, DC: CQ Press, 1995.

Hinkley Barbara. *Congressional Elections*. Washington, DC: CQ Press, 1981.

Jacob, Charles E. "The Congressional Elections." In *The Election of 1980*, ed. Gerald Pomper. Chatham, NJ: Chatham House, 1981.

———. "The Congressional Elections and Outlook." In *The Election of 1976*, ed. Gerald Pomper. New York: McKay, 1977.

Jacobson, Gary C. "Congress: Politics After a Landslide without Coattails." In *The Elections of 1984*, ed. Michael Nelson. Washington, DC: CQ Press, 1985.

———. *The Politics of Congressional Elections*. 3rd ed. New York: HarperCollins, 1992.

Jones, Charles O. *Every Second Year*. Washington, DC: Brookings Institution, 1967.

Maisel, Louis Sandy, and Joseph Cooper, eds. *Congressional Elections*. Beverly Hills, CA: Sage, 1981.

Mann, Thomas E., and Norman J. Ornstein. *The American Elections of 1982*. Washington, DC: American Enterprise Institute, 1983.

Mayhew, David R. "Congressional Elections: The Case of the Vanishing Marginals." *Polity* 6 (1974): 295–317.

Wilcox, Clyde. *The Latest American Revolution? The 1994 Elections and Their Implications for Governance*. New York: St. Martin's Press, 1995.

Congressional Party Leadership

Along with committees, political parties are the central organizing institutions in the Congress. Although political parties are traditionally more important in the House of Representatives, they are important in the Senate as well. In the House, it is along party lines that the Speaker is selected and House rules are adopted. In both the House and the Senate, parties organize competition, aid in building coalitions, and provide formal leadership.

PARTIES IN CONGRESS: PROCEDURAL AND SUBSTANTIVE COALITIONS

Political parties are central to the organization of the Congress. Two-party politics in the United States usually allows for a clear majority and minority within both houses of Congress. Charles O. Jones has identified two kinds of majorities in congressional parties: procedural and substantive majorities. Although substantive majorities—those "necessary to pass legislation"—vary greatly from issue to issue (and thus are not necessarily congruent with partisan majorities), "normally, membership of procedural majorities and minorities coincides with that of the two political parties" (Jones 1992, 233). Elsewhere, Jones makes this organizational role of parties more explicit: "the party willingly assumes the responsibility for organizing the process—providing personnel (including leadership), making rules, establishing committees" (Jones 1964, 5). Through procedural organization, political parties gain control of the House Speakership, the administra-

tion of Congress, as well as the schedules and committee systems in both chambers.

As much as there were parties in the First Congress, the Democratic-Republicans (who would become the Democratic Party) represented the oppositional minority in both the House and the Senate. Although they would remain a minority in the Senate until the election of Thomas Jefferson as president in 1800, the Democratic-Republicans briefly enjoyed majority status in the House of Representatives during the Third Congress (1793–1795). From the Fourth through the Sixth Congresses, Federalists enjoyed a narrow majority in the House. But the election of Jefferson in 1800 ushered in an era in which the Democratic-Republicans would control both the House and the Senate for a quarter of a century. Similarly, the popular election of President Andrew Jackson reaffirmed the party's control of both chambers until 1841. From 1841 to 1855, Democrats would lose control of the House to the Whigs in both the 27th and 30th Congresses, although Democrats would retain Senate control until 1860.

During the Civil War era and until the elections of 1874, Democrats were relegated to minority status in both chambers as the Lincoln and early Reconstruction Republicans controlled the national government. From the 44th to the 53rd Congresses, Democrats controlled the House (except for the 47th and 51st Congresses), while Republicans controlled the Senate (with the exception of the 46th and 53rd Congresses). Democrats languished in the minority in both the House and the Senate for eight consecutive Congresses from 1895 to 1911.

For most of the twentieth century, however, Democrats have been the majority party in both houses of Congress. Since the election of Woodrow Wilson in 1912, Democrats have held a majority of House seats in 33 of 42 Congresses. The Republicans controlled the House for six Congresses from 1919 to 1931, as well as the 80th, 83rd, and 104th Congresses. Democrats have controlled the Senate for much of this time as well, having a majority of Senate seats in 29 of 42 Congresses. Democrats only lost control of the Senate during the Republican 1920s, the 80th and 83rd Congresses, the first six years of the Reagan administration, and the midterm elections of the Clinton administration.

Aside from this procedural role, parties also help to organize both the House and Senate as floor voting coalitions. Although substantive majorities do vary, Melissa Collie and David W. Brady (1985) claim that from "a historical perspective the congressional parties have proved the broadest and most stable basis of coalition formation in the Congress" (p. 284). Perhaps more important than party in building coalitions, however, are personal ideology, constituency, and the numerous other factors that cause one to be either a Republican or a Democrat. Cooper, Brady, and Hurley (1977) found that, from 1887 to 1969, electoral factors were "a highly influential determinant of party voting" in Congress (p. 159). Indeed, electoral factors in addition to a changing issue agenda can have an impact on the extent to which party is important in creating and maintaining substantive majorities; at times in U.S. history, party voting in Congress has been relatively high while at other times factors such as region have predominated (Sinclair 1978).

For most of the twentieth century, party has been a less important consideration in congressional floor voting. Examining data from 1887 to 1969, Cooper, Brady, and Hurley (1977) found that over "the course of this century there has been a clear and substantial decline in the strength of party as a determinant of voting" (p. 137). Extending this analysis through the 1970s, Collie and Brady (1985) found that "the salience of the partisan cleavage declined in the 1950s and again in the 1970s" (p. 282). There has been "a striking resurgence of partisanship" in the 1980s, however. Pointing to extremely high unity among House Democrats in 1987 and 1988, David W. Rohde says: "To find a Congress in which Democratic unity was higher than that, one has to go back to the Sixty-first Congress (1909–1911), when 'Boss' Cannon was Speaker. Republican unity also increased, albeit not so sharply, from 71 percent in 1969 to 80 percent in 1988" (Rohde 1991, 14).

LEADERSHIP POSITIONS AND ACTIVITIES: AGENCY AND CONTEXT

Any examination of leadership in Congress must examine the methods and norms that govern parties' selection of leaders. Robert L. Peabody found that Republican succession in the House is marked by "open competition and even revolt against established leadership" (1976, 291). In the Senate, Republican succession has involved much less conflict and much more stability than in the House. Examining seven case studies of leadership change, Peabody finds external variables to have the least impact on leadership selection; he says: "Leadership selection is primarily, although not exclusively, determined by individual competition played out within positional and institutional restraints" (1976, 469).

Congressional party leaders are selected, often on internal and interpersonal criteria, by the majority of their party in the House and Senate, respectively.

Thus, the congressional party caucus represents each leader's constituency. One valuable way of studying congressional party leadership views leaders as "agents of the members who select them and charge them with advancing members' goals" (Sinclair 1995, 9). In attempting to further members' collective goals, party leaders throughout history have had to accomplish different tasks while enjoying varying levels of resources. Joseph Cooper and David W. Brady (1981) offer a contextualist view of party leadership that helps explain the variability of leadership activity; they suggest that "the impact of institutional context on leadership power and style is determined primarily by party strength" (p. 424). By comparing the leadership styles of Speakers Cannon and Rayburn, Cooper and Brady find that "institutional context rather than personal skill is the primary determinant of leadership power" as well as leadership style (p. 423). Thus it is within varying contexts and as agents of their fellow partisans in Congress that party leaders can best be understood.

House Leaders

In the House, the core party leadership posts are the Speaker, the floor leaders, and the whips within each party. The House Speaker serves the dual role of leader and spokesperson for both the House as an institution and his or her (historically the former) party within the House. Mary Parker Follett suggests that American Speakers have unique parliamentary powers beyond those powers typically afforded Speakers in legislative assemblies. Speakers have the political powers of appointment and control of the Rules Committee, the political power of attempting to influence party followers, and the rights commonly afforded any member of the House (Follett 1896, 299–301). As Barbara Sinclair suggests, the Speaker's parliamentary and political powers are used in tandem, one reinforcing the power of the other: "The Speaker wears two hats; he is an officer of the House and the leader of his party in the chamber. The two roles are neither clearly separable nor of equal importance. The Speakership is predominantly a partisan position; within the limits of fairness, he is expected to use the resources provided by the first role to help him perform the second" (Sinclair 1983, 34).

Second in command in the majority party and first in the minority party are the House floor leaders. The majority leader's position is defined by the leader's relationship to the Speaker and thus varies depending on the desires of the Speaker and the implicit or explicit negotiation of that role by the Speaker and the majority leader. Traditionally, majority leaders are "responsible for scheduling legislation for floor consideration" as well as acting as the party's leader on the floor, and taking "the lead on issues that are important to the party but that are politically too risky for the Speaker" (Sinclair 1983, 42). The minority floor leader is the leader of his party in the House. "Minority leaders promote unity among party colleagues, monitor the progress of bills through committees and subcommittees, and forge coalitions with like-minded members of the opposition party" (Davidson and Oleszek 1994, 175).

Parties in the House also employ party whips and rather elaborate whip systems that aid Speakers and floor leaders by providing a conduit of information from leaders to followers and vice versa. Whips also attempt to persuade colleagues, encourage and facilitate attendance for floor votes, and count votes that often provide leaders with the knowledge of the outcome before a vote even takes place.

Senate Leaders

The Senate—described as "an institution rife with rampant individualism (Davidson and Oleszek 1994, 177)—has considerably weaker party leadership than does the House. In the Senate, the floor leaders are the heads of both parties. Formal party floor leadership did not exist in the Senate until the early twentieth century. In the Senate as in the House, majority and minority whips assist floor leaders in carrying out leadership tasks. As in the House, the Senate whip's chief functions are relaying information and counting votes.

THE HOUSE DEMOCRATS: A PERMANENT MAJORITY?

Democratic control of the House of Representatives from 1955 to 1994 represented the longest stretch of one-party control in American history. In contrast to the frustrated House Republicans, House Democrats enjoyed majority status and, in many ways, showed signs that they expected to be in power for a long time. For example, compared to House Republicans, who regularly had rancorous intraparty leadership races, House Democrats had a rather orderly pattern of leadership succession. If a party leader was to wait his turn, he would assuredly move up the leadership ladder.

Democratic leaders in this time confronted different leadership tasks. Sam Rayburn of Texas was Speaker from the 76th to the 79th Congress, the 81st to the 82nd Congress, and the 84th to the 87th Congress, spanning the years 1940 to 1961. Certainly in term of both

longevity and success, Speaker Rayburn was the most effective Speaker of the Democratic era. Although institutional context precluded him from having the kind of power enjoyed by Speakers of a stronger party era (Cooper and Brady 1981), Rayburn used personal prestige and friendship to orchestrate and negotiate with the strong committee chairs in the House. In many ways, Speakers John McCormack of Massachusetts and Carl Albert of Oklahoma attempted to lead Congress modeling Rayburn's style. Not only did these leaders not have the personal skills of Rayburn, but the House was changing as well. More liberal Democrats demanded more active party leadership to counterbalance the extensive powers of the more conservative Democratic committee chairs. Speaker Thomas "Tip" O'Neill of Massachusetts enjoyed considerable success leading the Democrats as he was liked by both the senior Democrats and the liberal reformers within the party.

In relationship to House Republicans, many claim that the House Democratic leadership in the 1980s grew increasingly arrogant with power. Much like, although not to the extent of, Republican Speakers Reed and Cannon, Democratic leaders used institutional prerogatives to further the policy goals of the majority party. Through the use of multiple committee referral, restrictive rules limiting debate and floor amendments, and other institutional powers, Democrats attempted to make the legislative process in the House more conducive to majority action and, perhaps, less sensitive to the rights of the minority party.

SENATE DEMOCRATIC LEADERSHIP: CENTRALIZATION TO COLLEGIALITY

Senate party leaders on both sides of the aisle were strong in the 1950s. Since that time, only five Democrats have served as the Democratic leader in the Senate: Lyndon Johnson, Mike Mansfield, Robert Byrd, George Mitchell, and Tom Daschle. Lyndon Johnson's Senate leadership was highly personalized, much like the House leadership of his mentor, Speaker Sam Rayburn. Johnson's "pragmatic outlook, domineering style, and arm-twisting abilities made him the premier vote gatherer in the Senate" (Davidson and Oleszek 1994, 180).

With an influx of more independent and assertive Democrats in the Senate in 1958 and after, this strong leadership style was increasingly inappropriate and ineffective. From 1960 and well into the 1990s, a more collegial and participatory leadership style developed. Although earlier leaders developed this style, Majority

Leader George Mitchell's actions in 1989 typified this leadership style. Mitchell "dispers[ed] to partisan colleagues power that previously had been consolidated in the majority leader's office. He named a senior Democrat, Daniel K. Inouye of Hawaii, to chair the Steering Committee, a panel heretofore always headed by the majority leader. Mitchell also appointed Tom Daschle of South Dakota to co-chair with him the Democratic Policy Committee" (Davidson and Oleszek 1994, 182).

NEW STYLES OF CONGRESSIONAL LEADERSHIP

Students of congressional party leadership focus on the internal tools party leaders have at their disposal. Indeed, these scholars have explained a great deal of leadership activity by focusing on party leaders' use of the whip system, power over committee appointments (both standing committees and conference committees), power over the Rules Committee, power to refer bills, and many other significant internal tools. But scholars have paid little attention to the external leadership strategies party leaders employ.

Perhaps the most significant new strategy is the use of the media to build coalitions within the House. On the Democratic side, Speaker Jim Wright used media strategies in 1987 to set not only the congressional agenda but the national agenda as well in both domestic and foreign policy. Wright reflected on this new duty of Speakers of the House: "Like an evangelist, the Speaker must use the pulpit to promote the Congress and its role to the public while selling the legislative program to both the public and the members. By open advocacy and vocal defense of the institution, the Speaker sometimes can make doing the right thing more palatable for the members by making it more generally understood and publicly acceptable" (Wright 1994, 223). Increasingly, members of Congress "have come to expect their party leaders to function as outward-oriented public leaders" (Sinclair 1995, 260). Progressively, party leaders have met these increasing expectations to shape the public debate through the mass media.

Douglas Harris

BIBLIOGRAPHY
Collie, Melissa P., and David W. Brady. "The Decline of Partisan Voting Coalitions in the House of Representatives." In *Congress Reconsidered*, 3rd ed., ed. Lawrence C. Dodd and Bruce I. Oppenheimer. Washington, DC: CQ Press, 1985.

Cooper, Joseph, and David W. Brady. "Institutional Context and Leadership Style: The House from Cannon to Rayburn." *American Political Science Review* 75 (1981): 411–425.

Cooper, Joseph, David W. Brady, and Patricia A. Hurley. "The Electoral Basis of Party Voting: Patterns and Trends in the U.S. House of Representatives, 1887–1969." In *The Impact of the Electoral Process*, ed. Louis Maisel and Joseph Cooper, 133–165. Beverly Hills, CA: Sage, 1977.

Davidson, Roger H., and Walter J. Oleszek. *Congress and Its Members*. 4th ed. Washington, DC: CQ Press, 1994.

Follett, Mary Parker. *The Speaker of the House of Representatives*. New York: Longmans, Green, 1896.

Jones, Charles O. *Party and Policy-Making: The House Republican Policy Committee*. New Brunswick, NJ: Rutgers University Press, 1964.

———. "Joseph G. Cannon and Howard W. Smith: The Limits of Leadership in the House of Representatives." In *New Perspectives on the House of Representatives*, 4th ed., ed. Robert L. Peabody and Nelson W. Polsby, 233–259. Baltimore: Johns Hopkins University Press, 1992.

Peabody, Robert L. *Leadership in Congress: Stability, Succession and Change*. Boston: Little, Brown, 1976.

Rohde, David W. *Parties and Leaders in the Postreform House*. Chicago: University of Chicago Press, 1991.

Sinclair, Barbara. "From Party Voting to Regional Fragmentation, 1933–1956." *American Politics Quarterly* 6 (1978): 125–146.

———. *Majority Leadership in the U.S. House*. Baltimore: Johns Hopkins University Press, 1983.

———. *Legislators, Leaders and Lawmaking*. Baltimore: Johns Hopkins University Press, 1995.

Wright, Jim. "Challenges That Speakers Face." In *The Speaker: Leadership in the U.S. House of Representatives*, ed. Ronald M. Peters Jr., 222–246. Washington, DC: CQ Press, 1994.

Crime

Until the dawn of the twentieth century and the social problems that accompanied urbanization and industrialization, crime policy was often viewed as properly belonging to state and local authorities. The U.S. Constitution, combined with a tradition of federalism, reserved police powers for the states, and both the federal and state governments were satisfied to keep it that way, at least until the twentieth century. Before the 1900s, most of the federal government's forays into crime policy involved regulating interstate commerce and the railroads, protecting the mails, combating counterfeiting, and conducting such moral purity crusades as those against pornography and lotteries. With the Sherman Antitrust Act in the late 1800s, Congress struck out against monopolies.

After the turn of the century, Congress increasingly turned to passing legislation to solve a growing crime problem. And while many Democrats played important roles in moving anticrime legislation through Congress, several stand out as key players as the war against crime unfolded. Democratic President Franklin D. Roosevelt launched a war on crime as part of his New Deal. During Roosevelt's administration, Democratic Representative Hatton W. Sumners of Texas, chairman of the House Judiciary Committee, helped guide anticrime legislation through Congress. In subsequent years, conservative southern Democrats often led the fight in Congress against crime. For instance, during the 1950s and 1960s, Senator John L. McClellan, a conservative Democrat from Arkansas, led a committee that produced several landmark pieces of anticrime legislation. In the mid-1990s, Democratic President Bill Clinton fought to bolster federal antiterrorism laws in the wake of bombings at New York's World Trade Center and the Federal Building in Oklahoma City.

Many of the battles among Democrats over anticrime legislation took place not so much over the need for the acts but over to whom—state governments or local authorities—federal funds should be distributed, battles that frequently divided the Democratic Party. Southern conservative Democrats have tended to favor allocating federal anticrime funds to state governments, while their northern, liberal, and urban counterparts have campaigned to give the money to city and other local administrations. Members of the Democratic Party have also been divided over such issues as broadening police powers and spending on crime prevention versus repression, again with conservative southern Democrats taking a harder line than other elected members of the party by favoring an expansion of search-and-seizure laws and a focus on repressing crime.

In 1908, Republican President Theodore Roosevelt helped increase the federal government's anticrime role by proposing the creation of a Bureau of Investigation within the Department of Justice. But recalling allegations that Roosevelt had misused the Secret Service for his political ends and wary of the president's motives, Congress rejected his proposal. The president reacted by establishing the bureau by executive order.

Then, in 1910, Congress passed a piece of landmark legislation, the Mann Act, officially the White Slave-Trade Act, prohibiting the transportation of women across state lines for prostitution. A few years later, Congress passed the Webb–Kenyon Act over Republican William H. Taft's veto. The act forbade the use of interstate commerce for the movement of liquor into dry states.

In 1914 the seeds of the drug war of the 1980s were planted as Congress passed the Harrison Narcotics Act, which regulated professionals dealing with narcotic drugs. Enforcement of the legislation increasingly criminalized drug trafficking and the use of narcotics, which in turn prompted still more legislation.

As the century moved on, crime increasingly moved into the spotlight as a political issue, and the Prohibition period brought yet more attention to it. During the presidential election of 1928, Prohibition was a major point of contention between Democratic candidate Alfred E. Smith and the Republican nominee, Herbert Hoover, who went on to win the election and to focus the nation's attention further on crime.

As part of his New Deal, Democratic President Franklin D. Roosevelt expanded Hoover's drive against criminals into a war on crime. The president's attorney general, Homer S. Cummings, teamed up with Democratic Representative Hatton W. Sumners of Texas to push ten pieces of anticrime legislation through Congress, with much of their enforcement responsibilities going to the Federal Bureau of Investigation (FBI).

Although organized crime had certainly existed in American before World War I, federal legislators had generally considered the problem to be the province of state and local authorities. But as organized crime increasingly pervaded the national consciousness, Congress began to react—first with antiracketeering statutes enacted in 1934 and 1946 and later with the proceedings of the Senate Special Committee to Investigate Organized Crime in Interstate Commerce, otherwise known as the Kefauver Crime Committee, after its chairman, Estes Kefauver, a Tennessee Democrat. The committee, formed in 1950, also included Democrats Lester C. Hunt of Wyoming and Herbert R. O'Conor of Maryland.

During the second half of the twentieth century, growing concern over organized crime, drug abuse, and violent crime, as well as the advent of the civil rights movement, brought a massive increase in federal involvement in law-and-order issues. From 1957 through 1960, Senator John L. McClellan, a conservative Democrat from Arkansas, ran the hearings of the Senate Select Committee on Improper Activities in the Labor and Management Field that was investigating labor–management racketeering—meaning organized crime. The committee uncovered a close relationship between members of the underworld and the heads of several unions, most notably the Teamsters. The hearings eventually led Robert F. Kennedy, Democratic President John F. Kennedy's attorney general and former chief counsel for the McClellan labor racketeering hearings, to gain passage in the early 1960s of several anticrime statutes aimed at curbing the gambling activities of the underworld. Robert Kennedy also led a drive against racketeering.

In the mid-1960s, a dramatic shift in national attitude took place: crime began to be viewed as a national problem warranting a national solution. In 1964 the Democratic Party's platform, which for years had made little mention of crime, commented that lawlessness must be eradicated.

The 1964 presidential campaign battle among Republican Senator Barry Goldwater, Independent candidate George Wallace, and Democrat Lyndon B. Johnson further brought crime into the national spotlight as a policy issue. In reaction to civil rights demonstrations and a rising crime rate, both Goldwater and Wallace included a strong law-and-order plank in their campaigns, with Goldwater often referring to "crime in the streets." Both accused Johnson of fostering a leniency that abetted crime. In the conservative tradition, Goldwater and Wallace promised to repress crime with a stricter enforcement of the criminal code.

Johnson responded with not so much a war on crime as a War on Poverty, hoping to reduce the crime rate by ameliorating what such Democratic liberals as Johnson saw as its root cause. Indeed, even by as early as the 1960s, the Democrats had focused on attacking the root causes of crime. In fact, references to such an approach appear as early as the 1940 Democratic Party platform, when the party noted its work in clearing the slums that, it said, were breeding grounds of crime.

The difference between the approaches of how to resolve the crime problem reveals the fundamental tenets of the conservative and liberal positions. The conservative position, including that taken by many in a long line of southern Democrats, seeks to resolve crime directly through repressing it. The liberal position, often taken up by many northern, urban members of the Democratic Party, seeks to solve the crime problem by alleviating what they see as its source: poverty, discrimination, and inequality. The conservative position emphasizes individual responsibility, while the liberal view centers on social welfare. Hence Johnson's Great Society programs.

In 1967, as the next presidential election was approaching, the crime issue remained alive, kept to the fore of public and political consciousness by a high crime rate and continuing racial tensions. In February, President Johnson presented a detailed message to Congress on crime that included a landmark proposal for the enactment of the Safe Streets and Crime Control Act of 1967, one of the biggest pieces of federal legislation yet proposed to help combat crime. The

measure proposed to implement a large-scale program of grants to cities and other communities to aid their fight against crime.

The president's bill, however, encountered formidable opposition in Congress, not only from Republicans, but also from southern Democrats, both of which groups were becoming increasingly disenchanted with Johnson's Great Society program, which, they believed, had made big promises but had fulfilled few of them. The objection to the president's bill, though, was not over the need for it, but over how the funds should be allocated. Johnson's bill would distribute money to the cities; Republicans and southern Democrats wanted the grants delivered to the states. In the wake of the assassinations of John F. Kennedy and Martin Luther King Jr. and amid rioting in such cities as Newark and Detroit, a subcommittee of the House Judiciary Committee held hearings on the bill.

Meantime, as the debate over Johnson's proposal continued into spring 1968, law and order again rose as a central point of contention in the presidential election. Richard M. Nixon, seeking the presidency for the Republican Party, employed the issue in his campaign, as did Wallace, who was again running for the presidency as an Independent candidate. Both Nixon and Wallace argued that decisive action needed to be taken against crime—and that action meant enforcing the criminal laws more forcefully. The voting public, having its attention further focused on crime by the campaign messages of Nixon and Wallace, waited to see what Congress would do with Johnson's proposal.

Despite the lack of enthusiasm among Republicans and, perhaps more important, conservative southern Democrats for the administration's bill, the House Judiciary Committee reported out a bill that, in accordance with the president's proposal, provided direct grants to local authorities. The committee's chairman, Democrat Emanuel Celler, was instrumental in guiding the bill through committee. Yet 12 of the 15 Republicans on the Judiciary Committee lobbied strongly against the bill when it was introduced to the floor, where it met strong opposition not only from House Republicans but also from conservative southern Democrats. The southern Democrats joined the Republicans in arguing that the bill would usurp states' rights and allow the central government to dictate the law enforcement policies of local authorities.

The Republicans counterattacked with an alternative named the Cahill Amendment, after its sponsor. It proposed distributing block grants to state agencies rather than grants-in-aid to local authorities. Besides House Republicans and many southern Democrats, 47 of the 50 governors, many of whom were members of the Democratic Party, supported the Cahill Amendment. In contrast, big-city majors, again including many Democrats, backed the administration's bill. Thus, a deeper division arose within the Democratic Party over the Safe Streets and Crime Control Act. Democratic city majors as well as liberal northern Democrats in the House held fast to the administration's plan, while state governors and southern Democrats generally opposed it, favoring the Republicans' alternative instead.

A fault line had also developed within Johnson's Democratic administration. The president's Crime Commission, for one, did not strongly support grants to local authorities. Instead, it identified lack of coordination as among the problems of U.S. crime policy, which some interpreted as an endorsement of the need to include state governments better in law enforcement. Second, many other mid-level administration officials quietly favored the Republicans' block-grant approach.

These fractures within the Democratic Party, both within and outside the administration, helped influence the House of Representatives to reject the administration's bill in favor of a bill sanctioning a strong state role.

During this period, the Senate Judiciary Committee was considering the administration's bill. The committee's chairman, conservative Democrat John McClellan of Arkansas, frowned on Johnson's proposal, causing an early party fissure in the Senate. Backed by three other southern Democrats on the Judiciary Committee, Democrat McClellan joined committee Republicans to rewrite the administration's bill to emphasize a strong state role in fighting crime. But some of the more liberal Senate Democrats, arguing that the revised bill was anti-city, obtained a compromise stipulating that states had to funnel percentages of the grants to local government units. In the end, as in the House, southern Democrats joined forces with Republicans to rout the administration's bill and substitute a state-oriented version for it.

Over the objections of some liberal Democrats, President Johnson reluctantly signed the Omnibus Crime Control and Safe Streets Act of 1968 into law, saying that it contained "more good than bad." The act, which included the establishment of the Law Enforcement Assistance Administration, was a victory for critics of the Great Society, including some conservative southern Democrats. The enforcement administration survived into the 1980s, when battles over the federal budget led to its demise. The act also included gun-control provisions initially proposed by Johnson, though they had been weakened by Republicans during their revision of the bill. In the act, conservative Democrat McClellan succeeded in winning expanded authority for wiretapping without warrants, despite objections from his fellow, albeit more liberal, Democrats, including President Johnson.

In the late 1960s and early 1970s, the administration of Republican President Richard Nixon continued the full-scale attack against crime begun by Johnson, but with an emphasis on law and order. Nixon's policy, however, came under attack, largely from liberals, who saw Nixon's law-and-order campaign as an attempt to put down civil rights activists and antiwar demonstrators. President Nixon used the rising public sentiment that criminals were out of control and city streets unsafe to assail members of the Democratic Party as being "soft on crime."

Yet, during the Nixon administration, several pieces of anticrime legislation became law, including the landmark Organized Crime Control Act of 1970. Sponsored by Senator McClellan, the conservative southern Democrat, and Senator Samuel J. Ervin, a conservative Democrat from North Carolina, the act included Title IX, the Racketeer Influenced and Corrupt Organizations statute, which helped launch a concerted drive against organized crime. The statute established severe criminal and civil penalties for using racketeering money or procedures in authentic businesses. But it also led to numerous civil lawsuits, which in turn prompted Congress to review the statute.

In 1970 President Nixon also helped encourage passage of the Comprehensive Drug Abuse and Control Act, which reinforced narcotics penalties. Yet the act did not stop the issue of drug abuse from reappearing in nearly every election year thereafter; the issue eventually culminated during the 1980s in conservative Ronald Reagan's "war on drugs" and, later, with passage of the 1988 Anti–Drug Abuse Act, which further increased penalties for both users and dealers, established a cabinet-level drug czar, and set aside additional federal funds to fight drugs.

But Nixon's criticism of the Democrats as soft on crime and his anticrime crusade soon ended, as he found himself accused of perpetuating criminal acts as part of the Watergate affair. Several of his high-ranking administration officials, including Attorney General John N. Mitchell, were convicted of crimes.

The 1980 campaign of conservative Republican presidential candidate Ronald Reagan revived the Republican Party's law-and-order theme and reinvigorated crime as a national political issue after it had flagged slightly during the latter half of the 1970s. After being elected president, Reagan's anticrime policies focused on repressing, rather than preventing, crime, and in so doing drew widespread criticism from Democrats. During Reagan's tenure, fighting crime translated into combating drug trafficking and abuse. He expanded the federal government's drug interdiction effort, while Nancy Reagan, the first lady, led a "Just Say No" campaign that equated drug use with immorality. In 1986 Congress passed the Anti–Drug Abuse Act, which greatly expanded Reagan's war against trafficking and abuse. Republican President George Bush continued Reagan's antidrug drive among his crime-fighting efforts.

In the 1990s crime has remained a dominant political issue. Following the bombing of the World Trade Center in New York City and the attack on the Federal Building in Oklahoma City, President Bill Clinton, a moderate Democrat, fought for a crime bill aimed at combating terrorism. Clinton also sought to address the crime problem with such crime-prevention proposals as the establishment of "drug courts" that obtain treatment for addicts and midnight basketball leagues that give teenagers an alternative to hanging out on city streets. The programs have been popular with Democrats and backed by many moderate Republicans—but not conservatives. In late 1994, conservative Republicans, led by Representative Newt Gingrich of Georgia, the Speaker of the House, tendered a plan to reduce crime prevention spending by $5 billion, starting a conflict that polarized Congress. Conservatives maintained that such spending is wasteful, while Democrats as well as Republican moderates argued that spending money on crime prevention is cheaper than building prisons. Yet the ultraconservative Gingrich insisted that crime prevention proposals were "pork."

The Grand Old Party's anticrime proposal of 1995 included a provision that would require violent criminals to serve 85% of their prison terms. Such hardline policies as determinate sentencing advocated by conservative Republicans have not been without their costs, however, resulting in a U.S. prison population proportionately larger than that of any other country.

Besides seeking to cut federal money for crime prevention, conservatives in Congress, especially the authors of the Contract with America, sought to alter President Clinton's "community policing" drive to emphasize hiring more police officers and buying more crime-fighting hardware.

But the Clinton administration has resisted the attacks on its crime policies. Attorney General Janet Reno, appointed by President Clinton, has argued forcibly for the effectiveness of community policing, adding that it has the overwhelming support of the public. Other major points of contention over crime policy during the mid-1990s have included search-and-seizure rights and, as always, the level of federal aid.

In 1995, after reports showed the overall level of crime declining slightly for the third year in a row, President Clinton set up a National Commission on Crime Control and Prevention and charged it with developing a strategy for controlling and preventing crime and violence.

In the presidential election of 1996, the issue of crime, whether it focuses on drug control, prison sentences, or prevention, promises to remain an issue of paramount social importance that will continue to distinguish the ideologies of the Republican Party from those of the Democratic Party.

Steve Hoenisch

SEE ALSO Gun Control

BIBLIOGRAPHY

Bacon, Donald C., Roger H. Davidson, and Morton Keller, eds. *The Encyclopedia of the United States Congress.* New York: Simon and Schuster, 1995.

Barnes, Fred. "Dopey." *New Republic*, May 23, 1988.

Feeley, Malcolm M., and Austin D. Sarat. *The Policy Dilemma: Federal Crime Policy and the Law Enforcement Assistance Administration.* Minneapolis: University of Minnesota Press, 1980.

Gest, Ted. "Congress and Cops." *U.S. News & World Report*, December 26, 1994.

Harris, Richard. *Justice: The Crisis of Law, Order, and Freedom in America.* New York: Dutton, 1970.

Porter, Kirk H., and Donald Bruce Johnson. *National Party Platforms: 1840–1964.* Urbana: University of Illinois Press, 1966.

Tromanhauser, Edward D. *The Shaping of Crime Policy.* Chicago: Union Institute, 1990.

Defense

The philosophical basis for the congressional Democrats' position on defense was effectively characterized by Paul Kennedy (1987) in his work *The Rise and Fall of Great Powers*: "Great Powers in relative decline instinctively respond by spending more on 'security,' and thereby divert potential resources from 'investment' and compound their long term dilemma."

In general, congressional Democrats staunchly believe that national security cannot be measured by simply counting the number of planes, divisions, and submarines (information available on the Internet). On the contrary, they assert that long-term national security is ultimately a function of the nation's overall economic power. Furthermore, the Democrats perceive the budget process as a zero-sum game. Every dollar spent on defense constitutes a drain on domestic investment that, if neglected, will eventually erode America's economic security (Dellums 1995).

Advocating a position that defense and domestic spending are diametrically opposed, the Democrats are not, however, naive. They do not promote unilateral disarmament. Instead, they suggest a three-pronged national security strategy mandating "a right-sized military, an engaged foreign policy, and a determined effort to rebuild the nation's communities" (Dellums 1995).

The Democrats champion military and acquisition reform that could produce a smaller yet more effective force structure capable of meeting any real threat to the vital national interest. The resulting optimized military force structure would be capable of independently countering any direct threat to the United States, as well as leading multilateral efforts to stop aggression, maintain the peace, and provide humanitarian assistance around the world (Dellums 1995).

Consistent with their efforts to reduce the size of the military budget, Democrats argue that spending beyond what is absolutely necessary on the military serves only to exacerbate the security dilemma. Robert Jervis (1976) explains how a nation's efforts to protect itself simultaneously threaten others. The United States must resist the temptation to maintain the overwhelming military superiority that fosters a threatening global environment, compels our adversaries to pursue military modernization, and ultimately results in the erosion of international stability. Therefore, the United States security interests are best served by the thoughtful restraint of defense spending (Dellums 1995).

To reinforce the "right-sized military," the Democrats support an aggressive, engaged foreign policy that encourages both arms-control negotiations and multilateral cooperation. Through arms-control negotiations the United States should seek "prompt, significant reductions in its nuclear arsenal, which will eventually lead to global nuclear disarmament (Dellums 1995). In addition, by promoting multilateral cooperation the United States could nurture the proactive resolution of regional disputes, reducing the need for crisis intervention. Finally, by "funding our fair share" of international development, leading peace-keeping and humanitarian operations, and supporting international organizations, the United States could help limit and defuse ethnic and religious tension around the world. The emphasis on multilateral cooperation would facilitate distribution of the defense burden more equally among our allies and eliminate the domestic financial stress of attempting to "go it alone" as the world's policeman.

The windfall from the Democratic strategy of military reform and international engagement would be invested in our domestic economy, providing the foundation for our long-term national security (information available on the Internet). Defense savings would be redirected to rebuild the nation's infrastructure, revitalize the educational system, and strengthen community institutions. The result would ensure that the United States sustains the best educated, most productive, and highest-paid workforce in the world. Instead of mortgaging the future on unnecessary and destabilizing weapons systems, the Democrats would finance programs enhancing America's civic, industrial, and global competitiveness in the twenty-first century. Reducing the income gap between rich and poor and expanding the middle class would reduce the potential for social instability and civil strife at home (Dellums 1995). Likewise, the Democrats believe that ensuring economic security is essential to defending the long-term national interest. Therefore, establishing defense spending priorities requires a delicate balance between building the right military for today while promoting the economic vitality necessary to meet the threats of tomorrow.

The Democratic leadership's advancement of the three-pronged defense strategy is apparent in their current battles with the Republican majority and their disputes with President Clinton. First, they oppose the spending priorities established by the defense department's bottom-up review (BUR). Congressional Democrats assert that the BUR unnecessarily retains much of the outdated Cold War military force structure while neglecting to train and equip U.S. forces optimally to meet the realistic security challenges of the post–Cold War international environment (information available on the Internet). These broad philosophical differences with their colleagues across the aisle and at the White House were evident in the struggle over the 1996 defense appropriations and authorization bills. Specifically, the battle lines were drawn over the B-2 bomber, the Seawolf submarine, and, most important, national missile defense.

In early fall the Republican Congress voted to fund an additional 20 B-2 bombers, despite the Pentagon's official desire to forego additional procurement of the 500 million aircraft. The Democrats quickly pointed out that the Republicans were funding systems the military did not want or need (information available on the Internet). The Republicans argued that the Clinton budget priorities had effectively tied the military's hands, preventing top military officials from expressing their true opinions on what was required for the national security. Seemingly supporting these assertions, the Clinton administration did not vigorously fight the B-2 procurement, perceiving a possible political gain in crucial elections in California, where much of the B-2 is built. The president even briefly flirted with increasing the B-2 procurement to 30.

After losing the fight over the B-2, congressional Democrats were equally frustrated by the debate over acquiring a third Seawolf submarine. In 1992 the Bush administration terminated the Seawolf program, but the Clinton administration revived the program, insisting that the Seawolf was critical to maintaining viability of America's two nuclear submarine shipyards. The third Seawolf would provide the necessary shipbuilding continuity to enable production of the New Attack Submarine (NSSN). The Democrats in Congress argued that the end of the Cold War had rendered the Seawolf's mission obsolete and that submarine construction could be easily reconstituted in the future. Likewise, by shifting overhauls and modernizations from public shipyards to Electric Boat and Newport News, the navy could easily maintain a dual nuclear submarine construction capability. Funding for the third Seawolf passed the House and the Senate along basically partisan lines.

The congressional Democrats' crusade to limit defense expenditures and reduce international tensions finally caught some life over the issue of national missile defense. The Republicans attempted to increase funding for the Strategic Defense Initiative (SDI) by $7 billion and include language in both defense bills that would mandate deployment of national missile defense by the year 2001. Democrats believed that such language would constitute a breakout from the 1972 ABM treaty and reduce the chances for additional strategic arms reduction agreements with the Russian Federation. In the midst of an intense budget battle, the Democratic leadership convinced the president to veto the defense bills and forced the Republicans to reduce the funding for SDI and adopt less aggressive language concerning missile defense. Finally, they pushed a vote through House of Representatives establishing defense spending priorities that emphasize combat readiness and modernization over the deployment of National Missile Defense (information available on the Internet).

These debates over spending priorities illustrate the Democratic position that for the United States to retain its status as a Great Power, it must redirect today's "excessive and unwarranted" military spending toward domestic investment. Only by right sizing the military, reducing international tensions through arms-control negotiations, multilateral operations, and burden sharing can the country foster economic security through the appropriate investment in infrastructure, education, and civic programs. According to the congressional Democrats, the resulting economic prowess is the only guarantor of long-term national security.

Cynthia J. Levy

SEE ALSO Arms Control

BIBLIOGRAPHY

Dellums, Ronald. "Military Excess and the Progressive Alternative." *The Nation*, October 2, 1995.

Jervis, Robert. *Perceptions and Misperceptions in International Politics.* Princeton: Princeton University Press, 1976.

Kennedy, Paul. *The Rise and Fall of Great Powers.* New York: Vintage Books, 1987.

Democratic Leadership Council

Formed in 1985 by southern moderates, the Democratic Leadership Council (DLC) has developed into a significant factor in Democratic Party politics. Although southern Democrats such as Senator Sam Nunn of Georgia and Senator Charles Robb of Virginia were instrumental in establishing the DLC, the DLC's membership is now more geographically and ideologically diverse. Nonsouthern Democratic politicians, including Senator Joe Lieberman of Connecticut, have assumed leadership posts in the organization. In addition, during the 1990s the DLC became active in policy research. The DLC retains its moderate heritage, however, claiming the role of promoter of a "new Democrat" philosophy.

The origins of the DLC are traceable to the rift between traditional Democratic liberals, claiming to represent the poor, working class, and minorities, and neoliberals, claiming to represent the middle class. In 1984 Walter Mondale, a traditional liberal, handily defeated neoliberal Gary Hart for the Democratic presidential nomination. The Mondale nomination and the party's landslide defeat in 1984 by Ronald Reagan led many Democrats to reassess the party's direction, and from this reassessment came the founding of the DLC. Southern Democrats played a key role in this reassessment (Quirk and Hinchliffe 1996, 265).

Given the influence of southern political figures in the DLC, the organization aimed at enhancing the prospectives of a southern presidential candidate. In 1984 southern party leaders expressed dismay over the lack of southern representation in the party's presidential nominating process. By 1988, the DLC unveiled programs designed to enhance the South's role in selecting a Democratic presidential candidate.

Super Tuesday, the holding of southern primaries on the same day, was promoted by the DLC as an effective way to enhance the prospects of a southern presidential candidate (Rae 1992, 145).

After 1988, the DLC focused on policy research. In 1989 the DLC established a policy planning group conceived as a Democratic version of the conservative Heritage Foundation. The DLC's Progressive Policy Institute (PPI) played a role in defining the "new Democrat" philosophy in terms of opportunity, responsibility, and community. Former DLC chairperson Bill Clinton used these ideas in his 1992 "new Democrat" presidential campaign. Clinton's New Covenant speech of October 23, 1991, referred to the need to balance rights with responsibilities and to rebuild a sense of community (Milkis 1993, 311). Most notably, Clinton's campaign discussed the need to move beyond the traditional divisions between liberalism and conservatism by developing a nonideological "third way." PPI recommendations formed the basis for Clinton's welfare reform proposal, his national service plan, and his campaign pledge of a middle-class tax cut (Stoesz 1996, 214–216).

Nevertheless, the Clinton administration disassociated its domestic policy from the DLC-PPI approach. Although DLC-PPI leaders anticipated that President Clinton would appoint DLC-PPI policy analysts to the White House staff, the new administration included relatively few "new Democrats." Moreover, for the first two years of the Clinton administration, domestic policy moved in the direction of traditional Democratic liberalism. This, in turn, caused tensions between the DLC-PPI and the Clinton administration (Bennett 1996; Stoesz 1996, 214–216).

Michael E. Meagher

BIBLIOGRAPHY

Bennett, W. Lance. *The Governing Crisis*. New York: St. Martin's Press, 1996.

Kearny, Edward N., and Robert A. Heineman. "Scenario for a Centrist Revolt: Third Party Prospects in a Time of Ideological Polarization." *Presidential Studies Quarterly* 22 (Winter 1992): 107–118.

Milkis, Sidney. *The President and the Parties: The Transformation of the American Party System since the New Deal*. New York and London: Oxford University Press, 1993.

Quirk, Paul J., and Joseph Hinchcliffe. "Domestic Policy: The Trials of a Centrist Democrat." In *The Clinton Presidency: First Appraisals*, ed. Colin Campbell and Bert A. Rockman. Chatham, NJ: Chatham House, 1996.

Rae, Nicol. "The Democrats' 'Southern Problem' in Presidential Politics." *Presidential Studies Quarterly* 22 (Winter 1992): 135–151.

Stoesz, David. *Small Change: Domestic Policy under the Clinton Presidency*. White Plains, NY: Longman, 1996.

The Democratic National Committee

The Democratic National Committee (DNC) was created during the Democratic National Convention of 1848 to organize and direct the presidential campaign and tend to the details of future conventions and election campaigns. Since then, it has grown from an ad hoc organization with a limited set of purposes to an influential body involved in many facets of American politics. Nevertheless, its central mission remains the election of Democratic candidates to public office, and its influence in the political system has not reached that enjoyed by national party committees in most other modern democracies.

DEVELOPMENT

Throughout most of its history, the DNC devoted most of its energies to organizing the Democratic National Convention and electing Democrats to the presidency. From its founding through the early twentieth century, the committee had little organizational permanence. Its major function was to meet every four years to make arrangements for the Democratic National Convention and to help its presidential nominee campaign for the White House. In 1928 the DNC opened its first professionally staffed year-round headquarters. In doing so, it laid the groundwork for two developments that would alter the structure of the committee and change its relationships with Democratic candidates and state and local party organizations.

The first major phase of modern Democratic Party development has been labeled *party reform*. Following the tumultuous 1968 Democratic National Convention, the party undertook a number of efforts to change its governance and nomination process. The party chartered the Commission on Party Structure and Delegate Selection (also known as the McGovern–Fraser Commission) to suggest ways to heal the rifts that had divided the party and to enhance the representation of Democratic voters on the DNC and at the party's national convention. The commission introduced myriad reforms that altered the composition of the DNC, changed the party's methods for selecting national convention delegates, and created a series of guidelines for state party operations. It also mandated that the Democratic National Committee implement and enforce the reforms.

The reforms established regulations prohibiting state and local Democratic Party committees from arbitrarily shutting out registered Democratic voters from party proceedings. The reforms also enlarged and increased the demographic representativeness of the DNC and Democratic National Convention, ensuring that women, minorities, and youths would have seats on both. New rules mandated that states open to all registered Democratic voters the processes they use to select delegates to the national convention. The rules encouraged most states to adopt presidential primaries, but a few states opted to use participatory caucuses and state convention systems for delegate selection. The new rules also banned the use of winner-take-all primaries, requiring states to allocate convention delegates in accordance with the proportion of primary or caucus votes that each nomination candidate received. The old rules favored large states, front-runner candidates, and individuals who had a long period of service in Democratic Party politics; the new rules benefited smaller states, less-well-known candidates, minorities, women, youths, ideological activists, and those who did not have long histories of involvement in the Democratic Party.

By empowering the DNC to enforce the party's new rules, the reforms created a significant shift in the flow of power within the Democratic Party organization. Before their passage, power flowed up from local party committees to state Democratic committees to the DNC. The reforms partially reversed this flow of power. They gave the national committee broad regulatory powers over Democratic state committees that in some ways parallel those that the federal government has over the states.

The second major phase of national party development, sometimes called *party renewal*, refers to the institutionalization of the DNC, the Democratic congressional and sentorial campaign committees, and Democratic state party organizations. After the party's crushing defeat in the 1980 elections, the DNC chairman, Charles Manatt, embarked on a program to rebuild and strengthen the DNC's organizational apparatus and increase its role in election campaigns. Under his leadership and that of his successors Paul Kirk and Ron Brown, the DNC created new direct-mail and large-donor fund-raising programs to improve its finances, and it enlarged and professionalized its staff. In 1985 the committee moved into its first privately owned building, which provides a secure working environment for DNC staff, computer equipment, and records.

The committee also developed a number of programs to strengthen state and local Democratic committees. DNC money and professional staff were used to help Democratic state committees improve their fund raising, develop computerized voter lists, and modernize their organizations. The DNC is credited with helping state and local Democratic committees develop the financial means and professional know-how to assist their candidates and run more modern and more effective campaigns.

Finally, the DNC became more directly active in the campaigns of presidential and other Democratic candidates. As noted below, its financial support, campaign services, candidate recruitment efforts, and training seminars have helped Democratic candidates wage more competitive bids for public office.

The DNC's party renewal program has been very successful. By 1992 the committee collected $136 million (including private and public funds to finance its national convention), employed 270 full-time staffers, distributed $14.3 million to state Democratic committees, and participated directly or indirectly in the campaigns of thousands of Democratic candidates, mainly through its funding of voter registration and get-out-the-vote drives. This new level of activity has made the committee more influential with Democratic candidates and other Democratic Party organizations. The DNC's ability to distribute or withhold money, technical expertise, and other party-building and campaign-oriented resources also enhanced its clout within the party structure. The DNC's ability to distribute its resources to states that follow its lead in campaigning and organizational development bears similarities to the way that the federal government distributes grants-in-aid to induce states to carry out certain programs.

ORGANIZATION

The DNC is located below the national convention in the party hierarchy, but because the convention meets only for a short time every four years, the committee is responsible for carrying out the convention's mandates and tending to much of the national party's day-to-day business. Although the Democratic state and local party organizations are located below the national party committee, giving the Democratic Party organization the appearance of having a hierarchical structure, power is not and has never been concentrated in the DNC. Party reform and renewal greatly strengthened the DNC, but power within the party remains decentralized similar to the distribution of power within the larger political system.

Before 1968, seats on the DNC were distributed in accordance with the principle of federalism: each state was afforded equal representation. Following the party reform movement, the DNC enlarged its membership from 165 men and women in 1968 to 431 in 1995. Two hundred seats are divided among the states and American territories using a formula that considers the size of each state's population and its level of electoral support for Democratic candidates. An additional 157 seats are reserved for each state and territorial party's chair, the next-highest-ranking party officer of the opposite sex, and others who are selected by virtue of their political office or membership in an affiliated Democratic organization, such as the Democratic Governors' Association or the National Conference of Democratic Mayors. The Young Democrats, College Democrats, and National Federation of Democratic Women each elect three members. The final 65 seats are reserved for individuals who serve in an at-large capacity to help ensure broad representation of the party's constituencies. States are allowed to choose from several methods the procedures they use to select their representatives to the DNC. The most commonly used methods are selection in a primary election, by a state party delegation to the national convention, by a state party central committee, and at a state party convention.

DNC chairmen are not required to be committee members, and they rarely are. They are officially selected by committee, but in reality, chairs are chosen by the party's presidential nominee and then ratified by the committee's members. If the nominee wins the general election, then the DNC chair continues to serve at the president's pleasure. In the event the nominee loses the election, DNC members typically select a new chair to replace their nominee's choice. DNC members also select the committee's other officers, including its vice chair, secretary, treasurer, and executive committee members. Many but not all of these officials are drawn from the DNC's ranks.

In addition to its members, which generally meet twice a year, the DNC has a professional staff of campaign strategists, public relations experts, attorneys, fund raisers, and other political operatives who carry out most of the committee's activities. Some DNC research and strategic activities are carried out by a network of private consultants hired on retainer and by interest groups that donate polls, sponsor conferences, and provide other political services. The size of the DNC's staff expands and contracts with the four-year

presidential election cycle, as does the level of services it purchases or receives from outside groups.

ELECTION ACTIVITIES

Most of the DNC's election efforts are concentrated on presidential elections. Federal law and custom limit the committee's activities in elections. The DNC neither selects nor backs candidates for the Democratic nomination, but it plays a major role in establishing the guidelines under which Democratic presidential nominations are contested. It is also responsible for organizing and making most of the financial arrangements for the party's national convention.

Once the convention adjourns, the DNC works to help elect its nominee in the general election. Major-party presidential nominees have their own campaign organizations, and those who accept public subsidies (all have done so since the funds from the presidential election campaign fund were first made available in 1976) are prohibited from accepting money from a national committee or any other source. As a result, national committees are relegated to supporting roles in their presidential election committees. The DNC provides its presidential nominee with issue research and technical, strategic, and legal advice. In addition, the DNC spearheads a "coordinated campaign" designed to mobilize Democratic voters on behalf of the entire party ticket. The coordinated campaign consists mainly of strategically targeted voter registration and get-out-the-vote drives. It also includes television, radio, and other advertisements that the DNC uses to reinforce the Democratic presidential nominee's message and to communicate an overall image of the Democratic Party to voters. In 1992 the DNC spent $10.4 million directly on behalf of its presidential nominee, Bill Clinton, plus another $30.2 million on the coordinated campaign.

The DNC is less active in subpresidential elections, leaving the bulk of the election activities in these races to the candidates' campaign organizations, the congressional and senatorial campaign committees, and state and local party organizations. The national committee helps to recruit Democratic candidates for the House, Senate, and statewide offices and runs training seminars for candidates and campaign managers. It also finances public opinion polls, contracts for focus-group research, and distributes valuable information on major campaign issues. In 1992 the DNC spent over $1.1 million on campaign services for individual Democratic House and Senate candidates and $148,000 on services for state-level candidates. These and other Democratic candidates also benefited from the money the committee spent on its coordinated campaign and party-building activities.

OTHER ACTIVITIES

When a Democrat occupies the Oval Office, the DNC plays an important supporting role for his administration. The committee provides polling information and strategic advice, and finances the president's and other White House officials' travel to politically oriented events. In recent years, it has also run public relations campaigns to support the president's major legislative initiatives. In 1993, for example, the DNC aired television advertisements in support of President Clinton's health care package.

Paul S. Herrnson

BIBLIOGRAPHY

Beck, Paul Allen, and Frank J. Sorauf. *Party Politics in America*. New York: HarperCollins, 1992.

Bibby, John F. *Politics, Parties, and Elections in America*. Chicago: Nelson-Hall, 1987.

Epstein, Leon D. *Political Parties in the American Mold*. Madison: University of Wisconsin Press, 1986.

Herrnson, Paul S. *Party Campaigning in the 1980s*. Cambridge: Harvard University Press, 1989.

Maisel, L. Sandy, ed. *The Parties Respond*. Boulder, CO: Westview Press, 1994.

Drug Policy

Members of the Democratic Party, with their big-city constituency, have long had a vested interest in federal drug-control policy. They have, at times, played forceful roles in this often bipartisan issue. Many in the Democratic Party have stood firmly behind the need for drug control; splits within the party usually have taken place over the priorities, funding levels, or strategies for controlling drugs. Most moderate and liberal Democrats have favored an approach that emphasizes prevention and treatment over interdiction and enforcement, while the more conservative southern Democrats have often favored a tougher, law-and-order approach to the problem.

During the 1990s, some members of the Democratic Party increasingly began to speak in favor of the legalization of drugs, arguing that the drug war had failed and that legalization, coupled with extensive treatment programs, would be the best policy for controlling drug abuse.

From 1976 through the 102d Congress, the three Democrats who served as chairmen of the House Select Narcotics Abuse and Control Committee played important roles in drug policy. They were Representatives Lester L. Wolff, Leo C. Zeferetti, and Charles B. Rangel, all from New York City.

Yet, despite the involvement of many Democrats in drug policy, it was conservative Republican President Ronald Reagan who elevated the issue to the national spotlight with his war on drugs of the early 1980s. Since then, the issue has remained of paramount public and political importance, arising during every presidential election since 1980 as members of both parties articulated their approaches to handling the problem. The issue became particularly heated during the 1988 presidential campaigns. Jesse Jackson, a candidate in the 1988 Democratic Party presidential primaries, tried to make drug control into a major foreign policy issue. Jackson called for a drug czar to coordinate the efforts of the agencies fighting the drug war, more money for the coast guard, and possible use of the military. Michael Dukakis, the eventual 1988 Democratic presidential candidate, made similar demands.

Unfortunately for the Democrats, it was Republican George Bush who won the 1988 presidential election, and he lost no time in continuing former President Reagan's war on drugs. Passage of the Anti–Drug Abuse Act of 1988 created a cabinet-level drug czar, and Bush appointed ultraconservative William J. Bennett to the post. He focused on combating street sales of drugs and on financing antidrug efforts in the countries from which the drugs were originating.

Elected members of the Democratic Party have often opposed the law-and-order tactics used by previous Republican administrations such as those of Bush, Reagan, and Richard M. Nixon, who helped encourage the 1970 passage of the Comprehensive Drug Abuse Prevention and Control Act, which reinforced narcotics penalties. The Democrats instead favor expanding education and other prevention programs along with treatment and rehabilitation facilities.

In the mid-1990s, the administration of Democratic President Bill Clinton emphasized treatment for addicts while limiting support for overseas antidrug campaigns. Republicans, led by conservative Newt Gingrich of Georgia, the Speaker of the House, have argued that the administration's approach fails to diminish effectively the supply of illicit drugs. Yet such hardline policies as determinate sentencing, advocated by Republicans, have resulted in a U.S. prison population proportionately larger than that of any other country.

Steve Hoenisch

BIBLIOGRAPHY

Bacon, Donald C., Roger H. Davidson, and Morton Keller, eds. *The Encyclopedia of the United States Congress*. New York: Simon and Schuster, 1995.

Barnes, Fred. "Dopey." *New Republic*, May 23, 1988.

Feeley, Malcolm M., and Austin D. Sarat. *The Policy Dilemma: Federal Crime Policy and the Law Enforcement Assistance Administration*. Minneapolis: University of Minnesota Press, 1980.

Gest, Ted. "Congress and Cops." *U.S. News & World Report*, December 26, 1994.

Treaster, Joseph B. "Missing the Glory: Clinton's Opportunity on Drug Policy Seems to Fade into Political Setback." *New York Times*, October 22, 1993.

Education

The Democratic Party, its candidates, and elected politicians have established a consistent record of initiating and supporting federal aid for education. Although the party began its early years by opposing federal educational assistance, the party soon altered its position, taking a favorable stance toward education that has endured, albeit in changing policies, through the first half of the 1990s.

Before the party turned to supporting education, one Democrat attempted to thwart an early piece of historic legislation. The Morrill Act, introduced by Vermont Representative Justin Morrill in 1857 to donate land to states and territories for colleges, was among the first attempts to provide federal aid for education. The measure was vetoed in 1857 by Democratic President James Buchanan, who maintained that it unconstitutionally interfered with states' rights. Although the objection that federal involvement in education interferes with states' rights has been a refrain often repeated, usually by the Republican Party, the constitutionality of federal aid for public schooling is considered by many to have been settled by precedent. Legally, the argument that the federal government's involvement is unconstitutional also seems to hold little validity. Indeed, even in the early years of the battle over aid for education, the constitutionality argument failed to persuade Congress. A resubmitted Morrill Act was passed in 1862 and signed into law by President Abraham Lincoln.

The constitutionality issue aside, the proper role of the federal government in public education was increasingly to become a point of contention between Democrats and Republicans and at times among Democrats themselves. But first the stage had to be set.

After the Civil War, President Andrew Johnson, a Democrat nominated by the Union Party, approved a federal Department of Education in March 1867. The department was soon demoted and renamed the Office of Education from 1870 to 1939, when it was subsumed under the Federal Security Agency, later the Department of Health, Education, and Welfare. Congress established the U.S. Department of Education on May 4, 1980.

In 1870 Republican President Ulysses S. Grant implored Congress to support primary education, an entreaty that became a precursor to the future struggles over federal aid to education. The battle lines, however, would typically, though not necessarily, be drawn along partisan lines, with Republicans opposing and Democrats favoring federal involvement in education. During the year of Grant's request, the struggle in Congress, but not yet the partisanship, began when George F. Hoar, a Republican representative from Massachusetts, introduced a bill to provide general aid to public schools. Although Hoar's bill never came to a vote, it served to focus attention on the issue.

In 1876 the Democratic Party took a view that the party and its candidates would repudiate after having remained nearly silent on the issue for several election years: the platform declared that the establishment and support of public schools belonged exclusively to the states. Then, as the Republican platforms of 1880, 1884, and 1888 and the Republican presidents of 1880 and 1888 endorsed national support for education, the Democrats kept quiet. From 1880 to 1920, the Democratic Party platforms made little mention of the subject. Grover Cleveland, the Democratic president from 1884 to 1888 and again from 1892 to 1896, also had little to say on the matter. After the 1888 presidential election, the Republicans also dropped the issue.

The issue did not resurface significantly until 1920, when the positions of the parties had been reversed: the Democrats favored federal aid to education, while the Republicans condemned all aid except that for vocational and agricultural training. The Democratic Party platform called for "co-operative federal assistance to the states" for the removal of illiteracy, the increase of teachers' salaries, and instruction in citizenship. The reversal completed the requisite conditions for partisan conflict and, in general, established the positions that the two parties would henceforth take.

Meanwhile, the twentieth century brought social crises that manifested themselves in bills, often proposed by Democrats, for new federal legislation on education. The rate of Selective Service rejections, for instance, prompted demands for aid in 1918, just as rejections during the World War II draft rekindled the debate over federal aid. World War II also brought legislation to supplement education in communities affected by the war effort. The teacher shortage after World War II inspired the aid proposals of the late 1940s. The Great Depression of the 1930s led to emergency aid to education. And the baby boom of the 1950s spawned school construction bills. The Cold War and the Soviet Union's launching of *Sputnik* in 1957 helped spur the National Defense Education Act. The civil rights demonstrations of the 1960s encouraged legislation to help equalize educational opportunity. Yet to a degree beyond that established by any one of these social crises, initiatives—first from Congress and later from Democratic presidents—emerged for general federal assistance for education, though they were not to arise in earnest until the 1930s.

In fact, despite the Democrats' pro-education platform of 1920, the issue had lost much of its poignancy by 1924 among the Democratic Party, which by now merely held that the "federal government should offer to the states such counsel, advice, and aid as may be available through the federal agencies for the general improvement of our schools." Four years later, during the election year of 1928, the Democratic Party reiterated the stance of 1924.

The 1930s found the Democratic Party avoiding endorsement of an expanded education program, even though Democrats took credit for helping youths stay in school and for the construction of school buildings with public works funds. Other than endorsing the original Americanization bill, Woodrow Wilson, the Democratic president from 1912 to 1920, did little of major significance regarding education.

Beginning with his election in 1932, President Franklin D. Roosevelt, the first Democrat in the White House since Wilson's term of 1916 to 1920, renewed the failed struggle of Republican Herbert Hoover, president from 1928 to 1932, to reduce appropriations for vocational education in the states. Congress, however, rejected Roosevelt's appeal and sought an increase, passing a measure in 1936 that expanded the program. Roosevelt signed the bill, but he appointed a Committee on Vocational Education to review the program. Responding to pressure from Congress for a general federal aid bill, Roosevelt expanded the committee's sphere to include all aspects of federal education policy. In February 1938, the committee, now renamed the Advisory Committee on Education, recommended a multimillion-dollar education-assistance program. Roosevelt did not endorse the report, prompting Congressman John J. Cochran, a Missouri Democrat, to say that "the president of the United States has in no way expressed himself as either for or against the recommendations of the committee he appointed."

Roosevelt soon found himself hard-pressed to take a stance. To the Thomas–Harrison bill of 1939, prepared on the basis of the Advisory Committee's report and approved by the Senate's Education and Labor Committee, the administration responded that the legislation did not fit the president's program. Roosevelt said in speeches that he would only accept an aid program that limited assistance to those states unable to fulfill their own educational needs. Roosevelt continued to avoid endorsing federal aid through 1943.

But Roosevelt's cool attitude toward federal aid for education did not stop the Democratic Party from taking up the issue with renewed force in 1944, even though the Republicans included no mention of the school aid issue in their platform. The Democratic Party platform called for federal aid to education administered by the states.

During his final year in office, Roosevelt extended a partial commitment to education. He wrote in his budget message to Congress in 1945 that Selective Service records exposed shortcomings in elementary and secondary education. "If a suitable standard is to be maintained in all parts of the country," Roosevelt wrote, "the federal government must render aid where needed—but only where it is needed."

Democrat Harry S. Truman, vice president during Roosevelt's final term and his successor after Roosevelt died in April 1945, took a more active position toward education than did Roosevelt. In fact, Truman made aid for education one of his campaign issues in 1948. And Truman's first budget called for legislation to supplement the resources of the states to help them equalize educational opportunities and achieve satisfactory standards. Subsequent Truman budgets also set aside money for education.

While Truman turned aid to education into a campaign issue in 1948, the Democratic Party repeated its 1944 call for federal aid—this time with a direct attack on the Republicans: "We vigorously support the authorization, which was so shockingly ignored by the Republican 80th Congress, for the appropriation of $300 million as a beginning of federal aid to the states to assist them in meeting the present educational needs." The challenge was a precursor to the partisan conflicts over education that surfaced during the next presidential election year. For the time being, however, the Republicans generally avoided the issue.

By the election of 1952, the education aid issue had moved farther into the spotlight, and the Democratic and Republican parties took sharply contrasting positions. The Democratic Party refined its position of the previous elections by outlining school construction, teachers' salaries, and school maintenance and repair as the specific purposes for which federal support should be allocated. The Republican Party's platform maintained that the responsibility for sustaining popular education rested with local communities and the states.

But by 1956 the two parties were again backing away from their differences. The Republican administration had proposed a school construction program, and it was now supported by the Republican Party. Meanwhile, the Democrats, taking a position not largely different from that of the Republicans, endorsed legislation to help states and local communities build schools, to educate migratory workers, to set up programs for gifted children, and to train teachers in technical and scientific fields.

In 1958, the National Defense Education Act was approved by Congress at the urging of Republican President Dwight D. Eisenhower. Even though the act was advocated by a Republican president and sanctioned by bipartisan support in Congress, its passage signaled an expanded role for the federal government in education, prompted in part by concerns over the country's national defense and rate of scientific advancement, which had arisen after the Soviets launched *Sputnik* the previous year and in response to the Cold War in general. The measure supported science, math, and foreign language programs in public schools.

With the election of 1960, however, partisan controversy returned. Although the platforms of both parties supported federal aid in principle in 1960, the kind of support the two parties had in mind was radically different. The Democrats called for generous financial support for, among other educational programs, teachers' salaries and construction of classrooms and other facilities, spurring the Republicans to counter that aid for teachers' salaries could lead only to federal domination and control of schools. The Republicans supported only limited assistance for school construction. The contrast between the two parties' policies blossomed into a major domestic issue of the presidential campaign—a campaign that also compelled the two parties in Congress to solidify their positions.

Senator John F. Kennedy, the Democratic presidential candidate in 1960, seized on federal support for schools and attempted to make it a major issue in the election. He blasted President Eisenhower for giving only limited support to the issue and attacked the Republican candidate for president, Vice President Richard M. Nixon, for backing only a limited construction program and for referring to federal aid for education as "too extreme."

Kennedy is often regarded as being the first president to make federal aid to education a major component of his domestic program and to back it forcefully. After taking office in the White House, Kennedy handed Congress a proposal in 1961 asking for a three-year, $2.3 billion aid-to-education program. As embodied in Oregon Senator Wayne E. Morse's School Assistance Act of 1961, the bill sought, among other initiatives, to provide increases for teacher salaries, assistance in constructing classrooms, and aid to children in depressed areas. Though passed by the Senate and approved by the House Education and Labor Committee, the School Assistance Act died in the House Rules Committee. The bill is significant, however, in demonstrating the assertive role that Democrat Morse, then chairman of the Subcommittee on Education, took in advocating federal involvement in education. Senator Morse introduced numerous bills as he fought unrelentingly to expand federal aid to education. Unfortunately for Morse and the Democratic Party, the School Assistance Act's death was hastened, in part, by the fight over aid to parochial schools; Catholics had lobbied for such support.

Even President Kennedy, despite his crusade for school aid, stopped short of allowing public funding for private schooling. "There can be no question of federal funds being used for support of private and parochial schools. It is unconstitutional under the First Amendment as interpreted by the Supreme Court," Kennedy said. In 1947 the Supreme Court had ruled in *Emerson* v. *Board of Education* that "no tax in any amount . . . can be levied to support any religious activities or institutions, whatever they may be called, or whatever form they may adopt to teach or practice religion." Kennedy's comments notwithstanding, the administration eventually weakened its stance against aid for parochial schools in the hopes of achieving a compromise on a major aid bill.

In 1962 Kennedy tried again, asking Congress in his State of the Union speech to pass his aid-to-education bill, which he modified to give priority to aid to higher education, advancement of teaching standards, and adult literacy. Congress took little action on the bill, and it withered. Again, the controversy over aid to parochial schools helped squelch the bill.

Kennedy tried yet again in 1963—a year that was to become a prolific one for the Democrats in their campaign for federal aid to education. Kennedy put forth an omnibus education bill called the National Education Improvement Act of 1963. It died in the House.

Although President Kennedy failed to get an omnibus education aid bill through Congress, several education bills, some of which embodied parts of Kennedy's proposals, did become law either during the Kennedy–Johnson administration or in the years to come. Two major 1963 bills that became law and the Democrats who helped push them were the following:

The Vocational Education Act of 1963, otherwise known as the Perkins–Morse bill, after Democrat Carl Perkins, a representative from Kentucky, and Democrat Wayne Morse, a senator from Oregon. The act, signed by President Johnson, a Democrat, on December 18, 1963, was aimed at strengthening and expanding vocational education.

The Higher Education Facilities Act of 1963, also known as the Morse–Green bill, after Senator Morse and Representative Edith Green, also an Oregon Democrat. The purpose of the act, signed by Johnson on December 16, 1963, was to help colleges construct facilities. Green, like Morse, was a tireless and innovative advocate for education, earning herself the title "mother of higher education." During her 18 years on the Committee on Education and Labor, she played major roles in much of the educational legislation that took place in the House, even though she did not always agree with or support her fellow Democrats. Also in 1963, Green, herself formerly a schoolteacher, published a study called *The Federal Government and Education* that took issue with a long-standing Republican criticism of federal aid: that it lacked sufficient historical precedent. Green's study found the precedent to be 100 years old.

The rift between the parties only grew during the 1964 presidential campaign, which was characterized by vast differences in ideological positions among the candidates and their parties. Presidential candidate Senator Barry Goldwater, Republican from Arizona, a long-time critic of the expanding role of the federal government, maintained that support for education was a step toward subordinating state and local governments to administrative divisions of the central government in Washington. He also held that there was no educational problem requiring federal aid. In contrast, Democratic President Lyndon B. Johnson was a strong advocate of the strengthened role of the federal government and the strongest supporter of federal aid for education yet to occupy the White House. Johnson's platform promised additional and expanded aid to supplement those programs enacted by what had been dubbed the "Education Congress of 1963."

Johnson, after winning the election, fought to fulfill those campaign promises. Indeed, the greatest amount of educational legislation yet followed the election of 1964. Pushed by such Democratic members of Congress as John Brademas of Indiana and Carl Perkins of Kentucky, both serving on the House Education and Labor Committee, and signed into law by President Johnson, several major pieces of educational legislation became law.

On January 12, 1965, President Johnson called for a new federal initiative to support elementary and secondary education. The same day, Representative Perkins, then senior member of the House Committee on Education and Labor, introduced a bill that embodied Johnson's goals. Meantime, Senator Morse, Democrat of Oregon, proposed an identical bill in the Senate. On April 9, Congress approved the Elementary and Secondary Education Act of 1965, doubling the federal share of elementary and secondary education expenditures. At the act's core is Title 1, renamed Chapter 1 in 1981, which assists school districts with large numbers of low-income children. Johnson signed the act on April 11, 1965.

Another major bill enacted during the Kennedy–Johnson years is the Economic Opportunity Act of 1964, also known as the War on Poverty bill. Although not an education act per se, the measure, presented to Congress by Johnson, included education among its ammunition to be used in the war. The bill earmarked money for such programs as a Job Corps for youth, job training and vocational rehabilitation, and basic education for adults. The Civil Rights Act of 1964 also had a strong impact on education. It was passed to foster desegregation of public schools and to ensure equal rights to students regardless of race, color, religion, or national origin. The Higher Education Act of 1965, written and moved through Congress by Representative Green, provided students with federal aid. In 1966 the International Education Act, which approved grants to colleges for international studies and research, was signed into law by President Johnson. Representative Adam Clayton Powell Jr., a New York Democrat who was chairman of the House Education and Labor Committee at the time, created a task force to steer the legislation through the House and appointed as its chairman Representative John Brademas, Democrat of Indiana, who was instrumental in winning passage of the bill.

Other education-related acts, many of which were components of President Johnson's War on Poverty and aimed in particular at helping children from low-income families, included Project Head Start, the Job Corps, the Neighborhood Youth Corps, and Upward Bound.

Many in the Democratic Party—including Presidents Kennedy, Johnson, and Carter and Representative Brademas—also fought to establish research foundations. For example, although it was Republican President Richard M. Nixon who urged the establishment of a National Institute of Education in a speech to

Congress in 1970, it was Brademas who introduced the bill, which became law in 1972.

Besides Nixon's call for the institute, the Nixon administration initiated few other proposals to help education. As a result, Congress, especially certain of its Democratic members, took an increasingly active role in proposing educational legislation. For instance, Democratic Senator Claiborne Pell of Rhode Island, chairman since 1969 of the Education Subcommittee of the Labor and Public Welfare Committee, worked to develop a direct form of financial assistance to college students. Pell's grants for needy undergraduate students eventually became law.

The years 1973 and 1974 saw legislators from large, industrial states pitted against those from smaller, rural states over the allocation formulas of Title 1 of the Elementary and Secondary Education Act. Representative Brademas's compromise formula became law in 1973.

Another measure of note during the 1970s is the Middle Income Student Assistance Act of 1978, which sought to aid middle-class students who needed assistance in paying for college. The measure was proposed in response to a tuition tax-credit bill. According to Representative John Brademas, he and Democratic Congressman William D. Ford of Michigan, both of whom were on the Education and Labor Committee, told Joseph A. Califano Jr., the secretary of health, education, and welfare in the Carter administration, that an alternative to the tax credit was needed. Their initiative helped induce President Jimmy Carter, himself a Democrat, to propose in 1978 a Middle Income Student Assistance bill, which became law. The measure, however, only postponed additional calls for a tuition tax credit, made by Republican President George Bush.

The 12 years following the Carter administration were dominated by Republican Presidents Ronald Reagan and George Bush. Former Democratic Representative Brademas has written that the Reagan administration "has been more hostile to education than any other administration in the nation's history." It reduced or attempted to reduce many federal education programs, from Chapter 1 to student aid.

President Bill Clinton, the first Democrat in the White House since Carter, has taken decisive action to support education. After taking office, he signed the Goals 2000: Educate America Act, which passed Congress with strong bipartisan support. The act seeks to improve teaching and learning by providing a national framework for educational reform. More recently, Clinton signed into law the Improving America's Schools Act of 1994, which extends for five years the authorizations of appropriations for the programs

under the Elementary and Secondary Education Act of 1965. President Clinton has also fought, often with the threat of vetoes, to keep a Republican-controlled Congress from slashing funds for various education programs. In addition, the Clinton administration has chosen education as a battleground in its budget battles with Congress.

Democratic Party members in Congress have also taken action against the Republicans' Contract with America, which seeks to cut funding from such social programs as education and job training. Senator Edward Kennedy, a Massachusetts Democrat on the Labor and Human Relations Committee, has attempted to shield education from budget cuts. Senator Paul Simon, an Illinois Democrat, and Senator Barbara Mikulski, a Maryland Democrat, have fought against Republican-proposed cuts to the Americorps program, which provides thousands of students with a way to earn money for education.

As the presidential election of 1996 approaches, the issue has surfaced over whether parents should be provided with school vouchers to send their children to private, public, or religious schools. Clinton says that while he backs public school choice and charter schools, he does not support using public funds to pay for private schools.

Steve Hoenisch

BIBLIOGRAPHY

Brademas, John, with Lynne P. Brown. *The Politics of Education: Conflict and Consensus on Capital Hill.* Norman: University of Oklahoma Press, 1987.

Meranto, Philip. *The Politics of Federal Aid to Education in 1965: A Study in Political Innovation.* Syracuse, NY: Syracuse University Press, 1967.

Mitchell, Douglas E., and Margaret E. Goertz, eds. *Education Politics for the New Century.* Bristol, PA: Falmer Press, Taylor and Francis, Inc., 1990.

Munger, Frank J., and Richard F. Fenno Jr. *National Politics and Federal Aid to Education.* Syracuse, NY: Syracuse University Press, 1962.

Spring, Joel. *Conflicts of Interest: The Politics of American Education.* White Plains, NY: Longman, 1988.

Tiedt, Sidney W. *The Role of the Federal Government in Education.* New York: Oxford University Press, 1966.

Wirt, Frederick M., and Michael W. Kirst. *The Political Web of American Schools.* Boston: Little, Brown, 1972.

Fiscal Policy

Most Democrats are followers of John Maynard Keynes when it comes to dealing with the economy and the problems of unemployment and inflation.

Fiscal policy uses the spending habits of the government as a way to control the cycles of the economy. In periods when the economy is in a recession, Democrats recommend increasing government spending to stimulate the economy. While the effect of deficit spending could be accomplished by either a cut in taxes—freeing more money to be spent by consumers—or increasing government expenditures, Democrats have historically preferred the latter to the former. In periods when the economy is growing too fast and there is inflation, Keynesian theory recommends that the government decrease its spending—dropping demand—or increasing taxes—removing discretionary spending by consumers. In so doing, Democrats hope to control the demand for goods and services. This program is distinct from the Republican supply-side theories that focus on monetary policy.

For most Democrats, who are Keynesians, monetary policy plays no important part of their economic modeling except to the extent that it accommodates their fiscal policy. Rather than control the money supply, as most Republicans suggest, Democrats use deficit spending as a way to stimulate the economy.

Jeffrey D. Schultz
Diane L. Schultz

Foreign Policy

A "thread of consistency" is present in Democratic foreign policy, which corresponds to the party's liberal tradition. Democrats customarily have believed in "U.S. exceptionalism," that the United States is inherently different from other countries. Democrats also typically have favored exporting America's interpretations of democracy, personal freedoms, and political equality. Consequently, the party's foreign policy is grounded in idealism and altruism. Conversely, the Republican Party and its predecessors usually followed the principles of Realpolitik and national self-interest that correspond to the conservative tradition of the party.

The division between the two parties has its roots in the early days of the U.S. political system when the nascent parties, Democratic-Republicans and the Federalists, had competing visions of the French Revolution and the proper response of the United States to the subsequent European war. While party leaders such as Thomas Jefferson endorsed President Washington's Proclamation of Neutrality, rank-and-file Democratic-Republicans were disappointed that the United States did not side with the French. Jeffersonian Republicans saw themselves as defenders of liberty at home and supporters of the revolutionary cause of republicanism abroad. Consequently, Democratic foreign policy has been grounded in U.S. exceptionalism since the early days of the party.

Obviously, this characterization is not a perfect means for differentiating between the parties. Democratic Party leaders often use both idealistic and Realpolitik justifications for foreign policy. Based on historical analyses, however, this generalization is accurate enough to be useful in assessing Democratic foreign policy.

Critics often have charged that the Democratic Party has been the party of expansion and war. But the Democratic Party's endorsement of U.S. exceptionalism did not necessarily translate into a partywide support of an internationalist and interventionist foreign policy. Since there is a Democratic belief that the United States should be better than other countries, some party leaders have asserted that isolationism was preferable to imperialism or misguided interventionism. The internal division between idealistic interventionists and idealistic isolationists surfaced before World War I. While idealistic isolationists traditionally have been a minority faction in the party, during the 1970s and 1980s these "doves" dominated Democratic foreign policy.

The development of the Democratic Party's foreign policy can be roughly categorized into four historical phases based on the policies of the dominant leaders of the party: expansionism (1800 to 1859), anti-imperialism (1865 to 1913), idealistic internationalism (1914 to 1968), and the legacy of the Vietnam War (1968 to 1995).

EXPANSIONISM (1800–1859)

Democratic foreign policy centered on expansionism after the party came to power in 1800. Initially, the party's advocation of expanding the territories of the United States was relatively benign. During the War of 1812, however, party members advocated the use of military force to acquire new territory. Later, the Monroe Doctrine and the spirit of Manifest Destiny provided the ideological justification for the proposed seizures of additional territory on the North American continent and adjacent islands. Besides expanding the territory and power of the United States, expansionism was used to unite diverse elements of the Democratic Party. Southern Democrats were anxious to increase the representation of slave states, while western Democrats and immigrants were eager for land. Consequently, a Democratic foreign policy based on expansionism was a key element of party unity and political strength.

After the Democratic-Republicans came to power in 1800, leaders asserted that the party's foreign policy would center on neutrality and rely on state militias rather than a standing army for national defense. Jefferson and Madison also believed the strength of U.S. trade would provide an alternative to war with European nations. In 1803, President Jefferson started the expansionistic phase of Democratic foreign policy when he used his treaty-making power to purchase 800,000 square miles from France.

President Jefferson declared a complete trade embargo on foreign trade after the French and English had seized U.S. ships. While the embargo did impose some hardships on Europeans, it created a nationwide depression in the United States. A new breed of nationalistic Republicans, including Henry Clay and John C. Calhoun, was elected in 1811. These "war hawks" advocated a war with Great Britain to gain new territories. Democratic-Republican foreign policy changed because of the War of 1812, when the party recognized the necessity of a peacetime army and tariffs.

In 1823 President James Monroe articulated the Monroe Doctrine, which is one foundation of Democratic foreign policy. President Monroe stated that European powers could no longer colonize the American continents or interfere with independent Spanish American countries. He also asserted that the United States would not interfere in existing European colonies or European affairs. Subsequent Democratic Party leaders used the Monroe Doctrine and the Louisiana Purchase to justify U.S. expansion in the 1840s.

President Andrew Jackson continued the pattern of expansionism when he removed all Indian tribes to lands west of the Mississippi River. Democratic expansionism reached its zenith during the administration of James Polk (1845–1849), the Great Expansionist. President Polk combined the expansionist desires of southern Democrats with those of western Democrats under a Manifest Destiny platform. According to this ideology, Providence had given the United States the North American continent to develop its great experiment of liberty and popular self-government. Expansion was a way to extend the area of freedom by bringing more land and people under U.S. jurisdiction.

In 1846 Polk negotiated a compromise with Great Britain to divide Oregon at the 49th parallel and launched the Mexican-American War. Based on U.S. military successes, Polk secured the Mexican cession of 1848 by which the United States obtained California, New Mexico, and the Rio Grande bound-

ary for $15 million. The Democrats' foreign policy under President Polk was extremely controversial, since critics accused the party of trying to create a large southern slave empire to increase its domestic political power.

During the Pierce administration (1853–1857) the Democratic Party continued to rely on expansionism to unite its diverse followers. President Pierce and his supporters believed the United States would annex Canada and Mexico eventually. Democrats also focused their attention on Cuba, Central America, and Hawaii. Under the Pierce administration the United States acquired a 45,000-square-mile strip of desert land from Mexico for $10 million in the Gadsden Purchase.

ANTI-IMPERIALISM (1865–1913)

After 1865, domestic affairs preoccupied Democrats as they tried to regain lost political strength. Party leaders advocated "continentalism," the belief that the United States should not acquire any territory outside the continental limits of the United States, and were very critical of the Alaska purchase in 1867 and Republican imperialists.

The party adopted a new trend in foreign policy, anti-imperialism, under Grover Cleveland. President Cleveland announced in 1885 that Democrats would follow the foreign policy advocated by George Washington against entangling alliances and oppose the acquisition of new and distant territories. During his two terms in office Cleveland resisted Republican efforts to intervene in Cuba and annex Hawaii, which led to a foreign policy dispute between the parties. The month after he lost the election of 1896, however, President Cleveland stated that U.S. intervention in Cuba was inevitable if the Cuban struggle for independence should continue to degenerate into "senseless slaughter."

Democrats vigorously opposed U.S. imperialism based on a variant of U.S. exceptionalism during the McKinley, Theodore Roosevelt, and Taft administrations. William Jennings Bryan and other leaders asserted that U.S. imperialism violated the primary principles underlying the U.S. political system. The United States should act as a model for other civilized nations and refrain from military conquest for material gain. Moreover, since Americans had fought a revolution to gain a government based on consent of the governed, the United States should not force its government on conquered territories. Democrats also argued that overseas expansion violated the Monroe Doctrine.

Democrats were outspoken critics of the Spanish-

American War in 1898, which they interpreted as a war of plundering and spoils. When the Spanish surrendered control over Cuba, Guam, Puerto Rico, and the Philippine Islands to the United States at the end of the war, party leaders united to oppose ratification of the treaty in the Senate. But Bryan eventually decided that his party should approve the treaty to keep the peace and to give the Philippines an opportunity to win self-government through pacific means. Democrats also resisted the annexation of Hawaii in 1898 and repeatedly demanded independence for the Philippines.

IDEALISTIC INTERNATIONALISM
(1914–1968)

With the election of Woodrow Wilson, the Democratic Party entered another era of idealistic international foreign policy analogous to the earlier expansionist period. Wilson set the parameters for an international foreign policy based on U.S. exceptionalism and national interest concerns that his successors followed. Ultimately, Democratic foreign policy was so successful after World War II that containment served as the basis for a bipartisan U.S. foreign policy during the 1950s and 1960s. Nevertheless, there also was consistent, though limited, opposition to idealistic internationalism from within the Democratic Party in this period.

The debate over imperialism polarized the two parties in the early twentieth century. At the beginning of the Wilson administration, it appeared that Democratic foreign policy would continue the course set by anti-imperialists, particularly when William Jennings Bryan became Wilson's first secretary of state. Wilson and Bryan believed that the United States had the force of moral principle and should set the example for the rest of the world. The United States had a mission to teach semideveloped countries to live according to the kind of legal and constitutional system that existed in the United States and to respect international law. This idealistic policy set the framework for an active, internationalist, and extremely controversial Democratic foreign policy.

The road to World War I revealed a major split in both U.S. parties between isolationists and internationalists as the Democratic Party had to create a clear-cut foreign policy concerning the "European war." Initially, Wilson based Democratic foreign policy on "the existing rules of international law and the treaties of the United States." Wilson insisted that the United States had neutral rights to trade and use the ocean. When European countries, most notably the Germans with submarine warfare, violated these rights, Wilson

wanted a tough response to European aggression. Consequently, he tried to create a middle ground between hardline Republicans and isolationistic Democrats. Wilson also publicly favored a league of nations (initially proposed by Progressive Republicans) during the 1916 Democratic Party convention and won approval from the membership. Therefore, from 1916 onward, Wilson dominated Democratic foreign policy despite vigorous opposition within the party.

Bryan and his supporters and Progressive Republicans opposed Wilson's declaration of war against Germany "to make the world safe for democracy." Bryan invoked Washington's Farewell Address and Jefferson's prescription on "entangling alliances" as infallible guides for twentieth-century foreign policy and resigned from the Wilson administration in protest. Though Wilson tried to make the 1918 congressional elections a referendum on Democratic foreign policy, he also set the framework for bipartisanship during U.S. military actions when he declared that "politics is adjourned in 1918" and appointed administrators from both parties to manage the war effort.

After World War I, the differences between interventionists and isolationists deeply divided the Democratic Party. During the interwar period, the Democrats appeared to return to a noninterventionist foreign policy and supported continued disarmament efforts. But internationalism prevailed when Franklin D. Roosevelt was elected. FDR did as much as possible to prepare the country for war and an internationalist foreign policy in the late 1930s and early 1940s. He also relied on Wilson's idealistic legacy and national interests before and during World War II. For example, Roosevelt's Four Freedoms (Freedom of Speech and Worship and Freedom from Want and Fear) and the Atlantic Charter (1941) provided an idealistic justification for an aggressive U.S. foreign policy.

One of the major issues dividing the Democratic Party after World War II was how to treat the Soviet Union. President Truman continued an international Democratic foreign policy and responded to the Soviets' moves into Eastern Europe with the containment policy. Democratic foreign policy was grounded in the belief that the United States should act militarily and politically to contain the power of the Soviet Union "for a long time to come." Left-wing Democrats such as former Vice President Henry Wallace maintained that the containment policy undermined the chance to create a harmonious international community. Wallace believed Stalin's moves into Eastern Europe grew out of a sense of the Soviet Union's vulnerability to attack and were not a threat to the United States. This division over the Soviet Union caused a deep split in the Democratic Party that never fully healed. Nonetheless, most Democrats and conservative Republicans supported containment. The Democrats enacted the Marshall Plan to facilitate economic recovery in Europe, sent U.S. troops to defend Western Europe, and resisted communist expansion into South Korea under their global policy. Democrats also believed that protectionism was one cause of World War II and moved toward a comprehensive reshaping of the international political economy based on free trade.

Truman committed the Democratic Party (and the Republicans) to an active involvement in world politics to establish a liberal international political economy and contain the expansionist totalitarian Soviet empire. After Truman left office, President Eisenhower, with widespread Democratic support, institutionalized a global containment policy using military alliances and air power. President Kennedy proposed the Flexible Response Policy, a military force structure designed to give U.S. leaders containment options, which President Johnson used during the Vietnam War. Though left-wing Democrats denounced containment, particularly during the 1970s and 1980s, it remained the guiding principle of U.S. foreign policy until the Soviet Union collapsed in 1990 and the principal legacy of Democratic foreign policy.

THE LEGACY OF THE VIETNAM WAR (1968–1995)

Containment dominated Democratic foreign policy until the Vietnam War. As U.S. involvement in the Vietnam War became more controversial, however, consensus within the Democratic Party on the basic elements of U.S. foreign policy disintegrated. Again the split between Democratic internationalists (hawks) and isolationists (doves) surfaced in the 1960s. Both sides relied on moral arguments and U.S. exceptionalism to justify their positions. To the doves, the Vietnam War was unworthy of this exceptional nation. Hawks argued that containment and American support of the South Vietnamese reflected the party's basic commitments to individual dignity and freedom, racial equality, and social justice for all.

The Democratic Party has been searching for a coherent foreign policy since the end of the Vietnam War. In the 1970s and 1980s, Democrats were more divided than at any other time in the party's history. The Democrats' main thrust was antimilitary, anti-interventionist, and pro–human rights. "No more Vietnams" was the major theme of Democratic foreign policy. Democrats advocated a variation of isolationism in the sense that military force and violence were to be avoided even as the party focused on new international issues. Nevertheless, the party could not agree on the basic outlines of a new Democratic foreign policy to replace containment.

Many Democratic leaders viewed the world from a new internationalist perspective based on the increasing interdependency of countries. They believed that the key issues of U.S. foreign policy should focus on transnational problems such as overpopulation, hunger, and environmental issues, rather than a preoccupation with the Soviet Union. These Democrats' chief concern was the North–South axis rather than the East–West axis, which was consistent with the Democrats' focus on domestic social policies. They saw the Soviet Union as a traditional great power and viewed Russian expansionism as mainly defensive. Other Democrats continued to support a strict containment policy.

The division between elements of the Democratic Party was apparent in the Carter administration. Carter denounced past Democratic foreign policy as an overreaction to an exaggerated threat and condemned containment for its lack of morality. Carter and his followers believed that the United States had linked itself with too many right-wing dictatorships and called for a new concern with human rights. Carter used a trilateral approach, which stressed an active pursuit of better political and economic relations with all nations. But members of the administration were still deeply divided about a new Democratic foreign policy, most notably the proper U.S. response to the Soviet Union's invasion of Afghanistan in 1979. Carter embraced containment at the end of his administration and announced a new "doctrine" when he warned that an attempt by any outside force to gain control of the Persian Gulf region would be regarded as an assault on U.S. interests and repelled by any means necessary, including military force.

The legacy of Vietnam continued to haunt the Democratic Party in the 1980s. Whenever the United States was involved in an international struggle, Democrats encouraged the Reagan and Bush administrations either to avoid military involvement or to use limited military force to open negotiations. Democratic reaction to the Persian Gulf War demonstrates this foreign policy position. Democrats argued that President Bush should not "rush into war" and supported an economic embargo on Iraq instead of troop deployments to Saudi Arabia. They also wanted to stick with economic sanctions for at least a year to give them sufficient time to work. Military force would be considered only after sanctions proved ineffectual. Only ten Democrats in the Senate voted for the president's request for congressional approval of the use of force. The vast majority of Democrats in Congress, including the senior leadership, voted against the measure.

The Clinton administration inherited a curious Democratic foreign policy. On the one hand, many party leaders are still very internationalistic and idealistic even as they renounce the use of military force. Some analysts, however, assert that Democrats have lost their fear of using military intervention to support humanitarian and idealistic goals since the Persian Gulf War and the collapse of the Soviet Union. Therefore, President Clinton could send U.S. troops to Somalia, Haiti, and Bosnia-Herzegovinia. When he visited soldiers in Bosnia in 1996, Clinton used Manifest Destiny, idealism, and national interests to justify his policy, stating, "around the world people look to America, not just because of our size and strength, but because of what we stand for and what we're willing to stand against. We can't be everywhere. . . . But where we can make a difference, where our values and our interests are at stake, we must act." Based on the rhetoric and foreign policy actions of the Clinton administration, Democratic foreign policy may be returning to its Wilsonian heritage as the legacy of the Vietnam War begins to fade.

Janet B. Manspeaker

SEE ALSO The Cold War

BIBLIOGRAPHY

Goldman, Ralph. *Search for Consensus.* Philadelphia: Temple University Press, 1979.

Kovler, Peter B., ed. *Democrats and the American Idea.* Washington, DC: Center for National Policy Press, 1992.

Nathan, James, and James Oliver. *United States Foreign Policy and World Order.* 3rd ed. Boston: Little, Brown, 1985.

Reichley, A. James. *The Life of the Parties.* New York: Free Press, 1992.

Spanier, John, and Eric Uslaner. *American Foreign Policy Making and the Democratic Dilemmas.* 6th ed. New York: Macmillan, 1994.

Freedom of Speech

The Democratic Party's approach to First Amendment guarantees of freedom of speech and expression has not always been as liberal as it is today. While postwar Democrats have tended to be much less likely to oppose expression without limitation than Republicans, earlier members of the Democratic Party took strong action against free speech.

Before World War II, the party's record includes such blemishes as President Woodrow Wilson's appointment in 1919 of A. Mitchell Palmer as attorney general, whose communist-hunting measures were akin to the witch hunts carried out in the 1950s by Republican Senator Joseph McCarthy of Wisconsin.

The World War I era stands out for its repressive antispeech policies, often proposed by leading Democrats, and subsequent violations of personal liberties. The Sedition Act of 1918 was a flagrant example. Introduced into the House by Democratic Representative Martin Davey of Ohio at the urging of Palmer, the bill defined as punishable sedition any activity aimed at changing the government or the laws of the United States. Endorsed by Democratic President Wilson, the act passed both houses to become law.

The Congress of 1919 and 1920 introduced more than 70 measures aimed at restricting, among other activities, peacetime sedition, the display of the Red flag, and the sending of seditious material in the mail. A Senate committee headed by Less S. Overman, a North Carolina Democrat, attempted to suppress radical and Bolshevik activities with restrictive legislation such as the Overman bill, which did not pass.

On January 2, 1920, the Department of Justice, under Palmer's direction, carried out what have come to be known as the Palmer raids—perhaps the most repressive actions of the "Red scare" period in U.S. history. More than 4,000 people labeled as communists or associated with communist labor parties were arrested in 33 cities. Palmer said they were plagued with a "disease of evil thinking."

The Alien Registration Act, otherwise known as the Smith Act, after Democrat Howard W. Smith of Virginia, was introduced in 1939. The act forbade advocating the violent overthrow of the government and the publication of writing toward that end. It passed both houses in 1940 and was signed into law by Democratic President Franklin D. Roosevelt. In 1948 the act was used by the Roosevelt administration's Justice Department to indict leaders of the American Communist Party.

While Democratic policy on free speech issues has been characterized by intraparty splits, often between conservative southern Democrats and their more liberal, prolabor northern colleagues, the advent of public radio created partisan conflict between Republicans and Democrats. The Radio Act of 1927, passed at the suggestion of Republican Secretary of Commerce Herbert Hoover, himself appointed by Republican President Warren G. Harding, required broadcasters to act in the "public interests"—a phrase that allowed a

Republican-appointed commission to evaluate program content when considering the renewal of stations' licenses. In 1931 the committee rejected the Chicago Federation of Labor's renewal application based on the station's programming content.

Though the decision started a battle between the Republicans and the Democrats that culminated in 1934 with the New Deal Democrats' passage of the Communications Act, Democrats were acting partly in their own interest. After seeing how newspapers had in general supported Republicans, the New Deal Democrats wanted to ensure that radio and television would be nonpartisan. The act, which rewrote the Radio Act and established the Federal Communications Commission (FCC), also strengthened the provisions of the law applying to equal time for candidates and ballot measures. But it was not until 1949 that the FCC promulgated the Fairness Doctrine, which required the presentation of contrasting viewpoints on controversial issues of public consequence. Yet partisan conflict over the broadcasting policy did not end there. Five decades later, the FCC repealed the Fairness Doctrine under pressure from conservative Republican President Ronald Reagan. Soon after, South Carolina Senator Ernest Hollings, a moderate conservative Democrat, fought to reinstate the rule.

More recently, wide-ranging public access to the Internet has prompted calls for restrictive legislation. Following the pattern of the twentieth century, politicians reacted with regulatory fervor to the unknown effects of new technology. The bipartisan Exon–Coats Amendment, proposed as part of the telecommunications reform bill, aimed to prohibit the transmission of "indecent communication" to cyberspace users younger than 18 years of age. It was drafted by Senators Jim Exon, a Nebraska Democrat, and Daniel R. Coats, an Indiana Republican.

Steve Hoenisch

BIBLIOGRAPHY

Bacon, Donald C., Roger H. Davidson, and Morton Keller, eds. *The Encyclopedia of the United States Congress.* New York: Simon and Schuster, 1995.

Hentoff, Nat. *The First Freedom: The Tumultuous History of Free Speech in America.* New York: Delacorte Press, 1980.

Maisel, L. Sandy, ed. *Political Parties and Elections in the United States: An Encyclopedia.* New York: Garland, 1991.

Murphy, Paul L. *The Meaning of Freedom of Speech: First Amendment Freedoms from Wilson to FDR.* Westport, CT: Greenwood Press, 1972.

Porter, Kirk H., and Donald Bruce Johnson. *National Party Platforms: 1840–1964.* Urbana: University of Illinois Press, 1966.

Smith, Craig R. *Freedom of Expression and Partisan Politics.* Columbia: University of South Carolina Press, 1989.

Gun Control

The Democratic Party's handling of the issue of gun control is frequently cautious and sometimes ambivalent. Although much more supportive of gun-control legislation than the Republicans, Democrats find they must tread carefully in confronting the constitutional questions and political opposition that such legislation invites. It is an issue that some Democrats simply wish would go away. Other members of the party, however, have taken on the issue with a missionary zeal, thus securing the party's image as friendly toward gun control. Certainly the party has used the issue for political advantage with some segments of the electorate.

Gun control did not become a sustained national issue until increasing violence and a wave of assassinations prompted a political response that resulted in the Gun Control Act of 1968. From that time forward, gun control has been a highly emotional and partisan issue. The debate revolves around two primary questions. First, how intrusive should the government be in the regulation of private possession of handguns? Answers run the gamut from disallowing any governmental restrictions to prohibiting private ownership altogether. Possible answers between those two extremes include mandatory handgun registration, mandatory waiting periods for purchase, and prohibitions on gun ownership by certain people (such as convicted felons). The other dimension of the gun-control issue centers on the distinction between types of guns. Rifles are typically presumed less concealable than handguns, and thus less potentially dangerous. Automatic weapons are considered more destructive and less justifiable as weapons for sport or self-defense. Although governmental policy has established some basic principles on both these dimensions of the gun-control issue, a vociferous debate continues at the boundaries of that limited consensus.

That the Democratic Party more readily accepts the need for gun control stems partly from the party's weighing of individual and societal interests. Democrats tend to place a higher value on societal standards and needs and thus envision more opportunities for government to protect society from individuals. The restriction of access to guns is seen as a legitimate manifestation of this function. It is construed as consistent with governmental restrictions on other potentially dangerous commodities, including (legal) drugs and various toxic substances. Gun control can also be justified by the party's desire to prevent individual members of society from acquiring grossly disproportionate power.

Although advocacy of gun control has fit comfortably within the larger Democratic philosophy, surmounting the constitutional arguments against gun control has proved more difficult. Along with other gun-control advocates, the Democratic Party has emphasized the first words of the Second Amendment, which refer to "a *well-regulated* militia" (emphasis added). These words have been interpreted alternatively to justify gun control as a form of "regulation" and to weaken the amendment's applicability to individuals (as opposed to "militias," construed as quasi-governmental organizations). These interpretations, however, as well as those offered by gun-control opponents, remain largely unsubstantiated by Supreme Court decisions.

Constitutional questions about gun control at times have caused friction between the Democratic Party and the American Civil Liberties Union (ACLU), which generally are allied on a whole range of domestic issues. The ACLU's "liberal" interpretation of the Constitution has led it to side with the National Rifle Association (NRA) in some cases. Motivated perhaps by different concerns, the ACLU and NRA have opposed some Democratic efforts to restrict access to guns and to maintain centralized files on gun owners. These cases have turned on issues of privacy and due process.

Outside the courts, public opinion poses additional problems for the Democratic Party's stand on gun control. Substantial opposition to certain types of gun control exists in large segments of the population, including some of the party's traditional bases of support. Opinion polls consistently reveal a solid majority of Americans opposing any general ban on guns. A 1995 poll showed that three-quarters of all American voters believe that the Constitution guarantees them the right to own a gun. With opposition to gun control especially strong in the South, the split in the Democratic Party between northern liberals and southern conservatives is intensified.

These factors may explain the mildness of the party's "firearms" plank in its 1992 platform: "We support a reasonable waiting period to permit background checks for purchases of handguns, as well as assault weapons controls to ban . . . the most deadly assault weapons. We do not support efforts to restrict weapons used for legitimate hunting and sporting purposes." This plank represents the lowest common denominator of Democrats' ideology. The party is, of course, known for a number of high-profile propo-

nents of gun control, including Representative Charles Schumer of New York.

The attempted assassination of Republican President Ronald Reagan in 1981 provided the Democrats with a powerful issue to secure bipartisan support for gun control. But Reagan, as well as his Republican successor, George Bush, refused to support major gun-control legislation while in office. With the election of Democrat Bill Clinton to the White House in 1992, Democrats had the institutional strength to push through legislation to require a waiting period and background check for handgun purchases. This "Brady Bill" (named after Reagan's press secretary, who was severely injured in the assassination attempt) was signed into law in 1993. A year later, the Democrats succeeded in enacting legislation to ban certain assault weapons. Although the party lost its majorities in the House and Senate in 1994, a terrorist attack on a federal office building the following year derailed Republican efforts to repeal the assault weapons ban.

In the eyes of Democratic leaders, the opportunity to enact gun-control legislation arises only when the public has been adequately outraged by some high-profile crime wave or act of terrorism. The Democratic Party is sensitive to charges that it concerns itself more with defendants than crime victims—that it is "soft on crime." The party's advocacy of gun control is perhaps one of its strongest weapons to combat that image. It is ironic, therefore, that the NRA and Republicans have been so successful in frightening the party away from taking an unequivocal stand on the issue of gun control.

Steve D. Boilard

BIBLIOGRAPHY

Idelson, Holly. "Gun Rights and Restructuring: The Territory Reconfigured." *Congressional Quarterly* 51 (April 24, 1993): 21–26.

Nisbet, Lee, ed. *The Gun Control Debate: You Decide.* Buffalo, NY: Prometheus Books, 1990.

"Party Positions on National Issues." *Congressional Digest,* October 1992, pp. 234–255.

Robin, Gerald D. *Violent Crime and Gun Control.* Cincinnati: Anderson, 1991.

Health Care

Although the early proposals for federal health care were tendered by Republicans, health legislation soon became the domain of Democrats, who increasingly encountered opposition from Republicans weary of enlarging the central government. With his proposals to expand the Public Health Service in the 1920s,

Democratic Senator Joseph E. Ransdell opened the way for later generations of Democrats to fight for augmenting the federal government's role in health care. But these later generations of Democrats, often composed of northern, liberal, and prolabor congressmen, found significant and often decisive resistance from their conservative southern Democratic brethren.

Federal health care began in 1798 with an Act for Relief of Sick and Disabled Seamen, which created the Marine Hospital Service, the progenitor of the Public Health Service, the name that the agency took following passage of the Public Health and Marine Service Act of 1902. The bill was enacted after Republican Senator John C. Spooner of Wisconsin asked for changes in the public health service. But partisan politics over health care did not take hold with full force until the beginning of the twentieth century.

In 1926 Democratic Senator Ransdell of Louisiana, chairman of the Public Health Committee, introduced a bill to create a national institute of health. The proposal, however, languished in Congress for four years, encountering indifference from many members of Congress and facing determined opposition from Republican President Calvin Coolidge's Bureau of the Budget. During 1928, the Ransdell bill was also being kicked around the Senate, but Republican Senator Reed Smoot of Utah, an early opponent of federal health care, prevented its passage.

Also in 1926, Republican Representative James S. Parker of New York introduced a bill to expand the authority and services of the Public Health Service. In 1928, the Parker bill passed both houses only to be vetoed by Republican President Calvin Coolidge over the question of executive authority.

In 1930, both the Parker and Ransdell acts became law, determining the direction of the Public Health Service for the next 40 years. The Parker Act, officially known as the Public Health Service Amendments of 1930, enhanced the authority and operations of the service. The Ransdell Act was officially known as the National Institute of Health Act. The passage of the acts helped open the door for the more extensive health care proposals that were to follow.

In 1937, several Democrats teamed up to pass an act establishing and funding a cancer institute. The National Cancer Institute Act, which passed both houses unanimously, was proposed by Representatives Maury Maverick, a Texas Democrat, and Warren G. Magnuson, a Washington Democrat, as well as Senator Homer T. Bone, also a Washington Democrat.

Democratic President Franklin D. Roosevelt, with the backing of other Democrats in his administration, brought up the subject of a government health insurance program when he proposed his Social Security bill in 1935. But Roosevelt, fearing that such a controversial issue could endanger the overall Social Security bill and his chances of reelection, let the issue wither. Despite the lobbying efforts of some progressive Democrats for an expansion of federal health services and compulsory insurance, Roosevelt's New Deal included few other attempts to expand federal health care significantly, though it did manage to get aid for maternal and children's health and matching grants for state health departments. Yet it was Roosevelt's vision of a government health insurance program that formed the progenitor of the 1965 Medicare Act.

Further into the years of the New Deal, a rift emerged on health care among elected members of the Democratic Party. Between 1939 and 1943, three northern Democrats—Senators Robert F. Wagner of New York and James E. Murray of Montana and Representative John D. Dingell of Michigan—repeatedly introduced measures for national health insurance. The bills, however, did not have strong support from the Roosevelt administration, which continued to be fearful that such controversial legislation could doom other aspects of the president's agenda. But the absence of administrative backing was not the cause of the bills' demise. Instead, they were blocked by conservative southern Democrats, who had formed a strong coalition with Republicans.

The next battle over health care came in 1946 when Democratic Senator Joseph Lister Hill of Alabama and Republican Senator Harold H. Burton of Ohio introduced a bill to help defray the costs of hospital construction.

Senator Hill dedicated much of his congressional career to proposing and fighting for health care legislation. As chairman of the Senate Committee on Labor and Public Welfare, Hill, working with Democratic Representative John E. Fogarty of Rhode Island, persuaded Congress to expand the National Institutes of Health into a comprehensive facility for medical research. Along with Representative J. Percy Priest, Democrat of Tennessee, and Senator Claude Pepper, Democrat of Florida, Hill was instrumental in moving the National Mental Health Act of 1946 through Congress.

But the influential Senator Robert A. Taft, an Ohio Republican, frowned upon the Hill–Burton bill because, he believed, it allowed for too much federal control. In order to gain his backing, Senator Taft wanted the measure to contain assurances of states' rights and local control, money set aside according to state assessments of need, and matching funds for local hospital boards.

Within the Democratic Party, it was significant that Senator Hill, a southerner, had introduced the bill. The measure appealed to many southern conservatives in Congress, both Democrat and Republican, because it promised to funnel aid to their states. Even Senator Taft was eventually persuaded to back the bill by a funding formula that awarded the largest sums to the poorest states. The Hill–Burton Act, officially known as the Hospital Survey and Construction Act, became law in 1946.

Democratic President Harry S. Truman was a strong advocate of health care legislation. In his State of the Union speech in 1948, Truman announced that his goal was "to enact a comprehensive insurance system which would remove the money barrier between illness and therapy." For Truman, national health insurance was an issue of equality.

In early 1949, President Truman urged Congress to act on medical insurance. Soon thereafter, a bill drafted by Democratic Senators Wagner and Murray, along with Democratic Representative Dingell, was again presented to Congress, as it had been during previous years, when it usually met with congressional refusal to hold hearings on it. The fate of the 1949 bill was much the same. Despite backing from President Truman, the bill met with strong opposition from a coalition of anti-Truman conservative southern Democrats. They combined forces with Republicans to block the insurance proposal; it was never reported out of committee.

Despite the dashed hopes for President Truman's insurance legislation, a group of Democrats teamed up with a Republican to gain passage of two acts that provided funding for medical research. Surgeon General Leonard Scheele joined Democrats Mary Lasker, Murray, and Pepper, as well as Republican H. Styles Bridges of New Hampshire, to pass the National Heart Institute Act in 1948 and the Omnibus Medical Research Act of 1950, which established new institutes for health research. The acts are indicative of Congress's strong bipartisan support at the time for medical research, which continued through the 1950s, resulting in increased funding for the National Institutes of Health in 1957 and 1958.

In 1950, 1951, and 1952, President Truman continued to push for compulsory health insurance. But the prospects for passage appeared bleak after 1949, as even Truman's advisers acknowledged, especially after the elections of 1950 reduced the Democrats' House majority from 263–171 to 235–199 and scarcely allowed them to maintain control of the Senate.

The 1952 election that installed Republican Dwight D. Eisenhower as president shattered all possibility of a northern Democratic–supported compulsory insurance bill. In fact, under President Eisenhower, no substantial medical bill had a chance. Even after the Democrat Party regained control of Congress in 1954, the Democrats still lacked enough votes to ensure a favorable majority.

The year 1958 rekindled the debate over a national health insurance program. During that year, Aime J. Forand, a Rhode Island Democrat and a member of the House Ways and Means Committee, where at least one earlier proposal for national health insurance had died a quiet death, reintroduced an insurance bill. During the 1950s, statistics began to show that the aged had health and financial problems. Despite the statistics, the Forand bill drew opposition from conservative members of Congress, including some Democrats, who argued that it was regressive and limited. They objected that it would not offer substantial assistance to those who needed it most while covering those who did not. Opponents further argued that Americans were not poor enough to warrant compulsory government health insurance. They added that the bill would encroach on states' rights, an oft-used objection by Republicans. Many southern Democrats, though, also held states' rights in high regard, one reason they often found themselves voting with Republicans on issues of social welfare policy. Although Forand's bill was rejected by the House Ways and Means Committee in 1959 by a 17–8 vote, it did serve to revive the battle over federal health care.

In the wake of the Forand bill, Senator Robert S. Kerr, an Oklahoma Democrat, and Democratic Representative Wilbur D. Mills of Arkansas, the powerful chairman of the Ways and Means Committee, sponsored and gained passage of a compromise bill in 1960 that gave states matching funds to help the needy.

An increasingly significant federal role in health care emerged with the dawn of the 1960s and the presidential election of Democrat John F. Kennedy, who campaigned on a strong social welfare platform. The Democratic Party platform of 1960 included a section on health that proposed to use the Social Security system to cover the hospital bills of those in need and to make it available to all retired persons without a means test.

In February 1961, true to his party's campaign promises, President Kennedy called for an extension of Social Security benefits to cover hospital and nursing home costs but not surgical expenses for those over age 65. Senator Clinton P. Anderson, a New Mexico Democrat who was a high-ranking member of the Finance Committee, and Representative Cecil R. King, a California Democrat who sat on the Ways and

Means Committee, introduced the president's proposal as the King–Anderson bill.

The bill, however, lacked bipartisan backing, and Representative Mills, though a Democrat, was determined to consider in the crucial Ways and Means Committee only a proposal that had bipartisan support. Besides, the Kerr–Mills program was already in place, and it was unlikely they would cave in to the president's plans. Of course, President Kennedy could have chosen to pressure Chairman Mills into supporting the King–Anderson bill, but Medicare was only one of the president's priorities. As Mills had agreed to introduce several of the president's other measures, Kennedy could not demand Mills's support for the health bill. Democratic Representative Sam Rayburn of Texas, the Speaker of the House, did support the president's proposal, but that support would not be enough to overcome the influential Mills.

Besides Mills, there was another significant barrier to passage of the King–Anderson Bill. It was a coalition of five other southern Democrats on the House Ways and Means Committee who, together with Republicans, formed a bloc strong enough to override the favorable votes of the committee's urban, prolabor Democrats. The six "swing" southern Democrats on the committee who opposed or were likely to oppose the Medicare bill in 1961 were Mills, a publicly announced opponent; Burr Harrison of Virginia, a conservative; John Watts of Kentucky; Frank Ikard of Texas, who had conservative tendencies; A. Sydney Herlong of Florida, who also tended to vote conservatively; and Representative Frazier, another conservative.

The aggregation of these factors—opposition from the committee's southern Democrats, especially Chairman Mills, President Kennedy's focus on other priorities, and the fact that the Kerr–Mills program was already in place—effectively killed the Medicare bill without a formal committee vote. But the battle for a national program of health insurance was not over yet; it was only postponed.

Following the assassination of President Kennedy, the ascendancy of Democrat Lyndon B. Johnson to the White House brought a liberal administration committed to social reforms as part of a War on Poverty. The Democratic Party's platform in 1964 contained a demand for including hospital care for older Americans in the Social Security program. More specifically, President Johnson's dramatic victory over Republican candidate Senator Barry Goldwater of Arizona could be seen as a popular mandate for Medicare, for Johnson had included a strong Medicare plank in his campaign, while Goldwater had not.

The 1964 Democratic landslide also placed in Congress liberal Democrats who not only firmly supported the administration but also were interested in health legislation, greatly improving the prospects for a Medicare bill.

More important, the composition of the House Ways and Means Committee had changed during the preceding elections; three of the conservative southern Democrats who had opposed Medicare in 1961 had been replaced by fellow southern Democrats willing to back the King–Anderson bill. Richard Fulton, Pat Jennings, and Clark Thompson supplanted Frazier, Harrison, and Ikard. Moreover, following the 1964 election, the committee's ratio was changed to reflect the strength of the parties in the House as a whole, increasing the number of Democrats on the committee. Thus, in 1965, the Ways and Means Committee shifted from 15 Democrats and 10 Republicans to 17 Democrats and 8 Republicans, further ensuring a bloc favorable to Medicare. The fate of the reintroduced King–Anderson bill had changed from being a possibility to a certainty. The bill continued to include coverage of the aged, limited hospitalization and nursing home insurance benefits, and Social Security financing.

Republicans reacted to the reintroduction of the King–Anderson measure by starting to talk about alternative programs that they saw as more positive. The Republicans put forth the following arguments as grounds for opposing the King–Anderson bill in favor of an alternative: it contained inadequate benefits, with too many exclusions and limits; it was too costly; and it did not distinguish between the poor and wealthy among the aged. To address these concerns, Republican Representative John W. Byrnes of Wisconsin, the ranking Republican on the Ways and Means Committee, proposed a bill for a voluntary system. Byrnes's bill was also driven by the desires of Republicans on the Ways and Means Committee to prevent the Democrats from taking exclusive credit for health insurance legislation.

Representative Mills, foreseeing that passage of the King–Anderson bill was now inevitable, sought to build bipartisan consensus for it. In a brilliant legislative move that at once strengthened the proposal and brought Republican backing to it, Mills moved to draft legislation combining the King–Anderson hospital insurance bill with Byrnes's voluntary plan and an expanded state-administered Kerr–Mills program for all medically needy people. Thus Mills succeeded in winning bipartisan support for his combination bill because it appealed to the Republicans, many of whom wanted, at most, a voluntary plan.

And Mills continued to guide the legislation through the House with expertise and diplomacy.

Throughout the drafting of the combination bill, Theodore R. Marmor writes in *The Politics of Medicare,* "Mills left no doubt that he was first among equals—he acted as the conciliator, the negotiator, the manager of the bill, always willing to praise others, but guiding the 'marking up' of H.R. 6675 through persuasion, entreaty, authoritative expertise, and control of the agenda." The combination measure became known as the Mills bill, and when the House convened on April 8 to vote on it, Mills received a standing ovation.

Yet Despite Mills's labors, in October 1964, a deadlock over the entire Social Security bill again postponed the possibility of Medicare until the following year.

In 1965, the Social Security Amendments of 1965 passed both houses and were signed into law by Democratic President Johnson, establishing Medicare and Medicaid and ending with victory for the Democratic Party—a long, bitter fight for health insurance that began with the Roosevelt administration and spanned the administrations of Presidents Truman and Kennedy and part of Johnson's. Perhaps the most far-reaching health care legislation passed in U.S. history, the amendments included a hospital insurance program for Social Security recipients over age 65, funded from payroll taxes, and voluntary medical service insurance for the same group, funded by small premiums and general revenues. It also expanded the Kerr–Mills program for all medically needy people.

The battle of a federal health insurance program did not end with the passage of Medicare and Medicaid. The battle merely shifted—to what the appropriate level of funding for such programs should be. The origins of Medicare during the 1960s also shaped the dispute over national health insurance in the 1970s, an era during which health policy continued to have strong appeal in Congress. Senator Edward M. Kennedy, a Massachusetts Democrat, and Representative Paul G. Rogers, a Florida Democrat, played key leadership roles on health legislation. Kennedy in particular has been the leading congressional advocate during the past quarter century for a universal health care system. In the 1970s, Senator Kennedy focused his efforts on passing a universal health care measure, but his attempts failed because a compromise could not be reached on the issue.

In 1971 President Nixon suggested a plan to cut health care costs and spur development of health maintenance organizations (HMOs) for providing care for Medicare and Medicaid recipients. Although the plan eventually lost favor with the White House, it was embraced by several influential congressional Republicans and Democrats, notably Senator Kennedy

and Representative Rogers. Working with several key Republicans in Congress, they adopted Nixon's plan. After three years of legislative effort, the Health Maintenance Organization Act of 1973 established an experimental program to underwrite HMO development, becoming a forerunner to the debate over stimulating HMO development and use during the 1990s.

In 1972 President Nixon announced that he intended to end federal backing for the Hill–Burton Act and several other programs and to cut funding for other programs. He also said he would revoke funds already appropriated to certain health care programs. Congress reacted with anger, passing amendments to secure appropriations. Congress eventually secured the grant programs at least temporarily in the Special Health Revenue Sharing Act of 1975, passed over Republican President Ford's veto. Many members of Congress, resenting Ford's tactics, backed the congressional health care leaders.

The late 1970s saw the election of Democrat Jimmy Carter to the presidency and a simultaneous respite from the health care debate. During the 1970s, however, many in Congress, particularly Republicans, became increasingly concerned over the rising costs of health care and voiced those concerns during hearings.

Republican President Ronald Reagan, soon after his election in 1981, launched an assault on the federal health care system, announcing that he planned to consolidate all 26 health services programs into two block grants. He also announced plans to slash spending on health by 25%. The president's announcement set off a battle in Congress, with Senator Kennedy, the Massachusetts Democrat, and Representative Henry A. Waxman, a California Democrat who was the new chairman of the House Health Subcommittee, leading the charge to retain federal health programs.

Despite formidable opposition from both conservative Republicans and conservative Democrats, Representative Waxman managed to negotiate three block grants and to retain several programs as categorical grants in the Omnibus Budget Reconciliation Act of 1981. But in the end the conservatives had won. The act reduced funding for all health services programs, collapsed funding for many categorical grant programs into block grants to states, and increased local and state governance over remaining programs.

One of the few victories during the conservative era that spanned the 12 years of the Reagan and Bush administrations came in 1991 when a coalition of three congresswomen joined forces to pass the Women's Health and Equity Act. Olympia Snowe, a Maine Republican, Senator Barbara Mikulski, a Maryland Democrat, and Representative Patricia Schroeder, an influential Colorado Democrat, were instrumental in securing passage of the bill, which created an office for research on women's health at the National Institutes of Health.

The election of Democratic President Bill Clinton returned health care to the fore of national politics in 1992. Clinton ran on a plank of reforming the nation's health care system. Once elected, Clinton's goal soon became universal coverage, arguing that it was necessitated by rising costs of care and large numbers of people without insurance. True to his campaign promise, he unveiled a health care reform proposal in a speech to Congress and the nation on September 22, 1993, saying that Hillary Rodham Clinton had consulted with government leaders of both parties and that many of the plan's principles had been embraced by Republicans as well as Democrats. He proposed a concept first conveyed by Republican President Richard M. Nixon—that every employer and individual would be asked to contribute to health care.

Clinton's proposal would require that all legal residents be insured by choosing from at least three plans providing standard medical benefits: an HMO, a fee-for-service, or a combination plan. The plans would be administered by large corporate employers or by regional purchasing alliances. Employers would pay 80% of the insurance cost, while individuals would pay up to 20%. There would be subsidies for small, low-wage employers and poor individuals. Clinton maintained that his plan would deliver security, simplicity, savings, and quality while retaining freedom of choice.

Also among the principles of Clinton's plan was an expansion of states' responsibilities. Other Democrats, however, have been distrustful of states' abilities to ensure high-quality health care. For example, Democratic Representatives Pete Stark and Henry Waxman of California have written during the 1990s detailed laws outlining states' responsibilities to help low-income earners, nursing home residents, pregnant women, and children.

Despite Clinton's assurances of support for his plan from Democrats and Republicans alike, rifts soon developed not only between the two parties but also, and significantly, within the Democratic Party, spawning three separate Democratic proposals, including Clinton's, and three additional Republican ones.

A major split within the Democratic Party was between the backers of the administration plan and backers of a single-payer system, meaning a government-run universal health care system like Canada's. The split was significant because many analysts believed that for the Democrats to pass a plan, they needed to include those committed to extensive reform.

Backers of the single-payer system—generally liberal Democrats—argued against Clinton's plan on the grounds that managed competition was untested, overly complex, and possibly inefficient compared with a single-payer system. Many liberal Democrats also feared that money would be diverted from Medicaid and Medicare to help pay for Clinton's plan.

The single-payer system was proposed by Representative Jim McDermott, a Washington Democrat who had been pushing for a government-run program for some time. McDermott's plan would give all legal residents access to a standard medical benefits package, administered by the states, with the government paying the bills. It would cover all medically necessary procedures. The program would be funded through payroll taxes on employers; individuals would pay nothing. Supporters of McDermott's plan included Representative Stark, the California Democrat who was chairman of the House Ways and Means Subcommittee on Health. Among the 60 other advocates of a single-payer system in Congress is Democratic Senator Paul Wellstone of Minnesota, a cosponsor of the legislation. Wellstone and the other backers argue that Canada's system, in which federal and provincial governments share costs, is a proven and generally successful way of providing citizens with fairly high-quality care. They also argue that taxpayers would be willing to back a single-payer system once they realized that it would replace all other health insurance costs, adding that managed competition will actually prove more burdensome for consumers. The proposal for the single-payer system, however, led many in Congress to raise questions about rationing. Conservative Democrats and Republicans alike consider a single-payer system akin to socialized medicine.

A third plan was proposed by a conservative Democrat, Representative Jim Cooper of Tennessee. It would establish purchasing cooperatives to reduce the cost of insurance and make it more affordable. The government would pay premiums of those below the poverty line and subsidize others in need. Cooper believed the virtues of his more conservative plan lay in less federal bureaucracy and control. Conservative Democrats had criticized Clinton's plan as containing excessive controls. They also had concerns over requiring small businesses to buy insurance for their employees. Cooper's alternative would require no payments by employers.

But along with the other plans, Clinton's initiative died in Congress, unable to survive challenges from the strong Republican minority, which had garnered frequent support from conservative Democrats. The nearly century-old split in the Democratic Party between conservatives and liberals that had for so long undermined Medicare and stalled other federal health care proposals by liberal Democrats had struck again. Indeed, the death of Clinton's plan left unresolved the issue of health care and extent of government involvement, as it has remained since the early days of the twentieth century.

Steve Hoenisch

BIBLIOGRAPHY

Bacon, Donald C., Roger H. Davidson, and Morton Keller, eds. *The Encyclopedia of the United States Congress.* New York: Simon and Schuster, 1995.

Eckholm, Erik, ed. *Solving America's Health-Care Crisis: A Guide to Understanding the Greatest Threat to Your Family's Economic Security.* New York: Times Books, 1993.

"Health Care: Clinton's Plan and the Alternatives." *New York Times*, October 17, 1993, p. 22.

Johnson, Donald Bruce. *National Party Platforms: Volume II, 1960–1976.* Urbana: University of Illinois Press, 1978.

Maisel, L. Sandy, ed. *Political Parties and Elections in the United States: An Encyclopedia.* New York: Garland, 1991.

Marmor, Theodore R. *The Politics of Medicare.* Chicago: Aldine, 1973.

Porter, Kirk H., and Donald Bruce Johnson. *National Party Platforms: 1840–1964.* Urbana: University of Illinois Press, 1966.

Stevens, Robert, and Rosemary Stevens. *Welfare Medicine in America: A Case Study in Medicaid.* New York: Macmillan, 1974.

Immigration

Throughout American history, immigration has encompassed a vast array of people and experiences. There is no single motive that all immigrants share. Nor is there a common path that all immigrants follow. Immigrants do not necessarily wish to become citizens or to remain in America indefinitely. Many maintain citizenship in their native country and live in the United States as resident aliens. Still others enter the country illegally or move back and forth following seasonal work.

Debate over immigration in the United States has historically addressed three distinct categories of immigrants: legal immigrants, refugees, and illegal immigrants. At various moments in American history these categories have been given different meanings or have referred to different groups of people. For example, the term *refugee* has been used in different eras to describe people fleeing genocide, ideological conflict, or even economic crisis. In each era, however, immigration policy has prioritized offering asylum to refugees.

Arguments for and against immigration are made on economic, political, and moral grounds. People opposed to immigration, or those favoring a more restrictive immigration policy, argue that immigrants take away much-needed jobs from Americans and become dependent on the generous welfare system of the United States. Immigrants are portrayed as a drain on the U.S. economy because they send their earnings to relatives in their native countries. At times, immigrants have been depicted as agents of foreign powers, who vote according to whatever foreign policy is best for their families back home. Moreover, immigrants are accused of diluting American culture and of a moral depravity that threatens the values essential to American life.

Politicians who favor a more liberal immigration policy argue that, historically, immigrant labor has contributed greatly to U.S. expansion and industrialization. Today, they add, immigrants play a necessary role in the division of labor by taking jobs American workers will not accept. Proponents of immigration point out that immigrants contribute tax dollars and Social Security payments in amounts that far outnumber the social services they consume. Immigration, they point out, is a net gain for the U.S. economy.

Moreover, they explain that immigrants have made invaluable contributions to the political and cultural development of the country. Individuals who emigrate to the United States are often fleeing repressive regimes or extreme poverty, and they tend to be not only ambitious but also ardent supporters of American democracy. Democratic politicians have employed a combination of these arguments to defend their pro-immigration policy.

Whereas the Republican Party is often associated with a restrictionist platform and the Democratic Party with a liberal immigration policy, their respective party positions have changed over time in response to shifts in the economic and political climate of the United States. The result is an extremely diverse set of policies that, over the course of U.S. immigration history, have failed to articulate a consistent position.

THREE PHASES OF U.S. IMMIGRATION POLICY

The history of U.S. immigration policy can be divided into three phases, each with very different objectives and each resulting in new patterns of immigration. The first, leading up to the 1880s, was a time of relatively few restrictions on immigration. The country was expanding rapidly, and it was generally understood that a growing population was necessary to push the frontier forward. From 1880 to 1965, the

United States developed ever more restrictive policies on the number of immigrants that could enter in any given year. This period is marked by the creation of a national-origin quota system. It was a time of intense anti-immigrant sentiment, but also a period of rapid advancement in the standard of living for newly arrived immigrants. With the 1965 amendments to U.S. immigration law, an era of liberal policy began, and the national-origin system was altered so as to create equity between groups seeking to emigrate.

Pre-1880s

From its inception, the United States has truly been a nation of immigrants. The colonies were founded by refugees fleeing religious and ideological persecution. The early U.S. economy was fueled by the forced immigration of slave labor and the contract labor of indentured servants.

Despite a deeply ingrained ideology of openness and freedom, forged as each new wave of immigrants was integrated into American society, there was a great deal of nativism in the political rhetoric of the time. In particular, during the development of the two-party system, immigration policy played an important role in articulating opposing national party platforms.

The Democratic Party has often been considered the party of and for immigrants. Not only did Democratic politicians during this period tend to advocate a more liberal immigration policy but as new immigrants entered the country and settled in urban centers such as New York and Chicago, they funneled these newcomers into the party machine. Immigrant communities quickly became a rock bed of support. Irish and German immigrants established themselves as powerful voting blocs and were thus able to exercise some control over the direction of the Democratic Party platform (Daniels 1990).

1880–1965

Until the 1880s, U.S. immigration policy remained relatively open and, in the case of contract laborers, often encouraged immigration. In 1882, this era of openness came to an end. Economic instability brought on by rapid industrialization combined with social instability resulting from rapid urbanization caused increased unrest among many Americans. This unrest resulted in several important pieces of anti-immigrant legislation. While Democratic politicians attempted to protect the country's open immigration policy, there was overwhelming support for restrictive measures. The Chinese Exclusion Act of 1882, for example, resulted in the elimination of almost all Chinese migration to the

United States. The act, which was demanded by the Democratic Party's other growing source of support, the labor unions, was the first of several measures restricting Asian immigration; for example, the National Origins Act completely blocked Japanese immigration for the next 40 years (Mink 1986).

The Immigration Act of 1924, or National Origins Act, created an entirely new system for controlling the flow of immigrants into the country. Under the new law, visas were allocated based on national origin and determined as 2% of the U.S. population originating from that same nation according to 1890 census data. The 1924 measure effectively limited immigration to around 300,000 and controlled the composition of that immigration so that a majority of the newcomers were European (Daniels 1990).

While most immigration during this period was severely restricted, one category flourished. At the end of World War II, Europe was ravaged, and a large refugee population had been created. Victory in Europe left many Americans with renewed faith in democracy and a sense of moral responsibility for the rest of the world. As a result, there was a great deal of public support for resettling refugees in the United States. A bipartisan coalition in Congress passed the Displaced Persons Act of 1948, which admitted 205,000 refugees. The act was an extremely popular piece of legislation, so when Republicans claimed sole responsibility for the bill during that year's presidential campaign, the Democrats called for even more refugees to be admitted (Cafferty et al. 1983).

During the Cold War, refugees from political repression were also admitted in large numbers. This group of immigrants was met with ambivalence, though, as suspicions about Soviet infiltration increased. The Immigration and Nationality Act of 1952, also referred to as the McCarran–Walter Act, essentially continued the national-origin quota system but added a provision excluding communists. President Harry Truman vetoed the bill, arguing that the national-origin aspect "discriminates, deliberately and intentionally, against many of the peoples of the world" (Daniels 1990). The McCarran–Walter Act passed over Truman's veto, and it was another 13 years before a policy was enacted that did not discriminate on the basis of national origin.

1965–Present

The liberal politics of the 1960s and the resulting advances made during the civil rights movement led to a corresponding change in Americans' attitudes toward immigrants. Increased awareness of race and a growing national dialogue about institutional racism resulted in calls for a more enlightened immigration policy. By 1964, President Lyndon Johnson, in his State of the Union speech, was urging reform of federal immigration laws (Cafferty et al. 1983).

The next year, a series of amendments to the Immigration and Nationality Act drastically changed U.S. immigration policy by doing away with the national-origin quota system. The 1965 amendments, which ended years of strict limits on Asian immigration, caused a dramatic shift in immigration patterns and the racial makeup of America's immigrant population (Cafferty et al. 1983). The new policy also allowed immediate relatives of U.S. citizens to enter the country with very few restrictions. Current patterns of immigration to the United States are a direct result of the 1965 amendments.

One consequence of this more liberal immigration policy was that all attention became focused on the issue of illegal immigrants. In November 1986 a Democratic Congress enacted the Immigration Reform and Control Act (IRCA). Introduced by Senator Alan Simpson (R-Wyoming) and Representative Romano Mazzoli (D-Kentucky), the bill was a bipartisan effort to strengthen enforcement of existing immigration law. The most important aspect of the legislation, however, was that it combined sanctions for companies that employed illegal aliens with amnesty for illegal immigrants residing in the United States since 1981. Through IRCA, over 3 million illegal immigrants were accepted into the amnesty program and began the naturalization process (Daniels 1990).

Current debate on immigration policy centers on the issue of illegal immigrants. Nevertheless, campaign rhetoric in both parties has responded to growing public sentiment that restrictions even on legal immigration might be necessary. Measures such as the 1994 California state referendum Proposition 187 represent the first time that anti-immigrant sentiment has turned into the legislated denial of social services such as health care and education to the children of illegal immigrants.

The Democratic Party continues to advocate a liberal immigration policy and to oppose such restrictionist anti-immigrant measures as Proposition 187. But economic instability and a steady decline in real wages among middle-class Americans has caused many Democrats to question the party's immigration platform.

Edward W. Siskel

BIBLIOGRAPHY

Abrams, F. "American Immigration Policy: How Strait the Gate?" In *U.S. Immigration Policy*, ed. Richard Hofstetter. Durham: Duke University Press, 1984.

Cafferty, P., B. Chiswick, A. Greeley, and T. Sullivan. *The Dilemma of American Immigration: Beyond the Golden Door.* New Brunswick, NJ: Transaction Books, 1983.

Daniels, Roger. *Coming to America: A History of Immigration and Ethnicity in American Life.* New York: HarperCollins, 1990.

Foner, E. *Free Soil, Free Labor, Free Men: The Ideology of the Republican Party Before the Civil War.* New York: Oxford University Press, 1970.

Higham, J. *Strangers in the Land.* New York: Oxford University Press, 1977.

Kasinitz, P. *Caribbean New York: Immigrants and the Politics of Race.* Ithaca: Cornell University Press, 1992.

Mink, G. *Old Labor and New Immigrants in American Political Development: Union, Party, and State, 1875–1920.* Ithaca: Cornell University Press, 1986.

Seller, M. "Historical Perspectives on American Immigration Policy: Case Studies and Current Implications." In *U.S. Immigration Policy*, ed. Richard Hofstetter. Durham: Duke University Press, 1984.

Jews

Despite numbers of Jews that are moving toward the Republican Party, traditionally and continually Jews, as a voting bloc, vote Democratic. The Clinton position on the Middle East gives him much support among Jewish voters.

The likelihood of Dole's winning the Republican candidacy may make for even stronger Jewish Democratic ties, given the anti-Israel voting record of Dole, who, while supporting millions to Iraq in 1990, opposed loan guarantees to Israel to help Soviet Jewish settlers.

The age factor may also work against Dole in attracting the Jewish vote. Dole can do nothing about his age, but he is seeking to shore up his image with American Jewry with proposing the shift of the American Embassy from Tel Aviv to Jerusalem.

Jewish money is still mainly going to the Democrats, but with the Gingrich and Dole positions about relocating the embassy in Israel, the Democrats may be losing some of the shekels.

The National Jewish Democratic Council (NJDC), which claims representation of Jewry within the Democratic Party, seeks to influence politics within the areas of U.S.-Israeli relations, of course, but also in the area of school prayer, human rights, and social issues.

The NJDC has attacked the Dole legislation vis-à-vis the establishment of the embassy at Jerusalem as pure political pandering. But as this issue, important to all Jewry in either party, is being successfully addressed by the Republicans, the NJDC attack may be viewed by Jews as support of the Democratic Party over support of Jewish interests.

The Clinton Iranian embargo and ordered U.S. veto of the UN resolution concerning Israeli expropriation of land around Jerusalem, however, has helped the Democrats retain Jewish voters and contributors.

The growing dissatisfaction with governmental influence in business, Democratic tax-and-spend politics, and the decline of traditional values, held dear to Jewry (i.e., family and education), may be making for at least a partial switch of political allegiance.

There is growing Jewish support for the Republican political agenda and its exponents. Articles in Jewish newspapers are reappraising the Religious Right, long allies of the Republican Party, insofar as it concerns their perceived anti-Semitism and threat to Jewish ideals.

The Republican-oriented National Jewish Coalition has appeared to be more loyal to Jewish interests than the aforesaid NJDC, and as the younger and more conservative Jewish voters reexamine their views on the Republican Party, it is possible that there will be a weakening in the relationship between Jews and the Democrats.

W. Adam Mandelbaum

SEE ALSO Other Minorities

Labor

From the birth of the United States, labor and the Democratic Party seemed to have been a perfect fit.

In Thomas Jefferson and the Democratic-Republicans, the discontented artisans, mechanics, and laborers of the early Republic found a voice. They saw the young United States being controlled by money interests—wealthy merchants, speculators, and the landed gentry—and looked to the Jeffersonians, who espoused the virtues of the common man, for leadership. Jefferson's support of the Bill of Rights won him labor's favor, as did his nullification of the Alien and Sedition Acts.

Although the voting franchise was limited in 1800, in at least one state, where workers who met certain property qualifications could vote for the state assembly, labor made a difference in Jefferson's election. With labor's help, the Democratic-Republicans won control of New York City and with it control of the presidential electors of that state, which went to Jefferson. Winning New York was crucial to Jefferson's election.

During Jefferson's administration, democracy was extended in several states by the elimination of property qualifications for voting. As a voice of the common man, Jeffersonian Democracy was able to unite agrarian interests that were close to Jefferson's heart with those of the budding urban workers. It was a coalition that would carry the Democrats for a quarter century as James Madison and James Monroe followed Jefferson as president for two terms.

Labor was not enthusiastic at first with Andrew Jackson. But when he vetoed the Second Bank of the United States, labor became a major supporter of Jacksonian Democracy. The bank was viewed by labor as a tool for the rich against the working man, and when Jackson took his stand against the bank, labor enthusiastically endorsed him and his successor, Martin Van Buren. At this time, the Democratic-Republicans split along the line of the bank. Those in favor formed the Whig Party, while Jacksonians simply called themselves Democrats.

During the 1850s the newly formed Republican Party was able to make some gains among labor when it took charge of the antislavery movement. There was a fear that the extension of slavery would threaten some of the freedoms enjoyed by labor. Many laborers sided with the Republicans on the moral grounds that slavery in any form was wrong. Those who stayed with Democrats believed that Stephen Douglas and his party could deal with the slavery issue just as well as the Republicans and without threatening war.

As the Industrial Revolution hit full stride in the United States in the second half of the nineteenth century, labor was more interested in organizing and improving working conditions than in politics. The first national union was the Noble Order of the Knights of Labor, formed in Philadelphia in December 1869. It was an offshoot of the Philadelphia garment workers.

The Knights enjoyed early success in organizing labor, reaching a membership of 700,000 by the mid-1880s. The order, though, would lose its influence as a result of the Haymarket Square riot in Chicago on May 4, 1886. When one of the eight anarchists found guilty of inciting the riot had ties to the Knights, it crippled the union's reputation and ability to represent its members.

As the Knights' influence waned, the American Federation of Labor, headed by Samuel Gompers, became labor's most powerful union. The AFL differed from the Knights fundamentally in that they were more concerned with skilled than unskilled laborers. The AFL practiced craft unionism, an attempt to unionize only skilled workers by trade. In a time when the machine was costing more and more skilled laborers their jobs, this was leaving out a lot of unskilled workers.

The early goals of the Knights and AFL were higher

wages, workers' compensation, the 10-hour day, and child labor laws. Under Gompers, the AFL wanted to be politically neutral. He thought the best way for unions to achieve their goals was by staying out of politics and trying to change things from within. Unions saw both the Democratic and Republican parties as tools for big business and not at all interested in labor's needs. Neither party was taking up any of labor's concerns. That caused a flirtation with the idea of a third party, the Labor Party. At the height of this movement, Eugene V. Debs, the Socialist Party candidate for president, received 900,000 votes in the 1912 election. Beginning with the 1896 election, when William Jennings Bryan was the Democratic candidate for president and the platform he ran on took up populist cause, unions began to identify with the Democrats.

Labor began to turn to politics in the first years of the twentieth century when big business was able successfully to circumvent strikes through injunctions. The use of the injunction was crippling the unions' ability to organize and to use the strike as leverage. When the courts began to uphold the injunction, the unions looked for a political solution.

In the election of 1906, labor organizations made their first presidential endorsement, that of Bryan, who was committed to anti-injunction legislation. At the time when organized labor was struggling with what direction to take, urban liberalism was taking center stage. Responding to the excesses of industrial capitalism (the power of monopolies and wretched working conditions laborers had to deal with), the urban liberal reformers looked to a more interventionist government to come to the defense of the less fortunate in society. This interventionist government would take up many of labor's causes.

Democrat Woodrow Wilson, who had labor's support, was one of the leading reformers, and when he won the 1912 election, he ushered in the new era. Labor saw their support for Wilson pay off with the passing of the Clayton Act in 1914, which recognized labor's right to organize.

Labor did not move forward very far despite the legislation as World War I was followed by the prosperous 1920s. But that came crashing to an end with the Great Depression.

Before the New Deal, labor unions in the United States operated under heavy handicaps. Whenever labor faced off with management, as in the Homestead strike of the 1890s and the steel strike of 1919, the government either looked the other way or intervened on the side of management.

All that changed with Franklin Delano Roosevelt and the New Deal. Labor made significant progress with the National Industrial Recovery Act (NIRA) of 1933, but the real breakthrough came when Congress adopted the National Labor Relations Acts of 1935. The Wagner Act (named after its sponsor, Senator Robert F. Wagner of New York) strengthened the provisions of the NIRA. It declared that workers engaged in interstate commerce had the right to join labor unions and bargain collectively with employers. A new regulatory agency was created, the National Labor Relations Board, and was empowered to conduct elections by secret ballot within corporations so that workers could choose their own bargaining agents. The act required employers to recognize unions and bargain in good faith.

The rise of Big Labor, with its huge assist from the federal government, was another major step toward a mixed economy. Business would never again have the degree of autonomy it had enjoyed before the New Deal.

In the 1936 election, organized labor gave FDR more support than the movement had given earlier Democratic contenders. Labor liked the social welfare programs and government protection for the labor movement and wanted additional benefits. John L. Lewis's United Mine Workers contributed heavily to FDR's campaign. About 80% of union members voted for FDR. The New Deal profoundly altered industrial relations by throwing the weight of government behind the efforts to unionize workers. At the outset of the Great Depression, the American labor movement was an anachronism in the world with a tiny minority of factory workers unionized.

In a short period of time under the New Deal a new pattern emerged. Under the umbrella of the NIRA and Wagner Act, union organizers gained millions of recruits in such industries as steel, textiles, and automobiles. Employees won wage rises, reduction in hours, greater job security, freedom from tyranny of the company guard, and protection against arbitrary punishment. Workers, who were working seven days a week 12 hours a day, won concessions for paid vacations and sabbatical leaves.

Labor took advantage of its New Deal gains to reach unprecedented heights. In the late 1940s, led by Walter Reuther, the United Auto Workers was able to unionize Chevrolet and then Ford.

Not all was fine within organized labor as the conflict between craft unionism (which wanted to organize by craft; putting painters, electricians, welders or machinists in one union) and industrial unionism (which called for the mass production industries to organize everyone working within a plant, skilled and unskilled) led in 1935 to a split in the AFL. Led by Lewis and his Mine Workers United, the Congress of Industrial Organizations (CIO) was formed. It enjoyed immediate success because it included the unskilled and skilled laborers. It was also more politically active than the AFL. The first organizing manual for politics was published by the CIO in 1938 and it formed the first political action committee (PAC) in 1943.

The New Deal would align the Democrats and organized labor for the remainder of the century. The war years saw cooperation between labor and the government. Roosevelt sought to keep the home front running smoothly so that war production could reach its maximum. The president asked for and received a no-strike pledge from the unions to be honored while America was still at war. That pledge was kept except for two minor coal strikes. The blue-collar war effort was largely underappreciated. Workers agreed to longer hours and speed-ups, volunteered for swing shifts, and put their savings in war bonds to keep the war effort going.

When the war came to an end in 1945, labor was ready to regain the earnings and purchasing power it had lost during the war years. Anxious to get its workers pay raises and other benefits to make up for the sacrifices that had been made, unions became militant. By 1946, nearly 5 million workers were on strike at one time or another, creating serious problems for Harry Truman's administration. The turning point was the coal and railroad strike that threatened to bring the nation's transportation system to a standstill, forcing Truman to act. He earned the wrath of labor when, to stop the coal and railroad strikes of 1946, he threatened to draft all strikers into the military. He forced Lewis's hand and brought the strikes to an end. Despite their shaky start, Truman and labor would get along, and he won union support for reelection in 1948. It was veto of the restrictive Taft–Hartley Act, approved by a Republican-controlled Congress that was antiunion, that won Truman labor's favor. Repeal of the act became one of labor's major goals.

In the 1950s labor became very active politically and remained open to the party that best picked up its cause. The Democratic platforms of 1952 and 1956 called for a repeal of Taft–Hartley, putting the Democrats in line with labor. The Republicans paid no attention to that demand.

George Meany, president of the AFL, and Reuther, president of the CIO, both came to power in the early 1950s recognizing the need for labor to have a stronger voice, and the best way to achieve that goal was to merge the AFL-CIO. That happened on December 5, 1955. Labor now had a strong single voice. Meany

would become the first president of the AFL-CIO. While the Democrats did not win the White House against Eisenhower in 1952 and 1956, the party did gain control of Congress, and with labor's support, John F. Kennedy narrowly won the presidency in 1960. Labor was beginning to identify itself with the Democratic Party.

During this time, organized labor was at the height of its influence with more workers than ever unionized. During the administrations of Kennedy and Lyndon Johnson, progressive legislation such as Medicare, federal grants for rebuilding urban centers, federal aid to education, raising of the minimum wage, and civil rights laws were passed by Congress. The AFL-CIO's first official endorsement of a presidential candidate was the Democrat Hubert H. Humphrey in 1968.

With Republicans regaining the White House in 1968 with the election of Richard M. Nixon and controlling it for all but four years through 1992, organized labor saw its influence decreasing. With its power on the wane, union membership also declined. Unions became more concerned about solidifying the gains they had made in the previous 30 years than adding to membership. The low point was the Reagan era, when the White House was clearly antiunion. Early in his administration, Reagan fired the air traffic controllers who went on strike; that sent a message of hostility toward organized labor that would remain through the 1980s. Recession and restructural changes combined with the hostile political climate to diminish labor's influence.

Labor became more tied to the Democratic Party than ever in the 1980s and continued to support Democratic candidates for president and Congress. In 1984 AFL-CIO president Lane Kirkland decided that if labor was going to support the Democratic candidate for president, it would best serve its interest to be involved in the nominating process. Thus, labor lent its support to Walter Mondale during the primary season and used its power to deliver the vote to help nominate him. One-quarter of the delegates to the 1984 convention were from labor.

Labor helped elect Bill Clinton in 1992. Although the unions came out against the North American Free Trade Agreement (NAFTA) that Clinton pushed through Congress in 1992, he was generally on labor's side. Among his first acts as president were to pass a family leave bill and one prohibiting the practice of replacement workers. He also called for an increase in the minimum wage.

In 1995, with its numbers and influence continuing to dwindle, organized labor decided to strike back and return to its militancy of the 1930s. John Sweeney, president of the service workers union, challenged incumbent Lane Kirkland, who was seen as representing the old guard, and won the presidency of the AFL-CIO. Sweeney, who was looked upon as a militant in the way he aggressively ran his service workers union, ran on a platform demanding more unity and action on the part of labor and a drive to increase membership. With workers' wages stagnating over a period of years and downsizing by large corporations threatening job security, Sweeney saw the perfect scenario for labor's comeback.

Later in the year, the nation's Big Three unions, the automobile workers, the steel workers, and the machinists, announced that they were going to merge over a five-year period. This would create one giant union with 2.1 million members. The sheer numbers would give the union a lot of leverage.

Tim Morris

BIBLIOGRAPHY

Foner, Philip S. *The Policies and Practices of the American Federation of Labor, 1900–1909*. New York: International Publishers, 1964.

———. *Labor in the Progressive Era, 1910–1915*. New York: International Publishers, 1980.

Gould, Jean, and Lorena Hickok. *Walter Reuther—Labor's Rugged Individualist*. New York: Dodd, Mead, 1972.

Rayback, Joseph G. *A History of American Labor*. New York: Macmillan, 1966.

Robinson, Archie. *George Meany and His Times*. New York: Simon and Schuster, 1981.

Rubin, Richard L. *Party Dynamics—The Democratic Coalition and the Politics of Change*. New York: Oxford University Press, 1976.

Sitkoff, Harvard. *Fifty Years Later: The New Deal Evaluated*. New York: Knopf, 1985.

Shostak, Arthur B. *Robust Unionism*. Ithaca, NY: ILR Press, 1991.

The McGovern–Fraser Commission

Formally known as the Commission on Party Structure and Delegate Selection, the McGovern–Fraser Commission was established by the Democratic National Convention in 1968 to recommend reforms in the way the party selected its presidential nominees. South Dakota Senator George McGovern and Minnesota Representative Donald Fraser successively chaired the commission, from 1968 through 1972.

The commission emerged largely as a response by liberal, reform-minded Democrats to the party's em-

battled 1968 nomination contest. Vice President Hubert H. Humphrey of Minnesota won the party's nomination, despite vigorous protests from more liberal Democrats who charged that Humphrey had locked up the nomination by currying favor with party insiders. The reformers sought to open the nomination process to more democratic influences—fostering greater popular participation in the delegate selection process—through such devices as party primaries and caucuses. Their intent was to wrest control from party "bosses," who had frustrated the popular challenges mounted in 1968 by Robert Kennedy and Eugene McCarthy.

The commission's recommendations led to a sea change in Democratic presidential politics, completing a shift in the locus of party decision making from the traditional party regulars in convention to more rank-and-file Democratic activists and voters. It also established quotas for bringing minorities, women, and young people more fully into the party structure. These reforms undermined the strength of the party insiders, leading to conditions in which presidential candidates had to develop popularly based followings in order to secure the Democratic nomination.

Russell L. Riley

Media

Like the Republican Party, the Democratic Party has had a changing relationship with the media—sometimes feeling that its leaders could manipulate the media and that Democrats were well represented in the media; at other times fearing that the media were a hostile outside enemy out to destroy the Democratic Party and its leaders. The changes are attributable in part to changes in the Democratic Party and in part to changes in the media.

Among the issues that led to the Democratic Party's concern with the media were perceived incompatibility between national security and media independence, regulation of pornographic and indecent material, attempts to ensure fairness in the political process, and regulation of new forms of technology. The record generally reflects James Madison's inclination that "*absolute* restrictions in cases that are doubtful, or where emergencies may override them, ought to be avoided."

During its first years, after the Democratic-Republican Party was founded by Antifederalists in 1794, the Democratic-Republican Party defended the media, especially its party media, against Federalist attack. The origins of what we today refer to as the Democratic Party may be traced to a breach between the Federalist Alexander Hamilton and Thomas Jefferson. The breach was more than personal: the Federalists would generally advocate the manufacturing interests of people in the North, the Democratic-Republicans agrarian interests and the South.

Indeed, the First Amendment to the Constitution, under which the media claim independence from government interference, resulted from pressure by Thomas Jefferson, a leading promoter of independence from Britain, vice president under his rival and Federalist President John Adams (1797–1801), and president from 1801 to 1809. (It is important to remember, however, that the First Amendment was not applied to state and local governments until 1925; hence party differences at state and local levels remained very significant until that date.)

On a trip to New York in 1791 Jefferson and James Madison had persuaded the poet Philip Freneau to come to Philadelphia to start an opposition (to the Federalist, and later Democratic-Republican) newspaper. They also gained the support of an important civic organization, Tammany Hall, and of politicians who would later be the bulwark of the Democratic-Republican Party in New York, including Governor George Clinton.

The Alien and Sedition Acts of 1798 were passed because of concern with a possible war with France and were supported by members of the Federalist Party, with the notable exception of John Marshall, who thought that the Sedition Act would not be constitutional. Every single Democratic-Republican legislator, with the exception of James Sullivan, thought that it would be unconstitutional. That act made it punishable by a fine or imprisonment, among other things to "write, print, utter, or publish . . . any false, scandalous, or malicious writing or writings against the government . . . with the intent to defame."

Democratic-Republican editors of four leading newspapers as well as some Democratic-Republican officeholders were indicted and prosecuted under the act, which lapsed the day before Jefferson's inauguration. The outgoing Federalist secretary of state, Timothy Pickering, had planned to shut down all leading pro-Jefferson newspapers in the country.

It would be tempting to label Jefferson and the precursors of today's Democratic Party as the advocates of unqualified press freedom, but it would not be accurate. Indeed, not long after all those prosecuted under the Sedition Act were pardoned by the Jefferson administration, six of Jefferson's political opponents were charged with common-law seditious libel. And part of the Democrat-Republican argument against the

Sedition Act was that prosecutions were appropriately brought at the state and not the federal level.

Restrictions on the media in the name of "national security" were again pronounced during the Civil War. (In the intervening years there were few restrictions, although Democratic-Republican President Andrew Jackson tried without success to ban the abolitionist newspaper, *Liberator*, edited by William Garrison, from the mails.) Again the Democrats (there was now a separate Republican Party which believed in the Union's fighting a civil war against southern secessionists) generally criticized the restrictions. Papers were closed, editors were jailed, and presses were confiscated. The invention of the telegraph sped communication from the battlefield to home newpapers; hence the government's fear that reporting would damage national security was heightened.

Typical of congressional votes was a May 1864 motion to suspend the House Rules, allowing consideration of a resolution condemning the seizure of two New York newspapers' offices. The motion failed, but every Democrat voted for it. During Reconstruction, government controls on southern newspapers continued, lest their editors try to foment a new rebellion.

Democrats joined Republicans in supporting the Spanish-American War, dubbed by Secretary of State John Hay as "a splendid little war." Indeed the vote on appropriations to support that war was unanimous. William Jennings Bryan, a prominent Democrat, was colonel of a National Guard regiment, and former members of the Confederate militia played leading roles in the U.S. effort.

Critics held the "yellow press," and especially the influential Republican William Randolph Hearst, responsible. The claim that the media could incite violence has been echoed by pacifists, who claim that the media stir up passions for war, then sound caution during a later phase. A minority of Democrats agreed with Senator George Hoar of Massachussetts and explicitly opposed imperialism, in which they contended the media played a large role.

During most of the major U.S. wars of the twentieth century, by contrast, Democratic presidents were in office. During World War I, most Democrats supported the Wilson administration in setting up a federal censorship board; the majority Democratic Congress passed a Sedition Act (to control media criticism of the government) and an Espionage Act (to control media reports that enemies might find useful), which are still in force today. There were approximately 2,000 prosecutions brought under the Espionage Act; about 45% of those prosecuted were convicted. In addition,

President Wilson authorized the seizure of all wireless communication.

During World War II, a voluntary press code limited the reporting of war and economic information. The Smith Act (Howard W. Smith was a member of Congress from Virginia) was enacted to prevent the promulgation of doctrines aimed at overthrowing the U.S. government, but received little use against the media (although much use in paving the way for the internment of Japanese Americans) until after the war. And during the wars in Korea and Indochina, many Democrats supported censorship, infiltration, or disinformation to stop what they viewed as unfair criticisms.

Democratic as well as Republican administrations continued COINTELPRO (counterintelligence program), whose tactics included the fabrication of letters to the editor of newspapers of suspicious organizations, infiltration, and the use of agents provocateurs. The program originated during the Eisenhower administration but was used by both Democratic and Republican leaders against opponents of U.S. policies in Indochina. It was eventually investigated by a legislative committee led by Democratic Senator Frank Church of Idaho. Acts carried out during the Johnson administration included a break-in at the headquarters of the Socialist Workers Party, reported in party organs but given scant coverage in the major media. The attacks on dissident media at the national level were accompanied by similar police activities in several cities, including Los Angeles, Minneapolis, Memphis, New York, Chicago, Detroit, and Seattle.

To cover the war, a reporter had to be accredited, and there were fifteen types of information (including unannounced troop movements and casualty figures) that could not be reported without government approval.

The 1968 election found friends and enemies in both major political parties. The Democratic convention was held in Chicago, where the mayor, Richard Daley, accused the media of giving comfort to the enemy. The respected Columbia Broadcasting System anchor Walter Cronkite referred to the Chicago police, who had arrested or attacked more than 20% of the reporters covering the convention, as "thugs." Cynics saw so little difference between Humphrey and Nixon that they thought an appropriate response to the Republican campaign slogan "Nixon's the One" was "Hubert's the Other."

Nixon won the election, and his mutual animosity with the media continued. It reached its height when the administration sought unsuccessfully to stop publication of the "Pentagon Papers"; the attempt failed in part because Democratic Senator Mike Gravel read from the papers at length (as a member of Congress, Gravel enjoyed immunity from prosecution). The Supreme Court did not argue that prior restraint of the newspapers was unconstitutional; instead, they argued that the Nixon administration had not met its heavy burden of proof. At the Senate impeachment hearings, Democratic Senator Sam Ervin emerged as a champion of constitutional rights, including press freedom.

Reaction to what were perceived as the excessive actions of a Republican administration out of control led to new protections for the media. Largely in response to a search of the newsroom of the *Stanford Daily*, Democrats enacted the Privacy Protection Act of 1980.

With Republican leadership of the last stages of the war in Indochina, and of the interventions in Grenada, Panama, and the Persian Gulf, most Democrats became critics of controls on the media, and also of many covert operations, to which media access was impossible. In 1982 many Democrats tried unsuccessfully to block the passage of legislation making it a federal crime to publish anything they have reason to know will disclose the identity of U.S. intelligence agents.

When the Reagan administration invaded Grenada in 1983, it ordered an unprecedented 48-hour news blackout. Criticism of the blackout from Democrats and others led to the appointment of a panel recommending that press pools accompany future U.S. interventions, and news not be blacked out.

During the Gulf War, press pools were used with general support but some criticism from Democratic leaders. Similarly, press pools were used when the Democrat-led Clinton administration intervened in Somalia, Haiti, and Bosnia.

Notable Democrats were, therefore, proponents as well opponents of control of the media in the name of national security. They were also proponents and opponents of attempts to use the media to promote perceived national security interests. Democratic administrations favored the use of the media for propaganda during World War II and during the Cold War, especially through Radio Free Europe and Radio Liberty. Today one can find Democrats who support the funding of foreign radio broadcasts, including Radio Marti, which broadcasts to Cuba.

For the majority of American history, Democratic politicians endorsed the principles codified in the Comstock Laws (for one-star Union General Anthony Comstock) and previously defined through the English *Hicklin* case of 1868, whereby material was obscene if isolated passages could produce prurient or lustful thoughts in a particularly susceptible person.

Indecent or pornographic material was a local matter unless interstate commerce was involved, as it was when the mails were used or material was broadcast on radio or television. Attitudes toward indecent material and pornography became a litmus test for Supreme Court justices, with Democratic senators more likely to allow the media to disseminate questionable materials. Indecent material may not be obscene. The key is that it is "patently offensive" and either sexual or excretory.

William Brennan was nominated by a Republican, Dwight Eisenhower, partly to attract bipartisan support in the 1956 election. Brennan's working to fashion wider bounds for free expression came as a disappointment to Eisenhower. Another Democratic justice who worked to widen the bounds of permissible expression was Abe Fortas, nominated by President Lyndon Johnson. Antipornography forces worked against Fortas's confirmation, and when they were unsuccessful, pressured him into resigning.

The election of Richard Nixon partly represented public endorsement of his pledge to appoint Supreme Court judges who, in marked contrast to Democratic appointees, would allow less latitude for pornographers. Democratic legislators were more likely than Republicans to object to attacks on the media by Nixon and his first vice president, Spiro Agnew, and to object to child pornography legislation and the report issued by a commission headed by Edwin Meese, President Ronald Reagan's attorney general, linking pornography to crime. It was, however, during Carter's Democratic administration that the Protection of Children Against Sexual Exploitation Act of 1977 was adopted (with support from both major parties), and some Democrats in Minneapolis supported an ordinance proposed by local feminists that would have allowed for civil suits against pornographers. (Mayor Donald Fraser, also a Democrat, vetoed the measure.)

Given the restrictive mood in the country, prominent Democrats urged the media to be "prudent." When the National Endowment for the Arts was attacked, Robert Byrd of West Virginia, who was then Senate majority leader, declared: "if the endowments and the institutions they fund do not take heed . . . the Congress will just have to stop its funding. . . ."

Current concerns include the dissemination of "cyberporn" over the Internet, to which minors have access, and pornography on television and in the movies. Democrats and Republicans have tended to endorse media efforts to find a "safe haven," hours during which children are usually not in the audience; hence more explicit materials can be disseminated. There is also some protective concern with truth in ad-

vertising and with misleading though true advertising, primarily expressed through the Federal Trade Commission. But the general trend within both major political parties has been to advocate deregulation.

Attempts to make the political process more fair included the Fairness Doctrine of the 1950s, codified by Congress in 1959 amendments to the Communications Act, the Equal Opportunity Doctrine, the Zapple Doctrine, and right-of-reply laws. At the national level, the desire for political fairness was embodied in the 1934 Communications Act (although that act makes explicit reference instead to national defense, and safety of life and property in requiring that broadcasters operate in the "public interest") adopted during a Democratic administration, that of Franklin Roosevelt.

The act superseded the Radio Act of 1927 and established the Federal Communications Commission, which, in theory, although not in practice, is immune to partisan pressure. At the point the statute was adopted, the isssue was not whether communication should be regulated, but how, since the number and strength of radio stations were proliferating rapidly.

The Fairness Doctrine referred to the obligation of broadcasters to "provide reasonable opportunity for the discussion of conflicting views." There were two parts to the obligation: (1) to spend a reasonable amount of time discussing controversial issues; and (2) to do so fairly, that is, to give some coverage to every side of the controversy. It assumed that there was a scarcity of radio frequencies and that there could be a limited number of television stations. Because advances in cable television technology created new possibilities for many more stations, and because members of the commission felt uncomfortable with regulating the content of broadcasters that did not comply, it was not enforced after 1985, when the Federal Communications Commission issued a report critical of the doctrine. That report was bolstered by judicial decisions, and by President Reagan with his veto of an attempt by the then majority Democratic Congress, which sought to reinstate it. Despite the repeal, licensees were still obligated to serve the "public interest."

Similarly, equal rates are to be charged political candidates for advertising, and if one candidate is allowed to use the airwaves, her or his opponents can demand equal time. Democrats have tended to argue for a wide definition of "use"; some unsuccessfully argued when Ronald Reagan was a candidate that each showing of one of his movies was a "use."

In 1971, despite Democratic opposition, the requirements that candidates be allowed to advertise at the lowest unit cost were loosened so that the rules applied only to a short period before elections.

Food and drug advertising through the media is regulated by the Federal Trade Commission. In general, Democrats have been less willing than Republicans to apply free speech arguments to commercial speech and more willing to regulate advertising, particularly advertising directed toward children.

Democrats as well as Republicans could object to what they perceived to be unfair media attacks. During the 1990s, Democratic President Bill Clinton objected to attacks from conservative talk radio and talk television hosts, including the Republican Rush Limbaugh.

Many Democrats saw public broadcasting as a guarantor of fairness. Spokespeople for controversial causes had difficulty competing in the marketplace and gaining access to the media. Most Democratic members of Congress therefore would consistently vote to continue or increase government funding of broadcasting. But Republican leaders, including Speaker of the House Newt Gingrich, argued that with new technology people had access to many sources of information, and controversial viewpoints had many outlets in the media. The original rationale for public broadcasting was therefore no longer valid.

The concern about the impact of the media on the political process (indeed, the saying that the four branches of the American government are ABC, NBC, CBS, and CNN is probably incorrect only in that it excludes Fox) reflects the importance of new technology. Radio brought with it a need to regulate the number of stations and how they would be used. Motion pictures brought concerns about where and how explicit sexual material would be shown.

With the arrival of new media came increasing concern with the susceptibility of children, reflected in advertising legislation as well as antipornography legislation. Although a simple analysis would suggest that Democrats made more use of Fair Trade Commission than Republicans, on closer analysis deregulation took place both in the Democratic Carter administration and in the Republican Reagan administration.

A facile conclusion would be that Democrats have been friends to the media. The reality is more complex, with the media being allied with Democratic politicians when the Democrats were not in control. In general, the advent of new media contributed to a decline in the influence of the Democratic Party and party government. No longer was it possible to make secret deals in a smoke-filled room. Now, if officeholders were blackballed for not following the party line, the public would know about it. Leaders were expected to

hold regular press conferences, to be on the Internet, and to deliver major speeches when the television audience was large. A candidate who hid things (for instance, drug experimentation, finances, or a war record) was thought to have something to hide.

The media have changed, but some elements have remained the same. In general, those at the bottom of the media hierarchy are likely to be Democrats; those at the top are not. We can generally expect that most reporters and correspondents will be Democrats, although only a minority of publishers and owners will be. In this respect, the media are similar to American society in general.

Arthur Blaser

BIBLIOGRAPHY

Carter, T. Barton, Juliet Lushbough Dee, Martin J. Gaynes, and Harvey L. Zuckman. *Mass Communication Law in a Nutshell.* 4th ed. St. Paul, MN: West, 1994.

Emerson, Thomas. *The System of Free Expression.* New York: Vintage, 1970.

Lemert, James B. *News Verdicts, the Debates and Presidential Campaigns.* Westport, CT: Greenwood, 1991.

Levy, Leonard W. *Emergence of a Free Press.* New York: Simon and Schuster, 1985.

Linfield, Michael. *Freedom under Fire: U.S. Civil Liberties in Times of War.* Boston: South End Press, 1990.

Nacos, Brigitte L. *The Press, Presidents and Crises.* New York: Columbia University Press, 1989.

Press, Charles, and Kenneth VerBurg. *American Politicians and Journalists.* Glenview, IL: Scott, Foresman, 1989.

Sabato, Larry J. *Feeding Frenzy: How Attack Journalism Has Transformed American Politics.* New York: Free Press, 1991.

The Minimum Wage

In 1938 Democratic President Franklin D. Roosevelt introduced the minimum wage as part of his New Deal with the Fair Labor Standards Act. Since then, Congress has significantly revised and expanded its terms, relying not only on general bipartisan backing but also on loyal support from elected members of the Democratic Party.

Despite frequent bipartisan backing, Democrats have found themselves fighting for increases in the minimum wage over objections from conservative Republicans, free-market libertarians, and business groups, who argue that a higher wage will raise unemployment and inflate prices, actually hurting the people that proponents say would be helped. Opponents of increasing the minimum wage also say it will drive up all wages. Many conservative

Republican members of Congress favor a policy of letting the free market establish wages, and some maintain there should be no minimum wage at all.

Most Democrats reject this reasoning. They maintain that raising the minimum wage does not result in higher unemployment or inflation. Neither does it push up all wages, they say. In fact, the Democrats point out, a recent increase in California's minimum wage actually led to less unemployment. Democrats also argue that every worker has the right to earn a subsistence wage.

President Bill Clinton has led the Democrats' drive during the mid-1990s to raise the minimum wage. He proposed that it be raised by 90 cents over two years, from its current $4.25 an hour to $5.15 an hour.

Principal Democratic sponsors of minimum-wage legislation in Congress have included Senator Edward M. Kennedy, a Massachusetts Democrat who is on the Committee on Labor and Human Resources, and Representative Augustus Hawkins, a California Democrat on the House Committee on Education and Labor. Senator Kennedy, in particular, has long fought to increase the minimum wage. He and his fellow Democrats argue that inflation has undermined the purchasing power of the minimum wage and that many entry-level workers will be condemned to a less-than-subsistence wage unless the minimum is expanded.

Kennedy and Hawkins's chief opponents in the battle over raising the minimum wage have been Senator Orrin Hatch, a conservative Republican from Utah who sits on the Committee on Labor and Human Resources, and Representative Steve Bartlett, a Texas Republican on the House Committee on Education and Labor.

Representative Martin Olav Sabo of Minnesota, the ranking Democrat on the House Budget Committee, has taken President Clinton's proposal even further. He introduced a measure that would not only raise the rate by more than the president's proposal but also would limit the tax deductibility of executive compensation at 25 times that of the company's lowest-paid employee.

Steve Hoenisch

BIBLIOGRAPHY

"An Honest Day's Pay?" *The Economist*, September 3, 1988.
Du Pont, Pete. "Pay Hazard." *National Review*, May 1, 1995.
McClenahen, John S. "Take a Hike: A Rise in the Minimum Wage Is Unlikely in 1995." *Industry Week*, March 6, 1995.
Mencimer, Stephanie. "Take a Hike: The Minimum Wage and Welfare Reform." *New Republic*, May 23, 1994.
"Wages of Politics." *The Economist*, March 18, 1989.

Nominating Conventions

Political scientist V.O. Key Jr. once said that "the national convention represents the solution by American parties of the problem of uniting scattered points of political leadership in support of candidates for the Presidency and Vice Presidency. Thus, it is the basic element of national party apparatus" (Key 1964, 396). National conventions were first used by parties to nominate presidential candidates in 1831, and, with some variation, national conventions remain an important institution in presidential nominating politics.

In the early days of the republic, congressional caucuses—meetings of a party's members of Congress—were the predominant means by which nominees for the presidency and vice presidency were selected. In 1831, as part of the democratizing spirit of the Jacksonian era, the first national party conventions were held. The first such convention was held by the Antimasonic Party in 1831; this relatively inconsequential party established the institution and many procedures that would be adopted by future party conventions (David, Goldman, and Bain 1960, 18).

The Democratic-Republican Party (which would become the Democratic Party) held its first national convention on May 21 and 22, 1832. The agenda of this convention really had little to do with the nomination of the Democratic-Republican presidential candidate; President Andrew Jackson was assured the renomination of his party. Instead, the convention was held to decide who would receive the vice presidential nomination. President Jackson had sought to dump Vice President John C. Calhoun in favor of Secretary of State Martin Van Buren. Under the congressional caucus system, Calhoun would most assuredly have secured renomination as the vice presidential candidate, but Jackson used the convention to circumvent the prior method of selecting nominees as well as to legitimate his own choice for vice president (Shafer 1988, 10).

Conventions would soon flex their capacity as authoritative party organizations by exercising the definitive power over presidential nominations. In 1844, the Democratic Convention, unable to reach consensus on any favored candidate, selected the first "dark-horse" candidate in James K. Polk of Tennessee. Polk's "nomination marked the coming of age of the convention as an institution capable of creating as well as of ratifying consensus within the party" (Key 1964, 398). And in 1856, the Democratic Party deposed a sitting president, replacing President Franklin Pierce with James Buchanan as the party's nominee.

FUNCTIONS AND RULES OF DEMOCRATIC CONVENTIONS

Through conventions, parties attempted to build consensus around both the party's nominations and its program. Furthermore, conventions represented a democratic and more representative alternative to the congressional caucus system. Many convention rules have been aimed at these goals of intraparty consensus and democratic representativeness. The basic rules of conventions concern the apportionment of delegates among states, the manner in which delegate votes are registered, and the number of votes needed to secure a candidate's nomination.

Until the 1944 Democratic Convention, Democrats apportioned delegates to the convention based on the number of representatives and senators each state had in Congress. In 1940, the Democrats approved a rule for the 1944 convention in which they would give two bonus votes to each state that the Democratic candidate for president had carried in the previous election; the number of bonus votes was increased to four in the succeeding convention. This system of bonus votes was instituted to reward states in which Democratic performance was strong. A system of bonus votes represents an attempt to reward stronger party organization at the expense of equal representation for each state.

From its first convention in 1831, the Democratic Party employed what was known as the "unit rule," which allowed a state delegation to cast all its votes for the candidate supported by the majority of the delegation. Because minority interests within state delegations have their voices muted by this rule, it has proven to be quite controversial. In 1960, Paul T. David and colleagues reported that the unit rule had been "abandoned by a number of states that formerly practiced it" (David, Goldman, and Bain 1960, 202). In 1968, the Democratic Convention in Chicago voted to abolish this rule.

Finally, in an effort to achieve and maintain consensus around its nominees, the Democratic Party instituted a "two-thirds rule," which required that a candidate receive two-thirds of the party's delegates in order to receive the nomination. This requirement made for many long, multiballot—often acrimonious—Democratic conventions. The two-thirds rule was, however, "viewed as a boon to the South since it allowed that region a virtual veto power over any possible nominee" (Congressional Quarterly 1983, 13). This rule was eliminated in 1936. In exchange for losing its virtual veto over party nominations, the southern wing of the party was given the concession of a bonus system of delegate apportionment (discussed above).

NOMINATION BATTLES

Through much of American history, party conventions performed that primary function of nominating presidential and vice presidential candidates. These rules, as well as a traditional lack of cohesion in the Democratic Party, conspired to create many significant nomination battles. The Democratic National Convention of 1844 provided a notable contest. A former president, Martin Van Buren, was favored to receive his third nomination in the 1844 convention. Two factors—one substantive, one structural—worked against Van Buren, however. The substantive factor concerned an untimely letter published by Van Buren opposing the annexation of Texas. This issue, coupled with the Democrats' continuation of the convention's two-thirds rule, would keep Van Buren from securing the Democratic nomination. Knowing two-thirds was going to be a difficult burden to meet, Van Burenites sought to do away with the rule. But Van Buren lost some critical support on this structural matter as a result of the letter on annexation. On the convention vote on the two thirds rule, "the critical vote was Virginia's. Virginia had come to the convention predominantly pro–Van Buren but was turning away from him as a result of his position against annexation. . . . When Virginia returned to the floor [after deliberation], the vote stood 131 for and 116 against the [two-thirds] rule. Virginia's 17 votes were added to the 131 rather than to the 116 as expected and the two thirds rule carried" (David, Goldman, and Bain 1960, 22). Van Buren received a majority of the delegates on the first seven ballots at the 1844 convention, but was unable to muster enough support to meet the two-thirds requirement. Although he had not received any votes on the first seven ballots, James K. Polk was offered as a compromise choice, receiving 44 votes on the eighth ballot. By the ninth ballot, Polk secured the two-thirds needed for nomination and thus became the first "dark-horse" candidate in the history of American conventions.

Sectional differences over the issue of slavery marked the Democratic National Convention of 1860. This convention has been described as "one of the longest, most turbulent and mobile conventions in Democratic history" (Congressional Quarterly 1983, 16). The convention first met in Charleston, South Carolina. After a platform battle between supporters of front-runner Senator Stephen Douglas and southern Democrats was won by the Douglas faction, several southern delegations bolted the convention. But Douglas was unable to secure the nomination of the convention. After 57 ballots, the Charleston convention was deadlocked; Democrats adjourned to meet two months later in Baltimore. After fights in Baltimore over the credentials of delegations from Alabama and Louisiana, the delegations of several southern states left the convention. Douglas would receive the nomination of the remaining Democrats, while these "seceders" held their own convention and nominated Vice President John C. Breckinridge as their presidential candidate. Although Douglas would finish second to Lincoln in the popular vote, he would finish fourth—behind Breckinridge and John Bell of the Constitutional Union Party—in the Electoral College vote.

After selecting its nominee on the 44th ballot in 1920, the Democratic Party convened its 1924 convention, which would prove even more contentious. According to V.O. Key Jr., the 1924 Democratic convention "was a savage bout beautiful to behold." The battle for the 1924 Democratic nomination was between Alfred E. Smith and William G. McAdoo. "Behind Smith were arrayed the urban, Catholic, and 'liberal' . . . elements of the party. McAdoo had the support of the southern, rural, dry, Protestant sectors" (Key 1964, 184). Seventeen days and 103 roll calls later, the bitterly divided convention nominated John W. Davis as its compromise choice. Smith would get the party's nomination in 1928, but the divisions evident in the 1924 convention would help Herbert Hoover secure victory over Smith in the 1928 general election.

One convention illustrative of the limitations of nominating conventions as political institutions was the Democratic Convention of 1948. Because of a civil rights plank in the Democratic platform, half of the Alabama delegation and the entire Mississippi delegation walked out of the convention. In addition to this bolt, the convention "found itself unable to make a nomination that all the state organizations regarded as binding. The Democratic parties of Mississippi, South Carolina, Louisiana, and Alabama had a 'Democratic' candidate other than that of the national convention" (Key 1964, 431). These states nominated J. Strom Thurmond as the "Dixiecratic" presidential candidate.

The Democrats conducted one of the first drafts of a nominee in 1952 by selecting Adlai Stephenson as their candidate. This convention is significant not only for this reason but also because it seems to have been—along with the Republican's 1952 convention—one of the last conventions wherein the presidential nomina-

tion was not decided prior to the convention. After 1952, "no convention was to construct a nominating majority within its confines; no nominating majority was to require so much as a second ballot to confirm its existence" (Shafer 1988, 8–9).

THE 1968 CONVENTION AND THE REFORM ERA

This is not to say that nominating conventions have been uneventful or unimportant since 1952. Few conventions in American history have been as acrimonious as the 1968 Democratic National Convention in Chicago. The controversies involved both procedural and substantive matters. Procedurally, there were "an unprecedented number of [credential] challenges, involving delegates from fifteen states." The battles over credentials often involved the seating of McCarthy supporters, but most often the real points of controversy were "racial imbalance, the party loyalty issue, or a combination of both" (Congressional Quarterly 1983, 109). In most cases, the traditional delegations were seated. Another procedural battle—this one won by the more liberal forces of McCarthy and McGovern—was the defeat of the unit rule for the convention.

The substantive controversies of the 1968 convention centered on the Vietnam War and the conflicts between young Democratic protesters and the Chicago police outside the convention hall. This bitter division in Chicago was in many ways a portrait of the division within the Democratic Party at the time. This division manifested itself inside the convention hall as well. Comparing the convention to the riots in the streets of Chicago, Norman Ornstein said: "Inside, the scene at the most famously divisive convention in modern times was only slightly more civil" (Ornstein 1995).

The history of Democratic conventions since 1968 has been one of perpetual reform. A number of reform commissions have sought to balance the need for consensus and party with the desire for representativeness. The first such commission was the McGovern–Fraser Commission, "which rewrote Democratic delegation rules prior to the 1972 elections." The purpose of this commission "was to take control of the presidential nomination away from state and local party officials as well as from national officeholders, and give it over to party activists attached to candidates" (Polsby and Wildavsky 1988, 107).

In an effort to redress some of the more controversial actions of the McGovern–Fraser Commission, a commission chaired by Baltimore City Councilwoman Barbara Mikulski was established to alter the rules for the 1976 Democratic Convention. Although the Mikulski Commission abolished quotas for various demographic groups, "the anticipated gutting of the [McGovern–Fraser] reforms never took place" (Crotty 1978, 252). In fact, by making the reforms of McGovern–Fraser less controversial, the Mikulski Commission solidified the position of these reforms within the party. The Winograd Commission, established four years later, enhanced the party's commitment to affirmative action, mandating that half the 1980 convention delegates be women. Each of these commissions placed an emphasis on increased representativeness at the potential cost of a loss of party control.

For the first time since the McGovern–Fraser Commission, the Hunt Commission, which established rules for the 1984 convention, attempted to secure more power for party officials in the nominating process by establishing a system of rewarding delegates for primary elections winners and superdelegate positions for party and elected officials. Since the Hunt Commission, changes have been made in the proportion of superdelegates, but the increased role of party officials in the convention seems to mark the 1980s as the Democrats' commitment to more representation in convention decision making marked the 1970s.

CONTEMPORARY CONVENTIONS

The most crucial change in conventions since World War II has been the lack of power to nominate candidates. Continuing the democratizing trends in the presidential nominating process, both the Democratic and the Republican parties have increasingly employed presidential primaries to determine the party's nominee. Often by the time of the convention, one candidate has secured the party's nomination. Thus, conventions no longer nominate presidential candidates. At best, they legitimize the choice made by primary voters. Nelson Polsby notes: "The institution of the national party convention . . . has been transformed. Instead of a body of delegates from the state parties meeting to ratify the results of a complex series of negotiations conducted by party leaders at the convention, the convention is now a body dominated by candidate enthusiasts and interest group delegates who meet to ratify a choice made prior to the convention mostly through primary elections" (Polsby 1983, 75–76).

Simply because they no longer have the power to nominate candidates does not mean that conventions are unimportant. They still represent a forum in which party disputes can be resolved and, perhaps more important, they represent a highly publicized campaign commercial for the party's nominee. Polsby claims that "today national conventions survive primarily as spectacle—an ingathering of the multitudes who by their good behavior can reward their foreordained nominee with favorable publicity, or by their bad behavior can cripple the party's ensuing presidential campaign" (Polsby 1983, 77). Norman Ornstein has echoed this point: "in the television age, the convention has also become an easy way for voters who normally tune out politics to judge the nominees and assess their mettle and the state of their organization." Ornstein claims that, at least since 1964, the party that has the smoothest, least acrimonious convention is victorious in the general election (Ornstein 1995).

Whether it is, as Ornstein implies, that smooth conventions lead to success as a result of their television value is still in question. An alternative hypothesis is that smooth conventions are indicative of the intraparty consensus and stability requisite for general election success. Perhaps the convention reflects the state of the national party. When the party is relatively homogeneous, the convention will be orderly. But when there is deep division within the party, that division will likely be reflected in the party's convention. And it is this division, rather than or in addition to the public's perception of division, that harms a party's attempt to win the general election.

Douglas Harris

SEE ALSO Presidential Nominations and Elections, Primary Elections

BIBLIOGRAPHY
Congressional Quarterly. *National Party Conventions, 1831–1980*. Washington, DC: CQ Press, 1983.
Crotty, William J. *Decision for the Democrats: Reforming the Party Structure*. Baltimore: Johns Hopkins University Press, 1978.
David, Paul T., Ralph M. Goldman, and Richard C. Bain. *The Politics of National Party Conventions*. Washington, DC: Brookings Institution, 1960.
Davis, James W. *National Conventions in an Age of Party Reform*. Westport, CT: Greenwood Press, 1983.
Key, V.O., Jr. *Politics, Parties and Pressure Groups*. 5th ed. New York: Crowell, 1964.
Ornstein, Norman. "Who Will Win the White House?" *Fortune*, October 30, 1995.
Polsby, Nelson W. *Consequences of Party Reform*. Oxford: Oxford University Press, 1983.
Polsby, Nelson W., and Aaron Wildavsky. *Presidential Elections*. 7th ed. New York: Free Press, 1988.
Shafer, Byron E. *Bifurcated Politics: Evolution and Reform in the National Party Convention*. Cambridge: Harvard University Press, 1988.

Other Minorities

The inclusion of religious and ethnic minorities has always been an important, though paradoxical, aspect of the Democratic Party. Democrats have been more likely to accept and recruit groups at the outer edge of U.S. society than have their opponents. While Federalists, Whigs, and Republicans emphasized the need for public order and economic growth, Democrats demanded social and economic equality. Though the party's belief in equality was a radical idea in the eighteenth century, it was limited to white men. It is ironic that as the Democratic Party championed the revolutionary philosophy of full equality for white male ethnic minorities and immigrants, it also became the foundation for white supremacy during the nineteenth century. In the late twentieth century, most Democrats rejected the premise of white male supremacy and expanded the party's emphasis on political and social equality to include all citizens. Consequently, most Hispanic and Asian Americans have gravitated to the Democratic Party, expanding its diverse base of supporters.

There is another irony about the role of minorities in the Democratic Party. While the party has benefited from the support of new religious and/or ethnic minority groups, this support has often been transitory. As religious or ethnic minority groups acculturate and gain acceptance, they lose a sense of being a minority and fall into the core culture advocated by conservatives. These former minority groups then move to the opposing party. (African Americans have been the only exception, moving from the Republican to the Democratic Party.) One major dilemma of the Democratic Party has been how to keep the support of older minority groups, such as Catholics and Jews, while including new ethnic and/or social minority groups. While they largely confined this trend to European religious and ethnic minority groups in the past, if racial barriers are dismantled, many Hispanic and Asian Americans could also follow this historical pattern.

EARLY INCLUSION: ETHNORELIGIOUS IMMIGRANTS AND WHITE MINORITY GROUPS

In the presidential election of 1800, the Democratic-Republicans initiated their fundamental belief in social and political equality as Jefferson specifically welcomed immigrants and scorned Yankee clerics. While the state-established churches were predominately Federalist, religious minority groups such as Baptists, Methodists, and Catholics were overwhelmingly Republican. During the Jeffersonian era, as its opponents stressed the development of hierarchical governmental and societal structures, the Democratic-Republicans advocated equalitarian individualism and supported the liberalization of voting qualifications. By 1824, nearly all adult white males could vote in most states.

Strong support from the rapidly growing number of evangelical Protestants was a key part of the coalition that brought Andrew Jackson to power in 1928. Methodists, Baptists, disciples of Christ, and campbellite Presbyterians became devout Democrats. During his tenure, Jackson viewed the Democratic Party as the voice of liberty against power and wealth. Democrats also attacked property requirements for the right to hold office and advocated full political participation for foreign-born white male Americans.

There was a surge of immigration to the United States throughout the mid-1800s from predominately Catholic regions in Ireland and Germany. Democrats actively recruited these strangers, stressing that a person's devotion to democratic principles, and not religion, language, or nativity, defined a good U.S. citizen. According to Jacksonian Democrats, the equality of white males was indivisible, and the newcomers were entitled to all the privileges of citizenship. Democrats also opened their party organizations and machines to white immigrants, particularly Irishmen and Germans, and actively supported their candidacies. Simultaneously, Democrats were indifferent to the political and social claims of women, African Americans, and Indians, asserting that the white man was master in his own house and would not submit to dependency on a woman or another white man. The only conceivable role of women and nonwhites was to obey the orders of white men. This message was popular in the South and with northern workers and immigrants who struggled against "wage slavery."

As the Democratic Party welcomed the flood of Catholic immigrants, an explosion of nativism and anti-Catholicism gripped the United States in the 1850s. Many evangelical Protestants fled to the Whig-Republican Party or joined the Know-Nothings. This realignment started the long-term trend in U.S. politics of minority groups leaving the party that initially welcomed them as they become part of the mainstream American political culture. Until slavery divided the party, Democrats could lessen the impact of these mass defections because of the waves of European immigration into U.S. cities.

During the Gilded Age (1870s to 1890s) the Democratic Party benefited from another surge of immigration, which came mainly from southern and eastern Europe. While Republicans tried to recruit immigrants, most newcomers joined the Democratic Party. The new voters enabled Democratic machines to challenge the dominant Republican Party in many northern states. But Progressives instituted a series of electoral reforms in the late 1800s and early 1900s, such as the Australian ballot, registration laws, and naturalization requirements, designed to restrict the electoral power of immigrants. Party loyalty and voter turnout began to decline as these reforms reduced the ability of local party organizations to mobilize voters. In the 1890s another partisan realignment occurred as many traditionally Democratic urban ethnic groups crossed over to the Republican Party, dramatically weakening the party. Simultaneously, the Democratic Party's power to recruit new immigrant voters was restricted. Consequently, the political base of the Democratic Party shrank dramatically in the northeastern states until the 1930s.

Ethnic and religious minority groups were a significant part of the New Deal coalition. Franklin Roosevelt actively sought the support of diverse ethnic Catholic groups and immigrant, first-generation, and old-stock white minority working-class voters. These ethnoreligious minority groups remained faithful Democratic voters during the Roosevelt, Truman, Kennedy, and Johnson administrations. But in the past 25 years many ethnoreligious white minority groups have moved to the Republican Party. For example, in 1972 Richard Nixon became the first Republican to receive most of the Catholic vote. By 1988, the Democratic presidential candidate, Michael Dukakis, received only 47% of the Catholic vote, and in 1992 only 44% of American Catholics voted for Bill Clinton.

THE RELATIONSHIP BETWEEN HISPANICS AND THE DEMOCRATIC PARTY

Hispanics are the second-largest ethnic minority group in the United States, constituting 9.5% of the U.S. population and 24 million people. Hispanic Americans are a very diverse minority group, consisting of three main subgroups: Mexican Americans (approximately 64%), Puerto Ricans (approximately 11%), and Cuban Americans (approximately 5%), and clusters of groups from the Caribbean and Central and Latin America. Today 75% of Hispanic Americans are concentrated in the metropolitan areas of California, Texas, New York, and Florida, with the remaining 45% residing primarily in Illinois, New Mexico, New Jersey, Arizona, Colorado, and Michigan. Hispanics constitute more than 25% of the population of California, New Mexico, and Texas, and from 1980 to 1992 the number of Hispanics in ten midwestern states increased from 1.2 million to 1.8 million. The socioeconomic status of Hispanics, except Cuban Americans, is considerably below that of Anglo Americans. For example, in 1992, the median incomes for Mexican Americans and Puerto Ricans were $23,714 and $20,301 respectively, compared with median incomes of $31,015 for Cuban Americans and $38,909 for Anglo Americans.

Despite the rapid increase in the Hispanic population, the Hispanic vote has been called the "sleeping giant," since this minority group has lower registration and voting rates than other groups. The main reason for reduced electoral participation is that about one-third of all Hispanics are resident aliens. Hispanic citizens also have been reluctant to register and vote. As an illustration, from 1980 to 1992, Hispanic registration figures were relatively low, averaging 36.7% for presidential election years and 31.5% for congressional election years, while Hispanic voter turnout averaged 30% and 23% respectively.

Generalizations about the party loyalty of Hispanic voters are difficult because only summary voting statistics are recorded, but Hispanics are not a cohesive political bloc. Most Mexican Americans and Puerto Ricans are Democrats, while Cuban Americans are predominately Republicans. Mexican Americans and Puerto Ricans also have much lower registration and voting rates than do Cuban Americans. Moreover, many analysts believe that Mexican and Puerto Rican Democrats are only moderately attached to the party and younger Cuban Americans are leaning away from the Republican Party.

Before the 1960s, voting and racial barriers instituted by both political parties were able essentially to limit the electoral power of Hispanic Americans to New Mexico. Nonetheless, Hispanics established a strong association with the Democratic Party in the 1930s because of the Great Depression. From 1929 to 1934, however, more than 400,000 Mexican Americans and Mexican immigrants working in southwestern and midwestern states were "voluntarily repatriated" back to Mexico to reduce welfare roles. Consequently, Mexican Americans and Hispanics became very distrustful of the U.S. government and did not develop an enduring predilection for the Democratic Party.

In the 1960s the Chicano movement increased the politicalization of Hispanics as organizational skills developed during a series of grape and lettuce boycotts were applied to voter registration drives and political campaigns. Hispanics became involved in the 1960 presidential election and formed "Viva Kennedy" organizations. Additional "Viva" organizations were created to support Lyndon Johnson and other Democratic candidates in 1964 and 1968. The party benefited from the increased participation by Hispanics during the 1960s, since 80% to 90% of Spanish-speaking voters supported Democratic candidates.

The Voting Rights Act of 1965 and subsequent amendments increased the potential political power of Hispanics during the 1970s. Between 1970 and 1980, the Hispanic American population increased from 9 million to 14.6 million people. Consequently, the Democratic Party became increasingly aware of the potential impact of Hispanic voters and took steps to incorporate their interests. Mexican Americans and Puerto Ricans were represented at Democratic state and national conventions and on steering committees. In 1972, the Democratic Party also organized the multistate Hispanic American Democrats (HAD); several state-level organizations registered new voters, addressed Hispanic issues, and supported Hispanic candidates. These Democratic initiatives were mutually beneficial. For example, Jimmy Carter received more than 81% of the Hispanic American vote and appointed 107 Hispanic Americans to administrative posts and 68 to boards and commissions. Nevertheless, it was estimated that only 32% of qualified Hispanics actually voted in 1976, compared with 61% of non-Hispanic voters.

During the 1980s the Hispanic population increased by another 47%, to 21.4 million. The number of Hispanic representatives, predominately Democratic, increased dramatically, with the most notable gains occurring in Arizona, California, Florida, New Mexico, New York, and Texas. Nevertheless, the strength of Hispanic votes for Democratic presidential candidates declined to approximately 55% in the 1980 and 1984 elections before increasing to 62% for Michael Dukakis in 1988 and approximately 70% for Bill Clinton in 1992.

Two major sources of tension between the Democratic Party and Hispanic political leaders should be noted. First, Hispanics have accused the Democratic Party of paternalism and taking the Hispanic vote for granted. Consequently, Hispanic leaders believe that Democrats have failed to address Hispanic issues and support Hispanic candidates. Second, the alliance between Hispanics and Democratic Party leadership has been strained over the creation of Hispanic majority districts during reapportionments. Hispanics have argued that Anglo Democratic leaders fragment Hispanic communities into several districts to ensure that loyal Democratic Hispanic voters help elect many Democratic representatives. For example, Hispanic groups actively participated in the 1971, 1981, and 1991 redistricting processes and often had to seek relief in the courts against Democratic state legislatures to increase the number of Hispanic majority districts. In several cases, Hispanics were successful in overturning apportionment plans with Republican assistance.

Hispanic representation in the U.S. political system has increased over the past five years. For example, after the 1990 census, six new Hispanic congressional districts were created and 19 Hispanics were elected to Congress in 1992, compared to ten before the election. Seventeen Hispanic representatives are serving in the 104th Congress. On state and local levels, 2,332 Hispanics representing both political parties served in elected city and county positions in 1993, primarily in Texas, California, and New Mexico.

Therefore, the relationship between Hispanics and the Democratic Party, except for Cuban Americans, is relatively strong. Hispanic political leaders have questioned the commitment of Democratic leaders to Hispanic interests and issues; nonetheless, the politicalization of Hispanics continues to benefit the Democratic Party.

ASIAN/PACIFIC ISLAND AMERICANS AND THE DEMOCRATIC PARTY

Asian Americans are the third-largest minority group in the United States with a population of 8.4 million people, representing 3.3% of the total population. Despite low fertility rates, immigration has made Asian Americans the fastest-growing minority group in the United States. The Asian American population is projected to increase to 7% of the total population by the year 2020. Like Hispanics, Asian Americans are a diverse minority group with different ethnic subdivisions. Currently, there are 1.6 million Chinese Americans, 1.4 Filipinos, and 847,000 Japanese Americans living in the United States. Other significant Asian/Pacific Islander minority groups include Indian Asians, Korean Americans, and Vietnamese citizens.

Asian Americans also tend to reside in concentrated areas. California has the most Asians and Pacific Islanders with 2.84 million, followed by New York and Hawaii with approximately 694,000 and 685,000 Asian/Pacific Islanders, respectively. Texas, Illinois, New Jersey, and Washington also have relatively large

Asian/Pacific Island American populations. The Asian American vote could have a significant impact in these states, particularly in California, where Asian Americans constitute almost 10% of the population.

Asian Americans have been reluctant to join either political party, since neither has served them well in the past. For example, the Democratic Party in California attempted to rehabilitate itself after the Civil War by exploiting anti-Chinese sentiment in the 1870s. After the Democrats swept California in 1867, they made the "Chinese question" a national issue, which contributed to the passage of the Chinese Exclusion Act in 1882, which suspended the immigration of Chinese laborers. Open Democratic and Republican racism and restrictions against Chinese and Japanese laborers and Asian immigrants continued until 1945. In 1942 President Franklin Roosevelt with Democratic congressional support signed Executive Order 9066, which empowered the military to transport 70,000 Japanese American citizens and 42,000 Japanese resident aliens on the West Coast to relocation camps and led to the confiscation of much of their property.

Democratic and Republican hostility toward Asian Americans began to lessen during and after World War II. They finally repealed the Chinese Exclusion Act in 1943, and a small number of Chinese were allowed to immigrate annually. In 1948 Japanese Americans lobbied for restitutions with only limited success. But the 1952 McCarran–Walter Act removed all racial and ethnic barriers to immigration and naturalization, and the 1965 Immigration Act abolished the national-origin system and substituted hemispheric quotas.

Most Asian Americans were politically apathetic during the post–World War II era with the exception of residents of Hawaii, who joined the state's Democratic Party. During the 1960s, politicalization began in the Asian American community. Since the mid-1970s, Asian Americans have tended to support the Democratic Party, which has worked harder than its opponents to win Asian American votes. Nevertheless, newer Asian immigrants and southeast Asian refugees are considered the "Cubans" of the Asian community because they have gravitated toward the Republican Party with its strident anticommunist and conservative political beliefs.

One important feature of Asian Americans' participation in the political process is that they have been a major source of money, particularly in California races, but a minor source of votes, which has limited their electoral impact. For example, Jimmy Carter was the first Democratic presidential candidate to solicit the

support of Asian American contributors and organized the Asian/Pacific American unit (APA Unit). Democratic Asian Americans contributed $2.5 million to the Carter campaign in 1980. Unfortunately, only about 30% to 35% of eligible Japanese, Chinese, and Filipino Americans registered to vote, and the registration rates for other groups of Asian/Pacific Island Americans were even lower. The low Asian voting rates reduced the impact of the campaign contributions. Consequently, many Asian Americans were frustrated that their large political contributions did not translate into political influence or Asian American appointments in the Carter administration.

According to many observers, Jesse Jackson was the first presidential candidate to take Asian American concerns seriously. Unlike other Democratic contenders in the 1980s, Jackson visited Asian American communities and addressed Asian American issues during campaign speeches. Asian American political activists were also an integral part of Jackson's campaign organization, and several were appointed to high-level staff positions.

The Asian Pacific Caucus (APC) was organized in 1983 to represent Asian American Democrats and presented an Asian Pacific Caucus platform at the 1984 convention. After the election, APC was terminated when the party leadership decided that separate caucuses were weakening party unity. Asian American Democrats were outraged because other minority Democratic caucuses were not dismantled; they responded with the creation of an independent national organization, the National Democratic Council of Asian and Pacific Americans (NDCAPA), in 1985. The NDCAPA held the first national convention of Asian American Democrats in Los Angeles in 1987 in preparation for the 1988 presidential election. Several presidential candidates addressed the convention and promised to appointment Asian Americans. The bipartisan Interim Coordinating Committee for Chinese Americans (ICCCA) also persuaded all of the 1988 Democratic presidential candidates to commit themselves to appoint at least three Chinese Americans to policymaking positions.

Currently, the political power of Asian Americans remains limited. With the exception of the Democratic Party in Hawaii, Asian American representation has been limited. For example, in 1990, less than 1% of locally elected officials were Asian American and only four Asian Americans were elected to the House of Representatives in 1994. Most Asian Americans are registered Democrats but tend to have a low level of voter turnout. Consequently, while the relationship between Asian Americans and the Democratic Party is relatively strong, the electoral impact of Asian Americans is still very limited.

Janet B. Manspeaker

SEE ALSO African Americans, Jews

BIBLIOGRAPHY

de la Garza, Rodolfo, et al. *Latino Voices: Mexican, Puerto Rican, and Cuban Perspectives on American Politics.* San Francisco: Westview Press, 1992.

Garcia, F. Chris, ed. *Latinos and the Political System.* Notre Dame: Notre Dame Press, 1988.

Kitano, Harry, and Roger Daniels. *Asian Americans: Emerging Minorities.* 2nd ed. Englewood Cliffs, NJ: Prentice Hall, 1995.

Vigil, Maurilio. *Hispanics in American Politics: The Search for Political Power.* New York: New York University Press, 1987.

Wei, William. *The Asian American Movement.* Philadelphia: Temple University Press, 1993.

Party Discipline

American humorist Will Rogers once quipped, "I am not a member of any organized political party. I am a Democrat." What Rogers observed was an enduring feature of the Democratic Party in the United States: an absence of party discipline.

As a general matter, the term *party discipline* has two closely related but distinct connotations. The first, to which Rogers referred, relates to the degree of internal cohesion characterizing a political party. Here discipline is thought of in its adjectival sense. Accordingly, a "disciplined" party is one that manifests a high degree of internal solidarity, usually in a coherent fashion across a wide range of domestic and foreign policies.

In the second definition, discipline is treated as a noun. In this sense, focus is on the *methods* the party has for achieving and maintaining unity. Party discipline may be exercised by those in leadership positions in the party so as to produce cohesion where it might not otherwise exist. Those empowered with the tools of discipline—the distribution of political rewards and punishments—may thus be able to conform the behavior of would-be nonconformists in the party. Accordingly, the exercise of party discipline may produce a disciplined political party.

The subject of party discipline is important because political parties are almost unique in their potential for giving unity of purpose to a government designed by the American framers to be divided against itself. Parties thus hold promise of binding together in common purpose that which the U.S. Constitution separates—if the parties themselves are not divided.

Indeed, many American observers see in the rigorously disciplined behavior of some parties, especially those of the English Parliament, a model for political behavior in the United States. Since at least the time of Democrat Woodrow Wilson (who was a scholar of American politics before he devoted his career to its practice), prominent political scientists have argued that the inherent inefficiencies of government in the United States can be remedied only through the emergence of strong, disciplined governing parties, which experts call *party government*.

In the main, however, party discipline has *not* been a defining characteristic of the American party system in general, nor of the Democratic Party in particular [see the companion essay in *The Encyclopedia of the Republican Party*]. Only rarely has the Democratic Party acted as a highly cohesive agent for crafting and adopting policy across the wide range of domestic and foreign issues confronting the American government.

Political parties in the United States have commonly existed as umbrella organizations interested principally in one major goal: the staffing of the government by winning elections. Unity on policy is at best a secondary concern. The decentralized character of American politics—"All politics is local" Speaker of the House Thomas P. "Tip" O'Neill (D-Mass.) often observed—places a premium on candidates and elected officials attending to local concerns in order to secure public office. There are accordingly powerful centrifugal forces acting on all American parties, impeding any efforts by party leaders to craft coherent public policy from a single vantage point. Moreover, the divided character of national political institutions in the United States—including a bicameral legislature with shared lawmaking authority and different constituencies in time and space, and an electorally independent executive—profoundly complicates the exercise of party discipline. Broadly defined ideological commitments generally *are* shared by those who claim a common party label, but American parties have seldom been successful over long stretches of time in getting their elected members to ignore the pull of localism or institutional prerogative in favor of voting the party line on policy exclusively.

During the mid-twentieth century, for example, the Democratic Party found itself subject to persistent tension on the question of race. By the 1930s, the effects of the so-called Great Migration—the massive movement of African Americans out of the agricultural South into the industrial North and Midwest—began to constrain some northern and urban Democrats to adopt a favorable posture toward black social and political equality. These same forces generated pressure on Democratic

Presidents Franklin D. Roosevelt and Harry S. Truman because black Americans were settling into states with heavy concentrations of electoral college votes. Consequently, Democratic Party leaders began advocating modest but historic advances in black civil rights. Their success in this regard, however, was largely limited to areas wherein a president could act alone (such as the signing of executive orders or the appointment of executive officials), because the Democratic Party in Congress was dominated by southern conservatives.

The Democratic Party at mid-century was not a disciplined party on civil rights because there was neither widespread consensus within the party on what the proper civil rights position should be nor were there sufficient carrots and sticks available to the party leaders—including the president—for them to enforce a common policy on a badly divided party with powerful dissenting southern congressional oligarchs. Some southerners did cast off their partisan attachments in 1948 to join a failed Dixiecrat bid for the White House, but for the most part the membership of the party agreed to disagree on that issue while holding on to the common party label. For southerners, the decision not to abandon the party in the face of leadership positions with which they strongly disagreed was rooted in long-time partisan attachments dating back to the politics of the Civil War and Reconstruction periods. Movement into the Republican Party was not a viable option for politicians in a region whose history had been so decisively influenced by Lincoln and Sherman and Grant.

Although American political parties have seldom acted in as disciplined a fashion as their English counterparts, they do in some ways reveal elements of party discipline in both senses of the term described earlier. This is especially true of the congressional parties. Extensive studies of Congress demonstrate that the party label is the single most important factor for explaining roll-call voting in both the House and the Senate. For example, one index—called a "party unity score," which measures the percentage of members who vote with the majority of their party on those roll-call votes on which a majority of the two parties divide—shows that Democrats voted together almost 80% of the time from 1954 to 1986. Such statistics, however, developed from roll-call voting patterns, tend to overstate the extent to which congressional policymaking is subjected to the influence of disciplined party decisions. Party unity at the final stage of the legislative process (i.e., on floor votes) in the American Congress is commonly the product of well-balanced compromises, representing what members of Congress can agree on, not what any one partisan prefers.

Such unity is of a different character from that produced by a disciplined party system, in which unity proceeds from partisan attachments alone, allowing party leaders to pass legislation without compromising on their concepts of what the most coherent policy should be. The "best" policy attainable under a system of divided powers—and thus that most likely to gain the broadest support—is likely to be a mix of policy compromises that departs substantially from what a single rational agent (such as a disciplined political party) would prescribe for dealing with a particular public problem. Thus, while a high level of cohesion may signify some measure of discipline on the part of party members, it may not be a signal of the kind of coherent policymaking usually associated with parliamentary parties.

Congressional parties also are the best place to see the tools of party discipline in practice in the United States, to the extent that they exist. The most prominent party power for congressional parties is the power to organize. Those leading the party have access to the appointment power for keeping their partisans in line by granting or denying committee or subcommittee appointments based on performance in relation to the party's standards. In recent history, however, the use of the appointment power by congressional party leadership for specific disciplinary purposes has been rare. Instead, at least in the awarding of committee and subcommittee chairs, the seniority rule has predominated, whereby those majority party members with the longest service on the committee assume its headship position, irrespective of their personal agendas. Nonetheless, a reserve power does exist for use in unseating those who clearly cannot serve the majority's interest in their committee chairs. In 1975, for example, reform-oriented Democrats (those elected in the wake of the Watergate scandals) unseated three committee chairs: Texan W. Robert Poage of Agriculture, Texan Wright Patman of Banking, and Louisianan F. Edward Hebert of Armed Services.

There are other tools congressional party leaders may employ to keep their forces unified on policy. They can use their control of the rules of each chamber to their advantage, including channeling floor action and establishing the agenda of the body. They can use their influence to see that certain bills get preferred attention or receive the majority party imprimatur vital to a measure's passage. They can work to see that a cooperative member's pet projects are favored in spending bills or other legislation. They also can control the flow of information to the party membership, keeping favored partisans up-to-date on the status of private negotiations and the likely scheduling of important votes.

Finally, party leaders can be useful sources of campaign money, assisting cooperative members with their reelection efforts. In recent times this support has commonly been channeled through official campaign committees—each party has a campaign committee established for each chamber of Congress—although the long-time practice of helping junior members make connections with sympathetic private funding sources remains an important mechanism for channeling party favors.

Yet missing from the arsenal of weapons available to party leaders in Washington are two crucial, integrated powers possessed by their disciplined parliamentary counterparts in London. At bottom, the carrots and sticks available to American party leaders are a relatively meager lot.

First, British parliamentary parties have a highly refined system for designating the degree of freedom an individual member of Parliament (MP) has on particular votes. According to British practice, party leaders may classify the party's position on an approaching vote with one of the following designations: a one-line, two-line, or three-line whip. An MP's freedom to exercise his or her individual discretion in accepting the party's position diminishes as the whip's lines increase. A three-line whip indicates the highest level of urgency, and that prior approval by a party member is required to miss the vote. It should be noted that in all instances the MP is expected to cast a vote for the party position; the latitude to act designated by the whip generally extends only to missing a vote or purposefully abstaining. Thus the party leadership has a well-regulated and widely accepted set of procedures for ensuring that the party position on various issues prevails.

A second tool is necessary to ensure that the whip system functions as intended, which is the power to enforce party unity through a disciplined set of sanctions levied against dissenters. Dissenters are at risk of severe punishments, including a temporary suspension from the party's legislative affairs. If the party leadership wishes, it may exercise the ultimate punishment: expulsion from the party. The denial of party affiliation is a severe punishment in Britain because local party organizations are so strongly integrated into the national party structure; thus, a national party endorsement is virtually essential to winning election. Further, the local electorates' commitment to the party itself is commonly so strong that expulsion is taken as a confirmed sign of bad faith.

The absence of disciplined governing parties in the United States may be traced directly to a fundamental difference in how the two electorates view the weight of partisan commitments on their legislators. In Great Britain, MPs are elected primarily because of their partisan attachments. Accordingly, the influence of those attachments on their legislative behavior is quite heavy because any departures from that standard are considered evidence of infidelity. American legislators are judged by a different standard. In the United States, a legislator's primary commitment is commonly to his or her constituency, which may or may not be well served, in specific instances, by the party's position on a host of complicated issues. Under this construction, a legislator's rejection of the party's position on specific issues may be easily defended to his or her constituency as a necessary service to them. In this environment, the ability of a party to discipline its members effectively is severely circumscribed.

In 1983, for example, House Democrats voted to remove one of their number—Texas Representative Phil Gramm—from the House Budget Committee. Gramm had defied the party leadership on a series of important budget votes during the first two years of Ronald Reagan's presidency and had provided sensitive intelligence to Republican policymakers gathered from confidential Democratic strategy sessions. The Democratic leadership of the House punished Gramm by giving his seat on that committee to someone more devoted to the party's legislative agenda. But that effort to exercise party discipline backfired. Gramm immediately resigned his House seat and his Democratic Party membership, returned to his conservative Texas district, registered as a Republican, and was reelected in a special election to the seat he had just vacated. Two years later the notoriety he achieved in defying the Democratic Party was instrumental in his election statewide to membership in the U.S. Senate. Since the reason most American parties exist is to staff the government, Gramm's abdication represented a signal failure in the Democrats' effort to impose discipline on one of its wayward members.

The presence of vigorous party discipline in a legislative body requires, then, the existence of a political culture amenable to its exercise. This precondition exists in Great Britain, where models of strong governing parties originated. The absence of that cultural precondition in the United States, however, furnishes serious problems for those who would make a disciplined Democratic Party the norm in the United States.

The Democratic Party *has* episodically acted as a strong governing party in the United States, in ways at least suggestive of Britain's parliamentary experience. The Democrats' first exercise as a governing party—

under its founder, Thomas Jefferson—was charged by its Federalist critics with too closely mimicking those British hierarchies against which the Americans had recently rebelled. Jefferson entered the presidency with congressional majorities in both chambers committed to a well-established program of governance. His partisans—the Democratic-Republicans—joined together in common purpose to advance the party's agenda. They worked as a disciplined unit, giving Jefferson almost everything he asked for and nothing to veto on a host of fronts: tax cuts, budget cuts, military retrenchment, and geographic expansion.

The unity of these Jeffersonians has been replicated by a few of their Democratic successors. Party leadership by a Democratic president of a remarkably cohesive Democratic congressional party can be identified under at least three subsequent administrations: Woodrow Wilson, Franklin Roosevelt, and Lyndon Johnson. In each of these four instances of cohesiveness, there are two common elements.

The first is that the unity characterizing these episodes was largely the product of a very broad consensus, freely formed, either about a wide range of policies or the need to defer to presidential leadership to deal with a pressing national emergency. The Jeffersonian Democrats flourished because they held a shared vision of a nation with a small, decentralized government, based in agriculture, strong by virtue of its massive expanse. The Wilsonian Democrats cohered in confronting the challenges of the world's first global war. Roosevelt's Democrats rallied to the president and party leader, first to defeat the nation's severest depression and then the specter of international fascism. Finally, Lyndon Johnson's Democrats, at least for a time, united both to honor the life of John Kennedy and to complete the unfinished business of the New Deal.

The second common feature of each of these regimes of party discipline, however, is that they all prevailed for only a brief time. All eventually failed. In no instance were the advantages of party unity so overwhelming that Americans decided to make government by a disciplined party the rule rather than the exception in American political life. Party government arose in these instances on what scholars have termed a contingency or conditional basis.

The cohesion of the Jeffersonian party collapsed before Jefferson himself left office, victim to Jefferson's decision to deal with an unexpected turn in international events by imposing an embargo on American business with European powers. Those Democrats representing commercial and agricultural interests hurt by the embargo elected to defy the party leader

rather than follow his lead. Wilson's mandate for leadership fell apart at war's end, as Congress, including many of his formerly loyal partisans, decided that the discipline of wartime was unnecessary in a time of peace. Roosevelt's Democrats refused to follow him in remaking the Supreme Court in 1937, defied his efforts to purge the party of its conservative elements in 1938, and labored to frustrate his early efforts to gird Europe for war before 1941. And Lyndon Johnson's Democratic Party disintegrated around him—conservatives challenging him on civil rights and liberals on Vietnam—leaving him too weak even to seek reelection in 1968.

In theory, the Democratic Party might have been able in these instances, in the absence of a spontaneous regeneration of consensus, to use a variety of political carrots and sticks to enforce party discipline, to employ skillfully political rewards and punishments in order to maintain the party's unity in the face of impending fragmentation. That this did not happen in any case testifies to the enormity of those obstacles American parties confront in perpetuating their governing powers in a disciplined fashion.

Russell L. Riley

BIBLIOGRAPHY

Bradshaw, Kenneth, and David Pring. *Parliament and Congress.* Austin: University of Texas Press, 1972.
Epstein, Leon. *Political Parties in the American Mold.* Madison: University of Wisconsin Press, 1986.
Jackson, Robert J. *Rebels and Whips: An Analysis of Dissension, Discipline and Cohesion in British Political Parties.* New York: Macmillan, 1968.
Ripley, Randall. *Congress: Process and Policy.* 4th ed. New York: Norton, 1988.
Stokes, Michael. "When Freedoms Conflict: Party Discipline and the First Amendment." *Journal of Law and Politics* 11 (1995).

Party Organization in Congress

The party organization of the Democrats in Congress has four parts: leadership position, caucus, whip system, and party committee. House and Senate Democrats operate with a similar overall structure, but some differences exist between the organizations in the two chambers. Differences also exist in the structure and operation of the majority and minority parties in Congress. Most of the Democrats' experience since 1933 has been as the majority party in the House and Senate.

When the House Democrats are in the majority, the main leadership positions are the Speaker, the majority leader, the majority whip, and the caucus chairman. When they are in the minority, the top positions are the minority leader, the minority whip, and the caucus chairman.

The Speaker is the leader of the House and the leader of the majority party. So a Speaker has powers and responsibilities to oversee the overall operation of the House and to promote the policies of the majority party. Each party elects a leader and then a vote is taken on the House floor to determine which party leader will be Speaker. Since this is usually a straight party-line vote, the majority party's leader becomes Speaker.

From 1933 through 1994, Democrats held the majority of House seats, and thus the Speaker's position, for all but four years. The Democratic Speaker for much of the first part of this period was Sam Rayburn. John McCormack, Carl Albert, Thomas "Tip" O'Neill, Jim Wright, and Thomas Foley followed Rayburn as Speaker.

A House Democratic minority leader performs the same party leadership functions as a Speaker, but without the powers and prestige of the Speaker's office. In 1995 Richard Gephardt had to adjust to the position of minority leader after spending his entire House career in the majority and being the majority leader in the previous Congress. Gephardt and his Democratic colleagues had to shift their focus from building majority coalitions in support of their programs to opposing the policies of the House Republican leadership.

The majority leader holds the number-two position in the majority party. The main job of the majority leader is to help the Speaker carry out the duties of the party leader. The majority leader is primarily concerned with scheduling legislation on the floor and building support for the legislation among party colleagues. The position of Democratic majority leader has become a steppingstone for the Speaker's office. For example, McCormack, Albert, O'Neill, Wright, and Foley were majority leaders before becoming Speaker.

The whip heads the organization (i.e., the whip system) that provides a communications network between the House Democratic leadership and the other House Democrats. The caucus chair leads the body that represents all the House Democrats. The whip and caucus chair work closely with the Speaker and majority leader (or minority leader if the party is in the minority) to maintain the party organization and promote party unity.

The House Democratic leadership had many oppor-

tunities to influence decisions on national public policies in recent decades because of the many years of majority control. But they also faced many difficulties trying to lead a group with such ideological and constituency differences as the House Democrats. Also, since the late 1960s, they had to deal with a decentralized power structure in the House and highly independent members. In their attempts to overcome these problems and forge majority coalitions, the House Democratic leadership utilized their powers (e.g., control over scheduling legislation on the floor) and provided services (e.g., help with committee assignments, legislation, and reelection) to party members.

In most cases, the House Democratic leadership allows the Democrats on the standing committees to formulate the policy agenda. Then the leadership coordinates the floor activities. But there have been exceptions to this pattern in recent decades. Speaker Jim Wright, for example, played a much bigger role than usual in developing the policy agenda for the House Democrats in 1987. Also, the congressional budget reforms of the 1970s and the partisan budget battles of the 1980s and 1990s provided the Democratic leadership with more opportunities than they had previously to influence the budget policy agenda.

All the House Democrats are members of the Democratic caucus. One of the functions of the caucus is to elect the leadership. When the Democrats are in the majority, the caucus actually chooses the Speaker through the process of electing a leader and nominating that person for Speaker. The following vote on the floor simply rubber-stamps the decision of the caucus. The caucus also selects the majority leader, majority whip (or minority leader and minority whip if the Democrats are in the minority), and the caucus chairman. During the period since the 1930s when the Democrats were usually in the majority, the caucus, in voting to select a new majority leader, was not only electing their number-two leader but also a future Speaker.

Additionally, the caucus makes policy recommendations on some occasions. But the caucus's role in setting policy for the House has generally not been very important. The Democratic leadership and the Democratic chairs and members of the standing committees shape policy positions much more than the caucus.

Finally, when the Democrats are in the majority, the caucus determines who will be the chairman of a standing committee if the chairman is challenged. This caucus challenge was one the reforms passed by the House Democrats in the 1970s. Before the challenge was adopted, committee chairs got and maintained their positions through the seniority system. By adopting the caucus challenge, its supporters hoped to make the committee chairs more accountable to the majority of House Democrats. Since the challenge was adopted, the caucus has rarely used this power to vote out committee chairs. In the mid-1970s, however, the caucus replaced three chairs with younger and more liberal members of the committee.

The House Democrats' whip organization is made up of the whip and several other House Democrats (chief deputy whips, deputy whips, at-large whips, and regional whips) who help the whip contact their party colleagues. The purpose of the organization is to provide a two-way communications system between the Democratic leadership and the rank-and-file Democratic representatives. The primary communication going out to the members is information about schedules, floor votes, and the policy positions of the leadership. The main information coming back to the leadership is vote counts on how House Democrats will likely vote on upcoming legislation. The leadership uses vote counts to plan strategy for building coalitions on floor votes and to decide when to schedule the votes.

Several party functions are administered by party committees. The Democratic Steering Committee decides on the assignment of Democrats to the standing committees, while the Policy Committee develops policy proposals. These two committees had previously been combined into a Steering and Policy Committee. Also, the Democratic Congressional Campaign Committee collects and distributes campaign funds for House Democratic candidates.

The Democratic leadership in the Senate consists of a majority leader and majority whip or a minority leader and minority whip. Just as with the House Democrats, the Senate Democrats also select a caucus (called a conference) chairman. The party leader (i.e., majority or minority leader), however, is usually given this position.

Similar to the Speaker of the House, a Senate majority leader is the overall leader of the chamber, as well as the leader of the majority party. He or she is responsible for the general operation of the Senate and for the program of the majority party.

As the Senate majority leader in the 1950s, Lyndon Johnson played a big role in shaping the position for the following decades. Johnson advanced the development of the position as the focus of the Senate's overall operation. While the Democratic majority leaders who followed Johnson were not as powerful as he was, they maintained the position as the key leadership post.

Mike Mansfield, a Democrat from Montana, became majority leader in 1961 after Johnson became vice president. Mansfield believed in a more decentralized power structure than his predecessor. He thought that the rank-and-file Senate Democrats should have more influence than they had previously and that the majority leader should have less power. By the time Robert Byrd (1977–1980, 1987–1988) and George Mitchell (1989–1994) followed Mansfield as Democratic majority leaders, the power structure in the Senate had become so decentralized that they would have had significant problems amassing the power Johnson had in the 1950s.

Like Democratic Speakers, Democratic majority leaders face difficult challenges in leading a diverse and highly independent group of Democratic colleagues and in managing the chamber overall. In fact, they often have had even more difficulties than Democratic Speakers during the past 30 years. Individual senators have more influence and thus more independence than individual representatives. Also, the greater power of individual senators combined with the possible use of the filibuster make the minority party more powerful in the Senate than in the House.

The majority (or minority) whip holds the number-two position among Senate Democrats. The majority/minority leader defines the role of this position. Whips head the whip organization and assist the leader's efforts to persuade other Senate Democrats to support the party's legislation.

The Democratic conference, the Senate Democrats' caucus, is the organization representing all Senate Democrats. The conference elects the majority/minority leader and the whip and occasionally makes policy recommendations.

The Democratic whip system in the Senate is a much smaller operation than its counterpart in the House. Also, with the smaller number of Democrats in the Senate, the need for a whip organization and its importance are less among Senate Democrats than among House Democrats. It is obviously much easier to communicate among 45 to 65 people than it is to communicate among 200 to 300 people.

Three of the four Senate Democrats' party committees are similar to those in the House. The Senate Democrats have a Policy Committee to analyze policy proposals, a Steering and Coordination Committee to make Democratic standing committee assignments, and a Democratic Senatorial Campaign Committee to provide campaign support. The fourth committee, the Technology and Communications Committee, was added in 1995 to communicate to the public information about the Democratic Party and its policy proposals.

Larry M. Schwab

BIBLIOGRAPHY

Burton, Larry. "Leadership Roles in the Senate: Function and Change." *In Congress and Public Policy*, ed. David C. Kozak and John D. Macartney, 2nd ed. Chicago: Dorsey Press, 1987.

Congressional Quarterly. *Players, Politics and Turf of the 104th Congress*. Washington, DC: CQ Press, 1995.

Duncan, Philip D., and Christine C. Lawrence. *Politics in America 1996*. Washington, DC: CQ Press, 1995.

Huitt, Ralph. "Democratic Party Leadership in the Senate." *American Political Science Review* 55 (1961): 333–344.

Matthews, Donald R. *U.S. Senators and Their World*. New York: Random House, 1960.

O'Neill, Thomas P., Jr. *Man of the House*. New York: Random House, 1987.

Oleszek, Walter J. *Majority and Minority Whips of the Senate: The History and Development of the Party Whip System in the U.S. Senate*. Washington, DC: Government Printing Office, 1979.

Peabody, Robert. *Leadership in Congress*. Boston: Little, Brown, 1976.

Rohde, David W. *Parties and Leaders in the Postreform House*. Chicago: University of Chicago Press, 1991.

Ripley, Randall. "The Party Whip Organization in the United States House of Representatives." *American Political Science Review* 58 (1964): 561–576.

———. *Majority Party Leadership in Congress*. New York: St. Martin's Press, 1969.

Smith, Steven S. "Forces of Change in the Senate Party Leadership and Organization." In *Congress Reconsidered*, ed. Lawrence C. Dodd and Bruce I. Oppenheimer, 5th ed. Washington, DC: CQ Press, 1993.

Sinclair, Barbara. *Majority Leadership in the U.S. House*. Baltimore: Johns Hopkins University Press, 1983.

———. "House Majority Party Leadership in an Era of Legislative Constraint." In *The Postreform Congress*, ed. Roger H. Davidson. New York: St. Martin's Press, 1992.

Stewart, John G. "Two Strategies of Leadership: Johnson and Mansfield." In *Congressional Behavior*, ed. Nelson W. Polsby. New York: Random House, 1971.

The Presidential Nomination Process

The framers of the Constitution, in designing the electoral college, established a system for electing the president of the United States. They did not foresee, however, the development of a party system or the growth of a complex presidential nomination process. At the Constitutional Convention in 1787, philosophical differences concerning the relationship between the states and the national government created factions among the political leadership of the new nation. The political party structure emerged from these factions during the mid-1790s. With George Washington's decision not to serve a third term in office, Federalist and Democratic-Republican members of Congress were forced to recommend candidates for the 1796 presidential election. The presidential nomination process has evolved since that time.

Beginning with the election of 1800, the party caucus served as the method by which presidential candidates were selected. This system, in which members of Congress met to pick the party's nominee, violated the spirit of the Constitution by creating legislative selection of the president. Because the party leadership often met in secret, the process was also unrepresentative. With the growth of party organizations at the state and local levels, this system began to decay and was last employed for the election of 1824.

By the 1830s, the national nominating convention had replaced the caucus system. While the initial conventions were rather informal, the Democratic Party established a process whereby the delegates fixed the rules and procedures of the convention and selected the presidential nominee. In this system, the states were generally granted delegates based on the size of their congressional delegation. Delegate selection at the state level was determined by the state party organization, usually through some combination of local and state conventions or caucuses. While this system was an improvement over its predecessor, the process remained unrepresentative of the party membership and the American public. Throughout the nineteenth century, the party leadership, particularly at the state level, acted as political brokers. Serving state and regional interests (in addition to fulfilling individual political agendas), this leadership generally conducted the most important business of the convention behind closed doors.

The presidential primary evolved from the public demand for wider popular participation in government, the expression of which resulted in numerous legal reforms during the 1880–1920 period. In the first decade of the new century, a large number of states enacted legislation providing for the direct election of party candidates for statewide office. The election of state party delegates to the national presidential nominating convention was a logical extension of the primary idea. The first Democratic statewide vote for convention delegates was held in Florida in 1904. The number of states holding Democratic primaries grew to 20 in 1916. Given the large number of uncommitted delegates at the national conventions, however, the party leadership was able to maintain its influence in the nomination process. In the following years, the number of primaries declined as some states reverted to previous methods of selecting delegates to the national conventions (i.e., caucuses and state conventions). In many states that continued to hold primaries, these were viewed as an advisory, rather than mandatory, means for selecting delegates. Thus, through the election of 1968, the primary was not considered the principal vehicle through which a candidate obtained the party nomination for president.

The bitterly contested Democratic National Convention of 1968 marked the demise of the leadership-controlled nomination process. The political fights and physical confrontations on the convention floor, combined with violent protest in the streets outside the convention hall, caused the party to address the issue of delegate selection. Beginning with the McGovern–Fraser Commission (1969), the party reformed the delegate selection process. Addressing charges that the convention delegates were not representative of the rank-and-file membership, a quota system was adopted. This arrangement provided for greater representation of women, minorities, and young people on state delegations. (This system gave way to affirmative action guidelines in 1976 and an "equal division" rule, adopted in 1980, requiring that state delegations be composed of an equal number of male and female delegates.) The commission also established rules that eliminated the practice of state party leaders' handpicking members of their state delegation.

The current system of nominating Democratic presidential candidates is characterized, most notably, by the importance of the primary election. The direct primary has become the principal means by which delegates are selected for the national convention. In an effort to avoid challenges concerning the composition of the state delegation, a number of states that had employed the caucus or convention system prior to 1969 changed to the primary election as a means of selecting delegates. In 1968, 17 states held Democratic presidential primaries in which approximately 48% of the delegates were selected. In contrast, 30 states staged primaries in 1976, selecting 72% of the delegates in this fashion. This trend, in general, has continued through the most recent election, with 40 states holding Democratic primaries in 1992.

The states that continue to hold conventions and/or caucuses have also been affected by the reform movement. Delegates cannot be selected until the calendar year of the national convention; state parties are required to publicize the time, place, and rules of meetings; and information concerning the presidential preferences of would-be delegates must be made public by the state party organization. These changes were designed to eliminate the backroom politics character-

istic of earlier times and dilute the influence of state party chairmen in the selection of delegates.

A second prominent feature of the current nomination system is the multifaceted nature of the process and the division of power among the national party organization, the state parties, and the state legislatures. While primaries have become the norm for the selection of delegates, these elections can take a number of forms. The form that primary elections (as well as conventions and caucuses) take is largely determined by the state party organizations. While the national party organization has some influence over the procedure, particularly with regard to rules, the state party organizations (in concert with state legislatures) determine the process by which delegates are chosen, that is, primary, convention, caucus (or some combination of these), the allocation of delegates (by congressional district or statewide), and the dates of caucuses and conventions. The state parties, however, do not operate in a vacuum and therefore cannot directly change their method of selecting delegates to the national convention. The state legislatures enact the laws governing the selection process and determine the dates of primary elections. In recent years, state legislation has generally provided the parties with the option of selecting the process by which delegates are chosen. (This serves to explain why, in some states, one party selects delegates by a primary election while the other party employs the caucus or convention system. Given the flexibility afforded state party organizations in determining the procedure, it is conceivable that there could be 50 different variations of this process, for each party.)

Given this division of power, however, state legislatures are sometimes at odds with the national party organization. For example, the New Hampshire legislature has threatened to pass legislation mandating that the state primary (for both parties) be held one week before any other state's primary. New Hampshire has traditionally held the first primary, and the legislature does not want the state to lose the political and economic benefits associated with this position. Similarly, the Iowa legislature does not wish to relinquish that state's distinction as the first caucus state. In each case, the Democratic National Committee has granted exceptions to the rules governing the time frame for the selection of delegates.

Another characteristic of the current system is the variable nature of the process. For example, in 1976 the Democratic Party abandoned the winner-take-all primary in favor of a proportional representation system. This change was instituted in order to avoid a repeat of the 1972 California primary in which George McGovern captured all of that state's delegates with a narrow popular-vote victory over Hubert Humphrey. Some states continue to employ winner-take-all systems at the district level, but generally the process has been modified so that the allocation of delegates more closely reflects the popular vote of the primaries.

The "superdelegate" is another recent feature of the nomination process. Since 1984, the Democrats have designated party leaders—members of Congress, governors, former presidents and vice presidents, and members of the Democratic National Committee—as superdelegates to the national convention. The introduction of the superdelegate was largely a reaction to the disastrous 1972 campaign and the general absence of party support for the Carter administration. In both elections, many of the party leaders and regulars (those who generally organize campaigns, raise money, and get out the vote at the state level) were excluded from the process or chose to watch from the sidelines. The inclusion of superdelegates ensures greater participation by party professionals at the convention and during the general election campaign.

The regional primary is yet another recent modification of the system. Following the lopsided defeat of Walter Mondale in the 1984 election, the Democratic Party encouraged the creation of a regional primary in the southern states—Super Tuesday. In 1988, 14 southern and border states (and six other states) held primaries or caucuses on the second Tuesday in March. The intent of the regional primary was to reduce the importance of the Iowa and New Hampshire contests (the first caucus and primary, respectively) and increase the likelihood of a moderate, centrist candidate winning the Democratic nomination. This, it was believed, would enhance the party's chances of winning the general election in November. The regional emphasis lost some steam in 1992; eight Democratic primaries were held on Super Tuesday. The results, however, were more in line with the original expectations of the party. Bill Clinton, a southern moderate, won decisive victories in each of the six southern or border states.

Also characteristic of the post-1968 nomination process is the trend toward shifting primary schedules. While the primary and caucus schedule is restricted to the March through June period (with notable exceptions granted to Iowa and New Hampshire), the early contests tend to have a greater impact on the selection process than those held in June. In 1992, several western states moved their primaries or caucuses to the week prior to Super Tuesday, a strategy designed to reflect regional concerns. This movement to a front-loaded primary schedule continued in 1996, with a number of states scheduling primaries or caucuses earlier in the political season. Most notable was California's switch

from a June to a March primary date. This move may further reduce the influence of the early contests in Iowa and New Hampshire while increasing the political importance of the California vote. With the largest state delegation at the Democratic convention, an early California primary may also temper the influence of the regional Super Tuesday contests. (This was a moot point in the 1996 Democratic nomination process in that President Clinton ran unopposed.)

In addition, the citizens of Iowa, New Hampshire, and the early March primary states generally have a broader slate of candidates to select from than do voters in the late primary states. For example, in 1984, eight Democrats contested the first primary but only three remained in the race by the beginning of June. Similarly, eight Democratic candidates were entered in the 1988 New Hampshire primary. By the time California, Montana, New Jersey, and New Mexico held their primaries in early June, this field had been reduced to two. This trend continued in 1992, with four of the six Democrats withdrawing their candidacies by the end of March.

Just as the debate pertaining to the role of political parties and the representative nature of the system shaped the transformation of the nomination process in the 1820s and the early 1900s, the current system is marked by these same concerns. The role of the Democratic Party and the degree to which this process represents the party membership and the American public is central to the changing rules and norms associated with the selection of presidential candidates.

William E. Dugan

BIBLIOGRAPHY

Asher, Herbert B. *Presidential Elections and American Politics: Voters, Candidates, and Campaigns since 1952.* 5th ed. Pacific Grove, CA: Brooks/Cole, 1992.

Chase, James S. *Emergence of the Presidential Nominating Convention, 1789–1832.* Urbana: University of Illinois Press, 1973.

Polsby, Nelson W. *Consequences of Party Reform.* New York: Oxford University Press, 1983.

Stanley, Harold W., and Richard G. Niemi. *Vital Statistics on American Politics.* 2nd ed. Washington, DC: CQ Press, 1990.

Wayne, Stephen J. *The Road to the White House: The Politics of Presidential Elections.* 5th ed. New York: St. Martin's Press, 1995.

Presidential Nominations and Elections

The second half of the twentieth century has seen the Democratic Party fundamentally transform its method of nominating presidential candidates. Because many of these changes were enacted into law, the Republican Party has, albeit less dramatically, followed along. Although the party convention still has the formal role of selecting the nominee, it is now the caucuses and primaries held by each state that actually make the choice. By the time the convention meets, everyone knows who will be the nominee.

This opening up of the process began with John Kennedy's nomination in 1960. Having to demonstrate to party leaders that a Catholic candidate could be elected, Kennedy had no choice but to contest the primaries. His use of television and political polling can be seen as the beginning of the modern media-oriented campaign. After primary victories against Hubert Humphrey in Wisconsin and largely Protestant West Virginia proved his electoral appeal, he was nominated. In the general election campaign, media, most notably the first televised debates, proved a major factor in Kennedy's narrow win against Vice President Richard Nixon.

Despite this use of primaries, most convention delegates continued to be chosen either in caucuses or by the party leadership until the upheaval of 1968. The 1964 election between Lyndon Johnson, who had succeeded to the presidency after Kennedy was assassinated, and Republican Senator Barry Goldwater had proven no contest as the Democrats successfully portrayed their conservative opponent as a dangerous radical. But what proved to be Johnson's only full term saw his popularity plunge as public discontent with an escalating Vietnam War grew. Opposition to that war led little-known Senator Eugene McCarthy to challenge the incumbent's nomination. After a narrow victory by Johnson in the New Hampshire primary, Senator Robert Kennedy, another opponent of the war, declared his candidacy. The president then surprised nearly everyone by withdrawing from the race, after which the Johnson forces rallied behind Vice President Hubert Humphrey. Humphrey did not enter any of the primaries, however, preferring to accumulate delegates chosen by party leaders. McCarthy and Kennedy contested a series of state primaries, but Kennedy was assassinated after winning in California. With only one-third of the delegates chosen by primary voters, Humphrey was able to win the nomination without having received a single vote in any primary. The Chicago convention was marred by riots in the streets and a divided party was defeated by Republican Richard Nixon in November despite a late Democratic comeback that narrowed the popular vote margin to less than .5%.

As a result of this debacle, the Democrats appointed a commission headed by Senator George McGovern to reform their presidential nomination process. Before finishing the job, McGovern decided to run for president himself and was replaced on the commission by Representative Donald Fraser. The main goal of the McGovern–Fraser Commission's recommendations was to open up the nomination process to greater participation by rank-and-file party members. By 1980 nearly three-fourths of the convention delegates, including those of the 11 largest states, were chosen in primaries. Neither caucuses nor primaries were allowed to award all of a state's delegates to the winner. Affirmative action requirements resulted in significant increases in the percentages of female, racial minority, and young (under the age of 30) delegates.

Whatever their value in democratizing the nomination process, these reforms failed to produce many winning candidates. McGovern was overwhelmed by incumbent Richard Nixon in 1972. Only one of the next four presidential elections resulted in a Democratic victory. Even that narrow win, by Jimmy Carter in 1976, was due in large part to the Watergate scandal, as indicated by Carter's defeat in his bid for reelection. Many Democrats believed that their party had gone too far in excluding its politically experienced leaders from having a say in choosing its presidential nominees. They pointed to events such as the exclusion of Chicago Mayor Richard Daley from the 1972 convention when his delegation failed to meet affirmative action requirements. The result, they believed, was a series of candidates who were either ideologically extreme (McGovern) or lacking in national political experience (Carter).

After Carter's defeat in 1980, another commission, headed by North Carolina Governor James Hunt, was appointed by the Democratic National Committee to review the nomination rules. It set aside approximately 15% of the convention seats for "superdelegates," a group of party leaders and elected officials, hoping that their influence would produce candidates who were more electable. In 1984, Walter Mondale, a thorough political professional who had served as a state attorney general, U.S. senator, and vice president, prevailed over Colorado Senator Gary Hart. Hart's promotion of his "new ideas," as a contrast to Mondale's support from traditional Democratic allies such as labor unions (derided by Hart as "special interests"), might have gained independent voters in a general election but was not as appealing to those Democrats who participated in the nomination process. A surprising win in the New Hampshire primary keyed an early Hart surge but, in the long haul, he fell well short of the nomination. Trailing badly in the polls, Mondale tried the dramatic gesture of nominating Representative Geraldine Ferraro for vice president, the first woman chosen by a major party for its national ticket. Such efforts proved futile, however, as Mondale was soundly defeated in November by incumbent President Ronald Reagan.

Moderate and conservative Democrats attributed that defeat to Mondale's liberalism. Hoping to increase the chances of less liberal candidates, they convinced 20 states, most in the South, to hold their primaries on a single day early in the process. But the first such "Super Tuesday," March 8, 1988, proved less useful to their favored candidate, Senator Al Gore, than to liberals Michael Dukakis and Jesse Jackson. Dukakis added this effective showing to his preceding victory in New Hampshire to create an unstoppable momentum that resulted in his nomination. But he, too, proved an unsuccessful nominee, losing in November to George Bush despite polls taken shortly after the convention giving Dukakis a significant lead.

Yet in 1992 the Democrats did triumph. At first the scenario seemed even less promising than the previous three elections. As a result of the successful invasion of Panama and the quick victory over Iraq in the Gulf War, President Bush's approval ratings soared over the 90% mark early in 1991. Seeing little prospect of victory, the best-known of the potential Democratic candidates renounced the possibility of running. Without stalwarts such as New York's governor Mario Cuomo, 1984 and 1988 contender Jesse Jackson, House Majority Leader Richard Gephardt, and Senators Bill Bradley, Sam Nunn, and Jay Rockefeller, the field was left to such little-known figures as Arkansas Governor Bill Clinton, former Massachusetts Senator Paul Tsongas, Virginia Governor Douglas Wilder, and Senators Bob Kerry and Tom Harkin. The better-known Jerry Brown, a former governor of California, had been so widely perceived as a political eccentric during his tenure in office as well as previous runs for the nomination that he was given little chance of winning the nomination, let alone the general election.

But Bush proved more vulnerable than anyone had imagined. The bloom of foreign policy success quickly wore off as the economy declined. Bush's popularity dropped even more quickly, setting a new record with a 57% decline between the end of the Gulf War and the start of the Republican convention. As Bush lost stature, several of the Democrats began to gain it. Rejecting any contributions of more than $100, Brown made reform of campaign finance the centerpiece of his campaign. Tsongas took advantage of his lack of

charisma by stating that, unlike his opponents, he was "no Santa Claus." Instead of making extravagant promises, he would tell the voters the unvarnished truth about the necessity of making hard choices to reduce an out-of-control budget deficit. The high point of Tsongas's campaign was his solid win in the New Hampshire primary. Prior to that, many experts had viewed Bill Clinton as the likely nominee. Portraying himself as a "new kind of Democrat," he proposed a middle-class tax cut, less severe budget reductions than Tsongas favored, and government programs ("investments") to increase economic growth. But as his program gained in popularity, questions arose about his personal life. After a series of evasions, he admitted to having smoked marijuana. His answers to questions about his avoidance of military service in Vietnam by use of a student deferment failed to quiet criticism. Most dramatically, he and his wife appeared on the nationally televised program *60 Minutes* just before the New Hampshire vote to counter charges that he had engaged in an adulterous affair. Trumpeting his ensuing second-place finish in a state so close to Tsongas's Massachusetts home base, Clinton styled himself the "comeback kid." His strong showing on Super Tuesday vindicated the hopes of its founders by propelling the southern moderate on his way to an eventual nomination.

Bush tried to counter Clinton's edge on economic issues by changing the subject to his opponent's character. But on-again, off-again third-party candidate Ross Perot kept the focus on the administration's weakness. As Clinton's staff stressed their strategy that "It's the economy, stupid," Clinton maintained his sometimes tenuous lead in the polls, winning the three-way contest with 43.4% to Bush's 37.7%. At the same time, however, the Democratic Party lost ten seats in the House of Representatives, while the Senate ratio remained unchanged. And in 1994 the party was swamped as the Republicans won control of both houses of Congress for the first time since 1952.

Thus it was unclear whether Clinton's victory was a real comeback or simply a one-term aberration in a long-term Republican string of victories, as Carter's had been in 1976. Had the Democrats' constant nomination rule tinkering finally resulted in an open process that made it likely that good candidates would emerge? Or would the party's various factions prove unable to unite for the long term? Perhaps Will Rogers's observation that he was not a member of an organized political party, he was a Democrat, still holds considerable relevance.

Bruce E. Altschuler

SEE ALSO Nominating Conventions, Primary Elections

BIBLIOGRAPHY

Nelson, Michael, ed. *The Elections of 1992*. Washington, DC: CQ Press, 1993.

Polsby, Nelson W., and Aaron Wildavsky. *Presidential Elections*. 8th ed. New York: Free Press, 1991.

Rose, Gary L., ed. *Controversial Issues in Presidential Selection*. Albany, NY: SUNY Press, 1994.

Wayne, Stephen J. *The Road to the White House 1992*. New York: St. Martin's Press, 1992.

Primary Elections

The primary election, also referred to as the direct primary, is the process whereby voters choose a political party's candidates for public office. This process is contrasted with the party caucus or convention, where candidates are chosen by party leaders and activists. At present, all states employ the primary process, sometimes in conjunction with caucuses or conventions or both, to nominate candidates for a variety of public posts.

The adoption of the primary election as the principal means of nominating party candidates for public office grew out of the reforms of the Progressive era. During the last two decades of the nineteenth century, the party convention and caucus (indirect methods of nomination) came under increasing attack from party membership. Combined with public demand for wider popular participation in government, the direct election of candidates became a central element in the crusade for responsible party government.

The first state legislation pertaining to primary elections was enacted in California in 1866, but the reform of the nomination process was sporadic and incomplete until after the turn of the century. Through 1889, state laws regulating the conduct of party primaries were generally limited in scope (addressing certain kinds of fraudulent activity) or optional (with the party deciding whether to invoke the legal protections and abide by statutory provisions). Several states enacted mandatory laws, but these applied only to major metropolitan areas. For the most part, primary elections were conducted by the political parties beyond the effective regulation of the state.

This situation began to change during the 1890s as states enacted more complete and effective statutes. Following the turn of the century, support for primary elections gained widespread acceptance across the country. State primary laws passed during the first two decades of the twentieth century were character-

ized by the statewide application of mandatory regulations. In other words, the political parties (in most states) no longer had the option of orchestrating the manner in which these elections were conducted. The statutes governing general elections were also enforced with respect to primary elections. Furthermore, an increasing number of states embraced the direct primary as a means of nominating party candidates for a wide range of public offices. For example, in 1904 only Wisconsin and Oregon held mandatory, legally regulated direct primaries covering nominations for state offices; by 1917, 32 of the 48 states held such elections.

The expansion of the primary election in the old "Solid South" was largely a product of changes in state Democratic Party rules, rather than legislative activity. As the dominant party, the Democrats controlled nearly every elective position (local and statewide) throughout the region. The Democratic primary thus became more significant in determining who would hold elective office than the general election, in which the Democratic nominee frequently ran uncontested or was pitted against a noncompetitive Republican candidate.

Another practice found throughout the Old South was the white primary. In this variation of the nomination process, the state Democratic parties prescribed requirements for party membership. By limiting membership to "whites only," the Democrats effectively disenfranchised the African American population. This violated the intent of the 15th Amendment, and state laws supporting the practice undermined the "equal protection of the law" clause of the 14th Amendment. The practice was challenged in court on a number of occasions and several important Supreme Court decisions (e.g., *Nixon* v. *Herndon*, 273 U.S. 536 [1927] and *Nixon* v. *Condon*, 286 U.S. 73 [1932]) overturned state laws supporting the white primary. Nevertheless, the state parties were able to circumvent these rulings by claiming to be private and not governmental organizations, which could restrict membership in the same fashion as private clubs. It was not until 1944, with the Court's decision in *Smith* v. *Allwright* (321 U.S. 649), that the white primary was invalidated.

At present, primary elections take one of several forms, depending on state law. A majority of states hold closed primaries, where participation is limited to those voters who are registered with or declare a preference for one of the major parties. For example, only registered Democrats can vote in the Democratic primary in this system. One criticism of the closed primary is that it restricts participation of those voters who identify themselves as Independents. Some states employ the open primary, a system in which registered voters may vote in either party's primary regardless of registration status. While the open primary provides the voter increased flexibility, in both the open and closed primary, the voter is restricted to voting for only one party's slate of candidates for a variety of public offices. A variation of the open primary known as the blanket or wide-open primary allows voters to cast a ballot for each office in either party's primary. In this system a voter may vote for a gubernatorial candidate from one party's slate while choosing among candidates for the state legislature from the other party. The blanket primary has been employed in Alaska, Louisiana, and Washington. Party leaders and activists are generally opposed to the blanket and open primary, arguing that Independents and members of one party may vote for weaker candidates of the other party.

A number of states also have provisions for runoff primaries. A runoff election is held when several candidates (three or more) for a given elective office run in the party primary and none receives a majority of the vote. The runoff election pits the two highest vote-getters in the primary against each other for the party nomination. The runoff primary was particularly important in the southern states prior to the time when the Republican Party began to compete effectively for public office. With the Democratic Party virtually assured of winning the general election, the party primary took on added significance. The large number of Democratic primary candidates for any given office frequently necessitated a runoff election to select the party's nominee.

The presidential primary, that is, the direct election of state party delegates to the national presidential nominating convention, was a logical extension of the primary idea sweeping the country in the early years of the twentieth century. Florida was the first state to provide political parties with this option, which the Democrats employed in 1904. A year later, Wisconsin passed legislation providing for a presidential primary and was followed in succession by Pennsylvania (1906), South Dakota (1909), and Oregon (1910). By 1916, 20 states held Democratic presidential primaries.

In part, the intent of the presidential primary was to reduce the influence of the state party bosses by removing the delegate selection process from their control. While a majority of the delegates to the 1916 Democratic National Convention were selected in primaries, many of these delegates were not bound to vote for specific candidates. These uncommitted delegates were, in large part, coopted into dominant coalitions by the party leadership. While the primary vote did not determine the outcome of the 1916 convention, this method of delegate selection posed a threat to the party leadership.

Contending that these elections were expensive and turnout was generally low, the leaders of both parties were successful in reducing the impact of the primary in the selection of presidential nominees. The number of Democratic primaries declined as some states reverted to previous methods of selecting delegates (i.e., caucuses and state conventions). In many states that continued to hold primaries, these were viewed as an advisory, rather than mandatory, means for selecting delegates. The party leadership continued to wield considerable influence in the nomination process through the 1968 elections. During this period, the presidential primary was not considered the principal means by which a candidate obtained the party's nomination. Instead, support of the party leadership remained the most decisive element in this process.

Following the divisive national convention of 1968, successive Democratic commissions have modified party rules pertaining to the presidential nomination process. Most notable were rule changes concerning the composition of state delegations. Addressing charges that delegates were not representative of the rank-and-file membership, the party first adopted a quota system (1972), later replaced by affirmative action guidelines and an "equal division" rule (1976), which ensured greater representation of women and minorities on state delegations. The new rules subsequently made the presidential primary the preferred method of delegate selection in that this process satisfied the criteria of openness and equal representation. In 1968, 17 states held Democratic presidential primaries in which approximately 48% of the delegates were selected. In contrast, 30 states staged primaries in 1976, selecting 72% of the delegates in this fashion. This trend, in general, has continued through the most recent election, with 40 states holding Democratic primaries in 1992.

These numbers reflect the increasing impact of presidential primaries on the nomination process over the course of the past 20 years. The process, however, is by no means uniform; these elections can take a number of forms. For example, one type of primary may involve the election of delegates that are pledged to a particular candidate, while a second type may provide an expression of nominee preference with no delegates elected. Other forms include the election of unpledged delegates, with no presidential candidates on the ballot, and an election that reflects presidential preference followed by a separate election for delegates. Furthermore, primary rules in the various states allow delegates to be allocated by two separate methods: at the substate level (usually apportioned by congressional district) and at-large (statewide).

While the presidential primary has become a crucial element in the nomination of candidates, there are objections to this process as well. One criticism of the system pertains to increasing campaign expenditures. In order to compete in a large number of front-loaded and regional primaries, a candidate must spend large sums of money for televised campaign messages. This requires effective fund-raising activities. Critics contend that the $1,000-a-plate dinners and special-interest contributions buy political influence. Another objection is that direct primaries reduce the power of party officials in the nomination process. While this was the original intent of the primary process, critics argue that candidates are no longer accountable to the party. The consequences of this development include decreasing levels of party discipline, which result in less coherent legislation and ineffective leadership. Another criticism of this system is that presidential primaries have become media events that detract from the serious discussion of issues. Instead, media coverage focuses on candidate personalities and treats the process much like a horserace. Finally, many observers note that the low turnout in primary elections has not expanded the scope of political participation in the nomination process. Despite these objections, primaries are likely to remain an important feature in the nomination of presidential candidates.

William E. Dugan

SEE ALSO Nominating Conventions, Presidential Nominations and Elections

BIBLIOGRAPHY

Aldrich, John H. *Before the Convention*. Chicago: University of Chicago Press, 1980.

Overacker, Louise. *The Presidential Primary*. New York: Macmillan, 1926.

Polsby, Nelson W. *Consequences of Party Reform*. New York: Oxford University Press, 1983.

Stanley, Harold W., and Richard G. Niemi. *Vital Statistics on American Politics*. 2nd ed. Washington, DC: CQ Press, 1983.

Wayne, Stephen J. *The Road to the White House: The Politics of Presidential Elections*. 5th ed. New York: St. Martin's Press, 1995.

Public Perception of Parties and Candidates

In his ground-breaking work on public opinion, Walter Lippmann (1922) pointed out that people's behavior is usually in response to a pseudo environment, based on perceptions of reality. Especially for abstract, intangible objects, such as political parties, these "pictures in our heads" are often simplified models of a very complex reality. Today, politicians and scholars agree that public perceptions of candidates, parties, and policies are crucial determinants of political success.

Public opinion research has uncovered several rules and limitations related to public perceptions of parties and candidates. First, one has to keep in mind that public perceptions are in constant flux. Since candidates change frequently, their role is quite volatile in regard to public opinion. Accordingly, studies have found that candidate evaluation is an important source of short-run change in election outcomes, with candidates either assets or liabilities for parties (Converse, Clausen, and Miller 1965). While party images are more resistant to change, they are not carved in stone. During Dwight Eisenhower's administration, the Democratic Party lost most of the advantage it had enjoyed, being perceived as the party of prosperity. Moreover, during the past 30 years, Democrats and Republicans have exchanged their public image in regard to which party is better able to keep the country out of war. For the future, it might even be possible that the Republicans will replace the Democrats as the party of the South, a label the Democrats held for more than 100 years.

Second, to talk of a (*single*) public perception is misleading, since different parts of the public have different views of the parties and candidates. The main reason for those differences is the fact that perceptual signals cannot by themselves serve as a basis for understanding. People first have to give those signals meaning by putting them into the appropriate categories of their *conceptual framework*. The pioneer work on how people conceptualize political signals was done in the late 1950s by the Center for Political Studies (CPS) of the University of Michigan. A series of questions about what people liked or disliked about parties and candidates revealed four main levels of conceptualization (Campbell et al. 1960). On the lowest level (about 22% of respondents), people seemed to have little to no understanding of political issues or events and either had no evaluation, or could not defend their evaluation, of candidates or parties. Almost 24% of respondents were found to refer to the *nature of times* ("times are good, so why change?") when evaluating parties and candidates. The biggest group (42%) referred to *group benefits*. Respondents on this level liked or disliked parties and candidates because they thought they were good or bad for a group they identified with (farmers, working people, middle class). Finally, only about 10% of all answers indicated a deeper, more structured understanding of the political world. People in this category used ideological labels to describe their political preferences. The levels of conceptualization/sophistication have led to an intensive debate over the limits of public understanding and knowledge (Converse 1964; Nie, Verba, and Petrocik 1979), but it seems fair to say that a large proportion of the public has only a rudimentary understanding of political issues and processes.

On top of the cognitive limitations of public perceptions, people's beliefs and attitudes about politics are strongly "colored" by their membership in groups and social categories and their identification with a party. V.O. Key (1966) claimed that public perceptions echo the alternatives and outlooks presented to them. This might be justified insofar as historical reality cannot be changed, but political issues or events are often subject to perceptual distortion (Campbell et al. 1960) Thus, we find that people's perceptions are strongly influenced by membership in primary groups (family, colleagues, friends) and, to a lesser degree, social categories such as race, class, or religion (Conover 1984). Party identification, the sense of attachment a person feels to a party, has been identified as the main point of reference for making sense of political events, issues, or personalities. The relationship between those different factors has been studied intensively and is one of interdependence. But it seems that the intensity of one's party identification can explain the direction of many other political perceptions (Niemi and Weisberg 1984). Thus, what a white male executive, living in a suburb and identifying strongly with the Republicans, will perceive when he looks at the Democratic Party or candidate will likely be very different from a poor, inner-city, African American female's view.

Keeping the above limitations in mind, one can try to identify the pattern of perceptions voters seem to hold about the Democratic Party and its candidates. Historically, very little empirical evidence exists about public perceptions before the onset of public opinion research. From its beginning, the Democratic Party presented itself as the party of the common man. Jacksonian Democrats supported reductions in the price of public land and a policy of cheaper money and credit. As a result, laborers, immigrants, and settlers west of the Alleghenies became attracted to it (Sundquist 1980). In 1860, the issue of slavery split the party. In the South, many Democrats served in the Confederate government. As a result of the Civil War, the Democrats became the "party of treason" and the party of the South. It took them until the Great Depression and 1932 to shake fully the former image, and the latter lingers on.

Franklin D. Roosevelt and his New Deal policies had a dramatic impact on the image of the Democratic Party. Roosevelt's reforms helped the poor, aged, unemployed, and labor unions, and the Democratic Party was more and more perceived as the party of "the common man" and economic prosperity. At the same time, an increased regulation of business became associated with Democratic administrations. Throughout the post–New Deal period—the first time national opinion surveys were conducted—an increasing proportion of the public favored (within the framework of a capitalist economy) an active role for the federal government in the areas of labor–management disputes, assistance with jobs, education, medical care, and welfare for the needy. Yet there remained an undercurrent of reverence for individual rights and a mistrust of big government (Page 1978).

In foreign affairs, where public interest and knowledge is even lower than in national politics, the Democratic government had to abandon the interwar isolationism of the 1930s to defeat the Axis powers and then to oppose the Soviet Union. By 1952, the Democrats were indeed perceived as the party of war, and there was some blame for the handling of the early Cold War conflict in Europe and China. This issue might have helped Eisenhower gain the presidency in 1952, since people believed that he might end the Korean War and avoid further conflict.

Public perceptions of the Democrats changed again dramatically during the late 1960s as a result of the combined effect of the Vietnam War and the civil rights movement. A majority of the public thought that racial integration was pushed too fast and too far and wanted the government to stay out of issues such as school integration. By 1967–1968, most people were tired of the Vietnam War, and 63% disapproved of President Lyndon B. Johnson's handling of the war (Page 1978, 33). After the crucial election of 1968, the Democrats were more and more seen as the party of minority interests, and African Americans became loyal Democrats, which alienated many of the white southern Democrats. Increasingly, the Democrats were seen as softer on issues of law and order and more willing to accept a variety of lifestyles. The fact that the image of the Democratic Party changed more than that of the opposition confirms that the actions of the incumbent party are more likely to be known and evaluated than the words of the opposition. Thus, incumbents will usually have a sharper image.

Despite discernible differences in some areas, Page's (1978) analysis of Republican and Democratic Party identifiers finds few sharp differences in 1968. On about half of the 63 issues he analyzed, he did not find any appreciable difference between party positions. On most others, the differences were very moderate. This finding supports the familiar claim that the two major parties are often indistinguishable, mainly because they try to be all things to all people. While party conflict was strongest and most obvious before and during the Civil War and again during the New Deal, Democrats and Republicans stood for much of the same things even during the late 1960s, when American society seemed quite polarized.

These similarities are reflected in public perceptions of parties and candidates. Between 1952 and 1976, around 45% of the public could not see any important differences between the two major parties. This proportion declined about 10% during the 1980s, probably as a result of the Reagan presidency. Several other measures, however, show a long-term decline in the relevance of parties, especially when it comes to evaluations (Wattenberg 1990) and problem-solving capacity. While in 1964 almost 70% of a national sample named one of the two major parties as "likely to do a better job in dealing with this [the most important] problem," this proportion had declined to 44% by 1988. Wattenberg (1991) shows that citizens are more and more likely to conceptualize issues in terms of candidates and less in terms of parties. This also means that the perceptual link between parties and candidates has deteriorated. Bill Clinton ran in 1992 as a "different kind of Democrat" mainly to avoid the "liberal Democrat" label.

With the increasing use of the mass media and political action committees (PACs), candidates have come to assume a more prominent role in the public mind. While earlier studies (Goldberg 1966) found that party identification influenced candidate choice directly and indirectly via its impact on issue evaluations, more recent analyses affirm the crucial role of candidates in the dynamics of electoral choice (Markus and Converse 1984). Starting with Eisenhower, the perception of presidential candidates' personality, experience, skills, and "attractiveness" has been crucial for electoral outcomes. Eisenhower, Nixon, and Reagan were all elected by a public in which Democrats clearly outnumbered Republicans. They also changed the image of their party. Eisenhower helped the Republicans to overcome the negative economic association, Nixon damaged his party with Watergate, and Reagan helped to give the Republicans a big advantage in the area of defense politics.

While the media have helped candidates to gain direct access to the electorate, they also seem to have lowered the quality of public discourse. Television, especially, often prefers images over issues, and tends to emphasize the negative, sensational, or theatrical. This has added to increasing public frustration and negativity about politics in general (Patterson 1994; Graber 1993).

Public confidence in the parties has declined, but the Democrats still retain a core image that shows more than marginal differences to the Republican Party. When asked which political party would do a better job, Democrats in 1992 held a more than 30% advantage over Republicans on the issues of economic conditions, unemployment, health care, environmental protection, race relations, education, and abortion. The public also thought that Democrats would be more likely to keep the United States out of World War III. But on issues such as foreign affairs, national defense, public order, moral decay, and a balanced budget, the Republicans are perceived as the party doing a better job (*Gallup Poll Monthly*, April 1992, July 1992). While these assessments might change in the future, they are much more likely to be persistent than public evaluations of candidates. The fact that President Bush's level of public approval fell from an unprecedented 91% in January 1991 to less than 50% one year later is proof of the volatile nature of public support for candidates.

Christian Goergen

BIBLIOGRAPHY

Campbell, Angus, Philip Converse, Warren Miller, and Donald Stokes. *The American Voter.* New York: Wiley, 1960.

Conover, Pamela J. "The Influence of Group Identification on Political Perception and Evaluation." *Journal of Politics* 46 (1984): 761–785.

Converse, Philip E. "The Nature of Belief Systems in Mass Publics." In *Ideology and Discontent*, ed. David E. Apter. New York: Free Press, 1964.

Converse, Philip E., Aage R. Clausen, and Warren Miller. "Electoral Myth and Reality: The 1964 Election." *American Political Science Review* 59 (1965): 321–334.

Converse, Philip E., and Gregory B. Markus. "Plus ça change . . . : The New CPS Election Study Panel." In *Controversies in Voting Behavior*, 2nd ed. Washington, DC: CQ Press, 1984.

Goldberg, Arthur S. "Discerning a Causal Pattern among Data on Voting Behavior." *American Political Science Review* 60 (1966): 913–922.

Graber, Doris. *Mass Media and American Politics.* 4th ed. Washington, DC: CQ Press, 1993.

Key, V.O., Jr. *The Responsible Electorate.* Cambridge: Harvard University Press, 1966.

Lippmann, Walter. *Public Opinion.* New York: Macmillan, 1922.

Nie, Norman H., S. Verba, and J. Petrocik. *The Changing American Voter.* Cambridge: Harvard University Press, 1979.

Niemi, Richard G., and Herbert F. Weisberg, eds. *Controversies in Voting Behavior.* 2nd ed. Washington, DC: CQ Press, 1984.

Page, Benjamin I. *Choices and Echoes in Presidential Elections: Rational Man and Electoral Democracy.* Chicago: University of Chicago Press, 1978.

Patterson, Thomas E. *Out of Order*. New York: Random House, 1994.

Sundquist, James. *Dynamics of the Party System: Alignments and Realignments of Political Parties in the United States*. Washington, DC: Brookings Institution, 1980.

Wattenberg, Martin P. *The Decline of American Political Parties, 1952–1988*. Cambridge: Harvard University Press, 1990.

———. *The Rise of Candidate-Centered Politics*. Cambridge: Harvard University Press, 1991.

Realignment and Dealignment

While the term *realignment* describes an enduring change in the relative strength of parties, *dealignment* refers to a decline in political party loyalty and a rise in political independence. The increasing number of voters who do not identify with any of the parties, increased split-ticket voting, and the shift from party politics toward candidate-centered politics are all signs of a party dealignment in contemporary American politics. A realignment, in contrast, would be indicated by a complete change in the identity of the major parties (as when the Republicans replaced the Whigs in the 1850s) or a significant change in the party balance (as when the Democrats became the majority party in the 1930s).

Central to an understanding of both realignment and dealignment is the concept of party identification, which has been set firmly in the minds of political scientists ever since the publication of *The American Voter* (Campbell et al. 1960). *The American Voter* defines party identification as a long-term stable influence on voters' decision-making processes. Further, it is a psychological attachment to one of the two major parties that is the result of a childhood socialization process. While party identification is a relatively strong and stable influence on voters' decisions, political scientists and historians have noted that there appear to be periodic shifts in party identification that change the political environment for decades at a time.

The first work to note these shifts was V.O. Key's "A Theory of Critical Elections" (1955). Key argued that critical elections were the signal that a realignment was occurring within the electorate that was "both sharp and durable" (1955, 11) and altered the preexisting cleavages within the electorate. Key identified the elections of 1896 and 1932 as examples of two such critical elections. Additionally, the 1860 election can be characterized as a landmark in American politics. The 1860 realignment left the Democrats with a stronghold in the Solid South, but made the Republicans the dominant party in the North. The Democratic Party was further weakened in the 1896 election of President William McKinley, which solidified Republican dominance. Further Democratic losses occurred mostly in the industrialized areas of the North. The probusiness Republican Party remained in firm control of national government, holding a majority in one or both houses of Congress except for the tenure of Democratic President Woodrow Wilson.

The major realigning electoral period, which, according to some scholars (Sundquist 1983), continues to influence the current cycle of electoral politics, occurred during the 1932, 1934, and 1936 elections. The Great Depression and the failure of the Hoover administration to take decisive efforts to alleviate the economic crisis brought massive switches in party identification in almost all classes of voters. Additionally, a whole new generation of voters, including many first-time women voters, acquired a strong allegiance to the Democratic Party and identified with the Democrats by a 2-to-1 margin (Andersen 1979). Thus the New Deal realignment seems to have been caused by the mobilization of new voters, as well as the conversion of long-standing party allegiances (Erikson and Tedin 1981). The New Deal coalition broadened the Democratic Party's base from its traditional stronghold in the South to the industrial areas in the North, Midwest, and New England.

Lasting rearrangements of party support are driven by policy; in other words, by ideals about what the government should and should not do. Thus realignments are issue centered. The issues causing realignment have been moral (slavery in the 1850s) or economic (as in the 1890s and 1930s).

For the past 30 years, election analysts have debated the question of a new realignment. For instance, Carmines, Renten, and Stimson (1984) argue that racial issues caused a realignment during the 1960s. According to Carmines et al., Democratic identification decreased among southern whites. Black voters, in contrast, became more firmly Democratic. Although these changes did not affect total party identification figures, the coalitional makeup of the parties was altered. Yet there is much scholarly disagreement on the question of whether or not a realignment occurred in 1964. Sundquist (1983) argues strongly against such a realignment. He sees the South belatedly conforming to class-based patterns of party identification that were adopted by the rest of the nation during the New Deal realignment (see also Silbey 1991).

The possibility of a new realignment at the expense of the Democrats was raised again by the victories of Republican Presidents Ronald Reagan and George Bush in 1980, 1984, and 1988. Similar to Roosevelt's success in 1932, Reagan's election was the result of widespread dissatisfaction with incumbent President Carter. Reagan's economic and social policies constituted a significant departure from previous policies, and Bush's electoral victory constituted the first time in four decades that the incumbent party has won the White House for two consecutive elections. Yet the realignment process seems to be incomplete because Republicans were unable to capture both houses of Congress. Although Republicans continued to dominate in presidential elections, they actually lost House seats in 1988. Bush won the presidency with a solid margin of 54% to 46%, yet Democrats were able to capture the House and the Senate. Further, there has been little discernible movement in state and local politics toward the kind of ideological division needed for party realignment (Huckshorn 1984).

It is possible that a new realignment favorable to the conservatives is in the making. The impressive gains of conservatives in the 1994 midterm election could signal the end of the New Deal realignment and the emergence of a new coalition of conservative voters. Democrats controlled the House of Representatives since 1952. As a result of the 1994 midterm election, they are now the minority party in the House, as well as in the Senate. Thirty-five Democratic incumbents, including House Speaker Tom Foley, had to surrender their seats to Republican challengers. Yet it remains to be seen if the conservative gains from 1994 will be followed up in the 1996 presidential election. In sum, scholarly work on realignment rejects the idea that Democratic losses in the presidential elections in the 1980s and the 1994 midterm elections should be interpreted as signs of a major nationwide realignment. Much of the speculation on realignment has focused on the South. Although formerly the stronghold of the Democratic Party, Democratic Presidents Jimmy Carter and Bill Clinton were unable to capture the southern white vote, and southern Democrats suffered significant losses in Congress.

An alternative to the realignment thesis is dealignment, and many scholars argue that the question of whether or not a realignment has occurred in the past 30 years is moot because the political system has experienced dealignment during that period. The dealignment argument contends that, instead of people changing from one party to another or new voters joining one party in large numbers, the American political system is characterized by voters' rejection of parties and a move toward independent status. Where once the great majority of Americans closely identified with a political party, strong attachments to the parties and support for the party system generally have fallen to all-

time historical lows. Survey data collected by the Center for Political Studies at the University of Michigan document the erosion of support for the parties.

Throughout the 1950s, only about 21% of the electorate considered themselves to be Independents. From 1964 on, the situation changed dramatically. Independent voters increased in the 1960s to 25.8%, and in the 1970s to 34.8%. The number of Independents has remained relatively stable throughout the 1980s and 1990s. Although the numbers of both Democratic and Republican identifiers decreased, losses for the Democrats have been more severe. In 1954, 22% of Americans identified strongly with the Democratic Party, and 25% considered themselves to be weak Democrats. Twenty years later, only 17% strongly identified with the Democrats and 21% weakly identified with Democrats. These numbers remained relatively constant throughout the 1980s and 1990s.

What have been the consequences of this process of dealignment? Throughout the 1950s, party identification was the key predictor of an individual's vote. For instance, 83% of American voters who identified with a party voted consistently with that identification in the 1956 election (Nie, Verba, and Petrocik 1984). In contrast, in 1972 about half the voters were not guided by their party identification. Although the Democrats can claim more party identifiers than Republicans, Democrats are more likely to defect than strong Republicans (Crotty 1984). In the 1988 election, 82% of Democrats voted for Dukakis; however, 91% of Republicans voted for Bush. Not only have there been marked increases in partisan defection in voting, but also concomitant increases in ticket splitting. Ticket splitting occurs when a voter casts his or her ballot for candidates of two or more parties for different offices in the same election. As recently as 1960, almost two-thirds of the electorate reported voting a straight party ballot in presidential elections. By 1972, these percentages nearly reversed as 62% of the electorate reported voting a split ticket.

What is behind the steady and dramatic decline in partisanship since 1964? Norpoth and Rusk's analysis (1982) indicates that the decline was caused by the entrance of new voters, who came with a discernible lower partisanship level than voters who entered the electorate between 1952 and 1964, as well as the desertion of parties by those already in the electorate. Thus, dealignment has occurred in all age groups since 1964, although the generations that entered the electorate after 1964 are much less likely to have ties to one of the political parties. These generational differences in the strength of party attachment point toward an incomplete transmission of partisanship from parents to children. In other words, parental partisanship was either less salient or was rejected in the generations entering the electorate after 1964.

Additional causes of party dealignment can be found by investigating citizens' attitudes toward the parties, as well as structural changes in the parties that have taken place throughout the past 30 years. More than ever before, voters distrust parties. Confidence in the parties is particularly low among the young. In 1984, 56% of those under age 35 felt better represented by interest groups; only 25% chose parties. Clyde Wilcox (1995) reports an exit poll showing that 31% of Americans were fed up with both political parties.

As far as structural changes in the parties are concerned, scholars point toward the decline of the urban political machine, the parties' diminished role in the recruitment and nomination of candidates, as well as the emergence of new campaign technologies as sources of dealignment. While changes in the Democratic presidential nomination process (McGovern–Frazer Commission 1972) resulted in an opening up and democratization of the selection process, the introduction of open primaries virtually eliminated the party's primary function—the control over who is running under its party label.

The introduction of new campaign technologies contributed to a further shift in the balance of power away from the parties and to the candidates. Campaign assets once received from the party organization (i.e., skills, manpower, information, and campaign funds) are now often provided by pollsters, fund raisers, the media, and public relations experts (Sorauf 1976). Consequently, a candidate's success depends on his or her ability to attract financial support from organized interests and create a favorable media image. The modern candidate is relatively independent from the party, and candidates are forced to proclaim allegiance to their party only when it seems politically expedient to do so (Bennett 1996).

Regardless of its causes or extent, the weakening of the parties and the growing alienation of the electorate from the major U.S. parties has produced significant changes in political behavior and the political system. For the past 30 years, American politics has been characterized by an increase in political independence among both citizens and politicians that manifests itself in personality-oriented politics and a decreased reliance on party cues.

Frauke Schnell

SEE ALSO Voting Behavior

BIBLIOGRAPHY

Andersen, Kristi. *The Creation of a Democratic Majority, 1928–1936.* Chicago: University of Chicago Press, 1979.

Bennett, Lance B. *The Governing Crisis: Media, Money, and Marketing in American Elections.* New York: St. Martin's Press, 1996.

Burnham, Walter D. *Critical Elections and the Mainsprings of American Politics.* New York: Norton, 1970.

Campbell, Angus, Philip E. Converse, Warren E. Miller, and Donald E. Stokes. *The American Voter.* New York: Wiley, 1960.

Carmines, Edward G., Steven H. Renten, and James A. Stimson. "Events and Alignments: The Party Image Link." In *Controversies in Voting Behavior*, ed. Richard G. Niemi and Herbert F. Weisberg. Washington, DC: CQ Press, 1984.

Converse, Philip E. *The Dynamics of Party Support.* Beverly Hills, CA: Sage, 1976.

Crotty, William. *American Parties in Decline.* Glenview, IL: Scott, Foresman, 1984.

Erikson, Robert S., and Kent L. Tedin. "The 1928–1936 Partisan Realignment: The Case for the Conversion Hypothesis." *American Political Science Review* 75 (1981): 951–962.

Huckshorn, Robert J. *Political Parties in America.* Monterey, CA: Brooks/Cole, 1984.

Key, V.O. "A Theory of Critical Elections." *Journal of Politics* 17 (1955): 3–18.

Nie, Norman, Sidney Verba, and John R. Petrocik. *The Changing American Voter.* Cambridge: Harvard University Press, 1979.

Norpoth, Helmut, and Jerold Rusk. "Partisan Dealignment in the American Electorate." *American Political Science Review* 76 (1982): 522–537.

Silbey, Joel H. "Beyond Realignment and Realignment Theory: American Political Eras, 1789–1989." In *The End of Realignment? Interpreting American Electoral Eras*, ed. Byron E. Shafer. Madison: University of Wisconsin Press, 1991.

Sorauf, Frank J. *Party Politics in America.* Boston: Little, Brown, 1976.

Sundquist, James L. *Dynamics of the Party System.* Washington, DC: Brookings Institution, 1983.

Wilcox, Clyde. *The Latest American Revolution? The 1994 Elections and Their Implications for Governance.* New York: St. Martin's Press, 1995.

Religion

The U.S. Constitution contains two passages strictly divorcing religion from the government. Article VI maintains that "no religious Test shall ever be required as a Qualification to any Office or public Trust under the United States," and the First Amendment begins "Congress shall make no law respecting an establishment of religion, or prohibiting the free exercise thereof." These provisions do not, however, remove religion from the arena of politics, and they cannot force citizens and voters to forget their religious affiliations and biases. In practice, American politics are often intricately interwoven with religious concerns, though the largely Protestant makeup of the United States often conceals the blatantly religious elements of public life that have been given official sanction: presidents traditionally take the oath of office with their hand resting on a Bible; since the 1860s, U.S. currency has borne the motto In God We Trust, made the national motto in 1956; and the Pledge of Allegiance, given federal sanction for recitation in public schools, has included the phrase "one nation, under God" since 1954; Christmas, but no other major religious holiday of any creed, is both a federal holiday and a state holiday in all fifty states.

The United States is undoubtedly a Christian nation, as these facts attest, yet significant and often influential elements of society do not adhere to one of the sects of the dominant form of Christianity in America, Protestantism. Struggles over the inclusion of certain moral precepts in legislation, the imposition of certain religious rites in public functions and institutions, and the issue of religious tolerance, religious separation, and religious privilege have made religion a central feature of electoral and partisan politics. Without artificially drawing lines, the two major parties can be readily identified with certain attitudes about religion: since World War II, both Roman Catholics and Jews have consistently voted Democratic, while white Protestants have consistently voted Republican. These voting patterns have deep historical roots and have been reinforced by the recent movement of the Religious Right into the mainstream of the Republican Party and the corresponding reaction of the Democratic Party against moralistic legislation and judgments in Republican-dominated courts.

Early in American history, immigration of diverse religious and ethnic groups forced the political parties to handle the issue of religious pluralism and toleration as they attempted to build broad-based voting coalitions directed at electoral success and control of government bodies. The Democratic Party has had to face these difficulties more directly than its opponents the Whigs and, later, the Republicans, for the Democratic Party began, early in its history, to draw on the support of the less privileged, which included poor farmers and urban laborers, most of whom were Catholic and, later, Jewish immigrants. In its opposition to the Whig Party, the Democratic Party of the early 1800s often relied on religious affiliation to generate loyalty. Initially, these loyalties divided along Protestant sectarian lines, with New England Congregationalists generally supporting the Whigs, while less-established denominations such as Baptists and Methodists backed the Democrats. The Democrats were also able to draw the support of early Catholic immigrants, as the Whig Party came to be associated with an evangelical Protestantism that aggressively pressed for Prohibition and legislation outlawing activities on Sunday. Hard-drinking natives, often poor urban laborers, joined Germans and Irishmen in opposing the temperance crusade of the Whigs.

But the diverse elements in the Democratic coalition brought difficulties for the party, as Protestant resentment of Catholic influence within the party and Catholic demands for separate, tax-supported schools constantly threatened to split the party, as it did, for example, in 1843, when dissident anti-Catholic Democrats broke from the party and formed the American Republican Party, which expressed concern over the number of Catholic officeholders. The Democrats also had difficulties sustaining immigrant support, as the diversity of groups coming to the United States in the mid-nineteenth century complicated the process of political integration. Some evangelical Protestant immigrants favored temperance and blue laws, but the strong nativism of certain Republican elements drove them into the Democratic fold. There were also Protestant immigrants from Germany, Ireland, and Wales who feared the Catholic church and despised their fellow countrymen who belonged to it, but these men were unwilling to support the moralism of temperance or sabbatarian campaigning, and they likewise supported the Democratic Party.

The Republican Party's steady support of pious issues such as temperance and blue laws, and that party's general anti-Catholicism, suspicion of immigrants, and opposition to parochial education, helped the Democrats maintain their uneasy alliance with Catholics and immigrants. The Democratic Party, in the mid- and late 1800s, actually offered little economically or politically to the poor immigrants it attracted, but the puritanical moralism and deep prejudice of many Republicans frightened these new Americans and, they felt, threatened their way of life. Thus the Democratic Party was able to continue to draw support from this sector simply by advocating, often merely tacitly or negatively, religious and ethnic toleration and by portraying, without much difficulty, the Republicans as a party that desired to Christianize society and abolish immorality.

By the turn of the twentieth century, Catholics, largely of Irish descent, occupied important positions in the Democratic Party, and their loyalty and discipline, as well as their status as immigrants (or immigrants' children) helped them draw most of the new immigrants from southern and eastern Europe, many of whom were Jewish, into the Democratic fold. But tensions once again arose in the coalition in the 1920s. Many of the Protestants in the party, by this time mostly from the rural areas of the South and West, were growing concerned about the decidedly urban base of the party. This rural, agrarian wing of the party, led by William Jennings Bryan, sought to give the Democrats a moralistic cast and attempted to rescue "traditional American virtue" from the corruption of the city, with its political machines, saloons, and Catholic and Jewish religions.

These conflicting wings of the Democratic Party crippled its presidential chances in the Republican-dominated 1920s, as the battles between urban-supported Alfred E. Smith and the rural-supported heir of Bryan, William G. McAdoo, attempted to take control of the party. The battle reached its climax at the 1924 Democratic convention in New York City, where Smith and McAdoo fought for the nomination, both in vain, as neither faction could marshal the necessary two-thirds, and on the 103rd ballot, a compromise candidate, a colorless lawyer and former solicitor general under Wilson, was selected.

By 1928, Smith had consolidated his position in the Democratic Party and, on the first ballot, became the first non-Protestant candidate for president of the United States. With Smith heading the Democratic ticket, religion became one of the central issues in the 1928 campaign. "If you vote for Al Smith," one Baptist pastor warned, "you're voting against Christ and you'll all be damned." Smith was easily defeated by Hoover, and though the Republican candidate was popular and the party was at one of its highest peaks of popularity at the time, Smith's Catholicism must have been a major factor in his defeat. Before the election, the *New York Times* had predicted that Smith would lose at least a million votes because of his religion. Senator George Norris, representing the farming state of Nebraska, put the case bluntly: "The greatest element involved in the landslide was religion. Regret it and conceal it as we may, religion had more to do with the defeat of Governor Smith than any other one thing."

Despite his loss, the Smith candidacy, and the Republican attacks on his religion, helped forge a lasting Democratic coalition between agrarian elements in the party and urban ethnic groups—an alliance that brought Democrat Franklin Delano Roosevelt an unprecedented four presidential victories. Roosevelt did much to strengthen this coalition, and the Democratic Party has been able to maintain it, with some defection, until the present, when Catholics and Jews still vote overwhelming Democratic. Thirty-two years after Smith's run for the White House, the Democratic Party fielded the first and only successful non-Protestant presidential candidate, John F. Kennedy. Though the Democratic coalition containing Catholics, Jews, and Protestants had been an established fact of American politics since FDR, the Democratic candidate's Catholicism was once again made an issue in the election, and fears of the pope running America were once again voiced. According to the Survey Research Center of the University of Michigan study of the 1960 election, Kennedy lost 16.5% of the vote in the normally Democratic South because of his religion.

After Kennedy, the specific religious preferences of presidential candidates was no longer an issue—at least for those of Christian denomination. When Michael Dukakis, a member of the Greek Orthodox church, ran for president, little was made of his affiliation (whereas his membership in the nonsectarian American Civil Liberties Union was made into a major issue by his opponent, George Bush). Nevertheless, the Democratic Party has yet to nominate a Jewish or other non-Christian presidential candidate, and national politics continues to be dominated by Protestants.

The Democratic National Committee, despite its reliance on diverse religious groups, has assiduously avoided the issue of religion in its official party platform. Neither religion nor religious toleration was specifically mentioned in the Democratic platform between 1876 (when the separation of church and state was mentioned in passing) and 1984, when the platform read as follows: "The current administration has consistently sought to reverse in the courts or overrule by constitutional amendment a long line of Supreme Court decisions that preserve our historic commitment to religious tolerance and church/state separation. The Democratic Platform affirms its support of the principles of religious liberty, religious tolerance and church/state separation and of the Supreme Court decisions forbidding violation of those principles. We pledge to resist all efforts to weaken those decisions."

Thus it was that the Democratic Party's generally liberal policies, particularly regarding toleration of diverse groups within the population, led the party to react strongly to the growing moralism and religious timber of Republican politics in the 1980s. The Democratic coalition, containing Catholics and Jews as well as Protestants, has associated that party with a more tolerant attitude toward religious practice and a stricter separation of church and state, and by the time the First Amendment's religion clauses were challenged in the Supreme Court, in the 1940s, Democratically appointed justices dominated the Court and would continue to do so until the early 1980s.

The Democrat-dominated Court adopted and stuck to a strict interpretation of the Establishment Clause, which bars "an establishment of religion." The precedent for Establishment cases was set in *Emerson* v. *Board of Education* (1947) in an opinion written by Roosevelt appointee Hugo Black (a bastion of liberal opinion on the Court for over 30 years). This ruling held that the Establishment Clause prohibits any aid to religion and requires a strict neutrality not only among religions but also between religion and irreligion.

The *Emerson* precedent was followed by the Court throughout the coming decades and used to strike down a variety of legislation that allegedly supported religion in one way or another, many of which were related, like *Emerson*, to nonpublic education. The Court invalidated state requirements for Bible reading and the recitation of the Lord's Prayer in public schools (1963), overturned an Arkansas law prohibiting the teaching of evolution (1968), invalidated a Maryland constitutional provision that established a religious test for public office (1961), struck down a Tennessee law that disqualified clergy from serving as state legislators (1978), invalidated North Carolina's practice of publishing a "motorist's prayer" on its official highway map (1981), struck down a Kentucky law directing that a copy of the Ten Commandments be posted in public school classrooms (1980), invalidated New York's establishment of a nondenominational prayer for public school children (1962), and disallowed an Illinois program that allowed students to be released from classes for religious instruction on school premises (1948). The Court also invalidated many state laws intended to aid parents and students associated with nonpublic schools, many of which offered religious instruction, overturning state programs that gave grants and tax benefits to parents attending nonpublic schools, state funding for the upkeep of nonpublic school facilities, state payment of salaries for teachers of secular subjects in nonpublic schools, lending of instructional materials (excluding textbooks) to pupils in nonpublic schools, provision of counseling, testing, and psychological services for pupils in nonpublic schools, and reimbursement to parents for field-trip transportation costs incurred by children attending nonpublic schools.

These interpretations of the First Amendment's religion clauses have been under attack since Nixon- and Reagan-appointed justices have come to dominate the Court (since 1981), bringing the sympathies toward organized religion of the Republican Party into the majority and enabling the enactment of a different program of constitutional interpretation. Religion, either the practice or the free expression of, has not otherwise

been a major issue for the Democratic Party, particularly in recent years as the Republicans have come more and more under the influence of religious interest groups and are adopting a stance that is continually informed by the moral precepts of evangelical Protestantism.

Jack J. Miller

SEE ALSO School Prayer

BIBLIOGRAPHY

Maisel, L. Sandy, ed. *Political Parties and Elections in the United States.* New York: Garland, 1991.

Noll, Mark A., ed. *Religion and American Politics: From the Colonial Period to the 1980s.* New York: Oxford University Press, 1990.

Schlesinger, Arthur M., Jr., ed. *History of U.S. Political Parties.* Broomall, PA: Chelsea House, 1973.

Wald, Kenneth D. *Religion and Politics in the United States.* Washington, DC: CQ Press, 1992.

School Prayer

Members of the Democratic Party have been far less inclined to support school prayer than their Republican brethren, with the majority of Democrats strongly aligned against it. One faction within the Democratic Party, however, has included some divergent members who favor an amendment to allow prayer in public schools: southern conservatives.

Yet it should be noted that on an issue as deeply personal as religion, elected Democrats, including both those in Congress and in past administrations, have often been impelled by personal reasons, ideologies, or beliefs to either support or denounce school prayer. Their positions have also been swayed by historical or legal arguments.

The issue, long at the margins of U.S. political history, took center stage after the 1982 election of conservative Republican President Ronald Reagan, who proposed an amendment to remove the legal barrier to prayer in public schools, making him the first chief executive to turn the country's attention to the issue. The Supreme Court banned prayer from public schools in the 1960s.

After Reagan's proposal, some of the most intensive lobbying of the 1980s took place as right-wing Christian fundamentalists rallied behind the amendment. But fierce opposition from Democrats and liberal, Protestant, and Jewish organizations kept proponents from amassing the required votes to secure passage.

Leading the school prayer charge for conservative southern Democrats was Senator Ernest F. Hollings of

South Carolina. He argued that the Court rulings of the 1960s banning school prayer were a misinterpretation of the Constitution, necessitating an amendment to neutralize what he and other conservatives saw as a hostile government policy toward religion. Yet for many Democrats, protecting the sanctity of the Constitution outweighed any personal inclinations for favoring school prayer.

The majority of Senate Democrats forcefully opposed Reagan's proposal. Senator Howard M. Metzenbaum of Ohio played a strong role for the Democrats in criticizing the amendment. The Democrats maintained that it would violate the country's tradition of separation between church and state and that the Constitution should be amended only in the most clear-cut cases and for the most pressing reasons. Senator Bill Bradley, Democrat of New Jersey, summed up the opposition of many Democrats when he stated that no prayer would ever be found acceptable for the array of diverse religions represented in America's schools. Other Democrats voiced fears that school prayer would be used as religious indoctrination by a community's dominant majority. Besides, they said, the amendment would, for all practical purposes, be impossible to implement.

Conservative Republicans, the chief supporters of the amendment, cited the omnipresence of God in the classroom and the right of students to pray to Him. And they rebutted the Democrats and moderate Republicans by maintaining that local communities could be entrusted to resolve the problem of implementing the amendment and the possibility of trivializing prayer. They contended that the federal government should not place limits of expression on local communities.

Although Congress rejected the school prayer amendment, it passed the Equal Access Act of 1984, which prohibits school districts from discriminating against high school religious clubs. Religious Right lobbyists and ultraconservatives viewed the act as a partial victory.

In the mid-1990s, the Christian Coalition revived the issue of school prayer, pushing a Religious Equality Amendment to the Constitution that would allow expression of religion in such public forums as schools. The amendment received the blessing of ultraconservative Republican Representative Newt Gingrich of Georgia, the Speaker of the House, and his more moderate Republican colleague Robert Dole of Kansas, the Senate majority leader until June 1996 and a 1996 presidential candidate. The Democratic administration of President Bill Clinton and most Democratic Party members opposed it.

Steve Hoenisch

SEE ALSO Religion

BIBLIOGRAPHY

Bacon, Donald C., Roger H. Davidson, and Morton Keller, eds. *The Encyclopedia of the United States Congress.* New York: Simon and Schuster, 1995.

Fenwick, Lynda Beck. *Should the Children Pray: A Historical, Judicial, and Political Examination of Public School Prayer.* Waco, TX: Baylor University Press, 1989.

Social Security

The Democratic Party takes credit for Social Security as a program of the U.S. government, and for efforts to make the program a priority when facing budget constraints. Prior to the enactment of Social Security as a government program, most Democrats argued that providing social services was a responsibility of the private sector. Social welfare programs are still a patchwork of national efforts, state efforts, and private efforts. Leaders of the Democratic Party have tried to increase the proportion of the federal government's contribution.

The founders of the Democratic Party (then the Democrat-Republican Party) saw social welfare more as something to be provided by individuals free of government interference than as something to be provided by government. Their rivals, the Federalists, were more likely to be the advocates of government action.

Indeed, the notion that ours was a nation of joiners, many of whom came to America because individual initiative was valued and government interference was not, was important in American culture. But during the Great Depression many people saw the limits to individual initiative and voluntary organization. People who thought of themselves as great successes realized just how vulnerable they were to the whims of the marketplace.

Most increases in spending on social services came during periods of social unrest, the Progressive era at the beginning of the twentieth century, the New Deal period of the 1930s, and the Great Society of the 1960s. Thus the Democratic Party's support of spending on social services is sometimes viewed as "saving capitalism."

One social welfare program that Democrats were less likely to support than Republicans was the old-age and disability pension given to veterans of the Civil War. As the veterans died, so too did the programs. Democrats were likely to oppose other schemes for having the government aid unemployed people of the 1800s as "wild-eyed" and "impractical." These included an Independent Party proposal in 1876 that workers without jobs settle western lands and be employed on government improvement projects; an 1878 Greenback–Labor Party proposal that the unemployed be aided through loans, public works programs, and settlement in the West; and various ideas of the influential American socialist Edward Bellamy.

During World War I, Britain, perhaps America's staunchest ally, extended unemployment insurance to cover munitions workers and others involved in support of the war effort. Eventually, benefits were extended to cover all British workers, who came to see them as an entitlement, rather than a privilege.

The advancement of industrialism and capitalism was accompanied by the declining influence of families, churches, and even civic-mindedness, so many Democrats were skeptical about the ability of the nongovernmental "social safety net" to provide for the social welfare of all Americans. Certain risks and obligations would not be borne by private insurance companies or by other institutions; in the face of this vacuum, government was a last and necessary resort.

Social welfare was guaranteed or proposed for limited groups of Americans by several Democrat-supported laws enacted or introduced prior to the Social Security Act of 1935. In 1917, the Robinson–Keating Bill proposed federal grants-in-aid and a cooperative federal–state–local administration. In 1933, the Wagner–Peyser Act created the U.S. Employment Service, which would later be transferred to the Social Security Board, within the Department of Labor.

The congressional election of 1934 saw a decisive Democratic victory. Third parties to the left of the Democrats now held ten seats in the House of Representatives and two in the Senate. The question was no longer whether the government should be involved in promoting social welfare, but how. The election was in part a mandate for the New Deal policies of Franklin Delano Roosevelt, but in part a sign that there was public sentiment for more decisive change.

The Social Security Act was passed in 1935 and was signed into law by then President Franklin Roosevelt. Originally it meant a 1% tax on payrolls, since increased to many times that amount.

When passed, the Social Security Act was even viewed by some of the Democrats who were its staunchest advocates as a temporary relief measure and a response to a crisis, rather than as a permanent entitlement. Instead of withering away, in later years of the twentieth century, demands for public assistance became greater, and leaders of the Democratic Party were generally responsive. Indeed, rather than limit the program, Roosevelt's successor, Democratic President Harry Truman, broadened it.

Within the Roosevelt administration, many people could give input on Social Security, and eventually the program sunk to the least common denominator. An interdepartmental Cabinet Committee on Economic Security helped shape the legislation, as did an advisory council of public, labor, and management representatives.

Finally, on January 17, 1935, a proposal was submitted to Congress. It represented a victory for proponents of a cautious approach such as Secretary of the Treasury Morgenthau or those especially concerned with the program's financial integrity. In a phone call to Roosevelt aide Harry Hopkins, Morgenthau complained that supplementing payroll taxes with general revenues would be a "bad curve."

Thanks to a proposal by Representative Lundeen, Roosevelt was able to portray his as a centrist one. In March 1935, Lundeen's bill received a favorable vote from the House Labor Committee and was sent to the full House. Roosevelt, though, viewed his bill as more politically pragmatic. He told a critic, "With those taxes in there, no damn politician can ever scrap my social security program."

A major issue has always been what percentage of Social Security revenues should come from the worker, and what percentage from the government. This helps determine the degree to which income is redistributed or the program functions like a bank account, with those with higher incomes putting in more and taking out more. Among the two major parties, Democrats have leaned toward the former view, Republicans the latter.

The battle between Social Security as an assistance program, redistributing wealth, and as an insurance program, serving essentially as a bank account, was a divisive one, within and between the major parties. Since the program's enactment, members of the Democratic Party were more likely to be protective of the assistance features of the program, members of the Republican Party of the insurance features. For instance, when Republican President Gerald Ford proposed a small increase in payroll taxes in 1976, Democratic legislative leaders balked because an increase in the payroll tax, while it might make for a sounder insurance program, would not redistribute wealth. Similarly, Ford once proposed a ceiling on increases in benefits, which was rejected by Democratic leaders in the Senate because the proposed increase was less than the rate of inflation. Because Social Security was a popular program, Ford reversed himself.

Indeed, when Ford proposed in his 1976 State of the Union address that Social Security taxes be increased, Democratic Congressman Al Ullman of Oregon countered that there should instead be a new tax on commercial transactions.

Because the act did little to redistribute wealth, there has always been a minority within the Democratic Party feeling that it should have gone further. That was the feeling of Huey Long of Louisiana. In 1934 he unsuccessfully proposed a means-tested federal pension to be financed by a progressive tax on wealth. He criticized the sum appropriated for federal old-age assistance as too meager to "pay for the ribbons of the typewriters it will take to mail out the envelopes."

Particularly influential in the act's adoption were President Roosevelt, who had observed in his 1933 inaugural, "I see a third of a nation ill-fed, ill-clad, and ill-housed," and Roosevelt's secretary of labor, Francis Perkins. Roosevelt's "Four Freedoms" speech also indicated that "freedom from want" was a major reason for fighting World War II. He felt that enactment of the Social Security Act had been a significant step toward providing that freedom at home.

Partly because a federal government guarantee was new in the United States, Democratic supporters were branded as communists, or at least as dupes helping to establish an important step on the agenda of Karl Marx. Indeed, some in the administration did see the act as an important step forward in establishing a Bill of Economic Rights, to accompany the civil and political guarantees of the Bill of Rights.

Changes at the national level were followed by programs in the states, most of them spearheaded by Democrats. In general the states were slow to act (Wisconsin was the only state with an unemployment insurance program) and, as with the federal Social Security statute, did very little to redistribute wealth.

Democratic leaders sponsored several amendments to the Social Security Act to broaden coverage; in many cases, these were successful. They include the 1956 introduction of disability insurance (blindness was covered in the original legislation) and Medicare for senior citizens. Earlier amendments, made in 1939, were also designed to ensure that benefits were not strictly proportioned to contributions.

The payroll tax also faced opposition from some Democrats in the Senate, including Hugo Black, then a senator from Alabama.

Partly in response to the recession of 1937–1938, which some allege was partly caused by the program's reliance on payroll taxes, the 1939 amendments called for some governmental subsidy. The revisions received large majorities from Democratic and Republican members of Congress, passing 364 to 2 in the House and 57 to 8 in the Senate.

In 1972 Democrats led efforts to index Social Security benefits to inflation. In fact, because benefits were to rise 1% faster than the Consumer Price Index, it was charged that they, too, were a source of inflation.

In practice, Social Security benefits did tend to rise at a rate greater than the rate of inflation. Between 1970 and 1975, for example, the Consumer Price Index increased 40%, while Social Security benefits increased 58%.

Key constituencies of the Democratic Party are supportive of government efforts to provide social services. Most labor unions provide retirement pensions for their members, but the amounts are insufficient if not accompanied by government funds. Many members of the ethnic groups that traditionally support the Democratic Party, including Italian, Irish, and African Americans, view government efforts to guarantee a minimum level of Social Security favorably. And senior citizens, many members of interest groups such as the American Association of Retired Persons and the Gray Panthers, are a potent political force.

When the Social Security Act was adopted, important pressure groups argued that the Democrats should have gone further. These included the American Association for Old Age Security, later the American Association for Social Security (AASS). The AASS wanted a more comprehensive system, one like the British one. Earlier the AASS complained: "Our present American doles are degrading and niggardly; British insurance payments are self-respecting and three times as adequate." For its part, the *London Times* welcomed the act's passage, saying that if it had been in force before the depression, the effects would not have been as swift or severe.

When the act was adopted, there was serious question whether it, and similar statutes introduced in various states, would be consistent with state and federal constitutions. But just as other federal institutions became more accepting of the increased governmental role, so too did the judiciary. Many federal judges were appointed by the Roosevelt administration and tended to find provisions of the act constitutional. State judges appointed by Democratic governors had every incentive to find the act consistent with their state constitutions because if they did not, it would only mean that other states, and not theirs, would receive federal funds.

Particularly significant were two cases, *Steward Machine Company* v. *Davis*, and *Helvering* v. *Davis*, for both of which Justice Cardozo wrote the majority (5–4) opinion. In the latter case Justice Cardozo agreed with many Democrats who argued that there were lessons to be learned from 1929 and that one of these was that the federal Congress must be able to legislate for the general welfare.

A later legal question concerned the applicability of the Due Process Clause of the Constitution to Social Security benefits. For example, was there a constitutional right to property in money paid into the Social Security fund, and was there a constitutional right to an evidentiary hearing prior to the termination of Social Security benefits? The answer of the Supreme Court, expressed in *Flemming* v. *Nestor* and *Mathews* v. *Eldridge*, was no. Speaking for a majority of the Court in the latter case, Justice Powell differentiated between welfare benefits and Social Security benefits, contending that "the disabled worker's need is likely to be less than that of a welfare recipient." Significantly, the two dissenters in the *Mathews* case, Justices Brennan and Marshall, argued that in many cases, Social Security benefits can be very significant, and an evidentiary hearing should be available prior to their termination. Most Democrats would agree with them.

In comparison to other industrialized countries, the Social Security Act in the United States is rather meager. Indeed, many Democrats would like to see additional protections granted and existing protections widened. They would like a system more like New Zealand's, for instance, in which medical care is guaranteed, and that has the effect of redistributing income downward. In the United States, by contrast, most medical care is privately paid for and provided, and some individuals go without, choosing to use their limited income for other things.

Cross-national comparisons lend support to the idea that the Democratic Party would be supportive of government Social Security guarantees. Labor and Social Democratic parties and governments tend to be more supportive of government programs than are parties and governments representing business or propertied classes.

Programs have very seldom given rights to the powerless. Indeed it is precisely because many recipients of Social Security benefits demand that the benefits be retained or broadened that most Democratic officeholders will adapt their policies to get reelected. Especially those representing an aging constituency, as did Representative Claude Pepper of Florida, have their political futures determined by how they vote on Social Security. And because most voters hope to be recipients of Social Security benefits, most Democratic politicians will have self-interested motivations, rather than charitable ones, for voting that appropriations be continued or increased.

Some of the differences are no doubt cultural, but others have to do with the political structure. In the United States, power is divided so that even if key constituencies placing a priority on comprehensive social services are able to obtain positions of leadership within the Democratic Party, their opponents are able to block change.

One important difference is in competing notions of civil rights and human rights. The French Declaration of the Rights of Man of 1789 describes public assistance as a "sacred debt." By contrast, the American Declaration of Independence proclaimed individuals' inalienable rights to "life, liberty, and the pursuit of happiness," and the Bill of Rights emphasizes freedom from government. Even when Democratic President Jimmy Carter urged (unsuccessfully) that the United States join most other industrial nations by ratifying the United Nations Covenant on Economic, Social and Cultural Rights, he proposed reservations indicating that in the United States many social services were to be provided by individuals or agencies other than the federal government.

In the 1990s, many Democrats joined Republicans in their concern over the budget deficit. A bipartisan commission, chaired by Bob Kerrey, an influential Democratic senator from Nebraska, and Missouri Republican senator John Danforth, proposed in 1993, among other things, that the minimum age for receiving old-age Social Security benefits from the government be raised from 65 to 67. This change, the commission indicated, would save $70 billion per year. The commission's proposed changes were induced largely by demographic factors; there were more people considered to be of "old age" than ever before, thanks to advances in health care; they were likely to live longer; and there were not enough people of "working age" to support them.

Another major change was the popularity of work requirements, less popular among Democrats than among Republicans. In the United States, unlike in most other industrialized countries, the Social Security system deals with those labeled as "beyond working age" and people with disabilities. People without disabilities who are considered of working age are handled by welfare systems administered by the states, many of which have work requirements for eligibility.

Just as Democratic politicians at the national level were likely to argue that government programs of social welfare should be given high priority, so too were Democratic politicians at state and local levels outside the South. In the rhetoric of the political battlefield that meant that they were "bleeding hearts," but in turn they accused their opponents of being "heartless." They were likely to cite examples of individuals who ate dog food or died of heat exhaustion because they could not afford other groceries or to purchase a fan on their meager Social Security earnings. They were likely to argue that less should be spent on the military, and the money reallocated to social services. Or, like Democratic President Lyndon Johnson and his followers, they could argue that we could have both "guns and butter."

Certain prominent politicians came to be identified in the public mind as "friends" or "enemies" of Social Security. Ronald Reagan, before and during his presidency, was identified with remarks he had made early in his political career suggesting that Social Security should be made voluntary. In other words, an individual could choose not to participate, not to have contributions deducted from his or her paycheck, and not to have them matched by the employer. Many prominent Democrats sought to be identified as "friends" of the Social Security program. One who succeeded was New York Senator Daniel Patrick Moynihan, who engaged in many legislative efforts to keep the program viable. On the other hand, Moynihan took the unpopular position that the Social Security Administration be taken "off the budget," in other words, that the program not be allowed to operate at a deficit, to be made up for elsewhere.

Other leading Democratic politicians, though, called for new initiatives with government involvement in areas considered as "social security" elsewhere, but not in the United States. President Bill Clinton and Senator Edward Kennedy sought unsuccessfully to increase the federal government's involvement massively in health care. Others, concerned about the great disparity in state programs of workers' compensation and unemployment, sought to move them to the federal level.

A basic question was how Social Security programs could best be administered, especially as they got bigger. With the creation of a separate Department of Education, the Department of Health, Education, and Welfare became the Department of Health and Human Services. Eventually, in the 1990s, the Social Security Administration became an independent agency. Although there was bipartisan support for the changes, leadership came from members of the Democratic Party. Coordination of the monumental tasks of Social Security had long been recognized as a problem. Soon after the Social Security Act became law, President Franklin Roosevelt formed a special interdepartmental coordinating committee, including administrators from the Public Health Service and the departments of the Interior, Agriculture, and Labor.

As voters toward the end of the twentieth century were likely to complain that their taxes were too high, leading Democratic politicians sought to ensure that Social Security programs would not be rolled back or frozen. Importantly, though, the debate was no longer over whether government had a role in guaranteeing Social Security; it was instead over how great that role should be.

Most voters made a distinction between Social Security, which they liked, and welfare programs, which they did not. In both cases, Democrats were likely to favor changes taking into account the rising cost of living and were likely to portray attempts to cut benefits as "mean." Democrats also argued that it was unrealistic to expect churches and voluntary agencies to do everything that government did not. At the close of the twentieth century, they tended to find Social Security to be one of their most effective campaign issues.

Arthur Blaser

SEE ALSO Welfare

BIBLIOGRAPHY

Epstein, Abraham. *Insecurity: A Challenge to America; A Study of Social Insurance in the U.S. and Abroad.* New York: H. Smith and R. Hoar, 1933.

Lampmann, Robert J., ed. *Social Security Perspectives: Essays in Honor of Edwin E. Witte.* Madison: University of Wisconsin Press, 1962.

Lubove, Roy. *The Struggle for Social Security, 1900–1935.* Cambridge: Harvard University Press, 1968.

Richards, Raymond. *Closing the Door to Destitution: The Shaping of the Social Security Acts of the United States and New Zealand.* University Park: Pennsylvania State University Press, 1994.

States' Rights

Thomas Jefferson, Andrew Jackson, and other founders of the Democratic Party viewed local and state governments as the proper locus of political power to preserve individual liberty, promote social and economic equality, and reduce tyranny. Early Democrats considered the expansion of national governmental power vis-à-vis the state governments to be the manifestation of political corruption. They saw the national government as the instrument used by wealthy elites to promote their particular interests. Conversely, since state and local governments were closer to the common man, they should be the primary institutions of representative government. A strict interpretation of the U.S. Constitution should rigorously limit the national government's role. Beginning with William Jennings Bryan, however, modern Democratic leaders (except for many white southern Democrats) reversed the party's position on states' rights and the proper role of the national government. They argued that the expansion of national government power is necessary to combat the overwhelming resources available to corporate leaders and provide for the common good. Therefore, though the underlying goals of the Democratic Party have remained constant, the means used to promote those goals have been reversed. The Democratic Party is now using the means originally promoted by its opponents to achieve its historical objectives. Paradoxically, since the early 1970s, the Republican Party has been promoting the ideology and means advocated by early Democrats to achieve its historical ends, public order and economic growth.

One major division between the first two U.S. political parties concerned the proper role of the national government. Shortly after he became secretary of the treasury in 1789, Alexander Hamilton proposed an ambitious economic reform program to develop a strong national government. Hamilton argued that if the United States was to prosper, the national government should pay all state and national governmental debts, encourage foreign and domestic investments, and establish a national bank. Moreover, Hamilton maintained, the national government should support manufacturing interests that would further the long-term interests of the nation. Thomas Jefferson and James Madison distrusted Hamilton and considered his plans an unconstitutional threat to liberty. They asserted that a strong, centralized government was the enemy of freedom and favored a limited government.

After Jefferson lost the presidency in 1796, his supporters charged that the Federalists were subservient to money power and were trying to establish a monarchy at the expense of liberty. Their fears seemed to be substantiated when the Federalist majority in Congress passed the Alien and Sedition Acts in 1798. Jefferson and Madison drafted resolutions for the Kentucky and Virginia legislatures, respectively, declaring the acts unconstitutional and asserting that a state had the right to make that determination. In 1799 the Kentucky legislature passed an additional resolution holding that a state could "interpose" its authority when the federal government assumed powers not granted by the Constitution and formally nullify unconstitutional laws. While other state governments did not support these resolutions, they were the first formal declaration of states' rights by the Democratic-Republican Party.

After the Democratic-Republican Party assumed control of the national government in 1800, leaders advocated a limited role for the central government. Jefferson asserted that the states were the most competent administration for domestic concerns and the defense against anti-Republican tendencies. After the

War of 1812, however, party leaders recognized the necessity of a standing army, supported a limited federal program of internal improvements, and created a new national bank. Disagreements over the proper role of the federal government and states' rights divided the Democratic-Republican Party during the Monroe administration. National Republicans supported the American system, which called for national government power to protect U.S. industry and commerce with federally financed internal improvements and a national bank.

Andrew Jackson and his supporters attacked these nationalist policies and supported states' rights. Jackson asserted that the moment the sovereignty of states was overwhelmed by the central government, "we may bid adieu to our freedom." Jacksonian Democrats advocated a country governed by small, frugal governments, close to the people and under their direct daily supervision. The party advocated a policy of localism, where local issues should be decided by state and local governments without national government interference. They believed that federal banks, tariffs, and federally sponsored internal improvements were hazards to freedom because federal government activism was inevitably based on special treatment for the wealthy.

When Jackson became president in 1828, he promised to adhere "to a just respect for state rights and the maintenance of state sovereignty as the best check of the tendencies to consolidate." Jackson killed the national bank because it had favored the wealthy elite and was unconstitutional. In addition, he supported Georgia's states' rights position regarding the Cherokee Indians and ignored two U.S. Supreme Court rulings. Nonetheless, since many western Democrats favored internal improvements, Jackson increased, rather than decreased, federal spending for road, canal, and harbor construction. He also expanded the powers of the presidency by claiming to be the representative of all the American people, exercising his veto powers, issuing executive orders, and removing federal employees.

During the Jackson administration, the Democratic Party faced a states' rights controversy. Right before the election of 1828, Congress passed a tariff that southerners charged was unconstitutional and discriminatory. When Jackson's tariff revision in 1832 did not substantially alter the original law, South Carolina, led by Vice President John C. Calhoun, passed an ordinance nullifying the tariff acts and forbidding the collection of duties in the state. Jackson replied that the tariff was constitutional and denied the power of a state to block enforcement of a federal law. He threatened to intervene to collect the duties and warned that nullification meant insurrection and war. Jackson pressured Congress to pass both a Force Act to compel compliance and a compromise tariff in 1833. Though South Carolina nullified the Force Act, it accepted the tariff. But this nullification incident strengthened southern Democrats' fear of federal interference over slavery and heightened their support of states' rights. Calhoun later supplemented the nullification doctrine with his theory of concurrent majority. Calhoun asserted that democratic decisions could be enacted only with the concurrence of all segments of society affected by the decision. If a group did not concur with the decision, it was not binding for them.

The states' rights doctrine supported by nullification and concurrent majority positions supported the secession of eleven southern states in 1860. Ironically, states' rights plagued the Confederate States of America throughout the Civil War, since southerners' loyalties and revenues were directed to their respective states rather than the Confederacy. During the Civil War, northern Democratic representatives continued to support states' rights and voted as a bloc against a national banking system and the Homestead Act. After the war, Democrats advocated "closing our lips upon the questions of the past" and supported the return of southern states to white control, the removal of federal troops, amnesty for Confederate soldiers, and no national interference with the local authority. The party continued to view the central government as the major agent of special interests. To reestablish its control over the South, Democrats agreed to accept equal rights for blacks in the early 1870s but insisted that each state should enforce the new rights. This position was very effective because many northerners were also opposed to federal interference in southern affairs. By 1877, all southern states were controlled by white southern Democrats. Systematic black disfranchisements under the guise of state voting reforms began in the 1880s.

From 1896 to 1912, William Jennings Bryan, a former populist, became the leading Democratic spokesperson. Bryan began to transform the traditional Democratic view of government. Bryan retained Jackson's distrust of governmental favoritism to business and corporations, but rejected his prescription for a limited government. Bryan argued that since businesses and monopolies had been allowed to flourish under Republican administrations, only the central government would be able to control these great concentrations of economic power and restore liberty and equality. He asserted that the federal government could be used to remove barriers to individual

achievement, especially those built by capitalists. Consequently, Bryan converted the Democratic Party to a positive theory of government in which the federal government must use its power to ensure that people receive an equal chance to succeed.

During his administration, Woodrow Wilson stated that the federal government should help enterprising individuals get started and adopted many of Bryan's positions in his "New Freedom Programs." From 1912 to 1916, the Democratic majority in Congress passed the Federal Reserve Act, antitrust laws, and the income tax amendment, and created the Federal Trade Commission. In World War I, the economy was subject to unprecedented governmental control, and the power of the national government increased.

President Franklin Roosevelt's response to the Great Depression continued the Democratic Party's transformation concerning states' rights and a limited role for the central government, over the objections of southern Democrats. Roosevelt's New Deal extended governmental regulation over the economy, accepted some federal responsibility for the public welfare, developed resource projects, championed the cause of organized labor, expanded the role of the presidency, and most important, broadened the authority of the federal government at the expense of the states. Southern Democrats initially supported FDR's policies but broke away after the 1936 election due to their traditional suspicion of centralized government and their support of states' rights. Some southern leaders also feared that a strong federal government would eventually take action against segregation. But southerners did not leave the Democratic Party because of their control over state party machinery and influence in Congress.

During and after World War II, civil rights violations in the South highlighted the Democratic Party's internal division regarding states' rights; however, Roosevelt refused to take an active civil rights position for fear of losing southern support. When Harry Truman inherited the presidency, to the surprise of many southerners, he called for the enactment of an extensive package of civil rights legislation based on federal enforcement. At the national party convention, northern Democrats inserted a plank into the party's platform supporting the civil rights legislation. Southern "States' Rights" Democrats walked out of the convention and nominated South Carolina Governor Strom Thurmond to run for the presidency as a third-party candidate. While the "Dixiecrats" failed to spoil the election for Truman, Thurmond won 39 electoral votes and 22.5% of the popular vote in the South. After his victory, as a result of the rise of McCarthyism and the Korean War, Truman refused to retaliate against the former Dixiecrats or lessen their power in Congress at the expense of his Fair Deal programs and civil rights proposals.

The persistence of poverty and racial discrimination in the United States led to the most wide-ranging Democratic limitations on states' rights, the Civil Rights Act of 1964 and Lyndon Johnson's Great Society programs. The Civil Rights Act and the Voting Rights Act of 1965 contained a broad national government offensive against discrimination and segregation at the expense of state and local governments. Southern state and local Democratic parties were transformed from all-white bastions of states' rights and segregation to racially integrated, socially liberal organizations as many white southerners fled to the Republican Party. The Great Society programs used federal monies and regulations to supersede state policies with federal goals.

Since 1968, the Democratic Party's limitation of states' rights and promotion of a positive role for government have had mixed results. While the party maintained its majorities in Congress until 1994 and controlled many state and local governments, the Republican Party has embraced the traditional Jeffersonian view of states' rights and limited government with effective results. Moreover, Republicans assert that the Democrats are now using the federal government to promote special interests, bloated bureaucracies, and wasteful social programs at the expense of the public good and a large federal deficit. It will be interesting to note if the current political climate will lead to resurgence of states' rights and limited government advocates in the Democratic Party as well.

Janet B. Manspeaker

BIBLIOGRAPHY

Goldman, Ralph. *Search for Consensus*. Philadelphia: Temple University Press, 1979.
Kovler, Peter B., ed. *Democrats and the American Idea*. Washington, DC: Center for National Policy Press, 1992.
Reichley, A. James. *The Life of the Parties*. New York: Free Press, 1992.

Term Limits

The Democratic Party has generally opposed term limits on public officeholders. The first successful target for term limitations at the national level, the presidency, was in response to the four elections of Democrat Franklin Delano Roosevelt (1933–1945). Beginning with George Washington and up to and including Roosevelt's predecessor, Republican Herbert

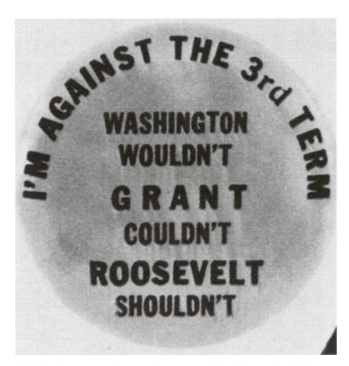

Willkie Campaign Button Opposes a Third Term for FDR. *Source:* Franklin Delano Roosevelt Library.

Hoover, no president had served more than two terms, even though there was no constitutional restriction keeping presidents from seeking more than two terms.

This situation changed in 1947 when congressional Republicans proposed a constitutional amendment limiting presidents to two full elected terms. In 1951 the amendment was ratified by the states. Similarly, governors, the states' chief executives, face limits in 40 states, the most restrictive of which, Kentucky and Virginia, permit only one four-year term. Prior to 1990, state legislators and members of the U.S. Congress did not face term limitations.

As the term-limits movement began to coalesce in the late 1980s, most Democratic officeholders, especially leaders within the party, moved to oppose what they believed to be artificial and harmful restrictions on a voter's choice of candidate. Since the Democrats had majority control of most of the nation's state legislative chambers, as well as the U.S. House of Representatives and the Senate, they viewed term limits as an attack on their service records and as partisan maneuvers designed to end their dominance. Control was threatened because many officeholders then served longer than the proposed limits would permit. Over time, therefore, passage of term limits would create many "open seats" (races without incumbents seeking reelection), jeopardizing Democratic hegemony.

Will He Bite? Newspaper Cartoon, 1903. Question of President Cleveland Running for Third Term. *Source:* Library of Congress.

According to many observers of elections, incumbents possessed advantages in constituency visibility, staffing assistance, and fund raising, which, except in a few cases, together made these officeholders difficult to defeat and consequently gave voters little realistic choice at election time (see Petracca 1990).

Where Democrats had majority control of legislatures, it was unlikely that they would limit their own terms. Citizen movements favoring term limits thus began in states that permitted the use of direct democracy tools such as the initiative. In 1990, the first proposals to limit terms were placed on ballots in three states: California, Colorado, and Oklahoma. In each, voters attempted to amend their state laws against the opposition of many of their sitting state legislators.

Despite differences in the proposed term limits (California: three 2-year terms for its Assembly and two 4-year terms for its senators; Colorado: four 2-year terms for its House and two 4-year terms for its Senate; and Oklahoma: a combined 12 years of service allowed in both chambers), and differences in majority party control (Democrats controlled the legislatures in California and Oklahoma, Republicans had majorities in Colorado), each proposal passed, emboldening advocates nationwide.

In 1991 a new tactic was tried out in the state of Washington (for a thorough description of this case, Olson 1992). Term-limit supporters placed on the ballot I-553, a proposal to limit state representatives to three 2-year terms and senators to two 4-year terms, with a combined limit of 10 consecutive years for both chambers. The new wrinkles were that I-553 also limited national members of Congress to three 2-year terms for representatives and two 6-year terms for senators, with a combined 12 consecutive years allowed. The limits would take effect retroactively, meaning incumbents' cumulative service would count toward the limit. For these officials, the initiative permitted just one more reelection attempt.

Democrats viewed the retroactive provision as the most serious threat to date both because of its immediacy and because the top legislative Democrat in the House, Speaker Thomas Foley, was from Washington. The resulting saliency of the election attracted national attention, and money given by traditional supporters of both national parties. While public opinion polls indicated I-553 would pass, and many political commentators predicted certain victory for the initiative, the measure in the end failed by 54% to 46%. Opponents like Foley played on Washingtonians' fears that passage of the measure would limit their choice, cost Washington's members of Congress needed seniority in the House and Senate, and cost the state Foley, its powerful representative (Olson 1992, 85).

Just a year later, term-limit proponents reversed the momentary setback in Washington, passing I-573, a nonretroactive provision limiting House members to three 2-year terms over 12 years, and Senators to two 6-year terms over 18 years. In 13 other states term limits on state and national officeholders passed by an average margin of two to one, despite the opposition of successful Democratic presidential candidate Bill Clinton. Ironically, in that same election voters elected 110 new members to the House of Representatives (more than one-fourth of the chamber), the most in decades, highlighting the point that individual district elections may sometimes add up to national change.

About the same time, Speaker Foley and other Democrats began the process of challenging term limits in federal courts. California Democrats had already tried to have limits on state officeholders ruled unconstitutional in the California Supreme Court, but it ruled six to one that state limits were consistent with California's constitution. State term limits on national officials was another matter entirely, however.

In 1993 and 1994, two U.S. district court judges ruled that term limits imposed by state voters on members of Congress, first in Arkansas and then in Washington, were unconstitutional because they added a nonincumbency qualification for office, something that only a constitutional amendment could achieve. Democrats had their court victory. Proponents quickly appealed.

The victory for Democrats was brief; in November 1994 voters in seven additional states imposed term limits and, surprising almost everyone, voters in districts and states across the nation took away Democratic control of the U.S. House and the Senate. Part of the 52-seat Democratic loss in the House was Speaker Foley, whose opponent had used Foley's suit against Washington's 1992 initiative with great effect.

While losing at the ballot box, opponents ultimately prevailed in the U.S. Supreme Court. In May 1995, it ruled in *U.S. Term Limits, Inc.* v. *Thornton* that state-imposed term limits were unconstitutional, leaving a constitutional amendment as the only viable route.

Stephen D. Van Beek

BIBLIOGRAPHY

Benjamin, Gerald, and Michael J. Malbin. *Limited Legislative Terms.* Washington, DC: CQ Press, 1992.

Galvin, Thomas. "Limits Score a Perfect 14-for-14, but Court Challenges Loom." *Congressional Quarterly Weekly Report,* November 7, 1992, pp. 3593, 3994.

Glaser, Susan B. "After Their Impressive Victories in 14 States, Term-Limit Backers Plan Next Steps on Hill." *Roll Call,* January 18, 1993, pp. 24, 26.

Greenhouse, Linda. "Administration Tells Justices That Term Limits Defy Constitution." *New York Times,* September 9, 1994.

Katz, Jeffrey L. "The Uncharted Realm of Term Limitation." *Governing,* January 1991, pp. 34–39.

Olson, David J. "Term Limits Fail in Washington." In *Limiting Legislative Terms,* ed. Gerald Benjamin and Michael Malbin. Washington, DC: CQ Press, 1992.

Petracca, Mark P. "Term Limits Will Put an End to Permanent Government by Incumbents." *Public Affairs Report* 31 (November 1990).

U.S. Term Limits, Inc. v. *Thornton* (115 S.Ct. 1842), 1995.

Third Parties

The Democratic Party is a coalition of diverse interests. Both U.S. major parties exist as big tents serving primarily electoral objectives. Third parties, in contrast, often expend more of their energies on articulating ideas, even exposing visions of a nation transformed. Some of America's noblest policy innovations first were ideas either conceived by third parties or taken up and pushed by third parties years before Democrats or Republicans grasped their political profitability.

Women were among those who created the Prohibition Party, this nation's oldest still-living third party, in 1869, and women took seats at Prohibition's first national convention. Democrats and Republicans finally placed woman suffrage planks into their 1916 platforms. Their tardy act had been preceded by the more timely suffrage activism of a half dozen or more third parties. The National Woman's Party (NWP), founded in 1913, became the militant wing of the suffrage movement. Using demonstration tactics primarily, since most of its members could not vote, NWP did seek also to influence election outcomes. NWPers were inclined in particular to punish Wilsonian Democrats, as the ruling party, the party with the power, though it lacked the will, to enact woman suffrage.

People who build, lead, and take part in third parties sometimes are motivated by hopes of altering the character of U.S. party politics or of surmounting the barriers that peripheralize them. Desires notwithstanding, third parties have been relegated to the margins, sometimes influencing but rarely if ever entering the political mainstream.

Unloved though they may be, the two relatively nonideological and undifferentiated major parties are ingenious in coopting the ideological space occupied by a large majority of the U.S. electorate. Direct primaries and other procedures for open participation encourage dissidents to enter into major parties rather than pursue "quixotic" third-party strategies. It has been suggested too that Americans have tended toward neat division on policy issues (business vs. labor, segregation vs. civil rights, pro-choice vs. pro-life), a bifurcation rationalizing a system of just two major parties.

Structural barriers also disadvantage third parties. Multiparty competition would be encouraged by proportional representation (PR) election systems; it is deterred instead by single-member district, winner-take-all elections, the norm in America. The 1992 electoral college produced no electoral votes for H. Ross Perot, despite the 19% the voters gave him. The Federal Election Campaign Act and other campaign finance laws discriminate substantially against third-party participants. State-imposed barriers to ballot access may be the most formidable structural obstacles in the way of third-party access to the mainstream. Finance and ballot-access legislation is, after all, the creation of Democratic and Republican lawmakers.

Third parties themselves may be characterized by reference to relative distance from the main thrust of political life. *Continuing doctrinal parties* (sometimes designated "minor" parties) exist for decades far removed, their longevity undergirded by commitment to, and the radicalism of, party doctrine. Communists, Libertarians, and other doctrinal parties sometimes *have* claimed loyalty among important sectors of the body politic. Issues raised by doctrinal parties are occasionally appropriated by one or both major parties, thus influencing the policy process. Socialist Party demands influenced the creation of Social Security and of depression-era public works programs. But doctrinal party voter strength has determined electoral outcomes only rarely. Never has the presidential tally of a doctrinal party candidate exceeded the 6% taken in 1912 by Socialist Eugene V. Debs.

There also are *non-national parties*. This is the kind of third party that may become significant, even a *major* party, in the politics of a community or an entire state, but that either does not seek or does not attain a significant presence in national politics (except perhaps in the U.S. congressional delegation from the particular state). Historic examples abound: the Minnesota Farmer–Labor Party, the Progressive Party of Wisconsin, the American Labor Party in New York. The Farmer–Labor Party, founded at the close of World War I, managed in the 1920s to supplant the Democrats as Minnesota's major opposition to the ruling state GOP. For several of the depression years,

Farmer–Labor enjoyed the status of ruling party in Minnesota.

The electoral strength and influence of the Progressive Coalition of Burlington, Vermont, produced in that city the only true three-party system existing in the United States in the 1980s and 1990s. Burlington's Democrats and Republicans, known to some as Republicrats, sometimes coalesce, offering a single nominee in opposition to the Progressives. The significance of partisan New York Liberals, Conservatives, and Right-to-Lifers late in the twentieth century has been largely the result of an extraordinary New York state cross-endorsement provision allowing a candidate's name to appear on the ballot as the nominee of more than one party.

Some non-national parties have existed as satellite parties, maintaining in-state autonomy while attaching themselves to the national Democratic Party. New York's American Labor was such a satellite party, but a purer example of a Democratic satellite was Minnesota Farmer–Labor. Farmer–Labor gave support to Franklin Roosevelt and his New Deal program; for their part, the national Democrats on occasion backed Farmer–Labor electoral campaigns and siphoned patronage to Minnesota through Farmer–Labor rather than through the state Democratic Party. In 1944, the Minnesota Democratic and Farmer–Labor parties formally merged. To this day, Minnesota Democrats as well as the Democratic nominee for president run in Minnesota on the ballot line of the DFL.

The Communist Party enjoyed some influence in both the Farmer–Labor and American Labor parties, and communists may have tried to use the connection to make a link with the Democratic Party. Though having previously endorsed the Roosevelt campaigns, American Labor in 1948 opposed Democrat Harry Truman and supported instead the communist-backed Progressive candidacy of Henry Wallace.

The most formidable partisan challenge to Democratic and Republican domination of mainstream politics comes from the nationally organized *transient or short-lived parties*. These parties' rise is meteoric, often indicating dysfunction or failure in major-party ranks. The Know-Nothings of the 1850s and the Populists four decades later almost achieved national major-party status.

Some transient parties originate as protest movements. Others, like the 1948 Dixiecrats, secede from one or the other major party. The participation of the southern Democrats, a secessionist splinter from the national Democratic Party, in the presidential election of 1860 helped secure the defeat of national Democrat Stephen A. Douglas by Republican Abraham Lincoln.

The secession of Theodore Roosevelt's Bull Moose Progressives from the GOP sealed the 1912 victory of Democrat Woodrow Wilson; Bull Moose was the only third party ever to beat a major party for second place in a presidential vote.

The short lives of these parties, their defining characteristic, indicates vulnerability but also their clout. Voter appeal by a transient party often poses the threat that it will determine election outcome. Neutralizing the threat means appropriating what appeals. Democrats held their first quadrennial national convention in 1832; major-party Whigs and then Republicans would follow suit. This method of presidential nomination, more democratic than the previously used closed caucus, was first conceived by the Antimasonic third party.

Major parties also gobble up transient parties' popular policy demands. The Republican Party adopted its southern strategy and began to redefine itself compatible with that strategy primarily to neutralize the 1968 threat from George Wallace's American Independent Party. AIP thus affected major-party relationships and the relative popularity and influence of Democrats and Republicans for all the years since.

In the nineteenth century, before state-printed secret ballots made it impossible to do so, a major party and a transient party sometimes fused in a unified presidential campaign. Democrats in 1872 nominated Liberal Republican nominee Horace Greeley and adopted the Liberal Republican platform verbatim. Populists in 1896 nominated the Democratic nominee William Jennings Bryan, thus charting their party's course to extinction. The classic case of big-fish-swallows-small, the Democratic-Populist story, also bears testimony to third-party clout and potential. Bryan-era Democrats devoured the Populists by incorporating almost every important element of the Populist platform. No other third party ever has matched Populist success in affecting the nation's public policy.

As the nation approached the twenty-first century, the window of third-party opportunity was more widely open than at any time since the 1930s. Opinion polls in the 1990s showed a breakdown in belief in public institutions, especially in the legitimacy of the major parties. Most Americans said they longed for a third *major* party in competition with Democrats and Republicans.

Connecticut and Maine elected third-party governors in 1990, and Maine an Independent in 1994. Ross Perot, who took the third-highest percentage ever for a non-major-party presidential candidate in 1992 (the highest for any such candidate not running as an ex-president), regrouped his forces and organized the Reform Party in

1996. Libertarians, Greens, Progressives, and Independents held elective offices in places scattered nationwide.

In the 1990s there was serious third-party talk by, or centered on, prominent people: Colin Powell, Bill Bradley, Paul Tsongas, Lowell Weicker, Pat Buchanan, Jesse Jackson, and others. Many of these people had come to politics through the Democratic or Republican Party. Some were well-known liberals or conservatives. But many of the most persistent advocates of third-party creation in the 1990s wanted a centrist party. As they saw it, it was no longer the age-old problem of Tweedledum and Tweedledee. Now, they said, the Democrats and Republicans had become *too* polarized, *too* partisan. Success seemed most likely to reach the grasp of some new party that would, in articulating its vision, combine fiscal conservatism with a liberal outlook on choice and lifestyle issues.

J. David Gillespie

BIBLIOGRAPHY

Black, Gordon S., and Benjamin D. Black. *Politics of American Discontent: How a New Party Can Make Democracy Work Again.* New York: Wiley, 1994.
Gillespie, J. David. *Politics at the Periphery: Third Parties in Two-Party America.* Columbia: University of South Carolina Press, 1993.
Hesseltine, William B. *Third-Party Movements in the United States.* Princeton: Princeton University Press, 1962.
Mazmanian, Daniel A. *Third Parties in Presidential Elections.* Washington, DC: Brookings Institution, 1973.
Rosenstone, Steven J., Roy L. Behr, and Edward H. Lazarus. *Third Parties in America: Citizen Response to Major Party Failure.* Princeton: Princeton University Press, 1984.

Tort Reform

The current tort system encompasses two general and previously separate categories of injuries. The first is when the injured and injurer have no prior relationship. The best example of this category is a car accident. The second category is when the injured and injurer have some previous relationship, such as doctor–patient, employer–employee, and manufacturer–consumer.

Until fairly recently, these two categories of injury cases had been handled differently. The former was under tort law—an area of the common law—while the latter was an aspect of contract law. But since the 1960s, in two state injury cases, *Henningsen* v. *Bloomfield Motors* in New Jersey and *Greenman* v. *Yuba Power Products Co.* in California, the contract aspect has given way to the tort law. In these cases, privity (a contrac-

tual term limiting damage payments to direct pur-
chasers of a product) was removed and replaced with
strict liability for product-related injuries, even if the
parties specified another standard for liability.

For more than a decade, Republicans have attempted to reform the tort system of the United States.
They have argued that the costs of litigation have driven up the cost of insurance and consumer goods. The
largest stumbling block for the Republican agenda of
tort reform had been Democratic control of Congress.
With the ascension of the Republican Party in the 1994
elections, prospects for reform looked good. As part of
the Contract with America, Republicans sought to
limit punitive damages, force courtroom losers to pay
winners' legal fees, and protect defendants from having to pay all the damages in cases where they were
only partly responsible for injuries.

Democratic opponents of tort reform believe that the
Republican agenda is an attempt to shield big business
from its responsiblity for faulty and dangerous products. In fact, they argue, the tort system is one of the
few places where the average citizen can pressure a
powerful corporation on nearly equal terms.

By imposing a loser-pays rule, Democrats argue,
middle-class Americans will be prevented from bring
suits against corporations. Businesses will not find this
rule burdensome because the number of lawsuits they
are involved in will likely result in a wash over time.
The average American, however, could hardly shoulder a legal bill of tens of thousands of dollars.
Democrats want to continue the "American Rule"
wherein each side pays for its own legal expenses.
Since most liability cases are taken on a contingency
basis, average citizens can afford to enter into litigation. In addition, Democratic senators such as Byron L.
Dorgan of North Dakota beleive that linking punitive
damages to concrete economic losses unfairly favors
rich plaintiffs.

Opposition to tort reform was led by the Association
of Trial Lawyers of America (ATLA) and consumer
groups, notably Public Citizen, a group founded by
consumer activist Ralph Nader. ATLA used its extensive lobbying power to convince enough senators, most
of them Democrats, not to support the measure. The
ATLA's influence is considerable among Democrats because it is one of the largest contributors to Democratic
campaign coffers. While it does not have a political action committee, ATLA contributed over $56 million to
Democratic candidates in 1990 alone. President Bill
Clinton considered vetoing any tort reform measure.
While ATLA and President Clinton argued that the
Republican bill would have hurt consumers and protected wrongdoers, it is hard to ignore the fact that 30%

to 40% of Clinton's 1992 campaign funds came from
trial lawyers.

Democrats attacked the Republican plan for tort reform because the GOP attempted to impose a single
federal standard on tort law. They cited the fact that
central to the Contract with America is the returning of
power to the states. Democrats believed that tort law
had been a fundamental area of state regulation and
that to change this situation was, at a minimum, inconsistent with the Republicans' stated philosophy. In
fact, they argue, many states have enacted legislation
that would limit punitive damages and frivolous lawsuits. According to Joan Claybrook of Public Citizen,
the Republican measures would create confusion and
take away the capacity of states to manage their own
laws. Larry Stewart, president of ATLA, argues that
"important thresholds are trying to be crossed, those
of states' rights and the Tenth Amendment."

In the end, the Democrats coopted the Republicans
states' rights argument in an attempt to protect both
consumers and their campaign coffers.

Jeffrey D. Schultz
Diane L. Schultz

BIBLIOGRAPHY

Abraham, Spencer. "The Federal Case for National Tort
Reform." *Policy Review*, no. 73 (Summer 1995).
Bogus, Carl T. "The Contract and the Consumer." *American
Prospect*, no. 21 (Spring 1995): 53–57.
Reske, Henry. "A Classic Battle of Loyalists." *ABA Journal* 81
(June 1, 1995): 22.
Rubin, Paul H. *Tort Reform by Contract*. Washington, DC: AEI
Press, 1993.

Trade Policy

Major partisan and sectional disagreements over trade
policy, particularly over the level of tariffs, have been
an important element of U.S. politics. While both parties recognized the necessity of tariffs after the War of
1812, Democrats favored low tariffs for revenue purposes, and their opponents advocated high tariffs to
stimulate industrialization. After 1934, Democrats promoted a managed international economic system
based on free trade through General Agreement on
Tariffs and Trade (GATT) negotiations. From 1934 to
the end of the 1960s, U.S. trade policy rested on bipartisan support as the economy prospered. When U.S.
imports exceeded exports in the early 1970s, partisan
internal and external disagreements undermined a
trade policy consensus. For the past 25 years,
Democrats have been unable to develop a uniform
trade position. Many congressional Democrats sup-

port protectionist measures designed to help U.S. workers; however, most Democratic legislators also approved the latest GATT treaty and regional free-trade agreements, and President Clinton generally supports free trade.

Partisan conflict over U.S. trade policy began in 1791 when Treasury Secretary Alexander Hamilton proposed an ambitious economic plan to strengthen the economy and the federal government. A major element of Hamilton's program was the establishment of a federal tariff to raise revenues and protect and subsidize manufacturers. Hamilton won the support of President Washington, but Thomas Jefferson and James Madison vigorously attacked his plan. They feared that protective tariffs would raise the price of manufactured goods, lead to retaliations against U.S. agricultural exports, and result in governmental corruption. Jefferson and Madison supported a *laissez-faire* policy in which manufacturers would compete without governmental assistance. While Jefferson and Madison limited the scope of the tariff, Congress passed duties on some imported goods in support of Hamilton.

After they came to power in 1800, the Democratic-Republicans, concerned that a shift in U.S. trade policy would destabilize the country, did not lower tariffs. When Great Britain and France began to seize U.S. ships in the early 1800s, Jefferson asserted that neutral American citizens were entitled to unrestricted trade under international law. After a British ship fired on an American frigate in 1807, Jefferson ordered British ships out of American waters and demanded reparations. Jefferson believed Europeans depended on U.S. exports and used trade as an instrument of foreign policy. Congress passed the Embargo Act, which suspended all U.S. exports. While the embargo did impose hardships on Europeans and strengthen U.S. manufacturers, it created a national depression, and Jefferson repealed the act in 1809.

Madison also supported several trade restriction bills aimed at Great Britain and France during his presidency. Though the measures were partially successful, Congress declared war against Britain in 1812. During and after the war, a new breed of nationalist Democratic-Republicans pushed the party toward protectionism as the American manufacturing sector expanded. Before he left office, Madison wholeheartedly adopted a Hamiltonian trade position. Democratic-Republican leaders such as Henry Clay advocated the American system during the Era of Good Feelings. A key element of the system was a protective tariff to stimulate U.S. manufacturing, create a domestic market for agricultural commodities, and finance internal improvements. In 1816, Congress increased the tariff du-

ties to an average of 20%. Nevertheless, Madison and Monroe refused to implement all of the American system for fear of unconstitutionally expanding the power of the national government.

Three sections of the United States began to develop different economic structures that affected U.S. trade policy in the early 1800s. The northeastern states advocated protectionism to support their expanding manufacturing sectors, while the southern states, who depended on British markets for their cotton exports, pressed for a low tariff policy. The western states wanted federally financed internal improvements and security but viewed tariffs with suspicion. Sectional differences divided the Democratic-Republican Party in the 1824 presidential election. After John Quincy Adams became president, Congress, which northerners dominated, raised the tariff to 36% and even higher in 1828. Southerners opposed the "tariffs of abominations," which they considered "peculiar" taxes on their region.

Andrew Jackson promised to reduce the power of the national government and eliminate governmental favoritism after he was elected in 1828. But Jackson wavered on tariffs and initially endorsed protective tariffs for essential products. He also declared that Congress was within its rights to levy high tariffs. By 1832, as southern opposition increased, Jackson shifted his position. He supported only temporary revenue tariffs and warned manufacturers that the people would not continue to pay high prices to support their expansion. Nevertheless, Jackson signed another highly protective tariff in 1832. South Carolina nullified the tariff with the support of Vice President John C. Calhoun. While Jackson promoted states' rights and sympathized with the southern position, he took strong actions to protect the Union. Jackson threatened military action to collect tariff duties but also pressured Congress to pass a tariff reduction measure that gradually returned the tariff to 1816 levels.

A series of panics hit President Van Buren's administration in the late 1830s and brought the Whig Party to power. Northern Whigs argued that by closing out foreign goods, protective tariffs would create a diversified industrial sector and more jobs for the poor. Despite his low-tariff position, President Tyler, a former Democrat, approved the Tariff of 1842, which reestablished the level of duties imposed in 1832.

The Democratic Party returned to national power in 1844 and passed the 1846 Walker Tariff, which significantly lowered tariffs. In the same year, Britain also lowered some of its tariffs against U.S. agricultural imports. From 1840 to 1860, the combined value of U.S. exports and imports increased from approximately

$220 billion to $690 billion as new markets for American raw materials opened in Europe. Though Northern American manufacturers protested as British goods competed with American-made products, Democrats lowered tariffs again in 1857.

During the Civil War, congressional Democrats objected as the Republican Party instituted tariffs averaging 47% to pay for the war and protect industries. After the war, most Republican leaders continued to support a high tariff to promote U.S. industrialization. Many Democrats, in contrast, adopted the economic policies of David A. Wells, a former Republican. Wells argued that technological advances would lead to U.S. agricultural and manufacturing surpluses that needed to be exported but that high tariffs prevented foreigners from selling goods in U.S. markets and using their profits to purchase U.S. exports. Wells also argued that reduced tariffs would lead to lower prices for raw materials, which would stimulate American manufacturing. Democrats also charged that tariffs were unfair privileges for manufacturers obtained by buying the votes of corrupt legislators. Republicans vigorously responded, branding Wells a traitor and labeling Democrats "internationalists" who were unconcerned about U.S. workers.

Congress made minor tariff reductions in 1780 and 1872 when dissident Republicans joined Democrats to reduce prices. But when the country plunged into a recession in 1873, the Republicans restored high tariff duties. In the 1880s, partisan debates over tariff policy became the central domestic policy issue. After his election in 1884, Grover Cleveland promised to reform America's economic system and launched an attack on the tariff. Throughout 1886, Cleveland tried to get a tariff reform bill passed as congressional Republicans blocked the bill and accused the president of being a British agent. Cleveland devoted his entire annual address to Congress in 1887 to an attack against high tariffs. While Cleveland won the popular vote in 1888, he lost in the electoral college to Benjamin Harrison.

In 1890 the Republicans reinstituted high tariffs under the McKinley Tariff. Cleveland and the Democratic Party returned to national power in 1888 after the public reacted to higher prices caused by the new tariff. Unfortunately, in 1893 the country entered its worst depression to date. Democrats in the House of Representatives attempted to reform the tariff by offering modest reductions under the Wilson–Gorman Act. Protectionists from both parties in the Senate gutted the bill with amendments, however, and actually raised tariffs.

Except during the Wilson years, Republican protectionism remained the basis of U.S. trade policy until Franklin Roosevelt was elected in 1932. With Wilson's

support, Congress passed the Underwood–Simmons bill, which gradually decreased tariffs and provided for an income tax to restore lost revenues in 1913. But Presidents Harding and Hoover reinstituted high tariffs in 1922 and 1930, triggering retaliatory actions against U.S. exports in several countries. Democrats argued that the United States was engaging in protectionism when world events dictated trade liberalization.

From 1934 to the end of the 1960s, the Democratic Party modified its position as it dominated U.S. trade policy. Under the leadership of Franklin Roosevelt and his secretary of state, Cordell Hull, the party promoted a managed international economy based on free trade. In 1934 Congress passed the Reciprocal Trade Agreements, which granted the president three years to negotiate foreign trade agreements that could reduce tariffs by 50%. By 1945, reciprocal trade agreements were in effect with 29 countries. After World War II, the United States and other noncommunist countries decided to establish a liberal international economic order based on the assumption that protectionism had contributed to the war. Under the Bretton Woods Agreement, the General Agreement on Tariffs and Trade (GATT) became the international forum for trade liberalization through multilateral tariff reductions.

In the 1950s and 1960s Democrats and Republicans supported the elimination of trade barriers through GATT as U.S. exports boomed and the nation's economy prospered. The largest tariff reductions occurred during the Kennedy administration, when the president received congressional authorization in 1962 to cut U.S. tariffs by 50% and to abolish tariffs for certain goods. The 1967 GATT agreement reduced tariffs by approximately 35% on industrial products.

By the end of the 1960s, many Democrats began to question their party's free-trade position as some American industries, such as textiles, steel, and automobiles, lost sales to foreign competitors. When President Johnson requested authority to participate in the 1968 GATT negotiations, congressional Democrats rejected his petition. President Nixon also failed to obtain congressional authority in the following year. From 1970 to 1992, Democrats charged that competitors were using unfair trading practices to distort the U.S. market. Consequently, congressional Democrats tried to shield U.S. workers from foreign competition with protectionist trade legislation. For example, in 1988 Congress passed the Omnibus Trade and Competitiveness Act, which contained the "Super 301" clause authorizing retaliatory trade restrictions against unfair trading partners. But congressional Democrats also ratified free-trade agreements that will eliminate U.S. tariffs and protections before 2020. As an illustration, during the Bush administration, congressional Democrats supported the U.S.–Canada Trade Agreement in 1988 and gave the president "fast track" authority to negotiate the North American Free Trade Agreement (NAFTA) in 1992. U.S. trade policy became an important issue in the 1992 presidential campaign. Democratic candidates proposed protectionist trade policies, while Bill Clinton promised to amend NAFTA to provide for retraining and environmental assistance to Mexico.

The Democratic Party has continued its schizophrenic trade position during the Clinton administration. In 1993 Congress ratified NAFTA, which calls for the elimination of trade barriers among the United States, Mexico, and Canada by 2009. There also was strong bipartisan approval of the 1994 GATT agreement, which established the World Trade Organization (WTO) and is expected to reduce tariffs substantially. In 1993 Clinton attended summit meetings of the Asia Pacific Economic Cooperation (APEC) forum, whose members account for approximately 50% of the world's exports. At the end of the summit, American and Japanese leaders pledged to remove all trade barriers by 2010; the other APEC members agreed to remove their barriers by 2020. Moreover, Clinton attended the 1994 Summit of the Americas and pledged to try to create a free-trade zone in the Western Hemisphere before 2005. Nevertheless, Clinton also has supported retaliatory trade initiatives. For example, Clinton reasserted the Super 301 provision in February 1994 against the Japanese and threatened to establish specific import and export limits against Japanese imports.

Democrats have been unable to develop a uniform trade position. On the one hand, the party is committed to GATT, the WTO, and regional free trade agreements. Conversely, many congressional Democrats support protectionist measures to assist U.S. workers.

Janet B. Manspeaker

BIBLIOGRAPHY

Frieden, Jeffry, and David A. Lake, eds. *International Political Economy*. New York: St. Martin's Press, 1991.

Spanier, John W., and Eric M. Uslaner. *American Foreign Policy Making and Democratic Dilemmas*. 6th ed. New York: Macmillan, 1994.

Blum, John M., et al. *The National Experience*. 4th ed. New York: Harcourt Brace, 1977.

Voting Behavior

The study of voting behavior seeks to explain the determinants of the individual vote choice, voting patterns, and trends. Voting is the most common act of political participation and for some citizens even the only form of political participation they engage in. Elections are the primary instrument of self-government in a democracy, and, once elected, the concern about reelection imposes a significant restraint on the elected leaders. Public officials who want to be reelected are likely to be responsive to broad segments of the citizenry. In addition, elections link public attitudes to public policy and confer legitimacy and authority on the government. Although elections usually do not determine the exact policy outcome, voting for one party is usually associated with distinct policy goals. Generally, voting Democratic usually means favoring liberal or labor views.

Systematic research on voting behavior emerged from the development of statistical sampling theory, which slowly led to the methodological refinement of political polling. The 1920s and 1930s saw the first reports of political polls in the media and political science research. For instance, in 1936 *Literary Digest*, a popular weekly magazine, sent out 10 million questionnaires asking respondents if they would vote for Democratic candidate Franklin D. Roosevelt or for Republican Alfred M. Landon. The sample utilized by the magazine was a nonrandom or haphazard sample. Because of the lack of comprehensive lists of voters, questionnaires were sent to car owners, as well as citizens listed in the telephone directories. The base of Roosevelt's support, the unemployed, underemployed, and poor, were excluded from the magazine's sample. Only 2 million questionnaires were returned. Not surprisingly, the *Literary Digest* predicted that only 45% of the vote would be cast for the Democratic candidate Roosevelt. Actual election results, however, gave Roosevelt an overwhelming margin of support of 61%. Commercial researchers such as George Gallup and Elmo Roper used systematic sampling procedures and predicted the right winner of the 1936 election.

In contrast to commercial polling, scientific studies of voting behavior, which began to emerge in the early 1940s, are less concerned about correct predictions of electoral outcomes, but focus on in-depth analyses of the determinants of the individual vote. The first major study of voting behavior was conducted by Columbia University's Bureau of Applied Statistics with a random sample of respondents from Erie County. *The People's Choice* (1944), the seminal work by Paul Lazarsfeld, Bernard Berelson, and Hazel Gaudet, relied on a sociological model to analyze voting behavior in the 1940 election. Lazarsfeld et al. argued that a person's vote decision was mainly determined by sociodemographic background variables, most importantly religious affiliation, socioeconomic status, and place of residence. For example, Catholics from urban areas and with low socioeconomic status were most likely to vote for the incumbent Democrat Roosevelt. The authors of *The People's Choice* concluded that "a person thinks politically, as he is, socially" (p. 27).

The basic findings of the sociological Columbia model were confirmed in a second major study, *Voting*, conducted in 1948 (Berelson, Lazarsfeld, and McPhee 1954). Similar to the first study, the authors of *Voting* concluded that social-group factors accounted for most of the differences in voting behavior. The most serious criticisms directed toward the Columbia model of voting behavior point toward the social determinism of the model and the lack of attention paid to the political aspects of an election. Further, the Columbia model is not useful in explaining political change across elections. Different parties are elected in different years even if social group characteristics do not change much.

The book that gives the most comprehensive analysis of electoral behavior and stands at the fore of academic research in the field is *The American Voter* by University of Michigan researchers Angus Campbell, Philip E. Converse, Warren E. Miller, and Donald E. Stokes. In contrast to the purely sociological Columbia model, Campbell et al.'s analysis of the 1952 and 1956 presidential elections emphasizes three psychological aspects of an individual's vote choice: the person's attachment to a party, orientation toward the major issues, and evaluation of the candidates. Central to an understanding of voting behavior is the concept of party identification, which acts as a long-term and stable influence on voters' decision-making processes. Party identification is a psychological attachment to one of the two major parties, which is the result of a childhood socialization process. Party identification predisposes individuals to vote for their own party's candidate. Although the influence of party identification has declined over the past 40 years, its impact on individual vote choices continues to be significant.

While party identification is a long-term influence affecting the vote, issues, candidate characteristics, and party images represent short-term factors specific to the election. As a result of these short-term influences, an individual's vote may "deviate" from his or her party identification and may be cast for the opposition political party's candidate. Despite the marked differences between the Columbia and Michigan models, both theories rest on the assumption that the electorate is apathetic and irrational. Issues do not have much impact on the vote because voters' interest in the

campaign is low, and their understanding of issue positions is shallow and superficial.

Yet, *The American Voter* relied on data from the 1950s, a period in which few political events agitated the electorate. Issue or policy voting became somewhat more important in the post-1960 elections, which centered on a new set of foreign policy and social issues, the Vietnam War, civil rights, and desegregation. According to Carmines and Stimson (1980), issue voting was especially prevalent during the 1972 electoral contest between Democratic challenger George McGovern and incumbent Republican Richard Nixon (see also Nie, Verba, and Petrocik 1976). In order for issues to matter, however, issues have to be salient and parties and candidates have to stake out distinguishable positions on this issue. Carmines and Stimson (1980) argue that desegregation fell into this category of "easy" issues. The Vietnam War issue, in contrast, did not induce issue voting because the candidates did not stake out sufficiently distinct positions on U.S. involvement in the war.

This implies that the lack of issue awareness cannot be solely attributed to an unsophisticated electorate. Carmines and Stimson show that voters choose candidates according to issues, provided the parties' different positions are discernible. Voting on the basis of issues continued to be important in the 1980s and 1990s. Citizens' dissatisfaction with the performance of the economy, the federal deficit, and national debt were important issues in the 1992 election, and voters unsatisfied with Bush's economic record were significantly more likely to endorse Democratic challenger Bill Clinton. Although voters were not able to compare Clinton's and Bush's economic platforms exactly, vote choices were made on the retrospective evaluation of the incumbent president's ability to handle the nation's economy. In a similar vein, Democrat Jimmy Carter lost the 1980 election because retrospective evaluations of his handling of foreign policy and economic matters were unfavorable.

The influence of party identification, the most important determinant of the vote choice in the 1950s, declined throughout the 1960s and 1970s, which were characterized by a decrease in political party loyalty and a rise in political independence, especially at the expense of the Democratic Party. The role of partisanship as a determinant of individual vote choices increased again in the 1988 and 1992 elections. Exit polls indicated that 89% of strong and weak Democrats cast their vote in favor of challenger Michael Dukakis, a higher percentage than in the 1980 or 1984 elections.

An entirely different approach to the study of voting behavior was taken by rational choice theorists

(Downs 1957). According to the economic theory of voting, the decision to cast a ballot and the decision for which candidate to vote is determined by an economic cost–benefit analysis. Voters will vote for the candidate closest to them on important issues and will cast a ballot only if the perceived benefits of voting outweigh the costs associated with voting.

This economic model of voting behavior is especially useful in explaining low electoral turnout in the United States. In 1960, turnout in presidential elections peaked at 63%, but it has since declined to about 50%, although it increased slightly in the 1992 presidential election to about 53%. Electoral turnout in off-year congressional elections, primaries, and local elections is substantially lower. These numbers are even more dramatic if one considers that the education of the electorate increased steadily since the 1960s and that educated citizens are more likely to vote than those with less education (Wolfinger and Rosenstone 1980). Thus, turnout should have increased and not decreased.

Downs's model of voting behavior explains electoral turnout by pointing toward the costs and benefits associated with casting a ballot. Registration, the act of voting itself, and the search for information needed to make an informed choice involves costs. These costs will induce the citizen to stay home unless he or she can see that the returns offered by becoming informed and voting are greater than the costs. Applying the cost–benefit model to the decline in electoral participation implies that many citizens perceive little benefit in voting. Costs associated with voting have actually declined since the 1960s. Registration is less an institutional obstacle course than 30 years ago. In particular, the "Motor Voter Law" that came into effect in 1995 and allows for voter registration when citizens apply for or renew their licenses has made registration significantly easier. Yet, it remains to be seen if this law will result in an increase in electoral participation.

This decline in the costs associated with voting, however, has not been accompanied by increases in the perceived benefits of citizen participation. Instead, the electorate's trust in the government decreased steadily since the early 1960s, reaching a low point in 1988 and staying at about this level throughout the early 1990s. In 1988, 58% of Americans indicated that government can never or only some of the times be trusted. Only 32.7% of the citizenry indicated that government is run for the benefit of all. Almost 70% believe that government is run by big interests. Obviously, citizens who feel alienated from the government are less likely to vote than those who place trust in the governing institutions. In a similar vein, citizens' likelihood of detecting differences between the parties' policy platforms has decreased. It must make a difference to the voter which candidate wins the election. The larger the party differential, that is, the ideological or performance-based difference between the parties, the greater the benefit derived from voting.

In comparison to research on voting conducted in the 1940s and 1950s, recent studies of electoral behavior rely on increasingly sophisticated methodologies and high-quality data. Yet a commonly accepted theory of voting behavior has still to evolve. The theoretical framework developed by *The American Voter* study (Campbell et al. 1960) continues to influence current investigations of voting patterns. Nevertheless, the major emphasis on the role of party identification as the main determinant of the individual vote choice has been replaced by more dynamic models of the electoral decision process (e.g., Page and Jones 1979). These models are trying to account for the fact that candidate, party, and issue factors interact. For instance, party loyalties do not function merely as a fixed determinant of the vote but are themselves influenced by issue and candidate factors.

The more complicated models developed throughout the 1970s, 1980s, and 1990s did not necessarily provide definite conclusions. There has been a great deal of electoral volatility during the postwar years. None of the discussed models can entirely account for change and stability in American electoral behavior. Yet their combined conclusions give a fairly comprehensive picture of the determinants of electoral choices.

Frauke Schnell

SEE ALSO Realignment and Dealignment

BIBLIOGRAPHY

Asher, Herbert B. *Presidential Elections and American Politics.* 5th ed. Chicago: University of Chicago Press, 1992.

Berelson, Bernard R., Paul F. Lazarsfeld, and William N. McPhee. *Voting.* Chicago: University of Chicago Press, 1954.

Campbell, Angus, Philip E. Converse, Warren E. Miller, and Donald E. Stokes. *The American Voter.* New York: Wiley, 1960.

Carmines, Edward G., and James A. Stimson. "The Two Faces of Issue Voting." *American Political Science Review* 74 (1980): 78–91.

Downs, Anthony. *An Economic Theory of Democracy.* New York: Harper and Row, 1957.

Key, V.O. (with Milton C. Cummings). *The Responsible Electorate: Rationality in Presidential Voting, 1936–1960.* New York: Vintage Books, 1966.

Lazarsfeld, Paul F., Bernard R. Berelson, and Helen Gaudet. *The People's Choice.* New York: Columbia University Press, 1948.

Miller, Warren E. "The Puzzle Transformed: Explaining Declining Turnout." *Political Behavior* 14 (1982): 1–40.

Nie, Norman H., Sidney Verba, and John R. Petrocik. *The Changing American Voter*. Cambridge: Harvard University Press, 1979.

Niemi, Richard G., and Herbert F. Weisberg. *Controversies in Voting Behavior*. Washington, DC: Congressional Quarterly, 1984.

Page, Benjamin I. *Choices and Echoes in Presidential Elections*. Chicago: University of Chicago Press, 1978.

Page, Benjamin I., and Calvin Jones. "Reciprocal Effects of Policy Preferences, Party Loyalties and the Vote." *American Political Science Review* 73 (1979): 1071–1089.

Piven, Frances E., and Richard A. Cloward. *Why Americans Don't Vote*. New York: Pantheon Books, 1988.

Pomper, Gerald M., ed. *The Election of 1988: Reports and Interpretations*. Chatham, NJ: Chatham House, 1993.

Teixeira, Ruy A. *The Disappearing American Voter*. Washington, DC: Brookings Institution, 1992.

Wolfinger, Raymond E., and Steven J. Rosenstone. *Who Votes?* New Haven: Yale University Press, 1980.

Welfare

WHAT IS WELFARE?

The term *welfare* is used broadly to refer to direct or indirect financial subsidies to individuals. People receive direct subsidies individually from the government by means of a check or other financial benefit. Social Security payments and subsidized student loans are direct subsidies. Indirect subsidies are not paid individually to beneficiaries. Instead, the government provides goods and services that are used collectively; for example, government supports education. Students receive a government service at far below its real cost because taxpayers in the school district, state, and nation pay. A third kind of subsidy is one provided through tax benefits. A tax-break subsidy permits some people and corporations to pay less in taxes than others of the same income. Most tax subsidies go directly to middle- and upper-income people through corporate tax breaks. Since shareholders of corporations are usually upper-income people, they profit the most from these tax subsidies.

THE AMERICAN WELFARE SYSTEM

The American welfare system is usually dated from the Social Security Act of 1935. After defeating the Republican president, Herbert Hoover, who opposed a federal response to the depression, the Democrat president, Franklin D. Roosevelt, enacted several temporary emergency relief programs for poor people and unemployed workers. Only with the passage of the 1935 Social Security Act did the United States begin to develop a nonemergency, permanent welfare act. That act established a "safety net" to catch those falling into poverty. It did so through a system of entitlements for the elderly, the unemployed, and poor fatherless children and created a program for maternal and child health care. Health insurance, originally part of the package, was removed to deflect strong opposition from business, the medical profession, and the insurance industry. In 1937 the Supreme Court upheld the constitutionality of the act, which made the federal government's responsibility for social welfare permanent. The fourth program created by the Social Security Act is actually a series of programs, now known as Supplemental Security Income (SSI) (Katz 1995).

The centerpiece of the Social Security Act was the establishment of a national pension program for retired workers—Old Age Insurance (OAI), popularly known as Social Security. The payments were available to many but not all workers who retired at age 62 or later. Agricultural workers, domestic workers, unpaid female homemakers, those employed by nonprofit religious, scientific, literary, and educational institutions, as well as employers covered by the Railroad Retirement Act were excluded from coverage (Abramovitz 1988). The 1939 amendments to the act extended coverage to include a retired or deceased worker's dependents. In subsequent years the act was modified by a series of amendments and court cases stretching from 1939 through the 1970s to include the most needy groups, for example, people of color, the very poor, unmarried mothers, and other workers not protected under the original act.

Social Security is financed through a payroll tax on employees and employers paid to a trust fund. In 1995 the tax was slightly over 7.6% of the first $61,200 of an employee's wages. Individuals who qualify collect their full Social Security benefits on reaching retirement age, although partial benefits may be collected before then. Individuals who receive Social Security do not believe they are collecting welfare since they are only getting back what they paid into the program through payroll deductions. This is not wholly accurate, however, because recipients receive back their contributions, with interest, in six years, while they typically receive Social Security for 14 years (Peters 1986).

The Social Security Act also included unemployment insurance to protect some workers against the loss of income caused by temporary or involuntary joblessness. States determine their own eligibility requirements, rules of coverage, benefit levels, waiting periods, and financing systems, within broad guidelines. Most states' regulations limit unemployment insurance benefits to persons who are actively seeking a job and who can establish that their unemployment is for a "good cause," that is, involuntary. Most state unemployment programs disqualify workers who quit a job voluntarily without good cause, are fired for work-related misconduct, refuse a suitable job, are directly involved in a strike, or make fraudulent claims.

Another program created by the Social Security Act was a public assistance program, Aid to Families with Dependent Children (AFDC). Commonly referred to as "welfare," this is the major welfare program that provides cash assistance for families below the official poverty line. It is a program for children deprived of parental care and support as a result of parental death, continued absence from the home, incapacity, or unemployment. Until recently, two-parent families were ineligible for benefits in most states. The caseload consists mainly of women and their children (Zopf 1989). Since the recipients are poor, they have been means tested; that is, individual recipients must periodically demonstrate eligibility by showing they are poor. In between times, any change, for example, births, deaths, or change of address, must be reported to the welfare bureaucracy. Almost every aspect of a welfare recipient's life is subject to scrutiny by welfare officials. Federal AFDC grants match state welfare and local general assistance expenditures up to specified amounts for individuals not already covered by old-age or Social Security insurance. This results in widely varying welfare grants in different states, ranging from a high of $924 a month for a family of three in Alaska to a low of $120 a month in Mississippi.

In the 1990s there has been a significant return of state authority over social and moral behavior of welfare recipients (Kleniewski 1995). Although under the federal grant-in-aid law, states retain a great deal of discretion over AFDC, states cannot generally impose additional eligibility requirements (such as denying aid for a child conceived while the mother was receiving AFDC) or withhold money for behavioral matters (such as failure to attend school). The Department of Health and Human Services (HSS) has been granting the states waivers to institute these policies (Savner and Greenberg 1995). This waiver practice has been going on since 1962, but it became increasingly popular during the Reagan and Bush administrations and increased during the Clinton administration. Now,

even more state control over AFDC under block grants, with or without federal restrictions, is a central feature of the debate over welfare reform in the new Republican-controlled Congress.

DEMOCRATIC PARTY APPROACH TO WELFARE

Democrats have argued since the 1930s that every citizen is entitled to the minimum conditions of a decent life as a matter of basic justice, and no citizens should be denied those minimum conditions because they cannot pay for them. Democrats do not agree, of course, on the exact type and level of benefits that ought to be guaranteed. Some, for example, would include complete health care from birth to death. Some would include only hospitalization insurance. Some would include free public education for students from kindergarten through graduate school. Others would limit the guarantee to the high school diploma. Most Democrats agree, however, that the appropriate function of government is to provide every citizen with some degree of formal education and health care even if it requires that the rich be taxed to provide benefits for the poor.

Democratic Party philosophy supports the idea that caring for people is a federal government responsibility because it believes that at the core of many poor people's problems is the lack of jobs paying wages adequate to support a family. While individual attributes may play some role in causing poverty, Democrats maintain that the main explanation for poverty is found in the nature of the opportunity structure that disadvantaged people face. Millions of U.S. citizens have little job security, few hopes of promotion, and work in low-paying, low-status jobs. Moreover, high unemployment, the decline of low and semiskilled jobs, an increase in part-time and contingent work and in jobs requiring at least a high school education, the falling value of real wages, and ongoing discrimination on the basis of race and gender make it difficult for many workers to earn enough money to keep a family above the poverty line (Cassidy 1995). About half of family heads of poor families are employed, but even working full-time at a minimum-wage job yields an income less than $10,000, far below the poverty line for a family.

With this diagnosis of the causes of poverty, the solution, according to Democrats, is generally twofold. First, a mammoth effort needs to be devoted to the problem of skill formation and education so that disadvantaged children are equipped to participate actively in the labor market. Second, effective jobs programs need to be created to employ people with marginal skills. In addition, Democrats support minimum-wage laws designed to keep pace automatically with changes in the standard of living and mandatory fringe benefit programs. Both solutions require an expansion of the "affirmative state" (Wright 1994). The Democratic Party thus concentrates its energies on trying to find ways to use government either to ease the burden of poverty or to assist the individual in adapting to prevailing institutions. Democrats generally reject exclusive reliance on the market to foster social mobility and attempt to use government to equalize opportunities with the market or assist individuals in coping with their poverty status by direct income transfers.

President Bill Clinton campaigned on a party platform to "end welfare as we know it" and, as president, introduced the Work and Responsibility Act of 1994. The act, which did not become law, would have imposed a cumulative two-year limit on welfare benefits, after which poor women and men would have to find paid jobs or participate in the WORK program, a government-sponsored jobs program. That program would entail states' creating jobs at a minimum of 15–35 hours for at least the minimum wage, through subsidized private-sector jobs, public-sector jobs, and community service jobs. The president's act would also have allowed states the option of limiting AFDC increases for children conceived while the mother was receiving assistance (family caps); created a nationwide, simplified paternity-establishment process to facilitate child support enforcement; made it easier for two-parent families to be eligible for AFDC payments; increased the earned income tax credit for poor working families (which reduces the taxes of the employed poor and gives them a check if they owe no taxes); and proposed spending $2.7 billion over five years to pay for child care for those in the mandatory education and training programs, the WORK slots, and for one year after welfare recipients join the wage labor force (Backer 1995).

Democrats used to argue that women with children receiving welfare had a responsibility to stay at home and take care of their children, but times have changed. Democrats today argue that because the majority of women, including mothers of young children, are now in the paid labor force, welfare recipients can no longer expect to stay home and take care of children. Just as middle-class women are now expected to work in the paid labor force, so too are women on welfare expected to work. This explains Democratic support for the Republican state work demonstration projects and the Job Opportunities and Basic Skills (JOBS) training pro-

gram, created by the Reagan administration's Family Support Act of 1988, the major welfare reform legislation passed into law in the 1980s (Miller 1989).

Susan L. Thomas

SEE ALSO Social Security

BIBLIOGRAPHY

Abramovitz, M. *Regulating the Lives of Women: Social Welfare Policy from Colonial Times to the Present.* Boston: South End Press, 1988.

Backer, L.C. "Welfare Reform at the Limit: The Futility of 'Ending Welfare as We Know It.' " *Harvard Civil Rights–Civil Liberties Law Review* 30 (1995): 339–405.

Cassidy, J. "Who Killed the Middle Class?" *New Yorker*, October 16, 1995, pp. 113–121.

Goodin, R.E. *Reasons for Welfare: The Political Theory of the Welfare State.* Princeton: Princeton University Press, 1988.

Katz, M. *Improving Poor People: The Welfare State, The "Underclass," and Urban Schools as History.* Princeton: Princeton University Press, 1995.

Kleniewski, N. "The War Against Welfare Moves to the States." *Research in Politics and Society* 5 (1995): 193–215.

Miller, D. *Women and Social Welfare.* New York: Praeger, 1989.

Peters, C. "Tilting at Windmills." *Washington Monthly*, June 1986, p. 10.

Savner, S., and M. Greenberg. *The CLASP Guide to Welfare Waivers: 1992–1995.* Washington, DC: Center for Law and Social Policy, May 1995.

Shogran, E. "Clinton Vetoes GOP's Welfare Overhaul Plan." *Los Angeles Times,* January 16, 1996.

Thomas, S.L. *Gender and Poverty.* New York: Garland, 1994a.

———. "From the Culture of Poverty to the Culture of Single Motherhood: The New Poverty Paradigm." *Women & Politics* 14 (1994b): 65–97.

Wright, E.O. *Interrogating Inequality: Essays on Class Analysis, Socialism and Marxism.* New York: Verso, 1994.

Zopf, P.E. *American Women in Poverty.* New York: Greenwood Press, 1989.

Women

For the past 150 years, American women have struggled for equality with men, fighting for and winning the right to vote and antidiscrimination legislation. Women have also fought for rights related to uniquely female biological functions, such as reproductive rights (abortion, contraception, family planning, counseling) and workplace rights such as paid maternity leave and punishment of sexual harassment. Women have also struggled against the traditional role of the "weaker" sex, and many of the political issues that have motivated women center on gaining freedom from the confining, male-imposed social place of women. Of course, not all women have been proponents of these causes, nor has one of the mainstream, male-dominated political parties consistently supported or opposed these movements. The Democratic Party was initially opposed to women's suffrage, but since the 1960s when the Democratic coalition came to include the New Left movements, one of which was feminism, the Democrats have pushed for equal rights and antidiscrimination policies and have supported reproductive rights. Democrats have also been more aggressive in putting women in high government positions and have sought to protect women who wish to lead nontraditional lives from the Reaganites' "traditional family values" crusade that would roll back many advances of the women's movement.

WOMEN'S SUFFRAGE

In the United States, women became active politically in the mid-nineteenth century in campaigns for social justice and to free the slaves, but out of these movements coalesced a women's suffrage movement that was active throughout the last half of the nineteenth century. The demand for the enfranchisement of American women was first seriously formulated at the Seneca Falls Convention in 1848. The Seneca Falls Convention, the first women's rights assembly in the United States, was organized by Lucretia Coffin Mott and Elizabeth Cady Stanton and met at Seneca Falls, New York, on July 19–20, 1848. The 68 women and 32 men present passed a Declaration of Sentiments, which paralleled the language of the Declaration of Independence and listed 16 forms of discrimination against women, including denial of suffrage and of control of their wages, their own persons, and their children. Twelve resolutions calling for various rights were passed. Eleven received unanimous approval, whereas one, advocating the vote for women, was adopted over Mott's opposition. The convention was moved to Rochester, New York, two weeks later to win broader support for its goals.

After the Civil War, agitation by women for the ballot became increasingly vociferous. In 1869, however, a rift developed among feminists over the proposed 15th Amendment, which gave the vote to black men. Susan B. Anthony, Elizabeth Cady Stanton, and others refused to endorse the amendment because it did not give women the ballot. Other suffragists, including Lucy Stone and Julia Ward Howe, argued that once the black man was enfranchised, women would achieve their goal. As a result of the conflict, two organizations emerged. Stone created the American Woman Suffrage Association, which aimed to secure the ballot through state legislation. Stanton and Anthony formed the National Woman Suffrage Association to work for suffrage on the federal level and to press for more extensive institutional changes, such as the granting of property rights to married women. In 1872, Anthony went to the polls and asked to be registered. While the two Republican members of the board agreed to receive her name, the Democratic members opposed it. Ultimately, Anthony and 13 other women were arrested when they voted but given an unconditional pardon. In 1878, Anthony wrote and submitted to Congress a proposed right-to-vote amendment that later became the 19th Amendment to the U.S. Constitution.

In 1890 the two groups united under the name National American Woman Suffrage Association (NAWSA). In the same year Wyoming entered the union, becoming the first state with general women's suffrage (which it had adopted as a territory in 1869). Initially the Democratic Party opposed women's suffrage. When in 1896 a Republican senator introduced a proposal in the Senate to give women the right to vote, the proposal was defeated in the Democrat-controlled Senate. The Democratic Party did not officially endorse women's right to vote until 1916.

The women's suffrage movement achieved its most notable successes during the Progressive era, when many women's groups were active in various battles aimed at liberating women from various tyrannies. To many Progressive-era women's activists, like Jane Addams and Florence Kelley, women's rights were merely a part of the larger cluster of rights to be fought for, particularly workers' rights (working conditions, pay). To other women reformers of the Progressive era, women's rights were the central issue. There was, however, great diversity among these reform groups. There were a few militant champions of sexual liberation, among whom was Emma Goldman, an immigrant later deported for her radical anarchist activities. Goldman advocated birth control and free love, saying that "women must no longer keep their mouths shut and their wombs open."

A less radical advocate of birth control was Margaret Sanger. Sanger's followers, largely middle class, did not favor free love or critique the nuclear family; some were conservatives who feared that Anglo-Saxon Protestants were committing "race suicide" through the immigration policies of the United States. They believed that birth control could reduce the population growth of immigrant masses. Others in the movement were not such xenophobes but merely wanted to give women a way out of the tyranny of unwanted pregnancy—a theme that would later be picked up by abortion rights advocates. By 1918, Sanger succeeded in getting the courts to permit doctors to distribute birth-control information—states, however, continued to prohibit the sale of contraceptives.

Other feminists opposed the traditional role of women not out of a desire for sexual freedom or in order to destroy marriage but to allow women to be liberated from the burdens of housework and motherhood and provide them with the opportunities afforded to men to pursue freedom and satisfaction through meaningful work and creative effort. Charlotte Perkins Gilman was a leading advocate of this position, and in her book *Women and Economics* (1898), which prefigured much of what the National Organization for Women (NOW) would say 70 years later, she called for a form of communalism featuring large housing units, day nurseries, central kitchens, and maid service to relieve women of domestic chores. Gilman's ideas were once again aimed at middle-class Anglo-Saxon Protestant women and as such had little widespread appeal, particularly among the large population of women already working not out of the desire to find fulfillment but because of economic necessity.

The suffrage movement did not suffer from the limited appeal of other women's movements of the time, though its leaders were largely middle-class women. The membership of NAWSA increased from 17,000 in 1905 to 75,000 in 1910, and by the end of 1917, NAWSA claimed 2 million members. With such overwhelming numbers, many of whom were visible in various protests and political actions, Democratic President Woodrow Wilson was forced to come out in support of the Equal Suffrage Amendment in 1918. Retaining the original language as drafted by Anthony, the 19th Amendment finally passed (304 to 88) Congress in 1919. Opposition was strongest among House Democrats, who comprised 72 of the 88 opposing votes. Democrat-controlled state legislatures also posed the most determined opposition: of the nine states that voted against ratification, eight were controlled by Democrats.

ANTIDISCRIMINATION POLICY

Women voters did not have a noticeable impact on state and federal elections for many years, and when women voted they tended to vote Republican. In the 1960 presidential election between John F. Kennedy and Richard Nixon, Democrats mobilized an increasingly aware women's vote, which helped Kennedy win one of the closest elections in American history.

Women were angered, however, when Kennedy failed to appoint women to high government positions, particularly in the case of the Labor Department's Women's Bureau. In response, Kennedy created the President's Commission on the Status of Women for the stated purpose of combating "the prejudices and outmoded customs" that serve as "barriers to the realization of women's basic rights."

The commission, following Kennedy's own position, rejected the ideas of the Equal Rights Amendment, claiming that the rights of women were adequately protected by the 5th and 14th amendments. The commission did, however, recommend a number of antidiscrimination measures, one of which was passed as the Equal Pay Act in 1963. This act, the first piece of federal legislation to prohibit discrimination on the basis of gender, requires equal compensation for women and men who perform equal work. Kennedy's successor, Lyndon Johnson, was more forceful in his support of women's rights. Johnson pushed for passage of the Civil Rights Act, and in an attempt to make passage of the act more difficult, Republican Congressman Howard Smith of Virginia proposed that women should be included in the protected groups. The act passed anyway, and Title VII established the Equal Employment Opportunity Commission to help battle discrimination based on sex, color, race, religion, and national origin. Johnson also issued an executive order banning the federal government and any federal contractor from discrimination based on sex.

In preparation for a 1977 National Conference on Women in observance of the United Nation's International Women's Year, Democratic President Carter appointed renowned feminist Bella Abzug to chair the President's Commission on the Status of Women, and he replaced the conservative Republican members appointed by Nixon and Ford with liberal Democrats.

Upon election, Bill Clinton became the strongest champion of women's rights ever to occupy the White House, appointing more women to his cabinet than any other president, as well as the first female attorney general, Janet Reno. He also supported the Family and Medical Leave Act of 1993, which requires companies with fifty or more employees to grant up to 12 weeks of unpaid leave annually for the birth or adoption of a child or to care for a spouse or immediate family member with a serious health condition. Although not limited to women, this act greatly contributed to women's ability to balance family and career. Clinton also instructed his secretary of defense, Les Aspin, to implement the congressional mandate on the assignment of women in the armed forces to all units excluding ground combat troops.

THE EQUAL RIGHTS AMENDMENT

Dissatisfied with continued gender-based discrimination, despite women's right to vote, the National Woman's Party, headed by Alice Paul, drafted a proposed amendment to the Constitution stating that "equality of rights under the law shall not be denied or abridged by the United States nor by any State on account of sex." The ERA was originally introduced in Congress in 1923, but it was opposed by both major parties, and it was not acted on until 1970, when the National Organization for Women (NOW) brought women's issues to the center of public attention with protests and calls for equality. NOW gained influence within the Democratic Party as many New Left groups of the 1960s were incorporated into the liberal Democratic coalition.

The ERA was finally approved by the House of Representatives in 1971 and by the Senate in 1972. The deadline for ratification was originally set at March 1979, but in 1978, with many states still delaying action, it was extended three years. Despite being endorsed by two Republican presidents, Nixon and Ford, the controversial ERA was strongly opposed by conservative Republican majorities in various state legislatures. Between 1979 and 1982, ERA supporters employed economic boycotts against states that did not ratify the amendment, but when Republican nominee Ronald Reagan opposed the ERA in 1980 and forced the Republican Party to drop support for the ERA from its platform, the ERA seemed doomed. Although national polls indicated that a majority of Americans favored passage of the ERA, with the aid of the newly elected president, the anti-ERA movement, spearheaded by STOP ERA, an organization founded by Phyllis Schlafly in 1972, managed to quash what support remained for the ERA. On June 30, 1982, ratification of the ERA fell three states short of the 38 needed. Efforts to regain congressional approval of the proposal, however, were defeated in the House on November 15, 1983.

The ERA would be rendered irrelevent if the United States would ratify the Convention on the Elimination of All Forms of Discrimination Against Women, adopted by the United Nations in 1979. Although President Carter signed the convention, it is not binding domestically until the Senate ratifies it. It has been before the Senate Judiciary Committee for several years, but little action is being taken to speed its ratification.

ABORTION

In recent years, with the death of the ERA and the success of antidiscrimination laws, the women's movement has concentrated on reproductive rights, which are viewed as fundamental to women's control of their lives. Margaret Sanger's birth-control movement had been an attempt to get women out from under the domination of the male-imposed "biologically determined" social roles. The right to abortion was a further step in women's liberation from the often confining position of wife and mother. Outlawed by most states since the mid-nineteenth century, abortion was made legal in one broad sweep in 1973, when the Supreme Court struck down a Texas abortion law in *Roe* v. *Wade*.

Although the *Roe* court was dominated by Republican-appointed justices (five of the seven justices in the majority belonged to the Republican Party), abortion rights has been a Democratic cause since 1980. Democrats largely supported *Roe* from the beginning, but the Democratic presidential candidate in 1976, Jimmy Carter, was a deeply religious sourthern Baptist who personally opposed abortion. He campaigned to end federal funding for abortions, but, like his opponent Ford, he opposed a constitutional amendment to overturn *Roe*. Carter's nomination by the Democratic convention in 1976 meant that the party's first post-*Roe* platform was a lukewarm concession to the pro-choice forces within the party; it read that "it is undesirable to amend the U.S. Constitution to overturn the Supreme Court decison [on abortion]." As the campaign progressed, Carter changed his position on the constitutional amendment, cutting the one thread that connected him to abortion rights elements of the Democratic Party. As president, Carter did little either to legitimize or to oppose the ruling in *Roe*. He mainly restricted himself to fighting federal funding of abortion by supporting the Hyde Amendment's restrictions on the use of Medicaid funds to pay for abortions. Carter maintained throughout his presidency that, though personally opposed to abortion, he had taken an oath to uphold the laws and Constitution of the United States, which included the Supreme Court's ruling in *Roe*.

In 1980, pro-choice forces within the Democratic Party were more active than they had been at the 1976 convention, and they managed to get a plank into the platform that more strongly supported abortion; the platform recognized "the belief of many Americans that a woman has a right to choose whether and when to have a child." This was a compromise between Carter's position and that of a faction of the Democratic Party, led by the feminist Gloria Steinem, that had called for federal funding of abortions through Medicaid. Throughout the 1980s and early 1990s, the party adopted stronger language in response to the Republican denunciation of *Roe* and calls for an amendment to overturn that ruling. The Democratic Party claimed that "reproductive freedom [is] a fundamental human right," a clause that would appear in later Democratic platforms.

Democratic members of the Senate were also instrumental in opposing the Supreme Court nominations of the Reagan and Bush administrations. Democratic Senator Joseph Biden, chairman of the Senate Judiciary Committee, spearheaded the successful opposition to Robert Bork, the controversial antiabortion Reagan nominee. Though both Reagan and Bush called for the overturning of *Roe*, they were often forced to appoint moderate candidates to the Supreme Court because of this Democratic opposition. Still, by 1989, with Rehnquist and White, the original two dissenters in *Roe*, reinforced by three Reagan appointees, the Court began rolling back the rulings of the 1970s that supported an almost unconditional abortion right. In the case of *Webster* v. *Reproductive Health Services*, the Court ruled, by a 5-to-4 margin, that some state-imposed restrictions on abortion are constitutionally permissible. The issue in *Webster* was a preamble to a Missouri law that declared that human life begins at the moment of conception. *Webster* did not overturn *Roe*, though Republican-appointed Justice Antonin Scalia urged the Court to do so, but it did invite state legislatures to write restrictive abortion laws that might pass constitutional muster.

The Reagan and Bush appointments had succeeded in swinging the attitude of the Court, but when Bill Clinton became the first post-*Roe* Democratic president to have a chance to make Supreme Court appointments, he quickly chose noted women's rights supporter Ruth Bader Ginsburg. His second Supreme Court appointment was Steven Breyer, a moderate with no public stand on abortion prior to his nomination. Breyer contributes to the growing middle on the Court and though not likely to be a strong supporter of women's rights is a sturdy bulwark against the overturn of *Roe* that many thought was presaged by *Webster*.

Jessamyn West

SEE ALSO Abortion

BIBLIOGRAPHY

Hecker, Eugene A. *A Short History of Women's Rights*. Westport, CT: Greenwood Press, 1971.

Langley, Winston E., and Vivian C. Fox, eds. *Women's Rights in the United States: A Documentary History*. Westport, CT: Greenwood Press, 1994.

Le Veness, Frank P., and Jane P. Sweeney, eds. *Women Leaders in Contemporary U.S. Politics*. Boulder, CO: Lynne Rienner, 1987.

BIOGRAPHIES

Presidents

JAMES BUCHANAN

James Buchanan, 15th president of the United States, took the oath of office repudiating sectionalism and determined to unify a nation that was breaking apart at the seams over the issue of slavery.

As one of the most accomplished and experienced statesmen ever to sit in the oval office—having served as a member of the House of Representatives (1820–1831) and the U.S. Senate (1834–1845), secretary of state under President James K. Polk (1845–1849), and minister to Russia (1831–1833) and Great Britain (1853–1856)—Buchanan appeared to be just the man who could best accomplish his goal.

Unfortunately, for all of his presidential qualifications, he was a man out of place and time when he won the election of 1856. His talents for compromise and foreign policy expertise were not required during a period when the nation was torn apart from within over slavery and secession. He tried to steer a neutral course that looked to preserve the status quo.

Buchanan was very much opposed to slavery personally but, as a strict constructionist, did not think that, constitutionally, the Union could force states to give it up. He denounced abolitionists as troublemakers, which won him critical support from the South.

Buchanan also has the distinction of being the only never-married person to be president (he was engaged to Ann Coleman in 1819, but she died before their wedding).

Born in Mercerburg, Pennsylvania, on April 23, 1791, Buchanan was the son of James Buchanan, a local businessman, and Elizabeth Speer. The elder James Buchanan owned the Stony Batter, a trading post in Cove Gap, a busy crossroads for travelers from Philadelphia and Baltimore who were headed for Pittsburgh.

In 1794, the Buchanans moved to Dunwoodie Farm, a 300-acre tract of land near Mercerburg. Life at Dunwoodie Farm would have a lasting impact on Buchanan and, in turn, on the country's future. He cherished his days on the farm, preferring the rural way of life to that of the city. Buchanan was at heart an agrarian and, as a result, felt a kinship with the southern plantation farmers. They would become his best friends in Washington, and he was drawn into their orbit.

Buchanan left Mercerburg at age 16 to attend Dickinson College, where he had an excellent record as a student and earned his law degree in 1809. He began his law career in the state capital in Lancaster, as an apprentice to James Hopkins. During the War of 1812, Buchanan was a military volunteer.

Buchanan started his political career as a Federalist at the state level, first being named to the Pennsylvania State Assembly in 1814. He was a Federalist by principle because he was a *laissez-faire* economist who didn't believe in government intervention. However, Buchanan was troubled by what he saw as his party's elitism and lack of concern for the poor. He would become a Jacksonian Democrat and later a driving force for the Democratic Party in his home state.

After serving in the House of Representatives from 1820 to 1831, Buchanan was President Andrew Jackson's minister to Russia from 1831 to 1833. While serving as minister, he orchestrated the first-ever commercial treaty with that nation. As Polk's secretary of state, Buchanan negotiated the treaty with Great Britain that settled the Oregon Territory dispute and supported the war with Mexico and the annexation of Texas.

Buchanan's selection as minister to Great Britain under President Franklin Pierce turned out to be a blessing in disguise. He wasn't in the United States at the time of the Kansas/Nebraska conflict and thus was away from the controversy. Largely because he had taken no stand on the divisive Kansas/Nebraska issue, Buchanan would win the Democratic nomination for president in 1856. He ran on a platform of popular sovereignty, free trade and free seas, and the ascendancy of the United States in the Gulf of Mexico.

In the election of 1856, Buchanan and his running

James Buchanan. *Source:* Library of Congress.

mate, John C. Breckinridge of Kentucky, won 45.28 % of the popular vote and 174 electoral votes, defeating John C. Frémont of California, the first Repub-lican presidential candidate, and former President Millard Fillmore, the candidate of the old Whig Party. Buchanan's win was the result of a sweep of the South and victory in five northern states, including his home state of Pennsylvania. Because he owed his electoral victory to the South, Buchanan was more indebted than ever to the southern leaders, which would have an impact on his presidency.

Before he even took the oath of office, a dark cloud hung over the Buchanan presidency. In March 1857, the Supreme Court decided the *Dred Scott* case. Buchanan considered the decision—which denied Scott, a slave who had lived in the North, his free-dom—the final word on the issue of slavery. However, he misjudged the northern reaction to *Dred Scott*. Politically, the decision was anything but the final word. It drew the battle lines between the two sides further apart, making it even more difficult for

Buchanan to keep the country from dividing and to keep his Democratic Party united.

Adding more fuel to the fire at his inauguration was "Bleeding Kansas." Buchanan had inherited the volatile Kansas Territory situation from President Franklin Pierce. There was a proslavery Lecompton Constitution, which had been drawn up by a proslav-ery legislature elected fraudulently. Although the resi-dents of Kansas were clearly antislavery, Buchanan would side with the South on the legality of Lecomp-ton, drawing the ire of the antislavery forces.

Buchanan's handling of Kansas proved fatal for his leadership of the Democratic Party. Although Kansas would enter the Union as a free state in 1858, the Democratic Party split as a result of Lecompton. Buchanan lost the northern Democrats, who believed in popular sovereignty, and the pro-Union Democrats in the South.

With Kansas entering the Union as a free state, the South was now more bitterly opposed to the Union than ever before and unhappy with Buchanan as well. He was losing on all fronts, and his chances to be the man who united the country had vanished.

As if the *Dred Scott* decision and Kansas were not enough for the new president, the nation's economy took a downward spiral, and he was greeted with the Panic of 1857. It is generally agreed that the panic was caused by unlimited credit during the expansion of the 1850s. Buchanan was true to his Jacksonian philoso-phy and offered no federal help. He thought it best to let nature take its course. That hands-off approach was not forgotten by the businessmen who were deeply af-fected by the economic downturn.

If Buchanan was seen as indecisive and as failing to provide bold leadership on domestic issues, the same cannot be said of his foreign policy. Had he not been overwhelmed by the internal conflicts dividing the na-tion, Buchanan would have been known as one of the most imperialistic and expansionist of American pres-idents. He clearly thought that America's future lay with South America. From his days as secretary of state and again as minister to Great Britain, Buchanan sought to purchase Cuba from Spain. As minster to London, he signed the Ostend Treaty (calling for the purchase of Cuba). Three times during his administra-tion, he tried to buy the island but never received ap-proval from Congress. He also initiated discussions with Russia for the purchase of Alaska.

Buchanan pursued an aggressive policy toward Great Britain that risked war. His goal in Central America was to clear it of European influence and then establish American control, either by purchase, by annexation or, if needed, by intervention. Buchanan was able to force territorial concessions from the British, who ceded the Mosquito Kingdom to Nicaragua and Bey Island to Honduras. He also persuaded the British to give up what they had long asserted was their right to search American ships at sea. England's active policing of the slave trade led to a near conflict with the United States because some slave vessels had been flying American flags to avoid being stopped and searched. Buchanan reacted strongly when American ships were detained by the British, suggesting that American ships would in the future defend themselves in such incidents.

During his administration, Buchanan used gunboat diplomacy against Paraguay to uphold the rights of Americans abroad, sending 19 warships to Asunción to demand payment for property lost by American citizens. Buchanan vastly expanded American commercial opportunities on three continents, including China, and opened the door to diplomatic relations in Asia. He made a deal with Mexico that gave the United States transit rights from the Gulf of Mexico to the Pacific and the right to police that route.

For all his aggressiveness in foreign policy, Buchanan lacked precisely that quality as the leader of the Democratic Party. His failure to unite the party led to two official presidential candidates in 1860, Stephen A. Douglas and Breckinridge (the choice of the southerners), all but guaranteeing a victory for the Republican Party and its candidate, Abraham Lincoln.

The South had threatened secession if Lincoln was elected president, and on December 20, 1860, South Carolina made good on its word and voted to secede from the Union. The country was inching toward disunion. On February 8, 1861, the South followed South Carolina's lead, and the Confederate States of America were organized.

Instead of quietly sitting out the final months of his term, Buchanan had to wrestle with the issue of secession. He was—and still is—criticized severely for what was seen as his inaction. Using federal power in a dictatorial fashion, à la Andrew Jackson, to coerce the South was simply not in Buchanan's nature. It would have violated everything on which he had based his political career—the rule of law. His actions in those final days would permanently mar his reputation.

Buchanan did not approve of secession but, as a man who believed in the power of the law and as a strict constructionist, did not see anything he could do about it that would have been constitutional. He would point out that he did not use federal troops to force obedience on the South because he never received a request for such an action from any state.

What Buchanan tried to do to ward off an all-out war was to pacify the South through compromise. He would support the Crittenden Plan, which called for extending the Missouri Compromise line prohibiting slavery to the Pacific but, at the same time, guaranteeing slavery's existence in the South and calling for full enforcement of the Fugitive Slave Act. Buchanan himself called for a constitutional convention to let the people decide the issue of slavery itself, and as a last resort, he tried to bring both sides to the table in a peace conference.

The goal for Buchanan was to limit the number of states joining in the secession movement. He thought that if secessionist states could be isolated and violence avoided, secession would run its course and fade away. But his peacemaking methods failed, first, because the Republican-controlled Congress would not support his proposals, not with their president-elect, Lincoln, set to take office, and second, because both sides had simply gone too far to turn back. Buchanan was a man of reason at a time when emotions were ruling the day. He would blame the uncompromising abolitionists for starting the war.

In addition to his peace efforts, Buchanan warned South Carolina that an attack on Fort Sumter would be tantamount to war. South Carolina waited until April 12, 1861, to fire the shots that started the conflict in earnest. Now that the war had begun, someone had to be blamed, and that someone was Buchanan. Buchanan retired to private life at his estate in Wheatland, Pennsylvania, following his presidency and spent the remainder of his life trying to clear his name. He died on June 1, 1867, never having fully absolved himself of those accusations and never having been fully appreciated for his strengths.

Tim Morris

SEE ALSO History

BIBLIOGRAPHY

Klein, Philip S. *President James Buchanan: A Biography.* Philadelphia: Pennsylvania State University Press, 1962.

Morison, Samuel Eliot. *The Oxford History of the American People, 1789 through Reconstruction.* New York: Oxford University Press, 1972.

Smith, Elbert B. *The Presidency of James Buchanan.* Lawrence: University Press of Kansas, 1975.

Stampp, Kenneth M. *America in 1857: A Nation on the Brink.* New York: Oxford University Press, 1990.

200 Years: A Bicentennial Illustrated History of the United States. Washington, DC: U.S. News and World Report, Inc., 1973.

JIMMY CARTER

Jimmy Carter was elected the 39th president of the United States in 1976. His career began in his home state of Georgia where he served in state politics. His

Jimmy Carter. *Source:* Library of Congress.

achievements include the creation of new departments of energy and education and a foreign policy grounded in a concern for human rights. His administration was marked by a peace accord signed by Israel and Egypt, as well as the seizing of U.S. citizens as hostages by Iran in 1979 and the Soviet invasion of Afghanistan. These latter two events, a troubled economy, and opposition within his own party led to his defeat for reelection by Ronald Reagan in 1980.

Early Life

James Earl Carter was born to Earl and Lillian Carter on October 1, 1924, in Plains, a small town in rural Georgia. His father was a well-respected businessman and farmer who worked hard to attain a successful middle-class life. Jimmy Carter's early life was spent on the family farm. He attended a rural school, where he was active in sports and an avid reader. Later he attended Georgia South Western, a local community college and Georgia Tech, each for a single year. At

Georgia Tech, Carter was active in the Naval Reserve Officers Training Corps (NROTC) in preparation for a military career. He was admitted to the U.S. Naval Academy in Annapolis, Maryland, in June 1943 and graduated in three years due to the shortened program necessitated by World War II. His record at Annapolis was solid but without distinction. In 1946 Jimmy Carter married Rosalynn Smith, also of Georgia.

Carter's naval career began with service on the USS *Wyoming* and the USS *Mississippi*, battleships on which he served a year each. As a competent and effective officer desiring advancement, Carter applied for and was given a transfer to the submarine service. He qualified for command of diesel submarines. Desiring to maximize his chances for a successful naval career, he applied for the new nuclear submarine program under the direction of Admiral Hymen Rickover. He was accepted and completed some graduate work in nuclear physics. In his autobiography *Why Not the Best*, Jimmy Carter acknowledged the impact Admiral Rickover had on his life and career. The title refers to an incident in which Rickover asked him if he had always done his best. Carter replied, "No sir, I didn't always do my best." Rickover asked, "Why not?" Carter admits that this incident, along with a later "born again" religious experience, were two of his most formative experiences.

The career prospects for naval officers in the postwar years were slim. This fact, coupled with a strong postwar economy, his father's death of cancer, and the need to help on the family farm led Carter to resign his commission in October 1953.

Entry into Politics

Jimmy Carter returned to Plains, Georgia, and took over the running of the family peanut business. As a successful businessman, Carter also took on the role of civic leader. From 1956 to 1962 he served as a member of the local school board and as its chairman during his last year. During these years, the nation, especially the South, was undergoing the deep social turmoil brought on by the desegregation of schools mandated by the Supreme Court and the emerging civil rights movement. Carter biographer Betty Glad notes that while Carter was not a civil rights activist, neither did he join the various white resistance groups that developed at that time.

In 1962 Jimmy Carter sought election to the Georgia state legislature. This was initially unsuccessful because of opposition by local party leaders, who preferred a candidate of their own. In a bitterly contested election marred by sharp political maneuvering on all sides, ballot irregularities, outright corruption, and the involvement of the courts, Carter won election as state senator from Georgia's 14th District.

Carter served in the state senate from 1962 until 1966. Though he had an uneventful first term, he was allied with the progressive or reform elements in Georgia politics. He was unopposed in 1964 and won reelection easily. He was generally seen as an effective politician with good political skills who quickly made himself a reputation as a reformer, especially in the area of education.

Campaigns for Governor

In 1966 Jimmy Carter, after briefly considering running for the U.S. House of Representatives, announced his candidacy for governor of Georgia. In a multicandidate race, Carter attempted to take a centrist compromise position. In spite of showing organizational and media skills, he lost this first attempt to achieve statewide office. He failed even to make the runoff election, which was finally won by Lester Maddox. The themes of this race remained a part of each subsequent Carter campaign. There was an emphasis on personal integrity, tough-minded pursuit of victory, and a generally nonideological pragmatism with a moral base.

In 1970 Carter entered the primary again in his second attempt to be elected governor. Aided by the statewide name recognition he obtained in 1966 and benefiting from the experiences of that campaign, Carter ran aggressively. He positioned himself as a new-style politician running against the traditional Georgia establishment. In a runoff election against former governor Carl Sanders, Jimmy Carter won 60% of the vote and a clear victory. He easily won over his Republican opponent, Hal Suit, a television newscaster, with over 59% of the statewide vote total.

Jimmy Carter served a single term as governor. His administration was marked by a generally successful attempt to reorganize state government. This was done to improve efficiency, increase the power of the executive, and minimize the power of the various special interests in Georgia politics. He introduced the concept of zero-based budgeting and increased state spending on conservation and natural resources. He also undertook to make reforms in the court and criminal justice system (he restored the death penalty) and in welfare and mental health areas. In spite of some setbacks, on balance his record as a reformer was substantial, especially given the inertia inherent in Georgia politics and the wide-ranging nature of his agenda. It was a pragmatic record, not easily labeled liberal or conservative. Politically, he developed management skills and honed his political talents in the often bitterly fought battles with the legislature.

Campaign for President

Jimmy Carter's record as governor earned him national recognition as a successful leader of the "new South." In 1972 Carter began what has been called a "marathon" campaign for his party's nomination for president in 1976. To understand why the opportunity for a one-term governor from the Deep South existed, it is necessary to look at the changes in campaign law and party organization that occurred in the early 1970s. The Watergate scandal and legislative changes precipitated change in the contours of the election process. The Federal Election Campaign Act, which took effect in 1976 after a major court challenge, set limits on fund raising and campaign spending. This had the effect of directing funding to candidates, rather than party organizations, and in general increased the money available to nontraditional candidates. It also made federal money available to candidates who surpassed a minimum of private fund raising. It also limited spending, which tended to level the playing field for all candidates. The climate of reform that existed also affected party organization. The number of primaries increased, leading to a corresponding decrease in the power of party regulars and the convention itself. And the Democratic Party in particular passed numerous internal reforms in response to the debacle of the Chicago convention in 1968. The most important of these was the elimination of "winner-take-all" contests in favor of apportionment by proportional representation and quotas for underrepresented groups in the various state delegations. These changes, coupled with an attitude that the time was ripe for a Democratic victory in the White House, produced an opportunity for a relative outsider like Carter to contest for the nomination.

There were numerous serious contenders for the Democratic nomination in 1976. These included Morris Udall, Henry Jackson, George Wallace (who, though paralyzed, retained a solid and enthusiastic base), Jerry Brown, Frank Church, Sargent Shriver, Birch Bayh, and Hubert Humphrey. The new party rules, especially the use of proportional selection of delegates, tactical and strategic errors by his opponents, shrewd campaigning by a Carter team that had begun its strategic planning as early as 1972, and the ability to straddle both the left and right wings of his party because of his pragmatic style and political record, gave Carter the nomination.

Popular dissatisfaction with President Ford because

of the pardon of President Nixon and the lingering effects of Watergate, coupled with divisions within the Republican Party exemplified by Ronald Reagan's challenge to Ford for the nomination and tactical blunders in the Ford campaign, gave Jimmy Carter, a relatively unknown southerner with an appealing folksy style, a close victory over Gerald Ford. Carter won with 51% of the popular vote and 297 electoral votes, having carried 23 states, often by narrow margins, and the District of Columbia.

The Carter Presidency

President Carter's administration was bedeviled by domestic and foreign events that ultimately limited him to one term. Party discipline had eroded in Congress because of the events of the 1960s, which made it difficult for Carter as an outsider inexperienced in the ways of Washington to exert effective leadership. Poor staff work and a management style that sought discussion and consensus through an enhanced role of the cabinet, which ultimately weakened his own leadership base, contributed to a perception of weakness and indecisiveness. Carter did have some domestic victories, including the establishment of new departments of energy and education, the building of an oil pipeline in Alaska, and a modest economic stimulus package, but these were overshadowed by economic weaknesses including a high inflation rate and a recession late in his term. He failed to persuade Congress to take on tax and welfare reform. Charges of financial improprieties involving his director of the OMB, Bert Lance, weakened his position as a partisan of moral integrity.

In foreign affairs he had more success. He successfully brokered a landmark peace agreement between Egypt and Israel through strong personal diplomacy. He successfully worked for the ratification of the Panama Canal Treaty, and he signed the second Strategic Arms Limitation Treaty (SALT II), though he failed to get Senate ratification. In spite of these achievements, foreign policy was eventually his undoing. He was unable to free American hostages seized by Iranian militants in 1979, a failure amplified by the collapse of a rescue mission in 1980. He responded to the Soviet invasion of Afganistan by canceling American participation in the Olympic games and instituting a limited trade embargo, a response that created an impression that he had weakened U.S resolve and military defenses.

These difficulties led to challenges to his renomination by his own party by Jerry Brown and Senator Edward Kennedy. Though these challenges failed, they further weakened Carter's chances for reelection. In 1980 the Republicans nominated a skilled consensus builder and effective campaigner, Ronald Reagan. President Carter lost in a three-man race (John Anderson had run an independent campaign). Reagan won with 489 electoral votes to Carter's 49. Carter received about 41% of the popular vote. Reagan received over 51%, with the remainder of the vote going to Anderson.

Carter's Legacy

Jimmy Carter was the first southern elected president (excepting the unique case of Lyndon Johnson) since the Civil War and the first governor to be elected since Franklin Roosevelt. He left a legacy of concern for human rights in foreign policy. His campaign and election signaled the advent of the personal campaign in a new political environment and a new era in southern politics. As a former president, Jimmy Carter has been active in the areas of conflict resolution and charity, notably Habitat for Humanity.

Melvin A. Kulbicki

SEE ALSO History

BIBLIOGRAPHY
Abernathy, M. Glenn. *The Carter Years*. New York: St. Martin's Press, 1984.
Fink, Gary M. *Prelude to the Presidency: The Political Character and Legislative Leadership Style of Governor Jimmy Carter*. Westport, CT: Greenwood Press, 1980.
Hargrove, Erwin C. *Jimmy Carter as President: Leadership and the Politics of the Public Good*. Baton Rouge: Louisiana State University Press, 1988.
Jones, Charles O. *The Trusteeship Presidency: Jimmy Carter and the United States Congress*. Baton Rouge: Louisiana State University Press, 1988.
Mollenhoff, Clark R. *The President Who Failed. Carter Out of Control*. New York: St. Martin's Press, 1980.

GROVER CLEVELAND

Grover Cleveland served as president of the United States from 1885 to 1889 and again from 1893 to 1897. As the 22nd and 24th president, he is the only president to have served two nonconsecutive terms. He was the first president elected from the Democratic Party after the American Civil War.

Cleveland was born in 1837 in Caldwell, New Jersey, the fifth of nine children of Ann and Richard Cleveland. He was named Steven Grover at birth. Richard Cleveland was a Presbyterian minister, who moved his family to upstate New York in 1841.

In 1854 Grover Cleveland settled in Buffalo, New York. Soon thereafter he took employment as a clerk in a law firm. Cleveland taught himself law while hold-

Grover Cleveland. *Source:* Library of Congress.

ing this position and was admitted to the New York bar in May 1859. During this time, he was becoming increasingly active in Democratic Party politics. In 1862 and 1863 he was elected to local posts within the party.

In 1863 Cleveland accepted an appointment as assistant district attorney. The same year, at the height of the Civil War, he was conscripted to serve in the Union army. Instead, as allowed by law, Cleveland paid a substitute to serve in his place; political opponents would later use this against him. In 1865 he received the Democratic Party nomination for district attorney but lost in the general election. In 1870 he was elected sheriff of Erie County, New York. In 1873 he completed his term and, along with two friends, established a successful Buffalo law firm.

In 1874 there began a series of events that would become a major scandal later in Cleveland's political career. A son was born out of wedlock to Buffalo widow Maria Halpin, who named Cleveland as the father. Cleveland did not dispute his paternity, but later in life he would allege uncertainty. At any rate, Cleveland assumed financial responsibility for the child. In 1876 Halpin sued Cleveland, asserting that he had promised

to marry her; she later dropped the suit. The same year, Cleveland gained custody of the child and had him placed in an orphanage until, three years later, he was able to have the child adopted into a family.

At the time, however, these events were of little public note. In 1881 Cleveland's political career began to skyrocket when he was elected mayor of Buffalo, defeating the local Republican political machine in a year when Republicans had done well in statewide races. He quickly established himself as a political reformer against machine politics.

In 1882 Cleveland was elected governor of New York. As governor, one of his main quarrels was with the New York City Democratic political machine, Tammany Hall. While this created problems for him as governor, it helped to solidify his popularity among other New York State Democrats and among Democrats throughout the country. It also curried favor with a growing nationwide movement of Republican political reformers known as "Mugwumps." Consequently, he gained sufficient national attention to become the Democratic nominee for president in 1884.

The 1884 presidential election was a rather vicious one. During the campaign, the Mugwumps circulated a series of letters suggesting that Cleveland's Republican opponent, James G. Blaine, had benefited financially from legislation passed while he was Speaker of the House that advanced his railroad interests. Soon afterward, the story broke concerning Cleveland's paternity of the child in Buffalo; the story, as reported, suggested that Cleveland had treated the mother and child harshly. From this the Republicans developed a chant: "Ma, Ma, where's my pa?" (After the election, the victorious Democrats would respond, "Gone to the White House, ha, ha, ha!") Cleveland successfully handled the matter by admitting that he might have been the father but denying that he had acted improperly after the child was born. In the last days of the campaign, Blaine attended a rally in New York in which a Protestant minister—noting the Democratic support from antiprohibitionists, Roman Catholics, and southerners—denounced the Democratic Party as the party of "rum, romanism, and rebellion." Blaine's slowness in repudiating the statement may have been decisive, because it angered many of New York's Irish Catholics, who—although typically Democratic—had been somewhat supportive of Blaine's candidacy. Cleveland carried New York by a margin of only 1,200 votes, but that gave Cleveland all of New York's 36 electoral votes. In an extremely close election, Cleveland received 219 electoral votes, a mere 18 votes more than he needed to win.

Thus, Cleveland became the first Democratic president after the Civil War. Throughout his first term, he faced a Democratic House but a Republican Senate. Not surprisingly, the first major battle of his presidency was with the Republicans, who resented Cleveland's attempts to replace Republican appointees with Democrats. In 1867, during the presidential administration of Andrew Johnson, the radical Republican Congress had passed the Tenure of Office Act. The act, which was of dubious constitutionality, required a president to obtain Senate approval before dismissing any official who had previously received Senate confirmation for appointment. In 1885, when Cleveland sought to dismiss the U.S. attorney in Alabama and replace him with someone of his own choosing, the Senate requested from Cleveland all papers relating to the dismissal. Cleveland refused, arguing that it would constitute an infringement upon his constitutional role as president. A political battle ensued. The angry Senate Republicans were forced to back down, however, when the public sided with the president. A few months later, the Tenure of Office Act was finally repealed.

Two economic issues dominated the remainder of Cleveland's first term. The first issue pitted Cleveland against a majority within his party: in order to keep the United States on the gold standard, Cleveland favored a law that would have ended the use of silver to back American currency. Cleveland, however, was unable to get the law passed. The second issue dealt with the protective American tariff. Although the tariff had not been a major issue in the 1884 campaign, Democrats generally favored lower tariff rates. As president, Cleveland grew increasingly concerned with this issue. In 1887 he delivered a message to Congress calling for lower rates. The tariff became one of the central issues of his first term, but Congress did not produce a bill for the president to sign.

The 1888 election was dominated by the tariff issue. Although Cleveland garnered more of the popular vote, he lost the election in the electoral college to the Republican nominee, Benjamin Harrison. Cleveland moved to New York City and temporarily returned to the practice of law. But in 1892 the Democrats again nominated Cleveland. This time Cleveland defeated Harrison.

The silver issue surfaced once again at the start of Cleveland's second term. The law at the time required the government to purchase and coin silver. Favoring an adherence to the gold standard alone, and believing that the silver purchase law was leading to the destabilization of U.S. currency, Cleveland called for its repeal. Although Democrats had a majority in both houses of Congress in 1893, the Democratic Party was divided on the issue while Republicans supported the

president. Congress gave Cleveland a major victory when it voted to repeal the law, but the matter left the Democratic Party deeply divided.

The tariff issue was also revisited in Cleveland's second term, with the president again calling for lower rates. Although Congress passed a tariff-reduction bill in 1894, it contained so many provisions protecting various interests that Cleveland let it become law without his signature.

In 1894 workers in the Pullman Palace Car Company went on strike. This was followed by a nationwide strike when the American Railway Union refused to work with any trains that pulled a Pullman car. The strike blocked the delivery of mail and stopped interstate commerce. When a skirmish between strikers and federal marshals occurred near Chicago, Cleveland sent federal troops to Illinois without waiting for the state to request assistance. Although the Supreme Court would later uphold Cleveland's action as a legitimate use of presidential emergency powers, it was politically costly because it alienated both the emerging labor movement and those Democrats who were proponents of states' rights.

In 1896 the Democratic Party convention nominated prosilver congressman William Jennings Bryan for the presidency, thus establishing the Democratic Party as the party favoring silver coinage. The Democrats further repudiated Cleveland by failing to pass a resolution commending him. The Republicans nominated William McKinley, who came out in favor of the gold standard. Unable to support Bryan, but not wanting to declare his support for McKinley publicly, Cleveland remained silent.

Three other aspects of Cleveland's presidencies also deserve mention. First, Cleveland vetoed a total of 584 bills in his two terms, making him second only to Franklin Roosevelt in this regard; many of his vetoes were against private pension bills for veterans of the Civil War and their dependents. Second, Cleveland began his first term by stopping the U.S. move to annex Hawaii, arguing that the Hawaiian people did not support it; annexation would not occur until 1898. Third, Cleveland successfully invoked the Monroe Doctrine against England in 1885 during a boundary dispute between Venezuela and British Guiana; the British backed down from a potential conflict and agreed to an arbitrated settlement.

After his presidency, Cleveland retired to Princeton, New Jersey, with his wife, Frances Folsum, whom he had married in 1886 during his first term as president. The couple had two sons and three daughters. In 1908 Cleveland died at his home in Princeton.

Michael J. Towle

SEE ALSO History

BIBLIOGRAPHY

Ford, Henry Jones. *The Cleveland Era*. New Haven, CT: Yale University Press, 1919.

Lynch, Denis Tilden. *Grover Cleveland: A Man Four-Square*. New York: Horace Liveright, 1932.

McElroy, Robert. *Grover Cleveland: The Man and the Statesman*. New York: Harper and Brothers, 1923.

Milkus, Sidney M., and Michael Nelson. *The American Presidency: Origins and Development, 1776–1990*. Washington, DC: CQ Press, 1990.

Nevins, Allan. *Grover Cleveland: A Study in Courage*. New York: Dodd, Mead, 1933.

Nevins, Allan, ed. *Letters of Grover Cleveland, 1850–1908*. New York: Da Capo Press, 1933; reprinted 1961.

Parker, George F. *Recollections of Grover Cleveland*. New York: Century, 1909.

Welch, Richard E. *The Presidencies of Grover Cleveland*. Lawrence: University of Kansas Press, 1988.

BILL CLINTON

The Prepresidential Years

William Jefferson "Bill" Clinton (b. August 19, 1946) began his political career in 1974 when, as a professor of constitutional law at the University of Arkansas, he decided to challenge Republican Congressman John Hammerschmidt in a historically Republican district. Using rhetoric emphasizing a liberal approach to policy, Clinton called for more federal funding of education, a national health insurance program, higher taxes on business, and public financing of presidential campaigns (English 1993).

Losing the campaign against Hammerschmidt, Clinton continued his pursuit of a political career. In 1976 Clinton was elected attorney general of Arkansas, and two years later he was elected governor of the state. As governor, he emphasized education reform. Clearly, Clinton's emphasis on education reform continues to be part of his political philosophy, for he has consistently supported federal education programs, including maintenance of the student loan and school lunch programs. As president, he has opposed Republican efforts to abolish the Department of Education and the national service program (English 1993).

The Presidential Years

With a primary interest in domestic policy, Clinton campaigned for president as a centrist "New Democrat." Claiming to support innovative approaches to welfare reform, job training, education, transportation, and reducing the budget deficit, Clinton's proposals were traceable to his association with the centrist Democratic Leadership Council (DLC). The DLC emerged in the mid-1980s as the leading voice of centrist Democrats, and in 1989 it established its own think tank, the Progressive Policy Institute, to develop proposals for domestic policy reform. Bill Clinton's involvement with the DLC was substantial, and during 1991 he served as chairman of the organization (Stoesz 1996).

After assuming office, Clinton's agenda faced opposition from liberal members of the House Democratic caucus, which complicated the strategic planning of the incoming administration. Clearly, developing budget recommendations posed the biggest dilemma. Clinton and his advisers were aware of the difficulties involved in designing a viable budget and economic strategy. Clinton's choice for treasury secretary, Lloyd Bentsen, and his choice for budget director, Leon Panetta, came to the administration with impeccable congressional credentials. Panetta warned Clinton of impending Republican opposition (Woodward 1994, 74). Without Republican congressional support, the president's proposals required overwhelming Democratic majorities in the House and Senate. This, however, required Clinton to modify his "New Democrat" agenda (Campbell 1996). According to political scientists Paul Quirk and Joseph Hinchliffe, "the same election that produced a New Democrat president . . .

Bill Clinton. *Source:* Library of Congress.

shifted the ideological balance within [the] congressional Democratic party away from the conservative or centrist Democrats . . . and toward the liberals" (Quirk and Hinchliffe 1996, 266). Yet Clinton, while needing the support of liberal members of the House Democratic caucus, could not ignore the concerns of conservative and centrist Democrats. Centrist House Democrats were an organized force, with three unofficial groups, the House Mainstream Forum, the Conservative Democratic Forum, and the Democratic Budget Group, representing moderate House Democrats (Quirk and Hinchliffe 1996).

Unveiled to Congress on February 17, 1993, the Clinton economic package contained spending cuts, spending increases in certain targeted areas, and tax increases. The program was designed to reduce the size of the nation's budget deficit by $700 billion over five years, with reductions in spending representing $375 billion and tax increases totaling $325 billion. Although the president proposed substantial cuts in federal spending, his economic package simultaneously called for $30 billion in new spending on highway construction and other infrastructure projects (Quirk and Hinchcliffe 1996, 269). Opposing the administration's infrastructure proposals, conservative and centrist Democrats joined the Republicans in claiming that the Clinton economic package did not include enough spending cuts. As Budget Director Panetta had predicted, the president's proposals passed with Democratic support alone. The proposals were passed by the House with a vote of 218 to 216; the close vote was indicative of the internal divisions in the Democratic Party. Indeed, the Senate vote on the economic package ended in a 50–50 tie, with Vice President Al Gore casting the tie-breaking vote. Although less ambitious than the original version, the final package contained spending cuts of $255 billion and tax increases of $241 billion (Quirk and Hinchliffe 1996; Woodward 1994).

Despite the difficulty in gaining congressional approval of the economic package, President Clinton achieved several legislative victories during his first year in office, including the Family and Medical Leave Act, the Motor Voter Law, the Brady Handgun Law, and a program of national service. During 1993, the Clinton administration developed a bipartisan coalition in support of the North American Free Trade Agreement (NAFTA). But the Clinton administration failed in its attempt to reform the nation's health care system.

In selecting the first lady, Hillary Rodham Clinton, as chair of a health care task force, Clinton revealed the high priority of health care reform to the administration. But the task force conducted its hearings in a se-

cret fashion. While collecting data and testimony from experts in the health care field, the special task force failed to include congressional leaders in the process (Quirk and Hinchliffe 1996, 275). Clearly, this was a major political error by the administration. When the administration submitted its Health Security Act to Congress in October 1993, the administration had alienated many members of Congress. And the Health Security Act contained several controversial measures, including a plan to require employers to provide health insurance to workers, which engendered substantial conservative and business opposition. The call for employer mandates, combined with a proposal for price controls on insurance products and the president's insistence on universal coverage, led to substantial interest-group opposition to the administration's plan. Given the necessity of securing conservative Democratic and Republican support for health care reform, the president's commitment to universal coverage proved to be an obstacle to achieving health care reform.

With the Republican takeover of Congress in the 1994 midterm elections, Clinton confronted a Congress hostile to his policy proposals. Given his preference for domestic affairs, this was a significant change for the administration. Policy differences with the Republican-controlled Congress led to a failure to produce a budget agreement in 1995. Unable to implement reforms in domestic policy, the Clinton administration has focused on foreign affairs, supporting military interventions in Haiti and Bosnia.

Michael E. Meagher

SEE ALSO History

BIBLIOGRAPHY

Campbell, Colin. "Management in a Sandbox: Why the Clinton White House Failed to Cope with Gridlock." In *The Clinton Presidency: First Appraisals*, ed. Colin Campbell and Bert A. Rockman. Chatham, NJ: Chatham House, 1996.

English, Art. "The Clinton Promise and Style." *American Review of Politics* 14 (1993): 229–248.

Quirk, Paul J., and Joseph Hinchliffe. "Domestic Policy: The Trials of a Centrist Democrat." In *The Clinton Presidency: First Appraisals*, ed. Colin Campbell and Bert A. Rockman. Chatham, NJ: Chatham House, 1996.

Stoesz, David. *Small Change: Domestic Policy under the Clinton Administration*. White Plains, NY: Longman, 1996.

Woodward, Bob. *The Agenda: Inside the Clinton White House*. New York: Simon and Schuster, 1994.

ANDREW JACKSON

Andrew Jackson, the seventh president of the United States, was born at Waxhaw, South Carolina, on March

Andrew Jackson. *Source:* Library of Congress.

16, 1767, the youngest of three sons of Andrew and Elizabeth Jackson, poor farmers who had emigrated from Ireland. The elder Jackson died a few days after his son's birth. At the age of 13 Andrew joined the militia along with his brother Robert. Their oldest brother, Hugh, had died in the Revolutionary War, and the two surviving brothers were wounded and captured by the British in 1781. As prisoners, the Jacksons were mistreated by the British. For refusing to clean the boots of a British officer, Andrew received a saber blow on the head that scarred him for life and left him with a lifelong hatred for the British. Andrew lost both his brother and mother soon after being released from a prisoner-of-war camp. In 1784 Jackson, then only 17, moved to Salisbury, North Carolina. There he studied law, supporting himself by gambling and horseracing. In 1788 he accepted the appointment of a public prosecutor in the turbulent frontier settlement of Nashville. About this time, Jackson met his future wife, Rachel, and they were married in 1791, even before her divorce from her first husband had become legal. Jackson be-

came a respected public prosecutor, restoring the rule of law in a frontier settlement and occasionally drawing his pistols to enforce his authority. He also speculated in lands and grew rich as a planter and merchant. His early political affiliations were with the "nabob" wing of the Jefferson Republicans. When Tennessee became a state in 1796, he was elected as its first representative in the House of Representatives. He declined to run for reelection but was named to fill a vacancy in the U.S. Senate, where he served from November 1797 to April 1798. He returned to Tennessee because of financial difficulties and the loneliness of Washington life. He accepted an appointment on the Tennessee superior court, serving on the bench until 1804. Possessed of a violent temper, he was involved in several duels and fights during this period. In 1796 he fought a duel with and killed a man who had slandered his wife. A bullet lodged near his heart during this duel caused him immense pain for the rest of his life.

When the War of 1812 against the British broke out, Jackson, who held the rank of major general in the Tennessee militia, took the field against the Creek Indians, allies of the British. After four pitched battles, he destroyed the enemy at Horseshoe Bend on March 27, 1814. Promoted as a major general in the regular army, he captured Pensacola in Florida from the British and then turned west to the defense of New Orleans. When the seasoned British army under Sir Edward Parkenham attacked, Jackson's motley troops, consisting mostly of backwoodsmen, free blacks, and pirates, laid down a deadly fire, killing or wounding over 2,000 British troops while losing only 40 of their own. This decisive victory against great odds made Jackson, now known as "Old Hickory," a folk hero to the nation. Jackson's military career ended with an unauthorized foray into Florida, which precipitated the transfer of the province from Spain to the United States. Both Secretary of State John Quincy Adams and President James Monroe retrospectively approved Jackson's invasion of Florida in the face of much political criticism.

Although Jackson disclaimed any political ambitions, his military successes obviously made him a candidate for the presidency. In 1823 he returned to Washington as a U.S. senator from Tennessee and soon became the front-runner in the 1824 presidential contest. As the votes were counted, Jackson received more popular votes than the other contenders, although in the electoral college, he commanded only 99, or 34 votes fewer than the 133 needed to secure the election. The election was thus thrown under constitutional provisions to the House of Representatives, where the second-place finisher, John Quincy Adams, received Henry Clay's support to be elected. Four years later, however, Jackson was able to sweep the polls to dislodge Adams and gain the White House.

Jackson's eight-year "reign," from 1829 to 1837, was one of the most notable in the annals of the presidency and inaugurated the era known as Jacksonian Democracy. He brought more power to the executive office than any presidenct except Lincoln and FDR. He achieved this by unflinching courage, utter disregard for his political future, and, above all, a natural gift of leadership. He was the people's president, at a time when the executive office was considered as the bastion of the established elite. Tens of thousands of Americans descended on Washington for Jackson's inauguration, and the jubilant throngs broke the china and furniture at the White House and muddied the carpets.

Jackson's term was marked by controversies that presaged the later conflicts of the 1850s. He boldly asserted presidential power, vetoing 12 measures during his term; in contrast, his six predecessors, among them, had cast only 12 vetoes. In 1832 Congress passed a high tariff over the opposition of the southern states. The tariff worked in favor of the manufacturing interests in the North, while the trade reprisals of European nations hurt the agricultural South. South Carolina moved to declare the law null and void in that state. Jackson denounced the nullification and obtained congressional authority to send troops to South Carolina. Thereupon Henry Clay fashioned a compromise that was acceptable to the president and to the South. But the incident led to bad feelings between Jackson and his vice president, John C. Calhoun. Jackson's populist sentiments led him to oppose the recharter of the Bank of the United States, a bastion of the Northeastern business establishment. It was headed at that time by Nicholas Biddle, a political opponent of Jackson. Jackson vetoed the recharter on the grounds that the bank was an unconstitutional monopoly that benefited only the rich. The disappearance of the bank left the country without a sound banking system and contributed to the severe depression that began in 1837, after Jackson had left office. In the field of foreign policy, Jackson enhanced the prestige of the new republic by paving the way for the acquisition of the Pacific Coast, collecting from France an old debt of 25 million francs, and recognizing the Republic of Texas established by Jackson's lieutenant, Sam Houston. In 1835 Jackson was the target of the first assassination attempt against a sitting president. Miraculously, he escaped both shots fired at him by an assailant who was later committed to an insane asylum. After he left office, Jackson retired to Hermitage, his estate near Nashville, where he died in 1845. But his influence was such that both Martin Van Buren in 1836 and James K. Polk in 1844 owed their victories to his support.

SEE ALSO History

BIBLIOGRAPHY

Bassett, Jean Spencer. *Life of Andrew Jackson*. Hamden, CT: Archon Books, 1911.

Davis, Burke. *Old Hickory: The Life of Andrew Jackson*. New York: Dial Press, 1977.

James, Marquis. *Andrew Jackson*. New York: Grosset, 1961.

Remini, Robert. *Andrew Jackson*. New York: Harper and Row, 1986.

Schlesinger, Arthur M., Jr. *The Age of Jackson*. Boston: Little, Brown, 1945.

Sellers, Charles G. *Andrew Jackson: A Profile*. New York: Hill and Wang, 1971.

LYNDON JOHNSON

Lyndon Baines Johnson, the 36th president of the United States, was born on August 27, 1908, in Stonewall, Texas, where his Baptist family was greatly involved in local politics. He endured an impoverished childhood in the isolated Texas hill country town of Stonewall, working on a road-grading crew that was building a local highway when he was in his teens. Later he attended Southwest Texas State Teachers College.

By the age of 21, Johnson had earned a reputation for being a superb politician, not unlike his father and grandfather before him. By the time Johnson was an adult, he was an imposing 6 feet 3 inches tall and weighed approximately 230 pounds. His massive bulk, fierce determination, outsized nose, and jutting jaw made him seem larger than life to those around him. Johnson's political track record and personal life underwent intense scrutiny decades later and reveal a man of contradictions: he was compassionate and ruthless, dominating, effective, often dishonest, and wholly devoted to politics.

Johnson supported himself through college, intent on becoming a teacher. As a 20-year-old in the predominantly Mexican town of Cotulla, Texas, he was one of the first teachers in his school to care whether or not the students could speak English. He arrived at school early and stayed late, persuaded the school board to buy supplies and gym equipment for the students, organized extracurricular activities, and formed a debate team. One of his students recalled decades later that Johnson's arriving at the school was "like a blessing from a clear sky."

When Johnson was 21 and participating in his first political campaign, State Senator Welly Hopkins concluded

Lyndon Johnson. *Source:* Library of Congress.

that he "had a gift—a very unusual ability to meet and greet the public." Johnson's hand would inevitably reach out to voters, and he knew the effect a kiss on the cheek would have to a grandmother. He worked as a congressman's secretary in Washington at the age of 23, where he was known as the "Boss of the Little Congress," the organization of congressional assistants.

At the age of 26, Johnson was the youngest of the 48 state directors of the National Youth Administration and possibly the youngest person ever trusted with statewide authority for a New Deal program. Johnson and President Roosevelt enjoyed an instant rapport. Upon meeting Johnson for the first time in May 1937, Roosevelt remarked to one of his Washington insiders, "I've just met the most remarkable young man. Help him with anything you can." Also in 1937, at the age of 28, Johnson was elected to the House of Representatives as a New Deal Democrat, in a race no one believed he could win.

When Johnson was elected, the 200,000 farmers and ranchers of the Tenth Congressional District in Texas had no electricity and were living a bleak existence. Johnson's victory literally "brought light" to his con-

stituents. He was a diligent, energetic, and creative representative, who financed and revitalized the Democratic Campaign Committee with money from Texas oilmen and contractors—people to which he alone had access. As a result, he had power over other congressmen.

Johnson was defeated in his first campaign for the U.S. Senate in June 1941. The unexpected death of Senator Morris Sheppard had opened up a Senate seat, and most politicians in Washington had assumed that Johnson, a bright young star, would take his place. In spite of spending money on a scale that Texas had never seen before, much of the funds generated by one man, Herman Brown, the recipient of many federal contracts, Johnson lost the race to Governor W. Lee "Pappy" O'Daniel. In the opening speech of Johnson's 1941 campaign, he said, "If the day ever comes when my vote must be cast to send your boy to the trenches—that day Lyndon Johnson will leave his Senate seat to go with him."

Johnson joined the U.S. Navy immediately following Pearl Harbor and was decorated with honors. While campaigning in the poor rural areas of Texas for the 1948 senatorial race, Johnson played on the fear of communism by portraying vivid horrors of germ warfare and the escalation of atomic bombs, adding, "Nobody would walk up and give Jack Dempsey a punch in the nose, and nobody is going to give us a punch in the nose if we're strong enough, too." While campaigning to wealthy listeners such as businesspeople and oilmen, Johnson would emphasize his plutocratic vocabulary, and increasing the wealth for the wealthy what was he emphasized. He was prolabor in labor districts, antilabor in antilabor districts and effectively said whatever his listeners wanted to hear. Johnson was masterful at knowing how to manipulate the political system. And he knew how to discredit and slander an opponent, which is significant because at the time he ushered in an entirely new way to approach elective office, one that would be copied for decades by politicians who followed him: the notion that the end victory justifies the means.

In 1948 Johnson was elected to the Senate by only 87 votes. For 40 years after that election, Johnson aides and ardent supporters steadfastly denied rumors that Johnson had stolen the election from Texas Governor Coke Robert Stevenson. Johnson managed to halt a federal court's investigation into the 1948 election, but decades later, a manuscript relating details of the theft of many thousands of crucial votes revealed that Johnson had, in fact, stolen the election.

In the 11 years that Johnson was a congressman, beginning in 1937, he voted against every civil rights bill—not only against legislation aimed at ending the poll tax and segregation in the armed services but also against legislation designed to end lynching. When Johnson ran for the Senate in 1948, he attacked President Truman's entire civil rights program, referring to it as "an effort to set up a police state." This earlier stance may have been a shrewd bid for the support of the southern bloc in the Senate; if so, it was successful. Johnson rose to leadership as a result of the overwhelming support of those in the Senate who wanted to preserve segregation.

A professional politician, Johnson had been majority leader in the Senate since 1955, and he became vice president under President John F. Kennedy in 1960. He was part of Kennedy's motorcade during the tragic presidential assassination in Dallas, Texas, in 1963, and was immediately sworn in as president. After he picked up the reins of the presidency, he enacted Kennedy's proposals on three fronts: civil rights; a cut in taxes, which was already well advanced toward passage; and something that had been under discussion among Kennedy's advisers called the War on Poverty. The centerpiece of the "War" was the Economic Opportunity Act, designed to create the Job Corps to train the long-term unemployed. The Economic Opportunity Act became law in August 1964. Johnson deferred Medicare and aid to education bills for future consideration.

The same congressional session that enacted the War on Poverty granted legislative protection to wilderness areas, enacted the food stamp program and the Urban Mass Transportation Act, and financed a major housing bill. Johnson's record shortly after Kennedy's death was remarkably impressive, especially compared to what Kennedy had achieved before his untimely death. Johnson's most impressive feat was simultaneously forcing a comprehensive civil rights bill on southern Democrats and retaining their votes on other issues. Johnson's southern connections enabled him to take advantage of the party system, and no president for decades after his time in office was able to duplicate Johnson's success.

Under his administration the Civil Rights Act introduced by Kennedy the previous year was passed in 1964, and the Voting Rights Act was passed in 1965. These two measures made effective improvements for black Americans in the United States, but many protest groups felt that Johnson could have assured the right to vote much sooner, and government protection could have been provided during the protest marches in the South in 1964 and 1965.

Johnson returned as president in the 1964 election by defeating Senator Barry Goldwater with an over-

whelming majority. Johnson corraled 61.1% of the votes cast, the largest share to date ever received by a presidential candidate in a contested election. Johnson's triumph underscored the public's interest in an activist, New Deal approach to the presidency and a nonmilitary, reasoned conduct in foreign affairs.

Johnson introduced a series of significant social welfare and economic reforms under the Great Society rubric; they included a Medicare program for the elderly and strident leaps to improve education. The Great Society was the most comprehensive legislative program since 1935. Johnson told the public that "the lights are still on in the White House tonight—preparing programs that will keep our country up with the times."

Riots in New York City's Harlem district seemed to mock Johnson's Civil Rights Act in 1964, and these riots were followed by larger and more terrifying riots in the Watts district of Los Angeles shortly after Johnson's Voting Rights Act in 1965. The Watts riot lasted six days and required 14,000 National Guardsmen to restore order. Property damage was estimated at $45 million, over 1,000 people were injured, and 34 people were killed. More than 100 American cities experienced race riots in 1967. A riot in Detroit was even more damaging than the riot in Watts in terms in casualties, people injured, and property damage.

Puzzled by the riots, Johnson appointed a National Advisory Commission on Civil Disorders, headed by Illinois Governor Otto Kerner, to investigate the problem of race relations. The Kerner Commission had a 1,400-page report finished by March 1968. It read: "Our Nation is moving toward two societies, one black, one white—separate and unequal. White institutions created it [the urban ghetto], white institutions maintain it, and white society condones it."

Johnson's financial success was as spectacular as his political success. Johnson had less than $1,000 in the bank in 1937. By 1963, his family assets totaled approximately $20 million. Johnson entered the Oval Office as arguably the richest man ever to occupy it; his empire included radio and television stations, cattle, banking, and real estate.

When Johnson became president, the number of American advisers—not combatants—in Vietnam was 16,000, and press coverage was relatively muted. During Johnson's 1964 campaign, he had pledged not to widen the war in Vietnam, saying, "They call upon us to supply American boys to do the job that Asian boys should do." By July 1965, there were 175,000 men in Vietnam; by August, 219,000; by December 1966, 385,000. By the time Johnson left the presidency, 549,000 American troops were in Vietnam. By the time the Vietnam War ended, 58,000 Americans had died there and 288,000 had been seriously wounded.

Because of a penchant for stretching the truth, or even outright lying, a new phrase entered the political dialogue during Johnson's administration: "credibility gap." It was printed in headlines and on buttons across the country. Johnson had seemingly not only misled the public about his intentions in Vietnam but lied about what the American ambassador to the Dominican Republic had said to him in order to send American troops into the country. Johnson claimed that American lives were at stake, that the ambassador had been shot at, and that 1,500 innocent people had been murdered, some by decapitation. None of this was true.

The continuation and ceaseless escalation of the Vietnam War led to widespread protests across the nation and contributed to Johnson's growing unpopularity throughout the mid- and late 1960s. The years 1966 through 1968 saw the most strident anti–Vietnam War protests, and the chant "Hey! Hey! LBJ! How many kids did you kill today?" became a slogan of the times for hundreds of thousands of young people. Johnson would remember this particular chant much later, after he had retired to his ranch in Texas. He could not forget it. In spite of the fact that new police regulations had limited the number of pickets allowed to parade on Pennsylvania Avenue, the last 45 months of Johnson's administration were marked by a steady stream of protests outside the White House that often involved burning draft cards.

In 1968 Johnson announced his decision not to run for another presidential term of office and to retire from active politics. He died in 1973.

B. Kim Taylor

SEE ALSO History

BIBLIOGRAPHY

Caro, Robert A. *Lyndon Johnson: Means of Ascent.* New York: Knopf, 1990.

Boller, Paul F., Jr. *Presidential Campaigns.* New York: Oxford University Press, 1984.

Polakoff, Keith J. *Political Parties in American History.* New York: Wiley, 1981.

Polsby, Nelson W. *Presidential Elections.* 6th ed. New York: Scribner's, 1980.

JOHN F. KENNEDY

The Prepresidential Years

According to historian James N. Giglio, "it was Jack's father who developed his son's interest in international issues, particularly after Joseph became Ambassador to Great Britain during the Roosevelt administration" (Giglio 1991, 3). In fact, Joe Kennedy had a substantial impact on his son's political career.

Majoring in political science with concentrations in the fields of international relations and political theory (Burns 1960; Hamilton 1992), Kennedy impressed his undergraduate instructors with his keen interest in international relations (Wild 1968). During his senior year he was given the opportunity to prepare a thesis on an international relations topic. Kennedy chose the subject of Britain's rearmament policy, the thesis was accepted by the political science faculty, and Jack graduated summa cum laude from Harvard. Jack's father insisted on having the senior thesis published, despite the efforts of Harold Laski, a political scientist at the London School of Economics, to convince Joe Kennedy not to proceed with publication of his son's manuscript. Joe Kennedy arranged for the publication of the essay by Wilfred Funk, Incorporated, and even convinced journalist Arthur Krock to edit Jack's original manuscript. The founder of *Time*, Henry Luce, wrote a foreword to Jack's book, which had been retitled *Why England Slept* (Giglio 1991, 4).

Returning from naval service in World War II, Jack Kennedy was encouraged by his father to enter politics. In 1946, Jack Kennedy announced his candidacy for the 11th Congressional District of Massachusetts,

John F. Kennedy. *Source:* Library of Congress.

an area that had once been the political base of his grandfather, John "Honey Fitz" Fitzgerald. But Jack did not rely on his grandfather's ties to the district in winning the Democratic nomination. Since Jack was not a resident of the 11th District, he faced critics who claimed he did not understand the district's needs. To overcome this liability, Joe Kennedy developed an elaborate public relations campaign highlighting Jack's war record (Parmet 1980).

Jack represented the 11th District for six years, compiling a voting record that was moderately conservative. Although he supported such measures as the school lunch program, raising the minimum wage, and building federal housing projects, he expressed opposition to deficit spending. On several measures, he voted to reduce expenditures, including votes to reduce the budgets of the agriculture and interior departments and the Tennessee Valley Authority (Giglio 1991, 8). On questions relating to foreign policy, Jack expressed strong anticommunist views. Indeed, his foreign policy views often ran counter to the policies of the Truman administration. Kennedy claimed that President Truman's defense spending requests were inadequate and that the Truman administration was partially responsible for the "loss" of China to the communists (Giglio 1991).

In 1952, despite the election of Dwight Eisenhower to the presidency and a Republican takeover of Congress, Jack won election to the U.S. Senate. Impressively, he won the Senate seat by defeating a popular Republican incumbent, Henry Cabot Lodge Jr. Kennedy's campaign strategy against Lodge emphasized Jack's foreign policy differences with President Truman. Criticizing Lodge for supporting Truman's foreign policy, Kennedy ran a campaign more conservative than that of his Republican opponent (Giglio 1991, 10).

Throughout his Senate career, Kennedy developed a reputation as a political moderate (Collier and Horowitz 1984, 106; Schlesinger 1965, 95). Although he recruited the support of Democratic Party liberals, the party's liberal wing viewed him with distrust. In part, this distrust was based on a dislike of his father. Still remembering Joe Kennedy's isolationism during his days as ambassador to Great Britain, and his friendship with Senator Joseph McCarthy, liberals, including Eleanor Roosevelt, saw Jack Kennedy as a threat to New Deal liberalism. While he tried to gain the support of liberals, Kennedy's voting record did not ease their suspicions of him. In 1957 Kennedy supported a moderate version of a civil rights bill and failed to support northern liberals who were trying to strengthen the legislation. In addition, as Jack seriously considered a campaign for president, he carefully recruited the support of leading southern politicians, including Alabama Governor John Patterson. Indeed, at the 1956 Democratic National Convention, when Jack was mentioned as a running mate for Adlai Stevenson, southern delegations enthusiastically supported a Kennedy vice presidential candidacy (Giglio 1991; Parmet 1980).

In 1955, Kennedy published his second book, *Profiles in Courage*, which won a Pulitzer Prize and strengthened Kennedy's position in the Democratic Party. Controversy exists over the authorship of the book, with some evidence indicating that Kennedy's aide Theodore C. Sorensen was heavily involved in the writing (Parmet 1980). Other Kennedy publications appeared during the decade, however, including an article in *Foreign Affairs*. Highlighting what would become an important theme of Kennedy's 1960 campaign for president, the *Foreign Affairs* article called for a new approach to foreign policy. This approach entailed a recognition that the Soviet Union was intent on achieving a worldwide communist victory, and the United States had to prepare its diplomatic and military resources to meet this challenge. Indeed, beginning in 1958, Kennedy referred to a "missile gap" between the United States and the Soviet Union and called for a dramatic rearmament policy in response to the alleged Soviet nuclear buildup. Although the missile gap never existed, it was an effective issue for Kennedy. Jack campaigned in 1960 by criticizing the "complacency" of the Eisenhower administration and by pledging to "get America moving again" (Giglio 1991; Miroff 1993). In November 1960 John F. Kennedy narrowly defeated Richard M. Nixon and became the nation's 35th president.

The Presidential Years: Foreign Policy

Emphasizing an anticommunist theme during his campaign, President Kennedy continued this message during his administration. Calling for a renewed Cold War effort against the Soviet Union in both his inaugural speech and first State of the Union address, President Kennedy seemingly rejected the idea of a negotiated relaxation of tensions with the Soviet bloc. Instead of a period of détente with Moscow, the Kennedy years were characterized by heightened international tensions and crisis events.

The first crisis confronting the Kennedy administration was in Cuba. Initially, Kennedy expressed sympathy for Castro, identifying the Cuban leader as a democratic reformer (Kennedy 1961). During the campaign, Kennedy's assessment of Castro became less favorable. Indeed, shortly after the election victory over Richard Nixon, Kennedy embraced the outgoing Eisenhower administration's plan to overthrow the Castro government. The plan, devised by the Central Intelligence Agency, involved training anti-Castro forces for an invasion of Cuba. Despite misgivings by Kennedy administration officials and former diplomats, the invasion of Cuba by Cuban exiles took place at the Bay of Pigs in April 1961. The operation was a military and political failure. Kennedy refused to commit American forces to the invasion, and this may have led the Soviet leadership to evaluate Kennedy as young, inexperienced, and weak. Clearly, the failure at the Bay of Pigs had far-reaching implications for American–Soviet relations (Giglio 1991; Parmet 1983).

In June 1961, Kennedy held a summit meeting with Soviet leader Nikita Khrushchev in Vienna, Austria. The meetings between Kennedy and Khrushchev were difficult, with Kennedy leaving Vienna convinced that a U.S.–Soviet confrontation was possible. The major issue dividing the two leaders involved the Occupation of American and Allied troops in West Berlin. At the end of World War II, the United States, Great Britain, and France shared Occupation responsibilities in the western areas of Berlin; however, the Soviet Union claimed that the three western powers no longer had valid claim to the Occupation. Khrushchev threatened to end the division of the former German capital unilaterally, while Kennedy maintained that the United States and its allies intended to stay in West Berlin (Parmet 1983, 191–192).

Although the Soviet Union eventually resolved the Berlin issue by building a wall separating East and West Berlin, the Kennedy administration took the Soviet attitude seriously and embarked on a major diplomatic and military response. Kennedy called for substantially higher defense expenditures and a large-scale civil defense program. The Berlin crisis was followed by an even more dangerous confrontation over nuclear missiles in Cuba.

In October 1962, the United States discovered that the Soviet Union was constructing nuclear bases in Cuba. The Cuban missile crisis represents the most dangerous U.S.–Soviet confrontation of the Cold War. Aware of the dangers involved in the crisis, Kennedy established an informal group called EXCOMM to evaluate options for dealing with the Soviet action. Although the president faced a difficult challenge by Khrushchev in Cuba, it is striking that EXCOMM and the president rejected a diplomatic solution to the confrontation (Miroff 1993, 288; Parmet 1983, 289). Instead of beginning the American response with a diplomatic initiative, EXCOMM presented Kennedy with three options: (1) an invasion of Cuba, (2) air strikes against the Soviet installations, and (3) a naval blockade of Cuba. Kennedy decided on a naval blockade, although under international law a blockade is an act of war. While the naval blockade was in progress, the United States continued to make preparations for an invasion of Cuba. Kennedy feared that an American invasion would lead the Soviets to begin military operations against Berlin, which would have led to a general war between the two superpowers (Miroff 1993, 288).

Following the Cuban missile crisis, Kennedy emphasized improving relations with the Soviet Union. In 1963 the Kennedy administration negotiated the Test Ban Treaty, which prohibited the atmospheric testing of nuclear devices. Also, agreements were signed providing for the establishment of improved communications between Washington and Moscow. In the summer of 1963 Kennedy delivered a speech at the American University calling for peaceful coexistence and cooperation between the two superpowers (Miroff 1993, 294).

The Presidential Years: Domestic Policy

Kennedy's domestic policy proposals faced opposition from Congress, despite Democratic control of the House of Representatives and Senate. Conservative, mainly southern, Democrats objected to many elements of the Kennedy legislative proposals. This was especially true in the area of civil rights.

As a presidential candidate, Kennedy supported expanded efforts to secure civil rights for black Americans. He pledged to end housing discrimination by issuing an executive order immediately on assuming office; however, he failed to issue the order until the fall of 1962. Kennedy's reluctance to issue the executive order on housing was tied to his need for southern Democratic support for his tax-cut plan (Parmet 1983, 258). Eventually, Kennedy received congressional approval for the tax cut, but the administration faced strong opposition from conservative Democrats on several other proposals. Kennedy secured congressional approval for an increase in the minimum wage. Nevertheless, Kennedy had to agree to several amendments to the legislation, with the result that only a modest number of additional people received an increase in wages (Bernstein 1991). Moreover, Kennedy proposed health insurance coverage for elderly Americans through Medicare. Here again, he had difficulty convincing Congress to approve Medicare, and with his death on November 22, 1963, Lyndon B. Johnson assumed the presidency.

Gaining congressional approval for Medicare, and for far-reaching civil rights reforms, Johnson was instrumental in implementing Kennedy's legislative package. In June 1963 Kennedy proposed legislation prohibiting discrimination in motel, hotel, and restaurant accommodations and employment. But Kennedy was having difficulty convincing Congress to approve his civil rights bill. Indeed, Kennedy's lack of legislative experience may have contributed to his failure on Medicare and his problems with civil rights. Although he was a former member of the House and Senate, Kennedy did not occupy leadership positions in either body. With Democratic presidents facing the need to cajole the liberal and conservative wings of the party, this was a crucial shortcoming. Lyndon Johnson, Senate majority leader before becoming Kennedy's vice president, had the legislative experience and used his legislative skills in supporting Medicare and civil rights.

The Kennedy Record

Since John F. Kennedy served as president from January 1961 until November 1963, he did not occupy the White House long enough to transform American life. Although the public usually ranks him as one of the nation's "great" presidents, his accomplishments were of a modest nature. While Lyndon Johnson achieved the accomplishments in domestic policy proposed by the Kennedy administration, the question that haunts Kennedy scholars is this: How would Kennedy have performed as a legislative leader? And in foreign policy the question is, How would Kennedy have handled the growing crisis in Vietnam?

Michael E. Meagher

SEE ALSO History

BIBLIOGRAPHY

Bernstein, Irving. *Promises Kept: John F. Kennedy's New Frontier*. New York: Oxford University Press, 1991.

Burns, James MacGregor. *John Kennedy: A Political Profile*. New York: Harcourt, Brace, 1960.

Collier, Peter, and David Horowitz. *The Kennedys: An American Drama*. New York: Summit Books, 1984.

Giglio, James N. *The Presidency of John F. Kennedy*. Lawrence: University Press of Kansas, 1991.

Hamilton, Nigel. *JFK: Reckless Youth*. New York: Random House, 1992.

Kennedy, John F. *The Strategy for Peace*. Edited by Allan Nevins. New York: Popular Library, 1961.

Miroff, Bruce. *Icons of Democracy: American Leaders as Heroes, Aristocrats, Dissenters and Democrats*. New York: McKay, 1993.

Parmet, Herbert. *Jack: The Struggles of John F. Kennedy*. New York: Dial Press, 1980.

———. *JFK: The Presidency of John F. Kennedy*. New York: Dial Press, 1983.

Schlesinger, Arthur M., Jr. *A Thousand Days: John F. Kennedy in the White House*. Boston: Houghton Mifflin, 1965.

Wild, Payson. "Recorded Interview by Larry J. Hackman." John F. Kennedy Library Oral History Program, November 25, 1968.

FRANKLIN PIERCE

In 1853, when Franklin Pierce took office as the nation's 14th president, little could he have known that history would find him on the wrong side of one of America's most controversial moral issues ever. Pierce came to the presidency after a rather undistinguished political and military career, and his support of the Kansas–Nebraska Act, which allowed slavery in the territory north of 36°30′ for the first time, made him look like a "doughface," a northerner with southern principles. After losing a bid for renomination in 1856 to fellow Democrat James Buchanan, Pierce withdrew from active politics.

Pierce was born in Hillsborough, New Hampshire, on November 23, 1804, to General Benjamin and Anna (Kendrick) Pierce. Franklin was the sixth of eight children and followed many of his father's deeply held democratic principles in his own public life. He received his early education in private academies and entered Bowdoin College in Brunswick, Maine, in 1820. As a college student, Pierce was not known for his scholarship, but his attention and obedience were such that he graduated with respectable grades. He was admitted to the New Hampshire bar in 1827, the very same year that his father was reelected governor of New Hampshire, and began his law practice in Hillsborough. To those who knew him well, though, it was obvious that Franklin's true interest was not in the practice of law but rather in politics. In 1829 he ran for and won a seat in the state legislature from Hillsborough and within two years had been elected speaker of that body.

In 1833 Pierce was elected to the U.S. House of Representatives and soon became a confidant of Andrew Jackson, who regarded Pierce as one of his closest advisers and staunchest supporters. It was while serving in the lower house of Congress that Pierce first publicly stated his position on slavery. While an easy stand to take in the 1830s, and one from which Pierce never wavered far, it was nevertheless a position that would later cloud his entire political career. He argued that the Constitution guaranteed the southern states certain rights that could not be taken away by the federal government. In 1837 he became a United States senator but retired from that body five

Franklin Pierce. *Source:* Library of Congress.

years later and returned to practice law full-time in Concord. Having married Jane Means in 1834, and with children to raise, Pierce realized that a senator's salary would not be enough to secure his future as adequately as he would prefer.

Back in New Hampshire, Pierce once again became active in state politics and, as one of the leading members of the Concord Cabal, strongly supported the Compromise of 1850, which included the Fugitive Slave Act. Several times during the next few years, Pierce was given the opportunity to leave private life and return to the public domain. In 1846 President James K. Polk offered Pierce the post of attorney general of the United States, and soon after, the governor of New Hampshire offered to appoint Pierce to the United States Senate again. Pierce respectfully declined those and other offers, saying that he planned never to be far from his family again unless his country called him in time of war. Little did Pierce know at the time that his country would soon call. In response to President Polk's declaration of war against Mexico in 1846, Pierce volunteered, was commissioned as a

brigadier general in the army, and was placed in charge of the Ninth Regiment, which was made up largely of New England volunteers.

After landing his regiment at Vera Cruz in June 1847, Pierce led the 2,500 men on a 150-mile march inland to meet up with and reinforce General Winfield Scott at Pueblo. Immediately, the American forces moved toward Mexico City, and in one of Pierce's first experiences leading troops into battle, his horse was frightened by artillery fire and threw him, causing the general to seriously injure his pelvis and left knee. Undeterred, Pierce resumed command of his regiment but fell ill and missed out on the final assault on Mexico City. With victory secured for the American force, Pierce returned to New Hampshire in early 1848 to resume his law practice in Concord and was received with a hero's welcome.

When the Democratic National Convention gathered in Baltimore in June 1852, *Franklin Pierce* was certainly not the name most often tossed around as a potential presidential nominee. In fact, several times during the previous months, Pierce had made it known that he was not interested in returning to public life as president, vice president or anything else. For the first 35 rounds of balloting, neither of the more prominent candidates could gain the needed two-thirds of the votes to win the nomination, and not once had Franklin Pierce's name appeared on a ballot. On the 36th round, however, his name appeared, and by the 49th round, he had become the Democratic Party's nominee. Pierce, who did not attend the convention, received the news in Concord with some hesitation but accepted the nomination as a matter of principle and patriotism.

Pierce won one of the least exciting presidential campaigns in history by 254 electoral votes over Winfield Scott's 42. Before he could celebrate much, though, a tragedy struck his family that more than likely darkened Pierce's entire presidency. Just days before Pierce moved to Washington, his 11-year-old son, Bennie, was crushed to death beneath a train as the family watched helplessly. Pierce was deeply depressed by the accident, feeling partially responsible, and Mrs. Pierce was so distraught that she withdrew from public life for some time. His emotional turmoil was worsened when both Pierce's close friend New Hampshire Senator Charles G. Atherton and his vice president, William R. King, died only months into his administration.

In his inaugural address, Pierce laid out the plans for his presidency, which included a foreign policy that would look toward the expansion of America and a domestic policy that promised to reform the government to make it more effective and economical and to adhere to the Compromise of 1850. He had a difficult time dealing with Congress, though, despite the fact that Democrats held the majority. The Congress was confronted with deep sectional divisions, with some issues falling along an east–west divide and others falling along a north–south divide. Pierce, who was not a strong leader in the first place, often found himself unable to bridge the sectional gaps and bring the Congress together. Many Democrats in Congress simply did not share a loyalty to Pierce and dissented whenever they felt the need. One group especially troublesome to Pierce was the Free Soilers, a northern faction that held antislavery and antisouthern views and disliked Pierce's reputation as sympathizer with the southern cause. In fact, it was the Free Soilers who kept alive the issue of slavery when most people thought that the Compromise of 1850 had settled it once and for all.

The Kansas–Nebraska Act of 1854, which was by far the most important piece of legislation passed during the Pierce administration, and Pierce's greatest liability thereafter, stirred the issue of slavery as it had not been stirred before. Missouri Senator David Rice Atchison was among the primary architects of the Kansas–Nebraska Bill, and his intentions were twofold. First, he wanted to see the vast territory to the west of Missouri settled, and second, he wanted the Missouri Compromise to be repealed so that slavery would be allowed in the newly settled territory. The bill, which later became the Kansas–Nebraska Act, was initially introduced by Stephen A. Douglas, and while it did not explicitly state that the Missouri Compromise would be repealed, it made the point clear enough that Free Soilers in the North became aroused. Southerners, however, rejected anything that did not explicitly overturn the Missouri Compromise, and an amendment to that effect was soon attached to Douglas's original bill.

Pierce, who had initially opposed the idea of repealing the Missouri Compromise even though he thought it unconstitutional, was soon persuaded by Douglas to support the bill. A deal was struck in which Pierce would receive support for his nominee for the post of collector of the Port of New York, Jeman J. Redfield, in return for his support of the Kansas–Nebraska Bill. While a frenzy of opposition erupted over the bill among Free Soilers and their supporters, it passed with a comfortable majority in the Senate and by a closer vote in the House. Pierce rejoiced in his first major legislative victory, but it would soon prove to be a hollow win. He had failed to fully consider the strength of public opinion against the slavery issue and the moral ramifications of his actions. His support

of the Kansas–Nebraska Act would continue to haunt Pierce for some time to come. His support forever cast him as a sympathizer with the South and slavery and as a result made him very unpopular.

The 34th Congress, which convened in January 1855, did not help matters. A group of congressmen from the North made up of antislavery and anti-Nebraska activists, among others, had joined in a coalition calling themselves Republicans and held a majority in the lower house of Congress. After fighting for nearly nine weeks, the new House voted in a decidedly antislavery Speaker, much to the dismay of Pierce.

Problems were also brewing for Pierce in the Kansas Territory, where Free Soilers and the advocates of slaveholders were deeply divided over the future of the territory. Pierce, who did not fully appreciate the complexity and explosive potential of the situation, appointed only proslavery officials to important posts in the territory and blamed much of the violence there on the Free Soil movement. By the time of the Democratic National Convention in 1856, Pierce was very unpopular with the majority of his party. Northern Democrats disliked his support for the repeal of the Missouri Compromise and blamed him for many of the problems in the Kansas Territory. Southern Democrats had reservations because they considered him fickle and wished that he had simply left the Kansas situation alone and allowed it to settle on its own. Instead, they complained, Pierce had brought the federal government into the situation.

In matters of foreign policy, the Pierce administration was as unsuccessful as it was with domestic policy, although the latter tended to complicate the former. While United States holdings were expanded with the purchase of land from Mexico and the annexation of several Pacific islands, and U.S. influence around the world continued to increase, sectional strife prevented many of Pierce's other expansionist ideas from becoming reality. Northerners opposed any expansion to the south, fearing that it would only benefit slaveholding interests, and southerners opposed attempts to acquire Canada, fearing that it would benefit Free Soilers in the North.

After the election of 1856, Pierce withdrew from public life for some time to care for his wife, who was suffering from bad health and four years later was still mourning the death of their son. They traveled to the island of Madeira and then later throughout Europe, finally returning to the United States in the summer of 1859. While away, Pierce kept up with the political news in the States and was always quick to express his opinion about matters. He was pleased with the presidency of James Buchanan, feeling that the country was in good hands with him, but was deeply troubled by the election of Abraham Lincoln. While Pierce felt his presidency had been a success, arguing that he had expanded the United States' territory, his major legislative accomplishment, the Kansas–Nebraska Act, set the stage for a civil war that was soon to come. Pierce blamed many of the nation's problems on the abolitionists and Free Soilers but failed to see the moral void left by slavery. He believed instead that respect for property, even slave property, was more important. He died on October 8, 1869.

Quentin Kidd

SEE ALSO History

BIBLIOGRAPHY

Gara, Larry. *The Presidency of Franklin Pierce*. Lawrence: University of Kansas Press, 1991.

Hawthorne, Nathaniel. *The Life of Franklin Pierce*. New York: Garrett Press, 1970.

Nichols, Roy Franklin. *Franklin Pierce: Young Hickory of the Granite Hills*. Philadelphia: University of Pennsylvania Press, 1931.

JAMES K. POLK

James Knox Polk, 11th president of the United States (1845–1849), was born on November 2, 1795, in Mecklenburg County, North Carolina. As a boy, he moved to what is now Maury County, Tennessee, with his parents. He returned to North Carolina for his university education, graduating in 1818 at the top of his University of North Carolina class. He returned to Tennessee to study law and to begin a political career.

The first "dark-horse" candidate in American political history, Polk was also unique in his announcement of only four goals for his administration and his vow to serve only a single term; remarkably, he fulfilled all of his goals and stuck to his promise not to run again, for which he is generally regarded as a near-great president. Although Polk is relatively unknown today, during his term the United States expanded its territory to the Pacific Ocean as a result of the Oregon Treaty with Britain and the Mexican cession.

Early Political Career

During the presidential campaign of 1844, the Whigs sought to undermine Polk's credibility by asking, "Who is James K. Polk?" This attempt to imply that Polk was an inexperienced nobody with little claim to the White House was misleading, for Polk had been active in politics since the age of 28; had served seven consecutive terms in the U.S. House of Representatives, from 1825 to

1839; and was Speaker of the House from 1835 to 1839. Polk was also a prominent and influential member of the Tennessee Democratic Party, having served as a member of the Tennessee legislature from 1823 to 1825 and as governor of that state from 1839 to 1841.

Polk left Washington, D.C., in 1839 to assume the governorship of Tennessee, but he had plans to return to the nation's capital in the office of the vice presidency. He had used his influence within the Democratic Party to push for a Democratic National Convention in 1836, even though many Democrats were against such a move as it was a foregone conclusion that Vice President Martin Van Buren, President Andrew Jackson's handpicked successor, would be nominated. Polk had influence, but he often overestimated his political appeal. Not only was he denied the vice presidential nomination, but the waning strength of the Democratic Party in Tennessee cost him reelection as governor in 1841. Local Democratic Party leaders blamed the unpopularity of Van Buren for Polk's defeat, citing the affinities between Polk's policies and those of the ex-president as well as Polk's departure from the Tennessee Democratic opposition to Van Buren in the election of 1840. Although prominent Tennessee Democrats tried to push Polk aside, he ran for governor again in 1843 but was again defeated by a narrow margin.

James K. Polk *Source:* Library of Congress.

Despite these political setbacks, which undermined the support of Tennessee Democrats, Polk was still shooting for the vice presidency in 1844. It was expected that the Democratic ticket would be headed by former President Van Buren, who had a majority of delegates going into the national convention in Baltimore in May 1844. The Texas question, however, cost Van Buren much of his support when he published a letter opposing the annexation of Texas shortly before the Democratic National Convention. This drastically changed the political situation, and expansionists, particularly southerners who wished to have Texas enter into the Union as a slave state, resolved to deny the former president the nomination. At the convention, pro-Texas delegates adopted a rule requiring a two-thirds majority to nominate the party's candidates, thus preventing the selection of Van Buren. Polk, who was a staunch backer of U.S. claims to Texas and a slave owner himself, won the party's endorsement on the ninth ballot, thereby becoming the first dark-horse presidential nominee.

The main issue in the election was the expansion of American territory—with the background of the slavery question, which had been tied to the question of southwestern movement, sharply dividing the northern and southern states. The Democratic platform called for "the reoccupation of Oregon and the reannexation of Texas." Both the Whigs and the Democrats conducted the election by a series of slogans on these themes, such as "Fifty-four Forty or Fight" and "All of Oregon or None" on the Democratic side and "Polk, Slavery, and Texas, or Clay, Union, and Liberty" on the Whig side. The two parties were matched almost entirely, and Polk won a narrow victory in the general election, edging out Henry Clay by 38,000 votes. New York, which Polk won by fewer than 5,000 votes, was the deciding state in the election, giving Polk the 35 electoral votes needed to defeat Clay 170 to 105. Ironically, it was the antislavery Liberty Party that took 16,000 votes in New York, most of which presumably would have gone to Clay, thereby helping Polk to victory in this key state. The issue of Texas, which had been so influential both at the National Democratic Convention and in the general election, was resolved just before Polk's inauguration in March 1845, when Congress passed a joint resolution offering the Texas Republic admission to the Union as the 28th state.

Presidency

Upon his election, Polk resolved to be a representative not of a party only but of the whole people of the United States, and in order to avoid the necessity for posturing to get reelected and the possibility of party favoritism, he became the first president to commit himself to serving only a single term. Equally resolute in the goals of his administration, he announced a four-point program for his term of office: a reduced tariff, reestablishment of the Independent Treasury System, settlement of the Oregon question, and the acquisition of California.

Polk's domestic program to reduce the tariff and reestablish the Independent Treasury System caused conflict within the Democratic Party, which was facing deepening ideological and sectional differences as a result of economic and territorial expansion as well as the slavery question, raised whenever the possibility of new American territories was broached. The Walker Tariff of 1846, which reduced the tariff for revenue from about 32% to 25%, was passed only after a fierce battle in Congress and largely because of overwhelming support in the South and West. Manufacturers in New England and the middle states worried that they would be ruined by the reduction, but they turned out to be wrong as the Walker Tariff proved to be an excellent generator of revenues, though largely because of the renewed boom in western movement and the corresponding increase in imports.

Polk faced similar troubles getting the Independent Treasury Act passed. The act, which had originally been passed in 1840 during the Democratic administration of Van Buren but repealed a year later during the Whig administration of John Tyler, displeased the same probanking interests in the Democratic Party that had opposed it in 1840. As a congressman, Polk had supported Jackson's battle against the Bank of the United States, and as Ways and Means Committee chair, he had led the defense of Jackson's policy of favoring some state banks (the "pet banks") for the deposit of federal funds; the collapse of some of these banks in the Panic of 1837, which had been partially caused by the use of federal funds to back speculation, resulted in the loss of federal funds and exposed the flaw in Jackson's banking policy. However, Polk's change of stance a decade later was not followed by all Democrats, many of whom were still "probanking" because of the beneficial uses to which federal moneys could be put by private interests. Nevertheless, in 1846 Polk succeeded in reestablishing this system, which placed federal funds in government-owned institutions in major cities.

Polk had to overcome fierce sectional differences to fulfill his two expansionist promises. During his presidential campaign, Polk had publicly reaffirmed the American claim to the entire Oregon Territory up to 54°40' north latitude, but early in his term he offered a compromise to the British that would bring the United States the Oregon Territory up to the 49th parallel. The British, who were claiming rights to the territory farther south to the Columbia River, spurned this offer, and Polk was faced with the possibility of having to come through on the "fight" portion of the "Fifty-four Forty or Fight" slogan adopted by the "All of Oregon" advocates in his party. The British, however—influenced by the antiexpansionists known as "Little Englanders," who opposed a faraway war over a wilderness that would only benefit the hated monopoly of the Hudson's Bay Company—changed their mind and decided to settle along the 49th parallel. Polk, angry over the original rejection, put the responsibility for handling the offer on the Senate, which, already war-wary because of the monthlong Mexican War, quickly approved.

Polk also attempted peaceful means in the acquisition of California. Even though Mexico had broken off diplomatic relations with the United States after the annexation of Texas, Polk sent John Slidell to Mexico with instructions to offer to purchase California and New Mexico for up to $25 million. Slidell was also instructed to propose that the United States would assume the claims of American citizens against Mexico in exchange for recognition of the Rio Grande as the southern boundary of Texas. When the Mexican government refused even to receive Slidell, Polk ordered General Zachary Taylor to cross the Nueces River into the disputed territory north of the Rio Grande, and when, several weeks later, reports reached Washington that Taylor's troops had been attacked, Polk asked for a declaration of war on the grounds that American blood had been shed on American soil. Congress passed a declaration of war in May 1846.

As commander in chief, Polk personally planned U.S. strategy during the war. Lacking confidence in Taylor's ability to force the Mexicans to sue for peace, Polk sent an army under General Winfield Scott and dispatched Nicholas P. Trist, chief clerk of the State Department, with authority to negotiate a peace treaty. Scott landed at Veracruz and marched on Mexico City, which he occupied in September 1847. Earlier, Trist had offered Mexican Emperor Santa Anna, who had been reinstalled from exile in Cuba with American military help, $10,000 to declare an armistice, but the emperor simply used the money to beef up his defenses. Polk, dissatisfied with Trist's lack of progress, recalled him, but Trist ignored the president and concluded the Treaty of Guadalupe Hidalgo, which the Senate passed in February 1848. The treaty recognized the U.S. claim to Texas and provided for the cession of California and New Mexico for the cost of $15 mil-

lion plus American assumption of approximately $3 million in claims by U.S. citizens against the Mexican government.

Polk's acquisitions from Britain and Mexico had come more cheaply, in terms of money and lives, than anyone, including Polk, had anticipated. However, they contributed to the increasing hostility between northern and southern states over the issue of slavery. Antislavery northerners were joined by northwesterners in condemning Polk for betraying them to the South: "Why all of Texas and not all of Oregon?" they asked. Abolitionists attacked Polk for the Mexican War, which they claim Polk had provoked as a means of adding slave states to the Union in the newly acquired territories of California and New Mexico. Efforts on the part of northerners to bar slavery from the Mexican cession, introduced into Congress by Representative David Wilmot of Pennsylvania, reopened the sectional controversy that Van Buren had succeeded in calming during his antiexpansionist administration.

Polk, having fulfilled his four goals, kept his promise not to seek reelection in 1848. Divisions within the Democratic Party, which had been exacerbated during Polk's term and for which Polk's economic and expansionist policies were significantly responsible, made it difficult for the Democrats to agree on a candidate. They finally settled on Lewis Cass, a hero of the War of 1812, who was defeated by his Whig opponent, Zachary Taylor, whom Polk had helped make a more recent and memorable war hero. The rigors of office and party politicking had taken their toll on Polk, and he died on June 15, 1849, in Nashville, only three months after leaving the White House.

Jack J. Miller

SEE ALSO History

BIBLIOGRAPHY

Bergeron, Paul H. *The Presidency of James K. Polk.* Lawrence: University Press of Kansas, 1987.

Hoyt, Edwin. *James Knox Polk.* New York: Reilly and Lee, 1965.

Sellers, Charles. *James K. Polk, Continentalist,* vol. 2, *1843–1846.* Princeton, NJ: Princeton University Press, 1966.

Williams, Frank B. *Tennessee's Presidents.* Knoxville: University of Tennessee Press, 1981.

FRANKLIN DELANO ROOSEVELT

Franklin Delano Roosevelt was elected the 32nd president of the United States in 1932 and served an unprecedented four terms in this office. His career began in New York State, where he was twice elected gover-

Franklin Delano Roosevelt. *Source:* Library of Congress.

nor. His presidency spanned two of the most critical and tumultuous events of the twentieth century. The first was the Great Depression, to which Roosevelt crafted a comprehensive response called the New Deal. The second was the active engagement in world affairs brought about by the Japanese attack on Pearl Harbor and the subsequent entry of the United States into World War II. During this period, Franklin Roosevelt helped orchestrate the Allied victory and shaped the outline of the postwar world. He died on April 12, 1945, of a cerebral hemorrhage.

Early Life

Franklin Delano Roosevelt was born to James Roosevelt and his second wife (his first wife, Rebecca, died in 1876), Sara Delano Roosevelt, on January 30, 1882, at Hyde Park, New York. Both parents were of wealthy patrician families. Young Franklin was educated at the family estate by a succession of governesses and tutors; he traveled widely and was active athletically. Eventually he attended Groton School in Massachusetts, where he developed an interest in public affairs and a sense of service and obligation. After Groton, he attended Harvard University, from which he graduated with a solid but undistinguished record. His political future may have been foreshadowed in his work for Harvard's newspaper, *The Crimson*. As editor, he was instrumental in giving it a focus on na-

tional and international affairs in addition to its local concerns. He graduated in 1904 and continued his studies at Columbia Law School. Though he did not complete his law degree, he was admitted to the New York bar in 1907. In 1904 Franklin married Anna Eleanor Roosevelt, a distant cousin and niece of President Theodore Roosevelt (he himself was a distant cousin of the president). In 1907 Roosevelt took a position with Carter, Ledyard and Milburn, a well-known law firm, which he found broadening but ultimately unsatisfying. It gave him an appreciation of and insight into the lives and problems of people who were not as privileged as he. The historian Kenneth S. Davis notes that it was during this period that Franklin Roosevelt announced to his friends and colleagues that his ultimate ambition was to become president of the United States and to follow in the footsteps of his Republican relative Theodore Roosevelt.

Entry into Politics

Franklin Roosevelt's opportunity to pursue a political career occurred in 1910. Nationally, the Republican Party of Theodore Roosevelt and his successor, William Howard Taft, was divided over issues of leadership, style, and a legislative program seen by many as Taft's betrayal of his predecessor's progressive agenda. This split was especially deep in New York. The state's Republicans were split among those who defended Taft, those who criticized him from the right, and those who wanted to turn to TR once again. This turmoil created opportunities for Democrats in New York's Republican Dutchess County. Franklin Roosevelt was encouraged to run for state senate because of his wealth, personality and personal style, and the Roosevelt name. After accepting the nomination in October, Franklin Roosevelt ran a campaign made distinctive by his extensive use of a rented automobile, which was at that time still a luxury item. By all accounts the campaign was intense, colorful, and exciting. The election was a landslide for the Democrats, who took control of both state houses and the governorship. Roosevelt ran ahead of his party's ticket in his district and so commenced his political career.

Franklin Roosevelt thus entered politics in a time of Progressivism and reform and of machine politics and patronage. He took the lead in a fight for control of the Senate nomination (this was before the 17th Amendment, which established the direct election of U.S. senators) between a group of party insurgents and the Tammany machine. Though the insurgents lost, Roosevelt emerged with a reputation of leadership and a large measure of public recognition. His successes in Albany led to involvement in national politics in 1912. He was an early and enthusiastic supporter of Woodrow Wilson at the party's nominating convention in Baltimore. For his efforts at the convention and in the subsequent campaign, Franklin Roosevelt was rewarded with an appointment as assistant secretary of the navy, a position he held from 1913 to 1920. His reputation as a reformer led to his nomination as vice president with Governor James Cox of Ohio in 1920. The Democratic ticket was defeated by Warren G. Harding, who promised a "return to normalcy."

Illness and Recovery

While vacationing during the summer of 1921, Franklin Roosevelt contracted poliomyelitis, which in spite of long and intensive therapy permanently cost him the use of his legs. Instead of opting to leave public life, Roosevelt returned to politics in New York and became prominent on the national scene. This occurred in part because of a very well received speech he gave at the party's national convention nominating New York Governor Alfred E. Smith for president in 1824. It was in this speech that Roosevelt labeled Smith the "Happy Warrior," a phrase taken from a poem by William Wordsworth. Smith failed to obtain the nomination and ran for reelection as governor. It is important to note that the Democratic Party was deeply and regionally divided at this time between party conservatives and those who advocated a more progressive stance. Though Roosevelt sided with the liberal faction, he began laying the groundwork to revitalize the party with a new and broader-based coalition that incorporated dissatisfied Republicans, organized labor and the cities, along with the traditional solidly Democratic South. Smith was renominated as his party's candidate in 1928, and Roosevelt was nominated for governor of New York, in part to help Smith, who was strongly identified with the Tammany machine, carry his home state. Smith lost both New York and the presidential race, but Roosevelt eked out a narrow victory, in part by running a vigorous campaign to erase doubts about his physical health.

Governor of New York

As governor of New York, Roosevelt honed his political skills. New York political life was dominated by the fact that the state had numerous diverse, well-organized interest groups. He was also confronted by a rural-dominated state legislature, which, though Democratic, differed with his progressive reputation and agenda. To deal with what was often a stalemate between him and the legislature, Roosevelt developed the tack of taking his case to the people directly with powerful rhetorical appeals. Though he had setbacks, Roosevelt's record as a two-term governor (he was reelected easily in 1930) was successful. He left a legacy of public power development, civil service reform, increased government support for farm issues and rural development, and awareness of the need for new approaches to new public problems and changing times.

The Election of 1932

Franklin Roosevelt's growing national visibility, progressive reputation, and popularity, coupled with the economic and social crises of the Great Depression, gained him his party's nomination for the presidency in 1932, in spite of opposition by his party's conservative wing, led by Alfred E. Smith. During his acceptance speech at the Democratic convention, he pledged a "New Deal for the American People." He defined the party in this speech as a party of "liberal thought, of planned action, of enlightened international outlook, and the greatest good for the greatest number of citizens." During the campaign he carried these themes to the nation speaking in favor of relief, conservation, and the responsibilities of business to society. He defeated President Herbert Hoover in a decisive victory, carrying 42 states and 472 electoral votes. Both the House and the Senate were won by the Democrats, giving him a legislative base on which to govern.

The New Deal coalition, assembled by Roosevelt's political acumen, that delivered this result was composed of intellectuals (Roosevelt made extensive use of academics as a "brain trust"), farmers, the unemployed middle class, organized labor, the traditionally Democratic South, and racial and urban ethnic minorities. This coalition continued to be the electoral backbone of the Democratic Party for nearly 50 years. It transformed what was essentially a sectional party into a nationally dominant force. It lasted as a coherent electoral force until the elections of President Richard Nixon in 1968 and 1972. Though it eventually unraveled, in part because of changing economic times and its own success, it remained a crucial element in Democratic Party politics for decades beyond the Nixon years.

The New Deal

The New Deal of Franklin Roosevelt marked a profound transformation of American public philosophy, politics, and policy. Roosevelt pledged an active government and delivered on this promise. In the famous

"100 days" and in subsequent months and years he established the contours of a new national political agenda that relied on planning, regulation, and government intervention to deal with the social and economic problems of the twentieth century. He addressed agricultural problems with the Agricultural Adjustment Act, and unemployment through the Civilian Conservation Corps and the Federal Emergency Relief Organization. A federal power system was created through the Tennessee Valley Authority. The gold standard was repealed in an effort to reinflate the currency. He established the Federal Deposit Insurance Corporation, the Securities and Exchange Commission, the Federal Power Commission, the Social Security Act, the Fair Labor Standards Act, and the Food, Drug and Cosmetics Act. Though he had promised a balanced budget during the campaign, he abandoned this goal because of strong pressure to provide economic relief and to resuscitate the economy by increasing demand through government spending. These initiatives marked a transformation of American politics. In spite of opposition and frustrations caused by a conservative Supreme Court (which led to his ill-fated attempt to enlarge the Court by packing it with his appointees), Franklin Roosevelt changed the political culture of the United States. He legitimized the ideas of an active government, national solutions to national problems, and "safety net" programs to protect those who were victims of economic dislocation.

Roosevelt achieved this though a unique combination of personal style, which was at once empathetic, witty, and inspiring, and sharp political and rhetorical skills, the effective use of the radio to reach people directly, solid political appointments, and a pragmatic cast of mind that made him open to policy experiments. These talents and the popularity of the New Deal gave Roosevelt an unprecedented four terms as president. He defeated Alfred M. Landon in 1936, Wendell L. Willkie in 1940, and Thomas E. Dewey in 1944.

The latter years of his presidency were dominated by the demands of World War II. Though he had hoped to avoid entanglement in European affairs, threats from Germany led him to adopt a position of preparedness and aid to threatened nations. This took the form of Lend–Lease, which provided arms for Britain and eventually the Soviet Union, along with a policy of escorting convoys of supply ships bound for England. During the war, Roosevelt was personally involved in shaping both military strategy and the decision to insist on unconditional surrender. He also attempted to structure the postwar era by a series of diplomatic initiatives involving Winston Churchill and Joseph Stalin. It was after the Yalta Conference in 1945 that a combination of exhaustion, failing health, and the pressures of bringing the war to a close led to his death of a cerebral hemorrhage on April 12 while on vacation in Warm Springs, Georgia.

Franklin Roosevelt's Legacy

Franklin Roosevelt's political career was one of the most eventful in U.S. history. His statesmanship preserved the American system during its most profound political and economic crisis. His politics led to the dominance of his party for over 50 years. He articulated and implemented a new public philosophy of governmental activism. His leadership in foreign affairs shaped the contours of the postwar world. Franklin Roosevelt has entered history as one the nation's most significant presidents.

Melvin A. Kulbicki

SEE ALSO History

BIBLIOGRAPHY

Abbott, Philip. *The Exemplary Presidency: Franklin D. Roosevelt and the American Political Tradition.* Amherst: University of Massachusetts Press, 1990.

Dallek, Robert. *Franklin D. Roosevelt and American Foreign Policy.* New York: Oxford University Press, 1979.

Davis, Kenneth S. *FDR: The New Deal Years.* New York: Random House, 1986.

Freidel, Frank. *Franklin D. Roosevelt: A Rendezvous with Destiny.* Boston: Little, Brown, 1990.

Graham, Otis L., Jr., and Meghan R. Wander. *Franklin D. Roosevelt: His Life and Times.* Boston: G.K. Hall, 1985.

Leuchtenberg, William E. *Franklin D. Roosevelt and the New Deal, 1932–40.* New York: Harper-Collins, 1983.

Simpson, Michael. *Franklin D. Roosevelt.* Cambridge, MA: Basil Blackwell, 1989.

Tugwell, Rexford G. *In Search of Roosevelt.* Cambridge, MA: Harvard University Press, 1972.

Ward, Geoffrey. *A First Class Temperament. The Emergence of Franklin Roosevelt.* New York: Harper-Collins, 1990.

HARRY S. TRUMAN

Harry S. Truman, the 33rd president of the United States, was born the eldest of three children on May 8, 1884, in Lamar, Missouri. Named after his Uncle Harrison, he was raised and educated in Independence, Missouri, just blocks from where his future wife, Bess Wallace, resided. Truman applied to West Point after graduating from high school but was turned down because of his poor eyesight. To help support his parents and siblings, he took a job in the mailroom of the *Kansas City Star*. After that, he took a job as a construction timekeeper for the Santa Fe

Railroad, working ten-hour days for six days a week for $30 a month. He had to live with the labor gangs in their tent camps along the river, which was a rough initiation for the scholarly young Truman.

In 1903 Truman was hired as a bank clerk at the National Bank of Commerce in Kansas City. His performance was considered outstanding, and as a foreshadowing of what was to come in the future, his superior at the bank wrote: "His appearance is good and his habits and character are of the best." He worked at the bank until 1905.

After 1905, he worked with his father as a farmer until 1917, when he joined the armed services. He turned 33 in the spring of 1917, which was two years beyond the age limit set by the Selective Service Act. He had been out of the National Guard for almost six years and was the sole support of his mother and sister. And as a farmer, he was expected to remain on the farm as part of his patriotic duty. Nevertheless, he chose to serve as an artillery captain on the Western Front during World War I. He said of the war: "It is the great adventure, and I am in it." Truman's experience as a captain during the war honed his leadership qualities and afforded him the opportunity to relate to a broad spectrum of people.

On his return home to Independence after the war, he resumed his life as a farmer and eventually went

Harry S. Truman. *Source:* Library of Congress.

into partnership in a Kansas City men's clothing store, called Truman & Jacobson, with a friend from the military named Eddie Jacobson. There were no signed agreements between the two men, and there was never a need for them. The business, a men's shirt and tie store, failed, but it taught Truman many valuable lessons that he later would be able to draw on in order to relate to the American business owner.

In 1922 Truman became judge for the Eastern District of Jackson County, Missouri, and in 1926 he became presiding judge, which was a post he held until 1934 when Missouri elected him to the U.S. Senate. While an eastern district judge, Truman was convinced that the soldier's vote plus the fact that he had failed in business were important influences on his popularity. He felt that people could sympathize with a man in politics who admitted his poor financial condition. Truman, at first, was one of the poorest of senators, a fact he felt intensely.

Truman's experiences while embroiled in local Missouri politics tested his integrity and character and opened his eyes to the corruption of politics. In spite of political pressure and thinly veiled threats, Truman would still not give in to powerful local politicians such as Thomas J. Pendergast, the "Big Boss" of Kansas City, who wanted to work against the law or to misuse power with contract favoritism and Truman's help. As a result of Truman's unfailing honesty, he quickly garnered a reputation for being stubborn, aboveboard, opinionated, and a man of principles.

Truman was reelected to the Senate in 1940, He was chairman of the seven-member Senate Special Committee to Investigate the National Defense Program, a committee that was unofficially dubbed "The Truman Committee." Largely as a result of Truman's efforts, the committee was reported to have saved the country more than $1 billion.

Truman was elected vice president in 1944 practically against his wishes. He had no desire to be President Franklin D. Roosevelt's vice president and felt that the vice presidency would be less riveting than his work in the Senate. It was only after Roosevelt informed Truman that it was his duty as a Democrat to accept the offer for vice president that Truman even considered it. Roosevelt initially had preferred James F. Byrnes or Henry A. Wallace as his vice president, but decided that Truman's popularity was too impressive and useful to overlook. Truman also had a good New Deal voting record and came from a key border state.

Truman became president on April 12, 1945, when Roosevelt died of a stroke. He was considered the "everyday American who became president" or "the man next door who became president," and he often stunned his critics by far surpassing their expectations. Truman had to make an unusual amount of historically significant decisions throughout his presidency—far more than most of his predecessors. He faced formidable challenges simply to keep his party together and the nation on a steady course.

Truman decided to drop the first atomic bomb on Japan after meeting with Prime Minister Winston Churchill and Russia's Joseph Stalin at Potsdam, Germany, in 1945. His headquarters during the Potsdam Conference was No. 2 Kaiserstrasse, a residence that he referred to as "the nightmare house" because of the difficult decision he had to make there.

America thrived during wartime, but after World War II ended, Truman was faced with constant prophecies of economic doom, fueled by memories of the Great Depression. He also had to grapple with a rise in the cost of living—which was up 30%—and a malady of labor union strikes in almost every imaginable field of industry, as well as severe housing shortages across the nation. Elevator operators, oil workers, coal workers, lumber workers, longshoremen, automobile and transit workers, all went on strike shortly after the war. Three weeks after the end of the war, Truman presented Congress with a 21-point program for planned reconversion. The prevailing postwar mood on Capitol Hill, however, was to scale back the role of government.

On May 25, 1946, Truman called on Congress for the power to draft striking rail workers into the army, thus avoiding a nationwide shutdown; however, the draft threat proved to be unnecessary after Truman appealed to the American public. Truman delivered a broadcast to the country on May 24, saying, "I am a friend of labor . . . [but] it is inconceivable that in our democracy . . . men should be placed in a position where they can completely stifle our economy and ultimately destroy our country." He compared the striking workers to a foreign enemy and said, "The crisis tonight is caused by a group of men within our own country who place their private interests above the welfare of the nation."

Truman was reelected in November 1948 in a surprise victory over Thomas E. Dewey, which rendered the Gallup poll useless. According to the press in practically every city across the nation, only a miracle or a series of unimaginable Republican blunders could save Truman from defeat. Truman received 49.5% of the votes to Dewey's 45.1%. Dewey's strategy was to appear presidential, and he never took a clear stand on most issues in order to avoid alienating his party's moderate–conservative schism. In stark contrast,

Truman was clear on where he stood and what he wanted to accomplish. Approximately 750,000 people filled the streets in Washington, D.C., to welcome Truman back to the White House, the largest outpouring for a president that the capital had ever seen.

Truman wanted his idea for a national health insurance plan to gain acceptance, but it never did. He pushed an enormous postwar loan to Britain through Congress and was the first president to recommend statehood for Alaska and Hawaii. Truman also crafted a major change in U.S. policy toward Russia, underscored by the Truman Doctrine, which highlighted communist containment and automatic support for free people resisting subjugation.

Truman established the North Atlantic Treaty Organization (NATO) in April 1949, providing a basis for West European collective security. The Marshall Plan, approved by Truman, was a plan to provide massive funding to Western Europe in order to avoid an economic collapse overseas that would, in turn, mean revolution and an economic tailspin for America. Truman also organized the Berlin Airlift in 1948 and 1949, thus saving thousands of Germans from starvation and succeeding in breaking the Soviet blockade of ground-access routes. Truman is also credited with recognizing Israel and is remembered as the first president to recommend Medicare.

On June 27, 1950, Truman announced that U.S. troops would be sent overseas on behalf of the United Nations to withstand the communist invasion of South Korea. In April 1951 Truman dismissed the much-lauded UN commander in Korea, General Douglas MacArthur, from all of his commands in order to take control of the military and bring it back to the Oval Office. After erroneously discounting the possibility of Chinese intervention in the Korean War, MacArthur had begun pleading in public for proposals that far exceeded the Security Council resolution under which the United States was acting, which would have meant a larger war.

As the 1952 elections approached, General Dwight D. Eisenhower, commander of NATO forces in Europe, was persuaded to become a Republican candidate. In 1951 Truman decided not to seek another term; he felt Governor Adlai E. Stevenson of Illinois would be a solid Democratic candidate. Truman embarked on a round of whistle-stop adventures on Stevenson's behalf, but the increasing unpopularity of the Korean War may have done Stevenson more harm than good. Eisenhower won the election, receiving 55.1% of the votes and carrying 39 states. Truman later became a strident critic of President Eisenhower's Republican administration.

In 1953, after Truman's presidency was over, a census report confirmed that the gains in income, standard of living, education, and housing since he took office were unparalleled in American history. In all, 11 million jobs were gained in seven years, unemployment had almost disappeared, and the postwar economic collapse that everyone expected had never happened. Yet Truman's most important accomplishments had been in world affairs. He was most proud of aid to Greece and Turkey and of NATO. Yet Truman had failed to do as much as he wanted for public housing, education, civil rights, and medical insurance.

Although Truman wanted to accomplish more in the area of civil rights, he had created the Commission on Civil Rights and had ordered the desegregation of the armed services and the federal Civil Service. Truman had altered the power structure in Washington in ways that surpassed even the drastic measures of Franklin D. Roosevelt with the establishment of the National Security Council, the CIA, and a unified Defense Department.

For seven historically crucial years, President Truman stressed unity for the American people as new alignments were forming around the globe. He liked to refer to himself as "the hired man of 150,000,000 people." He did not run for reelection in 1952 and retired to his home town of Independence, where he resided for the last twenty years of his life. Truman died at the age of 88 in a Kansas City hospital from complications relating to lung congestion, on December 26, 1972. He was buried in the courtyard of his library at home.

Truman's Monday night poker games, Masonic ring, bow ties, Main Street cronies, and dry Missouri twang were thoroughly middle American. He had an authentic pioneer background and, like many of those he guided, had to work hard for whatever he needed. He brought to office the language and value system of decent, common American citizens. He was a direct, determined, honest man, who said of his time as president, "I tried to never forget who I was and where I was going back to."

B. Kim Taylor

SEE ALSO History

BIBLIOGRAPHY

Boller, Paul F., Jr., *Presidential Campaigns*. New York: Oxford University Press, 1984.

McCullough, David. *Truman*. New York: Simon and Schuster, 1992.

Polakoff, Keith J. *Political Parties in American History*. New York: Wiley, 1981.

Polsby, Nelson W. *Presidential Elections*. 6th ed. New York: Scribner's, 1980.

MARTIN VAN BUREN

Martin Van Buren, born on December 5, 1782, in Kinderhook, New York, the son of a farmer and tavern keeper, was the first president born a U.S. citizen. Trained as a lawyer, he entered electoral politics in 1812 and played a key role in organizing the Democratic Party. He led the Albany Regency, a New York political machine, for many years. His skill as a party boss earned Van Buren, known as "The Little Magician" and "The Fox of Kinderhook," a reputation as a careerist and a crafty political tactician.

Elected in 1836, he was the eighth president of the United States (1837–1841) and held the highest office during the Panic of 1837, America's worst economic crisis to that time. Although he never again held elected office after his defeat in 1840, Van Buren continued to be active in politics for many years, running for president in 1844 and 1848. However, he was unable to secure the nomination of a major party, and after two losses, he retired from politics altogether.

Early Political Career

Soon after passing the bar exam in 1803 and joining the law practice of his half brother, James J. Van Alen, Van Buren established ties with the Democratic-Republican Party (later the Democratic Party) of New York. In 1804 Congressman William P. Van Ness was charged with being an accessory to murder for his involvement as a second in the famous duel between Aaron Burr and Alexander Hamilton, but Van Buren successfully defended the congressman in court and intervened on his behalf with the governor. The inside connections with the party that he subsequently developed helped launch Van Buren on a career in New York politics. He served as a state senator from 1812 to 1820 and as attorney general of New York from 1816 to 1819. The New York State legislature elected Van Buren to the U.S. Senate in 1821 and again in 1827.

During this time Van Buren was active in building the political machine known as the Albany Regency. When New York voters overwhelmingly endorsed a constitutional convention to revise the state constitution, Van Buren and his clique, known as the Bucktails, comprised more than three-fourths of the delegates. They seized the opportunity to strengthen their organization in Albany, and when Van Buren left New York in December to take his seat in the U.S. Senate, the Regency, which he now headed, was firmly in control of New York politics.

Van Buren adjusted readily to Washington society

Martin Van Buren. *Source:* Library of Congress.

and quickly used his skills as a behind-the-scenes schemer to become an important and prominent senator. Although he supported the unsuccessful presidential candidacy of William H. Crawford in 1824, during the administration of John Quincy Adams (1825–1829), he led Senate opposition to the president and played a major role in organizing the political coalition that elected Andrew Jackson president in 1828.

While in the Senate, Van Buren continued to dominate New York State politics through the Albany Regency, and upon the expiration of his second term as senator in 1828, he was elected governor of New York. Van Buren had made too many strong connections in Washington to remain outside national politics for long, though, and he resigned as governor after only a few months in office in order to accept appointment as Jackson's secretary of state.

In the cabinet Van Buren quickly became embroiled in a bitter power struggle with Vice President John C. Calhoun, but he used Jackson's disaffection with Calhoun to became a close companion and adviser to Jackson. Jackson's conflict with Calhoun was partly caused by the role of the vice president's wife in snubbing the bride of Secretary of War John Henry Eaton. Jackson also discovered that Calhoun had privately called for his censure in 1819 for his actions during the invasion of Florida. Allying himself closely with Jacksonian policies, Van Buren further ingratiated himself with Old Hickory by resigning from the cabinet in order to pave the way for a double move beneficial to Jackson's power—the quiet resignation from the cabinet of Eaton, who was a potential source of embarrassment, and the removal of the pro-Calhoun element. After forming a new cabinet decidedly hostile to Calhoun, Jackson appointed Van Buren minister to Great Britain, and Van Buren soon left for his new post.

Six months later, however, Van Buren was denied the nomination to this position, with Calhoun casting the tie-breaking vote in a deadlocked Senate. This proved beneficial to Van Buren, however, as it won him public sympathy and gained even stronger support from President Jackson, who, incensed, supported Van Buren for the vice presidential nomination at the 1832 Democratic National Convention. Serving as vice president, Van Buren acted as a cautious but faithful lieutenant to the president, and Jackson, deciding to follow George Washington's precedent of running for only two terms, gave the full measure of his support to Van Buren in the 1836 presidential election.

As Jackson's chosen successor, Van Buren easily won the Democratic presidential nomination. The Whig Party, badly divided and hurt by Jackson's extremely popular presidency, attempted a novel but ill-conceived political strategy: it ran William Henry Harrison in the West and South and Daniel Webster in the Northeast, hoping to scatter the vote and prevent Van Buren from getting a majority of electoral votes, forcing a deadlock that would have to be decided in the House of Representatives, where the Whigs would have a chance. Although some southern Democrats defected, Van Buren won the election with 170 electoral votes to 73 for runner-up Harrison; the popular vote, however, was far from overwhelming, with Van Buren beating Harrison by a margin of only 762,678 to 735,651.

Presidency

Shortly after his inauguration, Van Buren was forced to face the consequences of Jackson's economic and monetary policies, as the nation was hit with its first major depression, the Panic of 1837. Committed to the Jeffersonian principle of limited government and abysmally unprepared by his background to handle a situation never before faced by the young nation, Van

Buren refused to yield to pressure for federal intervention to relieve economic distress. He felt that restoration of full employment could only come from the efforts of private business and saw his responsibility as chief executive as being limited to preventing the further loss of federal funds that had occurred as a result of the collapse of certain "pet" banks.

Van Buren responded to these collapses by calling for the establishment of an Independent Treasury System. Such a system, in line with Van Buren's ideology of private initiative, would divorce government and banking by placing all public moneys in federally owned depositories. The Panic of 1837 had resulted largely from the boom in western land sales, a phenomenon that had occurred partly because of rapid American expansion and partly because banks with federal moneys deposited in them were able to use public funds as a basis for making loans and issuing notes. The Independent Treasury System was intended to separate the banking system from the administration of the government's finances and end the speculation that had been based on government deposits. Van Buren faced opposition not only from Whigs but also from conservative Democrats allied to state banking interests. Congress passed the bill in 1840, and though it was repealed in 1841, during the administration of Whig President John Tyler, it was reinstated in 1846 and lasted until 1863.

As president, Van Buren also sought to maintain the strength and solidarity of the Democratic Party in an age of heightening sectional conflict. He placated southern Democrats by adhering to a strict states' rights policy on slavery, opposed the abolition of the slave trade in the District of Columbia, and favored guarantees that the federal government would not interfere with slavery in the states. Though he opposed the expansion of slavery, Van Buren aroused the fears of northern Democrats anyway, conducting a protracted and costly war against the Seminole Indians in Florida in an attempt to move the Seminoles to Indian Territory (now Oklahoma). Gradually, most of them were captured and sent west, and Seminole resistance virtually ended in 1842, but many northerners felt that this action was a prelude to the admission of Florida as a slave state. Van Buren also offended many southerners by refusing to support the annexation of Texas, a move that cost him crucial support in the Democratic National Convention of 1844, when a proannexation candidate, James K. Polk, was chosen.

Despite these difficulties, Van Buren managed to hold the nation together during some of the sectional crises that began with the debate over slavery in Missouri and eventually ended in the Civil War. His failure to deal with the economic crisis, however, cost him most of his support and ultimately the election of 1840.

In addition to domestic economic and party problems, Van Buren faced several pressing issues of territory and expansion during his single term as president. In 1838 he had to conciliate Great Britain in the *Caroline* affair, which arose when loyalists in the Canadian militia crossed into U.S. territory and sank the *Caroline*, a small U.S. steamer based at Buffalo, New York, which was used to take men and supplies to Canadian rebels. One American life was lost, and the American press clamored for revenge. Van Buren sent Major General Winfield Scott to the border with orders to maintain the peace and prevent further disturbances.

Van Buren had other difficulties to deal with in the Northeast. In 1839 the Aroostook War once again threatened the peace with Britain. The war was a small border conflict between the inhabitants of Maine and New Brunswick, Canada, over the Aroostook Valley, an area whose possession was not made clear in the Treaty of Paris (1783) ending the American Revolution. General Scott halted the fighting in March 1839. Though Van Buren issued several neutrality proclamations, and General Scott was able to maintain the peace, the Canadian problems were not settled until the Webster–Ashburton Treaty of 1842, after Van Buren's term of office had ended.

Van Buren was generally cautious and conciliatory in his foreign policy, and his steady advocacy of nonexpansionist policies (excluding his position on the Seminole issue) helped keep the United States out of the kind of armed conflicts that might easily have befallen the growing nation.

Postpresidency

Despite his abilities as both chief executive and party leader, Van Buren's failure to take steps to alleviate the hardships of the Panic of 1837 undermined his popularity. Facing a Whig Party that had played on Van Buren's difficulties between northern and southern Democrats to regain strength and unity, and riding a wave of massive unpopularity for his ineptitude in managing the economic crisis, Van Buren was defeated for reelection in 1840 by William Henry Harrison. Though Harrison won 234 of the 294 electoral votes, the margin of victory was surprisingly close: only 1,275,016 to 1,129,102.

Van Buren was not stopped by his defeat in 1840. He sought the Democratic presidential nomination again in 1844 and went into the Democratic National

Convention in Baltimore with the support of a majority of the delegates. However, Van Buren had come out against the annexation of Texas, which cost him the support of Andrew Jackson along with the allegiance of many delegates who, prior to this announcement, had been pledged to him. To make matters worse, the convention adopted a two-thirds rule, and Van Buren did not possess enough delegates to win the nomination outright. His refusal to support the annexation of Texas proved fatal, and after nine ballots, the convention chose annexationist James K. Polk of Tennessee, the new favorite of fellow Tennessean Andrew Jackson.

Out of favor with the Democratic Party, Van Buren ran in 1848 as the Free Soil Party candidate. The Free Soil Party—an eclectic political alliance composed of former Liberty Party members, antislavery Whigs, and certain New York Democrats known as Barnburners—was organized in 1848 to oppose the extension of slavery into the territories newly acquired by the United States from Mexico. Van Buren ran a distant third in the election, failing to carry a single state, and his candidacy drew significant support away from the Democrats in New York, helping the Whigs defeat the Democrats in that crucial state, which won the presidency for Whig Zachary Taylor.

After that, Van Buren took no further part in active politics. He died at Kinderhook on July 24, 1862. His memoirs, which were written in 1833, were not published until 1920 (*The Autobiography of Martin Van Buren*).

Jack J. Miller

SEE ALSO History

BIBLIOGRAPHY

Cole, Donald B. *Martin Van Buren and the American Political System*. Princeton: Princeton University Press, 1984.

Curtis, James C. *The Fox at Bay: Martin Van Buren and the Presidency, 1837–1841*. Lexington: University Press of Kentucky, 1970.

Niven, John. *Martin Van Buren: The Romantic Age of American Politics*. New York: Oxford University Press, 1983.

Wilson, Major L. *The Presidency of Martin Van Buren*. Lawrence: University Press of Kansas, 1984.

WOODROW WILSON

Thomas Woodrow Wilson was the 28th president of the United States. Woodrow Wilson's presidency validated the progressive era and saw the United States emerge from World War I as a great power. His academic and religious background gave Wilson an austere, idealistic quality that is often seen as the defining signature of his presidency.

Woodrow Wilson's Image on a Campaign Button. *Source:* Three Lions.

Born in Staunton, Virginia, on December 28, 1856, Wilson was a child of the South. He grew up during the Reconstruction period and internalized the latent southern pride that manifested itself during that period. Throughout his life he believed that the South had a right to secede, and he believed in white supremacy.

After a brief stint at Davidson College, Wilson entered Princeton University in New Jersey, from which he graduated in 1879. He went on to the University of Virginia to study law, but health problems forced him to withdraw after two years. Nonetheless, while recuperating, Wilson continued his studies and passed the bar exam in 1882. He quickly grew bored with practicing law. Within a year, Wilson gave up his practice to go to graduate school at Johns Hopkins University and study political science. He received a Ph.D. in political science in 1886. Wilson met and married Ellen Louise Axson while in graduate school. The couple eventually had three daughters.

After graduate school, Wilson taught political economy and law at Bryn Mawr College and then went on to teach at Wesleyan University and Princeton. In 1902, he was selected as president of Princeton, a position he held until 1910. He enacted a number of reforms at the school that were soon adopted by other institutions. These efforts earned Wilson a reputation in New Jersey as a progressive. This reputation led the state Democratic Party bosses to urge Wilson to run for governor in 1910. He easily won the election and immediately turned on the political bosses by endorsing legislation that mandated party primaries for all elective positions in the state, limited campaign expenditures, and required candidates to file financial statements. Wilson also pushed through New Jersey's first workers' compensation law and enacted state antitrust laws.

These progressive reforms boosted Wilson into the national spotlight and made him a serious candidate for the Democratic Party's presidential nomination in 1912. However, at the party's convention in Baltimore, conservative elements blocked Wilson's nomination. Only after he received the endorsement of William Jennings Bryan and after 46 ballots did Wilson gain the nomination. Wilson chose Thomas R. Marshall of Indiana as his running mate. The party platform stressed progressive reforms such as a federal income tax, direct election of senators, regulation of business, banking reform and a diminution of tariffs.

Soon after the Republican National Convention, it became apparent to most that Wilson would win the election. When conservative Republicans renominated President William H. Taft for a second term without even allowing former President Theodore Roosevelt's name to be offered for consideration, Roosevelt broke ranks with the Republicans and launched a third-party candidacy, which attracted considerable popular support. Running as a progressive candidate of the "Bull Moose" Party, Roosevelt promised the country a "New Nationalism," which stressed increased government regulation of industry and major social reforms. Wilson countered with a "New Freedom" campaign, which emphasized antimonopoly measures and labor rights. The split in the Republican Party assured Wilson of victory, but even so, it was a close race: Wilson got 6,286,820 popular votes (42%) and 435 electoral votes; Roosevelt came in second, with 4,126,020 popular votes (27%) and 88 electoral votes; while Taft came in third, with 3,483,922 popular votes (23%) and 8 electoral votes. Upon entering office, Wilson clearly showed his southern roots by choosing five southerners for posts in his first cabinet.

Following his inauguration, Wilson immediately embarked upon a series of progressive reforms. In 1913, he became the first president to address Congress personally since John Adams. He urged the body to overturn the restrictive Payne–Aldrich Tariff. The legislature responded with the Underwood Tariff, which cut most existing tariffs in half and exempted a number of items such as iron and wool from any duties. This drastically reduced consumer prices. The new law compensated for lost tariff revenue by enacting a federal income tax (in accordance with the 16th Amendment). Also in 1913, the 17th Amendment, which mandated the direct election of senators, was ratified.

Wilson dramatically overhauled the nation's monetary system during the same year. The Federal Reserve Act gave the United States its first central banking system since 1832. The act created a system of 12 regional banks that controlled the money supply by adjusting the discount rate at which they loaned money to member banks. Wilson hoped this system would help eliminate some of the spectacular fluctuations in American business cycles.

The following year, Wilson continued to push his progressive policies with the passage of the Clayton Antitrust Act. This law forbade monopolistic practices such as unfair pricing and interlocking directorates. The Clayton Act also freed labor unions from antitrust restrictions and curbed the use of injunctions during strikes. This had the effect of galvanizing the American labor movement and dramatically increasing the number and size of unions in the United States.

The year 1914 also marked the death of Wilson's first wife due to Bright's disease. Though devastated, Wilson eventually remarried Mrs. Edith Bolling Galt, a widow, on December 18, 1915. Edith Wilson proved to be a strong and able companion for the president through the difficulties he would face.

Wilson tried to address the problem of child labor in the United States, but with little success. The Keating–Owen Act of 1916 outlawed the interstate transport of products manufactured by companies that used child labor. This law was eventually struck down by the Supreme Court in 1918, and a subsequent law, the Child Labor Act of 1919, suffered the same fate.

The president had much more success in the arena of workers' rights. Besides the Clayton Act, Wilson undertook such measures as providing workers' compensation for all federal employees and supporting the La Follete Seaman's Act of 1915, which mandated better conditions for merchant seamen, and the Adamson Act of 1916, which granted railroad workers an eight-hour day and time and a half for overtime. The Adamson Act laid the foundation for the eventual broad acceptance of these conditions by most businesses.

In the realm of foreign policy, Wilson carried on the interventionist policies of his Republican predecessors. He frequently used American troops to intervene in Latin America to ensure the stability of the region. He continued to station American troops in Nicaragua, making the nation a de facto American protectorate. In 1915, he sent troops to intervene in Haiti. A year later, American marines occupied Santo Domingo in an effort to forestall a revolution and maintain stability on the island of Hispaniola.

Wilson also undertook a very proactive policy toward Mexico, although he refused to invade Mexico and restore democracy when the Mexican Revolution brought Victoriano Huerta to power in 1913 and instead issued the Mobile Doctrine, which asserted that the United States would never again acquire territory through conquest. Nonetheless, after an incident in Tampico, Mexico, in which American sailors were arrested, Wilson sent marines to occupy Vera Cruz in 1914. This had the effect of turning many Mexicans, even anti-Huerta factions, against the United States. In 1916, the Mexican revolutionary Pancho Villa raided the American border town of Columbus, New Mexico, killing 17 Americans. Wilson responded by dispatching General John J. Pershing and 6,000 American troops to pursue Villa into Mexico. The futile expedition, which failed to capture Villa, did little more than worsen relations between the United States and Mexico.

With the beginning of World War I in 1914, Wilson tried to steer a course of careful neutrality for the United States. Privately, Wilson clearly favored the Allies (Great Britain, France and Russia), which he felt, especially in the case of Britain and France, were more democratic than the Central Powers (Germany, Austria–Hungary and the Ottoman Empire). A tight British naval blockade of the Central Powers soon forced Germany to turn to submarine warfare as a means of conducting naval strikes against the British. When a German submarine sank the British passenger liner *Lusitania* in 1915, with the loss of 1,200 civilians, including 120 Americans, Wilson demanded that Germany cease unrestricted submarine warfare. Wilson issued an ultimatum to the Germans a year later, when the French passenger ship *Sussex* was sunk, again with American casualties. The Germans responded in May 1916, with the *Sussex* pledge to end unrestricted submarine warfare.

In response to the increasing possibility that the United States would be pulled into the war, Wilson urged Congress to pass legislation such as the National Defense Act (1916), which increased the size of the army and brought state militias under federal control. Congress also authorized an increase in naval construction.

American involvement in World War I became the leading issue of the 1916 election. Wilson's campaign slogan was "He kept us out of War!" He pledged to continue both American neutrality and his domestic reforms. The Republican candidate, Supreme Court Justice Charles E. Hughes, condemned Wilson for not taking a strong enough stance on American neutrality and for failing to protect American interests abroad. Theodore Roosevelt endorsed Wilson and thereby healed the split that had plagued the Republican Party in the previous election. Up until election day, Hughes appeared to be the front-runner. However, Wilson tipped the scales in his favor by winning vote-rich California. Wilson won with 9,129,606 popular votes

(49%) and 277 electoral votes to Hughes's 8,538,221 popular votes (46%) and 254 electoral votes.

Soon after Wilson's second inauguration, events propelled the United States into World War I. In February 1917, Germany resumed unrestricted submarine warfare and quickly sank eight American merchant ships. In March of the same year, the Zimmermann message became public. This message contained pledges by the German government to aid Mexico in reconquering the lost territories of Texas, New Mexico and Arizona in exchange for Mexico's entry into the war on the side of the Central Powers. These two events aroused the American public and forced Wilson to ask Congress for a declaration of war. In April, the Senate voted 82 to 6 to go to war, and the House followed suit with a vote of 373 to 50. In May, Congress passed the Selective Service Act, which established conscription. In spite of his oft-touted idealism, Wilson signed the Espionage Act of 1917 and the Sedition Act of 1918, which gave the government broad powers to prosecute those who opposed the war.

The arrival of American troops in Europe in 1917 stopped Germany's last major offensive of the war and turned the tide against the Central Powers. With Allied victory in sight, Wilson announced his 14 Points for a just peace to Congress in January 1918. Wilson's 14-point vision for peace emphasized four major areas: the abolition of secret treaties, self-determination for nations, free and open trade, and the establishment of a broad collective security organization. After the armistice was signed on November 11, 1918, Wilson personally led the American delegation to the peace talks in Paris. The Treaty of Versailles, signed in 1919, contained many of Wilson's proposals. For instance, it created numerous independent nations—such as Poland, Czechoslovakia and Hungary—from the former empires of central Europe. It also called for the creation of a League of Nations to preserve the independence of the world's states. At the same time, the treaty contained provisions that helped set the stage for World War II.

Upon returning to the United States, Wilson campaigned vigorously for ratification of the treaty. He overexerted himself and suffered a physical collapse in September 1919. Soon after this episode, he suffered a stroke from which he never fully recovered. Since there were no constitutional guidelines to cover succession when a president was disabled, Wilson, aided by his second wife, served out his second term. Hampered by Republican control of both houses of Congress and his own fragile health, Wilson was ineffectual for the remainder of his time in office. The Senate refused to ratify the Treaty of Versailles; thus, the United States never joined the League of Nations.

After Wilson left office, his health continued to deteriorate. He died on February 3, 1924.

Tom Lansford

SEE ALSO History

BIBLIOGRAPHY

Braeman, John, ed. *Wilson.* Englewood Cliffs, NJ: Prentice-Hall, 1973.

Clements, Kendrick A. *Woodrow Wilson: World Statesman.* Boston: Twayne Publishers, 1987.

Knock, Thomas J. *To End All Wars: Woodrow Wilson and the Quest for a New World Order.* New York: Oxford University Press, 1992.

Link, Arthur S. *The Higher Realism of Woodrow Wilson.* Nashville: Vanderbilt University Press, 1971.

Vice Presidents

ALBEN W. BARKLEY

In 1912 Alben William Barkley (1877–1956) was elected to the United States House of Representatives from Kentucky after having served in a number of elected county positions. An ardent supporter of President Woodrow Wilson, Barkley remained a committed progressive and internationalist throughout his tenure in public office. In 1924 he served as chair of the Democratic National Convention. Elected to the Senate in 1926, he had strong, though unsuccessful, support for the vice presidential nomination in 1928. The keynote speaker at the 1932 Democratic National Convention, he was a major speaker at every convention through 1952, keynoting again in 1936 and 1948. Reelected to the Senate in 1932, he was an important ally of the Franklin D. Roosevelt administration, which suported him for majority leader in 1937. The administration also helped Barkley fend off a strong primary challenge by Governor A.B. "Happy" Chandler in 1938. Barkley approached his post of majority leader as a broker between his conservative colleagues and the more liberal White House. A committed liberal, he was willing to compromise to achieve ends. Barkley was slighted by Roosevelt when the president passed him over for the Supreme Court in 1943. Barkley resigned from the post of majority leader when Roosevelt vetoed a revenue bill that Barkley recommended. His fellow Democratic senators reelected him to the post. Though passed over for the number-two spot on the ticket, Barkley placed Roosevelt's name in nomination in 1944. When the Republicans gained control of the Senate in 1946, he became minority leader. Truman did not place much faith in Barkley's capabilities and rarely sought his advice, although in 1948 Truman selected Barkley to be his vice presidential candidate. During his tenure as vice president, Barkley was instrumental in building coalitions on Capitol Hill. Failing to win the Democratic presidential nomination in 1952, he was reelected to the Senate in 1954. He served there until his death in 1956.

Jeffrey D. Schultz

SEE ALSO Harry S. Truman

JOHN CABELL BRECKINRIDGE

At the age of 36, John Cabell Breckinridge, born in 1821, was the youngest man to become vice president; he was also the youngest contender for the presidency at age 39. Born near Lexington, Kentucky, on January 15, 1821, Breckinridge was the scion of a patrician family that included many lawyers and statesmen, among them, John Breckinridge, Jefferson's attorney general. A precocious boy, he studied at Centre College and Princeton and gained admission to the bar at the age of 20. During the Mexican War he volunteered to serve on the front as a major in 1847. Returning to Kentucky, he was elected to the state legislature and later to the U.S. House of Representatives as a proslavery Demo-

John Cabell Breckinridge. *Source:* Library of Congress.

crat. Handsome and immensely popular in his state, Breckinridge was chosen as Buchanan's running mate in 1856. As vice president, he worked for a compromise to avert the impending civil war. He was also a capable presiding officer in the U.S. Senate. Sixteen months before his term as vice president ended, he was elected U.S. senator from Kentucky. In 1860 Breckinridge was nominated by the southern Democrats for the presidency, Stephen A. Douglas by the northern Democrats, John Bell by the Constitutional Union Party, and Abraham Lincoln by the newly formed Republican Party. In the elections, Breckinridge came second with 72 votes from 11 southern slaveowning states. Although Lincoln received less than 40% of the popular vote, he won a clear majority of the 180 electoral votes. After Lincoln's inauguration, Breckinridge took his seat in the Senate, but opposed vigorously Lincoln's war efforts. Breckinridge defended the right of the southern states to secede and favored secession for Kentucky, although he later acquiesced in the state's declaration of neutrality. Following the expulsion of all Confederate forces from Kentucky, he left Washington and accepted a commission as brigadier general in the Confederate army and was indicted by the federal government. Breckinridge served with distinction at Shiloh, Vicksburg, Chickamauga, and Cold Harbor. He made an unsuccessful attack on Baton Rouge in August 1862 and commanded the right wing of Braxton Bragg's army at Murfreesboro in December 1862. Toward the end of the war he defeated Union forces at Newmarket and East Tennessee and took part in the battle near Nashville. In February 1865 he was appointed as the Confederate secretary of war. After the surrender of the South, Breckinridge fled to Cuba, Europe, and Canada, wandering for three and a half years as a stateless person. His exile ended on Christmas 1868 when President Andrew Johnson issued a general amnesty. Breckinridge returned to Kentucky in March 1869 to a great outpouring of popular support for a genuine southern hero. He never held public office again but was engaged in his latter days building railroads. He died in 1875.

SEE ALSO James Buchanan

BIBLIOGRAPHY

Davis, William C. *Breckinridge: Statesman, Soldier, Symbol.* Baton Rouge: Louisiana State University Press, 1974.

GEORGE MIFFLIN DALLAS

George Mifflin Dallas—a senator, diplomat and vice president of the United States—was born in Philadel-

George Mifflin Dallas. *Source:* Library of Congress.

phia on July 10, 1792. He was the son of Alexander Dallas, secretary of the treasury in the James Madison administration. Dallas graduated from the College of New Jersey (now Princeton University) in 1810 and then took a job at his father's law office. After serving briefly in the War of 1812, he was appointed private secretary to Albert Gallatin, the United States minister to Russia. Dallas returned from Russia in October 1814 and took the position of clerk in the Department of the Treasury, then headed by his father. In 1816 Dallas returned to Philadelphia and married Sophia Nicklin. He practiced law and in 1817 was appointed deputy attorney general of the city. Dallas was active in politics throughout the 1820s. In 1829 he was elected mayor of Philadelphia, and from 1829 to 1831 he served as district attorney for the eastern district of Pennsylvania.

In late 1831 Senator Isaac Barnard resigned his seat, and on December 13 Dallas was appointed to fill the vacancy. While serving in the Senate, he was active in banking issues and supported President Andrew Jackson's tariff policy in his fight with South Carolina. On March 13, 1833, Dallas left the Senate in order to advance his legal career. His move back to Pennsylvania reaped dividends when Governor George Wolf appointed him the state's attorney general, a position he held until 1835. After retiring as attorney general, Dallas was appointed minister to Russia by President Martin Van Buren in 1837. In 1839 Dallas found the assignment in Russia lacking in importance and asked to be relieved.

For the next five years, Dallas concentrated on his law practice and continued his unfriendly rivalry with fellow Pennsylvania politician James Buchanan. At the 1844 Democratic National Convention, James Polk was nominated for president and New York Senator Silas Wright was chosen for vice president. Wright declined the nomination, however, and on advice from Dallas's brother-in-law, Senator Robert Walker of Mississippi, Dallas was nominated as Polk's running mate.

During Dallas's term as vice president the country was in a process of great geographical expansion resulting from the popular perception of what is sometimes referred to as "Manifest Destiny." Dallas supported expansion and the 1846 war with Mexico. His main contribution, however, was his effort to find a compromise on the tariff issues that dominated his tenure as vice president. He opposed the low presidential tariff bill, but showing loyalty to Polk and his party, he cast the tie-breaking vote that passed the Walker Bill. Dallas made no attempt to run for president and retired to Pennsylvania in 1849. He practiced law until 1856, when he was appointed minister to Great Britain. There he obtained the renunciation of England's claims to the right to search ships on the high seas. He died in Philadelphia on December 3, 1864.

Daniel Stanhagen

SEE ALSO James K. Polk

JOHN NANCE GARNER

A long-time power in the House and vice president under two Franklin D. Roosevelt administrations, John Nance "Cactus Jack" Garner of Texas was instrumental in shepherding much of the New Deal legislation through the Senate but later broke with Roosevelt over various issues, including the "packing" of the Supreme Court and Roosevelt's decision to run for a third term, and he unsuccessfully challenged Roosevelt for the party nomination in 1940.

Having spent 30 years in the U.S. House of Representatives and risen to the speakership—a position from which he would advise younger legislators like Texan Sam Rayburn that "you've got to bloody your knuckles"—Garner ran for the Democratic nomination for president in 1932 with the backing of newspaper magnate William Randolph Hearst. After releasing his Texas and California delegates to Roosevelt at the Democratic National Convention, Garner reluctantly accepted the vice presidential nomination to help appeal to party conservatives. But he was dissatisfied with the limited role of the vice presidency, once

even saying that it wasn't worth "a bucket of warm spit," and Roosevelt neither sought nor received advice from Garner. Gradually, Garner became uncomfortable with much of Roosevelt's New Deal, and a break between the two came in 1937 over such issues as Roosevelt's desire to increase the size of the Supreme Court and "pack" it with New Dealers.

Garner's election as Speaker of the House in 1931 was the culmination of a nearly 30-year career that included being among the insurgents in the House in the 1910 battle to reduce the powers of Speaker Joe Cannon. His tenure included a failed early attempt to pass a graduated income tax, service on the House Ways and Means Committee, and acting as House liaison to President Woodrow Wilson. Garner was adept at backstage maneuvering to influence legislation, even persuading members with whiskey in his private office—"striking a blow for liberty," he would say.

Born on November 22, 1868, in Red River County, Texas, the son of a Confederate veteran, Garner began his career as a voice for west Texas. After practicing law in Uvalde and becoming editor of the Uvalde *Leader*, the ownership of which he obtained in lieu of

John Nance Garner. *Source:* Library of Congress.

legal fees, Garner was elected county judge of Uvalde County in 1895. In 1898 he joined the Texas House of Representatives, where he served two terms and rose to prominence for his efforts on railroad reform. He was elected to the U.S. House of Representatives in 1902, from a new congressional district along the Rio Grande that was larger than many states.

After his failed presidential attempt in 1940 and after serving out his second term as vice president, Garner made and kept a vow never to return east of the Potomac River. Instead, he retired to his ranch in Uvalde and devoted himself to business interests. On Garner's 95th birthday, on November 22, 1963, President John F. Kennedy telephoned him to wish him well from Fort Worth before leaving for the fateful trip to Dallas. Garner died in Uvalde on November 7, 1967.

John F. Yarbrough

SEE ALSO Franklin Delano Roosevelt

ALBERT GORE JR.

Albert "Al" Gore Jr. was born in Carthage, Tennessee, on March 31, 1948. He was raised in both Carthage and Washington, D.C. He is the son of former Democratic Senator Albert Gore Sr. Growing up in a world of privilege as well as political exposure, Gore was well prepared for his future role as a politician. Al Gore Jr. graduated with honors from Harvard University in 1969 with a degree in government. Upon graduating, he volunteered for military service in the U.S. Army and served in Vietnam.

Subsequent to his military service, Gore pursued a career as an investigative reporter for *The Tennessean*, a newspaper in Nashville. Gore worked as a journalist for seven years. During this time, he furthered his education by attending Vanderbilt University Divinity School and Vanderbilt Law School.

Following in the footsteps of his father, Gore decided to embark on a political career. In 1976 he ran for and was elected to the U.S. House of Representatives, representing his home state of Tennessee. Always a defender of the environment, Gore organized the first congressional hearings on toxic waste. He served for eight years in the House before winning a seat in the U.S. Senate in 1984. He was reelected in 1990 as the only candidate in modern state history—of either political party—to win all 95 of Tennessee's congressional districts.

While serving in the U.S. Senate, Gore wrote the book *Earth in Balance*. A natural blending of his journalistic background and his political savvy, this book emphasized what Gore referred to as "a global ecolog-

ical crisis." Gore was a passionate defender of the environment during his years of service in the U.S. Congress.

Gore was an unsuccessful candidate for the Democratic nomination for president in 1988. He did manage to win national attention and 3 million votes in the primary process before eventually losing the presidential nomination to Governor Michael Dukakis of Massachusetts.

On July 2, 1992, the presidential candidate, Governor Bill Clinton of Arkansas, chose Gore to be his vice presidential running mate. Gore was formally nominated as the Democratic Party nominee for vice president one week later at the Democratic National Convention in New York City. There was concern initially about the pair's age (both were baby boomers) and the fact that both men came from southern states. But Gore's experience and familiarity with Washington, D.C., foreign policy, and the environment, in addition to his Vietnam military service, balanced what were viewed as Clinton's weaknesses. Certainly Gore's prior national exposure in the 1988 campaign made him an asset in the 1992 general election. The Clinton–Gore ticket proved to be a winning combination.

On November 4, 1992, Al Gore was elected the 45th vice president of the United States. He officially assumed his duties on January 20, 1993. While serving as vice president, Gore's areas of responsibility included the environment, federal government efficiency, and information technology, among others.

Kimberly J. Pace

SEE ALSO Bill Clinton

BIBLIOGRAPHY

Becker, Jim. *Bill & Al's Excellent Adventure*. New York: St. Martin's Press, 1993.

Burford, Betty M. *Al Gore: United States Vice President*. Springfield, IL: Enslow Publishers, 1994.

Gore, Albert, Jr. *Earth in Balance*. Boston: Houghton Mifflin, 1992.

Hillin, Hank. *Al Gore Jr.: His Life & Career*. New York: Carol Publishing, 1992.

THOMAS A. HENDRICKS

Born in Muskingum County, Ohio, on September 7, 1819, Thomas Andrews Hendricks was raised in Indiana where he graduated in 1841 from Hanover College in Madison. After being admitted to the bar in 1844, Hendricks began his political career as a Democratic legislator in the Indiana state legislature and a delegate to the second state constitutional convention, 1850–1851. In 1851 he was elected to Congress and was named commissioner of the General Land Office in 1855. He lost the first of his three attempts to win the governor's mansion in 1860 but went on to win a U.S. Senate seat in 1863. In the Republican-dominated Senate, Hendricks continued to speak out against harsh Reconstruction measures. He was one of the 19 senators to oppose Andrew Johnson's impeachment. He attacked the Republicans for instituting a military draft and imposing heavy taxes to support the war effort. Like many other Democrats of his time, he opposed the 14th Amendment, which gave blacks citizenship rights, and claimed that the black slave was inferior and "that no good would come out of his freedom." He made a second run in 1868 for the governor's office, but failed by fewer than 1,000 votes. Four years later, he was successful, becoming the first Democratic governor in a northern state after the Civil War. While governor, he was nominated as Samuel Tilden's running mate in the 1876 presidential election. Nominated again in 1880 as Grover Cleveland's running mate, he was installed as vice president in March 1885. But he died within eight months of taking office, on November 25, 1885. He presided over only a single session of the Senate.

SEE ALSO Grover Cleveland

BIBLIOGRAPHY

Holcombe, John W., and Hubert M. Skinner. *Life and Public Service of Thomas A. Hendricks.* Indianapolis: Carlon and Hollenbeck, 1886.

HUBERT HUMPHREY

Hubert Horatio Humphrey Jr. was born in Wallace, South Dakota (population 600), on May 27, 1911. He was raised in Doland, South Dakota. He attended the Capitol College of Pharmacy in Denver, Colorado (he worked as a pharmacist on and off throughout his life), the University of Minnesota (earning an undergraduate degree in political science), and Louisiana State University (where he received a master's degree in political science and worked on a doctorate in the same field).

While Humphrey was an undergraduate, his interest in politics thrived. Continued studies at the graduate level only enhanced his love of the political world. He put his theoretical knowledge (and his graduate school friends) to work in the real world of politics when he was elected mayor of Minneapolis in 1945. Humphrey's margin of victory was larger than any other in the city's history.

In 1948 Humphrey was elected to the U.S. Senate. This was a large accomplishment considering that

Minnesota had never before sent a Democrat to the Senate and the fact that Humphrey was the only member of the Democratic Party to be elected from the Midwest. Reelected in 1954, he ran for another Senate term in 1960, in addition to seeking the 1960 Democratic presidential nomination. While Humphrey lost the presidential nomination, he was returned to the Senate by an overwhelming margin.

This was Humphrey's most productive time in the Senate. He served as majority whip and as an influential member of the Foreign Relations Committee and the Armed Services Committee during the Cuban missile crisis. He advised President Kennedy as the Soviets increased their pressure on Berlin.

Many Humphrey proposals were key components of Kennedy's New Frontier programs, including the Peace Corps, which Humphrey had proposed in 1957, when it was dismissed as unworkable. Humphrey, a long-term believer in civil rights, took the initiative and pushed civil rights legislation to the forefront of the national political agenda in the early 1960s.

Following the Kennedy assassination, President Lyndon Johnson teamed with Humphrey in the Senate to pass the most comprehensive piece of civil rights

Hubert Humphrey. *Source:* Library of Congress.

legislation in history. Humphrey called the passage of the Civil Rights Act in 1964 his "greatest achievement."

President Johnson selected Humphrey as his vice presidential running mate. On January 20, 1965, Humphrey became the 38th vice president of the United States, filling an office that had stood vacant for 13 months. The Johnson–Humphrey ticket lost the 1968 election, in large part because of their failure to live up to their campaign promise to stay out of the war in Vietnam.

Humphrey was reelected to the Senate in 1970 and was defeated by George McGovern in his bid for the 1972 Democratic presidential nomination. In 1976, Humphrey was elected to a fourth Senate term. He served as an adviser to President Carter in both domestic affairs and foreign policy matters.

Humphrey's health declined rapidly in the mid-1970s. He lapsed into a coma and died on January 13, 1978, at the age of 66.

Kimberly J. Pace

SEE ALSO Lyndon Johnson

BIBLIOGRAPHY

Humphrey, Hubert H. *The Education of a Public Man: My Life and Politics*. Garden City, NY: Doubleday, 1976.

Solberg, Carl. *Hubert Humphrey: A Biography*. New York: Norton, 1984.

RICHARD M. JOHNSON

The ninth vice president of the United States, Richard Mentor Johnson had a number of firsts. He was the first vice president to be elected by the U.S. Senate and the first native Kentuckian to be elected to the Kentucky legislature, the U.S. House of Representatives and the Senate, and the vice presidency. Johnson was born October 17, 1781, in the frontier settlement of Beargrass, now Louisville, Kentucky. He was admitted to the Kentucky bar in 1802 and established a lucrative legal practice. His political career began in 1802 when he was elected to the Kentucky legislature, followed by election as a Democrat at the age of 26 to the House of Representatives in 1804. As a War Hawk and member of the House Military Affairs Committee, Johnson supported the War of 1812 against Great Britain. When hostilities broke out, he took leave of his legislative duties and organized and commanded a voluntary regiment of Kentucky Riflemen. He was seriously wounded on the Canadian border in the Battle of the Thames, during which he reputedly killed the Indian chief and British ally Tecumseh. The claim, of course, made him a U.S. military hero and helped advance his political career. Johnson resigned his seat in the House

Richard M. Johnson. *Source:* Library of Congress.

in 1819, but was elevated to the Senate by the Kentucky legislature. Defeated for reelection in 1829, he returned to the House in 1829, where he remained for the next eight years. As a senator and representative, Johnson's fortunes were on the ascendant because of his role as Andrew Jackson's staunchest ally and confidant. Both men shared a common frontier and military background. Jackson used Johnson as his agent on various delicate personal missions, such as the Eaton Affair, and, in turn, Johnson defended Jackson in Congress for the invasion of Florida during the Seminole War of 1818. He also supported the president in his tariff policies and opposed rechartering the Bank of the United States. He also supported a number of progressive legislative measures, such as military pensions, government-sponsored education, and abolition of imprisonment for debt. He played an active role in the establishment of George Washington University and other institutions. Johnson was rewarded for his loyal support when Jackson hand-picked him as Martin Van Buren's running mate. Johnson campaigned on the slogan "Rumpsey, dumpsey, Colonel Johnson killed Tecumseh," and he toured the country displaying his battle scars. Unable to secure a majority of the votes in the electoral college, Johnson became the first vice president to be elected by the Senate. Toward the latter part of his life, he fell into disfavor with some voters because he kept a mulatto slave woman as his mistress. Johnson was not renominated in 1840. He returned to Kentucky in 1841 and served one more term in the state legislature before passing away on November 19, 1850.

SEE ALSO Martin Van Buren

BIBLIOGRAPHY

Emmons, William. *Authentic Biography of Colonel Richard M. Johnson of Kentucky*. New York: H. Mason, 1833.

Meyer, Leland Winfield. *The Life and Times of Colonel Richard M. Johnson of Kentucky*. New York: Columbia University Press, 1932.

WILLIAM RUFUS DE VANE KING

William Rufus de Vane King was born on April 7, 1786, in Sampson County, North Carolina, and graduated from the University of North Carolina. He was admitted to the bar in 1806 and elected to Congress in 1810. As a representative, he sided with the War Hawks in the War of 1812. King resigned from the House in 1816 to serve in the diplomatic service, as secretary to the U.S. legations in Naples and St. Petersburg. Returning from abroad, he was elected as the first U.S. senator from Alabama in 1819. He served in the Senate until 1844, when President Tyler appointed him minister to France, where he remained for two years. He regained his Senate seat in 1848. As a political moderate, he supported the Compromise of 1850 and worked for the ratification of the Clayton–Bulwer Treaty, which ensured U.S. participation in any Central American canal. He was one the prime backers of James Buchanan, but when Franklin Pierce won the nomination on the 49th ballot in 1852, King was placed on the ticket as his running mate. Although Pierce won the election, King was a sick man by the time of the inauguration. On medical advice he went to Havana, Cuba, to seek a dry climate to heal his tuberculosis. There, by special act of Congress, he was permitted to take the oath of office on March 4, 1853, the only vice president to do so in U.S. history. He returned to Alabama, where he died on April 18, 1853. He had been vice president for just 25 days. King never married, and his sharing of living quarters with Buchanan gave rise to rumors that he was a homosexual. He was also noted for his wig and fastidious dress, which earned him the nickname "Miss Nancy."

SEE ALSO Franklin Pierce

THOMAS R. MARSHALL

Thomas Riley Marshall is remembered less for the fact that he was vice president for eight years (1913–1921) than for his remark that "what this country needs is a really good five-cent cigar." Born in North Manchester, Indiana, on March 14, 1854, Marshall graduated from Wabash College in 1873. He was admitted to the bar in 1875 and established a lucrative legal practice. Although he had not sought any major public office until he was 54, he won his first election as governor of Indiana. The Republican Party was bitterly divided over the Prohibition issue and thus Marshall was able to win with a big majority in a conservative state. He opposed Prohibition and capital punishment and pushed important social and prolabor legislation. Marshall planned to leave politics in 1912 because the Indiana constitution barred him from succeeding himself, but, fortunately, he was nominated as Woodrow Wilson's running mate in 1912. The Republican rift of that year led to the first Democratic presidential victory in the twentieth century. Wilson and Marshall managed to stay together for the next eight years. Describing himself as a "progressive with the brakes on," Marshall presented a self-deprecating and pragmatic image. He resisted attempts to become an acting president when Wilson was stricken with illness. At the end of his second term, Marshall retired to Indiana where he published his *Recollections*, a collection of homey anecdotes. He died some months later, on June 1, 1925.

SEE ALSO Woodrow Wilson

BIBLIOGRAPHY

Marshall, Thomas. *Recollections of Thomas R. Marshall, Vice President and Hoosier Philosopher: A Hoosier Salad*. Indianapolis: Bobbs-Merrill, 1925.

Thomas, Charles Marlon. *Thomas Riley Marshall, Hoosier Statesman*. Oxford, OH: Mississippi Valley Press, 1939.

WALTER F. MONDALE

Walter Frederick "Fritz" Mondale (b. January 5, 1928, Ceylon, Minnesota) has had many jobs during his life, but he is probably best remembered as Jimmy Carter's vice president (1977–1981). He has also been a practicing attorney, attorney general of Minnesota (appointed and later elected to the post), U.S. senator (appointed when Hubert Humphrey became vice president and elected twice thereafter), and ambassador to Japan. Mondale tried unsuccessfully to capture the presidency himself in 1984; a bid for a second term as vice president in the 1980 election was also unsuccessful. Mondale had himself sought the 1976 presidential nomination, withdrawing from the race in November 1974. When Mondale withdrew, he indicated that he lacked the heart, and perhaps the stomach, for the grueling campaign grind.

Mondale's aptness for the job was not immediately apparent to presidential aspirant Jimmy Carter, although Mondale was the first one Carter asked to be his running mate and was nominated on the first ballot by the Democratic National Convention. Carter has indicated that he did not give much thought to who would be his running mate while running for the nomination, but if forced to make a choice, it probably would have been either Senator Henry M. Jackson of Washington or Senator Frank Church of Idaho. Since these two men had been among Carter's opponents for the nomination, he knew their positions well, and they were compatible.

Mondale was among many men Carter interviewed as prospective vice presidential candidates. In addition to Mondale, Senators Edmund Muskie and John Glenn were interviewed at Carter's home in Plains, Georgia; Representative Peter Rodino and Senators Church, Jackson, and Adlai Stevenson III were interviewed in New York City. All indicated a willingness to serve except Rodino, who requested not to be considered because his wife was in poor health.

Leading candidates were also asked to fill out a lengthy questionnaire. Mondale's indicated a tax audit, which he suspected, but could not prove, resulted from his having been on President Richard M. Nixon's "enemies list." It indicated very little else, other than that Mondale's family and financial background were stable.

One of the purposes of the questionnaire was to avoid an experience like 1972, in which it was generally believed that Democratic nominee George McGovern had failed to ask questions that could have uncovered the fact that his first running mate, Thomas Eagleton, had been voluntarily hospitalized several times for nervous exhaustion. By the time Eagleton was replaced by R. Sargent Shriver, McGovern had said of Eagleton, "I'm behind him one thousand percent." This led to public questioning of McGovern's credibility, which haunted him throughout the campaign.

Mondale's reputation was as a liberal: "a hardnosed dreamer" was the oxymoronic label the *New York Times* used for him. As attorney general of Minnesota and as a U.S. senator, he was known as a champion of the poor. He had fought for the right to public counsel for poor defendants in Minnesota, child nutrition, Indian education, and open housing. The selec-

tion of Mondale as a running mate made many Republicans, including President Gerald Ford, think that they could successfully attack Jimmy Carter as a "liberal" during the campaign.

Mondale's selection provided the ticket with several kinds of balance. Carter was a southerner, while Mondale was a northerner. Carter was a peanut farmer, while Mondale was a lawyer. Carter was an outsider, while Mondale, as a senator, had extensive experience inside the Washington beltway. Mondale was more liberal than Carter and so could assuage some members of the party who knew very little about their presidential nominee and did not like what they did know. On the other hand, the clear differences between Carter and Mondale—for instance, on the death penalty (Carter was a proponent, Mondale an opponent)— were not such as would keep the two men from working together. The selection, though, did not provide every kind of balance. Both men were Protestants, which led Carter to consider the potential advantages of instead running with Edmund Muskie, a Catholic.

Additionally, the selection of Mondale could satisfy several key Democratic constituencies that the nomination of Carter did not. Mondale was considered a friend of organized labor (including the United Auto Workers and the American Federation of Labor and Congress of Industrial Organizations). He was also respected by leaders of major Jewish organizations, while many felt that they could not trust Carter. And Mondale had strong civil rights credentials, which could satisfy many of those worried about the white southerner Carter.

In accepting the nomination at the Democratic National Convention in New York City, Mondale issued five pledges: truth, open government, efficiency, protection from our enemies, and an end to paralysis in democracy. The crowd applauded more loudly, however, when he attacked the incumbent president, Gerald Ford, "who pardoned the person [responsible for] the worst scandal in American history."

Mondale played a very active role in the 1976 campaign, criticizing the Ford administration for not caring and not being effective. Since Mondale was just 48 during the campaign (and Carter was 51), his relative youth was an advantage. Most observers thought that his televised debate with the Republican vice presidential nominee, Robert Dole, was either a victory for Mondale or a tie.

During and after the campaign, the fact that Mondale was not a member of the "Georgia mafia" that surrounded Carter was both an advantage and a disadvantage to Carter. People like Hamilton Jordan, Jody Powell, and Bert Lance could call upon their familiarity with Carter from Georgia days. That same familiarity, though, made the Georgians suspect to many northerners, while Mondale was not suspect.

Carter and Mondale intended for the latter to be an active vice president. He was given regular access to security briefings and often asked to perform tasks that Carter would have done himself if he could have been in two places at once. Often these were tasks involving international travel. Other tasks could be handled in Washington, D.C., but involved foreign policy matters. Given President Carter's consultative style, Mondale's opinion was often sought. He got along well personally with the president and so was sometimes the only non-Georgian trusted to provide candid political advice.

Partly with Mondale's influence, the country moved closer to China in early 1978. He had volunteered to take a trip to that country representing U.S. interests—a trip that was eventually taken by National Security Adviser Zbigniew Brzezinski.

Mondale contributed to the administration's giving greater attention to Africa than previous administrations had done. During a visit to South Africa, he angered whites with comments that were prescient in hindsight when he urged adoption of the "one man, one vote" principle. Mondale also visited Nigeria, which reflected the administration's desire not to ignore Africa on the American foreign policy agenda.

In early July 1979, President Carter abruptly canceled a scheduled energy speech. Mondale was among those who objected to the indecisiveness and urged that if something was wrong, incompatible cabinet members should be replaced. As a result of complaints about inconsistent policies, the secretary of energy, James Schlesinger, secretary of the treasury, Michael Blumenthal, and secretary of health, education, and welfare, Joseph Califano, resigned and were replaced.

One of the most controversial issues of the administration was the negotiation and ratification of the Panama Canal Treaty. Mondale's role in getting his former colleagues in the Senate to vote for ratification was vital. As President Carter wrote in his diary for March 14, 1978: "Fritz will be working full-time . . . personally with members of the Senate."

Certainly one of the proudest moments for the Carter administration was the signing of the Camp David Accords in September 1978. Mondale's role was both in negotiating the accords and in soothing the feelings of diverse constituencies in their aftermath.

As Carter and Mondale were campaigning for reelection in 1980, the Carter administration instituted a grain embargo against the Soviet Union as a response to that country's invasion of Afghanistan. Mondale ve-

hemently disagreed with the embargo. He also disagreed with the registration of young men for the draft. He nevertheless defended an administration position with which he disagreed many times during the campaign.

The last year of the Carter–Mondale administration was dominated by relations with Iran. Mondale was clearly "in the loop": along with the president, Secretary of State Cyrus Vance, and National Security Adviser Zbigniew Brzezinski, he was notified of every new development. Mondale expressed a preference that Shah Reza Pahlavi be taken from Mexico to Egypt for medical treatment, and not to the United States, as the Shah was (before he went to Panama). When hostages were taken at the U.S. Embassy in Teheran, and the United States attempted a rescue mission, Mondale advocated a maximum of secrecy and a minimum of notice. President Carter agreed with him; Secretary of State Cyrus Vance, who later resigned, was at the opposite pole.

Largely due to the influence of his wife, Joan, the vice president became an unofficial ambassador to the arts. This involved patronizing leading museums in the United States and abroad. In this, Mondale was returning to his childhood love of the arts. Walter and Joan Mondale were the parents of three children, teenagers during the campaign.

In personality, Mondale was quiet and thoughtful. This probably contributed to his effectiveness as vice president because President Carter would solicit his opinion and listen to it when it was offered. It also contributed to Mondale's respect in the Senate, of which he was once a member, and over which he presided as vice president.

In the 1976 election, during the Carter administration, and afterward, Mondale enjoyed more popularity than President Carter. Even in areas where his liberal ideology was unpopular, he was viewed as articulate and effective.

The Democrats nominated President Carter and Vice President Mondale to serve a second term. In accepting the nomination, Mondale voiced the human rights theme with which Carter is more often associated. In referring to his travels to the Middle East and Africa, Mondale declared: "Above all, above all, America's strength depends on American values."

The speech hit themes that Mondale had emphasized both during the 1976 campaign and during his career as a senator. He had criticized arms sales around the world and U.S. policies in Chile (including the overthrow of Salvador Allende) and Angola as not reflecting America's values.

By 1980, the country had turned more conservative, and the Republican ticket of Ronald Reagan and

George Bush defeated the Carter–Mondale ticket. Reagan and Bush succeeded in associating Democratic leaders, including Carter and Mondale, with "big government" and naïveté toward adversaries in the global arena.

The big defeat of the Carter–Mondale ticket indicated to many people that the Democratic Party was in trouble. Mondale was widely considered a potential choice for the chairmanship of the Democratic National Committee, a position he did not want. Because he was still relatively young when he left the vice presidency (Mondale could not yet even draw a government pension), he became an active and articulate commentator on foreign and domestic issues.

In the 1984 election, Mondale captured the top spot on the Democratic ticket, but he had no better luck. He and his running mate, Geraldine Ferraro, were badly defeated by Reagan and Bush. President Reagan was very popular, and the world *liberalism*, with which Mondale was associated, had negative connotations for many of the American people.

Prior to the United States' 1989 invasion of Panama, Mondale advocated in a newspaper column that a condition of the American aid be that the Panamanian military be placed under civilian control. This was very consistent with policies advocated during his vice presidency: Mondale always tended to look for more peaceful alternatives to military action.

By 1993, a Democrat, Bill Clinton, was again in the White House. By that time, Walter Mondale was revered as a "senior statesman." So when Mondale was nominated to be ambassador to Japan, the choice was welcomed by both Americans and Japanese.

Thus, Mondale is known both for serving his country well as an active vice president and for an active career in Minnesota, U.S., and international politics.

Arthur Blaser

SEE ALSO Jimmy Carter

BIBLIOGRAPHY

Carter, Jimmy. *Keeping Faith*. Toronto: Bantam Books, 1982.

Gillon, Steven M. *Walter F. Mondale and the Liberal Legacy.* New York: Columbia University Press, 1992.

Lewis, Finlay. *Mondale: Portrait of an American Politician*. New York: Harper and Row, 1980.

Republican National Committee. *Vice-President Malaise, Twenty Years of Walter Mondale: 1984 Mondale Fact Book.* Washington, DC: Republican National Committee, 1984.

ADLAI STEVENSON

Born in Christian County, Kentucky, in 1835, Adlai Ewing Stevenson established a dynasty of political lead-

Adlai Stevenson. *Source:* Library of Congress.

ers. The son of a planter, he attended Centre College in Kentucky and studied law in Illinois before being admitted to the bar in 1858. His first campaign was for Stephen A. Douglas against Abraham Lincoln in 1858 and 1860; later, he served as George McClellan's elector in 1864. He won his first congressional seat in 1874 in a heavily Republican district, lost it in 1876, and regained it in 1868. By this time, he had become identified as a leading soft-money and low-tariff Democrat. In 1885 Grover Cleveland appointed him as first assistant postmaster, in which capacity he removed 40,000 Republican postmasters and replaced them with Democrats. For this act, he earned the nickname "The Headsman" and the implacable hostility of Republicans. In 1892 he headed the Illinois delegation to the Democratic National Convention, where he was nominated as vice president to balance the ticket headed by Cleveland. As vice president, he was a good presiding officer of the Senate but not a close ally of the president. He was again the vice presidential choice on William Jennings Bryan's unsuccessful ticket in 1900 and lost his last election for governor of Illinois in 1908. He died on June 14, 1914.

SEE ALSO Grover Cleveland

HENRY A. WALLACE

Henry A. Wallace was born in Adair County, Iowa, on October 7, 1888. Active in agricultural research and reform, he was also a prominent, controversial politician who served as secretary of agriculture, secretary of commerce, and vice president. Wallace ran unsuccessfully for president in 1948.

Wallace came from a family of farm journalists, and he began his career in agriculture, attending Iowa State College and receiving a B.S. in agriculture in 1910. He wrote for the family paper, *Wallace's Farmer*, and engaged in research on plant genetics, developing the first commercial high-yield hybrid corn. His father was a Republican and served as secretary of agriculture from 1921 until his death in 1924. Disillusioned by Republican policies toward hard-pressed midwestern farmers, Wallace became a Democrat after his father's death and was appointed secretary of agriculture by Franklin D. Roosevelt in 1933.

Wallace presided over New Deal programs that attempted to aid the hard-hit midwestern farmers during the depression. He supported commodity prices and other assistance for farmers through his involvement in the Agricultural Adjustment Administration.

Henry A. Wallace. *Source:* Library of Congress.

Wallace was selected as FDR's running mate in 1940, but he served only one term as vice president (1941–1945). In 1944 the Democratic Party, bowing to an increasingly conservative Congress and concerned with wartime affairs, shifted toward the right and refused to renominate the liberal Wallace in favor of the more moderate Harry S. Truman. Roosevelt appointed Wallace secretary of commerce in January 1945, but he became one of the earliest victims of the emerging Cold War when, in September 1946, Truman fired him from this position for publicly criticizing the administration's hard-line policy toward the USSR. Wallace had said in a speech that the Russians were trying to "socialize their sphere of interest just as we try to democratize our sphere of interest. . . . Only mutual trust would allow the United States and Russia to live together peacefully, and such trust could not be created by an unfriendly attitude and policy."

In the 1948 Democratic primaries, Wallace ran against Truman. When he failed to secure the nomination over the incumbent, he broke away from the Democratic Party and, along with a few left-wing leaders, formed the Progressive Party. Running for president as a Progressive, Wallace advocated extensive social reform and friendship with the Soviet Union. Wallace was an easy target for anticommunist rhetoric, however, and his opponents, who included many liberal reformers, had little trouble derailing his campaign by branding him a dupe of Russia. He received no electoral votes and only slightly more than a million popular votes.

Afterward, Wallace seemed to take a right turn himself, leaving the Progressive Party in 1950 when it refused to support the Korean War and, two years later, publishing a book entitled *Why I Was Wrong*, which sharply criticized the policies of the Soviet Union and explained his new distrust of that nation. Wallace took no further active part in electoral politics, thereafter dedicating his life to agricultural research. He died November 18, 1965.

Jack J. Miller

SEE ALSO Franklin Delano Roosevelt

Losing Presidential Candidates

WILLIAM JENNINGS BRYAN

William Jennings Bryan was born in Salem, Illinois, on March 19, 1860. He graduated from Illinois College and Union Law School and practiced law for four

William Jennings Bryan Tired During the 1896 Campaign. *Source:* United Press International.

years before moving to Lincoln, Nebraska, in 1887. Bryan became a dynamic speaker for the agrarian movement during the populist revolt and won election to Congress in 1890 and again in 1892.

Bryan became popular in Congress among free-silver Democrats. At the Democratic National Convention in 1896, Bryan served on the Platform Committee and riveted the delegates with his "Cross of Gold" speech urging the free coinage of silver. This speech won him the presidential nomination of both the Democratic Party and the Populist Party. Bryan agreed with populist views that government should protect individuals and the democratic process against monopolistic corporations. His concern for the working people earned him the moniker "The Great Commoner."

His 1896 campaign was a turning point within the Democratic Party away from a Jacksonian-style interest in minimal government and toward a positive view of government as a tool to protect citizens. Bryan's campaign was an energetic nationwide speaking tour in which he appealed to farmers and workers against the high-tariff policies of William McKinley. He was defeated by a majority of fewer than 600,000 votes

from a total return of almost 14 million. He ran again against McKinley in 1900 on an anti-imperialist ticket, strongly attacking McKinley's policies in the Philippines. However, McKinley was able to turn the prosperity of America into the winning issue for the election, defeating Bryan by a wide margin.

Bryan had become a dominant figure in Democratic politics and continued to speak on issues such as his opposition to U.S. expansionism and the dangers of corporate monopolies. He founded his own newspaper, *The Commoner,* in Lincoln, Nebraska, in 1901 and used it as a platform for his political ideas. Bryan stayed out of the convention spotlight in 1904, when conservatives controlled the Democratic National Convention, but returned in 1908 to run against William Howard Taft. The slogan of his campaign was "Shall the People Rule?" Taft defeated Bryan.

Bryan used his party influence to help Woodrow Wilson gain the Democratic nomination in 1912, and after Wilson was elected, he made Bryan his secretary of state. Bryan was committed, like Wilson, to neutrality when the European war broke out in 1914. However, he went beyond Wilson by actually advocating restrictions on American citizens and companies to prevent them from drawing the nation into war. When Wilson objected in writing to Germany's sinking of the *Lusitania*, Bryan resigned from office because he could not approve of a message that he felt would draw the United States into the war.

After his resignation, Bryan worked for Prohibition, peace, and woman suffrage. In 1925 he sided with legislators and joined the prosecution in the trial of John Scopes, a schoolteacher charged with violating Tennessee State law by teaching evolution. Clarence Darrow, Scopes's lawyer, actually put Bryan on the witness stand to reveal his ignorance of science. Five days after the trial ended, on July 26, Bryan died.

Jessamyn West

LEWIS CASS

Born October 9, 1782, in Exeter, New Hampshire, Lewis Cass was educated at Phillips Exeter Academy. After studying law, he established a law practice in Marietta, Ohio. His political career began in 1806 when at the age of 24 he was elected to the Ohio legislature as a Jeffersonian Democrat. His opposition to the western plans of Aaron Burr drew the attention of Thomas Jefferson, who appointed Cass marshal for Ohio. Thereafter his rise was swift. Decorated for valor in the War of 1812, he was governor of Michigan Territory from 1813 to 1831, secretary of war under Andrew

Jackson from 1831 to 1836, minister to France in 1836, and senator from Michigan from 1845 to 1848. As governor of Michigan he was responsible for important treaties with Indians resulting in large acquisitions of land. As Jackson's secretary, he supported the president in the South Carolina nullification crisis and carried out the program of expelling all eastern Indian tribes to territories west of Mississippi. As a senator, he pushed for the occupation of Mexico, supported war with Great Britain over Oregon, and backed the Compromise of 1850 and the Kansas–Nebraska Act of 1854. He first sought the presidential nomination in 1844 against Martin Van Buren. He made a second attempt in 1847, advocating the notion of popular sovereignty by which each territory would decide the slavery question for itself. This position gained him the nickname "Doughface," a northern man with southern principles, and enabled him to secure the Democratic nomination in 1848. But the Democrats split before the elections, with disgruntled Democrats known as Backburners joining antislavery Conscience Whigs to back Martin Van Buren on the Free Soil ticket. As a result of this split, the Democrats lost. Cass lost his Senate seat in 1856 but was appointed by James Buchanan in 1857 as his secretary of state. Three years later, Cass resigned to protest Buchanan's waffling over the slavery issue and his inability to control the secessionists. The specific occasion for Cass's resignation was Buchanan's refusal to reinforce the forts at Charleston, South Carolina. Cass remained an ardent supporter of the Union during the Civil War. He was the author of several articles and books on Indian, western, and military themes.

BIBLIOGRAPHY

Woodford, Frank B. *Lewis Cass: The Last Jeffersonian.* New York: Octagon Books, 1973.

JAMES MIDDLETON COX

James Middleton Cox—publisher, governor of Ohio, and United States presidential candidate—was born in Jacksonburg, Ohio, on March 31, 1870. Cox left high school at 15 but, with tutoring from his brother-in-law, passed the examination for a teaching certificate. He taught school for a few years and then went to work at his brother-in-law's newspaper, the *Middleton Signal.* An impressive reporter, he was offered a job in 1892 with the *Cincinnati Enquirer.* Cox left the paper and became the private secretary to the newly elected congressman Paul Sorg. Sorg did not win reelection but did help Cox purchase the *Dayton Daily News* in 1896.

For ten years Cox built his newspaper business and expanded into radio.

Though successful at business, Cox decided to enter politics again and in 1908 was elected to the United States House of Representatives from Dayton as a progressive Democrat. He was reelected in 1910 but stepped down in 1912 to run successfully for governor of Ohio. As governor, Cox initiated school reform, workers' compensation and the minimum wage. In 1913, during massive flooding of the Ohio River, Cox was awarded the Red Cross Gold Medal of Merit for his swift and efficient action as executive. Cox was defeated in 1914 but won consecutive terms in 1916 and 1918.

In 1920 Cox decided that, as governor of a key electoral state, he would have a good chance to win the presidency. At the Democratic National Convention in San Francisco that year, he was nominated after 44 ballots and selected Franklin Roosevelt as his running mate. During the campaign Cox advocated a universalist role for the United States in world affairs and argued that the country should join the League of Na-

James Middleton Cox. *Source:* Library of Congress.

tions. His universalist approach to world involvement did not play well with voters tired of war and overseas commitments. Cox lost to Harding by the electoral margin of 404 to 127. After the defeat, Cox never ran for election again. In 1933 he accepted an appointment from President Roosevelt as a delegate to the London World Monetary and Economic Conference. He refused offers for all other positions, including head of the Federal Reserve and several ambassadorships. Cox retired to private life in 1934 and concentrated on building his business. By the time of his death, on July 15, 1957, he owned newspapers, radio stations and television stations in Ohio, Georgia and Florida.

Daniel Stanhagen

JOHN WILLIAM DAVIS

John William Davis was born in Clarksburg, West Virginia, on April 13, 1873, the son of John James Davis, member of the House of Representatives from 1871 to 1875. He graduated from Washington and Lee

John William Davis. *Source:* Library of Congress.

University in West Virginia in 1892, studied law, and was admitted to the bar in 1895. His political career began with his election to the Virginia House of Delegates in 1899 and to the U.S. House of Representatives in 1910. He left the House in 1913 to become Woodrow Wilson's solicitor general, serving with distinction in that post until 1919 when Wilson named him ambassador to the Court of St. James. When Republicans captured the White House in 1920, Davis joined a prominent Wall Street law firm in 1921 and became known as a high-profile corporate lawyer. The high point of his career was his selection as presidential candidate on the 103rd ballot in the hotly contested Democratic nomination of 1924. A probusiness conservative, he was alarmed by the New Deal and gravitated toward the Republican Party, supporting Alfred Landon and other Republican candidates after 1936.

BIBLIOGRAPHY
Harbaugh, William H. *Lawyer's Lawyer: The Life of John W. Davis.* New York: Oxford University Press, 1973.

STEPHEN A. DOUGLAS

Born in Brandon, Vermont, on April 23, 1813, Stephen Arnold Douglas received only a rudimentary education. After attending the Canandaigua Academy in Ontario County in New York and briefly studying law, he migrated to the West, settling in Winchester, Illinois, where he conducted a school. Elected state's attorney for the first judicial district, he helped to build the Democratic Party in Illinois and was elected as a Democrat to the state legislature. In 1840 he was appointed secretary of state and subsequently a judge in the state supreme court. His national political career began with his election to the House of Representatives in 1843 and to the U.S. Senate in 1847. As chairman of the Senate Committee on Territories he was in the center of a whirling storm of controversy regarding the extension of slavery, and he helped the passage of compromise bills establishing territorial governments in Utah and New Mexico in 1850. In the debates on the Kansas–Nebraska Bill of 1854, he originated the phrase with which he is clearly associated, "popular sovereignty." Under this principle, settlers in these territories were granted the right to decide on the slavery issue. Opposition to this bill stemmed from its repeal of the Missouri Compromise, outlawing slavery in the Louisiana Purchase territory. The Kansas–Nebraska Bill is notable as the triggering event for the formation of the Republican Party. The struggle for

Stephen A. Douglas. *Source:* Library of Congress.

Kansas between the proslavery faction and the antislavery faction dominated national politics for most of the 1850s. Despite his concession on the issue of outlawing slavery, Douglas took an uncompromising stand against the admission of Kansas as a state under the proslavery Lecompton Constitution. It signaled his break with the southern Democrats, a breach that was never healed. Over Douglas's opposition, Congress passed a compromise measure, the English Bill, which offered land grants to Kansans to persuade them to approve the Lecompton Constitution. In 1858, running for the U.S. Senate, he conducted his seven famous debates with Abraham Lincoln, which brought the latter to national attention although Douglas won the election. His positions alienated him further from the southern Democrats. At one point Horace Greeley even proposed that Douglas should ally with the new Republican Party. The highlight of his career was his nomination as the Democratic presidential candidate in the fateful election of 1860, in a second convention at Baltimore that was boycotted by the southern Democrats, who had withdrawn from the first deadlocked convention at Charleston. In the four-way race that followed, Douglas came second in popular vote,

gaining support from every state in the Union, but he gained only 12 electoral college votes from Missouri and New Jersey. After his loss, Douglas continued to work for the preservation of the Union. Upon the outbreak of the Civil War, he threw his full support behind Lincoln, but died on June 3, 1861, shortly after the firing on Fort Sumter. Only 5 feet 4 inches tall, he was known affectionately as the "Little Giant" and "Steam Engine in Britches."

BIBLIOGRAPHY

Johanssen, Robert W. *Stephen Arnold Douglas*. New York: Oxford University Press, 1973.

MICHAEL DUKAKIS

Michael Stanley Dukakis was born November 3, 1933, of Greek American parents. His father was the first Greek American to graduate from Harvard Medical School. When Dukakis was a child, his family moved to Brookline, an affluent suburb of Boston. He graduated from Swarthmore in 1955 and, following military service in Korea from 1955 to 1957, earned his law degree at Harvard Law School in 1960. His political career began with his election as the first Democrat in the Brookline town council, followed by an eight-year stint in the Massachusetts House of Representatives from 1963 to 1971. There he gained public attention for the introduction of no-fault automobile insurance. After leaving the legislature in 1971, he served for two years as moderator on Public Television's "The

Michael Dukakis and Lloyd Bentsen. *Source:* Library of Congress.

Advocates." Gaining statewide visibility on television, he was able to win election as governor in 1974. As governor, he represented a new breed of compassionate technocrats, on the one hand socially conscious, liberal, sensitive about women's and minority rights and environment friendly, and on the other fiscally conservative and prudent. His innate honesty led him to fight the kind of patronage and corruption and compromise associated with old-time politicians. As a result, the state budget, which had shown a deficit of over $500 million when he entered office, had a surplus of $200 million at the end of his term. But his much-vaunted competence came across as arrogance for many voters, and he lost his reelection primary in 1978. The four years of political wilderness that followed were used by Dukakis in a serious effort to change both his image and his tactics. Teaching at Harvard's Kennedy School of Government, he learned the value of cultivating political connections and allies. This helped him to recapture the governor's mansion in 1982. Fortunately, Massachusetts was entering a period of growth based on high technology, and he claimed credit as the author of the so-called Massachusetts Miracle. The mix of social liberalism and fiscal conservatism made him the idol of many progressive Democrats, and he was able to wrest the Democratic nomination in 1988 after outlasting seven plodding rivals. Early in the campaign he led President George Bush in the polls, but a series of negative attacks by the Republican strategists, led by Lee Atwater, whittled down this lead fairly rapidly. Further, Dukakis projected an image on television and in the media that was not calculated to arouse enthusiasm, and his apparent arrogance and technocratic mind-set came across as liabilities in a fast-paced campaign. He tried at first to disassociate himself from the liberal wing of the party by selecting the centrist Lloyd Bentsen as his running mate, but later the revelation that Dukakis was a card-carrying member of the American Civil Liberties Union had the opposite effect. The Republicans used the story of Willie Horton—a convict furloughed by Dukakis who committed another gruesome murder—to portray Dukakis as soft on crime. Unemotional and detached by nature, Dukakis tried to ignore these attacks until it was too late. In the last two weeks of the campaign, he tried to hit back in kind, drawing on old-time populist rhetoric, telling crowds, "I'm on your side." The resounding Republican victory in November 1988 was seen by Democrats as the result of a bungled campaign. The aftermath was particularly bitter for Dukakis, whose popularity plummeted even in Massachusetts. The economic miracle on which he had staked his campaign soon evaporated, and his personal life was touched by the tragedy of his wife's alcoholism and attempted suicide.

BIBLIOGRAPHY

Gaines, Richard, and Michael Segal. *Dukakis: The Man Who Would Be President*. New York: Avon, 1987.
Kenney, Charles. *Dukakis: An American Odyssey*. Boston: Houghton Mifflin, 1988.

HORACE GREELEY

Born in Amherst, New Hampshire, on February 3, 1811, Horace Greeley's formal education ended when he was apprenticed to the local print shop of the *Northern Spectator* in East Poultney, Vermont, at the age of 14. In 1831 he moved to New York City in search of typesetting work. He worked his way up from printer to reporter to publisher. In 1834, with Jonas Winchester as partner, he established a weekly, the *New Yorker*, in which he advised the unemployed to go West, later popularized in the phrase attributed to him, "Go West, young man, go West." An active Whig, he began editing in 1838 the weekly *Jeffersonian*, and three years later founded the Whig party's weekly newspaper, *Log Cabin*. His success as an editor led him to borrow money and found the *New York Tribune* in 1841. Within a decade, the *Tribune* became widely read with a national circulation exceeding 300,000 by 1861. A social reformer by instinct, Greeley used his paper as a forum to advocate a variety of causes including Fourierism, spiritualism, homesteadism, the abolition of capital punishment, and the establishment of copyright. His many crusades raised his moral stature among the educated, and he became a national figure. Among his staff members were such luminaries as Charles A. Dana, Margaret Fuller, George Ripley, and Bayard Taylor. Greeley also worked the lecture circuit, which increased his visibility. His radical opposition to slavery led him to join the Republican Party, which he was among the first to propose as a replacement for the Whigs. He was present at the national meeting in Philadelphia in 1856, when the party was born, and was one of Lincoln's earliest supporters. Although an extremist at the outbreak of the Civil War, and later favoring the passage of the 14th and 15th amendments and the impeachment of Andrew Johnson, he became more erratic in the course of time, making fumbling attempts at peace negotiations with Confederate agents in Canada and signing Jefferson Davis's bond on the latter's release from federal imprisonment. Greeley formally broke with President Grant over the issue of corruption and the annexation of Santo Domingo. In

1872 the newly formed Liberal Republican Party and the Democratic Party combined to nominate him against Grant. Even though Greeley fought a hard campaign, he carried only six states, all in the South. He died shortly after, on November 29, 1872. The strain of the unsuccessful campaign combined with the death of his wife is said to have made him insane. He was the author of numerous books, including *The American Conflict* (2 vols., 1864–66), and *Recollections of a Busy Life* (1868).

BIBLIOGRAPHY

Hale, William Harlan. *Horace Greeley: Voice of the People.* New York: Harper and Brothers, 1936.

Van Deusen, Glyndon G. *Horace Greeley: Nineteenth Century Crusader.* Philadelphia: University of Pennsylvania Press, 1953.

WINFIELD S. HANCOCK

A career soldier, Winfield Scott Hancock (b. February 14, 1824; d. February 9, 1886) had only a brief political career that peaked in 1880 with his unsuccessful bid for the presidency, which he lost to James Garfield by what was then the closest popular vote ever. A heroic Civil War general, Hancock received extensive support for the Democratic Party's nomination during its conventions of both 1868 and 1876. In 1880, Hancock easily won the nomination after no significant rivals materialized, before going on to wage what was regarded as a lackluster campaign.

Moreover, the entire 1880 presidential election contest has long been remembered for both major party nominees' ignoring issues while launching salvos of personal attacks. Hancock perhaps came closest to making an issue statement when he said that the nation needed a tariff "for revenue only" and that at its heart the issue was a "local question." However, even this effort backfired when Republicans charged him with incompetence and failing to understand basic issues such as the tariff question. Overall, the candidates relied on exchanging negative attacks about their rivals' honesty and competence.

Yet party unity appeared to be the most important factor determining the election's outcome. Initially, Democrats were optimistic. Going into the campaign, their party was comparatively united, nominating Hancock on just the second ballot, while it took rival Garfield 35 ballots to win the Republican nomination. But the keys to winning the election were New York and Indiana, two states whose Democratic divisions proved fatal for Hancock. Especially troubling was New York,

where Hancock was damaged by a feud between the leader of Tammany Hall and a former governor.

Finally, Hancock lost the popular vote by fewer than 10,000 out of the nearly 8.9 million cast while losing in the electoral college 155 to 214. However, the Democratic nominee would have captured the presidency had he won New York's 35 electoral votes.

Robert E. Dewhirst

GEORGE B. McCLELLAN

George Brinton McClellan was born in Philadelphia on December 3, 1856. After graduating from West Point in 1846, he entered the Engineer Corps and fought under General Winfield Scott in the Mexican War. Returning to West Point as an instructor, he was promoted to captain and in 1855 assigned to study new military strategies in Europe. One of his proposals was the adoption of a new type of saddle, known as the McClellan saddle. In 1857 he resigned his com-

George B. McClellan. *Source:* Library of Congress.

mission to join the Illinois Central Railroad and four years later became the president of the Ohio and Mississippi Railroad. On the outbreak of the Civil War, he was commissioned as a major general in command of the Department of the Ohio. His success in forcing the Confederate forces from western Virginia gained the attention of Abraham Lincoln, who named him commander of the Army of the Potomac after the Union defeat at Bull Run and, later, commander of all Union forces. Now at the pinnacle of his military career, he found that his natural caution made him indecisive and ill prepared to take the offensive when required. His great failing was overestimating the strength of the enemy and underestimating his own strength, coupled with a desire to reduce casualties through delaying tactics. In the spring of 1862 he flinched from launching an attack on Richmond even when the city was within his grasp. By summer, learning that Lincoln was about to issue the Emancipation Proclamation, McClellan expressed his opposition in the Harrison Landing letter. In September of the same year he gained the crucial victory at Antietam and halted Robert E. Lee's campaign in Maryland, but he did not pursue and destroy Lee's forces before they could escape. A month later, Lincoln relieved him of his command. Thereafter, he was courted by the Democrats to be their candidate in the 1864 presidential election. He was easily nominated, even though he repudiated the Copperhead plank (seeking a negotiated peace) that had been added to the platform. Ultimately he carried only three states and 45% of the popular vote. After the war, McClellan retired to private life, briefly emerging from it to serve as governor of New Jersey from 1878 to 1881. He died in 1885.

BIBLIOGRAPHY

Hassler, Warren W., Jr. *General George B. McClellan*. Baton Rouge: Louisiana State University Press, 1957.

McClellan, George B. *McClellan's Own Story*. New York: Charles L. Webster, 1887.

Sears, Stephen W. *George B. McClellan: The Young Napoleon*. New York: Ticknor and Fields, 1988.

GEORGE McGOVERN

Born George Stanley McGovern in Avon, South Dakota, in 1922, McGovern was the son of a Methodist minister. After serving with the U.S. Army Air Corps in World War II, he became a professor of history and government at Dakota Wesleyan University. From 1956 through 1961 he was a member of the House of Representatives, and from 1963 on, he was a senator for South Dakota. In July 1972, after a campaign that underscored his new radicalism, he was chosen as the Democratic candidate to oppose Richard Nixon in the presidential election, but was heavily defeated.

Shortly after Senator Fred Harris became national chairman in 1968, he appointed Senator McGovern to head a Commission on Party Structure and Delegate Selection. Few party regulars took the commission seriously, and as a result the membership consisted primarily of liberals who had been offended by the method of Hubert Humphrey's nomination. Most of the commission's recommendations were not controversial: the abolition of proxy voting, the unit rule, and financial assessments levied on delegates; requirements that delegates be chosen in the same year as the national convention and that party meetings be held in public places after adequate public notice; the requirement that at least 75% of the delegates in nonprimary states be selected at the congressional district level or below; and the proposal that winner-take-all primaries be eliminated after 1972. Less appealing to the regulars were rules stating that no more than 10% of any particular delegation could be appointed by the state committee and prohibiting *ex officio* delegates. These guidelines indicated that officeholders and party dignitaries would have to compete for the privilege of voting in a national convention. The commission also urged that state parties be required to "overcome the effects of past discrimination by affirmative steps to encourage" participation by minorities, women, and the young "in reasonable relationship" to each group's "presence in the population of the State." A footnote specified that "this was not to be accomplished by the mandatory imposition of quotas."

McGovern served as President Kennedy's Food for Peace administrator. He originally became a presidential candidate in order to provide an option for delegates who did not want to choose solely between Humphrey and Eugene McCarthy; he hoped to provide an option for the youthful voter and the minority voter who could eventually support the convention's nominee.

McGovern was a leading critic of the Vietnam War and of the military in general. His message of peace and reconciliation garnered most of the primaries in 1972, including California and New York. He also did well in nonprimary states and had an impressive force of student volunteers. He employed direct-mail solicitation to attract small contributions from hundreds of thousands of first-time political donors. One of McGovern's advantages was a thorough knowledge of the operation of the new party rules he had helped craft.

McGovern chose Senator Thomas F. Eagleton of Missouri as his vice presidential designee and then, af-

Alton B. Parker. *Source:* Library of Congress.

ter Eagleton's earlier hospitalization for exhaustion and depression became an issue, McGovern forced the Missourian off the ticket and replaced him with R. Sargent Shriver. Nixon outstripped McGovern in the presidential race by 18 million votes, sweeping everything but Massachusetts and the District of Columbia.

B. Kim Taylor

BIBLIOGRAPHY

Anson, Robert Sam. *McGovern: A Biography.* New York: Holt Rinehart and Winston, 1972.

McGovern, George. *Grassroots: The Autobiography of George McGovern.* New York: Random House, 1977.

MacLaine, Shirley. *McGovern: The Man and His Beliefs.* New York: Norton, 1972.

ALTON B. PARKER

Alton Brooks Parker was born in Cortland, New York, on May 14, 1852, and graduated from Albany Law School in 1873. He established a successful law practice in Kingston and became actively involved in the state's Democratic Party politics. He managed David B. Hill's successful 1885 campaign for governor and was re-

warded with a seat on the New York Supreme Court. In 1892 he was elected chief justice. A liberal in political ideology, but conservative in personal philosophy, Parker was noted for his integrity and honesty on the bench and for loyalty to his party. He thus was the natural choice of the kingmakers, who chose him as the party's standard-bearer in 1904 against the popular Theodore Roosevelt. Parker did nothing to promote his candidacy and accepted the nomination reluctantly. Until the last few months before the election, he conducted a front-porch campaign from Rosemount, his Hudson River estate in Esopus, New York, and spoke only occasionally. It was September when Parker decided to hit the stump and attack Roosevelt's "shameless" sellout to big business. He broke with the free-silver wing of the party and endorsed the gold standard as "firm and irrevocable." Parker was almost relieved to lose the election and resumed his private law practice without any regrets. He was president of the American Bar Association from 1906 to 1908 but remained active in Democratic Party politics until his death on May 10, 1926.

HORATIO SEYMOUR

Horatio Seymour was born in Pompey Hill, New York, on May 31, 1810, to a prosperous family. He was admitted to the bar in 1832 but never practiced. He began

Horatio Seymour. *Source:* Library of Congress.

his political career by entering the New York State assembly in 1841 and became speaker in 1845. After losing his first gubernatorial race in 1850, he went on to become governor twice, from 1852 to 1854 and from 1862 to 1864. The principal event during his second term was the draft riot. His attempts to placate the rioters cost him his office in 1864. He was deeply opposed to the Emancipation Proclamation and the assumption of extraconstitutional powers by the Lincoln administration. Although he was not an official candidate at the Democratic National Convention in 1968, and had openly stated that he would not accept the nomination if offered, he was chosen on the 22nd ballot as a compromise candidate. With Francis Blair of Missouri as his running mate, Seymour campaigned vigorously but lost to Ulysses S. Grant by over 300,000 votes. Seymour thereafter retired from public life. He died on February 12, 1886.

BIBLIOGRAPHY

Stewart, Mitchell. *Horatio Seymour.* Cambridge: Harvard University Press, 1938.
Wall, Alexander J. *A Sketch of the Life of Horatio Seymour, 1810–1866.* New York: New York Historical Society, 1929.

ALFRED E. SMITH

Alfred Emanuel Smith was born December 30, 1873, of poor Irish immigrants living in the shadow of the Brooklyn Bridge. He went to work at the age of 12 as a day laborer in the Fulton Fish Market. He became active in Democratic politics and obtained a political clerical appointment as a legal documents process server in 1895. He won his first election in 1905 to the state legislature. He rose rapidly, becoming floor leader in 1911 and speaker in 1913. In 1918 he was elected governor and served for four terms, losing only once in 1920 in the Republican landslide of that year. As governor, he championed industrial welfare legislation, woman suffrage, and Prohibition repeal. He instituted far-reaching reforms in the state government, established an executive budget, and authorized bond-financed reconstruction of infrastructure, expansion of the state park system, and the elimination of grade crossings. Smith first sought the presidential nomination in 1924, but the deadlock between him and W.G. McAdoo led to the selection of John W. Davis as a compromise candidate. In 1928, Smith won the nomination in a convention in which Franklin D. Roosevelt proposed his name, describing him as the "Happy Warrior" who would lead the Democrats to victory. Smith was the first Roman Catholic to be nom-

inated for the presidency by either Democrats or Republicans. Smith's nomination was significant as the first time a poor immigrant was able to contend for the highest political prize in the land, thus breaking the class barrier that had helped to keep power in the hands of WASP elites. Smith's Catholicism was a major issue in the campaign and the election. A majority of Protestants helped Smith's Republican rival, Herbert Hoover, to coast to an easy victory. But at the same time Smith won an overwhelming majority among Catholic voters, and it was the first time that the Catholic bloc emerged as a strong power at the polling booth. In Boston, Providence, and Hartford, heavily Catholic cities, Smith received 91%, 71%, and 60% of the vote, respectively. The idea of a Catholic president fired the imagination of Catholic voters. In Boston, for example, Smith was greeted by over 750,000 persons, the crowds outnumbering those that welcomed Charles Lindbergh in 1920. Smith tried again to win the 1932 Democratic nomination, but lost out to FDR, who had replaced him as New York governor in 1928. Although he supported FDR during the campaign, the two friends broke up over the New Deal. Together with Herbert Hoover, John W. Davis, and William Randolph Hearst, Smith joined the anti–New Deal Liberty League in 1934. He was thereafter ostracized by the Democratic Party, and he, in turn, attacked Roosevelt's "autocratic power." He supported Alfred M. Landon in 1936 and Wendell Willkie in 1940. Toward the latter part of his life, Smith served as president of Empire State, Inc., which owned and operated the Empire State Building in New York City. Smith made enduring contributions to the American political landscape. A reformer, he made New York a laboratory for social welfare reform, and many of his policies were adopted by FDR in the New Deal. A large number of New Deal administrators were Smith's protégés, and FDR himself had looked on Smith as a mentor. Smith also built up a successful and coherent coalition of immigrants, blacks, urbanites, and the middle class that eventually came to be the cornerstone of Roosevelt's power. Smith is remembered not only for his political accomplishments but also for his characteristically slanted derby hats and his broad New York City accent. He died October 4, 1944.

BIBLIOGRAPHY

Handlin, Oscar. *Al Smith and His America.* Boston: Little, Brown, 1958.
Josephson, Matthew, and Hannah Josefson. *Al Smith: Hero for the Cities.* Boston: Houghton Mifflin, 1969.
O'Connor, Richard. *The First Hurrah.* New York: Putnam, 1970.

Smith, Alfred E. *Up to Now: An Autobiography.* New York: Viking Press, 1929.

Warner, Emily. *The Happy Warrior: A Biography of My Father.* New York: Doubleday, 1956.

ADLAI STEVENSON II

Idealist, diplomat, political leader twice defeated in presidential bids in 1952 and 1956, Adlai Stevenson II of Illinois is remembered for his politics of honor and for his commitment to unpopular causes that later became widely accepted.

Having made his name as governor of Illinois and the first U.S. ambassador to the United Nations, Stevenson was recruited to run for the presidency against General Dwight Eisenhower in one of the few genuine drafts in American political history. Despite his refusals, he was nominated on the third ballot in 1952, and his vigorous campaigns of both 1952 and 1956 won support but could not overcome Eisenhower's appeal. Though some of Stevenson's ideas were criticized, many—such as his support for a nuclear test ban treaty and an end to the military draft—were later adopted, and his campaigns were admired both for raising the intellectual level and moral tone of the debate and for their wit.

"If the Republicans would stop telling lies about us," he once said on the campaign trail, "then we would stop telling the truth about them."

Born in Los Angeles in 1900 and raised in Bloomington, Illinois, Stevenson was the grandson of Adlai E. Stevenson, vice president to Grover Cleveland during his second term, and young Adlai's political consciousness began early. But tragedy also entered his early years, when a rifle young Stevenson was holding accidentally went off and killed a young girl. Some close to him have speculated that the incident might later have accounted in part for his calm acceptance of defeats for the presidency.

Following his service as an apprentice seaman in the navy, Stevenson entered Princeton University, and after graduation and two years at Harvard Law School, he returned to Illinois to work at the family-owned Bloomington *Daily Pantagraph.* While overseeing the affairs of the paper, he finished law school at Northwestern University and even reported from Russia before joining a Chicago law firm in 1927. After involvement in the law, civil rights, and international relations during the 1930s, Stevenson went to Washington and served in a number of capacities, including as special assistant to both Secretary of the Navy Frank Knox and Secretary of State Edward Stettinius. In 1945 he became the minister of the

United States delegation at the Preparedness Commission of the United Nations, helping to launch the organization, and served as a U.S. delegate to the United Nations from 1946 to 1947.

In 1948, with the backing of close friend Eleanor Roosevelt and others, Stevenson ran for the governorship of Illinois and won. During his tenure (1949–1953), he reformed the state police force and created a ten-year road-building program, and was frequently discussed as a presidential candidate, particularly in January 1952 after President Truman announced that he would not seek reelection and endorsed Stevenson. Events soon propelled him into the arena.

During the 1950s, Stevenson continued to practice law and gained prominence in foreign affairs after his presidential election defeats. Following the election of President John F. Kennedy in 1960, Stevenson was appointed ambassador to the United Nations, a position in which he continued to serve under President Lyndon Johnson. Stevenson died of a heart attack while in London on July 14, 1965.

John F. Yarbrough

SAMUEL J. TILDEN

Born in New Lebanon, New York, in 1814, Samuel Jones Tilden attended Yale and graduated from New York University. Admitted to the bar in 1841, he became a successful corporation lawyer and amassed a huge fortune through shrewd investments in railroads, mines, and real estate. He made an early foray into politics, serving a single term in the state legislature. A Jacksonian in the 1830s, Tilden became a leader of the Backburners, a Democratic antislavery group committed to free soil. But the party split before the Civil War left Tilden siding with the conservatives. He opposed Lincoln in 1860, remained neutral during the Civil War, and managed Horatio Seymour's campaign in the presidential election of 1868. As New York state party chair from 1866 to 1876, he purged the Democrats of the Tweed Ring, gaining a strong reputation as a doughty reformer. The image helped him to gain the governor's mansion in 1874. He was instrumental in smashing the Canal Ring, a group of contractors working on the Erie Canal who had defrauded the state of millions. He was able to project a clean image over the scandal-ridden Grant administration. The Democrats chose him to run against Rutherford Hayes in 1876. The election was marred by massive voter fraud in Louisiana, South Carolina, and Florida and disputes about vote counts in those states. An election commission controlled by Republicans awarded all the dis-

Samuel J. Tilden. *Source:* Library of Congress.

puted states to Hayes. Although Tilden received 250,000 more popular votes than Hayes, he lost in the electoral college by one vote. Before he died on August 4, 1886, Tilden left his vast fortune to the New York Public Library, where his name is inscribed in stone over the main entrance.

BIBLIOGRAPHY

Bigelow, John. *The Life of Samuel J. Tilden.* New York: Harper, 1895.
Flick, Alexander. *Samuel Jones Tilden.* New York: Dodd, Mead, 1939.

Speakers

CARL B. ALBERT

Carl Bert Albert represented Oklahoma's Third Congressional District (known as "Little Dixie" be-

cause of the dominance of the Democratic Party there) from 1946 to 1977. He rose in the Democratic Party's House leadership ranks quickly, being elevated to majority whip in 1955, majority leader in 1962, and in 1971 being elected the 46th Speaker of the House. Albert was a protégé of Sam Rayburn and was known as a gentle man with a solid work ethic—to work hard, go along, and get along. Given his leadership roles within the party, Albert had surprisingly few political enemies and was often a source of stability in Washington, D.C.

Albert was born in McAlester, Oklahoma, on May 10, 1908, one of five children of Earnest Homer and Leona Ann (Scott) Albert, who made their living in rural southeastern Oklahoma working in the coal mines and raising cotton. He was a bright and outgoing young man and was elected student body president his senior year at McAlester High School. At the University of Oklahoma, Albert majored in political science and participated in debate and oratory, winning the National Oratorical Championship in 1928. After graduating with a B.A. in 1931, he attended Oxford University on a Rhodes Scholarship and graduated in 1934 with a degree in law.

After Oxford, Albert returned to Oklahoma for a short time and worked as a lawyer for the Federal Housing Administration in Oklahoma City before taking a job with the Ohio Oil Company. He enlisted as a private in the army in 1941, serving in the Pacific theater, and was discharged with the rank of lieutenant colonel in 1946. After the war, he returned to McAlester to start a law practice, but before he could get settled, incumbent Representative Democrat Paul Stewart announced that he would not seek reelection, and Albert decided to run in his place. He won the Democratic nomination and was elected to the House despite the Republican wave sweeping the country in 1946.

As a leader in the House, Albert was known as a quiet persuader and firm believer in the committee system. He played an important role in the passage of President Lyndon B. Johnson's Great Society programs and was generally a hawk on the Vietnam War and American foreign policy toward the Soviet Union. Albert believed in internationalism abroad and generous redistribution at home and played a significant role in America's foreign policy, being the first Speaker to travel abroad and meet with foreign leaders.

Albert proved to be a stabilizing force in American politics during the early and mid-1970s when everything else seemed to be going wrong. Twice during these years, Albert was second in line to the presidency: when Richard Nixon's first vice president,

Spiro T. Agnew, resigned in scandal and again when Nixon himself resigned and Vice President Gerald Ford became president. It was Albert's cautious way of handling the impeachment inquiry in the House that allowed the constitutional crisis surrounding the Watergate affair to be resolved as smoothly as it was. Albert returned to his native Oklahoma when he retired from the House in 1977.

Quentin Kidd

BIBLIOGRAPHY

Albert, Carl B. *Little Giant: The Life and Times of Speaker Carl Albert.* Norman: University of Oklahoma Press, 1990.

Palazzolo, Daniel J. *The Speaker and the Budget.* Pittsburgh: University of Pittsburgh Press, 1992.

Peters, Ronald M., Jr. *The American Speakership.* (Baltimore: Johns Hopkins University Press, 1990.

WILLIAM B. BANKHEAD

After a brief period in New York City, where he considered a career as an actor and worked for the Tammany political machine, William Brockman Bankhead (1874–1940) returned to his native Alabama and was elected to the state House in 1900. After serving in several elected legal posts, he ran unsuccessfully for the United States House of Representatives in 1914. In 1916, with the backing of the conservative wing of the Alabama Democratic Party, he was successful in his second bid for a newly created district. Bankhead remained in the House until his death in 1940. Regarded by many in the House as a man who could forge important compromises, he was elected majority leader in 1934. In the House he generally supported the New Deal despite his more conservative personal sentiments. In 1936 he was elevated to the post of Speaker of the House. At the 1940 Democratic National Convention, he had wide support for the number-two spot on the ticket over the more liberal Henry Wallace.

Jeffrey D. Schultz

PHILIP P. BARBOUR

Philip Pendleton Barbour was born on May 25, 1783, at Frascati, a plantation near Gordonsville, Virginia. He attended the College of William and Mary, studied law, and set up legal practice in Kentucky. He returned to Virginia and was elected to the Virginia House of Delegates in 1812. Two years later, Barbour was elected to the House of Representatives to fill a vacancy and served as representative until 1825 and from

1827 to 1830. He was elected Speaker in the 17th Congress, but did not offer himself for reelection. At the end of his second term in the House, in 1830, he was named an associate justice in the U.S. Supreme Court. A strict constructionist and an advocate of states' rights, Barbour opposed the Missouri Compromise, the levy of tariffs as proposed by Henry Clay, and the extension of federal jurisdiction by the Supreme Court. He died on February 25, 1841.

LYNN BOYD

In 1819, at the age of 19, Lynn Boyd (b. November 22, 1800) was appointed to assist in the Jackson Purchase. In 1827 he was elected to the Kentucky State legislature, a post he held until 1832. In the following year, he ran unsuccessfully for the United States House of Representatives. In 1835 he successfully defeated the incumbent for a House seat but lost his reelection bid in 1837. Not giving up, Boyd was reelected in 1839 and served in the House continuously until 1855.

A loyal Democrat, Boyd was a staunch supporter of President Andrew Jackson. He played an important role in the resolutions favoring the annexation of Texas. During the Mexican War, Boyd chaired the Committee on Military Affairs. After the conflict, he served as chair of the Committee on Territories. A committed Unionist, he championed compromise measures when they reached the floor of the House.

Boyd served as Speaker of the House from 1851 to 1855, when he returned to Kentucky in order to build a base for election to the Senate. In 1859 he was elected as the state's lieutenant governor, though he had sought the governorship. He died later that year without having served in the post.

Robert Allen Rutland

JOSEPH W. BYRNS

Joseph Wellington Byrns was born July 20, 1869, on a farm near Cedar Hill, Tennessee. After earning a law degree from Vanderbilt University in 1890, he was admitted to the bar and established a legal practice in Nashville in 1891. His political career began with his election in 1894 to the Tennessee legislature, where he remained until he was elected in 1900 for a two-year term in the state senate. In 1908 he won a surprising bid for a seat in the House of Representatives. He retained the seat for the next 28 years. Serving on the House Appropriations Committee, Byrns honed his skills as a fiscal watchdog, cutting costs and championing frugality. One of his proposals later led to the consolidation of the war and navy departments into the Department of Defense. He was a strong supporter of Woodrow Wilson's legislative program. When Democrats gained control of the House in 1930, Byrns became chairman of the Appropriations Committee and was elevated to the position of majority leader in 1932. When Henry T. Rainey resigned as Speaker in 1934, Byrns defeated both Sam Rayburn and William Bankhead to become Speaker, although FDR himself favored him less than the others. Nevertheless, he proved to be a steadfast and loyal New Dealer and helped the passage of many critical bills in FDR's legislative program. He died June 4, 1936, after serving as Speaker for only two years.

BIBLIOGRAPHY

Ripley, Randall B. *Party Leaders in the House of Representatives*. Washington, DC: Brookings Institution, 1967.

JOHN G. CARLISLE

One of the most prominent Speakers in the history of the U.S. House of Representatives, John Griffin Carlisle (b. September 5, 1835; d. July 31, 1910) served in that chamber from 1877 to 1890, when he resigned to take a seat in the Senate, an office he held until 1893. He then served as secretary of the treasury in the Grover Cleveland administration until 1896.

Carlisle, a powerful House Speaker from 1883 to 1890, was especially known for his ability to control the chamber's floor proceedings. A respected expert on parliamentary procedure, Carlisle would often decline to recognize those whose views he opposed, even if the member was a fellow Democrat. Carlisle was known for treating minority party members fairly; he considered himself to be leader of the entire House and not just his party's delegation. The Speaker also dominated the chamber through his position as chair of the Rules Committee, where he employed special orders to control the flow of legislation. As Speaker, Carlisle often battled serious political obstacles, such as occasional deep divisions within the Democratic ranks or minority Republican disruptive tactics (filibusters, repeated quorum calls, and the like).

Concerning issues, Carlisle was best known for leading revenue and tariff reform efforts. An opponent of tariffs to protect domestic businesses, Carlisle favored tariffs for revenue only. However, divisions over financial policies ultimately led to his political downfall. As a new secretary of the treasury, Carlisle confronted a nationwide economic downturn coupled with a rapid decline in the gold reserves. He re-

sponded by promoting a tight "sound money" policy, which not only reversed his previous positions but alienated him from his fellow Democrats as well. His support for the gold standard so angered the growing majority of silver Democrats that Carlisle retired from politics in 1896 to practice law in New York City.

Robert E. Dewhirst

LANGDON CHEVES

Langdon Cheves (b. September 17, 1776; d. June 26, 1857) began his public service in 1810, when he was elected from South Carolina to fill a vacancy in the United States House of Representatives. In the House he served on the Committee on Naval Affairs and the Ways and Means Committee, chairing the latter.

In 1814 he was elected Speaker of the House of Representatives, replacing Henry Clay, who had been appointed to the delegation for the Treaty of Ghent. Cheves was regarded as one of the most effective debaters in the House. In 1814 he cast the tie-breaking vote that defeated the rechartering of the Bank of the United States. In that same year he declined to stand for reelection to Congress. Instead, he was appointed as a justice on the Court of Appeals for South Carolina.

Friends convinced Cheves to decline appointment to the United States Supreme Court in January 1819 in order to assume the post as a director of the United States Bank. He became its president on March 6, 1819. Cheves worked tirelessly to recapitalize the overextended organization. In 1822, when he had achieved full recapitalization, he resigned his post. Upon his resignation, Cheves was appointed as the chief commissioner of claims under the Treaty of Ghent.

Returning to South Carolina, Cheves found the state in the midst of the nullification controversies that would lead to South Carolina's eventual secession. While believing in the right of secession, Cheves argued that such a move was imprudent. However, the years of absence from his home state had limited his political influence. Rather than engage in the debate, Cheves removed himself from public life.

Robert Allen Rutland

JAMES B. "CHAMP" CLARK

James Beauchamp "Champ" Clark was born March 7, 1850, near Lawrenceburg, Kentucky, and attended Kentucky University, from which he was expelled in 1870 for firing a pistol at a fellow student. He graduated from Bethany College in Virginia in 1873 and

Cincinnati Law School in 1875. While in college, he shortened his middle name to Champ and was known by that name for the rest of his life. After serving for a year as president of Marshall College in Huntington, West Virginia, he moved to Missouri in 1875. His political career began in 1892 when he was elected to the House of Representatives, but he lost his seat in the next election in the Republican landslide of 1894. He was reelected in 1896 and served in the House without interruption until 1920. He was elected minority leader in 1908 and Speaker in 1911 when the Democrats gained control. A skillful leader, Clark built a coalition with disgruntled Republicans that led to the ouster of Speaker Joe Cannon. Clark also had a pivotal role in the reform of House rules that reduced the autocratic powers of the Speaker. He was a leading candidate for the Democratic presidential nomination in 1912 but lost out to Woodrow Wilson. After Wilson won the election, Clark helped shepherd a series of progressive legislative measures, including the Underwood Tariff, the Progressive Income Tax, the Federal Reserve Act, the Clayton Antitrust Act, and the Federal Trade Commission Act. He supported America's entry into World War I and loyally backed Wilson's war policies, except military conscription. He lost his reelection bid in 1920 and died before the end of his last term, on March 2, 1921.

BIBLIOGRAPHY

Clark, Champ. *My Quarter Century of American Politics*. New York: Harper, 1920.

HOWELL COBB

Howell Cobb (b. September 7, 1815; d. October 9, 1868), a member of a politically active family from Georgia, entered politics in 1837 as solicitor general for the Western Circuit of Georgia. After six years as solicitor, he was elected to the United States House of Representatives on the last general ticket. In 1844 he was reelected from the Sixth District of Georgia. He was regarded as one of the great debaters and scholars of constitutional questions. In 1848 Cobb was elected party leader in the House.

Throughout his tenure in the House, issues of expansion and slavery dominated public affairs. When the issue of the annexation of Texas brought forth Senator John C. Calhoun's "Southern Address" call for a united South to defend its interests, Cobb argued that membership in the Union offered better security. In December 1849 he was elected Speaker of the House on the 63rd ballot.

The passage of the Compromise of 1850 became the major issue for reelection in Georgia. The governor of Georgia called for a state convention to debate the course the state would pursue in light of the compromise. The state Democratic Party was divided between those led by the pro-Union forces, most notably Cobb, and the states' rights forces. Cobb took his message to the people and won the election of a majority of pro-Union Democrats to the convention.

The state convention saw the formal division of the Democratic Party into the Constitutional Unionists and the Southern States Party. In 1851 Cobb was nominated as the Constitutional Unionist candidate for governor. Using his gifted electioneering skills, he defeated the Southern Rights candidate. In 1854 he stood for election to the United States Senate but was defeated. The following year he was reelected to Congress.

At the Democratic National Convention in 1856, he played a critical role in securing the party's nomination for James Buchanan. After Buchanan's election, Cobb was appointed secretary of the treasury. His efforts in handling the crisis of 1857 were resoundingly praised.

When Abraham Lincoln was elected in 1860, Cobb urged the immediate secession of Georgia. Serving as chair of the convention of seceding states assembled in Montgomery in 1861, Cobb was a leading candidate for the presidency of the Confederacy. However, his lack of military leadership and former Unionist position prevented his selection. During the Civil War he served in the Confederate army, rising to the rank of major general and commander of the District of Georgia. After his surrender, Cobb retired from public life to practice law.

Robert Allen Rutland

CHARLES F. CRISP

At the age of 16, Charles Frederick Crisp (b. January 29, 1845) served as a soldier in the Confederate army for three years before becoming a prisoner of war in 1864. Upon his release from prison in 1865, Crisp studied law and was appointed solicitor general of the Southwestern Superior Court Circuit of Georgia in 1872. After five years of service, he became the circuit's judge.

In 1882 Crisp resigned from the bench in order to run for a seat in the United States House of Representatives, a post he held until his death in 1896. In the House he undertook an intense study of parliamentary procedure and was regarded as one of the great parliamentarians of his time. In 1891 he was elected

Speaker of the House, a post he held for four years. He is largely responsible for the passage of the Interstate Commerce Act of 1887 and the Sherman Act of 1890.

In 1896 Crisp sought the state party's nomination for the United States Senate. He would have won both the nomination and the seat; however, he died in October.

Robert Allen Rutland

JOHN WESLEY DAVIS

John Wesley Davis was born in New Holland, Pennsylvania, April 16, 1799. He graduated from Baltimore Medical College in 1821 and began the practice of medicine in Carlisle, Indiana. His political career began with his election to the Indiana House of Representatives in 1831, followed by election to the U.S. House of Representatives in 1835. His six terms in the Indiana legislature (1832–1833, 1841–1842, and 1851–1852) alternated with four nonconsecutive terms in the U.S. House of Representatives, during one of which he served as Speaker. He was chairman of the chaotic 1852 Democratic National Convention that nominated Franklin Pierce after 49 ballots. In addition to his legislative service, Davis was commissioner to China from 1848 to 1850 and governor of Oregon Territory from 1853 to 1854.

THOMAS S. FOLEY

Thomas Stephen Foley represented the state of Washington's Fifth District for 30 years in Congress. In that time he rose from junior member of the House Agriculture Committee to become the 49th Speaker of the House of Representatives. Foley's narrow defeat in the 1994 midterm elections was only the third time in history that a sitting Speaker had been voted out of office and came during a year when the Republicans broke a 40-year Democratic hold on the House.

Foley was born in Spokane, Washington, on March 6, 1929, the only son of Ralph E. and Helen Marrie (Higgins) Foley. Foley's father was the Spokane County prosecutor and later a state superior court judge. Young Tom Foley was not known for his academic work at Gonzaga High School but overcame a pronounced lisp and won the state debating championship during his senior year. In 1947 he began college in Spokane at Gonzaga University and later transferred to the University of Washington, from which he graduated in 1951. He earned a degree in law from the University of Washington Law School in 1957 and went into private practice in Spokane with his cousin Hank

Wiggins. In 1961 Foley was hired by Washington Senator Henry M. "Scoop" Jackson as a special counsel on the Senate Interior and Insular Affairs Committee.

In 1964 Scoop Jackson encouraged Foley to return home and challenge Republican Walt Horan for the Fifth District seat. Although reluctant, Foley decided at the last minute to give it a try and narrowly defeated Horan thanks to the long coattails of President Lyndon B. Johnson. As 1 of a freshman class of 71, Foley was appointed to the Agriculture Committee and the Interior Committee. He strongly supported Johnson's Great Society programs but opposed America's growing involvement in the Vietnam conflict.

Foley won his first leadership post in 1971, being elected chair of the Democratic Study Group. In 1976 he was elected chair of the Democratic Caucus but was never a very active leader. The Reagan landslide victory of 1980 proved to be a blessing in disguise for Foley. Although Foley almost lost reelection himself that year, several prominent leaders of the Democratic Party did lose their seats and Foley found himself the majority whip. He became the majority leader in 1986, when Thomas P. "Tip" O'Neill retired and Jim Wright won the speakership. When Wright resigned amid allegations of ethical misconduct in 1989, Foley was elected to succeed him. With the election of Bill Clinton as president in 1992, Foley worked tirelessly to see a new Democratic agenda enacted, but those efforts were cut short with Foley's defeat in the 1994 midterm elections.

Foley had a reputation for fairness and sensibility, together with a distaste for the mean-spirited nature of American politics. Although he was often criticized by colleagues for his cautious approach, his steady style and even-handed treatment were appreciated by members on both sides of the aisle. Foley once conceded that he was cursed with the ability to see the other point of view and try to understand it.

Quentin Kidd

BIBLIOGRAPHY

Congressional Quarterly Almanac, 1994. Washington, DC: CQ Press, 1994.
Current Biography Yearbook 1989. New York: W.H. Wilson, 1989.

ROBERT M.T. HUNTER

Robert Mercer Taliaferro Hunter, Speaker of the House and United States senator, was born in 1809 in Essex County, Virginia. His mother's family was influential in the area, helping him gain admittance to the

University of Virginia. A serious student of law and finance, he graduated in 1828 and was admitted to the bar in 1830.

From 1834 to 1837 Hunter served as an independent in the Virginia General Assembly. In 1838 he declared himself a Whig and was elected to the House of Representatives. In spite of his Whig affiliation, Hunter supported most of President Martin Van Buren's moderate Democratic proposals and supported the contested election of the Democratic candidates from New Jersey, but refrained from embracing any radical theory of states' rights. During his second term, Hunter was elected Speaker of the House as a moderate southern Democrat. Even after his election as Speaker, however, he continued his movement toward the Democratic states' rights position. Hunter was soon an ardent advocate of John C. Calhoun's extreme doctrine of states' rights. His one term as Speaker was filled with turmoil as Hunter became more radical and officially switched to the Democratic Party in 1840. His decision to become a Democrat eliminated Hunter from the contest for Speaker and cost him reelection from his Whig gerrymandered district.

Hunter spent the next two years reorganizing the Virginia Democrats around Calhoun's ideas and trying to extend his national influence by contacting the Tammany Society of New York. His efforts paid off, and in 1845 he was reelected to the House. Two years later he was appointed to fill the vacant Senate seat from Virginia. Hunter's support for states' rights and slavery was so staunch that he advocated secession as early as 1850 in response to Calhoun's defeat and the Wilmot Proviso. A decade later, in 1860, he was mentioned as a presidential candidate but instead threw his support behind the proslavery southern candidate, John Breckinridge. Hunter sought compromise after Abraham Lincoln's election but withdrew from the Senate one month before Virginia left the Union.

Hunter served as the Confederate secretary of state from July 1861 to February 1862 and as a member of the Confederate Senate until the war ended in 1865. He was one of the three Confederate politicians who attended negotiations with Lincoln in February 1865, but he remained convinced that the South would be destroyed by the war. After the war Hunter was arrested and held in prison for several months. His farm and property had been destroyed during the conflict. He served as treasurer of Virginia for six years and advocated a policy of full repayment of war debts. In 1885 President Grover Cleveland appointed Hunter to the post of collector of the port of Tappahannock, Virginia. Hunter died in that post on July 18, 1887.

Daniel Stanhagen

JOHN WINSTON JONES

John Winston Jones, Speaker of the House of Representatives, was born in 1791 in Amelia County, Virginia. His father died when he was young, and Jones was raised by his uncle. He attended public schools and in 1813 graduated from William and Mary College with a degree in law. Jones moved to Petersburg and for five years practiced law before being appointed prosecuting attorney for the Fifth Virginia Judicial Circuit. He continued in his capacity as prosecutor for 15 years. His political career started in 1829, when, against his wishes, Jones was chosen to attend the state constitutional convention. He enjoyed the atmosphere and decided to run for Congress, to which he was elected in 1834.

Jones served as a Jacksonian in his first term and won four more terms as a Democrat. He was the chairman of the Ways and Means Committee in the 27th Congress (1841–1843) and performed well during this period of financial instability. In 1843 Jones was elected Speaker of the House. In 1842 his election to Congress was contested, and Jones asked to be relieved from the task of naming the members who would investigate his own election results. This action established the precedent for a Speaker pro tempore to appoint members to committees in which the Speaker has a personal interest. Although not one of Jones's decisions as Speaker was reversed by the House, Representative John Quincy Adams (former president of the United States) did not vote for the traditional thank-you on the grounds that his leadership was too partisan. Others described him as "a clever politician who made but an indifferent presiding officer."

Jones retired from Congress in 1844 and went back to practicing law in Petersburg. Despite his retirement, the people of his district chose him to represent Chesterfield County in the state legislature. Soon after taking office in 1846, he was made speaker of the House. Jones would be elected to another term in 1848, but his health deteriorated so badly that he could not take his seat. A few weeks after leaving office, he died on January 29, 1848.

Daniel Stanhagen

MICHAEL C. KERR

Michael Crawford Kerr was born on March 15, 1827, in Titusville, Pennsylvania. He graduated from Erie Academy in 1845 and completed his law studies at the University of Louisville in 1851. He set up a law practice in New Albany, Indiana, where he became active in politics. His legislative career began when he was elected to the Indiana House of Representatives in 1857, followed by election to the U.S. House of Representatives in 1864. He served in four successive Congresses before losing his seat in 1872. He returned to the House in 1875 for his final term and was elected Speaker with the help of hard-money conservatives opposed to the inflationist plank of the Democratic Party. In poor health as the session began, he was not able to complete his term and died at a mountain spa in Virginia on August 19, 1876.

NATHANIEL MACON

While serving in the Continental army, Nathaniel Macon (b. 1758; d. 1837) was elected to the North Carolina State Senate in 1781, serving until 1785. In 1790 he was elected to the Continental Congress but refused to serve. Macon actively opposed the ratification of the United States Constitution. While a member of the state House, he was elected to the United States House of Representatives in 1791, serving until 1815, when he was elevated to the United States Senate.

Macon was Speaker of the House from 1801 until 1807. He was active in opposing almost all Federalist proposals. Generally a supporter of President Thomas Jefferson's policies, Macon did, however, oppose the building of a navy. Chairing the Foreign Relations Committee beginning in 1809, he actively supported the Jefferson and James Madison administrations. He opposed the recharter of the United States Bank and higher tariffs. Opposed to the Missouri Compromise, he was an ardent defender of slavery. Much of Macon's political career was based on his being opposed to various measures, which earned him the label of a negative radical.

Macon retired from the Senate in 1828. However, in 1832 he opposed nullification, believing secession was the appropriate response to usurpation of authority by the national government. In 1835 he was chosen as a delegate to the state's constitutional convention and served as the body's president. After aiding Martin Van Buren's election as president in 1836, Macon died suddenly at his home the following year.

Robert Allen Rutland

JOHN W. McCORMACK

A Boston Irishman and the first Roman Catholic to be elected Speaker of the House, John William McCormack was noted for his diligence as a legislator,

unswerving loyalty to his party and a barbed wit that made him a feared debater.

Elected Speaker pro tempore in the months before Speaker Sam Rayburn's death on October 2, 1961, and then drawing on his years of political favors to win the speakership, McCormack at the age of 70 became the second oldest man to hold the post. While some felt his age made him ineffective, he had influence with both the liberal and conservative wings of the Democratic Party. Though not close allies with President John F. Kennedy, despite their common bond of Boston, McCormack and the young president worked together, and McCormack was a consistent supporter of Kennedy's New Frontier domestic programs.

Born in Boston on December 21, 1891, into a poor family of 12 children, nine of whom died in infancy, McCormack grew up in the Irish community of South Boston. The grandson of immigrants who came to the United States during the Irish potato famine of the 1840s, McCormack's father, a bricklayer, died when McCormack was 13. The young McCormack left school to work as a newsboy and in other jobs for the family, eventually working in a law office for $4 a week and getting encouragement from his employer to pursue the law as a career. He passed the bar examination in 1913 at the age of 21 and, while practicing law in Boston, set his sights on a political career. After serving in the U.S. army stateside in World War I, McCormack was elected to the Massachusetts House of Representatives in 1920 and served one term, followed by three years in the state Senate, from 1923 to 1926.

After an unsuccessful run for the U.S. Congress in 1926, McCormack won a South Boston seat in 1928 following the death of the incumbent. Once in Congress, he was noted for working diligently and over time developed an expertise on tax matters. His strong loyalty to Democratic Party positions won him favor with then Minority Leader John Nance Garner and with Congressman Sam Rayburn. When the Democrats took control of the House, McCormack was appointed to the powerful Ways and Means Committee after less than two terms in office. He helped draw broad support for Rayburn's candidacy for majority leader, and when Rayburn moved up to the speakership, McCormack became majority leader. He was Rayburn's deputy and confidant for two decades, a consistent backer of the New Deal, and a heavy cigar smoker and an able poker player.

Immediately following the assassination of President Kennedy, McCormack was first in line to succeed President Lyndon Johnson under the Presidential Succession Act of 1947. By the late 1960s McCormack came under increasing fire for what some felt was ineffective leadership and for his support of the Vietnam War. In January 1970 his administrative assistant and a friend were indicted on influence-peddling charges, and later that year McCormack announced he would not seek reelection. After leaving Congress, McCormack resided in Boston until his death on November 22, 1980, in Dedham, Massachusetts.

John F. Yarbrough

THOMAS P. "TIP" O'NEILL

Thomas P. "Tip" O'Neill Jr., who coined the phrase "All politics is local," served as Speaker of the House of Representatives from 1977 to 1986. O'Neill was the Speaker during a difficult time for Democrats. He served under an unpopular Democrat, Jimmy Carter, and a popular Republican, Ronald Reagan.

O'Neill was continually at odds with Reagan, who tried to dismantle many of the social programs of the New Deal. O'Neill, a New Deal liberal, "believed that government has a moral responsibility to help people who can't help themselves" and was appalled at Reagan's social spending cuts.

O'Neill was born on December 9, 1912, in Cambridge, Massachusetts. His early political influences included his father, Thomas P. O'Neill, who was elected to the Cambridge City Council; the working-class neighborhoods of North Cambridge, his home; and Franklin Roosevelt and the New Deal. This background made him a government activist.

O'Neill, a Boston College graduate, began his political career in the Massachusetts legislature, to which he was first elected in 1936. He became one of Boston's and the state's leading Democrats and by 1948 was the first Democrat to be the speaker of the Massachusetts House. In 1952 O'Neill ran for Congress and was victorious, capturing the seat that had been held by John F. Kennedy.

As a congressman, O'Neill quickly became one of the leading Democrats in the House because of his political insight and savvy. He also received high marks for being a man of conscience (he was one of the first members of Congress to oppose the Vietnam War) and for his work as head of the Democratic Congressional Campaign Committee. He worked his way up from whip to majority leader and finally, upon the retirement of Carl Albert, to Speaker of the House in 1977.

One of O'Neill's first acts as Speaker was to push through a strong ethics bill that limited the outside income that members of Congress could earn. It was an important measure in the wake of the Watergate scandal. He was the first to permit live television coverage of the House when it was in session.

As Speaker, O'Neill took a hands-on approach, making himself available to all members of Congress. He was very active in fund raising and traveled across the country to support Democratic candidates, never forgetting the importance of local ties. This made him a very successful party leader.

O'Neill's greatest challenge came during the Reagan years, when the Republicans took control of the Senate and made huge gains in the House. The Democrats were no longer the dominant party, and Reagan's popularity enabled him to get his agenda (tax cuts and reductions in social spending) through Congress. O'Neill sometimes stood alone in opposition to what he saw as the meanness of the agenda and its attack on the poor. O'Neill did his best to save programs for the handicapped and limit the cuts in education and Social Security. He remained a voice for the powerless and was vindicated when the Democrats gained a working majority in the 1982 by-elections.

O'Neill retired following the 1986 term, having served in public office for 50 years. He died January 5, 1994.

Tim Morris

JAMES LAWRENCE ORR

James Lawrence Orr, Speaker of the House of Representatives and governor of South Carolina, was born in 1822 in Anderson, South Carolina. He graduated from the University of Virginia in 1842 and returned home to practice law. Orr worked briefly as a journalist before joining a prosperous law firm. In 1844, at the age of 22, Orr was elected to the state legislature and served until 1848. While in the state legislature, Orr fought for public school reform and spoke out against nullification and in favor of the Union.

Orr was elected to Congress in 1848 and became known as a powerful orator. During his 11 years in Congress, Orr was chairman of the Committee on Indian Affairs and advocated the cause of the displaced Indians. Against the wishes of his constituents, he worked against any suggestion of secession, but he opposed all attempts, including the Compromise of 1850, to limit slavery. In 1856 Orr headed the South Carolina delegation to the Democratic National Convention and worked for the nomination of Stephen Douglas, an opponent of secession. Orr's position on secession and his opposition to the Know-Nothings, a nativist and anti-Catholic party, made him popular with northern members. With their support, he was elected Speaker of the House in 1857.

After only one year as Speaker, Orr decided to return to South Carolina and run for the United States Senate. The strong feelings in his state for secession took him by surprise, and he was beaten by a pro-secession candidate. Because of his popularity in the North, Orr was briefly considered as a possible Democratic nominee for the 1860 presidential race. In April 1860 Orr, still advocating Union, dominated the state Democratic convention and restrained the delegates from voting to leave the Union.

Despite all his previous actions to the contrary, Orr abruptly changed his view on secession following the state convention. Orr's position on secession was so unpopular that at the Democratic National Convention he withdrew his delegates and championed a break from the Union. He signed the ordinance of secession but hoped for a peaceful split and was one of the commissioners sent to Washington to resolve the Fort Sumter dispute. When war broke out, Orr was elected to the Confederate Senate in 1861, after a short term commanding Orr's Regiment of Rifles. By 1864, with the war going badly, Orr recommended that the Confederacy settle for a negotiated peace. This suggestion, seen in light of his earlier reluctance to embrace secession, cast doubt upon his loyalty.

In 1865 Orr became a Republican and supported President Andrew Johnson's policies toward the South. By a small majority, Orr was elected governor in 1866. His embrace of the Republican Party and acceptance of the policies of radical Reconstruction were so unpopular with whites that he left office in 1868. Orr supported President Ulysses S. Grant's fight against the Ku Klux Klan and, as a reward, was appointed minister to Russia in 1872. He died several months later, in 1873, in St. Petersburg.

Daniel Stanhagen

HENRY T. RAINEY

Henry Thomas Rainey (b. August 20, 1860), a progressive Democrat from Illinois's traditionally one-term 20th District, was elected Speaker of the House of Representatives on March 9, 1933. He was the first Democrat since the Civil War from north of the Mason–Dixon Line to lead the lower house of Congress. Rainey was known as a ready reformer, and the fact that he served during 30 years of mostly Republican domination of Congress was an indication of his ability to balance constituency service with national service.

Rainey's congressional career was marked by a progressive and sometimes radical impulse. He supported such issues as water conservation, the income

tax, and railroad regulation in his first few years in Congress and later became one of President Woodrow Wilson's chief legislative lieutenants. In that role Rainey worked for the downward revision of tariffs and the establishment of the Federal Trade Commission, and was a vocal supporter of the League of Nations. In the 1920s he was a chief critic of the Republican administrations, and by the 1930s he had gained a reputation as a Democratic maverick.

Rainey came to be considered a potential Speaker because of his longevity in office and because he was a rather liberal northern Democrat who would work well with President Franklin D. Roosevelt. He worked hard to see Roosevelt's early emergency packages passed in the House and came to be known as the chief interpreter of those policies to the people. Following the adjournment of Congress in 1934, Rainey went on an extensive speaking tour in an effort to build momentum for Roosevelt's New Deal.

While on a speaking stop in St. Louis in 1934, Rainey suddenly fell ill of pneumonia and died, catching the nation by surprise. He was just one day short of his 74th birthday and was only the third Speaker to die while holding that office.

Quentin Kidd

SAMUEL J. RANDALL

Born in Philadlephia on October 10, 1828, Samuel Jackson Randall attended the University Academy. Coming from a prominent Whig family, he gravitated to politics and was elected to the House of Representatives in 1862 as a Democrat although, unlike most Democrats, he favored high tariffs. A man of independent means, Randall controlled the Democratic Party in Pennsylvania from 1875 to 1888. His influence in the Democratic Party led to his election as Speaker in 1876. Randall tried to use his power as Speaker to promote his own policies and thwart the passage of bills he opposed. But his efforts to change House rules to reinforce his authority were not always successful. He failed to bring all appropriations under the firm control of the Appropriations Committee. Similarly, the House overrode his attempts to make it tougher to pass water-project bills. Randall's fiscal conservatism and protectionist policies led to a revolt by the House Democrats in 1883 when he was deposed in favor of John G. Carlisle. Randall was demoted as chair of the Appropriations Committee, but there he used his powers to strangle bills he opposed. In 1885, Carlisle stripped the Appropriations Committee of half its spending authority by transferring several kinds of bills to other committees. Because of his refusal to support President Grover Cleveland's efforts to reduce the tariff in 1887, Randall was denied all further patronage appointments, His political fortunes declined thereafter. He died April 13, 1890.

SAM RAYBURN

Sam Rayburn, who rose up from rural poverty to become one of the most powerful Speakers of the House, was a major force in Democratic politics for almost half a century. He served in the House of Representatives from 1914 until his death in 1961 and was Speaker for almost 17 years, longer than any other Speaker in history. Known as "Mr. Democrat," Rayburn also had a major impact on the career of fellow Texan Lyndon Johnson.

Born Samuel Taliaferro Rayburn on January 6, 1882, Rayburn was one of the leading players in Congress, supporting Franklin Roosevelt's New Deal programs. He used his chairmanship of the Interstate and Foreign Commerce Committee to get much of the New Deal through Congress. In the process, he did a great deal to improve the way of life for his rural con-

Sam Rayburn. *Source:* Library of Congress.

stituency in Texas. The son of Will Rayburn and Martha Clementine Waller, Rayburn was born in Tennessee but grew up on a small farm in Bonham, Texas, where the family moved in 1887.

The ambitious Rayburn, who had early on showed an inclination for politics, worked his way through school, graduating from Mayo College in Commerce, Texas. He taught briefly before entering politics in 1906, when he was elected to the Texas legislature for the first of three terms. He was voted speaker of the Texas House in 1911.

In 1913, he won election to Congress. Rayburn represented the Fourth Congressional District in northeast Texas, which was largely agricultural, with cotton as its major crop, and was overwhelmingly Democratic.

The reason for his popularity and longevity was the Rayburn style. He was one of the last of the old-fashioned politicians who relied on personal contact with his constituents, friendship, honesty and trust. His integrity mattered most to Rayburn.

It didn't take long for Rayburn to make an impact in Congress. In his first term, he helped President Woodrow Wilson get the Underwood tariff reduction passed and the Federal Reserve System created. His early success made him a major player within the Democratic Party. He moved up to majority leader in 1937 thanks to his role in the New Deal and, finally, to Speaker of the House, his lifelong goal, in 1940. For almost 17 of the next 20 years, he was the Speaker. Under Rayburn, the House's highest post was transformed to one of power and influence.

To Rayburn, the American system of government worked best if there was a strong, independent legislature that asserted itself. He believed that relations between Congress and the president should be marked by cooperation and compromise.

Rayburn was the Speaker through World War II and was able to hold together a bipartisan coalition that gave FDR what he needed to run the war effort.

Known as a great legislator, Rayburn shepherded many major pieces of legislation through Congress, including rural electrification, soil conservation, regulation of the railroads and securities, antimonopoly laws, the oil-depletion allowance, and the 1957 Civil Rights Bill.

Rayburn died of cancer on November 16, 1961.

Tim Morris

ANDREW STEVENSON

Andrew Stevenson (b. January 21, 1784; d. January 25, 1857) was a member of the Virginia House of Delegates from 1809 to 1816 and from 1816 to 1821, serving as Speaker from 1812 to 1815. In 1814 and 1816 he ran unsuccessfully for the United States House of Representatives. On his third attempt, in 1820, Stevenson was elected and served until 1834, when he resigned.

A member of the powerful Richmond Junto, Stevenson was Speaker of the House from 1827 until 1834. He opposed nullification as a solution to the growing conflict between North and South. A strong supporter of Martin Van Buren, Stevenson was instrumental in the former's nomination as vice president in 1832. In 1835 he chaired the Democratic National Convention in Baltimore, which nominated Van Buren for the presidency.

Although Stevenson was appointed to be ambassador to Great Britain in 1834 by President Andrew Jackson, the Senate refused to confirm Stevenson until after the 1836 election. He served in that post until 1841. Stevenson remained a private citizen for the rest of his life.

Robert Allen Rutland

JOHN W. TAYLOR

Born in Charlton, New York, on March 26, 1784, John W. Taylor was educated at home and graduated from Union College, Schenectady. He was admitted to the bar in 1807. He was elected to the House of Representatives in 1812 and served in it until 1833. An abolitionist, he supported James Tallmadge's amendment to the Missouri Bill in 1819, which would have outlawed the expansion of slavery in Missouri and liberated the children of slaves at the age of 25. Taylor introduced a similar amendment to the Arkansas Territorial Bill, arguing that the power of Congress to admit states also gave it the power to prescribe the conditions for such admission. In 1820 he was elected to complete Henry Clay's term as Speaker. He was again elected Speaker in 1825, but the opposition of the proslavery states made him ineffective in promoting John Quincy Adams's legislative program. He supported Henry Clay in organizing the national Republican Party. He was defeated in the Speaker's election in 1827 and lost his seat in 1832. He was a member of the New York Senate in 1840–1841, but retired thereafter to Ohio, where he died on September 18, 1854.

JAMES CLAUDE WRIGHT JR.

James Claude Wright Jr. was born in Fort Worth, Texas, on December 22, 1922, and grew up in many different

small Texas towns. He attended Weatherford College and the University of Texas. During World War II he served in the army air force. Shortly after the war, Wright began his long career of public service. In 1946 he was elected to the Texas House of Representatives but was defeated for reelection following his first term. Wright served as mayor of Weatherford, Texas, from 1950 to 1954. He first sought election to the U.S. House of Representatives in 1954. His campaign was successful, and he was reelected to 16 consecutive terms. His only run for a Senate seat, in 1961, was unsuccessful. From that time he devoted his efforts to strengthening the power of the House through the leadership of the Democratic Party.

Wright's political views were shaped by the backdrop of the depression. He firmly believed that it was through the House of Representatives that the people's voice was heard. He endeavored to strengthen the House and raise its importance to be equal to that of the presidency. To that end, he was effective. Wright successfully elevated the position of Speaker of the House. During his tenure as Speaker, he wielded more power than any other member of Congress in this century up to that time, and perhaps at any time. He dictated domestic and foreign policy and determined what legislation would pass and fail in Congress. Under Wright's leadership, Republican governmental policy was redirected in the areas of trade, clean water, transportation, infrastructure, catastrophic illness insurance, farming credit, and the homeless population. Democratic members of the House were kept firmly in check during his tenure. At the height of Wright's power, the Reagan administration appeared weak by comparison.

Wright was elected to the position of majority leader by the Democrats in the House of Representatives in 1976. On January 6, 1987, he succeeded Thomas P. "Tip" O'Neill as Speaker of the House. Wright was determined to enlarge the capacity of that office and to elevate it to new levels of power. In doing so, he proved to be a domineering and aggressive force. However, in June 1988 the House Ethics Committee started an investigation that would rapidly lead to Wright's fall from eminence. In April 1989 the Ethics Committee unanimously accused Wright of five counts (totaling 69 separate instances) that violated the House's ethics rules. He was accused of receiving extremely high fees that violated limits placed on outside earned income. In addition, the committee accused him of receiving various other gifts that he failed to disclose publicly on his financial records. On May 31, 1989, Wright announced that he would be resigning as Speaker of the House and also giving up his seat in

Congress. On June 6, 1989, he officially stepped down, and Thomas Foley succeeded him as Speaker. Wright was the only Speaker in the history of the House of Representatives to resign in the middle of his term due to political scandal.

BIBLIOGRAPHY

Barry, John M. *The Ambition and the Power: The Fall of Jim Wright—A True Story of Washington. New York:* Penguin, 1989.

Kimberly J. Pace

Other Notable Democrats

Les Aspin (1938–1995)   Leslie Aspin Jr. began his political career as an aide to Wisconsin Senator William Proxmire in 1960. Three years later, he served as a staff assistant to Walter W. Heller, President John F. Kennedy's head of the Council of Economic Advisers. In 1968 he returned to Wisconsin to organize President Lyndon B. Johnson's presidential campaign in the state. However, when Johnson decided not to run, Aspin made an unsuccessful bid for the post of state treasurer. Campaigning on a liberal platform, he succeeded in defeating incumbent Republican Henry C. Shadeburg for the United States House of Representatives in 1970. Aspin made a name for himself on the Armed Services Committee by exposing cost overruns and other needless expenditures. During his first two terms, he released hundreds of stories about Defense Department waste. In a particularly bold move, he built a coalition of fiscal conservatives and liberals that cut the defense budget in 1973 over the objections of the Democratic chair of the Armed Services Committee, Representative F. Edward Herbert of Louisiana. As time passed, Aspin became less of a controversial figure—in part, because he was gaining power and respect on military issues. During the 1980s, he played a crucial role in the passage of military-spending bills by getting several of his Democratic colleagues to support projects like the MX missile system. In 1985 Aspin was rewarded for his understanding of defense issues by being tapped to be the chair of the Armed Services Committee. In this position, he worked to shape his party's defense agenda. Many of his Democratic colleagues were unhappy with Aspin's more conservative stands, which aligned him with most Republicans on defense issues. In 1992, after President Bill Clinton took office, Aspin was named secretary of defense. Applauded from all corners as the most experienced Democrat on Pentagon issues, he served in this post until his res-

ignation in 1993 because of health reasons and after he was criticized when 18 American servicemen were killed in Somalia.

Augustus O. Bacon (1835–1914)   Augustus Octavius Bacon, a former captain on the Confederate army's general staff, served two decades in the Senate from the state of Georgia. After the Civil War, Bacon practiced law in Macon, where in 1868 he was selected as a Democratic presidential elector. Two years later, he was elected to the Georgia House. He was a recognized legal scholar, having completed a digest of state Supreme Court decisions in 1872. Although an unsuccessful candidate for governor in 1883, Bacon was unanimously appointed to the U.S. Senate in 1895. Perhaps his most important distinction was to have been the first senator elected under the new direct-election mechanisms established in 1913.

Birch E. Bayh Jr. (1928–)   Birch Evans Bayh Jr. served four terms in the Indiana State House from 1954 to 1962. He was minority leader in 1957 and 1961 and speaker of the House in 1959. After winning the 1962 Democratic nomination for the United States Senate, Bayh faced three-term incumbent Republican Homer E. Capehart in the general election. The conservative Republican seemed likely to win reelection, in part, because of his outspoken criticism of the John F. Kennedy administration's Cuba policy. However, when the administration blockaded Cuba, the Republican's leading issue declined along with his electoral strength. In one of the year's most important upsets, Bayh combined the change in policy with a heavy media blitz to defeat Senator Capehart. In the Senate, Bayh, a moderate, supported the Kennedy and Lyndon B. Johnson administrations on most issues. When Johnson assumed the presidency, Bayh chaired the committee that drafted the 25th Amendment, on presidential succession. In 1964 he served as chair of the Young Citizens for Johnson. Reelected to the Senate in 1968 and 1974, he did not stand as a candidate for reelection in 1980. During his tenure in the Senate, Bayh gained a reputation as a skilled legislator.

Martin Behrman (1864–1926)   Martin Behrman began his 36-year political career in 1888 when he was elected to the post of secretary in the Algiers (New Orleans's district) Democratic committee. As secretary, he helped Francis T. Nicholas to win the governorship and was rewarded with an appointment as deputy assessor for the Fifth District, a post he held for four years until his political enemies captured the governorship. In 1896 he ran unsuccessfully for a seat in the Louisiana House of Representatives. When his political friends were elected in 1897, he was appointed assessor of the Fifth District. In the Louisiana constitutional convention of 1898, Behrman distinguished himself. He continued to join organizations and made contacts that he would use to advance himself and his party. In 1904 he was elected state auditor. The influential Choctow Club nominated Behrman for mayor of New Orleans. Behrman won a tough election, in large part because of the support of the Democratic Labor League. At his inauguration, he promised economy, clean streets, vigilant sanitation, and law and order. Behrman delivered on his promises. He was easily reelected in 1908, receiving 98.6% of the vote. Behrman was once again reelected in 1912 despite the opposition of the Good Government League's candidate, Judge Charles F. Claiborne. The league had attempted to limit the power of the mayor by changing the mayor–council form of government to a commission form. During his 1912 term, Behrman continued to centralize power in his own hands. He was easily reelected to another four-year term in 1916. This term was his most difficult. The War Department had decided to end segregation in a vice district. Rather than have the department's decision forced on the city, Behrman backed an ordinance that did away with the segregated area. Additionally, he became ill and was absent from New Orleans for periods in order to seek treatment. He was defeated for reelection in 1920 when past supporters turned to his opponent. In 1921 he was elected to the state constitutional convention where he served on committees responsible for housing, public education, taxation, and other important issues. Behrman used his political influence to aid the election of Governor Harry Fuqua in 1924. In an act of political patronage, he was elected chairman of the state central committee. Behrman successfully won a fifth term as mayor of New Orleans in 1924, campaigning on his record of public improvements. His fifth term was an impressive program of street paving, park building, and crime suppression. Although his death prevented him from seeing the completion of his ambitious program, Behrman's vision of New Orleans continued after he died in 1926.

Jeffrey D. Schultz

Thomas Hart Benton (1782–1858)   Thomas Hart Benton was first elected to the U.S. Senate in 1820. He served until 1850, when he was not reelected because of his opposition to the Compromise of 1850. During his tenure in the Senate, he served as the spokesman for the Andrew Jackson administration, championing the defeat of the National Bank. This position reflected his career-long concern with sound money policies. By 1828 he favored the gradual abolition of slavery,

believing that just compensation was due slave owners. Essentially a moderate, he strongly supported Martin Van Buren in the presidential election of 1840. As time passed, he came to the conclusion that compromises given to the secessionists would not solve the growing problem of slavery. He opposed the annexation of Texas, but when war broke out, he sought a military commission. He was offered a major generalship, though he was convinced to decline the offer. His failure to take sides in the Van Buren–Lewis Cass party split left him as a man without a party. While defeated for reelection to the Senate in 1850, he won a term in the House of Representatives in 1852. However, he was defeated when he stood for reelection. He retired from public life and wrote one of the greatest political autobiographies, *Thirty Years' View*. In addition to this 2-volume work, he labored to produce the 16-volume *Abridgment of the Debates of Congress*. He finished the final volume on April 9, 1858, the day before his death.

Lloyd M. Bentsen (1921–) Lloyd Millard Bentsen Jr. ran for the Democratic nomination to the United States Senate in 1970 to unseat incumbent Democrat Ralph W. Yarborough, who was too liberal for Bentsen's and his backers' tastes. Bensten painted Yarborough as a liberal out of touch with Texans. In the general election, he faced and defeated George Bush, a Republican congressman. Bentsen was reelected to the Senate in 1976, 1982, and 1988. During his first term, he decided to run for the Democratic nomination for president in 1976. However, he soon pulled out of the race after being unable to garner much support. Generally regarded as a conservative on defense and economic issues, Bentsen is more moderate on social issues. He has chaired several important Senate committees, including the Finance Committee, where he served the interests of oil and gas, earning the nickname "Loophole Lloyd," and later sponsored a $10,000-a-person breakfast with the chair—a political mistake dubbed "Eggs McBentsen." In his post as chair, he played a critical role in the tax bills of the Ronald Reagan and George Bush administrations. In 1988 Bensten was the vice presidential candidate on the Democratic ticket headed by Governor Michael S. Dukakis of Massachusetts. He was a sharp critic of President Bush, leading many to believe he was staking out campaign ground. However, Bentsen refused to run for president in 1992. Instead, he served as an adviser to Governor Bill Clinton's campaign. When Clinton won the presidency, Bentsen was appointed secretary of the treasury. Bentsen resigned his post in 1994 as a result of growing problems with Whitewater, a failed land-development deal involving President Clinton and his wife, and his seeming lack of influence on economic policy in the more liberal Clinton White House.

Richard W. Bolling (1916–)   After serving as midwestern director for Americans for Democratic Action and vice chair of the American Veterans Committee, Richard Walker Bolling was elected to the United States House of Representatives from Missouri in 1948. Bolling, a liberal, was instrumental in the passage of civil rights legislation. As early as 1956, he manuevered to have the issue brought to a floor vote by circumventing the Rules Committee chair Howard W. Smith of Virginia. He continued to work on behalf of civil rights issues throughout his tenure in the House. In 1965 he authored a book entitled *House Out of Order,* in which, among other things, he argued against the House's seniority system. In 1979 Bolling became chair of the powerful Rules Committee, a post he held until his retirement in 1983.

David L. Boren (1941–)   David Lyle Boren was elected to the Oklahoma House of Representatives in 1966 and was then reelected three times unopposed. He gained a reputation as a reformer because he sought to have legislators disclose their campaign finances and voting records. In 1974 he challenged incumbent Democratic Governor David Hall, who was under federal investigation, for the party nomination. Boren, who attracted attention by carrying a broom around as a symbol of his pledge to sweep out the old guard, defeated the two other candidates for the nomination in a runoff election, then easily won the general election. As governor, he worked to reorganize the government and limit its size. A close colleague of Governor Jimmy Carter of Georgia, Boren endorsed Carter early in the 1976 presidential race. While Carter was a candidate, Boren drafted many of his proposed energy policies. However, Carter did not enact the deregulation of oil and gas as promised, whereupon Boren became an outspoken critic. In 1978 he decided to run for the United States Senate. After defeating six other candidates in the Democratic primary, Boren was easily elected to the Senate in the general election. He was reelected in 1984 and 1990. In the Senate, he served on the Finance Committee and played a large role in the Gramm–Rudman–Hollings (deficit-reduction) Act of 1985. Generally a conservative, he has supported a constitutional amendment requiring a balanced budget, prayer in public schools, aid to the contras, and the rights of gun owners. In 1987 he was one of only two Democrats to vote for the confirmation of Judge Robert H. Bork as an associate justice on the United States Supreme Court. As chair of the Select Committee on Intelligence, he presided over the Iran–contra scandal hearings in 1987. Boren has championed the limitation of political action committee contributions to politicians. He resigned from the Senate in November 1994.

John Brademas (1927–)   John Brademas twice ran unsuccessfully for the United States House of Representatives from Indiana, in 1954 and 1956. During that time, he held several positions with prominent politicians, including Governor Adlai E. Stevenson of Illinois. On his third attempt at Congress, Brademas defeated the incumbent Republican F. Jay Nimtz in 1958. He retained his seat in the House until 1981, serving as majority whip from 1977 to 1981. In Congress he was active in the passage of many significant education acts, including the Higher Education Facilities Act of 1963, the Elementary and Secondary Education Act of 1965, and the Higher Education Act of 1972. A committed liberal, he generally supported the policies of the John F. Kennedy and Lyndon B. Johnson administrations while opposing most measures of the Dwight D. Eisenhower, Richard M. Nixon and Gerald R. Ford administrations. In foreign affairs, he supported every proposal to end the war in Indochina and favored the discontinuation of military aid to Turkey. He did not run for reelection in 1980 because he had accepted an offer to become president of New York University.

Jesse D. Bright (1812–1875)   Jesse David Bright served from 1843 to 1845 as lieutenant governor of Indiana as the proslavery half of a pro-/antislavery ticket. In 1845 he was elected to the United States Senate, to which he was reelected in 1851 and 1857. Bright used his power in the Senate to isolate and limit the power of antislavery senators such as Republican Charles Sumner of Massachusetts. On February 5, 1862, Bright was expelled from the Senate on the grounds of disloyalty to the Union. He had written a letter of introduction to Confederate President Jefferson Davis for a friend. While the Judiciary Committee recommended that Bright keep his seat, the whole Senate voted 32 to 14 to expel him. The Indiana legislature, despite its Democratic majority, did not send Bright back to Washington. Prior to his expulsion from the Senate for disloyalty, he was the most senior Democrat and had served as president pro tempore.

Edmund G. "Jerry" Brown Jr. (1938–)   The son of popular California Governor Edmund Gerald "Pat" Brown, Edmund G. "Jerry" Brown Jr. began his political career in 1970, when he was elected secretary of state in California. During his term in office, he fought against political corruption. In 1974, he ran successfully for governor of California as an unconventional liberal who opposed high taxes and wasteful government spending while supporting legislation to benefit minorities, the poor, and the environment. Brown was reelected in 1978 and served until 1983. He unsuccessfully sought the Democratic presidential nomination in 1976 and 1980. He also ran unsuccessfully for the United States Senate against Republican Pete Wilson in 1982. After this defeat, Brown left public life to travel, work with Mother Teresa, learn Zen Buddhism, and practice law. In 1992 he made a third unsuccessful bid for the Democratic presidential nomination, running as a reform candidate. His candidacy added controversy to the 1992 Democratic National Convention because the supporters of Bill Clinton did not want to allow Brown to address the delegates in prime time.

Ronald H. Brown (1941–1996)   Ronald Harmon Brown entered politics as a district leader for the Democratic Party in Westchester County, New York. He later moved to Washington, D.C., with the Urban League. Brown managed California for Senator Edward M. Kennedy's failed 1980 campaign for the Democratic presidential nomination. Brown's efforts resulted in his appointment as chief counsel to the Senate Judiciary Committee, which Kennedy chaired. He became deputy chair of the Democratic National Committee in 1982. In 1985, when his appointment to the committee ended, Brown returned to private law practice. In 1988, Brown returned to party politics at the Democratic National Convention, where he was floor manager for Jesse Jackson. In this post, he worked to unify the forces of Michael Dukakis and Jackson. On February 10, 1989, Brown became the first black to serve as chair of any major political party. He successfully increased the control of Democrats nationwide during his tenure. Additionally, he was critical to President Bill Clinton's campaign victory in 1992. When Clinton entered the White House, Brown was appointed secretary of commerce.

John A. Burns (1909–1975)   John Anthony Burns became an organizer for the Democratic Party in Hawaii, serving as chair of the state's Central Committee from 1952 to 1956. In 1956 he defeated the incumbent Republican, Elizabeth Farrington, to become the nonvoting territorial delegate to the United States House of Representatives. In Washington, Burns worked for statehood. Although there was a movement to combine Hawaii's statehood vote with that of Alaska, Burns succeeded in keeping the votes separate, fearing that the combination would be opposed

by too many members of Congress. Reelected in 1958, he continued to press for statehood. In March 1959 he was successful in steering the statehood bill through both houses of Congress and a presidential signing. In 1959 he was defeated in his quest to be the first governor of the state of Hawaii by the incumbent territorial governor, William F. Quinn. However, in 1962, he defeated Quinn to become governor, and was reelected in 1966 and 1970. Burns enjoyed a period of economic prosperity in Hawaii while maintaining a middle-of-the-road approach to policies. In his second term, the rapid growth of tourism and crime became issues because of their negative impact on the environment and traditional lifestyles. Burns held to the "big Hawaii" scheme, under which other island territories like the Mariana, Caroline, and Marshall Islands as well as Guam and Samoa would become part of the state.

Harry F. Byrd Jr. (1914–)   Harry Flood Byrd Jr., son of Senator Harry F. Byrd Sr., began his political career on the Virginia State Democratic Central Committee, on which he served from 1940 to 1945. In 1966 he was appointed to the United States Senate to replace his father. He was subsequently elected to serve the remainder of the term. Byrd's voting pattern continued his father's legacy as a fiscal conservative. When the party machine that elected his father and him to the Senate began to fall into more liberal hands, Byrd ran in 1970 as an independent. He was reelected in 1976, serving until his retirement in 1983.

Harry F. Byrd Sr. (1887–1966)   Harry Flood Byrd Sr. came from one of the very well connected first families of Virginia. In 1915 he was elected to the state Senate, serving there until 1925. He gained a reputation as a fiscal conservative and a social moderate. During this time he took a leadership role in the creation of a statewide system of highways and served as the state's fuel commissioner during World War I. In 1925, at the age of 38, he was elected over the objections of the Democratic Party regulars to become Virginia's youngest governor since Thomas Jefferson. As governor, he engaged in a number of successful reorganizations of the state's bureaucracy, turning a deficit into a surplus by the end of his first term. According to Virignia's Constitution, Byrd was limited to one term. In 1932 he received favorite-son support for president. After declining an offer to become secretary of agriculture, he was appointed to the United States Senate when Senator Claude Swanson was appointed secretary of the navy. He successfully stood for election to the Senate six times, serving until he retired because of failing health in 1965. During his tenure, he was the leader of a conservative coalition of southern Democrats. Byrd was one of the earliest Democratic critics of the Franklin D. Roosevelt administration. After supporting Roosevelt's reelection in 1936, he never again supported a Democratic ticket. He urged fiscal conservatism rather than the costly programs of the New Deal, a theme repeated throughout his tenure. On the foreign policy side, Byrd was generally an isolationist, although he did support United States membership in the North Atlantic Treaty Organization. An ardent opponent of civil rights reforms, he encouraged the Viriginia State legislature to close schools rather than comply with the 1954 decision in *Brown* v. *Board of Education* (of Topeka). He also opposed passage of the 24th Amendment, which outlawed the poll tax, a method used to limit black voter participation. In the 1960 presidential election, he received 15 electoral votes.

Robert C. Byrd (1917–)   While a fundamentalist preacher, Robert Carlyle Byrd was elected to the West Viriginia House of Delegates in 1946 and was re-elected in 1948 and 1950. In 1952 Byrd announced his candidacy for the United States House of Representatives. Despite controversy over his membership in and later support of the Ku Klux Klan, he was elected to the House. Easily reelected in 1954 and 1956, he is generally considered a liberal on economic issues, though quite conservative in all other areas. In 1958 he successfully challenged the Republican incumbent for a seat in the United States Senate. His mentors in the Senate were Lyndon B. Johnson of Texas and Richard B. Russell Jr. of Georgia. He joined the latter in an extended filibuster of the Civil Rights Act of 1964. He chaired the Senate Subcommittee on the District of Columbia from 1961 to 1969. When riots broke out in Washington in 1968 after the murder of Martin Luther King Jr., Byrd advocated the use of federal troops to put down the unrest. Eventually, he became a supporter of home rule for the district as a way of ending Congress's involvement with the city's problems. By the end of the 1960s, Byrd had become more conservative in his voting patterns. He supported the nominations of both G. Harrold Carswell and Clement F. Haynesworth Jr. to the Supreme Court. When these conservative Nixon appointees were not confirmed, Byrd bitterly chastised his liberal colleagues. An excellent parliamentarian, he converted the post of secretary of the Democratic caucus into an important stop on the legislative trail. In 1971 he defeated incumbent Senator Edward M. Kennedy of Massachusetts for the post of party whip. In the post as majority whip, Byrd's voting record began to moderate. In 1977 he became majority leader of the Senate. In this position,

Byrd was often criticized for his forceful tactics and parliamentary maneuvering to limit debate and achieve his objectives. During his tenure as majority leader, Byrd successfully funneled large amounts of federal funds and federal jobs to his home state, earning him the title "king of pork." When the Republicans controlled the Senate from 1986 to 1988, he served as minority leader, a post he has also held since the 1994 elections.

James F. Byrnes (1879–1972)   James Francis Byrnes of South Carolina ran successfully for the United States House of Representatives in 1910. He was an excellent legislator, understanding the art of compromise. In 1924 Byrnes decided to run for the Senate against the incumbent Democrat, Cole L. Blease. In a runoff election for the nomination, Blease supporters used Byrnes's childhood religion, Roman Catholicism, effectively as a campaign issue. Byrnes lost despite having left the Catholic Church in 1906. In 1930 he ran again for the Democratic nomination for Senator Blease's seat. Since his positions on white supremacy, lynching, and black enfranchisment were no different than Blease's, Byrnes decided to focus on economic issues. He succeeded in redefining the agenda. He worked well with President Franklin D. Roosevelt, to whom he had been close since the Woodrow Wilson administration. Byrnes acted as a whip for the administration in its attempts to pass New Deal legislation. Despite his staunch support of FDR, he distanced himself from the administration after his reelection in 1936. He supported Roosevelt for reelection in 1940, despite having been passed over for the number-two spot. As a consolation to Byrnes, Roosevelt appointed him to the Supreme Court to replace Justice C. McReynolds. Byrnes did not enjoy the post and left in order to venture back into politics. He was appointed director of economic stabilization and chair of the War Mobilization Board. Once again seeking the vice presidency, he was opposed because of his racist views and Catholicism. He attended the Yalta Conference with Roosevelt in February 1945, though he did not participate in the negotiations. Following Roosevelt's death, he became an important player in postwar international affairs. He attended the Potsdam Conference with President Harry S. Truman and represented the United States at the London Conference of Foreign Ministers, the December Big Three Conference in Moscow, and United Nations organizational meetings. In 1947 he resigned from the Truman administration, citing health reasons, though it was clear that he and Truman did not get along. In 1950 he ran successfully for governor of South Carolina. Two years later, he supported Dwight D. Eisenhower for president. Prevented by law from running for reelection in 1954, he retired from politics.

Hattie W. Caraway (1878–1950)   Hattie Ophelia Wyatt Caraway was appointed to fill the United States Senate seat vacated by her husband's death in 1931. Rather than leave politics, she decided to run for the seat herself. Given little chance of victory as six more-experienced Democrats sought the nomination, she was victorious in the primary and general election of 1932. The campaigning by Huey P. Long of Louisiana on her behalf in Arkansas had helped. With that election, she became the first woman ever elected to the United States Senate. Additionally, she was the first woman to chair a committee, to preside over the Senate, and to conduct a Senate committee hearing. She rarely spoke on the floor of the Senate, while compiling a progressive voting record. In 1938 she won reelection to the Senate after another bitter primary contest. However, she was defeated by J. William Fulbright in 1944. After her defeat, President Franklin D. Roosevelt appointed her to the Federal Employees' Compensation Commission.

Lewis Cass (1782–1866)   Lewis Cass began his long political career with his election to the Ohio legislature in 1806 at the age of 24. Moving to the Michigan Territory, he served as the territorial governor beginning in 1813 and gained national recognition. From 1831 to 1836, he served as President Andrew Jackson's secretary of war. Afterward, he accepted an appointment as minister to France, where a dispute with his childhood friend Daniel Webster over the Quintuple Treaty led to his resignation. In 1845 he was elected to the U.S. Senate from Michigan. Cass actively supported containment of the slavery issue by advocating a doctrine similar to, though prior to, Stephen A. Douglas's "squatter sovereignty." He was his party's standard-bearer in the election of 1848 but lost as Martin Van Buren divided the Democratic vote. In 1851 he was reelected to the Senate, serving until appointed secretary of state in President James Buchanan's cabinet. In 1860 he resigned from office because Buchanan refused to reinforce the forts in Charleston Harbor. Throughout his career, he was a strong nationalist and Union man.

A.B. "Happy" Chandler (1898–1991)   Albert Benjamin "Happy" Chandler was elected to the Kentucky state senate in 1929, serving a single term. In 1931 he was elected lieutenant governor and subsequently governor in 1935. As governor, he was responsible for eliminating 130 state agencies and wiping out the state's $20 million deficit. In addition, Chandler secured ratification of a child labor amendment to the state constitution and ordered national guardsmen to restore calm at a coal-mining strike. Chandler unsuccessfully challenged incumbent Senator Alben W. Barkley for the Democratic nomination in 1938. However, Senator M.M. Logan died in 1939, and Chandler was appointed to the vacant seat. In 1940 he was elected to fill the remainder of the term until 1943. Chandler easily won reelection to the Senate in 1942. Fearing that the Allies would not help with the war in the Pacific, Chandler urged prosecution of the Pacific theater first. A candidate for the vice presidential nomination in 1944, Chandler resigned from the Senate in 1945 to assume the post of baseball commissioner. In 1948 he supported Strom Thurmond's States' Rights Democratic presidential bid. He ended his term as baseball commissioner in 1950, when fewer than two-thirds of the managers voted for him. At the 1952 Democratic National Convention, he supported the candidacy of Senator Russell B. Long of Georgia. In a crowded field of Democratic hopefuls, Chandler was successful in securing the Democratic nomination for governor in 1955. He easily defeated the Republican challenger in the general election. As governor, he oversaw the integration of Kentucky schools as he had overseen the opening of the major leagues to the first black players. At the 1956 Democratic National Convention, Chandler received modest support for the presidential nomination. Prevented from running for reelection as governor in 1959, Chandler waged an unsuccessful bid for a third term as governor in 1963.

James P. Clarke (1854–1926)   James Paul Clarke served as governor of Arkansas from 1893 to 1895. In 1902 he was elected to the United States Senate, a post he held until 1917. In 1913 Clarke was selected as president pro tempore. Much to his party's displeasure, he broke with the rank and file to support President Theodore Roosevelt's Panama Canal legislation. In addition, he actively lobbied for the Bristow Amendment, which provided for the direct election of senators. Generally a conservative Democrat, he had little support in the progressive Democratic Party of the turn of the century.

Earle C. Clements (1896–1985)   Earle Chester Clements began his public service as sheriff of Union County, Kentucky, in 1922. Four years later, he became the county clerk. In 1934 Clements was elevated to county judge, a post he held until 1941. Elected to the state Senate in 1942, he served as majority leader in 1944. Later that year, he was elected to the United States House of Representatives and was reelected in 1946. In the House he sponsored a bill to support tobacco prices. He also supported many of the New Deal programs, including the Rural Electrification Administration and the Tennessee Valley Authority. He resigned from Congress in 1947 after his election as governor of Kentucky. Clements increased taxes on gasoline in order to improve Kentucky's highway system and increase spending on education. In 1950 he resigned from his post as governor in order to take the seat in the United States Senate vacated by the resignation of Alben W. Barkley. In 1952 he chaired the Senate Democratic Campaign Committee. The following year he was named party whip, a post he held until he left the Senate in 1957, having been defeated for reelection in 1956. He served as director of the United States Senate Democratic Campaign Committee from 1957 until he returned to Kentucky in 1959. In 1960 he served as a state highway commissioner before retiring to private life.

Anthony L. Coelho (1942–)   Anthony Lee "Tony" Coelho began his political career as a Capitol Hill staffer from 1965 to 1976. Active in California State Democratic politics, he has been a delegate to state conventions since 1977 and a delegate to the Democratic National Conventions in 1976, 1980, 1984, 1988 and 1992. Elected to Congress in 1978 from California, Coelho became majority whip in 1987. However, his tenure in the House and as whip ended on June 15, 1989, when he resigned because of the growing controversy surrounding his investments in junk bonds.

Erastus Corning II (1809–1883)   A successful businessman, Erastus Corning II served on the Board of Aldermen for Albany, New York, from 1834 to 1835. In that year, he was elected mayor of Albany. Reelected three times to the post, he resigned during 1837. Corning again entered politics in 1842, when he was elected to the state Senate, serving there until 1846. In 1856 he was elected to the United States House of Representatives. He was unsuccessful in his reelection bid in 1858 but was returned to Congress in 1860. Three years later he resigned from Congress because of ill health. He returned to Albany and his business interests, although he did serve as a delegate to the New York State Constitutional Convention in 1867.

Wilbur L. Cross (1862–1948)   After a full career at Yale University, Wilbur Lucius Cross was nominated by the Democratic Party to run for governor of Connecticut in 1930. Few expected him to do well in the polling, but to everyone's surprise, he was elected by a solid majority in the heavily Republican state. He fought against the Republican state legislature, which tried to limit his authority. A tough politician, he was reelected three times. Though he had not been person-

ally involved, scandals over highway construction and local city corruption in Waterbury prevented him from being elected to a fifth term. During his tenure, he worked to reorganize the government to make it more efficient and to build a modern system of highways. His efforts in Connecticut were labeled the "little New Deal."

Richard J. Daley (1902–1976)   At the young age of 21, Richard Joseph Daley was active in Democratic politics as a precinct captain in Chicago. Thirteen years later, in 1936, he would be elected to his first office, as a member of the Illinois House of Representatives, by a write-in vote. In 1938 he was elected to the state Senate, serving as minority leader from 1941 to 1946. Daley was unsuccessful in his 1946 bid for Cook County sheriff. Afterward, he served in appointed positions as controller of Cook County and then director of revenue for Governor Adlai E. Stevenson. He failed to win the Democratic nomination for president of the Cook County Commissioners. However, in 1949 he was appointed acting county clerk, a post he won for a full term in 1950. After Republicans won many state and county positions in 1950, Daley played a major role in the removal of Colonel Jacobs M. Arvey as Democratic chair. Taking control of the Democratic Central Committee in Cook County, he created a powerful political machine. Daley ran sucessfully for mayor of Chicago in 1955 against the two-term incumbent Democrat, Martin H. Kennelly. As mayor, he undertook a major building project to revitalize the city. He also controlled the strongest modern political machine, which, at its height, was responsible for the election of ten congressmen, the governor, and Democratic majorities in both houses of the state legislature as well as in the Chicago and Cook County governments. Daley easily won reelection in 1959, 1963, 1967, 1971 and 1975. At the 1960 Democratic National Convention, he provided John F. Kennedy the support he needed in order to win the nomination on the first ballot. He also helped Kennedy win the state in the general election against Richard M. Nixon, though voter fraud was likely. At the request of President Lyndon B. Johnson, Daley hosted the 1968 Democratic National Convention, which was marked by violence. At the convention, he was a leader of the draft–Edward M. Kennedy movement. By 1972, however, things had begun to change. At the Democratic National Convention, Daley's delegates were not seated because he had not followed the new selection guidelines. In addition, a noted Democratic critic of Daley won election as governor. A prominent supporter of Jimmy Carter's presidential bid in 1976, Daley failed to deliver Illinois for Carter. Daley died later that year. Currently, Daley's son, Richard J. Daley Jr., continues the family dynasty, serving as mayor of Chicago.

Henry G. Davis (1823–1916)   After running a series of very successful businesses, Henry Gassaway Davis was elected to the West Virginia House of Delegates in 1865 as a member of the Union–Conservative Party. In 1868 he was elected to the state Senate, being reelected two years later. From 1888 until 1908, he represented West Virginia at Democratic National Conventions. Though he was more in tune with the Republicans on policy issues such as a protective tariff, Davis could not bring himself to be a member of the party responsible for the harsh Reconstruction of the South. In 1870 he was elected to the U.S. Senate and was reelected in 1876. He refused to stand for reelection to a third term as he wanted to return to his railroad interests. He served as a delegate to the first two Pan-American Conferences. In 1904, at the age of 81, Davis was the vice presidential nominee on a ticket headed by Alton B. Parker.

Ronald V. Dellums (1935–)   In 1967 Ronald Vernie Dellums was elected to the Berkeley City Council, on which he served until 1971. He then challenged liberal Democratic incumbent Jeffery Cohelan for the United States House of Representatives in one of the most liberal districts in the country. Running as a self-declared radical, Dellums won the primary and the general election of 1970. He has been reelected easily in every congressional election since then. As a member of the Armed Services Committee, Dellums called for hearings into war crimes committed by Americans in Vietnam. When the full committee refused to investigate, he held his own hearings. He has gained a reputation as an ardent critic of the military. This was especially true during the Ronald Reagan administration, when he became the chief opponent of the arms buildup. In 1991 Dellums voted present on the resolution to engage in the Gulf War because he could not bring himself to vote in favor of the measure. During his career, he chaired the committee that oversaw the District of Columbia, using this post to limit the federal government's intervention in district affairs. In 1984 he was arrested for protesting apartheid outside the Embassy of South Africa. His bill sanctioning South Africa was passed in 1986. When Representative Les Aspin became secretary of defense in 1993, Dellums was elevated to chair of the Armed Services Committee. When the Pentagon placed all five of the bases in his district on the closure list in 1993, Dellums vowed to fight against their closure.

Richardson Dilworth (1898–1974)   After returning from service in World War II, Richardson Dilworth, who had been wounded during World War I, led a reform movement in Philadelphia that resulted in a new city charter in 1951. While an unsuccessful candidate for mayor in 1947, he exposed graft and corruption in Republican Mayor Bernard Samuel's administration, which led to a grand jury indictment of many key officials as well as nine suicides. In 1949 he was elected city treasurer. After running unsuccessfully for governor in 1950, he was elected district attorney in 1951. Dilworth focused his energies on organized crime and vigorously prosecuted police who used excessive force. In 1955 he was elected mayor of Philadelphia. During his tenure, he not only cleaned up city hall but also oversaw urban renewal of the city. Opponents used his comments that the United States should recognize the People's Republic of China to prevent him from running for governor in 1958. However, he resigned as mayor in 1962 to run as the Democratic nominee for governor against Republican William W. Scranton. Dilworth was defeated in the general election. In 1965, he was appointed to a six-year term on the Philadelphia Board of Education. Dilworth resigned in 1971 before Frank Rizzo took office as mayor.

Paul H. Douglas (1892–1976)   After serving on a number of state and national government appointed boards, mostly linked to his knowledge of economics, Paul Howard Douglas was elected to the Chicago Board of Aldermen in 1939, serving until 1942. He was defeated in his attempt to gain the Democratic nomination for Senate in 1942. After this loss, he enlisted as a private in the marines, seeing duty in the Pacific theater. In 1948 Douglas defeated incumbent Republican Senator C. Wayland Brooks. His independence and idealism kept him outside of the inner circles of power in Washington. He worked hard on economic issues for the disadvantaged and supported civil rights legislation, public housing, national health insurance, and expanded Social Security. Douglas was also a staunch anticommunist who favored the creation of the North Atlantic Treaty Organization. He was a delegate to the Democratic National Conventions in 1952, 1956, 1964 and 1968. Twice reelected to the Senate in 1954 and 1960, he was defeated in 1966 because of his defense of the Lyndon B. Johnson administration's Vietnam policies and backlash against his votes in favor of the Civil Rights Act of 1964 and the Voting Rights Act of 1965. Douglas continued to serve on commissions and write books on economic and budgetary issues.

Thomas F. Eagleton (1929–)   Thomas Francis Eagleton began his political career as attorney general of Missouri in 1960. He was elected lieutenant governor in 1964 and to the United States Senate in 1968.

However, he resigned that seat in order to be appointed to a seat that had been vacated by the death of Senator Edward V. Long in 1968. He was elected to the remainder of the term in 1969. In 1972 he was chosen as the Democratic vice presidential nominee on a ticket headed by liberal Senator George S. McGovern. However, after the convention ended, Eagleton disclosed that he had been voluntarily committed to a hospital three times between 1960 and 1966 for nervous exhaustion and had received electroshock therapy. Initially, McGovern defended his running mate. However, as time went on, it became clear that Eagleton would have to resign the nomination, a first in American history. McGovern announced that his choice to replace Eagleton was Ambassador to France R. Sargent Shriver of Maryland. Shriver had formerly directed the Peace Corps and the Office of Economic Opportunity. Despite the controversy, Eagleton was reelected to the Senate in 1974 and 1980. He retired from public life in 1987 after losing his 1986 reelection bid.

India Edwards (1895–1990)   After participating in the Democratic National Convention in 1944, India Edwards began her association with the Democratic Party as the executive secretary of the Women's Division in 1945. Later that year, she also attended the United Nations Conference on International Organization in San Francisco. She became associate director of the Women's Division in 1947, a post she held until mid-1948, when she became executive director of the division. She dramatically made inflation a key issue at the 1948 Democratic National Convention. When the party included a civil rights plank, she organized women to canvass the South championing the party's position. She traveled the campaign trail with President Harry S. Truman, helping to bring out the women's vote. While she ended her formal relationship with the Democratic National Committee in 1950, when she stepped down as executive director of the Women's Division, she remained active in Democratic politics until her death in 1990.

A. Michael Espy (1953–)   Albert Michael "Mike" Espy was the first black appointed to be an assistant secretary of state for Mississippi in 1978. After four years in that post, he managed the campaign of Ed Pittman for state attorney general. In 1984 he was a member of the Democratic National Committee. After serving as assistant attorney general for Mississippi, Espy ran for the United States House of Representatives in 1986. After barely winning the Democratic primary, Espy successfully unseated the Republican incumbent, Webb Franklin. He was reelected in 1988, 1990 and 1992. He gained the respect of many for his

service on the Agriculture Committee. Early in the 1992 Democratic presidential primaries, Espy endorsed Governor Bill Clinton of Arkansas for the party's nomination. After Clinton's victory, Espy was tapped to be secretary of agriculture, overseeing one of the nation's largest bureaucracies. Espy resigned from his post on December 31, 1993, after being indicted for taking gifts, including a $1,200 college scholarship for his girlfriend, from Tyson's Food and other companies regulated by the Department of Agriculture.

James A. Farley (1888–1976)   A lifelong Democrat, James Aloysius Farley entered politics in 1912 by winning a postcard campaign for town clerk of Stony Point, New York. He served three terms as clerk before becoming Rockland County Democratic Committee chair in 1918. When Alfred E. Smith won the governorship, Farley was appointed as post warden for New York City, serving until the position was abolished by a Republican legislature in 1920. In 1922 he was elected to the New York State Assembly, though he was defeated for reelection in 1924. In 1928 he began his service as secretary of the Democratic State Committee. In 1930 he was elected chair of the committee, being reelected in 1932. At the Democratic National Convention of 1932, he was the floor leader for the Franklin D. Roosevelt forces. He was elected Democratic National Committee chair that year. After Farley was appointed postmaster general in the Roosevelt administration, his critics charged him with using his post for political patronage. In 1936 he managed Roosevelt's reelection campaign. However, his support for the Roosevelt administration began to wane. In 1940 his name was placed in nomination as a competitor to Roosevelt. However, after FDR was renominated, Farley resigned as postmaster general and as chair of the Democratic National Committee. In 1944 he supported Senator Harry F. Byrd Sr. of Virginia for the presidential nomination, although when Roosevelt was renominated, he campaigned for the ticket. Farley remained active in Democratic politics until his death in 1976.

Orval E. Faubus (1910–)   Orval Eugene Faubus began his political career when he was appointed Arkansas state highway commissioner in 1949. He was elected governor of Arkansas in 1954 and then reelected to five additional terms. He gained national attention in 1957, when he used the Arkansas National Guard to block the integration of Little Rock Central High School. Although a court injunction forced Faubus to remove the guardsmen, violence ensued, which resulted in President Dwight D. Eisenhower's sending federal troops to enforce integration. The incident increased Faubus's popularity in the state. He served as governor until 1967, when he retired from public life.

Geraldine A. Ferraro (1935–)   Geraldine Anne Ferraro was born to Italian immigrant parents in Newburgh, New York, August 26, 1935. Educated at Marymount College and Fordham University Law School, she began her career as an assistant dictrict attorney, Queen's County, in 1974–1978. She was first elected as a Democrat to the U.S. House of Representatives in 1978 and served in the House for three terms. She voted the party line except for opposing busing and supporting tuition tax credits. Although a strong feminist, she moderated her stand on abortion in deference to her large Catholic constituency. In 1984 she became the surprise choice of Walter Mondale as his running mate, but went down in one of the worst defeats in modern political history. Her campaign was weakened by allegations of fraudulent land deals and illegal contributions against her husband. In 1994 she lost in the Democratic primary for the U.S. Senate seat held by Alphonse D'Amato.

BIBLIOGRAPHY

Ferraro, Geraldine, and Linda Bird Franke. *Ferraro: My Story.* New York: Bantam Books, 1985.

J. William Fulbright (1905–1995)   After graduating from law school, James William Fulbright joined the Antitrust Division of the Department of Justice in 1934. A year later he left his post to pursue a career in academia, including a stint from 1939 to 1942 as president of the University of Arkansas. In 1942 Fulbright ran a successful campaign for the United States House of Representatives. He served only one term because in 1944 he ran sucessfully for the United States Senate. While in the Senate, he was instrumental in establishing government grants for international exchange. These grants, which bear his name, were first instituted by the Fulbright Act in 1946 and expanded by the Fulbright–Hays Act of 1965. He chaired the powerful Senate Foreign Relations Committee from 1959 until 1974. During this time he urged coexistence with communists. A leading opponent of the Vietnam War, he was not reelected in 1974.

Walter F. George (1878–1957)   An associate justice of the Georgia Supreme Court, Walter Franklin George resigned his position in 1922 to run successfully for an unexpired term in the United States Senate. He served in the Senate from 1922 until his retirement in 1957, being elected to five full terms. An old-fashioned Democrat, he began his career supporting states' rights. Though he opposed Franklin D. Roosevelt's

nomination in 1932, he campaigned for the national ticket. Opposed to the prolabor legislation of the New Deal, he did support much of the remainder of the early agenda. George began to criticize the president's policies, especially the Court-packing plan. Roosevelt actively campaigned in Georgia against George's re-election in 1938. Back in the Senate, he cast the deciding vote against further consideration of Roosevelt's cash-and-carry policy. Later, George was supportive of the administration's foreign policies. In 1940 he became chair of the Senate Foreign Relations Committee and in 1941 chair of the Senate Finance Committee. He played a major role in the Roosevelt and Harry S. Truman administrations' conduct of World War II and the postwar peace settlement. When Dwight D. Eisenhower became president, George had extensive access to the administration, especially to Secretary of State John Foster Dulles. He supported the administration's Formosa policy, turning back opposition in his own party. Under increasing criticism from his fellow Democrats, George supported fewer and fewer of the Eisenhower foreign policies. Warned that he could not defeat the more segregationist Governor Herman Talmadge for reelection in 1956, he announced his retirement. Because of his strong bipartisan support in foreign affairs, President Eisenhower appointed him ambassador to the North Atlantic Treaty Organization in 1957. He died later that year.

Richard A. Gephardt (1941–)   Richard Andrew Gephardt became a Democratic committeeman for St. Louis, Missouri, in 1968. Three years later he was elected to the Board of Aldermen. When 12-term Democratic incumbent Leonor Sullivan announced her retirement in 1976, Gephardt won her seat in the United States House of Representatives. With the aid of Representative Richard Bolling of Missouri, Gephardt was placed on the most important committee in Congress, the House Ways and Means Committee. From 1979 until 1984, he held the distinction of serving on both the Ways and Means Committee and the Budget Committee. Party leaders often chose Gephardt to make Democratic responses to the Ronald Reagan administration's budget and tax proposals. In 1984 he was selected to be the chair of the party caucus, the fourth highest post. He has used his position to build coalitions between the older and younger members of Congress. A political centrist, Gephardt founded the Democratic Leadership Council with other younger members of the party. In 1988 Gephardt ran unsuccessfully for the party's presidential nomination, which went to the more liberal Governor Michael Dukakis. He was, however, chosen majority leader of the House in 1989. In 1994, when the Republicans recaptured control of the House, he became the minority leader.

Carter Glass (1858–1946)   A lifelong Democrat, Carter Glass used his position as a newspaper publisher to editorialize on political subjects ranging from the treatment of the South after the Civil War to the free coinage of silver, a position he later regretted. He served one term in the Virginia State Senate, from 1899 to 1903. During that time he was a delegate to the Virginia Constitutional Convention of 1901–1902. At the convention he led the movement for the adoption of literacy tests and poll taxes as curbs on voting, correctly believing that these would limit black and poor white suffrage. The adoption of these measures halved the number of eligible voters. In 1902 Glass was elected to the United States House of Representatives, serving eight terms. A recognized expert on banking and currency, he chaired the committee that dealt with these issues. He was responsible for drafting the Federal Reserve System after his private reserve system was rejected by President Woodrow Wilson. His work on the system earned him the title "Father of the Federal Reserve System." In 1919 President Wilson appointed Glass secretary of the treasury. He had served there only one year when he was appointed to fill a vacancy in the United States Senate. Later that year he was elected to a full term. At the 1920 Democratic National Convention, he championed the League of Nations, having support for the League made a plank in the platform. In 1932 Glass declined appointment as secretary of the treasury in the Franklin D. Roosevelt administration. Despite Glass's early support for the administration's banking policies, when it began inflationary practices, he broke with the administration. In his reelection bid in 1936, he openly ran against the New Deal. Roosevelt referred to him as an "unreconstructed old rebel." True to his Wilsonian internationalism, Glass supported American intervention in Europe. Reelected in 1942, he did not enter the Senate after June of that year because of ill health. He died four years later of heart failure.

Arthur P. Gorman (1839–1906)   Arthur Pue Gorman had a 56-year association with the U.S. Senate, ranging from page to party leader. He began his service to the Senate in 1852, when he became a page. In that role, he caught the attention of Stephen A. Douglas, who hired him as his private secretary. Because of his relationship to the powerful senator, he enjoyed several appointments, including messenger, assistant doorkeeper, assistant postmaster, and postmaster during the Civil War. However, his political ties

to President Andrew Johnson cost him his job in 1866. He was elected to the Maryland legislature in 1869 and served there until 1875, when he was chosen as a U.S. Senator. In 1893 he was selected by his fellow Democrats to be the first official chairman of the Democratic caucus. He was defeated for reelection in 1898 but returned to the Senate as the Democratic floor leader in 1903. Though he opposed the policies of President Grover Cleveland, he ran Cleveland's successful campaigns of 1884 and 1892.

Ella T. Grasso (1919–1980)   Ella Tambussi Grasso was born of immigrant parents on May 10, 1919, in Windsor Locks, Connecticut. She graduated with honors from Mount Holyoke College in 1940. She began her political career when she was elected in 1952 to the state House of Representatives, where she served two terms. She chaired the Democratic state committee for 12 years (1956–1968) and completed three terms as secretary of state (1958–1970). She was the Democratic floor leader in the 1965 Connecticut constitutional convention and chaired the commission that drafted the new constitution. At the end of her term as secretary of state, she was elected to the U.S. House of Representatives (1970–1974). She did not stand for reelection to the House, but was Democratic Party Chairman John M. Bailey's hand-picked choice as governor. She was the first American woman to be elected governor without having succeeded her husband. In her 28 years in public service she never lost an election. Although considered as a vice presidential choice in 1976, she never had a large national following, particularly because of her antiabortion stand and her disinclination to fight for affirmative action and the Equal Rights Amendment. She won a second term in office but did not stand again because of a physical disability. She died December 31, 1980.

George Gray (1840–1925)   George Gray, a staunch Democrat, was appointed attorney general of Delaware in 1879 and reappointed in 1884. He resigned, however, a year later upon his election to the United States Senate, where he remained until 1899. A national figure after his speech at the 1880 Democratic National Convention in Cincinnati, Ohio, Gray became a leader of his party in the Senate. He declined the post of attorney general in the Grover Cleveland administration. Instead, he was an invaluable supporter of the president in the Senate. President William McKinley, in recognition of Gray's talent, appointed him a member of the Joint High Commission in 1899 that was to resolve ongoing issues between the United States and Canada. Later that year, he served as a delegate to the Paris peace negotiations that ended the

Spanish-American War. After Gray's resignation from the Senate, McKinley appointed him to the United States Circuit Court. Gray put his formidable talents as a negotiator to good use by settling the Pennsylvania coal strike of 1902.

Theodore F. Green (1868–1966)   Theodore Francis Green began his involvement in Rhode Island politics when, with a group of fellow reformers, he merged with the Democratic Party in efforts to reform the state government in 1906. He was elected to the state House in 1907, though he failed in his bid for the governorship in 1912 and 1930 as well as his bid for Congress in 1920. In 1932 he was elected governor of Rhode Island in a Democratic landslide. Working with the Republican majority in the state House, he secured support for many relief measures. He was reelected in 1934, when the state House also went Democratic. In 1936 Green was elected to the United States Senate. He was a staunch supporter of Franklin D. Roosevelt, including the president's Court-packing plan. He also voted in favor of most of Harry S. Truman's Fair Deal legislation. His most important service was on the Senate Foreign Relations Committee, where he was instrumental in supporting the Truman administration's foreign policy. In 1951 he became chair of the committee, supporting President Dwight D. Eisenhower while tolerating Secretary of State John Foster Dulles. With his health failing, Green did not stand for reelection in 1960, having resigned as chair earlier because of hearing and vision problems.

Fred R. Harris (1930–)   As a student at the University of Oklahoma, Fred Roy Harris ran an unsuccessful campaign for the Oklahoma legislature, losing by only 35 votes. However, in 1956 he was successful in his bid for the Oklahoma Senate, becoming its youngest member at the age of 26. A productive legislator, he sponsored bills for local industrial financing and the creation of the Oklahoma Human Rights Commission. In 1962 he ran an unsuccessful campaign for governor while retaining his state Senate seat. In 1964 he decided to run for the United States Senate seat vacated by the death of Senator Robert S. Kerr. The seat was temporarily filled by J. Howard Edmondson, who had resigned as governor to take the appointment. In a Democratic primary field of four candidates, Edmondson and Harris finished in the top spots for the runoff election. To the suprise of many, Harris bested Edmondson by 100,000 votes. His opponent in the general election was the former University of Oklahoma football coach Charles "Bud" Wilkinson, who ran as a conservative opposed to big government. Harris campaigned as neither a conservative nor a lib-

eral, but he did align himself with the Lyndon B. Johnson administration. He defeated his Republican opponent by more than 21,000 votes. In the Senate, he was a consistent supporter of President Johnson's policies. He also worked to cut wasteful federal spending and to better scrutinize research projects funded by the government. Harris was reelected in 1966 to a full six-year term. In 1968 he cochaired Hubert Humphrey's unsuccessful bid for the presidency. In 1972 he did not stand for reelection to the United States Senate. He was unsuccessful in his attempt to win the 1976 Democratic presidential nomination.

Byron Patton Harrison (1881–1941)   Byron Patton "Pat" Harrison began his political career as an elected district attorney of Mississippi in 1906. After attending the 1908 Democratic National Convention, he was elected to the United States House of Representatives two years later. Harrison, a loyal supporter of President Woodrow Wilson's policies, served four terms in the House. In 1918 Harrison was elected to the Senate with the help of Senator John Sharp Williams, leader of one of the two major factions in the Mississippi Democratic Party. Harrison unseated incumbent Democratic Senator James K. Vardaman, leader of the other major faction. President Wilson appealed to Mississippi Democrats to defeat Vardaman, who was a major critic of the administration. Harrison supported United States entry into the League of Nations as well as the World Court. He was reelected without opposition in 1924, 1930 and 1936. When the White House was held by the Republicans during the 1920s, he was a critic of the failures of those administrations. Despite his conservative southern tendencies, Harrison was an aggressive campaigner for Alfred E. Smith and Franklin D. Roosevelt. When the latter took office, Harrison was made chair of the powerful Senate Finance Committee, where he shepherded many of the New Deal proposals through Congress. He began to disagree with the president, especially over tax rates. When the post of majority leader became available in 1937, Roosevelt supported Harrison's opponent, Alben W. Barkley, who was elected by a single vote over Harrison. While he did not formally break with the New Deal or the administration, the loss freed Harrison to move in other directions. He did, however, refuse to sign a bipartisan condemnation of the New Deal. In 1941 he was elected as president pro tempore, serving only months, as he died later that year.

Carl T. Hayden (1877–1972)   In 1912 Carl Trumbull Hayden was chosen as one of Arizona's first representatives to the United States House. He would spend 56 years in the House and Senate, earning the nickname

"Arizona's man in Washington." Hayden, a moderate, was most interested in the issues of water rights, use of public lands, and mining rights. In 1926 he was elected to the United States Senate, a position he held until his retirement in 1969. Despite his longevity, he was not an extremely powerful senator, though his power did grow because of his hard work and quiet solicitation of votes. From 1927 to 1947, he took the floor of the Senate only once. He played a major role in the creation of the federal highway aid program in the 1950s. In 1957 he became the dean of the Senate, being the body's most senior member. He served as president pro tempore during much of the 1960s.

David B. Hill (1843–1910)   An early associate of Boss William Marcy Tweed, David Bennett Hill was elected as a delegate to the Democratic State Conventions in New York from 1868 to 1881. In 1877 and 1881 he served as the presiding officer of the conventions. Samuel J. Tilden convinced him to expose the corruption of his former associate and Tammany Hall leader. With increasing political influence, Hill was elected to the state Assembly and selected as the speaker in 1872. From this post, he worked to have Tilden elected governor and was an important supporter of Tilden's 1876 run for the White House. In 1880 he returned to local politics, being elected an alderman of Elmira, New York, and then mayor of the city the following year. He resigned from that post to run for the post of lieutenant governor on the Grover Cleveland ticket. When Cleveland was elected president, Hill assumed the governorship and was elected on his own in 1888. The state legislature chose him as a U.S. senator in 1891, but he did not take the seat until 1892. Ironically, President Cleveland did not support his appointment to the Senate because of Hill's attempts to block the president's renomination in 1892. Hill retired from politics at the end of his senatorial term in 1897.

Harold E. Hughes (1922–)   Harold Everett Hughes entered politics as an Iowa State commerce commissioner in 1958, when he decided to run because of his personal dissatisfaction with the commission when he lodged a complaint in 1957. He unsuccessfully sought the 1960 Democratic nomination for governor. However, in 1962 he succeeded in securing the Democratic gubernatorial nomination and won the general election against incumbent Republican Governor Norman A. Erbe. He was the only Democrat to win state office that year and was reelected to a second two-year term in 1964. While governor, he served on the executive committee of the National Governors' Conference and as chair of the Democratic Governors' Conference. He was elected to the United States Senate in 1968 but did

not stand as a candidate for reelection in 1974. Hughes briefly sought the Democratic presidential nomination in 1972. After his retirement from the Senate, he served for one year as an outside consultant to the Senate Judiciary Committee.

James B. Hunt Jr. (1937–)   James Baxter Hunt Jr. was elected in 1972 as lieutenant governor of North Carolina, where he served as liaison between the Republican governor and the Democrat-controlled legislature. In 1976 he was a landslide winner in the gubernatorial race, being reelected in 1980. In 1978 he gained national attention when he was pressured to parole the Wilmington Ten, a group that had been convicted of violence during a 1971 race riot. Hunt, a moderate, sought a compromise position. He agreed with the convictions but reduced the sentences. Hunt focused much of his energy on education in an attempt to upgrade the North Carolina system. In addition, he worked both to create a better business climate in the state and to get a handle on crime. In 1980 he served on the National Democratic Party Commission on the Presidential Nomination, where he helped rewrite the rules for future primaries and conventions. Prohibited by state law from running for a third consecutive term, Hunt decided to challenge conservative Republican Senator Jesse Helms. After a heated campaign, Helms decisively defeated the moderate Democrat. Hunt retired to practice law until 1992, when he decided to run again for the governorship. He easily defeated his Democratic opponent in the primary and then the Republican candidate in the general election by a margin of 53% to 43% to become the first person elected to a third term as governor of North Carolina.

Henry M. "Scoop" Jackson (1912–1983)   Henry Martin "Scoop" Jackson entered public life in 1938 as the crusading prosecuting attorney for Snohomish County, Washington, where he gained the nickname "Soda Pop" for his efforts to clean up bordellos, speakeasies and gambling. In 1940 he was elected to the United States House of Representatives, defeating five other Democrats in the primary. Reelected to five additional terms, Jackson was the only Democrat from the Pacific Northwest to be reelected in 1946. Though generally a moderate, Jackson was more conservative on defense issues, supporting increased defense expenditures. In 1952 he defeated conservative Republican Senator Harry P. Cain for a seat in the U.S. Senate. An ardent anticommunist, Jackson was appointed to the committee headed by Wisconsin Senator Joseph McCarthy to investigate communism in the State Department. He played a key role in ending the investigation and in the censure of McCarthy. A leading proponent of the missile-gap theory, Jackson urged further expenditures on nuclear weapons. He served as chair of the Democratic National Committee and managed the 1960 presidential campaign of John F. Kennedy. However, he resigned from the committee post after the election. A strong believer in the domino theory, Jackson sought a more aggressive war effort in Vietnam to stop communism. President-elect Richard M. Nixon offered Jackson the post of secretary of defense. Fearing that he would be a Democratic scapegoat for a failed Vietnam policy, he refused. However, Jackson continued to be a strong supporter of increased defense measures, helping to secure the deployment of antiballistic missiles in 1969. Since that time, he supported the B-1 bomber, Trident submarine-launched ballistic missile, and C-5A transport projects. In 1972 Jackson ran for the Democratic presidential nomination but placed no better than third. In 1976 his campaign for the presidency started well, with victories in Massachusetts and New York. However, when he lost Pennsylvania to Jimmy Carter, his campaign began to flounder. He withdrew from the race and supported Carter. Reelected to the Senate in 1976, Jackson spent a lot of energy on conservation issues. Jackson continued to serve in the Senate—fighting for a strong defense, a sound energy policy, and preservation of the environment—until his death in 1983. Senator Jackson had earned the nickname "Scoop" as a newsboy who delivered 74,880 copies of the *Everett Daily Herald* without a single complaint.

Jesse L. Jackson (1941–)   Jesse Louis Jackson has been an active civic leader for three decades. In the mid-1960s, he was the national director of Operation Breadbasket, a program to secure better jobs and services for blacks through the use of boycotts and picketing. After the assassination of Martin Luther King Jr. in 1968, Jackson continued his work at the Southern Christian Leadership Conference. In 1971 he returned to Chicago and founded PUSH, an organization that tried to increase the political and economic power of the poor. Five years later, with a Ford Foundation grant, he founded PUSH–Excel (PUSH for Excellence), a program to curb vandalism, drug abuse, and teenage pregnancy. In 1979 Jackson entered into foreign causes by touring South Africa, where he encouraged nonviolent civil disobedience to apartheid, and the Middle East, where he advocated recognition by Israel of the Palestine Liberation Organization. In 1980 Jackson received a controversial $2 million grant from the Carter administration through the Department of Labor for PUSH–Excel and a new career development project. In late 1983 Jesse Jackson announced his plans to seek the Democratic presidential nomination. Black leaders were divided in their support for Jackson. Many feared that his candidacy would divide the Democratic Party and ensure the reelection of President Ronald Reagan. In New Hampshire, the first primary, he finished a dismal fourth, with only 5% of the vote. However, as the campaign continued, Jackson picked up support and delegates. Although he placed third in the balloting at the 1984 convention, the experience he gained during that year has shaped his participation ever since. Jackson formed the Rainbow Coalition in an attempt to increase voter registration among minority groups. He has also continued to play an active role in foreign controversies and domestic politics. In 1988 he ran his most competitive campaign for president. While the nomination went to Governor Michael Dukakis of Massachusetts, Jackson was successful in shaping the platform. In 1992 he was less influential because the Democratic Party had become more centrist since 1988. Some political commentators speculate that Jackson may use the Rainbow Coalition as a platform from which to launch a third-party run for the White House if the Democratic Party continues its centrist trend.

James K. Jones (1839–1908)   After infrequent service in the Confederate army because of illness, James Kimbrough Jones set up a law practice in Washington, Arkansas. In 1873 he entered politics as a state senator, serving until 1879, the last two years as president of the Senate. In 1878 he won election to the U.S. House of Representatives, serving there until 1885, when he was chosen to be a U.S. senator. As a senator, he gained a national reputation for his opposition to almost all tariff bills. President Grover Cleveland, knowing he had to have the support of Jones on a new tariff bill, urged Jones to pass the Wilson bill out of committee. After weeks of wrangling, the tariff measure passed the Senate with 634 amendments attached. The president was so angry over the bill that he sent Congress a message of dissatisfaction, which Jones took personally. Passing on a Jones-for-president movement in 1896, Jones instead served as chairman of the Democratic National Committee, a post he held once again in the election of 1900.

Estes Kefauver (1903–1963)   Running as a New Deal Democrat in a special election for Congress in 1939, (Carey) Estes Kefauver won the seat. He was liberal for a southern Democrat, supporting the creation of the Tennessee Valley Authority and civil rights legislation. He was also a strong supporter of the reform of Congress. Kefauver coauthored a book on congressional reform with Jack Levin, *A Twentieth-Century*

Congress (1947). In a bitter primary battle challenging Tennessee's Democratic political machine, Kefauver defeated incumbent Senator Arthur T. Stewart and easily won the general election of 1948 against the Republican candidate. He entered the 1952 Democratic National Convention with more committed delegates than any other presidential hopeful. However, his independence and liberalism limited his support among party regulars. While popular with voters, he would be denied the nomination in 1952 and 1956. In a hard-fought contest, he secured the nomination for vice president on the 1956 ticket headed by Adlai E. Stevenson. Reelected to the Senate in 1960, he died in 1963.

Edward M. "Ted" Kennedy (1932–) Edward Moore Kennedy began his long political career managing the reelection campaign of his brother John F. Kennedy to the United States Senate in 1958. In 1960 he organized the western states for John's successful presidential bid. After serving for several years as an assistant district attorney, Kennedy defeated Edward J. McCormack Jr. for the nomination to the U.S. Senate in a bitter Democratic primary during which Kennedy's expulsion from Harvard and maturity were questioned. In the general election, he defeated George Cabot Lodge by more than 300,000 votes. With this victory, Kennedy, at the age of 30, became the youngest person ever elected to the Senate. He was presiding over the Senate on November 22, 1963, when news reached him of his brother's assassination. In 1964 he was reelected to a full Senate term despite the fact that he was in the hospital recovering from injuries received in a plane crash. In the Senate he was generally a supporter of President Lyndon B. Johnson's agenda. While initially supporting the Vietnam conflict, Kennedy soon came to oppose it and worked to alter draft laws and to aid refugees. He withdrew from public life for more than ten weeks after the funeral of his brother Robert F. Kennedy. When he reentered the Senate, he worked to end the Vietnam War, condemning the Richard M. Nixon administration's escalation of the conflict. Declining the chance to be the Democratic standard-bearer in 1968, he was elected majority whip with the aid of liberal senators. Reelected in 1970 by a smaller margin than in 1964, Kennedy also lost the post of majority whip to Senator Robert C. Byrd of West Virginia. As time passed, and the Chappaquiddick incident (in which Kennedy pled guilty to leaving a scene of an accident when he drove his car off the road on Chappaquiddick Island into the water, drowning his passenger, Mary Jo Kopechne) became less important to voters and colleagues, Kennedy began to regain his

clout in the Senate. Reelected in 1976, he became chair of the powerful Senate Judiciary Committee. In 1980 he led a spirited campaign for the Democratic presidential nomination against incumbent President Jimmy Carter. Though he lost the nomination, his forces were critical in shaping the liberal platform of 1980. In 1984 he placed Walter F. Mondale's name in nomination as the party's standard-bearer. Reelected in 1982, 1988 and 1994, Kennedy has continued to be one of the most liberal senators. During his tenure, he has chaired many important committees, including the Labor and Education Committee.

Robert F. Kennedy (1925–1968) Robert Francis Kennedy began his life of public service as an attorney in the Department of Justice's Criminal Division in 1951. The following year he served as campaign manager for his brother John F. Kennedy's 1952 race for the United States Senate against Republican incumbent Henry Cabot Lodge Jr. of Massachusetts. After his brother's victory, Robert Kennedy served as counsel to various Senate committees, including the Hoover Commission (1953) and the Senate Select Committee on Improper Activities in the Labor and Management Field (1957–1960). In 1960 he left his post to become the national campaign manager for Senator Kennedy's bid for the White House. Robert Kennedy was rewarded for his efforts by being appointed attorney general in his brother's administration. He served in this post until 1964, when he resigned in order to run for the United States Senate from New York. Kennedy served in the Senate until his assassination in 1968 while he was campaigning for the Democratic presidential nomination.

John W. Kern (1849–1917) John Worth Kern was an ardent Democrat from boyhood, and when he settled as an adult in a Republican stronghold in Indiana, he worked to form a cohesive party apparatus. As a local leader of the party, he served in myriad minor posts until his election in 1892 to the Indiana State Senate, where he served until 1897. After twice losing his bids for governor of the state (in 1900 and 1904), he was nominated by acclamation as the party's vice presidential candidate in 1908. In 1910 he defeated Albert J. Beveridge for the U.S. Senate. In the Senate he was regarded as one of the leaders of the progressive wing of the party. When the Democrats took control of the Senate in 1912, he was chosen floor leader. However, he was beaten in his reelection bid in 1916. Kern retired from politics that year and died of tuberculosis the following year.

Edward I. Koch (1924–) Edward Irving Koch began his political career as an active member of the

Village Independent Democrats in 1956. This newly formed group sought to reform Democratic Party politics by ousting the Tammany machine. In 1962 he ran as the party's nominee for the state Assembly, securing only 32% of the votes. However, in 1963 he won the post of Democratic district leader by defeating the head of the Tammany organization. In 1966 Koch was elected to the city counsel as the first Democrat in 38 years. A committed liberal, he was elected to the United States House of Representatives in a hotly contested 1968 race in which his opposition to the Vietnam War and support for the presidential candidacy of Senator Eugene J. McCarthy were issues. He was reelected to four additional terms in 1970, 1972, 1974, and 1976 with growing majorities. In 1972 he was briefly a candidate for the office of mayor of New York City. He decided to run again for mayor, announcing his candidacy in 1976 while still a representative. New York City was in the midst of a financial crisis, and Koch used this issue to his advantage. He employed his dull political image and reputation for hard work to counter the more flamboyant and machinelike politics of his predecessors. With a field that included Representative Bella Abzug, Secretary of State Mario Cuomo, and incumbent Mayor Abe Beame, Koch led the primary after the first round and won the nomination after a runoff election, defeating Cuomo by nearly 80,000 votes. The first issue he had to face when he entered office in 1978 was the city's growing financial crisis. He worked with federal officials to establish a plan by which the city would have a balanced budget by 1983. His policies brought both praise and support as well as anger from city labor unions. However, he was successful in his endeavors. Still a committed liberal, he banned by executive order discrimination in city jobs on the basis of sexual orientation. Koch was reelected in 1981 and 1985 to the post of mayor, from which he continued his efforts to rebuild one of the world's great cities. He lost his bid for a fourth term as mayor in 1989 to the Democratic Primary winner, David Dinkins.

Fiorello H. La Guardia (1882–1947)   Born in New York City in 1882, Fiorello Henry La Guardia began his political career in the Republican Party as a precinct captain in 1912. In 1916 he was elected to the United States Congress, the first Republican from the Lower East Side since the Civil War. After a stint as a pilot on the Italian–Austrian front in World War I, he was reelected to the House. In 1919 he resigned from the post in order to run for president of the board of aldermen. Running for mayor of New York City in 1921, La Guardia lost the Republican primary. With the help of

newspaper magnate William Randolph Hearst, he won reelection to the House in 1922, being reelected four times. La Guardia, a progressive, began to break away from the Republican Party. In 1924 he endorsed Senator Robert M. La Follette for president. Additionally, he ran for reelection that year as a progressive. He regularly worked with Senator George W. Norris of Nebraska to curb the influence of monied interests. In 1932 he led the fight against President Hoover's sales tax initiative. After his defeat for reelection in 1932, an anti-Tammany faction of the Democratic Party nominated him as its candidate for mayor of New York City in 1933. He won the general election and was reelected in 1937 and 1941. During his tenure, he worked to reorganize the city's bureaucracy and balance its budget. He built the first sewage system and also unified the subway and took it public. La Guardia used federal funds to build and modernize the city. He built the first airport, which today bears his name, and improved schools, bridges, roads, and parks. As World War II began, La Guardia sought appointment as secretary of war. Instead, he was offered the post of director of civilian defense. He was never very loyal to any party, having been elected on the tickets of more than four in his career. He refrained from holding any party offices and also forbade his chief administrators from holding such offices. In 1946 he served as director of the United Nations Relief and Rehabilitation Administration, a post he did not enjoy. He died the following year, having garnered the reputation of having been "New York City's best mayor."

David Lawrence (1889–1966)   David Lawrence worked behind the scenes to create a powerful Democratic political machine in Pittsburgh. In 1934 he was instrumental in the election of George Earle as governor of Pennsylvania. Rewarded for his efforts, Lawrence served from 1935 until 1939 as secretary of the commonwealth, working to implement the state's "little New Deal." He also served as the chair of the state Democratic Party. In 1945 he was elected mayor of Pittsburgh and was reelected twice. During his tenure as mayor, Lawrence worked with business leaders to revitalize the city through an aggressive building program. After serving three terms as mayor, he was elected for a single term as governor of Pennsylvania. He then served on the President's Committee on Equal Opportunity in Housing.

Blair Lee (1857–1945)   Blair Lee, great-grandson of Richard Henry Lee, first ran for public office in 1896 as an unsuccessful candidate for the United States House of Representatives. From 1905 to 1913 he served in the Maryland State Senate. Lee lost his 1911 bid for the governorship. However, on November 4, 1913, he became the first directly elected United States senator from Maryland. His election was challenged by Senator William Jackson, whom he had been elected to replace. The dispute was over the length of Lee's term. Lee argued that since his election had taken place before the passage of the 17th Amendment, his temporary appointment lasted until the next election. The Senate Committee on Privileges and Elections agreed. However, Lee failed to win reelection in 1916. Leaving the Senate, he retired from politics to practice law until his death in 1945.

J. Hamilton Lewis (1863–1939)   James Hamilton Lewis was a member of the last legislature in Washington Territory from 1887 to 1888. In 1890 he presided over the first Democratic State Convention. Six years later he was elected to the House of Representatives, where he served a single term, being defeated for reelection. After military service in the Spanish-American War, Lewis ran unsuccessfully for the United States Senate in 1899. Moving to Chicago, he was active in the successful campaign of Edward F. Dunne for mayor in 1905. After serving as corporation counsel in the Dunne administration, he failed to win the Democratic nomination for governor of Illinois in 1908. Despite these electoral defeats, Lewis was finally elected to the United States Senate from Illinois in 1912. Upon his entry into the Senate, he was selected as the first Senate majority whip in party history. In this position he played a vital role in securing Senate support for the programs and policies of Woodrow Wilson. In 1918 he was defeated for reelection by Republican Medill McCormick. In 1920 he lost his bid for the post of governor and returned to the practice of law. In 1930 he returned to elected politics by defeating Representative Ruth Hanna McCormick, daughter of Mark Hanna and widow of Senator McCormick, in a run for the U.S. Senate. In 1933 he was again selected as party whip. Reelected in 1936 by a large margin, he died in 1939.

Earl K. Long (1895–1960)   A longtime and trusted political aide to his brother, Huey P. Long, Earl Kemp Long was defeated in his first bid for elected office, as lieutenant governor of Louisiana, because Huey did not endorse him. After they patched up their differences and Huey was assassinated in 1935, Earl was elected lieutenant governor in 1936. When Governor Richard W. Leche resigned because of graft and corruption charges in 1939, Long became governor and tried to mount a campaign for reelection in 1940. Despite being personally cleared of any wrongdoing, Long was defeated. Although he lost the nomination for lieutenant

governor in 1944, he won a bitter campaign battle for governor in 1948. As governor, he promoted the progressive and populist agenda that was the Long trademark. Long, however, continued to make political enemies in Louisiana. His handpicked successor was defeated for election in 1952. In 1956 he was successful in his bid for an unprecedented third term as governor. The term was marked by bitter battles with segregationists. In the end, Long's health began to fail, and he was hospitalized on three occasions. He failed in his 1956 run for lieutenant governor but surprised political pundits by winning a 1960 Democratic primary election for the United States House of Representatives over incumbent Harold Barnett McSween. Long died a week after this primary victory.

Huey P. Long (1893–1935)   In 1918, at the age of 25, Hugh Pierce Long Jr. was elected as a railroad commissioner—the only state office in Louisiana for which he met the minimum age requirement. Reelected in 1924 to the reorganized job of public service commissioner, he served as chair from 1921 to 1926. While failing in his 1924 bid for governor, he was elected in 1928. Despite not having control of the state legislature, Long pursued his populist agenda. In a special session of the legislature in 1929, he escaped impeachment by 15 votes on charges that ranged from bribing state legislators with government funds to plotting the assassination of political opponents. Long took his case to the people, claiming to be persecuted by the Standard Oil Company. He was elected to the United States Senate in 1930. He retained his post as governor of Louisiana to prevent a hostile lieutenant governor from taking control. Long, nicknamed "Kingfish," entered the Senate in 1932. Despite campaigning for Roosevelt that year, Long became an outspoken critic of the president because the latter did not support his more radical wealth-redistribution schemes. When his machine lost the New Orleans mayoral election in 1934, Long ordered the state legislature to reorganize the state government in order to consolidate and maintain his power. In March 1935 he announced his candidacy for the Democratic presidential nomination, pledging to bolt the convention if Roosevelt were nominated. However, on September 8, 1935, Dr. Carl A. Weiss shot Long, who died two days later.

Russell B. Long (1918–)   Russell Billiu Long, son of the charismatic Huey P. Long, served as a campaign assistant to his uncle, Earl K. Long, in the latter's successful 1948 bid for the governorship of Louisiana. Long then served as executive counsel to his uncle. In 1948 he decided to run for the United States Senate vacancy created by the death of Senator John H. Overton.

In his campaign he stressed his father's legacy and his desire to work for the little people. He was elected to the Senate on November 2, 1948, one day before his 30th birthday. He was subsequently elected to a six-year term in 1950, being reelected in 1956, 1962, 1968, 1974 and 1980. He did not stand for reelection in 1986. He compiled a moderate, independent voting record. In 1965 he became the party whip, a post he held until 1969. When he took that post, he continued to pledge that his would be a voice independent from the administration. In addition to serving as party whip, he chaired the influential Finance Committee, drafting key legislation in the area of tax reform.

Scott W. Lucas (1892–1968)   In 1932 Scott Wike Lucas unsuccessfully sought the Democratic nomination for a United States Senate seat from Illinois. However, the governor appointed him to the State Tax Commission while urging him to run for Congress in 1934. Successful in his bid for the House of Representatives, Lucas was a firm supporter of the New Deal. He was reelected to a second term in 1936. With the support of the southern Illinois political machine, Lucas again ran for the Democratic nomination for the United States Senate in 1938. He was successful in his quest and entered the Senate still a supporter of the Franklin D. Roosevelt administration. In 1946 he was elected party whip, and in 1949 he was unanimously elected majority leader. Despite a Democratic majority, Lucas did not command the votes the Harry S. Truman administration needed for its agenda because many southern Democrats were aligned with more conservative Republicans. The issue of communists in the government plagued Lucas. In an attempt to defuse the issue of registration of communists, Lucas sponsored a more restrictive internment bill that he thought would fail and put the issue to rest. However, both the registration bill and the internment bill passed. Furthermore, the committee he set up to investigate Senator Joseph McCarthy's charges failed to quiet the senator. He was defeated in 1950 by Everett McKinley Dirksen.

Warren G. Magnuson (1905–1989)   Warren Grant Magnuson entered public life as the special prosecutor of King County, Washington, in 1931. In 1933 he was elected to the state House of Representatives, serving only one term. Also in that year, he served as a delegate to the state Constitutional Convention. After serving as district attorney and prosecuting attorney, he was elected to the United States House of Representatives in 1936, serving until he resigned in 1944 to enter the United States Senate. In the House he gained a reputation as a progressive New Dealer who sup-

ported many of the Franklin D. Roosevelt administration's policies. In 1944 he was appointed to fill a vacancy in the Senate, where he remained until 1981. In part because of his longevity on Capitol Hill, Magnuson became one of Washington's most powerful figures. He served as chair of the influential Appropriations Committee, where he was instrumental in securing funding for the National Institutes of Health.

Michael J. Mansfield (1903–)   After placing third in the Democratic primary of 1940, Michael Joseph Mansfield ran a successful campaign for the United States House of Representatives in 1942, replacing retiring Republican Jeannette Rankin of Montana and serving there until his election to the United States Senate in 1952. The former professor of Far East and Latin American history was placed on the House Foreign Relations Committee. In 1944 he was sent to China on a confidential mission by President Franklin D. Roosevelt. Mansfield believed that the Nationalists could defeat the Communists, though he was impressed with the latter's strength. He was also instrumental in convincing President Harry S. Truman to retain Hirohito as emperor of Japan. Offered the post of assistant secretary of state for public affairs by Truman, Mansfield declined, as he preferred to remain in Congress. During his five terms in the House, he was generally regarded as a liberal. In 1952 he decided to challenge the conservative Republican incumbent, Zales N. Ecton, for the Senate. Despite the fact that Wisconsin Senator Joseph McCarthy campaigned for Ecton and despite the Dwight D. Eisenhower landslide, Mansfield defeated Ecton. A trusted ally to Senate Majority Leader Lyndon B. Johnson, Mansfield became majority whip in 1957. When Johnson became vice president, Mansfield became majority leader. His style was in stark contrast to that of the post's former occupant. Unlike Johnson, Mansfield was not willing to use strong-arm tactics. Many within the party were disappointed at the soft nature of his leadership. Mansfield worked with Democrats and Republicans in order to achieve legislative movement. His opposition to the war in Vietnam led him into conflict with the Johnson administration through his efforts to limit presidential authority by cosponsoring the War Powers Act. Mansfield announced his retirement from the Senate at the end of his 1970 term. President Jimmy Carter appointed Mansfield as United States ambassador to Japan in 1977, a post he continued to hold even during the Ronald Reagan administration. Mansfield retired from the post in 1988.

Thomas S. Martin (1849–1919)   During the Civil War, Thomas Staples Martin served a year in the Confederate army's infamous New Market Corps of Cadets. As a relative unknown, he announced that he would run for a U.S. Senate seat from Virginia in 1893 against the nephew of Robert E. Lee. To the surprise of almost everyone, he was elected. Martin remained in the Senate until his death in 1919, serving as majority leader for two years beginning in 1917. Late in his life, he became boss of the Virginia political machine. Martin, a staunch conservative, was not a forceful speaker. However, he was known for his hard work and common sense. From his dual posts of majority leader and chair of the Senate Appropriations Committee, he successfully guided much of President Woodrow Wilson's war legislation through the Senate.

Patrick A. McCarran (1876–1954)   Patrick Anthony McCarran served as an elected justice on the Nevada State Supreme Court from 1913 to 1918, the last two years as chief justice. He was, however, interested in the United States Senate and ran two unsuccessful campaigns for a Senate seat in 1916 and 1926. In 1932, on his third attempt, he was elected in a Democratic landslide. An independent voter, McCarran became part of the conservative coalition of southern Democrats and Republicans. His independence and his opposition to President Franklin D. Roosevelt's Court-packing plan won him reelection in 1938. He was also reelected in 1944 and 1950. He worked to eliminate or reduce the federal bureaucracy and agencies that had sprouted during the New Deal. A skilled parliamentarian, McCarran was well respected when he spoke on legislative issues. Prior to World War II, he sought to build the nation's defenses while staying out of the growing hostilities in Europe. An ardent anticommunist, he supported measures to aid Spain's right-wing regime. He blamed the Harry S. Truman administration for the fall of mainland China. He also advocated the adoption of the Bricker amendment, which would have limited the president's authority in foreign affairs. A supporter of Senator Joseph McCarthy, McCarran died before the resolution to censure McCarthy came to a vote.

Ernest W. McFarland (1894–1984)   Ernest William McFarland was appointed assistant attorney general of Arizona in 1923. Two years later he assumed the post of Pinal County attorney, a post he held until 1930. In 1934 he began a six-year tenure as judge on the Superior Court of Pinal County. McFarland was elected in 1940 to the United States Senate, where he served on a five-member subcommittee investigating the motion picture industry for warmongering. In the Senate he had a keen interest in issues such as price controls, water rights, and mining. Reelected in 1946, McFarland was elected majority leader in 1951 despite

his lack of seniority. In this post he tried to bridge the gap between the more liberal Harry S. Truman administration and the fiscally conservative southern Democrats who elected him. He was defeated in his reelection bid in 1952. Three years later he won the governorship of Arizona, a post he hoped to use as a springboard back into the Senate. However, in 1958 he was defeated in his bid to return to the Senate. In 1964 McFarland began his service on the Arizona Supreme Court, where in 1967 he became chief justice, a post he held until his retirement in 1971.

George J. Mitchell (1933–)   In 1960 George John Mitchell was hired as a trial attorney for the United States Department of Justice in the Antitrust Division. He resigned in 1962 to work for Senator Edmund S. Muskie of Maine. Leaving the senator's office in 1965, Mitchell returned to Maine to enter private practice. While in private practice, he served as state Democratic Committee chair from 1966 to 1968. In 1968 he worked as deputy director of Senator Muskie's vice presidential campaign. Mitchell was also the deputy director of Muskie's 1972 campaign for the Democratic presidential nomination. He ran unsuccessfully for chair of the Democratic National Committee in 1972 against Robert S. Strauss. He also failed in his 1974 bid for the governorship of Maine. Resuming his law practice, he served on the Democratic National Committee's Executive Committee from 1974 until 1977, when he was appointed United States attorney for Maine. In 1979 he was appointed to the United States District Court. When Senator Muskie entered Jimmy Carter's cabinet, Mitchell was appointed to the Senate to fill the vacancy. In a nasty campaign, Mitchell won election to the Senate in 1981, overcoming his opponent's 36-point lead in the polls. A liberal lawmaker, Mitchell opposed the Ronald Reagan administration's proposals supporting prayer in public schools, funding for the Strategic Defense Initiative, aid to the contras, and a constitutional amendment requiring a balanced budget. In 1986 he chaired the Democratic Senatorial Campaign Committee, which won back control from the Republicans. In recognition for this, he was appointed deputy president pro tempore. He served on the committee that investigated the Iran–contra scandal, giving a memorable closing statement on patriotism. In 1988, when Senator Robert C. Byrd of West Virginia stepped down as majority leader, Mitchell successfully campaigned for the post, beating Senator Daniel K. Inouye of Hawaii and Senator J. Bennett Johnston of Louisiana and serving until his retirement in 1994. Though not regarded as a great parliamentarian, Mitchell used his post effectively to shape the national agenda.

John T. Morgan (1824–1907)   John Tyler Morgan began his political career as an elector on the John C. Breckinridge ticket in 1860. In 1861 he was an active member of the secession convention. During the Civil War, he served in the Confederate army, rising from the rank of private to brigadier general. As the war was reaching its conclusion, he was raising Negro troops in his home state of Mississippi. As a white supremacist, he was elected to the U.S. Senate in 1876, serving until his death in 1907. Many of the Republican senators attempted to keep him from being seated in the Senate because of his racial views. Ironically, his first vote was for Frederick Douglass as marshal of the District of Columbia. While in the Senate, he was an ardent defender of the doctrine of states' rights and expansion. He actively worked for the admission of Cuba, Puerto Rico, and Hawaii to the Union as states because he believed that they would be aligned with his southern policies.

Wayne Morse (1900–1974)   More than anything else, maverick Wayne Lyman Morse served as a spur to his political party. In many ways, he forged this role as a constructive force within both his party and the U.S. Senate. He is the only U.S. senator of the twentieth century formally to switch his party affiliation three times. He began as a liberal Republican, became an Independent, and then changed to a Democrat, serving in political office longest while affiliated with the Democratic Party. Unfortunately for his party and his nation, Morse's positions were the road not taken.

His political transitions echoed his geographic and professional moves. Morse was born on a farm in Madison, Wisconsin, on October 20, 1900. Raised on a steady diet of the populist tradition in his native state, he attended the University of Wisconsin, gaining a reputation as a champion debater while majoring in labor economics. After receiving his undergraduate degree in 1923, he served the next year as a speech instructor and debate coach while earning his master's degree. From 1924 to 1928, he was an assistant professor of speech and a law student at the University of Minnesota, which granted him an LL.B. degree in 1928. That same year, he was awarded a teaching fellowship at Columbia University, which, in 1932, conferred on Morse only the fourth J.D. degree it ever awarded. Morse moved west in 1929 to become an assistant professor of law at the University of Oregon. He was promoted to associate professor after one year, and in 1931 was made full professor and dean of the School of Law. At age 31, he was the youngest dean of a law school. Louisiana Governor Huey P. Long offered the youthful Morse the deanship of the LSU Law School. Morse rejected the offer.

Before running for elective office, Morse established his national reputation as a prison expert and labor arbitrator. He was appointed special assistant to the U.S. attorney general in 1936, and in 1938, Labor Secretary Frances Perkins appointed Morse as an arbitrator. He served on the National War Labor Board until 1944. In virtually all these positions, Morse displayed his trademark maverick approach—challenging a university president in the same way that he later would challenge the five presidents of the United States who served during his tenure as a U.S. senator.

Though Morse had New Deal sympathies, he won Oregon's 1944 Republican nomination as the candidate for the U.S. Senate and won the fall election that year, carrying more counties than anyone else had up to that time. His maverick tendencies were evident from the start in Congress. During his first six months, he made more speeches than all the other freshmen senators, earning for himself the nickname "The Five O'Clock Shadow." He was an internationalist, supporting the UN Charter (1945), NATO (1949), and the Marshall Plan (1950). A poll of political scientists early in 1952 ranked the senator third out of 95 senators rated.

In late October 1952, Morse resigned from the Republican Party after candidate Dwight Eisenhower and his forces failed to denounce Senator Joseph R. McCarthy. Morse became an Independent. After the Republicans had stripped him of his seniority on the Armed Services and Labor committees, he performed major service on the District of Columbia Committee, emerging as one of the strongest advocates of home rule. It was during his senatorial service as an Independent that he delivered "the longest continuous oration in the history of the Senate," when in April 1953 he spoke for 22 hours and 26 minutes against off-shore-oil legislation that would give title to the adjacent coastal state. Morse switched his party affiliation for the third and final time in 1955, becoming a Democrat. He won reelection in 1956 by easily defeating Eisenhower's former secretary of the interior, who had resigned his cabinet post specifically to challenge Morse in an effort to "purge" the maverick senator. Senate Majority Leader Lyndon B. Johnson assigned Morse to the Foreign Relations Committee.

During the 1960 presidential campaign, Morse sought the Democratic nomination. The effort failed after successive primary defeats in the District of Columbia, Maryland, and Oregon. Morse's major domestic contributions to the Democratic Party were trade unionism, civil rights, and floor-managing President Lyndon Johnson's aid to education bill in 1965, sponsoring the Federal City College and the

Washington Institute. In 1964 he was the only senator to speak on the floor of the Senate against the Gulf of Tonkin resolution that allowed for America's involvement in the Vietnam War, and one of only two to vote against the legislation.

After a 24-year maverick career, Morse was defeated in 1968 by 3,000 votes by a liberal Republican, Robert W. Packwood. In August 1972 when the Democrats picked Thomas Eagleton's replacement as George McGovern's running mate on the Democratic ticket, four of Oregon's votes went to former Senator Morse. He won the 1974 Democratic primary bid to regain his U.S. Senate seat and was given a good chance to win back the seat, but Morse died late in the campaign.

William D. Pederson

BIBLIOGRAPHY

Broder, David S. "Former Senator Morse Dies." *Washington Post*, July 23, 1974, p. A16.
Smith, Arthur R. *The Tiger in the Senate. The Biography of Wayne Morse*. Garden City, NY: Doubleday, 1962.
Unruh, Gail Q. "Eternal Liberal: Wayne L. Morse and the Politics of Liberalism." Ph.D. dissertation, University of Oregon, 1987.
Wilkins, Lee. *Wayne Morse: A Bio-bibliography*. Westport, CT: Greenwood Press, 1985.

Edmund S. Muskie (1914–1996)   Edmund Sixtus Muskie was elected to the Maine House of Representatives in 1946. After that session, he ran unsuccessfully for mayor of Waterville. However, Muskie was reelected to the Maine legislature in 1948 and again in 1950, serving as Democratic floor leader from 1949 to 1951. He resigned from the House in 1951 to serve as district director for Maine of the Office of Price Stabilization. In 1952 he became a member of the Democratic National Committee. After a serious accident in 1953, Muskie was elected governor of Maine in 1954 over the Republican incumbent and was reelected in 1956. Rather than run for a third term, Muskie decided to run against the Republican incumbent Senator Frederick G. Payne for the United States Senate. He managed an upset victory by some 60,000 votes and was reelected in 1964, 1970 and 1976. Muskie was out of favor in the Senate because he opposed Democratic Senator Lyndon B. Johnson's attempt to defeat a liberal proposal to limit filibusters. Assigned by Johnson to minor committees in retaliation, Muskie became chair of the Senate Banking and Currency Committee. Concerned with the environment, he was the chief sponsor of the 1963 Clear Air Act and the Water Quality Act of 1965. In addition, he chaired the powerful Senate Budget Committee. Muskie was a committed party loyalist and liberal whose voting

record confirmed his positions. In 1968 he accepted the Democratic nomination for vice president on a ticket headed by Vice President Hubert H. Humphrey. He resigned from the Senate in 1980 to enter President Jimmy Carter's cabinet as secretary of state. In 1987 he served on the Tower Commission to investigate the Iran–contra scandal.

Claude D. Pepper (1900–1989)   Although he failed in his bid for election to the United States Senate in 1934, Claude Denson Pepper was elected unopposed to fill the unexpired term of Senator Duncan U. Fletcher of Florida in 1936. In his first speech, Pepper attacked fellow Democrats for not continuing their strong support of the Franklin D. Roosevelt administration. A fighting liberal, he won reelection to the Senate running on a pro–New Deal agenda in 1938. Upon his reelection, he championed such liberal causes as national health insurance, repeal of the poll tax, and a federal fine arts bureau. He worked for the passage of legislation to transfer destroyers to Great Britain and for the passage of lend–lease legislation to help America's World War II Allies. During the war he supported most of the Roosevelt administration's agenda. During Harry S. Truman's administration, Pepper continued to support the liberal elements of the Fair Deal. However, he opposed the growing Cold War because he believed that the Soviet Union was not aggressive. He opposed military aid to Greece and Turkey and U.S. support of Franco in Spain. In 1948 he tried to convince Dwight D. Eisenhower to run for the Democratic nomination for president against Truman. Pepper briefly offered himself as an alternative candidate. During Pepper's 1950 reelection bid, his Democratic opponent, Representative George A. Smathers, exploited Pepper's soft-on-communism record, labeling him "Red Pepper." Defeated, Pepper returned to the practice of law in Tallahassee. In 1958 he unsuccessfully challenged conservative Democrat Spessard L. Holland for his Senate seat. In 1962 he ran for and won a newly created seat in the United States House of Representatives. In the House he supported most of the John F. Kennedy and Lyndon B. Johnson administration proposals on the domestic front, including Medicare, federal aid to education, and civil rights legislation. While initially supporting the United States involvement in Vietnam, Pepper hesitated when hostilities escalated. He chaired the House Committee on Crime and the Committee on Aging. He was largely responsible for the bill that raised the retirement age from 65 to 70 during the Jimmy Carter administration. He was a vocal critic of President Ronald Reagan, largely because he believed Reagan's policies were detrimental to elderly Americans. He became chair of the House Rules Committee in 1983, replacing retired Representative Richard M. Bolling of Missouri. Pepper was still a member of the House when he died in 1989 at the age of 89.

Key Pittman (1912–1940)   After losing a close race to his Republican opponent, George S. Nixon, in 1910, Key Pittman was elected to the United States Senate from Nevada when Nixon died in 1912. He would serve in the Senate until his death after being reelected in 1940. In the Senate he displayed great abilities at using procedures and coalitions to achieve political ends. Pittman used his abilities to aid his home state's silver industry. In 1934 he worked out the compromise between the Franklin D. Roosevelt administration and more extreme inflationists that resulted in the Silver Purchase Act. He served as president pro tempore of the Senate from 1933 until his death.

William Proxmire (1915–)   William Proxmire was elected to the Wisconsin State Assembly in 1951, serving a single term. After three unsuccessful bids for governor in 1952, 1954, and 1956, he won the special election to fill the United States Senate seat vacated by the death of Senator Joseph McCarthy. He was reelected to full terms in 1958, 1964, 1970, 1976, and 1982. He announced in 1987 that he would not seek reelection in 1988. In the Senate he gained a reputation as a severe critic of wasteful spending. In 1975 he began issuing his famous "Golden Fleece Awards," which highlighted specific wasteful expenditures on research projects. He also chaired the Senate Banking, Housing, and Urban Affairs Committees. Having voted more than 12,000 times, Proxmire holds the record for the most votes cast. From April 20, 1966, until his retirement, he did not miss a single roll-call vote.

Joseph L. Rauh (1911–)   In 1936 Joseph Louis Rauh Jr. went to Washington, D.C., to serve as senior law secretary to Supreme Court Associate Justice Benjamin N. Cardozo as well as enforcement attorney for the Wage and Hour Administration. In addition he directed the Federal Communications Commission's investigation of monopoly in the radio industry. After Cardozo's death, Rauh served one year as senior law secretary to Justice Felix Frankfurter. From 1939 until his enlistment in the army in 1942, Rauh was counsel for the Lend–Lease Administration and other government agencies in the Franklin D. Roosevelt administration. In 1946 he founded the anticommunist, liberal organization Americans for Democratic Action. He served as the chair of its executive committee from 1947 to 1952. In 1952 he became chair of the District of Columbia Democratic Party. Rauh defended William Walter

Remington, who was accused of giving secrets to the Soviet Union, as well as writer Arthur Miller against the House Un-American Activities Committee. He served as the Americans for Democratic Action's chair from 1955 to 1956. A delegate to the 1960 Democratic National Convention, he supported Hubert H. Humphrey over John F. Kennedy. When Kennedy won, Rauh urged him to make strides on civil rights. Rauh played a major role in the founding of the National Association for the Advancement of Colored People. Although he never served in elected office, Rauh was an influential shaper of the liberal Democratic agenda.

Joseph T. Robinson (1872–1937)   After serving a single term (1894) in the Arkansas State legislature, where he supported measures to regulate the railroad industry, Joseph Taylor Robinson was elected to the United States House of Representatives in 1902. In his five terms in the House, he was regarded as a moderate progressive. In 1912 he left the House and ran successfully for the post of governor of Arkansas. When Senator Jeff Davis died in 1913, Robinson was appointed to the Senate. He was a strong supporter of President Woodrow Wilson's policies, including the Treaty of Versailles. He was elected Senate Democratic leader in 1923, a post he held until his death in 1937. At the Democratic National Convention of 1928, he was selected as the vice presidential candidate to balance the ticket headed by Governor Alfred E. Smith of New York. In the Senate, Robinson opposed many of the policies of the Republican administrations of the 1920s. When Franklin D. Roosevelt took office, Robinson worked to have much of the early New Deal legislation put into law.

Eleanor Roosevelt (1884–1962)   From a well-connected and financially secure background, (Anna) Eleanor Roosevelt found a life of public service rewarding. Her first experiences in this realm were during World War I as a volunteer at the Red Cross. She became more active with other women interested in issues of trade unions and the suffrage movement when she learned of the infidelity of her husband, Franklin D. Roosevelt, with her social secretary, Lucy Mercer. While her husband sought to recover the use of his legs after having contracted polio in 1921, she developed herself as a politician and an organizer. She was active in the League of Women Voters, the Women's Trade Union League and the Democratic Party. When Franklin was elected governor of New York, she continued to define her own set of priorities, dividing her time among her many projects. When her husband was elected president, she feared that the duties of first lady would prevent her from pursuing her agenda. However, she became an activist first lady, holding

Eleanor Roosevelt. *Source:* Library of Congress.

women-only press conferences. She dutifully performed the traditional functions of the first lady; however, she also made speeches advocating policy. In 1935 she wrote a daily column carried in more than 60 newspapers. During the Great Depression, she focused much of her attention on youth, including support for the communist-backed American Youth Congress, which shared many of her objectives. Eleanor did not favor a third term for her husband. However, when Franklin decided to run, she supported him by flying to the 1940 Democratic National Convention to defend the selection of Henry Wallace as vice president. She served as cochair of the Office of Civilian Defense but resigned because of growing criticism from the press and Congress. Eleanor accompanied her husband to international conferences. As her influence grew, she increased her lobbying for her liberal agenda, often acting as a spur to her husband. President Harry S. Truman appointed her to the United Nations Human Rights Commission, where she worked to draft an international bill of rights. In 1948 she addressed the U.N. General Assembly, which

adopted the Universal Declaration of Human Rights. She resigned from the United Nations when Dwight D. Eisenhower became president. Eleanor Roosevelt remained active in Democratic politics. At the Democratic National Conventions in 1952, 1956 and 1960, she supported Adlai E. Stevenson. President John F. Kennedy appointed her to the United Nations delegation. She also became a prolific writer, coauthoring several books. She died in 1962 of tuberculosis.

Richard B. Russell (1897–1971)   In 1920 Richard Bevard Russell Jr. began his political career with his election to the Georgia House of Representatives, where he served as speaker from 1927 to 1931. At the age of 33, he was elected governor, serving from 1931 to 1933. An incident involving an escaped prisoner from a chain gang whom the governor of New Jersey refused to extradite to Georgia at Russell's request brought him into the national spotlight. In 1932 he was elected to the United States Senate, being reelected six times. He served as president pro tempore from 1969 until his death in 1971. Although a supporter of the New Deal, he opposed President Harry S. Truman's Fair Deal, President John F. Kennedy's New Frontier, and President Lyndon B. Johnson's Great Society because he believed that they threatened individual liberty and states' rights. Russell opposed all of the civil rights legislation throughout his tenure. He even sponsored a bill to compensate blacks for relocating out of the South. A strong supporter of national defense, he chaired the Armed Services Committee and the committee investigating the firing of General Douglas MacArthur by Truman for insubordination.

Terry Sanford (1917–)   Terry Sanford was elected to the North Carolina State Senate in 1953, serving a single term. He served as the state manager for Governor W. Kerr Scott's successful 1954 campaign for the United States Senate. He remained active in Democratic politics, helping to build an effective county-by-county organization. In 1960 he was elected governor of the state, defeating a segregationist candidate. He played a major role in the nomination of Senator John F. Kennedy for the presidency in 1960, seconding the senator's nomination. As governor he was largely responsible for encouraging economic development in the Raleigh–Durham area. In 1969 Sanford became president of Duke University in Durham, North Carolina. He served in that post until 1985. The following year, he was elected to the United States Senate, where he served a single term, being defeated for reelection in 1992.

James Shields (1806 or 1810–1879)   James Shields is the only man to have served as a United States senator from three different states—Illinois, Minnesota, and Missouri. In 1836 he entered elected office as a state legislator in Illinois. He later served as state auditor when the state verged on bankruptcy because of panic and canal construction costs. In 1843 he was appointed to the state Supreme Court and reappointed in 1845. He resigned soon after, however, to accept the post of commissioner of general land from President James K. Polk. Shields resigned this post in 1846 to take command of a company of Illinois volunteers in the Mexican War. In 1848 he was elected to the United States Senate from Illinois. A strict party man, Shields also had an independent streak that allowed him the freedom to disagree with extremists. He was defeated for reelection in 1854 by Lyman Trumbull, who was supported by Abraham Lincoln in the Illinois legislature. He moved to the Minnesota Territory, from which, upon its admission as a state, he was elected to the United States Senate in 1858. He was not reelected by the Republican state legislature after serving the short term in 1859. He then left Minnesota for California. Later, while in business in Mexico, Shields offered his services to President Lincoln. Shields was appointed as brigadier general of volunteers in 1861. After two years of active service, he retired and returned to San Francisco, where he was appointed a state railroad commissioner. He next moved to Missouri, where he campaigned unsuccessfully for Congress and supported the Liberal–Republican ticket of 1872. In 1879 he was appointed to the United States Senate to fill an unexpired term. He declined to stand for reelection in 1880, citing health reasons.

Furnifold M. Simmons (1854–1940)   Elected to Congress from North Carolina in 1886, Furnifold McLendel Simmons was defeated for reelection in 1888 by a black Republican, Henry P. Cheatham. In the following congressional election, he withdrew from the race because more liberal forces wanted him out. However, by 1892 Simmons and his fellow conservatives had regained control of the party. As state chair, he developed well-disciplined county organizations. In 1898 he led a white supremacy campaign against the Republicans and their black members who had been victorious in 1894 and 1896. Simmons's campaign of racial intolerance worked, and his party swept into power. The Democrats passed a constitutional amendment that disenfranchised most of North Carolina's blacks. In 1900 Simmons was sent to the United States Senate. In 1913, through the seniority system, he became the chair of the Senate Finance Committee, despite opposition by more progressive Democrats. He proved to be a loyal supporter of

President Woodrow Wilson, even trying to find a compromise on the Treaty of Versailles. In 1930 Simmons was defeated in his primary campaign as the voters of North Carolina tired of his type of machine politics.

Howard W. Smith (1883–1976)   Howard Worth "Judge" Smith was elected to the United States House of Representatives in 1930. He was an opponent of many of Franklin D. Roosevelt's later New Deal proposals. In fact, Roosevelt supported Smith's Democratic opponent in the 1938 primary in hopes of ridding himself of Smith. The Smith Act of 1940 criminalized speech in the military that encouraged the overthrow of the government by force. In 1955 he became chair of the powerful House Rules Committee. He was also a leader of the conservative coalition of southern Democrats and Republicans. He used his position as chair of the Rules Committee to prevent legislation that he opposed from reaching the floor of the House. He tried to block the passage of Alaska's admission to the Union and the Civil Rights Act of 1964. Smith was out of step with his own party but unwilling to switch to the more conservative Republican Party. As a result, in 1966 he was defeated in the Democratic primary by a more liberal opponent, who, in turn, was defeated by a conservative Republican in the general election.

John Sparkman (1899–1985)   John Jackson Sparkman entered public life when he captured a seat in the United States House of Representatives from Alabama in 1936 after winning a tough Democratic primary. In Congress he was a regular supporter of President Franklin D. Roosevelt. He was a member of the Tuesday Night Group of young Democrats committed to helping get the New Deal policies through Congress, including expansion of the Tennessee Valley Authority, enlargement of the air force, and the Selective Service Act. He was elected party whip in 1946 in recognition of his leadership abilities. In that same year, he was elected to both the House of Representatives and the United States Senate. He resigned his House seat and took up his Senate one. While he generally supported President Harry S. Truman's policies, he took exception to the administration's civil rights agenda. In 1948 he advocated the drafting of Dwight D. Eisenhower as the party's candidate. Sparkman served as a representative to the Fifth General Assembly of the United Nations in 1950. In 1952 he was the vice presidential candidate on the losing Democratic ticket headed by Governor Adlai E. Stevenson of Illinois. Reelected to the Senate in 1954, 1960, 1966 and 1972, he did not stand for reelection in 1978. Among his posts in the Senate were chair of the

Banking and Currency Committee and chair of the Senate Foreign Relations Committee. In the latter position, he used his power to defend the president's executive authority in foreign policy.

John C. Stennis (1901–1995)   John Cornelius Stennis began his long political career in 1928, when he was elected to the Mississippi legislature. After serving four years in the state House, he became district prosecuting attorney, a post he held from 1932 until 1937. In that year, he was elected to the circuit court as a judge, remaining on the court until 1947, when he was elevated to the United States Senate in a special election to replace Senator Theodore G. Bilbo. Unlike his opponents in the 1947 election, Stennis did not focus on race as an election issue; rather, he emphasized agriculture. However, while in the Senate, he opposed every piece of civil rights legislation including the 1983 vote on the creation of a national holiday in honor of Martin Luther King Jr. Reelected to a full term in 1952, he was the first Democrat to denounce the activities of Senator Joseph McCarthy. Throughout his tenure he earned a reputation as a man of integrity. He chaired the special committee investigating influence peddling, which centered on Bobby Baker, a former aide to Vice President Lyndon B. Johnson, and oversaw the inquiry that led to the censure of Senator Thomas J. Dodd. President Richard M. Nixon even suggested Stennis as the man to verify the transcripts of the tapes prosecutors sought in connection with the Watergate investigation. Stennis chaired the Armed Services Committee beginning in 1969 and was instrumental in defining Pentagon programs for more than a decade. Reelected to his final term in 1982, he became chair of the Appropriations Committee in 1987. Serving as president pro tempore from 1987 until his retirement in 1989, Stennis did not stand for reelection in 1988 as age had finally caught up with him.

Carl Stokes (1927–1996)   Carl Burton Stokes became the first African American mayor of a major American city when he won the 1965 mayoral race in Cleveland. As a two-term mayor he won plaudits for creating a better city for all Cleveland residents.

Born June 21, 1927, Stokes was only two years old when his father died. He and his brother Lewis Stokes (later congressman) were brought up by their mother, who worked as a domestic when she was not on welfare. Stokes dropped out of school at the age of 17 and became a pool hustler. He joined the army in 1945 but returned to school after a tour of duty in Germany. After graduating from the University of Minnesota in 1954, he went to law school; he set up law practice in 1956.

Stokes began his political career in 1962 as the first African American Democrat to be elected to the Ohio legislature. He lost his first attempt to become mayor of Cleveland in 1965 but won on his second attempt in 1967. Cleveland at this time was about one-third black, and it had been the scene of racial riots in 1966. Stokes downplayed the race issue and tried to neutralize the fears of white voters by stressing his legal qualifications and his record as a legislator.

Stokes was able to keep Cleveland relatively strife-free during his early months in office. Cleveland was one of the few cities in the North that escaped riots in the aftermath of the assassination of Martin Luther King. Violence erupted in 1968, however, when a black nationalist group led by Fred Ahmed Evans fired on policemen in Glenville. The Ohio National Guard was called out, and by the time peace was restored seven people were dead. The incident tarnished Stokes's reputation among both blacks and whites. Despite this setback, Stokes won reelection in 1969 handily. Among his more impressive achievements during his two terms was the introduction of the Cleveland NOW urban renewal program under which thousands of public housing units were built. After refusing a third term, he turned to journalism as a newscaster and also won election to the bench as municipal court judge. Stokes died in 1996.

Robert S. Strauss (1918–)   Robert Schwarz Strauss put the political connections and savvy that he learned working for political candidates as a student at the University of Texas at Austin to good use when he was the chief fund-raiser for Governor John B. Connally in 1962. In 1968 he brought together the warring factions of the Texas Democratic Party to give the state to Hubert H. Humphrey, the 1968 party standard-bearer. Later that year, he assumed a post in the Democratic National Committee and within the year was elected to its Executive Committee. As party treasurer in 1970, he cut the Democrats' debt in half. When he was replaced in 1972 by a McGovern appointee, Strauss headed the National Committee to Reelect a Democratic Congress. Despite Richard M. Nixon's landslide victory, the Democrats, with the money Strauss was able to raise, maintained firm control of the House. He was elected chair of the Democratic Party by a coalition of conservatives, labor, and governors who were dismayed at the liberal wing's disastrous 1972 McGovern presidential campaign. Strauss was instrumental in rewriting delegate rules that removed the strict quotas for women and minorities. In 1976 he presided over a unified Democratic National Convention that nominated Jimmy Carter. While Carter kept Strauss as chair of the National Committee, the election was directed by Hamilton Jordan. Strauss defended George Bush, his counterpart at the Republican National Committee, when the latter was under extreme pressure during his confirmation hearings to head the Central Intelligence Agency. After Carter's inauguration, Strauss resigned as party chair to become special representative for trade negotiations. In 1979 he was President Carter's personal representative at the second round of Middle East peace talks. He resigned after five months to head the president's reelection bid. After Carter's defeat, Strauss returned to his lucrative law practice. When George Bush was elected president in 1988, Strauss again gained access to the chief executive, helping the president win the support of leading Democrats for the Gulf War. In 1991, President Bush appointed Strauss as ambassador to the USSR, a post in which he continued after the Soviet Union collapsed and Russia emerged as the most powerful of its former republics.

Stuart Symington (1901–1989)   After a successful career as an industrialist, William Stuart Symington entered public life as the assistant secretary of war for air in 1946. In 1947 he became the first secretary of the air force, a post he held until 1950. During his tenure, he urged the development of air power to counteract the growing threat of the Soviet Union. He resigned in protest because of cuts in programs that he believed to be essential. As chair of the National Security Resource Board, Symington was responsible for the early mobilization of American forces in Korea. When other organizations took control of the situation, he became administrator of the Reconstruction Finance Corporation, charged with cleaning up the lending agency. Elected to the United States Senate in 1952 from Missouri, he served in that body until 1977. Symington resigned from his committee assignment on the Government Operations Committee in protest over Senator Joseph McCarthy's tactics. A staunch anticommunist, he was a strong supporter of the defense department and military expenditures until the Vietnam War. He twice ran unsuccessfully for the Democratic presidential nomination, in 1956 and 1960.

Eugene Talmadge (1884–1946)   Eugene Talmadge's first elected office was as commissioner of agriculture in Georgia, a position he won by defeating the machine's candidate in 1926. Twice reelected, he was investigated for using commission funds in futures speculations on the Chicago hog market but was not impeached. Small farmers rallied behind Talmadge to elect him governor in 1932, once again defeating the party regulars. Talmadge came to oppose the New Deal and similar measures in Georgia, especially those

that he thought detrimental to his farming constituents. He supported Governor Huey P. Long of Louisiana as an alternative to President Franklin D. Roosevelt in 1936. However, after Long's assassination, Talmadge stood as a candidate for president from the newly formed Constitutional Jeffersonian Democratic Party. His candidacy did not last long. Ineligible to run for a fourth term as governor, he unsuccessfully challenged Senator Richard B. Russell Jr. for a seat in the United States Senate in 1936. He failed again in 1938 against Senator Walter F. George. reelected governor in 1940, Talmadge did not attack the Roosevelt administration but did attack the University of Georgia system, from which a crony had been released. Though he lost his bid for reelection to a four-year term in 1942, he was reelected governor in 1946 with the help of large corporate contributions. However, he died before he could assume office.

Lyman Trumbull (1813–1896)   Lyman Trumbull began his political career in the Illinois State legislature, having won election in 1840. However, in 1841 he resigned to become secretary of state, serving until removed in 1843. In 1848 he was elected as a justice to the state Supreme Court. He was reelected in 1852 to a nine-year term. Trumbull served only two years of the term because he was elected to the United States House of Representatives as an anti-Nebraska Democrat. However, before he could be seated, he was elevated to the United States Senate by the Illinois legislature. Abraham Lincoln, a Whig, supported Trumbull, a Democrat, in order to elect a Free Soiler to the Senate. In the Senate Trumbull continued his movement toward the Republican Party. He and fellow Illinoisan Stephen A. Douglas were on opposite sides of most issues of slavery that came before the body. When Lincoln was elected to the White House in 1860, Trumbull was often the president's chief aide in Congress. He supported many of the controversial actions that Lincoln took in the name of prosecuting the war. As chair of the Senate Judiciary Committee, Trumbull drafted much of the legislation that became the basis for the 13th Amendment. Trumbull became more radical as Reconstruction shifted from Lincoln to President Andrew Johnson. However, much of the radical Reconstruction plan of Senator Charles Sumner and Representative Thaddeus Stevens was objectionable to Trumbull, who, unlike his colleagues, felt that the Constitution placed greater limits on the scope of Reconstruction. His beliefs led him to vote against the impeachment of Johnson, one of only seven Republicans to do so. He retired from the Senate after the nomination and victory of President Ulysses S. Grant. Trumbull had supported Horace Greeley. In 1876 it became clear that Trumbull had returned to the Democratic Party because he was counsel to Samuel J. Tilden in the dispute over the results of the 1876 presidential election. Trumbull ran unsuccessfully as a Democrat for governor of Illinois in 1880. In 1894 he drafted the platform for the Populist Party, which convened in St. Louis.

Millard E. Tydings (1890–1961)   In 1916 Millard Evelyn Tydings was elected to the Maryland House of Delegates. Later that year, he entered the military as a private, subsequently rising to the rank of lieutenant colonel during World War I. In 1920 he was reelected to the House of Delegates, serving as speaker from 1920 to 1922. Serving two years in the Maryland Senate and the United States House of Representatives, Tydings was elected to the United States Senate in 1926. In the Senate he gained a reputation as a conservative opponent of President Franklin D. Roosevelt. Nicknamed "the goad of the Senate" because of his sharp mind and tongue, Tydings voted against almost every New Deal proposal. Roosevelt failed in his attempts to get the senator defeated in his third-term reelection bid in 1938. Tydings was a leader of the southern Democrat–Republican coalition that opposed the Roosevelt admistration's domestic agenda. He was a proponent of states' rights and fiscal conservatism. Appointed to the special committee to investigate the charges made by Senator Joseph McCarthy that communists were in the State Department, Tydings used his acidic tongue to denounce the Wisconsin senator. In Tydings's 1950 reelection bid, McCarthy countered by supporting the election of John Marshall Butler. The Senate later condemned McCarthy's activities in the election. Offered the 1956 Democratic nomination for the Senate, Tydings withdrew from the race because of failing health.

James K. Vardaman (1861–1930)   James Kimble Vardaman served three terms in the Mississippi state legislature, being speaker of the House in 1894. He failed in his bids to obtain the Democratic Party nomination for governor in 1895 and 1899. However, in 1903 his bid succeeded because of changes in the primary laws that made him more competitive. In order to win the election for governor, Vardaman played on the emotions of poor whites and farmers, who, he argued, were threatened by preferential treatment of blacks. In 1907 he failed to get the Democratic nomination for the United States Senate. After a bitter primary fight, which he lost, he succeeded in getting the people to back him over the party's nominee. In the Senate Vardaman was an ardent opponent of President Woodrow Wilson. He participated in a successful filibuster of the Armed Neutrality Act and was one of

only six senators to vote against entry into World War I. Vardaman was defeated for reelection in 1918 by Pat Harrison, who was aided by Wilson. Although Vardaman ran again for the Senate in 1922, his political career was over.

Robert F. Wagner (1877–1953)   In 1904 German immigrant Robert Ferdinand Wagner was elected to the New York Assembly. He was defeated in 1905 for reelection when he followed the Tammany machine in its opposition to a lower gas rate. In 1906, however, he was returned to the Assembly, where he served until 1911, when he was elevated to the state Senate. Serving as a skilled legislator and president pro tempore of that body, Wagner supported many reform measures to improve the conditions of working-class people. In 1918 he was elected to a 14-year term on the First District Supreme Court. He resigned from the bench in 1926 to run for the United States Senate, serving in the Senate until his death in 1953. While Washington reveled in the Roaring Twenties, Wagner warned of the growing problems of unemployment and inequality of prosperity in the nation. When Franklin D. Roosevelt was elected president, Wagner continued to press for national planning. He was responsible for the National Labor Relations Act, which established the National Labor Relations Board. A hardworking senator, he was able and willing to oppose New Deal programs he thought unwise. He urged Roosevelt and President Harry S. Truman to support a Jewish state in Palestine. In 1949 he convinced conservative Senators Allen J. Ellender and Robert A. Taft to sponsor the Public Housing Act. Wagner used his charms learned in the back rooms of the Tammany machine to win support for his reform agenda.

George C. Wallace (1919–1995)   George Corley Wallace, four-term Democratic governor of Alabama and three-time presidential candidate, was one of the most consequential figures in American politics in the 1960s and 1970s. Wallace built a national following among those frightened by the dramatic social transformations of that era. The currents of political conservatism that ascended in the United States decades later were in large part stirred by the antigovernment sentiment to which Wallace gave voice in Alabama and beyond.

Wallace was originally something of a southern liberal. He was a member of the Alabama delegation to the 1948 Democratic National Convention but remained loyal to the party in the face of the Dixiecrat revolt of that year. In 1958 Wallace lost the Democratic nomination for governor in Alabama to an opponent who stigmatized him as being soft on race. Afterward

Wallace allegedly declared that he would never again make that mistake.

In 1962 Wallace was elected governor and in his inaugural message pledged to defend segregation forever. He subsequently resisted efforts by John F. Kennedy's administration to promote integration in his state, and in a well-publicized act of defiance, physically stood in the door of the registration building at the University of Alabama to prevent the enrollment of black students there.

Wallace's popularity, however, was not limited to the Deep South. In 1964 he traveled throughout the Midwest as a Democratic candidate for president, speaking to enthusiastic gatherings in a host of states. In April he won 25% of the vote in the Wisconsin primary. More success followed, until the Republicans' nomination of Barry Goldwater co-opted his support among those opposed to intrusive federal government.

In 1968, buoyed by a popular backlash against antiwar protesters and race riots, Wallace again mounted a presidential campaign. He ran this time as an Independent, declaring that there was not "a dime's worth of difference between" the two major parties. For a period he ran ahead of Democrat Hubert Humphrey in some polls, and he finished with 46 electoral votes, the most of any outside candidate since 1912. Moreover, as a campaigner and governor, Wallace succeeded in moving Richard Nixon toward a "southern strategy," leaving his imprint on public policy despite losing the election.

Wallace ran again for president as a Democrat in 1972, winning large blocs of delegates, but a failed assassination attempt removed him from the race and left him permanently paralyzed. He refused to leave the political arena after recovering partially from the attack, briefly campaigning for president in 1976 and again winning the governorship of Alabama in 1974 and 1982. In that last campaign, Wallace survived a close Democratic challenge and overwhelmed his Republican opponent largely on the strength of African American votes. The lasting influence of federal voting-rights legislation made black voters a crucial component of Democratic electoral coalitions in the South, ironically placing Wallace's fate in the hands of those whose equality he had so long denied.

Russell L. Riley

Thomas J. Walsh (1859–1933)   Thomas James Walsh ran unsuccessfully for the United States House of Representatives from Montana in 1906 and the United States Senate in 1910. However, in 1912 he was elected to the Senate, where he served until his death in 1933. Walsh was a progressive Democrat who favored woman suffrage and child labor laws, and supported President Woodrow Wilson's positions with regard to the League of Nations and the Treaty of Versailles. He led the fight to confirm Louis D. Brandeis to the Supreme Court and denounced Attorney General A. Mitchell Palmer's Red scare tactics. Walsh, replacing Senator Burton K. Wheeler, headed the investigation of the Teapot Dome scandal, gaining a national reputation in the process. A delegate to every Democratic National Convention from 1908 to 1932, he was offered the post of vice president on a ticket headed by John W. Davis in 1924 but declined. He toyed with the possibility of seeking the presidential nomination in 1928 but decided not to run when he fared poorly in the California primary against Alfred E. Smith. President-elect Franklin D. Roosevelt offered Walsh the post of attorney general. He accepted but died suddenly on a train from Florida as he made his way north for the inauguration.

Burton K. Wheeler (1882–1975)   Burton Kendall Wheeler was elected in 1910 to the Montana State legislature, where he opposed the activities of the Anaconda Copper Mining Company. The company controlled Democratic politics in Montana, and when Wheeler ran for attorney general, the company heavily aided his opponent. President Woodrow Wilson appointed Wheeler United States district attorney in 1913, and he was regarded as a fair and effective prosecutor. Though defeated in a 1920 run for governor of Montana, he was elected to the United States Senate in 1922. He was chosen to lead the initial investigation of the Teapot Dome scandal after an impassioned speech attacking Attorney General Harry M. Daugherty for failing to do so. Daugherty was forced to resign because of the investigation. In an act of retaliation, the Justice Department unsuccessfully brought criminal indictments against Wheeler. In 1924 he was the Progressive Party's vice presidential candidate on a ticket headed by Wisconsin Senator Robert M. La Follette. An early supporter of the New Deal, he broke with the Franklin D. Roosevelt administration over the Court-packing plan. He led the opposition to the plan, which he saw as an unconstitutional power play. A leading isolationist, Wheeler voted against every measure he believed might have increased the possibility of U.S. involvement in the growing conflict in Europe. In 1941 Wheeler supplied the *Chicago Tribune* with a classified War Department document known as the "Victory Plan." No action was taken against Wheeler because, within a few days, the Japanese attacked Pearl Harbor. While he supported the war effort, he failed in his reelection bid in 1946.

Members of Congress

ABBITT, Watkins Moorman (Va.) May 21, 1908–; House Feb. 17, 1948–73.

ABBOTT, Joseph (Tex.) Jan. 15, 1840–Feb. 11, 1908; House 1887–97.

ABBOTT, Josiah Gardner (Mass.) Nov. 1, 1814–June 2, 1891; House July 28, 1876–77.

ABERCROMBIE, John William (Ala.) May 17, 1866–July 2, 1940; House 1913–17.

ABERCROMBIE, Neil (Hawaii) June 26, 1938–; House Sept. 23, 1986–87, 1991–.

ABERNETHY, Charles Laban (N.C.) March 18, 1872–Feb. 23, 1955; House Nov. 7, 1922–35.

ABERNETHY, Thomas Gerstle (Miss.) May 16, 1903–; House 1943–73.

ABOUREZK, James George (S.Dak.) Feb. 24, 1931–; House 1971–73; Senate 1973–79.

ABZUG, Bella Savitzky (N.Y.) July 24, 1920–; House 1971–77.

ACKER, Ephraim Leister (Pa.) Jan. 11, 1827–May 12, 1903; House 1871–73.

ACKERMAN, Gary Leonard (N.Y.) Nov. 19, 1942–; House March 1, 1983–.

ACKLEN, Joseph Hayes (La.) May 20, 1850–Sept. 28, 1938; House Feb. 20, 1878–81.

ADAIR, Jackson Leroy (Ill.) Feb. 23, 1887–Jan. 19, 1956; House 1933–37.

ADAIR, John Alfred McDowell (Ind.) Dec. 22, 1864–Oct. 5, 1938; House 1907–17.

ADAMS, Alva Blanchard (Colo.) Oct. 29, 1875–Dec. 1, 1941; Senate May 17, 1923–Nov. 30, 1924, 1933–Dec. 1, 1941.

ADAMS, Brockman "Brock" (Wash.) Jan. 13, 1927–; House 1965–Jan. 22, 1977; Chrmn. House Budget 1975–77; Senate 1987–93; Secy. of Transportation Jan. 23, 1977–July 22, 1979.

ADAMS, George Madison (nephew of Green Adams) (Ky.) Dec. 20, 1837–April 6, 1920; House 1867–75.

ADAMS, John Joseph (N.Y.) Sept. 16, 1848–Feb. 16, 1919; House 1883–87.

ADAMS, Stephen (Miss.) Oct. 17, 1807–May 11, 1857; House 1845–47; Senate March 17, 1852–57.

ADAMS, Wilbur Louis (Del.) Oct. 23, 1884–Dec. 4, 1937; House 1933–35.

ADAMSON, William Charles (Ga.) Aug. 13, 1854–Jan. 3, 1929; House 1897–Dec. 18, 1917.

ADDABBO, Joseph Patrick (N.Y.) March 17, 1925–April 10, 1986; House 1961–April 10, 1986.

ADDAMS, William (Pa.) April 11, 1777–May 30, 1858; House 1825–29.

ADDONIZIO, Hugh Joseph (N.J.) Jan. 31, 1914–Feb. 2, 1981; House 1949–June 30, 1962.

AHL, John Alexander (Pa.) Aug. 16, 1813–April 25, 1882; House 1857–59.

AIKEN, David Wyatt (father of Wyatt Aiken, cousin of William Aiken) (S.C.) March 17, 1828–April 6, 1887; House 1877–87.

AIKEN, William (cousin of David Wyatt Aiken) (S.C.) Jan. 28, 1806–Sept. 7, 1887; House 1851–57; Gov. 1844–46.

AIKEN, Wyatt (son of David Wyatt Aiken) (S.C.) Dec. 14, 1863–Feb. 6, 1923; House 1903–17.

AINSLIE, George (Idaho) Oct. 30, 1838–May 19, 1913; House (Terr. Del.) 1879–83.

AINSWORTH, Lucien Lester (Iowa) June 21, 1831–April 19, 1902; House 1875–77.

AKAKA, Daniel Kahikina (Hawaii) Sept. 11, 1924–; House 1977–May 16, 1990; Senate May 16, 1990–.

ALBERT, Carl Bert (cousin of Charles Wesley Vursell) (Okla.) May 10, 1908–; House 1947–77; House majority leader Jan. 10, 1962–71; Speaker Jan. 21, 1971–75, Jan. 14, 1975–77.

ALBERTSON, Nathaniel (Ind.) June 10, 1800–Dec. 16, 1863; House 1849–51.

ALBOSTA, Donald Joseph (Mich.) Dec. 5, 1925–; House 1979–85.

ALDERSON, John Duffy (Va.) Nov. 29, 1854–Dec. 5, 1910; House 1889–95.

ALESHIRE, Arthur William (Ohio) Feb. 15, 1900–March 11, 1940; House 1931–39.

ALEXANDER, Arrnstead Milton (Mo.) May 26, 1834–Nov. 7, 1892; House 1883–85.

ALEXANDER, Hugh Quincy (N.C.) Aug. 7, 1911–Sept. 17, 1989; House 1953–63.

ALEXANDER, Joshua Willis (Mo.) Jan. 22, 1852–Feb. 27, 1936; House 1907–Dec. 15, 1919; Secy. of Commerce Dec. 16, 1919–March 4, 1921.

ALEXANDER, Syndenham Benoni (cousin of Adlai Ewing Stevenson and John Sharp Williams) (N.C.) Dec. 8, 1840–June 14, 1921; House 1891–95.

ALEXANDER, William Vollie Jr. (Ark.) Jan. 16, 1934–; House 1969–93.

ALFORD, Thomas Dale (Ark.) Jan. 28, 1916–; House 1959–63.

ALLEN, Alfred Gaither (Ohio) July 23, 1867–Dec. 9, 1932; House 1911–17.

ALLEN, Asa Leonard (La.) Jan. 5, 1891–Jan. 5, 1969; House 1937–53.

ALLEN, Clifford Robertson (Tenn.) Jan. 6, 1912–June 18, 1978; House Nov. 25, 1975–June 18, 1978.

ALLEN, Henry Dixon (Ky.) June 24, 1854–March 9, 1924; House 1899–1903.

ALLEN, James Browning (husband of Maryon Pittman Allen) (Ala.) Dec. 28, 1912–June 1, 1978; Senate 1969–June 1, 1978.

ALLEN, James Cameron (Ill.) Jan. 29, 1822–Jan. 30 1912; House 1853–July 18, 1856, Nov. 4, 1856–57, 1863–65.

ALLEN, John Mills (Miss.) July 8, 1846–Oct. 30, 1917; House 1885–1901.

ALLEN, Judson (N.Y.) April 3, 1797–Aug. 6, 1880; House 1839–4l.

ALLEN, Maryon Pittman (wife of James Browning Allen) (Ala.) Nov. 30, 1925–; Senate June 8–Nov. 7, 1978.

ALLEN, Philip (R.I.) Sept. 1, 1785–Dec. 16, 1865; Senate July 20, 1853–59; Gov. May 6, 1851–July 20, 1853.

ALLEN, Robert Edward Lee (W.Va.) Nov. 28, 1865–Jan. 28, 1951; House 1923–25.

ALLEN, Robert Gray (Pa.) Aug. 24, 1902–Aug. 9, 1963; House 1937–41.

ALLEN, Thomas (Mo.) Aug. 29, 1813–April 8, 1882; House 1881–April 8, 1882.

ALLEN, William (Ohio.) Dec. 18 or Dec. 27,1803–July 11, 1879; House 1833–35 (Jacksonian); Senate 1837–49; Gov. Jan. 12, 1874–Jan. 10, 1876.

ALLEN, William (Ohio) Aug. 13, 1827–July 6, 1881; House 1859–63.

ALLEN, William Franklin (Del.) Jan. 19, 1883–June 14, 1946; House 1937–39.

ALLEN, William Joshua (son of Willis Allen) (Ill.) June 9, 1829–Jan. 26, 1901; House June 2, 1862–65.

ALLEN, Willis (father of William Joshua Allen) (Ill.) Dec. 15, 1806–April 15, 1859; House 1851–55.

ALLGOOD, Miles Clayton (Ala.) Feb. 22, 1878–March 4, 1977; House 1923–35.

ALMON, Edward Berton (Ala.) April 18, 1860–June 22, 1933; House 1915–June 22, 1933.

ALMOND, James Lindsay Jr. (Va.) June 15, 1898–April 14, 1986; House Jan. 2, 1946–April 17, 1948; Gov. Jan. 11, 1958–Jan. 13, 1962.

AMBRO, Jerome Anthony Jr. (N.Y.) June 27, 1928–March 4, 1993; House 1975–81.

AMERMAN, Lemuel (Pa.) Oct. 29, 1846–Oct. 7,1897; House 1891–93.

AMMERMAN, Joseph Scofield (Pa.) July 14, 1924–; House 1977–79.

ANCONA, Sydenham Einathan (Pa.) Nov. 20, 1824–June 20, 1913; House 1861–67.

ANDERSON, Alexander Outlaw (son of Joseph Anderson) (Tenn.) Nov. 10, 1794–May 23, 1869; Senate Feb. 26, 1840–41.

ANDERSON, Carl Carey (Ohio) Dec. 2, 1877–Oct. 1, 1912; House 1909–Oct. 1, 1912.

ANDERSON, Chapman Levy (Miss.) March 15, 1845–April 27, 1924; House 1887–91.

ANDERSON, Charles Arthur (Mo.) Sept. 26, 1899–April 26, 1977; House 1937–41.

ANDERSON, Charles Marley (Ohio) Jan. 5, 1845–Dec. 28, 1908; House 1885–87.

ANDERSON, Clinton Presba (N.Mex.) Oct. 23, 1895–Nov. 11, 1975; House 1941–June 30, 1945; Senate 1949–73; Chrmn. Senate Interior and Insular Affairs 1961–63; Chrmn. Senate Aeronautical and Space Sciences 1963–73; Secy. of Agriculture June 30, 1945–May 10, 1948.

ANDERSON, George Alburtus (Ill.) March 11, 1853–Jan. 31, 1896; House 1887–89.

ANDERSON, Glenn Malcolm (Calif.) Feb. 21, 1913–; House 1969–93; Chrmn. House Public Works and Transportation 1988–91.

ANDERSON, Hugh Johnston (Maine) May 10, 1801–May 31, 1881; House 1837–41; Gov. Jan. 5, 1844–May 12, 1847.

ANDERSON, James Patton (Wash.) Feb. 16, 1822–Sept. 20, 1872; House (Terr. Del.) 1855–57.

ANDERSON, Joseph Halstead (N.Y.) Aug. 25, 1800–June 23, 1870; House 1843–47.

ANDERSON, LeRoy Hagen (Mont.) Feb. 2, 1906–; House 1957–61.

ANDERSON, Thomas Lilbourne (Mo.) Dec. 8, 1808–March 6, 1885; House 1857–61 (1857–59 American Party).

ANDERSON, Wendell Richard (Minn.) Feb. 1, 1933–; Senate Dec. 30, 1976–Dec. 29, 1978; Gov. Jan. 4, 1971–Dec. 29, 1976.

ANDERSON, William Robert (Tenn.) June 17, 1921–; House 1965–73.

ANDREW, John Forrester (Mass.) Nov. 26, 1850–May 30, 1895; House 1889–93.

ANDREWS, Charles (Maine) Feb. 11, 1814–April 30, 1852; House 1851–April 30, 1852.

ANDREWS, Charles Oscar (Fla.) March 7, 1877–Sept. 18, 1946; Senate Nov. 4, 1936–Sept. 18, 1946.

ANDREWS, Elizabeth Bullock (widow of George William Andrews) (Ala.) Feb. 12, 1911–; House April 4, 1972–73.

ANDREWS, George William (husband of Elizabeth Bullock Andrews) (Ala.) Dec. 12, 1906–Dec. 25, 1971; House March 14, 1944–Dec. 25, 1971.

ANDREWS, Ike Franklin (N.C.) Sept. 2, 1925–; House 1973–85.

ANDREWS, John Tuttle (N.Y.) May 29, 1803–June 11, 1894; House 1837–39.

ANDREWS, Michael Allen (Tex.) Feb. 7, 1944–; House 1983–.

ANDREWS, Robert Ernest (N.J.) Aug. 4, 1957–; House 1991–1995.

ANDREWS, Thomas Hiram (Maine) March 22, 1953–1995.

ANFUSO, Victor L'Episcopo (N.Y.) March 10, 1905–Dec. 28, 1966; House 1951–53, 1955–63.

ANNUNZIO, Frank (Ill.) Jan. 12, 1915–; House 1965–93; Chrmn. House Administration 1985–91.

ANSBERRY, Timothy Thomas (Ohio) Dec. 24, 1871–July 5, 1943; House 1907–Jan. 9, 1915.

ANTHONY, Beryl Franklin Jr. (Ark.) Feb. 21, 1938–; House 1979–93.

ANTONY, Edwin Le Roy (Tex.) Jan. 5, 1852–Jan. 16, 1913; House June 14, 1892–93.

APPLEGATE, Douglas Earl (Ohio) March 27, 1928–; House 1977–1995.

APPLETON, John (Maine) Feb. 11, 1815–Aug. 22, 1864; House 1851–53.

ARCHER, Stevenson (Md.) Feb. 28, 1827–Aug. 2, 1898; House 1867–75.

ARMFIELD, Robert Franklin (N.C.) July 9, 1829–Nov. 9, 1898; House 1879–83.

ARMSTRONG, David Hartley (Mo.) Oct. 21, 1812–March 18, 1893; Senate Sept. 29, 1877–Jan. 26, 1879.

ARMSTRONG, Moses Kimball (Dakota) Sept. 19, 1832–Jan. 11, 1906; House (Terr. Del.) 1871–75.

ARMSTRONG, William (Va.) Dec. 23, 1782–May 10, 1865; House 1825–33.

ARNOLD, Laurence Fletcher (Ill.) June 8, 1891–Dec. 6, 1966; House 1937–43.

ARNOLD, Marshall (Mo.) Oct. 21, 1845–June 12, 1913; House 1891–95.

ARNOLD, Samuel (Conn.) June 1, 1806–May 5, 1869; House 1857–59.

ARNOLD, William Wright (Ill.) Oct. 14, 1877–Nov. 23, 1957; House 1923–Sept. 16, 1935.

ARNOT, John (N.Y.) March 11, 1831–Nov. 20, 1886; House 1883–Nov. 20, 1886.

ARRINGTON, Archibald Hunter (uncle of Archibald Hunter Arrington Williams) (N.C.) Nov. 13, 1809–July 20, 1872; House 1841–45.

ARTHUR, Willams Evans (Ky.) March 3, 1825–May 18, 1897; House 1871–75.

ASHBROOK, William Albert (father of John Milan Ashbrook, father-in-law of Jean Spencer Ashbrook) (Ohio) July 1, 1867–Jan. 1, 1940; House 1907–21, 1935–Jan. 1, 1940.

ASHE, Thomas Samuel (nephew of John Baptista Ashe of N.C., cousin of John Baptista Ashe of Tenn. and William Shepperd Ashe) (N.C.) July 19, 1812–Feb. 4, 1887; House 1873–77.

ASHE, William Shepperd (brother of John Baptista Ashe of Tenn., nephew of John Baptista Ashe of N.C., cousin of Thomas Samuel Ashe) (N.C.) Sept. 14, 1814–Sept. 14, 1862; House 1849–55.

ASHLEY, Chester (Ark.) June 1, 1970–April 29, 1848; Senate Nov. 8, 1844–April 29, 1848.

ASHLEY, Thomas William Ludlow (great-grandson of James Mitchell Ashley) (Ohio) Jan. 11, 1923–; House 1955–81.

ASHMORE, John Durant (cousin of Robert Thomas Ashmore) (S.C.) Aug. 18, 1819–Dec. 5, 1871; House 1859–Dec. 21, 1860.

ASHMORE, Robert Thomas (cousin of John Durant Ashmore) (S.C.) Feb. 22, 1904–Oct. 4, 1989; House June 2, 1953–69.

ASHURST, Henry Fountain (Ariz.) Sept. 13, 1874–May 31, 1962; Senate March 27, 1912–41.

ASPIN, Leslie (Wis.) July 21, 1938–1995; House 1971–Jan. 20, 1993; Chrmn. House Armed Services 1985–93; Secy. of Defense Jan. 22, 1993–Feb. 2, 1994.

ASPINALL, Wayne Norviel (Colo.) April 3, 1896–Oct. 9, 1983; House 1949–73; Chrmn. House Interior and Insular Affairs 1959–73.

ASWELL, James Benjamin (La.) Dec. 23, 1869–March 16, 1931; House 1913–March 16, 1931.

ATHERTON, Charles Gordon (son of Charles Humphrey Atherton) (N.H.) July 4, 1804–Nov. 15, 1853; House 1837–43; Senate 1843–49 (also elected for the term beginning 1853 but never qualified).

ATHERTON, Gibson (Ohio) Jan. 19, 1831–Nov. 10, 1887; House 1879–83.

ATKINS, Chester Greenough (Mass.) April 14, 1948–; House 1985–93.

ATKINS, John DeWitt Clinton (Tenn.) June 4, 1825–June 2, 1908; House 1857–59, 1873–83.

ATKINSON, Archibald (Va.) Sept. 15, 1792–Jan. 7, 1872; House 1843–49.

ATKINSON, Richard Merrill (Tenn.) Feb. 6, 1894–April 29, 1947; House 1937–39.

AuCOIN, Les (Oreg.) Oct. 21, 1942–; House 1975–93.

AUF DER HEIDE, Oscar Louis (N.J.) Dec. 8, 1874–March 29, 1945; House 1925–35.

AVERETT, Thomas Hamlet (Va.) July 10, 1800–June 30, 1855; House 1849–53.

AVERY, William Tecumsah (Tenn.) Nov. 11, 1819–May 22, 1880; House 1857–61.

AXTELL, Samuel Beach (Calif.) Oct. 14, 1819–Aug. 6, 1891; House 1867–71; Gov. (Utah Terr.) 1874–June 1875; Gov. (N.Mex. Terr.) 1875–78.

AYERS, Roy Elmer (Mont.) Nov. 9, 1882–May 23, 1955; House 1933–37; Gov. Jan. 4, 1937–Jan. 6, 1941.

AYERS, Steven Beckwith (N.Y.) Oct. 27, 1861–June 1, 1929; House 1911–13.

AYERS, William Augustus (Kans.) April 19, 1867–Feb. 17, 1952; House 1915–21, 1923–Aug. 22, 1934.

BABBITT, Clinton (Wis.) Nov. 16, 1831–March 11, 1907; House 1891–93.

BABCOCK, Leander (N.Y.) March 1, 1811–Aug. 18, 1864; House 1851–53.

BABKA, John Joseph (Ohio) March 16, 1884–March 22, 1937; House 1919–21.

BACCHUS, James (Fla.) June 21, 1949–; House 1991–1995.

BACHMAN, Nathan Lynn (Tenn.) Aug. 2, 1878–April 23, 1937; Senate Feb. 28, 1933–April 23, 1937.

BACHMAN, Reuben Knecht (Pa.) Aug. 6, 1834–Sept. 19, 1911; House 1879–81.

BACON, Augustus Octavius (cousin of William Schley Howard) (Ga.) Oct. 20, 1839–Feb. 14, 1914; Senate 1895–Feb. 14, 1914; elected Pres. pro tempore Jan. 15, 1912 (to serve Jan. 15–Jan. 17, March 11–March 12, April 8, May 10, May 30–June 3, June 13–July 5, Aug. 1–Aug. 10, Aug. 27–Dec. 15, 1912; Jan. 5–Jan. 18, Feb. 2–Feb. 15, 1913).

BACON, Henry (N.Y.) March 14, 1846–March 25, 1915; House Dec. 6, 1886–89, 1891–93.

BADGER, De Witt Clinton (Ohio) Aug. 7, 1858–May 20, 1926; House 1903–05.

BADILLO, Herman (N.Y.) Aug. 21, 1929–; House 1971–Dec. 31, 1977.

BAESLER, Scotty (Ky.) July 9, 1941–; House 1993–.

BAGBY, Arthur Pendleton (Ala.) 1794–Sept. 21, 1858; Senate Nov. 24, 1841–June 16, 1848; Gov. Nov. 21, 1837–Nov. 22, 1841.

BAGBY, John Courts (Ill.) Jan. 24, 1819–April 4, 1896; House 1875–77.

BAGLEY, John Holroyd Jr. (N.Y.) Nov. 26, 1832–Oct. 23, 1902; House 1875–77, 1883–85.

BAILEY, Cleveland Monroe (W. Va.) July 15, 1886–July 13, 1965; House 1945–47, 1949–63.

BAILEY, David Jackson (Ga.) March 11, 1812–June 14, 1897; House 1851–55 (1851–53 State Rights Party).

BAILEY, Donald Allen (Pa.) July 21, 1945–; House 1979–83.

BAILEY, James Edmund (Tenn.) Aug. 15, 1822–Dec. 29, 1885; Senate Jan. 19, 1877–81.

BAILEY, Joseph (Pa.) March 18, 1810–Aug. 26, 1885; House 1861–65.

BAILEY, Joseph Weldon (father of Joseph Weldon Bailey Jr.) (Tex.) Oct. 6, 1862–April 13, 1929; House 1891–1901; Senate 1901–Jan. 3, 1913.

BAILEY, Joseph Weldon Jr. (son of Joseph Weldon Bailey) (Tex.) Dec. 15, 1892–July 17, 1943; House 1933–35.

BAILEY, Warren Worth (Pa.) Jan. 8, 1855–Nov. 9, 1928; House 1913–17.

BAIRD, Samuel Thomas (La.) May 5, 1861–April 22, 1899; House 1897–April 22, 1899.

BAKER, David Jewett (Ill.) Sept. 7, 1792–Aug. 6, 1869; Senate Nov. 12–Dec. 11, 1830.

BAKER, Jacob Thompson (N.J.) April 13, 1847–Dec. 7, 1919; House 1913–15.

BAKER, Jehu (Ill.) Nov. 4, 1822–March 1, 1903; House 1865–69 (Republican), 1887–89 (Republican), 1897–99.

BAKER, Robert (N.Y.) April 1862–June 15, 1943; House 1903–05.

BALDACCI, R. (Maine) House 1995–.

BALDUS, Alvin James (Wis.) April 27, 1925–; House 1975–81.

BALDWIN, Harry Streett (Md.) Aug. 21, 1894–Oct. 19, 1952; House 1943–47.

BALDWIN, Melvin Riley (Minn.) April 12, 1838–April 15, 1901; House 1893–95.

BALL, Thomas Henry (Tex.) Jan. 14, 1859–May 7, 1944; House 1897–Nov. 16, 1903.

BALLENTINE, John Goff (Tenn.) May 20, 1825–Nov. 23, 1915; House 1883–87.

BALTZ, William Nicolas (Ill.) Feb. 5, 1860–Aug. 22, 1943; House 1913–15.

BANDSTRA, Bert Andrew (Iowa) Jan. 25, 1922–; House 1965–67.

BANKHEAD, John Hollis (father of John Hollis Bankhead II and William Brockman Bankhead, grandfather of Walter Will Bankhead) (Ala.) Sept. 13, 1842–March 1, 1920; House 1887–1907; Senate June 18, 1907–March 1, 1920.

BANKHEAD, John Hollis II (son of John Hollis Bankhead, brother of William Brockman Bankhead, father of Walter Will Bankhead) (Ala.) July 8, 1872–June 12, 1946; Senate 1931–June 12, 1946.

BANKHEAD, Walter Will (son of John Hollis Bankhead II, grandson of John Hollis Bankhead, nephew of William Brockman Bankhead) (Ala.) July 21, 1897–; House Jan. 3–Feb. 1, 1941.

BANKHEAD, William Brockman (son of John Hollis Bankhead, brother of John Hollis Bankhead II, uncle of Walter Will Bankhead) (Ala.) April 12, 1874–Sept. 15, 1940; House 1917–Sept. 15, 1940; House majority leader 1935–June 4, 1936; Speaker June 4, 1936–37, Jan. 5, 1937–Sept. 15, 1940.

BANKS, Linn (Va.) Jan. 23, 1784–Jan. 13, 1842; House April 28, 1838–Dec. 6, 1841.

BANNING, Henry Blackstone (Ohio) Nov. 10, 1836–Dec. 10, 1881; House 1873–79 (1873–75 Liberal Republican).

BARBER, Laird Howard (Pa.) Oct. 25, 1848–Feb. 16, 1928; House 1899–1901.

BARBOUR, John Strode Jr (Va.) Dec. 29, 1820–May 14, 1892; House 1881–87; Senate 1889–May 14, 1892.

BARCA, Peter William (Wis.) Aug. 7, 1955–; House June 8, 1993–1995.

BARCIA, James A. (Mich.) Feb. 29, 1952–; House 1993–.

BARCLAY, David (Pa.) 1823–Sept. 10, 1889; House 1955–57.

BARDEN, Graham Arthur (N.C.) Sept. 25, 1896–Jan. 29, 1967; House 1935–61; Chrmn. House Education and Labor 1950–53, 1955–61.

BARING, Walter Stephan Jr. (Nev.) Sept. 9, 1911–July 13, 1975; House 1949–53, 1957–73.

BARKLEY, Alben William (Ky.) Nov. 24, 1877–April 30, 1956; House 1913–27; Senate 1927–Jan. 19, 1949, 1955–April 30, 1956; Senate majority leader July 22, 1937–47; Senate minority leader 1947–49; Vice President 1949–53.

BARKSDALE, Ethelbert (brother of William Barksdale) (Miss.) Jan. 4, 1824–Feb. 17, 1893; House 1883–87.

BARKSDALE, William (brother of Ethelbert Barksdale) (Miss.) Aug. 21, 1821–July 2, 1863; House 1853–Jan. 12, 1861.

BARLOW, Thomas Jefferson III (Ky.) Aug. 7, 1940–; House 1993–1995.

BARNARD, Druie Douglas Jr. (Ga.) March 20, 1922–; House 1977–93.

BARNES, Demas (N.Y.) April 4, 1827–May 1, 1888; House 1867–69.

BARNES, George Thomas (Ga.) Aug. 14, 1833–Oct. 24, 1901; House 1885–91.

BARNES, James Martin (Ill.) Jan. 9, 1899–June 8, 1958; House 1939–43.

BARNES, Lyman Eddy (Wis.) June 30, 1855–Jan. 16, 1904; House 1893–95.

BARNES, Michael Darr (Md.) Sept. 3, 1943–; House 1979–87.

BARNHART, Henry A. (Ind.) Sept. 11, 1858–March 26, 1934; House Nov. 3, 1908–19.

BARNUM, William Henry (Conn.) Sept. 17, 1818–April 30, 1889; House 1867–May 18, 1876; Senate May 18, 1876–79; Chrmn. Dem. Nat. Comm. 1877–89.

BARR, Joseph Walker (Ind.) Jan. 17, 1918–; House 1959–61; Secy. of the Treasury Dec. 21, 1968–Jan. 20, 1969.

BARRET, John Richard (Mo.) Aug. 21, 1825–Nov. 2, 1903; House 1859–June 8, 1860, Dec. 3, 1860–61.

BARRETT, Thomas Mark (Wis.) Dec. 8, 1953–; House 1933–.

BARRETT, William Aloysius (Pa.) Aug. 14, 1896–April 12, 1976; House 1945–47, 1949–April 12, 1976.

BARROW, Middleton Pope (grandson of Wilson Lumpkin) (Ga.) Aug. 1, 1839–Dec. 23, 1903; Senate Nov. 15, 1882–83.

BARRY, Frederick George (Miss.) Jan. 12, 1845–May 7, 1909; House 1885–89.

BARRY, William Bernard (N.Y.) July 21, 1902–Oct. 20, 1946; House Nov. 5, 1935–Oct. 20, 1946.

BARRY, William Taylor Sullivan (Miss.) Dec. 10, 1821–Jan. 29, 1868; House 1853–55.

BARTLETT, Charles Lafayette (Ga.) Jan. 31, 1853–April 21, 1938; House 1895–1915.

BARTLETT, Edward Lewis "Bob" (Alaska) April 20, 1904–Dec. 11, 1968; House (Terr. Del.) 1945–59; Senate 1959–Dec. 11, 1968.

BARTLETT, Franklin (N.Y.) Sept. 10, 1847–April 23, 1909; House 1893–97.

BARTLETT, George Arthur (Nev.) Nov. 30, 1869–June 1, 1951; House 1907–11.

BARTLETT, Thomas Jr. (Vt.) June 18, 1808–Sept. 12, 1876; House 1851–53.

BARTON, William Edward (cousin of Courtney Walker Hamlin) (Mo.) April 11, 1868–July 29, 1955; House 1931–33.

BARWIG, Charles (Wis.) March 19, 1837–Feb. 15, 1912; House 1889–95.

BASS, Ross (Tenn.) March 17, 1918–Jan. 1, 1993; House 1955–Nov. 3, 1964; Senate Nov. 4, 1964–Jan. 2, 1967.

BASSETT, Edward Murray (N.Y.) Feb. 7, 1863–Oct. 27, 1948; House 1903–05.

BATE, William Brimage (Tenn.) Oct. 7, 1826–March 9, 1905; Senate 1887–March 9, 1905; Gov. Jan. 15, 1883–Jan. 17, 1887.

BATES, Jim (Calif.) July 21, 1941–; House 1983–91.

BATES, Joseph Bengal (Ky.) Oct. 29, 1893–Sept. 10, 1965; Senate Jan. 14, 1857–59.

BATES, Martin Waltham (Del.) Feb. 24, 1786–Jan. 1, 1869; Senate Jan. 14, 1857–59.

BATHRICK, Elsworth Raymond (Ohio) Jan. 6, 1863–Dec. 23, 1917; House 1911–15, March 4–Dec. 23, 1917.

BATTLE, Laurie Calvin (Ala.) May 10, 1912–; House 1947–55.

BAUCUS, Max Sieben (Mont.) Dec. 11, 1941–; House 1975–Dec. 14, 1978; Senate Dec. 15, 1978–; Chrmn. Senate Environment and Public Works 1993–1995.

BAY, William Van Ness (Mo.) Nov. 23, 1818–Feb. 10, 1894; House 1849–51.

BAYARD, James Asheton Jr. (son of James Asheton Bayard Sr., brother of Richard Henry Bayard, grandson of Richard Bassett, father of Thomas Francis Bayard Sr., grandfather of Thomas Francis Bayard Jr.) (Del.) Nov. 15, 1799–June 13, 1880; Senate 1851–Jan. 29, 1864, April 5, 1867–69.

BAYARD, Thomas Francis Sr. (son of James Asheton Bayard J., father of Thomas Francis Bayard Jr.) (Del.) Oct. 29, 1828–Sept. 28, 1898; Senate 1869–March 6, 1885; elected Pres. pro tempore Oct. 10, 1881; Secy. of State March 7, 1885–March 6, 1889.

BAYARD, Thomas Francis Jr. (son of Thomas Francis Bayard Sr., grandson of James Asheton Bayard Jr.) (Del.) June 4, 1868–July 12, 1942; Senate Nov. 8, 1922–29.

BAYH, Birch Evan (Ind.) Jan. 22, 1928–; Senate 1963–81; Chrmn. Senate Select Committee on Intelligence Activities 1978–81.

BAYLY, Thomas Henry (son of Thomas Monteagle Bayly) (Va.) Dec. 11, 1810–June 23, 1856; House May 6, 1844–June 23, 1856.

BEACH, Lewis (N.Y.) March 30, 1835–Aug. 10, 1886; House 1881–Aug. 10, 1886.

BEAKES, Samuel Willard (Mich.) Jan. 11, 1861–Feb. 9, 1927; House 1913–March 3, 1917, Dec. 13, 1917–19.

BEALE, James Madison Hite (Va.) Feb. 7, 1786–Aug. 2, 1866; House 1833–37 (Jacksonian), 1849–53.

BEALE, Richard Lee Turbeville (Va.) May 22, 1819–April 21, 1893; House 1847–49, Jan. 23, 1879–81.

BEALL, James Andrew "Jack" (Tex.) Oct. 25, 1866–Feb. 12, 1929; House 1903–15.

BEAM, Harry Peter (Ill.) Nov. 23, 1892–Dec. 31, 1967; House 1931–Dec. 6, 1942.

BEARD, Edward Peter (R.I.) Jan. 20, 1940–; House 1975–81.

BEARDSLEY, Samuel (N.Y.) Feb. 6, 1790–May 6, 1860; House 1831–March 29, 1836 (Jacksonian), 1843–Feb. 29, 1844.

BEATTY, William (Pa.) 1787–April 12, 1851; House 1837–41.

BECERRA, Xavier (Calif.) Jan. 26, 1958–; House 1993–.

BECK, Erasmus Williams (Ga.) Oct. 21, 1833–July 22, 1898; House Dec. 2, 1872–73.

BECK, James Burnie (Ky.) Feb. 13, 1822–May 3, 1890; House 1867–75; Senate 1877–May 3, 1890.

BECKHAM, John Crepps Wickliffe (grandson of Charles Anderson Wickliffe, cousin of Robert Charles Wickliffe) (Ky.) Aug. 5, 1869–Jan. 9, 1940; Senate 1915–21; Gov. Feb. 3, 1900–Dec. 10, 1907.

BECKNER, William Morgan (Ky.) June 19, 1841–March 14, 1910; House Dec. 3, 1894–95.

BECKWORTH, Lindley Garrison "Gary" Sr. (Tex.) June 30, 1913–March 9, 1984; House 1939–53, 1957–67.

BEDELL, Berkley Warren (Iowa) March 5, 1921–; House 1975–87.

BEDINGER, Henry (nephew of George Michael Bedinger) (Va.) Feb. 3, 1812–Nov. 26, 1858; House 1845–49.

BEE, Carlos (Tex.) July 8, 1867–April 20, 1932; House 1919–21.

BEEBE, George Monroe (N.Y.) Oct. 28, 1836–March 1, 1927; House 1875–79.

BEEMAN, Joseph Henry (Miss.) Nov. 17, 1833–July 31, 1909; House 1891–93.

BEERS, Cyrus (N.Y.) June 21, 1786–June 5, 1850; House Dec. 3, 1838–39.

BEESON, Henry White (Pa.) Sept. 14, 1791–Oct. 28, 1863; House May 31, 1841–43.

BEGICH, Nicholas Joseph (Alaska) April 6, 1932–?; House 1971–72. (Disappeared on an airplane flight Oct. 16, 1972, and presumed dead; congressional seat declared vacant Dec. 29, 1972.)

BEILENSON, Anthony Charles (Calif.) Oct. 26, 1932–; House 1977–; Chrmn. House Permanent Select Committee on Intelligence 1989–91.

BEIRNE, Andrew (Va.) 1771–March 16, 1845; House 1837–41.

BEITER, Alfred Florian (N.Y.) July 7, 1894–March 11, 1974; House 1933–39, 1941–43.

BELCHER, Nathan (Conn.) June 23, 1813–June 2, 1891; House 1853–55.

BELL, Charles Jasper (Mo.) Jan. 16, 1885–Jan. 21, 1978; House 1935–49.

BELL, Charles Keith (nephew of Reese Bowen Brabson) (Tex.) April 18, 1853–April 21, 1913; House 1893–97.

BELL, Hiram Parks (Ga.) Jan. 19, 1827–Aug. 17, 1907; House 1873–75, March 13, 1877–79.

BELL, John Junior (Tex.) May 15, 1910–Jan. 24, 1963; House 1955–57.

BELL, Peter Hansbrough (Tex.) May 12, 1812–March 8, 1898; House 1853–57; Gov. Dec. 21, 1849–Nov. 23, 1853.

BELL, Samuel Newell (grandson of Samuel Bell, nephew of James Bell) (N.H.) March 25, 1829–Feb. 8, 1889; House 1871–73, 1875–77.

BELL, Theodore Arlington (Calif.) July 25, 1872–Sept. 4, 1922; House 1903–05.

BELL, Thomas Montgomery (Ga.) March 17, 1861–March 18, 1941; House 1905–31.

BELLAMY, John Dillard (N.C.) March 24, 1854–Sept. 25, 1942; House 1899–1903.

BELMONT, Oliver Hazard Perry (brother of Perry Belmont) (N.Y.) Nov. 12, 1858–June 10, 1908; House 1901–03.

BELMONT, Perry (brother of Oliver Hazard Perry Belmont) (N.Y.) Dec. 28, 1851–May 25, 1947; House 1881–Dec. 1, 1888.

BELSER, James Edwin (Ala.) Dec. 22, 1805–Jan. 16, 1859; House 1843–45.

BELTZHOOVER, Frank Eckels (Pa.) Nov. 6, 1841–June 2, 1923; House 1879–83, 1891–95.

BENEDICT, Charles Brewster (N.Y.) Feb. 7, 1828–Oct. 3, 1901; House 1877–79.

BENET, Christie (S.C.) Dec. 26, 1879–March 30, 1951; Senate July 6–Nov. 5, 1918.

BENJAMIN, Adam Jr. (Ind.) Aug. 6, 1935–Sept. 7, 1982; House 1977–Sept. 7, 1982.

BENJAMIN, Judah Philip (La.) Aug. 6, 1811–May 6, 1884; Senate 1853–Feb. 4, 1861 (1853–59 Whig).

BENNER, George Jacob (Pa.) April 13, 1859–Dec. 30, 1930; House 1897–99.

BENNETT, Charles Edward (Fla.) Dec. 2, 1910–; House 1949–93; Chrmn. House Standards of Official Conduct 1977–81.

BENNETT, Hendley Stone (Miss.) April 7, 1807–Dec. 15, 1891; House 1855–57.

BENNETT, Risden Tyler (N.C.) June 18, 1840–July 21, 1913; House 1883–87.

BENNY, Allan (N.J.) July 12, 1867–Nov. 6, 1942; House 1903–05.

BENSON, Carville Dickinson (Md.) Aug. 24, 1872–Feb. 8, 1929; House Nov. 5, 1918–21.

BENTLEY, Henry Wilbur (N.Y.) Sept. 30, 1838–Jan. 27, 1907; House 1891–93.

BENTON, Charles Swan (N.Y.) July 12, 1810–May 4, 1882; House 1843–47.

BENTON, Maecenas Eason (Mo.) Jan. 29, 1848–April 27, 1924; House 1897–1905.

BENTON, Thomas Hart (father-in-law of John Charles Fremont) (Mo.) March 14, 1782–April 10, 1858; Senate Aug. 10, 1821–51; House 1853–55.

BENTON, William (Conn.) April 1, 1900–March 18, 1973; Senate Dec. 17, 1949–53.

BENTSEN, Lloyd Millard Jr. (Tex.) Feb. 11, 1921–; House Dec. 4, 1948–55; Senate 1971–Jan. 20, 1993; Chrmn. Senate Finance 1987–93; Secy. of the Treasury Jan. 22, 1993–1995.

BERGEN, Teunis Garret (second cousin of John Teunis Bergen) (N.Y.) Oct. 6, 1806–April 24, 1881; House 1865–67.

BERGLAND, Robert Selmer (Minn.) July 22, 1928–; House 1971–Jan. 22, 1977; Secy. of Agriculture Jan. 23, 1977–Jan. 20, 1981.

BERLIN, William Markle (Pa.) March 29, 1880–Oct. 14, 1962; House 1933–37.

BERMAN, Howard Lawrence (Calif.) April 15, 1941–; House 1983–.

BERRY, Albert Seaton (Ky.) May 13, 1836–Jan. 6, 1908; House 1893–1901.

BERRY, Campbell Polson (cousin of James Henderson Berry) (Calif.) Nov. 7, 1834–Jan. 8, 1901; House 1879–83.

BERRY, George Leonard (Tenn.) Sept. 12, 1882–Dec. 4, 1948; Senate May 6, 1937–Nov. 8, 1938.

BERRY, James Henderson (cousin of Campbell Polson Berry) (Ark.) May 15, 1841–Jan. 30, 1913; Senate March 20, 1885–1907; Gov. Jan. 13, 1883–Jan. 17, 1885.

BERRY, John (Ohio) April 26, 1833–May 18, 1879; House 1873–75.

BESHLIN, Earl Hanley (Prohib. Pa.) April 28, 1870–July 12, 1971; House Nov. 8, 1917–19.

BEVILL, Tom (Ala.) March 27, 1921–; House 1967–.

BIAGGI, Mario (N.Y.) Oct. 26, 1917–; House 1969–Aug. 8, 1988.

BIBLE, Alan Harvey (Nev.) Nov. 20, 1909–Sept. 12, 1988; Senate Dec. 2, 1954–Dec. 17, 1974; Chrmn. Senate District of Columbia 1959–69; Chrmn. Senate Select Committee on Small Business 1969–75.

BICKNELL, Bennet (N.Y.) Nov. 14, 1781–Sept. 15, 1841; House 1837–39.

BICKNELL, George Augustus (Ind.) Feb. 6, 1815–April 11, 1891; House 1877–81.

BIDDLE, Charles John (nephew of Richard Biddle) (Pa.) April 30, 1819–Sept. 28, 1873; House July 2, 1861–63.

BIDEN, Joseph Robinette Jr. (Del.) Nov. 20, 1942–; Senate 1973–; Chrmn. Senate Judiciary 1987–1995.

BIDLACK, Benjamin Alden (Pa.) Sept. 8, 1804–Feb. 6, 1849; House 1841–45.

BIEMILLER, Andrew John (Wis.) July 23, 1906–April 3, 1982; House 1945–47, 1949–51.

BIERMANN, Frederick Elliott (Iowa) March 20, 1884–July 1, 1968; House 1933–39.

BIGELOW, Herbert Seely (Ohio) Jan. 4, 1870–Nov. 11, 1951; House 1937–39.

BIGGS, Asa (N.C.) Feb. 4, 1811–March 6, 1878; House 1845–47; Senate 1855–May 5, 1858.

BIGGS, Benjamin Thomas (Del.) Oct. 1, 1821–Dec. 25, 1893; House 1869–73; Gov. Jan. 18, 1887–Jan. 20, 1891.

BIGGS, Marion (Calif.) May 2, 1823–Aug. 2, 1910; House 1887–91.

BIGLER, William (brother of Gov. John Bigler of Calif.) (Pa.) Jan. 1, 1814–Aug. 9, 1880; Senate Jan. 14, 1856–61; Gov. Jan. 20, 1852–Jan. 15, 1855.

BILBO, Theodore Gilmore (Miss.) Oct. 13, 1877–Aug. 21, 1947; Senate 1935–Aug. 21, 1947; Gov. Jan. 18, 1916–Jan. 20, 1920. Jan. 17, 1928–Jan. 19, 1932.

BILBRAY, James Hubert (Nev.) May 19, 1938–; House 1987–1995.

BILLMEYER, Alexander (Pa.) Jan. 7, 1841–May 24, 1924; House Nov. 4, 1902–03.

BINDERUP, Charles Gustav (Nebr.) March 5, 1873–Aug. 19, 1950; House 1935–39.

BINGAMAN, Jesse Francis Jr. "Jeff" (N.Mex.) Oct. 3, 1943–; Senate 1983–.

BINGHAM, Jonathan Brewster (son of Hiram Bingham) (N.Y.) April 24, 1914–July 3, 1986; House 1965–83.

BIRD, John Taylor (N.J.) Aug. 16, 1829–May 6, 1911; House 1869–73.

BIRDSALL, Ausburn (N.Y.) ?–July 10, 1903; House 1847–49.

BIRDSALL, Samuel (N.Y.) May 14, 1791–Feb. 8, 1872; House 1837–39.

BISHOP, Sanford (Ga.) Feb. 4, 1947–; House 1993–.

BISHOP, William Darius (Conn.) Sept. 14, 1827–Feb. 4, 1904; House 1857–59.

BLACK, Edward Junius (father of George Robison Black) (Ga.) Oct. 30, 1806–Sept. 1, 1846; House 1839–41 (Whig), Jan. 3, 1842–45.

BLACK, Eugene (Tex.) July 2, 1879–May 22, 1975; House 1915–29.

BLACK, George Robison (son of Edward Junius Black) (Ga.) March 24, 1835–Nov. 3, 1886; House 1881–83.

BLACK, Hugo Lafayette (Ala.) Feb. 27, 1886–Sept. 25, 1971; Senate 1927–Aug. 19, 1937; Assoc. Justice Supreme Court Aug. 19, 1937–Sept. 17, 1971.

BLACK, James (Pa.) March 6, 1793–June 21, 1872; House Dec. 5, 1836–37 (Jacksonian), 1843–47.

BLACK, James Augustus (S.C.) 1793–April 3, 1848; House 1843–April 3, 1848.

BLACK, James Conquest Cross (Ga.) May 9, 1842–Oct. 1, 1928; House 1893–March 4, 1895, Oct. 2, 1895–97.

BLACK, John Charles (Ill.) Jan. 27, 1839–Aug. 17, 1915; House 1893–Jan. 12, 1895.

BLACK, Loring Milton Jr. (N.Y.) May 17, 1886–May 21, 1956; House 1923–35.

BLACKBURN, Joseph Clay Stiles (Ky.) Oct. 1, 1838–Sept. 12, 1918; House 1875–85; Senate 1885–97, 1901–07.

BLACKMON, Fred Leonard (Ala.) Sept. 15, 1873–Feb. 8, 1921; House 1911–Feb. 8, 1921.

BLACKWELL, Julius W. (Tenn.) ?–?; House 1839–41, 1843–45.

BLACKWELL, Lucien Edward (Pa.) Aug. 1, 1931–; House Nov. 13, 1991–.

BLAIR, Francis Preston Jr. (Mo.) Feb. 19, 1821–July 8, 1875; House 1857–59 (Republican), June 8–25, 1860, 1861–July 1862, 1863–June 10, 1864; Senate Jan. 20, 1871–73.

BLAKLEY, William Arvis (Tex.) Nov. 17, 1898–Jan. 5, 1976; Senate Jan. 15–April 28, 1957, Jan. 3–June 14, 1961.

BLANCHARD, James Johnston (Mich.) Aug. 8, 1942–; House 1975–83; Gov. Jan. 1, 1983–.

BLANCHARD, Newton Crain (La.) Jan. 29, 1849–June 22, 1922; House 1881–March 12, 1894; Senate March 12, 1894–97; Gov. May 10, 1904–May 18, 1908.

BLAND, Richard Parks (Mo.) Aug. 19, 1835–June 15, 1899; House 1873–95, 1897–June 15, 1899.

BLAND, Schuyler Otis (Va.) May 4, 1872–Feb. 16, 1950; House July 2, 1918–Feb. 16, 1950; Chrmn. House Merchant Marine and Fisheries 1949–50.

BLAND, William Thomas (grandson of John George Jackson, cousin of James Monroe Jackson) (Mo.) Jan. 21, 1861–Jan. 15, 1928; House 1919–21.

BLANTON, Leonard Ray (Tenn.) April 10, 1930–; House 1967–73; Gov. Jan. 18, 1975–Jan. 17, 1979.

BLANTON, Thomas Lindsay (Tex.) Oct. 25, 1872–Aug. 11, 1957; House 1917–29, May 20, 1930–37.

BLATNIK, John Anton (Minn.) Aug. 17, 1911–Dec. 17, 1991; House 1947–Dec. 31, 1974; Chrmn. House Public Works 1971–75.

BLEASE, Coleman Livingston (S.C.) Oct. 8, 1868–Jan. 19, 1942; Senate 1925–31; Gov. Jan. 17, 1911–Jan. 14, 1915.

BLISS, Archibald Meserole (N.Y.) Jan. 25, 1838–March 19, 1923; House 1875–83, 1885–89.

BLISS, George (Ohio) Jan. 1, 1813–Oct. 24, 1868; House 1853–55, 1863–65.

BLITCH, Iris Faircloth (Ga.) April 25, 1912–Aug. 19, 1993; House 1955–63.

BLODGETT, Rufus (N.J.) Oct. 9, 1834–Oct. 3, 1910; Senate 1887–93.

BLOOM, Sol (N.Y.) March 9, 1870–March 7, 1949; House 1923–March 7, 1949.

BLOUIN, Michael Thomas (Iowa) Nov. 7, 1945–; House 1975–79.

BLOUNT, James Henderson (Ga.) Sept. 12, 1837–March 8, 1903; House 1873–93.

BOARDMAN, Elijah (Conn.) March 7, 1760–Aug. 18, 1823; Senate 1821–Aug. 18, 1823.

BOATNER, Charles Jahleal (La.) Jan. 23, 1849–March 21, 1903; House 1889–95, June 10, 1896–97.

BOCOCK, Thomas Stanley (Va.) May 18, 1815–Aug. 5, 1891; House 1847–61.

BODINE, Robert Nall (Mo.) Dec. 17, 1837–March 16, 1914; House 1879–99.

BOEHNE, John William (father of John William Boehne Jr.) (Ind.) Oct. 28, 1856–Dec. 27, 1946; House 1909–13.

BOEHNE, John William Jr. (son of John William Boehne) (Ind.) March 2, 1895–July 5, 1973; House 1931–43.

BOGGS, Corinne Claiborne "Lindy" (widow of Thomas Hale Boggs Sr.) (La.) March 13, 1916–; House March 20, 1973–91.

BOGGS, Thomas Hale Sr. (husband of Corinne Claiborne Boggs) (La.) Feb. 15, 1914–?; House 1941–43, 1947–73; House majority leader 1971–73. (Disappeared on an airplane flight Oct. 16, 1972, and presumed dead; congressional seat declared vacant Jan. 3, 1973.)

BOGY, Lewis Vital (Mo.) April 9, 1813–Sept. 20, 1877; Senate 1873–Sept. 20, 1877.

BOLAND, Edward Patrick (Mass.) Oct. 1, 1911–; House 1953–89; Chrmn. House Permanent Select Committee on Intelligence 1977–85.

BOLAND, Patrick Joseph (husband of Veronica Grace Boland) (Pa.) Jan. 6, 1880–May 18, 1942; House 1931–May 18, 1942.

BOLAND, Veronica Grace (widow of Patrick Joseph Boland) (Pa.) March 18, 1899–June 19, 1982; House Nov. 19, 1942–43.

BOLLING, Richard Walker (great-great-grandson of John Williams Walker, great-great-nephew of Percy Walker) (Mo.) May 17, 1916–April 21, 1991; House 1949–83; Chrmn. House Rules 1979–83.

BOLTON, William P. (Md.) July 2, 1885–Nov. 22, 1964; House 1949–51.

BONE, Homer Truett (Wash.) Jan. 25, 1883–March 11, 1970; Senate 1933–Nov. 13, 1944.

BONER, William Hill (Tenn.) Feb. 14, 1945–; House 1979–Oct. 5, 1987.

BONHAM, Milledge Luke (S.C.) Dec. 25, 1813–Aug. 27, 1890; House 1857–Dec. 21, 1860; Gov. Dec. 17, 1862–Dec. 20, 1864 (Confederate Democrat).

BONIOR, David Edward (Mich.) June 6, 1945–; House 1977–.

BONKER, Don Leroy (Wash.) March 7, 1937–; House 1975–89.

BONNER, Herbert Covington (N.C.) May 16, 1891–Nov. 7, 1965; House Nov. 5, 1940–Nov. 7, 1965; Chrmn. House Merchant Marine and Fisheries 1955–66.

BOODY, David Augustus (N.Y.) Aug. 13, 1837–Jan. 20, 1930; House March 4–Oct. 13, 1891.

BOOHER, Charles Ferris (Mo.) Jan. 31, 1848–Jan. 21, 1921; House Feb. 19–March 3, 1889, 1907–Jan. 21, 1921.

BOON, Ratliff (Ind.) Jan. 18, 1781–Nov. 20, 1844; House 1825–27 (no party), 1829–39 (1829–37 Jacksonian); Gov. Sept. 12–Dec. 5, 1822 (Democrat).

BOONE, Andrew Rechmond (Ky.) April 4, 1831–Jan. 26, 1886; House 1875–79.

BORCHERS, Charles Martin (Ill.) Nov. 18, 1869–Dec. 2, 1946; House 1913–15.

BOREN, David Lyle (son of Lyle H. Boren) (Okla.) April 21, 1941–; Senate 1979–1995; Chrmn. Senate Select Committee on Intelligence Activities 1987–93; Gov. Jan. 13, 1975–Jan. 3, 1979.

BOREN, Lyle H. (father of David Lyle Boren) (Okla.) May 11, 1909–July 2, 1992; House 1937–47.

BORLAND, Solon (Ark.) Sept. 21, 1808–Jan. 1, 1864; Senate March 30, 1848–April 3, 1853.

BORLAND, William Patterson (Mo.) Oct. 14, 1867–Feb. 20, 1919; House 1909–Feb. 20, 1919.

BORSKI, Robert Anthony Jr. (Pa.) Oct. 20, 1948–; House 1983–.

BOSCO, Doublas Harry (Calif.) July 28, 1946–; House 1983–91.

BOSONE, Reva Zilpha Beck (Utah) April 2, 1895–July 21, 1983; House 1949–53.

BOSSIER, Pierre Evariste John Baptiste (La.) March 22, 1797–April 24, 1844; House 1843–April 24, 1844.

BOUCHER, Frederick C. (Va.) Aug. 1, 1946–; House 1983–.

BOUCK, Gabriel (nephew of Joseph Bouck) (Wis.) Dec. 16, 1828–Feb. 21, 1904; House 1877–81.

BOULDIN, James Wood (brother of Thomas Tyler Bouldin) (Va.) 1792–March 30, 1854; House March 15, 1834–35 (March 15, 1834–37 Jacksonian).

BOWDLE, Stanley Eyre (Ohio) Sept. 4, 1868–April 6, 1919; House 1913–15.

BOWDON, Franklin Welsh (uncle of Sydney Johnston Bowie) (Ala.) Feb. 17, 1817–June 8, 1957; House Dec. 7, 1846–51.

BOWEN, David Reece (Miss.) Oct. 21, 1932–; House 1973–83.

BOWEN, Rees Tate (father of Henry Bowen) (Va.) Jan. 10, 1809–Aug. 29, 1879; House 1873–75.

BOWER, Gustavus Miller (Va.) Dec. 12, 1790–Nov. 17, 1864; House 1843–45.

BOWER, William Horton (N.C.) June 6, 1850–May 11, 1910; House 1893–95.

BOWERS, Eaton Jackson (Miss.) June 17, 1865–Oct. 26, 1939; House 1903–11.

BOWIE, Sydney Johnston (nephew of Franklin Welsh Bowdon) (Ala.) July 26, 1865–May 7, 1928; House 1901–07.

BOWIE, Thomas Fielder (great-nephew of Walter Bowie, brother-in-law of Reverdy Johnson) (Md.) April 7, 1808–Oct. 30, 1869; House 1855–59.

BOWLER, James Bernard (Ill.) Feb. 5, 1875–July 18, 1957; House July 7, 1953–July 18, 1957.

BOWLES, Chester Bliss (Conn.) April 5, 1901–May 25, 1986; House 1959–61; Gov. Jan. 5, 1949–Jan. 3, 1951.

BOWLIN, James Butler (Mo.) Jan. 16, 1804–July 19, 1874; House 1843–51.

BOWLING, William Bismarck (Ala.) Sept. 24, 1870–Dec. 27, 1946; House Dec. 14, 1920–Aug. 16, 1928.

BOWMAN, Thomas (Iowa) May 25, 1848–Dec. 1, 1917; House 1891–93.

BOWNE, Samuel Smith (N.Y.) April 11, 1800–July 9, 1865; House 1841–43.

BOX, John Calvin (Tex.) March 28, 1871–May 17, 1941; House 1919–31.

BOXER, Barbara (Calif.) Nov. 11, 1940–; House 1983–93; Senate 1993–.

BOYCE, William Henry (Del.) Nov. 28, 1855–Feb. 6, 1942; House 1923–25.

BOYCE, William Waters (S.C.) Oct. 24, 1818–Feb. 3, 1890; House 1853–Dec. 21, 1860.

BOYD, Linn (Ky.) Nov. 22, 1800–Dec. 17, 1859; House 1835–37 (Jacksonian), 1839–55; Speaker Dec. 1, 1851–53, Dec. 5, 1853–55.

BOYER, Benjamin Markley (Pa.) Jan. 22, 1823–Aug. 16, 1887; House 1865–69.

BOYER, Lewis Leonard (Ill.) May 19, 1886–March 12, 1944; House 1937–39.

BOYKIN, Frank William (Ala.) Feb. 21, 1885–March 12, 1969; House July 30, 1935–63.

BOYLAN, John Joseph (N.Y.) Sept. 30, 1878–Oct. 5, 1938; House 1923–Oct. 5, 1938.

BOYLE, Charles Augustus (Ill.) Aug. 13, 1907–Nov. 4, 1959; House 1955–Nov. 4, 1959.

BOYLE, Charles Edmund (Pa.) Feb. 4, 1836–Dec. 15, 1888; House 1883–87.

BRADBURY, James Ware (Maine) June 10, 1802–Jan. 6, 1901; Senate 1847–53.

BRADEMAS, John (Ind.) March 2, 1927–; House 1959–81.

BRADFORD, Taul (grandson of Micah Taul) (Ala.) Jan. 20, 1835–Oct. 28, 1883; House 1875–77.

BRADLEY, Edward (Mich.) April 1808–Aug. 5, 1847; House March 4–Aug. 5, 1847.

BRADLEY, Michael Joseph (Pa.) May 24, 1897–Nov. 27, 1979; House 1937–47.

BRADLEY, Thomas Joseph (N.Y.) Jan. 2, 1870–April 1, 1901; House 1897–1901.

BRADLEY, William Warren "Bill" (N.J.) July 28, 1943–; Senate 1979–1995.

BRAGG, Edward Stuyvesant (Wis.) Feb. 20, 1827–June 20, 1912; House 1877–83, 1885–87.

BRAGG, John (Ala.) Jan. 14, 1806–Aug. 10, 1878; House 1851–53.

BRAGG, Thomas (N.C.) Nov. 9, 1810–Jan. 21, 1872; Senate 1859–March 6, 1861; Gov. Jan. 1, 1855–Jan. 1, 1859.

BRANCH, John (uncle of Lawrence O'Bryan Branch, great-uncle of William Augustus Blount Branch) (N.C.) Nov. 4, 1782–Jan. 3, 1863; Senate 1823–March 9, 1829; House May 12, 1831–33; Gov. Dec. 6, 1817–Dec. 7, 1820 (Democratic Republican); Secy. of the Navy March 9, 1829–March 12, 1831.

BRANCH, Lawrence O'Bryan (father of William Augustus Blount Branch, nephew of John Branch) (N.C.) Nov. 28, 1820–Sept. 17, 1862; House 1855–61.

BRANCH, William Augustus Blount (son of Lawrence O'Bryan Branch, great-nephew of John Branch) (N.C.) Feb. 26, 1847–Nov. 18, 1910; House 1891–95.

BRAND, Charles Hillyer (Ga.) April 20, 1861–May 17, 1933; House 1917–May 17, 1933.

BRANTLEY, William Gordon (Ga.) Sept. 18, 1860–Sept. 11, 1934; House 1897–1913.

BRASCO, Frank James (N.Y.) Oct. 15, 1932–; House 1967–75.

BRATTON, Robert Franklin (Md.) May 3, 1845–May 10, 1894; House 1893–May 10, 1894.

BRATTON, Sam Gilbert (N.Mex.) Aug. 19, 1888–Sept. 22, 1963; Senate 1925–June 24, 1933.

BRAWLEY, William Huggins (cousin of John James Hemphill, great-uncle of Robert Witherspoon Hemphill) (S.C.) May 13, 1841–Nov. 15, 1916; House 1891–Feb. 12, 1894.

BRAXTON, Elliott Muse (Va.) Oct. 8, 1823–Oct. 2, 1891; House 1871–73.

BREAUX, John Berlinger (La.) March 1, 1944–; House Sept. 30, 1972–87; Senate 1987–.

BREAZEALE, Phanor (La.) Dec. 29, 1858–April 29, 1934; House 1899–1905.

BRECKINRIDGE, Clifton Rodes (son of John Cabell Breckinridge, great-grandson of John Breckinridge) (Ark.) Nov. 22, 1846–Dec. 3, 1932; House 1883–Sept. 5, 1890, Nov. 5, 1890–Aug. 14, 1894.

BRECKINRIDGE, John Bayne (great-great-grandson of John Breckinridge, great-great-great-nephew of James Breckinridge, great-nephew of William Campbell Preston Breckinridge) (Ky.) Nov. 29, 1913–July 29, 1979; House 1973–79.

BRECKINRIDGE, John Cabell (grandson of John Breckinridge, father of Clifton Rodes Breckinridge, cousin of Henry Donnel Foster) (Ky.) Jan. 21, 1821–May 17, 1875; House 1851–55; Senate March 4–Dec. 4, 1861; Vice President 1857–61.

BRECKINRIDGE, William Campbell Preston (grandson of John Breckinridge, uncle of Levin Irving Handy, great-uncle of John Bayne Breckinridge) (Ky.) Aug. 28, 1837–Nov. 18, 1904; House 1885–95.

BREEDING, James Floyd (Kans.) Sept. 28, 1901–Oct. 17, 1977; House 1957–63.

BREEN, Edward G. (Ohio) June 10, 1908–; House 1949–Oct. 1, 1951.

BREESE, Sidney (Ill.) July 15, 1800–June 27, 1878; Senate 1843–49.

BREMNER, Robert Gunn (N.J.) Dec. 17, 1874–Feb. 5, 1914; House 1913–Feb. 5, 1914.

BRENNAN, Joseph Edward (Maine) Nov. 2, 1934–; House 1987–91; Gov. Jan 3, 1979–Jan. 7, 1987.

BRENNAN, Martin Adlai (Ill.) Sept. 21, 1879–July 4, 1941; House 1933–37.

BRENNER, John Lewis (Ohio) Feb. 2, 1832–Nov. 1, 1906; House 1897–1901.

BRETZ, John Lewis (Ind.) Sept. 21, 1852–Dec. 25, 1920; House 1891–95.

BREWER, Willis (Ala.) March 15, 1844–Oct. 30, 1912; House 1897–1901.

BREWSTER, Daniel Baugh (Md.) Nov. 23, 1923–; House 1959–63; Senate 1963–69.

BREWSTER, David P. (N.Y.) June 15, 1801–Feb. 20, 1876; House 1839–43.

BREWSTER, William (Okla.) Nov. 8, 1941–; House 1991–.

BRICE, Calvin Stewart (Ohio) Sept. 17, 1845–Dec. 15, 1898; Senate 1891–97; Chrmn. Dem. Nat. Comm. 1889–92.

BRICKNER, George H. (Wis.) Jan. 21, 1834–Aug. 12, 1904; House 1889–95.

BRIDGES, Samuel Augustus (Pa.) Jan. 27, 1802–Jan. 14, 1884; House March 6, 1848–49, 1853–55, 1877–79.

BRIGGS, Clay Stone (Tex.) Jan. 8, 1876–April 29, 1933; House 1919–April 29, 1933.

BRIGGS, Frank Parks (Mo.) Feb. 25, 1894–Sept. 23, 1992; Senate Jan. 18, 1945–47.

BRIGHT, Jesse David (Ind.) Dec. 18, 1812–May 20, 1875; Senate 1845–Feb. 5, 1862; elected Pres. pro tempore Dec. 5, 1854, June 11, 1856, June 12, 1860.

BRIGHT, John Morgan (Tenn.) Jan. 20, 1817–Oct. 3, 1911; House 1871–81.

BRINKERHOFF, Henry Roelif (cousin of Jacob Brinkerhoff) (Ohio) Sept. 23, 1787–April 30, 1844; House 1843–April 30, 1844.

BRINKERHOFF, Jacob (cousin of Henry Roelif Brinkerhoff) (Ohio) Aug. 31, 1810–July 19, 1880; House 1843–47.

BRINKLEY, Jack Thomas (Ga.) Dec. 22, 1930–; House 1967–83.

BRINSON, Samuel Mitchell (N.C.) March 20, 1870–April 13, 1922; House 1919–April 13, 1922.

BRISBIN, John (Pa.) July 13, 1818–Feb. 3, 1880; House Jan. 13–March 3, 1851.

BRITT, Charles Robin (N.C.) June 29, 1942–; House 1983–85.

BROADHEAD, James Overton (Mo.) May 29, 1819–Aug. 7, 1898; House 1883–85.

BROCK, Lawrence (Nebr.) Aug. 16, 1906–Aug. 28, 1968; House 1959–61.

BROCK, William Emerson (Tenn.) March 14, 1872–Aug. 5, 1950; Senate Sept. 2, 1929–31.

BROCKENBROUGH, William Henry (Fla.) Feb. 23, 1812–Jan. 28, 1850; House Jan. 24, 1846–47.

BROCKSON, Franklin (Del.) Aug. 6, 1865–March 16, 1942; House 1913–15.

BRODBECK, Andrew R. (Pa.) April 11, 1860–Feb. 27, 1937; House 1913–15, 1917–19.

BRODERICK, David Colbreth (cousin of Andrew Kennedy and Case Broderick) (Calif.) Feb. 4, 1820–Sept. 16, 1859; Senate 1857–Sept. 16, 1859.

BRODHEAD, John Curtis (N.Y.) Oct. 27, 1780–Jan. 2, 1859; House 1831–33 (Jacksonian), 1837–39.

BRODHEAD, William McNulty (Mich.) Sept. 12, 1941–; House 1975–83.

BRONSON, Isaac Hopkins (N.Y.) Oct. 16, 1802–Aug. 13, 1855; House 1837–39.

BROOCKS, Moses Lycurgus (Tex.) Nov. 1, 1864–May 27, 1908; House 1905–07.

BROOKS, Jack Bascom (Tex.) Dec. 18, 1922–; House 1953–1995; Chrmn. House Government Operations 1975–89; Chrmn. House Judiciary 1989–1995.

BROOKS, James (N.Y.) Nov. 10, 1810–April 30, 1873; House 1849–53 (Whig), 1863–April 7, 1866, 1867–April 30, 1873.

BROOKS, Joshua Twing (Pa.) Feb. 27, 1884–Feb. 7, 1956; House 1933–37.

BROOKS, Overton (nephew of John Holmes Overton) (La.) Dec. 21, 1897–Sept. 16, 1961; House 1937–Sept. 16, 1961; Chrmn. House Science and Astronautics 1959–61.

BROOKS, Preston Smith (S.C.) Aug. 5, 1819–January 27, 1857; House 1853–July 15, 1856, Aug. 1, 1856–Jan. 27, 1857.

BROOKSHIRE, Elijah Voorhees (Ind.) Aug. 15, 1856–April 14, 1936; House 1889–95.

BROUGHTON, Joseph Melville (N.C.) Nov. 17, 1888–March 6, 1949; Senate Dec. 31, 1948–March 6, 1949; Gov. Jan. 9, 1941–Jan. 4, 1945.

BROUSSARD, Edwin Sidney (brother of Robert Foligny Broussard) (La.) Dec. 4, 1874–Nov. 19, 1934; Senate 1921–33.

BROUSSARD, Robert Foligny (brother of Edwin Sidney Broussard) (La.) Aug. 17, 1864–April 12, 1918; House 1897–1915; Senate 1915–April 12, 1918.

BROWDER, Glen (Ala.) Jan. 15, 1943–; House April 18, 1989–.

BROWER, John Morehead (N.C.) July 19, 1845–Aug. 5, 1913; House 1887–91.

BROWN, Aaron Venable (Tenn.) Aug. 15, 1795–March 8, 1859; House 1839–45; Gov. Oct. 14, 1845–Oct. 16, 1847; Postmaster Gen. March 7, 1857–March 8, 1859.

BROWN, Albert Gallatin (Miss.) May 31, 1813–June 12, 1880; House 1839–41, 1847–53; Senate Jan. 7, 1854–Jan. 12, 1861; Gov. Jan. 10, 1844–Jan. 10, 1848.

BROWN, Bedford (N.C.) June 6, 1795–Dec. 6, 1870; Senate Dec. 9, 1829–Nov. 16, 1840.

BROWN, Charles (Pa.) Sept. 23, 1797–Sept. 4, 1883; House 1841–43, 1847–49.

BROWN, Charles Harrison (Mo.) Oct. 22, 1920–; House 1957–61.

BROWN, Corrine (Fla.) Nov. 11, 1946–; House 1993–.

BROWN, Fred Herbert (N.H.) April 12, 1879–Feb. 3, 1955; Senate 1933–39; Gov. Jan. 4, 1923–Jan. 1, 1925.

BROWN, George Edward Jr. (Calif.) March 6, 1920–; House 1963–71, 1973–; Chrmn. House Science, Space, and Technology 1991–1995.

BROWN, James Sproat (Wis.) Feb. 1, 1824–April 15, 1878; House 1863–65.

BROWN, Jason Brevoort (Ind.) Feb. 26, 1839–March 10, 1898; House 1889–95.

BROWN, John Brewer (Md.) May 13, 1836–May 16, 1898; House Nov. 8, 1892–93.

BROWN, John Young (nephew of Bryan Rust Young and William Singleton Young) (Ky.) June 28, 1835–Jan. 11, 1904; House 1859–61, 1873–77; Gov. Sept. 1, 1891–Dec. 10, 1895.

BROWN, John Young (Ky.) Feb. 1, 1900–June 16, 1985; House 1933–35.

BROWN, Joseph Emerson (Ga.) April 15, 1821–Nov. 30, 1894; Senate May 26, 1880–91; Gov. Nov. 6, 1857–June 17, 1865.

BROWN, Lathrop (N.Y.) Feb. 25, 1883–Nov. 28, 1959; House 1913–15.

BROWN, Paul (Ga.) March 31, 1880–Sept. 24, 1961; House July 5, 1933–61.

BROWN, Prentiss Marsh (Mich.) June 18, 1889–Dec. 19, 1973; House 1933–Nov. 18, 1936; Senate Nov. 19, 1936–43.

BROWN, Sherrod (Ohio) Nov. 9, 1952–; House 1953–.

BROWN, William Gay Jr. (son of William Gay Brown) (W. Va.) April 7, 1856–March 9, 1916; House 1911–March 9, 1916.

BROWN, William John (Ind.) Aug. 15, 1805–March 18, 1857; House 1843–45, 1849–51.

BROWNE, Charles (N.J.) Sept. 28, 1875–Aug. 17, 1947; House 1923–25.

BROWNING, Gordon Weaver (Tenn.) Nov. 22, 1889–May 23, 1976; House 1923–35; Gov. Jan. 15, 1937–Jan. 16, 1939, Jan 17, 1949–Jan. 15, 1953.

BRUCE, Terry L. (Ill.) March 25, 1944–; House 1985–93.

BRUCE, William Cabell (Md.) March 12, 1860–May 9, 1946; Senate 1923–29.

BRUCKER, Ferdinand (Mich.) Jan. 8, 1858–March 3, 1904; House 1897–99.

BRUCKNER, Henry (N.Y.) June 17, 1871–April 14, 1942; House 1913–Dec. 31, 1917.

BRUMBAUGH, Clement Laird (Ohio) Feb. 28, 1863–Sept. 28, 1921; House 1913–21.

BRUNDIDGE, Stephen Jr. (Ark.) Jan. 1, 1857–Jan. 14, 1938; House 1897–1909.

BRUNNER, David B. (Pa.) March 7, 1835–Nov. 29, 1903; House 1889–93.

BRUNNER, William Frank (N.Y.) Sept. 15, 1887–April 23, 1965; House 1929–Sept. 27, 1935.

BRUYN, Andrew DeWitt (N.Y.) Nov. 18, 1790–July 27, 1838; House 1837–July 27, 1838.

BRYAN, Guy Morrison (Tex.) Jan. 12, 1821–June 4, 1901; House 1857–59.

BRYAN, Nathan Philemon (brother of William James Bryan) (Fla.) April 23, 1872–Aug. 8, 1935; Senate 1911–17.

BRYAN, Richard Hudson (Nev.) July 16, 1937–; Senate 1989–; Chrmn. Select Senate Committee on Ethics 1993–1995; Gov. Jan. 3, 1983–Jan. 3, 1989.

BRYAN, William James (brother of Nathan Philemon Bryan) (Fla.) Oct. 10, 1876–March 22, 1908; Senate Dec. 26, 1907–March 22, 1908.

BRYAN, William Jennings (father of Ruth Bryan Owen) (Nebr.) March 19, 1860–July 26, 1925; House 1891–95; Secy. of State March 5, 1913–June 9, 1915.

BRYANT, John Wiley (Tex.) Feb. 22, 1947–; House 1983–.

BRYCE, Lloyd Stephens (N.Y.) Sept. 4, 1851–April 2, 1917; House 1887–89.

BUCHANAN, Andrew (Pa.) April 8, 1780–Dec. 2, 1848; House 1835–39 (1835–37 Jacksonian).

BUCHANAN, Frank (Ill.) June 14, 1862–April 18, 1930; House 1911–17.

BUCHANAN, Frank (husband of Vera Daerr Buchanan) (Pa.) Dec. 1, 1902–April 27, 1951; House May 21, 1946–April 27, 1951.

BUCHANAN, Hugh (Ga.) Sept. 15, 1823–June 11, 1890; House 1881–85.

BUCHANAN, James (Pa.) April 23, 1791–June 1, 1868; House 1821–31 (no party); Senate Dec. 6, 1834–March 5, 1845; Secy. of State March 10, 1845–March 7, 1849; President 1857–61.

BUCHANAN, James Paul (cousin of Edward William Pou) (Tex.) April 30, 1867–Feb. 22, 1937; House April 5, 1913–Feb. 22, 1937.

BUCHANAN, John Alexander (Va.) Oct. 7, 1843–Sept. 2, 1921; House 1889–93.

BUCHANAN, Vera Daerr (widow of Frank Buchanan) (Pa.) July 20, 1902–Nov. 26, 1955; House July 24, 1951–Nov. 26, 1955.

BUCK, Charles Francis (La.) Nov. 5, 1841–Jan. 5, 1918; House 1895–97.

BUCK, Frank Henry (Calif.) Sept. 23, 1887–Sept. 17, 1942; House 1933–Sept. 17, 1942.

BUCKALEW, Charles Rollin (Pa.) Dec. 28, 1821–May 19, 1899; Senate 1863–69; House 1887–91.

BUCKLEY, Charles Anthony (N.Y.) June 23, 1890–Jan. 22, 1967; House 1935–65; Chrmn. House Public Works 1951–53, 1955–65.

BUCKLEY, James Richard (Ill.) Nov. 18, 1870–June 22, 1945; House 1923–25.

BUCKLEY, James Vincent (Ill.) May 15, 1894–July 30, 1954; House 1949–51.

BUCKNER, Aylett Hawes (nephew of Aylett Hawes, cousin of Richard Hawes and Albert Gallatin Hawes) (Mo.) Dec. 14, 1816–Feb. 5, 1894; House 1873–85.

BUDD, James Herbert (Calif.) May 18, 1851–July 30, 1908; House 1883–85; Gov. Jan. 11, 1895–Jan. 3, 1899.

BUEL, Alexander Woodruff (Mich.) Dec. 13, 1813–April 19, 1868; House 1849–51.

BUELL, Alexander Hamilton (N.Y.) July 14, 1801–Jan. 29, 1853; House 1851–Jan. 29, 1853.

BULKLEY, Robert Johns (Ohio) Oct. 8, 1880–July 21, 1965; House 1911–15; Senate Dec. 1, 1930–39.

BULLOCK, Robert (Fla.) Dec. 8, 1828–July 27, 1905; House 1889–93.

BULOW, William John (S.Dak.) Jan. 13, 1869–Feb. 26, 1960; Senate 1931–43; Gov. Jan. 4, 1927–Jan. 6, 1931.

BULWINKLE, Alfred Lee (N.C.) April 21, 1883–Aug. 31, 1950; House 1921–29, 1931–Aug. 31, 1950.

BUMPERS, Dale Leon (Ark.) Aug. 12, 1925–; Senate 1975–; Chrmn. Senate Small Business 1987–1995; Gov. Jan. 12, 1971–Jan. 2, 1975.

BUNKER, Berkeley Lloyd (Nev.) Aug. 12, 1906–; Senate Nov. 27, 1940–Dec. 6, 1942; House 1945–47.

BUNN, Benjamin Hickman (N.C.) Oct. 19, 1844–Aug. 25, 1907; House 1889–95.

BUNTING, Thomas Lathrop (N.Y.) April 24, 1844–Dec. 27, 1898; House 1891–93.

BURCH, John Chilton (Calif.) Feb. 1, 1826–Aug. 31, 1885–; House 1859–61.

BURCH, Thomas Granville (Va.) July 3, 1869–March 20, 1951; House 1931–May 31, 1946; Senate May 31–Nov. 5, 1946.

BURCHARD, Samuel Dickinson (Wis.) July 17, 1836–Sept. 1, 1901; House 1875–77.

BURCHILL, Thomas Francis (N.Y.) Aug. 3, 1882–March 28, 1960; House 1943–45.

BURDICK, Jocelyn Birch (widow of Quentin Northrop Burdick, daughter-in-law of Usher Lloyd Burdick, sister-in-law of Robert Woodrow Levering) (N.Dak.) Feb. 6, 1922–; Senate Sept. 16–Dec. 14, 1992.

BURDICK, Quentin Northrop (son of Usher Lloyd Burdick, husband of Jocelyn Birch Burdick, brother-in-law of Robert Woodrow Levering) (N.Dak.) June 19, 1908–Sept. 8, 1992; House 1959–Aug. 8, 1960; Senate Aug. 8, 1960–Sept. 8, 1992; Chrmn. Senate Environment and Public Works 1987–92.

BURGESS, George Farmer (Tex.) Sept. 21, 1861–Dec. 31, 1919; House 1901–17.

BURGIN, William Olin (N.C.) July 28, 1877–April 11, 1946; House 1939–April 11, 1946.

BURKE, Edmund (N.H.) Jan. 23, 1809–Jan. 25, 1882; House 1839–45.

BURKE, Edward Raymond (Nebr.) Nov. 28, 1880–Nov. 4, 1968; House 1933–35; Senate 1935–41.

BURKE, Frank Welsh (Ky.) June 1, 1920–; House 1959–63.

BURKE, James Anthony (Mass.) March 30, 1910–Oct. 13, 1983; House 1959–79.

BURKE, John Harley (Calif.) June 2, 1894–May 14, 1951; House 1933–35.

BURKE, Michael Edmund (Wis.) Oct. 15, 1863–Dec. 12, 1918; House 1911–17.

BURKE, Robert Emmet (Tex.) Aug. 1, 1847–June 5, 1901; House 1897–June 5, 1901.

BURKE, Thomas A. (Ohio) Oct. 30, 1898–Dec. 5, 1971; Senate Nov. 10, 1953–Dec. 2, 1954.

BURKE, Thomas Henry (Ohio) May 6, 1904–Sept. 12, 1959; House 1949–51.

BURKE, Yvonne Brathwaite (Calif.) Oct. 5, 1932–; House 1973–79.

BURKHALTER, Everett Glen (Calif.) Jan. 19, 1897–May 24, 1975; House 1963–65.

BURLESON, Albert Sidney (Tex.) June 7, 1863–Nov. 24, 1937; House 1899–March 6, 1913; Postmaster Gen. March 5, 1913–March 4, 1921.

BURLESON, Omar Truman (Tex.) March 19, 1906–May 14, 1991; House 1947–Dec. 31, 1978; Chrmn. House Administration 1955–68.

BURLISON, William Dean (Mo.) March 15, 1933–; House 1969–81.

BURNES, Daniel Dee (Mo.) Jan. 4, 1851–Nov. 2, 1899; House 1893–95.

BURNES, James Nelson (Mo.) Aug. 22, 1827–Jan. 23, 1889; House 1883–Jan. 23, 1889.

BURNETT, Edward (Mass.) March 16, 1849–Nov. 5, 1925; House 1887–89.

BURNETT, Henry Cornelius (Ky.) Oct. 5, 1825–Oct. 1, 1866; House 1855–Dec. 3, 1861.

BURNETT, John Lawson (Ala.) Jan. 20, 1854–May 13, 1919; House 1899–May 13, 1919.

BURNEY, William Evans (Colo.) Sept. 11, 1893–Jan. 29, 1969; House Nov. 5, 1940–41.

BURNS, John Anthony (Hawaii) March 30, 1909–April 4, 1975; House (Terr. Del.) 1957–Aug. 21, 1959; Gov. Dec. 3, 1962–Dec. 2, 1974.

BURNS, Robert (N.H.) Dec. 12, 1792–June 26, 1866; House 1833–37.

BURNSIDE, Maurice Gwinn (W. Va.) Aug. 23, 1902–; House 1949–53, 1955–57.

BURR, Aaron (cousin of Theodore Dwight, father-in-law of Gov. Joseph Alston of S.C.) (N.Y.) Feb. 6, 1756–Sept. 14, 1836; Senate 1791–97; Vice President 1801–05.

BURR, Albert George (Ill.) Nov. 8, 1829–June 10, 1882; House 1867–71.

BURT, Armistead (S.C.) Nov. 13, 1802–Oct. 30, 1883; House 1843–53.

BURTON, Clarence Godber (Va.) Dec. 14, 1886–Jan. 18, 1982; House Nov. 2, 1948–53.

BURTON, John Lowell (brother of Phillip Burton, brother-in-law of Sala Burton) (Calif.) Dec. 15, 1932–; House June 25, 1974–83.

BURTON, Phillip (brother of John Lowell Burton, husband of Sala Burton) (Calif.) June 1, 1926–April 10, 1983; House Feb. 18, 1964–April 10, 1983.

BURTON, Sala (widow of Phillip Burton, sister-in-law of John Lowell Burton) (Calif.) April 1, 1925–Feb. 1, 1987; House June 21, 1983–Feb. 1, 1987.

BUSBY, George Henry (Ohio) June 10, 1794–Aug. 22, 1869; House 1851–53.

BUSBY, Thomas Jefferson (Miss.) July 26, 1884–Oct. 18, 1964; House 1923–35.

BUSEY, Samuel Thompson (Ill.) Nov. 16, 1835–Aug. 12, 1909; House 1891–93.

BUSHNELL, Allen Ralph (Wis.) July 18, 1833–March 29, 1909; House 1891–93.

BUSTAMANTE, Albert Garza (Tex.) April 8, 1935–; House 1985–93.

BUTLER, James Joseph (Mo.) Aug. 29, 1862–May 31, 1917; House 1901–June 28, 1902, Nov. 4, 1902–Feb. 26, 1903, 1903–05.

BUTLER, Matthew Calbraith (son of William Butler born in 1790, grandson of William Butler born in 1759, nephew of Andrew Pickens Butler) (S.C.) March 8, 1836–April 14, 1909; Senate 1877–95.

BUTLER, Mounce Gore (Tenn.) May 11, 1849–Feb. 13, 1917; House 1905–07.

BUTLER, Pierce (S.C.) July 11, 1744–Feb. 15, 1822; Senate 1789–Oct. 25, 1796, Nov. 4, 1802–Nov. 21, 1804; Cont. Cong. 1787.

BUTLER, Sampson Hale (S.C.) Jan. 3, 1803–March 16, 1948; House 1839–Sept. 27, 1842.

BUTLER, Walter Halben (Iowa) Feb. 13, 1852–April 24, 1931; House 1891–93.

BUTLER, William Orlando (Ky.) April 19, 1791–Aug. 6, 1880; House 1839–43.

BYNUM, Jesse Atherton (N.C.) May 23, 1797–Sept. 23, 1868; House 1833–41 (1833–37 Jacksonian).

BYNUM, William Dallas (Ind.) June 26, 1846–Oct. 21, 1927; House 1885–95.

BYRD, Adam Monroe (Miss.) July 6, 1859–June 21, 1912; House 1903–11.

BYRD, Harry Flood (father of Harry Flood Byrd Jr., nephew of Henry De La Warr Flood and Joel West Flood) (Va.) June 10, 1887–Oct. 20, 1966; Senate 1933–Nov. 10, 1965; Gov. Feb. 1, 1926–Jan. 15, 1930.

BYRD, Robert Carlyle (W.Va.) Nov. 20, 1917–; House 1953–59; Senate 1959–; Senate majority leader, 1977–81, 1987–89; Senate minority leader 1981–87; elected Pres. pro tempore Jan. 3, 1989; Chrmn. Senate Appropriations 1989–1995.

BYRNE, James Aloysius (Pa.) June 22, 1906–Sept. 3, 1980; House 1953–73.

BYRNE, Leslie Larkin (Va.) Oct. 27, 1946–; House 1993–1995.

BYRNE, William Thomas (N.Y.) March 6, 1876–Jan. 27, 1952; House 1937–Jan. 27, 1952.

BYRNES, James Francis (S.C.) May 2, 1879–April 9, 1972; House 1911–25; Senate 1931–July 8, 1941; Assoc. Justice Supreme Court July 8, 1941–Oct. 3, 1942; Secy. of State July 3, 1945–Jan. 21, 1947; Gov. Jan. 16, 1951–Jan. 18, 1955.

BYRNS, Joseph Wellington (father of Joseph Wellington Byrns, Jr.) (Tenn.) July 20, 1869–June 4, 1936; House 1909–June 4, 1936; House majority leader 1933–35; Speaker 1935–June 4, 1936.

BYRNS, Joseph Wellington Jr. (son of Joseph Wellington Byrns) (Tenn.) Aug. 15, 1903–March 8, 1973; House 1939–41.

BYRNS, Samuel (Mo.) March 4, 1848–July 9, 1914; House 1891–93.

BYRON, Beverly Barton Butcher (widow of Goodloe Edgar Byron, daughter-in-law of Katharine Edgar Byron and William Devereaux Byron) (Md.) July 26, 1932–; House 1979–93.

BYRON, Goodloe Edgar (son of Katharine Edgar Byron and William Devereaux Byron, great-grandson of Louis Emory McComas, husband of Beverly Barton Butcher Byron) (Md.) June 22, 1929–Oct. 11, 1978; House 1971–Oct. 11, 1978.

BYRON, Katharine Edgar (widow of William Devereaux Byron, mother of Goodloe Edgar Byron, granddaughter of Louis Emory McComas, mother-in-law of Beverly Barton Butcher Byron) (Md.) Oct. 25, 1903–Dec. 28, 1976; House May 27, 1941–43.

BYRON, William Devereaux (husband of Katharine Edgar Byron, father of Goodloe Edgar Byron, father-in-law of Beverly Barton Butcher Byron) (Md.) May 15, 1895–Feb. 27, 1941; House 1939–Feb. 27, 1941.

CABANISS, Thomas Banks (cousin of Thomas Chipman McRae) (Ga.) Aug. 31, 1835–Aug. 14, 1915; House 1893–95.

CABELL, Earle (Tex.) Oct. 27, 1906–Sept. 24, 1975; House 1965–73.

CABELL, George Craighead (Va.) Jan. 25, 1836–June 23, 1906; House 1875–87.

CABLE, Benjamin Taylor (Ill.) Aug. 11, 1853–Dec. 13, 1923; House 1891–93.

CABLE, Joseph (Ohio) April 17, 1801–May 1, 1880; House 1849–53.

CADMUS, Cornelius Andrew (N.J.) Oct. 7, 1844–Jan. 20, 1902; House 1891–95.

CADWALADER, John (Pa.) April 1, 1805–Jan. 26, 1879; House 1855–57.

CADWALADER, Claude Ernest (Mich.) May 28, 1878–Nov. 30, 1953; House 1933–35.

CAFFERY, Donelson (grandfather of Patrick Thomson Caffery) (La.) Sept. 10, 1835–Dec. 30, 1906; Senate Dec. 31, 1892–1901.

CAFFERY, Patrick Thomson (grandson of Donelson Caffery) (La.) July 6, 1932–; House 1969–73.

CALDWELL, Andrew Jackson (Tenn.) July 22, 1837–Nov. 22, 1906; House 1883–87.

CALDWELL, Ben Franklin (Ill.) Aug. 2, 1848–Dec. 29, 1924; House 1899–1905, 1907–09.

CALDWELL, Charles Pope (N.Y.) June 18, 1875–July 31, 1940; House 1915–21.

CALDWELL, George Alfred (Ky.) Oct. 18, 1814–Sept. 17, 1866; House 1843–45, 1849–51.

CALDWELL, Greene Washington (N.C.) April 13, 1806–July 10, 1864; House 1841–43.

CALDWELL, John Henry (Ala.) April 4, 1826–Sept. 4, 1902; House 1873–77.

CALDWELL, John William (Ky.) Jan. 15, 1837–July 4, 1903; House 1877–83.

CALDWELL, Millard Fillmore (Fla.) Feb. 6, 1897–Oct. 23, 1984; House 1933–41; Gov. Jan. 2, 1945–Jan. 4, 1949.

CALDWELL, Patrick Calhoun (S.C.) March 10, 1801–Nov. 22, 1855; House 1841–43.

CALDWELL, Robert Porter (Tenn.) Dec. 16, 1821–March 12, 1885; House 1871–73.

CALDWELL, William Parker (Tenn.) Nov. 8, 1832–June 7, 1903; House 1875–79.

CALKIN, Hervey Chittenden (N.Y.) March 23, 1828–April 20, 1913; House 1869–71.

CALL, Wilkinson (Fla.) Jan. 9, 1834–Aug. 24, 1910; Senate 1879–97.

CALLAN, Clair Armstrong (Nebr.) March 20, 1920–; House 1965–67.

CALLAWAY, Oscar (Tex.) Oct. 2, 1872–Jan. 31, 1947; House 1911–17.

CAMBRELENG, Churchill Caldom (N.Y.) Oct. 24, 1786–April 30, 1862; House 1821–39 (1821–29 no party, 1829–37 Jacksonian).

CAMDEN, Johnson Newlon (father of Johnson Newlon Camden Jr.) (W.Va.) March 6, 1828–April 25, 1908; Senate 1881–87, Jan 25, 1893–95.

CAMDEN, Johnson Newlon Jr. (son of Johnson Newlon Camden) (Ky.) Jan. 5, 1865–Aug. 16, 1942; Senate June 16, 1914–15.

CAMERON, Ronald Brooks (Calif.) Aug. 16, 1927–; House 1963–67.

CAMINETTI, Anthony (Calif.) July 30, 1854–Nov. 17, 1923; House 1891–95.

CAMP, Albert Sidney (Ga.) July 26, 1892–July 24, 1954; House Aug. 1, 1939–July 24, 1954.

CAMPBELL, Albert James (Mont.) Dec. 12, 1857–Aug. 9, 1907; House 1899–1901.

CAMPBELL, Brookins (Tenn.) 1808–Dec. 25, 1853; House March 4–Dec. 25, 1853.

CAMPBELL, Courtney Warren (Fla.) April 29, 1895–Dec. 22, 1971; House 1953–55.

CAMPBELL, Felix (N.Y.) Feb. 28, 1829–Nov. 8, 1902; House 1883–91.

CAMPBELL, James Edwin (nephew of Lewis Davis Campbell) (Ohio) July 7, 1843–Dec. 18, 1924; House June 20, 1884–89; Gov. Jan. 13, 1890–Jan. 11, 1892.

CAMPBELL, James Romulus (Ill.) May 4, 1853–Aug. 12, 1924; House 1897–99.

CAMPBELL, John (brother of Robert Blair Campbell) (S.C.) ?–May 19, 1845; House 1829–31 (Jacksonian), 1837–45 (1837–39 Nullifier).

CAMPBELL, John Goulder (Ariz.) June 25, 1827–Dec. 22, 1903; House (Terr. Del.) 1879–81.

CAMPBELL, Lewis Davis (uncle of James Edwin Campbell) (Ohio) Aug. 9, 1811–Nov. 26, 1882; House 1849–May 25, 1858 (1849–55 Whig, 1855–57 American Party, 1857–May 25, 1858 Republican), 1871–73.

CAMPBELL, Thompson (Ill.) 1811–Dec. 6, 1868; House 1851–53.

CAMPBELL, Timothy John (N.Y.) Jan. 8, 1840–April 7, 1904; House Nov. 3, 1855–89, 1891–95.

CANDLER, Allen Daniel (cousin of Ezekiel Samuel Candler Jr. and Milton Anthony Candler) (Ga.) Nov. 4, 1834–Oct. 26, 1910; House 1883–91; Gov. Oct. 29, 1898–Oct. 25, 1902.

CANDLER, Ezekiel Samuel Jr. (nephew of Milton Anthony Candler, cousin of Allen Daniel Candler) (Miss.) Jan. 18, 1862–Dec. 18, 1944; House 1901–21.

CANDLER, Milton Anthony (uncle of Ezekiel Samuel Candler Jr., cousin of Allen Daniel Candler) (Ga.) Jan. 11, 1837–Aug. 8, 1909; House 1875–79.

CANFIELD, Harry Clifford (Ind.) Nov. 22, 1875–Feb. 9, 1945; House 1923–33.

CANNON, Arthur Patrick (Fla.) May 22, 1904–Jan. 23, 1966; House 1939–47.

CANNON, Clarence Andrew (Mo.) April 11, 1879–May 12, 1964; House 1923–May 12, 1964; Chrmn. House Appropriations 1949–53, 1955–64.

CANNON, Howard Walter (Nev.) Jan. 26, 1912–; Senate 1959–83; Chrmn. Senate Rules and Administration 1973–77; Chrmn. Senate Select Committee on Standards and Conduct 1975–77; Chrmn. Senate Commerce, Science, and Transportation 1978–81.

CANNON, Raymond Joseph (Wis.) Aug. 26, 1894–Nov. 25, 1951; House 1933–39.

CANTOR, Jacob Aaron (N.Y.) Dec. 6, 1854–July 2, 1921; House Nov. 4, 1913–15.

CANTRILL, James Campbell (Ky.) July 9, 1870–Sept. 2, 1923; House 1909–Sept. 2, 1923.

CANTWELL, Maria (Wash.) Oct. 13, 1958–; House 1993–1995.

CAPEHART, James (W.Va.) March 7, 1847–April 28, 1921; House 1891–95.

CAPERTON, Allen Taylor (W.Va.) Nov. 21, 1810–July 26, 1876; Senate 1875–July 26, 1876.

CAPOZZOLI, Louis Joseph (N.Y.) March 6, 1901–Oct. 8, 1982; House 1941–45.

CARAWAY, Hattie Wyatt (widow of Thaddeus Horatius Caraway) (Ark.) Feb. 1, 1878–Dec. 21, 1950; Senate Nov. 13, 1931–Jan. 2, 1945.

CARAWAY, Thaddeus Horatius (husband of Hattie Wyatt Caraway) (Ark.) Oct. 17, 1871–Nov. 6, 1931; House 1913–21; Senate 1921–Nov. 6, 1931.

CARDEN, Cap Robert (Ky.) Dec. 17, 1866–June 13, 1935; House 1931–June 13, 1935.

CARDIN, Benjamin Louis (Md.) Oct. 5, 1943–; House 1987–.

CAREW, John Francis (nephew of Thomas Francis Magner) (N.Y.) April 16, 1873–April 10, 1951; House 1913–Dec. 28, 1929.

CAREY, Hugh Leo (N.Y.) April 11, 1919–; House 1961–Dec. 31, 1974; Gov. Jan. 1, 1975–Jan. 1, 1983.

CARLETON, Ezra Child (Mich.) Sept. 6, 1838–July 24, 1911; House 1883–87.

CARLEY, Patrick J. (N.Y.) Feb. 2, 1866–Feb. 25, 1936; House 1927–35.

CARLIN, Charles Creighton (Va.) April 8, 1866–Oct. 14, 1938; House Nov. 5, 1907–19.

CARLISLE, John Griffin (Ky.) Sept. 5, 1835–July 31, 1910; House 1877–May 26, 1890; Speaker Dec. 8, 1883–85, Dec. 7, 1885–87, Dec. 5, 1887–89; Senate May 26, 1890–Feb. 4, 1893; Secy. of the Treasury March 7, 1893–March 5, 1897.

CARLTON, Henry Hull (Ga.) May 14, 1835–Oct. 26, 1905; House 1887–91.

CARLYLE, Frank Ertel (N.C.) April 7, 1897–Oct. 2, 1960; House 1949–57.

CARMACK, Edward Ward (Tenn.) Nov. 5, 1858–Nov. 9, 1908; House 1897–1901; Senate 1901–07.

CARMICHAEL, Archibald Hill (Ala.) June 17, 1864–July 15, 1947; House Nov. 14, 1933–37.

CARNAHAN, Albert Sidney Johnson (Mo.) Jan. 9, 1897–March 24, 1968; House 1945–47, 1949–61.

CARNEY, Charles Joseph (Ohio) April 17, 1913–Oct. 7, 1987; House Nov. 3, 1970–79.

CARPENTER, Levi D. (N.Y.) Aug. 21, 1802–Oct. 27, 1856; House Nov. 5, 1844–45.

CARPENTER, Terry McGovern (Nebr.) March 28, 1900–April 27, 1978; House 1933–35.

CARPENTER, William Randolph (Kans.) April 24, 1894–July 26, 1956; House 1933–37.

CARPER, Thomas Richard (Del.) Jan. 23, 1947–; House 1983–93; Gov. Jan. 19, 1993–.

CARR, John (Ind.) April 9, 1793–Jan. 20, 1845; House 1831–37 (Jacksonian), 1839–41.

CARR, Milton Robert "Bob" (Mich.) March 27, 1943–; House 1975–81, 1983–.

CARR, Nathan Tracy (Ind.) Dec. 25, 1833–May 28, 1885; House Dec. 5, 1876–77.

CARR, Wooda Nicholas (Pa.) Feb. 5, 1871–June 28, 1953; House 1913–15.

CARROLL, James (Md.) Dec. 2, 1791–Jan. 16, 1873; House 1839–41.

CARROLL, John Albert (Colo.) July 30, 1901–Aug. 31, 1983; House 1947–51; Senate 1957–63.

CARROLL, John Michael (N.Y.) April 27, 1823–May 8, 1901; House 1871–73.

CARTER, Charles David (Okla.) Aug. 16, 1868–April 9, 1929; House Nov. 16, 1907–27.

CARTER, Steven V. (Iowa) Oct. 8, 1915–Nov. 4, 1959; House Jan. 3–Nov. 4, 1959.

CARTER, Timothy Jarvis (Maine) Aug. 18, 1800–March 14, 1838; House Sept. 4, 1837–March 14, 1838.

CARTTER, David Kellogg (Ohio) June 22, 1812–April 16, 1887; House 1849–53.

CARTWRIGHT, Wilburn (Okla.) Jan. 12, 1892–March 14, 1979; House 1927–43.

CARUTH, Asher Graham (Ky.) Feb. 7, 1844–Nov. 25, 1907; House 1887–95.

CARUTHERS, Samuel (Mo.) Oct. 13, 1820–July 20, 1860; House 1853–59 (1853–57 Whig).

CARVILLE, Edward Peter (Nev.) May 14, 1885–June 27,

1956; Senate July 25, 1945–47; Gov. Jan. 2, 1939–July 24, 1945.

CARY, George (Ga.) Aug. 7, 1789–Sept. 10, 1843; House 1823–27.

CARY, George Booth (Va.) 1811–March 5, 1850; House 1841–43.

CARY, Glover H. (Ky.) May 1, 1885–Dec. 5, 1936; House 1931–Dec. 5, 1936.

CARY, Jeremiah Eaton (N.Y.) April 30, 1803–June 1888; House 1843–45.

CARY, Shepard (Maine) July 3, 1805–Aug. 9, 1866; House May 10, 1844–45.

CASEY, John Joseph (Pa.) May 26, 1875–May 5, 1929; House 1913–17, 1919–21, 1923–25, 1927–May 5, 1929.

CASEY, Joseph Edward (Mass.) Dec. 27, 1898–Sept. 1, 1980; House 1935–43.

CASEY, Robert Randolph (Tex.) July 27, 1915–April 17, 1986; House 1959–Jan. 22, 1976.

CASKIE, John Samuels (Va.) Nov. 8, 1821–Dec. 16, 1869; House 1851–59.

CASS, Lewis (great-great-grandfather of Cass Ballenger) (Mich.) Oct. 9, 1782–June 17, 1866; Senate 1845–May 29, 1848, 1849–57; elected Pres. pro tempore Dec. 4, 1854; Gov. (Mich. Terr.) 1813–31; Secy. of War Aug. 1, 1831–Oct. 5, 1836; Secy. of State March 6, 1857–Dec. 14, 1860.

CASSERLY, Eugene (Calif.) Nov. 13, 1820–June 14, 1883; Senate 1869–Nov. 19, 1873.

CASSIDY, George Williams (Nev.) April 25, 1836–June 24, 1892; House 1881–85.

CASSINGHAM, John Wilson (Ohio) June 22, 1840–March 14, 1930; House 1901–05.

CASTELLOW, Bryant Thomas (Ga.) July 29, 1876–July 23, 1962; House Nov. 8, 1932–37.

CASTLE, James Nathan (Minn.) May 23, 1836–Jan. 2, 1903; House 1891–93.

CATCHINGS, Thomas Clendinen (Miss.) Jan. 11, 1847–Dec. 24, 1927; House 1885–1901.

CATE, George Washington (Wis.) Sept. 17, 1825–March 7, 1905; House 1875–77.

CATE, William Henderson (Ark.) Nov. 11, 1839–Aug. 23, 1899; House 1889–March 5, 1890, 1891–93.

CATHCART, Charles William (Ind.) July 24, 1809–Aug. 22, 1888; House 1845–49; Senate Dec. 6, 1852–53.

CATLIN, George Smith (Conn.) Aug. 24, 1808–Dec. 26, 1851; House 1843–45.

CAULFIELD, Bernard Gregory (Ill.) Oct. 18, 1828–Dec. 19, 1887; House Feb. 1, 1875–77.

CAUSEY, John Williams (Del.) Sept. 19, 1841–Oct. 1, 1908; House 1891–95.

CAVALCANTE, Anthony (Pa.) Feb. 6, 1897–Oct. 29, 1966; House 1949–51.

CAVANAUGH, James Michael (Mont.) July 4, 1823–Oct. 30, 1879; House May 11, 1858–59 (Minn.), 1867–71 (Terr. Del.).

CAVANNAUGH, John Joseph III (Nebr.) Aug. 1, 1945–; House 1977–81.

CELLER, Emanuel (N.Y.) May 6, 1888–Jan. 15, 1981; House 1923–73; Chrmn. House Judiciary 1949–53, 1955–73.

CHALMERS, Joseph Williams (father of James Ronald Chalmers) (Miss.) 1807–June 16, 1853; Senate Nov. 3, 1845–47.

CHAMBERLAIN, Ebenezer Mattoon (Ind.) Aug. 20, 1805–March 14, 1861; House 1853–55.

CHAMBERLAIN, George Earle (Oreg.) Jan. 1, 1854–July 9, 1928; Senate 1909–21; Gov. Jan. 14, 1903–Feb. 28, 1909.

CHAMPION, Edwin Van Meter (Ill.) Sept. 18, 1890–Feb. 11, 1976; House 1937–39.

CHANDLER, Albert Benjamin "Happy" (Ky.) July 14, 1898–June 15, 1991; Senate Oct. 10, 1939–Nov. 1, 1945; Gov. Dec. 10, 1935–Oct. 9, 1939, Dec. 13, 1955–Dec. 8, 1959.

CHANDLER, Walter "Clift" (Tenn.) Oct. 5, 1887–Oct. 1, 1967; House 1935–Jan. 2, 1940.

CHANEY, John (Ohio) Jan. 12, 1790–April 10, 1881; House 1833–39 (1833–37 Jacksonian).

CHANLER, John Winthrop (father of William Astor Chanler) (N.Y.) Sept. 14, 1826–Oct. 19, 1877; House 1863–69.

CHANLER, William Astor (son of John Winthrop Chanler) (N.Y.) June 11, 1867–March 4, 1934; House 1899–1901.

CHAPIN, Alfred Clark (grandfather of Hamilton Fish Jr., born in 1926) (N.Y.) March 8, 1848–Oct. 2, 1936; House Nov. 3, 1891–Nov. 16, 1892.

CHAPIN, Chester Williams (Mass.) Dec. 16, 1798–June 10, 1883; House 1875–77.

CHAPMAN, Andrew Grant (son of John Grant Chapman) (Md.) Jan. 17, 1839–Sept. 25, 1892; House 1881–83.

CHAPMAN, Augustus Alexandria (Va.) March 9, 1803–June 7, 1876; House 1843–47.

CHAPMAN, Bird Beers (Nebr.) Aug. 24, 1821–Sept. 21, 1871; House (Terr. Del.) 1855–57.

CHAPMAN, Henry (Pa.) Feb. 4, 1804–April 11, 1891; House 1857–59.

CHAPMAN, Jim (Tex.) March 8, 1945–; House Sept. 4, 1985–.

CHAPMAN, Reuben (Ala.) July 15, 1799–May 16, 1882; House 1835–47 (1835–37 Jacksonian); Gov. Dec. 16, 1847–Dec. 17, 1849.

CHAPMAN, Virgil Munday (Ky.) March 15, 1895–March 8, 1951; House 1925–29, 1931–49; Senate 1949–March 8, 1951.

CHAPMAN, William Williams (Iowa) Aug. 11, 1808–Oct. 18, 1892; House (Terr. Del.) Sept. 10, 1838–Oct. 27, 1840.

CHAPPELL, William Venroe Jr. (Fla.) Feb. 3, 1922–March 30, 1989; House 1969–89.

CHARLTON, Robert Milledge (Ga.) Jan. 19, 1807–Jan. 18, 1854; Senate May 31, 1852–53.

CHASE, Lucien Bonaparte (Tenn.) Dec. 5, 1817–Dec. 4, 1864; House 1845–49.

CHASTAIN, Elijah Webb (Ga.) Sept. 25, 1813–April 9, 1874; House 1851–55 (1851–53 Unionist).

CHATHAM, Richard Thurmond (N.C.) Aug. 16, 1896–Feb. 5, 1957; House 1949–57.

CHAVEZ, Dennis (N.Mex.) April 8, 1888–Nov. 18, 1962; House 1931–35; Senate May 11, 1935–Nov. 18, 1962; Chrmn. Senate Public Works 1949–53, 1955–62.

CHELF, Frank Leslie (Ky.) Sept. 22, 1907–Sept. 1, 1982; House 1945–67.

CHESNEY, Chester Anton (Ill.) March 9, 1916–Sept. 20, 1986; House 1949–51.

CHESNUT, James Jr. (S.C.) Jan. 18, 1815–Feb. 1, 1885; Senate Dec. 3, 1858–Nov. 10, 1860.

CHILES, Lawton Mainor Jr. (Fla.) April 3, 1930–; Senate 1971–89; Chrmn. Senate Budget 1987–89; Gov. Jan. 8, 1991–.

CHILTON, Horace (grandson of Thomas Chilton) (Tex.) Dec. 29, 1853–June 12, 1932; Senate June 10, 1891–March 22, 1892, 1895–1901.

CHILTON, William Edwin (W.Va.) March 17, 1858–Nov. 7, 1939; Senate 1911–17.

CHIPMAN, John Logan (grandson of Nathaniel Chipman, great-nephew of Daniel Chipman) (Mich.) June 5, 1830–Aug. 17, 1893; House 1887–Aug. 17, 1893.

CHIPMAN, John Smith (Mich.) Aug. 10, 1800–July 27, 1869; House 1845–47.

CHISHOLM, Shirley Anita (N.Y.) Nov. 30, 1924–; House 1969–83.

CHRISMAN, James Stone (Ky.) Sept. 14, 1818–July 29, 1881; House 1853–55.

CHRISTOPHER, George Henry (Mo.) Dec. 9, 1888–Jan. 23, 1959; House 1949–51, 1955–Jan. 23, 1959.

CHUDOFF, Earl (Pa.) Nov. 15, 1907–May 17, 1993; House 1949–Jan. 5, 1958.

CHURCH, Denver Samuel (Calif.) Dec. 11, 1862–Feb. 21, 1952; House 1913–19, 1933–35.

CHURCH, Frank Forrester (Idaho) July 25, 1924–April 7, 1984; Senate 1957–81; Chrmn. Senate Foreign Relations 1979–81.

CHURCHWELL, William Montgomery (Tenn.) Feb. 20, 1826–Aug. 18, 1862; House 1851–55.

CILLEY, Jonathan (brother of Joseph Cilley) (Maine) July 2, 1802–Feb. 24, 1838; House 1837–Feb. 24, 1838.

CILLEY, Joseph (nephew of Bradbury Cilley, brother of Jonathan Cilley) (N.H.) Jan. 4, 1791–Sept. 16, 1887; Senate June 13, 1846–47.

CITRON, William Michael (Conn.) Aug. 29, 1896–June 7, 1976; House 1935–39.

CLAIBORNE, James Robert (Mo.) June 22, 1882–Feb. 16, 1944; House 1933–37.

CLANCY, John Michael (N.Y.) May 7, 1837–July 25, 1903; House 1889–95.

CLANCY, John Richard (N.Y.) March 8, 1859–April 21, 1932; House 1913–15.

CLAPP, Asa William Henry (Maine) March 6, 1805–March 22, 1891; House 1847–49.

CLARDY, John Daniel (Ky.) Aug. 30, 1828–Aug. 20, 1918; House 1895–99.

CLARDY, Martin Linn (Mo.) April 26, 1844–July 5, 1914; House 1879–89.

CLARK, Alvah Augustus (cousin of James Nelson Pidcock) (N.J.) Sept. 13, 1840–Dec. 27, 1912; House 1877–81.

CLARK, David Worth (Idaho) April 2, 1902–June 19, 1955; House 1935–39; Senate 1939–45.

CLARK, Frank (Fla.) March 28, 1860–April 14, 1936; House 1905–25.

CLARK, Frank Monroe (Pa.) Dec. 24, 1915–; House 1955–Dec. 31, 1974.

CLARK, Franklin (Maine) Aug. 2, 1801–Aug. 24, 1874; House 1847–49.

CLARK, Henry Selby (N.C.) Sept. 9, 1809–Jan. 8, 1869; House 1845–47.

CLARK, James Beauchamp "Champ" (father of Joel Bennett Clark) (Mo.) March 7, 1850–March 2, 1921; House 1893–95, 1897–March 2, 1921; House minority leader 1908–11, 1919–21; Speaker April 4, 1911–13, April 7, 1913–15, Dec. 6, 1915–17, April 2, 1917–19.

CLARK, Jerome Bayard (N.C.) April 5, 1882–Aug. 26, 1959; House 1929–49.

CLARK, Joel Bennett (son of James Beauchamp Clark) (Mo.) Jan. 8, 1890–July 13, 1954; Senate Feb. 3, 1933–45.

CLARK, John Bullock (father of John Bullock Clark Jr., nephew of Christopher Henderson Clark and James Clark (Mo.) April 17, 1802–Oct. 29, 1885; House Dec. 7, 1857–July 13, 1861.

CLARK, John Bullock Jr. (son of John Bullock Clark, great-nephew of Christopher Henderson Clark and James Clark) (Mo.) Jan. 14, 1831–Sept. 7, 1903; House 1873–83.

CLARK, Joseph Sill (Pa.) Oct. 21, 1901–Jan. 12, 1990; Senate 1957–69.

CLARK, Lincoln (Iowa) Aug. 9, 1800–Sept. 16, 1886; House 1851–53.

CLARK, Richard Clarence (Iowa) Sept. 14, 1929–; Senate 1973–79.

CLARK, Samuel (Mich.) Jan. 1800–Oct. 2, 1870; House 1833–35 (N.Y.), 1853–55.

CLARK, William Andrews (Mont). Jan. 8, 1839–March 2, 1925; Senate Dec. 4, 1899–May 15, 1900, 1901–07.

CLARKE, Beverly Leonidas (Ky.) Feb. 11, 1809–March 17, 1860; House 1847–49.

CLARKE, James McClure (N.C.) June 12, 1917–; House 1983–85, 1987–91.

CLARKE, James Paul (Ark.) Aug. 18, 1854–Oct. 1, 1916; Senate 1903–Oct. 1, 1916; elected Pres. pro tempore March 13, 1913, Dec. 6, 1915; Gov. Jan. 18, 1895–Jan. 12, 1897.

CLARKE, John Blades (Ky.) April 14, 1833–May 23, 1911; House 1875–79.

CLARKE, Richard Henry (Ala.) Feb. 9, 1843–Sept. 26, 1906; House 1889–1897.

CLAY, Alexander Stephens (Ga.) Sept. 25, 1853–Nov. 13, 1910; Senate 1897–Nov. 13, 1910.

CLAY, Clement Claiborne Jr. (son of Clement Comer Clay) (Ala.) Dec. 13, 1816–Jan. 3, 1882; Senate Nov. 29, 1853–Jan. 21, 1861.

CLAY, James Brown (son of Henry Clay) (Ky.) Nov. 9, 1817–Jan. 26, 1864; House 1857–59.

CLAY, James Franklin (Ky.) Oct. 29, 1840–Aug. 17, 1921; House 1883–85.

CLAY, William Lacy Sr. (Mo.) April 30, 1931–; House 1969–; Chrmn. House Post Office and Civil Service 1991–1995.

CLAYPOOL, Harold Kile (son of Horatio Clifford Claypool, cousin of John Barney Peterson) (Ohio) June 2, 1886–Aug. 2, 1958; House 1937–43.

CLAYPOOL, Horatio Clifford (father of Harold Kile Claypool, cousin of John Barney Peterson) (Ohio) Feb. 9, 1859–Jan. 19, 1921; House 1911–15, 1917–19.

CLAYTON, Bertram Tracy (brother of Henry De Lamar Clayton (N.Y.) Oct. 19, 1862–May 30, 1918; House 1899–1901.

CLAYTON, Eva (N.C.) Sept. 16, 1934–; House 1993– (elected Nov. 3, 1992, to fill a vacancy in the 102d Congress and to the 103d Congress but was not sworn in until Jan. 5, 1993).

CLAYTON, Henry De Lamar (brother of Bertram Tracy Clayton) (Ala.) Feb. 10, 1857–Dec. 21, 1929; House 1897–May 25, 1914.

CLEARY, William Edward (N.Y.) July 20, 1849–Dec. 20, 1932; House March 5, 1918–21, 1923–27.

CLEMENS, Jeremiah (Ala.) Dec. 28, 1814–May 21, 1865; Senate Nov. 30, 1849–53.

CLEMENS, Sherrard (Va.) April 28, 1820–June 30, 1881; House Dec. 6, 1852–53, 1857–61.

CLEMENT, Robert Nelson (Tenn.) Sept. 23, 1943–; House Jan 25, 1988–.

CLEMENTE, Louis Gary (N.Y.) June 10, 1908–May 13, 1968; House 1949–53.

CLEMENTS, Earle Chester (Ky.) Oct. 22, 1896–March 12, 1985; House 1945–Jan. 6, 1948; Senate Nov. 27, 1950–57; Gov. Jan. 1948–Nov. 27, 1950.

CLEMENTS, Judson Claudius (Ga.) Feb. 12, 1846–June 18, 1917; House 1881–91.

CLEMENTS, Newton Nash (Ala.) Dec. 23, 1837–Feb. 20, 1900; House Dec. 8, 1880–81.

CLEVELAND, Chauncey Fitch (Conn.) Feb. 16, 1799–June 5, 1887; House 1849–53; Gov. May 4, 1842–May 1844.

CLEVELAND, Jesse Franklin (Ga.) Oct. 25, 1804–June 22, 1841; House Oct. 5, 1835–39 (Oct. 5, 1835–37 Jacksonian).

CLEVELAND, Orestes (N.J.) March 2, 1829–March 30, 1896; House 1869–71.

CLEVENGER, Raymond Francis (Mich.) June 6, 1926–; House 1965–67.

CLEVER, Charles P. (N.Mex.) Feb. 23, 1830–July 8, 1874; House (Terr. Del.) Sept. 2, 1867–Feb. 20, 1869.

CLINE, Cyrus (Ind.) July 12, 1856–Oct. 5, 1923; House 1909–17.

CLINGMAN, Thomas Lanier (N.C.) July 27, 1812–Nov. 3, 1897; House 1843–45 (Whig), 1847–May 7, 1858 (Whig); Senate May 7, 1858–March 28, 1861.

CLINTON, James Graham (half-brother of De Witt Clinton, cousin of George Clinton, nephew of Vice Pres. George Clinton) (N.Y.) Jan. 2, 1804–May 28, 1849; House 1841–45.

CLOPTON, David (Ala.) Sept. 29, 1820–Feb. 5, 1892; House 1859–Jan. 21, 1861.

CLUNIE, Thomas Jefferson (Calif.) March 25, 1852–June 30, 1903; House 1889–91.

CLYBURN, James Enos (S.C.) July 21, 1940–; House 1993–.

CLYMER, Hiester (nephew of William Hiester, cousin of Isaac Ellmaker Hiester) (Pa.) Nov. 3, 1827–June 12, 1884; House 1873–81.

COAD, Merwin (Iowa) Sept. 28, 1924–; House 1957–63.

COADY, Charles Pearce (Md.) Feb. 22, 1868–Feb. 16, 1934; House Nov. 4, 1913–21.

COBB, George Thomas (N.J.) Oct. 13, 1813–Aug. 12, 1870; House 1861–63.

COBB, Seth Wallace (Mo.) Dec. 5, 1838–May 22, 1909; House 1891–97.

COBB, Thomas Reed (Ind.) July 2, 1828–June 23, 1892; House 1877–87.

COBB, Williamson Robert Winfield (Ala.) June 8, 1807–Nov. 1, 1864; House 1847–Jan. 30, 1861.

COBURN, Frank Potter (Wis.) Dec. 6, 1858–Nov. 2, 1932; House 1891–93.

COCHRAN, Alexander Gilmore (Pa.) March 20, 1846–May 1, 1928; House 1875–77.

COCHRAN, Charles Fremont (Mo.) Sept. 27, 1846–Dec. 19, 1906; House 1897–1905.

COCHRAN, John Joseph (Mo.) Aug. 11, 1880–March 6, 1947; House Nov. 2, 1926–47.

COCHRANE, John (N.Y.) Aug. 27, 1813–Feb. 7, 1898; House 1857–61.

COCKERILL, Joseph Randolph (Ohio) Jan. 2, 1818–Oct. 23, 1875; House 1857–59.

COCKRAN, William Bourke (N.Y.) Feb. 28, 1854–March 1, 1923; House 1887–89, Nov. 3, 1891–95, Feb. 23, 1904–09, 1921–March 1, 1923.

COCKRELL, Francis Marion (brother of Jeremiah Vardaman Cockrell) (Mo.) Oct. 1, 1834–Dec. 13, 1915; Senate 1875–1905.

COCKRELL, Jeremiah Vardaman (brother of Francis Marion Cockrell) (Tex.) May 7, 1832–March 18, 1915; House 1893–97.

COELHO, Anthony Lee "Tony" (Calif.) June 15, 1942–; House 1979–June 15, 1989.

COFFEE, Harry Buffington (Nebr.) March 16, 1890–Oct. 3, 1972; House 1935–43.

COFFEE, John Main (Wash.) Jan. 23, 1897–; House 1937–47.

COFFEEN, Henry Asa (Wyo.) Feb. 14, 1841–Dec. 9, 1912; House 1893–95.

COFFEY, Robert Lewis Jr. (Pa.) Oct. 21, 1918–April 20, 1949; House Jan. 3–April 20, 1949.

COFFIN, Frank Morey (Maine) July 11, 1919–; House 1957–61.

COFFROTH, Alexander Hamilton (Pa.) May 18, 1828–Sept. 2, 1906; House 1863–65, Feb. 19–July 18, 1866–1879–81.

COHELAN, Jeffrey (Calif.) June 24, 1914–; House 1959–71.

COHEN, John Sanford (Ga.) Feb. 26, 1870–May 13, 1935; Senate April 25, 1932–Jan. 11, 1933.

COHEN, William Wolfe (N.Y.) Sept. 6, 1874–Oct. 12, 1940; House 1927–29.

COKE, Richard (Tex.) March 13, 1829–May 14, 1897; Senate 1877–95; Gov. Jan. 15, 1874–Dec. 1, 1876.

COLCOCK, William Ferguson (S.C.) Nov. 5, 1804–June 13, 1889; House 1849–53.

COLDEN, Charles J. (Calif.) Aug. 24, 1870–April 15, 1938; House 1933–April 15, 1938.

COLE, George Edward (Wash.) Dec. 23, 1826–Dec. 3, 1906; House (Terr. Del.) 1863–65; Gov. (Wash. Terr.) Nov. 1866–March 4, 1867.

COLE, William Hinson (Md.) Jan. 11, 1837–July 8, 1886; House 1885–July 8, 1886.

COLE, William Purington Jr. (Md.) May 11, 1889–Sept. 22, 1957; House 1927–29, 1931–Oct. 26, 1942.

COLEMAN, Ronald D'Emory (Tex.) Nov. 29, 1941–; House 1983–.

COLERICK, Walpole Gillespie (Ind.) Aug. 1, 1845–Jan. 11, 1911; House 1879–83.

COLES, Walter (son of Isaac Coles) (Va.) Dec. 8, 1790–Nov. 9, 1857; House 1835–45 (1835–37 Jacksonian).

COLLIER, James William (Miss.) Sept. 28, 1872–Sept. 28, 1933; House 1909–33.

COLLIN, John Francis (N.Y.) April 30, 1802–Sept. 16, 1889; House 1845–47.

COLLINS, Barbara-Rose (Mich.) April 13, 1939–; House 1991–.

COLLINS, Cardiss (widow of George Washington Collins) (Ill.) Sept. 24, 1931–; House June 5, 1973–.

COLLINS, Francis Dolan (Pa.) March 5, 1841–Nov. 21, 1891; House 1875–79.

COLLINS, George Washington (husband of Cardiss Collins) (Ill.) March 5, 1925–Dec. 8, 1972; House Nov. 3, 1970–Dec. 8, 1972.

COLLINS, Patrick Andrew (Mass.) March 12, 1844–Sept. 13, 1905; House 1883–89.

COLLINS, Ross Alexander (Miss.) April 25, 1880–July 14, 1968; House 1921–35, 1937–43.

COLLINS, William (N.Y.) Feb. 22, 1818–June 18, 1878; House 1847–49.

COLMER, William Meyers (Miss.) Feb. 11, 1890–Sept. 9, 1980; House 1933–73; Chrmn. House Rules 1967–73.

COLQUITT, Alfred Holt (son of Walter Terry Colquitt) (Ga.) April 20, 1824–March 26, 1894; House 1853–55 (no party); Senate 1883–March 26, 1894; Gov. Jan. 12, 1877–Nov. 4, 1882.

COLQUITT, Walter Terry (father of Alfred Holt Colquitt) (Ga.) Dec. 27, 1799–May 7, 1855; House 1839–July 21, 1840 (Whig), Jan. 3, 1842–43 (Van Buren Democrat); Senate 1843–Feb. 1848.

COMBS, George Hamilton Jr. (Mo.) May 2, 1899–Nov. 29, 1977; House 1927–29.

COMBS, Jesse Martin (Tex.) July 7, 1889–Aug. 21, 1953; House 1945–53.

COMER, Braxton Bragg (Ala.) Nov. 7, 1848–Aug. 15, 1927; Senate March 5–Nov. 2, 1920; Gov. Jan. 14, 1907–Jan. 17, 1911.

COMINGO, Abram (Mo.) Jan. 9, 1820–Nov. 10, 1889; House 1871–75.

COMPTON, Barnes (great-grandson of Philip Key) (Md.) Nov. 16, 1830–Dec. 4, 1898; House 1885–March 20, 1890, 1891–May 15, 1894.

COMSTOCK, Charles Carter (Mich.) March 5, 1818–Feb. 20, 1900; House 1885–87.

CONDIT, Gary (Calif.) April 21, 1948–; House Sept. 20, 1989–.

CONDON, Francis Bernard (R.I.) Nov. 11, 1891–Nov. 23, 1965; House Nov. 4, 1930–Jan. 10, 1935.

CONDON, Robert Likens (Calif.) Nov. 10, 1912–June 3, 1976; House 1953–55.

CONN, Charles Gerard (Ind.) Jan. 29, 1844–Jan. 5, 1931; House 1893–95.

CONNALLY, Thomas Terry "Tom" (Tex.) Aug. 19, 1877–Oct. 28, 1963; House 1917–29; Senate Foreign Relations 1949–53.

CONNELL, Richard Edward (N.Y.) Nov. 6, 1857–Oct. 30, 1912; House 1911–Oct. 30, 1912.

CONNELLY, John Robert (Kans.) Feb. 27, 1870–Sept. 9, 1940; House 1913–19.

CONNER, John Coggswell (Tex.) Oct. 14, 1842–Dec. 10, 1873; House March 31, 1870–73.

CONNERY, Lawrence Joseph (brother of William Patrick Connery Jr.) (Mass.) Oct. 17, 1895–Oct. 19, 1941; House Sept. 28, 1937–Oct. 19, 1941.

CONNERY, William Patrick Jr. (brother of Lawrence Joseph Connery) (Mass.) Aug. 24, 1888–June 15, 1937; House 1923–June 15, 1937.

CONNOLLY, Daniel Ward (Pa.) April 24, 1847–Dec. 4, 1894; House 1883–85.

CONNOLLY, Maurice (Iowa) March 13, 1877–May 28, 1921; House 1913–15.

CONNOR, Henry William (N.C.) Aug. 5, 1793–Jan. 6, 1866; House 1821–41 (1821–33 no party, 1833–37 Jacksonian).

CONRAD, Kent (N.Dak.) March 12, 1948–; Senate 1987–.

CONRY, Joseph Aloysius (Mass.) Sept. 12, 1868–June 22, 1943; House 1901–03.

CONRY, Michael Francis (N.Y.) April 2, 1870–March 2, 1917; House 1909–March 2, 1917.

CONSTABLE, Albert (Md.) June 3, 1805–Sept. 18, 1855; House 1845–47.

CONVERSE, George Leroy (Ohio) June 4, 1827–March 30, 1897; House 1879–85.

CONYERS, John Jr. (Mich.) May 16, 1929–; House 1965–; Chrmn. House Government Operations 1989–1995.

COOK, John Calhoun (Iowa) Dec. 26, 1846–June 7, 1920; House March 3, 1883, Oct. 9, 1883–85.

COOK, Philip (Ga.) July 30, 1817–May 24, 1894; House 1873–83.

COOK, Robert Eugene (Ohio) May 19, 1920–; House 1959–63.

COOK, Samuel Ellis (Ind.) Sept. 30, 1860–Feb. 22, 1946; House 1923–25.

COOLEY, Harold Dunbar (N.C.) July 26, 1897–Jan. 15, 1974; House July 7, 1934–67; Chrmn. House Agriculture 1949–53, 1955–67.

COOLIDGE, Frederick Spaulding (father of Marcus Allen Coolidge) (Mass.) Dec. 7, 1841–June 8, 1906; House 1891–93.

COOLIDGE, Marcus Allen (son of Frederick Spaulding Coolidge) (Mass.) (Oct. 6, 1865–Jan. 23, 1947; Senate 1931–37.

COOMBS, William Jerome (N.Y.) Dec. 24, 1833–Jan. 12, 1922; House 1981–95.

COONEY, James (Mo.) July 28, 1848–Nov. 16, 1904; House 1897–1903.

COOPER, Charles Merian (Fla.) Jan. 16, 1856–Nov. 14, 1923; House 1893–97.

COOPER, George Byran (Mich.) June 6, 1808–Aug. 29, 1866; House 1859–May 15, 1860.

COOPER, George William (Ind.) May 21, 1851–Nov. 27, 1899; House 1889–95.

COOPER, Henry (brother of Edmund Cooper) (Tenn.) Aug. 22, 1827–Feb. 4, 1884; Senate 1871–77.

COOPER, James Haynes Shofner (Tenn.) June 19, 1954–; House 1983–1995.

COOPER, Jere (Tenn.) July 20, 1893–Dec. 18, 1957; House 1929–Dec. 18, 1957; Chrmn. House Ways and Means 1955–57.

COOPER, Mark Anthony (cousin of Eugenius Aristides Nisbet) (Ga.) April 20, 1800–March 17, 1885; House 1839–41 (Whig), Jan. 3, 1842–June 26, 1843.

COOPER, Samuel Bronson (Tex.) May 30, 1850–Aug. 21, 1918; House 1893–1905, 1907–09.

COOPER, Thomas Buchecker (Pa.) Dec. 29, 1823–April 14, 1862; House 1861–April 4, 1862.

COOPER, William Raworth (N.J.) Feb. 20, 1793–Sept. 22, 1856; House 1839–41.

COPELAND, Royal Samuel (N.Y.) Nov. 7, 1868–June 17, 1938; Senate 1923–June 17, 1938.

COPPERSMITH, Sam (Ariz.) May 22, 1955–; House 1993–1995.

CORKER, Stephen Alfestus (Ga.) May 7, 1830–Oct. 18, 1879; House Dec. 22, 1870–71.

CORMAN, James Charles (Calif.) Oct. 20, 1920–; House 1961–81.

CORNELL, Robert John (Wis.) Dec. 16, 1919–; House 1975–79.

CORNING, Erastus (grandfather of Parker Corning) (N.Y.) Dec. 14, 1794–April 9, 1872; House 1857–59, 1861–Oct. 5, 1863.

CORNING, Parker (grandson of Erastus Corning) (N.Y.) Jan. 22, 1874–May 24, 1943; House 1923–37.

CORNISH, Johnston (N.J.) June 13, 1858–June 26, 1920; House 1893–95.

CORNWELL, David Lance (Ind.) June 14, 1945–; House 1977–79.

COSGROVE, John (Mo.) Sept. 12, 1839–Aug. 15, 1925; House 1883–85.

COSTELLO, Jerry Francis (Ill.) Sept. 25, 1949–; House Aug. 11, 1988–.

COSTELLO, John Martin (Calif.) Jan. 15, 1903–Aug. 28, 1976; House 1935–45.

COSTIGAN, Edward Prentiss (Colo.) July 1, 1874–Jan. 17, 1939; Senate 1931–37.

COTHRAN, James Sproull (S.C.) Aug. 8, 1830–Dec. 5, 1897; House 1887–91.

COTTER, William Ross (Conn.) July 18, 1830–Dec. 5, 1897; House 1887–91.

COTTRELL, James La Fayette (Ala.) Aug. 25, 1808–Sept. 7, 1885; House Dec. 7, 1846–47.

COURTNEY, William Wirt (Tenn.) Sept. 7, 1889–April 6, 1961; House May 11, 1939–49.

COVERT, James Way (N.Y.) Sept. 2, 1842–May 16, 1910; House 1877–81, 1889–95.

COVINGTON, George Washington (Md.) Sept. 12, 1838–April 6, 1911; House 1881–85.

COVINGTON, James Harry (Md.) May 3, 1870–Feb. 4, 1942; House 1909–Sept. 30, 1914.

COWAN, Jacob Pitzer (Ohio) March 20, 1823–July 9, 1895; House 1875–77.

COWEN, John Kissig (Md.) Oct. 28, 1844–April 26, 1904; House 1895–97.

COWHERD, William Strother (Mo.) Sept. 1, 1860–June 20, 1915; House 1897–1905.

COWLES, William Henry Harrison (uncle of Charles Holden Cowles) (N.C.) April 22, 1840–Dec. 30, 1901; House 1885–93.

COX, Edward Eugene (Ga.) April 3, 1880–Dec. 24, 1952; House 1925–Dec. 24, 1952.

COX, Isaac Newton (N.Y.) Aug. 1, 1846–Sept. 28, 1916; House 1891–93.

COX, James Middleton (Ohio) March 31, 1870–July 15, 1957; House 1909–Jan. 12, 1913; Gov. Jan. 13, 1913–Jan. 11, 1915, Jan. 8, 1917–Jan. 10, 1921.

COX, John W. Jr. (Ill.) July 10, 1947–; House 1991–93.

COX, Nicholas Nichols (Tenn.) Jan. 6, 1837–May 2, 1912; House 1891–1901.

COX, Samuel Sullivan (N.Y.) Sept. 30, 1824–Sept. 10, 1889; House 1857–65 (Ohio), 1869–73, Nov. 4, 1873–May 20, 1885, Nov. 2, 1886–Sept. 10, 1889.

COX, William Elijah (Ind.) Sept. 6, 1861–March 11, 1942; House 1907–19.

COX, William Ruffin (N.C.) March 11, 1831–Dec. 26, 1919; House 1881–87.

COYNE, William Joseph (Pa.) Aug. 24, 1936–; House 1981–.

CRAIG, Alexander Kerr (Pa.) Feb. 21, 1828–July 29, 1892; House Feb. 26–July 29, 1892.

CRAIG, James (Mo.) Feb. 28, 1818–Oct. 22, 1888; House 1857–61.

CRAIG, Robert (Va.) 1792–Nov. 25, 1852; House 1829–33 (Jacksonian), 1835–41.

CRAIG, William Benjamin (Ala.) Nov. 2, 1877–Nov. 27, 1925; House 1907–11.

CRAIGE, Francis Burton (N.C.) March 13, 1811–Dec. 30, 1875; House 1853–61.

CRAIN, William Henry (Tex.) Nov. 25, 1848–Feb. 10, 1896; House 1885–Feb. 10, 1896.

CRALEY, Nathaniel Nieman Jr. (Pa.) Nov. 17, 1927–; House 1965–67.

CRAMER, Bud (Ala.) Aug. 22, 1947–; House 1991–.

CRANFORD, John Walter (Tex.) 1862–March 3, 1899; House 1897–March 3, 1899.

CRANSTON, Alan (Calif.) June 19, 1914–; Senate 1969–93; Chrmn. Senate Veterans' Affairs 1977–81, 1987–93.

CRARY, Isaac Edwin (Mich.) Oct. 2, 1804–May 8, 1854; House Jan. 26, 1837–41 (Jan. 26–March 3, 1837 Jacksonian).

CRAVENS, James Addison (second cousin of James Harrison Cravens) (Ind.) Nov. 4, 1818–June 20, 1893; House 1861–65.

CRAVENS, Jordan Edgar (cousin of William Ben Cravens) (Ark.) Nov. 7, 1830–April 8, 1914; House 1877–83 (1877–79 Independent Democrat).

CRAVENS, William Ben (father of William Fadjo Cravens, cousin of Jordan Edgar Cravens) (Ark.) Jan. 17, 1872–Jan. 13, 1939; House 1907–13, 1933–Jan. 13, 1939.

CRAVENS, William Fadjo (son of William Ben Cravens) (Ark.) Feb. 15, 1889–April 16, 1974; House Sept. 12, 1939–49.

CRAWFORD, Martin Jenkins (Ga.) March 17, 1820–July 23, 1883; House 1855–Jan. 23, 1861.

CRAWFORD, William Thomas (N.C.) June 1, 1856–Nov. 16, 1913; House 1891–95, 1899–May 10, 1900, 1907–09.

CREAL, Edward Wester (Ky.) Nov. 20, 1883–Oct. 13, 1943; House Nov. 5, 1935–Oct. 13, 1943.

CREAMER, Thomas James (N.Y.) May 26, 1843–Aug. 4, 1914; House 1873–75, 1901–03.

CREBS, John Montgomery (Ill.) April 9, 1830–June 26, 1890; House 1869–73.

CRISP, Charles Frederick (father of Charles Robert Crisp) (Ga.) Jan. 29, 1845–Oct. 23, 1896; House 1883–Oct. 23, 1896; Speaker Dec. 8, 1891–93, Aug. 7, 1893–95.

CRITCHER, John (Va.) March 11, 1820–Sept. 27, 1901; House 1871–73.

CRITTENDEN, Thomas Theodore (nephew of John Jordan Crittenden) (Mo.) Jan. 1, 1832–May 29, 1909; House 1873–75, 1877–79; Gov. Jan. 10, 1881–Jan. 12, 1885.

CROCKETT, George William Jr. (Mich.) Aug. 10, 1909–; House Nov. 12, 1980–91.

CROFT, George William (father of Theodore Gaillard Croft)

(S.C.) Dec. 20, 1846–March 10, 1904; House 1903–March 10, 1904.

CROFT, Theodore Gaillard (son of George William Croft) (S.C.) Nov. 26, 1874–March 23, 1920; House May 17, 1904–05.

CROLL, William Martin (Pa.) April 9, 1866–Oct. 21, 1929; House 1923–25.

CROOK, Thurman Charles (Ind.) July 18, 1891–Oct. 23, 1981; House 1949–51.

CROSBY, Charles Noel (Pa.) Sept. 29, 1876–Jan. 26, 1951; House 1933–39.

CROSBY, John Crawford (Mass.) June 15, 1859–Oct. 14, 1943; House 1891–93.

CROSS, Edward (Ark.) Nov. 11, 1798–April 6, 1887; House 1839–45.

CROSS, Oliver Harlan (Tex.) July 13, 1868–April 24, 1960; House 1929–37.

CROSSER, Robert (Ohio) June 7, 1874–June 3, 1957; House 1913–19, 1923–55; Chrmn. House Interstate and Foreign Commerce 1949–53.

CROSSLAND, Edward (Ky.) June 30, 1827–Sept. 11, 1881; House 1871–75.

CROWE, Eugene Burgess (Ind.) Jan. 5, 1878–May 12, 1970; House 1931–41.

CROWLEY, Joseph Burns (Ohio) July 19, 1858–June 25, 1931; House 1899–1905.

CROWLEY, Miles (Tex.) Feb. 22, 1859–Sept. 22, 1921; House 1895–97.

CROXTON, Thomas (Va.) March 8, 1822–July 3, 1903; House 1885–87.

CRUMP, Edward Hull (Tenn.) Oct. 2, 1874–Oct. 16, 1954; House 1931–35.

CULBERSON, Charles Allen (son of David Browning Culberson) (Tex.) June 10, 1855–March 19, 1925; Senate 1899–1923; Gov. Jan. 15, 1895–Jan. 17, 1899.

CULBERSON, David Browning (father of Charles Allen Culberson) (Tex.) Sept. 29, 1830–May 7, 1900; House 1875–97.

CULLEN, Thomas Henry (N.Y.) March 29, 1868–March 1, 1944; House 1919–March 1, 1944.

CULLOM, Alvan (brother of William Cullom, uncle of Shelby Moore Cullom) (Tenn.) Sept. 4, 1797–July 20, 1877; House 1843–47.

CULLOP, William Allen (Ind.) March 28, 1853–Oct. 9, 1927; House 1909–17.

CULVER, John Chester (Iowa) Aug. 8, 1932–; House 1965–75; Senate 1975–81.

CUMMING, Thomas William (N.Y.) 1814 or 1815–Oct. 13, 1855; House 1853–55.

CUMMINGS, Amos Jay (N.Y.) May 15, 1841–May 2, 1902;

House 1887–89, Nov. 5, 1889–Nov. 21, 1894, Nov. 5, 1895–May 2, 1902.

CUMMINGS, Fred Nelson (Colo.) Sept. 18, 1864–Nov. 10, 1952; House 1933–41.

CUMMINGS, Herbert Wesley (Pa.) July 13, 1873–March 4, 1956; House 1923–25.

CUMMINS, John D. (Ohio) 1791–Sept. 11, 1849; House 1845–49.

CUNNINGHAM, Francis Alanson (Ohio) Nov. 9, 1804–Aug. 16, 1864; House 1845–47.

CURLEY, Edward Walter (N.Y.) May 23, 1873–Jan. 6, 1940; House Nov. 5, 1935–Jan. 6, 1940.

CURLEY, James Michael (Mass.) Nov. 20, 1874–Nov. 12, 1958; House 1911–Feb. 4, 1914, 1943–47; Gov. Jan. 3, 1935–Jan. 7, 1937.

CURLIN, William Prather Jr. (Ky.) Nov. 30, 1933–; House Dec. 4, 1971–73.

CURRY, Jabez Lamar Monroe (Ala.) June 5, 1825–Feb. 12, 1903; House 1857–Jan. 21, 1861.

CURTIN, Andrew Gregg (Pa.) April 22, 1815–Oct. 7, 1894; House 1881–87; Gov. Jan. 15, 1861–Jan. 15, 1867 (Republican).

CUSACK, Thomas (Ill.) Oct. 5, 1858–Nov. 19, 1926; House 1899–1901.

CUSHMAN, Samuel (N.H.) June 8, 1783–May 20, 1851; House 1835–39 (1835–37 Jacksonian).

CUTLER, Augustus William (N.J.) Oct. 22, 1827–Jan. 1, 1897; House 1875–79.

CUTTING, Francis Brockholst (N.Y.) Aug. 6, 1804–June 26, 1870; House 1853–55.

DADDARIO, Emilio Quincy (Conn.) Sept. 24, 1918–; House 1959–71.

DALE, Harry Howard (N.Y.) Dec. 3, 1868–Nov. 17, 1935; House 1913–Jan. 6, 1919.

D'ALESANDRO, Thomas Jr. (father of Nancy Pelosi) (Md.) Aug. 1, 1903–Aug. 23, 1987; House 1939–May 16, 1947.

DALLAS, George Mifflin (great-great-great-uncle of Claiborne de Borda Pell) (Pa.) July 10, 1792–Dec. 31, 1864; Senate Dec. 13, 1831–33; Vice President 1845–49.

DALY, John Burrwood (Pa.) Feb. 13, 1872–March 12, 1939; House 1935–March 12, 1939.

DALY, William Davis (N.J.) June 4, 1851–July 31, 1900; House 1899–July 31, 1900.

D'AMOURS, Norman Edward (N.H.) Oct. 14, 1937–; House 1975–85.

DANA, Amasa (N.Y.) Oct. 19, 1792–Dec. 24, 1867; House 1839–41, 1843–45.

DANA, Judah (Maine) April 25, 1772–Dec. 27, 1845; Senate Dec. 7, 1836–37.

DANIEL, Charles Ezra (S.C.) Nov. 11, 1895–Sept. 13, 1964; Senate Sept. 6–Dec. 23, 1954.

DANIEL, John Reeves Jones (N.C.) Jan. 13, 1802–June 22, 1868; House 1841–53.

DANIEL, John Warwick (Va.) Sept. 5, 1842–June 29, 1910; House 1885–87; Senate 1887–June 29, 1910.

DANIEL, Price Marion (Tex.) Oct. 10, 1910–Aug. 25, 1988; Senate 1953–Jan. 14, 1957; Gov. Jan. 15, 1957–Jan. 15, 1963.

DANIEL, Wilbur Clarence "Dan" (Va.) May 12, 1914–Jan. 23, 1988; House 1969–Jan. 23, 1988.

DANIELL, Warren Fisher (N.H.) June 26, 1826–July 30, 1913; House 1891–93.

DANIELS, Dominick Vincent (N.J.) Oct. 18, 1908–July 17, 1987; House 1959–77.

DANIELSON, George Elmore (Calif.) Feb. 20, 1915–; House 1971–March 9, 1982.

DANNER, Joel Buchanan (Pa.) 1804–July 29, 1885; House Dec. 2, 1850–51.

DANNER, Patsy Ann "Pat" (Mo.) Jan. 13, 1934–; House 1993–.

DARDEN, Colgate Whitehead Jr. (Va.) Feb. 11, 1897–June 9, 1981; House 1933–37, 1939–March 1, 1941; Gov. Jan. 21, 1942–Jan. 16, 1946.

DARDEN, George "Buddy" (Ga.) Nov. 22, 1943–; House Nov. 8, 1983–1995.

DARGAN, Edmund Strother (Ala.) April 15, 1805–Nov. 22, 1879; House 1845–47.

DARGAN, George William (great-grandson of Lemuel Benton (S.C.) May 11, 1841–June 29, 1898; House 1883–91.

DARLING, Mason Cook (Wis.) May 18, 1801–March 12, 1866; House June 9, 1848–49.

DASCHLE, Thomas Andrew (S.Dak.) Dec. 9, 1947–; House 1979–87; Senate 1987–; Senate minority leader 1995–.

DAUGHERTY, James Alexander (Mo.) Aug. 30, 1847–Jan. 26, 1920; House 1911–13.

DAUGHTON, Ralph Hunter (Va.) Sept. 23, 1885–Dec. 22, 1958; House Nov. 7, 1944–47.

DAVEE, Thomas (Maine) Dec. 9, 1797–Dec. 9, 1841; House 1837–41.

DAVENPORT, Harry James (Pa.) Aug. 28, 1902–Dec. 19, 1977; House 1949–51.

DAVENPORT, James Sanford (Okla.) Sept. 21, 1864–Jan. 3, 1940; House Nov. 16, 1907–09, 1911–17.

DAVENPORT, Stanley Woodward (Pa.) July 21, 1861–Sept. 26, 1921; House 1899–1901.

DAVEY, Martin Luther (Ohio) July 25, 1884–March 31, 1946; House Nov. 5, 1918–21, 1923–29; Gov. Jan. 14, 1935–Jan. 9, 1939.

DAVEY, Robert Charles (La.) Oct. 22, 1853–Dec. 26, 1908; House 1893–95, 1897–Dec. 26, 1908.

DAVIDSON, Alexander Caldwell (Ala.) Dec. 26, 1826–Nov. 6, 1897; House 1885–89.

DAVIDSON, Irwin Delmore (N.Y.) Jan. 2, 1906–Aug. 1, 1981; House 1955–Dec. 31, 1956.

DAVIDSON, Robert Hamilton McWhorta (Fla.) Sept. 23, 1832–Jan. 18, 1908; House 1877–91.

DAVIDSON, Thomas Green (La.) Aug. 3, 1805–Sept. 11, 1883; House 1855–61.

DAVIES, John Clay (N.Y.) May 1, 1920–; House 1949–51.

DAVIS, Alexander Mathews (Va.) Jan. 17, 1833–Sept. 25, 1889; House 1873–March 5, 1874.

DAVIS, Clifford (Tenn.) Nov. 18, 1897–June 8, 1970; House Feb. 15, 1940–65.

DAVIS, Ewin Lamar (Tenn.) Feb. 5, 1876–Oct. 23, 1949; House 1919–33.

DAVIS, Garrett (brother of Amos Davis) (Ky.) Sept. 10, 1801–Sept. 22, 1872; House 1839–47 (Whig); Senate Dec. 10, 1861–Sept. 22, 1872 (1861–67 Unionist).

DAVIS, Henry Gassaway (brother of Thomas Beall Davis, grandfather of Davis Elkins) (W.Va.) Nov. 16, 1823–March 11, 1916; Senate 1871–83.

DAVIS, Jacob Cunningham (Ill.) Sept. 16, 1820–Dec. 25, 1883; House Nov. 4, 1856–57.

DAVIS, Jacob Erastus (Ohio) Oct. 31, 1905–; House 1941–43.

DAVIS, James Curran (Ga.) May 17, 1895–Dec. 18, 1981; House 1947–63.

DAVIS, James Harvey "Cyclone" (Tex.) Dec. 24, 1853–Jan. 31, 1940; House 1915–17.

DAVIS, Jeff (Ark.) May 6, 1862–Jan. 3, 1913; Senate 1907–Jan. 3, 1913; Gov. Jan. 8, 1901–Jan. 8, 1907.

DAVIS, Jefferson Finis (Miss.) June 3, 1808–Dec. 6, 1889; House 1845–June 1846; Senate Aug. 10, 1847–Sept. 23, 1851, 1857–Jan. 21, 1861; Secy. of War March 7, 1853–March 6, 1857.

DAVIS, John (Pa.) Aug. 7, 1788–April 1, 1878; House 1839–41.

DAVIS, John James (father of John William Davis of W.Va.) (W.Va.) May 5, 1835–March 19, 1916; House 1871–75 (1871–73 Democrat).

DAVIS, John Wesley (Ind.) April 16, 1799–Aug. 22 1859; House 1835–37 (Jacksonian), 1839–41, 1843–47; Speaker Dec. 1, 1845–47; Gov. (Oreg. Terr.) 1853, 1854.

DAVIS, John William (son of John James Davis) (W.Va.) April 13, 1873–March 24, 1955; House 1911–Aug. 29, 1913.

DAVIS, John William (Ga.) Sept. 12, 1916–Oct. 3, 1992; House 1961–75.

DAVIS, Joseph Jonathan (N.C.) April 13, 1828–Aug. 7, 1892; House 1875–81.

DAVIS, Lowndes Henry (Mo.) Dec. 13, 1836–Feb. 4, 1920; House 1879–85.

DAVIS, Mendel Jackson (S.C.) Oct. 23, 1942–; House April 27, 1971–81.

DAVIS, Reuben (Miss.) Jan. 18, 1813–Oct. 14, 1890; House 1857–Jan. 12, 1861.

DAVIS, Richard David (N.Y.) 1799–June 17, 1871; House 1841–45.

DAVIS, Robert Wyche (Fla.) March 15, 1849–Sept. 15, 1929; House 1897–1905.

DAVIS, Thomas (R.I.) Dec. 18, 1806–July 26, 1895; House 1853–55.

DAVIS, Thomas Beall (brother of Henry Gassaway Davis) (W.Va.) April 25, 1828–Nov. 26, 1911; House June 6, 1905–07.

DAWSON, John Bennett (La.) March 17, 1798–June 26, 1845; House 1841–June 26, 1845.

DAWSON, John Littleton (Pa.) Feb. 7, 1813–Sept. 18, 1870; House 1851–55, 1863–67.

DAWSON, William (Mo.) March 17, 1848–Oct. 12, 1929; House 1885–87.

DAWSON, William Levi (Ill.) April 26, 1886–Nov. 9, 1970; House 1943–Nov. 9, 1970; Chrmn. House Expenditures in the Executive Departments 1949–52; Chrmn. House Government Operations 1952–53, 1955–71.

DEAL, Joseph Thomas (Va.) Nov. 19, 1860–March 7, 1942; House 1921–29.

DEAL, Nathan (Ga.) Aug. 25, 1942–; House 1993–.

DEAN, Benjamin (Mass.) Aug. 14, 1824–April 9, 1879; House March 28, 1878–79.

DEAN, Ezra (Ohio) April 9, 1795–Jan. 25, 1872; House 1841–45.

DEAN, Gilbert (N.Y.) Aug. 14, 1819–Oct. 12, 1870; House 1851–July 3, 1854.

DEANE, Charles Bennett (N.C.) Nov. 1, 1898–Nov. 24, 1969; House 1947–57.

DEAR, Cleveland (La.) Aug. 22, 1888–Dec. 30, 1950; House 1933–37.

DE ARMOND, David Albaugh (Mo.) March 18, 1844–Nov. 23, 1909; House 1891–Nov. 23, 1909.

DE BOLT, Rezin A. (Mo.) Jan. 20, 1828–Oct. 30, 1891; House 1875–77.

DeCONCINI, Dennis Webster (Ariz.) May 8, 1937–; Senate 1977–1995; Chrmn. Senate Select Committee on Intelligence Activities 1993–1995.

DEEN, Braswell Drue (Ga.) June 28, 1893–Nov. 28, 1981; House 1933–39.

DeFAZIO, Peter Anthony (Oreg.) May 27, 1947–; House 1987–.

DE FOREST, Robert Elliott (Conn.) Feb. 20, 1845–Oct. 1, 1924; House 1891–95.

DE GRAFF, John Isaac (N.Y.) Oct. 2, 1783–July 26, 1848; House 1827–29 (no party), 1837–39.

DE GRAFFENREID, Reese Calhoun (Tex.) May 7, 1859–Aug. 29, 1902; House 1897–Aug. 29, 1902.

deGRAFFENRIED, Edward (Ala.) June 30, 1899–Nov. 5, 1974; House 1949–53.

DEITRICK, Frederick Simpson (Mass.) April 9, 1875–May 24, 1948; House 1913–15.

DE JARNETTE, Daniel Coleman (Va.) Oct. 18, 1822–Aug. 20, 1881; House 1859–61.

DE LACY, Emerson Hugh (Wash.) May 9, 1910–Aug. 19, 1986; House 1945–47.

de la GARZA, Eligio "Kika" II (Tex.) Sept. 22, 1927–; House 1965–; Chrmn. House Agriculture 1981–1995.

DE LA MONTANYA, James (N.Y.) March 20, 1798–April 29, 1849; House 1839–41.

DELANEY, James Joseph (N.Y.) March 19, 1901–May 24, 1987; House 1945–47, 1949–Dec. 31, 1978; Chrmn. House Rules 1977–78.

DELANEY, John Joseph (N.Y.) Aug. 21, 1878–Nov. 18, 1948; House March 5, 1918–19, 1931–Nov. 18, 1948.

DELAPLAINE, Isaac Clason (N.Y.) Oct. 27, 1817–July 17, 1866; House 1861–63.

DeLAURO, Rosa (Conn.) March 2, 1943–; House 1991–.

DELLAY, Vincent John (N.J.) June 23, 1907–; House 1957–59 (1957 Republican).

DELLUMS, Ronald Vernie (Calif.) Nov. 24, 1935–; House 1971–; Chrmn. House District of Columbia 1979–93; Chrmn. House Armed Services 1993–1995.

de LUGO, Ron (V.I.) Aug. 2, 1930–; House (Delegate) 1973–79, 1981–.

DE MOTT, John (N.Y.) Oct. 7, 1790–July 31, 1870; House 1845–47.

DEMPSEY, John Joseph (N.Mex.) June 22, 1879–March 11, 1958; House 1935–41, 1951–March 11, 1958; Gov. Jan. 1, 1943–Jan. 1, 1947.

DE MUTH, Peter Joseph (Pa.) Jan. 1, 1892–; House 1937–39.

DENHOLM, Frank Edward (S.Dak.) Nov. 29, 1923–; House 1971–75.

DENISON, Charles (nephew of George Denison) (Pa.) Jan. 23, 1818–June 27, 1867; House 1863–June 27, 1867.

DENNIS, George Robertson (Md.) April 8, 1822–Aug. 13, 1882; Senate 1873–79.

DENNY, James William (Md.) Nov. 20, 1838–April 12, 1923; House 1899–1901, 1903–05.

DENNY, Walter McKennon (Miss.) Oct. 28, 1853–Nov. 5, 1926; House 1895–97.

DENSON, William Henry (Ala.) March 4, 1846–Sept. 26, 1906; House 1893–95.

DENT, John Herman (Pa.) March 10, 1908–April 9, 1988; House Jan. 21, 1958–79.

DENT, Stanley Hubert Jr. (Ala.) Aug. 16, 1869–Oct. 6, 1938; House 1909–21.

DENT, William Barton Wade (Ga.) Sept. 8, 1806–Sept. 7, 1855; House 1853–55.

DENTON, George Kirkpatrick (father of Winfield Kirkpatrick Denton) (Ind.) Nov. 17, 1864–Jan. 4, 1926; House 1917–19.

DENTON, Winfield Kirkpatrick (son of George Kirkpatrick Denton) (Ind.) Oct. 28, 1896–Nov. 2, 1971; House 1949–53, 1955–67.

DENVER, James William (father of Matthew Rombach Denver) (Calif.) Oct. 23, 1817–Aug. 9, 1892; House 1855–57; Gov. (Kansas Terr.) June 7, 1857–58.

DENVER, Matthew Rombach (son of James William Denver) (Ohio) Dec. 21, 1870–May 13, 1954; House 1907–13.

DE ROUEN, René Louis (La.) Jan. 7, 1874–March 27, 1942; House Aug. 23, 1927–41.

DERRICK, Butler Carson Jr. (S.C.) Sept. 30, 1936–; House 1975–1995.

DERSHEM, Franklin Lewis (Pa.) March 5, 1865–Feb. 14, 1950; House 1913–15.

DE SAUSSURE, William Ford (S.C.) Feb. 22, 1792–March 13, 1870; Senate May 10, 1852–53.

DEUSTER, Peter Victor (Wis.) Feb. 13, 1831–Dec. 31, 1904; House 1879–85.

DEUTSCH, Peter (Fla.) April 1, 1957–; House 1993–.

DE VRIES, Marion (Calif.) Aug. 15, 1865–Sept. 11, 1939; House 1897–Aug. 20, 1900.

DEWALT, Arthur Granville (Pa.) Oct. 11, 1854–Oct. 26, 1931; House 1915–21.

DEWART, William Lewis (son of Lewis Dewart) (Pa.) June 21, 1821–April 19, 1888; House 1857–59.

DE WITT, David Miller (N.Y.) Nov. 25, 1837–June 23, 1912; House 1873–75.

DIAL, Nathaniel Barksdale (S.C.) April 24, 1862–Dec. 11, 1940; Senate 1919–25.

DIBBLE, Samuel (S.C.) Sept. 16, 1837–Sept. 16, 1913; House June 9, 1881–May 31, 1882, 1883–91.

DIBRELL, George Gibbs (Tenn.) April 12, 1822–May 9, 1888; House 1875–85.

DICKERMAN, Charles Heber (Pa.) Feb. 3, 1843–Dec. 17, 1915; House 1903–05.

DICKERSON, Philemon (brother of Mahlon Dickerson) (N.J.) Jan. 11, 1788–Dec. 10, 1862; House 1833–Nov. 3, 1836 (Jacksonian), 1839–41; Gov. Nov. 3, 1836–Oct. 27, 1837 (Democrat).

DICKERSON, William Worth (Ky.) Nov. 29, 1851–Jan. 31, 1923; House June 21, 1890–93.

DICKEY, Henry Luther (Ohio) Oct. 29, 1832–May 23, 1910; House 1877–81.

DICKINSON, Clement Cabell (Mo.) Dec. 6, 1849–Jan. 14, 1938; House Feb. 1, 1910–21, 1923–29, 1931–35.

DICKINSON, Daniel Stevens (N.Y.) Sept. 11, 1800–April 12, 1866; Senate Nov. 30, 1844–51.

DICKINSON, Edward Fenwick (Ohio) Jan. 21, 1829–Aug. 25, 1891; House 1869–71.

DICKINSON, Rodolphus (Ohio) Dec. 28, 1797–March 20, 1849; House 1847–March 20, 1849.

DICKS, Norman De Valois (Wash.) Dec. 16, 1940–; House 1977–.

DICKSON, William Alexander (Miss.) July 20, 1861–Feb. 25, 1940; House 1909–13.

DICKSTEIN, Samuel (N.Y.) Feb. 5, 1885–April 22, 1954; House 1923–Dec. 30, 1945.

DIES, Martin (father of Martin Dies Jr.) (Tex.) March 13, 1870–July 13, 1922; House 1909–19.

DIES, Martin Jr. (son of Martin Dies) (Tex.) Nov. 5, 1900–Nov. 14, 1972; House 1931–45, 1953–59.

DIETERICH, William Henry (Ill.) March 31, 1876–Oct. 12, 1940; House 1931–33; Senate 1933–39.

DIETRICH, Charles Elmer (Pa.) July 30, 1889–May 20, 1942; House 1935–37.

DIFENDERFER, Robert Edward (Pa.) June 7, 1849–April 25, 1923; House 1911–15.

DIGGS, Charles Coles Jr. (Mich.) Dec. 2, 1922–; House 1955–June 3, 1980; Chrmn. House District of Columbia 1973–79.

DILL, Clarence Cleveland (Wash.) Sept. 21, 1884–Jan. 14, 1978; House 1915–19; Senate 1923–35.

DILLINGHAM, Paul Jr. (father of William Paul Dillingham) (Vt.) Aug. 10, 1799–July 26, 1891; House 1843–47; Gov. Oct. 13, 1865–Oct. 13, 1867 (Republican).

DILWEG, LaVern Ralph (Wis.) Nov. 1, 1903–Jan. 2, 1968; House 1943–45.

DIMMICK, Milo Melankthon (brother of William Harrison Dimmick) (Pa.) Oct. 30, 1811–Nov. 22, 1872; House 1849–53.

DIMMICK, William Harrison (brother of Milo Melankthon Dimmick) (Pa.) Dec. 20, 1815–Aug. 2, 1861; House 1857–61.

DIMOCK, Davis Jr. (Pa.) Sept. 17, 1801–Jan. 13, 1842; House 1841–Jan. 13, 1842.

DIMOND, Anthony Joseph (Alaska) Nov. 30, 1881–May 28, 1953; House (Terr. Del.) 1933–45.

DINGELL, John David (father of John David Dingell Jr.) (Mich.) Feb. 2, 1894–Sept. 19, 1955; House 1933–Sept. 19, 1955.

DINGELL, John David Jr. (son of John David Dingell)

(Mich.) July 8, 1926–; House Dec. 13, 1955–; Chrmn. House Energy and Commerce 1981–1995.

DINSMORE, Hugh Anderson (Ark.) Dec. 24, 1850–May 2, 1930; House 1893–1905.

DISNEY, David Tiernan (Ohio) Aug. 25, 1803–March 14, 1857; House 1849–55.

DISNEY, Wesley Ernest (Okla.) Oct. 31, 1883–March 26, 1961; House 1931–45.

DIX, John Adams (son-in-law of John Jordan Morgan) (N.Y.) July 24, 1798–April 21, 1879; Senate Jan. 27, 1845–49; Secy. of the Treasury Jan. 15–March 6, 1861; Gov. Jan. 1, 1873–Jan. 1, 1875 (Republican).

DIXON, Alan John (Ill.) July 7, 1927–; Senate 1981–93.

DIXON, Joseph Andrew (Ohio) June 3, 1879–July 4, 1942; House 1937–39.

DIXON, Julian Carey (Calif.) Aug. 8, 1934–; House 1979–; Chrmn. House Standards of Official Conduct 1985–91.

DIXON, Lincoln (Ind.) Feb. 9, 1860–Sept. 16, 1932; House 1905–19.

DIXON, William Wirt (Mont.) June 3, 1838–Nov. 13, 1910; House 1891–93.

DOAN, William (Ohio) April 4, 1792–June 22, 1847; House 1839–43.

DOBBIN, James Cochrane (grandson of James Cochran of North Carolina) (N.C.) Jan. 17, 1814–Aug. 4, 1857; House 1845–47; Secy. of the Navy March 8, 1853–March 6, 1857.

DOBBINS, Donald Claude (Ill.) March 20, 1878–Feb. 14, 1943; House 1933–37.

DOCKERY, Alexander Monroe (Mo.) Feb. 11, 1845–Dec. 26, 1926; House 1883–99; Gov. Jan. 14, 1901–Jan. 9, 1905.

DOCKWEILER, John Francis (Calif.) Sept. 19, 1895–Jan. 31, 1943; House 1933–39.

DODD, Christopher John (son of Thomas Joseph Dodd) (Conn.) May 27, 1944–; House 1975–81; Senate 1981–.

DODD, Thomas Joseph (father of Christopher John Dodd) (Conn.) May 15, 1907–May 24, 1971; House 1953–57; Senate 1959–Jan. 2, 1971.

DODDS, Ozro John (Ohio) March 22, 1840–April 18, 1882; House Oct. 8, 1872–73.

DODGE, Augustus Caesar (son of Henry Dodge) (Iowa) Jan. 2, 1812–Nov. 20, 1883; House (Terr. Del.) Oct. 28, 1840–Dec. 28, 1846; Senate Dec. 7, 1848–Feb. 22, 1855.

DODGE, Henry (father of Augustus Caesar Dodge) (Wis.) Oct. 12, 1782–June 19, 1867; House (Terr. Del.) 1841–45; Senate June 8, 1848–57; Gov. (Wis. Terr.) 1836–41, 1845–48.

DOIG, Andrew Wheeler (N.Y.) July 24, 1799–July 11, 1875; House 1839–43.

DOLLINGER, Isidore (N.Y.) Nov. 13, 1903–; House 1949–Dec. 31, 1959.

DOMENGEAUX, James (La.) Jan. 6, 1907–April 11, 1988; House 1941–April 15, 1944, Nov. 7, 1944–49.

DOMINICK, Frederick Haskell (S.C.) Feb. 20, 1877–March 11, 1960; House 1917–33.

DONAHEY, Alvin Victor (Ohio) July 7, 1873–April 8, 1946; Senate 1935–41; Gov. Jan. 8, 1923–Jan. 14, 1929.

DONNELLY, Brian Joseph (Mass.) March 2, 1946–; House 1979–93.

DONOHOE, Michael (Pa.) Feb. 22, 1864–Jan. 17, 1958; House 1911–15.

DONOHUE, Harold Daniel (Mass.) June 18, 1901–Nov. 4, 1984; House 1947–Dec. 31, 1974.

DONOVAN, Dennis D. (Ohio) Jan. 31, 1859–April 21, 1941; House 1891–95.

DONOVAN, James George (N.Y.) Dec. 15, 1898–April 6, 1987; House 1951–57.

DONOVAN, Jeremiah (Conn.) Oct. 18, 1857–April 22, 1935; House 1913–15.

DONOVAN, Jerome Francis (N.Y.), Feb. 1, 1872–Nov. 2, 1949; House March 5, 1918–21.

DOOLEY, Calvin (Calif.) Jan. 11, 1954–; House 1991.

DOOLING, Peter Joseph (N.Y.) Feb. 15, 1857–Oct. 18, 1931; House 1913–21.

DOOLITTLE, Dudley (Kans.) June 21, 1881–Nov. 14, 1957; House 1913–19.

DOREMUS, Frank Ellsworth (Mich.) Aug. 31, 1865–Sept. 4, 1947; House 1911–21.

DORGAN, Byron Leslie (N.Dak.) May 14, 1942–; House 1981–Dec. 14, 1992; Senate Dec. 15, 1992–.

DORN, William Jennings Bryan (S.C.) April 14, 1916–; House 1947–49, 1951–Dec. 31, 1974; Chrmn. House Veterans' Affairs 1973–75.

DORSEY, Frank Joseph Gerard (Pa.) April 26, 1891–July 13, 1949; House 1935–39.

DORSEY, John Lloyd Jr. (Ky.) Aug. 10, 1891–March 22, 1960; House Nov. 4, 1930–31.

DORSHEIMER, William (N.Y.) Feb. 5, 1832–March 26, 1888; House 1883–85.

DOUGHERTY, Charles (Fla.) Oct. 15, 1850–Oct. 11, 1915; House 1885–89.

DOUGHERTY, John (Mo.) Feb. 25, 1857–Aug. 1, 1905; House 1899–1905.

DOUGHTON, Robert Lee (N.C.) Nov. 7, 1863–Oct. 1, 1954; House 1911–53; Chrmn. House Ways and Means 1949–53.

DOUGLAS, Beverly Browne (Va.) Dec. 21, 1822–Dec. 22, 1878; House 1875–Dec. 22, 1878.

DOUGLAS, Emily Taft (wife of Paul Howard Douglas) (Ill.) April 10, 1899–Jan. 28, 1994; House 1945–47.

DOUGLAS, Helen Gahagan (Calif.) Nov. 25, 1900–June 28, 1980; House 1945–51.

DOUGLAS, Lewis Williams (Ariz.) July 2, 1894–March 7, 1974; House 1927–March 4, 1933.

DOUGLAS, Paul Howard (husband of Emily Taft Douglas) (Ill.) March 26, 1892–Sept. 24, 1976; Senate 1949–67.

DOUGLAS, Stephen Arnold (Ill.) April 23, 1813–June 3, 1861; House 1843–47; Senate 1847–June 3, 1861.

DOUGLASS, John Joseph (Mass.) Feb. 9, 1873–April 5, 1939; House 1925–35.

DOW, John Goodchild (N.Y.) May 6, 1905–; House 1965–69, 1971–73.

DOWD, Clement (N.C.) Aug. 27, 1832–April 15, 1898; House 1881–85.

DOWDELL, James Ferguson (Ala.) Nov. 26, 1818–Sept. 6, 1871; House 1853–59.

DOWDNEY, Abraham (N.Y.) Oct. 31, 1841–Dec. 10, 1886; House 1885–Dec. 10, 1886.

DOWDY, Charles Wayne (Miss.) July 27, 1943–; House July 9, 1981–89.

DOWDY, John Vernard (Tex.) Feb. 11, 1912–; House Sept. 23, 1952–73.

DOWNEY, Sheridan (son of Stephen Wheeler Downey) (Calif.) March 11, 1884–Oct. 25, 1961; Senate 1939–Nov. 30, 1950.

DOWNEY, Thomas Joseph (N.Y.) Jan. 28, 1949–; House 1975–93.

DOWNING, Finis Ewing (Ill.) Aug. 24, 1846–March 8, 1936; House 1895–June 5, 1896.

DOWNING, Thomas Nelms (Va.) Feb. 1, 1919–; House 1959–77.

DOWNS, Le Roy Donnelly (Conn.) April 11, 1900–Jan. 18, 1970; House 1941–43.

DOWNS, Solomon Weathersbee (La.) 1801–Aug. 14, 1854; Senate 1847–53.

DOX, Peter Myndert (grandson of John Nicholas) (Ala.) Sept. 11, 1813–April 2, 1891; House 1869–73.

DOXEY, Wall (Miss.) Aug. 8, 1892–March 2, 1962; House 1929–Sept. 28, 1941; Senate Sept. 29, 1941–43.

DOYLE, Clyde Gilman (Calif.) July 11, 1887–March 14, 1963; House 1945–47, 1949–March 14, 1963.

DOYLE, Michael (Pa.) House, 1995–.

DOYLE, Thomas Aloysius (Ill.) Jan. 9, 1886–Jan. 29, 1935; House Nov. 6, 1923–31.

DRANE, Herbert Jackson (Fla.) June 20, 1863–Aug. 11, 1947; House 1917–33.

DREW, Ira Walton (Pa.) Aug. 31, 1878–Feb. 12, 1972; House 1937–39.

DREWRY, Patrick Henry (Va.) May 24, 1875–Dec. 21, 1947; House April 27, 1920–Dec. 21, 1947.

DRIGGS, Edmund Hope (N.Y.) May 2, 1865–Sept. 27, 1946; House Dec. 6, 1897–1901.

DRINAN, Robert Frederick (Mass.) Nov. 15, 1920–; House 1971–81.

DRISCOLL, Daniel Angelus (N.Y.) March 6, 1875–June 5, 1955; House 1909–17.

DRISCOLL, Denis Joseph (Pa.) March 27, 1871–Jan. 18, 1958; House 1935–37.

DRIVER, William Joshua (Ark.) March 2, 1873–Oct. 1, 1948; House 1921–39.

DROMGOOLE, George Coke (uncle of Alexander Dromgoole Sims) (Va.) May 15, 1797–April 27, 1847; House 1835–41 (1835–37 Jacksonian), 1843–April 27, 1847.

DRUM, Augustus (Pa.) Nov. 26, 1815–Sept. 15, 1858; House 1853–55.

DUBOIS, Fred Thomas (Idaho) May 29, 1851–Feb. 14, 1930; House (Terr. Del.) 1887–July 3, 1890; Senate 1891–97, 1901–07 (1887–97 Republican, 1901 Silver Republican).

DU BOSE, Dudley McIver (Ga.) Oct. 28, 1834–March 2, 1883; House 1871–73.

DUFFEY, Warren Joseph (Ohio) Jan. 24, 1886–July 7, 1936; House 1933–July 7, 1936.

DUFFY, Francis Ryan (Wis.) June 23, 1888–Aug. 16, 1979; Senate 1933–39.

DUFFY, James Patrick Bernard (N.Y.) Nov. 25, 1878–Jan. 8, 1969; House 1935–37.

DUGRO, Philip Henry (N.Y.) Oct. 3, 1855–March 1, 1920; House 1881–83.

DULSKI, Thaddeus Joseph (N.Y.) Sept. 27, 1915–Oct. 11, 1988; House 1959–Dec. 31, 1974; Chrmn. House Post Office and Civil Service 1967–75.

DUNBAR, William (La.) 1805–March 18, 1861; House 1853–55.

DUNCAN, Alexander (Ohio) 1788–March 23, 1853; House 1837–41, 1843–45.

DUNCAN, Richard Meloan (Mo.) Nov. 10, 1889–Aug. 1, 1974; House 1933–43.

DUNCAN, Robert Blackford (Oreg.) Dec. 4, 1920–; House 1963–67, 1975–81.

DUNCAN, William Addison (Pa.) Feb. 2, 1836–Nov. 14, 1884; House 1883–Nov. 14, 1884.

DUNGAN, James Irvine (Ohio) May 29, 1844–Dec. 28, 1931; House 1891–93.

DUNHAM, Cyrus Livingston (Ind.) Jan. 16, 1817–Nov. 21, 1877; House 1849–55.

DUNLAP, Robert Pickney (Maine) Aug. 17, 1794–Oct. 20, 1859; House 1843–47; Gov. Jan. 1, 1834–Jan. 3, 1838.

DUNN, Aubert Culberson (Miss.) Nov. 20, 1896–Jan. 4, 1987; House 1935–37.

DUNN, John Thomas (N.J.) June 4, 1838–Feb. 22, 1907; House 1893–95.

DUNN, Matthew Anthony (Pa.) Aug. 15, 1886–Feb. 13, 1942; House 1933–41.

DUNN, Poindexter (Ark.) Nov. 3, 1834–Oct. 12, 1914; House 1879–89.

DUNPHY, Edward John (N.Y.) May 12, 1856–July 29, 1926; House 1889–95.

DUPRE, Henry Garland (La.) July 28, 1873–Feb. 21, 1924; House Nov. 8, 1910–Feb. 21, 1924.

DURAND, George Harman (Mich.) Feb. 21, 1838–June 8, 1903; House 1875–77.

DURBIN, Richard Joseph (Ill.) Nov. 21, 1944–; House 1983–.

DURBOROW, Allan Cathcart Jr. (Ill.) Nov. 10, 1857–March 10, 1908; House 1891–95.

DURGAN, George Richard (Ind.) Jan. 20, 1872–Jan. 13, 1942; House 1933–35.

DURHAM, Carl Thomas (N.C.) Aug. 28, 1892–April 29, 1974; House 1939–61.

DURHAM, Milton Jameson (Ky.) May 16, 1824–Feb. 12, 1911; House 1873–79.

DURKIN, John Anthony (N.H.) March 29, 1936–; Senate Sept. 18, 1975–Dec. 29, 1980.

DWYER, Bernard James (N.J.) Jan. 24, 1921–; House 1981–93.

DYAL, Kenneth Warren (Calif.) July 9, 1910–May 12, 1978; House 1965–67.

DYMALLY, Mervyn Malcolm (Calif.) May 12, 1926–; House 1981–93.

DYSON, Royden Patrick "Roy" (Md.) Nov. 15, 1948–; House 1981–91.

EAGAN, John Joseph (N.J.) Jan. 22, 1872–June 13, 1956; House 1913–21, 1923–25.

EAGLE, Joe Henry (Tex.) Jan. 23, 1870–Jan. 10, 1963; House 1913–21, Jan. 28, 1933–37.

EAGLETON, Thomas Francis (Mo.) Sept. 4, 1929–; Senate Dec. 28, 1968–87; Chrmn. Senate District of Columbia 1971–77.

EARHART, Daniel Scofield (Ohio) May 28, 1907–Jan. 2, 1976; House Nov. 3, 1936–37.

EARLE, Joseph Haynsworth (great-grandson of Elias Earle, cousin of John Laurens Manning Irby, nephew of William Lowndes Yancey) (S.C.) April 30, 1847–May 20, 1897; Senate March 4–May 20, 1897.

EARLL, Nehemiah Hezekiah (cousin of Jones Earll Jr.) (N.Y.) Oct. 5, 1787–Aug. 26, 1872; House 1839–41.

EARLY, Joseph Daniel (Mass.) Jan. 31, 1933–; House 1975–93.

EARTHMAN, Harold Henderson (Tenn.) April 13, 1900–; House 1945–47.

EASTLAND, James Oliver (Miss.) Nov. 28, 1904–Feb. 19, 1986; Senate June 30–Sept. 28, 1941, 1943–Dec. 27, 1978; Chrmn. Senate Judiciary 1956–78; elected Pres. pro tempore July 28, 1972.

EASTMAN, Ben C. (Wis.) Oct. 24, 1812–Feb. 2, 1856; House 1851–55.

EASTMAN, Ira Allen (N.H.) Jan. 1, 1809–March 21, 1881; House 1839–43.

EATON, William Wallace (Conn.) Oct. 11, 1816–Sept. 21, 1898; Senate Feb. 5, 1875–81; House 1883–85.

EBERHARTER, Herman Peter (Pa.) April 29, 1892–Sept. 9, 1958; House 1937–Sept. 9, 1958.

ECKART, Dennis Edward (Ohio) April 6, 1950–; House 1981–93.

ECKERT, Charles Richard (Pa.) Jan. 20, 1868–Oct. 26, 1959; House 1935–39.

ECKHARDT, Robert Christian (cousin of Richard Mifflin Kleberg Sr., great-nephew of Rudolph Kleberg, nephew of Harry McLeary Wurzbach) (Tex.) July 16, 1913–; House 1967–81.

EDDY, Norman (Ind.) Dec. 10, 1810–Jan. 28, 1872; House 1853–55.

EDELSTEIN, Morris Michael (N.Y.) Feb. 5, 1888–June 4, 1941; House Feb. 6, 1940–June 4, 1941.

EDEN, John Rice (Ill.) Feb. 1, 1826–June 9, 1909; House 1863–65, 1873–79, 1885–87.

EDGAR, Robert William (Pa.) May 29, 1943–; House 1975–87.

EDGERTON, Alfred Peck (brother of Joseph Ketchum Edgerton) (Ohio) Jan. 11, 1813–May 14, 1897; House 1851–55.

EDGERTON, Joseph Ketchum (brother of Alfred Peck Edgerton) (Ind.) Feb. 16, 1818–Aug. 25, 1893; House 1863–65.

EDMISTON, Andrew (W.Va.) Nov. 13, 1892–Aug. 28, 1966; House Nov. 28, 1933–43.

EDMONDSON, Edmond Augustus (brother of James Howard Edmondson) (Okla.) April 7, 1919–Dec. 8, 1990; House 1953–73.

EDMONDSON, James Howard (brother of Edmond Augustus Edmondson) (Okla.) Sept. 27, 1925–Nov. 17, 1971; Senate Jan. 7, 1963–Nov. 3, 1964; Gov. Jan. 12, 1959–Jan. 6, 1963.

EDMUNDS, Paul Carrington (Va.) Nov. 1, 1836–March 12, 1899; House 1889–95.

EDMUNDSON, Henry Alonzo (Va.) June 14, 1814–Dec. 16, 1890; House 1849–61.

EDSALL, Joseph E. (N.J.) 1789–1865; House 1845–49.

EDWARDS, Charles Gordon (Ga.) July 2, 1878–July 13, 1931; House 1907–17, 1925–July 13, 1931.

EDWARDS, Chet (Tex.) Nov. 24, 1951–; House 1991–.

EDWARDS, Don (Calif.) Jan. 6, 1915–; House 1963–.

EDWARDS, Edward Irving (N.J.) Dec. 1, 1863–Jan. 26, 1931; Senate 1923–29; Gov. Jan. 20, 1920–Jan. 15, 1923.

EDWARDS, Edwin Washington (husband of Elaine Schwartzenburg Edwards) (La.) Aug. 7, 1927–; House Oct.

18, 1965–May 9, 1972; Gov. May 9, 1972–March 10, 1980, March 12, 1984–May 14, 1988.

EDWARDS, Elaine Schwartzenburg (wife of Edwin Washington Edwards) (La.) March 8, 1929–; Senate Aug. 1–Nov. 13, 1972.

EDWARDS, John (N.Y.) Aug. 6, 1781–Dec. 28, 1850; House 1837–39.

EDWARDS, John Cummins (Mo.) June 24, 1804–Sept. 14, 1888; House 1841–43; Gov. Nov. 20, 1844–Nov. 27, 1848.

EGBERT, Albert Gallatin (Pa.) April 13, 1828–March 28, 1896; House 1875–77.

EGBERT, Joseph (N.Y.) April 10, 1807–July 7, 1888; House 1841–43.

EICHER, Edward Clayton (Iowa) Dec. 16, 1878–Nov. 29, 1944; House 1933–Dec. 2, 1938.

EICKHOFF, Anthony (N.Y.) Sept. 11, 1827–Nov. 5, 1901; House 1877–79.

EILBERG, Joshua (Pa.) Feb. 12, 1921–; House 1967–79.

ELAM, Joseph Barton (La.) June 12, 1821–July 4, 1885; House 1877–81.

ELDER, James Walter (La.) Oct. 5, 1882–Dec. 16, 1941; House 1913–15.

ELDREDGE, Charles Augustus (Wis.) Feb. 27, 1820–Oct. 26, 1896; House 1863–75.

ELDREDGE, Nathaniel Buel (Mich.) March 28, 1813–Nov. 27, 1893; House 1883–87.

ELIOT, Thomas Hopkinson (Mass.) June 14, 1907–Oct. 14, 1991; House 1941–43.

ELLENBOGEN, Henry (Pa.) April 3, 1900–July 4, 1985; House 1933–Jan. 3, 1938.

ELLENDER, Allen Joseph (La.) Sept. 24, 1890–July 27, 1972; Senate 1937–July 27, 1972; Chrmn. Senate Agriculture and Forestry 1951–53, 1955–71; elected Pres. pro tempore Jan. 22, 1971; Chrmn. Senate Appropriations 1971–72.

ELLERBE, James Edwin (S.C.) Jan. 12, 1867–Oct. 24, 1917; House 1905–13.

ELLETT, Henry Thomas (Miss.) March 8, 1812–Oct. 15, 1887; House Jan. 26–March 3, 1847.

ELLETT, Tazewell (Va.) Jan. 1, 1856–May 19, 1914; House 1895–97.

ELLIOTT, Alfred James (Calif.) June 1, 1895–Jan. 17, 1973; House May 4, 1937–49.

ELLIOTT, Carl Atwood (Ala.) Dec. 20, 1913–; House 1949–65.

ELLIOTT, John Milton (Ky.) May 20, 1820–March 26, 1879; House 1853–59.

ELLIOTT, Mortimer Fitzland (Pa.) Sept. 24, 1839–Aug. 5, 1920; House 1883–85.

ELLIOTT, William (S.C.) Sept. 3, 1838–Dec. 7, 1907; House

1887–Sept. 23, 1890, 1891–93, 1895–June 4, 1896, 1897–1903.

ELLIS, Chesselden (N.Y.) 1808–May 10, 1854; House 1843–45.

ELLIS, Clyde Taylor (Ark.) Dec. 21, 1908–Feb. 9, 1980; House 1939–43.

ELLIS, Ezekiel John (La.) Oct. 15, 1840–April 25, 1889; House 1875–85.

ELLIS, William Thomas (Ky.) July 24, 1845–Jan. 8, 1925; House 1889–95.

ELLISON, Andrew (Ohio) 1812–about 1860; House 1853–55.

ELLSBERRY, William Wallace (Ohio) Dec. 18, 1833–Sept. 7, 1894; House 1885–87.

ELLSWORTH, Samuel Stewart (N.Y.) Oct. 13, 1790–June 4, 1863; House 1845–47.

ELLZEY, Lawrence Russell (Miss.) March 20, 1891–Dec. 7, 1977; House March 15, 1932–35.

ELMER, Lucius Quintius Cincinnatus (N.J.) Feb. 3, 1793–March 11, 1883; House 1843–45.

ELMORE, Franklin Harper (S.C.) Oct. 15, 1799–May 29, 1850; House Dec. 10, 1836–39 (State Rights Democrat); Senate April 11–May 28, 1850.

ELY, John (N.Y.) Oct. 8, 1774–Aug. 20, 1849; House 1839–41.

ELY, Smith Jr. (N.Y.) April 17, 1825–July 1, 1911; House 1871–73, 1875–Dec. 11, 1876.

EMERICH, Martin (Ill.) April 27, 1846–Sept. 27, 1922; House 1903–05.

ENGEL, Eliot Lanze (N.Y.) Feb. 18, 1947–; House 1989–.

ENGLE, Clair (Calif.) Sept. 21, 1911–July 30, 1964; House Aug. 31, 1943–59; Chrmn. House Interior and Insular Affairs 1955–59; Senate 1959–July 30, 1964.

ENGLISH, Glenn Lee Jr. (Okla.) Nov. 30, 1940–; House 1975–Jan. 7, 1994.

ENGLISH, James Edward (Conn.) March 13, 1812–March 2, 1890; House 1861–65; Senate Nov. 27, 1875–May 17, 1876; Gov. May 1, 1867–May 5, 1869, May 4, 1870–May 16, 1871.

ENGLISH, Karan (Ariz.) March 23, 1949–; House 1993–1995.

ENGLISH, Thomas Dunn (N.J.) June 29, 1819–April 1, 1902; House 1891–95.

ENGLISH, Warren Barkley (Calif.) May 1, 1840–Jan. 9, 1913; House April 4, 1894–95.

ENGLISH, William Eastin (son of William Hayden English) (Ind.) Nov. 3, 1850–April 29, 1926; House May 22, 1884–85.

ENGLISH, William Hayden (father of William Eastin English) (Ind.) Aug. 27, 1822–Feb. 7, 1896; House 1853–61.

ENLOE, Benjamin Augustine (Tenn.) Jan. 18, 1848–July 8, 1922; House 1887–95.

EPES, James Fletcher (cousin of Sydney Parham Epes) (Va.) May 23, 1842–Aug. 24, 1910; House 1891–95.

EPES, Sydney Parham (cousin of James Fletcher Epes and William Bacon Oliver) (Va.) Aug. 20, 1865–March 3, 1900; House 1897–March 23, 1898 (no party), 1899–March 3, 1900.

ERDMAN, Constantine Jacob (grandson of Jacob Erdman) (Pa.) Sept. 4, 1846–Jan. 15, 1911; House 1893–97.

ERDMAN, Jacob (grandfather of Constantine Jacob Erdman) (Pa.) Feb. 22, 1801–July 20, 1867; House 1845–47.

ERDREICH, Ben (Ala.) Dec. 9, 1938–; House 1983–93.

ERICKSON, John Edward (Mont.) March 14, 1863–May 25, 1946; Senate March 13, 1933–Nov. 6, 1934; Gov. Jan. 5, 1925–March 13, 1933.

ERMENTROUT, Daniel (Pa.) Jan. 24, 1837–Sept. 17, 1899; House 1881–89, 1897–Sept. 17, 1899.

ERTEL, Allen Edward (Pa.) Nov. 7, 1936–; House 1977–83.

ERVIN, Joseph Wilson (brother of Samuel James Ervin Jr.) (N.C.) March 3, 1901–Dec. 25, 1945; House Jan. 3–Dec. 25, 1945.

ERVIN, Samuel James Jr. (brother of Joseph Wilson Ervin) (N.C.) Sept. 27, 1896–April 23, 1985; House Jan. 22, 1946–47; Senate June 5, 1954–Dec. 31, 1975; Chrmn. Senate Government Operations 1972–74.

ESHOO, Anna Georges (Calif.) Dec. 13, 1942–; House 1993–.

ESLICK, Edward Everett (husband of Willa McCord Blake Eslick) (Tenn.) April 19, 1872–June 14, 1932; House 1925–June 14, 1932.

ESLICK, Willa McCord Blake (widow of Edward Everett Eslick) (Tenn.) Sept. 8, 1878–Feb. 18, 1961; House Aug. 4, 1932–33.

ESPY, Albert Michael "Mike" (Miss.) Nov. 30, 1953–; House 1987–Jan. 22, 1993; Secy. of Agriculture Jan. 22, 1993–1995.

ESTOPINAL, Albert (La.) Jan. 30, 1845–April 28, 1919; House Nov. 3, 1908–April 28, 1919.

EUSTIS, James Biddle (brother of George Eustis Jr.) (La.) Aug. 27, 1834–Sept. 9, 1899; Senate Jan. 12, 1876–79, 1885–91.

EVANS, Billy Lee (Ga.) Nov. 10, 1941–; House 1977–83.

EVANS, Charles Robley (Nev.) Aug. 9, 1866–Nov. 30, 1954; House 1919–21.

EVANS, David Walter (Ind.) Aug. 17, 1946–; House 1975–83.

EVANS, Frank Edward (Colo.) Sept. 6, 1923–; House 1965–79.

EVANS, John Morgan (Mont.) Jan. 7, 1863–March 12, 1946; House 1913–21, 1923–33.

EVANS, Josiah James (S.C.) Nov. 27, 1786–May 6, 1858; Senate 1853–May 6, 1858.

EVANS, Lane Allen (Ill.) Aug. 4, 1951–; House 1983–.

EVANS, Lynden (Ill.) June 28, 1858–May 6, 1926; House 1911–13.

EVANS, Marcellus Hugh (N.Y.) Sept. 22, 1884–Nov. 21, 1953; House 1935–41.

EVERETT, Robert Ashton (Tenn.) Feb. 24, 1915–Jan. 26, 1969; House Feb. 1, 1958–Jan. 26, 1969.

EVERETT, Robert William (Ga.) March 3, 1839–Feb. 27, 1915; House 1891–93.

EVERETT, William (son of Edward Everett) (Mass.) Oct. 10, 1839–Feb. 16, 1910; House April 25, 1893–95.

EVINS, John Hamilton (S.C.) July 18, 1830–Oct. 20, 1884; House 1877–Oct. 20, 1884.

EVINS, Joseph Landon (Tenn.) Oct. 24, 1910–March 31, 1984; House 1947–77; Chrmn. House Select Committee on Small Business 1963–75; Chrmn. House Small Business 1975–77.

EWING, Andrew (brother of Edwin Hickman Ewing) (Tenn.) June 17, 1813–June 16, 1864; House 1849–51.

EXON, John James (Nebr.) Aug. 9, 1921–; Senate 1979–; Gov. Jan. 7, 1971–Jan. 3, 1979.

FADDIS, Charles Isiah (Pa.) June 13, 1890–April 1, 1972; House 1933–Dec. 4, 1942.

FAIR, James Graham (Nev.) Dec. 3, 1831–Dec. 28, 1894; Senate 1881–87.

FAIRFIELD, John (Maine) Jan. 30, 1797–Dec. 24, 1847; House 1835–Dec. 24, 1838; Senate 1843–Dec. 24, 1847; Gov. Jan. 2, 1839–Jan. 6, 1841, Jan. 5, 1842–March 7, 1843.

FAISON, John Miller (N.C.) April 17, 1862–April 21, 1915; House 1911–15.

FALEOMAVAEGA, Eni F.H. (Amer. Samoa) Aug. 15, 1943–; House (Delegate) 1991–.

FALLON, George Hyde (Md.) July 24, 1902–March 21, 1980; House 1945–71; Chrmn. House Public Works 1965–71.

FARAN, James John (Ohio) Dec. 29, 1808–Dec. 12, 1892; House 1845–49.

FARBSTEIN, Leonard (N.Y.) Oct. 12, 1902–; House 1957–71.

FARLEY, James Indus (Ind.) Feb. 24, 1871–June 16, 1948; House 1933–39.

FARLEY, James Thompson (Calif.) Aug. 6, 1829–Jan. 22, 1886; Senate 1879–85.

FARLEY, Michael Francis (N.Y.) March 1, 1863–Oct. 8, 1921; House 1915–17.

FARNSLEY, Charles Rowland Peaslee (Ky.) March 28, 1907–June 19, 1990; House 1965–67.

FARNUM, Billie Sunday (Mich.) April 11, 1916–Nov. 18, 1979; House 1965–67.

FARR, Sam (Calif.) July 4, 1941–; House June 16, 1993–.

FARRINGTON, James (N.H.) Oct. 1, 1791–Oct. 29, 1859; House 1837–39.

FARY, John George (Ill.) April 11, 1911–June 7, 1984; House July 8, 1975–83.

FASCELL, Dante Bruno (Fla.) March 9, 1917–; House 1955–93; Chrmn. House Foreign Affairs 1984–93.

FAULKNER, Charles James (father of Charles James Faulkner, below) (W.Va.) July 6, 1806–Nov. 1, 1884; House 1851–59 (1851–55 Whig) (Va.), 1875–77.

FAULKNER, Charles James (son of Charles James Faulkner, above) (W.Va.) Sept. 21, 1847–Jan. 13, 1929; Senate 1887–99.

FAUNTROY, Walter Edward (D.C.) Feb. 5, 1933–; House (Delegate) March 23, 1971–91.

FAVROT, George Kent (La.) Nov. 26, 1868–Dec. 26, 1934; House 1907–09, 1921–25.

FAY, James Herbert (N.Y.) April 29, 1899–Sept. 10, 1948; House 1939–41, 1943–45.

FAZIO, Victor Herbert Jr. (Calif.) Oct. 11, 1942–; House 1979–.

FEATHERSTON, Winfield Scott (Miss.) Aug. 8, 1820–May 28, 1891; House 1847–51.

FEAZEL, William Crosson (La.) June 10, 1895–March 16, 1965; Senate May 18–Dec. 30, 1948.

FEELY, John Joseph (Ill.) Aug. 1, 1875–Feb. 15, 1905; House 1901–03.

FEIGHAN, Michael Aloysius (uncle of Edward Farrell Feighan) (Ohio) Feb. 16, 1905–March 19, 1992; House 1943–71.

FEINGOLD, Russell Dana (Wis.) March 2, 1953–; Senate 1993–.

FEINSTEIN, Dianne (Calif.) June 22, 1933–; Senate Nov. 10, 1992–.

FELCH, Alpheus (Mich.) Sept. 28, 1804–June 13, 1896; Senate 1847–53; Gov. Jan. 5, 1846–March 3, 1847.

FELLOWS, John R. (N.Y.) July 29, 1832–Dec. 7, 1896; House 1891–Dec. 31, 1893.

FELTON, Rebecca Latimer (wife of William Harrell Felton) (Ga.) June 10, 1835–Jan. 24, 1930; Senate Nov. 21–Nov. 22, 1922.

FELTON, William Harrell (husband of Rebecca Latimer Felton) (Ga.) June 1, 1823–Sept. 24, 1909; House 1875–81.

FENN, Stephen Southmyd (Idaho) March 28, 1820–April 13, 1892; House (Terr. Del.) June 23, 1876–79.

FERGUSON, Fenner (Nebr.) April 25, 1814–Oct. 11, 1859; House (Terr. Del.) 1857–59.

FERGUSON, Phillip Colgan (Okla.) Aug. 15, 1903–Aug. 8, 1978; House 1935–41.

FERGUSSON, Harvey Butler (N.Mex.) Sept. 9, 1848–June 10, 1915; House (Terr. Del.) 1897–99, (Rep.) Jan. 8, 1912–15.

FERNANDEZ, Antonio Manuel (N.Mex.) Jan. 17, 1902–Nov. 7, 1956; House 1943–Nov. 7, 1956.

FERNANDEZ, Joachim Octave (La.) Aug. 14, 1896–Aug. 8, 1978; House 1931–41.

FERRARO, Geraldine Anne (N.Y.) Aug. 26, 1935–; House 1979–85.

FERRELL, Thomas Merrill (N.J.) June 20, 1844–Oct. 20, 1916; House 1883–85.

FERRIS, Charles Goadsby (N.Y.) about 1796–June 4, 1848; House Dec. 1, 1834–35 (Jacksonian), 1841–43.

FERRIS, Scott (Okla.) Nov. 3, 1877–June 8, 1945; House Nov. 16, 1907–21.

FERRIS, Woodbridge Nathan (Mich.) Jan. 6, 1853–March 23, 1928; Senate 1923–March 23, 1928; Gov. Jan. 1, 1913–Jan. 1, 1917.

FICKLIN, Orlando Bell (Ill.) Dec. 16, 1808–May 5, 1886; House 1843–49, 1851–53.

FIEDLER, William Henry Frederick (N.J.) Aug. 25, 1847–Jan. 1, 1919; House 1883–85.

FIELD, David Dudley (N.Y.) Feb. 13, 1805–April 13, 1894; House Jan. 11–March 3, 1877.

FIELD, Scott (Tex.) Jan. 26, 1847–Dec. 20, 1931; House 1903–07.

FIELDER, George Bragg (N.J.) July 24, 1842–Aug. 14, 1906; House 1893–95.

FIELDS, Cleo (La.) Nov. 22, 1962–; House 1993–.

FIELDS, William Jason (Ky.) Dec. 29, 1874–Oct. 21, 1954; House 1911–Dec. 11, 1923; Gov. Dec. 11, 1923–Dec. 13, 1927.

FIESINGER, William Louis (Ohio) Oct. 25, 1877–Sept. 11, 1953; House 1931–37.

FILNER, Robert (Calif.) Sept. 4, 1942–; House 1993–.

FINCK, William Edward (Ohio) Sept. 1, 1822–Jan. 25, 1901; House 1863–67, Dec. 7, 1874–75.

FINDLAY, John Van Lear (Md.) Dec. 21, 1839–April 19, 1907; House 1883–87.

FINE, John (N.Y.) Aug. 26, 1794–Jan. 4, 1867; House 1839–41.

FINE, Sydney Asher (N.Y.) Sept. 14, 1903–April 13, 1982; House 1951–Jan. 2, 1956.

FINGERHUT, Eric David (Ohio) May 6, 1959–; House 1993–1995.

FINLEY, David Edward (S.C.) Feb. 28, 1861–Jan. 26, 1917; House 1899–Jan. 26, 1917.

FINLEY, Ebenezer Byron (nephew of Stephen Ross Harris) (Ohio) July 31, 1833–Aug. 22, 1916; House 1877–81.

FINLEY, Jesse Johnson (Fla.) Nov. 18, 1812–Nov. 6, 1904; House April 19, 1876–77, Feb. 20–March 3, 1879, 1881–June 1, 1882.

FINNEGAN, Edward Rowan (Ill.) June 5, 1905–Feb. 2, 1971; House 1961–Dec. 6, 1964.

FISHBURNE, John Wood (cousin of Fontaine Maury Maverick) (Va.) March 8, 1868–June 24, 1937; House 1931–33.

FISHER, Hubert Frederick (Tenn.) Oct. 6, 1877–June 16, 1941; House 1917–31.

FISHER, Joseph Lyman (Va.) Jan. 11, 1914–Feb. 19, 1992; House 1975–81.

FISHER, Ovie Clark (Tex.) Nov. 22, 1903–; House 1943–Dec. 31, 1974.

FISHER, Spencer Oliver (Mich.) Feb. 3, 1843–June 1, 1919; House 1885–89.

FITCH, Ashbel Parmelee (N.Y.) Oct. 8, 1838–May 4, 1904; House 1887–Dec. 26, 1893 (1887–89 Republican).

FITCH, Graham Newell (grandfather of Edwin Denby) (Ind.) Dec. 5, 1809–Nov. 29, 1892; House 1849–53; Senate Feb. 4, 1857–61.

FITE, Samuel McClary (Tenn.) June 12, 1816–Oct. 23, 1875; House March 4–Oct. 23, 1875.

FITHIAN, Floyd James (Ind.) Nov. 3, 1928–; House 1975–83.

FITHIAN, George Washington (Ill.) July 4, 1854–Jan. 21, 1921; House 1889–95.

FITZGERALD, Frank Thomas (N.Y.) May 4, 1857–Nov. 25, 1907; House March 4–Nov. 4, 1889.

FITZGERALD, John Francis (grandfather of John Fitzgerald Kennedy, Robert Francis Kennedy and Edward Moore Kennedy, great-grandfather of Joseph Patrick Kennedy II) (Mass.) Feb. 11, 1863–Oct. 2, 1950; House 1895–1901, March 4–Oct. 23, 1919.

FITZGERALD, John Joseph (N.Y.) March 10, 1872–May 13, 1952; House 1899–Dec. 31, 1917.

FITZGERALD, Thomas (Mich.) April 10, 1796–March 25, 1855; Senate June 8, 1848–49.

FITZGERALD, William Joseph (Conn.) March 2, 1887–May 6, 1947; House 1937–39, 1941–43.

FITZGIBBONS, John (N.Y.) July 10, 1868–Aug. 4, 1941; House 1933–35.

FITZHENRY, Louis (Ill.) June 13, 1870–Nov. 18, 1935; House 1913–15.

FITZPATRICK, Benjamin (Ala.) June 30, 1802–Nov. 21, 1869; Senate Nov. 25, 1848–Nov. 30, 1849, Jan. 14, 1853–55, Nov. 26, 1855–Jan. 21, 1861; elected Pres. pro tempore Dec. 7, 1857, March 29, 1858, June 14, 1858, Jan. 25, 1859, March 9, 1859, Dec. 19, 1859, Feb. 20, 1860, June 26, 1860; Gov. Nov. 22, 1841–Dec. 10, 1845.

FITZPATRICK, James Martin (N.Y.) June 27, 1869–April 10, 1949; House 1927–45.

FITZPATRICK, Morgan Cassius (Tenn.) Oct. 29, 1868–June 25, 1908; House 1903–05.

FITZPATRICK, Thomas Young (Ky.) Sept. 20, 1850–Jan. 21, 1906; House 1897–1901.

FLAHERTY, Thomas Aloysius (Mass.) Dec. 21, 1898–April 27, 1965; House Dec. 14, 1937–43.

FLAKE, Floyd Harold (N.Y.) Jan. 30, 1945–; House 1987–.

FLANAGAN, De Witt Clinton (N.J.) Dec. 28, 1870–Jan. 15, 1946; House June 18, 1902–03.

FLANNAGAN, John William Jr. (Va.) Feb. 20, 1885–April 27, 1955; House 1931–49.

FLANNERY, John Harold (Pa.) April 19, 1898–June 3, 1961; House 1937–Jan. 3, 1942.

FLEGER, Anthony Alfred (Ohio) Oct. 21, 1900–July 16, 1963; House 1937–39.

FLEMING, William Bennett (Ga.) Oct. 29, 1803–Aug. 19, 1886; House Feb. 10–March 3, 1879.

FLEMING, William Henry (Ga.) Oct. 18, 1856–June 9, 1944; House 1897–1903.

FLETCHER, Duncan Upshaw (Fla.) Jan. 6, 1859–June 17, 1936; Senate 1909–June 17, 1936.

FLETCHER, Isaac (Vt.) Nov. 22, 1784–Oct. 19, 1842–; House 1837–41.

FLETCHER, Thomas Brooks (Ohio) Oct. 10, 1879–July 1, 1945; House 1925–29, 1933–39.

FLIPPO, Ronnie Gene (Ala.) Aug. 15, 1937–; House 1977–91.

FLOOD, Henry De La Warr (brother of Joel West Flood, uncle of Harry Flood Byrd) (Va.) Sept. 2, 1865–Dec. 8, 1921; House 1901–Dec. 8, 1921.

FLOOD, Joel West (brother of Henry De La Warr Flood, uncle of Harry Flood Byrd) (Va.) Aug. 2, 1894–April 27, 1964; House Nov. 8, 1932–33.

FLORENCE, Thomas Birch (Pa.) Jan. 26, 1812–July 3, 1875; House 1851–61.

FLORIO, James Joseph (N.J.) Aug. 29, 1937–; House 1975–Jan. 16, 1990; Gov. Jan. 16, 1990–Jan. 18, 1994.

FLOWER, Roswell Pettibone (N.Y.) Aug. 7, 1835–May 12, 1899; House Nov. 8, 1881–83, 1889–Sept. 16, 1891; Gov. Jan. 1, 1892–Jan. 1, 1895.

FLOWERS, Walter (Ala.) April 12, 1933–April 12, 1984; House 1969–79.

FLOYD, Charles Albert (N.Y.) 1791–Feb. 20, 1873; House 1841–43.

FLOYD, John Charles (Ark.) April 14, 1858–Nov. 4, 1930; House 1905–15.

FLOYD, John Gelston (grandson of William Floyd) (N.Y.) Feb. 5, 1806–Oct. 5, 1881; House 1839–43, 1851–53.

FLYNN, Gerald Thomas (Wis.) Oct. 7, 1910–; House 1959–61.

FLYNN, Joseph Vincent (N.Y.) Sept. 2, 1883–Feb. 6, 1940; House 1915–19.

FLYNT, John James Jr. (Ga.) Nov. 8, 1914–; House Nov. 2, 1954–79; Chrmn. House Standards of Official Conduct 1975–77.

FOGARTY, John Edward (R.I.) March 23, 1913–Jan. 10, 1967; House 1941–Dec. 7, 1944, Feb. 7, 1945–Jan. 10, 1967.

FOGLIETTA, Thomas Michael (Pa.) Dec. 3, 1928–; House 1981– (1981–83 Independent).

FOLEY, James Bradford (Ind.) Oct. 18, 1807–Dec. 5, 1886; House 1857–59.

FOLEY, John Robert (Md.) Oct. 16, 1917–; House 1959–61.

FOLEY, Thomas Stephen (Wash.) March 6, 1929–; House 1965–; Chrmn. House Agriculture 1975–81; House majority leader 1987–June 6, 1989; Speaker June 6, 1989–1995.

FOLGER, Alonzo Dillard (brother of John Hamlin Folger) (N.C.) July 9, 1888–April 30, 1941; House 1939–April 30, 1941.

FOLGER, John Hamlin (brother of Alonzo Dillard Folger) (N.C.) Dec. 18, 1880–July 19, 1963; House June 15, 1941–49.

FOLLETT, John Fassett (Ohio) Feb. 18, 1831–April 15, 1902; House 1883–85.

FOOTE, Henry Stuart (Miss.) Feb. 28, 1804–May 19, 1880; Senate 1847–Jan. 8, 1852; Gov. Jan. 10, 1852–Jan. 5, 1854.

FORAN, Martin Ambrose (Ohio) Nov. 11, 1844–June 28, 1921; House 1883–89.

FORAND, Aime Joseph (R.I.) May 23, 1895–Jan 18, 1972; House 1937–39, 1941–61.

FORD, Aaron Lane (Miss.) Dec. 21, 1903–July 8, 1983; House 1935–43.

FORD, George (Ind.) Jan. 11, 1846–Aug. 30, 1917; House 1885–87.

FORD, Harold Eugene (Tenn.) May 20, 1945–; House 1975–.

FORD, Melbourne Haddock (Mich.) June 30, 1849–April 20, 1891; House 1887–89, March 4–April 20, 1891.

FORD, Thomas Francis (Calif.) Feb. 18, 1873–Dec. 26, 1958; House 1933–45.

FORD, Wendell Hampton (Ky.) Sept. 8, 1924–; Senate Dec. 28, 1974–; Chrmn. Senate Rules and Administration 1987–1995; Gov. Dec. 7, 1971–Dec. 28, 1974.

FORD, William David (Mich.) Aug. 6, 1927–; House 1965–; Chrmn. House Post Office and Civil Service 1981–91; Chrmn. House Education and Labor 1991–1995.

FORD, William Donnison (N.Y.) 1779–Oct. 1, 1833; House 1819–21.

FORKER, Samuel Carr (N.J.) March 16, 1821–Feb. 10, 1900; House 1871–73.

FORMAN, William St. John (Ill.) Jan. 20, 1847–June 10, 1908; House 1889–95.

FORNANCE, Joseph (Pa.) Oct. 18, 1804–Nov. 24, 1852; House 1839–43.

FORNES, Charles Vincent (N.Y.) Jan. 22, 1844–May 22, 1929; House 1907–13.

FORNEY, William Henry (grandson of Peter Forney, nephew of Daniel Munroe Forney) (Ala.) Nov. 9, 1823–Jan. 16, 1894; House 1875–93.

FORRESTER, Elijah Lewis (Ga.) Aug. 16, 1896–March 19, 1970; House 1951–65.

FOSS, Eugene Noble (brother of George Edmund Foss) (Mass.) Sept. 24, 1858–Sept. 13, 1939; House March 22, 1910–Jan. 4, 1911; Gov. Jan. 5, 1911–Jan. 8, 1914.

FOSTER, George Peter (Ill.) April 3, 1858–Nov. 11, 1928; House 1899–1905.

FOSTER, Henry Allen (N.Y.) May 7, 1800–May 11, 1889; House 1837–39; Senate Nov. 30, 1844–Jan. 27, 1845.

FOSTER, Henry Donnel (cousin of John Cabell Breckinridge) (Pa.) Dec. 19, 1808–Oct. 16, 1880; House 1843–47, 1871–73.

FOSTER, Martin David (Ill.) Sept. 3, 1861–Oct. 20, 1919; House 1907–19.

FOSTER, Murphy James (cousin of Jared Young Sanders) (La.) Jan. 12, 1849–June 12, 1921; Senate 1901–13; Gov. May 16, 1892–May 21, 1900 (Anti-Lottery Democrat).

FOUKE, Philip Bond (Ill.) Jan. 23, 1818–Oct. 3, 1876; House 1859–63.

FOULKES, George Ernest (Mich.) Dec. 25, 1878–Dec. 13, 1960; House 1933–35.

FOUNTAIN, Lawrence H. (N.C.) April 23, 1913–; House 1953–83.

FOWLER, Hiram Robert (Ill.) Feb. 7, 1851–Jan. 5, 1926; House 1911–15.

FOWLER, Samuel (N.J.) March 22, 1851–March 17, 1919; House 1889–93.

FOWLER, Wyche Jr. (Ga.) Oct. 6, 1940–; House April 6, 1977–87; Senate 1987–93.

FOX, Andrew Fuller (Miss.) April 26, 1849–Aug. 29, 1926; House 1897–1903.

FOX, John (N.Y.) June 30, 1835–Jan. 17, 1914; House 1867–71.

FRANCIS, William Bates (Ohio) Oct. 25, 1860–Dec. 5, 1954; House 1911–15.

FRANK, Barney (Mass.) March 31, 1940–; House 1981–.

FRANKLIN, Benjamin Joseph (Mo.) March 1839–May 18, 1898; House 1875–79; Gov. (Ariz. Terr.) April 18, 1896–July 29, 1897.

FRAZIER, James Beriah (father of James Beriah Frazier Jr.) (Tenn.) Oct. 18, 1856–March 28, 1937; Senate March 21, 1905–11; Gov. Jan. 19, 1903–March 21, 1905.

FRAZIER, James Beriah Jr. (son of James Beriah Frazier) (Tenn.) June 23, 1890–Oct. 30, 1978; House 1949–63.

FREAR, Joseph Allen Jr. (Del.) March 7, 1903–Jan. 15, 1993; Senate 1949–61.

FREDERICK, Benjamin Todd (Iowa) Oct. 5, 1834–Nov. 3, 1903; House 1885–87.

FREMONT, John Charles (son-in-law of Thomas Hart Benton) (Calif.) Jan. 21, 1813–July 13, 1890; Senate Sept. 9, 1850–51; Gov. (Ariz. Terr.) 1878–81.

FRENCH, Carlos (Conn.) Aug. 6, 1835–April 14, 1903; House 1887–89.

FRENCH, Richard (Ky.) June 20, 1792–May 1, 1854; House 1835–37 (Jacksonian), 1843–45, 1847–49.

FREY, Oliver Walter (Pa.) Sept. 7, 1887–Aug. 26, 1939; House Nov. 7, 1933–39.

FRIEDEL, Samuel Nathaniel (Md.) April 18, 1898–March 21, 1979; House 1953–71; Chrmn. House Administration 1968–71.

FRIES, Frank William (Ill.) May 1, 1893–July 17, 1980; House 1937–41.

FRIES, George (Ohio) 1799–Nov. 13, 1866; House 1845–49.

FROST, Jonas Martin (Tex.) Jan. 1, 1942–; House 1979–.

FROST, Richard Graham (Mo.) Dec. 29, 1851–Feb. 1, 1900; House 1879–March 2, 1883.

FRY, Jacob Jr. (Pa.) June 10, 1802–Nov. 28, 1866; House 1835–39 (1835–37 Jacksonian).

FUGATE, Thomas Bacon (Va.) April 10, 1899–Sept. 22, 1980; House 1949–53.

FULBRIGHT, James Franklin (Mo.) Jan. 24, 1877–April 5, 1948; House 1923–25, 1927–29, 1931–33.

FULBRIGHT, James William (Ark.) April 9, 1905–; House 1943–45; Senate 1945–Dec. 31, 1974; Chrmn. Senate Banking and Currency 1955–59; Chrmn. Senate Foreign Relations 1959–74.

FULKERSON, Abram (Va.) May 13, 1834–Dec. 17, 1902; House 1881–83 (elected as a Readjuster Democrat).

FULLER, Benoni Stinson (Ind.) Nov. 13, 1825–April 14, 1903; House 1875–79.

FULLER, Claude Albert (Ark.) Jan. 20, 1876–Jan. 8, 1968; House 1929–39.

FULLER, George (Pa.) Nov. 7, 1802–Nov. 24, 1888; House Dec. 2, 1844–45.

FULLER, Thomas James Duncan (Maine) March 17, 1808–Feb. 13, 1876; House 1849–57.

FULMER, Hampton Pitts (husband of Willa Lybrand Fulmer) (S.C.) June 23, 1875–Oct. 19, 1944; House 1921–Oct. 19, 1944.

FULMER, Willa Lybrand (widow of Hampton Pitts Fulmer) (S.C.) Feb. 3, 1884–May 13, 1968; House Nov. 7, 1944–45.

FULTON, Elmer Lincoln (brother of Charles William Fulton) (Okla.) April 22, 1865–Oct. 4, 1939; House Nov. 16, 1907–09.

FULTON, Richard Harmon (Tenn.) Jan. 27, 1927–; House 1963–Aug. 14, 1975.

FULTON, William Savin (Ark.) June 2, 1795–Aug. 15, 1844; Senate Sept. 18, 1836–Aug. 15, 1844; Gov. (Ark. Terr.) 1835–36.

FUQUA, Don (Fla.) Aug. 20, 1933–; House 1963–87; Chrmn. House Science and Technology 1979–87.

FURCOLO, Foster (Mass.) July 29, 1911–; House 1949–Sept. 30, 1952; Gov. Jan. 3, 1957–Jan. 5, 1961.

FURLONG, Robert Grant (Pa.) Jan. 4, 1886–March 19, 1973; House 1943–45.

FURSE, Elizabeth (Oreg.) Oct. 13, 1936–; House 1993–.

FUSTER, Jaime B. (P.R.) Jan. 12, 1941–; House (Res. Comm.) 1985–March 3, 1992.

FYAN, Robert Washington (Mo.) March 11, 1835–July 28, 1896; House 1883–85, 1891–95.

GAINES, John Wesley (Tenn.) Aug. 24, 1860–July 4, 1926; House 1897–1909.

GALBRAITH, John (Pa.) Aug. 2, 1794–June 15, 1860; House 1833–37 (Jacksonian), 1839–41.

GALIFIANAKIS, Nick (N.C.) July 22, 1928–; House 1967–73.

GALLAGHER, Cornelius Edward (N.J.) March 2, 1921–; House 1959–73.

GALLAGHER, Thomas (Ill.) July 6, 1850–Feb. 24, 1930; House 1909–21.

GALLAGHER, William James (Minn.) May 13, 1875–Aug. 13, 1946; House 1945–Aug. 13, 1946.

GALLEGOS, José Manuel (N.Mex.) (Oct. 30, 1815–April 21, 1875; House (Terr. Del.) 1853–July 23, 1856, 1871–73.

GALLIVAN, James Ambrose (Mass.) Oct. 22, 1866–April 3, 1928; House April 7, 1914–April 3, 1928.

GALLUP, Albert (N.Y.) Jan. 30, 1796–Nov. 5, 1851; House 1837–39.

GAMBLE, James (Pa.) Jan. 28, 1809–Feb. 22, 1883; House 1851–55.

GAMBRELL, David Henry (Ga.) Dec. 20, 1929–; Senate Feb. 1, 1971–Nov. 7, 1972.

GAMBRILL, Stephen Warfield (Md.) Oct. 2, 1873–Dec. 19, 1938; House Nov. 4, 1924–Dec. 19, 1938.

GAMMAGE, Robert Alton (Tex.) March 13, 1938–; House 1977–79.

GANDY, Harry Luther (S.Dak.) Aug. 13, 1881–Aug. 15, 1957; House 1915–21.

GANLY, James Vincent (N.Y.) Sept. 13, 1878–Sept. 7, 1923; House 1919–21, March 4–Sept. 7, 1923.

GANSON, John (N.Y.) Jan. 1, 1818–Sept. 28, 1874; House 1863–65.

GANTZ, Martin Kissinger (Ohio) Jan. 28, 1862–Feb. 10, 1916; House 1891–93.

GARBER, Harvey Cable (Ohio) July 6, 1866–March 23, 1938; House 1903–07.

GARCIA, Robert (N.Y.) Jan. 9, 1933–; House Feb. 21, 1978–Jan. 7, 1990 (in Feb. 21, 1978, special election, registered as a Democrat but elected as a Republican-Liberal).

GARD, Warren (Ohio) July 2, 1873–Nov. 1, 1929; House 1913–21.

GARDNER, Edward Joseph (Ohio) Aug. 7, 1898–Dec. 7, 1950; House 1945–47.

GARDNER, Frank (Ind.) May 8, 1872–Feb. 1, 1937; House 1923–29.

GARDNER, Obadiah (Maine) Sept. 13, 1852–July 24, 1938; Senate Sept. 23, 1911–13.

GARLAND, Augustus Hill (Ark.) June 11, 1832–Jan. 26, 1899; Senate 1877–March 6, 1885; Gov. Nov. 12, 1874–Jan. 11, 1877; Atty. General March 6, 1885–March 5, 1889.

GARMATZ, Edward Alexander (Md.) Feb. 7, 1903–July 22, 1966; House July 15, 1947–73; Chrmn. House Merchant Marine and Fisheries 1966–73.

GARNER, John Nance (Tex.) Nov. 22, 1868–Nov. 7, 1967; House 1903–33; House minority leader 1929–31; Speaker Dec. 7, 1931–33; Vice President 1933–Jan. 20, 1941.

GARNETT, Muscoe Russell Hunter (grandson of James Mercer Garnett) (Va.) July 25, 1821–Feb. 14, 1864; House Dec. 1, 1856–61.

GARRETT, Abraham Ellison (Tenn.) March 6, 1830–Feb. 14, 1907; House 1871–73.

GARRETT, Clyde Leonard (Tex.) Dec. 16, 1885–Dec. 18, 1959; House 1937–41.

GARRETT, Daniel Edward (Tex.) April 28, 1869–Dec. 13, 1932; House 1913–15, 1917–19, 1921–Dec. 13, 1932.

GARRETT, Finis James (Tenn.) Aug. 26, 1875–May 25, 1956; House 1905–29; House minority leader 1923–29.

GARRISON, George Tankard (Va.) Jan. 14, 1835–Nov. 14, 1889; House 1881–83, March 20, 1884–85.

GARTH, William Willis (Ala.) Oct. 28, 1828–Feb. 25, 1912; House 1877–79.

GARTRELL, Lucius Jeremiah (uncle of Choice Boswell Randell) (Ga.) Jan. 7, 1821–April 7, 1891; House 1857–Jan. 23, 1861.

GARVIN, William Swan (Pa.) July 25, 1806–Feb. 20, 1883; House 1845–47.

GARY, Frank Boyd (S.C.) March 9, 1860–Dec. 7, 1922; Senate March 6, 1908–09.

GARY, Julian Vaughan (Va.) Feb. 25, 1892–Sept. 6, 1973; House March 6, 1945–65.

GASQUE, Allard Henry (husband of Elizabeth "Bessie" Hawley Gasque) (S.C.) March 8, 1873–June 17, 1938; House 1923–June 17, 1938.

GASQUE, Elizabeth "Bessie" Hawley (widow of Allard Henry Gasque) (Mrs. A.J. Van Exem) (S.C.) Feb. 26, 1896–; House Sept. 13, 1938–39 (Congress was not in session between election and expiration of term).

GASSAWAY, Percy Lee (Okla.) Aug. 30, 1885–May 15, 1937; House 1935–37.

GASTON, Athelston (Pa.) April 24, 1838–Sept. 23, 1907; House 1899–1901.

GATHINGS, Ezekiel Candler (Ark.) Nov. 10, 1903–May 2, 1979; House 1939–69.

GAUSE, Lucien Coatsworth (Ark.) Dec. 25, 1836–Nov. 5, 1880; House 1875–79.

GAVAGAN, Joseph Andrew (N.Y.) Aug. 20, 1892–Oct. 18, 1968; House Nov. 5, 1929–Dec. 30, 1943.

GAY, Edward James (grandfather of Edward James Gay, below) (La.) Feb. 3, 1816–May 30, 1889; House 1885–May 30, 1889.

GAY, Edward James (grandson of Edward James Gay, above) (La.) May 5, 1878–Dec. 1, 1952; Senate Nov. 6, 1918–21.

GAYDOS, Joseph Matthew (Pa.) July 3, 1926–; House Nov. 5, 1968–93.

GAYLE, June Ward (Ky.) Feb. 22, 1865–Aug. 5, 1942; House Jan. 15, 1900–01.

GEARIN, John McDermeid (Oreg.) Aug. 15, 1851–Nov. 12, 1930; Senate Dec. 13, 1905–Jan. 23, 1907.

GEARY, Thomas J. (Calif.) Jan. 18, 1854–July 6, 1929; House Dec. 9, 1890–95.

GEDDES, George Washington (Ohio) July 16, 1824–Nov. 9, 1892; House 1879–87.

GEELAN, James Patrick (Conn.) Aug. 11, 1901–Aug. 10, 1982; House 1945–47.

GEISSENHAINER, Jacob Augustus (N.J.) Aug. 28, 1839–July 20, 1917; House 1889–95.

GEJDENSON, Samuel (Conn.) May 20, 1948–; House 1981–.

GENTRY, Brady Preston (Tex.) March 25, 1896–Nov. 9, 1966; House 1953–57.

GEORGE, Henry Jr. (N.Y.) Nov. 3, 1862–Nov. 14, 1916; House 1911–15.

GEORGE, James Zachariah (Miss.) Oct. 20, 1826–Aug. 14, 1897; Senate 1881–Aug. 14, 1897.

GEORGE, Newell Adolphus (Kans.) Sypt. 24, 1904–; House 1959–61.

GEORGE, Walter Franklin (Ga.) Jan. 29, 1878–Aug. 4, 1957; Senate Nov. 22, 1922–57; Chrmn. Senate Finance 1949–53; elected Pres. pro tempore Jan. 5, 1955; Chrmn. Senate Foreign Relations 1955–57.

GEPHARDT, Richard Andrew (Mo.) Jan. 31, 1941–; House 1977–; House majority leader June 14, 1989–1995; House minority leader 1995–.

GERAN, Elmer Hendrickson (N.J.) Oct. 24, 1875–Jan. 12, 1954; House 1923–25.

GEREN, Preston M. "Pete" (Tex.) Jan. 29, 1952–; House Sept. 20, 1989–.

GERRY, Elbridge (Maine) Dec. 6, 1813–April 10, 1886; House 1849–51.

GERRY, James (Pa.) Aug. 14, 1796–July 19, 1873; House 1839–43.

GERRY, Peter Goelet (great-grandson of Elbridge Gerry) (R.I.) Sept. 18, 1879–Oct. 31, 1957; House 1913–15; Senate 1917–29, 1935–47.

GETTYS, Thomas Smithwick (S.C.) June 19, 1912–; House Nov. 3, 1964–Dec. 31, 1974.

GETZ, James Lawrence (Pa.) Sept. 14, 1821–Dec. 25, 1891; House 1867–73.

GEYER, Lee Edward (Calif.) Sept. 9, 1888–Oct. 11, 1941; House 1939–Oct. 11, 1941.

GHOLSON, Samuel Jameson (Miss.) May 19, 1808–Oct. 16, 1883; House Dec. 1, 1836–37 (Jacksonian), July 18, 1837–Feb. 5, 1838.

GIAIMO, Robert Nicholas (Conn.) Oct. 15, 1919–; House 1959–81; Chrmn. House Budget 1977–81.

GIBBONS, Sam Melville (Fla.) Jan. 20, 1920–; House 1963–.

GIBBS, Florence Reville (widow of Willis Benjamin Gibbs) (Ga.) April 4, 1890–Aug. 19, 1964; House Oct. 1, 1940–41.

GIBBS, Willis Benjamin (husband of Florence Reville Gibbs) (Ga.) April 15, 1889–Aug. 7, 1940; House 1939–Aug. 7, 1940.

GIBSON, Charles Hopper (cousin of Henry Richard Gibson) (Md.) Jan. 19, 1842–March 31, 1900; House 1885–91; Senate Nov. 19, 1891–97.

GIBSON, Eustace (W.Va.) Oct. 4, 1842–Dec. 10, 1900; House 1883–87.

GIBSON, John Strickland (Ga.) Jan. 3, 1893–Oct. 19, 1960; House 1941–47.

GIBSON, Paris (Mont.) July 1, 1830–Dec. 16, 1920; Senate March 7, 1901–05.

GIBSON, Randall Lee (La.) Sept. 10, 1832–Dec. 15, 1892; House 1875–83; Senate 1883–Dec. 15, 1892.

GIDDINGS, De Witt Clinton (Tex.) July 18, 1827–Aug. 19, 1903; House May 13, 1872–75, 1877–79.

GIDDINGS, Napoleon Bonaparte (Nebr.) Jan. 2, 1816–Aug. 3, 1897; House (Terr. Del.) Jan. 5–March 3, 1855.

GILBERT, Edward (Calif.) about 1819–Aug. 2, 1852; House Sept. 11, 1850–51.

GILBERT, George Gilmore (father of Ralph Waldo Emmerson Gilbert) (Ky.) Dec. 24, 1849–Nov. 9, 1909; House 1899–1907.

GILBERT, Jacob H. (N.Y.) June 17, 1920–Feb. 27, 1981; House March 8, 1960–1971.

GILBERT, Ralph Waldo Emerson (son of George Gilmore Gilbert) (Ky.) Jan. 17, 1882–July 30, 1939; House 1921–29, 1931–33.

GILDEA, James Hilary (Pa.) Oct. 21, 1890–June 5, 1988; House 1935–39.

GILES, William Fell (Md.) April 8, 1807–March 21, 1879; House 1845–47.

GILL, John Jr. (Md.) June 9, 1850–Jan. 27, 1918; House 1905–11.

GILL, Michael Joseph (Mo.) Dec. 5, 1864–Nov. 1, 1918; House 1909–11, Aug. 12, 1912–13.

GILL, Patrick Francis (Mo.) Aug. 15, 1868–May 21, 1923; House 1909–11, Aug. 12, 1912–13.

GILL, Thomas Ponce (Hawaii) April 21, 1922–; House 1963–65.

GILLEN, Courtland Craig (Ind.) July 3, 1880–Sept. 1, 1954; House 1931–33.

GILLESPIE, Eugene Pierce (Pa.) Sept. 24, 1852–Dec. 16, 1899; House 1891–93.

GILLESPIE, James Frank (Ill.) April 18, 1869–Nov. 26, 1954; House 1933–35.

GILLESPIE, Oscar William (Tex.) June 20, 1858–Aug. 23, 1927; House 1903–11.

GILLET, Ransom Hooker (N.Y.) Jan. 27, 1800–Oct. 24, 1876; House 1833–37.

GILLETTE, Guy Mark (Iowa) Feb. 3, 1879–March 3, 1973; House 1933–Nov. 3, 1936; Senate Nov. 5, 1936–45, 1949–55.

GILLIGAN, John Joyce (Ohio) March 22, 1921–; House 1965–67; Gov. Jan. 11, 1971–Jan. 13, 1975.

GILLIS, James Lisle (Pa.) Oct. 2, 1792–July 8, 1881; House 1857–59.

GILMER, Thomas Walker (Va.) April 6, 1802–Feb. 28, 1844; House 1841–Feb. 16, 1844 (1841–43 Whig); Gov. March 31, 1840–March 1, 1841 (Whig); Secy. of the Navy Feb. 19–Feb. 28, 1844.

GILMER, William Franklin "Dixie" (Okla.) June 7, 1901–June 9, 1954; House 1949–51.

GILMORE, Alfred (Pa.) June 9, 1812–June 29, 1890; House 1849–53.

GILMORE, Edward (Mass.) Jan. 4, 1867–April 10, 1924; House 1913–15.

GILMORE, Samuel Louis (La.) July 30, 1859–July 18, 1910; House March 30, 1909–July 18, 1910.

GINGERY, Don (Pa.) Feb. 19, 1884–Oct. 15, 1961; House 1935–39.

GINN, Ronald Bryan (Ga.) May 31, 1934–; House 1973–83.

GITTINS, Robert Henry (N.Y.) Dec. 14, 1869–Dec. 25, 1957; House 1913–15.

GLASCOCK, John Raglan (Calif.) Aug. 25, 1845–Nov. 10, 1913; House 1883–85.

GLASCOCK, Thomas (Ga.) Oct. 21, 1790–May 19, 1841; House Oct. 5, 1835–39 (Oct. 5, 1835–37 Jacksonian).

GLASS, Carter (Va.) Jan. 4, 1858–May 28, 1946; House Nov. 5, 1902–Dec. 16, 1918; Senate Feb. 2, 1920–May 28, 1945; elected Pres. pro tempore July 10, 1941, Jan. 5, 1943; Secy of the Treasury Dec. 16, 1918–Feb. 1, 1920.

GLASS, Presley Thornton (Tenn.) Oct. 18, 1824–Oct. 9, 1902; House 1885–89.

GLATFELTER, Samuel Feiser (Pa.) April 7, 1858–April 23, 1927; House 1923–25.

GLENN, John Herschel Jr. (Ohio) July 18, 1921–; Senate Dec. 24, 1974–; Chrmn. Senate Governmental Affairs 1987–1995.

GLICKMAN, Daniel Robert (Kans.) Nov. 24, 1944–; House 1977–1995; Chrmn. Select House Committee on Intelligence 1993–1995.

GLOSSBRENNER, Adam John (Pa.) Aug. 31, 1810–March 1, 1889; House 1865–69.

GLOVER, David Delano (Ark.) Jan. 18, 1868–April 5, 1952; House 1929–35.

GLOVER, John Milton (nephew of John Montgomery Glover) (Mo.) June 23, 1852–Oct. 20, 1929; House 1885–89.

GLOVER, John Montgomery (uncle of John Milton Glover) (Mo.) Sept. 4, 1822–Nov. 15, 1891; House 1873–79.

GLYNN, Martin Henry (N.Y.) Sept. 27, 1871–Dec. 14, 1924; House 1899–1901; Gov. Oct. 17, 1913–Jan. 1, 1915.

GODWIN, Hannibal Lafayette (N.C.) Nov. 3, 1873–June 9, 1929; House 1907–21.

GOEKE, John Henry (Ohio) Oct. 28, 1869–March 25, 1930; House 1911–15.

GOLDFOGLE, Henry Mayer (N.Y.) May 23, 1856–June 1, 1929; House 1901–15, 1919–21.

GOLDSBOROUGH, Thomas Alan (Md.) Sept. 16, 1877–June 16, 1951; House 1921–April 5, 1939.

GOLDTHWAITE, George Thomas (Ala.) Dec. 10, 1809–March 16, 1879; Senate 1871–77.

GOLDZIER, Julius (Ill.) Jan. 20, 1854–Jan. 20, 1925; House 1893–95.

GOLLADAY, Edward Isaac (brother of Jacob Shall Golladay) (Tenn.) Sept. 9, 1830–July 11, 1897; House 1871–73.

GOLLADAY, Jacob Shall (brother of Edward Isaac Golladay) (Ky.) Jan. 19, 1819–May 20, 1887; House Dec. 5, 1867–Feb. 28, 1870.

GONZALEZ, Henry Barbosa (Tex.) May 3, 1916–; House Nov. 4, 1961–; Chrmn. House Banking, Housing, and Urban Affairs 1989–1995.

GOOCH, Daniel Linn (Ky.) Oct. 28, 1853–April 12, 1913; House 1901–05.

GOODE, John Jr. (Va.) May 27, 1829–July 14, 1909; House 1875–81.

GOODE, William Osborne (Va.) Sept. 16, 1798–July 3, 1859; House 1841–43, 1853–July 3, 1859.

GOODIN, John Randolph (Kans.) Dec. 14, 1836–Dec. 18, 1885; House 1875–77.

GOODNIGHT, Isaac Herschel (Ky.) Jan. 31, 1849–July 24, 1901; House 1889–95.

GOODWIN, William Shields (Ark.) May 2, 1866–Aug. 9, 1937; House 1911–21.

GOODYEAR, Charles (N.Y.) April 26, 1804–April 9, 1876; House 1845–47, 1865–67.

GORDON, Barton Jennings (Tenn.) Jan. 24, 1949–; House 1985–.

GORDON, George Washington (Tenn.) Oct. 5, 1836–Aug. 9, 1911; House 1907–Aug. 9, 1911.

GORDON, John Brown (Ga.) Feb. 6, 1832–Jan. 9, 1904; Senate 1873–May 26, 1880, 1891–97; Gov. Nov. 9, 1886–Nov. 8, 1890.

GORDON, Robert Bryarly (Ohio) Aug. 6, 1855–Jan. 3, 1923; House 1899–1903.

GORDON, Samuel (N.Y.) April 28, 1802–Oct. 28, 1873; House 1841–43, 1845–47.

GORDON, Thomas Sylvy (Ill.) Dec. 17, 1893–Jan. 22, 1959; House 1943–59; Chrmn. House Foreign Affairs 1957–59.

GORDON, William (Ohio) Dec. 15, 1862–Jan. 16, 1942; House 1913–19.

GORE, Albert Arnold (father of Albert Arnold Gore, Jr.) (Tenn.) Dec. 26, 1907–; House 1939–Dec. 4, 1944, 1945–53; Senate 1953–71.

GORE, Albert Arnold Jr. (son of Albert Arnold Gore) (Tenn.) March 31, 1948–; House 1977–85; Senate 1985–Jan. 2, 1993; Vice President 1993–.

GORE, Thomas Pryor (Okla.) Dec. 10, 1870–March 16, 1949; Senate Dec. 11, 1907–21, 1931–37.

GORMAN, Arthur Pue (Md.) March 11, 1839–June 4, 1906; Senate 1881–99, 1903–June 4, 1906.

GORMAN, George Edmund (Ill.) April 13, 1873–Jan. 13, 1935; House 1913–15.

GORMAN, James Sedgwick (Mich.) Dec. 28, 1850–May 27, 1923; House 1891–95.

GORMAN, Willis Arnold (Ind.) Jan. 12, 1816–May 20, 1876; House 1849–53; Gov. (Minn. Terr.) 1853–57.

GORSKI, Chester Charles (N.Y.) June 22, 1906–April 25, 1975; House 1949–51.

GORSKI, Martin (Ill.) Oct. 30, 1886–Dec. 4, 1949; House 1943–Dec. 4, 1949.

GOSSETT, Charles Clinton (Idaho) Sept. 2, 1888–Sept. 20, 1974; Senate Nov. 17, 1945–47; Gov. Jan. 1–Nov. 17, 1945.

GOSSETT, Ed Lee (Tex.) Jan. 27, 1902–; House 1939–July 31, 1951.

GOULD, Samuel Wadsworth (Maine) Jan. 1, 1852–Dec. 19, 1935; House 1911–13.

GOULDEN, Joseph Aloysius (N.Y.) Aug. 1, 1844–May 3, 1915; House 1903–11, 1913–May 3, 1915.

GRABOWSKI, Bernard Francis (Conn.) June 11, 1923–; House 1963–67.

GRADY, Benjamin Franklin (N.C.) Oct. 10, 1831–March 6, 1914; House 1891–95.

GRAHAM, Daniel Robert "Bob" (Fla.) Nov. 9, 1936–; Senate 1987–; Gov. Jan. 2, 1979–Jan. 3, 1987.

GRAHAM, James McMahon (Ill.) April 14, 1852–Oct. 23, 1945; House 1909–15.

GRAHAM, John Hugh (N.Y.) April 1, 1835–July 11, 1895; House 1893–95.

GRANAHAN, Kathryn Elizabeth (widow of William Thomas Granahan) (Pa.) Dec. 7, 1906–July 10, 1979; House Nov. 6, 1956–63.

GRANAHAN, William Thomas (husband of Kathryn Elizabeth Granahan) (Pa.) July 26, 1895–May 25, 1956; House 1945–47, 1949–May 25, 1956.

GRANFIELD, William Joseph (Mass.) Dec. 18, 1889–May 28, 1959; House Feb. 11, 1930–37.

GRANGER, Daniel Larned Davis (R.I.) May 30, 1852–Feb. 14, 1909; House 1903–Feb. 14, 1909.

GRANGER, Miles Tobey (Conn.) Aug. 12, 1817–Oct. 21, 1895; House 1887–89.

GRANGER, Walter Keil (Utah) Oct. 11, 1888–April 21, 1978; House 1941–53.

GRANT, Abraham Phineas (N.Y.) April 5, 1804–Dec. 11, 1871; House 1837–39.

GRANT, George McInvale (Ala.) July 11, 1897–Nov. 4, 1982; House June 14, 1938–65.

GRANTLAND, Seaton (Ga.) June 8, 1782–Oct. 18, 1864; House 1835–39 (1835–37 Jacksonian).

GRASSO, Ella Tambussi (Conn.) May 10, 1919–Feb. 5, 1981; House 1971–75; Gov. Jan. 8, 1975–Dec. 31, 1980.

GRAVEL, Maurice Robert "Mike" (Alaska) May 13, 1930–; Senate 1969–Jan. 2, 1981.

GRAVES, Alexander (Mo.) Aug. 25, 1844–Dec. 23, 1916; House 1883–85.

GRAVES, Dixie Bibb (wife of Gov. David Bibb Graves of Ala.) (Ala.) July 26, 1882–Jan. 21, 1965; Senate Aug. 20, 1937–Jan. 10, 1938.

GRAY, Finly Hutchinson (Ind.) July 21, 1863–May 8, 1947; House 1911–17, 1933–39.

GRAY, George (Del.) May 4, 1840–Aug. 7, 1925; Senate March 18, 1885–99.

GRAY, Hiram (N.Y.) July 10, 1801–May 6, 1890; House 1837–39.

GRAY, Joseph Anthony (Pa.) Feb. 25, 1884–May 8, 1966; House 1935–39.

GRAY, Kenneth James (Ill.) Nov. 14, 1924–; House 1955–Dec. 31, 1974, 1985–89.

GRAY, Oscar Lee (Ala.) July 2, 1865–Jan. 2, 1936; House 1915–19.

GRAY, William Herbert III (Pa.) Aug. 20, 1941–Sept. 11, 1991; House 1979–Sept. 11, 1991; Chrmn. House Budget 1985–89.

GREEN, Edith Starrett (Oreg.) Jan. 17, 1910–April 21, 1987; House 1955–Dec. 31, 1975.

GREEN, Frederick William (Ohio) Feb. 18, 1816–June 18, 1879; House 1851–55.

GREEN, Henry Dickinson (Pa.) May 3, 1857–Dec. 29, 1929; House Nov. 7, 1899–1903.

GREEN, James Stephen (Mo.) Feb. 28, 1817–Jan. 19, 1870; House 1847–51; Senate Jan. 12, 1857–61.

GREEN, Raymond Eugene "Gene" (Tex.) Oct. 17, 1947–; House 1993–.

GREEN, Robert Alexis (Fla.) Feb. 10, 1892–Feb. 9, 1973; House 1925–Nov. 25, 1944.

GREEN, Robert Stockton (N.J.) March 25, 1831–May 7, 1895; House 1885–Jan. 17, 1887; Gov. Jan. 18, 1887–Jan. 21, 1890.

GREEN, Theodore Francis (great-nephew of Samuel Greene Arnold, great-great-nephew of Tristam Burges, great-grandson of James Burrill Jr., great-great-grandson of Jonathan Arnold, great-great-nephew of Lemuel Hastings Arnold) (R.I.) Oct. 2, 1867–May 19, 1966; Senate 1937–61; Chrmn. Senate Rules and Administration 1955–57; Chrmn. Senate Foreign Relations 1957–59; Gov. Jan. 3, 1933–Jan. 5, 1937.

GREEN, Wharton Jackson (grandson of Jesse Wharton, cousin of Matt Whitaker Ransom) (N.C.) Feb. 28, 1831–Aug. 6, 1910; House 1883–87.

GREEN, William Joseph (son of William Joseph Green Jr.) (Pa.) June 24, 1938–; House April 28, 1964–77.

GREEN, William Joseph Jr. (father of William Joseph Green III) (Pa.) March 5, 1910–Dec. 21, 1963; House 1945–47, 1949–Dec. 21, 1963.

GREENE, George Woodward (N.Y.) July 4, 1831–July 21, 1895; House 1869–Feb. 17, 1870.

GREENLEAF, Halbert Stevens (N.Y.) April 12, 1827–Aug. 25, 1906; House 1883–85, 1891–93.

GREENWAY, Isabella Selmes (later Mrs. Harry Orland King) (Ariz.) March 22, 1886–Dec. 18, 1953; House Oct. 3, 1933–37.

GREENWOOD, Alfred Burton (Ark.) July 11, 1811–Oct. 4, 1889; House 1853–59.

GREENWOOD, Arthur Herbert (Ind.) Jan. 31, 1880–April 26, 1963; House 1923–39.

GREENWOOD, Ernest (N.Y.) Nov. 25, 1884–June 15, 1955; House 1951–53.

GREEVER, Paul Ranous (Wyo.) Sept. 28, 1891–Feb. 16, 1943; House 1935–39.

GREGG, Alexander White (Tex.) Jan. 31, 1855–April 30, 1919; House 1903–19.

GREGG, Curtis Hussey (Pa.) Aug. 9, 1865–Jan. 18, 1933; House 1911–13.

GREGG, James Madison (Ind.) June 26, 1806–June 16, 1869; House 1857–59.

GREGORY, Noble Jones (brother of William Voris Gregory) (Ky.) Aug. 30, 1897–Sept. 26, 1971; House 1937–59.

GREGORY, William Voris (brother of Noble Jones Gregory) (Ky.) Oct. 21, 1877–Oct. 10, 1936; House 1927–Oct. 10, 1936.

GREIGG, Stanley Lloyd (Iowa) May 7, 1931–; House 1965–67.

GRESHAM, Walter (Tex.) July 22, 1841–Nov. 6, 1920; House 1893–95.

GRIDER, George William (Tenn.) Oct. 1, 1912–; House 1965–67.

GRIDER, Henry (Ky.) July 16, 1796–Sept. 7, 1866; House 1843–47 (Whig), 1861–Sept. 7, 1866 (1861–65 Unionist).

GRIFFIN, Anthony Jerome (N.Y.) April 1, 1866–Jan. 13, 1935; House March 5, 1918–Jan. 13, 1935.

GRIFFIN, Charles Hudson (great-great-grandson of Isaac Griffin) (Miss.) May 9, 1926–Sept. 10, 1989; House March 12, 1968–73.

GRIFFIN, Daniel Joseph (N.Y.) March 26, 1880–Dec. 11, 1926; House 1913–Dec. 31, 1917.

GRIFFIN, John King (S.C.) Aug. 13, 1789–Aug. 1, 1841; House 1831–41 (1831–39 Nullifier).

GRIFFIN, Levi Thomas (Mich.) May 23, 1837–March 17, 1906; House Dec. 4, 1893–95.

GRIFFITH, Francis Marion (Ind.) Aug. 21, 1849–Feb. 8, 1927; House Dec. 6, 1897–1905.

GRIFFITH, John Keller (La.) Oct. 16, 1882–Sept. 25, 1942; House 1937–41.

GRIFFITH, Samuel (Pa.) Feb. 14, 1816–Oct. 1, 1893; House 1871–73.

GRIFFITHS, Martha Wright (Mich.) Jan. 29, 1912–; House 1955–Dec. 31, 1974.

GRIGGS, James Mathews (Ga.) March 29, 1861–Jan. 5, 1910; House 1897–Jan. 5, 1910.

GRIGSBY, Geoge Barnes (Alaska) Dec. 2, 1874–May 9, 1962; House (Terr. Del.) June 3, 1920–March 1, 1921.

GRIMES, Thomas Wingfield (Ga.) Dec. 18, 1844–Oct. 28, 1905; House 1887–91.

GRISWOLD, Glenn Hasenfratz (Ind.) Jan. 20, 1890–Dec. 5, 1940; House 1931–39.

GRISWOLD, John Ashley (N.Y.) Nov. 18, 1822–Feb. 22, 1902; House 1869–71.

GROESBECK, William Slocum (Ohio) July 24, 1815–July 7, 1897; House 1857–59.

GROOME, James Black (Md.) April 4, 1838–Oct. 5, 1893; Senate 1879–85; Gov. March 4, 1874–Jan. 12, 1876.

GROVER, Asa Porter (Ky.) Feb. 18, 1819–July 20, 1887; House 1867–69.

GROVER, La Fayette (Oreg.) Nov. 29, 1823–May 10, 1911; House Feb. 15–March 3, 1859; Senate 1877–83; Gov. Sept. 14, 1870–Feb. 1, 1877.

GROVER, Martin (N.Y.) Oct. 20, 1811–Aug. 23, 1875; House 1845–47.

GRUENING, Ernest (Alaska) Feb. 6, 1887–June 26, 1974; Senate 1959–69; Gov. (Alaska Terr.) 1939–53.

GRUNDY, Felix (Tenn.) Sept. 11, 1777–Dec. 19, 1840; House 1811–14 (Republican); Senate Oct. 19, 1829–July 4, 1838 (Jacksonian), Nov. 19, 1839–Dec. 19, 1840; Atty. Gen. Sept. 1–Dec. 1, 1838.

GUARINI, Frank Joseph Jr. (N.J.) Aug. 20, 1924–; House 1979–93.

GUDGER, James Madison Jr. (father of Katherine Gudger Langley, father-in-law of John Wesley Langley) (N.C.) Oct. 22, 1855–Feb. 29, 1920; House 1903–07, 1911–15.

GUDGER, Vonno Lamar Jr. (N.C.) April 30, 1919–; House 1977–81.

GUFFEY, Joseph F. (Pa.) Dec. 29, 1870–March 6, 1959; Senate 1935–47.

GUION, Walter (La.) April 3, 1849–Feb. 7, 1927; Senate April 22–Nov. 5, 1918.

GUNTER, Thomas Montague (Ark.) Sept. 18, 1826–Jan. 12, 1904; House June 16, 1874–83.

GUNTER, William Dawson Jr. (Fla.) July 16, 1934–; House 1973–75.

GUSTINE, Amos (Pa.) 1789–March 3, 1844; House May 4, 1841–43.

GUTHRIE, James (Ky.) Dec. 5, 1792–March 13, 1869; Senate 1865–Feb. 7, 1868; Secy. of the Treasury March 7, 1853–March 6, 1857.

GUTIERREZ, Luis Vincente (Ill.) Dec. 10, 1954–; House 1993–.

GWIN, William McKendree (Calif.) Oct. 9, 1805–Sept. 3, 1885; House 1841–43 (Miss.); Senate Sept. 9, 1850–55, Jan. 13, 1857–61.

HACKETT, Richard Nathaniel (N.C.) Dec. 4, 1866–Nov. 22, 1923; House 1907–09.

HACKETT, Thomas C. (Ga.) ?–Oct. 8, 1851; House 1849–51.

HACKNEY, Thomas (Mo.) Dec. 11, 1861–Dec. 24, 1946; House 1907–09.

HAGAN, George Elliott (Ga.) May 24, 1916–; House 1961–73.

HAGEN, Harlan Francis (Calif.) Oct. 8, 1914–; House 1953–67.

HAGER, John Sharpenstein (Calif.) March 12, 1818–March 19, 1890; Senate Dec. 23, 1873–75.

HAIGHT, Charles (N.J.) Jan. 4, 1838–Aug. 1, 1891; House 1867–71.

HAIGHT, Edward (N.Y.) March 26, 1817–Sept. 15, 1885; House 1861–63.

HAILEY, John (Idaho) Aug. 29, 1835–April 10, 1921; House (Terr. Del.) 1873–75, 1885–87.

HAINES, Charles Delemere (N.Y.) June 9, 1856–April 11, 1929; House 1893–95.

HAINES, Harry Luther (Pa.) Feb. 1, 1880–March 29, 1947; House 1931–39, 1941–43.

HALDEMAN, Richard Jacobs (Pa.) May 19, 1831–Oct. 1, 1886; House 1869–73.

HALE, John Blackwell (Mo.) Feb. 27, 1831–Feb. 1, 1905; House 1885–87.

HALEY, Elisha (Conn.) Jan. 21, 1776–Jan. 22, 1860; House 1835–39 (1835–37 Jacksonian).

HALEY, James Andrew (Fla.) Jan. 4, 1899–Aug. 6, 1981; House 1953–77; Chrmn. House Interior and Insular Affairs 1973–77.

HALL, Augustus (Iowa) April 29, 1814–Feb. 1, 1861; House 1855–57.

HALL, Benton Jay (Iowa) Jan. 13, 1835–Jan. 5, 1894; House 1885–87.

HALL, David McKee (N.C.) May 16, 1918–Jan. 29, 1960; House 1959–Jan. 29, 1960.

HALL, James Knox Polk (Pa.) Sept. 30, 1844–Jan. 5, 1915; House 1899–Nov. 29, 1902.

HALL, Katie Beatrice Green (Ind.) April 3, 1938–; House Nov. 2, 1982–85.

HALL, Lawrence Washington (Ohio) 1819–Jan. 18, 1863; House 1857–59.

HALL, Norman (Pa.) Nov. 17, 1829–Sept. 29, 1917; House 1887–89.

HALL, Osee Matson (Minn.) Sept. 10, 1847–Nov. 26, 1914; House 1891–95.

HALL, Ralph Moody (Tex.) May 3, 1923–; House 1981–.

HALL, Robert Samuel (Miss.) March 10, 1879–June 10, 1941; House 1929–33.

HALL, Sam Blakeley Jr. (Tex.) Jan. 11, 1924–April 10, 1994; House June 19, 1976–May 27, 1985.

HALL, Tim Lee (Ill.) June 11, 1925–; House 1975–77.

HALL, Tony Patrick (Ohio) Jan. 16, 1942–; House 1979–.

HALL, Uriel Sebree (son of William Augustus Hall, nephew of Willard Preble Hall) (Mo.) April 12, 1852–Dec. 30, 1932; House 1893–97.

HALL, Willard Preble (brother of William Augustus Hall, uncle of Uriel Sebree Hall) (Mo.) May 9, 1820–Nov. 3, 1882; House 1847–53; Gov. Jan. 31, 1864–Jan. 2, 1865 (Unionist).

HALL, William Augustus (father of Uriel Sebree Hall,

brother of Willard Preble Hall) (Mo.) Oct. 15, 1815–Dec. 15, 1888; House Jan. 20, 1862–65.

HALL, Wilton Earle (S.C.) March 11, 1901–Feb. 25, 1980; Senate Nov. 20, 1944–45.

HALLOCK, John Jr. (N.Y.) July 1783–Dec. 6, 1840; House 1825–29.

HALLOWELL, Edwin (Pa.) April 2, 1844–Sept. 13, 1916; House 1891–93.

HALSELL, John Edward (Ky.) Sept. 11, 1826–Dec. 26, 1899; House 1883–87.

HAMBLETON, Samuel (Md.) Jan. 8, 1812–Dec. 9, 1886; House 1869–73.

HAMBURG, Daniel Eugene (Calif.) Oct. 6, 1948–; House 1993–1995.

HAMER, Thomas Lyon (Ohio) July 1800–Dec. 2, 1846; House 1833–39 (1833–37 Jacksonian).

HAMILL, James Alphonsus (N.J.) March 30, 1877–Dec. 15, 1941; House 1907–21.

HAMILL, Patrick (Md.) April 28, 1817–Jan. 15, 1895; House 1869–71.

HAMILTON, Andrew Holman (Ind.) June 7, 1834–May 9, 1895; House 1875–79.

HAMILTON, Daniel Webster (Iowa) Dec. 20, 1861–Aug. 21, 1936; House 1907–09.

HAMILTON, Finley (Ky.) June 19, 1886–Jan. 10, 1940; House 1933–35.

HAMILTON, John M. (W.Va.) March 16, 1855–Dec. 27, 1916; House 1911–13.

HAMILTON, John Taylor (Iowa) Oct. 16, 1843–Jan. 25, 1925; House 1891–93.

HAMILTON, Lee Herbert (Ind.) April 20, 1931–; House 1965–; Chrmn. House Permanent Select Committee on Intelligence 1985–87; Chrmn. House Foreign Affairs 1993–1995.

HAMILTON, Norman Rond (Va.) Nov. 13, 1877–March 26, 1964; House 1937–39.

HAMILTON, Robert (N.J.) Dec. 9, 1809–March 14, 1878; House 1873–77.

HAMILTON, William Thomas (Md.) Sept. 8, 1820–Oct. 26, 1888; House 1849–55; Senate 1869–75; Gov. Jan. 14, 1880–Jan. 9, 1884.

HAMLIN, Courtney Walker (cousin of William Edward Barton) (Mo.) Oct. 27, 1858–Feb. 16, 1950; House 1903–05, 1907–19.

HAMLIN, Simon Moulton (Maine) Aug. 10, 1866–July 27, 1939; House 1935–37.

HAMMER, William Cicero (N.C.) March 24, 1865–Sept. 26, 1930; House 1921–Sept. 26, 1930.

HAMMETT, William Henry (Miss.) March 25, 1799–July 9, 1861; House 1843–45.

HAMMOND, Edward (Md.) March 17, 1812–Oct. 19, 1882; House 1849–53.

HAMMOND, James Henry (S.C.) Nov. 15, 1807–Nov. 13, 1864; House 1835–Feb. 26, 1836 (Nullifier); Senate Dec. 7, 1857–Nov. 11, 1860; Gov. Dec. 8, 1842–Dec. 7, 1844 (Democrat).

HAMMOND, Nathaniel Job (Ga.) Dec. 26, 1833–April 20, 1899; House 1879–87.

HAMMOND, Peter Francis (Ohio) June 30, 1887–April 2, 1971; House Nov. 3, 1936–37.

HAMMOND, Robert Hanna (Pa.) April 28, 1791–June 2, 1847; House 1837–41.

HAMMOND, Thomas (Ind.) Feb. 27, 1843–Sept. 21, 1909; House 1893–95.

HAMMOND, Winfield Scott (Minn.) Nov. 17, 1863–Dec. 30, 1915; House 1907–Jan. 6, 1915; Gov. Jan. 7–Dec. 30, 1915.

HAMMONS, David (Maine) May 12, 1808–Nov. 7, 1888; House 1847–49.

HAMPTON, Wade (S.C.) March 28, 1818–April 11, 1902; Senate 1879–91; Gov. Dec. 14, 1876–Feb. 26, 1879.

HANCE, Kent Ronald (Tex.) Nov. 14, 1942–; House 1979–85.

HANCOCK, Franklin Wills Jr. (N.C.) Nov. 1, 1894–Jan. 23, 1969; House Nov. 4, 1930–39.

HANCOCK, John (Tex.) Oct. 24, 1824–July 19, 1893; House 1871–77, 1883–85.

HAND, Augustus Cincinnatus (N.Y.) Sept. 4, 1803–March 8, 1878; House 1839–41.

HANDLEY, William Anderson (Ala.) Dec. 15, 1834–June 23, 1909; House 1871–73.

HANDY, Levin Irving (nephew of William Campbell Preston Breckenridge) (Del.) Dec. 24, 1861–Feb. 3, 1922; House 1897–99.

HANKS, James Millander (Ark.) Feb. 12, 1833–May 24, 1909; House 1871–73.

HANLEY, James Michael (N.Y.) July 19, 1920–; House 1965–81; Chrmn. House Post Office and Civil Service 1979–81.

HANNA, Richard Thomas (Calif.) June 9, 1914–; House 1963–Dec. 31, 1974.

HANNAFORD, Mark Warren (Calif.) Feb. 7, 1925–June 2, 1985; House 1975–79.

HANNEGAN, Edward Allen (Ind.) June 25, 1807–Feb. 25, 1859; House 1833–37; Senate 1843–49.

HANSEN, John Robert (Iowa) Aug. 24, 1901–Sept. 23, 1974; House 1965–67.

HANSEN, Julia Butler (Wash.) June 14, 1907–May 3, 1988; House Nov. 8, 1960–Dec. 31, 1974.

HARALSON, Hugh Anderson (Ga.) Nov. 13, 1805–Sept. 25, 1854; House 1843–51.

HARDEMAN, Thomas Jr. (Ga.) Jan. 12, 1825–March 6, 1891; House 1859–Jan. 23, 1861 (Opposition), 1883–85.

HARDENBERGH, Augustus Albert (N.J.) May 18, 1830–Oct. 5, 1889; House 1875–79, 1881–83.

HARDING, Aaron (Ky.) Feb. 20, 1805–Dec. 24, 1875; House 1861–67 (1861–65 (Unionist).

HARDING, Benjamin Franklin (Oreg.) Jan. 4, 1823–June 16, 1899; Senate Sept. 12, 1862–65.

HARDING, Ralph R. (Idaho) Sept. 9, 1929–; House 1961–65.

HARDWICK, Thomas William (Ga.) Dec. 9, 1872–Jan. 31, 1944; House 1903–Nov. 2, 1914; Senate Nov. 4, 1914–19; Gov. June 25, 1921–June 30, 1923.

HARDY, John (N.Y.) Sept. 19, 1835–Dec. 9, 1913; House Dec. 5, 1881–85.

HARDY, Porter Jr. (Va.) June 1, 1903–; House 1947–69.

HARDY, Rufus (Tex.) Dec. 16, 1855–March 13, 1943; House 1907–23.

HARE, Butler Black (father of James Butler Hare) (S.C.) Nov. 25, 1875–Dec. 30, 1967; House 1925–33, 1939–47.

HARE, Darius Dodge (Ohio) Jan. 9, 1843–Feb. 10, 1897; House 1891–95.

HARE, James Butler (son of Butler Black Hare) (S.C.) Sept. 4, 1918–July 16, 1966; House 1949–51.

HARE, Silas (Tex.) Nov. 13, 1827–Nov. 26, 1907; House 1887–91.

HARGIS, Denver David (Kans.) July 22, 1921–; House 1959–61.

HARKIN, Thomas Richard (Iowa) Nov. 19, 1939–; House 1975–85; Senate 1985–.

HARLAN, Andrew Jackson (cousin of Aaron Harlan) (Ind.) March 29, 1815–May 19, 1907; House 1849–51, 1853–55.

HARLAN, Byron Berry (Ohio) Oct. 22, 1886–Nov. 11, 1949; House 1931–39.

HARLESS, Richard Fielding (Ariz.) Aug. 6, 1905–Nov. 24, 1970; House 1943–49.

HARMAN, Jane (Calif.) June 28, 1945–; House 1993–.

HARMANSON, John Henry (La.) Jan. 15, 1803–Oct. 24, 1850; House 1845–Oct. 24, 1850.

HARMON, Randall S. (Ind.) July 19, 1903–Aug. 18, 1982; House 1959–61.

HARPER, Francis Jacob (Pa.) March 5, 1800–March 18, 1837; House March 4–18, 1837.

HARPER, James Clarence (N.C.) Dec. 6, 1819–Jan. 8, 1890; House 1871–73.

HARRIES, William Henry (Minn.) Jan. 15, 1843–July 23, 1921; House 1891–93.

HARRINGTON, Henry William (Ind.) Sept. 12, 1825–March 20, 1882; House 1863–65.

HARRINGTON, Michael Joseph (Mass.) Sept. 2, 1936–; House Sept. 30, 1969–79.

HARRINGTON, Vincent Francis (Iowa) May 16, 1903–Nov. 29, 1943; House 1937–Sept. 5, 1942.

HARRIS, Benjamin Gwinn (Md.) Dec. 13, 1805–April 4, 1895; House 1863–67.

HARRIS, Charles Murray (Ill.) April 10, 1821–Sept. 20, 1896; House 1863–65.

HARRIS, Christopher Columbus (Ala.) Jan. 28, 1842–Dec. 28, 1935; House May 11, 1914–15.

HARRIS, Claude Jr. (Ala.) June 29, 1940–; House 1987–93.

HARRIS, Fred Roy (Okla.) Nov. 13, 1930–; Senate Nov. 4, 1964–Jan. 2, 1973; Chrmn. Dem. Nat. Comm. 1969–70.

HARRIS, Henry Richard (Ga.) Feb. 2, 1828–Oct. 15, 1909; House 1873–79, 1885–87.

HARRIS, Henry Schenck (N.J.) Dec. 27, 1850–May 2, 1902; House 1881–83.

HARRIS, Herbert Eugene II (Va.) April 14, 1925–; House 1975–81.

HARRIS, Isham Green (Tenn.) Feb. 10, 1818–July 8, 1897; House 1849–53; Senate 1877–July 8, 1897; elected Pres. pro tempore March 22, 1893, Jan. 10, 1895; Gov. Nov. 3, 1857–March 12, 1862.

HARRIS, John Thomas (cousin of John Hill of Virginia) (Va.) May 8, 1823–Oct. 14, 1899; House 1859–61 (Independent Democrat), 1871–81.

HARRIS, Oren (Ark.) Dec. 20, 1903–; House 1941–Feb. 2, 1966; Chrmn. House Interstate and Foreign Commerce 1957–66.

HARRIS, Sampson Willis (Ala.) Feb. 23, 1809–April 1, 1857; House 1847–57.

HARRIS, Thomas Langrell (Ill.) Oct. 29, 1816–Nov. 24, 1858; House 1849–51, 1855–Nov. 24, 1858.

HARRIS, Wiley Pope (Miss.) Nov. 9, 1818–Dec. 3, 1891; House 1853–55.

HARRIS, William Alexander (Va.) Aug. 24, 1805–March 28, 1864; House 1841–43.

HARRIS, William Julius (great-grandson of Charles Hooks) (Ga.) Feb. 3, 1868–April 18, 1932; Senate 1919–April 18, 1932.

HARRIS, Winder Russell (Va.) Dec. 3, 1888–Feb. 24, 1973; House April 8, 1941–Sept. 15, 1944.

HARRISON, Albert Galliton (Mo.) June 26, 1800–Sept. 7, 1839; House 1835–39 (1835–37 Jacksonian).

HARRISON, Burr Powell (son of Thomas Walter Harrison) (Va.) July 2, 1904–Dec. 29, 1973; House Nov. 6, 1946–63.

HARRISON, Byron Patton "Pat" (Miss.) Aug. 29, 1881–June 22, 1941; House 1911–19; Senate 1919–June 22, 1941; elected Pres. pro tempore Jan. 6, 1941.

HARRISON, Carter Henry (Ill.) Feb. 15, 1825–Oct. 28, 1893; House 1875–79.

HARRISON, Francis Burton (N.Y.) Dec. 18, 1873–Nov. 21, 1957; House 1903–05, 1907–Sept. 1, 1913.

HARRISON, Frank Girard (Pa.) Feb. 2, 1940–; House 1983–85.

HARRISON, George Paul (Ala.) March 19, 1841–July 17, 1922; House Nov. 6, 1894–97.

HARRISON, Thomas Walter (father of Burr Powell Harrison) (Va.) Aug. 5, 1856–May 9, 1935; House Nov. 7, 1916–Dec. 15, 1922, 1923–29.

HART, Archibald Chapman (N.J.) Feb. 27, 1873–July 24, 1935; House Nov. 5, 1912–March 3, 1913, July 22, 1913–17.

HART, Edward Joseph (N.J.) March 25, 1893–April 20, 1961; House 1935–55; Chrmn. House Merchant Marine and Fisheries 1950–53.

HART, Elizur Kirke (N.Y.) April 8, 1841–Feb. 18, 1893; House 1877–79.

HART, Emanuel Bernard (N.Y.) Oct. 27, 1809–Aug. 29, 1897; House 1851–53.

HART, Gary Warren (Colo.) Nov. 28, 1936–; Senate 1975–87.

HART, Joseph Johnson (Pa.) April 18, 1859–July 13, 1926; House 1895–97.

HART, Michael James (Mich.) July 16, 1877–Feb. 14, 1951; House Nov. 3, 1931–35.

HART, Philip Aloysius (Mich.) Dec. 10, 1912–Dec. 26, 1976; Senate 1959–Dec. 26, 1976.

HARTER, Dow Watters (Ohio) Jan. 2, 1885–Sept. 4, 1971; House 1933–43.

HARTER, Michael Daniel (grandson of Robert Moore) (Ohio) April 6, 1846–Feb. 22, 1896; House 1891–95.

HARTKE, Rupert Vance (Ind.) May 31, 1919–; Senate 1959–77; Chrmn. Senate Veterans' Affairs 1971–77.

HARTRIDGE, Julian (Ga.) Sept. 9, 1829–Jan. 8, 1879; House 1875–Jan. 8, 1879.

HARTZELL, William (Ill.) Feb. 20, 1837–Aug. 14, 1903; House 1875–79.

HASKELL, Floyd Kirk (Colo.) Feb. 7, 1916–; Senate 1973–79.

HASTINGS, Alcee Lamar (Fla.) Sept, 5, 1936–; House 1993–.

HASTINGS, George (N.Y.) March 13, 1807–Aug. 29, 1866; House 1853–55.

HASTINGS, John (Ohio) 1778–Dec. 8, 1854; House 1839–43.

HASTINGS, Serranus Clinton (Iowa) Nov. 22, 1813–Feb. 18, 1893; House Dec. 28, 1846–47.

HASTINGS, William Wirt (Okla.) Dec. 31, 1866–April 8, 1938; House 1915–21, 1923–35.

HATCH, Carl Atwood (N.Mex.) Nov. 27, 1889–Sept. 15, 1963; Senate Oct. 10, 1933–Jan. 2, 1949.

HATCH, Israel Thompson (N.Y.) June 30, 1808–Sept. 24, 1875; House 1857–59.

HATCH, William Henry (Mo.) Sept. 11, 1833–Dec. 23, 1896; House 1879–95.

HATCHER, Charles Floyd (Ga.) July 1, 1939–; House 1981–93.

HATCHER, Robert Anthony (Mo.) Feb. 24, 1819–Dec. 4, 1886; House 1873–79.

HATFIELD, Paul Gerhart (Mont.) April 29, 1928–; Senate Jan. 22–Dec. 14, 1978.

HATHAWAY, William Dodd (Maine) Feb. 21, 1924–; House 1965–73; Senate 1973–79.

HAUN, Henry Peter (Calif.) Jan. 18, 1815–June 6, 1860; Senate Nov. 3, 1859–March 4, 1860.

HAVENNER, Frank Roberts (Calif.) Sept. 20, 1882–July 24, 1967; House 1937–41 (1937–39 Progressive), 1945–53.

HAVENS, James Smith (N.Y.) May 28, 1859–Feb. 27, 1927; House April 19, 1910–11.

HAWES, Harry Bartow (great-nephew of Albert Gallatin Hawes) (Mo.) Nov. 15, 1869–July 31, 1947; House 1921–Oct. 15, 1926; Senate Dec. 6, 1926–Feb. 3, 1933.

HAWKINS, Augustus Freeman (Calif.) Aug. 31, 1907–; House 1963–91; Chrmn. House Administration 1981–84; Chrmn. House Education and Labor 1984–91.

HAWKINS, George Sydney (Fla.) 1808–March 15, 1878; House 1857–Jan. 21, 1861.

HAY, James (Va.) Jan. 9, 1856–June 12, 1931; House 1897–Oct. 1, 1916.

HAYDEN, Carl Trumbull (Ariz.) Oct. 2, 1877–Jan. 25, 1972; House Feb. 19, 1912–27; Senate 1927–69; Chrmn. Senate Rules and Administration 1949–53; Chrmn. Senate Appropriations 1955–69; elected Pres. pro tempore Jan. 3, 1957.

HAYES, Charles Arthur (Ill.) Feb. 17, 1918–; House Aug. 23, 1983–93.

HAYES, James Alison "Jimmy" (La.) Dec. 21, 1946–; House 1987–.

HAYES, Philip Harold (Ind.) Sept. 1, 1940–; House 1975–77.

HAYES, Walter Ingalls (Iowa) Dec. 9, 1841–March 14, 1901; House 1887–95.

HAYMOND, William Summerville (Ind.) Feb. 20, 1823–Dec. 24, 1885; House 1875–77.

HAYNE, Arthur Peronneau (S.C.) March 12, 1788 or 1790–Jan. 7, 1867; Senate May 11–Dec. 2, 1858.

HAYNES, William Elisha (cousin of George William Palmer) (Ohio) Oct. 19, 1829–Dec. 5, 1914; House 1889–93.

HAYS, Lawrence Brooks (Ark.) Aug. 9, 1898–Oct. 11, 1981; House 1943–59.

HAYS, Samuel (Pa.) Sept. 10, 1783–July 1, 1868; House 1843–45.

HAYS, Samuel Lewis (Va.) Oct. 20, 1794–March 17, 1871; House 1841–43.

HAYS, Wayne Levere (Ohio) May 13, 1911–Feb. 10, 1989; House 1949–Sept. 1, 1976; Chrmn. House Administration 1971–76.

HAYWOOD, William Henry Jr. (N.C.) Oct. 23, 1801–Oct. 7, 1852; Senate 1843–July 25, 1846.

HAYWORTH, Donald (Mich.) Jan. 13, 1898–Feb. 25, 1982; House 1955–57.

HEALEY, Arthur Daniel (Mass.) Dec. 29, 1889–Sept. 16, 1948; House 1933–Aug. 3, 1942.

HEALEY, James Christopher (N.Y.) Dec. 24, 1909–Dec. 16, 1981; House Feb. 7, 1956–65.

HEALY, Ned Romeyn (Calif.) Aug. 9, 1906–Sept. 10, 1977; House 1945–47.

HEARD, John Thaddeus (Mo.) Oct. 29, 1840–Jan. 27, 1927; House 1885–95.

HEARST, George (father of William Randolph Hearst) (Calif.) Sept. 3, 1820–Feb. 28, 1891; Senate March 23–Aug. 4, 1886, 1887–Feb. 28, 1891.

HEARST, William Randolph (son of George Hearst) (N.Y.) April 29, 1863–Aug. 14, 1951; House 1903–07.

HEBERT, Felix Edward (La.) Oct. 12, 1901–Dec. 29, 1979; House 1941–77; Chrmn. House Armed Services 1971–75.

HECHLER, Ken (W.Va.) Sept. 20, 1914–; House 1959–77.

HEDRICK, Erland Harold (W.Va.) Aug. 9, 1894–Sept. 20, 1954; House 1945–53.

HEFFERNAN, James Joseph (N.Y.) Nov. 8, 1888–Jan. 27, 1967; House 1941–53.

HEFLIN, Howell Thomas (nephew of James Thomas Heflin) (Ala.) June 19, 1921–; Senate 1979–; Chrmn. Senate Select Committee on Ethics 1987–91.

HEFLIN, James Thomas (uncle of Howell Thomas Heflin, nephew of Robert Stell Heflin) (Ala.) April 9, 1869–April 22, 1951; House May 10, 1904–Nov. 1, 1920; Senate Nov. 3, 1920–31.

HEFNER, Willie Gathrel "Bill" (N.C.) April 11, 1930–; House 1975–.

HEFTEL, Cecil Landau (Hawaii) Sept. 30, 1924–; House 1977–July 11, 1986.

HEISKELL, John Netherland (Ark.) Nov. 2, 1872–Dec. 28, 1972; Senate Jan. 6–Jan. 29, 1913.

HELLER, Louis Benjamin (N.Y.) Feb. 10, 1905–Oct. 30, 1993; House Feb. 15, 1949–July 21, 1954.

HELM, Harvey (Ky.) Dec. 2, 1865–March 3, 1919; House 1907–March 3, 1919.

HELSTOSKI, Henry (N.J.) March 21, 1925–; House 1965–77.

HELVERING, Guy Tresillian (Kans.) Jan. 10, 1878–July 4, 1946; House 1913–19.

HEMPHILL, John James (cousin of William Huggins Brawley, nephew of John Hemphill, great-uncle of Robert Witherspoon Hemphill) (S.C.) Aug. 25, 1849–May 11, 1912; House 1883–93.

HEMPHILL, Robert Witherspoon (great-great-nephew of John Hemphill, great-nephew of John James Hemphill and William Huggins Brawley, great-great-grandson of Robert Witherspoon) (S.C.) May 10, 1915–Dec. 25, 1983; House 1957–May 1, 1964.

HENDERSON, Charles Belknap (Nev.) June 8, 1873–Nov. 8, 1954; Senate Jan. 12, 1918–21.

HENDERSON, David Newton (N.C.) April 16, 1921–; House 1961–77; Chrmn. House Post Office and Civil Service 1975–77.

HENDERSON, James Pinckney (Tex.) March 31, 1808–June 4, 1858; Senate Nov. 9–1857–June 4, 1858; Gov. Feb. 19, 1846–Dec. 21, 1847.

HENDERSON, John Steele (N.C.) Jan. 6, 1846–Oct. 9, 1916; House 1885–95.

HENDRICK, John Kerr (Ky.) Oct. 10, 1849–June 20, 1921; House 1895–97.

HENDRICKS, Joseph Edward (Fla.) Sept. 24, 1903–Oct. 20, 1974; House 1937–49.

HENDRICKS, Thomas Andrews (nephew of William Hendricks) (Ind.) Sept. 7, 1819–Nov. 25, 1885; House 1851–55; Senate 1863–69; Gov. Jan. 15, 1873–Jan. 8, 1877; Vice President Nov. 4–Nov. 25, 1885.

HENDRIX, Joseph Clifford (N.Y.) May 25, 1853–Nov. 9, 1904; House 1893–95.

HENKLE, Eli Jones (Md.) Nov. 24, 1828–Nov. 1, 1893; House 1875–81.

HENLEY, Barclay (son of Thomas Jefferson Henley) (Calif.) March 17, 1843–Feb. 15, 1914; House 1883–87.

HENLEY, Thomas Jefferson (father of Barclay Henley) (Ind.) April 2, 1810–Jan. 2, 1865; House 1843–49.

HENN, Bernhart (Iowa) 1817–Aug. 30, 1865; House 1851–55.

HENNEY, Charles William Francis (Wis.) Feb. 2, 1884–Nov. 16, 1969; House 1933–35.

HENNINGS, Thomas Carey Jr. (Mo.) June 25, 1903–Sept. 13, 1960; House 1935–Dec. 31, 1940; Senate 1951–Sept. 13, 1960; Chrmn. Senate Rules and Administration 1957–60.

HENRY, Daniel Maynadier (Md.) Feb. 19, 1823–Aug. 31, 1899; House 1877–81.

HENRY, Patrick (uncle of Patrick Henry, below) (Miss.) Feb. 12, 1843–May 18, 1930; House 1897–1901.

HENRY, Patrick (nephew of Patrick Henry, above) (Miss.) Feb. 15, 1861–Dec. 28, 1933; House 1901–03.

HENRY, Robert Lee (Tex.) May 12, 1864–July 9, 1931; House 1897–1917.

HENSLEY, Walter Lewis (Mo.) Sept. 3, 1871–July 18, 1946; House 1911–19.

HERBERT, Philemon Thomas (Calif.) Nov. 1, 1825–July 23, 1864; House 1855–57.

HEREFORD, Frank (W.Va.) July 4, 1825–Dec. 21, 1891; House 1871–Jan. 31, 1877; Senate Jan. 31, 1877–81.

HERLONG, Albert Sydney, Jr. (Fla.) Feb. 14, 1909–; House 1949–69.

HERNDON, Thomas Hord (Ala.) July 1, 1828–March 28, 1883; House 1879–March 28, 1883.

HERNDON, William Smith (Tex.) Nov. 27, 1835–Oct. 11, 1903; House 1871–75.

HERRICK, Anson (son of Ebenezer Herrick) (N.Y.) Jan. 21, 1812–Feb. 6, 1868; House 1863–65.

HERRICK, Joshua (Maine) March 18, 1793–Aug. 30, 1874; House 1843–45.

HERRING, Clyde La Verne (Iowa) May 3, 1879–Sept. 15, 1945; Senate Jan. 15, 1937–43; Gov. Jan. 12, 1933–Jan. 14, 1937.

HERSMAN, Hugh Steel (Calif.) July 8, 1872–March 7, 1954; House 1919–21.

HERTEL, Dennis Mark (Mich.) Dec. 7, 1948–; House 1981–93.

HEWITT, Abram Stevens (N.Y.) July 31, 1822–Jan. 18, 1903; House 1875–79, 1881–Dec. 30, 1886; Chrmn. Dem. Nat. Comm. 1876–77.

HEWITT, Goldsmith Whitehouse (Ala.) Feb. 14, 1834–May 27, 1895; House 1875–79, 1881–85.

HIBBARD, Ellery Albee (cousin of Harry Hibbard) (N.H.) July 31, 1826–July 24, 1903; House 1871–73.

HIBBARD, Harry (cousin of Ellery Albee Hibbard) (N.H.) June 1, 1816–July 28, 1872; House 1849–55.

HICKEY, John Joseph (Wyo.) Aug. 22, 1911–Sept. 22, 1970; Senate 1961–Nov. 6, 1962; Gov. Jan. 5, 1959–Jan. 2, 1961.

HICKS, Floyd Verne (Wash.) May 29, 1915–; House 1965–77.

HICKS, Louise Day (Mass.) Oct. 16, 1923–; House 1971–73.

HIGGINS, John Patrick (Mass.) Feb. 19, 1893–Aug. 2, 1955; House 1935–Sept. 30, 1937.

HIGHTOWER, Jack English (Tex.) Sept. 6, 1926–; House 1975–85.

HILDEBRANDT, Fred Herman (S.Dak.) Aug. 2, 1874–Jan. 26, 1956; House 1933–39.

HILL, Benjamin Harvey (cousin of Hugh Lawson White Hill) (Ga.) Sept. 14, 1823–Aug. 16, 1882; House May 5, 1875–77; Senate 1877–Aug. 16, 1882.

HILL, David Bennett (N.Y.) Aug. 29, 1843–Oct. 20, 1910; Senate Jan. 7, 1892–97; Gov. Jan. 6, 1885–Jan. 1, 1892.

HILL, Hugh Lawson White (cousin of Benjamin Harvey Hill) (Tenn.) March 1, 1810–Jan. 18, 1892; House 1847–49.

HILL, John (N.C.) April 9, 1797–April 24, 1861; House 1839–41.

HILL, Joseph Lister (Ala.) Dec. 29, 1894–Dec. 21, 1984; House Aug. 14, 1923–Jan. 11, 1938; Senate Jan. 11, 1938–Jan. 2, 1969; Chrmn. Senate Labor and Public Welfare 1955–69.

HILL, Knute (Wash.) July 31, 1876–Dec. 3, 1963; House 1933–43.

HILL, Robert Potter (Okla.) April 18, 1874–Oct. 29, 1937; House 1913–15 (Ill.), Jan. 3–Oct. 29, 1937.

HILL, Samuel Billingsley (Wash.) April 2, 1875–March 16, 1958; House Sept. 25, 1923–June 25, 1936.

HILL, William David (Ohio) Oct. 1, 1833–Dec. 26, 1906; House 1879–81, 1883–87.

HILL, William Luther (Fla.) Oct. 17, 1873–Jan. 5, 1951; Senate July 1–Nov. 3, 1936.

HILL, Wilson Shedric (Miss.) Jan. 19, 1863–Feb. 14, 1921; House 1903–09.

HILLEN, Solomon Jr. (Md.) July 10, 1810–June 26, 1873; House 1839–41.

HILLIARD, Benjamin Clark (Colo.) Jan. 9, 1868–Aug. 7, 1951; House 1915–19.

HILLIARD, Earl Frederick (Ala.) April 9, 1942–; House 1993–.

HILLYER, Junius (Ga.) April 23, 1807–June 21, 1886; House 1851–55 (1851–53 Unionist).

HINCHEY, Maurice Dudley (N.Y.) Oct. 27, 1938–; House 1993–.

HINDMAN, Thomas Carmichael (Ark.) Jan. 28, 1828–Sept. 27, 1868; House 1859–61.

HINDS, Thomas (Miss.) Jan. 9, 1780–Aug. 23, 1840; House Oct. 21, 1828–31.

HINES, William Henry (Pa.) March 15, 1856–Jan. 17, 1914; House 1893–95.

HINRICHSEN, William Henry (Ill.) May 27, 1850–Dec. 18, 1907; House 1897–99.

HISE, Elijah (Ky.) July 4, 1802–May 8, 1867; House Dec. 3, 1866–May 8, 1867.

HITCHCOCK, Gilbert Monell (Nebr.) Sept. 18, 1859–Feb. 3, 1934; House 1903–05, 1907–11; Senate 1911–23.

HITCHCOCK, Herbert Emery (S.Dak.) Aug. 22, 1867–Feb. 17, 1958; Senate Dec. 29, 1936–Nov. 8, 1938.

HOAG, Truman Harrison (Ohio) April 9, 1816–Feb. 5, 1870; House 1869–Feb. 5, 1870.

HOAGLAND, Moses (Ohio) June 19, 1812–April 16, 1865; House 1849–51.

HOAGLAND, Peter (Nebr.) Nov. 17, 1941–; House 1989–1995.

HOAR, Sherman (son of Ebenezer Rockwood Hoar, nephew of George Frisbee Hoar, cousin of Rockwood Hoar, grandson of Samuel Hoar) (Mass.) July 30, 1860–Oct. 7, 1898; House 1891–93.

HOBBS, Samuel Francis (Ala.) Oct. 5, 1887–May 31, 1952; House 1935–51.

HOBLITZELL, Fetter Schrier (Md.) Oct. 7, 1838–May 2, 1900; House 1881–85.

HOBSON, Richmond Pearson (Ala.) Aug. 17, 1870–March 16, 1937; House 1907–15.

HOCH, Daniel Knabb (Pa.) Jan. 31, 1866–Oct. 11, 1960; House 1943–47.

HOCHBRUECKNER, George Joseph (N.Y.) Sept. 20, 1938–; House 1987–1995.

HODGES, Charles Drury (Ill.) Feb. 4, 1810–April 1, 1884; House Jan. 4–March 3, 1859.

HODGES, Kaneaster Jr. (Ark.) Aug. 20, 1928–; Senate Dec. 10, 1977–79.

HOEPPEL, John Henry (Calif.) Feb. 10, 1881–Sept. 21, 1976; House 1933–37.

HOEY, Clyde Roark (N.C.) Dec. 11, 1877–May 12, 1954; House Dec. 16, 1919–21; Senate 1945–May 12, 1954; Gov. Jan. 7, 1937–Jan. 9, 1941.

HOGAN, Earl Lee (Ind.) March 13, 1920–; House 1959–67.

HOGAN, John (Mo.) Jan. 2, 1805–Feb. 5, 1892; House 1865–67.

HOGE, John Blair (W.Va.) Feb. 2, 1825–March 1, 1896; House 1881–83.

HOGE, Joseph Pendleton (Ill.) Dec. 15, 1810–Aug. 14, 1891; House 1843–47.

HOGG, Charles Edgar (father of Robert Lynn Hogg) (W.Va.) Dec. 21, 1852–June 14, 1935; House 1887–89.

HOIDALE, Elinar (Minn.) Aug. 17, 1870–Dec. 5, 1952; House 1933–35.

HOLBROCK, Greg John (Ohio) June 21, 1906–; House 1941–43.

HOLBROOK, Edward Dexter (Idaho) May 6, 1836–June 17, 1870; House (Terr. Del.) 1865–69.

HOLDEN, T. Timothy (Pa.) March 5, 1957–; House 1993–.

HOLFIELD, Chester Earl (Calif.) Dec. 3, 1903–; House 1943–Dec. 31, 1974; Chrmn. House Government Operations 1971–75.

HOLLADAY, Alexander Richmond (Va.) Sept. 18, 1811–Jan. 29, 1877; House 1849–53.

HOLLAND, Edward Everett (Va.) Feb. 26, 1861–Oct. 23, 1941; House 1911–21.

HOLLAND, Elmer Joseph (Pa.) Jan. 8, 1894–Aug. 9, 1968; House May 19, 1942–43, Jan. 24, 1956–Aug. 9, 1968.

HOLLAND, Kenneth Lamar (S.C.) Nov. 24, 1934–; House 1975–83.

HOLLAND, Spessard Lindsey (Fla.) July 10, 1892–Nov. 6, 1971; Senate Sept. 25, 1946–71; Gov. Jan. 7, 1941–Jan. 2, 1945.

HOLLEMAN, Joel (Va.) Oct. 1, 1799–Aug. 5, 1844; House 1839–40.

HOLLINGS, Ernest Frederick (S.C.) Jan. 1, 1922–; Senate Nov. 9, 1966–; Chrmn. Senate Budget 1979–81; Chrmn. Senate Commerce, Science and Transportation 1987–; Gov. Jan. 20, 1959–Jan. 15, 1963.

HOLLIS, Henry French (N.H.) Aug. 30, 1869–July 7, 1949; Senate March 13, 1913–19.

HOLMAN, William Steele (Ind.) Sept. 6, 1822–April 22, 1897; House 1859–65, 1867–77, 1881–95, March 4–April 22, 1897.

HOLMES, Isaac Edward (S.C.) April 6, 1796–Feb. 24, 1867; House 1839–51.

HOLSEY, Hopkins (Ga.) Aug. 25, 1779–March 31, 1859; House Oct. 5, 1835–39 (Oct. 5, 1835–37 Jacksonian).

HOLT, Orrin (Conn.) March 13, 1792–June 20, 1855; House Dec. 5, 1836–39 (Dec. 5, 1836–37 Jacksonian).

HOLT, Rush Dew (W.Va.) June 19, 1905–Feb. 8, 1955; Senate June 21, 1935–41.

HOLTZMAN, Elizabeth (N.Y.) Aug. 11, 1941–; House 1973–81.

HOLTZMAN, Lester (N.Y.) June 1, 1913–; House 1953–Dec. 31, 1961.

HONEYMAN, Nan Wood (Oreg.) July 15, 1881–Dec. 10, 1970; House 1937–39.

HOOD, George Ezekial (N.C.) Jan. 25, 1875–March 8, 1960; House 1915–19.

HOOK, Enos (Pa.) Dec. 3, 1804–July 15, 1841; House 1839–April 18, 1841.

HOOK, Frank Eugene (Mich.) May 26, 1893–June 21, 1982; House 1935–43, 1945–47.

HOOKER, Charles Edward (Miss.) 1825–Jan. 8, 1914; House 1875–83, 1887–95, 1901–03.

HOOKER, James Murray (Va.) Oct. 29, 1873–Aug. 6, 1940; House Nov. 8, 1921–25.

HOOPER, William Henry (Utah) Dec. 25, 1813–Dec. 30, 1882; House (Terr. Del.) 1859–61, 1865–73.

HOPKINS, Francis Alexander (Ky.) May 27, 1853–June 5, 1918; House 1903–07.

HOPKINS, George Washington (Va.) Feb. 22, 1804–March 1, 1861; House 1835–47 (1835–37 Jacksonian, 1837–39 Democrat, 1839–41 Conservative), 1857–59.

HOPKINS, James Herron (Pa.) Nov. 3, 1832–June 17, 1904; House 1875–77, 1883–85.

HORN, Joan Kelly (Mo.) Oct. 18, 1936–; House 1991–93.

HORNOR, Lynn Sedwick (W.Va.) Nov. 3, 1875–Sept. 23, 1933; House 1931–Sept. 23, 1933.

HOSTETLER, Abraham Jonathan (Ind.) Nov. 22, 1818–Nov. 24, 1899; House 1879–81.

HOTCHKISS, Julius (Conn.) July 11, 1810–Dec. 23, 1878; House 1867–69.

HOUCK, Jacob Jr. (N.Y.) Jan. 14, 1801–Oct. 2, 1857; House 1841–43.

HOUGH, William Jervis (N.Y.) March 20, 1795–Oct. 4, 1869; House 1845–47.

HOUK, George Washington (Ohio) Sept. 25, 1825–Feb. 9, 1894; House 1891–Feb. 9, 1894.

HOUSE, John Ford (Tenn.) Jan. 9, 1827–June 28, 1904; House 1875–83.

HOUSEMAN, Julius (Mich.) Dec. 8, 1832–Feb. 8, 1891; House 1883–85.

HOUSTON, Andrew Jackson (son of Samuel Houston) (Tex.) June 21, 1854–June 26, 1941; Senate April 21–June 26, 1941.

HOUSTON, George Smith (Ala.) Jan. 17, 1811–Dec. 31, 1879; House 1841–49, 1851–Jan. 21, 1861; Senate March 4–Dec. 31, 1879; Gov. Nov. 24, 1874–Nov. 28, 1878.

HOUSTON, Henry Aydelotte (Del.) July 10, 1847–April 5, 1925; House 1903–05.

HOUSTON, John Mills (Kans.) Sept. 15, 1890–April 29, 1975; House 1935–43.

HOUSTON, Samuel (father of Andrew Jackson Houston, cousin of David Hubbard) (Tex.) March 2, 1793–July 26, 1863; House 1823–27 (no party Tenn.); Senate Feb. 21, 1846–59; Gov. Oct. 1, 1827–April 16, 1829 (Tenn.), Dec. 21, 1859–March 16, 1861.

HOUSTON, William Cannon (Tenn.) March 17, 1852–Aug. 30, 1931; House 1905–19.

HOWARD, Benjamin Chew (son of John Eager Howard) (Md.) Nov. 5, 1791–March 6, 1872; House 1829–33 (Jacksonian), 1835–39 (1835–37 Jacksonian).

HOWARD, Edgar (Nebr.) Sept. 16, 1858–July 19, 1951; House 1923–35.

HOWARD, Everette Burgess (Okla.) Sept. 19, 1873–April 3, 1950; House 1919–21, 1923–25, 1927–29.

HOWARD, James John (N.J.) July 24, 1927–March 25, 1988; House 1965–March 25, 1988; Chrmn. House Public Works and Transportation 1981–88.

HOWARD, Jonas George (Ind.) May 22, 1825–Oct. 5, 1911; House 1885–89.

HOWARD, Tilghman Ashurst (Ind.) Nov. 14, 1797–Aug. 16, 1844; House Aug. 5, 1839–July 1, 1840.

HOWARD, Volney Erskine (Tex.) Oct. 22, 1809–May 14, 1889; House 1849–53.

HOWARD, William (Ohio) Dec. 31, 1817–June 1, 1891; House 1859–61.

HOWARD, William Marcellus (Ga.) Dec. 6, 1857–July 5, 1932; House 1897–1911.

HOWARD, William Schley (cousin of Augustus Octavius Bacon) (Ga.) June 29, 1875–Aug. 1, 1953; House 1911–19.

HOWE, Allan Turner (Utah) Sept. 5, 1927–; House 1975–77.

HOWE, Thomas Y. Jr. (N.Y.) 1801–July 15, 1860; House 1851–53.

HOWELL, Charles Robert (N.J.) April 23, 1904–July 5, 1973; House 1949–55.

HOWELL, George (Pa.) June 28, 1859–Nov. 19, 1913; House 1903–Feb. 10, 1904.

HOXWORTH, Stephen Arnold (Ill.) May 1, 1860–Jan. 25, 1930; House 1913–15.

HOYER, Steny Hamilton (Md.) June 14, 1939–; House June 3, 1981–.

HUBARD, Edmund Wilcox (Va.) Feb. 20, 1806–Dec. 9, 1878; House 1841–47.

HUBBARD, Carroll Jr. (Ky.) July 7, 1937–; House 1975–93.

HUBBARD, David (cousin of Samuel Houston) (Ala.) 1792–Jan. 20, 1874; House 1839–41, 1849–51.

HUBBARD, Richard Dudley (Conn.) Sept. 7, 1818–Feb. 28, 1884; House 1867–69; Gov. Jan. 3, 1877–Jan. 9, 1879.

HUBBARD, Richard Dudley (Conn.) Sept. 7, 1818–Feb. 28, 1884; House 1867–69; Gov. Jan. 3, 1877–Jan. 9, 1879.

HUBBELL, Edwin Nelson (N.Y.) Aug. 13, 1815–?; House 1865–67.

HUBBEL, William Spring (N.Y.) Jan. 17, 1801–Nov. 16, 1873; House 1843–45.

HUBER, Walter B. (Ohio) June 29, 1903–Aug. 8, 1982; House 1945–51.

HUBLEY, Edward Burd (Pa.) 1792–Feb. 23, 1856; House 1835–39 (1835–37 Jacksonian).

HUCKABY, Thomas Jerald (La.) July 19, 1941–; House 1977–93.

HUDD, Thomas Richard (Wis.) Oct. 2, 1835–June 22, 1896; House March 8, 1886–89.

HUDDLESTON, George (father of George Huddleston Jr.) (Ala.) Nov. 11, 1869–Feb. 29, 1960; House 1915–37.

HUDDLESTON, George Jr. (son of George Huddleston) (Ala.) March 19, 1920–Sept. 14, 1971; House 1955–65.

HUDDLESTON, Walter Darlington (Ky.) April 15, 1926–; Senate 1973–85.

HUDSPETH, Claude Benton (Tex.) May 12, 1877–March 19, 1941; House 1919–31.

HUFFMAN, James Wylie (Ohio) Sept. 13, 1894–; Senate Oct. 8, 1945–Nov. 5, 1946.

HUGHES, Charles (N.Y.) Feb. 27, 1822–Aug. 10, 1887; House 1853–55.

HUGHES, Charles James Jr. (Colo.) Feb. 16, 1853–Jan. 11, 1911; Senate 1909–Jan. 11, 1911.

HUGHES, Dudley Mays (Ga.) Oct. 10, 1848–Jan. 20, 1927; House 1909–17.

HUGHES, George Wurtz (Md.) Sept. 30, 1806–Sept. 3, 1870; House 1859–61.

HUGHES, Harold Everett (Iowa) Feb. 10, 1922–; Senate 1969–75; Gov. Jan. 17, 1963–Jan. 1, 1969.

HUGHES, James (Ind.) Nov. 24, 1823–Oct. 21, 1873; House 1857–59.

HUGHES, James Frederic (Wis.) Aug. 7, 1883–Aug. 9, 1940; House 1933–35.

HUGHES, James Hurd (Del.) Jan. 14, 1867–Aug. 29, 1953; Senate 1937–43.

HUGHES, James Madison (Mo.) April 7, 1809–Feb. 26, 1861; House 1843–45.

HUGHES, William (N.J.) April 3, 1872–Jan. 30, 1918; House 1903–05, 1907–Sept. 27, 1912; Senate 1913–Jan. 30, 1918.

HUGHES, William John (N.J.) Oct. 17, 1932–; House 1975–1995.

HULBERT, George Murray (N.Y.) May 14, 1881–April 25, 1950; House 1915–Jan. 1, 1918.

HULL, Cordell (Tenn.) Oct. 2, 1871–July 23, 1955; House 1907–21, 1923–31; Senate 1931–March 3, 1933; Chrmn. Dem. Nat. Comm. 1921–24; Secy. of State March 4, 1933–Nov. 30, 1944.

HULL, Noble Andrew (Fla.) March 11, 1827–Jan. 28, 1907; House 1879–Jan. 22, 1881.

HULL, William Raleigh Jr. (Mo.) April 27, 1906–Aug. 15, 1977; House 1955–73.

HUMPHREY, Hubert Horatio Jr. (husband of Muriel Buck Humphrey) (Minn.) May 27, 1911–Jan. 13, 1978; Senate 1949–Dec. 29, 1964, 1971–Jan. 13, 1978; Vice President 1965–69.

HUMPHREY, James Morgan (N.Y.) Sept. 21, 1819–Feb. 9, 1899; House 1865–69.

HUMPHREY, Muriel Buck (widow of Hubert Horatio Humphrey Jr.) (Minn.) Feb. 20, 1912–; Senate Jan. 25–Nov. 7, 1978.

HUMPHREYS, Andrew (Ind.) March 30, 1821–June 14, 1904; House Dec. 5, 1876–77.

HUMPHREYS, Benjamin Grubb (father of William Yerger Humphreys) (Miss.) Aug. 17, 1865–Oct. 16, 1923; House 1903–Oct. 16, 1923.

HUMPHREYS, Robert (Ky.) Aug. 20, 1893–Dec. 31, 1977; Senate June 21–Nov. 6, 1956.

HUMPHREYS, William Yerger (son of Benjamin Grubb Humphreys) (Miss.) Sept. 9, 1890–Feb. 26, 1933; House Nov. 27, 1923–25.

HUNGATE, William Leonard (Mo.) Dec. 24, 1922–; House Nov. 3, 1964–77.

HUNGERFORD, Orville (N.Y.) Oct. 29, 1790–April 6, 1851; House 1843–47.

HUNT, Carleton (nephew of Theodore Gaillard Hunt) (La.) Jan. 1, 1836–Aug. 14, 1921; House 1883–85.

HUNT, James Bennett (Mich.) Aug. 13, 1799–Aug. 15, 1857; House 1843–47.

HUNT, John Thomas (Mo.) Feb. 2, 1860–Nov. 30, 1916; House 1903–07.

HUNT, Jonathan (Vt.) Aug. 12, 1787–May 15, 1832; House 1827–May 15, 1832.

HUNT, Lester Callaway (Wyo.) July 8, 1892–June 19, 1954; Senate 1949–June 19, 1954; Gov. Jan. 4, 1943–Jan. 3, 1949.

HUNTER, Andrew Jackson (Ill.) Dec. 17, 1831–Jan. 12, 1913; House 1893–95, 1897–99.

HUNTER, John Feeney (Ohio) Oct. 19, 1896–Dec. 19, 1957; House 1937–43.

HUNTER, Richard Charles (Nebr.) Dec. 3, 1884–Jan. 23, 1941; Senate Nov. 7, 1934–35.

HUNTER, William H. (Ohio) ?–1842; House 1837–39.

HUNTON, Eppa (Va.) Sept. 22, 1822–Oct. 11, 1908; House 1873–81; Senate May 28, 1892–95.

HUOT, Joseph Oliva (N.H.) Aug. 11, 1917–Aug. 5, 1983; House 1965–67.

HURD, Frank Hunt (Ohio) Dec. 25, 1840–July 10, 1896; House 1875–77, 1879–81, 1883–85.

HUSTING, Paul Oscar (Wis.) April 25, 1866–Oct. 21, 1917; Senate 1915–Oct. 21, 1917.

HUTCHESON, Joseph Chappell (Tex.) May 18, 1842–May 25, 1924; House 1893–97.

HUTCHINS, Waldo (N.Y.) Sept. 30, 1822–Feb. 8, 1891; House Nov. 4, 1879–85.

HUTCHINS, Wells Andrews (Ohio) Oct. 8, 1818–Jan. 25, 1895; House 1863–65.

HUTCHINSON, John Guiher (W.Va.) Feb. 4, 1935–; House June 3, 1980–81.

HUTTO, Earl Dewitt (Fla.) May 12, 1925–; House 1979–1995.

HUTTON, John Edward (Mo.) March 28, 1828–Dec. 28, 1893; House 1885–89.

HUYLER, John (N.J.) April 9, 1808–Jan. 9, 1870; House 1857–59.

ICHORD, Richard Howard II (Mo.) June 27, 1926–Dec. 25, 1992; House 1961–81; Chrmn. House Internal Security 1969–74.

IGOE, James Thomas (Ill.) Oct. 23, 1883–Dec. 2, 1971; House 1927–33.

IGOE, Michael Lambert (Ill.) April 16, 1885–Aug. 21, 1967; House Jan. 3–June 2, 1935.

IGOE, William Leo (Mo.) Oct. 19, 1879–April 20, 1953; House 1913–21.

IKARD, Frank Neville (Tex.) Jan. 30, 1913–; House Sept. 8, 1951–Dec. 15, 1961.

IKIRT, George Pierce (Ohio) Nov. 3, 1852–Feb. 12, 1927; House 1893–95.

IMHOFF, Lawrence E. (Ohio) Dec. 28, 1895–April 18, 1988; House 1933–39, 1941–43.

INGE, Samuel Williams (nephew of William Marshall Inge) (Ala.) Feb. 22, 1817–June 10, 1868; House 1847–51.

INGERSOLL, Charles Jared (brother of Joseph Reed Ingersoll) (Pa.) Oct. 3, 1782–May 14, 1862; House 1813–15 (Republican), 1841–49.

INGERSOLL, Colin Macrae (son of Ralph Isaacs Ingersoll) (Conn.) March 11, 1819–Sept. 13, 1903; House 1851–55.

INGHAM, Samuel (Conn.) Sept. 5, 1793–Nov. 10, 1881; House 1835–39 (1835–37 Jacksonian).

INOUYE, Daniel Ken (Hawaii) Sept. 7, 1924–; House Aug. 21, 1959–63; Senate 1963–; Chrmn. Senate Select Committee on Intelligence Activities 1976–78; Chrmn. Senate Select Committee on Indian Affairs 1987–93; Chrmn. Senate Indian Affairs 1993–1995.

INSLEE, Jay Robert (Wash.) Feb. 9, 1951–; House 1993–1995.

IRBY, John Laurens Manning (great-grandson of Elias Earle) (S.C.) Sept. 10, 1854–Dec. 9, 1900; Senate 1891–97.

IRION, Alfred Briggs (La.) Feb. 18, 1833–May 21, 1903; House 1885–87.

IRVING, Theodore Leonard (Mo.) March 24, 1898–March 8, 1962; House 1949–53.

IRWIN, Donald Jay (Conn.) Sept. 7, 1926–; House 1959–61, 1965–69.

IVERSON, Alfred Sr. (Ga.) Dec. 3, 1798–March 4, 1873; House 1847–49; Senate 1855–Jan. 28, 1861.

IVES, Willard (N.Y.) July 7, 1806–April 19, 1896; House 1851–53.

IZAC, Edouard Victor Michel (Calif.) Dec. 18, 1891–; House 1937–47.

IZLAR, James Ferdinand (S.C.) Nov. 25, 1832–May 26, 1912; House April 12, 1894–95.

JACK, William (Pa.) July 29, 1788–Feb. 28, 1852; House 1841–43.

JACKSON, Alfred Metcalf (Kans.) July 14, 1860–June 11, 1924; House 1901–03.

JACKSON, David Sherwood (N.Y.) 1813–Jan. 20, 1872; House 1847–April 19, 1848.

JACKSON, Henry Martin (Wash.) May 31, 1912–Sept. 1, 1983; House 1941–53; Senate 1953–Sept. 1, 1983; Chrmn. Senate Interior and Insular Affairs 1963–77; Chrmn. Senate Energy and Natural Resources 1977–81; Chrmn. Dem. Nat. Comm. 1960–61.

JACKSON, Howell Edmunds (Tenn.) April 8, 1832–Aug. 8, 1895; Senate 1881–April 14, 1886; Assoc. Justice Supreme Court March 4, 1893–Aug. 8, 1895.

JACKSON, Jabez Young (son of James Jackson born in 1757, uncle of James Jackson born in 1819) (Ga.) July 1790–?; House Oct. 5, 1835–39 (1835–37 Jacksonian).

JACKSON, James (grandson of James Jackson above, nephew of Jabez Young Jackson) (Ga.) Oct. 18, 1819–Jan. 13, 1887; House 1857–Jan. 23, 1861.

JACKSON, James Monroe (cousin of William Thomas Bland) (W. Va.) Dec. 3, 1825–Feb. 14, 1901; House 1889–Feb. 3, 1890.

JACKSON, Samuel Dillon (Ind.) May 28, 1895–March 8, 1951; Senate Jan. 28–Nov. 13, 1944.

JACKSON, Thomas Birdsall (N.Y.) March 24, 1797–April 23, 1881; House 1837–41.

JACOBS, Andrew (father of Andrew Jacobs Jr., father-in-law of Martha Elizabeth Keys) (Ind.) Feb. 22, 1906–; House 1949–51.

JACOBS, Andrew Jr. (son of Andrew Jacobs, husband of Martha Elizabeth Keys) (Ind.) Feb. 24, 1932–; House 1965–73, 1975–.

JACOBSEN, Bernhard Martin (father of William Sebastian Jacobsen) (Iowa) March 26, 1862–June 30, 1936; House 1931–June 30, 1936.

JACOBSEN, William Sebastian (son of Bernhard Martin Jacobsen) (Iowa) Jan. 15, 1887–April 10, 1955; House 1937–43.

JACOBSTEIN, Meyer (N.Y.) Jan. 25, 1880–April 18, 1963; House 1923–29.

JACOWAY, Henderson Madison (Ark.) Nov. 7, 1870–Aug. 4, 1947; House 1911–23.

JAMES, Charles Tillinghast (R.I.) Sept. 15, 1805–Oct. 17, 1862; Senate 1851–57.

JAMES, Hinton (N.C.) April 24, 1884–Nov. 3, 1948; House Nov. 4, 1930–31.

JAMES, Ollie Murray (Ky.) July 27, 1871–Aug. 28, 1918; House 1903–13; Senate 1913–Aug. 28, 1918.

JAMES, Rorer Abraham (Va.) March 1, 1859–Aug. 6, 1921; House June 15, 1920–Aug. 6, 1921.

JAMESON, John (Mo.) March 6, 1802–Jan. 24, 1857; House Dec. 12, 1839–41, 1843–45, 1847–49.

JAMIESON, William Darius (Iowa) Nov. 9, 1873–Nov. 18, 1949; House 1909–11.

JARMAN, Pete (Ala.) Oct. 31, 1892–Feb. 17, 1955; House 1937–49.

JARRETT, William Paul (Hawaii) Aug. 22, 1877–Nov. 10, 1929; House (Terr. Del.) 1923–27.

JARVIS, Thomas Jordan (N.C.) Jan. 18, 1836–June 17, 1915; Senate April 19, 1894–Jan. 23, 1895; Gov. Feb. 5, 1879–Jan. 21, 1885.

JEFFERS, Lamar (Ala.) April 16, 1888–June 1, 1983; House June 7, 1921–35.

JEFFERSON, William J. (La.) March 14, 1947–; House 1991–.

JENCKES, Virginia Ellis (Ind.) Nov. 6, 1877–Jan. 9, 1975; House 1933–39.

JENKINS, Albert Gallatin (Va.) Nov. 10, 1830–May 21, 1864; House 1857–61.

JENKINS, Edgar Lanier (Ga.) Jan. 4, 1933–; House 1977–93.

JENKINS, Timothy (N.Y.) Jan. 29, 1799–Dec. 24, 1859; House 1845–49, 1851–53.

JENKS, George Augustus (Pa.) March 26, 1836–Feb. 10, 1908; House 1875–77.

JENNINGS, William Pat (Va.) Aug. 20, 1919–Aug. 2, 1994; House 1955–67.

JENRETTE, John Wilson Jr. (S.C.) May 19, 1936–; House Nov. 5, 1975–Dec. 10, 1980.

JETT, Thomas Marion (Ill.) May 1, 1862–Jan. 10, 1939; House 1897–1903.

JEWETT, Hugh Judge (brother of Joshua Husband Jewett) (Ohio) July 1, 1817–March 6, 1898; House 1873–June 23, 1874.

JEWETT, Joshua Husband (brother of Hugh Judge Jewett) (Ky.) Sept. 30, 1815–July 14, 1861; House 1855–59.

JOELSON, Charles Samuel (N.J.) Jan. 27, 1916–; House 1961–Sept. 4, 1969.

JOHNSON, Ben (Ky.) May 20, 1858–June 4, 1950; House 1907–27.

JOHNSON, Byron Lindberg (Colo.) Oct. 12, 1917–; House 1959–61.

JOHNSON, Cave (Tenn.) Jan. 11, 1793–Nov. 23, 1866; House 1829–37 (Jacksonian), 1839–45; Postmaster Gen. March 7, 1845–March 5, 1849.

JOHNSON, Charles Fletcher (Maine) Feb. 14, 1859–Feb. 15, 1930; Senate 1911–17.

JOHNSON, Clete Donald "Don" (Ga.) Jan. 30, 1948–; House 1993–1994.

JOHNSON, Eddie Bernice (Tex.) Dec. 3, 1935–; House 1993–.

JOHNSON, Edwin Carl (Colo.) Jan. 1, 1884–May 30, 1970; Senate 1937–55; Chrmn. Senate Interstate and Foreign Commerce 1949–53; Gov. Jan. 10, 1933–Jan. 2, 1937, Jan. 11, 1955–Jan. 8, 1957.

JOHNSON, Edwin Stockton (S.Dak.) Feb. 26, 1857–July 19, 1933; Senate 1915–21.

JOHNSON, George William (W.Va.) Nov. 10, 1869–Feb. 24, 1944; House 1923–25, 1933–43.

JOHNSON, Glen Dale (Okla.) Sept. 11, 1911–Feb. 10, 1983; House 1947–49.

JOHNSON, Harold Terry (Calif.) Dec. 2, 1907–March 16, 1988; House 1959–81; Chrmn. House Public Works and Transportation 1977–81.

JOHNSON, Harvey Hull (Ohio) Sept. 7, 1808–Feb. 4, 1896; House 1853–55.

JOHNSON, Herschel Vespasian (Ga.) Sept. 18, 1812–Aug. 16, 1880; Senate Feb. 4, 1848–49; Gov. Nov. 9, 1853–Nov. 6, 1857.

JOHNSON, James Augustus (Calif.) May 16, 1829–May 11, 1896; House 1867–71.

JOHNSON, James Hutchins (N.H.) June 3, 1802–Sept. 2, 1887; House 1845–49.

JOHNSON, Jed Joseph (father of Jed Joseph Johnson Jr.) (Okla.) July 31, 1888–May 8, 1963; House 1927–47.

JOHNSON, Jed Joseph Jr. (son of Jed Joseph Johnson) (Okla.) Dec. 17, 1939–Dec. 16, 1993; House 1965–67.

JOHNSON, Joseph (uncle of Waldo Porter Johnson) (Va.) Dec. 19, 1785–Feb. 27, 1877; House 1823–27 (no party), Jan. 21–March 3, 1833 (no party), 1835–41 (1835–37 Jacksonian), 1845–47; Gov. Jan. 16, 1852–Dec. 31, 1856.

JOHNSON, Joseph Travis (S.C.) Feb. 28, 1858–May 8, 1919; House 1901–April 19, 1915.

JOHNSON, Lester Roland (Wis.) June 16, 1901–July 24, 1975; House Oct. 13, 1953–65.

JOHNSON, Luther Alexander (Tex.) Oct. 29, 1875–June 6, 1965; House 1923–July 17, 1946.

JOHNSON, Lyndon Baines (Tex.) Aug. 27, 1908–Jan. 22, 1973; House April 10, 1937–49; Senate 1949–Jan. 3, 1961; Senate minority leader 1953–55; Senate majority leader 1955–61; Chrmn. Senate Aeronautical and Space Sciences 1958–61; Vice President 1961–Nov. 22, 1963; President Nov. 22, 1963–69.

JOHNSON, Paul Burney (Miss.) March 23, 1880–Dec. 26, 1943; House 1919–23; Gov. Jan. 16, 1940–Dec. 26, 1943.

JOHNSON, Philip (Pa.) Jan. 17, 1818–Jan. 29, 1867; House 1861–Jan. 29, 1867.

JOHNSON, Robert Davis (Mo.) Aug. 12, 1883–Oct. 23, 1961; House Sept. 29, 1931–33.

JOHNSON, Robert Ward (nephew of James Johnson born in 1774, John Telemachus Johnson and Richard Mentor Johnson) (Ark.) July 22, 1814–July 26, 1979; House 1847–53; Senate July 6, 1853–61.

JOHNSON, Thomas Francis (Md.) June 26, 1909–Feb. 1, 1988; House 1959–63.

JOHNSON, Timothy Peter (S.Dak.) Dec. 28, 1946–; House 1987–.

JOHNSON, Tom Loftin (Ohio) July 18, 1854–April 10, 1911; House 1891–95.

JOHNSON, Waldo Porter (nephew of Joseph Johnson) (Mo.) Sept. 16, 1817–Aug. 14, 1885; Senate March 17, 1861–Jan. 10, 1862.

JOHNSTON, David Emmons (W.Va.) April 10, 1845–July 7, 1917; House 1899–1901.

JOHNSTON, Harry Allison II (Fla.) Dec. 2, 1931–; House 1989–.

JOHNSTON, John Bennett Jr. (La.) June 10, 1932–; Senate Nov. 14, 1972–; Chrmn. Senate Energy and Natural Resources 1987–1995.

JOHNSTON, John Brown (N.Y.) July 10, 1882–Jan. 11, 1960; House 1919–21.

JOHNSTON, John Warfield (uncle of Henry Bowen, nephew of Charles Clement Johnston and Joseph Eggleston Johnston) (Va.) Sept. 9, 1818–Feb. 27, 1889; Senate Jan. 26, 1870–March 3, 1871, March 15, 1871–83.

JOHNSTON, Joseph Eggleston (brother of Charles Clement Johnston, uncle of John Warfield Johnston) (Va.) Feb. 3, 1807–March 21, 1891; House 1879–81.

JOHNSTON, Joseph Forney (Ala.) March 23, 1843–Aug. 8, 1913; Senate Aug. 5, 1907–Aug. 8, 1913; Gov. Dec. 1, 1896–Dec. 1, 1900.

JOHNSTON, Olin DeWitt Talmadge (father of Elizabeth Johnston Patterson) (S.C.) Nov. 18, 1896–April 18, 1965; Senate 1945–April 18, 1965; Chrmn. Senate Post Office and Civil Service 1949–53, 1955–65; Gov. Jan. 15, 1935–Jan. 17, 1939, Jan. 19, 1943–Jan. 2, 1945.

JOHNSTON, Rienzi Melville (cousin of Benjamin Edward Russell) (Tex.) Sept. 9, 1849–Feb. 28, 1926; Senate Jan. 4–29, 1913.

JOHNSTON, Thomas Dillard (N.C.) April 1, 1840–June 22, 1902; House 1885–89.

JOHNSTON, William (Ohio) 1819–May 1, 1866; House 1863–65.

JOHNSTONE, George (S.C.) April 18, 1846–March 8, 1921; House 1891–93.

JONAS, Benjamin Franklin (La.) July 19, 1834–Dec. 21, 1911; Senate 1879–85.

JONES, Andrieus Aristieus (N.Mex.) May 16, 1862–Dec. 20, 1927; Senate 1917–Dec. 20, 1927.

JONES, Ben (Ga.) Aug. 30, 1941–; House 1989–93.

JONES, Burr W. (Wis.) March 9, 1846–Jan. 7, 1935; House 1883–85.

JONES, Charles William (Fla.) Dec. 24, 1834–Oct. 11, 1897; Senate 1875–87.

JONES, Daniel Terryll (N.Y.) Aug. 17, 1800–March 29, 1861; House 1851–55.

JONES, Ed (Tenn.) April 20, 1912–; House March 25, 1969–89.

JONES, Frank (N.H.) Sept. 15, 1832–Oct. 2, 1902; House 1875–79.

JONES, George Wallace (Iowa) April 12, 1804–July 22, 1896; House (Terr. Del.) 1835–April 1836 (no party Mich.), 1837–Jan. 14, 1839 (no party Wis.); Senate Dec. 7, 1848–59.

JONES, George Washington (Tenn.) March 15, 1806–Nov. 14, 1884; House 1843–59.

JONES, Hamilton Chamberlain (N.C.) Sept. 26, 1884–Aug. 10, 1957; House 1947–53.

JONES, James Henry (Tex.) Sept. 13, 1830–March 22, 1904; House 1883–87.

JONES, James Kimbrough (Ark.) Sept. 29, 1839–June 1, 1908; House 1881–Feb. 19, 1885; Senate March 4, 1885–1903; Chrmn. Dem. Nat. Comm. 1896–1904.

JONES, James Robert (Okla.) May 5, 1939–; House 1973–87; Chrmn. House Budget 1981–85.

JONES, James Taylor (Ala.) July 20, 1832–Feb. 15, 1895; House 1877–79, Dec. 3, 1883–89.

JONES, Jehu Glancy (Pa.) Oct. 7, 1811–March 24, 1878; House 1851–53, Feb. 4, 1854–Oct. 30, 1858.

JONES, John James (Ga.) Nov. 13, 1824–Oct. 19, 1898; House 1859–Jan. 23, 1861.

JONES, John Marvin (Tex.) Feb. 26, 1886–March 4, 1976; House 1917–Nov. 20, 1940.

JONES, John Winston (Va.) Nov. 22, 1791–Jan. 29, 1848; House 1835–45 (1835–37 Jacksonian); Speaker Dec. 4, 1843–45.

JONES, Morgan (N.Y.) Feb. 26, 1830–July 13, 1894; House 1865–67.

JONES, Nathaniel (N.Y.) Feb. 17, 1788–July 20, 1866; House 1837–41.

JONES, Owen (Pa.) Dec. 29, 1819–Dec. 25, 1878; House 1857–59.

JONES, Paul Caruthers (Mo.) March 12, 1901–Feb. 10, 1981; House Nov. 2, 1948–69.

JONES, Robert Emmett Jr. (Ala.) June 12, 1912–; House Jan. 28, 1947–77; Chrmn. House Public Works and Transportation 1975–77.

JONES, Roland (La.) Nov. 18, 1813–Feb. 5, 1869; House 1853–55.

JONES, Seaborn (Ga.) Feb. 1, 1788–March 18, 1864; House 1833–35 (Jacksonian), 1845–47.

JONES, Thomas Laurens (Ky.) Jan. 22, 1819–June 20, 1887; House 1867–71, 1875–77.

JONES, Walter Beaman (N.C.) Aug. 19, 1913–Sept. 15, 1992; House Feb. 5, 1966–Sept. 15, 1992; Chrmn. House Merchant Marine and Fisheries 1981–92.

JONES, William Atkinson (Va.) March 21, 1849–April 17, 1918; House 1891–April 17, 1918.

JONES, Woodrow Wilson (N.C.) Jan. 26, 1914–; House Nov. 7, 1950–57.

JONTZ, James Prather (Ind.) Dec. 18, 1951–; House 1987–93.

JORDAN, Barbara Charline (Tex.) Feb. 21, 1936–; House 1973–79.

JORDAN, Benjamin Everett (N.C.) Sept. 8, 1896–March 15, 1974; Senate April 19, 1958–73; Chrmn. Senate Rules and Administration 1963–72.

JORDAN, Isaac M. (Ohio) May 5, 1835–Dec. 3, 1890; House 1883–85.

JOSEPH, Antonio (N.Mex.) Aug. 25, 1846–April 19, 1910; House (Terr. Del.) 1885–95.

JOST, Henry Lee (Mo.) Dec. 6, 1873–July 13, 1950; House 1923–25.

KALBFLEISCH, Martin (N.Y.) Feb. 8, 1804–Feb. 12, 1873; House 1863–65.

KANE, Nicholas Thomas (N.Y.) Sept. 12, 1846–Sept. 14, 1887; House March 4–Sept. 14, 1887.

KANJORSKI, Paul Edmund (Pa.) April 2, 1937–; House 1985–.

KAPTUR, Marcia Carolyn "Marcy" (Ohio) June 17, 1946–; House 1983–.

KARCH, Charles Adam (Ill.) March 17, 1875–Nov. 6, 1932; House 1931–Nov. 5, 1932.

KARST, Raymond Willard (Mo.) Dec. 31, 1902–Oct. 4, 1987; House 1949–51.

KARSTEN, Frank Melvin (Mo.) Jan. 7, 1913–; House 1947–69.

KARTH, Joseph Edward (Minn.) Aug. 26, 1922–; House 1959–77.

KASEM, George Albert (Calif.) April 6, 1919–; House 1959–61.

KASTENMEIER, Robert William (Wis.) Jan. 24, 1924–; House 1959–91.

KAUFMAN, David Spangler (Tex.) Dec. 18, 1813–Jan. 31, 1851; House March 30, 1846–Jan. 31, 1851.

KAVANAUGH, William Marmaduke (Ark.) March 3, 1866–Feb. 21, 1915; Senate Jan. 29–March 3, 1913.

KAZEN, Abraham Jr. (Tex.) Jan. 17, 1919–Nov. 29, 1987; House 1967–85.

KEATING, Edward (Colo.) July 9, 1875–March 18, 1965; House 1913–19.

KEE, James (son of John Kee and Maude Elizabeth Kee) (W.Va.) April 15, 1917–March 11, 1989; House 1965–73.

KEE, John (husband of Maude Elizabeth Kee, father of James Kee) (W.Va.) Aug. 22, 1874–May 8, 1951; House 1933–May 8, 1951; Chrmn. House Foreign Affairs 1949–51.

KEE, Maude Elizabeth (widow of John Kee, mother of James Kee) (W.Va.) ?–Feb. 16, 1975; House July 17, 1951–65.

KEFAUVER, Carey Estes (Tenn.) July 26, 1903–Aug. 10, 1963; House Sept. 13, 1939–49; Senate 1949–Aug. 10, 1963.

KEHOE, James Nicholas (Ky.) July 15, 1862–June 16, 1945; House 1901–05.

KEHOE, James Walter (Fla.) April 25, 1870–Aug. 20, 1938; House 1917–19.

KEHR, Edward Charles (Mo.) Nov. 5, 1837–April 20, 1918; House 1875–77.

KEIM, George May (uncle of William High Keim) (Pa.) March 23, 1805–June 10, 1861; House March 17, 1838–43.

KEITT, Laurence Massillon (S.C.) Oct. 4, 1824–June 4, 1864; House 1853–July 16, 1856, Aug. 6, 1856–Dec. 1860.

KELIHER, John Austin (Mass.) Nov. 6, 1866–Sept. 20, 1938; House 1903–11.

KELLER, Kent Ellsworth (Ill.) June 4, 1867–Sept. 3, 1954; House 1931–41.

KELLEY, Augustine Bernard (Pa.) July 9, 1883–Nov. 20, 1957; House 1941–Nov. 20, 1957.

KELLY, Edna Flannery (N.Y.) Aug. 20, 1906–; House Nov. 8, 1949–69.

KELLY, Edward Austin (Ill.) April 3, 1892–Aug. 30, 1969; House 1931–43, 1945–47.

KELLY, George Bradshaw (N.Y.) Dec. 12, 1900–June 26, 1971; House 1937–39.

KELLY, James Kerr (Oreg.) Feb. 16, 1819–Sept. 15, 1903; Senate 1871–77.

KELLY, John (N.Y.) April 20, 1822–June 1, 1886; House 1855–Dec. 25, 1858.

KEMBLE, Gouverneur (N.Y.) Jan. 25, 1786–Sept. 16, 1875; House 1837–41.

KEMP, Bolivar Edwards (La.) Dec. 28, 1871–June 19, 1933; House 1925–June 19, 1933.

KENDALL, Charles West (Nev.) April 22, 1828–June 25, 1914; House 1871–75.

KENDALL, John Wilkerson (father of Joseph Morgan Kendall) (Ky.) June 26, 1834–March 7, 1892; House 1891–March 7, 1892.

KENDALL, Joseph Morgan (son of John Wilkerson Kendall) (Ky.) May 12, 1863–Nov. 5, 1933; House April 21, 1892–93, 1895–Feb. 18, 1897.

KENDRICK, John Benjamin (Wyo.) Sept. 6, 1857–Nov. 3, 1933; Senate 1917–Nov. 3, 1933; Gov. Jan. 4, 1915–Feb. 26, 1917.

KENNA, John Edward (W.Va.) April 10, 1848–Jan. 11, 1893; House 1877–83; Senate 1883–Jan. 11, 1893.

KENNEDY, Ambrose Jerome (Md.) Jan. 6, 1893–Aug. 29, 1950; House Nov. 8, 1932–41.

KENNEDY, Andrew (cousin of Case Broderick) (Ind.) July 24, 1810–Dec. 31, 1847; House 1841–47.

KENNEDY, Edward Moore (brother of John Fitzgerald Kennedy and Robert Francis Kennedy, grandson of John Francis Fitzgerald, uncle of Joseph Patrick Kennedy II) (Mass.) Feb. 22, 1932–; Senate Nov. 7, 1962–; Chrmn. Senate Judiciary 1979–81; Chrmn. Senate Labor and Human Resources 1987–1995.

KENNEDY, John Fitzgerald (brother of Edward Moore Kennedy and Robert Francis Kennedy, grandson of John Francis Fitzgerald, uncle of Joseph Patrick Kennedy II) (Mass.) May 29, 1917–Nov. 22, 1963; House 1947–53; Senate 1953–Dec. 22, 1960; President 1961–Nov. 22, 1963.

KENNEDY, Joseph Patrick II (son of Robert Francis Kennedy, nephew of Edward Moore Kennedy and John Fitzgerald Kennedy, great-grandson of John Francis Fitzgerald) (Mass.) Sept. 24, 1952–; House 1987–.

KENNEDY, Martin John (N.Y.) Aug. 29, 1892–Oct. 27, 1955; House March 11, 1930–45.

KENNEDY, Michael Joseph (N.Y.) Oct. 25, 1897–Nov. 1, 1949; House 1939–43.

KENNEDY, Patrick (R.I.) House 1995–.

KENNEDY, Robert Francis (brother of Edward Moore Kennedy and John Fitzgerald Kennedy, grandson of John Francis Fitzgerald, father of Joseph Patrick Kennedy II) (N.Y.) Nov. 20, 1925–June 6, 1968; Senate 1965–June 6, 1968; Atty. Gen. Jan. 21, 1961–Sept. 3, 1964.

KENNEDY, William (Conn.) Dec. 19, 1854–June 19, 1918; House 1913–15.

KENNELLY, Barbara Bailey (Conn.) July 10, 1936–; House Jan. 25, 1982–.

KENNEY, Edward Aloysius (N.J.) Aug. 11, 1884–Jan. 27, 1938; House 1933–Jan. 27, 1938.

KENNEY, Richard Rolland (Del.) Sept. 9, 1856–Aug. 14, 1931; Senate 1897–1901.

KENNON, William Jr. (cousin of William Kennon Sr.) (Ohio) June 12, 1802–Oct. 19, 1867; House 1847–49.

KENT, Everett (Pa.) Nov. 15, 1888–Oct. 13, 1963, House 1923–25, 1927–29.

KEOGH, Eugene James (N.Y.) Aug. 30, 1907–May 26, 1989; House 1937–67.

KERN, Frederick John (Ill.) Sept. 6, 1864–Nov. 9, 1931; House 1901–03.

KERN, John Worth (Ind.) Dec. 20, 1849–Aug. 17, 1917; Senate 1911–17; Senate majority leader 1913–17.

KERNAN, Francis (N.Y.) Jan. 14, 1816–Sept. 7, 1892; House 1863–65; Senate 1875–81.

KERR, James (Pa.) Oct. 2, 1851–Oct. 31, 1908; House 1889–91.

KERR, John Hosea (great-nephew of John Kerr) (N.C.) Dec. 31, 1873–June 21, 1958; House Nov. 6, 1923–53.

KERR, Michael Crawford (Ind.) March 15, 1827–Aug. 19, 1876; House 1865–73, 1875–Aug. 19, 1876; Speaker Dec. 6, 1875–Aug. 19, 1876.

KERR, Robert Samuel (Okla.) Sept. 11, 1896–Jan. 1, 1963; Senate 1949–Jan. 1, 1963; Chrmn. Senate Aeronautical and Space Sciences 1961–63; Gov. Jan. 11, 1943–Jan. 13, 1947.

KERREY, Robert (Nebr.) Aug. 27, 1943–; Senate 1989–; Gov. Jan. 6, 1983–Jan. 9, 1987.

KERRIGAN, James (N.Y.) Dec. 25, 1828–Nov. 1, 1899; House 1861–63.

KERRY, John Forbes (Mass.) Dec. 22, 1943–; Senate 1985–.

KETTNER, William (Calif.) Nov. 20, 1864–Nov. 11, 1930; House 1913–21.

KEY, David McKendree (Tenn.) Jan. 27, 1824–Feb. 3, 1900; Senate Aug. 18, 1875–Jan. 19, 1877; Postmaster Gen. March 13, 1877–Aug. 24, 1880.

KEY, John Alexander (Ohio) Dec. 30, 1871–March 4, 1954; House 1913–19.

KEYS, Martha Elizabeth (wife of Andrew Jacobs Jr., daughter-in-law of Andrew Jacobs Sr.) (Kans.) Aug. 10, 1930–; House 1975–79.

KIDWELL, Zedekiah (Va.) Jan. 4, 1814–April 27, 1872; House 1853–57.

KILDAY, Paul Joseph (Tex.) March 29, 1900–Oct. 12, 1968; House 1939–Sept. 24, 1961.

KILDEE, Dale Edward (Mich.) Sept. 16, 1929–; House 1977–.

KILGORE, Constantine Buckley (Tex.) Feb. 20, 1835–Sept. 23, 1897; House 1887–95.

KILGORE, Daniel (Ohio) 1793–Dec. 12, 1851; House Dec. 1, 1834–July 4, 1838 (Dec. 1, 1834–37 Jacksonian).

KILGORE, Harley Martin (W.Va.) Jan. 11, 1893–Feb. 28, 1956; Senate 1941–Feb. 28, 1956; Chrmn. Senate Judiciary 1955–56.

KILGORE, Joe Madison (Tex.) Dec. 10, 1918–; House 1955–65.

KILLE, Joseph (N.J.) April 12, 1790–March 1, 1865; House 1839–41.

KIMBALL, William Preston (Ky.) Nov. 4, 1857–Feb. 24, 1926; House 1907–09.

KIMMEL, William (Md.) Aug. 15, 1812–Dec. 28, 1886; House 1877–81.

KINCHELOE, David Hayes (Ky.) April 9, 1877–April 16, 1950; House 1915–Oct. 5, 1930.

KINDEL, George John (Colo.) March 2, 1855–Feb. 28, 1930; House 1913–15.

KINDRED, John Joseph (N.Y.) July 15, 1864–Oct. 23, 1937; House 1911–13, 1921–29.

KING, Andrew (Mo.) March 20, 1812–Nov. 18, 1895; House 1871–73.

KING, Cecil Rhodes (Calif.) Jan. 13, 1898–March 17, 1974; House Aug. 25, 1942–69.

KING, David Sjodahl (son of William Henry King) (Utah) June 20, 1917–; House 1959–63, 1965–67.

KING, John Floyd (son of Thomas Butler King, nephew of Henry King) (La.) April 20, 1842–May 8, 1915; House 1879–87.

KING, William Henry (father of David Sjodahl King) (Utah) June 3, 1863–Nov. 27, 1949; House 1897–99, April 2, 1900–01; Senate 1917–41; elected Pres. pro tempore Nov. 19, 1940.

KING, William Rufus de Vane (Ala.) April 7, 1786–April 18, 1853; House 1811–Nov. 4, 1816 (no party N.C.); Senate Dec. 14, 1819–April 15, 1844 (Dec. 14, 1819–21 Republican, 1821–April 15, 1844 Republican/Jacksonian), July 1, 1848–Dec. 20, 1852; elected Pres. pro tempore July 1, 1836, Jan. 28, 1837, March 7, 1837, Oct. 13, 1837, July 2, 1838, Feb. 25, 1839, July 3, 1840, March 3, 1841, March 4, 1841, May 6, 1850; Vice President March 4–April 18, 1853.

KINGSBURY, William Wallace (Minn.) June 4, 1828–April 17, 1892; House (Terr. Del.) 1857–May 11, 1858.

KINKEAD, Eugene Francis (N.J.) March 27, 1876–Sept. 6, 1960; House 1909–Feb. 4, 1915.

KINNEY, John Fitch (Utah) April 2, 1816–Aug. 16, 1902; House (Terr. Del.) 1863–65.

KINSELLA, Thomas (N.Y.) Dec. 31, 1832–Feb. 11, 1884; House 1871–73.

KIPP, George Washington (Pa.) March 28, 1847–July 24, 1911; House 1907–09, March 4–July 24, 1911.

KIRBY, William Fosgate (Ark.) Nov. 16, 1867–July 26, 1934; Senate Nov. 8, 1916–21.

KIRKPATRICK, Littleton (N.J.) Oct. 19, 1797–Aug. 15, 1859; House 1843–45.

KIRKPATRICK, Sanford (Iowa) Feb. 11, 1842–Feb. 13, 1932; House 1913–15.

KIRWAN, Michael Joseph (Ohio) Dec. 2, 1886–July 27, 1970; House 1937–July 27, 1970.

KITCHENS, Wade Hampton (Ark.) Dec. 26, 1878–Aug. 22, 1966; House 1937–41.

KITCHIN, Alvin Paul (nephew of Claude Kitchin and William Walton Kitchin, grandson of William Hodges Kitchin) (N.C.) Sept. 13, 1908–Oct. 22, 1983; House 1957–63.

KITCHIN, Claude (son of William Hodges Kitchin, brother of William Walton Kitchin, uncle of Alvin Paul Kitchin) (N.C.) March 24, 1869–May 31, 1923; House 1901–May 31, 1923; House majority leader 1915–19; House minority leader 1921–23.

KITCHIN, William Hodges (father of Claude Kitchin and William Walton Kitchin, grandfather of Alvin Paul Kitchin) (N.C.) Dec. 22, 1837–Feb. 2, 1901; House 1879–81.

KITCHIN, William Walton (son of William Hodges Kitchin, brother of Claude Kitchin, uncle of Alvin Paul Kitchin) (N.C.) Oct. 9, 1866–Nov. 9, 1924; House 1897–Jan. 11, 1909; Gov. Jan. 12, 1909–Jan. 15, 1913.

KITTREDGE, George Washington (N.H.) Jan. 31, 1805–March 6, 1881; House 1853–55.

KLEBERG, Richard Mifflin Sr. (nephew of Rudolph Kleberg, cousin of Robert Christian Eckhardt) (Tex.) Nov. 18, 1887–May 8, 1955; House Nov. 24, 1931–45.

KLEBERG, Rudolph (great-uncle of Robert Christian Eckhardt, uncle of Richard Mifflin Kleberg Sr.) (Tex.) June 26, 1847–Dec. 28, 1924; House April 7, 1896–1903.

KLECZKA, Gerald Daniel (Wis.) Nov. 26, 1943–; House April 10, 1984–.

KLEIN, Arthur George (N.Y.) Aug. 8, 1904–Feb. 20, 1968; House July 29, 1941–45, Feb. 19, 1946–Dec. 31, 1956.

KLEIN, Herbert Charles (N.J.) June 24, 1930–; House 1993–1995.

KLEINER, John Jay (Ind.) Feb. 8, 1845–April 8, 1911; House 1883–87.

KLINE, Marcus Charles Lawrence (Pa.) March 26, 1855–March 10, 1911; House 1903–07.

KLINGENSMITH, John Jr. (Pa.) 1785–?; House 1835–39 (1835–37 Jacksonian).

KLINK, Ron (Pa.) Sept. 23, 1951–; House 1993–.

KLOEB, Frank Le Blond (grandson of Francis Celeste Le Blond) (Ohio) June 16, 1890–March 11, 1976; House 1933–Aug. 19, 1937.

KLOTZ, Robert (Pa.) Oct. 27, 1819–May 1, 1895; House 1879–83.

KLUCZYNSKI, John Carl (Ill.) Feb. 15, 1896–Jan. 26, 1975; House 1951–Jan. 26, 1975.

KLUTTZ, Theodore Franklin (N.C.) Oct. 4, 1848–Nov. 18, 1918; House 1899–1905.

KNAPP, Anthony Lausett (brother of Robert McCarty Knapp) (Ill.) June 14, 1828–May 24, 1881; House Dec. 12, 1861–65.

KNAPP, Robert McCarty (brother of Anthony Lausett Knapp) (Ill.) April 21, 1831–June 24, 1889; House 1873–75, 1877–79.

KNIFFIN, Frank Charles (Ohio) April 26, 1894–April 30, 1968; House 1931–39.

KNOTT, James Proctor (Ky.) Aug. 29, 1830–June 18, 1911; House 1867–71, 1875–83; Gov. Sept. 4, 1883–Aug. 30, 1887.

KOCH, Edward Irving (N.Y.) Dec. 12, 1924–; House 1969–Dec. 31, 1977.

KOCIALKOWSKI, Leo Paul (Ill.) Aug. 16, 1882–Sept. 27, 1958; House 1933–43.

KOGOVSEK, Raymond Peter (Colo.) Aug. 19, 1941–; House 1979–85.

KOHL, Herbert (Wis.) Feb. 7, 1935–; Senate 1989–.

KOLTER, Joseph Paul (Pa.) Sept. 3, 1926–; House 1983–93.

KONIG, George (Md.) Jan. 26, 1865–May 31, 1913; House 1911–May 31, 1913.

KONOP, Thomas Frank (Wis.) Aug. 17, 1879–Oct. 17, 1964; House 1911–17.

KOPETSKI, Michael (Oreg.) Oct. 27, 1949–; House 1991–.

KOPPLEMANN, Herman Paul (Conn.) May 1, 1880–Aug. 11, 1957; House 1933–39, 1941–43, 1945–47.

KORBLY, Charles Alexander (Ind.) March 24, 1871–July 26, 1937; House 1909–15.

KORNEGAY, Horace Robinson (N.C.) March 12, 1924–; House 1961–69.

KOSTMAYER, Peter Houston (Pa.) Sept. 27, 1946–; House 1977–81, 1983–93.

KOWALSKI, Frank (Conn.) Oct. 18, 1907–Oct. 11, 1974; House 1959–63.

KRAMER, Charles (Calif.) April 18, 1879–Jan. 20, 1943; House 1933–43.

KREBS, John Hans (Calif.) Dec. 17, 1926–; House 1975–79.

KREBS, Paul Joseph (N.J.) May 26, 1912–; House 1965–67.

KREIDLER, Myron Bradley "Mike" (Wash.) Sept. 28, 1943–; House 1993–.

KRIBBS, George Frederic (Pa.) Nov. 8, 1846–Sept. 8, 1938; House 1891–95.

KRUEGER, Robert Charles (Tex.) Sept. 19, 1935–; House 1975–79; Senate-Jan. 21–June 14, 1993.

KRUSE, Edward H. (Ind.) Oct. 22, 1918–; House 1949–51.

KUNKEL, Jacob Michael (Md.) July 13, 1822–April 7, 1870; House 1857–61.

KUNZ, Stanley Henry (Ill.) Sept. 26, 1864–April 23, 1946; House 1921–31, April 5, 1932–33.

KURTZ, William Henry (Pa.) Jan. 31, 1804–June 24, 1868; House 1851–55.

KYLE, John Curtis (Miss.) July 17, 1851–July 6, 1913; House 1891–97.

KYROS, Peter N. (Maine) July 11, 1925–; House 1967–75.

LA BRANCHE, Alcee Louis (La.) 1806–Aug. 17, 1861; House 1843–45.

LA DOW, George Augustus (Oreg.) March 18, 1826–May 1, 1875; House March 4–May 1, 1875.

LaFALCE, John Joseph (N.Y.) Oct. 6, 1939–; House 1975; Chrmn. House Small Business 1987–1995.

LAFFOON, Polk (Ky.) Oct. 24, 1844–Oct. 22, 1906, House 1885–89.

LAGAN, Matthew Diamond (La.) June 20, 1829–April 8, 1901; House 1887–89, 1891–93.

LAHM, Samuel (Ohio) April 22, 1812–June 16, 1876; House 1847–49.

LAIRD, William Ramsey III (W.Va.) June 2, 1916–Jan. 7, 1974; Senate March 13–Nov. 6, 1956.

LAMAR, James Robert (Mo.) March 28, 1866–Aug. 11, 1923; House 1903–05, 1907–09.

LAMAR, John Basil (Ga.) Nov. 5, 1812–Sept. 15, 1862; House March 4–July 29, 1843.

LAMAR, Lucius Quintus Cincinnatus (uncle of William Bailey Lamar, cousin of Absalom Harris Chappell) (Miss.) Sept. 17, 1825–Jan. 23, 1893; House 1857–Dec. 1860, 1873–77; Senate 1877–March 6, 1885; Secy. of the Interior March 6, 1885–Jan. 10, 1888; Assoc. Justice Supreme Court Jan. 18, 1888–Jan. 23, 1893.

LAMAR, William Bailey (nephew of Lucius Quintus

Cincinnatus Lamar) (Fla.) June 12, 1853–Sept. 26, 1928; House 1903–09.

LAMB, Alfred William (Mo.) March 18, 1824–April 29, 1888; House 1853–55.

LAMB, John (Va.) June 12, 1840–Nov. 21, 1924; House 1897–1913.

LAMB, John Edward (Ind.) Dec. 26, 1852–Aug. 23, 1914; House 1883–85.

LAMBERT, Blanche (Ark.) Sept. 30, 1960–; House 1993–.

LAMBETH, John Walter (N.C.) Jan. 10, 1896–Jan. 12, 1961; House 1931–39.

LAMISON, Charles Nelson (Ohio) 1826–April 24, 1896; House 1871–75.

LAMNECK, Arthur Philip (Ohio) March 12, 1880–April 23, 1944; House 1931–39.

LANCASTER, Columbia (Wash.) Aug. 26, 1803–Sept. 15, 1893; House (Terr. Del.) April 12, 1854–55.

LANCASTER, Harold Martin (N.C.) March 24, 1943–; House 1987–1995.

LANDERS, Franklin (Ind.) March 22, 1825–Sept. 10, 1901; House 1875–77.

LANDERS, George Marcellus (Conn.) Feb. 22, 1813–March 27, 1895; House 1875–79.

LANDES, Silas Zephaniah (Ill.) May 15, 1842–May 23, 1910; House 1885–89.

LANDRUM, John Morgan (La.) July 3, 1815–Oct. 18, 1861; House 1859–61.

LANDRUM, Phillip Mitchell (Ga.) Sept. 10, 1907–Nov. 19, 1990; House 1953–77.

LANDY, James (Pa.) Oct. 13, 1813–July 25, 1875; House 1857–59.

LANE, Edward (Ill.) March 27, 1842–Oct. 30, 1912; House 1887–95.

LANE, Harry (grandson of Joseph Lane, nephew of LaFayette Lane) (Oreg.) Aug. 28, 1855–May 23, 1917; Senate 1913–May 23, 1917.

LANE, Joseph (father of LaFayette Lane, grandfather of Harry Lane) (Oreg.) Dec. 14, 1801–April 19, 1881; House (Terr. Del.) June 2, 1851–Feb. 14, 1859 (no party); Senate Feb. 14, 1859–61; Gov. (Oreg. Terr.) 1849–50, May 16–May 19, 1853.

LANE, LaFayette (son of Joseph Lane, uncle of Harry Lane) (Oreg.) Nov. 12, 1842–Nov. 23, 1896; House Oct. 25, 1875–77.

LANE, Thomas Joseph (Mass.) July 6, 1898–June 14, 1994; House Dec. 30, 1941–63.

LANHAM, Fritz Garland (son of Samuel Willis Tucker Lanham) (Tex.) Jan. 3, 1880–July 31, 1965; House April 19, 1919–47.

LANHAM, Henderson Lovelace (Ga.) Sept. 14, 1888–Nov. 10, 1957; House 1947–Nov. 10, 1957.

LANHAM, Samuel Willis Tucker (father of Fritz Garland Lanham) (Tex.) July 4, 1846–July 29, 1908; House 1883–93, 1897–Jan. 15, 1903; Gov. Jan. 20, 1903–Jan. 15, 1907.

LANKFORD, Richard Estep (Md.) July 22, 1914–; House 1955–65.

LANKFORD, William Chester (Ga.) Dec. 7, 1877–Dec. 10, 1964; House 1919–33.

LANTAFF, William Courtland (Fla.) July 31, 1913–Jan. 28, 1970; House 1951–55.

LANTOS, Thomas Peter (father-in-law of Richard Swett) (Calif.) Feb. 1, 1928–; House 1981–.

LANZETTA, James Joseph (N.Y.) Dec. 21, 1894–Oct. 27, 1956; House 1933–35, 1937–39.

LAPHAM, Oscar (R.I.) June 29, 1837–March 29, 1926; House 1891–95.

LARCADE, Henry Dominique Jr. (La.) July 12, 1890–March 15, 1966; House 1943–53.

LaROCCO, Larry (Idaho) Aug. 25, 1946–; House 1991–1995.

LARRABEE, Charles Hathaway (Wis.) Nov. 9, 1820–Jan. 20, 1883; House 1859–61.

LARRABEE, William Henry (Ind.) Feb. 21, 1870–Nov. 16, 1960; House 1931–43.

LARSEN, William Washington (Ga.) Aug. 12, 1871–Jan. 5, 1938; House 1917–33.

LA SERE, Emile (La.) 1802–Aug. 14,1882; House Jan. 29, 1846–51.

LASSITER, Francis Rives (great-nephew of Francis Everod Rives) (Va.) Feb. 18, 1866–Oct. 31, 1909; House April 19, 1900–03, 1907–Oct. 31, 1909.

LATHAM, Louis Charles (N.C.) Sept. 11, 1840–Oct. 16, 1895; House 1881–83, 1887–89.

LATHAM, Milton Slocum (Calif.) May 23, 1827–March 4, 1882; House 1853–55; Senate March 5, 1860–63; Gov. Jan. 9–Jan. 14, 1860.

LATIMER, Asbury Churchwell (S.C.) July 31, 1851–Feb. 20, 1908; House 1893–1903; Senate 1903–Feb. 20, 1908.

LATTA, James Polk (Nebr.) Oct. 31, 1844–Sept. 11, 1911; House 1909–Sept. 11, 1911.

LAUGHLIN, Greg H. (Tex.) Jan. 21, 1942–; House 1989–.

LAUSCHE, Frank John (Ohio) Nov. 14, 1895–April 21, 1990; Senate 1967–69; Gov. Jan. 8, 1945–Jan. 13, 1947, Jan. 10, 1949–Jan. 3, 1957.

LAW, Charles Blakeslee (N.Y.) Feb. 5, 1872–Sept. 15, 1929; House 1905–11.

LAW, John (son of Lyman Law, grandson of Amasa Learned) (Ind.) Oct. 28, 1796–Oct. 7, 1873; House 1861–65.

LAWLER, Frank (Ill.) June 25, 1842–Jan. 17, 1896; House 1885–91.

LAWRENCE, Effingham (cousin of Cornelius Van Wyck Lawrence) (La.) March 2, 1820–Dec. 9, 1878; House March 3, 1875.

LAWRENCE, John Watson (N.Y.) Aug. 1800–Dec. 20, 1888; House 1845–47.

LAWRENCE, Sidney (N.Y.) Dec. 31, 1801–May 9, 1892; House 1847–49.

LAWRENCE, William (Ohio) Sept. 2, 1814–Sept. 8, 1895; House 1857–59.

LAWSON, John William (Va.) Sept. 13, 1837–Feb. 21, 1905; House 1891–93.

LAWSON, Thomas Graves (Ga.) May 2, 1835–April 16, 1912; House 1891–97.

LAY, Alfred Morrison (Mo.) May 20, 1836–Dec. 8, 1879; House March 4–Dec. 8, 1879.

LAYTON, Fernando Coello (Ohio) April 11, 1847–June 22, 1926; House 1891–97.

LAZARO, Ladislas (La.) June 5, 1872–March 30, 1927; House 1913–March 30, 1927.

LAZEAR, Jesse (Pa.) Dec. 12, 1804–Sept. 2, 1877; House 1861–65.

LEA, Clarence Frederick (Calif.) July 11, 1874–June 20, 1964; House 1917–49.

LEA, Luke (Tenn.) April 12, 1879–Nov. 18, 1945; Senate 1911–17.

LEACH, Anthony Claude "Buddy" Jr. (La.) March 30, 1934–; House 1979–81.

LEACH, James Madison (N.C.) Jan. 17, 1815–June 1, 1891; House 1859–61 (Opposition Party), 1871–75.

LEADBETTER, Daniel Parkhurst (Ohio) Sept. 10, 1797–Feb. 26, 1870; House 1837–41.

LEAHY, Edward Laurence (R.I.) Feb. 9, 1886–July 22, 1953; Senate Aug. 24, 1949–Dec. 18, 1950.

LEAHY, Patrick Joseph (Vt.) March 31, 1940–; Senate 1975–; Chrmn. Senate Agriculture, Nutrition, and Forestry 1987–1995.

LEAKE, Eugene Walter (N.J.) July 13, 1877–Aug. 23, 1959; House 1907–09.

LEATH, James Marvin (Tex.) May 6, 1931–; House 1979–91.

LEAVY, Charles Henry (Wash.) Feb. 16, 1884–Sept. 25, 1952; House 1937–Aug. 1, 1942.

LE BLOND, Francis Celeste (grandfather of Frank Le Blond Kloeb) (Ohio) Feb. 14, 1821–Nov. 9, 1902; House 1863–67.

LEDERER, Raymond Francis (Pa.) May 19, 1938–; House 1977–April 29, 1981.

LEE, Blair (great-grandson of Richard Henry Lee) (Md.) Aug. 9, 1857–Dec. 25, 1944; Senate Jan. 28, 1914–17.

LEE, Frank Hood (Mo.) March 29, 1873–Nov. 20, 1952; House 1933–35.

LEE, Gordon (Ga.) May 29, 1859–Nov. 7, 1927; House 1905–27.

LEE, Joshua Bryan (Okla.) Jan. 23, 1892–Aug. 10, 1967; House 1935–37; Senate 1937–43.

LEE, Robert Emmett (Pa.) Oct. 12, 1868–Nov. 19, 1916; House 1911–15.

LEE, Robert Quincy (Tex.) Jan. 12, 1869–April 18, 1930; House 1929–April 18, 1930.

LEE, William Henry Fitzhugh (grandson of Henry Lee) (Va.) May 31, 1837–Oct. 15, 1891; House 1887–Oct. 15, 1891.

LEEDOM, John Peter (Ohio) Dec. 20, 1847–March 18, 1895; House 1881–83.

LEET, Isaac (Pa.) 1801–June 10, 1844; House 1839–41.

LeFANTE, Joseph Anthony (N.J.) Sept. 8, 1928–; House 1977–Dec. 14, 1978.

LE FEVRE, Benjamin (Ohio) Oct. 8, 1838–March 7, 1922; House 1879–87.

LEFFLER, Shepherd (brother of Isaac Leffler) (Iowa) April 24, 1811–Sept. 7, 1879; House Dec. 28, 1846–51.

LEFTWICH, John William (Tenn.) Sept. 7, 1826–March 6, 1870; House July 24, 1866–67.

LEGARE, George Swinton (S.C.) Nov. 11, 1869–Jan. 31, 1913; House 1903–Jan. 31, 1913.

LEGARE, Hugh Swinton (S.C.) Jan. 2, 1797–June 20, 1843; House 1837–39; Atty. Gen. Sept. 13, 1841–June 20, 1843.

LEGGETT, Robert Louis (Calif.) July 26, 1926–; House 1963–79.

LEHMAN, Herbert Henry (N.Y.) March 28, 1878–Dec. 5, 1963; Senate Nov. 9, 1949–57; Gov. Jan. 1, 1933–Dec. 3, 1942.

LEHMAN, Richard Henry (Calif.) July 20, 1948–; House 1983–1995.

LEHMAN, William (Fla.) Oct. 4, 1913–; House 1973–93.

LEHMAN, William Eckart (Pa.) Aug. 21, 1821–July 19, 1895; House 1861–63.

LEHR, John Camillus (Mich.) Nov. 18, 1878–Feb. 17, 1958; House 1933–35.

LEIB, Owen D. (Pa.) ?–June 17, 1848; House 1845–47.

LEIDY, Paul (Pa.) Nov. 13, 1813–Sept. 11, 1877; House Dec. 7, 1857–59.

LELAND, George Thomas "Mickey" (Tex.) Nov. 27, 1944–Aug. 7, 1989; House 1979–Aug. 7, 1989.

LE MOYNE, John Valcoulon (Ill.) Nov. 17, 1828–July 27, 1918; House May 6, 1876–77.

LENAHAN, John Thomas (Pa.) Nov. 15, 1852–April 28, 1920; House 1907–09.

L'ENGLE, Claude (Fla.) Oct. 19, 1868–Nov. 6, 1919; House 1913–15.

LENNON, Alton Asa (N.C.) Aug. 17, 1906–Dec. 28, 1986; Senate July 10, 1953–Nov. 28, 1954; House 1957–73.

LENTZ, John Jacob (Ohio) Jan. 27, 1856–July 27, 1931; House 1897–1901.

LEONARD, Moses Gage (N.Y.) July 10, 1809–March 20, 1899; House 1843–45.

LEONARD, Stephen Banks (N.Y.) April 15, 1793–May 8, 1876; House 1835–37 (Jacksonian), 1839–41.

LESHER, John Vandling (Pa.) July 27, 1866–May 3, 1932; House 1913–21.

LESINSKI, John (father of John Lesinski Jr.) (Mich.) Jan. 3, 1885–May 27, 1950; House 1933–May 27, 1950.

LESINSKI, John Jr. (son of John Lesinski) (Mich.) Dec. 28, 1914–; House 1951–65; Chrmn. House Education and Labor 1949–50.

LESTER, Posey Green (Va.) March 12, 1850–Feb. 9, 1929; House 1889–93.

LESTER, Rufus Ezekiel (Ga.) Dec. 12, 1837–June 16, 1906; House 1889–June 16, 1906.

LETCHER, John (Va.) March 29, 1813–Jan. 26, 1884; House 1851–59; Gov. Jan. 1, 1860–Dec. 31, 1863.

LEVER, Asbury Francis (S.C.) Jan. 5, 1875–April 28, 1940; House Nov. 5, 1901–Aug. 1, 1919.

LEVERING, Robert Woodrow (son-in-law of Usher Lloyd Burdick, brother-in-law of Quentin Northrop Burdick, brother-in-law of Jocelyn Birch Burdick) (Ohio) Oct. 3, 1914–; House 1959–61.

LEVIN, Carl Milton (brother of Sander Martin Levin) (Mich.) June 28, 1934–; Senate 1979–.

LEVIN, Sander Martin (brother of Carl Milton Levin) (Mich.) Sept. 6, 1931–; House 1983–.

LEVINE, Meldon Edises "Mel" (Calif.) June 7, 1943–; House 1983–93.

LEVITAS, Elliott Harris (Ga.) Dec. 26, 1930–; House 1975–85.

LEVY, Jefferson Monroe (N.Y.) April 16, 1852–March 6, 1924; House 1899–1901, 1911–15.

LEVY, William Mallory (La.) Oct. 31, 1827–Aug. 14, 1882; House 1875–77.

LEWIS, Burwell Boykin (Ala.) July 7, 1838–Oct. 11, 1885; House 1875–77, 1879–Oct. 1, 1880.

LEWIS, Charles Swearinger (Va.) Feb. 26, 1821–Jan. 22, 1878; House Dec. 4, 1854–55.

LEWIS, Clarke (Miss.) Nov. 8, 1840–March 13, 1896; House 1889–93.

LEWIS, David John (Md.) May 1, 1869–Aug. 12, 1952; House 1911–17, 1931–39.

LEWIS, Dixon Hall (Ala.) Aug. 10, 1802–Oct. 25, 1848; House 1829–April 22, 1844 (State Rights Democrat); Senate April 22, 1844–Oct. 25, 1848.

LEWIS, Edward Taylor (La.) Oct. 26, 1834–April 26, 1927; House 1883–35.

LEWIS, Elijah Banks (Ga.) March 27, 1854–Dec. 10, 1920; House 1897–1909.

LEWIS, James Hamilton (Ill.) May 18, 1863–April 9, 1939; House 1897–99 (Wash.); Senate March 26, 1913–19, 1931–April 9, 1939.

LEWIS, John R. (Ga.) Feb. 21, 1940–; House 1987–.

LEWIS, Joseph Horace (Ky.) Oct. 29, 1824–July 6, 1904; House May 10, 1870–73.

LEWIS, Lawrence (Colo.) June 22, 1879–Dec. 9, 1943; House 1933–Dec. 9, 1943.

LEWIS, William J. (Va.) July 4, 1766–Nov. 1, 1828; House 1817–19.

LIBONATI, Roland Victor (Ill.) Dec. 29, 1900–; House Dec. 31, 1957–65.

LICHTENWALNER, Norton Lewis (Pa.) June 1, 1889–May 3, 1960; House 1931–33.

LIEB, Charles (Ind.) May 20, 1852–Sept. 1, 1928; House 1913–17.

LIEBEL, Michael Jr. (Pa.) Dec. 12, 1870–Aug. 8, 1927; House 1915–17.

LEIBERMAN, Joseph I. (Conn.) Feb. 24, 1942–; Senate 1989–.

LIGON, Robert Fulwood (Ala.) Dec. 16, 1823–Oct 11, 1901; House 1877–79.

LIGON, Thomas Watkins (Md.) May 10, 1810–Jan. 12, 1881; House 1845–49; Gov. Jan. 11, 1854–Jan. 13, 1858.

LILLY, Samuel (N.J.) Oct. 28, 1815–April 3, 1880; House 1853–55.

LILLY, Thomas Jefferson (W.Va.) June 3, 1878–April 2, 1956; House 1923–25.

LIND, James Francis (Pa.) Oct. 17, 1900–; House 1949–53.

LIND, John (Minn.) March 25, 1854–Sept. 18, 1930; House 1887–93 (Republican), 1903–05; Gov. Jan. 2, 1899–Jan. 7, 1901.

LINDSAY, George Henry (father of George Washington Lindsay) (N.Y.) Jan. 7, 1837–May 25, 1916; House 1901–13.

LINDSAY, George Washington (son of George Henry Lindsay) (N.Y.) March 28, 1865–March 15, 1938; House 1923–35.

LINDSAY, William (Ky.) Sept. 4, 1835–Oct. 15, 1909; Senate Feb. 15, 1893–1901.

LINDSLEY, William Dell (Ohio) Dec. 25, 1812–March 11, 1890; House 1853–55.

LINEHAN, Neil Joseph (Ill.) Sept. 23, 1895–Aug. 23, 1967; House 1949–51.

LINK, Arthur Albert (N.Dak.) May 24, 1914–; House 1971–73; Gov. Jan. 2, 1973–Jan. 7, 1981.

LINK, William Walter (Ill.) Feb. 12, 1884–Sept. 23, 1950; House 1945–47.

LINTHICUM, John Charles (Md.) Nov. 26, 1867–Oct. 5, 1932; House 1911–Oct. 5, 1932.

LIPINSKI, William Oliver (Ill.) Dec. 22, 1937–; House 1983–.

LISLE, Marcus Claiborne (Ky.) Sept. 23, 1862–July 7, 1894; House 1893–July 7, 1894.

LITTLE, Chauncey Bundy (Kans.) Feb. 10, 1877–Sept. 29, 1952; House 1925–27.

LITTLE, Edward Preble (Mass.) Nov. 7, 1791–Feb. 6, 1875; House Dec. 13, 1852–53.

LITTLE, John Sebastian (Ark.) March 15, 1853–Oct. 29, 1916; House Dec. 3, 1894–Jan. 1907; Gov. Jan. 8–Feb. 11, 1907.

LITTLE, Joseph James (N.Y.) June 5, 1841–Feb. 11, 1913; House Nov. 3, 1891–93.

LITTLEFIELD, Nathaniel Swett (Maine) Sept. 20, 1804–Aug. 15, 1882; House 1841–43, 1849–51.

LITTLEPAGE, Adam Brown (W.Va.) April 14, 1859–June 29, 1921; House 1911–13, 1915–19.

LITTLETON, Martin Wiley (N.Y.) Jan. 12, 1872–Dec. 19, 1934; House 1911–13.

LITTON, Jerry Lon (Mo.) May 12, 1937–Aug. 3, 1976; House 1973–Aug. 3, 1976.

LIVELY, Robert Maclin (Tex.) Jan. 6, 1855–Jan. 15, 1929; House July 23, 1910–11.

LIVERNASH, Edward James (subsequently Edward James de Nivernais) (UL Calif.) Feb. 14, 1866–June 1, 1938; House 1903–05.

LIVINGSTON, Leonidas Felix (Ga.) April 3, 1832–Feb. 11, 1912; House 1891–1911.

LLOYD, James Frederick (Calif.) Sept. 27, 1922–; House 1975–81.

LLOYD, James Tilghman (Mo.) Aug. 28, 1857–April 3, 1944; House June 1, 1897–1917.

LLOYD, Marilyn Laird (also known as Marilyn Laird Lloyd Bouquard) (Tenn.) Jan. 3, 1929–; House 1975–1995.

LLOYD, Wesley (Wash.) July 24, 1883–Jan. 10, 1936; House 1933–Jan. 10, 1936.

LOBECK, Charles Otto (Nebr.) April 6, 1852–Jan. 30, 1920; House 1911–19.

LOCHER, Cyrus (Ohio) March 8, 1878–Aug. 17, 1929; Senate April 5–Dec. 14, 1928.

LOCKHART, James (Ind.) Feb. 13, 1806–Sept. 7, 1857; House 1851–53, March 4–Sept. 7, 1857.

LOCKHART, James Alexander (N.C.) June 2, 1850–Dec. 24, 1905; House 1895–June 5, 1896.

LOCKWOOD, Daniel Newton (N.Y.) June 1, 1844–June 1, 1906; House 1877–79, 1891–95.

LOFT, George William (N.Y.) Feb. 5, 1865–Nov. 6, 1943; House Nov. 4, 1913–17.

LOFTIN, Scott Marion (Fla.) Sept. 14, 1878–Sept. 22, 1953; Senate May 26–Nov. 3, 1936.

LOGAN, Henry (Pa.) April 14, 1784–Dec. 26, 1866; House 1835–39 (1835–37 Jacksonian).

LOGAN, Marvel Mills (Ky.) Jan. 7, 1874–Oct. 3, 1939; Senate 1931–Oct. 3, 1939.

LOGAN, William Turner (S.C.) June 21, 1874–Sept. 15, 1941; House 1921–25.

LOGUE, James Washington (Pa.) Feb. 22, 1863–Aug. 27, 1925; House 1913–15.

LONERGAN, Augustine (Conn.) May 20, 1874–Oct. 18, 1947; House 1913–15, 1917–21, 1931–33; Senate 1933–39.

LONG, Alexander (Ohio) Dec. 24, 1816–Nov. 28, 1886; House 1863–65.

LONG, Catherine (widow of Gillis William Long) (La.) Feb. 7, 1924–; House April 4, 1985–87.

LONG, Clarence Dickinson (Md.) Dec. 11, 1908–; House 1963–85.

LONG, Edward Vaughn (Mo.) July 18, 1908–Nov. 6, 1972; Senate Sept. 23, 1960–Dec. 27, 1968.

LONG, George Shannon (brother of Huey Pierce "the Kingfish" Long, brother-in-law of Rose McConnell Long, uncle of Russell Billiu Long, cousin of Gillis William Long) (La.) Sept. 11, 1883–March 22, 1958; House 1953–March 22, 1958.

LONG, Gillis William (husband of Catherine Long, cousin of Huey Pierce "the Kingfish" Long, Rose McConnell Long, Russell Billiu Long and George Shannon Long) (La.) May 4, 1923–Jan. 20, 1985; House 1963–65, 1973–Jan. 20, 1985.

LONG, Huey Pierce "the Kingfish" (husband of Rose McConnell Long, father of Russell Billiu Long, brother of George Shannon Long, cousin of Gillis William Long) (La.) Aug. 30, 1893–Sept. 10, 1935; Senate Jan. 25, 1932–Sept. 10, 1935; Gov. May 21, 1928–Jan. 25, 1932.

LONG, Jill (Ind.) July 15, 1952–; House April 5, 1989–1995.

LONG, John Benjamin (Tex.) Sept. 8, 1843–April 27, 1924; House 1891–93.

LONG, Lewis Marshall (Ill.) June 22, 1883–Sept. 9, 1957; House 1937–39.

LONG, Oren Ethelbirt (Hawaii) March 4, 1889–May 6, 1965; Senate (Terr. Sen.) 1956–59, (Sen.) Aug. 21, 1959–63; Gov. (Hawaii Terr.) 1951–53.

LONG, Rose McConnell (widow of Huey Pierce "the Kingfish" Long, mother of Russell Billiu Long, sister-in-law of George Shannon Long) (La.) April 8, 1892–May 27, 1970; Senate Jan. 31, 1936–Jan. 2, 1937.

LONG, Russell Billiu (son of Huey Pierce "the Kingfish" Long and Rose McConnell Long, nephew of George Shannon Long) (La.) Nov. 3, 1918–; Senate Dec. 31, 1948–87; Chrmn. Senate Finance 1965–81.

LONG, Speedy Oteria (La.) June 16, 1928–; House 1965–73.

LOOMIS, Arphaxed (N.Y.) April 9, 1798–Sept. 15, 1885; House 1837–39.

LORD, Frederick William (N.Y.) Dec. 11, 1800–May 24, 1860; House 1847–49.

LORD, Scott (N.Y.) Dec. 11, 1820–Sept. 10, 1885; House 1875–77.

LORE, Charles Brown (Del.) March 16, 1831–March 6, 1911; House 1883–87.

LOSER, Joseph Carlton (Tenn.) Oct. 1, 1892–July 31, 1984; House 1957–63.

LOUNSBERY, William (N.Y.) Dec. 25, 1831–Nov. 8, 1905; House 1879–81.

LOVE, Peter Early (Ga.) July 7, 1818–Nov. 8, 1866; House 1859–Jan. 23, 1861.

LOVE, Rodney Marvin (Ohio) July 18, 1908–; House 1965–67.

LOVE, William Franklin (Miss.) March 29, 1850–Oct. 16, 1898; House 1897–Oct. 16, 1898.

LOVERING, Henry Bacon (Mass.) April 8, 1841–April 5, 1911; House 1883–87.

LOWELL, Joshua Adams (Maine) March 20, 1801–March 13, 1874; House 1839–43.

LOWENSTEIN, Allard Kenneth (N.Y.) Jan. 16, 1929–March 14, 1980; House 1969–71.

LOWEY, Nita Melnikoff (N.Y.) July 5, 1937–; House 1989–.

LOWREY, Bill Green (Miss.) May 25, 1862–Sept. 2, 1947; House 1921–29.

LOWRIE, Walter (Pa.) Dec. 10, 1784–Dec. 14, 1868; Senate 1819–25.

LOWRY, Michael Edward (Wash.) March 8, 1939–; House 1979–89; Gov. Jan. 13, 1993–.

LOWRY, Robert (Ind.) April 2, 1824–Jan. 27, 1904; House 1883–87.

LOZIER, Ralph Fulton (Mo.) Jan. 28, 1866–May 28, 1945; House 1923–35.

LUCAS, Scott Wike (Ill.) Feb. 19, 1892–Feb. 22, 1968; House 1935–39; Senate 1939–51; Senate majority leader 1949–51.

LUCAS, William (brother of Edward Lucas) (Va.) Nov. 30, 1800–Aug. 29, 1877; House 1839–41, 1843–45.

LUCAS, Wingate Hezekiah (Tex.) May 1, 1908–May 26, 1989; House 1947–55.

LUCKEY, Henry Carl (Nebr.) Nov. 22, 1868–Dec. 31, 1956; House 1935–39.

LUCKING, Alfred (Mich.) Dec. 18, 1856–Dec. 1, 1929; House 1903–05.

LUDLOW, Louis Leon (Ind.) June 24, 1873–Nov. 28, 1950; House 1929–49.

LUECKE, John Frederick (Mich.) July 4, 1889–March 21, 1952; House 1937–39.

LUKEN, Charles (son of Thomas Andrew Luken) (Ohio) July 18, 1951–; House 1991–93.

LUKEN, Thomas Andrew (father of Charles Luken) (Ohio) July 9, 1925–; House March 5, 1974–75, 1977–91.

LUMPKIN, Alva Moore (S.C.) Nov. 13, 1886–Aug. 1, 1941; Senate July 22–Aug. 1, 1941.

LUMPKIN, John Henry (nephew of Wilson Lumpkin) (Ga.) June 13, 1812–July 10, 1860; House 1843–49, 1855–57.

LUNDINE, Stanley Nelson (N.Y.) Feb. 4, 1939–; House March 2, 1976–87.

LUNN, George Richard (N.Y.) June 23, 1873–Nov. 27, 1948; House 1917–19.

LUSK, Georgia Lee (N.Mex.) May 12, 1893–Jan. 5, 1971; House 1947–49.

LUSK, Hall Stoner (Oreg.) Sept. 21, 1883–May 15, 1983; Senate March 16–Nov. 8, 1960.

LUTTRELL, John King (Calif.) June 27, 1831–Oct. 4, 1893; House 1873–79.

LYLE, John Emmett Jr. (Tex.) Sept. 4, 1910–; House 1945–55.

LYNCH, John (Pa.) Nov. 1, 1843–Aug. 17, 1910; House 1887–89.

LYNCH, Thomas (Wis.) Nov. 21, 1844–May 4, 1898; House 1891–95.

LYNCH, Walter Aloysius (N.Y.) July 7, 1894–Sept. 10, 1957; House Feb. 20, 1940–51.

LYNDE, William Pitt (Wis.) Dec. 16, 1817–Dec. 18, 1885; House June 5, 1848–49, 1875–79.

LYON, Homer Le Grand (N.C.) March 1, 1879–May 31, 1956; House 1921–29.

LYON, Lucius (Mich.) Feb. 25, 1800–Sept. 24, 1851; House (Terr. Del.) 1833–35, (Rep.) 1843–45; Senate Jan. 26, 1837–39.

MacDONALD, John Lewis (Minn.) Feb. 22, 1838–July 13, 1903; House 1887–89.

MACDONALD, Moses (Maine) April 8, 1815–Oct. 18, 1869; House 1851–55.

MACDONALD, Torbert Hart (Mass.) June 6, 1917–May 21, 1976; House 1955–May 21, 1976.

MACHEN, Hervey Gilbert (Md.) Oct. 14, 1916–; House 1965–69.

MACHEN, Willis Benson (Ky.) April 10, 1810–Sept. 29, 1893; Senate Sept. 27, 1872–73.

MACHROWICZ, Thaddeus Michael (Mich.) Aug. 21, 1899–Feb. 17, 1970; House 1951–Sept. 18, 1961.

MACIEJEWSKI, Anton Frank (Ill.) Jan. 3, 1893–Sept. 25, 1949; House 1939–Dec. 8, 1942.

MacINTYRE, Archibald Thompson (Ga.) Oct. 27, 1822–Jan. 1, 1900; House 1871–73.

MACIORA, Lucien John (Conn.) Aug. 17, 1902–; House 1941–43.

MACK, Peter Francis Jr. (Ill.) Nov. 1, 1916–July 4, 1986; House 1949–63.

MacKAY, James Armstrong (Ga.) June 25, 1919–; House 1965–67.

MacKAY, Kenneth Hood "Buddy" Jr. (Fla.) March 22, 1933–; House 1983–89.

MACKEY, Levi Augustus (Pa.) Nov. 25, 1819–Feb. 8, 1889; House 1875–79.

MACKIE, John C. (Mich.) June 1, 1920–; House 1965–67.

MACLAY, William Brown (N.Y.) March 20, 1812–Feb. 19, 1882; House 1843–49, 1857–61.

MACON, Robert Bruce (Ark.) July 6, 1859–Oct. 9, 1925; House 1903–13.

MACY, John B. (Wis.) March 26, 1799–Sept. 24, 1856; House 1853–55.

MADDEN, Ray John (Ind.) Feb. 25, 1892–Sept. 28, 1987; House 1943–77; Chrmn. House Rules 1973–77.

MADDOX, John W. (Ga.) June 3, 1848–Sept. 27, 1922; House 1893–1905.

MAGEE, Clare (Mo.) March 31, 1899–Aug. 7, 1969; House 1949–53.

MAGEE, John Alexander (Pa.) Oct. 14, 1827–Nov. 18, 1903; House 1873–75.

MAGINNIS, Martin (Mont.) Oct. 27, 1841–March 27, 1919; House (Terr. Del.) 1873–85.

MAGNER, Thomas Francis (uncle of John Francis Carew) (N.Y.) March 8, 1860–Dec. 22, 1945; House 1889–95.

MAGNUSON, Donald Hammer (Wash.) March 7, 1911–Oct. 5, 1979; House 1953–63.

MAGNUSON, Warren Grant (Wash.) April 12,1905–May 20, 1989; House 1937–Dec. 13, 1944; Senate Dec., 14, 1944–81; Chrmn. Senate Interstate and Foreign Commerce 1955–61; Chrmn. Senate Commerce 1961–77; Chrmn. Senate Commerce, Science, and Transportation 1977–78; Chrmn. Senate Appropriations 1978–81; elected Pres. pro tempore Jan. 15, 1979.

MAGRUDER, Allan Bowie (La.) 1775–April 15, 1822; Senate Sept. 3, 1812–13.

MAGUIRE, Gene Andrew (N.J.) March 11, 1939–; House 1975–81.

MAGUIRE, James George (Calif.) Feb. 22, 1853–June 20, 1920; House 1893–99.

MAGUIRE, John Arthur (Nebr.) Nov. 29, 1870–July 1, 1939; House 1909–15.

MAHAN, Bryan Francis (Conn.) May 1, 1856–Nov. 16, 1923; House 1913–15.

MAHER, James Paul (N.Y.) Nov. 3, 1865–July 31, 1946; House 1911–21.

MAHON, Gabriel Heyward Jr. (S.C.) Nov. 11, 1889–June 11, 1962; House Nov. 3, 1936–39.

MAHON, George Herman (Tex.) Sept. 22, 1900–Nov. 19, 1985; House 1935–79; Chrmn. House Appropriations 1964–77.

MAHONEY, Peter Paul (N.Y.) June 25, 1848–March 27, 1889; House 1885–89.

MAHONEY, William Frank (Ill.) Feb. 22, 1856–Dec. 27, 1904; House 1901–Dec.27, 1904.

MAISH, Levi (Pa.) Nov. 22, 1837–Feb. 26, 1899; House 1875–79, 1887–91.

MAJOR, James Earl (Ill.) Jan. 5, 1887–Jan. 4, 1972; House 1923–25, 1927–29, 1931–Oct. 6, 1933.

MAJOR, Samuel Collier (Mo.) July 2, 1869–July 28, 1931; House 1919–21, 1923–29, March 4–July 28, 1931.

MALLORY, Meredith (N.Y.) ?–?; House 1839–41.

MALLORY, Stephen Russell (father of Stephen Russell Mallory, below) (Fla.) 1813–Nov. 9, 1873; Senate 1851–Jan. 21, 1861.

MALLORY, Stephen Russell (son of Stephen Russell Mallory, above) (Fla.) Nov. 2, 1848–Dec. 23, 1907; House 1891–95; Senate May 15, 1897–Dec. 23, 1907.

MALONEY, Carolyn Bosher (N.Y.) Feb. 19, 1948–; House 1993–.

MALONEY, Francis Thomas (Conn.) March 31, 1894–Jan. 16, 1945; House 1933–35; Senate 1935–Jan. 16, 1945.

MALONEY, Paul Herbert (La.) Feb. 14, 1876–March 26, 1967; House 1931–Dec. 15, 1940, 1943–47.

MANASCO, Carter (Ala.) Jan. 3, 1902–Feb. 5, 1992; House June 24, 1941–49.

MANKIN, Helen Douglas (Ga.) Sept. 11, 1896–July 25, 1956; House Feb. 12, 1946–47.

MANN, David Scott (Ohio) Sept. 25, 1939–; House 1993–1995.

MANN, Edward Coke (S.C.) Nov. 21, 1880–Nov. 11, 1931; House Oct. 7, 1919–21.

MANN, James (La.) June 22, 1822–Aug. 26, 1868; House July 18–Aug. 26, 1868.

MANN, James Robert (S.C.) April 27, 1920–; House 1969–79.

MANN, Job (Pa.) March 31, 1795–Oct. 8, 1873; House 1835–37 (Jacksonian), 1847–51.

MANNING, John Jr. (N.C.) July 30, 1830–Feb. 12, 1899; House Dec. 7, 1870–71.

MANNING, Vannoy Hartrog (Miss.) July 26, 1839–Nov. 3, 1892; House 1877–83.

MANSFIELD, Joseph Jefferson (Tex.) Feb. 9, 1861–July 12, 1947; House 1917–July 12, 1947.

MANSFIELD, Michael Joseph (Mont.) March 16, 1903–; House 1943–53; Senate 1953–77; Chrmn. Senate Rules and Administration 1961–63; Senate majority leader 1961–77.

MANSON, Mahlon Dickerson (Ind.) Feb. 20, 1820–Feb. 4, 1895; House 1871–73.

MANSUR, Charles Harley (Mo.) March 6, 1835–April 16, 1895; House 1887–93.

MANTON, Thomas J. (N.Y.) Nov. 3, 1932–; House 1985–.

MANZANARES, Francisco Antonio (N.Mex.) Jan. 25, 1843–Sept. 17, 1904; House (Terr. Del.) March 5, 1884–85.

MARCHAND, Albert Gallatin (son of David Marchand) (Pa.) Feb. 27, 1811–Feb. 5, 1848; House 1839–43.

MARCY, Daniel (N.H.) Nov. 7, 1809–Nov. 3, 1893; House 1863–65.

MARGOLIS-MEZVINSKY, Marjorie (wife of Edward Maurice Mezvinsky) (Pa.) June 21, 1942–; House 1993–1995.

MARKEY, Edward John (Mass.) July 11, 1946–; House Nov. 2, 1976–.

MARLAND, Ernest Whitworth (Okla.) May 8, 1874–Oct. 3, 1941; House 1933–35; Gov. Jan. 14, 1935–Jan. 9, 1939.

MARSALIS, John Henry (Colo.) May 9, 1904–June 26, 1971; House 1949–51.

MARSH, John Otho Jr. (Va.) Aug. 7, 1926–; House 1963–71.

MARSHALL, Alfred (Maine) about 1797–Oct. 2, 1868; House 1841–43.

MARSHALL, Edward Colston (Calif.) June 29, 1821–July 9, 1893; House 1851–53.

MARSHALL, Fred (Minn.) March 13, 1906–June 5, 1985; House 1949–63.

MARSHALL, George Alexander (Ohio) Sept. 14, 1851–April 21, 1899; House 1897–99.

MARSHALL, James William (Va.) March 31, 1844–Nov. 27, 1911; House 1893–95.

MARSHALL, Samuel Scott (Ill.) March 12, 1821–July 26, 1890; House 1855–59, 1865–75.

MARTIN, Augustus Newton (Ind.) March 23, 1847–July 11, 1901; House 1889–95.

MARTIN, Barclay (uncle of Lewis Tillman) (Tenn.) Dec. 17, 1802–Nov. 8, 1890; House 1845–47.

MARTIN, Benjamin Franklin (W.Va.) Oct. 2, 1828–Jan. 20, 1895; House 1877–81.

MARTIN, Charles (Ill.) May 20, 1856–Oct. 28, 1917; House March 4–Oct. 28, 1917.

MARTIN, Charles Drake (Ohio) Aug. 5, 1829–Aug. 27, 1911; House 1859–61.

MARTIN, Charles Henry (Oreg.) Oct. 1, 1863–Sept. 22, 1946; House 1931–35; Gov. Jan. 14, 1935–Jan. 9, 1939.

MARTIN, Edward Livingston (Del.) March 29, 1837–Jan. 22, 1897; House 1879–83.

MARTIN, George Brown (grandson of John Preston Martin) (Ky.) Aug. 18, 1876–Nov. 12, 1945; Senate Sept. 7, 1918–19.

MARTIN, John (Kans.) Nov. 12, 1833–Sept. 3, 1913; Senate 1893–95.

MARTIN, John Andrew (Colo.) April 10, 1868–Dec. 23, 1939; House 1909–13, 1933–Dec. 23, 1939.

MARTIN, John Cunningham (Ill.) April 29, 1880–Jan. 27, 1952; House 1939–41.

MARTIN, John Mason (son of Joshua Lanier Martin) (Ala.) Jan. 20, 1837–June 16, 1898; House 1885–87.

MARTIN, John Preston (brother of Elbert Sevier Martin, grandfather of George Brown Martin) (Ky.) Oct. 11, 1811–Dec. 23, 1862; House 1845–47.

MARTIN, Joshua Lanier (father of John Mason Martin) (Ala.) Dec. 5, 1799–Nov. 2, 1856; House 1835–39 (1835–37 Jacksonian); Gov. Dec. 10, 1845–Dec. 16, 1847 (Independent).

MARTIN, Lewis J. (N.J.) Feb. 22, 1844–May 5, 1913; House March 4–May 5, 1913.

MARTIN, Morgan Lewis (cousin of James Duane Doty) (Wis.) March 31, 1805–Dec. 10, 1887; House (Terr. Del.) 1845–47.

MARTIN, Thomas Staples (Va.) July 29, 1847–Nov. 12, 1919; Senate 1895–Nov. 12, 1919; Senate minority leader 1911–13, March 4–Nov. 12, 1919; Senate majority leader 1917–19.

MARTIN, Whitmell Pugh (La.) Aug. 12, 1867–April 6, 1929; House 1915–April 6, 1929 (1915–19 Progressive).

MARTIN, William Harrison (Tex.) May 23, 1823–Feb. 3, 1898; House Nov. 4, 1887–91.

MARTINE, James Edgar (N.J.) Aug. 25, 1850–Feb. 26, 1925; Senate 1911–17.

MARTINEZ, Matthew Gilbert (Calif.) Feb. 14, 1929–; House July 15, 1982–.

MASON, Harry Howland (Ill.) Dec. 16, 1873–March 10, 1946; House 1935–37.

MASON, James Murray (Va.) Nov. 3, 1798–April 28, 1871; House 1837–39 (Jacksonian); Senate Jan. 21, 1847–March 28, 1861; elected Pres. pro tempore Jan. 6, 1857, March 4, 1857.

MASON, John Calvin (Ky.) Aug. 4, 1802–Aug. 1865; House 1849–53, 1857–59.

MASON, John Thomson (Md.) May 9, 1815–March 28, 1873; House 1841–43.

MASSINGALE, Samuel Chapman (Okla.) Aug. 2, 1870–Jan. 17, 1941; House 1935–Jan. 17, 1941.

MATHEWS, Harlan (Tenn.) Jan. 17, 1927–; Senate Jan. 5, 1993–1995.

MATHEWS, James (Ohio) June 4, 1805–March 30, 1887; House 1884–45.

MATHIS, Marvin Dawson (Ga.) Nov. 30, 1940–; House 1971–81.

MATSON, Courtland Cushing (Ind.) April 25, 1841–Sept. 4, 1915; House 1881–89.

MATSUI, Robert Takeo (Calif.) Sept. 17, 1941–; House 1979–.

MATSUNAGA, Spark Masayuki (Hawaii) Oct. 8, 1916–April 15, 1990; House 1963–77; Senate 1977–April 15, 1990.

MATTHEWS, Donald Ray "Billy" (Fla.) Oct. 3, 1907–; House 1953–67.

MATTOX, James Albon (Tex.) Aug. 29, 1943–; House 1977–83.

MAURICE, James (N.Y.) Nov. 7, 1814–Aug. 4, 1884; House 1853–55.

MAVERICK, Fontaine Maury (cousin of Abram Poindexter Maury, nephew of James Luther Slayden, cousin of John Wood Fishburne) (Tex.) Oct. 23, 1895–June 7, 1954; House 1935–39.

MAVROULES, Nicholas (Mass.) Nov. 1, 1929–; House 1979–93.

MAXEY, Samuel Bell (Tex.) March 30, 1825–Aug. 16, 1895; Senate 1875–87.

MAXWELL, Augustus Emmett (grandfather of Emmett Wilson) (Fla.) Sept. 21, 1820–May 5, 1903; House 1853–57.

MAY, Henry (Md.) Feb. 13, 1816–Sept. 25, 1866; House 1853–55, 1861–63.

MAY, Mitchell (N.Y.) July 10, 1870–March 24, 1961; House 1899–1901.

MAY, William L. (Ill.) about 1793–Sept. 29, 1849; House Dec. 1, 1834–39 (Dec. 1, 1834–37 Jacksonian).

MAYALL, Samuel (Maine) June 21, 1816–Sept. 17, 1892; House 1853–55.

MAYBANK, Burnet Rhett (S.C.) March 7, 1899–Sept. 1, 1954; Senate Nov. 5, 1941–Sept. 1, 1954; Chrmn. Senate Banking and Currency 1949–53; Gov. Jan. 17, 1939–Nov. 4, 1941.

MAYBURY, William Cotter (Mich.) Nov. 20, 1848–May 6, 1909; House 1883–87.

MAYFIELD, Earle Bradford (Tex.) April 12, 1881–June 23, 1964; Senate 1923–29.

MAYHAM, Stephen Lorenzo (N.Y.) Oct. 8, 1826–March 3, 1908; House 1869–71, 1877–79.

MAYNARD, Harry Lee (Va.) June 8, 1861–Oct. 23, 1922; House 1901–11.

MAYS, Dannite Hill (Fla.) April 28, 1852–May 9, 1930; House 1909–13.

MAYS, James Henry (Utah) June 29, 1868–April 19, 1926; House 1915–21.

MAZZOLI, Romano Louis (Ky.) Nov. 2, 1932–; House 1971–.

McADOO, William (N.J.) Oct. 25, 1853–June 7, 1930; House 1883–91.

McADOO, William Gibbs (Calif.) Oct. 31, 1863–Feb. 1, 1941; Senate 1933–Nov. 8, 1938; Secy. of the Treasury March 6, 1913–Dec. 15, 1918.

McALEER, William (Pa.) Jan. 6, 1838–April 19 1912; House 1891–95 (1891–93 Democrat, 1893–95 Independent Democrat), 1897–1901.

McALLISTER, Archibald (grandson of John Andre Hanna) (Pa.) Oct. 12, 1813–July 18, 1883; House 1863–65.

McANDREWS, James (Ill.) Oct. 22, 1862–Aug. 31, 1942; House 1901–05, 1913–21, 1935–41.

McARDLE, Joseph A. (Pa.) June 29, 1903–Dec. 27, 1967; House 1939–Jan. 5, 1942.

McCANDLESS, Lincoln Loy (Hawaii) Sept. 18, 1859–Oct. 5, 1940; House (Terr. Del.) 1933–35.

McCARRAN, Patrick Anthony (Nev.) Aug. 8, 1876–Sept. 28, 1954; Senate 1933–Sept. 28, 1954; Chrmn. Senate Judiciary 1949–53.

McCARTHY, Eugene Joseph (Minn.) March 29, 1916–; House 1949–59; Senate 1959–71.

McCARTHY, John Henry (N.Y.) Nov. 16, 1850–Feb. 5, 1908; House 1889–Jan. 14, 1891.

McCARTHY, Richard Dean (N.Y.) Sept. 24, 1927–; House 1965–71.

McCAUSLEN, William Cochran (Ohio) 1796–March 13, 1863; House 1843–45.

McCLAMMY, Charles Washington (N.C.) May 29, 1839–Feb. 26, 1896; House 1887–91.

McCLEAN, Moses (Pa.) June 17, 1804–Sept. 30, 1870; House 1845–47.

McCLELLAN, Abraham (Tenn.) Oct. 4, 1789–May 3, 1866; House 1837–43.

McCLELLAN, Charles A.O. (Ind.) May 25, 1835–Jan. 31, 1898; House 1889–93.

McCLELLAN, George (N.Y.) Oct. 10, 1856–Feb. 20, 1927; House 1913–15.

McCLELLAN, George Brinton (N.Y.) Nov. 23, 1865–Nov. 30, 1940; House 1895–Dec. 21, 1903.

McCLELLAN, John Little (Ark.) Feb. 25, 1896–Nov. 28, 1977; House 1935–39; Senate 1943–Nov. 28, 1977; Chrmn. Senate Expenditures in the Executive Departments 1949–52; Chrmn. Senate Government Operations 1952–53, 1955–72; Chrmn. Senate Appropriations 1972–77.

McCLELLAN, Robert (N.Y.) Oct. 2, 1806–June 28, 1860; House 1837–39, 1841–43.

McCLELLAND, Robert (Mich.) Aug. 1, 1807–Aug. 30, 1880; House 1843–49; Gov. Jan. 1, 1851–March 7, 1853; Secy. of the Interior March 8, 1853–March 9, 1857.

McCLELLAND, William (Pa.) March 2, 1842–Feb. 7, 1892; House 1871–73.

McCLERNAND, John Alexander (Ill.) May 30, 1812–Sept. 20, 1900; House 1843–51, Nov. 8, 1859–Oct. 28, 1861.

McCLINTIC, James Vernon (Okla.) Sept, 8, 1878–April 22, 1948; House 1915–35.

McCLOSKEY, Augustus (Tex.) Sept. 23, 1878–July 21, 1950; House 1929–Feb. 10, 1930.

McCLOSKEY, Francis Xavier (Ind.) June 12, 1939–; House 1983–85, May 1, 1985–.

McCLURE, Charles (Pa.) 1804–Jan. 10, 1846; House 1837–39, Dec. 7, 1840–41.

McCONNELL, Felix Grundy (Ala.) April 1, 1809–Sept. 10, 1846; House 1843–Sept. 10, 1846.

McCORD, James Nance (Tenn.) March 17, 1879–Sept. 2, 1968; House 1943–45; Gov. Jan. 16, 1945–Jan. 17, 1949.

McCORKLE, Joseph Walker (Calif.) June 24, 1819–March 18, 1884; House 1851–53.

McCORKLE, Paul Grier (S.C.) Dec. 19, 1863–June 2, 1934; House Feb. 24–March 3, 1917.

McCORMACK, John William (Mass.) Dec. 21, 1891–Nov. 22, 1980; House Nov. 6, 1928–71; House majority leader Sept. 26, 1940–47, 1949–53, 1955–Jan. 10, 1962; Speaker Jan. 10, 1962–63, Jan. 9, 1963–65, Jan. 4, 1965–67, Jan. 10, 1967–71.

McCORMACK, Mike (Wash.) Dec. 14, 1921–; House 1971–81.

McCORMICK, James Robinson (Mo.) Aug. 1, 1824–May 19, 1897; House Dec. 17, 1867–73.

McCOY, Walter Irving (N.J.) Dec. 8, 1859–July 17, 1933; House 1911–Oct. 3, 1914.

McCRATE, John Dennis (Maine) Oct. 1, 1802–Sept. 11, 1879; House 1845–47.

McCREARY, James Bennett (Ky.) July 8, 1838–Oct. 8, 1918; House 1885–97; Senate 1903–09; Gov. Aug. 31, 1875–Aug. 31, 1879, Dec. 12, 1911–Dec. 7, 1915.

McCREERY, Thomas Clay (Ky.) Dec. 12, 1816–July 10, 1890; Senate Feb. 19, 1868–71, 1873–79.

McCULLOCH, George (Pa.) Feb. 22, 1792–April 16, 1861; House Nov. 20, 1839–41.

McCULLOCH, Philip Doddridge Jr. (Ark.) June 23, 1851–Nov. 26, 1928; House 1893–1903.

McCULLOUGH, Hiram (Md.) Sept. 26, 1813–March 4, 1885; House 1865–69.

McCURDY, David Keith (Okla.) March 30, 1950–; House 1981–1995; Chmn. House Permanent Select Committee on Intelligence 1991–93.

McDANIEL, William (Mo.) ?–Dec. 14, 1866; House Dec. 7, 1846–47.

McDANNOLD, John James (Ill.) Aug. 29, 1851–Feb. 3, 1904; House 1893–95.

McDEARMON, James Calvin (Tenn.) June 13, 1844–July 19, 1902; House 1893–97.

McDERMOTT, Allan Langdon (N.J.) March 30, 1854–Oct. 26, 1908; House Dec. 3, 1900–07.

McDERMOTT, James Thomas (Ill.) Feb. 13, 1872–Feb. 7, 1938; House 1907–July 21, 1914, 1915–17.

McDERMOTT, James (Wash.) Dec. 28, 1936–; House 1989–; Chrmn. House Standards of Official Conduct 1993–1995.

McDONALD, Edward Francis (N.J.) Sept. 21, 1844–Nov. 5, 1892; House 1891–Nov. 5, 1892.

McDONALD, Joseph Ewing (Ind.) Aug. 29, 1819–June 21, 1891; House 1849–51; Senate 1875–81.

McDONALD, Lawrence Patton (Ga.) April 1, 1935–Sept. 1, 1983; House 1975–Sept. 1, 1983.

McDOUGALL, James Alexander (Calif.) Nov. 19, 1817–Sept. 3, 1867; House 1953–55; Senate 1861–67.

McDOWELL, Harris Brown Jr. (Del.) Feb. 10, 1906–; House 1955–57, 1959–67.

McDOWELL, James (Va.) Oct. 13, 1795–Aug. 24, 1851; House March 6, 1846–51; Gov. Jan. 1, 1843–Jan. 1, 1846.

McDOWELL, James Foster (Ind.) Dec. 3, 1825–April 18, 1887; House 1863–65.

McDOWELL, John Anderson (Ohio) Sept. 25, 1853–Oct. 2, 1927; House 1897–1901.

McDOWELL, Joseph Jefferson (son of Joseph McDowell) (Ohio) Nov. 13, 1800–Jan. 17, 1877; House 1843–47.

McDUFFIE, George (father-in-law of Wade Hampton) (S.C.) Aug. 10, 1790–March 11, 1851; House 1821–34 (no party); Senate Dec. 23, 1842–Aug. 17, 1846; Gov. Dec. 11, 1834–Dec. 10, 1836 (State Rights Democrat).

McDUFFIE, John (Ala.) Sept. 25, 1883–Nov. 1, 1950; House 1919–March 2, 1935.

McENERY, Samuel Douglas (La.) May 28, 1837–June 28, 1910; Senate 1897–June 28, 1910; Gov. Oct. 16, 1881–May 20, 1888.

McETTRICK, Michael Joseph (Mass.) June 22, 1848–Dec. 31, 1921; House 1893–95.

McFADDEN, Obadiah Benton (Wash.) Nov. 18, 1815–June 25, 1875; House (Terr. Del.) 1873–75.

McFALL, John Joseph (Calif.) Feb. 20, 1918–; House 1957–Dec. 31, 1978.

McFARLAND, Ernest William (Ariz.) Oct. 9, 1894–June 8, 1984; Senate 1941–53; Senate majority leader 1951–53; Gov. Jan. 3, 1955–Jan. 5, 1959.

McFARLAND, William (Tenn.) Sept. 15, 1821–April 12, 1900; House 1875–77.

McFARLANE, William Doddridge (Tex.) July 17, 1894–Feb. 15, 1980; House 1933–39.

McGANN, Lawrence Edward (Ill.) Feb. 2, 1852–July 22, 1928; House 1891–Dec. 27, 1895.

McGEE, Gale William (Wyo.) March 17, 1915–April 9, 1992; Senate 1959–77; Chrmn. Senate Post Office and Civil Service 1969–77.

McGEHEE, Daniel Rayford (Miss.) Sept. 10, 1883–Feb. 9, 1962; House 1935–47.

McGILL, George (Kans.) Feb. 12, 1879–May 14, 1963; Senate Dec. 1, 1930–39.

McGILLICUDDY, Daniel John (Maine) Aug. 27, 1859–July 30, 1936; House 1911–17.

McGINLEY, Donald Francis (Nebr.) June 30, 1920–; House 1959–61.

McGLENNON, Cornelius Augustine (N.J.) Dec. 10, 1878–June 13, 1931; House 1919–21.

McGLINCHEY, Herbert Joseph (Pa.) Nov. 7, 1904–; House 1945–47.

McGOVERN, George Stanley (S.Dak.) July 19, 1922–; House 1957–61; Senate 1963–81.

McGRANERY, James Patrick (Pa.) July 8, 1895–Dec. 23, 1962; House 1937–Nov. 17, 1943; Atty. Gen. May 27, 1952–Jan. 20, 1953.

McGRATH, Christopher Columbus (N.Y.) May 15, 1902–July 7, 1986; House 1949–53.

McGRATH, James Howard (R.I.) Nov. 28, 1903–Sept. 2, 1966; Senate 1947–Aug. 23, 1949; Chrmn. Senate District of Columbia 1949–51; Gov. Jan. 7, 1941–Oct. 6, 1945; Chrmn. Dem. Nat. Comm. 1947–49; Atty. Gen. Aug. 24, 1949–April 7, 1952.

McGRATH, John Joseph (Calif.) July 23, 1872–Aug. 25, 1951; House 1933–39.

McGRATH, Thomas Charles Jr. (N.J.) April 22, 1927–Jan. 15, 1994; House 1965–67.

McGROARTY, John Steven (Calif.) Aug. 20, 1862–Aug. 7, 1944; House 1935–39.

McGUIRE, John Andrew (Conn.) Feb. 28, 1906–May 28, 1976; House 1949–53.

McHALE, Paul (Pa.) July 26, 1950–; House 1993–.

McHENRY, Henry Davis (son of John Hardin McHenry) (Ky.) Feb. 27, 1826–Dec. 17, 1890; House 1871–73.

McHENRY, John Geiser (Pa.) April 26, 1868–Dec. 27, 1912; House 1907–Dec. 27, 1912.

McHUGH, Matthew Francis (N.Y.) Dec. 6, 1938–; House 1975–93.

McINTYRE, John Joseph (Wyo.) Dec. 17, 1904–Nov. 30, 1974; House 1941–43.

McINTYRE, Thomas James (N.H.) Feb. 20, 1915–Aug. 9, 1992; Senate Nov. 7, 1962–79.

McKAIG, William McMahon (Md.) July 29, 1845–June 6, 1907; House 1891–95.

McKAY, James Iver (N.C.) 1793–Sept. 4, 1853; House 1831–49 (1831–37 Jacksonian).

McKAY, Koln Gunn (Utah) Feb. 23, 1925–; House 1971–81.

McKELLAR, Kenneth Douglas (Tenn.) Jan. 29, 1869–Oct. 25, 1957; House Nov. 9, 1911–17; Senate 1917–53; elected Pres. pro tempore Jan. 6, 1945, Jan. 3, 1949; Chrmn. Senate Appropriations 1949–53.

McKENNEY, William Robertson (Va.) Dec. 2, 1851–Jan. 3, 1916; House 1895–May 2, 1896.

McKENTY, Jacob Kerlin (Pa.) Jan. 19, 1827–Jan. 3, 1866; House Dec. 3, 1860–61.

McKENZIE, Charles Edgar (La.) Oct. 3, 1896–June 7, 1956; House 1943–47.

McKENZIE, James Andrew (Ky.) Aug. 1, 1840–June 25, 1904; House 1877–83.

McKEON, John (N.Y.) March 29, 1808–Nov. 22, 1883; House 1835–37 (Jacksonian), 1841–43.

McKEOUGH, Raymond Stephen (Ill.) April 29, 1888–Dec. 16, 1979; House 1935–43.

McKEOWN, Thomas Deitz (Okla.) June 4, 1878–Oct. 22, 1951; House 1917–21, 1923–35.

McKIBBIN, Joseph Chambers (Calif.) May 14, 1824–July 1, 1896; House 1857–59.

McKIM, Isaac (nephew of Alexander McKim) (Md.) July 21, 1775–April 1, 1838; House Jan. 4, 1823–25 (no party), 1833–April 1, 1838 (1833–37 Jacksonian).

McKINIRY, Richard Francis (N.Y.) March 23, 1878–May 30, 1950; House 1919–21.

McKINNEY, Cynthia (Ga.) March 17, 1955–; House 1993–.

McKINNEY, John Franklin (Ohio) April 12, 1827–June 13, 1903; House 1863–65, 1871–73.

McKINNEY, Luther Franklin (N.H.) April 25, 1841–July 30, 1922; House 1887–89, 1891–93.

McKINNON, Clinton Dotson (Calif.) Feb. 5, 1906–; House 1949–53.

McLAIN, Frank Alexander (Miss.) Jan. 29, 1852–Oct. 10, 1920; House Dec. 12, 1898–1909.

MELANAHAN, James Xavier (grandson of Andrew Gregg) (Pa.) 1809–Dec. 16, 1861; House 1849–53.

McLANE, Patrick (Pa.) March 14, 1875–Nov. 13, 1946; House 1919–Feb. 25, 1921.

McLANE, Robert Milligan (son of Louis McLane) (Md.) June 23, 1815–April 16, 1898; House 1847–51, 1879–83; Gov. Jan. 9, 1884–March 27, 1885; Chrmn. Dem. Nat. Comm. 1852–54.

McLAUGHLIN, Charles Francis (Nebr.) June 19, 1887–Feb. 5, 1976; House 1935–43.

McLAURIN, Anselm Joseph (Miss.) March 26, 1848–Dec. 22, 1909; Senate Feb. 7, 1894–95, 1901–Dec. 22, 1909; Gov. Jan. 20, 1896–Jan. 16, 1900.

McLAURIN, John Lowndes (S.C.) May 9, 1860–July 29, 1934; House Dec. 5, 1892–May 31, 1897; Senate June 1, 1897–1903.

McLEAN, Samuel (Mont.) Aug. 7, 1826–July 16, 1877; House (Terr. Del.) Jan. 6, 1865–67.

McLEAN, William Pinkney (Tex.) Aug. 9, 1836–March 13, 1925; House 1873–75.

McLEMORE, Atkins Jefferson (Tex.) March 13, 1857–March 4, 1929; House 1915–19.

McMAHON, James O'Brien (born James O'Brien) (Conn.) Oct. 6, 1903–July 28, 1952; Senate 1945–July 28, 1952.

McMAHON, John A. (nephew of Clement Laird Vallandigham) (Ohio) Feb. 19, 1833–March 8, 1923; House 1875–81.

McMILLAN, Clara Gooding (widow of Thomas Sanders McMillan) (S.C.) Aug. 17, 1894–Nov. 8, 1976; House Nov. 7, 1939–41.

McMILLAN, John Lanneau (S.C.) April 23, 1898–Sept. 3, 1979; House 1939–73; Chrmn. House District of Columbia 1949–53, 1955–73.

McMILLAN, Thomas Sanders (husband of Clara Gooding McMillan) (S.C.) Nov. 27, 1888–Sept. 29, 1939; House 1925–Sept. 29, 1939.

McMILLEN, Charles Thomas (Md.) May 26, 1952–; House 1987–93.

McMILLEN, Benton (Tenn.) Sept. 11, 1845–Jan. 8, 1933; House 1879–Jan. 6, 1899; Gov. Jan. 16, 1899–Jan. 19, 1903.

McMULLEN, Chester Bartow (Fla.) Dec. 6, 1902–Nov. 3, 1953; House 1951–53.

McMULLEN, Fayette (Va.) May 18, 1805–Nov. 8, 1880; House 1849–57; Gov. (Wash. Terr.) 1857–61.

McMURRAY, Howard Johnstone (Wis.) March 3, 1901–Aug. 14, 1961; House 1943–45.

McNAGNY, William Forgy (Ind.) April 19, 1850–Aug. 24, 1923; House 1893–95.

McNAIR, John (Pa.) June 8, 1800–Aug. 12, 1861; House 1851–55.

McNAMARA, Patrick Vincent (Mich.) Oct. 4, 1894–April 30, 1966; Senate 1955–April 30, 1966; Chrmn. Senate Public Works 1963–66.

McNARY, William Sarsfield (Mass.) March 29, 1863–June 26, 1930; House 1903–07.

McNEELY, Thompson Ware (Ill.) Oct. 5, 1835–July 23, 1921; House 1869–73.

McNULTY, Frank Joseph (N.J.) Aug. 10, 1872–May 26, 1926; House 1923–25.

McNULTY, James Francis Jr. (Ariz.) Oct. 18, 1925–; House 1983–85.

McPHERSON, John Rhoderic (N.J.) May 9, 1833–Oct. 8, 1897; Senate 1877–95.

McQUEEN, John (S.C.) Feb. 9, 1804–Aug. 30, 1867; House Feb. 12, 1849–Dec. 21, 1860.

McRAE, John Jones (Miss.) Jan. 10, 1815–May 31, 1868; Senate Dec. 1, 1851–March 17, 1852; House Dec. 7, 1858–Jan. 12, 1861; Gov. Jan. 10, 1854–Nov. 16, 1857.

McRAE, Thomas Chipman (cousin of Thomas Banks Cabaniss) (Ark.) Dec. 21, 1851–June 2, 1929; House Dec. 7, 1885–1903; Gov. Jan. 11, 1921–Jan. 13, 1925.

McREYNOLDS, Samuel Davis (Tenn.) April 16, 1872–July 11, 1939; House 1923–July 11, 1939.

McROBERTS, Samuel (Ill.) April 12, 1799–March 27, 1843; Senate 1841–March 27, 1843.

McSHANE, John Albert (Nebr.) Aug. 25, 1850–Nov. 10, 1923; House 1887–89.

McSPADDEN, Clem Rogers (Okla.) Nov. 9, 1925–; House 1973–75.

McSWAIN, John Jackson (S.C.) May 1, 1875–Aug. 6, 1936; House l1921–Aug. 6, 1936.

McSWEEN, Harold Barnett (La.) July 19, 1926–; House 1959–63.

McSWEENEY, John (Ohio) Dec. 19, 1890–Dec. 13, 1969; House 1923–29, 1937–39, 1949–51.

McVICKER, Roy Harrison (Colo.) Feb. 20, 1924–Sept. 15, 1973; House 1965–67.

McWILLIE, William (Miss.) Nov. 17, 1795–March 3, 1869; House 1849–51; Gov. Nov. 16, 1857–Nov. 21, 1859.

MEAD, James Michael (N.Y.) Dec. 27, 1885–March 15, 1964; House 1919–Dec. 2, 1938; Senate Dec. 3, 1938–47.

MEADE, Edwin Ruthven (N.Y.) July 6, 1836–Nov. 28, 1889; House 1875–77.

MEADE, Hugh Allen (Md.) April 4, 1907–July 8, 1949; House 1947–49.

MEADE, Richard Kidder (Va.) July 29, 1803–April 20, 1862; House Aug. 5, 1847–53.

MEDILL, William (Ohio) Feb. 1802–Sept. 2, 1865; House 1839–43; Gov. July 13, 1853–Jan. 14, 1856.

MEECH, Ezra (Vt.) July 26, 1773–Sept. 23, 1856; House 1810–21, 1825–27.

MEEDS, Lloyd (Wash.) Dec. 11, 1927–; House l965–79.

MEEHAN, Martin Timothy (Mass.) Dec. 30, 1956–; House 1993–.

MEEK, Carrie (Fla.) April 29, 1926–; House l993–.

MEEKISON, David (Ohio) Nov. 14, 1849–Feb. 12, 1915; House 1897–1901.

MEEKS, James Andrew (Ill.) March 7, 1864–Nov. 10, 1946; House 1933–39.

MELCHER, John (Mont.) Sept. 6, 1924–; House June 24, 1969–77; Senate 1977–89.

MENENDEZ, Robert (N.J.) Jan. 1, 1954–; House 1993–.

MEREDITH, Elisha Edward (Va.) Dec. 26, 1848–July 29, 1900; House Dec. 9, 1891–97.

MERIWETHER, David (Ky.) Oct. 30, 1800–April 4, 1893; Senate July 6–Aug. 31, 1852; Gov. (N.M. Terr.) 1853–55.

MERRICK, William Matthew (son of William Duhurst Merrick) (Md.) Sept. 1, 1818–Feb. 4, 1889; House 1871–73.

MERRIMAN, Truman Adams (N.Y.) Sept. 5, 1839–April 16, 1892; House 1885–89 (1885–87 Independent Democrat).

MERRIMON, Augustus Summerfield (N.C.) Sept. 15, 1830–Nov. 14, 1892; Senate 1873–79.

MERRITT, Matthew Joseph (N.Y.) April 2, 1895–Sept. 29, 1946; House 1935–45.

MERRITT, Samuel Augustus (Idaho) Aug. 15, 1827–Sept. 8, 1910; House (Terr. Del.) 1871–73.

METCALF, Lee Warren (Mont.) Jan. 28, 1911–Jan. 12, 1978; House 1953–61; Senate 1961–Jan. 12, 1978.

METCALFE, Henry Bleecker (N.Y.) Jan. 20, 1805–Feb. 7, 1881; House 1875–77.

METCALFE, Ralph Harold (Ill.) May 29, 1910–Oct. 10, 1978; House 1971–Oct. 10, 1978.

METZ, Herman August (N.Y.) Oct. 19, 1867–May 17, 1934; House 1913–15.

METZENBAUM, Howard Morton (Ohio) June 4, 1917–; Senate Jan. 4–Dec. 23, 1974, Dec. 29, 1976–1995.

MEYER, Adolph (La.) Oct. 19, 1842–March 8, 1908; House 1891–March 8, 1908.

MEYER, John Ambrose (Md.) May 15, 1899–Oct. 2, 1969; House 1941–43.

MEYER, William Henry (Vt.) Dec. 29, 1914–Dec. 16, 1983; House 1959–61.

MEYERS, Benjamin Franklin (Pa.) July 6, 1833–Aug. 11, 1918; House 1871–73.

MEYNER, Helen Stevenson (N.J.) March 5, 1929–; House 1975–79.

MEZVINSKY, Edward Maurice (husband of Marjorie Margolies-Mezvinsky) (Iowa) Jan. 17, 1937–; House 1973–77.

MFUME, Kweisi (Md.) Oct. 24, 1948–; House 1987–1995.

MICA, Daniel Andrew (brother of John L. Mica) (Fla.) Feb. 4, 1944–; House 1979–89.

MICKEY, J. Ross (Ill.) Jan. 5, 1856–March 20, 1928; House 1901–03.

MIDDLETON, George (N.J.) Oct. 14, 1800–Dec. 31, 1888; House 1863–65.

MIERS, Robert Walter (Ind.) Jan. 27, 1848–Feb. 20, 1930; House 1897–1905.

MIKULSKI, Barbara Ann (Md.) July 20, 1936–; House 1977–87; Senate 1987–.

MIKVA, Abner Joseph (Ill.) Jan. 21, 1926–; House 1969–73, 1975–Sept. 26, 1979.

MILES, John Esten (N.Mex.) July 28, 1884–Oct. 7, 1971; House 1949–51; Gov. Jan. 1, 1939–Jan. 1, 1943.

MILES, Joshua Weldon (Md.) Dec. 9, 1858–March 4, 1929; House 1895–97.

MILES, William Porcher (S.C.) July 4, 1822–May ll, 1899; House 1857–Dec.1860.

MILFORD, Dale (Tex.) Feb. 18, 1926–; House 1973–79.

MILLEN, John (Ga.) 1804–Oct. 15, 1843; House March 4–Oct. 15, 1843.

MILLER, Bert Henry (Idaho) Dec. 15, 1879–Oct. 8, 1949; Senate Jan. 3–Oct. 8, 1949.

MILLER, Clement Woodnutt (nephew of Thomas Woodnutt Miller) (Calif.) Oct. 28, 1916–Oct. 7, 1962; House 1959–Oct. 7, 1962.

MILLER, George (Calif.) May 17, 1945–; House 1975–; Chrmn. House Interior and Insular Affairs 1991–93; Chrmn. House Natural Resources 1993–1995.

MILLER, George Paul (Calif.) Jan. 15, 1891–Dec. 29, 1982; House 1945–73; Chrmn. House Science and Astronautics 1961–73.

MILLER, Homer Virgil Milton (Ga.) April 29, 1814–May 31, 1896; Senate Feb. 24–March 3, 1871.

MILLER, Howard Shultz (Kans.) Feb. 27, 1879–Jan. 2, 1970; House 1953–55.

MILLER, James Francis (Tex.) Aug. 1, 1830–July 3, 1902; House 1883–87.

MILLER, John (Mo.) Nov. 25, 1781–March 18, 1846; House 1837–43; Gov. Jan. 20, 1826–Nov. 14, 1832 (Jacksonian).

MILLER, John Elvis (Ark.) May 15, 1888–Jan. 30, 1981; House 1931–Nov. 14, 1937; Senate Nov. 15, 1937–March 31, 1941.

MILLER, John Krepps (Ohio) May 25, 1819–Aug. 11, 1863; House 1847–51.

MILLER, Joseph (Ohio) Sept. 9, 1819–May 27, 1862; House 1857–59.

MILLER, Lucas Miltiades (Wis.) Sept. 15, 1824–Dec. 4, 1902; House 1891–93.

MILLER, Smith (Ind.) May 30, 1804–March 21, 1872; House 1853–57.

MILLER, William Henry (son of Jesse Miller) (Pa.) Feb. 28, 1829–Sept. 12, 1870; House 1863–65.

MILLIGAN, Jacob Le Roy (Mo.) March 9, 1889–March 9, 1951; House Feb. 14, 1920–21, 1923–35.

MILLIKEN, Charles William (Ky.) Aug. 15, 1827–Oct. 16, 1915; House 1873–77.

MILLS, Newt Virgus (La.) Sept. 27, 1899–; House 1937–43.

MILLS, Roger Quarles (Tex.) March 30, 1832–Sept. 2, 1911; House 1873–March 28, 1892; Senate March 29, 1892–99.

MILLS, Wilbur Daigh (Ark.) May 24, 1909–May 2, 1992; House 1939–77; Chrmn. House Ways and Means 1958–75.

MILLSON, John Singleton (Va.) Oct. 1, 1808–March 1, 1874; House 1849–61.

MILTON, John Gerald (N.J.) Jan. 21, 1881–April 14, 1977; Senate Jan. 18–Nov. 8, 1938.

MILTON, William Hall (Fla.) March 2, 1864–Jan. 4, 1942; Senate March 27, 1908–09.

MINAHAN, Daniel Francis (N.J.) Aug. 8, 1877–April 29, 1947; House 1919–21, 1923–25.

MINER, Henry Clay (N.Y.) March 23, 1842–Feb. 22, 1900; House 1895–97.

MINETA, Norman Yoshio (Calif.) Nov. 12, 1931–; House 1975–; Chrmn. House Public Works and Transportation 1993–1995.

MINGE, David (Minn.) March 19, 1942–; House 1993–.

MINISH, Joseph George (N.J.) Sept. 1, 1916–; House 1963–85.

MINK, Patsy Takemoto (Hawaii) Dec. 6, 1927–; House 1965–77, Sept. 27, 1990–.

MINTON, Sherman (Ind.) Oct. 20, 1890–April 9, 1965; Senate 1935–41; Assoc. Justice Supreme Court Oct. 12, 1949–Oct. 15, 1956.

MITCHEL, Charles Burton (Ark.) Sept. 19, 1815–Sept. 20, 1864; Senate March 4–July 11, 1861.

MITCHELL, Alexander (father of John Lendrum Mitchell) (Wis.) Oct. 18, 1817–April 19, 1887; House 1871–75.

MITCHELL, Arthur Wergs (Ill.) Dec. 22, 1883–May 9, 1968; House 1935–43.

MITCHELL, Charles Le Moyne (Conn.) Aug. 6, 1844–March 1, 1890; House 1883–87.

MITCHELL, George John (Maine) Aug. 20, 1933–; Senate May 19, 1980–1995; Senate majority leader 1989–1995.

MITCHELL, Harlan Erwin (Ga.) Aug. 17, 1924–; House Jan. 8, 1958–61.

MITCHELL, Hugh Burnton (Wash.) March 22, 1907–; Senate Jan. 10, 1945–Dec. 25, 1946; House 1949–53.

MITCHELL, John Joseph (Mass.) May 9, 1873–Sept. 13, 1925; House Nov. 8, 1910–11, April 15, 1913–15.

MITCHELL, John Lendrum (son of Alexander Mitchell) (Wis.) Oct. 19, 1842–June 29, 1904; House 1891–93; Senate 1893–99.

MITCHELL, John Ridley (Tenn.) Sept. 25, 1877–Feb. 26, 1962; House 1931–39.

MITCHELL, Parren James (Md.) April 29, 1922–; House 1971–87; Chrmn. House Small Business 1981–87.

MOAKLEY, John Joseph (Mass.) April 27, 1927–; House 1973– (elected as an Independent Democrat, changed party affiliation to Democrat effective Jan. 2, 1973); Chrmn. House Rules 1989–1995.

MOBLEY, William Carlton (Ga.) Dec. 7, 1906–; House March 2, 1932–33.

MOELLER, Walter Henry (Ohio) March 15, 1910–; House 1959–63, 1965–67.

MOFFET, John (Pa.) April 5, 1831–June 19, 1884; House March 4–April 9, 1869.

MOFFETT, Anthony John "Toby" Jr. (Conn.) Aug. 18, 1944–; House 1975–83.

MOLLOHAN, Alan Bowlby (son of Robert Homer Mollohan) (W.Va.) May 14, 1943–; House 1983–.

MOLLOHAN, Robert Homer (father of Alan Bowlby Mollohan) (W.Va.) Sept. 18, 1909–; House 1953–57, 1969–83.

MOLONY, Richard Sheppard (Ill.) June 28, 1811–Dec. 14, 1891; House 1851–53.

MONAGAN, John Stephen (Conn.) Dec. 23, 1911–; House 1959–73.

MONAGHAN, Joseph Patrick (Mont.) March 26, 1906–July 4, 1985; House 1933–37.

MONDALE, Walter Frederick "Fritz" (Minn.) Jan. 5, 1928–; Senate Dec. 30, 1964–Dec. 30, 1976; Vice President 1977–81.

MONEY, Hernando De Soto (Miss.) Aug. 26, 1839–Sept. 18, 1912; House 1875–85, 1893–97; Senate Oct. 8, 1897–1911.

MONRONEY, Almer Stillwell Mike (Okla.) March 2, 1902–Feb. 13, 1980; House 1939–51; Senate 1951–69; Chrmn. Senate Post Office and Civil Service 1965–69.

MONTAGUE, Andrew Jackson (Va.) Oct. 3, 1862–Jan. 24, 1937; House 1913–Jan. 24, 1937; Gov. Jan. 1, 1902–Feb. 1, 1906.

MONTET, Numa Francois (La.) Sept. 17, 1892–Oct. 12, 1985; House Aug. 6, 1929–37.

MONTGOMERY, Alexander Brooks (Ky.) Dec. 11, 1837–Dec. 27, 1910; House 1887–95.

MONTGOMERY, Gillespie V. "Sonny" (Miss.) Aug. 5, 1920–; House 1967–; Chrmn. House Veterans' Affairs 1981–1995.

MONTGOMERY, John Gallagher (Pa.) June 27, 1805–April 24, 1857; House March 4–April 24, 1857.

MONTGOMERY, William (N.C.) Dec. 29, 1789–Nov. 27, 1844; House 1835–41 (1835–37 Jacksonian).

MONTGOMERY, William (Pa.) April 11, 1818–April 28, 1870; House 1857–61.

MONTOYA, Joseph Manuel (N.Mex.) Sept. 24, 1915–June 5, 1978; House April 9, 1957–Nov. 3, 1964; Senate Nov. 4, 1964–77.

MOODY, Arthur Edson Blair (Mich.) Feb. 13, 1902–July 20, 1954; Senate April 23, 1951–Nov. 4, 1952.

MOODY, Jim (Wis.) Sept. 2, 1935–; House 1983–93.

MOON, John Austin (Tenn.) April 22, 1855–June 26, 1921; House 1897–1921.

MOONEY, Charles Anthony (Ohio) Jan. 5, 1879–May 29, 1931; House 1919–21, 1923–May 29, 1931.

MOOR, Wyman Bradbury Seavy (Maine) Nov. 11, 1811–March 10, 1869; Senate Jan. 5–June 7, 1848.

MOORE, Arthur Harry (N.J.) July 3, 1879–Nov. 18, 1952; Senate 1935–Jan. 17, 1938; Gov. Jan. 19, 1926–Jan. 15, 1929, Jan. 19, 1932–Jan. 3, 1935, Jan. 18, 1938–Jan. 21, 1941.

MOORE, Ely (N.Y. July 4, 1798–Jan. 27, 1860; House 1835–39 (1835–37 Jacksonian).

MOORE, Herman Allen (Ohio) Aug. 27, 1809–April 3, 1844; House 1843–April 3, 1844.

MOORE, Horace Ladd (Kans.) Feb. 25, 1837–May 1, 1914; House Aug. 2, 1894–95.

MOORE, John Matthew (Tex.) Nov. 18, 1862–Feb. 3, 1940; House June 6, 1905–13.

MOORE, John William (Ky.) June 9, 1877–Dec. 11, 1941; House Nov. 3, 1925–29, June 1, 1929–33.

MOORE, Littleton Wilde (Tex.) March 25, 1835–Oct. 29, 1911; House 1887–93.

MOORE, Paul John (N.J.) Aug. 5, 1868–Jan. 10, 1938; House 1927–29.

MOORE, Robert Lee (Ga.) Nov. 27, 1867–Jan. 14, 1940; House 1923–25.

MOORE, Robert Walton (Va.) Feb. 5, 1859–Feb. 8, 1941; House May 27, 1919–31.

MOORE, Sydenham (Ala.) May 25, 1817–May 31, 1862; House 1857–Jan. 21, 1861.

MOORHEAD, William Singer (Pa.) April 8, 1923–Aug. 3, 1987; House 1959–81.

MOORMAN, Henry DeHaven (Ky.) June 9, 1880–Feb. 3, 1939; House 1927–29.

MORAN, Edward Carleton Jr. (Maine) Dec. 29, 1894–July 12, 1967; House 1933–37.

MORAN, James Patrick Jr. (Va.) May 16, 1945–; House 1991–.

MOREHEAD, John Henry (Nebr.) Dec. 3, 1861–May 31, 1942; House 1923–35; Gov. Jan. 9, 1913–Jan. 4, 1917.

MORGAN, George Washington (Ohio) Sept. 20, 1820–July 26, 1893; House 1867–June 3, 1868, 1869–73.

MORGAN, James Bright (Miss.) March 14, 1833–June 18, 1892; House 1885–91.

MORGAN, John Tyler (Ala.) June 20, 1824–June 11, 1907; Senate 1877–June 11, 1907.

MORGAN, Lewis Lovering (La.) March 2, 1876–June 10, 1950; House Nov. 5, 1912–17.

MORGAN, Robert Burren (N.C.) Oct. 5, 1925–; Senate 1975–81.

MORGAN, Thomas Ellsworth (Pa.) Oct. 13, 1906–; House 1945–77; Chrmn. House Foreign Affairs 1959–75; Chrmn. House International Relations 1975–77.

MORGAN, William Stephen (Va.) Sept. 7, 1801–Sept. 3, 1878; House 1935–39 (1835–37 Jacksonian).

MORITZ, Theodore Leo (Pa.) April 18, 1868–March 13, 1982; House 1935–37.

MORRIS, Isaac Newton (son of Thomas Morris of Ohio, brother of Jonathan David Morris) (Ill.) Jan. 22, 1812–Oct. 29, 1879; House 1857–61.

MORRIS, James Remley (son of Joseph Morris) (Ohio) Jan. 10, 1819–Dec. 24, 1899; House 1861–65.

MORRIS, Jonathan David (son of Thomas Morris of Ohio, brother of Isaac Newton Morris) (Ohio) Oct. 8, 1804–May 16, 1875; House 1847–51.

MORRIS, Joseph (father of James Remley Morris) (Ohio) Oct. 16, 1795–Oct. 23, 1854; House 1843–47.

MORRIS, Joseph Watkins (Ky.) Feb. 26, 1879–Dec. 21, 1937; House Nov. 30, 1923–25.

MORRIS, Samuel Wells (Pa.) Sept. 1, 1786–May 25, 1847; House 1837–41.

MORRIS, Thomas Gayle (N.Mex.) Aug. 20, 1919–; House 1959–69.

MORRIS, Toby (Okla.) Feb. 28, 1899–Sept. 1, 1973; House 1947–53, 1957–61.

MORRISON, Bruce Andrew (Conn.) Oct. 8, 1944–; House 1983–91.

MORRISON, Cameron A. (N.C.) Oct. 5, 1869–Aug. 20, 1953; Senate Dec. 13, 1930–Dec. 4, 1932; House 1943–45; Gov. Jan. 12, 1921–Jan. 14, 1925.

MORRISON, George Washington (N.H.) Oct. 16, 1809–Dec. 21, 1888; House Oct. 8, 1850–51, 1853–55.

MORRISON, James Hobson (La.) Dec. 8, 1908–; House 1943–67.

MORRISON, James Lowery Donaldson (Ill.) April 12, 1816–Aug. 14, 1888; House Nov. 5, 1856–67.

MORRISON, John Alexander (Pa.) Jan. 31, 1814–July 25, 1904; House 1851–53.

MORRISON, Martin Andrew (Ind.) April 15, 1862–July 9, 1944; House 1909–17.

MORRISON, William Ralls (Ill.) Sept. 14, 1824–Sept. 29, 1909; House 1863–65, 1873–87.

MORRISSEY, John (N.Y.) Feb. 12, 1831–May 1, 1878; House 1867–71.

MORROW, John (N.Mex.) April 19, 1865–Feb. 25, 1935; House 1923–29.

MORSE, Isaac Edward (La.) May 22, 1809–Feb. 11, 1866; House Dec. 2, 1844–51.

MORSE, Wayne Lyman (Oreg.) Oct. 20, 1900–July 22, 1974; Senate 1945–69 (1945–57 Republican).

MOSELEY-BRAUN, Carol (Ill.) Aug. 16, 1947–; Senate 1993–.

MOSER, Guy Louis (Pa.) Jan. 23, 1866–May 9, 1961; House 1937–43.

MOSES, Charles Leavell (Ga.) May 2, 1856–Oct. 10, 1910; House 1891–97.

MOSES, John (N.Dak.) June 12, 1885–March 3, 1945; Senate Jan. 3–March 3, 1945; Gov. Jan. 5, 1939–Jan. 4, 1945.

MOSIER, Harold Gerard (Ohio) July 24, 1889–Aug. 7, 1971; House 1937–39.

MOSS, Frank Edward (Utah) Sept. 23, 1911–; Senate 1959–77; Chrmn. Senate Aeronautical and Space Sciences 1973–77.

MOSS, John Emerson (Calif.) April 13, 1915–; House 1953–Dec. 31, 1978.

MOSS, Ralph Wilbur (Ind.) April 21, 1862–April 26, 1919; House 1909–17.

MOTTL, Ronald Milton (Ohio) Feb. 6, 1934–; House 1975–83.

MOULDER, Morgan Moore (Mo.) Aug. 31, 1904–Nov. 12, 1976; House 1949–63.

MOULTON, Mace (N.H.) May 2, 1796–May 5, 1867; House 1845–47.

MOULTON, Samuel Wheeler (Ill.) Jan. 20, 1821–June 3, 1905; House 1865–67 (Republican), 1881–85.

MOUTON, Alexander (La.) Nov. 19, 1804–Feb. 12, 1885; Senate Jan. 12, 1837–March 1, 1842; Gov. Jan. 30, 1843–Feb. 12, 1846.

MOUTON, Robert Louis (La.) Oct. 20, 1892–Nov. 26, 1956; House 1937–41.

MOYNIHAN, Daniel Patrick (N.Y.) March 16, 1927–; Senate 1977–; Chrmn. Senate Environment and Public Works 1992–93; Chrmn. Senate Finance 1993–1995.

MRAZEK, Robert Jan (N.Y.) Nov. 6, 1945–; House 1983–93.

MUHLENBERG, Henry Augustus (son of Henry Augustus Philip Muhlenberg, grandson of Joseph Hiester) (Pa.) July 21, 1823–Jan. 9, 1854; House 1853–Jan. 9, 1854.

MUHLENBERG, Henry Augustus Philip (father of Henry Augustus Muhlenberg, nephew of John Peter Gabriel Muhlenberg and Frederick Augustus Conrad Muhlenberg) (Pa.) May 13, 1782–Aug. 11, 1844; House 1829–Feb. 9, 1838 (1829–37 Jacksonian).

MULDROW, Henry Lowndes (Miss.) Feb. 8, 1837–March 1, 1905; House 1877–85.

MULKEY, William Oscar (Ala.) July 27, 1871–June 30, 1943; House June 29, 1914–15.

MULLER, Nicholas (N.Y.) Nov. 15, 1836–Dec. 12, 1917; House 1877–81, 1883–87, 1899–Dec. 1, 1902.

MULTER, Abraham Jacob (N.Y.) Dec. 24, 1900–Nov. 4, 1986; House Nov. 4, 1947–Dec. 31, 1967.

MUNGEN, William (Ohio) May 12, 1821–Sept. 9, 1887; House 1867–71.

MURDOCK, John Robert (Ariz.) April 20, 1885–Feb. 14, 1972; House 1937–53; Chrmn. House Interior and Insular Affairs 1951–53.

MURDOCK, Orrice Abram Jr. "Abe" (Utah) July 18, 1893–Sept. 15, 1979; House 1933–41; Senate 1941–47.

MURPHY, Austin John (Pa.) June 17 1927–; House 1977–.

MURPHY, Edward Jr. (N.Y.) Dec. 15, 1836–Aug. 3, 1911; Senate 1893–99.

MURPHY, Henry Cruse (N.Y.) July 5, 1810–Dec. 1, 1882; House 1843–45, 1847–49.

MURPHY, James Joseph (N.Y.) Nov. 3, 1898–Oct. 19, 1962; House 1949–53.

MURPHY, James William (Wis.) April 17, 1858–July 11, 1927; House 1907–09.

MURPHY, Jeremiah Henry (Iowa) Feb. 19, 1835–Dec. 11, 1893; House 1883–87.

MURPHY, John Michael (N.Y.) Aug. 3, 1926–; House 1963–81; Chrmn. House Merchant Marine and Fisheries 1977–81.

MURPHY, John William (Pa.) April 26, 1902–March 28, 1962; House 1943–July 17, 1946.

MURPHY, Morgan Francis (Ill.) April 16, 1932–; House 1971–81.

MURPHY, Richard Louis (Iowa) Nov. 6, 1876–July 16, 1936; Senate 1933–July 16, 1936.

MURPHY, William Thomas (Ill.) Aug. 7, 1899–Jan. 29, 1978; House 1959–71.

MURRAY, James Cunningham (Ill.) March 16, 1917–; House 1955–57.

MURRAY, James Edward (Mont.) May 3, 1876–March 23, 1961; Senate Nov. 7, 1934–61; Chrmn. Senate Labor and Public Welfare 1951–53; Chrmn. Senate Interior and Insular Affairs 1955–61.

MURRAY, John L. (Ky.) Jan. 25, 1806–Jan. 31, 1842; House 1837–39.

MURRAY, Patty (Wash.) Oct. 11, 1950–; Senate 1993–.

MURRAY, Robert Maynard (Ohio) Nov. 28, 1841–Aug. 2, 1913; House 1883–85.

MURRAY, Thomas Jefferson (Tenn.) Aug. 1, 1894–Nov. 28, 1971; House 1943–67; Chrmn. House Post Office and Civil Service 1949–53, 1955–67.

MURRAY, William (brother of Ambrose Spencer Murray) (N.Y.) Oct. 1, 1803–Aug. 25, 1875; House 1851–55.

MURRAY, William Francis (Mass.) Sept. 7, 1881–Sept. 21, 1918; House 1911–Sept. 28, 1914.

MURRAY, William Henry David (Okla.) Nov. 21, 1869–Oct. 15, 1956; House 1913–17; Gov. Jan. 12, 1931–Jan. 14, 1935.

MURTHA, John Patrick Jr. (Pa.) Jan. 17, 1932–; House Feb. 5, 1974–.

MUSKIE, Edmund Sixtus (Maine) March 28, 1914–; Senate 1959–May 7, 1980; Chrmn. Senate Budget 1975–79; Gov. Jan. 5, 1955–Jan. 3, 1959, Secy. of State May 8, 1980–Jan. 18, 1981.

MUSSELWHITE, Harry Webster (Mich.) May 23, 1868–Dec. 14, 1955; House 1933–35.

MUSTO, Raphael John (Pa.) March 30, 1929–; House April 15, 1980–81.

MUTCHLER, Howard (son of William Mutchler) (Pa.) Feb. 12, 1859–Jan. 4, 1916; House Aug. 7, 1893–95, 1901–03.

MUTCHLER, William (father of Howard Mutchler) (Pa.) Dec. 21, 1831–June 23, 1893; House 1875–77, 1881–85, 1889–June 23, 1893.

MYERS, Francis John (Pa.) Dec. 18, 1901–July 5, 1956; House 1939–45; Senate 1945–51.

MYERS, Henry Lee (Mont.) Oct. 9, 1862–Nov. 11, 1943; Senate 1911–23.

MYERS, Michael Joseph "Ozzie" (Pa.) May 4, 1943–; House Nov. 2, 1976–Oct. 2, 1980.

MYERS, William Ralph (Ind.) June 12, 1836–April 18, 1907; House 1879–81.

NADLER, Jerrold Lewis (N.Y.) June 13, 1947–; House 1993– (elected Nov. 3, 1992, to fill a vacancy in the 102d Congress and to the 103d Congress but was not sworn in until Jan. 5, 1993).

NAGLE, David Ray (Iowa) April 15, 1943–; House 1987–93.

NAPHEN, Henry Francis (Mass.) Aug. 14, 1852–June 8, 1905; House 1899–1903.

NATCHER, William Huston (Ky.) Sept. 11, 1909–March 29, 1994; House Aug. 1, 1953–March 29, 1994; Chrmn. House Appropriations 1993–94.

NEAL, John Randolph (Tenn.) Nov. 26, 1836–March 26, 1889; House 1885–89.

NEAL, Lawrence Talbot (Ohio) Sept. 22, 1844–Nov. 2, 1905; House 1873–77.

NEAL, Richard Edmund (Mass.) Feb. 14, 1949–; House 1989–.

NEAL, Stephen Lybrook (N.C.) Nov. 7, 1934–; House 1975–1995.

NEDZI, Lucien Norbert (Mich.) May 28, 1925–; House Nov. 7, 1961–81; Chrmn. House Select Committee on Intelligence 1975–.

NEECE, William Henry (Ill.) Feb. 26, 1831–Jan. 3, 1909; House 1883–87.

NEELEY, George Arthur (Kans.) Aug. 1, 1879–Jan. 1, 1919; House Nov. 11, 1912–15.

NEELY, Matthew Mansfield (W.Va.) Nov. 9, 1874–Jan. 18, 1958; House Oct. 14, 1913–21, 1945–47; Senate 1923–29, 1931–Jan. 12, 1941, 1949–Jan. 18, 1958; Chrmn. Senate District of Columbia 1951–53, 1955–59; Gov. Jan. 13, 1941–Jan. 15, 1945.

NEILL, Robert (Ark.) Nov. 12, 1838–Feb. 16, 1907; House 1893–97.

NELSON, Clarence William "Bill" (Fla.) Sept. 29, 1942–; House 1979–91.

NELSON, Gaylord Anton (Wis.) June 4, 1916–; Senate Jan. 8, 1963–81; Chrmn. Senate Select Committee on Small Business 1975–81; Gov. Jan. 5, 1959–Jan. 7, 1963.

NELSON, Homer Augustus (N.Y.) Aug. 31, 1829–April 25, 1891; House 1863–65.

NELSON, William Lester (Mo.) Aug. 4, 1875–Dec. 31, 1946; House 1919–21, 1925–33, 1935–43.

NESBIT, Walter (Ill.) May 1, 1878–Dec. 6, 1938; House 1933–35.

NESMITH, James Willis (cousin of Joseph Gardner Wilson, grandfather of Clifton Nesmith McArthur) (Oreg.) July 23, 1820–June 17, 1885; Senate 1861–67; House Dec. 1, 1873–75.

NEUBERGER, Maurine Brown (widow of Richard Lewis Neuberger) (Oreg.) Jan. 9, 1907–; Senate Nov. 9, 1960–67.

NEUBERGER, Richard Lewis (husband of Maurine Brown Neuberger) (Oreg.) Dec. 26, 1912–March 9, 1960; Senate 1955–March 9, 1960.

NEW, Jeptha Dudley (Ind.) Nov. 28, 1830–July 9, 1892; House 1875–77, 1879–81.

NEWBERRY, Walter Cass (Ill.) Dec. 23, 1835–July 20, 1912; House 1891–93.

NEWHARD, Peter (Pa.) July 26, 1783–Feb. 19, 1860; House 1839–43.

NEWLANDS, Francis Griffith (Nev.) Aug. 28, 1848–Dec. 24, 1917; House 1893–1903; Senate 1903–Dec. 24, 1917.

NEWMAN, Alexander (Va.) Oct. 5, 1804–Sept. 8, 1849; House March 4–Sept. 8, 1849.

NEWSOME, John Parks (Ala.) Feb. 13, 1893–Nov. 10, 1961; House 1943–45.

NEWTON, Cherubusco (La.) May 15, 1848–May 26, 1910; House 1887–89.

NIBLACK, Silas Leslie (cousin of William Ellis Niblack) (Fla.) March 17, 1825–Feb. 13, 1883; House Jan. 29–March 3, 1873.

NIBLACK, William Ellis (cousin of Silas Leslie Niblack) (Ind.) May 19, 1822–May 7, 1893; House Dec. 7, 1857–61, 1865–75.

NICHOLAS, Robert Carter (nephew of John Nicholas and Wilson Cary Nicholas) (La.) 1793–Dec. 24, 1857; Senate Jan. 13, 1836–41.

NICHOLLS, John Calhoun (Ga.) April 25, 1834–Dec. 25, 1893; House 1879–81, 1883–85.

NICHOLLS, Samuel Jones (S.C.) May 7, 1885–Nov. 23, 1937; House Sept. 14, 1915–21.

NICHOLLS, Thomas David (Pa.) Sept. 16, 1870–Jan. 19, 1931; House 1907–11.

NICHOLS, John Conover (Okla.) Aug. 31, 1896–Nov. 7, 1945; House 1935–July 3, 1943.

NICHOLS, William Flynt (Ala.) Oct. 16, 1918–Dec. 13, 1988; House 1967–Dec. 13, 1988.

NICHOLSON, Alfred Osborn Pope (Tenn.) Aug. 31, 1808–March 23, 1876; Senate Dec. 25, 1840–Feb. 7, 1842, 1859–61.

NICHOLSON, John Anthony (Del.) Nov. 17, 1827–Nov. 4, 1906; House 1865–69.

NICOLL, Henry (N.Y.) Oct. 23, 1812–Nov. 28, 1879; House 1847–49.

NILES, John Milton (Conn.) Aug. 20, 1787–May 31, 1856; Senate Dec. 21, 1835–39, 1843–49; Postmaster Gen. May 26, 1840–March 3, 1841.

NIVEN, Archibald Campbell (N.Y.) Dec. 8, 1803–Feb. 21, 1882; House 1845–47.

NIX, Robert Nelson Cornelius Sr. (Pa.) Aug. 9, 1905–June 22, 1987; House May 20, 1958–79; Chrmn. House Post Office and Civil Service 1977–79.

NOBLE, David Addison (Mich.) Nov. 9, 1802–Oct. 13, 1876; House 1853–55.

NOBLE, Warren Perry (Ohio) June 14, 1820–July 9, 1903; House 1861–65.

NOBLE, William Henry (N.Y.) Sept. 22, 1788–Feb. 5, 1850; House 1837–39.

NOBELL, Thomas Estes (son of John William Nobell) (Mo.) April 3, 1839–Oct. 3, 1867; House 1865–Oct. 3, 1867 (1865–67 Republican).

NOLAN, Michael Nicholas (N.Y.) May 4, 1833–May 31, 1905; House 1881–83.

NOLAN, Richard Michael (Minn.) Dec. 17, 1943–; House 1975–81.

NOLAND, James Ellsworth (Ind.) April 22, 1920–; House 1949–51.

NOONAN, Edward Thomas (Ill.) Oct. 23, 1861–Dec. 19, 1923; House 1899–1901.

NORRELL, Catherine Dorris (widow of William Frank Norrell) (Ark.) March 30, 1901–Aug. 26, 1981; House April 18, 1961–63.

NORRELL, William Frank (husband of Catherine Dorris Norrell) (Ark.) Aug. 29, 1896–Feb. 15, 1961; House 1939–Feb. 15, 1961.

NORRIS, Moses Jr. (N.H.) Nov. 8, 1799–Jan. 11, 1855; House 1843–47; Senate 1849–Jan. 11, 1855.

NORTON, Eleanor Holmes (D.C.) June 13, 1937–; House (Delegate) 1991–.

NORTON, Elijah Hise (Mo.) Nov. 24, 1821–Aug. 6, 1914; House 1861–63.

NORTON, James (S.C.) Oct. 8, 1843–Oct. 14, 1920; House Dec. 6, 1897–1901.

NORTON, James Albert (Ohio) Nov. 11, 1843–July 24, 1912; House 1897–1903.

NORTON, John Nathaniel (Nebr.) May 12, 1878–Oct. 5, 1960; House 1927–29, 1931–33.

NORTON, Mary Teresa (N.J.) March 7, 1875–Aug. 2, 1959; House 1925–51; Chrmn. House Administration 1949–51.

NORTON, Richard Henry (Mo.) Nov. 16, 1849–March 15, 1918; House 1889–93.

NORVELL, John (Mich.) Dec. 21, 1789–April 24, 1850; Senate Jan. 25, 1837–41.

NORWOOD, Thomas Manson (Ga.) April 26, 1830–June 19, 1913; Senate Nov. 14, 1871–77; House 1885–89.

NOWAK, Henry James (N.Y.) Feb. 21, 1935–; House 1975–93.

NUCKOLLS, Stephen Friel (Wyo.) Aug. 16, 1825–Feb. 14, 1879; House (Terr. Del.) Dec. 6, 1869–71.

NUGEN, Robert Hunter (Ohio) July 16, 1809–Feb. 28, 1872; House 1861–63.

NUGENT, John Frost (Idaho) June 28, 1868–Sept. 18, 1931; Senate Jan. 22, 1918–Jan. 14, 1921.

NUNN, Samuel Augustus (great-nephew of Carl Vinson) (Ga.) Sept. 8, 1938–; Senate Nov. 8, 1972–1997; Chrmn. Senate Armed Services 1987–1995.

OAKAR, Mary Rose (Ohio) March 5, 1940–; House 1977–93.

OATES, William Calvin (Ala.) Nov. 30, 1835–Sept. 9, 1910; House 1881–Nov. 5, 1894; Gov. Dec. 1, 1894–Dec. 1, 1896.

OBERSTAR, James Louis (Minn.) Sept. 10, 1934–; House 1975–.

OBEY, David Ross (Wis.) Oct. 3, 1938–; House April 1, 1969–; Chrmn. House Appropriations 1994–.

OBRIEN, Charles Francis Xavier (N.J.) March 7, 1897–Nov. 15, 1940; House 1921–25.

OBRIEN, George Donoghue (Mich.) Jan. 1, 1900–Oct. 25, 1957; House 1937–39; 1941–47, 1949–55.

OBRIEN, James (N.Y.) March 13, 1841–March 5, 1907; House 1879–81.

OBRIEN, James Henry (N.Y.) July 15, 1860–Sept. 2, 1924; House 1913–15.

O'BRIEN, Leo William (N.Y.) Sept. 21, 1900–May 4, 1982; House April 1, 1952–67.

O'BRIEN, Thomas Joseph (Ill.) April 30, 1878–April 14, 1964; House 1933–39, 1943–April 14, 1964.

O'BRIEN, William James (Md.) May 28, 1836–Nov. 13, 1905; House 1873–77.

O'BRIEN, William Smith (W.Va.) Jan. 8, 1862–Aug. 10, 1948; House 1927–29.

O'CONNELL, David Joseph (N.Y.) Dec. 25, 1868–Dec. 29, 1930; House 1919–21, 1923–Dec. 29, 1930.

O'CONNELL, Jeremiah Edward (R.I.) July 8, 1883–Sept. 18, 1964; House 1923–27, 1929–May 9, 1930.

O'CONNELL, Jerry Joseph (Mont.) June 14, 1909–Jan. 16, 1956; House 1937–39.

O'CONNELL, John Matthew (R.I.) Aug. 10, 1872–Dec. 6, 1941; House 1933–39.

O'CONNELL, Joseph Francis (Mass.) Dec. 7, 1872–Dec. 10, 1942; House 1907–11.

O'CONNOR, James (La.) April 4, 1870–Jan. 7, 1941; House June 5, 1919–31.

O'CONNOR, James Francis (Mont.) May 7, 1878–Jan. 15, 1945; House 1937–Jan. 15, 1945.

O'CONNOR, John Joseph (N.Y.) Nov. 23, 1885–Jan. 26, 1960; House Nov. 6, 1923–39.

O'CONNOR, Michael Patrick (S.C.) Sept. 29, 1831–April 26, 1881; House 1879–81 (received credentials for the term beginning 1881 but died pending a contest).

O'CONOR, Herbert Romulus (Md.) Nov. 17, 1896–March 4, 1960; Senate 1947–53; Gov. Jan. 11, 1939–Jan. 3, 1947.

O'DANIEL, Wilbert Lee "Pappy" (Tex.) March 11, 1890–May 11, 1969; Senate Aug. 4, 1941–49; Gov. Jan. 17, 1939–Aug. 4, 1941.

O'DAY, Caroline Love Goodwin (N.Y.) June 22, 1875–Jan. 4, 1943; House 1935–43.

ODELL, Moses Fowler (N.Y.) Feb. 24, 1818–June 13, 1866; House 1861–65.

ODELL, Nathaniel Holmes (N.Y.) Oct. 10, 1823–Oct. 30, 1904; House 1875–77.

O'FERRALL, Charles Triplett (Va.) Oct. 21, 1840–Sept. 22, 1905; House May 5, 1884–Dec. 28, 1893; Gov. Jan. 1, 1894–Jan. 1, 1898.

OGDEN, Henry Warren (La.) Oct. 21, 1842–July 23, 1905; House May 12, 1894–99.

OGLESBY, Woodson Ratcliff (cousin of Richard James Oglesby) (N.Y.) Feb. 9, 1867–April 30, 1955; House 1913–17.

O'HAIR, Frank Trimble (Ill.) March 12, 1870–Aug. 3, 1932; House 1913–15.

O'HARA, Barratt (Ill.) April 28, 1882–Aug. 11, 1969; House 1949–51, 1953–69.

O'HARA, James Grant (Mich.) Nov. 8, 1925–March 13, 1989; House 1959–77.

OHLIGER, Lewis Philip (Ohio) Jan. 3, 1843–Jan. 9, 1923; House Dec. 5, 1892–93.

OLDFIELD, Pearl Peden (widow of William Allan Oldfield) (Ark.) Dec. 2, 1876–April 12, 1962; House Jan. 9, 1929–31.

OLDFIELD, William Allan (husband of Pearl Peden Oldfield) (Ark.) Feb. 4, 1874–Nov. 19, 1928; House 1909–Nov. 19, 1928.

OLDS, Edson Baldwin (Ohio) June 3, 1802–Jan. 24, 1869; House 1849–55.

O'LEARY, Denis (N.Y.) Jan. 22, 1863–Sept. 27, 1943; House 1913–Dec. 31, 1914.

O'LEARY, James Aloysius (N.Y.) April 23, 1889–March 16, 1944; House 1935–March 16, 1944.

OLIN, James R. (Va.) Feb. 28, 1920–; House 1983–93.

OLIVER, Andrew (N.Y.) Jan. 16, 1815–March 6, 1889; House 1853–57.

OLIVER, Daniel Charles (N.Y.) Oct. 6, 1865–March 26, 1924; House 1917–19.

OLIVER, Frank (N.Y.) Oct. 2, 1883–Jan. 1, 1968; House 1923–June 18, 1934.

OLIVER, James Churchill (Maine) Aug. 5, 1895–Dec. 25, 1986; House 1937–43 (Republican), 1959–61.

OLIVER, William Bacon (cousin of Sydney Parham Epes) (Ala.) May 23, 1867–May 27, 1948; House 1915–37.

OLIVER, William Morrison (N.Y.) Oct. 15, 1792–July 21, 1863; House 1841–43.

OLNEY, Richard (Mass.) Jan. 5, 1871–Jan. 15, 1939; House 1915–21.

O'LOUGHLIN, Kathryn Ellen (later married and served as Kathryn O'Loughlin McCarthy) (Kans.) April 24, 1894–Jan. 16, 1952; House 1933–35.

OLSEN, Arnold (Mont.) Dec. 17, 1916–Oct. 9, 1990; House 1961–71.

OLIVER, John Walter (Mass.) Sept. 3, 1936–; House June 18, 1991–.

O'MAHONEY, Joseph Christopher (Wyo.) Nov. 5, 1884–Dec. 1, 1962; Senate Jan. 1, 1934–53, Nov. 29, 1954–61; Chrmn. Senate Interior and Insular Affairs 1949–53.

O'MALLEY, Matthew Vincent (N.Y.) June 25, 1878–May 26, 1931; House March 4–May 26, 1931.

O'MALLEY, Thomas David Patrick (N.Y.) March 24, 1903–Dec. 19, 1979; House 1933–39.

O'NEAL, Emmet (Ky.) April 14, 1887–July 18, 1967; House 1935–47.

O'NEAL, Maston Emmett Jr. (Ga.) July 19, 1907–Jan. 9, 1990; House 1965–71.

O'NEALL, John Henry (Ind.) Oct. 30, 1838–July 15, 1907; House 1887–91.

O'NEIL, Joseph Henry (Mass.) March 23, 1853–Feb. 19, 1935; House 1889–95.

O'NEILL, Edward Leo (N.J.) July 10, 1903–Dec. 12, 1948; House 1937–39.

O'NEILL, Harry Patrick (Pa.) Feb. 10, 1889–June 24, 1953; House 1949–53.

O'NEILL, John (Ohio) Dec. 17, 1822–May 25, 1905; House 1863–65.

O'NEILL, John Joseph (Mo.) June 25, 1846–Feb. 19, 1898; House 1883–89, 1891–93, April 3, 1894–95.

O'NEILL, Thomas Phillip "Tip" Jr. (Mass.) Dec. 9, 1912–Jan. 5, 1994; House 1953–87; House majority leader 1973–77; Speaker Jan. 4, 1977–79, Jan. 15, 1979–81, Jan. 5, 1981–87.

O'REILLY, Daniel (N.Y.) June 3, 1838–Sept. 23, 1911; House 1879–81.

ORR, James Lawrence (S.C.) May 12, 1822–May 5, 1873; House 1849–59; Speaker Dec. 7, 1857–59; Gov. Nov. 29, 1865–July 6, 1868 (Republican).

ORTIZ, Solomon Porfirio (Tex.) June 3, 1938–; House 1983–.

ORTON, William (Utah) Sept. 22, 1949–; House 1991–.

OSBORNE, John Eugene (Wyo.) June 19, 1858–April 24, 1943; House 1897–99; Gov. Jan. 2, 1893–Jan. 7, 1895.

O'SHAUNESSY, George Francis (R.I.) May 1, 1868–Nov. 28, 1934; House 1911–19.

O'SULLIVAN, Eugene Daniel (Nebr.) May 31, 1883–Feb. 7, 1968; House 1949–51.

O'SULLIVAN, Patrick Brett (Conn.) Aug. 11, 1887–Nov. 10, 1978; House 1923–25.

OTERO, Miguel Antonio (uncle of Mariano Sabino Otero) (N.Mex.) June 21, 1829–May 30, 1882; House (Terr. Del.) July 23, 1856–61.

OTEY, Peter Johnston (Va.) Dec. 22, 1840–May 4, 1902; House 1895–May 4, 1902.

O'TOOLE, Donald Lawrence (N.Y.) Aug. 1, 1902–Sept. 12, 1964; House 1937–53.

OTTINGER, Richard Lawrence (N.Y.) Jan. 27, 1929–; House 1965–71, 1976–85.

OURY, Granville Henderson (Ariz.) March 12, 1825–Jan. 11, 1891; House (Terr. Del.) 1881–85.

OUTHWAITE, Joseph Hodson (Ohio) Dec. 5, 1841–Dec. 9, 1907; House 1885–95.

OUTLAND, George Elmer (Calif.) Oct. 8, 1906–March 2, 1981; House 1943–47.

OVERMAN, Lee Slater (N.C.) Jan. 3, 1854–Dec. 12, 1930; Senate 1903–Dec. 12, 1930.

OVERMYER, Arthur Warren (Ohio) May 31, 1879–March 8, 1952; House 1915–19.

OVERSTREET, James Whetstone (Ga.) Aug. 28, 1866–Dec. 4, 1938; House Oct. 3, 1906–07, 1917–23.

OVERTON, John Holmes (uncle of Overton Brooks) (La.) Sept. 17, 1875–May 14, 1948; House May 12, 1931–33; Senate 1933–May 14, 1948.

OWEN, Emmett Marshall (Ga.) Oct. 19, 1877–June 21, 1939; House 1933–June 21, 1939.

OWEN, Robert Dale (Ind.) Nov. 7, 1801–June 24, 1877; House 1843–47.

OWEN, Robert Latham (Okla.) Feb. 3, 1856–July 19, 1947; Senate Dec. 11, 1907–25.

OWEN, Ruth Bryan (later Mrs. Borge Rohde, daughter of William Jennings Bryan) (Fla.) Oct. 2, 1885–July 26, 1954; House 1929–33.

OWENS, Douglas Wayne (Utah) May 2, 1937–; House 1973–75, 1987–93.

OWENS, George Welshman (Ga.) Aug. 29, 1786–March 2, 1856; House 1835–39 (1835–37 Jacksonian).

OWENS, James W. (Ohio) Oct. 24, 1837–March 30, 1900; House 1889–93.

OWENS, Major Robert Odell (N.Y.) June 28, 1936–; House 1983–.

OWENS, William Claiborne (Ky.) Oct. 17, 1849–Nov. 18, 1925; House 1895–97.

PACE, Stephen (Ga.) March 9, 1891–April 5, 1970; House 1937–51.

PACKER, Asa (Pa.) Dec. 29, 1805–May 17, 1879; House 1853–57.

PADGETT, Lemuel Phillips (Tenn.) Nov. 28, 1855–Aug. 2, 1922; House 1901–Aug. 2, 1922.

PAGE, Charles Harrison (R.I.) July 19, 1843–July 21, 1912; House Feb. 21–March 3, 1887, 1891–93, April 5, 1893–95.

PAGE, Henry (Md.) June 28, 1841–Jan. 7, 1913; House 1891–Sept. 3, 1892.

PAGE, Robert Newton (N.C.) Oct. 26, 1859–Oct. 3, 1933; House 1903–17.

PAIGE, David Raymond (Ohio) April 8, 1844–June 30, 1901; House 1883–85.

PAINE, William Wiseham (Ga.) Oct. 10, 1817–Aug. 5, 1882; House Dec. 22, 1870–71.

PALLONE, Frank Jr. (N.J.) Oct. 30, 1951–; House Nov. 8, 1988–.

PALMER, Alexander Mitchell (Pa.) May 4, 1872–May 11, 1936; House 1909–15; Atty. Gen. March 5, 1919–March 5, 1921.

PALMER, John (uncle of George William Palmer) (N.Y.) Jan. 29, 1785–Dec. 8, 1840; House 1817–19 (Republican), 1837–39.

PALMER, John McAuley (Ill.) Sept. 13, 1817–Sept. 25, 1900; Senate 1891–97; Gov. Jan. 11, 1869–Jan. 13, 1873 (Republican).

PALMISANO, Vincent Luke (Md.) Aug. 5, 1882–Jan. 12, 1953; House 1923–39.

PANETTA, Leon Edward (Calif.) June 28, 1938–; House 1977–Jan. 21, 1993; Chrmn. House Budget 1989–93.

PARK, Frank (Ga.) March 3, 1864–Nov. 20, 1925; House Nov. 5, 1913–25.

PARKER, Amasa Junius (N.Y.) June 2, 1807–May 13, 1890; House 1837–39.

PARKER, Andrew (Pa.) May 21, 1805–Jan. 15, 1864; House 1851–53.

PARKER, Homer Cling (Ga.) Sept. 25, 1885–June 22, 1946; House Sept. 10, 1931–35.

PARKER, Hosea Washington (N.H.) May 30, 1833–Aug. 21, 1922; House 1871–75.

PARKER, Paul Michael "Mike" (Miss.) Oct. 31, 1949–; House 1989–.

PARKER, Richard (Va.) Dec. 22, 1810–Nov. 10, 1893; House 1849–51.

PARKS, Tilman Bacon (Ark.) May 14, 1872–Feb. 12, 1950; House 1921–37.

PARMENTER, William (Mass.) March 30, 1789–Feb. 25, 1866; House 1837–45.

PARRETT, William Fletcher (Ind.) Aug. 10, 1825–June 30, 1895; House 1889–93.

PARRISH, Isaac (Ohio) March 1804–Aug. 9, 1860; House 1839–41, 1845–47.

PARRISH, Lucian Walton (Tex.) Jan. 10, 1878–March 27, 1922; House 1919–March 27, 1922.

PARSONS, Claude VanCleve (Ill.) Oct. 7, 1895–May 23, 1941; House Nov. 4, 1930–41.

PARSONS, Edward Young (Ky.) Dec. 12, 1841–July 8, 1876; House 1875–July 8, 1876.

PARTRIDGE, Samuel (N.Y.) Nov. 29, 1790–March 30, 1883; House 1841–43.

PASCHAL, Thomas Moore (Tex.) Dec. 15, 1845–Jan. 28, 1919; House 1893–95.

PASCO, Samuel (Fla.) June 28, 1834–March 13, 1917; Senate May 19, 1887–April 18, 1899.

PASSMAN, Otto Ernest (La.) June 27, 1900–Aug. 13, 1988; House 1947–77.

PASTOR, Edward Lopez (Ariz.) June 28, 1943–. House Oct. 3, 1991–.

PASTORE, John Orlando (R.I.) March 17, 1907–; Senate Dec. 19, 1950–Dec. 28, 1976; Gov. Oct. 6, 1945–Dec. 19, 1950.

PATMAN, John William Wright (father of William Neff Patman) (Tex.) Aug. 5, 1893–March 7, 1976; House 1929–March 7, 1976; Chrmn. House Select Committee on Small Business 1949–53, 1955–63; Chrmn. House Banking and Currency 1963–75.

PATMAN, William Neff (son of John William Wright Patman) (Tex.) March 26, 1927–; House 1981–85.

PATRICK, Luther (Ala.) Jan. 23, 1894–May 26, 1957; House 1937–43, 1945–47.

PATTEN, Edward James (N.J.) Aug. 22, 1905–; House 1963–81.

PATTEN, Harold Ambrose (Ariz.) Oct. 6, 1907–Sept. 6, 1969; House 1949–55.

PATTEN, Thomas Gedney (N.Y.) Sept. 12, 1861–Feb. 23, 1939; House 1911–17.

PATTERSON, David Trotter (Tenn.) Feb. 28, 1818–Nov. 3, 1891; Senate May 4, 1865–69.

PATTERSON, Edward White (Kans.) Oct. 4, 1895–March 6, 1940; House 1935–39.

PATTERSON, Elizabeth Johnston (daughter of Olin DeWitt Talmadge Johnston (S.C.) Nov. 18, 1939–; House 1987–93.

PATTERSON, Ellis Ellwood (Calif.) Nov. 28, 1897–Aug. 25, 1985; House 1945–47.

PATTERSON, Gilbert Brown (N.C.) May 29, 1863–Jan. 26, 1922; House 1903–07.

PATTERSON, James O'Hanlon (S.C.) June 25, 1857–Oct. 25, 1911; House 1905–11.

PATTERSON, Jerry Mumford (Calif.) Oct. 25, 1934–; House 1975–85.

PATTERSON, Josiah (father of Malcolm Rice Patterson) (Tenn.) April 14, 1837–Feb. 10, 1904; House 1891–97.

PATTERSON, Lafayette Lee (Ala.) Aug. 23, 1888–March 3, 1987; House Nov. 6, 1928–33.

PATTERSON, Malcolm Rice (son of Josiah Patterson) (Tenn.) June 7, 1861–March 8, 1935; House 1901–Nov. 5, 1906; Gov. Jan. 17, 1907–Jan. 26, 1911.

PATTERSON, Thomas MacDonald (Colo.) Nov. 5, 1839–July 23, 1916; House (Terr. Del.) 1875–Aug. 1, 1876 (Rep.) Dec. 13, 1877–79; Senate 1901–07.

PATTISON, Edward Worthington (N.Y.) April 29, 1932–Aug. 22, 1990; House 1975–79.

PATTISON, John M. (Ohio) June 13, 1847–June 18, 1906; House 1891–93; Gov. Jan. 8–June 18, 1906.

PATTON, David Henry (Ind.) Nov. 26, 1837–Jan. 17, 1914; House 1891–93.

PATTON, John Denniston (Pa.) Nov. 28, 1829–Feb. 22, 1904; House 1883–85.

PATTON, John Mercer (Va.) Aug. 10, 1797–Oct. 29, 1858; House Nov. 25, 1830–April 7, 1838 (Nov. 25, 1830–37 Jacksonian); Gov. March 18–March 31, 1841 (State Rights Whig).

PATTON, Nat (Tex.) Feb. 26, 1884–July 27, 1957; House 1935–45.

PAYNE, Donald Milford (N.J.) July 16, 1934–; House 1989–.

PAYNE, Henry B. (grandfather of Frances Payne Bolton, great-grandfather of Oliver Payne Bolton) (Ohio) Nov. 30, 1810–Sept. 9, 1896; House 1875–77; Senate 1885–91.

PAYNE, Lewis Franklin Jr. (Va.) July 9, 1945–; House June 21, 1988–.

PAYNE, William Winter (Ala.) Jan. 2, 1807–Sept. 2, 1874; House 1841–47.

PAYNTER, Lemuel (Pa.) 1788–Aug. 1, 1863; House 1837–41.

PAYNTER, Thomas Hanson (Ky.) Dec. 9, 1851–March 8, 1921; House 1889–Jan. 5, 1895; Senate 1907–13.

PEACE, Roger Craft (S.C.) May 19, 1889–Aug. 20, 1968; Senate Aug. 5–Nov. 4, 1941.

PEARCE, James Alfred (Md.) Dec. 8, 1805–Dec. 20, 1862; House 1835–39 (Whig) 1841–43 (Whig); Senate 1843–Dec. 20, 1862 (1843–61 Whig.).

PEARSON, Albert Jackson (Ohio) May 20, 1846–May 15, 1905; House 1891–95.

PEARSON, Herron Carney (Tenn.) July 31, 1890–April 24, 1953; House 1935–43.

PEASE, Donald James (Ohio) Sept. 26, 1931–; House 1977–93.

PEASLEE, Charles Hazen (N.H.) Feb. 6, 1804–Sept. 18, 1866; House 1847–53.

PECK, George Washington (Mich.) June 4, 1818–June 30, 1905; House 1855–57.

PECK, Jared Valentine (N.Y.) Sept. 21, 1816–Dec. 25, 1891; House 1853–55.

PECK, Lucius Benedict (Vt.) Nov. 17, 1802–Dec. 28, 1866; House 1847–51.

PECKHAM, Rufus Wheeler (N.Y.) Dec. 20, 1809–Nov. 22, 1873; House 1853–55.

PEDEN, Preston Elmer (Okla.) June 28, 1914–June 27, 1985; House 1947–49.

PEEL, Samuel West (Ark.) Sept. 13, 1831–Dec. 18, 1924; House 1883–93.

PEERY, George Campbell (Va.) Oct. 28, 1873–Oct. 14, 1952; House 1923–29; Gov. Jan. 17, 1934–Jan. 19, 1938.

PELL, Claiborne de Borda (son of Herbert Claiborne Pell Jr., great-great grandson of John Francis Hamtramck Claiborne, great-great-great-nephew of George Mifflin Dallas, great-great-great-greatnephew of William Charles Cole Claiborne and Nathaniel Herbert Claiborne) (R.I.) Nov. 22, 1918–; Senate 1961–1996, Chrmn. Senate Rules and Administration 1978–81; Chrmn. Senate Foreign Relations 1987–1995.

PELL, Herbert Claiborne Jr. (great-grandson of John Francis Hamtramck Claiborne, great-great-greatnephew of William Charles Cole Claiborne and Nathaniel Herbert Claiborne, father of Claiborne de Borda Pell) (N.Y.) Feb. 16, 1884–July 17, 1961; House 1919–21.

PELOSI, Nancy (daughter of Thomas D'Alesandro Jr.) (Calif.) March 26, 1940–; House June 9, 1987–.

PENDLETON, George Cassety (Tex.) April 23, 1845–Jan. 19, 1913; House 1893–97.

PENDLETON, George Hunt (son of Nathanael Greene Pendleton) (Ohio) July 19, 1825–Nov. 24, 1889; House 1857–65; Senate 1879–85.

PENDLETON, John Overton (W.Va.) July 4, 1851–Dec. 24, 1916; House 1889–Feb. 26, 1890, 1891–95.

PENINGTON, John Brown (Del.) Dec. 20, 1825–June 1, 1902; House 1887–91.

PENN, Alexander Gordon (La.) May 10, 1799–May 7, 1866; House Dec. 30, 1850–53.

PENNY, Timothy Joseph (Minn.) Nov. 19, 1951–; House 1983–1995.

PENNYBACKER, Isaac Samuel, (cousin of Green Berry Samuels) (Va.) Sept. 3, 1805–Jan. 12, 1847; House 1837–39; Senate Dec. 3, 1845–Jan. 12, 1847.

PEPPER, Claude Denson (Fla.) Sept. 8, 1900–May 30, 1989; Senate Nov. 4, 1936–51; House 1963–May 30, 1989; Chrmn. House Rules 1983–89.

PEPPER, Irvin St. Clair (Iowa) June 10, 1876–Dec. 22, 1913; House 1911–Dec. 22, 1913.

PERCY, Le Roy (Miss.) Nov. 9, 1860–Dec. 24, 1929; Senate Feb. 23, 1910–13.

PERKINS, Bishop (N.Y.) Sept. 5, 1787–Nov. 20, 1866; House 1853–55.

PERKINS, Carl Christopher "Chris" (son of Carl Dewey Perkins) (Ky.) Aug. 6, 1954–; House 1985–93 (elected Nov. 6, 1984, to fill a vacancy in the 98th Congress and to the 99th Congress but was not sworn in until Jan. 3, 1985).

PERKINS, Carl Dewey (father of Carl Christopher "Chris" Perkins) (Ky.) Oct. 15, 1912–Aug. 3, 1984; House 1949–Aug. 3, 1984; Chrmn. House Education and Labor 1967–84.

PERKINS, John Jr. (La.) July 1, 1819–Nov. 28, 1885; House 1853–55.

PERKY, Kirtland Irving (Idaho) Feb. 8, 1867–Jan. 9, 1939; Senate Nov. 18, 1912–Feb. 5, 1913.

PERRILI, Augustus Leonard (Ohio) Jan. 20, 1807–June 2, 1882; House 1845–47.

PERRY, Eli (N.Y.) Dec. 25, 1799–May 17, 1881; House 1871–75.

PERRY, Nehemiah (N.J.) March 30, 1816–Nov. 1, 1881; House 1861–65.

PERRY, Thomas Johns (Md.) Feb. 17, 1807–June 27, 1871; House 1845–47.

PERRY, William Hayne (S.C.) June 9, 1839–July 7, 1902; House 1885–91.

PERSONS, Henry (Ga.) Jan. 30, 1834–June 17,1910; House 1879–81.

PETERS, Andrew James (Mass.) April 3, 1872–June 26, 1938; House 1907–Aug. 15, 1914.

PETERSON, Collin Clark (Minn.) June 29, 1944–; House 1991–.

PETERSON, Douglas Brian "Pete" (Fla.) June 26, 1935–; House 1991–.

PETERSON, Hugh (Ga.) Aug. 21, 1898–Oct. 3, 1961; House 1935–47.

PETERSON, James Hardin (Fla.) Feb. 11, 1894–March 28, 1978; House 1933–51; Chrmn. House Public Lands 1949–51.

PETERSON, John Barney (cousin of Horatio Clifford Claypool and Harold Kile Claypool) (Ind.) July 4, 1850–July 16, 1944; House 1913–15.

PETERSON, Morris Blaine (Utah) March 26, 1906–July 15, 1985; House 1961–63.

PETRIKIN, David (Pa.) Dec. 1, 1788–March 1, 1847; House 1837–41.

PETTENGILL, Samuel Barrett (nephew of William Horace Clagett) (Ind.) Jan. 19, 1886–March 20, 1974; House 1931–39.

PETTIT, John (Ind.) June 24, 1807–Jan. 17, 1877; House 1843–49; Senate Jan. 11, 1853–55.

PETTUS, Edmund Winston (Ala.) July 6, 1821–July 27, 1907; Senate 1897–July 27, 1907.

PEYSER, Peter A. (N.Y.) Sept. 7, 1921–; House 1971–77 (Republican), 1979–83.

PEYSER, Theodore Albert (N.Y.) Feb. 18, 1873–Aug. 8, 1937; House 1933–Aug. 8, 1937.

PEYTON, Samuel Oldham (Ky.) Jan. 8, 1804–Jan. 4, 1870; House 1847–49, 1857–61.

PFEIFER, Joseph Lawrence (N.Y.) Feb. 6, 1892–April 19, 1974; House 1935–51.

PFOST, Gracie Bowers (Idaho) March 12, 1906–Aug. 11, 1965; House 1953–63.

PHELAN, James (Tenn.) Dec. 7, 1856–Jan. 30, 1891; House 1887–Jan. 30, 1891.

PHELAN, James Duval (Calif.) April 20, 1861–Aug. 7, 1930; Senate 1915–21.

PHELAN, Michael Francis (Mass.) Oct. 22, 1875–Oct. 12, 1941; House 1913–21.

PHELPS, James (son of Lancelot Phelps) (Conn.) Jan. 12, 1822–Jan. 15, 1900; House 1875–83.

PHELPS, John Smith (son of Elisha Phelps) (Mo.) Dec. 22, 1814–Nov. 20, 1886; House 1845–63; Gov. Jan. 8, 1877–Jan. 10, 1881.

PHELPS, Lancelot (father of James Phelps) (Conn.) Nov. 9, 1784–Sept. 1, 1866; House 1835–39 (1835–37 Jacksonian).

PHELPS, William Wallace (Minn.) June 1, 1826–Aug. 3, 1873; House May 11, 1858–59.

PHELPS, William Walter (N.J.) Aug. 24, 1839–June 17, 1894; House 1873–75 (no party), 1883–89.

PHILBIN, Philip Joseph (Mass.) May 29, 1898–June 14, 1972; House 1943–71.

PHILIPS, John Finis (Mo.) Dec. 31, 1834–March 1919; House 1875–77, Jan. 10, 1880–81.

PHILLIPS, Alfred Noroton (Conn.) April 23, 1894–Jan. 18, 1970; House 1937–39.

PHILLIPS, Henry Myer (Pa.) June 30, 1811–Aug. 28, 1884; House 1857–59.

PHILLIPS, Philip (Ala.) Dec. 13, 1807–Jan. 14, 1884; House 1853–55.

PHISTER, Elijah Conner (Ky.) Oct. 8, 1822–May 16, 1887; House 1879–83.

PICKENS, Francis Wilkinson (grandson of Andrew Pickens) (S.C.) April 7, 1805–Jan. 25, 1869; House Dec. 8, 1834–43 (Dec. 8, 1834–39 Nullifier); Gov. Dec. 14, 1860–Dec. 17, 1862 (State Rights Democrat).

PICKETT, Owen Bradford (Va.) Aug. 31, 1930–; House 1987–.

PICKETT, Thomas Augustus (Tex.) Aug. 14, 1906–June 7, 1980; House 1945–June 30, 1952.

PICKLE, James Jarrell "Jake" (Tex.) Oct. 11, 1913–; House Dec. 21, 1963–.

PIDCOCK, James Nelson (cousin of Alvah Augustus Clark) (N.J.) Feb. 8, 1836–Dec. 17, 1899; House 1885–89.

PIERCE, Franklin (N.H.) Nov. 23, 1804–Oct. 8, 1869; House 1833–37; Senate 1837–Feb. 28, 1842; President 1853–57.

PIERCE, Rice Alexander (Tenn.) July 3, 1848–July 12, 1936; House 1883–85, 1889–93, 1897–1905.

PIERCE, Walter Marcus (Oreg.) May 30, 1861–March 27, 1954; House 1933–43; Gov. Jan. 8, 1923–Jan. 10, 1927.

PIGOTT, James Protus (Conn.) Sept. 11, 1852–July 1, 1919; House 1893–95.

PIKE, Otis Grey (N.Y.) Aug. 31, 1921–; House 1961–79; Chrmn. House Select Committee on Intelligence 1975–76.

PILCHER, John Leonard (Ga.) Aug. 27, 1898–Aug. 20, 1981; House Feb. 4, 1958–65.

PILSBURY, Timothy (Tex.) April 12, 1789–Nov. 23, 1858; House March 30, 1846–49.

PINCKNEY, John McPherson (Tex.) May 4,1845–April 24, 1905; House Nov. 17, 1903–April 24, 1905.

PINDAR, John Sigsbee (N.Y.) Nov. 18, 1835–June 30, 1907; House 1885–87, Nov. 4, 1890–91.

PIPER, William Adam (Calif.) May 21, 1826–Aug. 5, 1899; House 1875–77.

PITTMAN, Key (Nev.) Sept. 19, 1872–Nov. 10, 1940; Senate Jan. 29, 1912–Nov. 10, 1940; elected Pres. pro tempore March 9, 1933, Jan. 7, 1935.

PLAUCHE, Vance Gabriel (La.) Aug. 25, 1897–April 2, 1976; House 1941–43.

PLOWMAN, Thomas Scales (Ala.) June 8, 1843–July 26, 1919; House 1897–Feb. 9, 1898.

PLUMER, Arnold (Pa.) June 6, 1801–April 28, 1869; House 1837–39, 1841–43.

POAGE, William Robert (Tex.) Dec. 28, 1899–Jan. 3, 1987; House 1937–Dec. 31, 1978; Chrmn. House Agriculture 1967–75.

PODELL, Bertram L. (N.Y.) Dec. 27, 1925–; House Feb. 20, 1968–75.

POEHLER, Henry (Minn.) Aug. 22, 1833–July 18, 1912; House 1879–81.

POINSETT, Joel Roberts (S.C.) March 2, 1779–Dec. 12, 1851; House 1821–March 7, 1825; Secy. of War March 7, 1837–March 5, 1841.

POLK, Albert Fawcett (Del.) Oct, 11, 1869–Feb. 14, 1955; House 1917–19.

POLK, James Gould (Ohio) Oct. 6, 1896–April 28, 1959; House 1931–41, 1949–April 28, 1959.

POLK, James Knox (Tenn.) Nov. 2, 1796–June 15, 1849; House 1825–39 (1825–27 no party, 1827–37 Jacksonian); Speaker Dec. 7, 1835–37, Sept. 4, 1837–39; Gov. Oct. 14, 1839–Oct. 15, 1841; President 1845–49.

POLK, Rufus King (Pa.) Aug. 23, 1866–March 5, 1902; House 1899–March 5, 1902.

POLK, Trusten (Mo.) May 29, 1811–April 16, 1876; Senate 1857–Jan. 10, 1862; Gov. Jan. 6–Feb. 27, 1857.

POLLOCK, William Pegues (S.C.) Dec. 9, 1870–June 2, 1922; Senate Nov. 6, 1918–19.

POMERENE, Atlee (Ohio) Dec. 6, 1863–Nov. 12, 1937; Senate 1911–23.

POMEROY, Earl Ralph (N.Dak.) Sept. 2, 1952–; House 1993–.

POOL, Joe Richard (Tex.) Feb. 18, 1911–July 14, 1968; House 1963–July 14, 1968.

POPE, James Pinckney (Idaho) March 31, 1884–Jan. 23, 1966; Senate 1933–39.

POPPLETON, Earley Franklin (Ohio) Sept. 29, 1834–May 6, 1899; House 1875–77.

PORTER, Charles Orlando (Oreg.) April 4, 1919–; House 1957–61.

POSHARD, Glenn (Ill.) Oct. 30, 1945–; House 1989–.

POST, George Adams (Pa.) Sept. 1, 1854–Oct. 31, 1925; House 1883–85.

POST, James Douglass (Ohio) Nov. 25, 1863–April 1, 1921; House 1911–15.

POST, Morton Everel (Wyo.) Dec. 25, 1840–March 19, 1933; House (Terr. Del.) 1881–85.

POTTER, Allen (Mich.) Oct. 2, 1818–May 8, 1885; House 1875–77.

POTTER, Charles Edward (Mich.) Oct. 30, 1916–Nov. 23, 1979; House Aug. 26, 1947–Nov. 4, 1952; Senate Nov. 5, 1952–59.

POTTER, Clarkson Nott (N.Y.) April 25, 1825–Jan. 23, 1882; House 1869–75, 1877–79.

POTTER, Emery Davis (Ohio) Oct. 7, 1804–Feb. 12, 1896; House 1843–45, 1849–51.

POTTER, Orlando Brunson (N.Y.) March 10, 1823–Jan. 2, 1894; House 1883–85.

POTTER, William Wilson (Pa.) Dec. 18, 1792–Oct. 28, 1839; House 1837–Oct. 28, 1839.

POU, Edward William (cousin of James Paul Buchanan) (N.C.) Sept. 9, 1863–April 1, 1934; House 1901–April 1, 1934.

POWELL, Adam Clayton Jr. (N.Y.) Nov. 29, 1908–April 4, 1972; House 1945–Feb. 28, 1967, 1969–71; Chrmn. House Education and Labor 1961–67.

POWELL, Joseph (Pa.) June 23, 1828–April 24, 1904; House 1875–77.

POWELL, Lazarus Whitehead (Ky.) Oct. 6, 1812–July 3, 1867; Senate 1859–65; Gov. Sept. 2, 1851–Sept. 1, 1855.

POWELL, Paulus (Va.) 1809–June 10, 1874; House 1849–59.

PRALL, Anning Smith (N.Y.) Sept. 17, 1870–July 23, 1937; House Nov. 6, 1923–35.

PRATT, Eliza Jane (N.C.) March 5, 1902–May 13, 1981; House May 25, 1946–47.

PRATT, James Timothy (Conn.) Dec. 14, 1802–April 11, 1887; House 1853–55.

PRATTA, Le Gage (N.J.) Dec. 14, 1852–March 9, 1911; House 1907–09.

PRATT, Zadock (N.Y.) Oct. 30, 1790–April 6, 1871; House 1837–39, 1843–45.

PRENTISS, John Holmes (brother of Samuel Prentiss) (N.Y.) April 17, 1784–June 26, 1861; House 1837–41.

PRESTON, Prince Hulon Jr. (Ga.) July 5, 1908–Feb. 8, 1961; House 1947–61.

PREYER, Lunsford Richardson (N.C.) Jan. 11, 1919–; House 1969–81.

PRICE, Andrew (La.) April 2, 1854 -Feb. 5, 1909; House Dec. 2, 1889–97.

PRICE, Charles Melvin (Ill.) Jan. 1, 1905–April 22, 1988; House 1945–April 22, 1988; Chrmn. House Standards of Official Conduct 1969–75; Chrmn. House Armed Services 1975–85.

PRICE, David Eugene (N.C.) Aug. 17, 1940–; House 1987–1995.

PRICE, Emory Hilliard (Fla.) Dec. 3, 1899–Feb. 11, 1976; House 1943–49.

PRICE, Jesse Dashiell (Md.) Aug. 15, 1863–May 14, 1939; House Nov. 3, 1914–19.

PRICE, Rodman McCamley (N.J.) May 5, 1816–June 7, 1894; House 1851–53; Gov. Jan. 17, 1854–Jan. 20, 1857.

PRICE, Sterling (Mo.) Sept. 20, 1809–Sept. 29, 1867; House 1845–Aug. 12, 1846; Gov. Jan. 3, 1853–Jan. 5, 1857.

PRICE, Thomas Lawson (Mo.) Jan. 19, 1809–July 15, 1870; House Jan. 21, 1862–63.

PRICE, William Pierce (Ga.) Jan. 29, 1835–Nov. 4, 1908; House Dec. 22, 1870–73.

PRIDEMORE, Auburn Lorenzo (Va.) June 27, 1837–May 17, 1900; House 1877–79.

PRIEST, James Percy (Tenn.) April 1, 1900–Oct. 12, 1956; House 1941–Oct. 12, 1956 (1941–43 Independent Democrat); Chrmn. House Interstate and Foreign Commerce 1955–57.

PROKOP, Stanley A. (Pa.) July 29, 1909–Nov. 11, 1977; House 1959–61.

PROXMIRE, William (Wis.) Nov. 11, 1915–; Senate Aug. 28, 1957–89; Chrmn. Senate Banking, Housing, and Urban Affairs 1975–81, 1987–89.

PRUYN, John Van Schaick Lansing (N.Y.) June 22, 1811–Nov. 21, 1877; House Dec. 7, 1863–65, 1867–69.

PRYOR, David Hampton (Ark.) Aug. 29, 1934–; House Nov. 8, 1966–73; Senate 1979–; Gov. Jan. 14, 1975–Jan. 3, 1979.

PRYOR, Luke (Ala.) July 5, 1820–Aug. 5, 1900; Senate Jan. 7–Nov. 23, 1880 (no party); House 1883–85.

PRYOR, Roger Atkinson (Va.) July 19, 1828–March 14, 1919; House Dec. 7, 1859–61.

PUCINSKI, Roman Conrad (Ill.) May 13, 1919–; House 1959–73.

PUGH, George Ellis (Ohio) Nov. 28, 1822–July 19, 1876; Senate 1855–61.

PUGH, James Lawrence (Ala.) Dec. 12, 1820–March 9, 1907; House 1859–Jan. 21, 1861 (no party); Senate Nov. 24, 1880–97.

PUGSLEY, Cornelius Amory (N.Y.) July 17, 1850–Sept. 10, 1936; House 1901–03.

PUJO, Arsene Paulin (La.) Dec. 16, 1861–Dec. 31, 1939; House 1903–13.

PULITZER, Joseph (N.Y.) April 10, 1847–Oct. 29, 1886–April 10, 1886.

PURCELL, Graham Boynton Jr. (Tex.) May 5, House Jan. 27, 1962–73.

PURCELL, William Edward (N.Dak.) Aug. 3, 1856–Nov. 3, 1928; Senate Feb. 1, 1910–Feb. 1, 1911.

PURDY, Smith Meade (N.Y.) July 31, 1796–March 30, 1870; House 1843–45.

PUSEY, William Henry Mills (Iowa) July 29, 1826–Nov. 15, 1900; House 1883–85.

QUARLES, Julian Minor (Va.) Sept. 25, 1848–Nov. 18, 1929; House 1899–1901.

QUAYLE, John Francis (N.Y.) Dec. 1, 1868–Nov. 27, 1930; House 1923–Nov. 27, 1930.

QUIGLEY, James Michael (Pa.) March 30, 1918–; House 1955–57, 1959–61.

QUIN, Percy Edwards (Miss.) Oct. 30, 1872–Feb. 4, 1932; House 1913–Feb. 4, 1932.

QUINN, James Leland (Pa.) Sept. 8, 1875–Nov. 12, 1960; House 1935–39.

QUINN, John (N.Y.) Aug. 9, 1839–Feb. 23, 1903; House 1889–91.

QUINN, Peter Anthony (N.Y.) May 10, 1904–Dec. 23, 1974; House 1945–47.

QUINN, Terence John (N.Y.) Oct. 16, 1836–June 18, 1878; House 1877–June 18, 1878.

QUINN, Thomas Vincent (N.Y.) March 16, 1903–March 1, 1982; House 1949–Dec. 30, 1951.

QUITMAN, John Anthony (Miss.) Sept. 1, 1799–July 17, 1858; House 1855–July 17, 1858; Gov. Dec. 3, 1835–Jan. 7, 1836, Jan. 10, 1850–Feb. 3, 1851.

RABAUT, Louis Charles (Mich.) Dec. 5, 1886–Nov. 12, 1961; House 1935–47, 1949–Nov. 12, 1961.

RABIN, Benjamin J. (N.Y.) June 3, 1896–Feb. 22, 1969; House 1945–Dec. 31, 1947.

RACE, John Abner (Wis.) May 12, 1914–Nov. 10, 1983; House 1965–97.

RADCLIFFE, George Lovic Pierce (Md.) Aug. 22, 1877–July 29, 1974; Senate 1935–47.

RADFORD, William (N.Y.) June 24, 1814–Jan. 18, 1870; House 1863–67.

RAGON, Heartsill (Ark.) March 20, 1885–Sept. 15, 1940; House 1923–June 16, 1933.

RAGSDALE, James Willard (S.C.) Dec. 14, 1872–July 23, 1919; House 1913–July 23, 1919.

RAHALL, Nick Joe II (W.Va.) May 20, 1949–; House 1977–.

RAINEY, Henry Thomas (Ill.) Aug. 20, 1860–Aug. 19, 1934; House 1903–21, 1923–Aug. 19, 1934; House majority leader 1931–33; Speaker March 9, 1933–Aug. 19, 1934.

RAINEY, John William (Ill.) Dec. 21, 1880–May 4, 1923; House April 2, 1918–May 4, 1923.

RAINEY, Lilius Bratton (Ala.) July 27, 1876–Sept. 27, 1959; House Sept. 30, 1919–23.

RAINS, Albert McKinley (Ala.) March 11, 1902–March 22, 1991; House 1945–65.

RAKER, John Edward (Calif.) Feb. 22, 1863–Jan. 22, 1926; House 1911–Jan. 22, 1926.

RALSTON, Samuel Moffett (Ind.) Dec. 1, 1857–Oct 14, 1925; Senate 1923–Oct. 14, 1925; Gov. Jan. 13, 1913–Jan. 8, 1917.

RAMSAY, Robert Lincoln (W.Va.) March 24, 1877–Nov. 14, 1956; House 1933–39, 1941–43, 1949–53.

RAMSEY, William (Pa.) Sept. 7, 1779–Sept. 29, 1831; House 1827–Sept. 29, 1831 (1827–29 no party).

RAMSEY, William Sterrett (Pa.) June 12, 1810–Oct. 17, 1840; House 1839–Oct. 17, 1840.

RAMSPECK, Robert C. Word (Ga.) Sept. 5, 1890–Sept. 10, 1972; House Oct. 2, 1929–Dec. 31, 1945.

RANDALL, Samuel Jackson (Pa.) Oct. 10, 1828–April 13, 1890; House 1863–April 13, 1890; Speaker Dec. 4, 1876–77, Oct. 15, 1877–79, March 18, 1879–81.

RANDALL, William Joseph (Mo.) July 16, 1909–; House March 3, 1959–77.

RANDELL, Choice Boswell (nephew of Lucius Jeremiah Gartrelf) (Tex.) Jan. 1, 1857–Oct. 19, 1945; House 1901–13.

RANDOLPH, Jennings (W.Va.) March 8, 1902–; House 1933–47; Senate Nov. 5, 1958–85; Chrmn. Senate Public Works 1966–77; Chrmn. Senate Environment and Public Works 1977–81.

RANDOLPH, Theodore Fitz (son of James Fitz Randolph) (N.J.) June 24, 1826–Nov. 7, 1883; Senate 1875–81; Gov. Jan. 19, 1869–Jan. 16, 1872.

RANGEL, Charles Bernard (N.Y.) June 1, 1930–; House 1971–.

RANKIN, John Elliott (Miss.) March 29, 1882–Nov 26, 1960; House 1921–53; Chrmn. House Veterans' Affairs 1949–53.

RANKIN, Joseph (Wis.) Sept. 25, 1833–Jan. 24, 1886; House 1883–Jan. 24, 1886.

RANSDELL, Joseph Eugene (La.) Oct. 7. 1868–July 27, 1954; House Aug. 29, 1899–1913; Senate 1913–31.

RANSOM, Matt Whitaker (cousin of Wharton Jackson Green) (N.C.) Oct. 8, 1826–Oct. 8, 1904; Senate Jan. 30, 1872–95; elected Pres. pro tempore Jan. 7, 1895.

RANTOUL, Robert Jr. (Mass.) Aug. 13, 1805–Aug. 7, 1852; Senate Feb. 1–March 3, 1851; House March 4, 1851–Aug. 7, 1852.

RARICK, John Richard (La.) Jan. 29, 1924–; House 1967–75.

RATCHFORD, William Richard (Conn.) May 24, 1934–; House 1979–85.

RATHBUN, George Oscar (N.Y.) 1803–Jan. 5, 1870; House 1843–47.

RAUCH, George Washington (Ind.) Feb. 22, 1876–Nov. 4, 1940; House 1907–17.

RAWLINS, Joseph Lafayette (Utah) March 28, 1850–May 24, 1926; House (Terr. Del.) 1893–95; Senate 1897–1903.

RAWLS, Morgan (Ga.) June 29, 1829–Oct. 18, 1906; House 1873–March 24, 1874.

RAY, Richard Belmont (Ga.) Feb. 2, 1927–; House 1983–93.

RAYBURN, Samuel Taliaferro (Tex.) Jan. 6, 1882–Nov. 16, 1961; House 1913–Nov. 16, 1961; House majority leader 1937–Sept. 16, 1940; House minority leader 1947–49, 1953–55; Speaker Sept. 16, 1940–43, Jan. 6, 1943–47, 1949–53, Jan. 5, 1955–59, Jan. 7, 1959–Nov. 16, 1961.

RAYFIEL, Leo Frederick (N.Y.) March 22, 1888–Nov. 18, 1978; House 1945–Sept. 13, 1947.

RAYNER, Isidor (Md.) April 11, 1850–Nov. 25, 1912; House 1887–89, 1891–95; Senate 1905–Nov. 25, 1912.

REA, David (Mo.) Jan. 19, 1831–June 13, 1901; House 1875–79.

READ, Almon Heath (Pa.) June 12, 1790–June 3, 1844; House March 18, 1842–June 3, 1844.

READ, William Brown (Ky.) Dec. 14, 1817–Aug. 5, 1880; House 1871–75.

READING, John Roberts (Pa.) Nov. 1, 1826–Feb. 14, 1886; House 1869–April 13, 1870.

REAGAN, John Henninger (Tex.) Oct. 8, 1818–March 6, 1905; House 1857–61, 1875–87; Senate 1887–June 10, 1891.

REAMES, Alfred Evan (Oreg.) Feb. 5, 1870–March 4, 1943; Senate Feb. 1–Nov. 8, 1938.

REDDEN, Monroe Minor (N.C.) Sept. 24, 1901–; House 1947–53.

REDFIELD, William Cox (N.Y.) June 18, 1858–June 13, 1932; House 1911–13; Secy. of Commerce March 5, 1913–Oct. 31, 1919.

REDING, John Randall (N.H.) Oct. 18, 1806–Oct. 8, 1892; House 1841–45.

REDLIN, Rolland W. (N.Dak.) Feb. 29, 1920–; House 1965–67.

REED, Eugene Elliott (N.H.) April 23, 1866–Dec. 15, 1940; House 1913–15.

REED, James Alexander (Mo.) Nov. 9, 1861–Sept. 8, 1944; Senate 1911–29.

REED, James Byron (Ark.) Jan. 2, 1881–April 27, 1935; House Oct. 20, 1923–29.

REED, John Francis (R.I.) Nov. 12, 1949–; House 1991–.

REES, Thomas Mankell (Calif.) March 26, 1925–; House Dec. 15, 1965–77.

REESE, Seaborn (Ga.) Nov. 28, 1846–March 1, 1907; House Dec. 4, 1882–87.

REEVES, Henry Augustus (N.Y.) Dec. 7, 1832–March 4, 1916; House 1869–71.

REGAN, Kenneth Mills (Tex.) March 6, 1893–Aug. 15, 1959; House Aug. 23, 1947–55.

REID, Charles Chester (Ark.) June 15, 1868–May 20, 1922; House 1901–11.

REID, David Settle (nephew of Thomas Settle) (N.C.) April 19, 1813–June 19, 1891; House 1843–47; Senate Dec. 6, 1854–59; Gov. Jan. 1, 1851–Dec. 6, 1854.

REID, Harry (Nev.) Dec. 2, 1939–; House 1983–87; Senate 1987–.

REID, James Wesley (N.C.) June 11, 1849–Jan. 1, 1902; House Jan. 28, 1885–Dec. 31, 1886.

REID, John William (Mo.) June 14, 1821–Nov. 22, 1881; House March 4–Dec. 2, 1861.

REID, Ogden Rogers (N.Y.) June 24, 1925–; House 1963–75 (1963–March 22, 1972, Republican).

REILLY, James Bernard (Pa.) Aug. 12, 1845–May 14, House 1875–79, 1889–95.

REILLY, John (Pa.) Feb. 22, 1836–April 19, 1904; 1875–77.

REILLY, Michael Kieran (Wis.) July 15, 1869–Oct. 14, 1944; House 1913–17, Nov. 4, 1930–39.

REILLY, Thomas Lawrence (Conn.) Sept. 20, 1858–July 6, 1924; House 1911–15.

REILY, Luther (Pa.) Oct. 17, 1794–Feb. 20, 1854; House 1837–39.

RELFE, James Hugh (Mo.) Oct. 17, 1791–Sept. 14, 1863; House 1843–47.

RESA, Alexander John (Ill.) Aug. 4, 1887–July 4, 1964; House 1945–47.

RESNICK, Joseph Yale (N.Y.) July 13, 1924–Oct. 6, 1969; House 1965–69.

REUSS, Henry Schoellkopf (Wis.) Feb. 22, 1912–; House 1955–83; Chrmn. House Banking, Currency, and Housing 1975–77; Chrmn. House Banking, Housing, and Urban Affairs 1977–81.

REYNOLDS, John (Ill.) Feb. 26, 1788–May 8, 1865; House Dec. 1, 1834–37 (Jacksonian), 1839–43 (Democrat); Gov. Dec. 6, 1830–Nov. 17, 1834.

REYNOLDS, Melvin Jay "Mel" (Ill.) Jan. 8, 1952–; House 1993–1995.

REYNOLDS, Robert Rice (N.C.) June 18, 1884–Feb. 13, 1963; Senate Dec. 5, 1932–45.

RHEA, John Stockdale (Ky.) March 9, 1855–July 29, 1924; House 1897–March 25, 1902, 1903–05.

RHEA, William Francis (Va.) April 20, 1858–March 23, 1931; House 1899–1903.

RHETT, Robert Barnwell (formerly Robert Barnwell Smith) (S.C.) Dec. 24, 1800–Sept. 14, 1876; House 1837–49; Senate Dec. 18, 1850–May 7, 1852.

RHINOCK, Joseph Lafayette (Ky.) Jan. 4, 1863–Sept. 20, 1926; House 1905–11.

RHODES, George Milton (Pa.) Feb. 24, 1898–Oct. 23, 1978; House 1949–60.

RIBICOFF, Abraham Alexander (Conn.) April 9, 1910–; House 1949–53; Senate 1963–81; Chrmn. Senate Government Operations 1975–77; Chrmn. Senate Governmental Affairs 1977–81; Gov. Jan. 5, 1955–Jan. 21, 1961; Secy. of Health, Education and Welfare Jan. 21, 1961–July 13, 1962.

RICE, Americus Vespucius (Ohio) Nov. 18, 1835–April 4, 1904; House 1875–79.

RICE, Edmund (brother of Henry Mower Rice) (Minn.) Feb. 14, 1819–July 11, 1889; House 1887–89.

RICE, Edward Young (Ill.) Feb. 8, 1820–April 16, 1883; House 1871–73.

RICE, Henry Mower (brother of Edmund Rice) (Minn.) Nov. 29, 1817–Jan. 15, 1894; House (Terr. Del.) 1853–57; Senate May 11, 1858–63.

RICE, John McConnell (Ky.) Feb. 19, 1831–Sept. 18, 1895; House 1869–73.

RICHARDS, Charles Lenmore (Nev.) Oct. 3, 1877–Dec. 22, 1953; House 1923–25.

RICHARDS, James Alexander Dudley (Ohio) March 22, 1845–Dec. 4, 1911; House 1893–95.

RICHARDS, James Prioleau (S.C.) Aug. 31, 1894–Feb. 21, 1979; House 1933–57; Chrmn. House Foreign Affairs 1951–53, 1955–57.

RICHARDSON, George Frederick (Mich.) July 1, 1850–March 1, 1923; House 1893–95.

RICHARDSON, James Daniel (Tenn.) March 10, 1843–July 24, 1914; House 1885–1905; House minority leader 1899–1903.

RICHARDSON, James Montgomery (Ky.) July 1, 1858–Feb. 9, 1925; House 1905–07.

RICHARDSON, John Smythe (S.C.) Feb. 29, 1828–Feb. 24, 1894; House 1879–83.

RICHARDSON, William (Ala.) May 8, 1839–March 31, 1914; House Aug. 6, 1900–March 31, 1914.

RICHARDSON, William Alexander (Ill.) Jan. 16, 1811–Dec. 27, 1875; House Dec. 6, 1847–Aug. 25, 1866, 1861–Jan. 29, 1863; Senate Jan. 30, 1863–65.

RICHARDSON, William Blaine (N.Mex.) Nov. 15, 1947–; House 1983–.

RICHARDSON, William Emanuel (Pa.) Sept. 3, 1886–Nov. 3, 1948; House 1933–37.

RICHMOND, Frederick William (N.Y.) Nov. 15, 1923–; House 1975–August 25, 1982.

RICHMOND, James Buchanan (Va.) Feb. 27, 1842–April 30, 1910; House 1879–81.

RIDDLE, George Read (Del.) 1817–March 29, 1867; House 1851–55; Senate Feb. 2, 1864–March 29, 1867.

RIDDLE, Haywood Yancey (Tenn.) June 20, 1834–March 28, 1879; House Dec. 14, 1875–79.

RIDER, Ira Edgar (N.Y.) Nov. 17, 1868–May 29, 1906; House 1903–05.

RIEGLE, Donald Wayne Jr. (Mich.) Feb. 4, 1938–; House 1967–Dec. 30, 1976 (1967–73 Republican); Senate Dec. 30, 1976–1995; Chrmn. Senate Banking, Housing and Urban Affairs 1989–1995.

RIGGS, James Milton (Ill.) April 17, 1839–Nov. 18, 1933; House 1883–87.

RIGGS, Lewis (N.Y.) Jan. 16, 1789–Nov. 6, 1870; House 1841–43.

RIGNEY, Hugh McPheeters (Ill.) July 31, 1873–Oct. 12, 1950; House 1937–39.

RILEY, Corinne Boyd (widow of John Jacob Riley) (S.C.) July 4, 1893–April 12, 1979; House April 10, 1962–63.

RILEY, John Jacob (husband of Corinne Boyd Riley) (S.C.) Feb. 1, 1895–Jan. 1, 1962; House 1945–49, 1951–Jan. 1, 1962.

RIORDAN, Daniel Joseph (N.Y.) July 7, 1870–April 28, 1923; House 1899–1901, Nov. 6, 1906–April 28, 1923.

RIPLEY, Eleazar Wheelock (brother of James Wheelock Ripley) (La.) April 15, 1782–March 2, 1839; House 1835–March 2, 1839 (1835–37 Jacksonian).

RISENHOOVER, Theodore Marshall (Okla;) Nov. 3, 1934–; House 1975–79.

RITCHEY, Thomas (Ohio) Jan. 19, 1801–March 9, 1863; House 1847–49, 1853–55.

RITCHEY, Byron Foster (son of James Monroe Ritchie) (Ohio) Jan. 29, 1853–Aug. 22, 1928; House 1893–95.

RITCHIE, John (Md.) Aug. 12, 1831–Oct. 27, 1887; House 1871–73.

RITTER, Burwell Clark (uncle of Walter Evans) (Ky.) Jan. 6, 1810–Oct. 1, 1880; House 1865–67.

RITTER, John (Pa.) Feb. 6, 1779–Nov. 24, 1851; House 1843–47.

RIVERS, Lucius Mendel (S.C.) Sept. 28, 1905–Dec. 28, 1970; House 1941–Dec. 28, 1970; Chrmn. House Armed Services 1965–71.

RIVERS, Ralph Julian (Alaska) May 23, 1903–Aug. 14, 1976; House 1959–67.

RIVES, Francis Everod (great-uncle of Francis Rives Lassiter) (Va.) Jan. 14, 1792–Dec. 26, 1861; House 1837–41.

RIXEY, John Franklin (Va.) Aug. 1, 1854–Feb. 8, 1907; House 1897–Feb. 8, 1907.

ROACH, William Nathaniel (N.Dak.) Sept. 25, 1840–Sept. 7, 1902; Senate 1893–99.

ROANE, William Henry (Va.) Sept. 17, 1787–May 11, 1845; House 1815–17 (Republican); Senate March 14, 1837–41.

ROBB, Edward (Mo.) March 19, 1857–March 13, 1934; House 1897–1905.

ROBB, Charles Spittal (Va.) June 26, 1939–; Senate 1989–; Gov. Jan. 16, 1982–Jan. 18, 1986.

ROBBINS, Gaston Ahi (Ala.) Sept. 26, 1858–Feb. 22, 1902; House 1893–March 13, 1896, 1899–March 8, 1900.

ROBBINS, John (Pa.) 1808–April 27, 1880; House 1849–55, 1875–77.

ROBBINS, William McKendree (N.C.) Oct. 26, 1828–May 5, 1905; House 1873–79.

ROBERTS, Brigham Henry (Utah) March 13, 1857–Sept. 27, 1933; House 1899–Jan. 25, 1900.

ROBERTS, Charles Boyle (Md.) April 19, 1842–Sept. 10, 1899; House 1875–79.

ROBERTS, Herbert Ray (Tex.) March 28, 1913–April 13, 1992; House Jan. 30, 1962–81; Chrmn. House Veterans' Affairs 1975–81.

ROBERTS, Kenneth Allison (Ala.) Nov. 1, 1912–May 9, 1989; House 1951–65.

ROBERTS, Robert Whyte (Miss.) Nov. 28, 1784–Jan. 4, 1865; House 1843–47.

ROBERTS, William Randall (N.Y.) Feb. 6, 1830–Aug. 9, 1897; House 1871–75.

ROBERTSON, Absalom Willis (Va.) May 27, 1887–Nov. 1, 1971; House 1933–Nov. 5, 1946; Senate Nov. 6, 1946–Dec. 30, 1966; Chrmn. Senate Banking and Currency 1959–67.

ROBERTSON, Edward White (father of Samuel Matthews Robertson) (La.) June 13, 1823–Aug. 2, 1887; House 1877–83, March 4–Aug. 2, 1887.

ROBERTSON, Samuel Matthews (son of Edward White Robertson) (La.) Jan. 1, 1852–Dec. 24, 1911; House Dec. 5, 1887–1907.

ROBERTSON, Thomas Austin (Ky.) Sept. 9, 1848–July 18, 1892; House 1883–87.

ROBESON, Edward John Jr. (Va.) Aug. 9, 1890–March 10, 1966; House May 2, 1950–59.

ROBIE, Reuben (N.Y.) July 15, 1799–Jan. 21, 1872; House 1851–53.

ROBINSON, James Carroll (Ill.) Aug. 19, 1823–Nov. 3, 1886; House 1859–65, 1871–75.

ROBINSON, James McClellan (Ind.) May 31, 1861–Jan. 16, 1942; House 1897–1905.

ROBINSON, James William (Utah) Jan. 19, 1878–Dec. 2, 1964; House 1933–41.

ROBINSON, John Larne (Ind.) May 3, 1813–March 21, 1860; House 1847–53.

ROBINSON, John Seaton (Nebr.) May 4, 1856–May 25, 1903; House 1899–1901.

ROBINSON, Joseph Taylor (Ark.) Aug. 26, 1872–July 14, 1937; House 1903–Jan. 14, 1913; Senate 1913–July 14, 1937; Senate minority leader 1923–33; Senate majority leader 1933–July 14, 1937; Gov. Jan. 15–March 10, 1913.

ROBINSON, Leonidas Dunlap (N.C.) April 22, 1867–Nov. 7, 1941; House 1917–21.

ROBINSON, Orville (N.Y.) Oct. 28, 1801–Dec. 1, 1882; House 1843–45.

ROBINSON, Thomas Jr. (Del.) 1800–Oct. 28, 1843; House 1839–41.

ROBINSON, William Erigena (N.Y.) May 6, 1814–Jan. 23, 1892; House 1867–69, 1881–85.

ROCHESTER, William Beatty (N.Y.) Jan. 29, 1789–June 14, 1838; House 1821–April 1823.

ROCKEFELLER, John Davison "Jay" IV (great-grandson of Nelson Wilmarth Aldrich, great-nephew of Richard Steere Aldrich, nephew of Vice Pres. Nelson Aldrich Rockefeller and Gov. Winthrop Rockefeller of Ark., son-in-law of Charles Harting Percy) (W.Va.) June 18, 1937–; Senate Jan. 15, 1985–; Chrmn. Senate Veterans' Affairs 1993–1995; Gov. Jan. 17, 1977–Jan. 14, 1985.

ROCKHILL, William (Ind.) Feb. 10, 1793–Jan. 15, 1865; House 1847–49.

ROCKWELL, Hosea Hunt (N.Y.) May 31, 1840–Dec. 18, 1918; House 1891–93.

RODDENBERY, Seaborn Anderson (Ga.) Jan. 12, 1870–Sept. 25, 1913; House Feb. 16, 1910–Sept. 25, 1913.

RODINO, Peter Wallace Jr. (N.J.) June 7, 1909–; House 1949–89; Chrmn. House Judiciary 1973–89.

ROE, Dudley George (Md.) March 23, 1881–Jan. 4, 1970; House 1945–47.

ROE, James A. (N.Y.) July 9, 1896–April 22, 1967; House 1945–47.

ROE, Robert A. (N.J.) Feb. 28, 1924–; House Nov. 4, 1969–93; Chrmn. House Science, Space, and Technology 1987–91; Chrmn. House Public Works and Transportation 1991–93.

ROEMER, Charles Elson III "Buddy" (La.) Oct. 4, 1943–; House 1981–March 14, 1988; Gov. March 14, 1988– (March 11, 1991–Republican).

ROEMER, Timothy John (son-in-law of John Bennett Johnston Jr.) (Ind.) Oct. 30, 1956–; House 1991–.

ROGERS, Andrew Jackson (N.J.) July 1, 1828–May 22, 1900; House 1863–67.

ROGERS, Anthony Astley Cooper (Ark.) Feb. 14, 1821–July 27, 1899; House 1869–71.

ROGERS, Byron Giles (Colo.) Aug. 1, 1900–Dec. 31, 1983; House 1951–71.

ROGERS, Dwight Laing (father of Paul Grant Rogers) (Fla.) Aug. 17, 1886–Dec. 1, 1954; House 1945–Dec. 1, 1954.

ROGERS, Edward (N.Y.) May 30, 1787–May 29, 1857; Hous 1839–41.

ROGERS, George Frederick (N.Y.) March 19, 1887–Nov. 20, 1948; House 1945–47.

ROGERS, James (S.C.) Oct. 24, 1795–Dec. 21, 1873; House 1835–37 (Jacksonian), 1839–43.

ROGERS, John (N.Y.) May 9, 1813–May 11, 1879; House 1871–73.

ROGERS, John Henry (Ark.) Oct. 9, 1845–April 16, 1911; House 1883–91.

ROGERS, Paul Grant (son of Dwight Laing Rogers) (Fla.) June 4, 1921–; House Jan. 11, 1955–79.

ROGERS, Sion Hart (N.C.) Sept. 30, 1825–Aug. 14, 1874; House 1853–59 (Whig), 1871–73.

ROGERS, Walter Edward (Tex.) July 19, 1908–; House 1951–67.

ROGERS, Will (Okla.) Dec. 12, 1898–Aug. 3, 1983; House 1933–43.

ROGERS, William Findlay (son of Thomas Jones Rogers) (N.Y.) March 1, 1820–Dec. 16, 1899; House 1883–85.

ROGERS, William Nathaniel (N.H.) Jan. 10, 1892–Sept. 25, 1945; House 1923–25, Jan. 5, 1932–37.

ROGERS, William Vann Jr. (Calif.) Oct. 20, 1911–July 9, 1993; House 1943–May 23, 1944.

ROMJUE, Milton Andrew (Mo.) Dec. 5, 1874–Jan. 23, 1968; House 1917–21, 1923–43.

RONAN, Daniel John (Ill.) July 13, 1914–Aug. 13, 1969; House 1966–Aug. 13, 1969.

RONCALIO, Teno (Wyo.) March 23, 1916–; House 1965–67, 1971–Dec. 30, 1978.

ROONEY, Frederick Bernard (Pa.) Nov. 6, 1925–; House July 30, 1963–79.

ROONEY, John James (N.Y.) Nov. 29, 1903–Oct. 26, 1975; House June 6, 1944–Dec. 31, 1974.

ROOSEVELT, Franklin Delano Jr. (son of Pres. Franklin Delano Roosevelt, brother of James Roosevelt) (N.Y.) Aug. 17, 1914–Aug. 17, 1988; House May 17, 1949–55 (1949–51 Liberal).

ROOSEVELT, James (son of Pres. Franklin Delano Roosevelt, brother of Franklin Delano Roosevelt Jr.) (Calif.) Dec. 23, 1907–Aug. 13, 1991; House 1955–Sept. 30, 1965.

ROOSEVELT, James I. (uncle of Robert Barnwell Roosevelt) (N.Y.) Dec. 14, 1795–April 5, 1875; House 1841–43.

ROOSEVELT, Robert Barnwell (nephew of James I. Roosevelt, uncle of Theodore Roosevelt) (N.Y.) Aug. 7, 1829–June 14, 1906; House 1871–73.

ROSE, Charles Grandison III (N.C.) Aug. 10, 1939–; House 1973–; Chrmn. House Administration 1991–1995.

ROSECRANS, William Starke (Calif.) Sept. 6, 1819–March 11, 1898; House 1881–85.

ROSENTHAL, Benjamin Stanley (N.Y.) June 8, 1923–Jan. 4, 1983; House Feb. 20, 1962–Jan. 4, 1983.

ROSIER, Joseph (W.Va.) Jan. 24, 1870–Oct. 7, 1951; Senate Jan. 3, 1941–Nov. 17, 1942.

ROSS, Lewis Winans (Ill.) Dec. 8, 1812–Oct, 20, 1895; House 1863–69.

ROSS, Miles (N.J.) April 30, 1827–Feb. 22, 1903; House 1875–83.

ROSS, Thomas (son of John Ross) (Pa.) Dec. 1, 1806–July 7, 1865; House 1849–53.

ROSS, Thomas Randolph (Ohio) Oct. 26, 1788–June 28, 1869; House 1819–25.

ROSTENKOWSKI, Daniel David "Dan" (Ill.) Jan. 2, 1928–; House 1959–1995, Chrmn. House Ways and Means 1981–1995.

ROTHERMEL, John Hoover (Pa.) March 7, 1856–Aug. 1922; House 1907–15.

ROTHWELL, Gideon Frank (Mo.) April 24, 1836–Jan. 18, 1894; House 1879–81.

ROUSE, Arthur Blythe (Ky.) June 20, 1874–Jan. 25, 1956; House 1911–27.

ROUSH, John Edward (Ind.) Sept. 12, 1920–; House 1959–69, 1971–77.

ROWAN, Joseph (N.Y.) Sept. 8, 1870–Aug. 3, 1930; House 1919–21.

ROWAN, William A. (Ill.) Nov. 24, 1882–May 31, 1961; House 1943–47.

ROWE, Peter (N.Y.) March 10, 1807–April 17, 1876; House 1853–55.

ROWLAND, Alfred (N.C.) Feb. 9, 1844–Aug. 2, 1898; House 1887–91.

ROWLAND, James Roy Jr. (Ga.) Feb. 3, 1926–; House 1983–1995.

ROY, Alphonse (N.H.) Oct. 26, 1897–Oct. 5, 1967; House June 9, 1938–39.

ROY, William Robert (Kans.) Feb. 23, 1926–; House 1971–75.

ROYBAL, Edward Ross (father of Lucille Roybal-Allard) (Calif.) Feb. 10, 1916–; House 1963–93.

ROYBAL-ALLARD, Lucille (daughter of Edward Ross Roybal) (Calif.) June 12, 1941–; House 1993–.

RUBEY, Thomas Lewis (Mo.) Sept. 27, 1862–Nov. 2, 1928; House 1911–21, 1923–Nov. 2, 1928.

RUCKER, Atterson Walden (Colo.) April 3, 1847–July 19, 1924; House 1909–13.

RUCKER, Tinsley White (Ga.) March 24, 1848–Nov. 18, 1926; House Jan. 11–March 3, 1917.

RUCKER, William Waller (Mo.) Feb. 1, 1855–May 30, 1936; House 1899–1923.

RUDD, Stephen Andrew (N.Y.) Dec. 11, 1874–March 31, 1936; House 1931–March 31, 1936.

RUFFIN, James Edward (Mo.) July 24, 1893–April 9, 1977; House 1933–35.

RUFFIN, Thomas (N.C.) Sept. 9, 1820–Oct. 13, 1863; House 1853–61.

RUNNELS, Harold Lowell (N.Mex.) March 17, 1924–Aug. 5, 1980; House 1971–Aug. 5, 1980.

RUPPERT, Jacob Jr. (N.Y.) Aug. 6, 1867–Jan. 13, 1939; House 1899–1907.

RUSH, Bobby Lee (Ill.) Nov. 23, 1946–; House 1993–.

RUSK, Harry Welles (Md.) Oct. 17, 1852–Jan. 28, 1926; House Nov. 21, 1886–97.

RUSK, Thomas Jefferson (Tex.) Dec. 5, 1803–July 29, 1857; Senate Feb. 21, 1846–July 29, 1857; elected Pres. pro tempore March 14, 1857.

RUSSELL, Benjamin Edward (cousin of Rienzi Melville Johnston) (Ga.) Oct. 5, 1845–Dec. 4, 1909; House 1893–97.

RUSSELL, Donald Stuart (S.C.) Feb. 22, 1906–; Senate April 22, 1965–Nov. 8, 1966; Gov. Jan. 15, 1963–April 22, 1965.

RUSSELL, Gordon James (Tex.) Dec. 22, 1859–Sept. 14, 1919; House Nov. 4, 1902–June 14, 1910.

RUSSELL, Jeremiah (N.Y.) Jan. 26, 1786–Sept. 30, 1867; House 1843–45.

RUSSELL, John Edwards (Mass.) Jan. 20, 1834–Oct. 28, 1903; House 1887–89.

RUSSELL, Joseph (N.Y.) ?–?; House 1845–47, 1851–53.

RUSSELL, Joseph James (Mo.) Aug. 23, 1854–Oct. 22, 1922; House 1907–09, 1911–19.

RUSSELL, Richard Brevard Jr. (Ga.) Nov. 2, 1897–Jan. 21, 1971; Senate Jan. 12, 1933–Jan. 21, 1971; elected Pres. pro tempore Jan. 3, 1969; Chrmn. Senate Armed Services 1951–53, 1955–69; Chrmn. Senate Appropriations 1969–71; Gov. June 27, 1931–Jan. 10, 1933.

RUSSELL, Richard Manning (Mass.) March 3, 1891–Feb. 27, 1977; House 1935–37.

RUSSELL, Sam Morris (Tex.) Aug. 9, 1889–Oct. 19, 1971; House 1941–47.

RUSSELL, William Fiero (N.Y.) Jan. 14, 1812–April 29, 1896; House 1857–59.

RUSSO, Martin Anthony (Ill.) Jan. 23, 1944–; House 1975–93.

RUST, Albert (Ark.) ?–April 3, 1870; House 1855–57, 1859–61.

RUTHERFORD, J. T. (Tex.) May 30, 1921–; House 1955–63.

RUTHERFORD, Samuel (Ga.) March 15, 1870–Feb. 4, 1932; House 1925–Feb. 4, 1932.

RYALL, Daniel Bailey (N.J.) Jan. 30, 1798–Dec. 17, 1864; House 1839–41.

RYAN, Elmer James (Minn.) May 26, 1907–Feb. 1, 1958; House 1935–41.

RYAN, Harold Martin (Mich.) Feb. 6, 1911–; House Feb. 13, 1962–65.

RYAN, James Wilfrid (Pa.) Oct. 16, 1858–Feb. 26, 1907; House 1899–1901.

RYAN, Leo Joseph (Calif.) May 5, 1925–Nov. 18, 1978; House 1973–Nov. 18, 1978.

RYAN, William (N.Y.) March 8, 1840–Feb. 18, 1925; House 1893–95.

RYAN, William Fitts (N.Y.) June 28, 1922–Sept. 17, 1972; House 1961–Sept. 17, 1972.

RYAN, William Henry (N.Y.) May 10, 1860–Nov. 18, 1939; House 1899–1909.

RYON, John Walker (Pa.) March 4, 1825–March 12, 1901; House 1879–81.

RYTER, John Francis (Conn.) Feb. 4, 1914–Feb. 5, 1978; House 1945–47.

SABATH, Adolph Joachim (Ill.) April 4, 1866–Nov. 6, 1952; House 1907–Nov. 6, 1952; Chrmn. House Rules 1949–52.

SABO, Martin Olav (Minn.) Feb. 28, 1938–; House 1979–; Chrmn. House Budget 1993–1995.

SACKS, Leon (Pa.) Oct. 7, 1902–March 11, 1972; House 1937–41.

SADLER, Thomas William (Ala.) April 17, 1831–Oct. 29, 1896; House 1885–87.

SADOWSKI, George Gregory (Mich.) March 12, 1903–Oct. 9, 1961; House 1933–39, 1943–51.

ST. GERMAIN, Fernand Joseph (R.I.) Jan. 9, 1928–; House 1961–89; Chrmn. House Banking, Housing, and Urban Affairs 1981–89.

ST. JOHN, Henry (Ohio) July 16, 1783–May 1869; House 1843–47.

ST. MARTIN, Louis (La.) May 17, 1820–Feb. 9, 1893; House 1851–53, 1885–87.

ST. ONGE, William Leon (Conn.) Oct. 9, 1914–May 1, 1970; House 1963–May 1, 1970.

SALINGER, Pierre Emil George (Calif.) June 14, 1925–; Senate Aug. 4–Dec. 31, 1964.

SALMON, Joshua S. (N.J.) Feb. 2, 1846–May 6, 1902; House 1899–May 6, 1902.

SALMON, William Charles (Tenn.) April 3, 1868–May 13, 1925; House 1923–25.

SAMFORD, William James (Ala.) Sept. 16, 1844–June 11, 1901; House 1879–81; Gov. Dec. 26, 1900–June 11, 1901.

SAMUELS, Green Berry (cousin of Isaac Samuels Pennybacker) (Va.) Feb. 1, 1806–Jan. 5, 1859; House 1839–41.

SANDERS, Jared Young (father of Jared Young Sanders Jr., cousin of Murphy James Foster) (La.) Jan. 29, 1867–March 23, 1944; House 1917–21; Gov. May 18, 1908–May 14, 1912.

SANDERS, Jared Young Jr. (son of Jared Young Sanders) (La.) April 20, 1892–Nov. 29, 1960; House May 1, 1934–37, 1941–43.

SANDERS, Morgan Gurley (Tex.) July 14, 1878–Jan. 7, 1956; House 1921–39.

SANDIDGE, John Milton (La.) Jan. 7, 1817–March 30, 1890; House 1855–59.

SANDLIN, John Nicholas (La.) Feb. 24, 1872–Dec. 26, 1957; House 1921–37.

SANFORD, John (N.Y.) June 3, 1803–Oct. 4, 1857; House 1841–43.

SANFORD, John W. A. (Ga.) Aug. 28, 1798–Sept. 12, 1870; House March 4–July 25, 1835.

SANFORD, Nathan (N.Y.) Nov. 5, 1777–Oct. 17, 1838; Senate 1815–21, Jan. 14, 1826–31.

SANFORD, Terry (N.C.) Aug. 20, 1917–; Senate Nov. 4, 1986–93; Chrmn. Select Senate Committee on Ethics 1991–93; Gov. Jan. 5, 1961–Jan. 8, 1965.

SANGMEISTER, George Edward (Ill.) Feb. 16, 1931–; House 1989–1995.

SANTANGELO, Alfred Edward (N.Y.) June 4, 1912–March 30, 1978; House 1957–63.

SANTINI, James David (Nev.) Aug. 13, 1937–; House 1975–83.

SARBANES, Paul Spyros (Md.) Feb. 3, 1933–; House 1971–77; Senate 1977–.

SARPALIUS, William "Bill" (Tex.) Jan. 10, 1948–; House 1989–1995.

SASSCER, Lansdale Ghiselin (Md.) Sept. 30, 1893–Nov. 6, 1964; House Feb. 3, 1939–53.

SASSER, James Ralph (Tenn.) Sept. 30, 1936–; Senate 1977–1995; Chrm. Senate Budget 1989–1995.

SATTERFIELD, Dave Edward Jr. (father of David Edward Satterfield III (Va.) Sept. 11, 1894–Dec. 27, 1946; House Nov. 2, 1937–Feb. 15, 1945.

SATTERFIELD, David Edward III (son of Dave Edward Satterfield Jr.) (Va.) Dec. 2, 1920–Sept. 30, 1988; House 1965–81.

SAULSBURY, Eli (brother of Willard Saulsbury, uncle of Willard Saulsbury Jr.) (Del.) Dec. 29, 1817–March 22, 1893; Senate 1871–89.

SAULSBURY, Willard Sr. (brother of Eli Saulsbury, father of Willard Saulsbury Jr., below) (Del.) June 2, 1820–April 6, 1892; Senate 1859–71.

SAULSBURY, Willard Jr. (son of Willard Saulsbury Sr., above, nephew of Eli Saulsbury) (Del.) April 17, 1861–Feb. 20, 1927; Senate 1913–19; elected Pres. pro tempore Dec. 14, 1916.

SAUND, Daliph Singh (Calif.) Sept. 20, 1899–April 22, 1973; House 1957–63.

SAUNDERS, Edward Watts (Va.) Oct. 20, 1860–Dec. 16, 1921; House Nov. 6, 1906–Feb. 29, 1920.

SAUNDERS, Romulus Mitchell (N.C.) March 3, 1791–April 21, 1867; House 1821–27 (Republican), 1841–45.

SAVAGE, Charles Raymon (Wash.) April 12, 1906–Jan. 14, 1976; House 1945–47.

SAVAGE, Gus (Ill.) Oct. 30, 1925–; House 1981–93.

SAVAGE, John Houston (Tenn.) Oct. 9, 1815–April 5, 1904; House 1849–53, 1855–59.

SAVAGE, John Simpson (Ohio) Oct. 30, 1841–Nov. 24, 1884; House 1875–77.

SAWTELLE, Cullen (Maine) Sept. 25, 1805–Nov. 10, 1887; House 1845–47, 1849–51.

SAWYER, Lewis Ernest (Ark.) June 24, 1867–May 5, 1923; House March 4–May 5, 1923.

SAWYER, Samuel Locke (Mo.) Nov. 27, 1813–March 29, 1890; House 1879–81.

SAWYER, Thomas Charles (Ohio) Aug. 15, 1945–; House 1987–.

SAWYER, William (Ohio) Aug. 5, 1803–Sept. 18, 1877; House 1845–19.

SAYERS, Joseph Draper (Tex.) Sept. 23, 1841–May 15, 1929; House 1885–Jan. 16, 1899; Gov. Jan. 17, 1899–Jan. 20, 1903.

SAYLER, Milton (cousin of Henry Benton Sayler) (Ohio) Nov. 4, 1831–Nov. 17, 1892; House 1873–79.

SCALES, Alfred Moore (N.C.) Nov. 26, 1827–Feb. 9, 1892; House 1857–59, 1875–Dec. 30, 1884; Gov. Jan 21, 1885–Jan. 17, 1889.

SCAMMAN, John Fairfield (Maine) Oct. 24, 1786–May 22, 1858; House 1845–47.

SCANLON, Thomas Edward (Pa.) Sept. 18, 1896–Aug. 9, 1955; House 1941–45.

SCARBOROUGH, Robert Bethea (S.C.) Oct. 29, 1861–Nov. 23, 1927; House 1901–05.

SCHAEFER, Edwin Martin (Ill.) May 14, 1887–Nov. 8, 1950; House 1933–43.

SCHELL, Richard (N.Y.) May 15, 1810–Nov. 10, 1879; House Dec. 7, 1874–75.

SCHENK, Lynn (Calif.) Jan. 5, 1945–; House 1993–1995.

SCHERMERHORN, Simon Jacob (N.Y.) Sept. 26, 1827–July 21, 1901; House 1893–95.

SCHEUER, James Haas (N.Y.) Feb. 6, 1920–; House 1965–73, 1975–93.

SCHISLER, Darwin Gale (Ill.) March 2, 1933–; House 1965–67.

SCHLEICHER, Gustave (Tex.) Nov. 19, 1823–Jan. 10, 1879; House 1875–Jan. 10, 1879.

SCHMIDHAUSER, John Richard (Iowa) Jan. 3, 1922–; House 1965–67.

SCHROEDER, Patricia Scott (Colo.) July 30, 1940–; House 1973–.

SCHUETZ, Leonard William (Ill.) Nov. 16, 1887–Feb. 13, 1944; House 1931–Feb. 13, 1944.

SCHULTE, William Theodore (Ind.) Aug. 19, 1890–Dec. 7, 1966; House 1933–43.

SCHUMAKER, John Godfrey (N.Y.) June 27, 1826–Nov. 23, 1905; House 1869–71, 1873–77.

SCHUMER, Charles Ellis (N.Y.) Nov. 23, 1950–; House 1981–.

SCHWARTZ, Henry Herman "Harry" (Wyo.) May 18, 1869–April 24, 1955; Senate 1937–43.

SCHWELLENBACH, Lewis Baxter (Wash.) Sept. 20, 1894–June 10, 1948; Senate 1935–Dec. 16, 1940; Secy. of Labor July 1, 1945–June 10, 1948.

SCHWERT, Pius Louis (N.Y.) Nov. 22, 1892–March 11, 1941; House 1939–March 11, 1941.

SCOTT, Byron Nicholson (Calif.) March 21, 1903–; House 1935–39.

SCOTT, Charles Lewis (Calif.) Jan. 23, 1827–April 30, 1899; House 1857–61.

SCOTT, John Guier (Mo.) Dec. 26, 1819–May 16, 1892; House Dec. 7, 1863–65.

SCOTT, Owen (Ill.) July 6, 1848–Dec. 21, 1928; House 1891–93.

SCOTT, Ralph James (N.C.) Oct. 15, 1905–Aug. 6, 1983; House 1957–67.

SCOTT, Robert Cortez (Va.) April 30, 1947–; House 1993–.

SCOTT, Thomas (Pa.) 1739–March 2, 1796; House 1789–91, 1793–95.

SCOTT, William Kerr (N.C.) April 17, 1896–April 16, 1958; Senate Nov. 29, 1954–April 16, 1958; Gov. Jan. 6, 1949–Jan. 8, 1953.

SCOTT, William Lawrence (Pa.) July 2, 1828–Sept. 19, 1891; House 1885–89.

SCOVILLE, Jonathan (N.Y.) July 14, 1830–March 4, 1891; House Nov. 12, 1880–83.

SCRUGHAM, James Graves (Nev.) Jan. 19, 1880–June 23, 1945; House 1933–Dec. 7, 1942; Senate Dec. 7, 1942–June 23, 1945; Gov. Jan. 11, 1923–Jan. 3, 1927.

SCUDDER, Townsend (nephew of Henry Joel Scudder) (N.Y.) July 26, 1865–Feb. 22, 1960; House 1899–1901, 1903–05.

SCULLY, Thomas Joseph (N.J.) Sept. 19, 1868–Dec. 14, 1921; House 1911–21.

SCURRY, Richardson (Tex.) Nov. 11, 1811–April 9, 1862; House 1851–53.

SEARING, John Alexander (N.Y.) May 14, 1805–May 6, 1876; House 1857–59.

SEARS, William Joseph (Fla.) Dec. 4, 1874–March 30, 1944; House 1915–29, 1933–37.

SEBASTIAN, William King (Ark.) 1812–May 20, 1865; Senate May 12, 1848–July 11, 1861.

SECREST, Robert Thompson (Ohio) Jan. 22, 1904–May 15, 1994; House 1933–Aug. 3, 1942, 1949–Sept. 26, 1954, 1963–67.

SEDDON, James Alexander (Va.) July 13, 1815–Aug. 19, 1880; House 1845–47, 1849–51.

SEERLEY, John Joseph (Iowa) March 13, 1852–Feb. 23, 1931; House 1891–93.

SEIBERLING, John Frederick (cousin of Francis Seiberling) (Ohio) Sept. 8, 1918–; House 1971–87.

SELBY, Thomas Jefferson (Ill.) Dec. 4, 1840–March 10, 1917; House 1901–03.

SELDEN, Armistead Inge Jr. (Ala.) Feb. 20, 1921–Nov. 14, 1985; House 1953–69.

SELDOMRIDGE, Harry Hunter (Colo.) Oct. 1, 1864–Nov. 2, 1927; House 1913–15.

SEMPLE, James (Ill.) Jan. 5, 1798–Dec. 20, 1866; Senate Dec. 4, 1843–47.

SENEY, George Ebbert (Ohio) May 29, 1832–June 11, 1905; House 1883–91.

SENNER, George Frederick Jr. (Ariz.) Nov. 24, 1921–; House 1963–67.

SERRANO, Jose Enrique (N.Y.) Oct. 24, 1943–; House March 28, 1990–.

SETTLE, Evan Evans (Ky.) Dec. 1, 1848–Nov. 16, 1899; House 1897–Nov. 16, 1899.

SEVIER, Ambrose Hundley (cousin of Henry Wharton Conway) (Ark.) Nov. 4, 1801–Dec. 31, 1848; House (Terr.

Del.) Feb. 13, 1828–June 15, 1836; Senate Sept. 18, 1836–March 15, 1848; elected Pres. pro tempore Dec. 27, 1845.

SEWALL, Charles S. (Md.) 1779–Nov. 3, 1848; House Oct. 1, 1832–33 (Jacksonian), Jan. 2–March 3, 1843.

SEWARD, James Lindsay (Ga.) Oct. 30, 1813–Nov. 21, 1886; House 1853–59.

SEYMOUR, David Lowrey (N.Y.) Dec. 2, 1803–Oct. 11, 1867; House 1843–45, 1851–53.

SEYMOUR, Edward Woodruff (son of Origen Storrs Seymour) (Conn.) Aug. 30, 1832–Oct. 16, 1892; House 1883–87.

SEYMOUR, Origen Storrs (father of Edward Woodruff Seymour, nephew of Horatio Seymour) (Conn.) Feb. 9, 1804–Aug. 12, 1881; House 1851–55.

SEYMOUR, Thomas Hart (Conn.) Sept. 29, 1807–Sept. 3, 1868; House 1843–45; Gov. May 4, 1850–Oct. 13, 1853.

SHACKELFORD, John Williams (N.C.) Nov. 16, 1844–Jan. 18, 1883; House 1881–Jan. 18, 1883.

SHACKLEFORD, Dorsey William (Mo) Aug. 27, 1853–July 15, 1936; House Aug. 29, 1899–1919.

SHAFER, Jacob K. (Idaho) Dec. 26, 1823–Nov. 22, 1876; House (Terr. Del.) 1869–71.

SHAFROTH, John Franklin (Colo.) June 9, 1854–Feb. 22, 1922, House 1895–Feb. 15, 1904 (1895–97 Republican, 1897–1903 Silver Republican, Senate 1913–19; Gov. Jan. 12, 1909–Jan. 14, 1913.

SHALLENBERGER, Ashton Cokayne (Nebr.) Dec. 23, 1862–Feb. 22, 1938; House 1901–03, 1915–19, 1923–29, 1931–35; Gov. Jan. 7, 1909–Jan. 5, 1911.

SHAMANSKY, Robert Norton (Ohio) April 18, 1927–; House 1981–83.

SHANKLIN, George Sea (Ky.) Dec. 23, 1807–April 1, 1883; House 1865–67.

SHANLEY, James Andrew (Conn.) April 1, 1896–April 4, 1965; House 1935–43.

SHANNON, James Michael (Mass.) April 4, 1952–; House 1979–85.

SHANNON, Joseph Bernard (Mo.) March 17, 1867–March 28, 1943; House 1931–43.

SHANNON, Wilson (brother of Thomas Shannon) (Ohio) Feb. 24, 1802–Aug. 30, 1877; House 1853–55; Gov. Dec. 13, 1838–Dec. 16, 1840, Dec. 14, 1842–April 15, 1844, Aug. 10, 1855–Aug. 18, 1856 (Kans. Terr.).

SHARP, Philip Riley (Ind.) July 15, 1942–; House 1975–1995.

SHARP, William Graves (Ohio) March 14, 1859–Nov. 17, 1922; House 1909–July 23, 1914.

SHAW, Aaron (Ill.) Dec. 19, 1811–Jan. 7, 1887; House 1857–59, 1883–85.

SHAW, Frank Thomas (Md.) Oct. 7, 1841–Feb. 24, 1923; House 1885–89.

SHAW, Henry Marchmore (N.C.) Nov. 20, 1819–Nov. 1, 1864; House 1853–55, 1857–59.

SHAW, John Gilbert (N.C.) Jan. 16, 1859–July 21, 1932; House 1895–97.

SHAW, Tristram (N.H.) May 23, 1786–March 14, 1843; House 1839–43.

SHEAKLEY, James (Pa.) April 24, 1829–Dec. 10, 1917; House 1875–77; Gov. (Alaska Terr.) 1893–97.

SHEFFER, Daniel (Pa.) May 24, 1783–Feb. 16, 1880; House 1837–39.

SHELBY, Richard Craig (Ala.) May 6, 1934–; House 1979–87; Senate 1987–.

SHELL, George Washington (S.C.) Nov. 13, 1831–Dec.15, 1899; House 1891–95.

SHELLEY, Charles Miller (Ala.) Dec. 28, 1833–Jan. 20, 1907; House 1877–81, Nov. 7, 1882–Jan. 9, 1885.

SHELLEY, John Francis (Calif.) Sept. 3, 1905–Sept. 1, 1974; House Nov. 8, 1949–Jan. 7, 1964.

SHEPARD, Charles Biddle (N.C.) Dec. 5, 1808–Oct. 25, 1843; House 1837–41 (1837–39 Whig).

SHEPHERD, Karen (Utah) July 5, 1940–; House 1993–1995.

SHEPLER, Matthias (Ohio) Nov. 11, 1790–April 7, 1863; House 1837–39.

SHEPPARD, Harry Richard (Calif.) Jan. 10, 1885–April 28, 1969; House 1937–65.

SHEPPARD, John Levi (father of Morris Sheppard, great-grandfather of Connie Mack III) (Tex.) April 13, 1852–Oct. 11, 1902; House 1899–Oct. 11, 1902.

SHEPPARD, Morris (son of John Levi Sheppard) (Tex.) May 28, 1876–April 9, 1941; House Nov. 15, 1902–Feb. 3, 1913; Senate Feb. 3, 1913–April 9, 1941.

SHERIDAN, John Edward (Pa.) Sept. 15, 1902–Nov. 12, 1987; House Nov. 7, 1939–47.

SHERLEY, Joseph Swagar (Ky.) Nov. 28, 1871–Feb. 13, 1941; House 1903–19.

SHERROD, William Crawford (Ala.) Aug. 17, 1835–March 24, 1919; House 1869–71.

SHERWOOD, Henry (Pa.) Oct. 9, 1813–Nov. 10, 1896; House 1871–73.

SHERWOOD, Isaac R. (Ohio) Aug. 13, 1835–Oct. 15, 1925; House 1873–75 (Republican), 1907–21, 1923–25.

SHIEL, George Knox (Oreg.) 1825–Dec. 12, 1893; House July 30, 1861–63.

SHIELDS, Benjamin Glover (Ala.) 1808–?; House 1841–43.

SHIELDS, James (Mo.) May 10, 1810–June 1, 1879; Senate March 6–15, 1848 (Ill.) Oct. 27, 1849–55 (Ill.), May 11, 1858–59 (Minn.) Jan. 27–March 3, 1879.

SHIELDS, John Knight (Tenn.) Aug. 15, 1858–Sept. 30, 1934; Senate 1913–25.

SHIPLEY, George Edward (Ill.) April 21, 1927–; House 1959–79.

SHIVELY, Benjamin Franklin (Ind.) March 20, 1857–March 14, 1916; House Dec. 1, 1884–85 (National Anti-Monopolist), 1887–93; Senate 1909–March 14, 1916.

SHOBER, Francis Edwin (father of Francis Emanuel Shober) (N.C.) March 12, 1831–May 29, 1896; House 1869–73.

SHOBER, Francis Emanuel (son of Francis Edwin Shober) (N.Y.) Oct. 24, 1860–Oct. 7, 1919; House 1903–05.

SHORTER, Eli Sims (Ala.) March 15, 1823–April 29, 1879; House 1855–59.

SHOUSE, Jouett (Kans.) Dec. 10, 1879–June 2, 1968; House 1915–19.

SHOWER, Jacob (Md.) Feb. 22, 1803–May 25, 1879; House 1853–55.

SHUFORD, George Adams (N.C.) Sept. 5, 1895–Dec. 8, 1962; House 1953–59.

SHULL, Joseph Horace (Pa.) Aug. 17, 1848–Aug. 9, 1944; House 1903–05.

SICKLES, Carlton Ralph (Md.) June 15, 1921–; House 1963–67.

SICKLES, Daniel Edgar (N.Y.) Oct. 20, 1819–May 3, 1898; House 1869–61, 1893–95.

SIEMINSKI, Alfred Dennis (N.J.) Aug. 23, 1911–Dec. 13, 1990; House 1951–59.

SIKES, Robert Lee Fulton (Fla.) June 3, 1906–; House 1941–Oct. 19, 1944, 1945–79.

SILSBEE, Nathaniel (Mass.) Jan. 14, 1773–July 14, 1850; House 1817–21; Senate May 31, 1826–35.

SIMMONS, Furnifold McLendel (N.C.) Jan. 20, 1854–April 30, 1940; House 1887–89; Senate 1901–31.

SIMMS, William Emmett (Ky.) Jan. 2, 1822–June 25, 1898; House 1859–61.

SIMON, Paul Martin (Ill.) Nov. 29, 1928–; House 1975–85; Senate 1985–.

SIMONS, Samuel (Conn.) 1792–Jan. 13, 1847; House 1843–45.

SIMONTON, Charles Bryson (Tenn.) Sept. 8, 1838–June 10, 1911; House 1879–83.

SIMPSON, Richard Franklin (S.C.) March 24, 1798–Oct. 28, 1882; House 1843–49.

SIMS, Alexander Dromgoole (nephew of George Coke Dromgoole) (S.C.) June 12, 1803–Nov. 22, 1848; House 1845–Nov. 22, 1848.

SIMS, Hugo Sheridan Jr. (S.C.) Oct. 14, 1921–; House 1949–51.

SIMS, Leonard Henly (Mo.) Feb. 6, 1807–Feb. 28, 1886; House 1845–47.

SIMS, Thetus Willrette (Tenn.) April 25, 1852–Dec. 17, 1939; House 1897–1921.

SINGLETON, James Washington (Ill.) Nov. 23, 1811–April 4, 1892; House 1879–83.

SINGLETON, Otho Robards (Miss.) Oct. 14, 1814–Jan. 11, 1889; House 1853–56, 1857–Jan. 12, 1861, 1875–87.

SIPE, William Allen (Pa.) July 1, 1844–Sept. 10, 1935; House Dec. 5, 1892–95.

SIROVICH, William Irving (N.Y.) March 18, 1882–Dec. 17, 1939; House 1927–Dec. 17, 1939.

SISISKY, Norman (Va.) June 9, 1927–; House 1983–.

SISK, Bernice Frederic (Calif.) Dec. 14, 1910–; House 1955–79.

SISSON, Frederick James (N.Y.) March 31, 1879–Oct. 20, 1949; House 1933–37.

SISSON, Thomas Upton (Miss.) Sept. 22, 1869–Sept. 26, 1923; House 1909–23.

SITES, Frank Crawford (Pa.) Dec. 24, 1864–May 23, 1935; House 1923–25.

SITGREAVES, Charles (N.J.) April 22, 1803–March 17, 1878; House 1865–69.

SKAGGS, David Evans (Colo.) Feb. 22, 1943–; House 1987–.

SKELTON, Charles (N.J.) April 19, 1806–May 20, 1879; House 1851–55.

SKELTON, Isaac Newton "Ike" IV (Mo.) Dec. 20, 1931–; House 1977–.

SKINNER, Thomas Gregory (brother of Harry Skinner) (N.C.) Jan. 22, 1842–Dec. 22, 1907; House Nov. 20, 1883–87, 1889–91.

SLACK, John Mark Jr. (W.Va.) March 18, 1915–March 17, 1980; House 1959–March 17, 1980.

SLATER, James Harvey (Oreg.) Dec. 28, 1826–Jan. 28, 1899; House 1871–73; Senate 1879–85.

SLATTERY, James Charles (Kans.) Aug. 4, 1948–; House 1983–1995.

SLATTERY, James Michael (Ill.) July 29, 1878–Aug. 28, 1948; Senate April 14, 1939–Nov. 21, 1940.

SLAUGHTER, Louise M. (N.Y.) Aug. 14, 1929–; House 1987–.

SLAUGHTER, Roger Caldwell (Mo.) July 17, 1905–June 2, 1974; House 1943–47.

SLAYDEN, James Luther (uncle of Fontaine Maury Maverick) (Tex.) June 1, 1853–Feb. 24, 1924; House 1897–1919.

SLEMONS, William Ferguson (Ark.) March 15, 1830–Dec. 10, 1918; House 1875–81.

SLIDELL, John (La.) 1793–July 26, 1871; House 1843–Nov. 10, 1845; Senate Dec. 5, 1853–Feb. 4, 1861.

SLOCUM, Henry Warner (N.Y.) Sept. 24, 1827–April 14, 1894; House 1869–73, 1883–85.

SLOSS, Joseph Humphrey (Ala.) Oct. 12, 1826–Jan. 27, 1911; House 1871–75.

SMALL, John Humphrey (N.C.) Aug. 29, 1858–July 13, 1946; House 1899–1921.

SMART, Ephraim Knight (Maine) Sept. 3, 1813–Sept. 29, 1872; House 1847–49, 1851–53.

SMATHERS, George Armistead (nephew of William Howell Smathers) (Fla.) Nov. 14, 1913–; House 1947–51; Senate 1951–69; Chrmn. Senate Select Committee on Small Business 1967–69.

SMATHERS, William Howell (uncle of George Armistead Smathers) (N.J.) Jan. 7, 1891–Sept. 24, 1955; Senate April 15, 1937–43.

SMITH, Albert (Maine) Jan. 3, 1793–May 29, 1867; House 1839–41.

SMITH, Benjamin A. II (Mass.) March 26, 1916–; Senate Dec. 27, 1960–Nov. 6, 1962.

SMITH, Charles Bennett (N.Y.) Sept. 14, 1870–May 21, 1939; House 1911–19.

SMITH, David Highbaugh (Ky.) Dec. 19, 1854–Dec. 17, 1928; House 1897–1907.

SMITH, Delazon (Oreg.) Oct. 5, 1816–Nov. 19, 1860; Senate Feb. 14–March 3, 1959.

SMITH, Edward Henry (N.Y.) May 5, 1809–Aug. 7, 1885; House 1861–63.

SMITH, Ellison DuRant (S.C.) Aug. 1, 1866–Nov. 17, 1944; Senate 1909–Nov. 17, 1944.

SMITH, Frances Ormand Jonathan (Maine) Nov. 23, 1806–Oct. 14, 1876; House 1833–39 (1833–37 Jacksonian).

SMITH, Francis Raphael (Pa.) Sept. 25, 1911–Dec. 9, 1982; House 1941–43.

SMITH, Frank Ellis (Miss.) Feb. 21, 1918–; House 1951–Nov. 14, 1962.

SMITH, Frank Owens (Md.) Aug. 27, 1859–Jan. 29, 1924; House 1913–15.

SMITH, Gomer Griffith (Okla.) July 11, 1896–May 26, 1953; House Dec. 1937–39.

SMITH, Hezekiah Bradley (N.J.) July 24, 1816–Nov. 13, 1887; House 1879–81.

SMITH, Hoke (Ga.) Sept. 2, 1855–Nov. 27, 1931; Senate Nov. 16, 1911–21; Secy. of the Interior March 6, 1893–Sept. 1, 1896; Gov. June 29, 1907–June 26, 1909, July 1–Nov. 16, 1911.

SMITH, Howard Worth (Va.) Feb. 2, 1883–Oct. 3, 1976; House 1931–67; Chrmn. House Rules 1955–67.

SMITH, James Jr. (N.J.) June 12, 1851–April 1, 1927; Senate 1893–99.

SMITH, John (father of Worthington Curtis Smith) (Vt.) Aug. 12, 1789–Nov. 26, 1858; House 1839–41.

SMITH, John Joseph (Conn.) Jan. 25, 1904–Feb. 16, 1980; House 1935–Nov. 4, 1941.

SMITH, John T. (Pa.) ?–?; House 1843–45.

SMITH, Joseph Francis (Pa.) Jan. 24, 1920–; House July 28, 1981–83.

SMITH, Joseph Luther (W.Va.) May 22, 1880–Aug. 23, 1962; House 1929–45.

SMITH, Joseph Showalter (Oreg.) June 20, 1824–July 13, 1884; House 1869–71.

SMITH, Lawrence Jack (Fla.) April 25, 1941–; House 1983–93.

SMITH, Madison Roswell (Mo.) July 9, 1850–June 18, 1919; House 1907–09.

SMITH, Marcus Aurelius (Ariz.) Jan. 24, 1851–April 7, 1924; House (Terr. Del.) 1887–95, 1897–99, 1901–03, 1905–09; Senate March 27, 1912–21.

SMITH, Martin Fernand (Wash.) May 28, 1891–Oct. 25, 1954; House 1933–43.

SMITH, Neal Edward (Iowa) March 23, 1920–; House 1959–1995; House Small Business 1977–81.

SMITH, Perry (Conn.) May 12, 1783–June 8, 1852; Senate 1837–43.

SMITH, Robert (nephew of Jeremiah Smith and Samuel Smith of N.H.) (Ill.) June 12, 1802–Dec. 21, 1867; House 1843–49 (1843–47 Democrat, 1847–49 Independent Democrat), 1857–59.

SMITH, Robert Barnwell. (*See* **RHETT,** Robert Barnwell.)

SMITH, Samuel Axley (Tenn.) June 26, 1822–Nov. 25, 1863; House 1853–59.

SMITH, Thomas (Ind.) May 1, 1799–April 12, 1876; House 1839–41, 1843–47.

SMITH, Thomas Alexander (Md.) Sept. 3, 1850–May 1, 1932; House 1905–07.

SMITH, Thomas Francis (N.Y.) July 24, 1865–April 11, 1923; House April 12, 1917–21.

SMITH, Thomas Vernor (Ill.) April 26, 1890–May 24, 1964; House 1939–41.

SMITH, William (Va.) Sept. 6, 1797–May 18, 1887; House 1841–43, 1853–61; Gov. Jan. 1, 1846–Jan. 1, 1849 (Democrat), Jan. 1, 1864–April 1, 1865 (Confederate Democrat).

SMITH, William Ephraim (Ga.) March 14, 1829–March 11, 1890; House 1875–81.

SMITH, William Robert (Tex.) Aug. 18, 1863–Aug. 16, 1924; House 1903–17.

SMITH, Willis (N.C.) Dec. 19, 1887–June 26, 1953; Senate Nov. 27, 1950–June 26, 1953.

SMITHWICK, John Harris (Fla.) July 17, 1872–Dec. 2, 1948; House 1919–27.

SMYTH, George Washington (Tex.) May 16, 1803–Feb. 21, 1866; House 1853–55.

SNODGRASS, Charles Edward (nephew of Henry Clay Snodgrass) (Tenn.) Dec. 28, 1866–Aug. 3, 1936; House 1899–1903.

SNODGRASS, Henry Clay (uncle of Charles Edward Snodgrass) (Tenn.) March 29, 1848–April 22, 1931; House 1891–95.

SNODGRASS, John Fryall (Va.) March 2, 1804–June 5, 1854; House 1853–June 5, 1854.

SNOOK, John Stout (Ohio) Dec. 18, 1862–Sept. 19, 1952; House 1901–05, 1917–19.

SNOW, Herman Wilber (Ill.) July 3, 1836–Aug. 25, 1914; House 1891–93.

SNOW, William W. (N.Y.) April 27, 1812–Sept. 3, 1886; House 1851–53.

SNYDER, Adam Wilson (Ill.) Oct. 6, 1799–May 14, 1842; House 1837–39.

SNYDER, Charles Philip (W. Va.) June 9, 1847–Aug. 21, 1915; House May 15, 1883–89.

SNYDER, John Buell (Pa.) July 30, 1877–Feb. 24, 1946; House 1933–Feb. 24, 1946.

SOLARZ, Stephen Joshua (N.Y.) Sept. 12, 1940–; House 1975–93.

SOMERS, Andrew Lawrence (N.Y.) March 21, 1895–April 6, 1949; House 1925–April 6, 1949; Chrmn. House Public Lands 1949.

SOMERS, Peter J. (Wis.) April 12, 1850–Feb. 15, 1924; House Aug. 27, 1893–95.

SORG, Paul John (Ohio) Sept. 23, 1840–May 28, 1902; House May 21, 1894–97.

SOULE, Pierre (La.) Aug. 31, 1801–March 26, 1870; Senate Jan. 21–March 3, 1847, 1849–April 11, 1853.

SOUTH, Charles Lacy (Tex.) July 22, 1892–Dec. 20, 1965; House 1935–43.

SOUTHALL, Robert Goode (Va.) Dec. 26, 1852–May 25, 1924; House 1903–07.

SOUTHARD, Milton Isaiah (Ohio) Oct. 20, 1836–May 4, 1905; House 1873–79.

SOWDEN, William Henry (Pa.) June 6, 1840–March 3, 1907; House 1885–89.

SPARKMAN, John Jackson (Ala.) Dec. 20, 1899–Nov. 16, 1986; House 1937–Nov. 5, 1946; Senate Nov. 6, 1946–79; Chrmn. Senate Select Committee on Small Business 1950–53, 1955–67; Chrmn. Senate Banking and Currency 1967–71; Chrmn. Senate Banking, Housing, and Urban Affairs 1971–75; Chrmn. Senate Foreign Relations 1975–78.

SPARKMAN, Stephen Milancthon (Fla.) July 29, 1849–Sept. 26, 1929; House 1895–1917.

SPARKS, William Andrew Jackson (Ill.) Nov. 19, 1828–May 7, 1904; House 1875–83.

SPEARING, James Zacharie (La.) April 23, 1864–Nov. 2, 1942; House April 22, 1924–31.

SPEER, Robert Milton (Pa.) Sept. 8, 1838–Jan. 17, 1890; House 1871–75.

SPEIGHT, Jesse (Miss.) Sept. 22, 1795–May 1, 1847; House 1829–37 (no party N.C.); Senate 1845–May 1, 1847.

SPELLMAN, Gladys Noon (Md.) March 1, 1918–June 19, 1988; House 1975–Feb. 24, 1981.

SPENCE, Brent (Ky.) Dec. 24, 1874–Sept. 18, 1967; House 1931–63; Chrmn. House Banking and Currency 1949–53, 1955–63.

SPENCER, George Lloyd (Ark.) March 27, 1893–Jan. 14, 1981; Senate April 1, 1941–43.

SPENCER, James Bradley (N.Y.) April 26, 1781–March 26, 1848; House 1837–39.

SPENCER, James Grafton (Miss.) Sept. 13, 1844–Feb. 22, 1926; House 1895–97.

SPENCER, William Brainerd (La.) Feb. 5, 1835–Feb. 12, 1882; House June 8, 1876–Jan. 8, 1877.

SPERRY, Lewis (Conn.) Jan. 23, 1848–June 22, 1922; House 1891–95.

SPIGHT, Thomas (Miss.) Oct. 25, 1841–Jan. 5, 1924; House July 5, 1898–1911.

SPINOLA, Francis Barretto (N.Y.) March 19, 1821–April 14, 1891; House 1887–April 14, 1891.

SPONG, William Belser, Jr. (Va.) Sept. 29, 1920–; Senate Dec. 31, 1966–73.

SPRATT, John McKee Jr. (S.C.) Nov. 1, 1942–; House 1983–.

SPRIGGS, John Thomas (N.Y.) April 5, 1825–Dec. 23, 1888; House 1883–87.

SPRINGER, William McKendree (Ill.) May 30, 1836–Dec. 4, 1903; House 1875–95.

STACK, Edmund John (Ill.) Jan. 31, 1874–April 12, 1957; House 1911–13.

STACK, Edward John (Fla.) April 29, 1910–Nov. 3, 1989; House 1979–81.

STACK, Michael Joseph (Pa.) Sept. 29, 1888–Dec. 14, 1960; House 1935–39.

STACKHOUSE, Eli Thomas (S.C.) March 27, 1824–June 14, 1892;

STAEBLER, Neil Oliver (Mich.) July 11, 1905–; House 1963–65.

STAGGERS, Harley Orrin (father of Harley Orrin Staggers Jr.) (W.Va.) Aug. 3, 1907–Aug. 20, 1991; House 1949–81; Chrmn. House Interstate and Foreign Commerce 1966–81.

STAGGERS, Harley Orrin Jr. (son of Harley Orrin Staggers) (W.Va.) Feb. 22, 1951–; House 1983–93.

STAHLNECKER, William Griggs (N.Y.) June 20, 1849–March 26, 1902; House 1885–93.

STALBAUM, Lynn Ellsworth (Wis.) May 15, 1920–; House 1965–67.

STALLINGS, Jesse Francis (Ala.) April 4, 1856–March 18, 1928; House 1893–1901.

STALLINGS, Richard Howard (Idaho) Oct. 10, 1940–; House 1985–93.

STALLWORTH, James Adams (Ala.) April 7, 1822–Aug. 31, 1861; House 1857–Jan. 21, 1861.

STANDIFORD, Elisha David (Ky.) Dec. 28, 1831–July 26, 1887; House 1873–75.

STANLEY, Augustus Owsley (Ky.) May 21, 1867–Aug. 12, 1958; House 1903–15; Senate May 19, 1919–25; Gov. Dec. 7, 1915–May 19, 1919.

STANLEY, Thomas Bahnson (Va.) July 16, 1890–July 10, 1970; House Nov. 5, 1946–Feb. 3, 1953; Chrmn. House Administration 1951–53; Gov. Jan. 20, 1954–Jan. 11, 1958.

STANTON, Frederick Perry (Tenn.) Dec. 22, 1814–June 4, 1894; House 1845–55; Gov. (Kans. Terr.) 1858–61.

STANTON, James Vincent (Ohio) Feb. 27, 1932–; House 1971–77.

STANTON, Richard Henry (Ky.) Sept. 9, 1812–March 20, 1891; House 1849–55.

STANTON, William Henry (Pa.) July 28, 1843–March 28, 1900; House Nov. 7, 1876–77.

STARK, Benjamin (Oreg.) June 26, 1820–Oct. 10, 1898; Senate Oct. 29, 1861–Sept. 12, 1862.

STARK, Fortney Hillman "Pete" Jr. (Calif.) Nov. 11, 1931–; House 1973–; Chrmn. House District of Columbia 1993–1995.

STARKEY, Frank Thomas (Minn.) Feb. 18, 1892–May 14, 1968; House 1945–47.

STARKWEATHER, David Austin (Ohio) Jan. 21, 1802–July 12, 1876; House 1839–41, 1845–47.

STARKWEATHER, George Anson (N.Y.) May 19, 1794–Oct. 15, 1879; House 1847–49.

STARNES, Joe (Ala.) March 31, 1895–Jan. 9, 1962; House 1935–45.

STEAGALL, Henry Bascom (Ala.) May 19, 1873–Nov. 22, 1943; House 1915–Nov. 22, 1943.

STEBBINS, Henry George (N.Y.) Sept. 15, 1811–Dec. 9, 1881; House 1863–Oct. 24, 1864.

STECK, Daniel Frederic (Iowa) Dec. 16, 1881–Dec. 31, 1950; Senate April 12, 1926–31.

STEDMAN, Charles Manly (N.C.) Jan. 29, 1841–Sept. 23, 1930; House 1911–Sept. 23, 1930.

STEED, Thomas Jefferson (Okla.) March 2, 1904–June 8, 1983; House 1949–81.

STEELE, Henry Joseph (Pa.) May 10, 1860–March 19, 1933; House 1915–21.

STEELE, John Benedict (N.Y..) March 28, 1814–Sept. 24, 1866; House 1861–65.

STEELE, Leslie Jasper (Ga.) Nov. 21, 1868–July 24, 1929; House 1927–July 24, 1929.

STEELE, Thomas Jefferson (Iowa) March 19, 1853–March 20, 1920; House 1915–17.

STEELE, Walter Leak (N.C.) April 18, 1823–Oct. 16, 1891; House 1877–8l.

STEELE, William Gaston (N.J.) Dec. 17, 1820–April 22, 1892; House 1861–65.

STEELE, William Randolph (Wyo.) July 24, 1842–Nov. 30, 1901; House (Terr. Del.) 1873–77.

STEENROD, Lewis (Va.) May 27, 1810–Oct. 3, 1862; House 1839–45.

STENGER, William Shearer (Pa.) Feb. 13, 1840–March 29, 1918; House 1875–79.

STENGLE, Charles Irwin (N.Y.) Dec. 5, 1869–Nov. 23, 1953; House 1923–25

STENHOLM, Charles Walter (Tex.) Oct. 26, 1938–; House 1979–.

STENNIS, John Cornelius (Miss.) Aug. 3, 1901–; Senate Nov. 5, 1947–89; Chrmn. Senate Select Committee on Standards and Conduct 1966–75; Chrmn. Senate Armed Services 1969–81; elected Pres. pro tempore Jan. 6, 1987; Chrmn. Senate Appropriations 1987–89.

STEPHENS, Abraham P. (N.Y.) Feb. 18, 1796–Nov. 25, 1859; House 1851–53.

STEPHENS, Alexander Hamilton (great-great-uncle of Robert Grier Stephens Jr.) (Ga.) Feb. 11, 1812–March 4, 1883; House Oct. 2, 1843–59 (Oct. 2, 1843–51 Whig, 1851–53 Unionist, 1853–55 Whig), Dec. 1, 1873–Nov. 4, 1882; Gov. Nov. 4, 1882–March 4, 1883.

STEPHENS, Dan Voorhees (Nebr.) Nov. 4, 1868–Jan. 13, 1939; House Nov. 7, 1911–19.

STEPHENS, Hubert Durrett (Miss.) July 2, 1875–March 14, 1946; House 1911–21; Senate 1923–35.

STEPHENS, John Hall (Tex.) Nov. 22, 1847–Nov. 18, 1924; House 1897–1917.

STEPHENS, Robert Grier Jr. (great-great-nephew of Alexander Hamilton Stephens) (Ga.) Aug. 14, 1913–; House 1961–77.

STEPHENSON, Benjamin (Ill.) ?–Oct. 10, 1822; House (Terr. Del.) Sept. 3, 1814–17.

STERLING, Bruce Foster (Pa.) Sept. 28, 1870–April 26, 1945; House 1917–19.

STETSON, Charles (Maine) Nov. 2, 1801–March 27, 1863; House 1849–51.

STETSON, Lemuel (N.Y.) March 13, 1804–May 17, 1868; House 1843–45.

STEVENS, Bradford Newcomb (Ill.) Jan. 3, 1813–Nov. 10, 1885; House 1871–73.

STEVENS, Hestor Lockhart (Mich.) Oct. 1, 1803–May 7, 1864; House 1853–55.

STEVENS, Hiram Sanford (Ariz.) March 20, 1832–March 22, 1893; House (Terr. Del.) 1875–79.

STEVENS, Isaac Ingalls (cousin of Charles Abbot Stevens and Moses Tyler Stevens) (Wash.) March 25, 1818–Sept. 1, 1862; House (Terr. Del.) 1857–61; Gov. (Wash. Terr.) 1853–57.

STEVENS, Moses Tyler (brother of Charles Abbot Stevens, cousin of Isaac Ingalls Stevens) (Mass.) Oct. 10, 1825–March 25, 1907; House 1891–95.

STEVENS, Raymond Bartlett (N.H.) June 18, 1874–May 18, 1942; House 1913–15.

STEVENS, Robert Smith (N.Y.) March 27, 1824–Feb. 23, 1893; House 1883–85.

STEVENSON, Adlai Ewing (great-grandfather of Adlai Ewing Stevenson III, grandfather of Gov. Adlai Ewing Stevenson II of Ill.) (Ill.) Oct. 23, 1835–June 14, 1914; House 1875–77, 1879–81; Vice President 1893–97.

STEVENSON, Adlai Ewing III (great-grandson of Adlai Ewing Stevenson, son of Adlai Ewing Stevenson II of Ill.) (Ill.) Oct. 10, 1930–; Senate Nov. 17, 1970–81; Chrmn. Senate Select Committee on Ethics 1977–81.

STEVENSON, John White (son of Andrew Stevenson) (Ky.) May 4, 1812–Aug. 10, 1886; House 1857–61; Senate 1871–77; Gov. Sept. 8, 1867–Feb. 13, 1871.

STEVENSON, William Francis (S.C.) Nov. 23, 1861–Feb. 12, 1942; House 1917–33.

STEWARD, Lewis (Ill.) Nov. 21, 1824–Aug. 27, 1896; House 1891–93.

STEWART, Arthur Thomas "Tom" (Tenn.) Jan. 11, 1892–Oct. 10, 1972; Senate Jan. 16, 1939–49.

STEWART, Bennett McVey (Ill.) Aug. 6, 1912–; House 1979–81.

STEWART, Charles (Tex.) May 30, 1836–Sept. 21, 1895; House 1883–93.

STEWART, Donald Wilbur (Ala.) Feb. 8, 1940–; Senate Nov. 7, 1978–81.

STEWART, James Augustus (Md.) Nov. 24, 1808–April 3, 1879; House 1855–61.

STEWART, John (Conn.) Feb. 10, 1795–Sept. 16, 1860; House 1843–45.

STEWART, John David (Ga.) Aug. 2, 1833–Jan. 28, 1894; House 1887–91.

STEWART, Paul (Okla.) Feb. 27, 1892–Nov. 13, 1950; House 1943–47.

STEWART, Percy Hamilton (N.J.) Jan. 10, 1867–June 30, 1951; House Dec. 1, 1931–33.

STIGLER, William Grady (Okla.) July 7, 1891–Aug. 21, 1952; House March 28, 1944–Aug. 21, 1952.

STILES, John Dodson (Pa.) Jan. 15, 1822–Oct. 29, 1896; House June 3, 1862–65, 1869–71.

STILES, William Henry (grandson of Joseph Clay) (Ga.) Jan. 1, 1808–Dec. 20, 1865; House 1843–45.

STOCKDALE, Thomas Ringland (Miss.) March 28, 1828–Jan. 8, 1899; House 1887–95.

STOCKSLAGER, Strother Madison (Ind.) May 7, 1842–June 1, 1930; House 1881–85.

STOCKTON, John Potter (son of Robert Field Stockton, grandson of Richard Stockton) (N.J.) Aug. 2, 1826–Jan. 22, 1900; Senate March 15, 1865–March 27, 1866, 1869–75.

STOCKTON, Robert Field (son of Richard Stockton, father of John Potter Stockton) (N.J.) Aug. 20, 1795–Oct. 7, 1866; Senate 1851–Jan. 10, 1853.

STOKES, James William (S.C.) Dec. 12, 1853–July 6, 1901; House 1895–June 1, 1896, Nov. 3, 1896–July 6, 1901.

STOKES, Louis (Ohio) Feb. 23, 1925–; House 1969–; Chrmn. House Standards of Official Conduct 1981–85, 1991–93; Chrmn. House Permanent Select Committee on Intelligence 1987–89.

STOLL, Philip Henry (S.C.) Nov. 5, 1874–Oct. 29, 1958; House Oct. 7, 1919–23.

STONE, Alfred Parish (Ohio) June 28, 1813–Aug. 2, 1865; House Oct. 8, 1844–45.

STONE, Claudius Ulysses (Ill.) May 11, 1879–Nov. 13, 1957; House 1911–17.

STONE, Frederick (grandson of Michael Jenifer Stone) (Md.) Feb. 7, 1820–Oct. 17, 1899; House 1867–71:

STONE, James W. (Ky.) 1813–Oct. 13, 1854; House 1843–45, 1851–53.

STONE, Richard Bernard (Fla.) Sept. 22, 1928–; Senate Jan. 1, 1975–Dec. 31, 1980.

STONE, William Henry (Mo.) Nov. 7, 1828–July 9, 1901; House 1873–77.

STONE, William Joel (Mo.) May 7, 1848–April 14, 1918; House 1885–91; Senate 1903–April 14, 1918; Gov. Jan. 9, 1893–Jan. 11, 1897.

STONE, William Johnson (Ky.) June 26, 1841–March 12, 1923; House 1885–95.

STORKE, Thomas More (Calif.) Nov. 23, 1876–Oct. 12, 1971; Senate Nov. 9, 1938–39.

STORM, John Brutzman (Pa.) Sept. 19, 1838–Aug. 13, 1901; House 1871–75, 1883–87.

STOUT, Byron Gray (Mich.) Jan. 12, 1829–June 19, 1896; House 1891–93.

STOUT, Lansing (Oreg.) March 27, 1828–March 4, 1871; House 1859–61.

STOUT, Tom (Mont.) May 20, 1879–Dec. 26, 1965; House 1913–17.

STRADER, Peter Wilson (Ohio) Nov. 6, 1818–Feb. 25, 1881; House 1869–71.

STRAIT, Thomas Jefferson (S.C.) Dec. 25, 1846–April 18, 1924; House 1893–99.

STRANGE, Robert (N.C.) Sept. 20, 1796–Feb. 19, 1854; Senate Dec. 5, 1836–Nov. 16, 1840.

STRATTON, Nathan Taylor (N.J.) March 17, 1813–March 9, 1887; House 1851–55.

STRATTON, Samuel Studdiford (N.Y.) Sept. 27, 1916–Sept. 13, 1990; House 1959–89.

STRAUB, Christian Markle (Pa.) 1804–?, House 1853–55.

STRAUS, Isidor (N.Y.) Feb. 6, 1845–April 15, 1912; House Jan. 30, 1894–95.

STRICKLAND, Ted (Ohio) Aug. 4, 1941–; House 1993–1995.

STRINGER, Lawrence Beaumont (Ill.) Feb. 24, 1866–Dec. 5, 1942; House 1913–15.

STRONG, Selah Brewster (N.Y.) May 1, 1792–Nov. 29, 1872; House 1843–45.

STRONG, Stephen (N.Y.) Oct. 11, 1791–April 15, 1866; House 1845–47.

STRONG, Sterling Price (Tex.) Aug. 17, 1862–March 28, 1936; House 1933–35.

STRONG, Theron Rudd (cousin of William Strong of Pa.) (N.Y.) Nov. 7, 1802–May 14, 1873; House 1839–41.

STRONG, William (cousin of Theron Rudd Strong) (Pa.) May 6, 1808–Aug. 19, 1895; House 1847–51; Assoc. Justice Supreme Court March 14, 1870–Dec. 14, 1880.

STROUSE, Myer (Pa.) Dec. 16, 1825–Feb. 11, 1878; House 1863–67.

STUART, Andrew (Ohio) Aug. 3, 1823–April 30, 1872; House 1853–55.

STUART, Archibald (cousin of Alexander Hugh Holmes Stuart) (Va.) Dec. 2, 1795–Sept. 20, 1855; House 1837–39.

STUART, Charles Edward (Mich.) Nov. 25, 1810–May 19, 1887; House Dec. 6, 1847–49, 1851–53; Senate 1853–59; elected Pres. pro tempore June 9, 1856.

STUART, David (Mich.) March 12, 1816–Sept. 12, 1868; House 1853–55.

STUART, John Todd (Ill.) Nov. 10, 1807–Nov. 23, 1885; House 1839–43 (Whig), 1863–65.

STUBBLEFIELD, Frank Albert (Ky.) April 5, 1907–Oct. 14, 1977; House 1959–Dec. 31, 1974.

STUBBS, Henry Elbert (Calif.) March 4, 1881–Feb. 28, 1937; House 1933–Feb. 28, 1937.

STUCKEY, Williamson Sylvester Jr. (Ga.) May 25, 1935–; House 1967–77.

STUDDS, Gerry Eastman (Mass.) May 12, 1937–; House 1973–; Chrmn. House Merchant Marine and Fisheries 1992–1995.

STUDLEY, Elmer Ebenezer (N.Y.) Sept. 24, 1869–Sept. 6, 1942; House 1933–35.

STUMP, Herman (Md.) Aug. 8, 1837–Jan. 9, 1917; House 1889–93.

STUPAK, Bart (Mich.) Feb. 29, 1952–; House 1993–.

STURGEON, Daniel (Pa.) Oct. 27, 1789–July 3, 1878; Senate Jan. 14, 1840–51.

SULLIVAN, Christopher Daniel (N.Y.) July 14, 1870–Aug. 3, 1942; House 1917–41.

SULLIVAN, John Andrew (Mass.) May 10, 1868–May 31, 1927; House 1903–07.

SULLIVAN, John Berchmans (husband of Leonor Kretzer Sullivan) (Mo.) Oct. 10, 1897–Jan. 29, 1951; House 1941–43, 1945–47, 1949–Jan. 29, 1951.

SULLIVAN, Leonor Kretzer (wife of John Berchmans Sullivan) (Mo.) Aug. 21, 1902–Sept. 1, 1988; House 1953–77; Chrmn. House Merchant Marine and Fisheries 1973–77.

SULLIVAN, Maurice Joseph (Nev.) Dec. 7, 1884–Aug. 9, 1953; House 1943–45.

SULLIVAN, Timothy Daniel (N.Y.) July 23, 1862–Aug. 31, 1913; House 1903–July 27, 1906 (also elected to the term beginning 1913 but never took his seat).

SULLIVAN, William Van Amberg (Miss.) Dec. 18, 1857–March 21, 1918; House 1897–May 31, 1898; Senate May 31, 1898–1901.

SULZER, Charles August (brother of William Sulzer) (Alaska) Feb. 24, 1879–April 28, 1919; House (Terr. Del.) 1917–Jan. 7, 1919, March 4–April 28, 1919.

SULZER, William (brother of Charles August Sulzer) (N.Y.) March 18, 1863–Nov. 6, 1941; House 1895–Dec. 31, 1912; Gov. Jan. 1–Oct. 17, 1913.

SUMNER, Charles Allen (Calif.) Aug. 2, 1835–Jan. 31, 1903; House 1883–85.

SUMNER, Daniel Hadley (Wis.) Sept. 15, 1837–May 29, 1903; House 1883–85.

SUMNERS, Hatton William (Tex.) May 30, 1875–April 19, 1962; House 1913–47.

SUMTER, Thomas De Lage (grandson of Thomas Sumter) (S.C.) Nov. 14, 1809–July 2, 1874; House 1839–43.

SUNIA, Fofo Iosefa Fiti (Amer. Samoa) March 13, 1937–; House 1981–89.

SUTHERLAND, Jabez Gridley (Mich.) Oct. 6, 1825–Nov. 20, 1902; House 1871–73.

SUTHERLAND, Josiah (N.Y.) June 12, 1804–May 25, 1887; House 1851–53.

SUTPHIN, William Halstead (N.J.) Aug. 30, 1887–Oct. 14, 1972; House 1931–43.

SUTTON, James Patrick "Pat" (Tenn.) Oct. 31, 1915–; House 1949–55.

SWANK, Fletcher B. (Okla.) April 24, 1875–March 16, 1950; House 1921–29, 1931–35.

SWANN, Edward (N.Y.) March 10, 1862–Sept. 19, 1945; House Nov. 4, 1902–03.

SWANN, Thomas (Md.) Feb. 3, 1809–July 24, 1883; House 1869–79; Gov. Jan. 10, 1866–Jan. 13, 1869 (Union Democrat).

SWANSON, Claude Augustus (Va.) March 31, 1862–July 7, 1939; House 1893–Jan. 30, 1906; Senate Aug. 1, 1910–33; Gov. Feb. 1, 1906–Feb. 1, 1910; Secy. of the Navy March 4, 1933–July 7, 1939.

SWEARINGEN, Henry (Ohio) about 1792–?; House Dec. 3, 1838–41.

SWEAT, Lorenzo De Medici (Maine) May 26, 1818–July 26, 1898; House 1863–65.

SWEENEY, David McCann "Mac" (Tex.) Sept. 15, 1955–; House 1985–89.

SWEENEY, Martin Leonard (father of Robert E. Sweeney) (Ohio) April 15, 1885–May 1, 1960; House Nov. 3, 1931–43.

SWEENEY, Robert E. (son of Martin Leonard Sweeney) (Ohio) Nov. 4, 1924–; House 1965–67.

SWEENEY, William Northcut (Ky.) May 5, 1832–April 21, 1895; House 1869–71.

SWEENY, George (Ohio) Feb. 22, 1796–Oct. 10, 1877; House 1839–43.

SWEET, Edwin Forrest (Mich.) Nov. 21, 1847–April 2, 1935; House 1911–13.

SWEETSER, Charles (Ohio) Jan. 22, 1808–April 14, 1864; House 1849–53.

SWETT, Richard (son-in-law of Thomas Peter Lantos) (N.H.) May 1, 1957–; House 1991–1995.

SWIFT, Allen Byron (Wash.) Sept. 12, 1935–; House 1979–1995.

SWIFT, George Robinson (Ala.) Dec. 19, 1887–Sept. 10, 1972; Senate June 16–Nov. 5, 1946.

SWOPE, Guy Jacob (Pa.) Dec. 26, 1892–July 25, 1969; House 1937–39; Gov. (P.R.) Feb. 3–Aug. 6, 1941.

SWOPE, John Augustus (Pa.) Dec. 25, 1827–Dec. 6, 1910; House Dec. 23, 1884–85, Nov. 3, 1885–87.

SYKES, George (N.J.) Sept. 20, 1802–Feb. 25, 1880; House 1843–49, Nov. 4, 1845–47.

SYMINGTON, James Wadsworth (son of Stuart Symington, grandson of James Wolcott Wadsworth Jr., great-grandson of James Wolcott Wadsworth) (Mo.) Sept. 28, 1927–; House 1969–77.

SYMINGTON, William Stuart (father of James Wadsworth Symington, son-in-law of James Wolcott Wadsworth Jr.) (Mo.) June 26, 1901–Dec. 14, 1988; Senate 1953–Dec. 27, 1976.

SYNAR, Michael Lynn (Okla.) Oct. 17, 1950–; House 1979–1995.

TABER, Stephen (son of Thomas Taber II) (N.Y.) March 7, 1821–April 23, 1886; House 1865–69.

TACKETT, Boyd Anderson (Ark.) May 9, 1911–Feb. 23, 1985; House 1949–53.

TAGGART, Joseph (Kans.) June 15, 1867–Dec. 3, 1938; House Nov. 7, 1911–17.

TAGGART, Thomas (Ind.) Nov. 17, 1856–March 6, 1929; Senate March 20–Nov. 7, 1916; Chrmn. Dem. Nat. Comm. 1904–08.

TAGUE, Peter Francis (Mass.) June 4, 1871–Sept. 17, 1941; House 1916–19, Oct. 23, 1919–25.

TALBERT, William Jasper (S.C.) Oct. 6, 1846–Feb. 5, 1931; House 1893–1903.

TALBOTT, Albert Gallatin (uncle of William Clayton Anderson) (Ky.) April 4, 1808–Sept. 9, 1887; House 1855–59.

TALBOTT, Joshua Frederick Cockey (Md.) July 29, 1843–Oct. 5, 1918; House 1879–85, 1893–95, 1903–Oct. 5, 1918.

TALCOTT, Charles Andrew (N.Y.) June 10, 1857–Feb. 27, 1920; House 1911–15.

TALIAFERRO, James Piper (Fla.) Sept. 30, 1847–Oct. 6, 1934; Senate April 20, 1899–1911.

TALLMADGE, Nathaniel Pitcher (N.Y.) Feb. 8, 1795–Nov. 2, 1864; Senate 1833–June 17, 1844 (1833–39 Jacksonian); Gov. (Wis. Terr.) 1844–45.

TALLON, Robert Mooneyhan Jr. "Robin" (S.C.) Aug. 8, 1946–; House 1983–93.

TALMADGE, Herman Eugene (Ga.) Aug. 9, 1913–; Senate 1957–81; Chrmn. Senate Agriculture and Forestry 1971–77; Chrmn. Senate Agriculture, Nutrition, and Forestry 1977–81; Gov. Jan. 14–March 18, 1947, Nov. 17, 1948–Jan. 11, 1955.

TANNER, John (Tenn.) Sept. 22, 1944–; House 1989–.

TAPPAN, Benjamin (Ohio) May 25, 1773–April 20, 1857; Senate 1839–45.

TARBOX, John Kemble (Mass.) May 6, 1838–May 28, 1887; House 1875–77.

TARSNEY, John Charles (Mo.) Nov. 7, 1845–Sept. 4, 1920; House 1889–Feb. 17, 1896.

TARSNEY, Timothy Edward (Mich.) Feb. 4, 1849–June 8, 1909; House 1885–89.

TARVER, Malcolm Connor (Ga.) Sept. 25, 1885–March 5, 1960; House 1927–47.

TATE, Farish Carter (Ga.) Nov. 20, 1856–Feb. 7, 1922; House 1893–1905.

TAULBEE, William Preston (Ky.) Oct. 22, 1851–March 11, 1890; House 1885–89.

TAURIELLO, Anthony Francis (N.Y.) Aug. 14, 1899–Dec. 21, 1983; House 1949–51.

TAUZIN, Wilbert Joseph "Billy" (La.) June 14, 1943–; House May 17, 1980–.

TAVENNER, Clyde Howard (Ill.) Feb. 4, 1882–Feb. 6, 1942; House 1913–17.

TAYLOR, Arthur Herbert (Ind.) Feb. 29, 1852–Feb. 20, 1922; House 1893–95.

TAYLOR, Benjamin Irving (N.Y.) Dec. 21, 1877–Sept. 5, 1946; House 1913–15.

TAYLOR, Chester William (son of Samuel Mitchell Taylor) (Ark.) July 16, 1883–July 17, 1931; House Oct. 31, 1921–23.

TAYLOR, Edward Thomas (Colo.) June 19, 1858–Sept. 3, 1941; House 1909–Sept. 3, 1941.

TAYLOR, Gary Eugene "Gene" (Miss.) Sept. 17, 1953–; House Oct. 24, 1989–.

TAYLOR, George (N.Y.) Oct. 19, 1820–Jan. 18, 1894; House 1857–59.

TAYLOR, George Washington (Ala.) Jan. 16, 1849–Dec. 21, 1932; House 1897–1915.

TAYLOR, Glen Hearst (Idaho) April 12, 1904–April 28, 1984; Senate 1945–51.

TAYLOR, James Alfred (W.Va.) Sept. 25, 1878–June 9, 1956; House 1923–27.

TAYLOR, John Clarence (S.C.) March 2, 1890–March 26, 1983; House 1933–39.

TAYLOR, John James (N.Y.) April 27, 1808–July 1, 1892; House 1853–65.

TAYLOR, John May (Tenn.) May 18, 1838–Feb. 17, 1911; House 1883–87.

TAYLOR, Jonathan (Ohio) 1796–April 1848; House 1839–41.

TAYLOR, Miles (La.) July 16, 1805–Sept. 23, 1873; House 1855–Feb. 5, 1861.

TAYLOR, Nelson (N.Y.) June 8, 1821–Jan. 16, 1894; House 1865–67.

TAYLOR, Robert Love (son of Nathaniel Green Taylor, brother of Alfred Alexander Taylor) (Tenn.) July 31, 1850–March 31, 1912; House 1879–81; Senate 1907–March 31, 1912; Gov. Jan. 17, 1887–Jan. 19, 1891, Jan. 21, 1897–Jan. 16, 1899.

TAYLOR, Roy Arthur (N.C.) Jan. 31, 1910–; House June 25, 1960–77.

TAYLOR, Samuel Mitchell (father of Chester William Taylor) (Ark.) May 25, 1852–Sept. 13, 1921; House Jan. 15, 1913–Sept. 13, 1921.

TAYLOR, William (N.Y.) Oct. 12, 1791–Sept. 16, 1865; House 1833–39.

TAYLOR, William (Va.) April 5, 1788–Jan. 17, 1846; House 1843–Jan. 17, 1846.

TEAGUE, Olin Earl (Tex.) April 6, 1910–Jan. 23, 1981; House Aug. 24, 1946–Dec. 31, 1978; Chrmn. House Veterans' Affairs 1955–73; Chrmn. House Science and Astronautics 1973–75; Chrmn. House Science and Technology 1975–79.

TEESE, Frederick Halstead (N.J.) Oct. 21, 1823–Jan. 7, 1894; House 1875–77.

TEJEDA, Frank Mariano (Tex.) Oct. 2, 1945–; House 1993–.

TELLER, Henry Moore (Colo.) May 23, 1830–Feb. 23, 1914; Senate Nov. 15, 1876–April 17, 1882 (Republican), 1885–1909 (1885–97 Republican, 1897–1903 Silver Republican); Secy. of the Interior April 18, 1882–March 3, 1885.

TELLER, Ludwig (N.Y.) June 22, 1911–Oct. 4, 1965; House 1957–61.

TEMPLE, William (Del.) Feb. 28, 1814–May 28, 1863; House March 4–May 28, 1863.

TENEROWICZ, Rudolph Gabriel (Mich.) June 14, 1890–Aug. 31, 1963; House 1939–43.

TEN EYCK, Peter Gansevoort (N.Y.) Nov. 7, 1873–Sept. 2, 1944; House 1913–15, 1921–23.

TENZER, Herbert (N.Y.) Nov. 1, 1905–; House 1965–69.

TERRELL, George Butler (Tex.) Dec. 5, 1862–April 18, 1947; House 1933–35.

TERRELL, Joseph Meriwether (Ga.) June 6, 1861–Nov. 17, 1912; Senate Nov. 17, 1910–July 14, 1911; Gov. Oct. 25, 1902–June 29, 1907.

TERRY, David Dickson (son of William Leake Terry) (Ark.) Jan. 31, 1881–Oct. 7, 1963; House Dec. 19, 1933–Jan. 2, 1943.

TERRY, William (Va.) Aug. 14, 1824–Sept. 5, 1888; House 1871–73, 1875–77.

TERRY, William Leake (father of David Dickson Terry) (Ark.) Sept. 27, 1850–Nov. 4, 1917; House 1891–1901.

THACHER, Thomas Chandler (Mass.) July 20, 1858–April 11, 1945; House 1913–15.

THAYER, Andrew Jackson (Oreg.) Nov. 27, 1818–April 28, 1873; House March 4–July 30, 1861.

THAYER, John Alden (son of Eli Thayer) (Mass.) Dec. 22, 1857–July 31, 1917; House 1911–13.

THAYER, John Randolph (Mass.) March 9, 1845–Dec. 19, 1916; House 1899–1905.

THOM, William Richard (Ohio) July 7, 1885–Aug. 28, 1960; House 1933–39, 1941–43, 1945–47.

THOMAS, Albert (husband of Lera Millard Thomas) (Tex.) April 12, 1898–Feb. 15, 1966; House 1937–Feb. 15, 1966.

THOMAS, Charles Randolph (N.C.) Aug. 21, 1861–March 8, 1931; House 1899–1911.

THOMAS, Charles Spalding (Colo.) Dec. 6, 1849–June 24, 1934; Senate Jan. 15, 1913–21; Gov. Jan. 10, 1899–Jan. 8, 1901.

THOMAS, Elbert Duncan (Utah) June 17, 1883–Feb. 11, 1953; Senate 1933–51; Chrmn. Senate Labor and Public Welfare 1949–51.

THOMAS, James Houston (Tenn.) Sept. 22, 1808–Aug. 4, 1876; House 1847–51, 1859–61.

THOMAS, John William Elmer (Okla.) Sept. 8, 1876–Sept. 19, 1965; House 1923–27; Senate 1927–51; Chrmn. Senate Agriculture and Forestry 1949–51.

THOMAS, Lera Millard (widow of Albert Thomas) (Tex.) Aug. 3, 1900–; House March 26, 1966–67.

THOMAS, Phillip Francis (Md.) Sept. 12, 1810–Oct. 2, 1890; House 1839–41, 1875–77; Gov. Jan. 3, 1848–Jan. 6, 1951; Secy. of the Treasury Dec. 12, 1860–Jan. 14, 1861.

THOMAS, Robert Lindsay (Ga.) Nov. 20, 1943–; House 1983–93.

THOMAS, Robert Young Jr. (Ky.) July 13, 1855–Sept. 3, 1925; House 1909–Sept. 3, 1925.

THOMASON, Robert Ewing (Tex.) May 30, 1879–Nov. 8, 1973; House 1931–July 31, 1947.

THOMPSON, Bennie G. (Miss.) Jan. 28, 1948–; House April 20, 1993–.

THOMPSON, Charles James (Ohio) Jan. 24, 1862–March 27, 1932; House 1919–31.

THOMPSON, Charles Perkins (Mass.) July 30, 1827–Jan. 19, 1894; House 1875–77.

THOMPSON, Charles Winston (Ala.) Dec. 30, 1860–March 20, 1904; House 1901–March 20, 1904.

THOMPSON, Chester Charles (Ill.) Sept. 19, 1893–Jan. 30, 1971; House 1933–39.

THOMPSON, Clark Wallace (Tex.) Aug. 6, 1896–Dec. 16, 1981; House June 24, 1933–35, Aug. 23, 1947–67.

THOMPSON, Fountain Land (N.Dak.) Nov. 18, 1854–Feb. 4, 1942; Senate Nov. 10, 1909–Jan. 31, 1910.

THOMPSON, Frank Jr. (N.J.) July 26, 1918–July 22, 1989; House 1955–Dec. 29, 1980; Chrmn. House Administration 1976–80.

THOMPSON, George Western (Va.) May 14, 1806–Feb. 24, 1888; House 1851–July 30, 1852.

THOMPSON, Jacob (Miss.) May 15, 1810–March 24, 1885; House 1839–51; Secy. of the Interior March 10, 1857–Jan. 8, 1861.

THOMPSON, James (Pa.) Oct. 1, 1806–Jan. 28, 1874; House 1845–51.

THOMPSON, Joseph Bryan (Okla.) April 29, 1871–Sept. 18, 1919; House 1913–Sept. 18, 1919.

THOMPSON, Philip Burton Jr. (Ky.) Oct. 15, 1845–Dec. 15, 1909; House 1879–85.

THOMPSON, Robert Augustine (father of Thomas Larkin Thompson) (Va.) Feb. 14, 1805–Aug. 31, 1876; House 1847–49.

THOMPSON, Theo Ashton (La.) March 31, 1916–July 1, 1965; House 1953–July 1, 1965.

THOMPSON, Thomas Larkin (son of Robert Augustine Thompson) (Calif.) May 31, 1838–Feb. 1, 1898; House 1887–89.

THOMPSON, William (Iowa) Nov. 10, 1813–Oct. 6, 1897; House 1847–June 29, 1850.

THOMPSON, William Henry (Nebr.) Dec. 14, 1853–June 6, 1937; Senate May 24, 1933–Nov. 6, 1934.

THOMPSON, William Howard (Kans.) Oct. 14, 1871–Feb. 9, 1928; Senate 1913–19.

THOMSON, John Renshaw (N.J.) Sept. 25, 1800–Sept. 12, 1862; Senate 1853–Sept. 12, 1862.

THORNBERRY, William Homer (Tex.) Jan. 9, 1909–; House 1949–Dec. 20, 1963.

THORNTON, Anthony (Ill.) Nov. 9, 1814–Sept. 10, 1904; House 1865–67.

THORNTON, John Randolph (La.) Aug. 25, 1846–Dec. 28, 1917; Senate Dec. 7, 1910–15.

THORNTON, Raymond Hoyt Jr. (Ark.) July 16, 1928–; House 1973–79, 1991–.

THROCKMORTON, James Webb (Tex.) Feb. 1, 1825–April 21, 1894; House 1875–79, 1883–87; Aug. 9, 1866–Aug. 8, 1867.

THURMAN, Allen Granberry (Ohio) Nov. 13, 1813–Dec. 12, 1895; House 1845–47; Senate 1869–81; elected Pres. pro tempore April 15, 1879, April 7, 1880, May 6, 1880.

THURMAN, Karen Loveland (Fla.) Jan. 12, 1951–; House 1993–.

THURSTON, Samuel Royal (Oreg.) April 15, 1816–April 9, 1851; House (Terr. Del.) 1849–51.

TIBBATTS, John Wooleston (Ky.) June 12, 1802–July 5, 1852; House 1843–47.

TIERNAN, Robert Owens (R.I.) Feb. 24, 1929–; House March 28, 1967–75.

TIERNEY, William Laurence (Conn.) Aug. 6, 1876–April 13, 1958; House 1931–33.

TIFT, Nelson (Ga.) July 23, 1810–Nov. 21, 1891; House July 25, 1868–69.

TILLMAN, Benjamin Ryan (brother of George Dionysius Tillman) (S.C.) Aug. 11, 1847–July 3, 1918; Senate 1895–July 3, 1918; Gov. Dec. 4, 1890–Dec. 4, 1894.

TILLMAN, George Dionysius (brother of Benjamin Ryan Tillman) (S.C.) Aug. 21, 1826–Feb. 2, 1902; House 1879–June 19, 1882, 1883–93.

TILLMAN, John Newton (Ark.) Dec. 13, 1859–March 9, 1929; House 1915–29.

TIPTON, John (Ind.) Aug. 14, 1786–April 5, 1839; Senate Jan. 3, 1832–39.

TITUS, Obadiah (N.Y.) Jan. 20, 1789–Sept. 2, 1854; House 1837–39.

TOD, John (Pa.) 1779–March 27, 1830; House 1821–24.

TODD, Albert May (Mich.) June 3, 1850–Oct. 6, 1931; House 1897–99.

TODD, John Blair Smith (Dakota) April 4, 1814–Jan. 5, 1872; House (Terr. Del.) Dec. 9, 1861–63, June 17, 1864–65.

TODD, Paul Harold Jr. (Mich.) Sept. 22, 1921–; House 1965–67.

TOLAN, John Harvey (Calif.) Jan. 15, 1877–June 30, 1947; House 1935–47.

TOLL, Herman (Pa.) March 15, 1907–July 26, 1967; House 1959–67.

TONRY, Richard Alvin (La.) June 25, 1935–; House Jan. 3–May 4, 1977.

TONRY, Richard Joseph (N.Y.) Sept. 30, 1893–Jan. 17, 1971; House 1935–37.

TOOLE, Joseph Kemp (Mont.) May 12, 1851–March 11, 1929; House (Terr. Del.) 1885–89; Gov. Nov. 8, 1889–Jan. 2, 1893, Jan. 7, 1901–April 1, 1908.

TOOMBS, Robert (Ga.) July 2, 1810–Dec. 15, 1885; House 1845–53 (Whig); Senate 1853–Feb. 4, 1861.

TORRENS, James H. (N.Y.) Sept. 12, 1874–April 5, 1952; House Feb. 29, 1944–47.

TORRES, Esteban Edward (Calif.) Jan. 27, 1930–; House 1983–.

TORRICELLI, Robert Guy (N.J.) Aug. 26, 1951–; House 1983–.

TOUCEY, Isaac (Conn.) Nov. 15, 1792–July 30, 1869; House 1835–39; Senate May 12, 1852–57; Gov. May 6, 1846–May 5, 1847; Atty. Gen. June 21, 1848–March 3, 1849; Secy. of the Navy March 7, 1857–March 6, 1861.

TOUVELLE, William Ellsworth (Ohio) Nov. 23, 1862–Aug. 14, 1951; House 1907–11.

TOWEY, Frank William Jr. (N.J.) Nov. 5, 1895–Sept. 4, 1979; House 1937–39.

TOWNE, Charles Arnette (N.Y.) Nov. 21, 1868–Oct. 22, 1928; House 1895–97 (Republican Minn.), 1905–07; Senate Dec. 5, 1900–Jan. 28, 1901 (Minn.).

TOWNS, Edolphus "Ed" (N.Y.) July 21, 1934–; House 1983–.

TOWNS, George Washington Bonaparte (Ga.) May 4, 1801–July 15, 1854; House 1835–Sept. 1, 1836 (Jacksonian), 1837–39, Jan. 6, 1846–47; Gov. Nov. 3, 1847–Nov. 5, 1851.

TOWNSEND, Dwight (N.Y.) Sept. 26, 1826–Oct. 29, 1899; House Dec. 5, 1864–66, 1871–73.

TOWNSEND, Edward Waterman (N.J.) Feb. 10, 1855–March 15, 1942; House 1911–15.

TOWNSHEND, Norton Strange (Ohio) Dec. 25, 1816–July 13, 1895; House 1851–53.

TOWNSHEND, Richard Wellington (Ill.) April 30, 1840–March 9, 1889; House 1877–March 9, 1889.

TRACEY, Charles (N.Y.) May 27, 1847–March 24, 1905; House Nov. 8, 1887–95.

TRAFICANT, James Anthony Jr. (Ohio) May 8, 1941–; House 1985–.

TRAMMELL, Park (Fla.) April 9, 1876–May 8, 1936; Senate 1917–May 8, 1936; Gov. Jan. 7, 1913–Jan. 2, 1917.

TRANSUE, Andrew Jackson (Mich.) Jan. 12, 1903–; House 1937–39.

TRAXLER, Jerome Bob (Mich.) July 21, 1931–; House April 16, 1974–93.

TRAYNOR, Philip Andrew (Del.) May 31, 1874–Dec. 5, 1962; House 1941–43, 1945–47.

TREADWAY, Allen Towner (Mass.) Sept. 16, 1867–Feb. 16, 1947; House 1913–45.

TREADWAY, William Marshall (Va.) Aug. 24, 1807–May 1, 1891; House 1845–47.

TRIBBLE, Samuel Joelah (Ga.) Nov. 15, 1869–Dec. 8, 1916; House 1911–Dec. 9, 1916.

TRIGG, Connally Findlay (Va.) Sept. 18, 1847–April 23, 1907; House 1885–87.

TRIMBLE, James William (Ark.) Feb. 3, 1894–March 10, 1972; House 1945–67.

TRIMBLE, Lawrence Strother (Ky.) Aug. 26, 1825–Aug. 9, 1904; House 1865–71.

TRIMBLE, South (Ky.) April 13, 1864–Nov. 23, 1946; House 1901–07.

TROTTER, James Fisher (Miss.) Nov. 5, 1802–March 9, 1866; Senate Jan. 22–July 10, 1838.

TROTTI, Samuel Wilds (S.C.) July 18, 1810–June 24, 1856; House Dec. 17, 1842–43.

TROUT, Michael Carver (Pa.) Sept. 30, 1810–June 25, 1873; House 1853–55.

TRUAX, Charles Vilas (Ohio) Feb. 1, 1887–Aug. 9, 1935; House 1933–Aug. 9, 1936.

TRUMAN, Harry S. (Mo.) May 8, 1884–Dec. 26, 1972; Senate 1935–Jan. 17, 1945; Vice President Jan. 20–April 12, 1945; President April 12, 1945–53.

TSONGAS, Paul Efthemios (Mass.) Feb. 14, 1941–; House 1975–79; Senate 1979–85.

TUCK, William Munford (Va.) Sept. 28, 1896–June 9, 1983; House April 14, 1953–69; Gov. June 16, 1946–Jan. 18, 1960.

TUCKER, Henry St. George (Va.) April 5, 1853–July 23, 1932; House 1889–97, March 21, 1922–July 23, 1932.

TUCKER, James Guy Jr. (Ark.) June 13, 1943–; House 1977–79; Gov. Dec. 12, 1992–.

TUCKER, John Randolph (son of Henry St. George Tucker born in 1780, father of Henry St. George Tucker born in 1853) (Va.) Dec. 24, 1823–Feb. 13, 1897; House 1875–87.

TUCKER, Tilghman Mayfield (Miss.) Feb. 5, 1802–April 3, 1859; House 1843–45; Gov. Jan. 10, 1842–Jan. 10, 1844.

TUCKER, Walter Rayford III (Calif.) May 28, 1957–; House 1993–.

TULLY, Pleasant Britton (Calif.) March 21, 1829–March 24, 1897; House 1883–85.

TUMULTY, Thomas James (N.J.) March 2, 1913–Nov. 23, 1981; House 1955–57.

TUNNELL, James Miller (Del.) Aug. 2, 1879–Nov. 14, 1957; Senate 1941–47.

TUNNEY, John Varick (Calif.) June 26, 1934–; House 1965–Jan. 2, 1971; Senate Jan. 2, 1971–Jan. 1, 1977.

TURLEY, Thomas Battle (Tenn.) April 5, 1845–July 1, 1910; Senate July 20, 1897–1901.

TURNBULL, Robert (Va.) Jan. 11, 1850–Jan. 22, 1920; House March 8, 1910–13.

TURNER, Charles Henry (N.Y.) May 26, 1861–Aug. 31, 1913; House Dec. 9, 1889–91.

TURNER, Clarence Wyly (Tenn.) Oct. 22, 1866–March 23, 1939; House Nov. 7, 1922–23, 1933–March 23, 1939.

TURNER, Henry Gray (Ga.) March 20, 1839–June 9, 1904; House 1881–97.

TURNER, Oscar (Ky.) 1867–July 17, 1902; House 1899–1901.

TURNER, Smith Spangler (Va.) Nov. 21, 1842–April 8, 1898; House Jan. 30, 1894–97.

TURNER, Thomas (Ky.) Sept. 10, 1821–Sept. 11, 1900; House 1877–81.

TURNER, Thomas Johnston (Ill.) April 5, 1815–April 4, 1874; House 1847–49.

TURNEY, Hopkins Lacy (Tenn.) Oct. 3, 1797–Aug. 1 1857; House 1837–43; Senate 1845–51.

TURNEY, Jacob (Pa.) Feb. 18, 1825–Oct. 4, 1891; House 1875–79.

TURPIE, David (Ind.) July 8, 1828–April 21, 1909; Senate Jan. 14–March 3, 1863, 1887–99.

TURPIN, Louis Washington (Ala.) Feb. 22, 1849–Feb. 3, 1903; House 1889–June 4, 1890, 1891–95.

TUTEN, James Russell (Ga.) July 23, 1911–Aug. 16, 1968; House 1963–67.

TUTHILL, Joseph Hasbrouck (nephew of Selah Tuthill) (N.Y.) Feb. 25, 1811–July 27, 1877; House 1871–73.

TUTTLE, William Edgar Jr. (N.J.) Dec. 10, 1870–Feb. 11, 1923; House 1911–15.

TWEED, William Marcy (N.Y.) April 3, 1823–April 12, 1878; House 1853–55.

TYDINGS, Joseph Davies (adoptive son of Millard Evelyn Tydings) (Md.) May 4, 1928–; Senate 1965–71; Chrmn. Senate District of Columbia 1969–71.

TYDINGS, Millard Evelyn (adoptive father of Joseph Davies Tydings) (Md.) April 6, 1890–Feb. 9, 1961; House 1923–27; Senate 1927–51; Chrmn. Senate Armed Services 1949–51.

TYLER, David Gardiner (son of John Tyler, grandson of Gov.

John Tyler of Va.) (Va.) July 12, 1846–Sept. 5, 1927; House 1893–97.

TYSON, John Russell (Ala.) Nov. 28, 1856–March 27, 1923; House 1921–March 27, 1923.

TYSON, Lawrence Davis (Tenn.) July 4, 1861–Aug. 24, 1929; Senate 1925–Aug. 24, 1929.

UDALL, Morris King (brother of Stewart Lee Udall) (Ariz.) June 15, 1922–; House May 2, 1961–May 1991; Chrmn. House Interior and Insular Affairs 1977–91.

UDALL, Stewart Lee (brother of Morris King Udall) (Ariz.) Jan. 31, 1920–; House 1955–Jan. 18, 1961; Secy. of the Interior Jan. 21, 1961–Jan. 20, 1969.

ULLMAN, Albert Conrad (Oreg.) March 9, 1914–Oct. 11, 1986; House 1957–81; Chrmn. House Ways and Means 1975–81.

UMSTEAD, William Bradley (N.C.) May 13, 1895–Nov. 7, 1954; House 1933–39; Senate Dec. 18, 1946–Dec. 30, 1948; Gov. Jan. 8, 1953–Nov. 7, 1954.

UNDERHILL, Edwin Stewart (N.Y.) Oct. 7, 1861–Feb. 7, 1929; House 1911–15.

UNDERHILL, John Quincy (N.Y.) Feb. 19, 1848–May 21, 1907; House 1899–1901.

UNDERWOOD, John William Henderson (Ga.) Nov. 20, 1816–July 18, 1888; House 1859–Jan, 23, 1861.

UNDERWOOD, Mell Gilbert (Ohio) Jan. 30, 1892–March 8, 1972; House 1923–April 10, 1936.

UNDERWOOD, Oscar Wilder (grandson of Joseph Rogers Underwood, great-nephew of Warner Lewis Underwood) (Ala.) May 6, 1862–Jan. 25, 1929; House 1895–June 9, 1896, 1897–1915; House majority leader 1911–15; Senate 1915–27; Senate minority leader April 27, 1920–23.

UNDERWOOD, Robert Anacletus (Guam) July 13, 1948–; House (Delegate) 1993–.

UNDERWOOD, Thomas Rust (Ky.) March 3, 1898–June 29, 1956; House 1949–March 17, 1951; Senate March 19, 1951–Nov. 4, 1952.

UNSOELD, Jolene (Wash.) Dec. 3, 1931–; House 1989–1995.

UPSHAW, William David (Ga.) Oct. 15, 1866–Nov. 21, 1952; House 1919–27.

UPSON, Christopher Columbus (Tex.) Oct. 17, 1829–Feb. 8, 1902; House April 15, 1879–83.

UTTERBACK, Hubert (cousin of John Gregg Utterback) (Iowa) June 28, 1880–May 12, 1942; House 1935–37.

UTTERBACK, John Gregg (cousin of Hubert Utterback) (Maine) July 12, 1872–July 11, 1955; House 1933–35.

VAIL, George (N.J.) July 21, 1809–May 23, 1876; House 1853–67.

VAIL, Henry (N.Y.) 1782–June 25, 1853; House 1837–39.

VALENTINE, Itimous Thaddeus Jr. "Tim" (N.C.) March 16, 1926–; House 1983–1995.

VALLANDIGHAM, Clement Laird (uncle of John A. McMahon) (Ohio) July 29, 1820–June 17, 1871; House May 25, 1858–63.

VAN ALSTYNE, Thomas Jefferson (N.Y.) July 25, 1827–Oct. 26, 1903; House 1883–85.

VAN AUKEN, Daniel Myers (Pa.) Jan. 15, 1826–Nov. 7, 1908; House 1867–71.

VAN BUREN, John (N.Y.) May 13, 1799–Jan. 16, 1855; House 1841–43.

VAN BUREN, Martin (half-brother of James Isaac Van Alen) (N.Y.) Dec. 5, 1782–July 24, 1862; Senate 1821–Dec. 20, 1828; Gov. Jan. 1–March 12, 1829 (Jeffersonian Republican); Secy. of State March 28, 1829–March 23, 1831; Vice President 1833–37 (Democrat); President 1837–41 (Democrat).

VANCE, John Luther (Ohio) July 19, 1839–June 10, 1921; House 1875–77.

VANCE, Robert Brank (brother of Zebulon Baird Vance) (N.C.) April 24, 1828–Nov. 28, 1899; House 1873–85.

VANCE, Robert Johnstone (Conn.) March 15, 1854–June 15, 1902; House 1887–89.

VANCE, Zebulon Baird (brother of Robert Brank Vance born in 1828, nephew of Robert Brank Vance born in 1793) (N.C.) May 13, 1830–April 14, 1894; House Dec. 7, 1858–61; Senate 1879–April 14, 1894; Gov. Sept. 8, 1862–May 29, 1865, Jan. 1, 1877–Feb. 6, 1879.

VAN DEERLIN, Lionel (Calif.) July 25, 1914–; House 1963–81.

VANDERGRIFF, Tommy Joe "Tom" (Tex.) Jan. 29, 1926–; House 1983–85.

VANDERPOEL, Aaron (N.Y.) Feb. 5, 1799–July 18, 1870; House 1833–37 (Jacksonian), 1839–41.

VANDER VEEN, Richard Franklin (Mich.) Nov. 26, 1922–; House Feb. 18, 1974–77.

VANDERVEER, Abraham (N.Y.) 1781–July 21, 1839; House 1837–39.

VANDIVER, Willard Duncan (Mo.) March 30, 1854–May 30, 1932; House 1897–1905.

VAN DUZER, Clarence Dunn (Nev.) May 4, 1866–Sept. 28, 1947; House 1903–07.

VAN DYKE, Carl Chester (Minn.) Feb. 18, 1881–May 20, 1919; House 1915–May 20, 1919.

VAN EATON, Henry Smith (Miss.) Sept. 14, 1826–May 30, 1898; House 1883–87.

VAN HORN, George (N.Y.) Feb. 5, 1850–May 3, 1904; House 1891–93.

VANIK, Charles Albert (Ohio) April 7, 1913–; House 1955–81.

VAN NUYS, Frederick (Ind.) April 16, 1874–Jan. 25, 1944; Senate 1933–Jan. 25, 1944.

VAN SANT, Joshua (Md.) Dec. 31, 1803–April 8, 1884; House 1853–55.

VAN TRUMP, Philadelph (Ohio) Nov. 15, 1810–July 31, 1874; House 1867–73.

VARDAMAN, James Kimble (Miss.) July 26, 1861–June 25, 1930; Senate 1913–19; Gov. Jan. 19, 1904–Jan. 21, 1908.

VAUGHAN, Horace Worth (Tex.) Dec. 2, 1867–Nov. 10, 1922; House 1913–15.

VAUGHAN, William Wirt (Tenn.) July 2, 1831–Aug. 19, 1878; House 1871–73.

VAUX, Richard (Pa.) Dec. 19, 1816–March 22, 1895; House May 20, 1890–91.

VEEDER, William Davis (N.Y.) May 19, 1835–Dec. 2, 1910; House 1877–79.

VEHSLAGE, John Herman George (N.Y.) Dec. 20, 1842–July 21, 1904; House 1897–99.

VELAZQUEZ, Nydia Margarita (N.Y.) March 22, 1953–; House 1993–.

VENABLE, Abraham Watkins (nephew of Abraham Bedford Venable) (N.C.) Oct. 17, 1799–Feb. 24, 1876; House 1847–53.

VENABLE, Edward Carrington (Va.) Jan. 31, 1853–Dec. 8, 1908; House 1889–Sept. 23, 1890.

VENABLE, William Webb (Miss.) Sept. 25, 1880–Aug. 2, 1948; House Jan. 4, 1916–21.

VEST, George Graham (Mo.) Dec. 6, 1830–Aug. 9, 1904; Senate 1879–1903.

VIBBARD, Chauncey (N.Y.) Nov. 11, 1811–June 5, 1891; House 1861–63.

VICKERS, George (Md.) Nov. 19, 1801–Oct. 8, 1879; Senate March 7, 1868–73.

VIELE, Egbert Ludoricus (N.Y.) June 17, 1825–April 22, 1902; House 1885–87.

VIGORITO, Joseph Phillip (Pa.) Nov. 10, 1918–; House 1965–77.

VILAS, William Freeman (Wis.) July 9, 1840–Aug. 27, 1908; Senate 1891–97; Postmaster Gen. March 7, 1885–Jan. 16, 1888; Secy. of the Interior Jan. 16, 1888–March 6, 1889.

VINCENT, Beverly Mills (Ky.) March 28, 1890–Aug. 15, 1980; House 1937–45.

VINSON, Frederick Moore (Ky.) Jan. 22, 1890–Sept. 8, 1953; House Jan. 12, 1924–29, 1931–May 12, 1938; Secy. of the Treasury July 23, 1945–June 23, 1946; Chief Justice United States June 24, 1946–Sept. 8,

VISCLOSKY, Peter (Ind.) Aug. 13, 1949–; House 1985–.

VIVIAN, Weston Edward (Mich.) Oct. 25, 1924–; House 1965–67.

VOLKMER, Harold Lee (Mo.) April 4, 1931; House 1977–.

VOLLMER, Henry (Iowa) July 28, 1867–Aug. 25, 1930; House Feb. 10, 1914–15.

VOORHEES, Charles Stewart (son of Daniel Wolsey Voorhees) (Wash.) June 4, 1853–Dec. 26, 1909; House (Terr. Del.) 1885–89.

VOORHEES, Daniel Wolsey (father of Charles Stewart Voorhees) (Ind.) Sept. 26, 1827–April 10, 1897; House 1861–Feb. 23, 1866, 1869–73; Senate Nov. 6, 1877–97.

VOORHIS, Horace Jeremiah "Jerry" (Calif.) April 6, 1901–Sept. 11, 1984; House 1937–47.

VROOM, Peter Dumont (N.J.) Dec. 12, 1791–Nov. 18, 1873; House 1839–41; Gov. Nov. 6, 1829–Oct. 26, 1832, Oct. 25, 1833–Oct. 28, 1836.

WADDEL, Alfred Moore (N.C.) Sept. 16, 1834–March 17, 1912; House 1871–79.

WADDILL, James Richard (Mo.) Nov. 22, 1842–June 14, 1917; House 1879–81.

WADE, Martin Joseph (Iowa) Oct. 20, 1861–April 16, 1931; House 1903–05.

WAGENER, David Douglas (Pa.) Oct. 11, 1792–Oct. 1, 1860; House 1833–41 (1833–37 Jacksonian).

WAGGONNER, Joseph David Jr. (La.) Sept. 7, 1918; House Dec. 19, 1961–79.

WAGNER, Earl Thomas (Ohio) April 27, 1908–March 6, 1990; House 1949–51.

WAGNER, Robert Ferdinand (N.Y.) June 8, 1877–May 4, 1953; Senate 1927–June 28, 1949.

WALBRIDGE, Hiram (cousin of Henry Sanford Walbridge) (N.Y.) Feb. 2, 1821–Dec. 6, 1870; House 1853–55.

WALDEN, Hiram (N.Y.) Aug. 21, 1800–July 21, 1880; House 1849–51.

WALDIE, Jerome Russell (Calif.) Feb. 15, 1925–; House June 7, 1966–75.

WALDO, Loren Pinckney (Conn.) Feb. 2, 1802–Sept. 8, 1881; House 1849–51.

WALDON, Alton R. Jr. (N.Y.) Dec. 21, 1936–; House July 29, 1986–87.

WALGREN, Douglas (Pa.) Dec. 28, 1940–; House 1977–91.

WALKER, Charles Christopher Brainerd (N.Y.) June 27, 1824–Jan. 26, 1888; House 1875–77.

WALKER, E.S. Johnny (N.Mex.) June 18, 1911–; House 1965–69.

WALKER, Gilbert Carlton (Va.) Aug. 1, 1833–May 11, 1885; House 1875–79; Gov. (Provisional) Sept. 21, 1869–Jan. 1, 1870, Jan. 1, 1870–Jan. 1, 1874 (Conservative).

WALKER, Isaac Pigeon (Wis.) Nov. 2, 1815–March 29, 1872; Senate June 8, 1848–55.

WALKER, James David (grandson of David Walker, nephew of Finis Ewing McLean and John McLean born in 1791, cousin of Wilkinson Call, great-nephew of George Walker) (Ark.) Dec. 13, 1830–Oct. 17, 1906; Senate 1879–85.

WALKER, James Peter (Mo.) March 14, 1851–July 19, 1890; House 1887–July 19, 1890.

WALKER, John Randall (Ga.) Feb. 23, 1874–?; House 1913–19.

WALKER, John Williams (father of Percy Walker, great-great-grandfather of Richard Walker Bolling) (Ala.) Aug. 12, 1783–April 23, 1823; Senate Dec. 14, 1819–Dec. 12, 1822.

WALKER, Robert John (Miss.) July 19, 1801–Nov. 11, 1869; Senate 1835–March 5, 1845; Secy. of the Treasury March 8, 1845–March 5, 1849; Gov. (Kans. Terr.) April–Dec. 1857.

WALKER, Walter (Colo.) April 3, 1883–Oct. 8, 1956; Senate Sept. 26–Dec. 6, 1932.

WALKER, William Adams (N.Y.) June 5, 1805–Dec. 18, 1861; House 1853–55.

WALL, James Walter (son of Garret Dorset Wall) (N.J.) May 26, 1820–June 9, 1872; Senate Jan. 14–March 3, 1863.

WALLACE, Daniel (S.C.) May 9, 1801–May 13, 1859; House June 12, 1848–53.

WALLACE, Jonathan Hasson (Ohio) Oct. 31, 1824–Oct. 28, 1892; House May 27, 1884–85.

WALLACE, Nathaniel Dick (La.) Oct. 27, 1845–July 16, 1894; House Dec. 9, 1886–87.

WALLACE, Robert Minor (Ark.) Aug. 6, 1856–Nov. 9, 1942; House 1903–11.

WALLACE, Rodney (Mass.) Dec. 21, 1823–Feb. 27, 1903; House 1889–91.

WALLACE, William Andrew (Pa.) Nov. 28, 1827–May 22, 1896; Senate 1875–81.

WALLGREN, Monrad Charles (Wash.) April 17, 1891–Sept. 18, 1961; House 1933–Dec. 19, 1940; Senate Dec. 19, 1940–Jan. 9, 1945; Gov. Jan. 1945–Jan. 10, 1949.

WALLING, Ansel Tracy (Ohio) Jan. 10, 1824–June 22, 1896; House 1875–77.

WALSH, Allan Bartholomew (N.J.) Aug. 29, 1874–Aug. 5, 1953; House 1913–15.

WALSH, Arthur (N.J.) Feb. 26, 1896–Dec. 13, 1947; Senate Nov. 26, 1943–Dec. 7, 1944.

WALSH, David Ignatius (Mass.) Nov. 11, 1872–June 11, 1947; Senate 1919–25, Dec. 6, 1926–47; Gov. Jan. 8, 1914–Jan. 6, 1916.

WALSH, James Joseph (N.Y.) May 22, 1858–May 8, 1909; House 1895–June 2, 1896.

WALSH, John Richard (Ind.) May 22, 1913–Jan. 23, 1975; House 1949–51.

WALSH, Michael (N.Y.) March 8, 1810–March 17, 1859; House 1853–55.

WALSH, Patrick (Ga.) Jan. 1, 1840–March 19, 1899; Senate April 2, 1894–95.

WALSH, Thomas James (Mont.) June 12, 1869–March 2, 1933; Senate 1913–March 2, 1933.

WALSH, William (Md.) May 11, 1828–May 17, 1892; House 1875–79.

WALTER, Francis Eugene (Pa.) May 26, 1894–May 31, 1963; House 1933–May 31, 1963; Chrmn. House Un-American Activities 1955–63.

WALTERS, Herbert Sanford (Tenn.) Nov. 17, 1891–Aug. 17, 1973; Senate Aug. 20, 1963–Nov. 3, 1964.

WALTHALL, Edward Cary (Miss.) April 4, 1831–April 21, 1898; Senate March 9, 1885–Jan. 24, 1894, 1895–April 21, 1898.

WALTON, William Bell (N.Mex.) Jan. 23, 1871–April 14, 1939; House 1917–19.

WAMPLER, Fred (Ind.) Oct. 15, 1909–; House 1959–61.

WARD, Aaron (uncle of Elijah Ward) (N.Y.) July 5, 1790–March 2, 1867; House 1825–29 (no party), 1831–37 (Jacksonian), 1841–43.

WARD, Andrew Harrison (Ky.) Jan. 3, 1815–April 16, 1904; House Dec. 3, 1866–67.

WARD, David Jenkins (Md.) Sept. 17, 1871–Feb. 18, 1961; House June 6, 1939–45.

WARD, Elijah (nephew of Aaron Ward) (N.Y.) Sept. 16, 1816–Feb. 7, 1882; House 1857–59, 1861–65, 1875–77.

WARD, Hallett Sydney (N.C.) Aug. 31, 1870–March 31, 1956; House 1921–25.

WARD, James Hugh (Ill.) Nov. 30, 1853–Aug. 15, 1916; House 1885–87.

WARD, Matthias (Tex.) Oct. 13, 1805–Oct. 5, 1861; Senate Sept. 27, 1858–Dec. 5, 1859.

WARD, Thomas Bayless (Ind.) April 27, 1835–Jan. 1, 1892; House 1883–87.

WARE, Orie Solomon (Ky.) May 11, 1882–Dec. 16, 1974; House 1927–29.

WARNER, Adoniram Judson (Ohio) Jan. 13, 1834–Aug. 12, 1910; House 1879–81, 1883–87.

WARNER, Hiram (Ga.) Oct. 29, 1802–June 30, 1881; House 1855–57.

WARNER, John De Witt (N.Y.) Oct. 30, 1851–May 27, 1925; House 1891–95.

WARNER, Levi (brother of Samuel Larkin Warner) (Conn.) Oct. 10, 1831–April 12, 1911; House Dec. 4, 1876–79.

WARNER, Richard (Tenn.) Sept. 19, 1835–March 4, 1915; House 1881–85.

WARREN, Edward Allen (Ark.) May 2, 1818–July 2, 1875; House 1853–55, 1857–59.

WARREN, Joseph Mabbett (N.Y.) Jan. 28, 1813–Sept. 9, 1896; House 1871–73.

WARREN, Lindsay Carter (N.C.) Dec. 16, 1889–Dec. 28, 1976; House 1925–Oct. 31, 1940.

WARREN, William Wirt (Mass.) Feb. 27, 1834–May 2, 1880; House 1875–77.

WARWICK, John George (Ohio) Dec. 23, 1830–Aug. 14, 1892; House 1891–Aug. 14, 1892.

WASHINGTON, Craig (Tex.) Oct. 12, 1941–; House Jan. 23, 1990–.

WASHINGTON, Harold (Ill.) April 15, 1922–Nov. 25, 1987; House 1981–April 30, 1983.

WASHINGTON, Joseph Edwin (Tenn.) Nov. 10, 1851–Aug. 28, 1915; House 1887–97.

WASIELEWSKI, Thaddeus Francis Boleslaw (Wis.) Dec. 2, 1904–April 25, 1976; House 1941–47.

WASKEY, Frank Hinman (Alaska) April 20, 1875–Jan. 18, 1964; House (Terr. Del.) Aug. 14, 1906–07.

WATERS, Maxine (Calif.) Aug. 31, 1938–; House 1991–.

WATKINS, Albert Galiton (Tenn.) May 6, 1818–Nov. 9, 1895; House 1849–53 (Whig), 1855–59.

WATKINS, Elton (Oreg.) July 6, 1881–June 24, 1956; House 1923–25.

WATKINS, John Thomas (La.) Jan. 15, 1854–April 25, 1925; House 1905–21.

WATKINS, Wesley Wade (Okla.) Dec. 15, 1938–; House 1977–91.

WATSON, Clarence Wayland (W.Va.) May 8, 1864–May 24, 1940; Senate Feb. 1, 1911–13.

WATSON, Thomas Edward (Ga.) Sept. 5, 1856–Sept. 26, 1922; House 1891–93 (Populist); Senate 1921–Sept. 26, 1922.

WATSON, Walter Allen (Va.) Nov. 25, 1867–Dec. 24, 1919; House 1913–Dec. 24, 1919.

WATT, Melvin (N.C.) Aug. 26, 1945–; House 1993–.

WATTERSON, Harvey Magee (father of Henry Watterson) (Tenn.) Nov. 23, 1811–Oct. 1, 1891; House 1839–43.

WATTERSON, Henry (son of Harvey Magee Watterson, nephew of Stanley Matthews) (Ky.) Feb. 16, 1840–Dec. 22, 1921; House Aug. 12, 1876–77.

WATTS, John Clarence (Ky.) July 9, 1902–Sept. 24, 1971; House April 14, 1951–Sept. 24, 1971.

WAXMAN, Henry Arnold (Calif.) Sept. 12, 1939–; House 1975–.

WEADOCK, Thomas Addis Emmet (Mich.) Jan. 1, 1850–Nov. 18, 1938; House 1891–95.

WEARIN, Otha Donner (Iowa) Jan. 10, 1903–April 3, 1990; House 1933–39.

WEATHERFORD, Zadoc Lorenzo (Ala.) Feb. 4, 1888–; House Nov. 5, 1940–41.

WEAVER, Claude (Okla.) March 19, 1867–May 19, 1954; House 1913–15.

WEAVER, James Howard (Oreg.) Aug. 8, 1927–; House 1975–87.

WEAVER, Zebulon (N.C.) May 12, 1872–Oct. 29, 1948; House 1917–March 1, 1919, March 4, 1919–29, 1931–47.

WEBB, Edwin Yates (N.C.) May 23, 1872–Feb. 7, 1955; House 1903–Nov. 10, 1919.

WEBB, William Robert (grandson of Richard Stanford) (Tenn.) Nov. 11, 1842–Dec. 19, 1926; Senate Jan. 24–March 3, 1913.

WEBSTER, Taylor (Ohio) Oct. 1, 1800–April 27, 1876; House 1833–39 (1833–37 Jacksonian).

WEEKS, Joseph (grandfather of Joseph Weeks Babcock) (N.H.) Feb. 13, 1773–Aug. 4, 1845; House 1835–39 (1835–37 Jacksonian).

WEIDEMAN, Carl May (Mich.) March 5, 1898–March 5, 1972; House 1933–35.

WEIGHTMAN, Richard Hanson (N.Mex.) Dec. 28, 1816–Aug. 10, 1861; House (Terr. Del.) 1851–53.

WEISS, Samuel Arthur (Pa.) April 15, 1902–Feb. 1, 1977; House 1941–Jan. 7, 1946.

WEISS, Theodore S. (N.Y.) Sept. 17, 1927–Sept. 14, 1992; House 1977–Sept. 14, 1992.

WEISSE, Charles Herman (Wis.) Oct. 24, 1866–Oct. 8, 1919; House 1903–11.

WELCH, Philip James (Mo.) April 4, 1895–April 26, 1963; House 1949–53.

WELLBORN, Marshall Johnson (Ga.) May 29, 1808–Oct. 16, 1874; House 1849–51.

WELLBORN, Olin (Tex.) June 18, 1843–Dec. 6, 1921; House 1879–87.

WELLER, John B. (Calif.) Feb. 22, 1812–Aug. 17, 1875; House 1839–45 (Democrat Ohio); Senate Jan. 30, 1852–57; Gov. Jan. 8, 1858–Jan. 9, 1860.

WELLER, Royal Hurlburt (N.Y.) July 2, 1881–March 1, 1929; House 1923–March 1, 1929.

WELLING, Milton Holmes (Utah) Jan. 25, 1876–May 28, 1947; House 1917–21.

WELLS, Daniel Jr. (Wis.) July 16, 1808–March 18, 1902; House 1853–57.

WELLS, Erastus (Mo.) Dec. 2, 1823–Oct. 2, 1893; House 1869–77, 1879–81.

WELLS, Owen Augustine (Wis.) Feb. 4, 1844–Jan. 29, 1935; House 1893–95.

WELLSTONE, Paul (Minn.) July 21, 1944–; Senate 1991–.

WELSH, George Austin (Pa.) Aug. 9, 1878–Oct. 22, 1970; House 1923–May 31, 1932.

WELTNER, Charles Longstreet (Ga.) Dec. 17, 1927–Aug. 31, 1992; House 1963–67.

WELTY, Benjamin Franklin (Ohio) Aug. 9, 1870–Oct. 23, 1962; House 1917–21.

WEMPLE, Edward (N.Y.) Oct. 23, 1843–Dec. 18, 1920; House 1883–85.

WENE, Elmer H. (N.J.) May 1, 1892–Jan. 25, 1957; House 1937–39, 1941–45.

WERNER, Theodore B. (S.Dak.) June 2, 1892–; House 1933–37.

WEST, Charles Franklin (Ohio) Jan. 12, 1895–Dec. 27, 1956; House 1931–35.

WEST, Milton Horace (Tex.) June 30, 1888–Oct. 28, 1948; House April 22, 1933–Oct. 28, 1948.

WESTBROOK, John (Pa.) Jan. 9, 1789–Oct. 8, 1852; House 1841–43.

WESTBROOK, Theodoric Romeyn (N.Y.) Nov. 20, 1821–Oct. 6, 1885; House 1853–55.

WESTCOTT, James Diament Jr. (Fla.) May 10, 1802–Jan. 19, 1880; Senate July 1, 1845–49.

WHALEY, Richard Smith (S.C.) July 15, 1874–Nov. 8, 1951; House April 29, 1913–21.

WHEAT, Alan Dupree (Mo.) Oct. 16, 1951–; House 1983–.

WHEATON, Horace (N.Y.) Feb. 24, 1803–June 23, 1882; House 1843–47.

WHEELER, Burton Kendall (Mont.) Feb. 27, 1882–Jan. 6, 1975; Senate 1923–47.

WHEELER, Charles Kennedy (Ky.) April 18, 1863–June 15, 1933; House 1897–1903.

WHEELER, Ezra (Wis.) Dec. 23, 1820–Sept. 19, 1871; House 1863–65.

WHEELER, Harrison H. (Mich.) March 22, 1839–July 28, 1896; House 1891–93.

WHEELER, John (N.Y.) Feb. 11, 1823–April 1, 1906; House 1853–57.

WHEELER, Joseph (Ala.) Sept. 10, 1836–Jan. 25, 1906; House 1881–June 3, 1882, Jan. 15–March 3, 1883, 1885–April 20, 1900.

WHEELER, William McDonald (Ga.) July 11, 1915–; House 1947–55.

WHELCHEL, Benjamin Frank (Ga.) Dec. 16, 1895–May 11, 1954; House 1935–45.

WHITACRE, John Jefferson (Ohio) Dec. 28, 1860–Dec. 2, 1938; House 1911–15.

WHITAKER, John Albert (grandson of Addison Davis James) (Ky.) Oct. 31, 1901–Dec. 15, 1951; House April 17, 1948–Dec. 15, 1951.

WHITCOMB, James (Ind.) Dec. 1, 1795–Oct. 4, 1852; Senate 1849–Oct. 4, 1852; Gov. Dec. 6, 1843–Dec. 27, 1849.

WHITE, Allison (Pa.) Dec. 21, 1816–April 5, 1886; House 1857–59.

WHITE, Benjamin (Maine) May 13, 1790–June 7, 1860; House 1843–45.

WHITE, Cecil Fielding (Calif.) Dec. 12, 1900–; House 1949–51.

WHITE, Chilton Allen (Ohio) Feb. 6, 1826–Dec. 7, 1900; House 1861–65.

WHITE, Compton Ignatius (father of Compton Ignatius White Jr.) (Idaho) July 31, 1877–March 31, 1956; House 1933–47, 1949–51.

WHITE, Compton Ignatius Jr. (son of Compton Ignatius White) (Idaho) Dec. 19, 1920–; House 1963–67.

WHITE, Edward Douglass (grandson of James White, son of Edward Douglas White Sr.) (La.) Nov. 3, 1845–May 19, 1921; Senate 1891–March 12, 1894; Assoc. Justice Supreme Court March 12, 1894–Dec. 19, 1910; Chief Justice United States Dec. 19, 1910–May 19, 1921.

WHITE, Francis Shelley "Frank" (Ala.) March 13, 1847–Aug. 1, 1922; Senate May 11, 1914–15.

WHITE, Frederick Edward (Iowa) Jan. 19, 1844–Jan. 14, 1920; House 1891–93.

WHITE, George (Ohio) Aug. 21, 1872–Dec. 15, 1953; House 1911–15, 1917–19; Chrmn. Dem. Nat. Comm. 1920–21; Gov. Jan. 12, 1931–Jan. 14, 1935.

WHITE, James Bamford (Ky.) June 6, 1842–March 25, 1931; House 1901–03.

WHITE, Joseph Worthington (Ohio) Oct. 2, 1822–Aug. 6, 1892; House 1863–65.

WHITE, Richard Crawford (Tex.) April 29, 1923–; House 1965–83.

WHITE, Sebastian Harrison (Colo.) Dec. 24, 1864–Dec. 21, 1945; House Nov. 15, 1927–29.

WHITE, Stephen Mallory (Calif.) Jan. 19, 1853–Feb. 21, 1901; Senate 1893–99.

WHITEAKER, John (Oreg.) May 4, 1820–Oct. 2, 1902; House 1879–81; Gov. March 3, 1859–Sept. 10, 1862.

WHITEHEAD, Joseph (Va.) Oct. 31, 1867–July 8, 1938; House 1925–31.

WHITEHEAD, Thomas (Va.) Dec. 27, 1825–July 1, 1901; House 1873–75.

WHITEHOUSE, John Osborne (N.Y.) July 19, 1817–Aug. 24, 1881; House 1873–77.

WHITELAW, Robert Henry (Mo.) Jan. 30, 1854–July 27, 1937; House Nov. 5, 1890–91.

WHITELEY, William Gustavus (Del.) Aug. 7, 1819–April 23, 1886; House 1857–61.

WHITENER, Basil Lee (N.C.) May 14, 1915–; House 1957–69.

WHITFIELD, John Wilkins (Kans.) March 11, 1818–Oct. 27, 1879; House (Terr. Del.) Dec. 20, 1854–Aug. 1, 1856, Dec. 9, 1856–57.

WHITING, Justin Rice (Mich.) Feb. 18, 1847–Jan. 31, 1903; House 1887–95.

WHITLEY, Charles Orville (N.C.) Jan. 3, 1927–; House 1977–Dec. 31, 1986.

WHITTEN, Jamie Lloyd (Miss.) April 18, 1910–; House Nov. 4, 1941–1995; Chrmn. House Appropriations 1978–93.

WHITTHORNE, Washington Curran (Tenn.) April 19, 1825–Sept. 21, 1891; House 1871–83, 1887–91; Senate April 16, 1886–87.

WHITTINGTON, William Madison (Miss.) May 4, 1878–Aug. 20, 1962; House 1925–51; Chrmn. House Public Works 1949–51.

WHITTLESEY, Thomas Tucker (cousin of Elisha Whittlesey and Frederick Whittlessey) (Conn.) Dec. 8, 1798–Aug. 20, 1868; House April 29, 1836–39 (April 29, 1836–37 Jacksonian).

WHITTLESEY, William Augustus (nephew of Elisha Whittlesey) (Ohio) July 14, 1796–Nov. 6, 1866; House 1849–51.

WHYTE, William Pinkney (Md.) Aug. 9, 1824–March 17, 1908; Senate July 13, 1868–69, 1875–81, June 8, 1906–March 17, 1908; Gov. Jan. 10, 1872–March 4, 1874.

WICK, William Watson (Ind.) Feb. 23, 1796–May 19, 1868; House 1839–41, 1845–49.

WICKERSHAM, Victor Eugene (Okla.) Feb. 9, 1906–March 16, 1988; House April 1, 1941–47, 1949–57, 1961–65.

WICKLIFFE, Robert Charles (grandson of Charles Anderon Wickliffe, cousin of John Crepps Wickliffe Beckham) (La.) May 1, 1874–June 11, 1912; House 1909–June 11, 1912.

WIER, Roy William (Minn.) Feb. 25, 1888–June 27, 1963; House 1949–61.

WIGFALL, Louis Tresvant (Tex.) April 21, 1816–Feb. 18, 1874; Senate Dec. 5, 1859–March 23, 1861.

WIGGINTON, Peter Dinwiddie (Calif.) Sept. 6, 1839–July 7, 1890; House 1875–77, Feb. 7, 1878–79.

WIKE, Scott (Ill.) April 6, 1834–Jan. 15, 1901; House 1876–77, 1889–93.

WILCOX, James Mark (Fla.) May 21, 1890–Feb. 3, 1956; House 1933–39.

WILCOX, Leonard (son of Jeduthun Wilcox) (N.H.) Jan. 29, 1799–June 18, 1850; Senate March 1, 1842–43.

WILDRICK, Isaac (N.J.) March 3, 1803–March 22, 1892; House 1849–53.

WILEY, Ariosto Appling (brother of Oliver Cicero Wiley) (Ala.) Nov. 6, 1848–June 17, 1908; House 1901–June 17, 1908.

WILEY, James Sullivan (Maine) Jan. 22, 1808–Dec. 21, 1891; House 1847–49.

WILEY, John McClure (N.Y.) Aug. 11, 1846–Aug. 13, 1912; House 1889–91.

WILEY, Oliver Cicero (brother of Ariosto Appling Wiley) (Ala.) Jan. 30, 1851–Oct. 18, 1917; House Nov. 3, 1908–09.

WILFLEY, Xenophon Pierce (Mo.) March 18, 1871–May 4, 1931; Senate April 30–Nov. 5, 1918,

WILKINS, Beriah (Ohio) July 10, 1846–June 7, 1905; House 1883–89.

WILKINS, William (Pa.) Dec. 20, 1779–June 23, 1865; Senate 1831–June 30, 1834 (Jacksonian); House 1843–Feb. 14, 1844; Secy. of War Feb. 15, 1844–March 4, 1845.

WILKINSON, Theodore Stark (La.) Dec. 18, 1847–Feb. 1, 1921; House 1887–91.

WILLCOX, Washington Frederick (Conn.) Aug. 22, 1834–March 8, 1909; House 1889–93.

WILLETT, William Forte Jr. (N.Y.) Nov. 27, 1869–Feb. 12, 1938; House 1907–11.

WILLFORD, Albert Clinton (Iowa) Sept. 21, 1877–March 10, 1937; House 1933–35.

WILLIAMS, Alpheus Starkey (Mich.) Sept. 20, 1810–Dec. 21, 1878; House 1875–Dec. 21, 1878.

WILLIAMS, Archibald Hunter Arrington (nephew of Archibald Hunter Arrington) (N.C.) Oct. 22, 1842–Sept. 5, 1895; House 1891–93.

WILLIAMS, Clyde (Mo.) Oct. 13, 1873–Nov. 12, 1954; House 1927–29, 1931–43.

WILLIAMS, George Fred (Mass.) July 10, 1852–July 11, 1932; House 1891–93.

WILLIAMS, Guinn (Tex.) April 22, 1871–Jan. 9, 1948; House May 13, 1922–33.

WILLIAMS, Harrison Arlington Jr. (N.J.) Dec. 10, 1919–; House Nov. 3, 1953–57; Senate 1959–March 11, 1982; Chrmn. Senate Labor and Public Welfare 1971–77; Chrmn. Senate Human Resources 1977–79; Chrmn. Senate Labor and Human Resources 1979–81.

WILLIAMS, Henry (Mass.) Nov. 30, 1805–May 8, 1887; House 1839–41, 1843–45.

WILLIAMS, Hezekiah (Maine) July 28, 1798–Oct. 23, 1856; House 1845–49.

WILLIAMS, James (Del.) Aug. 4, 1825–April 12, 1899; House 1875–79.

WILLIAMS, James Douglas (Ind.) Jan. 16, 1808–Nov. 20, 1880; House 1875–Dec. 1, 1876; Gov. Jan. 8, 1877–Nov. 20, 1880.

WILLIAMS, James Robert (Ill.) Dec. 27, 1850–Nov. 8, 1923; House Dec. 2, 1889–95, 1899–1905.

WILLIAMS, James Wray (Md.) Oct. 8, 1792–Dec. 2, 1842; House 1841–Dec. 2, 1842.

WILLIAMS, Jared Warner (N.H.) Dec. 22, 1796–Sept. 29, 1864; House 1837–41; Senate Nov. 29, 1853–July 15, 1854; Gov. June 3, 1847–June 7, 1849.

WILLIAMS, Jeremiah Norman (Ala.) May 29, 1829–May 8, 1915; House 1875–79.

WILLIAMS, John (N.Y.) Jan. 7, 1807–March 26, 1875; House 1855–57.

WILLIAMS, John Bell (Miss.) Dec. 4, 1918–March 25, 1983; House 1947–Jan. 16, 1968; Gov. Jan. 16, 1968–Jan. 18, 1972.

WILLIAMS, John Patrick (Mont.) Oct. 30, 1937–; House 1979–.

WILLIAMS, John Sharp (grandson of Christopher Heris Williams) (Miss.) July 30, 1854–Sept. 27, 1932; House 1893–1909; House minority leader 1903–08; Senate 1911–23.

WILLIAMS, John Stuart (Ky.) July 10, 1818–July 17, 1898; Senate 1879–85.

WILLIAMS, Reuel (Maine) June 2, 1783–July 25, 1862; Senate 1837–Feb. 15, 1843.

WILLIAMS, Thomas (Ala.) Aug. 11, 1825–April 13, 1903; House 1879–85.

WILLIAMS, Thomas Hickman (Miss.) Jan. 20, 1801–May 3, 1851; Senate Nov. 12, 1838–39.

WILLIAMS, William (N.Y.) Sept. 6, 1815–Sept. 10, 1876; House 1871–73.

WILLIAMS, William Elza (Ill.) May 5, 1857–Sept. 13, 1921; House 1899–1901, 1913–17.

WILLIAMSON, Ben Mitchell (Ky.) Oct. 16, 1864–June 23, 1941; Senate Dec. 1, 1930–31.

WILLIE, Asa Hoxie (Tex.) Oct. 11, 1829–March 16, 1899; House 1873–15.

WILLIS, Albert Shelby (Ky.) Jan. 22, 1843–Jan. 6, 1897; House 1877–87.

WILLIS, Benjamin Albertson (N.Y.) March 24, 1840–Oct. 14, 1886; House 1875–79.

WILLIS, Edwin Edward (La.) Oct. 2, 1904–Oct. 24, 1972; House 1949–69; Chrmn. House Un-American Activities 1963–69.

WILSHIRE, William Wallace (Ark.) Sept. 8, 1830–Aug. 19, 1888; House 1873–June 16, 1874 (Republican), 1875–77.

WILSON, Benjamin (W.Va.) April 30, 1825–April 26, 1901; House 1875–83.

WILSON, Charles (Tex.) June 1, 1933–; House 1973–.

WILSON, Charles Herbert (Calif.) Feb. 15, 1917–July 21, 1984; House 1963–81.

WILSON, Emmett (grandson of Augustus Emmett Maxwell) (Fla.) Sept. 17, 1882–May 29, 1918; House 1913–17.

WILSON, Ephraim King (Md.) Dec. 22, 1821–Feb. 24, 1891; House 1873–75; Senate 1885–Feb. 24, 1891.

WILSON, Eugene McLanahan (son of Edgar Campbell Wilson, grandson of Thomas Wilson of Va., great-grandson of Isaac Griffin) (Minn.) Dec. 25, 1833–April 10, 1890; House 1869–71.

WILSON, Frank Eugene (N.Y.) Dec. 22, 1857–July 12, 1935; House 1899–1905, 1911–15.

WILSON, George Howard (Okla.) Aug. 21, 1905–July 16, 1985; House 1949–51.

WILSON, James Clifton (Tex.) June 21, 1874–Aug. 3, 1951; House 1917–19.

WILSON, John Frank (Ariz.) May 7, 1846–April 7, 1911; House (Terr. Del.) 1899–1901, 1903–05.

WILSON, John Haden (Pa.) Aug. 20, 1867–Jan. 28, 1913–March 4, 1921.

WILSON, Joseph Franklin (Tex.) March 18, 1901–Oct. 13, 1968; House 1947–55.

WILSON, Riley Joseph (La.) Nov. 12, 1871–Feb. 23, 1946; House 1915–37.

WILSON, Robert Patterson Clark (Mo.) Aug. 8, 1834–Dec. 21, 1916; House Dec. 2, 1889–93.

WILSON, Stanyarne (S.C.) Jan. 10, 1860–Feb. 14, 1928; House 1895–1901.

WILSON, Thomas (Minn.) May 16, 1827–April 3, 1910; House 1887–89.

WILSON, Thomas Webber (Miss.) Jan. 24, 1893–Jan. 31, 1948; House 1923–29.

WILSON, William Bauchop (Pa.) April 2, 1862–May 25, 1934; House 1907–13; Secy. of Labor March 4, 1913–March 4, 1921.

WILSON, William Edward (Ind.) March 9, 1870–Sept. 29, 1948; House 1923–25.

WILSON, William Lyne (W.Va.) May 3, 1843–Oct. 17, 1900; House 1883–95; Postmaster Gen. April 4, 1895–March 5, 1897.

WINANS, Edward Baruch (Mich.) May 16, 1826–July 4, 1894; House 1883–87; Gov. Jan. 1, 1891–Jan. 1, 1893.

WINANS, John (Wis.) Sept. 27, 1831–Jan. 17, 1907; House 1883–85.

WINCHESTER, Boyd (Ky.) Sept. 23, 1836–May 18, 1923; House 1869–73.

WINFIELD, Charles Henry (N.Y.) April 22, 1822–June 10, 1888; House 1863–67.

WINGATE, Joseph Ferdinand (Maine) June 29, 1786; House 1827–31.

WINGO, Effiegene Locke (widow of Otis Theodore Wingo, great-great-great-granddaughter of Matthew Locke) (Ark.) April 13, 1883–Sept. 19, 1962; House Nov. 4, 1930–33.

WINGO, Otis Theodore (husband of Effiegene Locke Wingo) (Ark.) June 18, 1877–Oct. 21, 1930; House 1913–Oct. 21, 1930.

WINN, Thomas Elisha (Ga.) May 21, 1839–June 5, 1925; House 1891–93.

WINSLOW, Warren (N.C.) Jan. 1, 1810–Aug. 16, 1862; House 1855–61; Gov. Dec. 6, 1854–Jan. 1, 1855.

WINSTEAD, William Arthur (Mass.) Jan. 6, 1904–; House 1943–65.

WIRTH, Timothy Endicott (Colo.) Sept. 22, 1939–; House 1975–87; Senate 1987–93.

WISE, George Douglas (cousin of John Sergeant Wise and Richard Alsop Wise, nephew of Henry Alexander Wise) (Va.) June 4, 1831–Feb. 4, 1898; House 1881–April 10, 1890, 1891–95.

WISE, Henry Alexander (father of John Sergeant Wise and Richard Alsop Wise, uncle of George Douglas Wise, son-in-law of John Sergeant) (Va.) Dec. 3, 1806–Sept. 12, 1876; House 1833–Feb. 12, 1844 (1833–37 Jacksonian, 1837–43 Whig); Gov. Jan. 1, 1856–Dec. 31, 1859.

WISE, James Walter (Ga.) March 3, 1868–Sept. 8, 1925; House 1915–25.

WISE, Morgan Ringland (Pa.) June 7, 1825–April 13, 1903; House 1879–83.

WISE, Robert Ellsworth Jr. (W.Va.) Jan. 6, 1948–; House 1983–.

WITHERS, Garrett Lee (Ky.) June 21, 1884–April 30, 1953; Senate Jan. 20, 1949–Nov. 26, 1950; House Aug. 2, 1952–April 30, 1953.

WITHERS, Robert Enoch (cousin of Thomas Withers Chinn) (Va.) Sept. 18, 1821–Sept. 21, 1907; Senate 1875–81.

WITHERSPOON, Samuel Andrew (Miss.) May 4, 1855–Nov. 24, 1915; House 1911–Nov. 24, 1915.

WITTE, William Henry (Pa.) Oct. 4, 1817–Nov. 24, 1876; House 1853–55.

WOFFORD, Harris Llewellyn (Pa.) April 9, 1926–; Senate May 9, 1991–1994.

WOFFORD, Thomas Albert (S.C.) Sept. 27, 1908–1978; Senate April 5–Nov. 6, 1956.

WOLCOTT, Josiah Oliver (Del.) Oct. 31, 1877–Nov. 11, 1938; Senate 1917–July 2, 1921.

WOLF, Harry Benjamin (Md.) June 16, 1880–Feb. 17, 1944; House 1907–09.

WOLF, Leonard George (Iowa) Oct. 29, 1925–March 28, 1970; House 1959–61.

WOLFE, Simeon Kalfius (Ind.) Feb. 14, 1824–Nov. 18, 1888; House 1873–75.

WOLFF, Joseph Scott (Mo.) June 14, 1878–Feb. 27, 1958; House 1923–25.

WOLFF, Lester Lionel (N.Y.) Jan. 4, 1919–; House 1965–81.

WOLFORD, Frank Lane (Ky.) Sept. 2, 1817–Aug. 2, 1895; House 1883–87.

WOLPE, Howard Eliott III (Mich.) Nov. 2, 1939–; House 1979–93.

WOLVERTON, Simon Peter (Pa.) Jan. 28, 1837–Oct. 25, 1910; House 1891–95.

WON PAT, Antonio Borja (Guam) Dec. 10, 1908–May 1, 1987; House 1973–85.

WOOD, Amos Eastman (Ohio) Jan. 2, 1810–Nov. 19, 1850; House Dec. 3, 1849–Nov. 19, 1850.

WOOD, Benjamin (brother of Fernando Wood) (N.Y.) Oct. 13, 1820–Feb. 21, 1900; House 1861–65, 1881–83.

WOOD, Bradford Ripley (N.Y.) Sept. 3, 1800–Sept. 26, 1889; House 1845–47.

WOOD, Ernest Edward (Mo.) Aug. 24, 1875–Jan. 10, 1952; House 1905–June 23, 1906.

WOOD, Fernando (brother of Benjamin Wood) (N.Y.) June 14, 1812–Feb. 14, 1881; House 1841–43, 1863–65, 1867–Feb. 14, 1881.

WOOD, John Stephens (Ga.) Feb. 8, 1885–Sept. 12, 1968; House 1931–35, 1945–53; Chrmn. House Un-American Activities 1949–53.

WOOD, Reuben Terrell (Mo.) Aug. 7, 1884–July 16, 1955; House 1933–41.

WOOD, Thomas Jefferson (Ind.) Sept. 30, 1844–Oct. 13, 1908; House 1883–85.

WOODARD, Frederick Augustus (N.C.) Feb. 12, 1854–May 8, 1915; House 1893–97.

WOODBURY, Levi (N.H.) Dec. 22, 1789–Sept. 4, 1851; Senate March 16, 1825–31 (no party), 1841–Nov. 20, 1845; Gov. June 5, 1823–June 2, 1824 (Democratic Republican); Secy. of the Navy May 23, 1831–June 30, 1834; Secy. of the Treasury July 1, 1834–March 2, 1841; Assoc. Justice Supreme Court Sept. 23, 1845–Sept. 4, 1851.

WOODHOUSE, Chase Going (Conn.) 1890–Dec. 12, 1984; House 1945–47, 1949–51.

WOODRUFF, George Catlin (Conn.) Dec. 1, 1805–Nov. 21, 1885; House 1861–63.

WOODRUM, Clifton Alexander (Va.) April 27, 1887–Oct. 6, 1950; House 1923–Dec. 31, 1945.

WOODS, James Pleasant (Va.) Feb. 4, 1868–July 7, 1948; House Feb. 25, 1919–23.

WOODWARD, George Washington (Pa.) March 26, 1809–May 10, 1875; House Nov. 21, 1867–71.

WOODWARD, Gilbert Motier (Wis.) Dec. 25, 1835–March 13, 1913; House 1883–85.

WOODWARD, Joseph Addison (son of William Woodward) (S.C.) April 11, 1806–Aug. 3, 1885; House 1843–53.

WOODWORTH, William W. (N.Y.) March 16, 1807–Feb. 13, 1873; House 1845–47.

WOOLSEY, Lynn (Calif.) Nov. 3, 1937–; House 1993–.

WOOTEN, Dudley Goodall (Tex.) June 19, 1860–Feb. 7, 1929; House July 13, 1901–03.

WORLEY, Francis Eugene (Tex.) Oct. 10, 1908–Dec. 17, 1974; House 1941–April 3, 1950.

WORTENDYKE, Jacob Reynier (N.J.) Nov. 27, 1818–Nov. 7, 1868; House 1857–59.

WORTHINGTON, John Tolley Hood (Md.) Nov. 1, 1788–April 27, 1849; House 1831–31 (Jacksonian).

WORTHINGTON, Nicholas Ellsworth (Ill.) March 30, 1836–March 4, 1916; House 1883–87.

WRIGHT, Augustus Romaldus (Ga.) June 16, 1813–March 31, 1891; House 1857–59.

WRIGHT, Daniel Boone (Miss.) Feb. 17, 1812–Dec. 27, 1887; House 1853–57.

WRIGHT, Edwin Ruthvin Vincent (N.J.) Jan. 2, 1812–Jan. 21, 1871; House 1865–67.

WRIGHT, James Assion (Pa.) Aug. 11, 1902–Nov. 7, 1963; House 1941–45.

WRIGHT, James Claude Jr. (Tex.) Dec. 22, 1922–; House 1955–June 30, 1989; House majority leader 1977–87; Speaker Jan. 6, 1987–June 6, 1989.

WRIGHT, John Vines (Tenn.) June 28, 1828–June 11, 1908; House 1855–61.

WRIGHT, William (N.J.) Nov. 13, 1794–Nov. 1, 1866; House 1843–47 (Whig); Senate 1853–59, 1863–Nov. 1, 1866.

WRIGHT, William Carter (Ga.) Jan. 6, 1866–June 11, 1933; House Jan. 24, 1918–33.

WYATT, Joseph Peyton Jr. (Tex.) Oct. 12, 1941; House 1979–81.

WYDEN, Ronald Lee (Oreg.) May 3, 1949–; House 1981–.

WYNN, Albert Russell (Md.) Sept. 10, 1951–; House 1993–.

WYNN, William Joseph (Calif.) June 12, 1860–Jan. 4, 1935; House 1903–05.

YANCEY, William Lowndes (uncle of Joseph Haynsworth Earle) (Ala.) Aug. 10, 1814–July 28, 1863; House Dec. 2, 1844–Sept. 1, 1846.

YAPLE, George Lewis (Mich.) Feb. 20, 1851–Dec. 16, 1939; House 1883–85.

YARBOROUGH, Ralph Webster (Tex.) June 8, 1903–; Senate April 29, 1957–; Chrmn. Senate Labor and Public Welfare 1969–71.

YATES, Sidney Richard (Ill.) Aug. 27, 1909–; House 1949–63, 1965–.

YATRON, Gus (Pa.) Oct. 16, 1927–; House 1969–93.

YEATES, Jesse Johnson (N.C.) May 29, 1829–Sept. 5, 1892; House 1875–79, Jan. 29–March 3, 1881.

YELL, Archibald (Ark.) 1797–Feb. 22, 1847; House Aug. 1, 1836–39 (Aug. 1, 1836–37 Jacksonian), 1845–July 1, 1846; Gov. Nov. 4, 1840–April 29, 1844.

YOAKUM, Charles Henderson (Tex.) July 10, 1849–Jan. 1, 1909; House 1895–97.

YODER, Samuel S. (Ohio) Aug. 16, 1841–May 11, 1921; House 1887–91.

YON, Thomas Alva (Fla.) March 14, 1882–Feb. 16, 1971; House 1927–33.

YORK, Tyre (N.C.) May 4, 1836–Jan. 28, 1916; House 1883–85.

YORTY, Samuel William (Calif.) Oct. 1, 1909–; House 1951–55.

YOST, Jacob Senewell (Pa.) July 29, 1801–March 7, 1872; House 1843–47.

YOUMANS, Henry Melville (Mich.) May 15, 1832–July 8, 1920; House 1891–93.

YOUNG, Andrew Jackson Jr. (Ga.) March 12, 1932–; House 1973–Jan. 29, 1977.

YOUNG, Hiram Casey (Tenn.) Dec. 14, 1828–Aug. 17, 1899; House 1875–81, 1883–85.

YOUNG, James (Tex.) July 18, 1866–April 29, 1942; House 1911–21.

YOUNG, John Andrew (Tex.) Nov. 10, 1916–; House 1957–79.

YOUNG, John Duncan (Ky.) Sept. 22, 1823–Dec. 26, 1910; House 1873–75.

YOUNG, John Smith (La.) Nov. 4, 1834–Oct. 11, 1916; House Nov. 5, 1878–79.

YOUNG, Pierce Manning Butler (Ga.) Nov. 15, 1836–July 6, 1896; House July 25, 1868–69, Dec. 22, 1870–75.

YOUNG, Richard Montgomery (Ill.) Feb. 20, 1798–Nov. 28, 1861; Senate 1837–43.

YOUNG, Robert Anton III (Mo.) Nov. 27, 1923–; House 1977–87.

YOUNG, Stephen Marvin (Ohio) May 4, 1889–Dec. 1, 1984; House 1933–37, 1941–43, 1949–51; Senate 1959–71.

YOUNG, Timothy Roberts (Ill.) Nov. 19, 1811–May 12, 1898; House 1849–51.

YULEE, David Levy (formerly David Levy) (Fla.) June 12, 1810–Oct. 10, 1886; House (Terr. Del.) 1841–45 (Whig Democrat); Senate July 1, 1845–51, 1855Jan. 21, 1861.

ZABLOCKI, Clement John (Wis.) Nov. 18, 1912–Dec. 3, 1983; House 1949–Dec. 3, 1983; Chrmn. House International Relations 1977–79; Chrmn. House Foreign Affairs 1979–83.

ZEFERETTI, Leo C. (N.Y.) July 15, 1927–; House 1975–83.

ZELENKO, Herbert (N.Y.) March 16, 1906–Feb. 23 1979; House 1955–63.

ZENOR, William Tayor (Ind.) April 30, 1846–June 2, 1916; House 1897–1907.

ZIEGLER, Edward Danner (Pa.) March 3, 1844–Dec. 21, 1931; House 1899–1901.

ZIMMERMAN, Orville (Mo.) Dec. 31, 1880–April 7, 1948; House 1935–April 7, 1948.

ZIONCHECK, Marion Anthony (Wash.) Dec. 5, 1901–Aug. 7, 1936; House 1933–Aug. 7, 1936.

ZORINSKY, Edward (Nebr.) Nov. 11, 1928–March 6, 1987; Senate Dec. 28, 1976–March 6, 1987.

Governors

ALABAMA

(became a state December 14, 1819)

MOORE, Samuel B. 1789–Nov. 7, 1846; March 3–Nov. 26, 1831.

GAYLE, John. Sept. 11, 1792–July 21, 1859; Nov. 26, 1831–Nov. 21, 1835; House 1847–49 (Whig).

CLAY, Clement Comer. Dec. 17, 1789–Sept. 7, 1866; Nov. 21, 1835–July 17, 1837; House 1829–35 (no party); Senate June 19, 1837–Nov. 15, 1841.

McVAY, Hugh. 1788–May 9, 1851; July 17–Nov. 21, 1837.

BAGBY, Arthur Pendleton. 1794–Sept. 21, 1858; Nov. 21, 1837–Nov. 22, 1841; Senate Nov. 24, 1841–June 16, 1848.

FITZPATRICK, Benjamin. June 30, 1802–Nov. 21, 1869; Nov. 22, 1841–Dec. 10, 1845; Senate Nov. 25, 1848–Nov. 30, 1849, Jan. 14, 1853–55, Nov. 26, 1855–Jan. 21, 1861; elected Pres. pro tempore Dec. 7, 1857, March 29, 1858, June 14, 1858, Jan. 25, 1859, March 9, 1859, Dec. 19, 1859, Feb. 20, 1860, June 26, 1860.

CHAPMAN, Reuben. July 15, 1799–May 16, 1882; Dec. 16, 1847–Dec, 17, 1849; House 1835–47 (1835–37 Jacksonian).

COLLIER, Henry Watkins. Jan. 17, 1801–Aug. 28, 1855; Dec. 17, 1849–Dec. 20, 1853.

WINSTON, John Anthony (brother-in-law of Robert Burns Lindsay, below). Sept. 4, 1812–Dec. 21, 1871; Dec. 20, 1853–Dec. 1, 1857.

SHORTER, John Gill. April 23, 1818–May 29, 1872; Dec. 2, 1861–Dec. 1, 1863.

SMITH, William Hugh. April 26, 1826–Jan. 1, 1899; July 14, 1868–Nov. 26, 1870.

LINDSAY, Robert Burns (brother-in-law of John Anthony Winston, above). July 4, 1824–Feb. 13, 1902; Nov. 26, 1870–Nov. 17, 1872.

HOUSTON, George Smith. Jan. 17, 1811–Dec. 31, 1879; Nov. 24, 1874–Nov. 28, 1878; House 1841–49, 1851–Jan. 21, 1861; Senate March 4–Dec. 31, 1879.

COBB, Rufus Wills. Feb. 25, 1829–Nov. 26, 1913; Nov. 28, 1878–Dec. 1, 1882.

O'NEAL, Edward Asbury (father of Emmet O'Neal, below). Sept. 20, 1818–Nov. 7, 1890; Dec. 1, 1882–Dec. 1, 1886.

SEAY, Thomas. Nov. 20, 1846–March 30, 1896; Dec. 1, 1886–Dec. 1, 1890.

JONES, Thomas Goode. Nov. 26, 1844–April 28, 1914; Dec. 1, 1890–Dec. 1, 1894.

OATES, William Calvin. Nov. 30, 1835–Sept. 9, 1910; Dec. 1, 1894–Dec. 1, 1896; House 1881–Nov. 5, 1894.

JOHNSTON, Joseph Forney. March 23, 1843–Aug. 8, 1913; Dec. 1, 1896–Dec. 1, 1900; Senate Aug. 6, 1907–Aug. 8, 1913.

JELKS, William Dorsey. Nov. 7, 1855–Dec. 13, 1931; Dec. 1–Dec. 26, 1900, June 11, 1901–April 25, 1904, March 5, 1905–Jan. 14, 1907.

Governors are listed in chronological order by state. Listed first are their birth and, if applicable, death dates, if available. Term or terms as governor are listed next, followed by any other government service.

SAMFORD, William James. Sept. 16, 1844–June 11, 1901; Dec. 26, 1900–June 1, 1901; House 1879–81.

JELKS, William Dorsey. June 11, 1901–April 25, 1904 (for previous term see above).

CUNNINGHAM, Russell McWhortor. Aug. 25, 1855–June 6, 1921; April 25, 1904–March 5, 1905.

JELKS, William Dorsey. March 5, 1905–Jan. 14, 1907 (for previous terms see above).

COMER, Braxton Bragg. Nov. 7, 1848–Aug. 15, 1927; Jan. 14, 1907–Jan. 17, 1911; Senate March 5–Nov. 2, 1920.

O'NEAL, Emmet (son of Edward Asbury O'Neal, above). Sept. 23, 1853–Sept. 7, 1922; Jan. 17, 1911–Jan. 18, 1915.

HENDERSON, Charles. April 26, 1860–Jan. 7, 1937; Jan. 18, 1916–Jan. 20, 1919.

KILBY, Thomas Erby. July 9, 1865–Oct. 22, 1943; Jan. 20, 1919–Jan. 15, 1923.

BRANDON, William Woodward. June 5, 1868–Dec. 7, 1934; Jan. 15, 1923–Jan. 17, 1927.

McDOWELL, Charles Samuel. Oct. 17, 1871–May 22, 1943; (Acting) July 10–July 11, 1924.

GRAVES, David Bibb. April 1, 1873–March 14, 1942; Jan. 17, 1927–Jan. 19, 1931, Jan. 14, 1935–Jan. 17, 1939.

MILLER, Benjamin Meek. March 13, 1864–Feb. 6, 1944; Jan. 19, 1931–Jan. 14, 1935.

GRAVES, David Bibb. Jan. 14, 1935–Jan. 17, 1939 (for previous term see above).

DIXON, Frank Murray. July 25, 1892–Oct. 11, 1965; Jan. 17, 1939–Jan. 19, 1943.

SPARKS, George Chauncey. Oct. 8, 1884–Nov. 6, 1968; Jan. 19, 1943–Jan. 20, 1947.

FOLSOM, James Elisha "Big Jim" (father of James Elisha Folsom Jr., below). Oct. 9, 1908–Nov. 21, 1987; Jan. 20, 1947–Jan. 15, 1951, Jan. 17, 1955–Jan. 19, 1959.

PERSONS, Seth Gordon. Feb. 5, 1902–May 29, 1965; Jan. 15, 1951–Jan. 17, 1955.

FOLSOM, James Elisha. Jan. 17, 1955–Jan. 19, 1959 (for previous term see above).

PATTERSON, John Malcolm. Sept. 27, 1921–; Jan. 19, 1959–Jan. 14, 1963.

WALLACE, George Corley (husband of Lurleen Burns Wallace, below). Aug. 25, 1919–; Jan. 14, 1963–Jan. 16, 1967, Jan. 18, 1971–June 5, 1972, July 7, 1972–Jan. 15, 1979, Jan. 17, 1983–Jan. 19, 1987.

WALLACE, Lurleen Burns (wife of George Corley Wallace, above). Sept. 19, 1926–May 7, 1968; Jan. 16, 1967–May 7, 1968.

BREWER, Albert Preston. Oct. 26, 1928–; May 7, 1968–Jan. 18, 1971.

WALLACE, George Corley. Jan. 18, 1971–June 5, 1972 (for previous term see above).

BEASLEY, Jere Locke. Dec. 12, 1935–; June 5–July 7, 1972.

WALLACE, George Corley. July 7, 1972–Jan. 15, 1979 (for previous terms see above).

JAMES, Forrest Hood "Fob" Jr. Sept. 15, 1934–; Jan. 15, 1979–Jan. 17, 1983.

WALLACE, George Corley. Jan. 17, 1983–Jan. 19, 1987 (for previous terms see above).

FOLSOM, James Elisha Jr. (son of James Elisha "Big Jim" Folsom, above) May 14, 1949–; April 22, 1993–1995.

ALASKA

(became a state January 3, 1959)

EGAN, William Allen. Oct. 8, 1914–May 6, 1984; Jan. 3, 1959–Dec. 5, 1966, Dec. 5, 1970–Dec. 2, 1974.

EGAN, William Allen. Dec. 5, 1970–Dec. 2, 1974 (for previous term see above).

SHEFFIELD, William Jennings. June 26, 1928–; Dec. 6, 1982–Dec. 1, 1986.

COWPER, Steve Camberling. Aug. 21, 1938–Dec. 1, 1986–Dec. 3, 1990.

KNOWLES, Tony. Jan. 1, 1943–; 1995–.

ARIZONA

(became a state February 14, 1912)

HUNT, George Wylie Paul. Nov. 1, 1859–Dec. 24, 1934; Feb. 14, 1912–Jan. 1, 1917, Dec. 25, 1917–Jan. 6, 1919, Jan. 1, 1923–Jan. 7, 1929, Jan. 5, 1931–Jan. 2, 1933.

HUNT, George Wylie Paul. Dec. 25, 1917–Jan. 6, 1919 (for previous term see above).

HUNT, George Wylie Paul. Jan. 1, 1923–Jan. 7, 1929 (for previous terms see above).

HUNT, George Wylie Paul. Jan. 5, 1931–Jan. 2, 1933 (for previous terms see above).

MOEUR, Benjamin Baker. Dec. 22, 1869–March 16, 1937; Jan. 2, 1933–Jan. 4, 1937.

STANFORD, Rawghlie Clement. Aug. 2, 1879–Dec. 15, 1963; Jan. 4, 1937–Jan. 2, 1939.

JONES, Robert Taylor. Feb. 8, 1884–June 11, 1958; Jan. 2, 1939–Jan. 6, 1941.

OSBORN, Sidney Preston. May 17, 1884–May 25, 1948; Jan. 6, 1941–May 25, 1948.

GARVEY, Daniel E. June 19, 1886–Feb. 5, 1974; May 25, 1948–Jan. 1, 1951.

McFARLAND, Ernest William. Oct. 9, 1894–June 8, 1984;

Jan. 3, 1955–Jan. 5, 1959; Senate 1941–53; Senate majority leader 1951–53.

FANNIN, Paul Jones. Jan. 29, 1907–; Jan. 5, 1959–Jan. 4, 1965; Senate 1965–77.

GODDARD, Samuel Pearson Jr. Aug. 8, 1919–; Jan. 4, 1965–Jan. 2, 1967.

CASTRO, Raul Hector. June 12, 1916–; Jan. 6, 1975–Oct. 20, 1977.

BOLIN, Wesley H. July 1, 1908–March 4, 1978; Oct. 20, 1977–March 4, 1978.

BABBITT, Bruce Edward. June 27, 1938–; March 4, 1978–Jan. 5, 1987; Secy. of the Interior Jan. 22, 1993–.

MOFFORD, Rose. June 10, 1922–; April 5, 1988–March 6, 1991.

ARKANSAS

(became a state June 15, 1836)

CONWAY, James Sevier (brother of Elias Nelson Conway, below). Dec. 9, 1798–March 3, 1855; Sept. 13, 1836–Nov. 4, 1840.

YELL, Archibald. Aug. 1797–Feb. 22, 1847; Nov. 4, 1840–April 29, 1844; House Aug. 1, 1836–39 (Aug. 1, 1836–37 Jacksonian), 1845–46.

ADAMS, Samuel. June 5, 1805–Feb. 27, 1850; April 29–Nov. 5, 1844.

DREW, Thomas Stevenson. Aug. 25, 1802–1879; Nov. 5, 1844–Jan. 10, 1849.

BYRD, Richard C. 1805–June 1, 1854; Jan. 11–April 19, 1849.

ROANE, John Selden. Jan. 8, 1817–April 17, 1867; April 19, 1849–Nov. 15, 1852.

CONWAY, Elias Nelson (brother of James Sevier Conway, above). May 17, 1812–Feb. 28, 1892; Nov. 15, 1852–Nov. 16, 1860.

FLETCHER, Thomas. April 8, 1819–Feb. 21, 1900; Nov. 4–Nov. 15, 1862.

FLANAGIN, Harris. Nov. 3, 1817–Sept. 23, 1874; Nov. 15, 1862–April 18, 1864.

GARLAND, Augustus Hill. June 11, 1832–Jan. 26, 1899; Nov. 12, 1874–Jan. 11, 1877; Senate 1877–March 6, 1885; Atty. Gen. March 6, 1885–March 5, 1889.

MILLER, William Read. Nov. 23, 1823–Nov. 29, 1887; Jan. 11, 1877–Jan. 13, 1881.

CHURCHILL, Thomas James. March 10, 1824–March 10, 1905; Jan. 13, 1881–Jan. 13, 1883.

BERRY, James Henderson. May 15, 1841–Jan. 30, 1913; Jan. 13, 1883–Jan. 11, 1885; Senate March 20, 1885–1907.

HUGHES, Simon P. April 14, 1830–June 29, 1906; Jan. 17, 1885–Jan. 1889.

EAGLE, James Philip. Aug. 10, 1837–Dec. 20, 1904; Jan. 17, 1889–Jan. 1 1893.

FISHBACK, William Meade. Nov. 5, 1831–Feb. 9, 1903; Jan. 10, 1893–Jan. 18, 1895.

CLARKE, James Paul. Aug. 18, 1854–Oct. 1, 1916; Jan. 18, 1895–Jan. 12, 1897; Senate 1903–Oct. 1, 1916; elected Pres. pro tempore March 13, 1913, Dec. 6, 1915.

JONES, Daniel Webster. Dec. 15, 1839–Dec. 25, 1918; Jan. 12, 1897–Jan. 8, 1901.

DAVIS, Jeff. May 6, 1862–Jan. 3, 1913; Jan. 8, 1901–Jan. 8, 1907; Senate 1907–Jan. 3, 1913.

LITTLE, John Sebastian. March 15, 1853–Oct. 29, 1916; Jan. 8–Feb. 11, 1967; House Dec. 3, 1894–Jan. 1907.

MOORE, John I. Feb. 7, 1856–March 18, 1937; Feb. 11–May 11, 1907.

PINDALL, Xenophon Overton. Aug. 21, 1873–Jan. 2, 1935; May 15, 1907–Jan. 11, 1909.

MARTIN, Jesse M. March 1, 1877–Jan. 22, 1915; Jan. 11–Jan. 14, 1909.

DONAGHEY, George W. July 1, 1856–Dec. 15, 1937; Jan. 14, 1909–Jan. 15, 1913.

ROBINSON, Joseph Taylor. Aug. 26, 1872–July 14, 1937; Jan. 15–March 10, 1913; House 1903–Jan. 14, 1913; Senate 1913–July 14, 1937; Senate minority leader 1923–33; Senate majority leader 1933–July 14, 1937.

OLDHAM, William Kavanaugh. May 29, 1865–May 6, 1938; March 10–March 13, 1913.

FUTRELL, Junius Marion. Aug. 14, 1870–June 20, 1955; March 13–July 23, 1913, Jan. 10, 1933–Jan. 12, 1937.

HAYS, George Washington. Sept. 23, 1863–Sept. 15, 1927; July 23, 1913–Jan. 9, 1917.

BROUGH, Charles Hillman. July 9, 1876–Dec. 26, 1935; Jan. 9, 1917–Jan. 11, 1921.

McRAE, Thomas Chipman. Dec. 21, 1851–June 2, 1929; Jan. 11, 1921–Jan. 13, 1925; House Dec. 7, 1885–1903.

TERRAL, Thomas Jefferson. Dec. 21, 1882–March 9, 1946; Jan. 13, 1925–Jan. 11, 1927.

MARTINEAU, John Ellis. Dec. 2, 1873–March 6, 1937; Jan. 11, 1927–March 4, 1928.

PARNELL, Harvey. Feb. 28, 1880–Jan. 16, 1936; March 14, 1928–Jan. 10, 1933.

FUTRELL, Junius Marion. Jan. 10, 1933–Jan. 12, 1937 (for previous term see above).

BAILEY, Carl Edward. Oct. 8, 1894–Oct. 23, 1948; Jan. 12 , 1937–Jan. 14, 1941.

ADKINS, Homer Martin. Oct. 15, 1890–Feb. 26, 1964; Jan. 14, 1941–Jan. 1945.

LANEY, Benjamin Travis. Nov. 25, 1896–Jan. 21, 1977; Jan. 9, 1945–Jan. 11 1949.

McMATH, Sidney Sanders. June 14, 1912–; Jan. 11, 1949–Jan. 13, 1953.

CHERRY, Francis Adams. Sept. 5, 1908–July 15, 1965; Jan. 13, 1953–Jan. 11, 1955.

FAUBUS, Orval Eugene. Jan. 7, 1910–; Jan. 11, 1955–Jan. 10, 1967.

BUMPERS, Dale Leon. Aug. 12, 1925–; Jan. 12, 1971–Jan. 2, 1975; Senate 1975–.

RILEY, Robert Cowley. Sept. 18, 1924–; Jan. 2–Jan. 14, 1975.

PRYOR, David Hampton. Aug. 29, 1934–; Jan. 14, 1975–Jan. 3, 1979; House Nov. 8, 1966–73; Senate 1979–.

PURCELL, Joe. July 29, 1923–; Jan. 3–Jan. 9, 1979.

CLINTON, William Jefferson "Bill." Aug. 19, 1946–; Jan. 9, 1979–Jan. 19, 1981, Jan. 11, 1983–Dec. 12, 1992; President 1993–.

CLINTON, William Jefferson "Bill." Jan. 11, 1983–Dec. 12, 1992 (for previous term see above).

TUCKER, James Guy Jr. June 13, 1943–; Dec. 12, 1992–; House 1977–79.

CALIFORNIA

(became a state September 9, 1850)

BIGLER, John (brother of William Bigler of Pa.). Jan. 8, 1805–Nov. 29, 1871; Jan. 8, 1852–Jan. 9, 1856.

WELLER, John B. Feb. 22, 1812–Aug. 17, 1875; Jan. 8, 1858–Jan. 9, 1860; House 1839–45 (Ohio); Senate Jan. 30, 1852–57.

LATHAM, Milton Slocum. May 23, 1827–March 4, 1882; Jan. 9–Jan. 14, 1860; House 1853–55; Senate March 5, 1860–63.

DOWNEY, John Gately. June 24, 1827–March 1, 1894; Jan. 14, 1860–Jan. 10, 1862.

HAIGHT, Henry Huntly. May 20, 1825–Sept. 2, 1878; Dec. 5, 1867–Dec. 8, 1871.

IRWIN, William. 1827–March 15, 1886; Dec. 9, 1875–Jan. 8, 1880.

STONEMAN, George. Aug. 8, 1822–Sept. 5, 1894; Jan. 10, 1883–Jan. 8, 1887.

BARTLETT, Washington. Feb. 29, 1824–Sept. 12, 1887; Jan. 8–Sept. 12, 1887.

BUDD, James Herbert. May 18, 1851–July 30, 1908; Jan. 11, 1895–Jan. 3, 1899; House 1883–85.

OLSON, Culbert Levy. Nov. 7, 1876–April 13, 1962; Jan. 2, 1939–Jan. 4, 1943.

BROWN, Edmund Gerald "Pat" Sr. (father of Edmund Gerald "Jerry" Brown Jr., below). April 21, 1905–; Jan. 5, 1959–Jan. 2, 1967.

BROWN, Edmund Gerald "Jerry" Jr. (son of Edmund Gerald "Pat" Brown Sr., above). April 7, 1938–; Jan. 6, 1975–Jan. 3, 1983.

COLORADO

(became a state August 1, 1876)

GRANT, James Benton. Jan. 2, 1848–Nov. 1, 1911; Jan. 9, 1883–Jan. 13, 1885.

ADAMS, Alva (brother of William Herbert Adams, below). May 14, 1850–Nov. 1, 1922; Jan. 11, 1887–Jan. 10, 1889, Jan. 12, 1897–Jan. 10, 1899, Jan. 10–March 17, 1905.

ADAMS, Alva. Jan. 12, 1897–Jan. 10, 1899 (for previous term see above).

THOMAS, Charles Spaulding. Dec. 6, 1849–June 24, 1934; Jan. 10, 1899–Jan. 8, 1901; Senate Jan. 15, 1913–21.

ORMAN, James B. Nov. 4, 1849–July 21, 1919; Jan. 8, 1901–Jan. 13, 1903.

ADAMS, Alva. Jan. 10–March 17, 1905 (for previous terms see above).

SHAFROTH, John Franklin. June 9, 1854–Feb. 20, 1909–Jan. 14, 1913; House 1895–Feb. 15, 1904 (1895–97 Republican, 1897–1903 Silver Republican); Senate 1913–19.

AMMONS, Elias Milton (father of Teller Ammons, below). July 28, 1860–May 20, 1925; Jan. 14, 1913–Jan. 12, 1915.

GUNTER, Julius Caldeen. Oct. 31, 1858–Oct. 26, 1940; Jan. 9, 1917–Jan. 14, 1919.

SWEET, William Ellery. Jan. 27, 1869–May 9, 1942; Jan. 9, 1923–Jan. 13, 1925.

ADAMS, William Herbert (brother of Alva Adams, above). Feb. 15, 1861–Feb. 4, 1954; Jan. 11, 1927–Jan. l0, 1933.

JOHNSON, Edwin Carl. Jan. 1, 1884–May 30, 1970; Jan. 10, 1933–Jan. 2, 1937, Jan. 11, 1955–Jan. 8, 1957; Senate 1937–55.

TALBOT, Ray H. Aug. 19, 1896–Jan. 31, 1955; Jan. 3–Jan. 12, 1937.

AMMONS, Teller (son of Elias Milton Ammons, above). Dec. 3, 1895–Jan. 16, 1972; Jan. 12, 1937–Jan. 10, 1939.

KNOUS, William Lee. Feb. 2, 1889–Dec. 13, 1959; Jan. 14, 1947–April 19, 1950.

JOHNSON, Walter Walfred. April 16, 1904–March 23, 1987; April 15, 1950–Jan. 9, 1951.

JOHNSON, Edwin Carl. Jan. 11, 1955–Jan. 8, 1957 (for previous term see above).

McNICHOLS, Stephen L.R. March 17, 1914–; Jan. 8, 1957–Jan. 8, 1963.

LAMM, Richard David. Aug. 3, 1935–; Jan. 14, 1975–Jan. 13, 1987.

ROMER, Roy. Oct. 31, 1928–; Jan. 13, 1987–.

CONNECTICUT

(ratified the Constitution January 9, 1788)

EDWARDS, Henry Waggaman. Oct. 1779–July 22, 1847; May 4, 1833–May 7, 1834, May 6, 1835–May 2, 1838; House 1819–23; Senate Oct. 8, 1823–27.

EDWARDS, Henry Waggaman. May 6, 1835–May 2, 1838 (for previous term see above).

CLEVELAND, Chauncey Fitch. Feb. 16, 1799–June 6, 1887; May 4, 1842–May 1844; House 1849–53.

TOUCEY, Isaac. Nov. 15, 1792–July 30, 1869; May 6, 1846–May 5, 1847; House 1835–39; Senate May 12, 1852–57; Atty. Gen. June 21, 1848–March 3, 1849; Secy. of the Navy March 7, 1857–March 6, 1861.

SEYMOUR, Thomas Hart. Sept. 29, 1807–Sept. 3, 1868; May 4, 1850–Oct. 13, 1853; House 1843–45 (Democrat).

POND, Charles Hobby. April 26, 1781–April 28, 1861; Oct. 13, 1853–May 1854.

ENGLISH, James Edward. March 13, 1812–March 2, 1890; May 1, 1867–May 5, 1869, May 4, 1870–May 16, 1871; House 1861–65; Senate Nov. 27, 1875–May 17, 1876.

ENGLISH, James Edward. May 4, 1870–May 16, 1871 (for previous term see above).

INGERSOLL, Charles Roberts. Sept. 16, 1821–Jan. 25, 1903; May 7, 1873–Jan. 3, 1877.

HUBBARD, Richard Dudley. Sept. 7, 1818–Feb. 28, 1884; Jan. 3, 1877–Jan. 9, 1879; House 1867–69.

WALLER, Thomas MacDonald. 1839–Jan. 24, 1924; Jan. 3, 1883–Jan. 8, 1885.

MORRIS, Luzon Burritt. April 16, 1827–Aug. 22, 1895; Jan. 4, 1893–Jan. 9, 1895.

BALDWIN, Simeon Eben. Feb. 5, 1840–Jan. 30, 1927; Jan. 4, 1911–Jan. 6, 1915.

CROSS, Wilber Lucius. April 10, 1862–Oct. 5, 1948; Jan. 7, 1931–Jan. 4, 1939.

HURLEY, Robert Augustine. Aug. 25, 1895–May 3, 1968; Jan. 8, 1941–Jan. 6, 1943.

SNOW, Charles Wilbert. April 6, 1884–Sept. 28, 1977; Dec. 27, 1946–Jan. 8, 1947.

BOWLES, Chester Bliss. April 5, 1901–May 25, 1986; Jan. 5, 1949–Jan. 3, 1951; House 1959–61.

RIBICOFF, Abraham Alexander. April 9, 1910–; Jan. 5, 1955–Jan. 21, 1961; House 1949–53; Senate 1963–81; Secy. of Health, Education and Welfare. Jan. 21, 1961–July 13, 1962.

DEMPSEY, John Noel. Jan. 3, 1915–July 16, 1989; Jan. 21, 1961–Jan. 6, 1971.

GRASSO, Ella Tambussi. May 10, 1919–Feb. 5, 1981; Jan. 8, 1975–Dec. 31, 1980; House 1971–75.

O'NEILL, William Atchinson. Aug. 11, 1930–; Dec. 31, 1980–Jan. 8. 1991.

DELAWARE

(ratified the Constitution December 7, 1787)

HAZZARD, David. May 18, 1781–July 8, 1864; Jan. 19, 1830–Jan. 15, 1833.

BENNETT, Caleb Prew. Nov. 11, 1758–May 9, 1836; Jan. 15, 1833–May 9, 1836.

THARP, William (grandfather of William T. Watson, below). Nov. 27, 1803–Jan. 1, 1865; Jan. 19, 1847–Jan. 21, 1851.

ROSS, William Henry Harrison. June 2, 1814–June 29, 1887; Jan. 21, 1851–Jan. 16, 1855.

BURTON, William. Oct. 16, 1789–Aug. 5, 1866; Jan. 18, 1859–Jan. 20, 1863.

SAULSBURY, Gove. May 29, 1815–July 31, 1881; March 1, 1865–Jan. 17, 1871.

PONDER, James. Oct. 31, 1819–Nov. 5, 1897; Jan. 17, 1871–Jan. 19, 1875.

COCHRAN, John P. Feb. 7, 1809–Dec. 27, 1898; Jan. 19, 1875–Jan. 21, 1879.

HALL, John Wood. Jan. 1, 1817–Jan. 23, 1892; Jan. 21, 1879–Jan. 16, 1883.

STOCKLEY, Charles Clark. Nov. 6, 1819–April 20, 1901; Jan. 16, 1883–Jan. 18, 1887.

BIGGS, Benjamin Thomas. Oct. 1, 1821–Dec. 25, 1893; Jan. 18, 1887–Jan. 20, 1891; House 1869–73.

REYNOLDS, Robert John. March 17, 1838–June 10, 1909; Jan. 20, 1891–Jan. 15, 1895.

WATSON, William T. (grandson of William Tharp, above). June 6, 1849–April 14, 1917; April 8, 1895–Jan. 19, 1897.

TUNNELL, Ebe Walter. Dec. 31, 1844–Dec. 13, 1917; Jan. 19, 1897–Jan. 15, 1901.

McMULLEN, Richard Cann. Jan. 2, 1868–Feb. 18, 1944; Jan. 19, 1937–Jan. 21, 1941.

CARVEL, Elbert Nostrand. Feb. 9, 1910–; Jan. 18, 1949–Jan. 20, 1953, Jan. 17, 1961–Jan. 19, 1965.

CARVEL, Elbert Nostrand. Jan. 17, 1961–Jan. 19, 1965 (for previous term see above).

TERRY, Charles Laymen Jr. Sept. 17, 1900–Feb. 6, 1970; Jan. 19, 1965–Jan. 21, 1969.

TRIBBITT, Sherman Willard. Nov. 9, 1922–; Jan. 16, 1973–Jan. 18, 1977.

CARPER, Thomas Richard. Jan. 23, 1947–; Jan. 19, 1993–; House 1983–93.

FLORIDA

(became a state March 3, 1845)

MOSELEY, William Dunn. Feb. 1, 1795–Jan. 4, 1863; June 25, 1845–Oct. 1, 1849.

BROOME, James E. Dec. 15, 1808–Nov. 23, 1883; Oct. 3, 1853–Oct. 5, 1857.

PERRY, Madison Stark. 1814–March 1865; Oct. 5, 1857–Oct. 7, 1861.

MILTON, John. April 20, 1807–April 1, 1865; Oct. 7, 1861–April 1, 1865.

MARVIN, William. April 14, 1808–July 9, 1902; July 13–Dec. 20, 1865.

DREW, George Franklin. Aug. 6, 1827–Sept. 26, 1900; Jan. 2, 1877–Jan. 4, 1881.

BLOXHAM, William Dunnington. July 9, 1835–March 15, 1911; Jan. 4, 1881–Jan. 6, 1885, Jan. 5, 1897–Jan. 8, 1901.

PERRY, Edward Alysworth. March 15, 1831–Oct. 15, 1889; Jan. 6, 1885–Jan. 8, 1889.

FLEMING, Francis Philip. Sept. 28, 1841–Dec. 20, 1908; Jan. 8, 1889–Jan. 3, 1893.

MITCHELL, Henry Laurens. Sept. 3, 1831–Oct. 14, 1903; Jan. 3, 1893–Jan. 5, 1897.

BLOXHAM, William Dunnington. Jan. 5, 1897–Jan. 8, 1901 (for previous term see above).

JENNINGS, William Sherman. March 24, 1863–Feb. 28, 1920; Jan. 8, 1901–Jan. 3, 1905.

BROWARD, Napoleon Bonaparte. April 19, 1857–Oct. 1, 1910; Jan. 3, 1905–Jan. 5, 1909.

GILCHRIST, Albert Waller. Jan. 15, 1858–May 15, 1926; Jan. 5, 1909–Jan. 7, 1913.

TRAMMELL, Park. April 9, 1876–May 8, 1936; Jan. 7, 1913–Jan. 2, 1917; Senate 1917–May 8, 1936.

HARDEE, Cary Augustus. Nov. 13, 1876–Nov. 21, 1957; Jan. 4, 1921–Jan. 6, 1925.

MARTIN, John Wellborn. June 21, 1884–Feb. 22, 1958; Jan. 6, 1925–Jan. 8, 1929.

CARLTON, Doyle Elam. July 6, 1887–Oct. 25, 1972; Jan. 8, 1929–Jan. 3, 1933.

SHOLTZ, David. Oct. 6, 1891–March 21, 1953; Jan. 3, 1933–Jan. 5, 1937.

CONE, Frederick Preston. Sept. 28, 1871–July 28, 1948; Jan. 5, 1937–Jan. 7, 1941.

HOLLAND, Spessard Lindsey. July 10, 1892–Nov. 6, 1971; Jan. 7, 1941–Jan. 2, 1945; Senate Sept. 25, 1946–71.

CALDWELL, Miliard Fillmore. Feb. 6, 1897–Oct. 23, 1984; Jan. 2, 1945–Jan. 4, 1949; House 1933–41.

WARREN, Fuller. Oct. 3, 1905–Sept. 23, 1973; Jan. 4, 1949–Jan. 6, 1963.

McCARTY, Daniel Thomas. Jan. 18, 1912–Sept. 28, 1953; Jan. 6–Sept. 28, 1953.

JOHNS, Charley Eugene. Feb. 27, 1905–; Sept. 28, 1953–Jan. 4, 1955.

COLLINS, Thomas LeRoy. March 19, 1909–March 12, 1991; Jan. 4, 1955–Jan. 3, 1961.

BRYANT, Cecil Farris. July 26, 1914–; Jan. 3, 1961–Jan. 5, 1965.

BURNS, William Haydon. March 17, 1912–; Jan. 5, 1965–Jan. 3, 1967.

ASKEW, Reubin O'Donovan. Sept. 11, 1928–; Jan. 5, 1971–Jan. 2, 1979.

GRAHAM, Daniel Robert "Bob." Nov. 9, 1936–; Jan. 2, 1979–Jan. 3, 1987; Senate 1987–.

MIXON, John Wayne. June 16, 1922–; Jan. 3–Jan. 6, 1987.

CHILES, Lawton Mainor Jr. April 3, 1930–; Jan. 8, 1991–.

GEORGIA

(ratified the Constitution January 2, 1788)

McDONALD, Charles James. July 9, 1793–Dec. 16, 1860; Nov. 6, 1839–Nov. 8, 1843.

TOWNS, George Washington Bonaparte. May 4, 1801–July 15, 1854; Nov. 3, 1847–Nov. 5, 1951; House 1835–Sept. 1, 1836 (Jacksonian), 1837–39, Jan. 5, 1846–47.

JOHNSON, Herschel Vespasian. Sept. 18, 1812–Aug. 16, 1880; Nov. 9, 1853–Nov. 6, 1857; Senate Feb. 4, 1848–49.

BROWN, Joseph Emerson (father of Joseph Mackey Brown, below). April 15, 1821–Nov. 30, 1894; 1857–June 17, 1865; Senate May 26, 1880–91.

JOHNSON, James. Feb. 12, 1811–Nov. 20, 1891; (Provisional) June 17–Dec. 14, 1865; House 1851–53 (Unionist).

JENKINS, Charles Jones. Jan. 6, 1805–June 14, 1883; Dec. 14, 1865–Jan. 3, 1868.

SMITH, James Milton. Oct. 24, 1823–Nov. 25, 1890; Jan. 12, 1872–Jan. 12, 1877.

COLQUITT, Alfred Holt. April 20, 1824–March 26, 1894; Jan. 12, 1877–Nov. 4, 1882; House 1853–55 (no party); Senate 1883–March 26, 1894.

STEPHENS, Alexander Hamilton. Feb. 11, 1812–March 4, 1883; Nov. 4, 1882–March 4, 1883; House Oct. 2, 1843–59 (1843–51 Whig, 1851–53 Unionist, 1853–55 Whig), Dec. 1, 1873–Nov. 4, 1882.

BOYNTON, James Stoddard. May 7, 1833–Dec. 22, 1902; March 5–May 10, 1883.

McDANIEL, Henry Dickerson. Sept. 4, 1836–July 25, 1926; May 10, 1883–Nov. 9, 1886.

GORDON, John Brown. Feb. 6, 1832–Jan. 9, 1904; Nov. 9, 1886–Nov. 8, 1890; Senate 1873–May 26, 1880, 1891–97.

NORTHEN, William Jonathan. July 9, 1835–March 25, 1913; Nov. 8, 1890–Oct. 27, 1894.

ATKINSON, William Yates. Nov. 11, 1854–Aug. 8, 1899; Oct. 27, 1894–Oct. 29, 1898.

CANDLER, Allen Daniel. Nov. 4, 1834–Oct. 26, 1910; Oct. 29, 1898–Oct. 25, 1902; House 1883–91.

TERRELL, Joseph Meriwether. June 6, 1861–Nov. 17, 1912; Oct. 25, 1902–June 29, 1907; Senate Nov. 17, 1910–July 14, 1911.

SMITH, Hoke. Sept. 2, 1855–Nov. 27, 1931; June 29, 1907–June 26, 1909, July 1–Nov. 16, 1911; Senate, Nov. 16, 1911–21; Secy. of the Interior March 6, 1893–Sept. 1, 1896.

BROWN, Joseph Mackey (son of Joseph Emerson Brown, above). Dec. 28, 1851–March 3, 1932; June 26, 1909–July 1, 1911, Jan. 25, 1912–June 28, 1913.

SMITH, Hoke. July 1–Nov. 16, 1911 (for previous term see above).

SLATON, John Marshall. Dec. 25, 1866–Jan. 11, 1955; Nov. 16, 1911–Jan. 25, 1912, June 28, 1913–June 26, 1915.

BROWN, Joseph Mackey. Jan. 25, 1912–June 28, 1913 (for previous term see above).

SLATON, John Marshall. June 28, 1913–June 26, 1915 (for previous term see above).

HARRIS, Nathaniel Edwin. Jan. 21, 1846–Sept. 21, 1929; June 26, 1915–June 30, 1917.

DORSEY, Hugh Manson. July 10, 1871–June 11, 1948; June 30, 1917–June 25, 1921.

HARDWICK, Thomas William. Dec. 9, 1872–Jan. 31, 1944; June 25, 1921–June 30, 1923; House 1903–Nov. 2, 1914; Senate Nov. 4, 1914–19.

WALKER, Clifford Mitchell. July 4, 1877–Nov. 9, 1954; June 30, 1923–June 25, 1927.

HARDMAN, Lamartine Griffin. April 14, 1856–Feb. 18, 1937; June 25, 1927–June 27, 1931.

RUSSELL, Richard Brevard Jr. Nov. 2, 1897–Jan. 21, 1971; June 27, 1931–Jan. 10, 1933; Senate Jan. 12, 1933–Jan. 21, 1971; elected Pres. pro tempore Jan. 3, 1969.

TALMADGE, Eugene (father of Herman Eugene Talmadge, below). Sept. 23, 1884–Dec. 21, 1946; Jan. 10, 1933–Jan. 12, 1937, Jan. 14, 1941–Jan. 12, 1943.

RIVERS, Eurith Dickinson. Dec. 1, 1895–June 11, 1967; Jan. 12, 1937–Jan. 14, 1941.

TALMADGE, Eugene. Jan. 14, 1941–Jan. 12, 1943 (for previous term see above).

ARNALL, Ellis Gibbs. March 20, 1907–Dec. 13, 1992; Jan. 12, 1943–Jan. 14, 1947.

TALMADGE, Herman Eugene (son of Eugene Talmadge, above). Aug. 9, 1913–; Jan. 14–March 18, 1947, Nov. 17, 1948–Jan. 11, 1955; Senate 1957–81.

THOMPSON, Melvin Ernest. May 1, 1903–Oct. 3, 1980; March 18, 1947–Nov. 17, 1948.

TALMADGE, Herman Eugene. Nov. 17, 1948–Jan. 11, 1955 (for previous term see above).

GRIFFIN, Samuel Marvin. Sept. 4, 1907–June 13, 1982; Jan. 11, 1955–Jan. 13, 1959.

VANDIVER, Samuel Ernest Jr. July 3, 1918–; Jan. 13, 1959–Jan. 15, 1963.

SANDERS, Carl Edward. July 15, 1925–; Jan. 15, 1963–Jan. 10, 1967.

MADDOX, Lester Garfield. Sept. 30, 1915–; Jan. 11, 1967–Jan. 12, 1971.

CARTER, James Earl "Jimmy" Jr. Oct. 1, 1925–; Jan. 12, 1971–Jan. 14, 1975; President 1977–81.

BUSBEE, George Dekle. Aug. 7, 1927–; Jan. 14, 1975–Jan. 11, 1983.

HARRIS, Joe Frank. Feb. 26, 1936–; Jan. 11, 1983–Jan. 14, 1991.

MILLER, Zell. Feb. 24, 1932–; Jan. 14, 1991–.

HAWAII

(became a state August 21, 1959)

BURNS, John Anthony. Nov. 30, 1909–April 5, 1975; Dec. 3, 1962–Dec. 2, 1974; House (Terr. Del.) 1957–Aug. 21, 1959.

ARIYOSHI, George Ryoichi. March 12, 1926–; Dec. 2, 1974–Dec. 1, 1986.

WAIHEE, John III. May 19, 1946–; Dec. 1, 1986–.

CAYETANO, Benjamin J. November 14, 1939–; 1995–.

IDAHO

(became a state July 3, 1890)

STEUNENBERG, Frank. Aug. 8, 1861–Dec. 30, 1905; Jan. 4, 1897–Jan. 7, 1901.

HUNT, Frank Williams. Dec. 16, 1871–Nov. 25, 1906; Jan. 7, 1901–Jan. 5, 1903.

HAWLEY, James Henry. Jan. 17, 1847–Aug. 3, 1929; Jan. 2, 1911–Jan. 6, 1913.

ALEXANDER, Moses. Nov. 15, 1853–Jan 4, 1932; Jan. 4, 1915–Jan. 6 1919.

ROSS, C. Ben. Dec. 27, 1876–March 31, 1946; Jan. 5, 1931–Jan. 4, 1937.

CLARK, Barzilla Worth. Dec. 22, 1880–Sept. 21, 1943; Jan. 4, 1937–Jan. 2, 1939.

CLARK, Chase Addison (brother of Barzilla Worth Clark above). Aug. 20, 1883–Dec. 29, 1966; Jan. 6, 1941–Jan. 4, 1943.

GOSSETT, Charles Clinton. Sept. 2, 1888–Sept. 20, 1974; Jan. 1–Nov. 17, 1945; Senate Nov. 17, 1945–47.

WILLIAMS, Arnold. May 21, 1898–May 25, 1970; Nov. 17, 1945–Jan. 6, 1947.

ANDRUS, Cecil Dale. Aug. 25, 1931–; Jan. 4, 1971–Jan. 24, 1977, Jan. 5, 1987–; Secy. of the Interior Jan. 23, 1977–Jan. 20, 1981.

EVANS, John Victor. Jan. 18, 1925–; Jan. 24, 1977–Jan. 5, 1987.

ANDRUS, Cecil Dale. Jan. 5, 1987–1995 (for previous term see above).

ILLINOIS

(became a state December 3, 1818)

REYNOLDS, John (brother of Thomas Reynolds of Mo.). Feb. 26, 1788–May 8, 1865; Dec. 6, 1830–Nov. 17, 1834; House 1834–Dec. 1, 1837 (Jacksonian), 1839–43.

CARLIN, Thomas. July 18, 1789–Feb. 14, 1852; Dec. 7, 1838–Dec. 8, 1842.

FORD, Thomas. Dec. 5, 1800–Nov. 3, 1850; Dec. 8, 1842–Dec. 9, 1846.

FRENCH, Augustus C. Aug. 2, 1808–Sept. 4, 1864; Dec. 9, 1846–Jan. 10, 1853.

MATTESON, Joel Aldrich. Aug. 2, 1808–Jan. 31, 1873; Jan. 10, 1853–Jan. 12, 1857.

ATGELD, John Peter. Dec. 30, 1847–March 12, 1902; Jan. 10, 1893–Jan. 11, 1897.

DUNNE, Edward Fitzsimmons. Oct. 12, 1853–May 14, 1937; Feb. 3, 1913–Jan. 8, 1917.

HORNER, Henry. Nov. 30, 1879–Oct. 6, 1940; Jan. 9, 1933–Oct. 6, 1940.

STELLE, John Henry. Aug. 10, 1891–July 5, 1962; Oct. 6, 1940–Jan. 13, 1941.

STEVENSON, Adlai Ewing II (grandson of Vice President Adlai Ewing Stevenson, father of Sen. Adlai Ewing Stevenson III). Feb. 5, 1900–July 14, 1965; Jan. 10, 1949–Jan. 12, 1953.

KERNER, Otto. Aug. 15, 1908–May 8, 1976; Jan. 9, 1961–May 22, 1968.

SHAPIRO, Samuel Harvey. April 25, 1907–; May 22, 1968–Jan. 13, 1969.

WALKER, Daniel. Aug. 6, 1922–; Jan. 8, 1973–Jan. 10, 1977.

INDIANA

(became a state December 11, 1816)

BOON, Ratliff. Jan. 18, 1781–Nov. 20, 1844; Sept. 12–Dec. 4, 1822; House 1825–27 (no party), 1829–39 (1829–37 Jacksonian).

WHITCOMB, James (father-in-law of Claude Matthews, below). Dec. 1, 1795–Oct. 4, 1852; Dec. 6, 1843–Dec. 27, 1848; Senate 1849–Oct. 4, 1852.

DUNNING, Paris Chipman. March 15, 1806–May 9, 1884; Dec. 27, 1848–Dec. 5, 1849.

WILLARD, Ashbel Parsons. Oct. 31, 1820–Oct. 4, 1860; Jan. 12, 1857–Oct. 4, 1860.

HAMMOND, Abram Adams. March 21, 1814–Aug. 27, 1875; Oct. 4, 1860–Jan. 14, 1861.

HENDRICKS, Thomas Andrews. Sept. 7, 1819–Nov. 25, 1885; Jan. 13, 1873–Jan. 8, 1877; House 1851–55; Senate 1863–69; Vice President Nov. 4–Nov. 25, 1885.

WILLIAMS, James Douglas. Jan. 16, 1808–Nov. 20, 1880; Jan. 8, 1877–Nov. 20, 1880; House 1875–Dec. 1, 1876.

GRAY, Isaac Pusey. Oct. 18, 1828–Feb. 14, 1895; Nov. 20, 1880–Jan. 10, 1881, Jan. 12, 1885–Jan. 14, 1889.

GRAY, Isaac Pusey. Jan. 12, 1885–Jan. 14, 1889 (for previous term see above).

MATTHEWS, Claude (son-in-law of James Whitcomb, above). Dec. 14, 1845–April 28, 1898, Jan. 9, 1893–Jan. 11, 1897.

MARSHALL, Thomas Riley March 14, 1854–June 1, 1925; Jan. 11, 1909–Jan. 13, 1913; Vice President 1913–21.

RALSTON, Samuel Moffett. Dec. 1, 1857–Oct. 14, 1925; Jan. 13, 1913–Jan. 8, 1917; Senate 1923–Oct. 14, 1925.

McNUTT, Paul Vories. July 19, 1891–March 24, 1955; Jan. 9, 1933–Jan. 11, 1937.

TOWNSEND, Maurice Clifford. Aug. 11, 1884–Nov. 11, 1954; Jan. 11, 1937–Jan. 13, 1941.

SCHRICKER, Henry Frederick. Aug. 30, 1883–Dec. 11, 1966; Jan. 13, 1941–Jan. 8, 1945, Jan. 10, 1949–Jan. 12, 1953.

SCHRICKER, Henry Frederick. Jan. 10, 1949–Jan. 12, 1953 (for previous term see above).

WELSH, Matthew Empson. Sept. 16, 1912–; Jan. 9, 1961–Jan. 11, 1965.

BRANIGIN, Roger Douglas. July 26, 1902–Nov. 19, 1975; Jan. 11, 1965–Jan. 13, 1969.

BAYH, Evan. Dec. 26, 1955–; Jan. 9, 1989–.

IOWA

(became a state December 28, 1846)

BRIGGS, Ansel. Feb. 3, 1806–May 5, 1881; Dec. 3, 1846–Dec. 4, 1850.

HEMPSTEAD, Stephen P. Oct. 1, 1812–Feb. 16, 1883; Dec. 4, 1850–Dec. 9, 1854.

BOIES, Horace. Dec. 7, 1827–April 4, 1923; Feb. 27, 1890–Jan. 11, 1894.

HERRING, Clyde LaVerne. May 3, 1879–Sept. 15, 1945; Jan. 12, 1933–Jan. 14, 1937; Senate Jan. 15, 1937–43.

KRASCHEL, Nelson George. Oct. 27, 1889–March 15, 1957; Jan. 14, 1937–Jan. 12, 1939.

LOVELESS, Herschel Celiel. May 5, 1911–May 4, 1989; Jan. 17, 1957–Jan. 12, 1961.

HUGHES, Harold Everett. Feb. 10, 1922–; Jan. 17, 1963–Jan. 1, 1969; Senate 1969–75.

FULTON, Robert David. May 13, 1929–; Jan. 1–Jan. 16, 1969.

KANSAS

(became a state January 29, 1861)

GLICK, George Washington. July 4, 1827–April 13, 1911; Jan. 8, 1883–Jan. 13, 1885.

HODGES, George Hartshorn. Feb. 6, 1866–Oct. 7, 1947; Jan. 13, 1913–Jan. 11, 1915.

DAVIS, Jonathan McMillan. April 27, 1871–June 27, 1943; Jan. 8, 1923–Jan. 12, 1925.

WOODRING, Harry Hines. May 31, 1890–Sept. 9, 1967; Jan. 12, 1931–Jan. 9, 1933; Secy. of War Sept. 25, 1936–June 30, 1940.

HUXMAN, Walter Augustus. Feb. 16, 1887–June 26, 1972; Jan. 11, 1937–Jan. 9, 1939.

DOCKING, George (father of Robert Blackwell Docking, below). Feb. 23, 1904–Jan. 20, 1964; Jan. 14, 1957–Jan. 9, 1961.

DOCKING, Robert Blackwell (son of George Docking, above). Oct. 9, 1925–Oct. 8, 1983; Jan. 9, 1967–Jan. 13, 1975.

CARLIN, John. Aug. 3, 1940–; Jan. 8, 1979–Jan. 12, 1987.

FINNEY, Joan. Feb. 12, 1925–; Jan. 14, 1991–1995.

KENTUCKY

(became a state June 1, 1792)

BREATHITT, John. Sept. 9, 1786–Feb. 21, 1834; June 1, 1832–Feb. 21, 1834.

MOREHEAD, James Turner (cousin of John Motley Morehead of N.C.). May 24, 1797–Dec. 28, 1854; Feb. 22, 1834–June 1, 1836; Senate 1841–47 (Whig).

HELM, John Larue. July 4, 1802–Sept. 8, 1867; July 31, 1850–Sept. 2, 1851 (Whig), Sept. 3–Sept. 8, 1867.

POWELL, Lazarus Whitehead. Oct. 6, 1812–July 3, 1867; Sept. 2, 1851–Sept. 1, 1855; Senate 1859–65.

MAGOFFIN, Beriah. April 18, 1815–Feb. 28, 1885; Aug. 30, 1859–Aug. 16, 1862.

ROBINSON, James Fisher. Oct. 4, 1800–Oct. 31, 1882; Aug. 18, 1862–Sept. 1, 1863.

HELM, John Larue. Sept. 3–Sept. 8, 1867 (for previous term see above).

STEVENSON, John White. May 4, 1812–Aug. 10, 1886; Sept. 8, 1867–Feb. 13, 1871; House 1857–61; Senate 1871–77.

LESLIE, Preston Hopkins. March 8, 1819–Feb. 7, 1907; Feb. 13, 1871–Aug. 31, 1875.

McCREARY, James Bennett. July 8, 1838–Oct. 8, 1918; Aug. 31, 1875–Aug. 31, 1879, Dec. 12, 1911–Dec. 7, 1915; House 1885–97; Senate 1903–09.

BLACKBURN, Luke Pryor. June 16, 1816–Sept. 14, 1887; Sept. 2, 1879–Sept. 4, 1883.

KNOTT, James Procter. Aug. 29, 1830–June 18, 1911; Sept. 4, 1883–Aug. 30, 1887; House 1867–71,1875–83.

BUCKNER, Simon Bolivar. April 1, 1823–Jan. 8, 1914; Aug. 30, 1887–Sept. 1, 1891.

BROWN, John Young. June 28, 1835–Jan. 11, 1904; Sept. 1, 1891–Dec. 16, 1895; House 1859–61, 1873–77.

GOEBEL, William. Jan. 4, 1856–Feb. 3, 1900; Jan. 31–Feb. 3, 1900.

BECKHAM, John Crepps Wickliffe (grandson of Charles Anderson Wickliffe, cousin of Robert Charles Wickliffe of La.). Aug. 5, 1869–Jan. 9, 1940; Feb. 3, 1900–Dec. 10, 1907; Senate 1915–21.

McCREARY, James Bennett. Dec. 12, 1911–Dec. 7, 1915 (for previous term see above).

STANLEY, Augustus Owsley. May 21, 1867–Aug. 12, 1958; Dec. 7, 1916–May 19, 1919; House 1903–15; Senate May 19, 1919–25.

BLACK, James Dixon. Sept. 24, 1849–Aug. 4, 1938; May 19–Dec. 9, 1919.

FIELDS, William Jason. Dec. 29, 1874–Oct. 21, 1954; Dec. 11, 1923–Dec. 13, 1927; House 1911–Dec. 11, 1923.

LAFOON, Ruby. Jan. 15, 1869–March 1, 1941; Dec. 8, 1931–Dec. 10, 1935.

CHANDLER, Albert Benjamin "Happy." July 14, 1898–June 15, 1991; Dec. 10, 1935–Oct. 9, 1939, Dec. 13, 1955–Dec. 8, 1959; Senate Oct. 10, 1939–Nov. 1, 1945.

JOHNSON, Keen. Jan. 12, 1896–Feb. 7, 1970; Oct. 9, 1939–Dec. 7, 1943.

CLEMENTS, Earle Chester. Oct. 22, 1896–March 12, 1985; Jan. 1948–Nov. 27, 1950; House 1945–Jan. 6, 1948; Senate Nov. 27, 1950–57.

WETHERBY, Lawrence Winchester. Jan. 2, 1908–March 27, 1994; Nov. 27, 1950–Dec. 13, 1955.

CHANDLER, Albert Benjamin "Happy." Dec. 13, 1955–Dec. 8, 1959 (for previous term see above).

COMBS, Bertram Thomas. Aug. 13, 1911–Dec. 4, 1991; Dec. 8, 1959–Dec. 10, 1963.

BREATHITT, Edward Thompson. Nov. 26, 1926–; Dec. 10, 1963–Dec. 12, 1967.

FORD, Wedell Hampton. Sept. 8, 1924–; Dec. 7, 1971–Dec. 28, 1974; Senate Dec. 28, 1974–.

CARROLL, Julian Morton. April 16, 1931–; Dec. 28, 1974–Dec. 11, 1979.

BROWN, John Young Jr. Dec. 28, 1933–; Dec. 11, 1979–Dec. 13, 1983.

COLLINS, Martha Layne. Dec. 7, 1936–; Dec. 13, 1983–Dec. 8, 1987.

WILKINSON, Wallace G. Dec. 12, 1941–; Dec. 8, 1987–Dec. 10, 1991.

JONES, Brereton Chandler. June 27, 1939–; Dec. 10, 1991–.

LOUISIANA

(became a state April 30, 1812)

MOUTON, Alexander. Nov. 19, 1804–Feb. 12, 1886; Jan. 30, 1843–Feb. 12, 1846; Senate Jan. 12, 1837–March 1, 1842.

JOHNSON, Isaac. Nov. 1, 1803–March 15, 1853; Feb. 12, 1846–Jan. 27, 1850.

WALKER, Joseph Marshall. July 1, 1784–Jan. 21, 1856; Jan. 28, 1850–Jan. 17, 1853.

HEBERT, Paul Octave. Dec. 12, 1818–Aug. 29, 1880; Jan. 18, 1853–Jan. 28, 1856.

WICKLIFFE, Robert Charles (son of Charles Anderson Wickliffe of Ky., uncle of John Crepps Wickliffe Beckham of Ky.). Jan. 6, 1819–April 18, 1895; Jan. 28, 1856–Jan. 22, 1860.

MOORE, Thomas Overton. April 10, 1804–June 25, 1876; Jan. 23, 1860–Jan. 25, 1864.

SHEPLEY, George Foster. Jan. 1, 1819–July 20, 1878; (Military) June 10, 1862–March 4, 1864.

ALLEN, Henry Watkins. April 29, 1820–April 22, 1866; Jan. 25, 1864–June 2, 1865.

NICHOLLS, Francis Redding Tillou. Aug. 20, 1834–Jan. 4, 1912; Jan. 8, 1877–Jan. 13, 1880, May 21, 1888–May 10, 1892.

WILTZ, Louis Alfred. Jan. 21, 1843–Oct. 16, 1881; Jan. 14, 1880–Oct. 16, 1881.

McENERY, Samuel Douglas. May 28, 1837–June 28, 1910; Oct. 16, 1881–May 20, 1888; Senate 1897–June 28, 1910.

NICHOLLS, Francis Redding Tillou. May 2l, 1888–May 10, 1892 (for previous term see above).

HEARD, William Wright. April 28, 1849–June 22, 1922; May 10, 1904–May 18, 1908; House 1881–March 12, 1894; Senate March 12, 1894–97.

BLANCHARD, Newton Crain. Jan. 29, 1849–June 22, 1922; May 10, 1904–May 18, 1908; House 1881–March 12, 1894; Senate March 12, 1894–97.

SANDERS, Jared Young. Jan. 29, 1867–March 23, 1944; May 18, 1908–May 14, 1912; House 1917–21.

HALL, Luther Egbert. Aug. 30, 1869–Nov. 6, 1921; May 20, 1912–May 15, 1916.

PLEASANT, Ruffin Golson. June 2, 1871–Sept. 12, 1937; May 15, 1916–May 17, 1920.

PARKER, John Milliken. March 16, 1863–May 20, 1939; May 17, 1920–May 19, 1924.

FUQUA, Henry Luce. Nov. 8, 1865–Oct. 11, 1926; May 19, 1924–Oct. 11, 1926.

SIMPSON, Oramel Hinckley. March 20, 1870–Nov. 17, 1932; Oct. 11, 1926–May 21, 1928.

LONG, Huey Pierce "the Kingfish" (father of Sen. Russell B. Long, brother of Earl Kemp Long, below). Aug. 30, 1893–Sept. 10, 1935; May 21, 1928–Jan. 25, 1932; Senate Sept. 25, 1932–Sept. 10, 1935.

KING, Alvin Olin. June 21, 1890–Feb. 21, 1958; Jan. 25–May 16, 1932.

ALLEN, Oscar Kelly. Aug. 8, 1882–Jan. 28, 1936; May 16, 1932–Jan. 28, 1936.

NOE, James Albert. Dec. 21, 1893–April 2, 1976; Jan. 28–May 12, 1936.

LECHE, Richard Webster. May 17, 1898–Feb. 22, 1965; May 12, 1936–June 26, 1939.

LONG, Earl Kemp (brother of Huey Pierce "the Kingfish" Long, above, uncle of Sen. Russell B. Long). Aug. 26, 1895–Sept. 5, 1960; June 26, 1939–May 14, 1940, May 11, 1948–May 13, 1952, May 15, 1956–May 10, 1960.

JONES, Sam Houston. July 15, 1897–Feb. 8, 1978; May 14, 1940–May 9, 1944.

DAVIS, James Houston. Sept. 11, 1902–; May 9, 1944–May 11, 1948, May 10, 1960–May 12, 1964.

LONG, Earl Kemp. May 11, 1948–May 13, 1952 (for previous terms see above).

KENNON, Robert Floyd. Aug. 21, 1902–; May 13, 1952–May 8, 1956.

LONG, Earl Kemp. May 15, 1956–May 10, 1960 (for previous terms see above).

DAVIS, James Houston. May 10, 1960–May 12, 1964 (for previous term see above).

McKEITHEN, John Julian. May 28, 1918–; May 12, 1964–May 9, 1972.

EDWARDS, Edwin Washington. Aug. 7, 1927–; May 9, 1972–March 10, 1980, March 12, 1984–March 14, 1988, Jan. 8, 1992–; House Oct. 18, 1965–May 9, 1972.

EDWARDS, Edwin Washington. March 12, 1984–March 14, 1988 (for previous term see above).

EDWARDS, Edwin Washington. Jan. 8, 1992– (for previous term see above).

MAINE

(became a state March 15, 1820)

CUTLER, Nathan. May 29, 1775–June 8, 1861; Oct. 12, 1829–Feb. 5, 1830.

HALL, Joshua. Oct. 22, 1768–Dec. 25, 1862; Feb. 5–Feb. 10, 1830.

DUNLAP, Robert Pinckney. Aug. 17, 1794–Oct. 20, 1859; Jan. 1, 1834–Jan. 3, 1838; House 1843–47.

FAIRFIELD, John. Jan. 30, 1797–Dec. 24, 1847; Jan. 2, 1839–Jan. 6, 1841, Jan. 5, 1842–March 7, 1843; House 1835–Dec. 24, 1838; Senate 1843–Dec. 24, 1847.

FAIRFIELD, John. Jan. 5, 1842–March 7, 1843 (for previous term see above).

KAVANAGH, Edward. April 27, 1795–Jan. 22, 1844; 1843–Jan. 1, 1844; House 1831–35 (Jacksonian).

DUNN, David. Jan. 17, 1811–Feb. 17, 1894; Jan.1–Jan. 3, 1844.

DANA, John Winchester. June 21, 1808–Dec. 22, 1867; Jan. 3–Jan. 5, 1844, May 13, 1847–May 8, 1850.

ANDERSON, Hugh Johnston. May 10, 1801–May 1, 1881; Jan. 5, 1844–May 12, 1847; House 1837–41.

DANA, John Winchester. May 13, 1847–May 8, 1850 (for previous term see above).

HUBBARD, John. March 22, 1794–Feb. 6, 1869; May 8, 1850–Jan. 5, 1853.

WELLS, Samuel. Aug. 15, 1801–July 15, 1868; Jan. 2, 1856–Jan. 8, 1857.

GARCELON, Alonzo. May 6, 1813–Dec. 8, 1906; Jan. 8, 1879–Jan. 17, 1880.

PLAISTED, Harris Merrill (father of Frederick William Plaisted, below). Nov. 2, 1828–Jan. 31, 1898; Jan. 13, 1881–Jan. 3, 1883; House Sept. 13, 1875–77 (Republican).

PLAISTED, Frederick William (son of Harris Merrill Plaisted, above). July 26, 1865–March 4, 1943; Jan. 4, 1911–Jan. 1, 1913.

CURTIS, Oakley Chester. March 29, 1865–Feb. 22, 1924; Jan. 6, 1915–Jan. 3, 1917.

BRANN, Louis Jefferson. July 6, 1876–Feb. 3, 1948; Jan. 4, 1933–Jan. 6, 1937.

MUSKIE, Edmund Sixtus. March 28, 1914–; Jan. 5, 1955–Jan. 3, 1959; Senate 1959–May 7, 1980; Secy. of State May 8, 1980–Jan. 18, 1981.

CLAUSON, Clinton Amos. March 24, 1898–Dec. 30, 1959; Jan. 8–Dec. 30, 1959.

CURTIS, Kenneth M. Feb. 8, 1931–; Jan. 5, 1967–Jan. 1, 1975; Chrmn. Dem. Nat. Comm. 1977–78.

BRENNAN, Joseph Edward. Nov. 2, 1934–; Jan. 3, 1979–Jan. 7, 1987; House 1987–91.

MARYLAND

(ratified the Constitution April 28, 1788)

GRASON, William. March 11, 1788–July 2, 1868; Jan. 7, 1839–Jan. 3, 1842.

THOMAS, Francis (son-in-law of James McDowell of Va.). Feb. 3, 1799–Jan. 22, 1876; Jan. 3, 1841–Jan. 6, 1845; House 1831–41 (1831–37 Jacksonian, 1837–41 Republican), 1861–69 (1861–63 Unionist, 1863–67 Unconditional Unionist, 1867–69 Republican).

THOMAS, Philip Francis. Sept. 12, 1810–Oct. 2, 1890; Jan. 3, 1848–Jan. 6, 1851; House 1839–41, 1875–77; Secy. of the Treasury Dec. 12, 1860–Jan. 14, 1861.

LOWE, Enoch Louis. Aug. 10, 1820–Aug. 23, 1892; Jan. 6, 1851–Jan. 11, 1854.

LIGON, Thomas Watkins. May 10, 1810–Jan. 12, 1881; Jan. 11, 1854–Jan. 13, 1858; House 1845–49.

BOWIE, Oden. Nov. 10, 1826–Dec. 4, 1894; Jan. 13, 1869–Jan. 10, 1872.

WHYTE, William Pinkney. Aug. 9, 1824–March 17, 1908; Jan. 10, 1872–March 4, 1874; Senate July 13, 1868–69, 1875–81, June 8, 1906–March 17, 1908.

GROOME, James Black. April 4, 1838–Oct. 5, 1893; March 4, 1874–Jan. 12, 1876; Senate 1879–85.

CARROLL, John Lee. Sept. 30, 1830–Feb. 27, 1911; Jan. 12, 1876–Jan. 14, 1880.

HAMILTON, William Thomas. Sept. 8, 1820–Oct. 26, 1888; Jan. 14, 1880–Jan. 9, 1884; House 1849–55; Senate 1869–75.

McLANE, Robert Milligan. June 23, 1815–April 16, 1898; Jan. 9, 1884–March 27, 1885; House 1847–51, 1879–83; Chrmn. Dem. Nat. Comm. 1852–54.

LLOYD, Henry (grandson of Edward Lloyd, greatgrandson of John Henry). Feb. 21, 1852–Dec. 30, 1920; March 27, 1885–Jan. 11, 1888.

JACKSON, Elihu Emory. Nov. 3, 1836–Dec. 27, 1907; Jan. 11, 1888–Jan. 13, 1892.

BROWN, Frank. Aug. 8, 1846–Feb. 3, 1920; Jan. 13, 1892–Jan. 8, 1896.

SMITH, John Walter. Feb. 5, 1845–April 19, 1925; Jan. 10, 1900–Jan. 13, 1904; House 1899–Jan. 12, 1900; Senate March 25, 1908–21.

WARFIELD, Edwin. May 7, 1848–March 31, 1920; Jan. 13, 1904–Jan. 8, 1908.

CROTHERS, Austin Lane. May 17, 1860–May 25, 1912; Jan. 8, 1908–Jan. 10, 1912.

HARRINGTON, Emerson Columbus. March 26, 1864–Dec. 15, 1945; Jan. 12, 1916–Jan. 14, 1920.

RITCHIE, Albert Cabell. Aug. 29, 1876–Feb. 24, 1936; Jan. 14, 1920–Jan. 9, 1935.

O'CONOR, Herbert Romulus. Nov. 17, 1896–March 4, 1960; Jan. 11, 1939–Jan. 3, 1947; Senate 1947–53.

LANE, William Preston Jr. May 12, 1892–Feb. 7, 1967; Jan. 3, 1947–Jan. 10, 1951.

TAWES, John Millard. April 8, 1894–June 25, 1979; Jan. 14, 1959–Jan. 25, 1967.

MANDEL, Marvin. April 19, 1920–; Jan. 7, 1969–June 1977.

LEE, Blair III. May 19, 1916–Oct. 25, 1985; June 1977–Jan. 15, 1979.

MANDEL, Marvin. Jan. 15–Jan. 17, 1979 (for previous term see above).

HUGHES, Harry R. Nov. 13, 1926–; Jan. 17, 1979–Jan. 20, 1987.

SCHAEFER, William Donald. Nov. 2, 1921–; Jan. 21, 1987–1995.

GLENDENING, Parris. June 11, 1942–; 1995–.

MASSACHUSETTS

(ratified the Constitution February 6, 1788)

MORTON, Marcus. Dec. 19, 1784–Feb. 16, 1864; Jan. 18, 1840–Jan. 7, 1841; Jan. 17, 1843–Jan. 3, 1844.

BOUTWELL, George Sewel. Jan. 28, 1818–Feb. 27, 1905; Jan. 11, 1851–Jan. 14, 1853; House 1863–March 12, 1869 (Republican); Senate March 17, 1873–77.

GASTON, William. Oct. 3, 1820–Jan. 19, 1894; Jan. 6, 1875–Jan. 5, 1876.

RUSSELL, William Eustis. Jan. 6, 1857–July 14, 1896; Jan. 7, 1891–Jan. 3, 1894.

DOUGLAS, William Lewis. Aug. 22, 1845–Sept. 17, 1924; Jan. 5, 1905–Jan. 4, 1906.

FOSS, Eugene Noble. Sept. 24, 1858–Sept. 13, 1939; Jan. 5, 1911–Jan. 8, 1914; House March 22, 1910–Jan. 4, 1911.

WALSH, David Ignatius. Nov. 11, 1872–June 11, 1947; Jan. 8, 1914–Jan. 6, 1916; Senate 1919–25, Dec. 6, 1926–47.

ELY, Joseph Buell. Feb. 22, 1881–June 13, 1956; Jan. 8, 1931–Jan. 3, 1935.

CURLEY, James Michael. Nov. 20, 1874–Nov. 12, 1958; Jan. 3, 1935–Jan. 7, 1937; House 1911–Feb. 4, 1914, 1943–47.

HURLEY, Charles Francis. Nov. 24, 1893–March 24, 1946; Jan. 7, 1937–Jan. 5, 1939.

TOBIN, Maurice Joseph. May 22, 1901–July 19, 1953; Jan. 3, 1945–Jan. 2, 1947; Secy. of Labor Aug. 13, 1948–Jan. 20, 1953.

DEVER, Paul Andrew. Jan. 15, 1903–April 11, 1958; Jan. 6, 1949–Jan. 8, 1953.

FURCOLO, Foster. July 29, 1911–; Jan. 3, 1957–Jan. 5, 1961; House 1949–Sept. 30, 1952.

PEABODY, Endicott "Chub." Feb. 15, 1920–; Jan. 3, 1963–Jan. 7, 1965.

DUKAKIS, Michael Stanley. Nov. 3, 1933–; Jan. 2, 1975–Jan. 4, 1979, Jan. 6, 1983–Jan. 3, 1991.

KING, Edward J. May 11, 1925–; Jan. 4, 1979–Jan. 6, 1983.

DUKAKIS, Michael Stanley. Jan. 6, 1983–Jan. 3, 1991 (for previous term see above).

MICHIGAN

(became a state January 26, 1837)

MASON, Stevens Thomson. Oct. 22, 1811–Jan. 4, 1843; Nov. 3, 1835–Jan. 1840.

BARRY, John Stewart. Jan. 29, 1802–Jan. 14, 1870; Jan. 3, 1842–Jan. 5, 1846, Jan. 7, 1850–Jan. 1, 1851.

FELCH, Alpheus. Sept. 28, 1804–June 13, 1896; Jan. 5, 1846–March 3, 1847; Senate 1847–53.

GREENLY, William L. Sept. 18, 1813–Nov. 29, 1883; March 3, 1847–Jan. 3, 1848.

RANSOM, Epaphroditus. Feb. 1787–Nov. 9, 1859; Jan. 3, 1848–Jan. 7, 1850.

BARRY, John Stewart. Jan. 7, 1850–Jan. 1, 1851 (for previous term see above).

McCLELLAND, Robert. Aug. 1, 1807–Aug. 30, 1880; Jan. 1, 1851–March 7, 1853; House 1843–49; Secy. of the Interior March 8, 1853–March 9, 1857.

PARSONS, Andrew. July 22, 1817–June 6, 1855; March 7, 1853–Jan. 3, 1855.

BEGOLE, Josiah William. Jan. 20, 1815–June 5, 1896; Jan. 1, 1883–Jan. 1, 1887; House 1873–75.

WINANS, Edwin Baruch. May 16, 1826–July 4, 1894; Jan. 1, 1891–Jan. 1, 1893; House 1883–87.

FERRIS, Woodbridge Nathan. Jan. 6, 1853–March 23, 1928; Jan. 1, 1913–Jan. 1, 1917; Senate 1923–March 23, 1928.

COMSTOCK, William Alfred. July 2, 1877–June 16, 1949; Jan. 1, 1933–Jan. 1, 1935.

MURPHY, Francis William. April 13, 1890–July 19, 1949; Jan. 1, 1937–Jan. 1, 1939; Atty. Gen. Jan. 17, 1939–Jan. 18, 1940; Assoc. Justice Supreme Court Feb. 5, 1940–July 19, 1949.

VAN WAGONER, Murray Delos. March 18, 1898–June 12, 1986; Jan. 1, 1941–Jan. 1, 1943.

WILLIAMS, Gerhard Mennen. Feb. 23, 1911–Feb. 2, 1988; Jan. 1, 1949–Jan. 2, 1961.

SWAINSON, John Burley. July 30, 1925–May 13, 1994; Jan. 2, 1961–Jan. 1, 1963.

BLANCHARD, James Johnston. Aug. 8, 1942–; Jan. 1, 1983–Jan. 1, 1991; House 1975–83.

MINNESOTA

(became a state May 11, 1858)

SIBLEY, Henry Hastings. Feb. 20, 1811–Feb. 18, 1891; May 24, 1858–Jan. 2, 1860; House (Terr. Del.) Oct. 30, 1848–49 (Wis.), July 7, 1849–53.

LIND, John. March 25, 1854–Sept. 18, 1930; Jan. 2, 1899–Jan. 7, 1901; House 1887–93 (Republican), 1903–05.

JOHNSON, John Albert. July 28, 1861–Sept. 21, 1909; Jan. 4, 1906–Sept. 21, 1909.

HAMMOND, Winfield Scott. Nov. 17, 1863–Dec. 30, 1915; Jan. 7–Dec. 30, 1915; House 1907–Jan. 6, 1915.

MISSISSIPPI

(became a state December 10, 1817)

QUITMAN, John Anthony. Sept. 1, 1799–July 17, 1858; Dec. 3, 1835–Jan. 7, 1836, Jan. 10, 1850–Feb. 3, 1851; House 1855–July 17, 1858.

McNUTT, Alexander Gallatin. Jan. 3, 1802–Oct. 22, 1848; Jan. 8, 1838–Jan. 10, 1842.

TUCKER, Tilghman Mayfield. Feb. 5, 1802–April 3, 1859; Jan. 10, 1842–Jan. 10, 1844; House 1843–45.

BROWN, Albert Gallatin. May 31, 1813–June 12, 1880; Jan. 10, 1844–Jan. 10, 1848; House 1839–41, 1847–53; Senate Jan. 7, 1854–Jan. 12, 1861.

MATTHEWS, Joseph W. 1812–Aug. 27, 1862; Jan. 10, 1848–Jan. 10, 1850.

QUITMAN, John Anthony. Jan. 10, 1850–Feb. 3, 1851 (for previous term see above).

GUION, John Isaac. Nov. 18, 1802–June 26, 1855; Feb. 3–Nov. 4, 1851.

WHITFIELD, James. Dec. 15, 1791–June 25, 1875; Nov. 24, 1851–Jan. 10, 1852.

FOOTE, Henry Stuart. Feb. 28, 1804–May 19, 1880; Jan. 10, 1852–Jan. 5, 1854; Senate 1847–Jan. 8, 1852.

PETTUS, John Jones. Oct. 9, 1813–Jan. 28, 1867; Jan. 5–Jan. 10, 1854, Nov. 21, 1859–Nov. 16, 1863.

McRAE, John Jones. Jan. 10, 1815–May 31, 1868; Jan. 10, 1854–Nov. 16, 1857; Senate Dec. 1, 1851–March 17, 1852; House Dec. 7, 1858–Jan. 12, 1861.

McWILLIE, William. Nov. 17, 1795–March 3, 1869; Nov. 16, 1857–Nov. 21, 1859; House 1849–51.

PETTUS, John Jones. Nov. 21, 1859–Nov. 16, 1863 (for previous term see above).

CLARK, Charles. Feb. 19, 1810–Dec. 18, 1877; Nov. 16, 1863–May 22, 1865.

HUMPHREYS, Benjamin Grubb. Aug. 26, 1808–Dec. 20, 1822; Oct. 16, 1865–June 15, 1868.

STONE, John Marshall. April 30, 1830–March 2, 1900; March 29, 1876–Jan. 29, 1882, Jan. 13, 1890–Jan. 20, 1896.

LOWRY, Robert. March 10, 1831–Jan. 18, 1910; Jan. 29, 1882–Jan. 13, 1890.

STONE, John Marshall. Jan. 13, 1890–Jan. 20, 1896 (for previous term see above).

McLAURIN, Anselm Joseph. March 26, 1848–Dec. 22, 1909; Jan. 20, 1896–Jan. 16, 1900; Senate Feb. 7, 1894–95, 1901–Dec. 22, 1909.

LONGINO, Andrew Houston. May 16, 1855–Feb. 24, 1942; Jan. 16, 1900–Jan. 19, 1904.

VARDAMAN, James Kimble. July 26, 1861–June 25, 1930; Jan. 19, 1904–Jan. 21, 1908; Senate 1913–19.

NOEL, Edmond Favor. March 4, 1856–July 30, 1927; Jan. 21, 1908–Jan. 16, 1912.

BREWER, Earl LeRoy. Aug. 11, 1869–March 10, 1942; Jan. 16, 1912–Jan. 18, 1916.

BILBO, Theodore Gilmore. Oct. 13, 1877–Aug. 21, 1947; Jan. 18, 1916–Jan. 20, 1920, Jan. 17, 1928–Jan. 19, 1932; Senate 1935–Aug. 21, 1947.

RUSSELL, Lee Maurice. Nov. 16, 1875–May 16, 1943; Jan. 20, 1920–Jan. 22, 1924.

WHITFIELD, Henry Lewis. June 20, 1868–March 18, 1927; Jan. 22, 1924–March 18, 1927.

MURPHREE, Herron Dennis. Jan. 6, 1886–Feb. 9, 1949; March 18, 1927–Jan. 17, 1928, Dec. 26, 1943–Jan. 18, 1944.

BILBO, Theodore Gilmore. Jan. 17, 1928–Jan. 19, 1932 (for previous term see above).

CONNER, Martin Sennett "Mike." Aug. 31, 1891–Sept. 16, 1950; Jan. 19, 1932–Jan. 21, 1936.

WHITE, Hugh Lawson. Aug. 19, 1881–Sept. 20, 1965; Jan. 21, 1936–Jan. 16, 1940, Jan. 22, 1952–Jan. 17, 1956.

JOHNSON, Paul Burney (father of Paul Burney Johnson Jr., below). March 23, 1880–Dec. 26, 1943; Jan. 16, 1940–Dec. 26, 1943; House 1919–23.

MURPHREE, Herron Dennis. Dec. 26, 1943–Jan. 18, 1944 (for previous term see above).

BAILEY, Thomas Lowry. Jan. 6, 1888–Nov. 2, 1946; Jan. 18, 1944–Nov. 2, 1946.

WRIGHT, Fielding Lewis. May 16, 1895–May 4, 1956; Nov. 2, 1946–Jan. 22, 1952.

WHITE, Hugh Lawson. Jan. 22, 1952–Jan. 17, 1956 (for previous term see above).

COLEMAN, James Plemon. Jan. 9, 1914–Sept. 28, 1991; Jan. 17, 1956–Jan. 19, 1960.

BARNETT, Ross Robert. Jan. 22, 1898–Nov. 6, 1987–Jan. 19, 1960–Jan. 21, 1964.

JOHNSON, Paul Burney Jr. (son of Paul Burney Johnson, above). Jan. 23, 1916–Oct. 14, 1985; Jan. 21, 1964–Jan. 16, 1968.

WILLIAMS, John Bell. Dec. 4, 1918–March 25, 1983; Jan. 16, 1968–Jan. 18, 1972; House 1947–Jan. 16, 1968.

WALLER, William Lowe. Oct. 21, 1926–; Jan. 18, 1972–Jan. 20, 1976.

FINCH, Charles Clifton. April 4, 1927–April 22, 1986; Jan. 20, 1976–Jan. 22, 1980.

WINTER, William Forrest. Feb. 21, 1923–; Jan. 22, 1980–Jan. 10, 1984.

ALLAIN, William A. Feb. 14, 1928–; Jan. 10, 1984–Jan. 12, 1988.

MABUS, Ray Jr. Oct. 11, 1948–; Jan. 12, 1988–Jan. 14, 1992.

MISSOURI

(became a state August 10, 1821)

DUNKLIN, Daniel. Jan. 14, 1790–July 25, 1844; Nov. 14, 1832–Sept. 13, 1836.

BOGGS, Lilburn W. Dec. 14, 1792–March 14, 1860; Sept. 13, 1836–Nov. 16, 1840.

REYNOLDS, Thomas (brother of John Reynolds of Ill.). March 12, 1796–Feb. 9, 1844; Nov. 16, 1840–Feb. 9, 1844.

MARMADUKE, Meredith Miles (father of John Sappington Marmaduke, brother-in-law of Claiborne Fox Jackson). Aug. 26, 1791–March 26, 1864; Feb. 9–Nov. 20, 1944.

EDWARDS, John Cummins. June 24, 1804–Sept. 14, 1888; Nov. 20, 1844–Nov. 27, 1848; House 1841–43.

KING, Austin Augustus. Sept. 21, 1802–April 22, 1870; Nov. 27, 1848–Jan. 3, 1853; House 1863–65 (Unionist).

PRICE, Sterling. Sept. 20, 1809–Sept. 29, 1867; Jan. 3, 1853–Jan. 5, 1857; House 1846–Aug. 12, 1846.

POLK, Trusten (nephew of Peter Foster Causey of Del.). May 29, 1811–April 16, 1876; Jan. 5–Feb. 27, 1857; Senate 1857–Jan. 10, 1862.

JACKSON, Hancock Lee. May 12, 1796–March 19, 1876; Feb. 27–Oct. 22, 1857.

STEWART, Robert Marcellus. March 12, 1815–Sept. 21, 1871; Oct. 22, 1857–Jan. 3, 1861.

JACKSON, Claiborne Fox (brother-in-law of Meredith Miles Marmaduke, above). April 4, 1806–Dec. 6, 1862; Jan. 3–July 30, 1861.

WOODSON, Silas. May 18, 1819–Oct. 9, 1896; Jan. 8, 1873–Jan. 12, 1875.

HARDIN, Charles Henry. July 15, 1820–July 29, 1892; Jan. 12, 1875–Jan. 8, 1877.

PHELPS, John Smith. Dec. 22, 1814–Nov. 20, 1886; Jan. 8, 1877–Jan. 16, 1881; House 1845–63.

CRITTENDEN, Thomas Theodore (nephew of John Jordan Crittenden of Ky.). Jan. 1, 1832–May 29, 1909; Jan. 10, 1881–Jan. 12, 1885; House 1873–75, 1877–79.

MARMADUKE, John Sappington (son of Meredith Miles Marmaduke, great-grandson of John Breathitt of Ky.). March 14, 1833–Dec. 28, 1887; Jan. 12, 1886–Dec. 28, 1887.

MOREHOUSE, Albert Pickett. July 11, 1835–Sept. 30, 1891; Dec. 28, 1887–Jan. l4, 1889.

FRANCIS, David Rowland. Oct. 1, 1850–Jan. 15, 1927; Jan. 14, 1889–Jan. 9, 1893; Secy. of the Interior Sept. 3, 1896–March 5, 1897.

STONE, William Joel. May 7, 1848–April 14, 1918; Jan. 9, 1893–Jan. 11, 1897; House 1885–91; Senate 1903–April 14, 1918.

STEPHENS, Lawrence Vest "Lon." Dec. 21, 1858–Jan. 10, 1923; Jan. 11, 1897–Jan. 14, 1901.

DOCKERY, Alexander Monroe. Feb. 11, 1845–Dec. 26, 1926; Jan. 14, 1901–Jan. 9, 1905; House 1883–99.

FOLK, Joseph Wingate. Oct. 28, 1869–May 28, 1923; Jan. 9, 1905–Jan. 11, 1909.

MAJOR, Elliot Woolfolk. Oct. 20, 1864–July 9, 1949; Jan. 13, 1913–Jan. 8, 1917.

GARDNER, Frederick D. Nov. 6, 1869–Dec. 18, 1933; Jan. 8, 1917–Jan. 10, 1921.

PARK, Guy Brasfield. June 10, 1872–Oct. 1, 1946; Jan. 9, 1933–Jan. 11, 1937.

STARK, Lloyd Crow. Nov. 23, 1886–Sept. 17, 1972; Jan. 11, 1937–Jan. 13, 1941.

DONNELLY, Philip Matthew. March 6, 1891–Sept. 12, 1961; Jan. 8, 1945–Jan. 10, 1949, Jan. 12, 1953–Jan. 14, 1957.

SMITH, Forrest. Feb. 14, 1886–March 8, 1962; Jan. 10, 1949–Jan. 1953.

DONNELLY, Philip Matthew. Jan. 12, 1953–Jan. 14, 1957 (for previous term see above).

BLAIR, James Thomas Jr. March 15, 1902–July 12, 1962; Jan. 14, 1957–Jan. 9, 1961.

DALTON, John Montgomery. Nov. 9, 1900–July 7, 1972; Jan. 9, 1961–Jan. 11, 1965.

HEARNES, Warren E. July 24, 1923–; Jan. 11, 1965–Jan. 8, 1973.

TEASDALE, Joseph P. March 29, 1936–; Jan. 10, 1977–Jan. 12, 1981.

CARNAHAN, Mel Eugene. Feb. 11, 1934–; Jan. 11, 1993–.

MONTANA

(became a state November 8, 1889)

TOOLE, Joseph Kemp. May 12, 1851–March 11, 1929; Nov. 8, 1889–Jan. 2, 1893, Jan. 7, 1901–April 1, 1908; House (Terr. Del.) 1885–89.

SMITH, Robert Burns. Dec. 29, 1854–Nov. 16, 1908; Jan. 4, 1897–Jan. 7, 1901.

TOOLE, Joseph Kemp. Jan. 7, 1901–April 1, 1908 (for previous term see above).

NORRIS, Edwin Lee. Aug. 16, 1865–April 25, 1924; April 1, 1908–Jan. 5, 1913.

STEWART, Samuel Vernon. Aug. 2, 1872–Sept. 15, 1939; Jan. 6, 1913–Jan. 2, 1921.

ERICKSON, John Edward. March 14, 1863–May 25, 1946; Jan. 5, 1925–March 13, 1933; Senate March 13, 1933–Nov. 6, 1934.

COONEY, Frank Henry. Dec. 31, 1872–Dec. 15, 1935; March 13, 1933–Dec. 15, 1935.

HOLT, William Elmer. Oct. 14, 1884–March 1, 1945; Dec. 16, 1935–Jan. 4, 1937.

AYERS, Roy Elmer. Nov. 9, 1882–May 23, 1955; Jan. 4, 1937–Jan. 6, 1941; House 1933–37.

BONNER, John Woodrow. July 16, 1902–March 28, 1970; Jan. 3, 1949–Jan. 5, 1953.

ANDERSON, Forrest Howard. Jan. 30, 1913–July 20, 1989; Jan. 6, 1969–Jan. 1, 1973.

JUDGE, Thomas Lee. Oct. 12, 1934–; Jan. 1, 1973–Jan. 5, 1981.

SCHWINDEN, Ted. Aug. 31, 1925–; Jan. 5, 1981–Jan. 2, 1989.

NEBRASKA

(became a state March 1, 1867)

BOYD, James E. Sept. 9, 1834–April 30, 1906; Jan. 15–May 5, 1891, Feb. 8, 1892–Jan. 13, 1893.

BOYD, James E. Feb. 8, 1892–Jan. 13, 1893 (for previous term see above).

SHALLENBERGER, Ashton Cockayne. Dec. 23, 1862–Feb. 22, 1938; Jan. 7, 1909–Jan. 5, 1911; House 1901–03, 1915–19, 1923–29, 1931–35.

MOREHEAD, John Henry. Dec. 3, 1861–May 31, 1942; Jan. 9, 1913–Jan. 4, 1917; House 1923–35.

NEVILLE, M. Keith. Feb. 25, 1884–Dec. 4, 1959; Jan. 4, 1917–Jan. 9, 1919.

BRYAN, Charles Wayland. Feb. 10, 1867–March 4, 1945; Jan. 4, 1923–Jan. 8, 1925, Jan. 8, 1931–Jan. 3, 1935.

BRYAN, Charles Wayland. Jan. 8, 1931–Jan. 3, 1935 (for previous term see above).

COCHRAN, Robert LeRoy. Jan. 28, 1886–Feb. 23, 1963; Jan. 3, 1935–Jan. 9, 1941.

BROOKS, Ralph Gilmour. July 6, 1898–Sept. 9, 1960; Jan. 8, 1959–Sept. 9, 1960.

BURNEY, Dwight Willard. Jan. 7, 1892–; Sept. 9, 1960–Jan. 5, 1961.

MORRISON, Frank Brenner. May 20, 1905–; Jan. 5, 1961–Jan. 5, 1967.

EXON, John James. Aug. 9, 1921–; Jan. 7, 1971–Jan. 3, 1979; Senate 1979–.

KERREY, Robert. Aug. 27, 1943–; Jan. 6, 1983–Jan. 9, 1987; Senate 1989–.

NELSON, Earl Benjamin "Ben." May 17, 1941–; Jan. 9, 1991–.

NEVADA

(became a state October 31, 1864)

BRADLEY, Lewis Rice. Feb. 18, 1805–March 21, 1879; Jan. 3, 1871–Jan. 6, 1879.

ADAMS, Jewett William. Aug. 6, 1835–June 18, 1920; Jan. 2, 1883–Jan. 3, 1887.

BOYLE, Emmet Derby. July 26, 1879–Jan. 3, 1926; Jan. 4, 1915–Jan. 1, 1923.

SCRUGHAM, James Graves. Jan. 19, 1880–June 23, 1945; Jan. 1, 1923–Jan. 3, 1927; House 1933–Dec. 7, 1942; Senate Dec. 7, 1942–June 23, 1945.

KIRMAN, Richard Sr. Jan. 14, 1877–Jan. 19, 1959; Jan. 7, 1935–Jan. 2, 1939.

CARVILLE, Edward Peter. May 14, 1885–June 27, 1956; Jan. 2, 1939–July 24, 1945; Senate July 25, 1945–47.

PITTMAN, Vail Montgomery. Sept. 17, 1883–Jan. 29, 1964; July 24, 1945–Jan. 1, 1951.

SAWYER, Grant "Frank." Dec. 14, 1918–; Jan. 5, 1959–Jan. 2, 1967.

O'CALLAGHAN, Donald Neil "Mike." Sept. 10, 1929–; Jan. 4, 1971–Jan. 1, 1979.

BRYAN, Richard Hudson. July 16, 1937–; Jan. 3, 1983–Jan. 3, 1989; Senate 1989–.

MILLER, Robert Joseph "Bob." March 30, 1945–; Jan. 3, 1989–.

NEW HAMPSHIRE

(ratified the Constitution June 21, 1788)

BADGER, William. Jan. 13, 1779–Sept. 21, 1852; June 5, 1834–June 2, 1836.

PAGE, John. May 21, 1787–Sept. 8, 1865; June 5, 1839–June 2, 1842; Senate June 8, 1836–37 (Whig).

HUBBARD, Henry. May 3, 1784–June 5, 1857; June 2, 1842–June 6, 1844; House 1829–35 (Jacksonian); Senate 1835–41 (Jacksonian).

STEELE, John Hardy. Jan. 4, 1789–July 3, 1864; June 6, 1844–June 4, 1846.

WILLIAMS, Jared Warner. Dec. 22, 1796–Sept. 29, 1864; June 1, 1847–June 7, 1849; House 1837–41; Senate Nov. 29, 1853–July 15, 1854.

DINSMOOR, Samuel Jr. May 8, 1799–Feb. 24, 1869; June 7, 1849–June 3, 1852.

MARTIN, Noah. July 26, 1801–May 28, 1863; June 3, 1852–June 8, 1854.

BAKER, Nathaniel Bradley. Sept. 29, 1818–Sept. 11, 1876; June 8, 1854–June 7, 1855.

WESTON, James Adams. Aug. 27, 1827–May 8, 1895; June 14, 1871–June 6, 1872, June 3, 1874–June 10, 1875.

WESTON, James Adams. June 3, 1874–June 10, 1875 (for previous term see above).

FELKER, Samuel Demeritt. April 16, 1859–Nov. 14, 1932; Jan. 2, 1913–Jan. 7, 1915.

BROWN, Fred Herbert. April 12, 1879–Feb. 3, 1955; Jan. 4, 1923–Jan. 1, 1925; Senate 1933–39.

KING, John William. Oct. 10, 1918–; Jan. 3, 1963–Jan. 2, 1969.

GALLEN, Hugh J. July 30, 1924–Dec. 29, 1982; Jan. 4, 1979–Nov. 11, 1982.

MONIER, Robert B. March 5, 1922–; Nov. 11–30, 1982.

GARDNER, William Michael. Oct. 26, 1948–; Nov. 30–Dec. 1, 1982.

NEW JERSEY

(ratified the Constitution December 18, 1787)

VROOM, Peter Dumont. Dec. 12, 1791–Nov. 18, 1873; Nov. 6, 1829–Oct. 26, 1832, Oct. 25, 1833–Oct. 28, 1836; House 1839–41.

VROOM, Peter Dumont. Oct. 25, 1833–Oct. 28, 1836 (for previous term see above).

DICKERSON, Philemon. Jan. 11, 1788–Dec. 10, 1862; Nov. 3, 1836–Oct. 27, 1837; House 1833–Nov. 3, 1836 (Jacksonian), 1839–41 (Democrat).

HAINES, Daniel. Jan. 6, 1801–Jan. 26, 1877; Oct. 27, 1843–Jan. 21, 1845, Jan. 18, 1848–Jan. 20, 1851.

HAINES, Daniel. Jan. 18, 1848–Jan. 20, 1851 (for previous term see above).

FORT, George Franklin. March 1809–April 22, 1872; Jan. 21, 1851–Jan. 17, 1854.

PRICE, Rodman McCamley. May 5, 1816–June 7, 1894; Jan. 17, 1854–Jan. 20, 1857; House 1851–53.

PARKER, Joel. Nov. 24, 1816–Jan. 2, 1888; Jan. 20, 1863–Jan. 16, 1866, Jan. 16, 1872–Jan. 19, 1875.

RANDOLPH, Theodore Fitz. June 24, 1826–Nov. 7, 1883; Jan. 19, 1869–Jan. 16, 1872; Senate 1875–81.

PARKER, Joel. Jan. 16, 1872–Jan. 19, 1875 (for previous term see above).

BEDLE, Joseph Dorsett. Jan. 5, 1821–Oct. 21, 1894; Jan. 19, 1875–Jan. 15, 1878.

McCLELLAN, George Brinton. Dec. 3, 1826–Oct. 29, 1885; Jan. 15, 1878–Jan. 18, 1881.

LUDLOW, George Craig. April 6, 1830–Dec. 18, 1900; Jan. 18, 1881–Jan. 15, 1884.

ABBETT, Leon. Oct. 8, 1836–Dec. 4, 1894; Jan. 15, 1884–Jan. 18, 1887, Jan. 21, 1890–Jan. 17, 1893.

GREEN, Robert Stockton. March 25, 1831–May 7, 1895; Jan. 18, 1887–Jan. 21, 1890; House 1885–Jan. 17, 1887.

ABBETT, Leon. Jan. 21, 1890–Jan. 17, 1893 (for previous term see above).

WERTS, George Theodore. March 24, 1846–Jan. 17, 1910; Jan. 17, 1893–Jan. 21, 1896.

WILSON, Thomas Woodrow. Dec. 28, 1856–Feb. 3, 1924; Jan. 17, 1911–March 1913; President 1913–21.

FIELDER, James Fairman. Feb. 26, 1867–Dec. 2, 1954; March 1–Oct. 28, 1943, Jan. 20, 1914–Jan. 15, 1917.

TAYLOR, Leon R. Oct. 26, 1883 April 1, 1924; Oct. 28, 1913–Jan. 20, 1914.

FIELDER, James Fairman. Jan. 20, 1914–Jan. 15, 1917 (for previous term see above).

EDWARDS, Edward Irving. Dec. 1, 1863–Jan. 26, 1931; Jan. 20, 1920–Jan. 15, 1923; Senate 1923–29.

SILZER, George Sebastian. April 14, 1870–Oct. 16, 1940; Jan. 15, 1923–Jan. 19, 1926.

MOORE, Arthur Harry. July 3, 1879–Nov. 18, 1952; Jan. 19, 1926–Jan. 15, 1929, Jan. 19, 1932–Jan. 3, 1935, Jan. 18, 1938–Jan. 21, 1941; Senate 1935–Jan. 17, 1938.

MOORE, Arthur Harry. Jan. 19, 1932–Jan. 3, 1935 (for previous term see above).

MOORE, Arthur Harry. Jan. 18, 1938–Jan. 21, 1941 (for previous terms see above).

EDISON, Charles. Aug. 3, 1890–July 31, 1969; Jan. 21, 1941–Jan. 18, 1944; Secy. of the Navy Jan. 2–June 24, 1940.

MEYNER, Robert Baumle. July 3, 1908–May 27, 1990; Jan. 19, 1954–Jan. 16, 1962.

HUGHES, Richard Joseph. Aug. 10, 1909–Dec. 7, 1992; Jan. 16, 1962–Jan. 25, 1970.

BYRNE, Brendan Thomas. April 1, 1924–; Jan. 15, 1974–Jan. 19, 1982.

FLORIO, James Joseph. Aug. 29, 1937–; Jan. 16, 1990–Jan. 18, 1994; House 1975–Jan. 16, 1990.

NEW MEXICO

(became a state January 6, 1912)

McDONALD, William C. July 25, 1858–April 11, 1918; Jan. 6, 1912–Jan. 1, 1917.

DE BACA, Ezequiel Cabeza. Nov. 1, 1864–Feb. 18, 1917; Jan. 1–Feb. 18, 1917.

HINKLE, James Fielding. Oct. 20, 1862–March 26, 1951; Jan. 1, 1923–Jan. 1, 1925.

HANNETT, Arthur Thomas. Feb. 17, 1884–March 18, 1966; Jan. 1, 1925–Jan. 1, 1927.

SELIGMAN, Arthur. June 14, 1871–Sept. 25, 1933; Jan. 1, 1931–Sept. 25, 1933.

HOCKENHULL, Andrew W. Jan. 16, 1877–June 20, 1974; Sept. 25, 1933–Jan. 1, 1935.

TINGLEY, Clyde. Jan. 5, 1883–Dec. 24, 1960; Jan. 1, 1935–Jan. 1, 1939.

MILES, John Esten. July 28, 1884–Oct. 7, 1971; Jan. 1, 1939–Jan. 1, 1943; House 1949–51.

DEMPSEY, John Joseph. June 22, 1879–March 11, 1958; Jan. 1, 1943–Jan. 1, 1947; House 1935–41, 1951–March 11, 1958.

MABRY, Thomas Jewett. Oct. 17, 1884–Dec. 23, 1962; Jan. 1, 1947–Jan. 1, 1951.

SIMMS, John Field Jr. Dec. 18, 1916–April 11, 1975; Jan. 1, 1955–Jan. 1, 1957.

BURROUGHS, John. April 7, 1907–May 21, 1978; Jan. 1, 1959–Jan. 1, 1961.

CAMPBELL, John M. "Jack." Sept. 10, 1916–; Jan. 1, 1963–Jan. 1, 1967.

KING, Bruce. April 6, 1924–; Jan. 1, 1971–Jan. 1, 1975, Jan. 1, 1979–Jan. 1, 1983, Jan. 1, 1991–.

APODACA, Raymond S. "Jerry." Oct. 3, 1934–; Jan. 1, 1975–Jan. 1, 1979.

KING, Bruce. Jan. 1, 1979–Jan. 1, 1983 (for previous term see above).

ANAYA, Toney. April 29, 1941–; Jan. 1, 1983–Jan. 1, 1987.

KING, Bruce. Jan. 1, 1991–1995 (for previous terms see above).

NEW YORK

(ratified the Constitution July 26, 1788)

VAN BUREN, Martin (half-brother of Rep. James Isaac Van Alen). Dec. 5, 1782–July 24, 1862; Jan. 1–March 12, 1829; Senate 1821–Dec. 20, 1828 (no party); Secy. of State March 28, 1829–March 23, 1831; Vice President 1833–37 (Democrat); President 1837–41 (Democrat).

BOUCK, William C. Jan. 7, 1786–April 19, 1859; Jan. 1, 1843–Jan. 1, 1845.

SEYMOUR, Horatio. May 31, 1810–Feb. 12, 1886; Jan. 1, 1853–Jan. 1, 1855, Jan. 11, 1863–Jan. 1, 1865.

SEYMOUR, Horatio. Jan. 1, 1863–Jan. 1, 1865 (for previous term see above).

HOFFMAN, John Thompson. Jan. 10, 1828–March 24, 1888; Jan. 1, 1869–Jan. 1, 1873.

TILDEN, Samuel Jones. Feb. 9, 1814–Aug. 4, 1886; Jan. 1, 1875–Jan. 1, 1877.

ROBINSON, Lucius. Nov. 4, 1810–March 23, 1891; Jan. 1, 1877–Jan. 1, 1880.

CLEVELAND, Stephen Grover. March 18, 1837–June 24, 1908; Jan. 1, 1883–Jan. 6, 1885; President 1885–89, 1893–97.

HILL, David Bennett. Aug. 29, 1843–Oct. 20, 1910; Jan. 6, 1885–Jan. 1, 1892; Senate Jan. 7, 1892–97.

FLOWER, Roswell Pettibone. Aug. 7, 1835–May 12, 1899; Jan. 1, 1892–Jan. 1, 1895; House Nov. 8, 1881–83, 1889–Sept. 16, 1891.

DIX, John Alden. Dec. 25, 1860–April 9, 1928; Jan. 1, 1911–Jan. 1, 1913.

SULZER, William. March 18, 1863–Nov. 6, 1941; Jan. 1–Oct. 17, 1913; House 1895–Dec. 31, 1912.

GLYNN, Martin Henry. Sept. 27, 1871–Dec. 14, 1924; Oct. 17, 1913–Jan. 1, 1915; House 1899–1901.

SMITH, Alfred Emanuel. Dec. 30, 1873–Oct. 4, 1944; Jan. 1, 1919–Jan. 1, 1921, Jan. 1, 1923–Jan. 1, 1929.

SMITH, Alfred Emanuel. Jan. 1, 1923–Jan. 1, 1929 (for previous term see above).

ROOSEVELT, Franklin Delano. Jan. 30, 1882–April 12, 1945; Jan. 1, 1929–Jan. 1, 1933; President 1933–April 12, 1945.

LEHMAN, Herbert Henry. March 28, 1878–Dec. 5, 1963; Jan. 1, 1933–Dec. 3, 1942; Senate Nov. 9, 1949–57.

POLETTI, Charles. July 2, 1903–; Dec. 3, 1942–Jan. 1, 1943.

HARRIMAN, William Averell. Nov. 15, 1891–July 7, 1986; Jan. 1, 1955–Jan. 1, 1959.

CAREY, Hugh Leo. April 11, 1919–; Jan. 1, 1975–Jan. 1, 1983; House 1961–Dec. 31, 1974.

CUOMO, Mario Matthew. June 15, 1932–; Jan. 1, 1983–1995.

NORTH CAROLINA

(ratified the Constitution November 21, 1789)

STOKES, Montfort. March 12, 1762–Nov. 4, 1842; Dec. 18, 1830–Dec. 6, 1832; Senate Dec. 4, 1816–23.

SPAIGHT, Richard Dobbs Jr. 1796–Nov. 2, 1850; Dec. 10, 1835–Dec. 31, 1836; House 1823–25 (no party).

REID, David Settle. April 19, 1813–June 19, 1891; Jan. 1, 1851–Dec. 6, 1854; House 1843–47; Senate Dec. 6, 1854–59.

WINSLOW, Warren. Jan. 1, 1810–Aug. 16, 1862; (Acting) Dec. 6, 1854–Jan. 1, 1855; House 1855–61.

BRAGG, Thomas. Nov. 9, 1810–Jan. 21, 1872; Jan. 1, 1855–Jan. 1, 1859; Senate 1859–March 6, 1861.

ELLIS, John Willis. Nov. 23, 1820–July 7, 1861; Jan. 1, 1859–July 7, 1861.

CLARK, Henry Toole. Feb. 7, 1808–April 14, 1874; July 7, 1861–Sept. 8, 1862.

VANCE, Zebulon Baird. May 13, 1830–April 14, 1894; Sept. 8, 1862–May 29, 1865, Jan. 1, 1877–Feb. 5, 1879; House Dec. 7, 1858–61; Senate 1879–April 14, 1894.

WORTH, Jonathan. Nov. 18, 1802–Sept. 6, 1869; Dec. 15, 1865–July 1, 1868.

VANCE, Zebulon Baird. Jan. 1, 1877–Feb. 6, 1879 (for previous term see above).

JARVIS, Thomas Jordan. Jan. 18, 1836–June 17, 1915; Feb. 5, 1879–Jan. 21, 1885; Senate April 19, 1894–Jan. 23, 1895.

SCALES, Alfred Moore. Nov. 26, 1827–Feb. 9, 1892; Jan. 21, 1885–Jan. 17, 1889; House 1857–59, 1875–Dec. 30, 1884.

FOWLE, Daniel Gould. March 3, 1831–April 7, 1891; Jan. 17, 1889–April 7, 1891.

HOLT, Thomas Michael. July 15, 1831–April 11, 1896; April 8, 1891–Jan. 18, 1893.

CARR, Elias. Feb. 25, 1839–July 22, 1900; Jan. 18 1893–Jan. 12, 1897.

AYCOCK, Charles Brantley. Nov. 1, 1859–April 4, 1912; Jan. 15, 1901–Jan. 11, 1905.

GLENN, Robert Brodnax. Aug. 11, 1854–May 16, 1920; Jan. 11, 1905–Jan. 12, 1909.

KITCHIN, William Walton. Oct. 9, 1866–Nov. 9, 1924; Jan. 12, 1909–Jan. 15, 1913; House 1897–Jan. 11, 1909.

CRAIG, Locke. Aug. 16, 1860–June 9, 1924; Jan. 15, 1913–Jan. 11, 1917.

BICKETT, Thomas Walter. Feb. 28, 1869–Dec. 28, 1921; Jan. 11, 1917–Jan. 12, 1921.

MORRISON, Cameron. A. Oct. 5, 1869–Aug. 20 1953; Jan. 12, 1921–Jan. 14, 1925; Senate Dec. 13, 1930–Dec. 4, 1932; House 1943–45.

MELEAN, Angus Wilton. April 20, 1870–June 21, 1935; Jan. 14, 1925–Jan. 11, 1929.

GARDNER, Oliver Max (brother-in-law of Clyde Roark Hoey, below). March 22, 1882–Feb. 6, 1947; Jan. 11, 1929–Jan. 5, 1933.

EHRINGHAUS, John Christoph Blocher. Feb. 5, 1882–July 31, 1949; Jan. 5, 1933–Jan. 7, 1937.

HOEY, Clyde Roark (brother-in-law of Oliver Max Gardner, above). Dec. 11, 1877–May 12, 1954; Jan. 7, 1937–Jan. 9, 1941; House Dec. 16, 1919–21; Senate 1945–May 12, 1954.

BROUGHTON, Joseph Melville. Nov. 17, 1888–March 6, 1949; Jan. 9, 1941–Jan. 4, 1945; Senate Dec. 31, 1948–March 6, 1949.

CHERRY, Robert Gregg. Oct. 17, 1891–June 25, 1957; Jan. 4, 1945–Jan. 6, 1949.

SCOTT, William Kerr (father of Robert Walter Scott, below). April 17, 1896–April 16, 1958; Jan. 6, 1949–Jan. 8, 1953; Senate Nov. 29, 1954–April 16, 1958.

UMSTEAD, William Bradley. May 13, 1895–Nov. 7, 1954; Jan. 8, 1953–Nov. 7, 1954; House 1933–39; Senate Dec. 18, 1946–Dec. 30, 1948.

HODGES, Luther Hartwell. March 9, 1898–Oct. 6, 1974; Nov. 7, 1954–Jan. 5, 1961; Secy. of Commerce Jan. 21, 1961–Jan. 15, 1965.

SANFORD, Terry. Aug. 20, 1917–; Jan. 5, 1961–Jan. 8, 1965; Senate Nov. 4, 1986–.

MOORE, Daniel Killian. April 2, 1906–Sept. 7, 1986; Jan. 8, 1965–Jan. 3, 1969.

SCOTT, Robert Walter (son of William Kerr Scott, above). June 13, 1929–; Jan. 3, 1969–Jan. 5, 1973.

HUNT, James Baxter Jr. May 16, 1937–; Jan. 8, 1977–Jan. 5, 1985, Jan. 9, 1993–.

HUNT, James Baxter Jr. Jan. 9, 1993– (for previous term see above).

NORTH DAKOTA

(became a state November 2, 1889)

BURKE, John. Feb. 25, 1859–May 14, 1937; Jan. 9, 1907–Jan. 8, 1913.

MOODIE, Thomas Hilliard. May 26, 1878–March 3, 1948; Jan. 7–Feb. 2, 1935.

MOSES, John. June 12, 1885–March 3, 1945; Jan. 5, 1939–Jan. 4, 1945; Senate Jan. 3–March 3, 1945.

GUY, William Lewis. Sept. 30, 1919–; Jan. 4, 1961–Jan. 2, 1973.

LINK, Arthur Albert. May 24, 1914–; Jan. 2, 1973–Jan. 7, 1981; House 1971–73.

SINNER, George. May 29, 1928–; Jan. 8, 1985–Jan. 5, 1993.

OHIO

(became a state March 1, 1803)

SHANNON, Wilson. Feb. 24, 1802–Aug. 30, 1877; Dec. 13, 1838–Dec. 16, 1840, Dec. 14, 1842–April 15, 1844, Aug. 10, 1855–Aug. 18, 1856 (Kansas Terr.); House 1853–55.

SHANNON, Wilson. Dec. 14, 1842–April 15, 1844 (for previous term see above).

BARTLEY, Thomas Welles. Feb. 11, 1812–June 20, 1885; April 15–Dec. 3, 1844.

WOOD, Reuben. 1792–Oct. 1, 1864; Dec. 12, 1850–July 13, 1853.

MEDILL, William. Feb. 1802–Sept. 2, 1865; July 13, 1853–Jan. 14, 1856; House 1839–43.

ALLEN, William. Dec. 18 or Dec. 27, 1803–July 11, 1879; Jan.

12, 1874–Jan. 10, 1876; House 1833–35 (Jacksonian); Senate 1837–49 (Democrat).

BISHOP, Richard Moore. Nov. 4, 1812–March 2, 1893; Jan. 14, 1878–Jan. 12, 1880.

HOADLY, George. July 31, 1826–Aug. 26, 1902; Jan. 14, 1884–Jan. 11, 1886.

CAMPBELL, James Edwin. July 7, 1843–Dec. 18, 1924; Jan. 13, 1890–Jan. 11, 1892; House Jan. 20, 1884–89.

PATTISON, John M. June 13, 1847–June 18, 1906; Jan. 8–June 18, 1906; House 1891–93.

HARMON, Judson. Feb. 3, 1846–Feb. 22, 1927; Jan. 11, 1909–Jan. 13, 1913.

COX, James Middleton. March 31, 1870–July 15, 1957; Jan. 13, 1913–Jan. 11, 1915, Jan. 8, 1917–Jan. 10, 1921; House 1909–Jan. 12, 1913.

COX, James Middleton. Jan. 8, 1917–Jan. 10, 1921 (for previous term see above).

DONAHEY, Alvin Victor. July 7, 1871–April 8, 1946; Jan. 8, 1923–Jan. 14, 1929; Senate 1935–41.

WHITE, George. Aug. 21, 1872–Dec. 15, 1953; Jan. 12, 1931–Jan. 14, 1935; House 1911–15, 1917–19; Chrmn. Dem. Nat. Comm. 1920–21.

DAVEY, Martin Luther. July 25, 1884–March 31, 1946; Jan. 14, 1935–Jan. 9, 1939; House Nov. 5, 1918–21, 1923–29.

LAUSCHE, Frank John. Nov. 14, 1895–April 21, 1990; Jan. 8, 1945–Jan. 13, 1947, Jan. 10, 1949–Jan. 3, 1957; Senate 1957–69.

LAUSCHE, Frank John. Jan. 10, 1949–Jan. 3, 1957 (for previous term see above).

DI SALLE, Michael Vincent. Jan. 6, 1908–Sept. 16, 1981; Jan. 12, 1959–Jan. 14, 1963.

GILLIGAN, John Joyce. March 22, 1921–; Jan. 11, 1971–Jan. 13, 1975; House 1965–67.

CELESTE, Richard F. Nov. 11, 1937–; Jan. 10, 1983–Jan. 14, 1991.

OKLAHOMA

(became a state November 16, 1907)

HASKEL, Charles Nathaniel. March 13, 1860–July 6, 1933; Nov. 16, 1907–Jan. 9, 1911.

CRUCE, Lee. July 8, 1863–Jan. 16, 1933; Jan. 9, 1911–Jan. 11, 1915.

WILLIAMS, Robert Lee. Dec. 20, 1868–April 10, 1948; Jan. 11, 1915–Jan. 13, 1919.

ROBERTSON, James Brooks Ayers. March 15, 1871–March 7, 1938; Jan. 13, 1919–Jan. 8, 1923.

WALTON, John Calloway "Jack." March 6, 1881–Nov. 25, 1949; Jan. 8–Nov. 19, 1923.

TRAPP, Martin Edwin. April 19, 1877–July 27, 1951; Nov. 19, 1923–Jan. 10, 1927.

JOHNSTON, Henry Simpson. Dec. 30, 1870–Jan. 7, 1965; Jan. 10, 1927–March 20, 1929.

HOLLOWAY, William Judson. Dec. 15, 1888–Jan. 28, 1970; March 20, 1929–Jan. 12, 1931.

MURRAY, William Henry David (father of Johnston Murray, below). Nov. 21, 1869–Oct. 15, 1956; Jan. 12, 1931–Jan. 14, 1935; House 1913–17.

MARLAND, Ernest Whitworth. May 8, 1874–Oct. 3, 1941; Jan. 14, 1935–Jan. 9, 1939; House 1933–35.

PHILLIPS, Leon Chase. Dec. 9, 1890–March 27, 1958; Jan. 9, 1939–Jan. 11, 1943.

KERR, Robert Samuel. Sept. 11, 1896–Jan. 1, 1963; Jan. 11, 1943–Jan. 13, 1947; Senate 1949–Jan. 1, 1963,

TURNER, Roy Joseph. Nov. 6, 1894–June 11, 1973; Jan. 13, 1947–Jan. 8, 1951.

MURRAY, Johnston (son of William Henry David Murray, above). July 21, 1902–April 16, 1974; Jan. 8, 1951–Jan. 10, 1955.

GARY, Raymond Dancel. Jan. 21, 1908–Dec. 11, 1993; Jan. 10, 1955–Jan. 19, 1959.

EDMONDSON, James Howard. Sept. 27, 1925–Nov. 17, 1971; Jan. 12, 1959–Jan. 6, 1963; Senate Jan. 7, 1963–Nov. 3, 1964.

NIGH, George Patterson. June 9, 1927–; Jan. 6–Jan. 14, 1963, Jan. 3, 1979–Jan. 12, 1987.

HALL, David. Oct. 20, 1930–; Jan. 11, 1971–Jan. 13, 1975.

BOREN, David Lyle. April 21, 1941–; Jan. 13, 1975–Jan. 3, 1979; Senate 1979–.

NIGH, George Patterson. Jan. 3, 1979–Jan. 12, 1987 (for previous term see above).

WALTERS, David. Nov. 20, 1951–; Jan. 14, 1991–1995.

OREGON

(became a state February 14, 1859)

WHITEAKER, John. May 4, 1820–Oct. 2, 1902; March 3, 1859–Sept. 10, 1862; House 1879–81.

GROVER, La Fayette. Nov. 29, 1823–May 10, 1911; Sept. 14, 1870–Feb. 1, 1877; House Feb. 15–March 13, 1859; Senate 1877–83.

CHADWICK, Stephen Fowler. Dec. 25, 1825–Jan. 15, 1895; Feb. 1, 1877–Sept. 11, 1878.

THAYER, William Wallace. July 15, 1827–Oct. 15, 1899; Sept. 11, 1878–Sept. 13, 1882.

CHAMBERLAIN, George Earle. Jan. 1, 1854–July 9, 1928; Jan. 14, 1903–Feb. 28, 1909; Senate 1909–21.

WEST, Oswald. May 20, 1873–Aug. 22, 1960; Jan. 10, 1911–Jan. 12, 1915.

PIERCE, Walter Marcus. May 30, 1861–March 27, 1954; Jan. 8, 1923–Jan. 10, 1927; House 1933–43.

MARTIN, Charles Henry. Oct. 1, 1863–Sept. 22, 1946; Jan. 14, 1935–Jan. 9, 1939; House 1931–35.

HOLMES, Robert Denison. May 11, 1909–June 6, 1976; Jan. 14, 1957–Jan. 12, 1959.

STRAUB, Robert William. May 6, 1920–; Jan. 13, 1975–Jan. 8, 1979.

GOLDSCHMIDT, Neil. June 16, 1940–; Jan. 12, 1987–Jan. 14, 1991; Secy. of Transportation July 27, 1979–Jan. 20, 1981.

ROBERTS, Barbara. Dec. 21, 1936–; Jan. 14, 1991–1995.

KITZHABER, John. March 5, 1947–; 1995–.

PENNSYLVANIA

(ratified the Constitution December 12, 1787)

PORTER, David Rittenhouse. Oct. 31, 1788–Aug. 6, 1867; Jan. 15, 1839–Jan. 21, 1845.

SHUNK, Francis Rawn. Aug. 7, 1788–July 20, 1848; Jan. 21, 1845–July 9, 1848.

BIGLER, William (brother of John Bigler of Calif.). Jan. 1, 1814–Aug. 9, 1880; Jan. 20, 1852–Jan. 16, 1855; Senate Jan. 14, 1856–61.

PACKER, William Fisher. April 2, 1807–Sept. 27, 1870; Jan. 19, 1858–Jan. 15, 1861.

PATTISON, Robert Emory. Dec. 8, 1850–Aug. 1, 1904; Jan. 16, 1883–Jan. 18, 1887, Jan. 20, 1891–Jan. 15, 1895.

PATTISON, Robert Emory. Jan. 20, 1891–Jan. 15, 1895 (for previous term see above).

EARLE, George Howard III. Dec. 5, 1890–Dec. 30, 1974; Jan. 15, 1935–Jan. 17, 1939.

LEADER, George Michael. Jan. 17, 1918–; Jan. 18, 1955–Jan. 20, 1959.

LAWRENCE, David Leo. June 18, 1889–Nov. 21, 1966; Jan. 20, 1959–Jan. 15, 1963.

SHAPP, Milton Jerrold. June 25, 1912–; Jan. 19, 1971–Jan. 16, 1979.

CASEY, Robert Patrok. Jan. 9, 1932–; Jan. 20, 1987–1995.

RHODE ISLAND

(ratified the Constitution May 29, 1790)

FRANCIS, John Brown. May 31, 1791–Aug. 9, 1864; May 1, 1833–May 2, 1838; Senate Jan. 25, 1844–45 (Whig).

ALLEN, Philip. Sept. 1, 1785–Dec. 16, 1865; May 6, 1851–July 20, 1853; Senate July 20, 1853–59.

DIMOND, Francis M. 1796–April 23, 1859; July 20, 1853–May 2, 1854.

DAVIS, John William. March 7, 1826–Jan. 26, 1907; May 31, 1887–May 29, 1888, May 27, 1890–May 26, 1891.

DAVIS, John William. May 27, 1890–May 26, 1891 (for previous term see above).

GARVIN, Lucius Fayette Clark. Nov. 13, 1841–Oct. 22, 1922; Jan. 6, 1903–Jan. 3, 1905.

HIGGINS, James Henry. Jan. 22, 1876–Sept. 16, 1927; Jan. 1, 1907–Jan. 5, 1909.

FLYNN, William Smith. Aug. 14, 1885–April 6, 1966; Jan. 2, 1923–Jan. 6, 1925.

GREEN, Theodore Francis. Oct. 2, 1867–May 19, 1966; Jan. 3, 1933–Jan. 5, 1937; Senate 1937–61.

QUINN, Robert Emmet. April 2, 1894–May 20, 1975; Jan. 5, 1937–Jan. 3, 1939.

McGRATH, James Howard. Nov. 28, 1903–Sept. 2, 1966; Jan. 7, 1941–Oct. 6, 1945; Senate 1947–Aug. 23, 1949; Chrmn. Dem. Nat. Comm. 1947–49; Atty. Gen. Aug. 24, 1949–April 7, 1952.

PASTORE, John Orlando. March 17, 1907–; Oct. 6, 1945–Dec. 19, 1950; Senate Dec. 19, 1950–Dec. 28, 1976.

McKIERNAN, John Sammon. Oct. 15, 1911–; Dec. 19, 1950–Jan. 2, 1951.

ROBERTS, Dennis Joseph. April 8, 1903–June 30, 1994; Jan. 2, 1951–Jan. 6, 1959.

NOTTE, John Anthony Jr. May 3, 1909–March 7, 1983; Jan. 3, 1961–Jan. 1, 1963.

LICHT, Frank. March 13, 1916–; Jan. 7, 1969–Jan. 2, 1973.

NOEL, Philip William. June 6, 1931–; Jan. 2, 1973–Jan. 4, 1977.

GARRAHY, John Joseph. Nov. 26, 1930–; Jan. 4, 1977–Jan. 1, 1985.

SUNDLUN, Bruce. Jan. 15, 1920–; Jan. 1, 1991–1995.

SOUTH CAROLINA

(ratified the Constitution May 23, 1788)

MILLER, Stephen Decatur. May 8, 1787–March 8, 1838; Dec. 10, 1828–Dec. 9, 1830; House Jan. 2, 1817–19 (no party); Senate 1831–March 2, 1833 (Nullifier).

HENAGAN, Barnabas Kelet. June 7, 1798–Jan. 10, 1855; April 7–Dec. 10, 1840.

HAMMOND, James Henry. Nov. 15, 1807–Nov. 13, 1864; Dec. 8, 1842–Dec. 7, 1844; House 1835–Feb. 26, 1836 (Nullifier); Senate Dec. 7, 1857–Nov. 11, 1860 (Democrat).

AIKEN, William. Jan. 28, 1806–Sept. 7, 1887; Dec. 7, 1844–Dec. 8, 1846; House 1851–57.

JOHNSON, David. Oct. 3, 1782–Jan. 7, 1855; Dec. 8, 1846–Dec. 12, 1848.

SEABROOK, Whitemarsh Benjamin. June 30, 1792–April 16, 1855; Dec. 12, 1848–Dec. 13, 1850.

ALLSTON, Robert Francis Withers. April 21, 1801–April 7, 1864; Dec. 9, 1856–Dec. 10, 1858.

HAMPTON Wade. March 28, 1818–April 11, 1902; Dec. 14, 1876–Feb. 26, 1879; Senate 1879–91.

SIMPSON, William Dunlap. Oct. 27, 1823–Dec. 26, 1890; Feb. 26, 1879–Sept. 1, 1880.

JETER, Thomas Bothwell. Oct. 13, 1827–May 20, 1883; Sept. 1–Nov. 30, 1880.

HAGOOD, Johnson. Feb. 21, 1829–Jan. 4, 1898; Nov. 30, 1880–Dec. 6, 1882.

THOMPSON, Hugh Smith. Jan. 24, 1836–Nov. 20, 1904; Dec. 5, 1882–July 10, 1886.

SHEPPARD, John Calhoun. July 5, 1850–Oct. 17, 1931; July 10–Nov. 30, 1886.

RICHARDSON, John Peter III (son of John Peter Richardson II, great-nephew of James Burchill Richardson, second cousin of Richard Ivine Manning I). Sept. 25, 1831–July 6, 1899; Nov. 30, 1886–Dec. 4, 1890.

TILLMAN, Benjamin Ryan. Aug. 11, 1847–July 3, 1918; Dec. 4, 1890–Dec. 4, 1894; Senate 1895–July 3, 1918.

EVANS, John Gary. Oct. 16, 1863–June 27, 1942; Dec. 4, 1894–Jan. 18, 1897.

ELLERBE, William Haselden. April 7, 1862–June 2, 1899; Jan. 18, 1897–June 2, 1899.

McSWEENEY, Miles Benjamin. April 18, 1855–Sept. 29, 1909; June 2, 1899–Jan. 20, 1903.

HEYWARD, Duncan Clinch. June 24, 1864–Jan. 23, 1943; Jan. 20, 1903–Jan. 15, 1907.

ANSEL, Martin Frederick. Dec. 12, 1850–Aug. 24, 1945; Jan. 15, 1907–Jan. 17, 1911.

BLEASE, Coleman Livingston. Oct. 8, 1868–Jan. 19, 1942; Jan. 17, 1911–Jan. 14, 1915; Senate 1925–31.

SMITH, Charles Aurelius. Jan. 22, 1861–April 1, 1916; Jan. 14–Jan. 19, 1915.

MANNING, Richard Irvine III (grandson of Richard Irvine Manning I, nephew of John Laurence Manning, great-great-nephew of James Burchill Richardson). Aug. 15, 1859–Sept. 11, 1931; Jan. 19, 1915–Jan. 21, 1919.

COOPER, Robert Archer. June 12, 1874–Aug. 7, 1953; Jan. 21, 1919–May 20, 1922.

HARVEY, Wilson Godfrey. Sept. 8, 1866–Oct. 7, 1932; May 20, 1922–Jan. 16, 1923.

McLEOD, Thomas Gordon. Dec. 17, 1868–Dec. 11, 1932; Jan. 16, 1923–Jan. 18, 1927.

RICHARDS, John Gardiner. Sept. 11, 1864–Oct. 9, 1941; Jan. 18, 1927–Jan. 20, 1931.

BLACKWOOD, Ibra Charles. Nov. 21, 1878–Feb. 12, 1936; Jan. 20, 1931–Jan. 15, 1935.

JOHNSTON, Olin Dewitt Talmadge. Nov. 18, 1896–April 18, 1965; Jan. 15, 1935–Jan. 17, 1939, Jan. 19, 1943–Jan. 2, 1945; Senate 1945–April 18, 1965.

MAYBANK, Burnet Rhett. March 7, 1899–Sept. 1, 1954; Jan. 17, 1939–Nov. 4, 1941; Senate Nov. 5, 1941–Sept. 1, 1954.

HARLEY, Joseph Emile. Sept. 14, 1880–Feb. 27, 1942; Nov. 4, 1941–Feb. 27, 1942.

JEFFRIES, Richard Manning. Feb. 27, 1889–April 20, 1964; March 2, 1942–Jan. 19, 1943.

JOHNSTON, Olin Dewitt Talmadge. Jan. 19, 1943–Jan. 2, 1945 (for previous term see above).

WILLIAMS, Ransome Judson. Jan. 4, 1892–Jan. 7, 1970; Jan. 2, 1945–Jan. 21, 1947.

THURMOND, James Strom. Dec. 5, 1902–; Jan. 21, 1947–Jan. 16, 1951; Senate Dec. 24, 1954–April 4, 1956 (Democrat), Nov. 7, 1956–; (Nov. 1, 1956–Sept. 16, 1964 Democrat, Sept. 16, 1964–Republican); elected Pres. pro tempore Jan. 5, 1981.

BYRNES, James Francis. May 2, 1879–April 9, 1972; Jan. 16, 1951–Jan. 18, 1955; House 1911–25; Senate 1931–July 8, 1941; Assoc. Justice Supreme Court July 8, 1941–Oct. 3, 1942; Secy. of State July 3, 1945–Jan. 21, 1947.

TIMMERMAN, George Bell Jr. Aug. 12, 1912–; Jan. 18, 1955–Jan. 20, 1959.

HOLLINGS, Ernest Frederick. Jan. 1, 1922–; Jan. 20, 1959–Jan. 15, 1963; Senate Nov. 9, 1966–.

RUSSELL, Donald Stuart. Feb. 22, 1906–; Jan. 15, 1963–April 22, 1965; Senate April 22, 1965–Nov. 8, 1966.

McNAIR, Robert Evander. Dec. 14, 1923–; April 22, 1965–Jan. 19, 1971.

WEST, John Carl. Aug. 27, 1922–; Jan. 19, 1971–Jan. 21, 1975.

RILEY, Richard Wilson. Jan. 2, 1933–; Jan. 10, 1979–Jan. 14, 1987; Secy. of Education Jan. 22, 1993–.

CAMPBELL, Carroll Ashmore Jr. July 24, 1940–; Jan. 14, 1987–1995; House 1979–87.

SOUTH DAKOTA

(became a state November 2, 1889)

BULOW, William John. Jan. 13, 1869–Feb. 26, 1960; Jan. 4, 1927–Jan. 6, 1931; Senate 1931–43.

BERRY, Thomas Matthew. April 23, 1879–Oct. 30, 1951; Jan. 3, 1933–Jan. 5, 1937.

HERSETH, Ralph E. July 2, 1909–Jan. 24, 1969; Jan. 6, 1959–Jan. 3, 1961.

KNEIP, Richard Francis. Jan. 7, 1933–March 9, 1987; Jan. 5, 1971–July 24, 1978.

WOLLMAN, Harvey L. May 14, 1935–; July 24, 1978–Jan. 1, 1979.

TENNESSEE

(became a state June 1, 1796)

CARROLL, William. March 3, 1788–March 22, 1844; Oct. 1, 1821–Oct. 1, 1827 (Democratic Republican), Oct. 1, 1829–Oct. 12, 1835.

HOUSTON, Samuel (father of Rep. Andrew Jackson Houston, cousin of Rep. David Hubbard). March 2, 1793–July 26, 1863; Oct. 1, 1827–April 16, 1829, Dec. 21, 1859–March 16, 1861 (Texas); House 1823–27 (no party); Senate Feb. 21, 1846–59 (Democrat Texas).

CARROLL William. Oct. 1, 1829–Oct. 12, 1835 (for previous term see above).

POLK, James Knox (brother of Rep. William Hawkins Polk). Nov. 2, 1795–June 15, 1849; Oct. 14, 1839–Oct. 15, 1841; House 1825–39 (1825–27 no party, 1827–37 Jacksonian, 1837–39 Democrat); Speaker Dec. 7, 1835–37, Sept. 4, 1837–39; President 1845–49.

BROWN, Aaron Venable. Aug. 15, 1795–March 8, 1859; Oct. 14, 1845–Oct. 16, 1847; House 1839–45; Postmaster Gen. March 7, 1857–March 8, 1859.

TROUSDALE, William. Sept. 23, 1790–March 27, 1872; Oct. 16, 1849–Oct. 16, 1851.

JOHNSON, Andrew (father-in-law of Sen. David Trotter Patterson). Dec. 29, 1808–July 31, 1875; Oct. 17, 1853–Nov. 3, 1857, (Military) March 12, 1862–March 4, 1865; House 1843–53 (Democrat); Senate Oct. 8, 1857–March 4, 1862 (Democrat), March 4–July 31, 1875 (Republican); Vice President March 4–April 15, 1865 (Republican); President April 15, 1865–69 (Republican).

HARRIS, Isham Green. Feb. 10, 1818–July 8, 1897; Nov. 3, 1857–March 12, 1862; House 1849–53; Senate 1877–July 8, 1897; elected Pres. pro tempore March 22, 1893, Jan. 10, 1895.

BROWN, John Calvin (brother of Neill Smith Brown, father-in-law of Benton McMillin). Jan. 6, 1827–Aug. 17, 1889; Oct. 10, 1871–Jan. 18, 1875.

PORTER, James Davis Jr. Dec. 7, 1828–May 18, 1912; Jan. 18, 1875–Feb. 16, 1879.

MARKS, Albert Smith. Oct. 16, 1836–Nov. 4, 1891; Feb. 16, 1879–Jan. 17, 1881.

BATE, William Brimage. Oct. 7, 1826–March 9, 1905; Jan. 15, 1883–Jan. 17, 1887; Senate 1887–March 9, 1905.

TAYLOR, Robert Love. July 31, 1850–March 31, 1912; Jan. 17, 1887–Jan. 19, 1891, Jan. 21, 1897–Jan. 16, 1899; House 1879–81; Senate 1907–March 31, 1912.

BUCHANAN, John Price. Oct. 24, 1837–May 14, 1930; Jan. 19, 1891–Jan. 16, 1893.

TURNEY, Peter. Sept. 27, 1827–Oct. 28, 1903; Jan. 16, 1893–Jan. 21, 1897.

TAYLOR, Robert Love. Jan. 21, 1897–Jan. 16, 1899 (for previous term see above).

McMILLIN, Benton (son-in-law of John Calvin Brown, above). Sept. 11, 1845–Jan. 8, 1933; Jan. 16, 1899–Jan. 19, 1903; House 1879–Jan. 6, 1899.

FRAZIER, James Beriah. Oct. 18, 1856–March 28, 1937; Jan. 19, 1903–March 21, 1905; Senate March 21, 1905–11.

COX, John Isaac. Nov. 23, 1855–Sept. 5, 1946; March 21, 1905–Jan. 17 1907.

PATTERSON, Malcolm Rice. June 7, 1861–March 8, 1935; Jan. 17, 1907–Jan. 26, 1911; House 1901–Nov. 5, 1906.

RYE, Thomas Clarke. June 2, 1863–Sept. 12, 1953; Jan. 17, 1915–Jan. 15, 1919.

ROBERTS, Albert Houston. July 4, 1868–June 25, 1946; Jan. 15, 1919–Jan. 15, 1921.

PEAY, Austin III. June 1, 1876–Oct. 2, 1927; Jan. 16, 1923–Oct. 2, 1927.

HORTON, Henry Hollis. Feb. 17, 1866–July 2, 1934; Oct. 3, 1927–Jan. 17, 1933.

McALISTER, Harry Hill. July 15, 1875–Oct. 30, 1959; Jan. 17, 1933–Jan. 15, 1937.

BROWNING, Gordon Weaver. Nov. 22, 1889–May 23, 1976; Jan. 15, 1937–Jan. 16, 1939, Jan. 17, 1949–Jan. 15, 1953; House 1923–35.

COOPER, William Prentice. Sept. 28, 1895–May 18, 1969; Jan. 16, 1939–Jan. 16, 1945.

McCORD, James Nance. March 17, 1879–Sept. 2, 1968; Jan. 16, 1945–Jan. 17, 1949; House 1943–45.

BROWNING, Gordon Weaver. Jan. 17, 1949–Jan. 15, 1953 (for previous term see above).

CLEMENT, Frank Goad. June 2, 1920–Nov. 4, 1969; Jan. 15, 1953–Jan. 16, 1959, Jan. 15, 1963–Jan. 16, 1967.

ELLINGTON, Earl Buford. June 27, 1907–April 3, 1972; Jan. 19, 1959–Jan. 15, 1963, Jan. 16, 1967–Jan. 16, 1971.

CLEMENT, Frank Goad. Jan. 15, 1963–Jan. 16, 1967 (for previous term see above).

ELLINGTON, Earl Buford. Jan. 16, 1967–Jan. 16, 1971 (for previous term see above).

BLANTON, Leonard Ray. April 10, 1930–; Jan. 18, 1975–Jan. 17, 1979; House 1967–73.

McWHERTER, Ned Ray. Oct. 15, 1930–; Jan. 17, 1987–1995.

TEXAS

(became a state December 29, 1845)

HENDERSON, James Pinckney. March 31, 1808–June 4, 1858; Feb. 19, 1846–Dec. 21, 1847; Senate Nov. 9, 1857–June 4, 1858.

WOOD, George Thomas. March 12, 1795–Sept. 3, 1858; Dec. 21, 1847–Dec. 21, 1849.

BELL, Peter Hansbrough. May 12, 1812–March 8, 1898; Dec. 21, 1849–Nov. 23, 1853; House 1853–57.

HENDERSON, James Wilson. Aug. 15, 1817–Aug. 30, 1880; Nov. 23–Dec. 21, 1853.

PEASE, Elisha Marshall. Jan. 3, 1812–Aug. 26, 1883; Dec. 21, 1853–Dec. 21, 1857, Aug. 8, 1867–Sept. 30, 1869.

RUNNELS, Hardin Richard (nephew of Hiram George Runnels of Miss.). Aug. 30, 1820–Dec. 25, 1873; Dec. 21, 1857–Dec. 21, 1859.

HOUSTON, Samuel (father of Rep. Andrew Jackson Houston, cousin of Rep. David Hubbard). March 2, 1793–July 26, 1863; Dec. 21, 1859–March 16, 1861, Oct. 1, 1827–April 16, 1829 (Tenn.); House 1823–27; (no party Tenn.); Senate Feb. 21, 1846–59 (Democrat).

CLARK, Edward (son of John Clark of Ga.). April 1, 1815–May 4, 1880; March 16–Nov. 7, 1861.

LUBBOCK, Francis Richard. Oct. 16, 1815–June 22, 1905; Nov. 7, 1861–Nov. 5, 1863.

MURRAH, Pendleton. 1824–Aug. 4, 1865; Nov. 5, 1863–June 11, 1865.

STOCKDALE, Fletcher S. 1823–1902; June 11–June 16, 1865.

PEASE, Elisha Marshall. Aug. 8, 1867–Sept. 30, 1869 (for previous term see above).

COKE, Richard. March 13, 1829–May 14, 1897; Jan. 15, 1874–Dec. 1, 1876; Senate 1877–95.

HUBBARD, Richard Bennett. Nov. 1, 1832–July 12, 1901; Dec. 1, 1876–Jan. 21, 1879.

ROBERTS, Oran Milo. July 9, 1816–May 19, 1898; Jan. 21, 1879–Jan. 16, 1883.

IRELAND, John. Jan. 21, 1827–March 5, 1896; Jan. 16, 1883–Jan. 18, 1887.

ROSS, Lawrence Sullivan "Sul." Sept. 27, 1838–Jan. 3, 1898; Jan. 18, 1887–Jan. 20, 1891.

HOGG, James Stephen. March 24, 1851–March 3, 1906; Jan. 20, 1891–Jan. 15, 1895.

CULBERSON, Charles Allen. June 10, 1855–March 19, 1925; Jan. 15, 1895–Jan. 17, 1899; Senate 1899–1923.

SAYERS, Joseph Draper. Sept. 23, 1841–May 15, 1929; Jan. 17, 1899–Jan. 20, 1903; House 1885–Jan. 16, 1899.

LANHAM, Samuel Willis Tucker. July 4, 1846–July 29, 1908; Jan. 20, 1903–Jan. 15, 1907; House 1883–93, 1897–Jan. 15, 1903.

CAMPBELL, Thomas Mitchell. April 22, 1866–April 1, 1923; Jan. 15, 1907–Jan. 17, 1911.

COLQUITT, Oscar Branch. Dec. 16, 1861–March 8, 1940; Jan. 17, 1911–Jan. 19, 1915.

FERGUSON, James Edward "Pa" (husband of Miriam Amanda "Ma" Ferguson, below). Aug. 31, 1871–Sept. 21, 1944; Jan. 19, 1915–Aug. 25, 1917.

HOBBY, William Pettus. March 26, 1878–June 7, 1964; Aug. 25, 1917–Jan. 18, 1921.

NEFF, Patrick Morris. Nov. 26, 1871–Jan. 20, 1952; Jan. 18, 1921–Jan. 20, 1925.

FERGUSON, Miriam Amanda "Ma" (wife of James Edward "Pa" Ferguson, above). June 13, 1875–June 25, 1961; Jan. 20, 1925–Jan.18, 1927, Jan. 17, 1933–Jan. 16, 1935.

MOODY, Daniel J. June 1, 1893–May 22, 1966; Jan. 18, 1927–Jan. 20, 1931.

STERLING, Ross Shaw. Feb. 11, 1875–March 25, 1949; Jan. 20, 1931–Jan. 17, 1933.

FERGUSON, Miriam Amanda "Ma." Jan. 17, 1933–Jan. 15, 1935 (for previous term see above).

ALLRED, James V. March 29, 1889–Sept. 24, 1959; Jan. 15, 1935–Jan. 17, 1939.

O'DANIEL, Wilbert Lee "Pappy." March 11, 1890–May 11, 1969; Jan. 17, 1939–Aug. 4, 1941; Senate Aug. 4, 1941–49.

STEVENSON, Coke Robert. March 20, 1888–June 28, 1975; Aug. 4, 1941–Jan. 21, 1947.

JESTER, Beauford Halbert. Jan. 12, 1893–July 11, 1949; Jan. 21, 1947–July 11, 1949.

SHIVERS, Allan. Oct. 5, 1907–Jan. 14, 1985; July 11, 1949–Jan. 15, 1957.

DANIEL, Price Marion. Oct. 10, 1910–Aug. 25, 1988; Jan. 15, 1957–Jan. 15, 1963; Senate 1953–Jan. 14, 1957.

CONNALLY, John Bowden. Feb. 27, 1917–June 15, 1993; Jan. 15, 1963–Jan. 21, 1969; Secy. of the Treasury Feb. 11, 1971–June 12, 1972.

SMITH, Preston Earnest. March 8, 1912–; Jan. 21, 1969–Jan. 16, 1973.

BRISCOE, Dolph Jr. April 23, 1923–; Jan. 16, 1973–Jan. 16, 1979.

WHITE, Mark. March 17, 1940–; Jan. 18, 1983–Jan. 20, 1987.

RICHARDS, Dorothy Ann Willis. Sept. 1, 1933–; Jan. 15, 1991–1995.

UTAH

(became a state January 4, 1896)

BAMBERGER, Simon. Feb. 27, 1846–Oct. 6, 1926; Jan. 1, 1917–Jan. 3, 1921.

DERN, George Henry. Sept. 8, 1872–Aug. 27, 1936; Jan. 5, 1925–Jan. 2, 1933.

BLOOD, Henry Hooper. Oct. 1, 1872–June 19, 1942; Jan. 2, 1933–Jan. 6, 1941.

MAW, Herbert Brown. March 11, 1893–Nov. 17, 1990; Jan. 6, 1941–Jan. 3, 1949.

RAMPTON, Calvin Lewellyn. Nov. 6, 1913–; Jan. 4, 1965–Jan. 3, 1977.

MATHESON, Scott Milne. Jan. 8, 1929–Oct. 7, 1990; Jan. 3, 1977–Jan. 7, 1985.

VERMONT

(became a state March 4, 1791)

ROBINSON, John Staniford. Nov. 10, 1804–April 25, 1860; Nov. 2, 1853–Oct. 13, 1854.

HOFF, Philip Henderson. June 29, 1924–; Jan. 10, 1963–Jan. 9, 1969.

SALMON, Thomas Paul. Aug. 19, 1932–; Jan. 4, 1973–Jan. 6, 1977.

KUNIN, Madeleine May. Sept. 28, 1933–; Jan. 10, 1985–Jan. 10, 1991.

DEAN, Howard. Nov. 17, 1948–; Aug. 14, 1991–.

VIRGINIA

(ratified the Constitution June 25, 1788)

FLOYD, John (father of John Buchanan Floyd, uncle of James McDowell, brother-in-law of James Patton Preston). April 24, 1783–Aug. 17, 1837; March 4, 1830–March 31, 1834; House 1817–29 (Republican).

TAZEWELL, Littleton Waller. Dec. 17, 1774–May 6, 1860; March 31, 1834–April 30, 1836; House Nov. 26, 1800–01 (no party); Senate Dec. 7, 1824–July 16, 1832 (no party); elected Pres. pro tempore July 9, 1832.

McDOWELL, James (nephew of James Patton Preston and John Floyd, cousin of John Buchanan Floyd, father-in-law of Francis Thomas of Md.). Oct. 13, 1795–Aug. 24, 1851; Jan. 1, 1843–Jan. 1, 1946; House March 6, 1846–51.

FLOYD, John Buchanan (son of John Floyd, nephew of James Patton Preston, cousin of James McDowell). June 1, 1806–Aug. 26, 1863; Jan. 1, 1849–Jan. 16, 1852; Secy. of War March 6, 1857–Dec. 29, 1860.

JOHNSON, Joseph. Dec. 19, 1785–Feb. 27, 1877; Jan. 16, 1852–Dec. 31, 1855; House 1823–27 (no party), Jan. 21–March 3, 1833 (no party), 1835–41 (1835–37 Jacksonian, 1837–41 Democrat), 1845–47 (Democrat).

WISE, Henry Alexander. Dec. 3, 1806–Sept. 12, 1876; Jan. 1, 1856–Dec. 31, 1859; House 1833–Feb. 12, 1844 (1833–37 Jacksonian, 1837–43 Whig, 1843–Feb. 12, 1844 Democrat).

LETCHER, John. March 29, 1813–Jan. 26, 1884; Jan. 1, 1860–Dec. 31, 1863; House 1851–59.

KEMPER, James Lawson. June 11, 1823–April 7, 1895; Jan. 1, 1874–Jan. 1, 1878.

HOLLIDAY, Frederick William Mackey. Feb. 22, 1828–May 29, 1899; Jan. 1, 1878–Jan. 1, 1882.

LEE, Fitzhugh. Nov. 19, 1835–April 28, 1905; Jan. 1, 1886–Jan. 1, 1890.

McKINNEY, Philip Watkins. May 1, 1832–March 1, 1899; Jan. 1, 1890–Jan. 1, 1894.

O'FERRALL, Charles Triplett. Oct. 21, 1840–Sept. 22, 1905; Jan. 1, 1894–Jan. 1, 1898; House May 5, 1884–Dec. 28, 1893.

TYLER, James Hoge. Aug. 11, 1846–Jan. 3, 1925; Jan. 1, 1898–Jan. 1, 1902.

MONTAGUE, Andrew Jackson. Oct. 3, 1862–Jan. 24, 1937; Jan. 1, 1902–Feb. 1, 1906; House 1913–Jan. 24, 1937.

SWANSON, Claude Augustus. March 31, 1862–July 7, 1939; Feb. 1, 1906–Feb. 1, 1910; House 1893–Jan. 30, 1906; Senate Aug. 1, 1910–33; Secy. of the Navy March 4, 1933–July 7, 1939.

MANN, William Hodges. July 30, 1843–Dec. 12, 1927; Feb. 1, 1910–Feb. 1, 1914.

STUART, Henry Carter. Jan. 18, 1855–July 24, 1933; Feb. 1, 1914–Feb. 1, 1918.

DAVIS, Westmoreland. Aug. 21, 1859–Sept 7, 1942; Feb. 1, 1918–Feb. 1, 1922.

TRINKLE, Elbert Lee. March 12, 1876–Nov. 25, 1939; Feb. 1, 1922–Feb. 1, 1926.

BYRD, Harry Flood. June 10, 1887–Oct. 20, 1966; Feb. 1, 1926–Jan. 15, 1930; Senate 1933–Nov. 10, 1965.

POLLARD, John Garland. Aug. 9, 1871–April 28, 1937; Jan. 15, 1930–Jan. 17, 1934.

PEERY, George Campbell. Oct. 28, 1873–Oct. 14, 1952; Jan. 17, 1934–Jan. 19, 1938; House 1923–29.

PRICE, James Hubert. Sept. 7, 1878–Nov. 22, 1943; Jan. 19, 1938–Jan. 21, 1942.

DARDEN, Colgate Whitehead Jr. Feb. 11, 1897–June 9, 1981; Jan. 21, 1942–Jan. 16, 1946; House 1933–37, 1939–March 1, 1941.

TUCK, William Munford. Sept. 28, 1896–June 9, 1983; Jan. 16, 1946–Jan. 18, 1950; House April 14, 1953–69.

BATTLE, John Stewart. July 11, 1890–April 9, 1972; Jan. 18, 1950–Jan. 20, 1954.

STANLEY, Thomas Bahnson. July 16, 1890–July 10 1970; Jan. 20, 1954–Jan. 11, 1958; House Nov. 5, 1946–Feb. 3, 1953.

ALMOND, James Lindsay Jr. June 15, 1898–April 14, 1986; Jan. 11, 1958–Jan. 11, 1962; House Jan. 22, 1946–April 17, 1948.

HARRISON, Albertis Sydney Jr. Jan. 11, 1907–; Jan. 13, 1962–Jan. 15, 1966.

ROBB, Charles Spittal. June 26, 1939–; Jan. 16, 1982–Jan. 18, 1986; Senate 1989–.

BALILES, Gerald L. July 8, 1940–; Jan. 18, 1986–Jan. 14, 1990.

WILDER, Lawrence Douglas. Jan. 17, 1931–; Jan. 14, 1990–Jan. 15, 1994.

WASHINGTON

(became a state November 11, 1889)

LISTER, Ernest. June 15, 1870–June 14, 1919; Jan. 11, 1913–June 14, 1919.

MARTIN, Clarence Daniel. June 29, 1887–Aug. 11, 1955; Jan. 9, 1933–Jan. 13, 1941.

WALLGREN, Monrad Charles. April 17, 1891–Sept. 18, 1961; Jan. 1945–Jan. 10 , 1949; House 1933–Dec. 19, 1940; Senate Dec. 19, 1940–Jan. 9, 1945.

ROSELLINI, Albert Dean. Jan. 21, 1910–; Jan. 14, 1957–Jan. 11, 1965.

RAY, Dixy Lee. Sept. 3, 1914–Jan. 2, 1994; Jan. 12, 1977–Jan. 14, 1981.

GARDNER, Booth. Aug. 21, 1936–; Jan. 16, 1985– Jan. 13, 1993.

LOWRY, Michael Edward. March 8, 1939– Jan. 13, 1993–; House 1979–89.

WEST VIRGINIA

(became a state June 19, 1863)

MATHEWS, Henry Mason. March 29, 1834–April 28, 1884; March 4, 1877–March 4, 1881.

JACKSON, Jacob Beeson. April 6, 1829–Dec. 11, 1893; March 4, 1881–March 4, 1885.

WILSON, Emanuel Willis. Aug. 11, 1844–May 28, 1909; March 4, 1885–Feb. 5, 1890.

FLEMING, Aretas Brooks. Oct. 15, 1839–Oct. 13, 1923; Feb. 5, 1890–March, 1893.

MacCORKLE, William Alexander. May 7, 1857–Sept. 24, 1930; March 4, 1893–March 4, 1897.

CORNWELL John Jacob. July 11, 1867–Sept. 8, 1953; March 4, 1917–March 4, 1921.

KUMP, Herinan Guy. Oct. 31, 1877–Feb. 14, 1962; March 4, 1933–Jan. 18, 1937.

HOLT, Homer Adams. March 1, 1898–Jan. 16, 1975; Jan. 18, 1937–Jan. 12, 1941.

NEELY, Matthew Mansfield. Nov. 9, 1874–Jan. 18, 1958; Jan. 13, 1941–Jan. 15, 1945; House Oct. 14, 1913–21, 1945–47; Senate 1923–29, 1931–Jan. 12, 1941, 1949–Jan. 18, 1958.

MEADOWS, Clarence Watson. Feb. 11, 1904–Sept. 12, 1961; Jan. 15, 1945–Jan. 17, 1949.

PATTESON, Okey Leonidas. Sept. 14, 1898–; Jan. 17, 1949–Jan. 19, 1953.

MARLAND, William Casey. March 26, 1918–Nov. 26, 1965; Jan. 19, 1953–Jan. 13, 1957.

BARRON, William Wallace. Dec. 8, 1911–; Jan. 16, 1961–Jan. 18, 1965.

SMITH, Hulett Carlson. Oct. 12, 1918–; Jan. 18, 1965–Jan. 13, 1969.

ROCKEFELLER, John Davidson "Jay" IV (nephew of Vice President Nelson Aldrich Rockefeller and Winthrop Rockefeller of Ark., great-grandson of Sen. Nelson Wilmarth Aldrich, great-uncle of Rep. Richard Steere Aldrich). June 18, 1937–; Jan. 17, 1977–Jan. 14, 1985; Senate Jan. 15, 1985–.

CAPERTON, Gaston. Feb. 21, 1940–; Jan. 16, 1989–.

WISCONSIN

(became a state May 29, 1848)

DEWEY, Nelson. Dec. 19, 1813–July 21, 1889; June 7, 1848–Jan. 5, 1852.

BARSTOW, William Augustus. Sept. 13, 1813–Dec. 13, 1865; Jan. 2, 1854–March 21, 1856.

MacARTHUR, Arthur. Jan. 26, 1815–Aug. 26, 1896; March 21–March 25, 1856.

TAYLOR, William Robert. July 10, 1820–March 17, 1909; Jan. 5, 1874–Jan. 3, 1876.

PECK, George Wilbur. Sept. 28, 1840–April 16, 1916; Jan. 5, 1891–Jan. 7, 1895.

SCHMEDEMAN, Albert George. Nov. 25, 1864–Nov. 26, 1946; Jan. 2, 1933–Jan.7, 1935.

NELSON, Gaylord Anton. June 4, 1916–; Jan. 5, 1959–Jan. 7, 1963; Senate Jan. 8, 1963–81.

REYNOLDS, John Whitcome. April 4, 1921–; Jan. 7, 1963–Jan. 4, 1965.

LUCEY, Patrick Joseph. March 21, 1918–; Jan. 4, 1971–July 7, 1977.

SCHREIBER, Martin James. April 8, 1939–; July 7, 1977–Jan. 1, 1979.

EARL, Anthony Scully. April 12, 1936–; Jan. 3, 1983–Jan. 5, 1987.

WYOMING

(became a state July 10, 1890)

OSBORNE, John Eugene. June 19, 1858–April 24, 1943; Jan. 2, 1893–Jan. 7, 1895; House 1897–99.

KENDRICK, John Benjamin. Sept. 6, 1857–Nov. 3, 1933; Jan. 4, 1915–Feb. 26, 1917; Senate 1917–Nov. 3, 1933.

HOUX, Frank L. Dec. 12, 1860–April 3, 1941; Feb. 26, 1917–Jan. 6, 1919.

ROSS, William Bradford (husband of Nellie Tayloe Ross, below). Dec. 4, 1873–Oct. 2, 1924; Jan. 1, 1923–Oct. 2, 1924.

ROSS, Nellie Tayloe (wife of William Bradford Ross, above). Nov. 29, 1876–Dec. 19, 1977; Jan. 5, 1925–Jan. 3, 1927.

MILLER, Leslie Andrew. Jan. 29, 1886–Sept. 29, 1970; Jan. 2, 1933–Jan. 2, 1939.

HUNT, Lester Calloway. July 8, 1892–June 19, 1954; Jan. 4, 1943–Jan. 3, 1949; Senate 1949–June 19, 1954.

HICKEY, John Joseph. Aug. 22, 1911–Sept. 22, 1970; Jan. 5, 1959–Jan. 2, 1961; Senate 1961–Nov. 6, 1962.

GAGE, Jack Robert. Jan. 13, 1899–March 14, 1970; Jan. 2, 1961–Jan. 6, 1963.

HERSCHLER, Edgar J. Oct. 27, 1918–Feb. 5, 1990; Jan. 6, 1975–Jan. 5, 1987.

SULLIVAN, Michael John. Sept. 22, 1939–; Jan. 5, 1987–1995.